D1236770

Elections, Politics, and Society
in Ireland 1832–1885

ELECTIONS, POLITICS, AND SOCIETY IN IRELAND 1832–1885

K. THEODORE HOPPEN

CLARENDON PRESS · OXFORD

1984

Oxford University Press, Walton Street, Oxford OX2 6DP

London New York Toronto
Delhi Bombay Calcutta Madras Karachi
Kuala Lumpur Singapore Hong Kong Tokyo
Nairobi Dar es Salaam Cape Town
Melbourne Auckland

and associated companies in
Beirut Berlin Ibadan Mexico City Nicosia

Oxford is a trade mark of Oxford University Press

Published in the United States by
Oxford University Press, New York

British Library Cataloguing in Publication Data
Hoppen, K. Theodore
Elections, politics, and society in
Ireland 1832-1885.
1. Ireland—Politics and government
—19th century
I. Title
320.9415   JN1411
ISBN 0-19-822630-6

Library of Congress Cataloging in Publication Data
Hoppen, K. Theodore, 1941-
Elections, politics, and society in Ireland 1832-1885.
Bibliography: p.
Includes index.
1. Ireland—Politics and government—1837-1901.
2. Elections—Ireland—History—19th century.
3. Ireland—Social conditions.   I. Title.
DA950.H68   1984   324.9415'081   84-4347
ISBN 0-19-822630-6

Typeset in Baskerville 11/12 by
Joshua Associates, Oxford
Printed in Great Britain
at the University Press, Oxford
by David Stanford
Printer to the University

For Alison

'And what are you to give us?' said the tatterdemalions headed by Bill-'i-the-Bowl.

'Why', replied the Young Ireland party, 'have you no soul—no spirit for universal freedom? Have you no lofty aspirations?—no humanity?—no fire?—no lightning?—no thunder?'

'No', said Billy, 'the devil a taste of anything o' the kind we have stronger than brimstone.'

William Carleton, *The Squanders of Castle Squander* (1852)

Preface

When I first thought of writing this book I immodestly pictured myself explaining the electoral system of Victorian Ireland along the lines so brilliantly pioneered by Norman Gash and H. J. Hanham across the sea in England.* It was not long before the very distinct nature of Irish politics and society, the exigencies of the evidence, and the various black holes which still litter even nineteenth-century Irish history turned the enterprise in an altogether different direction. Elections, certainly, have remained at the heart of the matter, for they and their associated events furnish unique insights into the concerns, behaviour, and values of the political classes of the time. It soon became apparent, however, that any study of elections and electoral techniques in isolation would, in the Irish context, make very little sense. These have, therefore, been depicted against a wider landscape in the hope that any loss in purely electoral detail might be more than made up for by contextual illumination. Hence the structure of the book—which opens with an examination of the formal electoral community called into being by the franchise legislation of the period and then moves on to confront directly the characteristics and the political impact of the most important groups and forces which helped shape Ireland in the half-century after 1832: landlords, tenants, labourers, priests, shopkeepers, artisans on the one hand, social change, violence, religious and cultural adjustment on the other. Although elections and party organization could not be—and are not—overlooked, this is, therefore, a study of politics in their social setting.

As the work proceeded two things struck me with particular force. The first—that in reality this was a hopelessly ambitious enterprise —I could do little about. The second—that a close examination of electoral and other developments within local communities revealed much that had previously been hidden—has, in the event, constituted something of a leitmotiv for the book as a whole. The more the detailed workings of individual political communities in Ireland were examined, the more striking and important seemed the gap between local realities and the rhetoric of national politics. Such communities, whether individual in the geographical or the social sense, often

* N. Gash, *Politics in the age of Peel: A study in the technique of parliamentary representation 1830-1850* (London, 1953); H. J. Hanham, *Elections and Party Management: Politics in the time of Disraeli and Gladstone* (London, 1959).

maintained a style of politics only intermittently in step with the
stated aims and methods of the movements generally held to have
dominated Irish history in the nineteenth century. Indeed, without
in any way dismissing the importance of national movements as such,
it is, none the less, necessary to amplify and to extend traditional
interpretations. Irish politics, whether operating upon the basis of
the pre-1850 franchise, the 1850–84 franchise, the post-1884
franchise, or even within the context of independent Ireland, were
often profoundly localist in both content and style. The two great
movements of 'national consciousness' led by O'Connell and Parnell
should not, therefore, be seen as the only true representations of
authentic political feeling, but rather as unusual superimpositions
upon the deeply pervasive and enduring localist traditions of Irish
political life. In this respect the period between about 1850 and
1870 represents Irish politics at their most typical, with the patina
of national movements stripped away and the underlying realities
revealed in an especially striking and immediate manner. In this
respect also, the comparatively long period of over fifty years with
which the book is concerned has allowed traditional historical
techniques to reveal more complex patterns of relationship between
the general and the particular than many valuable analyses of shorter
episodes have been able to do.

The materials and the conclusions presented are based on a wide
variety of sources. Statistical tables have been used to assess—in a
more succinct form than would otherwise have been possible—some
of the measurable aspects of electoral, political, social, and economic
change. In the end, however, the flavour of the work depends heavily
upon the examples and citations marshalled in the text. And here the
very nature of the general approach adopted, namely, the examination of intricate patterns and relationships at the local level, has
necessarily made this a book of some considerable length. My study
begins and ends in the two greatest reforming decades of the century:
the 1830s, which, elastically interpreted, can be said to encompass
Emancipation, and reforms in the franchise, the Church, the police,
education, poor relief, tithes, and local government; the 1880s,
which began the process towards 'peasant proprietorship' and thus
made Ireland safe for social conservatism for almost another hundred
years. Indeed, the essentially Janus-like nature of this last 'reform'
accurately reflects the modulating separation and kinship between
national and local politics throughout the period as a whole. In the
longer view, the bright political fireworks of O'Connell, of Parnell,
of the men of 1916–21, mark punctuations in the development of
a more penetrating and tenacious political culture in which limited

goals and local priorities could, more often than not, count for more than heroic principles or dramatic brilliance.

Throughout the book I have generally adopted the nomenclature used at the time. Thus, for example, Catholic means Roman Catholic and what is now known as Offaly is referred to as King's County. I hope none of this treads upon any delicate toes and I can only plead the justifications of contemporary usage and clarity of meaning in an area of Irish experience too long perhaps susceptible to religious and political sensitivities.

University of Hull   K. T. H.

Acknowledgements

I am grateful to the custodians and owners of the various collections of papers which have been cited or referred to in this book. Especially do I wish to acknowledge the gracious permission of Her Majesty Queen Elizabeth II to cite material in the Royal Archives and in the Melbourne Papers, and also my debt to the following: the Duke of Abercorn, the Marquess of Anglesey, Messrs Babington & Croasdaile (solicitors, Coleraine), the Earl of Belmore, the Trustees of the Broadlands Archive, Mrs Edwin Bryson, Messrs Carleton, Atkinson, & Sloan (solicitors, Portadown), the Trustees of the Chatsworth Settlement, the Earl of Clarendon, the Most Revd the Bishop of Clogher, the late Archibald Maxwell Close, Esq., Messrs Crawford & Lockhart (solicitors, Belfast), the Marquess of Downshire, the Earl of Dunraven, the Earl of Erne, Adrian FitzGerald, Esq., the Trustee of the Fitzwilliam (Wentworth) Estates, A. Foote, Esq., the Lord Gisborough, the Earl of Gosford, the Earl of Harewood, F. E. Hart, Esq., the Department of Irish Folklore of University College Dublin, William Johnston, Esq., Messrs L'Estrange & Brett (solicitors, Belfast), Messrs Longfield, Kelly, & Armstrong (solicitors, Dungannon), Messrs John McKee & Son (solicitors, Armagh), Messrs Martin & Henderson (solicitors, Downpatrick), Messrs Martin, King, French, & Ingram (solicitors, Limavady), Mrs Mayne-Reid, Captain Peter Montgomery, the Lord Moyola, the Lord O'Hagan, A. R. Pack-Beresford, Esq., the late Major J. R. Perceval-Maxwell and the Trustees of his Will, the Earl of Roden, the Lord Rossmore, Quentin Agnew Somerville, Esq., and the Board of Trinity College Dublin. I also acknowledge the kindness of libraries and individuals who have granted permission to make use of postgraduate dissertations, in particular those written by P. Connell, Esq., Dr S. J. Connolly, A. D. T. Fay, R. S. Gourlay, Esq., Dr Jacqueline Hill, R. F. Holmes, Esq., Dr J. P. Huttman, Dr D. S. Jones, A. McClelland, Esq., David M. Nolan, Esq., J. N. Qdurkene, Esq., Dr Cormac Ó Gráda, Dr Olive Robinson, Dr A. M. Tod, and Dr W. E. Vaughan.

The members of staff of the libraries and archives in which I have worked treated my sometimes importunate demands with exemplary patience and helpfulness: those at the Brynmor Jones Library of Hull University, the National Library of Ireland, and the Public Record Office of Northern Ireland deserve a special word of thanks. Financial assistance from the Social Science Research Council (as it then was), the Sir Philip Reckitt Educational Trust, and the University of Hull enabled me to undertake more extensive research than would otherwise have been possible.

Many individuals have helped me in various ways. Although I can only name a few, I am grateful to them all. Dr A. P. W. Malcomson placed his enormous knowledge of Irish family papers at my disposal and made my visits to Belfast a social as well as a scholarly delight. Professor J. H. Whyte gave generous help with respect to various archives in Rome. Conversations with Professor Sam Clark and Professor J. S. Donnelly, Jr.——who will I am sure not agree with many of my arguments——made me more aware of the complexities of nineteenth-century Irish society. Ann Barry was an invaluable guide to papers in the keeping of the Cork Archives Council. Dr J. J. N. Palmer manfully listened to my 'thoughts' over the years and deflated many an extravagance. Professor W. A. Speck read the typescript and made a number of extremely useful suggestions. Dr Tom Garvin, Mr Michael Millerick, Dr Cormac Ó Gráda, and Dr B. M. Walker all helped in various ways. I owe much to the stimulating teaching and friendship of Professor R. Dudley Edwards, Professor Hugh Kearney, and Professor T. Desmond Williams. Dr Angus Macintyre's encouragement was more valuable to me than he can possibly realize. The dedication of this book to my wife is a totally inadequate recognition of that love, help, and scholarly sympathy which she has always given to me throughout the happy years of our togetherness.

Contents

Maps

Tables

For notes on the sources and methods of Tables see the Appendix.

Abbreviations

Arch. Hib. xxx, xxxi, xxxii	'Irish College, Rome: Kirby Papers', ed. P. J. Corish, *Archivium Hibernicum*, xxx (1972), xxxi (1973), xxxii (1974)
B.L.	British Library, London
Catholic Directory 1836 [etc.]	[Battersby's] *Catholic Directory, Almanac, and Registry* (Dublin, 1836–) under various titles
C.C.	*Cork Constitution*
C.U.L.	Cambridge University Library
Paul Cullen	*Paul Cullen and his Contemporaries*, ed. P. Mac-Suibhne, 5 vols. (Naas, 1961–77)
D.E.P.	*Dublin Evening Post*
Devon Index	*Index to minutes of evidence taken before Her Majesty's Commissioners of Inquiry into the State of the Law and Practice in respect to the Occupation of Land in Ireland*, H.C. 1845 [673], xxii [Devon Commission]
Fictitious Votes, Ireland	Followed by series and report numbers, indicates reports from the *Select Committee on Fictitious Votes, Ireland*, 1st series, 1st report, H.C. 1837 (308), xi, part i, 1–739, 2nd report, 1837 (335), xi, part ii, 1–142, 3rd report, 1837 (480), xi, part ii, 143–761; 2nd series, 1st report, H.C. 1837–8 (259), xiii, part i, 1–338, 2nd report, 1837–8 (294), xiii, part i, 339–57, 3rd report, 1837–8 (643), xiii, part ii, 1–733
Hansard	*Hansard's Parliamentary Debates*, 3rd series
H.C.	House of Commons Paper
H.L.	House of Lords Paper
L.-B.	Letter-Book
N.L.I.	National Library of Ireland, Dublin
O.P.	Outrage Papers (in S.P.O.)
P.R.O.	Public Record Office, London
P.R.O.I.	Public Record Office of Ireland, Dublin
P.R.O.N.I.	Public Record Office of Northern Ireland, Belfast
R.I.A.	Royal Irish Academy, Dublin
R.P.	Registered Papers (in S.P.O.)
S.P.O.	State Paper Office, Dublin
Thom 1844 [etc.]	*Thom's Irish Almanac and Official Directory* (Dublin, 1844–)
U.C.D.	University College Dublin

NOTE ON THE CITATION OF MANUSCRIPTS

In cases where more than one collection (under the same name) pertains to a single individual, the larger collection is that referred to without elaboration of specific locations. Thus Cullen Papers = those in Dublin Diocesan Archives (not those in Irish College, Rome); Mayo Papers = those in N.L.I. (not those in C.U.L.); O'Hagan Papers = those in P.R.O.N.I. (not those in N.L.I.). See Bibliography.

Map A Parliamentary Constituencies 1832–1885

I

The Political Community

For most of the nineteenth century the United Kingdom was neither administratively united nor politically integrated. Its actual, as distinct from supposed, condition was one of informal devolution. The legacy of different histories and a tenderness towards tradition combined to preserve that chaotic half-understood collection of national anomalies known as the Victorian electoral system. Ireland, despite the Union, was allowed to maintain arrangements peculiar to itself. Even the traditional calendar of reform—1832, 1867, 1884-5 —becomes, in Hibernian metamorphosis, the more extended litany of 1801, 1829, 1832, 1850, 1868, and 1884-5. The Union had weeded out Ireland's Old Sarums so that almost two-thirds of the 100 (after 1832, 105) Irish Members of Parliament now came from counties, whereas in England, even after 1832, the situation was exactly the reverse. The pound of flesh demanded in return for Catholic Emancipation in 1829 ensured that the history of the Irish electorate was not to be a simple Whiggish tale of increase and multiplication. The number of county voters was slashed from about 216,000 to about 37,000[1] and Ireland entered the 'Age of Reform' bedecked with a set of unique, distinct, and obscure electoral traditions and experiences.

The aim of this chapter is to examine two simple problems: who were the Irish voters and how did they behave? This cannot be done without preliminary and rebarbative attention to property valuations and the haggling of lawyers. On the surface the Irish Reform Act of 1832 seems clear enough. The ten-pound freehold county electorate established in 1829 was augmented by various classes of leaseholders for years, and, although the government's information as to numbers was always vague, the one-in-ten presence of leaseholders by 1842 hardly constituted a dramatic intrusion.[2] The number of county voters rose to 60,597. The borough franchise, which (as in England)

---

[1] Nicholas Leader in *Hansard*, xiii, 580-5 (13 June 1832) suggests a drop to 26,000, but Peter Jupp in *British and Irish Elections 1784-1831* (Newton Abbot, 1973), p. 153 suggests c.37,000.

[2] *Hansard*, xiii, 816 and 1013-14 (18 and 25 June 1832); printed 'Statement of the number of parliamentary electors on the registries of Ireland, in January 1842', Derby Papers 28/3.

had varied from town to town, was co-ordinated upon the basis of occupation of a ten-pound property and produced 29,471 electors. In comparison with England this was small beer.

	Counties	Boroughs
Ireland	1 voter in every 116 inhabitants	1 in every 26
England and Wales	1 voter in every 24 inhabitants	1 in every 17
Scotland	1 voter in every 45 inhabitants	1 in every 27

But at least it seemed deliberate, careful, and, above all, rational. Beneath the surface gloss, however, lurked a nest of anomalies which qualified the whole affair, not for any prize that might have been awarded by philosophic radicals, but for Archbishop Lawrence of Cashel's strictures upon much Irish lawmaking of the time.

Unhappily Irish Acts are almost always slow in progress, and when they pass the legislature are seldom remarkably intelligible. Englishmen know little of this country, and Irishmen, when consulted, have . . . so irresistible an impulse to display their talents and acquirements, that, the moment a new act comes over, a thousand different opinions are here entertained of its meaning, and a thousand attempts made to defeat its provisions.[1]

That the ministry, and more specifically the brilliant and erratic Chief Secretary, E. G. Stanley (the future fourteenth Earl of Derby), should have had little idea of the mathematical effects of their proposals was nothing new. Captain Gipps, the chief Irish boundary commissioner, supplied estimates of projected borough electorates which proved wildly inaccurate.[2] Some minuscule bands of voters (Lisburn—91, New Ross—130, Portarlington—137, Tralee—180, Kinsale—206, Coleraine—207) emerged to greet the new reformist dawn, while the eight enormous counties of cities and towns (which now enjoyed a spatchcock franchise of borough householders and freemen together with 'county' freeholders and leaseholders) remained topographically untouched. In 1832 these eight constituencies, which returned only thirteen of the thirty-nine borough members but contained two-thirds of all borough voters, ranged in size from Dublin's 3,538 to Cork's massive 45,000 acres and included areas 'as much a country district as the most distant parts of the

---

[1] Archbishop Lawrence (writing about tithe legislation) to Edward Littleton, 17 June 1833, Hatherton Papers D260/M/01/6.

[2] *Copy of Instructions given by the chief secretary for Ireland with reference to the cities and boroughs in Ireland sending representatives to parliament,* H.C. 1831-2 (519), xliii, 8-11. For twenty-eight boroughs with an eventual electorate of 26,211 Gipps had estimated 41,858, and his individual estimates ranged from 40 per cent under (Carrick-fergus) to 58 per cent over (Wexford).

county'.[1] In comparison the 'pure' boroughs were drawn tightly around their built-up areas, many so tightly they covered less than a square mile of land.

The retention for life of the so-called 'ancient rights' voters and the lingering presence of five-pound householders and forty-shilling freeholders (who had not lost their *borough* votes in 1829) added a touch of impoverished colour to the supposedly strictly defined electorate of 1832.[2] And however much the reform acts may have been intended to establish a 'constituent body including all the intelligence and respectability of the independent classes of society' —a body 'uniform' in nature and homogeneous in composition— the Irish act produced something more akin to those pre-reform electorates comprehending all classes which Tories such as Peel and Ellenborough so much admired.[3] O'Connell too could never make up his mind as to the sort of electorate he wanted. At times he brayed loudly about the fate of the forty-shilling freeholders. At times he spoke publicly (and privately) of his belief that ten pounds was a more rational and—for him—politically advantageous point of exclusion.[4] O'Connell's conduct over reform, which he supported and indeed rescued at the crucial Commons division of 23 March 1831, shows the complexity of his political character, for, while the calculation of advantage urged one course of action, a concern for the 'operative classes' drove him into alliance with the Duke of Wellington to rescue the freemen voters from the ministerial axe.[5] In consequence the Irish freemen survived more luxuriantly than their English counterparts. Outside Galway they were almost all Protestants, often indigent, and open to the blandishments of electoral financiers. In Galway they were, in counterdistinction, almost all

[1] J. Besnard in *Fictitious Votes, Ireland*, 2nd series, 1st report, p. 15. They were Dublin, Drogheda, Waterford, Kilkenny, Carrickfergus, Galway, Limerick, and Cork.

[2] Of the borough electorate registered in 1832 11 per cent were qualified by ancient rights. In 1847 more than half of Dungarvan's and a fifth of Mallow's voters were still so qualified, and the forty-shilling freeholders of Dungarvan were a force to be reckoned with as late as 1857 (C. R. Dod, *Electoral Facts from 1832 to 1852*, 2nd edn. (London, 1853), pp. 101 and 203; F. E. Currey to Lord Carlisle, 2 Apr. 1857, Carlisle Papers L.-B. 85).

[3] *The Reform Act, 1832. The correspondence of the late Earl Grey with His Majesty King William IV*, ed. Henry George, 3rd Earl Grey, 2 vols. (London, 1867), i, 461-3; C. Seymour, *Electoral Reform in England and Wales: The development and operation of the parliamentary franchise 1832-1885* (New Haven, 1915), pp. 33 and 38; *Three early nineteenth-century diaries*, ed. A. Aspinall (London, 1952), pp. 92, 220, 257.

[4] O'Connell to his wife, 6 Mar. 1829, *The Correspondence of Daniel O'Connell*, ed. M. R. O'Connell, 8 vols. (Dublin, 1972-80), iv, 20-1; *Pilot*, 23 Dec. 1831; *Hansard*, iii, 868-72 (24 Mar. 1831).

[5] D. O'Connell, *Seven letters on the Reform Bill and the law of elections in Ireland* (Dublin, 1835), pp. 19-20; *Report of the Commissioners appointed by the act of the 32nd and 33rd Victoria, cap. 65, for the purpose of making inquiry into the existence of Corrupt Practices amongst the freemen electors of the City of Dublin*, H. C. 1870 [C 93], xxxiii, 4.

Catholics, often indigent, and open to the blandishments of electoral financiers. A series of those splendidly ingenious and rapidly contradictory judgements for which the nineteenth-century Irish bench was rightly renowned added to the freeman flood, especially in Dublin, where Chief Baron Joy's decisions in the 1830s ensured that, for a time, 'the process of registering [voters] . . . was a mere matter of form and dumb show. If a negro appeared,[1] he could hardly be asked a question, and must be admitted accordingly'.[2] Among the borough voters of 1832 no less than 22 per cent were freemen and as late as 1867 eight boroughs (including substantial places like Dublin, Galway, and Waterford) still had over a tenth of their electors so registered.[3] Mostly the freemen were poor artisans operating as electoral *condottieri* open to the highest bidder, establishing scales of prices for plumpers, double, or split votes,[4] writing semi-literate demands for cash and favours, and erratically prepared to take a lower bribe from someone whose local largesse or flamboyant personality appealed to them.[5] In Galway over half of them were to be found among nine occupations, notably shoemaking, tailoring, carpentering, weaving, butchering, and nailmaking, nearly all of them declining trades. In Dublin, shoemakers, tailors, and coopers were especially visible, while in Carrickfergus a large number of farmers and labourers were able to join the freeman roll. Everywhere the great majority were 'working tradesmen', not employer 'crafts-

---

[1] Among the Carrickfergus freemen of 1832 was James M'Key, a 'black servant' (*A Return of the names, occupations, and residences of the registered freeholders, leaseholders, and £10 householders, included in the return made to the House of Commons on the 25th day of February 1834, by the clerk of the County of the Town of Carrickfergus*, H.C. 1834 (329), xliii, 563).

[2] *Commissioners [on] . . . the freemen electors of the City of Dublin*, H.C. 1870 [C 93], xxxiii, 5; E. Bullen, *Five reports of the committee of the Precursor Association* (Dublin, 1839), pp. 55–6.

[3] *A Return of the electors registered in each county, county of a city, county of a town, and borough in Ireland*, H.C. 1833 (177), xxvii, 289–311; *Returns in tabular form of the different cities and boroughs in Ireland, in which the freeman franchise at present exists*, H.C. 1867–8 (305), lvi, 515–16.

[4] In two-member constituencies one could either 'plump' for a single candidate, vote for two candidates of the same party (a double), or split one's votes between opposing parties.

[5] See, e.g., *Report from the select committee on the Carrickfergus election petition*, H.C. 1833 (181), viii, 137–9; *D.E.P.* 8 Dec. 1835; *Fictitious Votes, Ireland*, 2nd series, 1st report, p. 169; M. Green to M. J. Blake, 16 July 1847, and E. Kelly to M. J. Blake, 27 July 1847, Blake of Ballyglunin Papers M6936/58; Lord Glengall to Lord Stanley, 16 Oct. 1849, Derby Papers 120/2; M. Morris to Lord Clanricarde, 23 Mar. 1857, T. Reid to Clanricarde, 27 Mar. 1857, T. Burke to Clanricarde, 19 Apr. [1857], Clanricarde Papers 40; *Report of the Commissioners appointed to investigate into the existence of corrupt practices in elections of members to serve in parliament for the County of the Town of Galway*, H.C. 1857–8 [2291], xxvi, 314 and 317; *Galway Vindicator*, 20, 23, 27 Apr. 1859; Bishop MacEvilly to Archbishop Cullen, 10 Nov. 1864, Cullen Papers; E. L. O'Malley and H. Hardcastle, *Reports of the decisions of the judges for the trial of election petitions in England and Ireland*, i (London, 1869), pp. 270–1.

men'.[1] Because of their Protestantism[2] the freemen acted as an important reservoir of Tory strength, for, although open to bribery, they were generally more receptive to Tory than to Liberal gold. Not that support could be relied upon gratuitously, as the Dublin Conservatives found to their cost in 1847 and 1865.[3] And although there were often tensions between more prosperous Protestants and their poorer brethren,[4] without the freeman bloc, Conservatives would never have been able to dominate the Dublin City seats or manage to gain those occasional victories in Catholic towns such as Cork (1835, 1849, 1876), Waterford (1832, 1841, 1857, 1859), Youghal (1852), Athlone (1835, 1841, 1856), and Kinsale (1835, 1847) which kept their cause alive until the last twenty years of the century.[5]

A final combination of unintentional oversight and intentional timidity further rendered the Irish Reform Act a highly unpredictable vehicle for the translation of intention into effect.[6] Anxious to let as many sleeping dogs as possible lie undisturbed, the ministry had simply continued the Irish system of voter registration established in 1727. This differed substantially from that introduced for the first time in England in 1832. In Ireland the voter was required to prove his title on registry, but, having once registered, he obtained a 'certificate' (a document unknown elsewhere) which entitled him to vote for eight years without further investigation and, in practice, regardless of whether he retained possession or occupation of the relevant property. Voters died or emigrated, yet their names remained on the registers and their certificates could be given to others, who, if

[1] See the Galway list for 1832 in Blake of Ballyglunin Papers M6935/5, and Dublin City Poll Book for 1842 (noted in Appendix—Tables 8, 9, and 10); *Return of the names, occupations, and residences of the registered freeholders . . . by the clerk of the County of the Town of Carrickfergus*, H.C. 1834 (329), xliii, 549-67; *Commissioners [on] . . . the freemen electors of the City of Dublin*, H.C. 1870 [C 93], xxxiii, 1103.

[2] *Hansard*, xxxi, 1035 (29 Feb. 1836); *Commissioners [on] . . . the freemen electors of the City of Dublin*, H.C. 1870 [C 93], xxxiii, 5; *First report of the commissioners appointed to inquire into the municipal corporations in Ireland: Appendix . . . Part I*, H.C. 1835 [27], xxvii, 298.

[3] Lord Clarendon to Lord John Russell, 5 Aug. 1847, Clarendon Papers L.-B. I; *Commissioners [on] . . . the freemen electors of the City of Dublin*, H.C. 1870 [C 93], xxxiii, 7-20.

[4] Jacqueline Hill, 'The Protestant response to Repeal: The case of the Dublin working class' in *Ireland under the Union: Varieties of tension: Essays in honour of T. W. Moody*, ed. F. S. L. Lyons and R. A. J. Hawkins (Oxford, 1980), pp. 35-68; I. d'Alton, *Protestant Society and Politics in Cork 1812-1844* (Cork, 1980). See also Chapter IV below.

[5] Overwhelmingly the freemen voted Tory. See *Commissioners [on] . . . the freemen electors of the City of Dublin*, H.C. 1870 [C 93], xxxiii, 6-11; T. M. Ray to O'Connell, 20 Feb. 1840, O'Connell Papers N.L.I. MS 13646; F. E. to W. Currey, 14 Feb. 1857, Lismore Papers MS 7188; *Drogheda Argus*, 30 Apr. 1859; *C.C.* 5 May 1859; *Central Conservative Society of Ireland: Report of the Sub-Committee 1859* (Mayo Papers MS 11025); *Report from the select committee on the Cork City election petition*, H.C. 1852-3 (528), xi, 97.

[6] For more detailed treatment of what follows, see K. T. Hoppen, 'Politics, the law, and the nature of the Irish electorate 1832-1850', *English Historical Review*, xcii (1977), 746-76.

prepared to perjure themselves, could not be prevented from voting in their stead. In addition, voters could not easily be prevented from acquiring more and more certificates at successive registration sessions. Impersonation became breathtakingly easy. At Belfast in the 1830s 618 certificates were issued to no more than 197 claimants and at the election of 1841 the Tories imported sixty men from Monaghan, provided them with 'plenty of whiskey, and all sorts of disguises, in the shape of wigs and different suits of clothes' and dispatched them to vote early and often on behalf of those who had departed to Glasgow, America, or to another world.[1] And although the Irish Franchise Act of 1850 made things less childishly easy, impersonation had by then become an integral part of Irish electoral life. The grand traditions of Belfast in 1841, Galway in 1847, and Cork in 1835 and 1837 were echoed in Co. Carlow in 1852, Lisburn in 1863, Co. Galway in 1872 (where 'the son thinks he has a right to vote if his name is the same as his father's'), Athlone in 1880, and North Fermanagh in 1885.[2]

The certificate system meant that after the first registration of 1832 no one could tell exactly how many voters there were at any one time until the reforms of 1850 made accurate enumeration possible. Virtually all the statistics tossed about by contemporaries and by historians are, therefore, utterly bogus. Sharp 'increases' and 'decreases' allegedly resulting from heightened political tensions or enfeebling torpor are mere chimeras. The best estimates that can be made suggest that between 1832 and 1850, at a time when the population as a whole was increasing, the electorate was declining, slowly at first and then more quickly.[3] 'Usually well-informed' local sources were driven to educated guesswork.[4]

[1] [Durham Dunlop], *A brief historical sketch of parliamentary elections in Belfast, from the first general election under the Reform Act till 1865* (Belfast, [1865]), p. 12; J. E. Tennent to Stanley, 22 July 1841, Derby Papers 131/7; *Hansard*, lxiii, 1534 (14 June 1842); *Report from the select committee on the Belfast election compromise*, H.C. 1842 (431), v, 308, 321-37.

[2] These are only selected cases. See John— to M. J. Blake, 12 Feb. 1847, Blake of Ballyglunin Papers M6936/58; *Fictitious Votes, Ireland*, 2nd series, 1st report, p. 200; J. D. Jackson to Sir Robert Peel, 28 Sept. 1837, Peel Papers Add. MS 40424; J. Lord, *Popery at the hustings: foreign and domestic legislation* (London, 1852), pp. 8-9; *Banner of Ulster*, 4 Apr. 1857; F. S. P. Wolferstan and S. Bristowe, *Reports of the decisions of election committees during the eighteenth parliament of the United Kingdom* (London, 1865), pp. 221-8; *Copy of the evidence taken at the trial of the Galway County election petition*, H.C. 1872 (241-I), xlviii, 826; E. L. O'Malley and H. Hardcastle, *Reports of the decisions of the judges*, iii (1881), pp. 55-60; P. M. Bottomley, 'The North Fermanagh elections of 1885 and 1886', *Clogher Record*, viii (1974), 174.

[3] K. T. Hoppen, 'Politics, the law, and the nature of the Irish electorate 1832-1850', p. 751. In the counties it is probable that the 'real' electorate dropped by more than 5 per cent between 1832 and 1840. By 1848 the drop was much greater, though the boroughs held their numbers more successfully (see Lord Farnham's memorandum of 1850, Clanricarde Papers 35).

[4] Clonmel: *D.E.P.* 29 July 1837; Belfast: *Hansard*, liii, 49 (25 Mar. 1840); Co. Longford,

	Nominal Electorate	'Real' Electorate
Clonmel (1837)	795	526
Belfast (1840)	6,000	1,900
Co. Cork (1840)	6,700	4,400
Dublin (1840)	18,000	9,000
Co. Dublin (1840)	4,000	2,900
Co. Longford (1840)	2,731	1,294
Co. Mayo (1840)	2,057	650
Waterford (1840)	2,654	1,148
Dundalk (1841)	559	300
Coleraine (1842)	368	240
Kinsale (1847)	429	213

If numbers did not respond smartly to the legislator's whip, even less so did the social composition of the electorate reflect the expectations of 1832. Negligent draughtsmanship made the assessment of freehold and leasehold values dependent more on judicial whim than legislative precept. And this was of crucial importance, because in Ireland an electoral freeholder was almost invariably not an owner in fee, but a tenant whose lease included one or more 'lives' as opposed to a fixed term of years. Confusions as to whether value should be assessed by the generous 'beneficial interest' test used before 1829 or the restrictive 'solvent tenant' test enforced thereafter led to what was politely called 'hard swearing', to a complete lack of accord among the assistant barristers appointed to hold registration sessions, and to appeals against exclusion aimed at the next circuit judge most likely to sympathize with the appellant's cause. As a Liberal barrister succeeded a Tory so the beneficial interest replaced the solvent tenant test. Of the forty-four election petitions tried between 1833 and 1840, twenty-four were concerned with value.[1] In boroughs too the assessment of household values created problems. In direct defiance of the act, claimants insisted that 'value' meant 'value to them' as traders or artisans. And barristers did not resist, one admitting eighty voters in Clonmel (15.4 per cent of the electorate) on the test case of a boatman who lived in the cellar of a house for which he paid 1*s*. 2*d*. a week, but who swore the cellar was worth ten pounds *to him* in his business, and that, in addition, 'his wife sold meat there'. Other barristers adopted rent as a criterion. Others again

Dublin, Co. Dublin, Waterford, Co. Cork: *Hansard*, liv, 191, 220, 1337–40 (18 May and 19 June 1840); Co. Mayo: *Hansard*, lvi, 290 (4 Feb. 1841); Dundalk: D. Molony to T. M. Ray, 13 Dec. 1841, O'Connell Papers N.L.I. MS 13623; Coleraine: Lord De Grey to Sir James Graham, 15 Oct. 1842, Graham Papers 1/Ir; Kinsale: *Minutes of evidence taken before the select committee on the Kinsale election petition*, H.C. 1847–8 (138), xiii, 12 and 145.

[1] *The Irish franchise and registration question* (London, 1841), pp. 18–23 (copy in R.I.A. Halliday Pamphlets 1816).

were driven to perambulating the streets to assess houses according to some unrevealed standard of their own. The judges, as usual, made matters worse and blandly continued to hand down contradictory decisions according to entirely political predilections.[1]

The result of all this was not to lower or raise the franchise, but to place it upon so unpredictable a base that admission and exclusion seemed merely arbitrary. Landlords, by refusing leases, could and did reduce the county electorate. Their reasons were partly political but mainly economic, for leases restricted the price-responsiveness of rent, a lesson bitterly learned during the Napoleonic boom. Leases became fewer throughout the 1830s and 1840s.[2] In Waterford the real electorate was halved between 1832 and 1841. In Meath even those landlords still prepared to grant leases were limiting their duration to thirteen years so as to undershoot the minimum required by franchise legislation.[3] By the mid-1840s almost two-thirds of the tenants on the estates of ten of the largest proprietors in Ireland had no leases of any kind, and the same was true elsewhere.[4] Although the standards of the poor-law valuators who began work in the late 1830s were not those of the assistant barristers, it is still an indication of the extent to which leasing and other technical problems had reduced the pool of potential electors that by 1840 only 7.1 per cent of those farmers with poor-law valuations of ten pounds and over actually had the vote, while the figure for those over twenty pounds (who could hardly have been excluded by any reasonable criterion of value) was still only 8.3 per cent.[5] Only the small minority of landlords prepared to sacrifice income to influence continued to grant leases in order, as Lord Downshire put it in 1838, to 'keep an imposing

[1] H. J. Perry and J. W. Knapp, *Cases of controverted elections in the eleventh parliament of the United Kingdom* (London, 1833), pp. 425–34; J. Alcock to Stanley, 25 Jan. 1841, Derby Papers 20/9.

[2] *Hansard*, lvi, 1114 (22 Apr. 1841); G. Lyne, 'The General Association of Ireland, 1836–7' (University College Dublin MA thesis, 1968), pp. 81–2; *Hansard*, lvi, 1104; D. Bullen, 'Statistics of an improved rural district (the Parish of Kilmurray) in the County of Cork', *Journal of the Statistical Society*, vi (1843), 352–4; Lord Ebrington to Russell, 19 Apr. 1841, Russell Papers 30/22/4A.

[3] *Hansard*, lvi, 808 (22 Feb. 1841); F. R. Bertolacci to Sir Charles Trevelyan, 21 Nov. 1848, Broadlands Archive 27M60, Box cxix; P. Q. Barron to T. M. Ray, 1 Nov. 1841, O'Connell Papers N.L.I. MS 13623 (Waterford); *Minutes of evidence taken before the select committee of the House of Lords, appointed to inquire into the state of Ireland since the year 1835 in respect to Crime and Outrage*, H.C. 1839 (486), xi and xii, Q. 1493 ff. (Meath).

[4] In the case of the ten landlords, only some estates in nine counties and all four provinces (totalling 149,059 acres) were examined by the government: see the Confidential Print in Derby Papers 32. The exact proportion without leases was 62.6 per cent. See also J. Evatt to Lord Ashburton, 8 Apr. 1840, Bath Papers Irish Box, apropos of the Bath estate in Monaghan.

[5] Calculated from figures relating to twenty-six unions in *Third General Report relative to the Valuations for poor rates, and to the registered elective franchise in Ireland*, H.C. 1841 [329], xxiii, 651–3.

number of voters'.[1] Some held rents artificially low in order to increase the 'interest' of reliable tenants and thus entitle them to register. Some even attended revision sessions and gave on-the-spot rent abatements to favoured claimants in danger of rejection on grounds of value—for the lower the rent the higher the 'interest'.[2] The arbitrariness of all this created considerable resentment.

Changes in the nature and distribution of different sizes of holding had an equal, though even less controllable, impact upon the electorate. The almost irresistible pressure towards subdivision pushed many farmers below the amount necessary for enfranchisement. On Viscount Palmerston's estate in Sligo the tenants' 'ruinous practice . . . of dividing and subdividing their holdings' had in one place left 236 out of 239 with rents 'considerably less than five pounds' and little hope of the vote. In the Donegal parish of Glencolumkille in 1837 only one tenant paid more than twelve pounds, the majority being rented between twelve and eighty shillings a year.[3] In any case, some three out of four members of the adult male agricultural labour force in 1841 were not even tenant farmers of any description, while in towns like Dublin, Drogheda, Galway, Cork, and Limerick the proportion of employed males over fifteen described as labourers, porters, or servants ranged from a quarter to almost two-fifths.[4] In the towns too, degrees of enfranchisement could depend crucially upon variables such as the local level of house prices and values. The failure of attempts to introduce a sliding franchise scale, with twenty pounds required for the vote in the large boroughs, fifteen in those between 500 and 1,000 voters, and ten in the smaller places,[5] meant that the qualification was effectively less exclusive in towns like Dublin (where 84.2 per cent of tenements were reckoned to be worth ten pounds) than in, for example, Ennis or Tralee (with proportions of 20.9 and 26.1 per cent respectively).[6]

---

[1] Downshire to W. E. Reilly, 18 Dec. 1838, in *Letters of a great Irish landlord: A selection from the estate correspondence of the third Marquess of Downshire, 1809–45*, ed. W. A. Maguire (Belfast, 1974), pp. 114–15. See also R. Smith to Lord Rossmore, 6 Oct. 1834, Rossmore Papers T2929/8/3; J. Pratt to Farnham, 8 Jan. 1835, Farnham Papers MS 18602; Johnston & Fawcett to J. Dicken, 4 Aug. 1847, Morley Papers Deposit 69.

[2] *Fictitious Votes, Ireland*, 2nd series, 3rd report, pp. 213, 262–3; *D.E.P.* 1 June 1837.

[3] I. Leister, *Das Werden der Agrarlandschaft in der Grafschaft Tipperary (Irland)*: Heft 18 in Marburger Geographische Schriften (Marburg, 1963), p. 206; J. Kincaid to Palmerston, 31 Oct. and 21 Nov. 1839, Broadlands Archive 27M60, Box cxix; *D.E.P.* 1 July 1837.

[4] See Chapter II, Table 22 below; also 1841 census under the respective towns.

[5] W. Paton to Archbishop Beresford, 4 June 1838, Peel Papers Add. MS 40425. See also L. G. Jones to O'Connell, 30 Dec. 1831, *Correspondence of Daniel O'Connell*, ed. M. R. O'Connell, iv, 390–4; *Hansard*, xiii, 1258 (2 July 1832).

[6] *Copy of Instructions*, H.C. 1831–2 (519), xliii, 8–13. Percentages elsewhere included Waterford 48.4, Galway 15.8, Limerick 26.2, Youghal 39.9, Sligo 30.4, Londonderry 36.0, Downpatrick 31.8, Lisburn 14.2—so size alone was no guide.

The size and composition of borough electorates were also at the mercy of the numerous conflicting interpretations placed upon the requirement that voters be up to date in the payment of local taxes. Dublin was notorious: expansionist Liberals tried to restrict things to grand-jury cess, pipe-water rent, paving and lighting tax, police tax, and wide-street tax, while exclusionist Tories insisted on another dozen payments—including exotics like Rutland Square tax, cholera tax, and Quay Wall tax—as essential prerequisites to registration and polling.[1] Municipal electors in Belfast were mown down by as much as one-half because of tax-payment failures in the 1840s. Youghal voters unable to pay seven shillings were disqualified in 1835. The Dublin election committee of 1847 spent seventy-two days untangling the problem which the then chief secretary, Sir William Somerville, thought amounted 'to something very like a disfranchisement as regards a very large proportion of the voters'.[2]

The weight of impressionistic evidence and the available statistical information make it clear, not only that large numbers of indigent men whom the legislators of 1832 had sought to exclude were able to register, but that even larger numbers who were universally considered qualified to vote were debarred. Reports shrieked into Dublin Castle and newspaper letter-columns to the effect that idiosyncratic assistant barristers were announcing that 'no one can know the value of land better than the applicant' and admitting hordes of 'shabbies' and 'smellies' to the registers.[3] In Kerry observers 'beheld the miserable, squalid wretches, some half washed, brought forward by their priests to vote'. In King's Co. 'fellows' were 'coming forward to register out of five or six acres of land they pay from a pound to thirty shillings an acre for'.[4] Anecdotes were exchanged by

[1] *Report of the committee, appointed at a public meeting held in Dublin, Thursday, March 19, 1840, to consider the effect of Lord Stanley's Registration Bill* (n.d.), pp. 11–12 (copy in Derby Papers 20/9); T. Smith to Graham, 22 Mar. 1844, Graham Papers 14/Ir.

[2] *Report of the committee . . . March 19, 1840, passim*; O'Connell to Lord Morpeth, 10 June 1838, *Correspondence of Daniel O'Connell*, ed. M. R. O'Connell, vi, 166–9; [D. Dunlop], *Brief historical sketch of parliamentary elections in Belfast*, p. 104; J. W. Knapp and E. Ombler, *Cases of controverted elections in the twelfth parliament of the United Kingdom* (London, 1837), pp. 444–50; D. Power, H. Rodwell, and E. L'E. Dew, *Reports of the decisions of committees of the House of Commons in the trial of controverted elections during the fifteenth parliament of the United Kingdom* (London, 1853), pp. 190–207; Sir William Somerville's memorandum on the franchise of Oct. 1848 in Somerville's Letter-Book T2982.

[3] E. M. Kelly to Downshire, 8 Feb. 1838, Downshire Papers D671/C/12/704; also H. J. Perry and J. W. Knapp, *Cases of controverted elections*, pp. 425–34; *Dublin Evening Mail*, 28 Jan. 1835; *D.E.P.* 3 Feb. 1838; Revd M. Beresford to Farnham, 12 Jan. 1837, Farnham Papers MS 18608; *Hansard*, lvi, 846 (22 Feb. 1841); *The Irish franchise and registration question* (1841), pp. 38–44, 59–61; *Fictitious Votes, Ireland*, 1st series, 1st report, pp. 18, 60, 135–41, 187, 216; ibid., 2nd series, 1st report, pp. 62–7.

[4] T. A. Ponsonby to Peel, 31 Jan. 1835, Peel Papers Add. MS 40412; Cutting of 18 Nov. 1832 in Earl of Charleville's scrap-book, Howard Bury Papers T3069/D/34.

scandalized Conservatives: the Waterford freeholder with three roods of ground at thirty-six shillings; the three-acre tenant on the Bath estate in Monaghan; the enfranchised Catholic 'peasants' of Meath 'in occupation of a miserable hut or a rood of land'; tenants in Co. Carlow with three-quarters of an acre rented at two guineas; farmers in King's Co. with a mere five acres for which they paid fifty-two shillings.[1] In the boroughs the story was pitched even more chillingly up the Tory spine. Most of the freeholders in Galway (a county of a town) were later found to have poor-law valuations below ten pounds. In Dungarvan pauperized fishermen formed a large element in the electorate. A single house in Dublin yielded three votes: 'one a carpenter, who had half the shop at ten shillings a week, the other a blacksmith holding the other half at seven shillings a week, and the third the occupant of the cellar who paid five shillings'. Half the 418 voters registered in Sligo were 'paupers who will take from £20 to £50 as their price'. In Cork about an eighth of the voters lived in houses valued at less than *five* pounds for local rating purposes.[2] 'I do not think' the house fit, said a Cork shopkeeper, 'for the habitation of any human being . . . it is without a roof . . . the rain must come in most parts and did.' In Longford the average voter's house was forty by sixteen by ten feet and built at a cost of ten pounds. At Kinsale in 1837 men set out to vote from two-roomed cabins with mud floors and mud walls.[3] More dramatic still, because more conclusive, was the situation at Youghal in 1835, where surviving rate books reveal a quite extraordinary state of things in that the mean valuation of the household voters (£16. 18s.) was actually lower than that of the rated inhabitants as a whole (£17. 14s.). This was not the mark either of an élite or of the 'competent and respectable constituency', which, in Stanley's view, it had been the purpose of the reform act to provide.[4]

[1] J. Alcock to Stanley, 29 June 1840, Derby Papers 20/9; J. Evatt to Lord Bath, 4 Dec. 1832, Bath Papers Irish Box; *Dublin Evening Mail*, 23 Jan. 1835; *Hansard*, xxx, 706 (19 Aug. 1835); *Fictitious Votes, Ireland*, 2nd series, 3rd report, p. 384.

[2] M. J. Finehy to M. J. Blake, 25 June 1841, Blake of Ballyglunin Papers M6936/46; Report of S. Jones, 30 July 1837, O.P. 1837/620/60, Box 53; *Fictitious Votes, Ireland*, 1st series, 3rd report, p. 283; *Dublin Evening Mail*, 6 Feb. 1835; J. Walker to Palmerston, 22 Nov. 1832, Broadlands Archive 27M60, Box cxxiii; *Hansard*, xxx, 776 (20 Aug. 1835), and liv, 1339–40 (19 June 1840); *Fictitious Votes, Ireland*, 2nd series, 1st report, pp. 62–7— most of the rural voters in Cork City had small fifty-shilling cabins and conacre plots (ibid. 14–15, 259, 278, 290).

[3] *Fictitious Votes, Ireland*, 2nd series, 1st report, pp. 118–19, also 78; *Minutes of evidence taken before the committee on the Longford County election petitions*, H.C. 1837 (319), x, 233; *Minutes of evidence taken before the select committee on the Kinsale election petition*, H.C. 1837–8 (332), xii, 91. Thus some of Kinsale's 180 supposedly 'respectable' household voters lived in the bottom third of houses in the town (see 1841 census).

[4] The 1835 poll book and the rate book for 1833 are among the Youghal Corporation Records at present in the keeping of Cork Archives Council. The former is printed with an

The nature of the electorate as a whole was finally pinned down by a government inquiry in 1841. Earlier impressions of arbitrary distribution and social mixing were fully confirmed. In fifteen boroughs 23.7 per cent of the voters had valuations below £10 and 12.7 per cent below even £8. In six boroughs where rent information was available 17.5 per cent paid less than £10 a year and 13.8 per cent less than £8. As ever, the figures varied greatly, with the percentage of voters valued under £10 ranging from 6.0 in Dublin, through 20.6 in Limerick and Cork, to 37.6 in Sligo and 44.3 in Armagh. In the county constituencies the majority of voters were of course farmers of one kind or another—more than three out of four by the 1860s.[1] At the December 1837 registration sessions for Armagh less than one in ten of those enrolled were anything else; much the same was true two years later in Roscommon. At Donegal in June 1837 all were farmers, and modest farmers at that: they paid on average below fifteen pounds rent and some of them held as little as five acres of poor land. Contemporaries were shocked by this, for even Repealers tended to believe that county voters should be men paying at least thirty pounds on holdings of not less than twenty acres or so.[2] Official investigations, out of which it is possible to construct a detailed profile of the pre-Famine county electorate (or, more strictly speaking, of its overwhelmingly dominant rural part), soon made the shock greater still (see Table 1).

Behind the solid averages lay great local differences. At the extremes were the poor law unions of Gort (in Galway and Clare), whose electors held a mean of 12 acres at £22. 19s. valuation, and Edenderry (in King's Co., Kildare, and Meath), where the comparable figures were 88 acres at £73. 13s. Most significant of all is the information on rent for twenty unions with 'representative' electorates. Here 23.4 per cent paid less than £10 a year, while 9.8 per cent paid under £5, and only 31.2 per cent more than £30. Such figures are striking indeed, for they show how mixed was the electorate and how improbable must be the suggestion that O'Connell found his 'political center [sic] of gravity located largely in the 100-acre

introduction in Ann Barry and K. T. Hoppen, 'Borough politics in O'Connellite Ireland: The Youghal poll books of 1835 and 1837', *Journal of the Cork Historical and Archaeological Society*, lxxxiii (1978), 106-46, and lxxxiv (1979), 15-43. For Stanley's remark, see *Hansard*, ix, 598 (19 Jan. 1832).

[1] Borough valuation figures calculated from *Third General Report relative to the Valuations*, H.C. 1841 [329], xxiii, 653-6 and 713. For proportion of farmers in county electorate, see Chapter II, Table 23.

[2] *Newry Telegraph*, 14 Dec. 1837; Clonalis Papers 9.2.HS.161; *Pilot*, 21 June 1837; F. W. B. Mullins in *Hansard*, xiii, 808 (18 June 1832).

TABLE 1
Profile of county electorate, 1840

	Under* £10 PLV per cent	Under* £15 PLV per cent	Under 10 acres per cent	10 acres to under 20 acres per cent	20 acres to under 50 acres per cent	50 acres and over per cent	Mean holding acres	Mean PLV £	Mean Rate £	Mean Rent per acre	N
Leinster	14.1	27.6	22.4	14.7	33.0	29.9	43	38	46	18s.	2,409
Munster	15.4	26.7	14.3	11.4	39.3	35.0	50	35	47	14s.	2,587
Ulster	10.3	30.3	8.2	26.7	50.3	14.8	33	24	28	14s.	2,403
Connacht	35.3	61.5	18.4	34.3	38.5	8.8	25	18	23	14s.	1,144
Ireland	16.0	32.4	15.4 (48.0)†	19.7 (24.4)†	40.5 (18.4)†	24.4 (9.2)†	40	30	38	15s.	8,543

PLV = Poor law valuation

* See also Table 4

† Figures in parentheses are for *all* 'persons holding land' with holdings in 1844–5 of one acre and more in this category (based on table in P. M. A. Bourke, 'The agricultural statistics of the 1841 Census of Ireland: A critical review', *Economic History Review*, 2nd series xviii (1965), 380).

farmer'.[1] In 1841 only one in fifteen ten-pound county freeholders came into so high a category, and 4,000 men, however spritely, could hardly have filled the front lawn at Darrynane let alone have provided the fulcrum with which to move the Irish countryside.

Proposals in the 1840s that the freehold franchise be based upon a fixed amount of poor-law valuation revealed further inconsistencies. Even O'Connell's Precursor Association admitted (as Table 1 reveals) that a ten-pound poor-law requirement would exclude many existing voters, and so did the sympathetic Whig Chief Secretary, Lord Morpeth. Even levels as low as eight and five pounds would still, experts conceded, 'deprive many of their votes'.[2] The principal attribute required of the existing heterogeneous collection of county voters was of course the possession of certain types of lease, and it was this (in addition to the complexities of registration law) which drove so haphazard a wedge between those admitted and those left out. Thus less than one in fifteen of those occupying tenements valued at eight pounds and above actually enjoyed the vote, while those who were registered included many valued at lower amounts.[3] Even at so high a valuation as forty pounds (equivalent roughly to a rent of fifty pounds) less than a quarter of occupiers were able to vote, with enormous county differences—7.6 per cent in Roscommon but 37.6 per cent in Wicklow—explicable only in terms of local tenurial and registration procedures. Certainly such substantial farmers constituted a surprisingly small proportion of the actual electorate. By 1842 less than 15 per cent of voters occupied farms valued at forty pounds, with county figures reflecting the heavy concentration of large farmers in areas such as Meath (36.5 per cent) and Wicklow (33.5 per cent) and of smaller agriculturalists in Monaghan (4.8 per cent) and Leitrim (2.7 per cent), though a residual element of unpredictability meant that the relative local strength of forty-pound voters was no simple function of the general ubiquity of such farmers in any particular county as a whole.[4]

The effects of the reforms of 1832 were not, therefore, to preserve existing voters and extend the franchise horizontally downwards through the broadening social pyramid of the time. Instead, electors

[1] E. Larkin, 'Church, state, and nation in modern Ireland', *American Historical Review*, lxxx (1975), 1247.

[2] E. Bullen, *Five reports of the committee of the Precursor Association*; *Hansard*, lvi, 287 (4 Feb. 1841); *Third General Report relative to the Valuations*, H.C. 1841 [329], xxiii, 613-15, 666; D. R. Pigot to Morpeth, 19 Jan. [1841], Carlisle Papers L.-B. 41.

[3] *Third General Report relative to the Valuations*, H.C. 1841 [329], xxiii, 651-3—based on a sample of twenty-six unions (none of which contained parliamentary boroughs) and 68,285 tenements.

[4] Based on data for seventeen counties only (seven in Ulster, three in Connacht, seven in Leinster) in the Confidential Print of Nov. 1843 by the Chief Secretary, Lord Eliot (Derby

were, to a remarkable extent, drawn from a similar social range as non-electors. No one, however, was satisfied with this. Tories and Whigs baulked at the unexpected presence of the great unwashed. O'Connellites too feared that marginal men were open to bribery and complained loudly that 'comfortable-looking' Repealers were being excluded to make room for the helots of the aristocracy.[1] All parties canvassed remedial legislation, and on the franchise alone no less than fourteen bills were printed between 1835 and 1850. The two most serious efforts were made by Stanley for the Tories in 1840-1 and Morpeth (then chief secretary) for the Whigs and Repealers in 1841. Stanley's bills,[2] which proposed annual registration along English lines, the abolition of certificates, and the definite adoption of the strict solvent tenant test, although undoubtedly partisan, were the work of one of the few men to understand the details of the problem. In 1841 they yielded precedence to Morpeth's government bill. This too proposed annual revision, the abolition of certificates, and appeal against admission as well as rejection to help expel the obviously unqualified. It also contained, however, the revolutionary proposal that the county franchise be put on the unequivocal basis of occupancy of property on a fourteen-year lease to the poor-law valuation of five (later eight) pounds.[3] Although a lease was still required, this was to prove an important step towards the solution adopted nine years later. O'Connell was enthusiastic, but the opposition managed to defeat the bill and it was abandoned.

What is most remarkable about all this is the ill-informed ingenuity behind so many of the proposals, as bored ministers grappled with the tedious but mildly pressing problems of the Irish electorate. Stanley's ideas alone had the merits of simplicity. The rest were based upon the endearing but already hopelessly exploded notion—exploded in England as well as Ireland[4]—that an ideal electorate could be created by a fine-tuning of complex sets of social and legislative

Papers 32), and in the printed 'Statement of the number of parliamentary electors on the registeries of Ireland, in January 1842' (ibid. 28/3).

[1] *D.E.P.* 7 Jan. 1837 and 2 Jan. 1841; Ebrington to Morpeth, 1 Mar. 1841, Carlisle Papers L.-B. 42; Same to Same, 17 Mar. 1841, Fortescue Papers 1262M/LI187; *Pilot*, 26 June 1837; *Kilkenny Journal*, 4 Jan. 1837; *Dublin Evening Mail*, 12 Jan. 1835; John O'Connell, *Recollections and Experiences during a parliamentary career from 1833 to 1848*, 2 vols. (London, 1849), i, 146-7.

[2] For the long debates in 1840, see *Hansard*, lii, 615-42; liii, 27-157; liv, 179-237, 323-460, 1049-99, 1306-65; lv, 120-59, 375-407, 458-63, when the bill foundered in committee.

[3] The debates are in *Hansard*, lvi, 274-312, 778-854, 862-939, 941-1016, 1024-131; lvii, 1073-137, 1167-242, 1252-89, when the bill foundered in committee.

[4] For a brilliant account of the unexpected turns taken by franchise matters in England, see J. Prest, *Politics in the age of Cobden* (London, 1977), which also contains an excellent discussion of Ireland (pp. 51-71) complementary to the present account.

variables. The palm for impractical intricacy must go to the brothers-in-law Charles Wood and Viscount Howick, who pressed, firstly, for a franchise based upon claimants having poor-law valuations at least five pounds higher than their rents, and, secondly, for one dependent upon ownership in fee simple of property valued at five pounds. The former would have been no better than existing arrangements, the latter was a triumph of hope over reality in a country where fee-simple owners were (apart from landlords themselves) virtually an extinct species.[1] The Tories too often behaved like some modern-day economist who still maintains, against all experience, that a little push here and a little pull there will somehow succeed when all previous adjustments have failed. Lord Clancarty wanted a combination of Chandos-type voters at £30 PLV [Poor Law Valuation], free-holders of £16 (a splendidly precise figure) with rents no higher than valuations, and freeholders under £16 if the gross annual value on the poor-law books exceeded rent by at least ten pounds. Sir James Graham, the home secretary, favoured a rental test but could not decide whether the point of exclusion should lie at twenty, twenty-five, thirty, thirty-five, or fifty pounds, while the Irish chief secretary, Lord Eliot, drew up plans of even more heroic complexity.[2] Only a few doughty extremists knew exactly what they wanted. The tiny Irish Universal Suffrage Association demanded votes for all (men), the ballot, annual parliaments, equal constituencies, payment of MPs, and other Chartist panaceas. A handful of Tory hard-liners demanded a system so exclusive as to disfranchise all but gentlemen farmers.[3] O'Connell's interventions were generally negative rather than constructive, while his Confederate rivals lived up to their élitist view of politics by nervously declaring the suffrage an 'open question' among the sword-waving ranks of Young Irelanders.[4]

Only the complete collapse of the electorate under the twin pressures of lease scarcity and the Great Famine made reform

[1] Ebrington to Russell, 19 Apr. 1841, Russell Papers 30/22/4A; C. Wood to Ebrington, 15 Mar. 1841, Fortescue Papers 1262M/LI186; Ebrington to Morpeth, 17 Mar, 1841, ibid. LI187; Ebrington to Wood, 21 Mar. 1841, ibid. LI188; Wood to Ebrington, 25 Mar. 1841, ibid. LI190; D. R. Pigot to Morpeth, [Feb. 1841], Carlisle Papers L.-B. 41.

[2] Clancarty reported in Eliot to Graham, 8 Dec. 1841, Graham Papers 8/Ir; Graham to Eliot, 5 Nov. 1841, ibid. 8/Ir; Eliot to Graham, 19 Dec. 1842, ibid. 1/Ir. By the so-called Chandos Clause in the *English* Reform Act of 1832 farmers paying £50 or more in rent were given the vote—even if they had no lease of any kind.

[3] *Civil and religious liberty: Address of the Irish Universal Suffrage Association to the Most Rev. and Right Rev. the Roman Catholic archbishops and bishops of Ireland* (Dublin, 1843)—copy in R.I.A. Halliday Pamphlets 1868; Glengall to Stanley, [1841], Derby Papers 120/2; Clancarty to Stanley, 13 Aug. 1841, ibid. 134/3.

[4] K. T. Hoppen, 'Politics, the law, and the nature of the Irish electorate 1832–1850', pp. 765–6; T. Davis to W. S. O'Brien, [1844], Smith O'Brien Papers MS 432; Irish Confederation Minute Book R. I. A. MS 23/H/44.

unavoidable. Voters simply melted away. Tipperary's effective electorate slumped from 2,369 in 1832 to about 200 in 1849. Armagh was down from 3,342 to 700, Tyrone from 1,151 to 800, Mayo from 1,350 to 250.[1] Even the total 'nominal' county electorate had fallen from 60,597 to 27,180, though the latter figure was still grossly inflated and a reasonable estimate of *effective* county voters in 1849-50 would probably lie in the region of 15,000 to 18,000. In the boroughs, where leasing was less important and the population dropped less rapidly, numbers held steady at about the 29,471 of 1832. Overall, however, the electorate had fallen from 121,194 to around 45,000.[2] Even Russell's government, never remarkable in its Irish policy for seeking to substitute action for anxious immobility, could hardly close its eyes. After a few half-hearted limbering-up exercises, Sir William Somerville, the chief secretary, introduced a bill in 1850, which, as the Irish Franchise Act (13 & 14 Vict., c. 69), was to become the single most important legislative influence upon the make-up of the electorate and the course of electoral politics in nineteenth-century Ireland. Two crucial changes were made. First, the whole system of registration was overhauled. Out went certificates and octennial revision, in came a so-called 'automatic' system in which voters' lists were officially maintained and no positive claim was necessary for inclusion. Second, although existing franchises were retained, they were in effect replaced, both in counties and boroughs, by a new franchise based solely on the *occupation* of property to a certain poor-law valuation together with some simple tax and residence requirements. The confusions of earlier tests of value disappeared, as did the notion that the *possession* (however theoretical) of property should be the sole indicator of fitness to vote in counties. A rugged rearguard action in the Lords led by Stanley and supported by some Peelites and Whigs had the effect of raising the new county level from the originally proposed eight to twelve pounds. A few unimpressive estimates were made as to how many voters would appear on the new rolls, all of them too high. Stanley wildly talked of 406,000 county voters. The Under-Secretary expected 205,000. Russell more accurately predicted 172,000. The actual result was 135,245

[1] Glengall to Stanley, 14 and 16 Oct. 1849, Derby Papers 120/2; *D.E.P.* 24 Oct. 1850; *Hansard*, cviii, 1357-8 (22 Feb. 1850); Lord Oranmore to Clarendon, 20 July [1850], Clarendon Papers Box 21.

[2] A good set of (mostly 'nominal') figures is available in a manuscript 'Return of the number of registered parliamentary electors in the several counties and boroughs in Ireland on 1st Jan. 1829 and 1830, 1st Feb. 1833, 1837, 1841, and 1845, and 1st Jan. 1850', compiled by the Under-Secretary, Sir Thomas Redington, on 2 Aug. 1850 (Clarendon Papers Box 25). See also the discussions in *Hansard*, cix, 263-8 (1 Mar. 1850).

in the counties and 28,301 in the boroughs, a total of 163,546 as compared with 45,000 just before the act—a substantial increase since 1832, from one voter in every 83 inhabitants to one in every 40.[1]

Who the new electors were was at first a matter of mystery. But while Tory Drs Frankenstein predicted 'an ignorant dependent class' and Whig Panglosses foresaw that 'they will all be subservient and they will vote each after his lord's orders', while the Tenant League told the 'Irish People' that they now possessed 'a franchise such as they never had since the forty-shilling freehold was abolished' and Catholic priests quivered with anticipation at the use the church might make of this heaven-sent 'instrument of terror',[2] more balanced assessment demands a digression into the murky world of property valuation, a world little understood by the gladiators of the time. What cannot be doubted is that the new electorate was chosen upon principles which effectively excluded many of the poor and marginal who had found it possible to get the vote before 1850. Between a fifth and a quarter of those registered in 1840 could not have been so ten years later, and of those, more than three-quarters were farmers holding less than twenty statute acres.[3] At the same time, prosperous farmers were no longer excluded for arbitrary reasons.

The new franchise was made possible by the establishment in 1838 of an Irish poor-law system and the consequent valuation of property for the purposes of levying a rate. The main characteristics of this valuation were its being locally supervised by individual boards of guardians and calculated upon the basis of net annual ('fair letting') value related to average rent on the assumption that insurance, repairs, and taxes were paid by the tenant (1 & 2 Vict., c. 56, s. 64). It all depended of course on what was meant by rent. With so many farmers involved in the valuing itself it is not surprising that a theoretically 'reasonable' standard of living was often adopted and

[1] Duke of Buccleuch to Aberdeen, 3 June 1850, Aberdeen Papers Add. MS 43201; Redington's Memo of 1 Aug. 1850, Clarendon Papers Box 25; Russell in *Hansard*, cxiii, 533-7 (30 July 1850). Because all previous writers have compared the results of the Franchise Act with the *nominal* electorate in 1847-8, they have failed to understand the act's importance even in the matter of increase.

[2] M. Toomey (Co. Wicklow Tory agent) to W. Owen, 31 May 1850, Downshire Papers D671/C/373/80; Lord Sligo to G. H. Moore, [1850], Moore Papers MS 891; Address of the Tenant League in *Nation*, 7 Feb. 1852; Father Cahill at a tenant-right meeting on 23 Jan. 1851 reported in an unnamed newspaper among cuttings relating to the political flamboyance of the clergy presented by the British Government to the Vatican and now in Vatican Secret Archives, Seg. di Stato 1852/278.

[3] These figures have been extracted from those in *Third General Report relative to the Valuations*, H.C. 1841 [329], xxiii, 618. My estimate of an exclusion of 22.1 per cent (of whom 76.9 per cent held below twenty and 41.4 per cent below ten acres) is based on the assumption that the distribution between £10 and £20 was uniform. It is broadly supported by information concerning a possible franchise at £12. 10s. (ibid. 669).

that value was then assumed to be whatever the tenant could thereafter afford to pay. 'That a valuation effected on this principle must in general be lower than the rent', reported two well-informed officials, 'follows from the valuator having adopted a scale of living for the tenant, above the ordinary situation of the peasantry . . . In every union the rents were above the valuation.'[1] With actual rents so variable ('one pound on one side of the fence and two pounds on the other'), this was almost inevitable, and the 'fair rents' adopted by most valuers turned out to be 'the rents of the proprietors in the district, whose rents are the lowest'.[2] From the start the poor-law valuators were subject to denunciation. Jobbery and incompetence were the commonest accusations.[3] Two countervailing forces were seen to be at work. The more powerful was the '*irresistible tendency* in all mankind who assist in the imposition of taxes which they bear, *to lower the valuation of the property* on which the taxes are to fall'. The other appeared about 1840 when the valuation became the official basis for certain local government franchises and, increasingly, the informal test for the assessment of parliamentary franchise requirements. As a result, particular guardians were to be seen raising and lowering valuations in accordance with the political views of the occupiers in question.[4]

This was the system adopted as the basis for the twelve-pound county and eight-pound borough franchise of 1850. Although the precise relationship between such amounts and actual rent remains obscure, all is not darkness. It seems to have been the case that valuations more nearly equalled actual rent in Ulster than in Connacht or Munster and that the shortfall below rent was greatest on small estates because larger proprietors tended to fix lower rents.[5] In parts

---

[1] *Hansard*, lvi, 284–7 (4 Feb. 1841), and 794 (22 Feb. 1841). See also *Report from the select committee on Townland Valuation of Ireland*, H.C. 1844 (513), vii, 496–7, 512, 585–8.

[2] *Third General Report relative to the Valuations*, H.C. 1841 [329], xxiii, 593–5, 607. See also Eliot to Graham, 13 Dec. 1841, Graham Papers 8/Ir; Ebrington to Wood, 21 Mar. 1841, Carlisle Papers L.-B. 42.

[3] For a sample garland, see T. Parry to E. Gulson, 26 Feb. 1841, Downshire Papers D671/C/12/773; Lord Farnham's Memo of 1850, Clanricarde Papers 35; Lord Devon to Ebrington, 26 Mar. 1839, Fortescue Papers 1262M/LI26; D. R. Pigot to Ebrington, 2 Mar. 1840, ibid. LI128; Graham to Eliot, 12 Oct. and 5 Nov. 1841, Graham Papers 8/Ir; Graham to De Grey, 19 Feb. 1843, ibid. 2/Ir.

[4] D. R. Pigot to Morpeth, 19 Jan. [1841], Carlisle Papers L.-B. 41; J. C. Besnard to Stanley, 15 Feb. 1841, Derby Papers 20/9; J. C. Besnard to Stanley, 19 Feb. 1841, Peel Papers Add. MS 40467; M. J. Finehy to M. J. Blake, 25 June 1841, Blake of Ballyglunin Papers M6936/46; J. Alcock to Stanley, 24 Apr. 1841, Derby Papers 20/9; Stanley to Clancarty, 26 July 1841, ibid. 172/1.

[5] See the comments of Edward Senior and R. M. Muggeridge (assistant poor-law commissioners) in *Committee on Townland Valuation*, H.C. 1844 (513), vii, 548–9, 566. Of 75 unions—out of a total of 130—Muggeridge assigned 19 to an equality of valuation to

of Carlow for which exact figures have survived the ratio of valuation to rent stood at 83 : 100.[1] County estimates of rent as a proportion of valuation in the mid-1840s produce an unweighted national mean of 125 per cent and provincial means of Ulster—118 per cent, Leinster —122 per cent, Connacht—131 per cent, and Munster—135 per cent.[2] Generally, therefore (and things were not in 1850 what they had been in 1844-5), the minimum rent exclusion point for the twelve-pound county voter established by the Franchise Act lay in the region of £14. 3s. in Ulster, £14. 13s. in Leinster, £15. 15s. in Connacht, and £16. 4s. in Munster. This was a much more highly priced admission ticket than had been exacted earlier.[3] But of course not all electors were poised at the precise point of inclusion. Three *broadly* consistent calculations can be made of the distribution of county voters shortly after the Franchise Act had come into effect (see Table 2).

Crucial to the make-up of the electorate was not the distribution of all farmers in a constituency, but the distribution of farmers valued at twelve pounds and above. As a result, counties with many small tenements, such as Donegal and Armagh, could have radically different electorates.[4]

	Donegal per cent	Armagh per cent
£12 and under £25	12.0	74.2
£25 and under £50	78.1	20.4
£50 and above	9.9	5.4

This helps to explain the problems encountered by the popular party in places like Carlow and Wicklow (with 58.7 and 52.1 per cent of

'letting value', 5 to 5 per cent below, 14 to 5-10 per cent below, 18 to 10-15 per cent below, 6 to 15-20 per cent below, and 13 to more than 20 per cent below. If one accepts those in equality and adopts midpoints for the other classes and 30 per cent for the last, an unweighted mean percentage deficiency of valuation as to rent of 11.2 per cent is obtained—not 11.8 as calculated by J. Stamp in *British incomes and property* (London, 1927), p. 149. If a perhaps more realistic 25 per cent is adopted for the last class, the mean deficiency falls to 10.3 per cent. See also Ebrington to Wood, 21 Mar. 1841, Fortescue Papers 1262M/LI188; *Third General Report relative to the Valuations*, H.C. 1841[329], xxiii, 595-9.

[1] *Committee on Townland Valuation*, H.C. 1844 (513), vii, 655-7. On Monaghan estates larger than 2,000 acres rent was almost 1.4 times PLV—on smaller estates about double (P. J. Duffy, 'Irish landholding structures and population in the mid-nineteenth century', *Maynooth Review*, iii (1977), 20).

[2] R. D. Crotty, *Irish agricultural production: Its volume and structure* (Cork, 1966), p. 303—based on an analysis of statements to the Devon Commission.

[3] Somerville's Memo of Oct. 1848 in Somerville Letter-Book T2982; *Hansard*, cix, 344-5 (4 Mar. 1850).

[4] See table in *Thom 1852*, p. 214; also sources in Appendix—Table 2, section A. The percentages of voters under £25 PLV in county constituencies were:

voters at and above £15) as well as in Donegal, for it seems to have been the case that O'Connellites, Independent Oppositionists, popular Liberals, and Home Rulers did not do well, either among the lumpen electors who had found their way on to the register before 1850 or among the highest reaches of rural prosperity. Furthermore, the bulk of those farmers with holdings of the requisite value were now enfranchised, so that, while in the 1840s less than a quarter of those with holdings of *forty pounds* and above had had the vote, a sample of eight counties in 1852–3 suggests that 76.1 per cent of all males with holdings of *twelve pounds* and above were now enrolled.[1] As most of the residue could be accounted for by surviving freehold and leasehold voters, by farmers under age, and by men excluded on various residence and taxation technicalities, it is clear that very few qualified persons were excluded from the electorate after 1850. In boroughs the same process was at work. Few were now arbitrarily shut out and the make-up of the 19,719 rated occupier voters in 1852–3 was as follows.[2]

	per cent
£8 to under £25	62.9
£25 to under £50	23.7
£50 and above	13.4

Yet the poor-law valuations themselves were still unsatisfactory. Eventually in 1852 Parliament passed 15 & 16 Vict., c. 63 which placed the matter on an entirely new basis. The first general valuation had been established in 1826 under the direction of Richard Griffith who was to dominate affairs for the next four decades. Only

Antrim	53	Carlow*	41	Clare	62	Galway	n.a.
Armagh	74	Dublin*	55	Cork	42	Leitrim	86
Cavan	75	Kildare*	35	Kerry	56	Mayo*	60
Donegal	12	Kilkenny	48	Limerick	44	Roscommon	66
Down	59	King's Co.	58	Tipperary	41	Sligo	73
Fermanagh	75	Longford	70	Waterford	34		
Londonderry	63	Louth*	53				
Monaghan	77	Meath*	n.a.				
Tyrone	74	Queen's Co.	53				
		Westmeath	53				
		Wexford	53				
		Wicklow*	47				

* Counties with at least 10 per cent of voters qualified as other than rated occupiers.

[1] Based on sources in Appendix—Table 2, section B. The proportion could rise as high as 85.7 per cent (Longford) and 90.0 per cent (Wicklow).

[2] Based on sources in Appendix—Table 2, section C.

TABLE 2
Valuation distribution of county electorate, 1851-2

A

	per cent
At £12	8.5
Above £12 to £15	18.0
Above £15 to £18	13.0
Above £18 to £20	7.7
Above £20 to £25	11.8
Above £25	41.0

B

	per cent
£12 to under £20	54.4
£20 to under £50	33.9
£50 and above	11.7

C

	Ireland per cent	Leinster per cent	Munster per cent	Connacht per cent	Ulster per cent
£12 to under £25	55.7	52.0	44.9	72.7	62.9
£25 to under £50	28.5	27.8	33.1	16.6	27.7
£50 and above	15.8	20.2	22.0	10.7	9.4

Note All three calculations underestimate the proportion of 'prosperous' voters, omitting as they do that small group still qualified under freehold and leasehold franchises. Total county electorate 135,245.

townlands (rather than individual tenements) were valued and the results 'applotted' locally for levying county cess and associated taxes.[1] The method of assessment for land was based upon the estimated output valued by means of a fixed scale of prices of the most important tillage and animal products, a scale left unchanged in the consolidating legislation of 1836. Buildings under five pounds were omitted altogether and the rest included at only two-thirds of a sum assessed by means of reference to net annual 'letting value'. This townland valuation was still in progress when the separate poor-law

[1] The history of valuation in Ireland badly needs detailed examination. One of the best available accounts is in a memorandum of 1897 by the Irish Local Government Board in *Appendix to minutes of evidence (volume I) taken before the Royal Commission on Local Taxation*, H.C. 1898 [C 8764], xlii, 127-42. See also *Committee on Townland Valuation*, H.C. 1844 (513), vii, 459-706; *Copy of a Letter addressed by the Commissioner for Valuation to the Lord Lieutenant of Ireland* [23 Dec. 1850], H.C. 1851 (4), l, 905-10 (and an earlier version in Clarendon Papers Box 68); *Report from the select committee on General Valuation etc. (Ireland)*, H.C. 1868-9 (362), ix, 1-303; W. F. Bailey, 'The government

valuation was started in 1838.[1] The government was moved by criticisms of the latter to order Griffith to complete the townland valuation in such a way as to render it of possible future use for the assessment of poor rates. In 1844 Griffith was instructed to value by tenements according to the 1826-36 scale of prices. Two years later a new act (9 & 10 Vict., c. 110) required him to conduct a curious tandem operation by which the counties still to be completed (Dublin, Cork, Kerry, Limerick, Tipperary, Waterford) were to be assessed in tenements both by means of the original scale for county cess and by means of net annual value for possible poor-law use. However, Griffith, an enormously forceful and energetic man, disliked the net value principle and mounted a powerful campaign against it.[2] He ingeniously argued that franchise requirements demanded an unchanging price-scale system and that because his valuation was 'made for the purposes of taxation it is immaterial if it be made high or low provided a relative scale be preserved throughout'.[3] In 1852 the government gave in and introduced—for both taxation and the franchise—an entirely new system. This (commonly called 'Griffith's Valuation') was to be under Griffith's central direction and executed along tenement lines with *all* buildings valued by net annual value and land by a new scale of prices allegedly based on those ruling during the depressed years of 1849-51 (see Table 3). But although Griffith organized vast teams of surveyors to whom he issued minute instructions regarding the digging of soil samples, the value added by the proximity of towns, the quality of manure, and so on,[4] the system was not without its vaguenesses. The

valuation of Ireland', *Journal of the Statistical and Social Inquiry Society of Ireland*, ix (1892-3), 651-63; *Richard Griffith 1784-1878*, ed. G. L. H. Davies and R. C. Mollan (Dublin, 1980), especially essays by W. E. Vaughan and John Lee.

[1] The townland valuation was lower than the poor-law valuation, though by varying amounts. Lord Farnham in 1850 (Clanricarde Papers 35) thought it a quarter lower. As regards the Navan area Griffith said he would add a third to obtain the PLV (to Eliot, 8 Jan. 1844, *Tenth annual report of the poor law commissioners with appendices* (London, 1844), p. 259). In 103 Carlow townlands the relationship was: Actual Rents = 100, PLV = 83, Townland Valuation = 71 (*Committee on Townland Valuation*, H.C. 1844 (513), vii, 655-7). The number of electors would, therefore, have been lower after 1850 had the franchise been based on the townland system.

[2] This (and some of what follows) is based on the sources in note 1 p. 23; and *Hansard*, cxiv, 771-2 (17 Feb. 1851); Griffith to Sir A. Shafto Adair, 7 June 1849, Monsell Papers MS 20693; Griffith to Lord St Germans, 20 and 24 May 1850, Ordnance Survey Letter-Book OL2/12; Griffith to Somerville, 22 Feb. 1850 and 4 Feb. 1852, ibid. OL2/12 and 13.

[3] Griffith to St Germans, 20 May 1850, Ordnance Survey Letter-Book OL2/12; Griffith to A. Caswell, 1 Oct. 1850, ibid. OL2/21 (cited by W. E. Vaughan in *Richard Griffith*, ed. G. L. H. Davies and R. C. Mollan, p. 121). By Oct. 1850 the Franchise Act was in force, and although Griffith's valuations were not being used for this purpose as yet, the possibility that they might soon be was already in his mind, and for franchise purposes relative values alone were quite unsatisfactory.

[4] [R. Griffith], *Instructions to the valuators and surveyors appointed under the 15th*

TABLE 3
Scales of agricultural prices in valuation acts
1826–36 and 1852 (per cwt.)

	1826–36	1852
Wheat	10*s*.	7*s*. 6*d*.
Oats	6*s*.	4*s*. 10*d*.
Barley	7*s*.	5*s*. 6*d*.
Flax	omitted	40*s*.
Potatoes	1*s*. 7*d*.	omitted
Butter	69*s*.	65*s*. 4*d*.
Beef	33*s*.	35*s*. 6*d*.
Mutton	34*s*. 6*d*.	41*s*.
Pork	25*s*. 6*d*.	32*s*.

proportions in which the several prices were to be used were left to
individual discretion and there was silence about such crucial matters
as the employment of capital, the rate of interest to be allowed, and
the price of labour.

Griffith began to issue his valuation county by county in 1853.
This at once became the basis for the next voters' register, so that, as
time went on, the franchise of individual counties was moved from
the poor-law to the Griffith standard. Most of the early counties issued
were either those Griffith had valued under the arrangements of
1844 or the two (Kilkenny and Queen's Co.) he had revised from the
original townland valuation in force before then.[1] The process, therefore, began in Munster and Leinster, moved to Connacht about
1856–7, to Ulster in 1857–8, and was finally completed with the
publication of Armagh as late as 1865. The effect upon the electorate
was determined by certain peculiarities of the new system: the
valuation of land (but not of buildings) was in practice *never* revised;
a variable deduction was made from the gross valuation for the rates
and taxes paid by tenants; the scale of prices remained entirely unchanged. The result was that land values (and hence the franchise)
became frozen into the profile laid down on first publication, that
(in theory at least) no account was taken of the rise in agricultural
prices after the early 1850s, and that deductions for rates were much
greater (and the resulting valuations lower) during the early years
when poor rates were historically high. Other things being equal, the
higher the valuation the larger the electorate. But, despite much

and 16th Vict., cap. 63, for the uniform valuation of lands and tenements in Ireland (Dublin,
1853)—copy in N.L.I. Ir658 u 2.

[1] The nature of the complicated and assumption-ridden methods by which this alignment of earlier valuations to the principles of 1852 must have been performed remains a
mystery.

agitated discussion at the time, the proportion by which valuation fell below actual rent (the latter taken to include the tenant-right payments made by incoming tenants in Ulster) did not vary widely between one part of the country and another. That, however, a *general* disparity did exist nationally cannot be doubted, so that, in order to match valuation with actual rent, it would, very roughly, be necessary to increase the former by percentages of about 15 for 1865, 20 for 1868, 25 for 1875, and 28 for 1880.[1] But individual prices rose at very different rates from the levels used in the scale of 1852. In particular, tillage prices fell more and more behind cattle prices: wheat up 42 per cent by 1877, oats by 66 per cent, beef by 103 per cent, mutton by 116 per cent. As time went on, therefore, the proportion of farmers whose *rent and income levels* should in theory have entitled them to a twelve-pound vote but who were excluded from the register because of the static nature of Griffith's valuation became much higher in cattle than in tillage districts.[2] But although in this sense the county electorate became 'distorted' and comparatively more exclusive—reaching its apogee of exclusivity during Parnell's early electoral successes between 1880 and 1884— the changing pattern of farm holdings after the Famine, the ability to acquire more land, and the consequent growth in the presence of twelve-pound-and-over farmers within the total farmer community steadily increased the proportion of that community able to claim the vote.[3] As it was, Griffith seems more often to have valued below

[1] B. L. Solow, *The land question and the Irish economy, 1870–1903* (Cambridge, Mass., 1971), pp. 60–72; J. Stamp, *British incomes and property*, pp. 150–2; evidence of H. Hutchings in *Committee on General Valuation*, H.C. 1868–9 (362), ix, 179–80 (although it should be recorded that a later valuation commissioner, J. G. Barton, claimed that Griffith *had* taken tenant-right payments into account: *Royal Commission on Local Taxation*, H.C. 1898 [C 8763], xli, 554). If one makes no allowance for tenant-right payments and accepts much of the contemporary argument (which Griffith and his successor, J. Ball Greene, fitfully supported) that Ulster *was* valued 'higher', it is possible, using the unweighted mean of Ball Greene's 1869 county estimates of the extent by which southern counties required increment to match Ulster levels (*Committee on General Valuation*, p. 228, also Greene's evidence, pp. 3–24), namely 20.8 per cent, to estimate roughly how many additional voters would have been on the rolls in the southern provinces *c*.1870 had they been valued as 'high' as Ulster. Rounding the mean to 20 per cent, the *total* county electorates would have been increased by a maximum of 8.6 per cent in Leinster, 10.9 per cent in Munster, 22.3 per cent in Connacht, and 11.9 per cent in the south generally, or a rise from 108,672 to 121,659 (calculated from *Return of the number of occupiers in Irish counties rated at £8 and under £10, and at £10 and under £12, in 1866*, H.C. 1867–8 (245), lvi, 507–8, and *Returns as respects each of the parliamentary boroughs in Ireland . . . [also] as respects each of the counties in Ireland, exclusive of the boroughs or parts of boroughs contained therein, of the following particulars, viz:- area, valuation, population*, H.C. 1874 (45), liii, 557–68). See also Griffith to Lord Mayo, 12 June 1868, Mayo Papers MS 11166.

[2] See Ball Greene's memorandum of Nov. 1880 (Printed Cabinet Paper, Gladstone Papers Add. MS 44625).

[3] See Chapter II, Table 17 below and related text.

than above the poor-law valuations he replaced. This had the gradual effect of making the electorate smaller and even more exclusive than would otherwise have been the case.[1] In some constituencies, such as Clonmel (where of course buildings formed the bulk of real property), the result could be devastating, for, as one local observer noted, 'In October [1853] over a hundred of Father Burke's men will lose their votes under Griffith's valuation'. In Dublin City, where in 1854 Griffith 'reduced' the valuation from £663,768 to £541,377, the electorate dropped from 11,290 in 1852 to 9,905 in 1857.[2] Thus every constituency in Ireland experienced not only the changes of 1850, but a second transformation produced by the gradual transfer from one valuation system to another.

In broader terms the profound changes which took place between 1840 and 1866 in the composition of the county electorate—more than three-quarters of which consisted of farmers—are demonstrated in Table 4, which, if anything, understates the dramatic movement towards economic homogeneity. Whereas in 1840 almost a third of the farmer voters occupied farms valued under £15, by 1866 little more than a fifth did so. In economic terms the electorate had become significantly more homogeneous. Connacht voters especially, once quite aberrantly poor, moved more into line as part of a post-Famine integration of Western society and politics into those of the nation as a whole. By 1866 the electorate varied from county to county, not because of arbitrary legal decisions or tenurial arrangements, but as a reflection of comparative wealth and local prosperity, with, for example, Limerick's 22.8 per cent of voters valued above fifty pounds contrasting with Leitrim's 5.8 per cent. Surviving electoral registers show also that, while the new voters were not marginal men, neither were they wealthy enough to be divorced from the concerns and preoccupations of substantial numbers of the farmer population as a whole (see Table 5).

Contemporary comments on the 'new' electors were quite different from those of earlier times. 'I was', wrote an Antrim Conservative

---

[1] A comparison of poor-law valuations in 1850 (which provided the electorate in 1852) in *Thom 1852*, p. 214 and Griffith's values in *Returns showing the counties in Ireland in which the tenement valuation has been completed*, H.C. 1857 (21 Sess. 2), xlii, 519–24, and *Return, in a tabular form, showing the area, population, and valuation of the several counties of cities, counties of towns, baronies, and half-baronies in Ireland*, H.C. 1872 (96), xlvii, 757–66 (although these of course include some changes as regards buildings since first publication) with movements in county electorates suggests that increases in voter numbers were substantially higher in counties where Griffith valued above poor-law valuation (e.g. Cork, Kilkenny, Louth) than in those where he valued below (e.g. Carlow, Tipperary, Kerry, Wicklow). These calculations are not without their problems and should be treated with caution.

[2] T. H. Barton to R. Bourke, [1853], Mayo Papers MS 11018 (the Clonmel electorate fell

TABLE 4

Valuation profile of county electorate, 1840,* 1850–1, 1866 (in percentages)

	Under	£12	£12 to under £15		£15 to under £20		£20 and over		£40 and over		£50 and over	
	1840	1866	1840	1866	1840	1866	1840	1866	1840	1866	1840	1866
Leinster	19.5	0.0	8.1	16.8	11.4	18.2	61.0	65.0	30.4	n.a.	n.a.	25.0
Munster	19.9	0.0	6.8	17.3	11.9	20.0	61.4	62.7	27.5	n.a.	n.a.	19.0
Ulster	18.3	0.0	12.0	27.4	17.5	25.7	52.2	46.9	11.6	n.a.	n.a.	9.1
Connacht	45.8	0.0	15.7	30.1	12.4	21.7	26.1	48.2	7.3	n.a.	n.a.	17.1
Ireland	22.6	0.0	9.8	22.0	12.8	21.7	54.8	56.3	21.0	n.a.	n.a.	17.0
Ireland (1850–1)	0.0		26.5		20.8		52.7		n.a.		n.a.	

* See also Table 1

TABLE 5

Valuation profile of electors in certain county constituencies
from electoral registers, 1852–70

	Mean PLV £	£12 to under £20 per cent	£20 to under £50 per cent	£50 and over per cent	N in sample
Armagh 1852*	22. 18s.	60.8	33.7	5.5	1,552
Down 1852*	32. 16s.	49.2	41.8	9.0	4,143
Louth‡ 1852*	36. 5s.	42.2	42.3	15.5	258
Sligo 1852*	34. 4s.	50.8	35.6	13.6	315
Galway 1857*	27. 3s.	61.4	28.0	10.6	378
Mayo 1857*	29. 19s.	61.9	26.3	11.8	1,681
Roscommon 1859†	36. 5s.	50.9	33.9	15.2	805
Armagh 1870†	22. 6s.	65.1	29.4	5.5	2,084

* Based on valuations undertaken by poor-law boards under 1838 Act etc.
† Based on valuations undertaken by Griffith under 1852 Act.
‡ Mean *size* of agricultural holdings occupied by Louth voters in 1852 = 35 statute acres.

in 1869, 'much struck with the respectability and enthusiasm of the farmers coming in to vote.' Voters in general were 'distinguished . . . for great respectability and quietness as well as wealth and intelligence'.[1] In Belfast, even after the lowering of the borough franchise in 1868, the voters' appearance 'bespoke comfort and personal respectability'.[2] Because valuations by the early 1870s were about a quarter under letting value (and up to a third below actual rent) the lowest class of enfranchised occupiers would have been those paying rents of sixteen to eighteen pounds in addition to rates and other taxes.[3] These were not to be counted among the poor. The mean valuation of all agricultural holdings nationally was only £20 in 1881: in Kerry, Galway, Sligo, Cavan, and Roscommon it was below £15, in Mayo, Donegal, and Leitrim below £10.[4] In 1866 only about a third (34.8 per cent) of such holdings were capable of yielding the

from 379 in 1852 to 318 in 1857); M. Daly, 'Late nineteenth and early twentieth century Dublin' in *The Town in Ireland*, ed. D. Harkness and M. O'Dowd (Belfast, 1981), p. 235.

[1] W. F. to Sir G. F. Seymour, 19 Aug. 1869, Seymour of Ragley Papers CR114A/538(3); J. E. Tennent to Stanley, 5 Dec. 1851, Derby Papers 131/7.

[2] *Belfast Election*, 24 Oct. 1868. The 1850 Franchise Act (s. 111) barred all who had received poor relief in the twelve months before 20 July from being registered.

[3] See p. 25 above; also (for various periods) *Freeman's Journal*, 6 Mar. 1860; *D.E.P.* 20 Mar. 1868; *Cork Examiner*, 23 Mar. 1868; *Hansard*, clii, 1287 (4 Mar. 1859); W. Kernaghan to Mayo, 27 June 1868, Mayo Papers MS 11168; *Minutes of evidence taken before Her Majesty's Commissioners on Agriculture*, H.C. 1881 [C 2778-I], xv, 590-1, 726-34, 852-60; W. F. Bailey, 'The government valuation of Ireland', pp. 657-63.

[4] T. W. Grimshaw, 'On some comparative statistics of Irish counties', *Journal of the Statistical and Social Inquiry Society of Ireland*, viii (1882-3), 444-58.

vote,[1] while of course labourers, farm servants, itinerants, and all non-householders were in any case excluded. The Tipperary farmer with eleven acres and two cows—with a rent reduced by agreement in 1882 to £11. 18s. and in debt to shopkeepers—would hardly have qualified. Nor would the ten-acre man west of Galway paying twelve pounds rent, thirty shillings poor rates and thirty-six shillings tax, despite his two-storied granite house.[2] Typical of those just admitted was the Kilkenny farmer, who in 1881 held 23 acres at £16. 13s. (unchanged since 1864), with seven acres in grass, a horse, five cows, pigs, poultry, five firkins of butter a year, and able to give his daughters dowries of sixty pounds each. On the Gosford estate in Armagh only a fifth of the 504 tenants in 1870 paid rents of sixteen pounds or more, while an even smaller proportion did so on the Londonderry estates of the Drapers' Company in 1856.[3] The really wealthy farmers, although they occupied a large fraction of the land, were simply too few to be able to overwhelm the post-Famine electorate. In Galway any man with eighty acres was thought a 'strong farmer' (over 500 'they begin to take the views of the land-lord class') and certainly no more than one in twenty rural electors could have matched the Waterford farmer of the 1880s paying £132 for 104 acres valued at £126, with his 'comfortable two-story build-ing and dining-room', his seventeen dairy cows, two servants, and three labourers.[4]

Informed observers commented on the intelligence and grasp of public affairs shown by the new county voters. In Limerick they were 'well versed in politics'; in Galway even those who only paid the lowest rents of fifteen to sixteen pounds were 'very intelligent, all the men of that kind have a great deal to do in the way of buying and selling, and they understand figures'.[5] Literacy was spreading,

[1] Calculated as in Table 4 above from data in *Thom 1870*, p. 842. Individual occupiers could combine separate holdings to qualify. The ratio of *holdings* under *fifteen* pounds valuation to *occupiers* of such holdings was 1.0 to 0.7 (*Returns showing the number of agricultural holdings in Ireland*, H.C. 1870 [C 32], lvi, 737–55).

[2] G. Pellew, *In Castle and Cabin or talks in Ireland in 1887* (New York and London, 1888), pp. 107–9, 166–7.

[3] *Commissioners on Agriculture*, H.C. 1881 [C 2778-I], xv, 526–30; R. S. Gourlay, 'The social and economic history of the Gosford estates 1610–1876' (Queen's University Belfast M.Sc.(Econ.) thesis, 1973), pp. 328–31; Olive Robinson, 'The economic significance of the London companies as landlords in Ireland during the period 1800–1870' (Queen's University Belfast Ph.D. thesis, 1957), pp. 258–60.

[4] *Galway County election petition*, H.C. 1872 (241-I), xlviii, 840; G. Pellew, *In Castle and Cabin*, pp. 105–6. In 1881, 6 per cent of all holdings of one acre and over exceeded a hundred acres (and some of these would have been on poor land). In 1854, although 74 per cent of all farmers held less than 30 acres, farmers with more than 50 acres occupied 60 per cent of the land (W. E. Vaughan, 'An assessment of the economic performance of Irish land-lords, 1851–81' in *Ireland under the Union*, ed. F. S. L. Lyons and R. A. J. Hawkins, p. 195).

[5] *Report from the select committee on parliamentary and municipal elections*, H.C.

but erratically and among the young rather than the old. Galway farmers paying fifty-nine-pound rents in 1872 could neither read nor write.[1] 'I hoop', wrote a substantial Co. Dublin farmer to his Liberal candidate in 1857, 'i am not intruuding to much on your honer—to send you a challing to no if yo will get 5 brothers . . . to vote for your honer.' A Tipperary farmer declared to a prospective candidate in 1865: 'Besids my forefather Back your forefathers Before now now I pledge . . . I will Never Back any won neither For Priest or Ministar or Any Won Els only as I think wel of it.'[2] Among voters generally, however, literacy had increased since pre-Famine days and increased more substantially than in the population as a whole. Indeed, the years between 1850 and 1885 constitute the high-point of electoral literacy in nineteenth-century Ireland. In 1837 about 14 per cent of borough voters were returned as 'marksmen' (unable to write their own names) in towns where the general percentage of males aged five and over who could not write was 46.5 per cent.[3] The arbitrariness of the contemporary franchise ensured that there was little connection between the two figures. Youghal, with a 51.4 per cent adult male illiteracy level, had only 4.9 per cent marksmen voters; Mallow with a 47.6 per cent level had 28.9 per cent. Liberal politicians, embarrassed by all this, nervously suggested that gout was responsible for the widespread giving of marks: 'Are the people that inhabit within the County of the City of Cork very much in the habit of having the gout?—There are a great number of respectable persons whose names appear as marksmen.'[4] Of perhaps greater significance, however, is the fact that, although the parliamentary boroughs together had a considerably lower male illiteracy rate than the rest of the country (43.5 per cent in 1841 as opposed to 65.1 per cent), the county *electorate* was no more illiterate than that in the boroughs and was not, therefore, composed largely of bumpkin farmers deficient in either articulateness, education, òr intelligence.[5] The

---

1868-9 (352), viii, 210–16; *Report from the select committee on parliamentary and municipal elections*, H.C. 1876 (162), xii, 67–70.

[1] *Galway County election petition*, H.C. 1872 (241-I), xlviii, 227; E. Larkin, 'Church, state, and nation in modern Ireland', p. 1263. For provincial and national literacy statistics 1841-81, see Chapter VI, Table 52 below.

[2] J. Hoey to Sir C. Domvile, [1857], Domvile Papers MS 9361 (contains other similar letters, e.g. 'i am annghiously waiting for your answer to me note & hopes you have not forgot'); M. Kennedy to R. J. Otway, 18 Feb. 1865, Otway Papers MS 13008.

[3] Unless otherwise stated the pre-Famine information has been (for general levels) taken from the 1841 *Census* (Miscellaneous Tables I: Parliamentary Boroughs) and (for voters) from figures in *Fictitious Votes, Ireland*, 1st series, 1st report, Appendix A; 2nd series, 2nd report, Appendix; 2nd series, 3rd report, Appendix No. 1. The borough marksmen figures are given for all boroughs save Dublin, Galway, and Waterford.

[4] *Fictitious Votes, Ireland*, 2nd series, 1st report, p. 75.

[5] Selected county figures are available (in sources cited in note 3 above) as proportions of

franchise reforms of 1850 accentuated the impact of the general rise in literacy. By 1868 'an excessively small proportion' of Co. Limerick voters was unable to write,[1] and by 1880 as few as 3.5 per cent of those voting at the general election were nationally classified as illiterate. This state of things was, however, dramatically changed by the Reform Act of 1884, so that at the general election of 1885 more than a fifth of the voters in Ireland were so classified.[2] Literacy statistics also shed important light on the locally variable nature of those excluded from the electorate between 1850 and 1884 but included thereafter— principally small farmers, labourers, and poorer urban householders. The number and the status of these differed greatly from county to county, so that the opening of electoral floodgates meant one thing in places like Armagh and Sligo, where the percentage of illiterate voters rose from 3.1 and 6.8 to 19.7 and 19.8, but something altogether more drastic in, for example, Cork and Donegal, which registered rises from 6.3 and 3.1 to no less than 38.5 and 43.9.[3]

The few (mostly abortive) attempts that were made to restructure the Irish franchise after 1850 had their origins, not in any significant Irish agitation, but as shamefaced appendages to English proposals. In 1851, 1852, 1860, and 1866 the Liberals pursued feeblenesses such as grouping boroughs on Scots lines, lowering the franchise to six pounds in boroughs and ten in counties, and giving the vote to the massed hordes with fifty pounds on deposit in the savings bank. The Irish Reform Act of 1868 was the suitably mouse-like outcome of all this. Even Disraeli declined to leap into the Hibernian dark and settled for leaving the counties alone, lowering the borough limit to 'over four pounds' (effectively a ratepayer rather than a householder franchise), and introducing a lodger vote. As a result the borough electorate went up from 30,955 to 45,625, but more than a third of this was because of boundary rather than franchise changes. Still, borough voters were being made to look less and less of an élite in comparison with their colleagues in the counties, and in constituencies

those *voting*, borough figures as proportions of those on the register. The county mean is 13.1 per cent, the borough 13.9 per cent. County figures stay close to the mean, but borough figures range widely (e.g. Lisburn 0.0, Wexford 1.1, Cork 13.0, Sligo 15.4, Drogheda 20.4, Carrickfergus 23.5, and Dungarvan—with its surviving forty-shilling freeholders—as high as 42.0).

[1] *Committee on parliamentary and municipal elections*, H.C. 1868-9 (352), viii, 213, 267.

[2] Calculated at 21.8 per cent from *Return showing with respect to each parliamentary constituency in England, Ireland, and Scotland respectively, the population, the total number of electors on the register then in force, the number of illiterate voters recorded . . . at the general election of 1880*, H.C. 1883 (327), liv, 293-303; the same for *the general election of 1885*, H.C. 1886 (165), lii, 605-17.

[3] Figures are available only for those counties contested in 1880 *all* of whose divisions

like Newry the new sub-eight-pound men soon provided almost a quarter of the total.[1] Yet, even if a four or five-pound house was nothing special, the very lowest were still excluded, men such as those described by a Newry Conservative as 'very little removed from pauperism being all weekly tenants'.[2]

Exclusion in 1868 meant, however, something very different from the haphazard exclusion of thirty years before. O'Connell's sustained and energetic campaigns for electoral success—an essential propellant both of parliamentary presence and popular mobilization—had been emasculated by the repeated necessity of diverting attention to franchise reform and fatally hampered by an electorate, which, because of its lack of social continuity and coherence, had rarely proved capable of sustained and united action. No group within it had been sufficiently powerful to provide a reliable constituency for anything other than flamboyant or sporadic success. The wealthy voters who supported the Conservatives and Whigs had been challenged, not by any solid opposition, but by fragmented groups ranging from prosperous shopkeepers to indigent labourers, from substantial farmers to cottiers at the margins of existence. Out of such disparate forces even O'Connell had not been able to fashion the politics of cohesion. And the insuperable difficulty of identifying the nature of his electoral 'centre of gravity' had provided O'Connell with perhaps the greatest of his political and organizational problems. With the Franchise Act of 1850 there came at last a coherent constituency chosen on a uniform principle, capable of sustained and consistent mobilization. Nothing, however, is changed overnight, least of all by legislation. It took time for politics to recover from the catastrophe of the Famine. The failures of the Independent Party of the 1850s were failures of personality and of that group's essentially inchoate nature. They also coincided with a dramatic intensification of the localist elements within Irish politics and with a brief but effective counter-attack by the landlord party,

---

were also contested in 1885 (though in some cases figures for the 1886 election (in *Return showing . . . the number of illiterate voters . . . at the general election of 1886*, H.C. 1886 (46 Sess. 2), lii, 627–39) have been used instead). Boroughs disenfranchised in 1885 have been included in the 1880 counties where necessary.

[1] *Newry Election. An alphabetically arranged list of electors who voted, and those who did not, at the election held in Newry, on the 20th of November 1868* (Newry, n.d.)—copy in P.R.O.N.I. T2336/1—reveals the following voter profile:

Under £8—   23.9 per cent   £20 and under £50—19.3 per cent
  £8 and under £12—28.8 per cent   £50 and over—   7.4 per cent
  £12 and under £20—20.6 per cent   (N = 796)

[2] Houses valued at eight pounds were auctioned for about fifty at Waterford in 1868 (calculated from figures for twenty-one houses in *Waterford Mail*, 30 Sept. 1868); Memorial

paradoxically strengthened by the Famine which had acted as a selector of the fittest among landed proprietors.[1] But the delay between cause and result should not disguise the importance of the Act, which, in effect, laid a time bomb into the nest of Irish politics. It was the electorate established in 1850 encompassing less than one in twenty of the population and less than one in five adult males that sustained the most important breakthroughs of the Nationalist movement: the by-elections of 1869-72, the general elections of 1874 and 1880, and the Parnellite triumphs at the by-elections of 1882, 1883, and 1884. Indeed, it was precisely this kind of electorate—compact, politically aware, shorn (at least in the counties) of the most bribable, the most fickle, and the most subservient, slowly expanding but still a recognizable élite—which gave particular prominence to those elements most likely to respond with enthusiasm and steadiness to the campaigns of the 1870s and 1880s. In electoral terms the crucial modernizing thrust was given in 1850, not in 1832 or 1884.

II VOTERS AND POLITICAL INFLUENCE

Electorates consist, not only of people stationed at various points along an economic scale, but of shopkeepers and carpenters, farmers and labourers, Catholics and Protestants. They consist, fundamentally, of individuals. All three aspects—the economic, the social, and the particular—are connected. The study of one illuminates the others. Without valuation data farmers would remain an undifferentiated mass. In towns occupation alone would tell a very imperfect story. Yet the sources which permit a study of behaviour as opposed to structure are predominantly couched in occupational terms. To know a man's job is to know at once something less and something more than to know the house in which he lived or the holding which he worked. Not everyone ran along a single track. Countrymen could be at once farmers and money-lenders, 'partly a farmer and partly a manufacturer', or a 'tailor and greengrocer'. A Clare butcher in 1852 was also a farm servant. A Galway man in 1872 ran 'a drapery and leather establishment' licensed to serve intoxicants. What, indeed, does 'gentleman' mean when voters so

of the Newry Registration Society, 11 Mar. 1868, Mayo Papers MS 11168. Of Newry's 2,933 houses, 1,452 (49.5 per cent) were then valued at or below four pounds.

[1] See Chapters II and VI below; also K. T. Hoppen, 'Landlords, society, and electoral politics in mid-nineteenth century Ireland', *Past and Present*, No. 75 (1977), 62-93, and 'National politics and local realities in mid-nineteenth century Ireland' in *Studies in Irish History presented to R. Dudley Edwards*, ed. A. Cosgrove and D. McCartney (Dublin, 1979), pp. 190-227.

designated could be successfully impersonated by drunken Monaghan labourers polling in fancy dress at Belfast in 1841?[1] But the bones of the skeleton stand out through the flesh: lawyers were not publicans, gentlemen did not make their own boots.

In the county constituencies, where the bulk of the population lived on the land, the occupational structure was clear enough. By the 1860s more than three out of every four county voters were farmers and many of the others were engaged in broadly agricultural activities. No less than 93 per cent of Louth voters in 1865 were tenants of one sort or another.[2] Opinions differed as to the political leanings of different sections of the farmer community, though the Tory vote seems to have contained a higher proportion of wealthy farmers than the non-Tory vote, whether O'Connellite, Liberal, or Home Rule. In 1832, for example, this was the case in counties like Dublin, Carlow, Leitrim, Kildare, and Cork.[3] At the Louth election of 1852 the mean valuation rose steadily the nearer one moved to the pure Tory faith, with anti-Tories at £30, split voters at £40, and Tory plumpers at £51. In Sligo too the mean valuation of Tories (£41) was noticeably higher than that of Liberals (£28).[4] But while in Sligo and Louth the nature of a man's holding seems to have had some kind of overarching impact upon his electoral behaviour, this was not so at the Down election of the same year. There the valuation profile of all four possible types of voter (Tory, Liberal, splitter, abstainer) was very similar, and the intensity of Tory support was evenly spread throughout the economic spectrum (see Table 6).

In Down Episcopalians and Presbyterians were, however, heavily Conservative, while the smaller Catholic electorate which tended to

---

[1] *A Return of the outrages specially reported by the constabulary as committed within the Barony of Kilmacrenan, County Donegal, during the last ten years*, H.C. 1861 (404), lii, 594; *Carrickfergus election petition*, H.C. 1833 (181), viii, 61, 71; *Minutes of evidence taken before the select committee on the Clare election petition*, H.C. 1852-3 (595), ix, 672-84; *Galway County election petition*, H.C. 1872 (241-I), xlviii, 516; *Belfast election compromise*, H.C. 1842 (431), v, 353. On 'gentlemen', see J. R. Vincent, *Pollbooks: How Victorians voted* (Cambridge, 1967), p. 54.

[2] See Chapter II, Table 23 below, and *An analysis of the parliamentary register of voters for the County of Louth, with the names of the landlords and their tenants on the register of voters, shewing the candidate for whom they voted at the election in April 1865* (Dublin, 1865)—copy N.L.I. P2491.

[3] *Galway County election petition*, H.C. 1872 (241-I), xlviii, 262, 430-1, 496, 743, 815; A. Macintyre, *The Liberator: Daniel O'Connell and the Irish party 1830-1847* (London, 1965), pp. 101-2.

[4] Calculated from a one-in-five Louth sample for four baronies (N = 258) from *A list of electors of the several baronies of the County of Louth, who voted at the general election of 1852* (Dundalk, 1852)—copy N.L.I. MS 1660—traced to Griffith's Valuation. For Sligo, see annotated poll book for 1852 (N.L.I. MS 3064): the 160 voters valued below £20 divided into 62 Tories, 77 Liberals, and 21 splitters.

TABLE 6

*Co. Down voters (1852) classified by party and by
valuation of holding*

| | N | Voting by party* | | Valuation profile of each party's vote | |
		Tory per cent	Liberal per cent	Tory per cent	Liberal per cent
£12 to under £20	1,890	53.1	17.3	46.4	45.5
£20 to under £50	1,819	52.1	17.6	43.8	44.5
£50 to under £100	348	48.3	18.7	7.8	9.0
£100 to under £200	66	50.0	6.1	1.5	0.6
£200 and over	20	60.0	15.0	0.5	0.4

* Splitters omitted

be somewhat (though only somewhat) poorer,[1] was predominantly Liberal. Of those voting a straight party ticket, 85.5 per cent of the Episcopalians, 79.7 per cent of the Presbyterians, but only 19.3 per cent of the Catholics supported the Conservatives. Yet of almost greater importance in Down were the various landlords, who, by underpinning or undermining the elements of religion and wealth, could confine electoral behaviour within very narrow limits indeed. Thus the voters of Dromara parish, whatever their religion or property, voted entirely along estate lines, while the 247 religiously mixed voters holding land from Lord Downshire in the Barony of Lower Iveagh polled virtually as a single entity—not one plumped for the tenant-right candidate and only eleven split their votes between him and one of the Conservatives.[2] Indeed, the great denominational divide was not always—in rural districts—quite so decisive as contemporaries and historians have generally assumed. Detailed geographical breakdowns of county election results show little consistent correlation between areas of Catholic concentration and anti-Tory success. And even if the electorate was a small élite,

[1] The percentage of each denomination with holdings at certain valuation levels was:

	£12 to under £20	£20 to under £50	£50 and over
Episcopalians (546)	45.9	37.5	16.6
Presbyterians (1,214)	49.3	43.9	6.8
Roman Catholics (184)	57.6	40.8	1.6

Religious affiliation is only available for certain voters in Lower Iveagh, Upper Castlereagh, and Newry, and not for most of the more Catholic areas in south Down. For sources, see Appendix—Table 6.

[2] Even though Downshire's voters were disproportionately Presbyterian and thus supposedly more likely to support tenant-right politics than were Episcopalians.

yet its denominational character cannot have been entirely isolated from that of the community at large. Sometimes the results are quite unexpected. The most Catholic parts of Donegal in 1852 were the most Tory. The same was true of Co. Wicklow in 1857 and Co. Dublin in 1865 but not in 1852.[1] Yet especially for Protestants denominational loyalty was often of profound electoral importance and helped to maintain a sense of cohesion and power within the heavily Catholic world of the south. The few Protestants in rural areas, though disproportionately enfranchised, clung together for mutual comfort. At the 1835 election many Kerry landlords were deserted by all save 'their few Protestants', while in Meath only seventeen Protestants went over to the Liberals. Protestant tenants in Wicklow in the 1830s voted overwhelmingly Conservative and in 1859 at Limerick they split their votes between a lone Tory and a 'respectable' Whig. Of the 663 Protestants on the Co. Sligo rolls in 1852, all but forty were staunch Conservatives. In Co. Dublin too the voting in 1852 followed denominational lines, an overspill perhaps of the heavily sectarian attitudes which dominated the city constituency.[2] In some cases sectarian loyalties could survive almost anything. 'It is a curious election', wrote Lord Lismore about Tipperary in 1866, 'all the Catholics supporting a Protestant candidate and the Protestants a Catholic.'[3]

Southern Protestantism was, however, predominantly an urban phenomenon, traditional iconography of the Big House and Hunt Balls notwithstanding. Whereas in the county constituencies outside Ulster, Protestants of all kinds formed only 7.2 per cent of the population in 1861, the figure for the twenty-three southern boroughs was 17.1 per cent. With such a comparatively strong demographic base, with the help of the freemen, and with, in general, a disproportionate share of wordly goods, urban Protestants were

[1] Detailed baronial voting statistics have been obtained for the following counties: Tyrone 1852 (P.R.O.N.I. D1604/9/1); Dublin 1852 (Domvile Papers MS 9361); Donegal 1852 (*Belfast Newsletter*, 2 Aug. 1852); Cavan 1855 (T. P. Cunningham, 'The Burrowes-Hughes by-election', *Breifne*, iii (1967), 203); Londonderry Mar. 1857, also 1859 (Wentworth Woodhouse Muniments T18); Antrim 1857 (*Northern Whig*, 14 Apr. 1857); Dublin 1865 (*D.E.P.* 22 July 1865); Antrim 1869 (*The Times*, 21 Aug. 1869)—and have been compared with religious breakdowns in the Censuses of 1861 and 1871, due allowance being made for the presence of parliamentary boroughs, etc.

[2] Revd A. B. Rowan to Knight of Kerry, 23 Jan. 1835, FitzGerald Papers; *Report from the select committee on Bribery at Elections*, H.C. 1835 (547), viii, 473; Lists of voters on Lord Downshire's Wicklow estate dated 17 Nov. 1832 and 18 July 1834, Downshire Papers D671/C/214/191, 234; List of voters on Dunraven estate, 1859, Dunraven Papers D3196; *Galway Vindicator*, 27 Mar. 1852; *Marked list of voters, Co. Dublin, July 1852*—copy U.C.D. Pamphlets 5328—religious affiliations are given for 343 voters in the four northern baronies: 93 of the 95 Protestants voted the straight Tory ticket, and 236 of the 248 Catholics the Liberal.

[3] Lord Lismore to Lady Donoughmore, 12 Oct. [1866], Mayo Papers MS 11144.

able to maintain a highly visible electoral presence in parts of the Catholic south (see Table 7). As a result, Tories were able to dominate places like Dublin, Bandon, and Portarlington, and to keep electoral hopes alive and even sometimes carry the day in seemingly unpromising boroughs such as Athlone, Carlow, Cork, Kinsale, Limerick, Mallow, New Ross, Sligo, Waterford, and Youghal. Religion indeed was itself a species of politics and in many towns provided the underlying point of reference for electoral action. In Derry 'Catholic and Protestant' was the 'division of parties' in 1846. Only two Catholic voters could be found to support Lord Naas at Coleraine in 1852. In Newry the Catholic vote acted as a united force.

TABLE 7

Proportion of Protestants in certain borough electorates, 1832–84

	Protestant voters per cent	Protestant population at nearest Census* per cent
Clonmel 1832	35.4	
Kilkenny 1832	12.5	
Portarlington 1835	60.9	
Athlone 1835	40.2	
Tralee 1835	35.3	
Dublin 1842	c.53.0	
Kinsale 1847	c.50.0	
Athlone 1852	36.5	
Limerick 1852	28.5	
New Ross 1852	30.7	
Waterford 1852	43.7	
Youghal 1852	34.9	
Dundalk 1859	35.5	17.5
Sligo 1859	52.6	21.7
Bandon 1863	70.0	30.3
Kinsale 1863	45.3	17.7
Limerick 1869	c.33.0	10.1
Cork 1884	c.30.0	13.8

* Available only from 1861. The religious statistics in *First Report of the commissioners of public instruction, Ireland*, H.C. 1835 [45], xxxiii cannot usefully be applied to parliamentary boroughs.

At Youghal, where the 'grand distinction' in 1851 was simply a religious one and where the Tories were all 'high Protestants', not a single Catholic came out to vote for Isaac Butt in 1852. Cashel Protestants acted as a group. Of the 411 Protestant votes cast at Limerick City in 1852, 323 went one way and only 88 the other. A Liberal canvasser at Dublin noted in 1874 how 'it runs very much Catholic and Protestant, and you find out a man's religion and you

are pretty safe'.[1] Conservative strength in Cork was heavily concentrated in those wards with the highest number of Protestants.[2] Of
the eighty-five Tralee voters who supported the victorious Liberal in
1835, only one was a Protestant, while twenty-four Catholics were to
be found among the eighty-one who preferred 'the blood-stained
Tithe system' to 'the Independence of Ireland'. In Ulster, although
Presbyterian radicalism was still in the 1860s supplying a thin stream
of non-Catholic Liberals, the increasing co-operation between Episcopalians and Presbyterians is revealed by the voting at Newry in 1868
and Derry City in 1870.[3]

	Newry	Derry
Percentage of all Protestants voting Tory	89.1	77.0
Percentage of Catholics voting Liberal	96.9	97.1

Religion was especially important for minority communities, like
southern Protestants or northern Catholics, though once the size of
the minority had diminished below a certain point (as with the rural
Protestants of the south) enthusiasm had a tendency to drain away.
But equally religion was no electoral juggernaut mowing down all
before its inexorable and predictable advance. Both the more
tangible imperatives of position, status, and cash, and the discreeter
charms of purely local needs retained their manifest and magnetic
attractions. Personal considerations and parochial pressures produced
substantial Catholic support for the Conservatives, not only in
counties, but in boroughs like Clonmel in 1835, Tralee in 1880, and
Kinsale in 1847, while at the Kinsale by-election of 1863 the more
reactionary of the two 'Liberal' candidates drew support from
Catholics, Dissenters, and members of the Church of Ireland alike.[4]

[1] Derry: B. Molloy to W. S. O'Brien, 28 Jan. 1846, Smith O'Brien Papers MS 436;
Coleraine: Autobiography of A. J. H. Moody, grocer, P.R.O.N.I. T2901/4/1; Newry: E. G.
Hallewell to Lord Naas, 31 May 1852, Mayo Papers MS 11019; Youghal: F. E. to W. Currey,
16 May 1849 and 26 Feb. 1851, Lismore Papers MSS 7183/2 and 7186, and J. Lord, *Popery
at the hustings*, p. 85; Cashel: Revd P. Leahy to Archbishop Cullen, 8 Mar. 1857, Cullen
Papers; Limerick: *Analysis of the late election of Limerick, showing the entire list of the
poll* (Limerick, 1852)—copy in Limerick City Library Bound Pamphlets kept in Office;
Dublin: *Report from the select committee on registration of parliamentary voters, Ireland*,
H.C. 1874 (261), xi, 239.

[2] R. B. Tooker to T. E. Taylor, 20 June 1868, Mayo Papers MS 11174; I. d'Alton,
'Southern Irish Unionism: A Study of Cork Unionists, 1884–1914', *Transactions of the
Royal Historical Society*, 5th series, xxiii (1973), 79.

[3] Printed List of Tralee voters, O.P. 1835/158, Box 47; *Newry Election. An alpha-
betically arranged list of electors . . . 1868; Names of the Voters at the election held in
Londonderry on Thursday, February 17th, 1870* (Londonderry, [1870])—copy at Magee
College, Londonderry. For a fuller discussion, see Chapter IV below.

[4] Lord Glengall to Sir Henry Hardinge, 15 Jan. [1835], O.P. 1835/157, Box 47; *The

As a shaper and indicator of electoral choice, religion often, therefore, melted into considerations of status and occupation. The relative strengths of the various occupational groups within borough electorates are best displayed by means of a table based on an analysis of poll books, voters' lists, and local directories (Table 8). The seven main occupational categories used, while not presenting a clear reflection of 'class' in any modern sense, provide insights into relative contemporary status and say something about class stratification. Apart from a handful of exceptions (often, like the large number of farmers and labourers in Cashel, Carrickfergus, and Cork, or of gentlemen and professionals in Dublin, explicable by local circumstances[1]), the occupational profile is remarkably consistent. Had, therefore, valuation records not indicated a significant increase in economic homogeneity, the important effects of the Franchise Act might have been entirely missed. Yet there are connections between occupation and wealth just as there were connections in nineteenth-century Ireland between what a man did and how he voted, and this in turn affected the occupational distribution of the support attracted by the various parties of the time. It is best here to talk simply of 'Tories' and 'anti-Tories', the second term encompassing that kaleidoscope of groups which adopted what was generally called the 'popular' stance. The proportion of each group voting Conservative (and therefore, by simple subtraction, the proportion voting anti-Conservative) and the respective occupational compositions of both the Conservative and anti-Conservative votes at various elections (see Tables 9 and 10) provide the best measure of the strengths and weaknesses of the relationships involved.

The preferences of the various groups, though clear enough, do not quite match expected stereotypes. Gentlemen (a particularly gnomic urban designation) were unsurprisingly Tory, in towns large and small. Professional men, despite the long years of Whig and Liberal patronage, stuck almost as closely to the Conservative cause. The mercantile class was mixed in its politics, with a slight tendency in the opposite direction. Artisans were more ambivalent than might have been supposed and provided the Tories with important support throughout the period, while the drink interest and retailers

reminiscences of an Irish land agent being those of S. M. Hussey, ed. H. Gordon (London, 1904), p. 98; *Kinsale election petition*, H.C. 1847–8 (138), xiii, 3, 145–9; lists of Kinsale voters *c.*1863 (O'Hagan Papers D2777/6), also *C.C.* 5 June 1863. See also Chapter VI, section I below.

[1] Carrickfergus and Cork as counties of towns included large rural hinterlands. Cashel, though a 'pure' borough, had been extended into the outlying 'Commons' in 1832 in order to give a sufficiently large electorate. Dublin contained many professional men, administrators, and *rentiers*.

TABLE 8

Occupations of voters in certain borough electorates, 1832-70

	Gentlemen per cent	Professionals per cent	Merchants, manufacturers, and commercial per cent	Shop-keepers per cent	Drink interest per cent	Artisans per cent	Farmers per cent	Labourers per cent	Others per cent
Cashel 1832	12.4	2.6	4.5	25.9	4.5	6.8	39.9	-	3.4
Clonmel 1832	9.8	5.0	15.0	32.2	8.6	22.1	2.1	-	5.2
Sligo 1832	15.1	4.7	10.1	27.2	8.6	15.8	8.6	-	9.9
Carrickfergus 1832*	2.8	1.6	2.4	9.4	3.1	20.0	33.6	23.3	3.8
Coleraine 1832	4.1	9.7	10.8	25.1	21.0	16.4	-	-	12.9
Belfast 1832	9.0	3.8	19.4	28.8	12.8	19.5	-	-	6.7
Belfast 1835	9.7	4.7	23.1	27.8	13.2	17.3	-	-	4.2
Belfast 1837	5.6	4.7	20.9	28.1	13.3	20.2	-	-	7.2
Cork 1835*	16.4	8.3	9.1	12.8	7.1	20.1	15.0	9.3	1.9
Tralee 1835	14.5	13.9	7.8	25.9	10.8	21.7	-	-	5.4
Youghal 1835*	15.4	6.4	10.9	25.1	13.5	19.1	-	-	9.6
Youghal 1837*	15.6	11.0	12.3	22.7	9.4	19.8	-	-	9.2

Dundalk 1847	0.4	9.5	15.2	35.5	12.6	20.3	–	–	6.5
Dublin 1832*	16.8	8.8	15.2	28.3	5.0	20.1	0.3	0.8	4.7
Dublin 1837*	20.3	12.1	12.4	24.5	6.1	19.1	0.2	1.5	3.8
Dublin 1841*	21.6	12.0	13.0	22.7	4.2	19.6	–	–	6.9
Dublin 1842*	26.1	11.2	11.1	22.6	5.0	17.3	–	–	6.7
Dublin 1857*	22.5	25.5	7.4	16.0	1.7	22.2	–	–	4.7
Dublin 1865*	25.7	26.6	8.6	13.0	1.2	20.7	–	–	4.2
Armagh 1859	7.5	19.4	22.3	27.6	11.9	11.3	–	–	0.0
Londonderry 1832*	9.2	8.2	14.7	26.4	12.8	21.2	–	–	7.5
Londonderry 1868	1.7	9.4	22.1	25.3	9.4	23.6	–	–	8.5
Londonderry 1870	1.6	9.0	21.6	20.7	12.0	26.8	–	–	8.3

* Boroughs where at least a tenth of voters were freemen.

– Category not used.

Note All figures (save those for Cashel, Clonmel, Sligo, Carrickfergus, Londonderry 1832 which are based on total electorates) are based on those actually voting, and are thus subject to differential turn-out by occupations. Overall turn-out was, however, generally high: 75 to 85 per cent or more.

constituted the most reliable forces within the anti-Tory camp.
Behaviour at the finer level of single occupations reveals ever more
detailed differences—the reasons for which are usually no longer
recoverable—as at Dublin in 1842 when the Tories were able to
attract almost three-quarters of the lawyers but less than three-fifths
of the physicians, only one in twenty-five coopers and one in twenty
grocers but half the carpenters and shoemakers, two-fifths of the
tailors, and a third of the painters.

What little evidence there is concerning the strictly economic
distribution of borough voting supports the reliability of occupational data as a measure of comparative standing in the local community. Tory voters at Dublin in 1857 were clearly wealthier than
their Liberal rivals: their properties had a mean valuation of £44. 7s.
as opposed to £24. 9s. and proportionately half as many lived in
houses under twelve pounds in value and twice as many in houses
worth fifty pounds or more.[1] At Youghal in 1835 the Tory voters'
mean local rating of £19. 6s. was noticeably, if not dramatically,
higher than the Liberals' £15. 8s.[2] In Ulster, however, the diminishing band of wealthy radical Presbyterians still added enough financial
muscle to the Liberal side to ensure that at both Lisburn in 1863
and Newry in 1868 the two parties were almost evenly matched.[3]
The religious distribution of occupations within the electorate,
though difficult to trace, was of equal importance. At Tralee in
1835 the Tory dominance among gentlemen and professional men
flowed in part from the fact that 32 of the 57 individuals involved
were Protestants, the Repealers doing best among the 79 shopkeepers
and artisans, all but 19 of whom were Catholics.[4] The disproportionate Protestant presence among the professional classes as a
whole—though less than a quarter of the population, Protestants
in 1861 supplied two out of every three lawyers and physicians[5]

---

[1] Calculated by tracing a one-in-five sample in six of the fifteen wards from the 1857–65
list of voters (see Appendix—Tables 8, 9, and 10) to Griffith's Valuation for Dublin.

[2] Calculated by tracing voters in the poll book (see Appendix—Tables 8, 9, and 10) to
the 1833 rate book for Youghal in the keeping of Cork Archives Council.

[3] Those in 'List of voters at the Lisburn election held on 21st February 1863' (P.R.O.N.I.
D1763/1) were traced to the relevant Griffith's Valuation. For Newry, see the poll book
cited in note 1 p. 32; also A. C. Hepburn, 'Catholics in the north of Ireland, 1850–1921:
The urbanization of a minority' in *Minorities in history*, ed. A. C. Hepburn (London, 1978),
p. 98. The percentages of voters in the various denominations (a) under £8, and (b) at £50
and over, were: Catholics (a) 32.3, (b) 3.2; Episcopalians (a) 24.2, (b) 6.4; Presbyterians (a)
12.4, (b) 3.2. At Downpatrick in 1857 the mean valuations of electors were: Catholics £17.
3s., Episcopalians £19. 16s., Presbyterians £21. 11s., Unitarians £26. 17s. (see annotated
list, P.R.O.N.I. D2223/21/10).

[4] See Tralee poll book noted in Appendix—Tables 8, 9, and 10. This is the only poll
book which gives occupations *and* religion.

[5] See the census-based table in *Thom 1876*, p. 633. In 1833, when more than four-fifths
of Cork City's inhabitants were Catholics, Protestants accounted for 12 of the 23 barristers,

TABLE 9

Occupational voting preferences in certain boroughs,
1832-70 (percentage voting Conservative)

	Gentle-men	Pro-fessionals	Merchants manu-facturers, and commercial	Shop-keepers	Drink interest	Artisans
Coleraine 1832	100.0	47.4	28.6	36.7	65.9	37.5
Belfast 1832	72.9	53.3	52.3	59.2	56.4	53.6
Belfast 1835	67.2	63.2	46.1	55.0	51.2	51.2
Belfast 1837	61.4	41.6	46.0	49.0	45.5	48.8
Cork 1835	75.2	71.2	35.6	37.8	17.1	51.3
Tralee 1835	70.8	69.6	30.8	39.5	16.7	47.2
Youghal 1835	87.8	76.5	58.6	35.8	11.1	60.8
Youghal 1837	75.0	70.6	47.4	34.3	10.3	62.3
Dublin 1832	71.7	77.4	26.3	17.7	5.3	33.1
Dublin 1837	73.6	74.8	41.7	31.1	12.7	54.4
Dublin 1841	78.2	71.9	39.1	31.8	7.5	50.0
Dublin 1842	80.1	71.1	42.2	36.7	15.2	40.4
Londonderry 1868	100.0	73.0	60.0	38.0	17.6	48.1
Londonderry 1870	100.0	70.3	61.0	38.8	15.3	54.1

Note Cross-party votes (splits) have been omitted in two-member constituencies.

—and among those likely to call themselves gentlemen, must clearly have helped to shape the voting habits of the wealthier electors. But, just as some lawyers were more successful than others, so some gentlemen were more equal than others. The majority of gentlemen and professionals who voted Tory at Youghal in 1835 were distinctly superior to the minority who supported Repeal, as were the Tory retailers and artisans more prosperous than their O'Connellite equivalents.[1]

In the end, although upper-income groups loomed larger in borough electorates than in the community as a whole, before 1850 the level of enfranchisement among the 'lower' groups could sometimes prove surprisingly high. At Sligo and Clonmel in 1832 almost a half and two-fifths respectively of all publicans and almost an eighth and a quarter respectively of all artisans and shopkeepers had the vote.[2] At Dublin ten years later grocers and provision dealers seem actually to

70 and 93 attorneys, 30 of the 53 physicians and surgeons, and 77 of the 131 large merchants and bankers (*C.C.* 24 Oct. 1833 cited in I. d'Alton, *Protestant Society and Politics in Cork 1812-1844*, p. 35).

[1] See note 2 p. 42 above. Only among merchants was the boot on the other foot.
[2] Calculated by comparing the lists of electors in *Fictitious Votes, Ireland*, 1st series, 3rd report, Appendix 6 with the occupational data for those males involved in the 'retail trade

TABLE 10

Occupational composition of party vote in certain boroughs, 1832–70 (in percentages)

	Gentlemen		Professionals		Merchants, manufacturers, and commercial		Shopkeepers		Drink interest		Artisans		Others	
	Tory	Anti-Tory	Tory	Anti-Tory	Tory	Anti-Tory	Tory	Anti-Tory	Tory	Anti-Tory	Tory	Anti-Tory	Tory	Anti-Tory
Coleraine 1832	8.2	0.0	9.2	10.3	6.1	15.5	18.4	32.0	27.6	14.4	12.2	21.6	18.3	6.2
Belfast 1832	11.1	5.2	3.3	3.9	17.1	21.5	30.2	28.5	12.6	13.4	18.1	21.5	7.6	6.0
Belfast 1835	11.3	6.3	3.9	4.6	19.9	22.2	30.1	27.0	12.5	15.0	16.4	17.4	5.9	7.5
Belfast 1837	8.8	6.5	2.5	5.8	20.4	21.5	32.0	24.3	11.0	15.7	17.9	21.5	7.4	4.7
Cork 1835	27.5	7.4	13.2	4.3	7.2	10.6	10.8	14.5	2.7	10.6	22.9	17.8	15.7*	34.8*
Tralee 1835	21.0	8.2	19.8	8.2	4.9	10.6	21.0	30.6	3.7	17.6	21.0	22.4	8.6	2.4
Youghal 1835	27.7	3.6	10.0	2.9	13.1	8.8	18.5	31.4	3.1	23.4	23.8	14.6	3.8	15.3
Youghal 1837	24.0	7.6	16.0	6.3	12.0	12.7	16.0	29.1	2.0	16.5	25.3	14.6	4.7	13.2
Dublin 1832	34.1	7.4	19.3	3.1	11.3	17.3	14.2	36.0	0.8	7.3	18.9	20.8	1.4	8.1
Dublin 1837	30.3	10.6	18.3	6.0	10.5	14.3	15.4	33.4	1.6	10.5	21.0	17.2	2.9	8.0
Dublin 1841	34.3	9.2	17.7	6.6	10.3	15.6	14.7	30.4	0.7	7.7	19.9	19.2	2.4	11.3
Dublin 1842	40.8	10.7	15.6	6.6	9.1	13.1	16.2	29.4	1.5	8.7	13.7	21.2	3.1	10.3
Dublin 1857	25.2	9.0	28.1	12.3	7.0	9.7	15.2	20.3	1.3	4.0	19.2	36.7	4.0	8.0
Dublin 1865	29.5	8.7	28.3	19.3	8.3	9.9	11.7	18.3	1.2	1.2	17.4	35.4	3.6	7.2
Londonderry 1868	3.3	0.0	13.6	5.1	26.4	17.8	19.2	31.6	3.3	15.6	22.6	24.7	11.6	5.2
Londonderry 1870	3.2	0.0	12.8	5.3	26.6	16.7	16.3	25.1	3.7	20.0	29.3	24.4	8.1	8.5

Note Cross-party votes (splits) have been omitted in two-member constituencies.
　* Predominantly farmers and labourers.

have had a greater chance of registration than lawyers and physicians, and the levels achieved by some craft trades were remarkable (see Table 11). Among those applying for registration at Armagh in the 1840s shopkeepers and publicans not only outnumbered gentlemen and professionals by almost four to one, but proved themselves more successful in pressing their claims.[1]

TABLE 11

Enfranchisement of certain occupations in the Dublin City constituency, 1842

	percentage enfranchised
Grocers and Provision dealers	32.3
Physicians	26.4
Lawyers	22.1
Coopers	10.5
Painters	6.2
Carpenters	6.0
Tailors	4.4
Shoemakers	4.1

Occupational and related analyses provide static snapshots of electorates constantly experiencing flux and change. The turnover of individual voters could be very swift. Some left the register completely; some left only to return again; new men appeared at every revision. Lord Downshire's tenants entered and left the Wicklow rolls with eye-deceiving rapidity in the 1830s.[2] A single revision could produce substantial changes: the Co. Waterford electorate of 3,408 lost 224 and gained 239 voters in 1868 alone. Annual percentage rates of loss and gain were always significant: 1.7 and 6.1 for Dublin City and 14.7 and 8.6 for Belfast in 1857; 6.5 and 1.9 for Co. Louth and 6.2 and 6.9 for Co. Londonderry in 1858; 1.7 and 4.7 for Co. Kilkenny in 1859; 11.2 and 10.8 for Coleraine in 1867.[3] Within four

or handicraft' sector in *Abstract of the returns made in pursuance of the acts for taking a census of the population of Ireland 1831*, H.C. 1833 (634), xxxix, 276–8, 400–2.

[1] Calculated from a series of printed lists of claimants for 1844–6 in Armagh Museum ('Armagh Borough Election File'). Of 262 applicants, 124 were successful, the percentage success rates being: Gentlemen 43.8, Professionals 41.2, Merchants, etc. 51.9, Shopkeepers 50.5, Drink interest 64.7, Artisans 39.0. Of those admitted, shopkeepers, publicans, and artisans constituted 67.7 per cent.

[2] List of Voters, 18 July 1834, Downshire Papers D671/C/214/234; J. Murray to Downshire, 5 Sept. 1837, ibid. D671/C/214/342.

[3] *Waterford Mail*, 11 Sept. 1868; *Dublin Evening Mail*, 9 Nov. 1857; *Banner of Ulster*, 10 Oct. 1857; *Central Conservative Society of Ireland: Report of the Sub-Committee 1859* (Mayo Papers MS 11025); *Kilkenny Journal*, 12 Oct. 1859; *Central Conservative Society of Ireland: Reports by agents of the revisions at the registration sessions of 1867* (Mayo Papers MS 11161).

months the new 1857 Co. Dublin electorate had lost 213 of its 6,123 members because of deaths and removals.[1] The cumulative effect was particularly marked. Of the 9,905 Dublin City voters in 1857, only 6,562 were still voters in 1864, so that almost two-fifths of Dublin's electorate in 1865 had been enfranchised for less than eight years. At Athlone only 48 of the 218 voters of 1866 had survived from the 181-strong register of 1852. The small overall drop in the Co. Carlow electorate from 2,539 in 1860 to 2,182 in 1873 conceals the departure of 2,964 and the arrival of 2,607 voters during that period.[2] But the passing of time marks out not only arrivals and departures, but also repeated occasions for remaining constant or for changing one's mind. The limited evidence available suggests that in the short term voters tended to stay within established political grooves, but whether out of 'conviction' or because the impact of influence, connection, and bribery also stayed constant is not clear. Certainly in the counties significant changes of pressure could produce substantial shifts.[3] But, in general, individual voting behaviour was not volatile, though trends in the longer term may well have been less stable. Of those who voted straight party tickets at neighbouring elections, the proportion who changed sides was generally small.[4]

	per cent
Dublin City 1832–5	4.0
Dublin City 1857–9	1.1
Belfast 1832–5	5.3
Belfast 1835–7	4.7
Youghal 1835–7	4.2
Derry City 1868–70	2.3

Such consistency could, however, be overwhelmed both by the high turnover of individuals and by abstentions. Almost a third of those who voted at Belfast in 1832 did not do so three years later, while nearly half the Youghal voters of 1835 had fallen into silence by 1837. But although electoral 'decay' could vary between different

[1] Calculated from figures in Domvile Papers MS 9361.

[2] Calculated from *The constituency of the City of Dublin as revised in the year 1864, arranged in street order and districts* [Dublin, 1864]—copy N.L.I. Ir94133 d 16; 'List of Voters' for Athlone (Burgess Papers in the Longford–Westmeath Library, Athlone); annual figures for Co. Carlow in *Committee on registration of parliamentary voters, Ireland*, H.C. 1874 (261), xi, 289.

[3] For a dramatic case in Co. Down between 1852 and 1857, see Chapter II, pp. 163–4 below.

[4] Calculated from a longitudinal study of the relevant poll books noted in Appendix— Tables 8, 9, and 10. In the two-member constituencies, split votes (which complicate the picture but were not in fact common at the Dublin and Belfast elections used) have been excluded.

occupational groups no general pattern can be said to emerge. At Youghal the best survivors were artisans, followed in descending order by gentlemen, professionals, shopkeepers, merchants, and publicans. At Belfast the order was quite different, with publicans first, and then merchants, shopkeepers, artisans, gentlemen, and professionals. Of course shifts of allegiance among individuals doubtless occurred dramatically in particular constituencies at particular times. Smaller boroughs especially could prove highly responsive to specific campaigns of a largely apolitical kind and English evidence suggests that the paucity of Irish sources may well disguise substantial if spasmodic switches in voting behaviour.[1]

Electoral influence, especially in the towns, was by no means confined to rarified levels of society, and political relationships were not simply a lightning-conductor for the conveyance of heavenly messages to earth-bound serfs. That the majority of voters in almost all the boroughs were shopkeepers, publicans, or artisans of various kinds, not only affected the electoral atmosphere, but exercised a powerful impact upon the nature of local politics. Both in this connection and in a more general sense the pre-Famine years can be called the time of the artisan, those thereafter the age of the shopkeeper.

Throughout the 1830s and 1840s the tradesmen (as artisans—rather than shopkeepers—were generally called in Ireland) maintained an active political involvement as voters and as members of political organisations. In the smaller towns such men depended heavily upon the prosperity of the surrounding agricultural hinterland. Comparatively flourishing rural districts could support an astonishing range of craftsmen. The parish of Kilmurray in Cork, with a population of 3,700 in 1841, gave some kind of livelihood, not only to 172 farmers, but also to 73 tradesmen who included 15 carpenters, 13 shoemakers, 12 smiths, 11 tailors, and 9 masons.[2] In country towns tradesmen were among the most prominent and enthusiastic depositors in the savings banks which were beginning to establish themselves.[3] Their income levels, though difficult to assess and

---

[1] See M. Drake, 'The mid-Victorian voter', *Journal of Interdisciplinary History*, i (1971), 473-90; J. C. Mitchell, 'Electoral change and the party system in England, 1832-1868' (Yale University Ph.D. thesis, 1976), Chs. V and VIII; J. C. Mitchell and J. Cornford, 'The political demography of Cambridge 1832-1868', *Albion*, ix (1977), 242-72.

[2] H. Mason, 'The development of the urban pattern in Ireland 1841-1881' (University of Wales Ph.D. thesis, 1969), pp. 112-13; D. Bullen, 'Statistics of an improved district (the Parish of Kilmurray) in the County of Cork', pp. 352-4. See also G. Alwill, 'The 1841 census of Killeshandra Parish', *Breifne*, v (1976), 32-4.

[3] G. L. Barrow, *The emergence of the Irish banking system 1820-1845* (Dublin, 1975), pp. 118-19. See also the list of investors from the Shirley estate in the Carrickmacross Savings Bank for 1835 in Shirley of Ettington Papers CR229/113/60.

affected by unemployment, were certainly higher than those of that desperate class, the agricultural labourers. Artisans in Dublin were more prosperous in the 1840s than they had been thirty years earlier. In 1840 the mean weekly wage for twenty-five Dublin trades was 19s. 2d. Wages were lower elsewhere, but in 1846 the mean weekly earnings of shoemakers, carpenters, blacksmiths, and nailers throughout the country were probably between twelve and thirteen shillings as compared with the four shillings and six pence of the agricultural labourer. By the mid-1850s, although some artisans like nailers were already under heavy industrial pressure, such differentials were in general still being maintained.[1] The artisans of the major towns in pre-Famine Ireland were actively engaged in politics. In Dublin, where many trades were well unionized, Catholic artisans constituted the most energetic proponents of Repeal and Protestant artisans the loudest and most volatile defenders of ascendancy.[2] But while Cork artisan Repealers in the Trades Association kept themselves separate from the O'Connellite merchants in the Chamber of Commerce, principles could sometimes be combined with self-interest, as when the Dublin Operative Coachmakers supported O'Connell's Protestant running-mate, Robert Hutton, at the election of 1837.

It is, and ever has been, in the factory of the Messrs Hutton, that the honest artisan always found the value of his labour, and every inducement to promote his enterprising genius . . . even the very children of coachmakers lisp the praise of the name of Hutton. Vote for Hutton and O'Connell.[3]

However, neither O'Connell's Lichfield House compact with the Whigs nor his attacks on combination provided Repeal tradesmen with much to enthuse about. And although Catholic artisans responded enthusiastically to the campaigns of the 1840s, this was

[1] F. A. D'Arcy, 'Dublin artisan activity, opinion, and organization, 1820-1850' (University College Dublin MA thesis, 1968), pp. 168-76. The 1846 figures have been calculated from *Sixth annual report of the commissioners for administering the laws for the relief of the poor in Ireland*, H.C. 1852-3 [1645], 1, 317-22. Adopting the labourers' national mean of 6s. 4d. for 1854-5 as base 100, we find weavers at 150, tailors 189, shoemakers 200, bakers 255, carpenters 282, bricklayers and masons 287 (F. Purdy, 'On the earnings of agricultural labourers in Scotland and Ireland', *Journal of the Statistical Society*, xxv (1862), 425-90).

[2] Lord Stuart de Decies to Clarendon, 8 Apr. 1848, Clarendon Papers Box 10. Unless otherwise stated, what follows is based on F. A. D'Arcy, 'Dublin artisan activity, opinion, and organization, 1820-1850', and 'The artisans of Dublin and Daniel O'Connell 1830-47: An unquiet liaison', *Irish Historical Studies*, xvii (1970), 221-43; Jacqueline Hill, 'The Protestant response to Repeal', pp. 35-68; Maura Murphy, 'Fenianism, Parnellism, and the Cork Trades 1860-1900', *Saothar*, No. 5 (1979), 27-38, and 'The economic and social structure of nineteenth century Cork' in *The Town in Ireland*, ed. D. Harkness and M. O'Dowd, pp. 125-54.

[3] *D.E.P.* 29 July 1837.

to prove an Indian summer rather than the shape of things to come. By the mid-century the Dublin tradesmen had become 'backward-looking men, dreaming dreams of a bygone world and attempting to restore it'. Their organizations became geared, not to the great issues of the day, but to 'catering for their particular concerns as working men'. In Cork too the trade society 'was in decline as a unit of political organization and expression', and although the Fenians were to involve themselves in artisan activities, the bread-and-butter issues of employment and pay were to achieve a greater and more exclusive prominence.[1]

The artisans of other towns, though less well organized, were not without political influence. At the Derry election of 1837 the Conservative candidate's diary records an unceasing round of attention.

McLaughlin shoemaker . . . Freeman the pavior . . . Several of the rope-spinners . . . promised their votes, gave them something to drink . . . Got a promise of vote from . . . Brennan a rope-spinner . . . Devine the coppersmith called, gave him a few shillings . . . Canvassed Evans the painter . . . Andrews the cabinet maker called . . . Canvassed J. Stewart the plaisterer, Thos. Quinn the soap-boiler.[2]

In towns like Galway and Limerick, where artisans had once been electorally active in opposition to 'Tory Despotism and Corporation Monopoly',[3] financial imperatives were leading to an emphasis upon the driving of hard sectional bargains in return for votes. By the 1850s the various Galway guilds and the Congregated Trades of Limerick had turned themselves into electoral banditti prepared to manœuvre deftly and rewardingly amidst the often corrupt world of local politics. For every occasion on which trades might march on an issue of 'principle', as they did at Limerick in 1867 to mourn the Fenian dead,[4] there were a hundred demonstrations, paid for by cash on the nail, in favour of parliamentary candidates with big purses. At Dungarvan in 1853 the 'respectable tradesmen' hung about while assorted hopefuls canvassed the town. At Ennis 'confidential arrangements' released the trade banners from pawn, and sweeteners of thirty pounds per trade ensured a lively demonstration along the principal streets. Bandon tradesmen showed publicly

[1] F. A. D'Arcy, 'Dublin artisan activity, opinion, and organization, 1820-1850', pp. i, 77-8; Maura Murphy, 'Fenianism, Parnellism, and the Cork Trades 1860-1900', p. 28. See also S. Daly, *Cork: A city in crisis, A history of labour conflict and social misery 1870-1872* (Cork, 1978), on the famous tailors' strike.

[2] G. R. Dawson's election diary T874.

[3] The words of a trades poster displayed at Galway enclosed in B. Warburton to H. Hardinge, 14 Jan. 1835, O.P. 1835, Box 46.

[4] B. Mac Giolla Choille, 'Mourning the Martyrs: A study of a demonstration in Limerick City, 8 December 1867', *North Munster Antiquarian Journal*, x (1967), 173-205.

on which side their bread was buttered by massing behind their banners to welcome the visiting Duke of Devonshire.[1] Artisans as a whole do not in any case seem to have been particularly radical in their electoral behaviour, and it is notable that in towns of all sizes —Dublin, Derry, Coleraine, Tralee, Youghal—they were second only to gentlemen and professionals in their lack of support for 'advanced' candidates. Merchants and shopkeepers, on the other hand, were more enthusiastic, so that pre-Famine Ireland (though its politics often reverberated to artisan excitement) may be said to have been the home, not of the radical shoemaker, but of the radical grocer.

After the Famine the crucial experience of artisan life was one of relative and absolute decline. As time went on, more and more crafts fell victim to mass production: nailing, shoemaking, carpentry, sawing, and many more. Already by 1851 the Dublin Trades Association was agitating against the 'Monster Houses' which impoverished 'the native artisan' and swelled 'the tide of pauperism'. By the 1870s the increasing number of import warehouses, especially in the footwear and furnishing businesses, had greatly reduced job opportunities in many localities.[2] Outside Belfast there were few large firms able to offer employment at a time when traditional crafts were declining and previously skilled jobs being 'replaced' by unskilled work in the transport, distribution, and building sectors.[3] And, because the differential between skilled and unskilled was probably higher in Ireland than in England, the outcome was even more serious than it might otherwise have been.[4] Under these circumstances artisans had little time for either the quasi-Chartism of Bertram Fullam's short-lived Irish Democratic Association of 1850 or for movements such as the Tenant League or the Independent Irish Party whose programmes seemed almost perversely remote. While shopkeepers, merchants, and publicans fought to put their names on the lengthy Cavan tenant-right petition of 1850, the local tradesmen held almost entirely aloof.[5]

---

[1] *Report from the select committee on the Dungarvan election petition*, H.C. 1854 (162), viii, 497; *Clare election petition*, H.C. 1852-3 (595), ix, 665-85, 712-13; *C.C.* 7 Oct. 1863.

[2] *Western Star*, 22 Feb. 1851; H. Mason, 'The development of the urban pattern in Ireland 1841-1881', p. 300; *Western Star*, 11 July, 1, 29 Aug. 1868; J. Lee, 'The Railways in the Irish Economy' in *The Formation of the Irish Economy*, ed. L. M. Cullen (Cork, 1969), pp. 77-87.

[3] Mary Daly, 'Late nineteenth and early twentieth century Dublin' in *The Town in Ireland*, ed. D. Harkness and M. O'Dowd, pp. 223-4. Even Guinness's employed only 2,000 wage-earners in 1886 as compared to the 4,000-5,000 employed in 1893 at the much less highly capitalized York Street Spinning Company in Belfast.

[4] J. Lee, 'Railway labour in Ireland 1833-1856', *Soathar*, No. 5 (1979), 17.

[5] *Nation*, 17 Jan. 1852; T. P. Cunningham, 'The Cavan tenant-right meeting of 1850', *Breifne*, iii (1969), 417-42.

Henceforth the electoral activity of artisans was to depend upon short-term needs and immediate influences. Occasionally working men would have themselves nominated and make speeches of iron cynicism, like the 'mechanic' at Kilkenny who in 1865 denounced any man who voted 'against the wishes of his landlord, when no good can be done by his doing so, [as] no better than a fool' or the tailor at Drogheda in 1859 whose chief political complaint concerned the price of whiskey.[1] Apart from the small band of dedicated Fenians, tradesmen seem to have confined themselves to intermittent electoral mobilization on behalf of favoured employers. The Liberal, Jonathan Pim, and the Tory, Sir Benjamin Lee Guinness, gained cross-party support at Dublin in 1865 from tradesmen 'on the ground of their being good employers and promoters of the manufactures of the country'. At Kilkenny W. J. Doherty, who provided a thousand local jobs, received the public support of the Operative Carpenters' Trade Union, the Operative Tailors' Society, the Operative Shoemakers, and the Nailers' Operative Society. Some tradesmen did of course eventually come to support Home Rule and to collaborate with farmers, especially in the west of the country.[2] But as a group artisans represented a declining force. By the mid-1880s a doleful queue of trade representatives told the select committee on industries of the depression caused by imports to everything from glovemaking to ironfounding.[3] The decline in numbers tells the same story. Towns like Mallow, heavily dependent on craft trades in 1841, experienced a severe fall in the numbers of cabinet makers, tailors, bootmakers, and the like in the decade after 1845. Nationally the number of shoemakers and dealers more than halved, from 52,000 in 1841 to 25,000 in 1881, although the overall population dropped by little more than a third. Even in Kilkenny there were less than half as many cabinet makers in 1881 as in 1841, while as a proportion of occupied adult males, the artisans of Cork registered a steady decline from 40.9 per cent in 1841 to 19.1 per cent forty years later.[4]

As artisans suffered, so publicans and shopkeepers prospered. Those designated as 'working and dealing in food and lodgings'

---

[1] *Tipperary Advocate*, 15 July 1865; *Drogheda Argus*, 7 May 1859.

[2] *Irish People*, 15 July 1865; *Kilkenny Journal*, 17, 24 Mar. 1880; *Freeman's Journal*, 16 Nov. 1885; S. Clark, *Social origins of the Irish Land War* (Princeton, 1979), pp. 268-9.

[3] G. Pellew, *In Castle and Cabin*, p. 194; *Report from the select committee on Industries (Ireland)*, H.C. 1884-5 (288), ix, 814-28.

[4] H. Mason, 'The development of the urban pattern in Ireland 1841-1881', pp. 203, 297-300; Maura Murphy, 'The economic and social structure of nineteenth century Cork', pp. 127, 137-8. See also *D.E.P.* 5 Nov. 1850.

(almost exclusively shopkeepers and publicans) grew from one in 166 of the population in 1841 to one in 78 in 1881. Whereas the eight million Irishmen of 1841 had enjoyed the services of 2,744 grocers selling tea, coffee, and the like, the five million of 1881 patronized no less than 11,776.[1] Publicans constituted one of the most powerful and permanent pressure groups in the country. Enfranchised at a high level, they supplied over one in ten of all voters in towns such as Coleraine, Belfast, Tralee, Youghal, Dundalk, Armagh, and Derry (see Table 8). Some places supported a positive flotilla of licensed traders, many of whom sold other things besides drink. More than one in ten of the *inhabitants* of Athlone, Bandon, Coleraine, and Newry held a licence in 1851-2 and one in twenty did so in Wexford, Sligo, and Drogheda.[2] Thirty-six of Youghal's hundred or so publicans voted at the general election of 1835. In 1870 Longford Town boasted sixty-six public houses, while Mallow's forty-seven publicans constituted over a fifth of that borough's total electorate.[3] This powerful interest was generally enthusiastic for Repeal, Liberalism, and Home Rule. In return, Repeal, Liberalism, and Home Rule were careful to keep tender watch over the political interests of alcohol and its distributors. 'They appealed to me', noted O'Connell in 1836, 'as their chief manager and supporter. I, of course, accepted that offer. Most of them were most active, useful, and valuable constituents.'[4] Yet the Dublin vintners who claimed to have 800 votes in 1865 were prepared to swallow even Conservatism when it came in the agreeable shape of Sir Benjamin Lee Guinness. Acting as a consistent pressure group, they denounced Sunday closing in 1874 and welcomed the Reform Act of 1884 in the belief that 'the admission

---

[1] S. Clark, 'The political mobilization of Irish farmers', *Canadian Review of Sociology and Anthropology*, xii (1975), 490, and *Social origins of the Irish Land War*, pp. 127-8, 268; H. Mason, 'The development of the urban pattern in Ireland 1841-1881', p. 301; Charles Booth, 'The economic distribution of population in Ireland' in *Ireland: Industrial and Agricultural*, ed. W. P. Coyne (Dublin, 1902), p. 65; A. W. Orridge, 'Who supported the Land War? An aggregate-data analysis of Irish agrarian discontent 1879-1882', *Economic and Social Review*, xii (1981), 210-14. Orridge adopts a more cautious approach, but even in his Table 2 on p. 211 the purely retail occupations of publican, butcher, and grocer show a rise from 22,456 to 34,274. See Chapter VI below.

[2] *Galway Vindicator*, 19 May 1852.

[3] *Poor Inquiry (Ireland) Appendix E containing baronial examinations relative to food, cottages and cabins, clothing and furniture, pawnbroking and savings banks, distillation*, H.C. 1836 [37], xxxii, 307; *Copy of the shorthand writer's notes of the judgement delivered by Mr Justice Fitzgerald, and of the minutes of evidence taken at the trial of the Longford election petition*, H.C. 1870 (178), lvi, 489; E. L. O'Malley and H. Hardcastle, *Reports of the decisions of the judges*, ii (1875), p. 18.

[4] O'Connell to Lord Duncannon, 23 June 1836, *Correspondence of Daniel O'Connell*, ed. M. R. O'Connell, v, 378-80. See also Ebrington to Morpeth, 26 May 1839, Carlisle Papers L.-B. 35.

of the working classes to the exercise of the franchise gives the trade an assurance that future legislation upon the liquor question will be founded upon a basis of fact rather than theory or fanaticism'.[1] In 1874 Cork publicans supported only candidates inimical to Sunday closing. Waterford publicans, who in 1868 constituted over a tenth of the electorate and had a 'good deal of influence', did the same. In 1880 publicans mounted organized attacks on the water-drinking MP, A. M. Sullivan, and helped, by means of five-hundred-pound cheques and personal canvassing, to keep the bibulous Philip Callan afloat in Louth, despite the fierce opposition of Parnell. In Cork the licensed vintners issued periodic endorsements of particular candidates. In Kilkenny they forced one who had been teetotal for thirty years to pledge himself to keep the pubs open on the Sabbath day.[2] In a curious way, both temperance and the drink interest were able to prop up nationalism in general and Repeal in particular, for both represented a characteristic aspect of Irish Catholic culture. Official reports in 1843 pointed to both pub conviviality and temperance meetings as occasions for the reinforcement of Repeal sentiment.[3] Thereafter, however, Catholic enthusiasm declined for a time and it was not until later in the century that the Pioneer Total Abstinence Association of the Sacred Heart was able once again to reintegrate temperance, Catholicism, and nationalism into a coherent political and cultural unity.

Occasional temperance hiccups left the drink interest unscathed. The per capita consumption of taxed spirits remained steady at about a gallon a year between 1857 and 1901. While the population fell the domestic sales of Guinness increased from 71,000 hogsheads in 1855 to 262,000 in 1875, mostly outside Dublin and not, it seems, at the expense of other brewers whose production rose also, though more slowly.[4] All the efforts of an extremely energetic landlord failed to do more than cut the number of pubs in Bandon from fifty in 1840 to 'a little over forty' in 1880: in effect

---

[1] *D.E.P.* 12 July 1865; *Irish Times*, 28 Jan. 1874; *C.C.* 11 Dec. 1885.

[2] *Cork Examiner*, 2 Feb. 1874; *Waterford Mail*, 25, 28, 30 Sept., 19, 23 Oct. 1868; *Drogheda Argus*, 10, 17 Apr. 1880; *C.C.* 19 Mar. 1880; *Kilkenny Journal*, 17, 20 Mar. 1880. At the Louth election 'wealthy and influential publicans proceeded to the scene of action from Dublin, Belfast, Drogheda, and other places, and aided in getting up the excitement throughout the county' (T. D. Sullivan, *A. M. Sullivan: A Memoir* (Dublin, 1885), pp. 134–5).

[3] Printed reports in Derby Papers 34; also T. Bolton to Stanley, 15 June 1843, ibid. 107/3.

[4] K. H. Connell, *Irish Peasant Society: Four historical essays* (Oxford, 1968), p. 46 (the decline of poteen would have affected mainly the shebeens); P. Lynch and J. Vaizey, *Guinness's Brewery in the Irish economy 1759–1876* (Cambridge, 1960), pp. 199–202. For production figures, see T. W. Grimshaw, *Facts and Figures about Ireland Part I* (Dublin, 1893), pp. 36–8.

not a cut at all but a rise from one for every 181 to one for every 100 inhabitants.[1] Of course some licensed houses were marginal places. Glasses of whiskey were sold over many a rural grocer's counter and many pubs were probably run as much for social as for commercial reasons.[2] Yet the larger publicans were politically well placed as men upon whom a wide variety of relationships converged. At the Clare election of 1859, for example, they acted as 'money-holders' for the six-pound bribes being offered. At Cashel in 1868 they behaved as informal clearing-houses for information, as brokers between the dispensers and receivers of favours.[3] As such, they themselves demanded and received favours usually in the form of extravagant hiring fees for their premises or huge orders for drink to be distributed among the electors and their hangers-on. At Derry in 1837 G. R. Dawson was persecuted by seventeen publicans angrily demanding settlement of a previous election's accounts: 'a general opinion seemed to prevail among my friends that great danger would ensue if they were not paid.' He did not hesitate long and the publicans, who in 1832 had formed an 'Independent Club' in order to extract as much cash from the candidates as possible, retired to count their winnings.[4] All twenty pubs in Carrickfergus kept open house at the candidates' expense in 1832. Two years later the organizational centre for bribery at Dungarvan was located in the local brewery. Limerick publicans successfully demanded larger and larger orders at the 1858 election. At Roscommon in 1859 enormous sums were spent on drink as much to please the publicans as the voters, for, as Judge Morris remarked of Mallow in 1870 (where twenty-two enfranchised licensees had suddenly switched sides *en bloc*), 'the case is . . . very often . . . that persons are afraid that if they do not provide entertainment and drink to secure the interests of the publicans . . . they will become unpopular'.[5] Publicans without votes could still 'command'

[1] W. Bence Jones in *Evidence taken before Her Majesty's Commissioners on Agriculture*, H.C. 1881 [C 2778-I], xv, 366.

[2] *Fictitious Votes, Ireland*, 1st series, 1st report, p. 378. J. M. Mogey's findings (*Rural life in Northern Ireland* (London, 1947), p. 116) that in Hilltown Co. Down in the 1940s (pop. 135) seven of the ten pubs did little business, but were kept 'as a method of maintaining contact with the outside world by their lonely owner' ring true of earlier years also.

[3] *Minutes of evidence taken before the select committee on the Clare election petition*, H.C. 1860 (178), xi, 103-5; *Minutes of evidence taken at the trial of the Cashel election petitions*, H.C. 1868-9 (121), xlix, 216-17.

[4] G. R. Dawson's election diary T874; G. R. Dawson's election expenses T1048/4; also H. J. Perry and J. W. Knapp, *Cases of controverted elections*, pp. 272-9.

[5] Ibid. 529-34; J. W. Knapp and E. Ombler, *Cases of controverted elections*, pp. 1-5; F. S. P. Wolferstan and E. L'E. Dew, *Reports of the decisions of committees of the House of Commons in the trial of controverted elections during the seventeenth parliament of the United Kingdom* (London, 1859), pp. 235-9; F. S. P. Wolferstan and S. B. Bristowe, *Reports*

others to do as they required and men who could influence publicans themselves were men of influence indeed.[1]

Shopkeepers represented more diverse interests. But what they lacked in cohesion they made up in numbers and influence. About a quarter of the electorate of most boroughs came from their ranks, as did a proportion of urban voters in the county constituencies. Their social role was not without its ambiguities. Especially in the smaller towns, where private acts were quick to become public knowledge, they were not simply the dispensers of credit, favours, and gossip, but the recipients of political pressures exerted by customers. Different kinds of retailer were open to different pressures from different directions: village hucksters from the poor, booksellers from the reading classes, colonial outfitters from the gentry. Exclusive dealing, as it was called, became a major Irish pastime and a prime means for transmuting disenfranchised attitudes into electoral power. The Tories flaunted purses and their opponents numbers. At Youghal in 1835 'men of the most abandoned habits and wretched circumstances . . . beset the shops' in the Repeal interest, while Tory ladies angrily cancelled their orders at stationers who had failed the cause.[2] O'Connell hypothesized for the people of Kerry and Tralee: 'Suppose a man took a stick and marked a line in the gutter before the door of the pitiful wretched Catholic [retailer] who would sell his vote against his country and his God to uphold tithes. That line would be found as impassable as a wall of brass.' And so it happened. Shopkeepers' doors were marked with a cross; bakers, clothiers, and publicans lost business; O'Connell assisted by clerical acolytes walked the streets to twist the arms of waverers.[3] The same was to happen again and again, with only minor grace notes to add variety to an old tune. Country shops in Kilkenny were festooned with notices in 1835 threatening their owners with desolation if they 'dont meak their fathers, brothers, and cusins vote for the people'. 'Who will deal with an Orangeman?' demanded a poster in neighbouring Carlow. At Bandon 'fellows with sticks, near the doors of the shops' kept a constant patrol. Meath priests paraphrased

of the decisions of election committees, pp. 102-13; E. L. O'Malley and H. Hardcastle, *Reports of the decisions of the judges*, ii (1875), pp. 18-22.

[1] Documents on Kildare election of 1847 in Mayo Papers MS 11028; Donoughmore to Naas, 9 Apr. [1857], ibid. MS 11036.

[2] M. Greene to W. Gossett, 6 Mar. 1835, O.P. 1835/166, Box 47; *C.C.* 7 Feb. 1835; *D.E.P.* 14 Feb. 1835; *Committee on Bribery at Elections*, H.C. 1835 (547), viii, 516-19.

[3] *Pilot*, 7 Jan. 1835; *Committee on Bribery at Elections*, H.C. 1835 (547), viii, 267; *Hansard*, xxvii, 1129-34 (15 May 1835); T. Dumas to Knight of Kerry, 29 Dec. 1834, Lord Kenmare to Knight of Kerry, 8 Jan. 1835, Lady Kenmare to Knight of Kerry, 13 Jan. 1835, all FitzGerald Papers; Stenographer's report of Repeal meeting, 12 Feb. 1835, O.P. 1835, Box 46.

O'Connell and demanded that circles 'be drawn round the door . . . they should get a calf's head, "Staggering Bob", they all knew what they meant, and nail it to the door'.[1] Twenty and thirty years later the same pressures were still being applied, if perhaps a little less flamboyantly.[2] The gentry too directed their purchasing power with electoral ends in view. 'He broke his solemn promise made to me last election . . . so Johnny and I with John paid our bills at his shop and walked over to Mr Hennessy, which was a loss of about a £100 a year.'[3] A Youghal Repealer who went bankrupt and a Dublin woollen draper who lost 'a large Conservative connection' demanded compensation from Repeal funds. In Drogheda a flour dealer's takings dropped from twenty-five pounds to twenty-seven shillings a week during the 1857 election because of exclusive dealing. Even large department stores like Cannock's in Limerick were sensitive to customers' complaints of shop assistants appearing on election platforms and only needing 'the *bonet rouge* to fully equal the most extreme red'.[4]

That integration of shopkeepers within local communities which laid them open to pressure also ensured that many were able to assume positions of influence and power. Buying and selling are reciprocal acts and, more often than not, involve a set of mutual rather than merely one-sided obligations. Already during the fifteen years before the Famine some retailers were beginning to establish themselves politically as well as economically. After the municipal reforms of 1840, shopkeepers, vintners, and merchants were able to dominate Cork corporation, while in Dublin the traditional corporation 'business élite' was being diluted by the arrival of pawnbrokers, publicans, and grocers. As early as 1837 the twenty-one elected Clonmel town commissioners included eight shopkeepers, four

[1] Report of Chief Inspector Cameron, 14 Jan. 1835, O.P. 1835, Box 46; of Constable Valentine, 15 Jan. 1835, O.P. 1835, Box 34; of Chief Constable Watkins, 18 Jan. 1835, O.P. 1835, Box 45; *Dublin Evening Mail*, 5 Jan. 1835.

[2] See, e.g., *D.E.P.* 20 Mar. 1851; *Nation*, 17 Apr. 1852; *Londonderry Standard*, 16 July 1852 and 19 July 1865; R. W. Stony to J. Wynne, 11 Aug. 1852, O.P. 1852/16/253; *Dublin Evening Mail*, 8 Apr. 1857; *Londonderry Sentinel*, 10 Apr. 1857; M. Battelle to C. W. Cooper, 13 Apr. 1857, O'Hara Papers MS 20355; Bishop Delany to Archbishop Cullen, 1 Feb. 1861, Cullen Papers; *Dundalk Democrat*, 14 Nov. 1868 ('Retailers of bread in the rural districts have been visited, and told not to deal with certain bakers in Drogheda. Drapers have been visited by sturdy persons, who told their customers to "clear out of the shop" ').

[3] A. W. Blake to Clanricarde, 12 Mar. 1857, Clanricarde Papers 40. See also *C.C.* 28 May 1859 and 28 Feb. 1863; *Dublin Evening Mail*, 1 Apr. 1857; *Galway County election petition*, H.C. 1872 (241-I), xlviii, 354-5, 411, 655.

[4] O'Connell to T. Drummond, 8 Apr. 1839, *Correspondence of Daniel O'Connell*, ed. M. R. O'Connell, vi, 231; Luke Dillon to O'Connell, 9 Sept. 1846, O'Connell Papers N.L.I. MS 13649; *Minutes of evidence taken before the select committee on the Drogheda election petitions*, H.C. 1857 (255 Sess. 2), vi, 96; *Limerick Chronicle*, 1 Apr. 1880.

publicans, and five merchants.[1] Retailers in Derry, Galway, Tipperary, Waterford, Dungarvan, and Queen's Co., to give only a few examples, had already established themselves as men of political weight able to influence votes other than their own.[2] And although there were many exceptions, the majority of southern shopkeepers seem to have supported O'Connell, most perhaps from conviction but some certainly from compulsion.[3]

After the Famine the shopkeeper entered his promised land.* Ill winds were blowing their goodness to men like the 'little ferrety shopkeeper' encountered by a dyspeptic Carlyle at Scariff in 1849: 'seemingly chief man of the place . . . he had got his house new floored; was prospering, I suppose, by workhouse grocery-and-meal trade, by secret pawnbroking—by *eating* the slain.'[4] Although the post-Famine recovery was not quite as swift as some have suggested, it was certainly well under way by the mid-1850s. In 1852 bank-note circulation began to climb again and bank deposits for the first time surpassed those of 1846. Between 1853 and 1875 (the longest period for which comparable figures are available) the annual value of income and property assessed for tax per head of the population rose by a half from 69s. to 103s. 6d.[5] As agriculture became more commercial so its marketed (though not its total) output rose between the 1840s and 1870, with money to be made for those who did the marketing. With the contraction of artisan crafts the economic base of country towns and villages was narrowing and retailing was becoming the main urban function.[6] Retailers prospered by selling

* For further aspects of Post-Famine retailing, see Chapter VI, section I below.

[1] Maura Murphy, 'The economic and social structure of nineteenth century Cork', p. 126; Mary Daly, 'Late nineteenth and early twentieth century Dublin', pp. 227-9; *Fictitious Votes, Ireland*, 1st series, 1st report, pp. 376-9.

[2] G. R. Dawson's election diary T874; J. H. Monohan to M. J. Blake, 2 Feb. 1847, Blake of Ballyglunin Papers M6936/58; Glengall to Clarendon, 9 Sept. 1847, Clarendon Papers Box 41; Carew to Clarendon, 19 Apr. 1848 and [Apr. 1848], ibid. Box 8; S. Jones to W. Gossett, 9 Feb. 1834, Hatherton Papers D260/M/01/2493; W. Shortt to Lord Farnham, 19 Mar. 1831, Farnham Papers MS 18612.

[3] Lord Eliot to Graham, 15 Nov. 1843, Graham Papers 11/Ir; Lord De Grey to Eliot, 8 Sept. 1843, ibid. 5/Ir; printed answers to Government questionnaire, May 1843, Derby Papers 34; Lord Stuart de Decies to Clarendon, 8 Apr. 1848, Clarendon Papers Box 10; Jacqueline Hill, 'The role of Dublin in the Irish national movement 1840-48' (University of Leeds Ph.D. thesis, 1973), pp. 69-78; Maura Murphy, 'The economic and social structure of nineteenth century Cork', pp. 140-2; *Fictitious Votes, Ireland*, 1st series, 2nd report, p. 24. See also Tables 9 and 10 above.

[4] Thomas Carlyle, *Reminiscences of my Irish journey in 1849* (London, 1882), pp. 181-2.

[5] J. Lee, 'The dual economy in Ireland 1800-1850', *Historical Studies*, viii (1971), 191-201. See also the memoranda of 1850 and 1851 made by Mr Murray of the Provincial Bank for Clarendon (Larcom Papers MS 7562); H. Mason, 'The development of the urban pattern in Ireland 1841-1881', p. 301.

[6] L. Kennedy, 'Farmers, traders, and agricultural politics in pre-Independence Ireland'

imported mass-produced goods at the expense of local tradesmen. By the early 1870s country shopkeepers in Cork were carrying 'on a trade such as was undreamt of twenty years ago'. Shops ranged from the magnificent to the squalid. Cannock's in Limerick, with its opulent décor, liveried attendants, and gaily varnished delivery carts, was only one great shop among many in a town which boasted two palatial chemists with medicines to 'physic the whole of Munster' and three 'enormous groceries and Italian warehouses'. More typical were the general stores 'where everything seems to be sold, from ironmongery and American sewing machines to sweetstuffs and national newspapers'.[1] In towns like Tuam and Ennis quite modest retailers were prepared in the 1870s to spend sums of £200 or even £500 improving their premises, while particularly successful entre-preneurs ruthlessly purchased the freeholds of rivals in order to force them out of business.[2] Yet, small establishments did survive, some profitable, many not. The atmosphere of the lowest was like that of the marginal pubs. Touring Donegal in the 1880s with a commercial traveller (who dealt in tea, sugar, drapery, spirits, cordials, and life insurance) George Pellew saw an old man digging. 'We called to him and went into his hut to try to sell him some tea. No sign was on the door, but one of the side rooms was a tiny shop, where eggs, butter, pipes, and tobacco were lying promiscuously on dingy shelves.' Horace Plunkett—espousing both the co-operative and the macro-biotic movements—was also offended by the 'clay pipes lolling their heads against the window sashes', the 'turf-laden atmosphere', the 'dirty meal moulding in rotten bins', and the 'few loaves for those whose style of living demands scientifically whitened bread'.[3]

Large employers of retailing, mercantile, and manufacturing labour could easily make political capital out of their positions. At the top of the tree, men like the Guinnesses, Jonathan Pim, the Dublin merchant, and William Martin Murphy, the retailing and transport magnate, mobilized employees at elections and behaved like the rural landlords which some of them were in the process of becoming. After Sir A. E. Guinness had topped the Dublin poll in 1874 fifteen hundred brewery workers were marshalled by the head

in *Irish peasants, violence, and political unrest 1780-1914*, ed. S. Clark and J. S. Donnelly Jr. (Manchester, 1983), pp. 339-73; T. W. Freeman, 'The Irish country town', *Irish Geography*, iii (1954), 7.

[1] W. Bence Jones, *The life's work in Ireland of a landlord who tried to do his duty* (London, 1880), p. 60 (written in 1871); A. I. Shand, *Letters from the west of Ireland 1884* (Edinburgh and London, 1885), pp. 167-70, 216.

[2] *Report from the select committee on town holdings*, H.C. 1886 (213), xii, 2-6, 72-9, 99-104.

[3] G. Pellew, *In Castle and Cabin*, pp. 232-9; H.C. Plunkett, 'Co-operative stores for Ireland', *Nineteenth Century*, xxiv (1888), 411.

foreman to give 'vent to their enthusiasm in round after round of the heartiest cheers. The well-trained band . . . forty strong were shortly afterwards on the ground, under the leadership of their efficient conductor, Mr Conliffe.' At Kilkenny in 1859 the gentrified merchant MP, Michael Sullivan, celebrated his victory with a banquet beyond the local newshounds' wildest superlatives. 'When we entered the mansion, we were dazzled with its magnificence. The reception room reminded us of an eastern palace . . . every luxury that could pander to the tastes was there, and the wines were in grand condition, and *ad libitum*.'[1] In vain did the declining artisans protest against what they thought the Manchester School face of Quaker philanthropists like Pim.[2] Everywhere the magnates were on the march. Sir Peter Tait, the army-clothing king, employed 1,800 people in Limerick and augmented his considerable influence by offering interest-free loans to political leaders. James Spaight could never have kept the Tory cause alive in Limerick (he actually won the 1858 by-election) without substantial business connections. Sir John Arnott (who had a little list of all the drapers in Kinsale who owed him favours) sat for that borough both as a charity-dispensing machine and as the employer of 1,100 people to whom he paid £90,000 a year.[3] The owners of many of the 'first establishments' in Cork crowded the polling booths in 1859 to keep their enfranchised employees up to the political mark, and Limerick merchants too issued electoral instructions to those on their payrolls.[4] The Richardsons of Lisburn, who won elections in the 1850s and 1860s, reminded voters of the £40,000 spent annually in the town, while Robert Webb collected a respectable Conservative vote at Mallow as late as 1880 largely because of the £14,000 his business dispensed each year in wages and railway charges. At Waterford in 1868 the Tories were shrewd enough to realize that 'any one unconnected with the trade of the town' stood no chance of success.[5]

---

[1] *D.E.P.* 10, 11 July 1865; *Irish Times*, 9 Feb. 1874; *Freeman's Journal*, 24 Nov. 1885; *Kilkenny Journal*, 14 May 1859.

[2] John Flint, *Mr Jonathan Pim and the Dublin Freemen* [Dublin, 1868]—copy N.L.I. J667: 'Demand and supply . . . are his governing principle . . . Pim Brothers know no man after they have paid his wages.'

[3] T. E. Taylor to Duke of Abercorn, 18 Oct. [1868], Abercorn Papers T2541/VR/266; Tait to W. Monsell, 7 July 1865, Monsell Papers MS 20676; Spaight's correspondence with Naas, Mayo Papers MS 11036; for Arnott, see O'Hagan Papers D2777/6, *C.C.* 3, 5 May 1859, and Chapter VI, section I below.

[4] *C.C.* 10 May 1859; *Committee on parliamentary and municipal elections*, H.C. 1868-9 (352), viii, 276.

[5] *Banner of Ulster*, 21 Mar. 1857 (Another Lisburn employer actually imprisoned enfranchised workers in his factory at the 1863 election: F. S. P. Wolferstan and S. B. Bristowe, *Reports of the decisions of election committees*, pp. 221-8); *C.C.* 31 Mar. 1880; G. F. Bloomfield to Mayo, 21 July 1868, Mayo Papers MS 11162.

The majority of small merchants and shopkeepers compensated for their comparative lack of individual wealth by their numbers and their strategic social and topographical locations. Like publicans, they provided clearing-houses for electoral bribes and favours. At Kinsale a hardware dealer acted as 'a sort of managing man at all elections'. Limerick shopkeepers were essential to the corrupt issuing of 'tickets' redeemable against goods from local stores. A Clare toyshop owner was the key negotiator between candidates and blocs of purchasable voters. In Cashel a modest fancy-goods dealer organized crucial support for a candidate who was an 'extensive customer' at all local shops. Above all, shops were meeting places for those with news, votes, and influence: 'It happened to be market day in Clifden, and in Casey's drapery and spirit shop a little circle of farmers sat and talked.'[1] Candidates liked to canvass amidst a cloud of shopkeepers and to be proposed or seconded by well-known local retailers on the hustings. In 1868 shopkeepers were the largest group within Dungarvan's radical élite and also provided the bulk of the candidates standing for election to the town council in Derry City. At the Tralee Town poor-law elections of 1881 two grocers headed the poll, one in the Nationalist and the other in the landlord interest.[2] Shopkeepers in Armagh successfully encouraged contested elections in order to 'push trade'. At Cookstown they operated as an electoral clique at the Tyrone by-election of 1873, while seven years later a rural Tyrone grocer and hardware dealer controlled no fewer than fifty votes among clients and dependants.[3] Monaghan shopkeepers organized tenant petitions on the Shirley estate, and shopkeepers' bills were often more successful than landlords' rent demands in extracting cash from farmers in difficult times.[4]

[1] *Kinsale election petition*, H.C. 1847-8 (138), xiii, 5; F. S. P. Wolferstan and E. L'E. Dew, *Reports of the decisions of committees of the House of Commons*, pp. 235-9; *Clare election petition*, H.C. 1860 (178), xi, 113-19; *Cashel election petitions*, H.C. 1868-9 (121), xlix, 141; G. Pellew, *In Castle and Cabin*, pp. 180-1.

[2] *Dublin Evening Mail*, 16 Feb. and 30 Mar. 1857; *D.E.P.* 3 July 1865; cutting in Flanagan scrap-book respecting Sligo, N.L.I. MS 14335; Clanricarde Papers 40; printed petition on behalf of Revd James Anderson O.S.A. in Cullen Papers; *Londonderry Sentinel*, 27 Oct. 1868 (occupations traced in 1868 poll book noted in Appendix—Tables 8, 9, and 10); W. L. Feingold, 'The Irish boards of poor law guardians 1872-86: A revolution in local government' (University of Chicago Ph.D. thesis, 1974), p. 163.

[3] F. McKee to Revd H. McKee, 11 Nov. 1868, McKee Papers D1821/1/8; J. C. Lowry to Lord Belmore, 15 Mar. 1873, Belmore Papers D3007/P/23; W. Renwick to J. W. Ellison Macartney, 10 Apr. 1880, Ellison Macartney Papers.

[4] J. Holland to E. P. Shirley, 5 May 1879, Shirley of Ettington Papers CR229/115/25; G. Molony, RM to Chief Secretary, Sligo, 19 June 1880, in printed Cabinet Papers CAB37/2/31; B. H. Becker, *Disturbed Ireland: Being the letters written during the winter of 1880-81* (London, 1881), pp. 213, 49-50, 107-8; B. L. Solow, *The land question and the Irish economy 1870-1903*, p. 87. For the credit relationship between shopkeepers and customers, see Chapter VI below.

Almost any position of power was capable of yielding electoral influence. Clerks to poor-law unions had some control over the drawing-up of election registers. Departments of state and local authorities spent money and awarded contracts with an eye to more than mere efficiency. Protestant employers sacked Catholic servants as a general protest against O'Connellite triumphalism.[1] In 1852 Galway poor-rate collectors, whose positions 'would enable them to exercise a great influence over the electors', were unashamedly canvassing the town, while other poor-law officials were active on behalf of the heroically corrupt Christopher Weguelin at Youghal in 1868. Even the police were not above making sophisticated use of their powers of detention to deprive candidates of votes.[2] Limerick's Church of Ireland dean forced choristers and vergers to vote Liberal in 1859, while the governor of Sligo Gaol made so energetic a song and dance of his electoral neutrality in 1868 as to suggest more partisan behaviour on previous occasions. Archbishop MacHale felt it necessary in 1852 to proclaim at the Galway hustings that voters needed no 'political godfathers to be answerable for the political creed and conduct of citizens often much more intelligent and enlightened than themselves'.[3] Prominent among such godfathers were the local representatives of the expanding commercial banks. As early as 1835 a Tralee director of the Provincial Bank was sacking staff and using his special business knowledge to oppose O'Connell's local interests. At Derry two years later agents for both the Provincial and the Bank of Ireland were prepared to discount bills for sympathetic voters and 'use their influence' among the tradesmen.[4] And the evidence for intervention by the Bank of Ireland on the Tory side at Dublin and Longford in 1837, by the Northern Bank on behalf of the Tories at Belfast and Coleraine in the 1850s, by the Provincial Bank at Sligo in 1857, and the National Bank at New Ross in 1863, clearly represents only the public face of a wider secret network of

[1] Papers of the Incorporated Society for Promoting English Protestant Schools in Ireland (henceforth cited as Incorporated Society Papers) MS 5805 (1850s); Eliot to Graham, 5 Jan. 1842, Graham Papers 7/Ir; Graham to Eliot, 16 Jan. 1842, ibid. 7/Ir; *C.C.* 7 Feb. 1835. In 1865 the Cashel town commissioners withdrew rent concessions from tenants who had voted against their wishes (*Tipperary Advocate*, 29 July 1865).

[2] *Galway Vindicator*, 10 July 1852; *Waterford Mail*, 9 Nov. 1868; *Central Conservative Society of Ireland: Report of the Sub-Committee 1859* (Mayo Papers MS 11025); C. F. Johnson to R. Bourke, 7 July 1852, ibid. MS 11019.

[3] J. Spaight to Naas, 9 May 1859, Mayo Papers MS 11036; E. Walsh to C. W. O'Hara, 13 Nov. 1868, O'Hara Papers MS 20348; B. O'Reilly, *John MacHale, Archbishop of Tuam. His life, times, and correspondence*, 2 vols. (New York, 1890), ii, 333.

[4] G. Lyne, 'Daniel O'Connell, intimidation, and the Kerry elections of 1835', *Journal of the Kerry Archaeological and Historical Society*, No. 4 (1971), 80, 96; G. R. Dawson's election diary T874.

political influence.[1] On the basis of his fraudulent Tipperary Joint Stock Bank (1838-56) John Sadleir was able to have himself, his brother, and two cousins returned to Parliament. So powerful was he that many Protestant voters in Carlow refused to support the Tories, 'being in money matters connected with the Tipperary Bank'. Although banks tried to restrain their senior staff and barred managers from running branches in their own native districts for fear of nepotism and other chicaneries, it seems generally to have been the case that the Bank of Ireland supported the Conservatives and the National Bank the O'Connellites or Liberals, while the others remained either neutral or unpredictable.[2] With the expansion of the branch network from 31 in 1829 to 404 (plus 147 sub-branches) in 1879, the local manager became a figure of increasing influence throughout the countryside. 'He is the man who has it in his power to accommodate farmers, and in doing so he acquires a knowledge of the farming class and those who have money . . . [so that he] can often be of service to a farmer, not alone in discounting for others, but in many matters of ordinary life.'[3]

At a less exalted level the growing number of pawnbrokers who operated only in towns and specialized in small loans of about half-a-crown at high rates (and high risks) were also able to make political capital out of their place within the local scheme of things. Even in a small town like Antrim the pawnbroker was issuing almost 12,000 tickets a year throughout the 1830s to a population of 2,655. Through contacts with the 'lowest class' (as a Youghal witness put it in 1835) pawnbrokers could organize those large mobs of 'bludgeon men' without which few Irish elections were complete. The great majority were Catholics and formed, together with publicans, a special kind of conduit for the movement of political sentiment, personal favours, and instant mobilization.[4] Three of the six Youghal pawnbrokers of the 1830s were themselves voters. They were all

[1] *D.E.P.* 20, 27 July 1837; Boyd to Naas, 27 Mar. 1852, Mayo Papers MS 11018; *Belfast election compromise*, H.C. 1842 (431), v, 271-86; *Dublin Evening Mail*, 8 Apr. 1857; *C.C.* 2 June 1863. The powerful director of a Kinsale bank was also active at the 1847 election (*Kinsale election petition*, H.C. 1847-8 (138), xiii, 12-17).

[2] J. Lord, *Popery at the hustings*, p. 9; *Waterford Mail*, 21 Sept. 1868; J. Kintore (of the Provincial Bank) to Sir C. Domvile, 8 Apr. 1857, Domvile Papers MS 9361. The policy of not appointing locally was a late development (*Report from the select committee on Industries (Ireland)*, H.C. 1884-5 (288), ix, 247).

[3] Evidence of a Cork land agent in *Minutes of evidence taken before Her Majesty's Commissioners on Agriculture*, H.C. 1881 [C 2778-I], xv, 842-3. For the growth of banking, see Chapter VI below, especially Table 53 and the sources there cited.

[4] R. J. Raymond, 'Pawnbrokers and pawnbroking in Dublin: 1830-1870', *Dublin Historical Record*, xxxii (1978), 15-26; *Ordnance Survey Memoir for the Parish of Antrim* (1838), ed. B. Trainor (Belfast, 1969), p. 103; *Poor Inquiry (Ireland) Appendix D*, H.C. 1836 [36], xxxi, 311; *Poor Inquiry (Ireland) Appendix E*, H.C. 1836 [37], xxxii, 307.

prosperous—and staunch O'Connellites.[1] At the Newry election of 1832 pawnbrokers were active as electoral go-betweens. In Co. Carlow they were prominent in the Liberal Club, while at the Dublin elections of 1868 a Protestant pawnbroker played havoc with party calculations by changing sides and taking with him his detailed list of those freemen most heavily in debt and most open to cash-on-the-nail persuasion.[2]

Electoral influence functioned not only by means of party organization or individual relationships between those with power and those in debt, but through the more complex mechanisms of groups of people bound together by mutual interests, shared obligations, or family bonds. Given sufficient time, political connections, even if built on the shifting sands of cash and favours, could sometimes achieve a remarkably coherent momentum of their own. Most obviously impressive were the large connections managed by landlords in the countryside or by wealthy merchants and urban proprietors in the towns. The latter were able to dominate some of the smaller boroughs virtually unaided, at least for short periods. At Athlone in the 1870s John Ennis 'and his father had been for years notoriously engaged, directly and thro' agents, in corrupting the electors by loans of money, which after young Ennis's election were to be instantly converted into gifts. Over *a hundred* electors were universally believed to be bound in this way.'[3] William Stacpoole at Ennis had been building up a connection long before his election in 1860, and so successfully, that it maintained him at Westminster until his death in 1879. Although he was nominally a Liberal, 'his relatives, who are numerous and influential', were able to secure the support of some twenty-five 'Tory' voters who preferred 'him to any candidate not locally connected'.[4] Sometimes two or three groups of virtually equal importance were locked in permanent combat, as at Enniskillen, where, after the 1850s, the landed Coles and the urban Collums (merchants) and Danes (lawyers), all of them Conservatives, fought a complicated game of musical chairs at contested and

---

[1] Youghal poll book for 1835 noted in Appendix—Tables 8, 9, and 10; Youghal rate book for 1833 in keeping of Cork Archives Council.

[2] *Report from the select committee on the Newry Borough election petition*, H.C. 1833 (76), x, 600; *Minutes of evidence taken before the committee on the Carlow County election petition*, H.C. 1837 (307), x, 91; *Commissioners [on] . . . the freemen electors of the City of Dublin*, H.C. 1870 [C 93], xxxiii, 13.

[3] Bishop Gillooly to Archbishop Cullen, 6 Feb. 1874, Cullen Papers. 'Mr Ennis has certain friends and dependants on the Leinster side of the town who will *certainly* vote for him' (Bishop Kilduff to Cullen, 4 Apr. 1856, ibid.).

[4] J. Kenny to Dr Carolly, [1863], O'Hagan Papers D2777/6; Bishop Flannery to Cullen, 19 Feb. 1860, Cullen Papers.

uncontested elections alike.[1] Other such powerful factions were led by Lord Portarlington in the borough of that name, the Protestant primate in Armagh, Lord Bandon in Bandon, the Bagwells in Clonmel, John Boyd in Coleraine, the Duke of Devonshire (or, more properly, his agent) in Dungarvan, and the Jephson-Norreys family in Mallow.

More numerous, however, were the smaller connections intent on trading a united support for individual or local favours. Too modest to merit the attentions of contemporary recording angels like Dod, they none the less provided perhaps the most pervasive means by which electors could combine for mutual benefit and protection. Some were entirely kin groups and most were constructed around a core of family relationships. Despite the increasing mobility of the people, the potential for kin co-operation is highlighted by the local dominance of a handful of surnames, especially in rural areas. 'Strong kinship links were important characteristics in these communities and undoubtedly the concentration of name-groups . . . in the mid-nineteenth century represented the operation of kinship at its height.'[2] Even in a town as large as Cork, election officials were constantly confused by the armies of Murphys and Macarthys coming up to poll. Of Derry's 1,521 borough voters in 1870 no less than 41 (all but two of them Catholics) were called Doherty.[3] Relatives voted and bargained together or coalesced with others to form a congeries of interlocking family groups. 'Thomas McColgan', noted G. R. Dawson at Derry in 1837, 'called in the evening and he agreed to give his own and brother's votes provided that I assisted his family . . . Mr John Hyndman called—promised his own vote and that of Quigley.' Thirty years later Lord Claud Hamilton trembled for his chances if Mr Colquhoun (who controlled 'the whole influence of his family') were not given the Crown Solicitorship which had been promised him. Many of the quarrels between leading Cork Repealers in the 1840s stemmed from 'certain personal and inter-family rivalries in the city'.[4] In Galway the pursuit of cash was fiercely contested by the party of Dr Browne, by the Fynns

[1] *Daily Express*, 20 Oct. 1852; Lord Enniskillen (head of the Coles) to Naas, 16 Dec. [1858], Mayo Papers MS 11026; Lord Erne to Mayo, 1, 11, 18 Aug. 1868, ibid. MS 11165; Duke of Abercorn to Mayo, 5 Feb. 1868, Abercorn Papers T2541/VR/85/37. Lord Naas succeeded to the earldom of Mayo on 12 Aug. 1867.

[2] P. J. Duffy, 'Irish landholding structures and population in the mid-nineteenth century', pp. 8–11. Six of the 309 surnames to be found on the electoral roll of Athlone Barony (Co. Roscommon) for 1858–9 (Incorporated Society Papers MS 5805) covered more than a fifth of the 843 voters. See also T. Jones Hughes, 'Landlordism in the Mullet of Mayo', *Irish Geography*, iv (1959), 16–34; W. Nolan, *Fassadinin: Land, settlement, and society in south-east Ireland 1600–1850* (Dublin, 1979), pp. 179–81.

[3] *Fictitious Votes, Ireland*, 2nd series, 1st report, p. 256; Derry poll book for 1870 noted in Appendix—Tables 8, 9, and 10.

[4] G. R. Dawson's election diary T874; Hamilton to Abercorn, 28 Nov. 1868, Abercorn

('the Fynns are with us' was a comforting cry), by the score of voters under Theobald Blake, by the 'Clare Militia' (an extended family of marble-cutters), by O'Connor the solicitor's connection, by the Barna voters under Henry Comerford, by the 'Lynch Party', and by various other *forces de frappe* based on a mixture of family and occupational identities: the bell-ringers, fishermen, printers, tailors.[1] In 1857 a butcher appeared before the select committee examining Galway's colourful election history.

Have you any relations who are in the same trade as yourself?—I have my brother and my sons-in-law. Are they voters?—They are; and my brother-in-law is too; we have three more; we have five, there are 23 in my family, all brothers-in-law. The whole 23 are connected with each other?—The whole of the 23. All those 23 of the trade that are connected with you, are they voters?—They are, every one of them.[2]

The trick was, as another witness remarked, to collect all 'the men who had influence as well as votes' and make them an offer they could not refuse. Failure to do so could prove dangerous, as one self-styled electoral 'strong man' threateningly informed Chichester Fortescue at the Louth election of 1854. Voters actively organized the flow of favours from candidates to voteless relatives. At Longford in 1869 the provision of free beer was extended to 'sons, brothers, and relations'.[3] In Kinsale half the voters belonged to personal factions, while many of the rest would, in the words of one local analyst, 'go with the crowd'. A certain police constable became widely courted in 1863 for 'having two or three publicans under his finger . . . for keeping irregular hours [which] will induce

Papers T2541/VR/299; Maura Murphy, 'Repeal and Young Ireland in Cork Politics 1830–1850', Abstract of University College Cork MA thesis, 1975, in *Bulletin of the Irish Committee of Historical Sciences: Thesis Abstracts No. 1* (1979), pp. 37–42. See also J. Hayes to O'Connell, 14 Aug. 1840, *Correspondence of Daniel O'Connell*, ed. M. R. O'Connell, vi, 352–3 ('Whenever a member of a [Cork] family has been started a candidate for public employ, the whole division of kindred deem it necessary to eschew Repeal, lest of its embarrassing the speculation'); C. Gavan Duffy, *Thomas Davis: Memoirs of an Irish patriot 1840–46* (London, 1870), p. 164.

[1] *Western Star*, 6 Mar. 1869; A. W. Blake to Clanricarde, 12, [14], 18 Mar. 1857, Clanricarde Papers 40; D. Perrse to Clanricarde, 27 Mar. 1857, ibid.; J. Blakeney to M. J. Blake, [July 1847], Blake of Ballyglunin Papers M6936/58; T. Lee to M. J. Blake, 1 Feb. 1859, ibid. M6936/81; H. Caddy to M. J. Blake, 7 July [1841], ibid. M6936/46; R. O'Gorman to W. S. O'Brien, [Feb. 1847], Smith O'Brien Papers MS 441; The Compositors of the *Galway Vindicator* to M. J. Blake, [1847], Blake of Ballyglunin Papers M6936/57; E. Kelly to M. J. Blake, 27 July 1847, ibid. M6936/58. See also F. S. P. Wolferstan and E. L'E. Dew, *Reports of the decisions of committees of the House of Commons*, pp. 136–44.

[2] *Minutes of evidence taken before the select committee on the Galway Town election petition*, H.C. 1857 (187 Sess. 2), vi, 556–7. Forty-eight butchers in all had the vote.

[3] *Galway Town corrupt practices commission*, H.C. 1857–8 [2991], xxvi, 425; P. M. Gartlan to C. Fortescue, 9 May [1854], Carlingford Papers CP3/19; E. L. O'Malley and H. Hardcastle, *Reports of the decisions of the judges*, ii (1875), pp. 12–15.

them to vote' as he wished.[1] At Bandon in the same year T. K. Sullivan led a 'phalanx' of relatives against the massed forces of the Bernards and the Shaws. A decade later his defeat was revenged when the thirty-odd Sullivans put the needle into William Shaw, the sitting member, by making highly 'unpleasant disclosures' as to his business dealings.[2] Examples of similar feuds and family cliques in other constituencies could be multiplied almost without end.[3]

The ties of kinship run like a leitmotiv through Irish life and politics. Outside the large cities they provided a standard against which it was possible to test the validity of economic, social, and political decisions. Especially in small to middling towns people often chose their grocer or shoemaker on grounds of family connection. 'Goodwill' as attached to premises rather than individuals had no meaning, as a Clonmel ironmonger explained in 1837: 'When you go to a person and know the person which is the case in all the small towns I am acquainted with, if that person moves into another corner of the town or street, he does just as much business in his establishment there as the one he left.'[4] Relationships and long-standing connections set off intricate reverberations in men's minds. A candidate at the Co. Cork election of 1841 was only allowed to canvass a certain family in Kanturk if accompanied by a Protestant magistrate who had been fostered out to them as a child. A Tory landlord at the Co. Galway by-election of 1872 (when the victorious Captain Nolan got forty-two votes from his own close family alone) was about to be attacked by a frenzied mob in Gort when 'a man of the name of James Coffin . . . a man who knows everything, came round, and he said "I carried this gentlemen as a child in my arms", and the men collected round me and said that nobody would touch me, and they said "We will see you up to your hotel" and there was immense cheering'. Another was accosted by a ragged mendicant on

[1] List of voters (1863) in O'Hagan Papers D2777/6; H. E. O'Donnell to T. O'Hagan, 5 Jan. 1863, ibid.

[2] *C.C.* 25 Feb. 1863; F. E. to W. Currey, 3 June 1863, Lismore Papers MS 7190; H. Law to Lord Hartington, 14 Nov. 1872, Devonshire Papers 340/513.

[3] See, for example, *Committee on Bribery at Elections*, H.C. 1835 (547), viii, 480 (Meath); Poster found in Co. Kilkenny outside shops, in Report of Chief Constable Cameron, 14 Jan. 1835, O.P. 1835, Box 46; Report of Sub-Inspector Brownrigg, 21 Jan. 1835, O.P. 1835, Box 46 (Kerry); Captain Jocelyn to [G. Studdart], 8 June 1852, Incorporated Society Papers MS 5848 (Dundalk); Archbishop Beresford to Naas, 14 Apr. 1859, Mayo Papers MS 11036 (Armagh);—to O'Hagan, 9 May 1863, O'Hagan Papers D2777/6 (Tralee); T. Slattery to Butt, 10 July 1865, Butt Papers MS 8687 (Youghal); *Tipperary Advocate*, 15 July 1865 (Cashel); *Commissioners [on] . . . the freemen electors of the City of Dublin*, H.C. 1870 [C 93], xxxiii, 1119; F. Ellis to Lord Belmore, 20 Mar. 1873, Belmore Papers D3007/P/533 (Tyrone).

[4] *Fictitious Votes, Ireland*, 1st series, 1st report, p. 269. Clonmel was then the tenth largest town in Ireland.

the road to Tuam. ' "Oh Sir, give me some assistance for I know you well", said he, "What do you know of me", said I. "I knew your family when you lived at Rathfake", said he.' Even the Marquess of Clanricarde (whose family name was De Burgh) was stopped by an aged man in the Mayo mountains 'who insisted upon my drinking goblets of raw whiskey with him because I was in his opinion and phraseology "the mother (!) of the Burkes, the old root" '.[1]

The promotion of such attitudes and of strong kin bonds within constituencies was encouraged by the intimate nature of Irish political life. Although not unrelated to the intensified localism of the immediate post-Famine years (for which it provided a necessary substructure),[2] this was a constant, distinct, and separate phenomenon. Much political discourse was a matter of reference and allusion, incomprehensible to outsiders. Most constituencies had local 'characters' who provided boisterous entertainment and hermetic dialogue. Youghal's court room boasted a Greek chorus which 'kept up a running fire of comments and pungent remarks'. Repeal meetings in Cork were graced by 'Bothered Dan' in 'military jacket and cocked hat'. The Newry hustings featured loud *badinage* about the wife-swapping proclivities of agents and voters. Derry had 'Hunter Gorman' the 'well-known independent non-elector', Dungarvan 'Nov Nov', a tediously articulate fisherman, Limerick 'Dirty Larry' Kelly, Waterford a character known as 'Red Lights' who specialized in arcane interjections of a broadly pessimistic flavour, such as 'What's the world to a man if his wife's a widow?'[3] A notice posted during the Meath election of 1835 called for vengeance against 'the old potteen man James Morgan . . . Morgan the shoemaker or snob. . . . George Reynolds Old Jokes . . . Henry Hazlewood apothecary that would poison his patient with the look of his eye'. Carlow Repealers singled out 'Snuffling Garret Kinsella . . . Black-eyed Martin Hughes . . . Gemmy Whitty . . . the tallow eater . . . and poor sweaty Kilbranish the driver'. A renegade Tory was execrated by his former associates as 'Doctor Judas' in

---

[1] *Minutes of the proceedings of the select committee on the Cork County election petition*, H.C. 1842 (271), vi, 78–9; *Galway County election petition*, H.C. 1872 (241-I), xlviii, 821, 362, 525; Clanricarde to Clarendon, [Nov. 1847], Clarendon Papers Box 9.

[2] See Chapter VI below; also K. T. Hoppen, 'National politics and local realities in mid-nineteenth century Ireland', pp. 190–227.

[3] J. O'Connell, *Recollections and Experiences*, i, 145; Maura Murphy, 'Municipal Reform and the Repeal Movement in Cork 1833-44', *Journal of the Cork Historical and Archaeological Society*, lxxxi (1976), 13; *Newry Borough election petition*, H.C. 1833 (76), x, 612; *Londonderry Sentinel*, 18 July 1865; *Waterford Mail*, 18 Sept. 1868; B. Cahir, 'Irish National By-Elections 1870–1874' (University College Dublin MA thesis, 1965), p. 50; P. H. Bagenal, *The Life of Ralph Bernal Osborne M.P.* (London, 1884), pp. 263–4.

a ballad sung at Youghal in 1837. Individual voters were woven
into song.[1]

> John Ellison, be careful John; on Porter's land right well
> We know what tenants got from you, when tenants had to sell;
> It was not much, now was it John? Our memory's somewhat sore,
> Just 'two years purchase' was the rule, 'two years, and nothing more'.

Digging out the dirt was, indeed, a minor election industry. Tory
candidates wrote to headquarters asking how best to discredit
their opponents. Partisans supplied the' information unprompted.
A prospective candidate at Coleraine had been 'a shopman or rather
a shop boy in . . . a linen . . . house', his father had 'died in a mad
house and . . . there was madness on his mother's side', his brother
was mad too and he himself up to his eyes in debt to a 'cent per
cent money lender'.[2] The hustings (abolished in 1872) provided a
splendid platform for the hitting of nails on local heads. 'Is he anything', demanded a speaker of a Waterford candidate in 1837, 'to
the notorious Reilly Cope, who in '98 was an active and efficient
supporter of the triangle and pitch-cap government of the day?'
Candidates and their supporters were accused of violating 'all and
every one' of their engagements (Mayo, 1847), watering the workhouse milk (Galway, 1852), evicting 'poor Mrs Grogan while in
fever' (Tipperary, 1865), turning but two leaves of their missal
at Sunday mass (Dungarvan, 1868), buying 'flax as cheap' as possible
(Tyrone, 1873), not paying Christmas or Easter dues to the priest
(Co. Limerick, 1874).[3] Radicals in danger of being outflanked were
fiercest of all. 'You may', remarked the nationalist Father Lavelle
in 1874, 'have often heard the question put—"Who is this Mr
O'Connor Power?" I often did but never could get an answer. I am,
however, now in a position to tell you that he is the bastard son of
a policeman named Fleming from Co. Cavan, and a house painter
by trade.'[4]

---

[1] Copies in Reports of Chief Constable Coghlan, 27 Jan. 1835, O.P. 1835, Box 47, and
Constable Valentine, 15 Jan. 1835, ibid. Box 34; 'Youghal Protestant Operatives Scrap-
book 1829-48' (Bradshaw Collection, C.U.L. Hib.1.844.1)—contains many similar items;
Ballad attacking J. Ellison Macartney in Belmore Papers D3007/P/154 (see also 'Adair's
Defeat' in Seymour of Ragley Papers CR114A/538/3).

[2] E. G. Hallewell to Naas, 31 May 1852, Mayo Papers MS 11019; J. Stephenson to Lord
Downshire, 19 Mar. 1852, ibid. MS 11018, sent by Downshire to the Tory Chief Secretary
(10 Apr. 1852, ibid.) in the belief that 'it may be useful if this fellow opposes you'.

[3] *D.E.P.* 3 Aug. 1837; *Telegraph or Connaught Ranger*, 18 Aug. 1847; *Galway Vindi-
cator*, 31 Mar. 1852; *Tipperary Advocate*, 16 Feb. 1865; *Waterford Mail*, 11 Sept. 1868;
J. F. Lowry to Belmore, 24 Mar, 1873, Belmore Papers D3007/P/68 ('Can you not get
Grey Porter's antecedents?'); *Daily Express*, 19 Jan. 1874.

[4] Lavelle to Butt, 12 Mar. 1874, Butt Papers cited in D. Thornley, *Isaac Butt and Home
Rule* (London, 1964), p. 184.

In such an atmosphere it was difficult to disguise actions or beliefs, especially as the intrinsically public nature of political life was intensified by exponents of electoral espionage who opened letters, intercepted telegrams, and forced meetings to adjourn to more leak-proof locations.[1] 'Blacklists' were posted of voters who had failed the cause in the certain knowledge that all would immediately be subjected to vociferous public abuse. 'Behold', ran one at Gorey in 1852, 'the men that eat meat on Friday and all for Mr George the Bobby Bawn.'[2] 'In Ireland every man's politics are just as well known as the noon-day' and 'everyone at bottom understands his neighbour's motives and his game'.[3] As a result, the outcome of elections could often be predicted with an accuracy quite different from the astrological guesswork normally associated with such undertakings.[4] But although this meant that many elections remained uncontested, the residuum of uncertainty which necessarily remained and the *amour propre* of individuals and parties ensured the continuing triumph of hope over experience.

Within the microcosm of individual constituencies there existed the yet smaller world of particular townlands or particular streets. That voting patterns in counties were localized is hardly surprising, but boroughs too were made up of communities with identifiable attitudes and values. Sometimes the distinctions were religious, sometimes economic, sometimes arbitrary. A Derryman's place of abode spoke strongly of his politics. At Cashel there was a division between town and suburbs. Coleraine's factions had firm topographical locations. Sligo was 'split up into little streets each having their own candidates'. Of those who in 1867 attended the large Limerick demonstration in memory of the 'Manchester Martyrs'

[1] H. E. O'Donnell to O'Hagan, 10 Jan. 1863, O'Hagan Papers D2777/6; P. F. French to M. J. Blake, 30 Aug. 1857, Blake of Ballyglunin Papers M6935/33; Downshire to J. W. Maxwell, 7 Apr. 1852, Perceval-Maxwell Papers D3244/G/1/156.
[2] See, for example, Report of W. Miller, 16 Feb. 1835, O.P. 1835, Box 46 (Kinsale); *D.E.P.* 6 Jan. 1835 (Waterford Borough); *Dublin Evening Mail*, 2 Feb. 1835 (Co. Carlow); *Kinsale election petition*, H.C. 1847–8 (138), xiii, 125–9; Letters from G. Brown, 10 Aug. 1852, J. Keady, 9 Aug. 1852, J. Hughes, 3 Aug. 1852, in Mayo Papers MS 11037 (Co. Wexford, King's Co., Co. Donegal).
[3] *Committee on parliamentary and municipal elections*, H.C. 1868–9 (352), viii, 180; W. Bence Jones, *The life's work in Ireland*, pp. 74–5.
[4] For some examples, see *D.E.P.* 11 Dec. 1834 (Tralee); ibid. 29 July 1837 (Clonmel); G. G. Aylmer to Naas, 7 Apr. 1851, Mayo Papers MS 11017 (Kildare); *Dublin Evening Mail*, 9 Nov. 1857 (Dublin City); *Central Conservative Society of Ireland: Report of the Sub-Committee 1859*, Mayo Papers MS 11025 (Waterford Borough); F. E. to W. Currey, 14 Feb. 1857, Lismore Papers MS 7188, and T. Slattery to Butt, 10 July 1865, Butt Papers MS 8687 (Youghal); *Central Conservative Society of Ireland: Reports by agents of the revisions at the registration sessions of 1867*, Mayo Papers MS 11161 (Newry); *Freeman's Journal*, 27 Nov. 1885 (Derry City).

over a third came from no more than ten streets.[1] In Belfast during
the 1830s 'Catholic streets' housed voters less socially elevated and
substantially less inclined to vote Tory than the constituency as a
whole.[2] In 1868 the heavily Protestant and working-class districts
voted overwhelmingly for the maverick Orangeman, William Johnston,
while the respectable residential and commercial centres remained
loyal to more orthodox Conservatism. At Lisburn in 1863, when
the overall vote was almost tied, particular streets split in proportions
of one to two and even one to three.[3] A study of the narrow Tory
victory at the Dublin City election of 1841 shows how localized
and class-bound party support *could* be. Almost two-fifths of those
voting lived in ninety-one streets divided by the census commissioners
into first and second-class private, and first, second, and third-class
shop streets (see Table 12).

TABLE 12

Voting by streets in the Dublin City constituency, 1841

	percentage voting Tory
1st class, private	77.8
2nd class, private	64.7
1st class, shop	63.6
2nd class, shop	37.4
3rd class, shop	34.8

The clear line of division running between the first- and second-class
shop streets demonstrates the Conservatives' hold on the more
exclusive retailing as well as the better residential areas. Residence
not only reflected a man's status, but perhaps also influenced his
politics. Lawyers in expensive areas were noticeably less Liberal
than lawyers in poorer areas. High-class shops harboured Tories,
low-class shops Repealers. Tradesmen serving the gentry at close

[1] G. R. Dawson's election diary T874; *Report of the Commissioners appointed for the purpose of making inquiry into the existence of Corrupt Practices at the last election for Cashel; with minutes of evidence*, H.C. 1870 [C 9], xxxii, 120; J. McFarland to Naas, 22 May 1858, Mayo Papers MS 11024; T. Mostyn to J. Whiteside, 14 Apr. 1859, ibid. MS 11036; B. Mac Giolla Choille, 'Mourning the Martyrs', p. 199.

[2] Comparing the percentages of those voting the straight Liberal ticket in Hercules St., Carrick Hill, and Smithfield with those of all voters doing so (latter in parentheses) we find—1832 (R. J. Tennent and W. S. Crawford being designated Liberals): 58.1 (37.8); 1835: 49.5 (41.0); 1837: 60.7 (49.2). In 1832 the proportion of gentlemen, professional, and mercantile etc. voters was 9.7 per cent in the 'Catholic area' as opposed to 32.2 per cent in the constituency as a whole (see poll book for 1832-7 noted in Appendix—Tables 8, 9, and 10).

[3] F. Wright, 'Protestant ideology and politics in Ulster', *Archives Européennes de Sociologie*, xiv (1973), 255. For Lisburn, see the list of voters, P.R.O.N.I. D1763/1.

quarters voted with their neighbours, and even the notoriously Liberal drink interest wavered when set amidst lusher pastures (see Table 13).

TABLE 13

Voting by streets and occupations in the Dublin City constituency, 1841

	1st class private streets	1st class shop streets	3rd class shop streets
	(percentage voting Tory)		
Gentlemen	90.8	88.9	60.7
Professionals	70.0	57.6	50.0
Merchants, etc.	67.9	63.8	25.0
Shopkeepers	70.0	58.1	26.0
Drink interest	—	37.5	6.7
Artisans	90.5	63.6	57.3

Electoral politics involved, however, not only a high proportion of voters, but many others also, attracted by connections of family, business, dependence, belief, love of crowds, or simple curiosity. The accurate turn-out figures which can be calculated for the general elections of 1832, 1857, 1859, and (to a lesser precision) 1852 demonstrate the high level of voter participation. Indeed, they under-estimate it, for deaths, absences, and double entries on the registers probably alone reduced nominal electorates by anything between 5 and 10 per cent (see Table 14). Individual constituencies were sometimes quite polled out, and the height of some figures (95 per cent or so at Longford and Newry in 1832, Leitrim in 1852, Mayo and Cashel in 1857, Louth and Carlow Town in 1859) suggests a certain liveliness among the recently deceased. Nor, on the basis of the information available, does turn-out seem to have suffered any significant fall during the quarter-century after 1859.[1] Non-electors too played a part because of their purchasing power, because of the force of mass opinion in small inward-looking con-stituencies, because (above all) of the impact of violence and threatened violence. 'The freehold', according to Archbishop MacHale in 1835, 'is held in trust for the benefit of the people.'

[1] Examples (in percentages) for two-member constituencies: Co. Cork 1868 = 74; Co. Waterford 1874 = 75, 1880 = 81 (kindly supplied by Dr. I. d'Alton); Belfast 1868 = 76 (*List of electors of the Borough of Belfast who voted at the general election, 1868* (Belfast: H. Adair, 1869); Co. Wexford 1874 = 82 (E. Carr to Lord Courtown, 19 Feb. 1874, Courtown Papers); Queen's Co. 1874 = 78 (*Leinster Express*, 14 Feb. 1874); Co. Carlow 1880 = 84 (*Daily Express*, 13 Apr. 1880). Single-member constituencies and by-elections present no difficulties, e.g. Co. Tyrone 1873 = 72; Mallow 1874 = 96; Dungannon 1874 = 91; Co. Leitrim 1876 = 85; Co. Down 1878 = 84; Dungarvan 1880 = 97; Co. Tyrone 1881 = 83; Co. Monaghan 1883 = 88.

TABLE 14

Voter turn-out, 1832, 1852, 1857, 1859

	1832 per cent	1852 per cent	1857 per cent	1859 per cent
Counties	81.5	73.2	74.2	82.2
Boroughs	88.3	72.9	80.9	80.6
All	85.4	73.0	77.7	81.1
N: Contested Constituencies*	44	43	36	27

* Excluding Dublin University

Dean Bourke in 1852 believed, 'as a general principle, that the non-electors of the county had a clear, strong, and undeniable claim'. A Galway priest twenty years later announced from the altar that 'in a village there would be only one voter, perhaps there might be 40 or 50 other people who would not have a vote; he said that that vote did not belong to that man any more than to the other men who had not a vote, and that he should go with the other men according to *their* conscience'. Frequent (and successful) appeals were made to non-electors 'to visit the electors and to use their influence', to 'brand' recalcitrant voters with the 'curse of scorn and indignation', to 'compel the electors to vote as *they* wished', indeed, to 'carry the election'.[1] The term 'non-elector' was almost a franchise in itself. Posters were addressed to 'The Electors and Non-Electors'. Money was distributed among particular non-electors considered influential. Meetings at which candidates were selected were not always confined to the enfranchised. Repeal or Home Rule candidates liked to canvass in the company of 'influential non-electors'.[2] Repeated thanks were publicly offered by successful candidates to all the non-electors who had helped 'by their exertions and had raised their voices'. 'This battle', announced the far-from-populist Chichester Fortescue after the Louth election of 1854, 'has been greatly assisted by the patriotic way in which the non-electors acted . . . by shaming the doubtful men.' Non-electors held meetings,

[1] B. O'Reilly, *John MacHale, Archbishop of Tuam*, i, 306–7; *Galway Vindicator*, 24 July 1852; *Galway County election petition*, H.C. 1872 (241–I), xlviii, 550 (also Bishop Blake of Dromore in *D.E.P.* 27 July 1837, and a Wexford priest in *Londonderry Sentinel*, 27 Oct. 1868); Diary of N. Browne, RM for 29 June 1841, S.P.O. Stipendiary Magistrates' Diaries No. 22; Report of H. Pollock, RM, 5 July 1852, O.P. 1852/15/152, Box 1218; Report of T. Cullagh, 12 July 1852, O.P. 1852/5/201, Box 1217.

[2] O.P. 1852/8/305, Box 1217; F. S. P. Wolferstan and S. B. Bristowe, *Reports of the decisions of election committees*, pp. 138–43; *Nation*, 10 Apr. 1852; J. J. Kelly to Archbishop Leahy, 2 Jan. 1874, Leahy Papers; *D.E.P.* 3 July 1865.

attended declarations of the poll, and were often fiercely partisan.[1] Persuasion shaded imperceptibly into something stronger and in the twilight zone between the two stood a mocking Daniel O'Connell in front of 40,000 non-electors at Mitchelstown in 1837.

> Let all of you who have not votes form yourselves into companies of twenty-five, let the whole company go to every neighbour who is registered, and let some one take off his hat and make him a low bow, and ask him, as politely as you'd ask your sweetheart to dance a jig, to go to Cork and vote for Roche and Barry . . . and no man will refuse you.[2]

Such attitudes clearly helped make the voting of a restricted electorate more representative than it might otherwise have been, and many leading politicians, including radicals as different as John Mitchel and Lord John Russell, opposed the ballot on the grounds that it would drive a wedge between those with and those without the vote.[3] Yet the arrival of secret voting in 1872 had little immediate effect. For a time few were entirely convinced that men of local influence— landlords, agents, priests—might not somehow penetrate the veil.[4] The many placards insisting on the absolute secrecy of the business were to a certain extent belied by a series of famous 'demonstrations' in which a leading Tory organizer purported to show otherwise and by a number of well-publicized procedural fiascos.[5] Many early secret voters were also far from expert and at one election in 1874 almost an eighth of the papers were incorrectly completed or left blank.[6] More important still was the fact that, in the case of an electorate confined—as late as 1884—to less than one person in every twenty-five, it was difficult for all but the eremitical to keep their political views concealed from the hawk-eyed gaze of neighbours in town and country alike.[7]

---

[1] *Londonderry Sentinel*, 17 Apr. 1857; *Drogheda Argus*, 21 May 1859; *Londonderry Sentinel*, 27 Oct. 1868 (also 30 July 1852); *C.C.* 17 Feb. 1835; *Tipperary Advocate*, 15 July 1865; *Sligo Champion*, 15 Aug. 1868.

[2] *D.E.P.* 27 July 1837 (also 20 July 1837). Violence proper is discussed in Chapter V below.

[3] Jacqueline Hill, 'The role of Dublin in the Irish national movement 1840–48', p. 19; J. Prest, *Lord John Russell* (London, 1972), p. 122.

[4] J. Greer to Belmore, 31 Mar. 1873, Belmore Papers D3007/P/93; also T. Sherry to Butt, 14 Feb. 1874, Butt Papers MS 8696. See also M. Hurst, 'Ireland and the Ballot Act of 1872', *Historical Journal*, viii (1965), 326–52.

[5] L'Estrange & Brett Papers D1905/2/3; J. S. Crawford Papers D1769/21/1; Perceval-Maxwell Papers D1556/23; *Belfast Newsletter*, 24 Mar. 1880; E. L. O'Malley and H. Hard-castle, *Reports of the decisions of the judges*, ii (1875), pp. 201–12; *Copies of the shorthand writers' notes, not already printed, of all judgements of the election judges*, H.C. 1880 (337-II), lvii, 76; J. Greer to Belmore, 9 Apr. 1873, Belmore Papers D3007/P/117; *Northern Whig*, 29 Nov. 1884.

[6] Athlone (E. L. O'Malley and H. Hardcastle, *Reports of the decisions of the judges*, ii (1875), pp. 186–90).

[7] As the Under-Secretary, T. H. Bourke, realized when writing about the proposed ballot legislation to his chief, Lord Hartington, 15 Feb. 1871, Devonshire Papers 387/2.

III CORRUPTION

The bond between voters and the community at large was further strengthened by that great amorphous business called corruption. This can be divided into two main types: the direct—that is actual cash payments and the like—and the indirect which included everything from subscriptions to local charities to providing jobs for voters and their relations. Both were more common in the boroughs than the counties; both fully withstood legislative assault until the passing of the Corrupt Practices Act of 1883.[1] Direct corruption was comparatively rare in the rural constituencies, not for reasons of superior morality but because the coercive power of landlords short-circuited the electric attractions of cash and because the large number of voters made bribery simply too expensive. A fairly determined trawl has yielded little more than peccadilloes: selling 'old cows and old mules' at inflated prices to Kerry candidates and the passing of greasy notes at Limerick in the 1830s, in the 1850s and 1860s some bogus expenses paid in Down, voters in Clare and Roscommon benefiting from 'reckless expenditure', Sligo Tories reminding each other to pay nothing 'until the time for petitioning elapses', Antrim mobs demanding shillings for intimidation, and anonymous priests handing out pound notes from behind shuttered windows at Longford in 1869.[2] The same exercise yielded at least twenty times as much relating to the boroughs. Yet before 1850 county voters outnumbered their borough counterparts by two to one and thereafter never by less than four to one. Whether or not the towns of Ireland were ever the bright centres of radical consciousness, they were certainly the home of the outstretched hand, the bulging pocket, and the floating voter adrift on seas of whiskey, beer, and stout. It was the rural not the urban elector who responded to the sentiments of an O'Connellite ballad sung at the Kilkenny election of 1837.

---

[1] Before 1883 even the judges who had begun to try petitions in 1868 had difficulty in defining corruption. See the solipsistic efforts in the Carrickfergus case (E. L. O'Malley and H. Hardcastle, *Reports of the decisions of the judges*, iii (1881), pp. 90-3) when numerous and baffling English decisions were cited. Baron Dowse in the Louth case (ibid. 161-77) settled for a tired pragmatism in which decisions 'will be found to depend very much upon the difference of the facts in each particular case'.

[2] M. J. Foley to Knight of Kerry, 29 Dec. 1834, FitzGerald Papers; J. O'Regan to Lord Dunraven, 22 Dec. 1832, Dunraven Papers D3196; T. Crozier to W. E. Teague, 12 Aug. 1857, Downshire Papers D671/C/164; F. S. P. Wolferstan and S. B. Bristowe, *Reports of the decisions of election committees*, pp. 102-13, 138-43; T. Mostyn to C. W. Cooper, 12 Apr. 1857, O'Hara Papers MS 20355; Dean Stannus to F. H. Seymour, 11 Sept. 1869, Seymour of Ragley Papers CR114A/724/2 (Antrim); Revd P. Moran to Revd Tobias Kirby, 13 Apr. 1870, Kirby Papers 1870(83a), and *Longford election petition*, H.C. 1870 (178), lvi, 286, 434.

> They knew that I was poor,
>> And they thought that I was base,
> And would readily endure
>> To be covered with disgrace;
> They judged me of their tribe,
>> Who on dirty Mammon dote,
> So they offered me a bribe
>> For my vote, boys, vote.[1]

Town elections were at all times supported upon a deep cushion of cash. Boroughs supplied three-quarters of the petitions alleging bribery or treating in the period 1832–50, four-fifths in 1851–68, and almost two-thirds in 1869–83. Towns sang a different song.

> Oh 'tis cash, 'tis cash, 'tis cash,
>> That makes the world go round,
> And with the cash, the cash, the cash,
>> Doth our candidate abound.
> When we return our friend,
>> He'll make our tyrant quake;
> His cash he'll freely spend
>> On us, for justice sake.[2]

Towns with electorates under five hundred were the corruptionist's native habitat, not only because they were cheaper, but because money could more effectively smother other considerations within their narrow and intimate political worlds. The *Nation*'s estimate that in 1859 at least twenty-seven of the thirty-three boroughs were significantly corrupt was not then and cannot now be refuted.[3]

The case of Galway, no more 'typical' than any other, must stand example for them all. In this large county of a town (electorate 1832 —2,062, 1852—1,038, 1874—1,444) a notoriously corrupt body of freemen constituted a significant minority (and in the 1850s a majority) of the voters. From an early date money percolated through the electorate: 'gentle and simple they all adopt the political economy notion, that all things, votes included, are worth just as much as they can bring in the market.' Attempts to conceal the elaborate paraphernalia of corruption were purely formal. Demands for money from the various trades were quite open. Publicans

---

[1] *Kilkenny Journal*, 2 Aug. 1837.

[2] Sung at Portarlington in 1832 (*A Farce. Portarlington Election: Intended in three parts. Part I - The Canvass* (printed at the Colombian Press, by M. Plattin, 1832), p. 15— copy in the Sir Thomas Gladstone Papers among the Glynne–Gladstone Papers at St Deiniol's Library, Hawarden).

[3] *Nation*, 16 Apr. 1859. Even the exceptions (Belfast, Carrickfergus [!], Cork, Dublin, Limerick, Waterford) were far from lilywhite. See A. K. Hanrahan, 'Irish electioneering 1850–1872' (University College Dublin MA thesis, 1965), pp. 138–41 where corruption in Waterford and Limerick is noted.

brazenly presented enormous bills for treating voters. Candidates threw open-house parties 'got up in a first-rate style'. In 1868 one alone 'employed' 133 election workers.[1] Even the cumberson e and inefficient investigatory techniques of 1852 identified twenty-three persons (including Sir Thomas Burke) guilty of giving money and sixty-seven of receiving it. Five years later twenty were found guilty of giving and 185 of receiving.[2] Typically the whole business was a mixture of high organization and casual incompetence. On the one hand, there was an elaborate system based on printed cards, which were 'officially' stamped once the requisite vote had been given and then taken to a 'secret' house where, behind a pigeon-hole in the hall, crouched J. V. Browne BA, MD, LRCSI, medical officer to the Galway Union and professor of surgery at the Queen's College, supplied with a large wad of bank notes. On the other, it all depended on being in the right place at the right time. 'I was', a nailer recalled, 'standing at a shop door with some other men . . . and we were discoursing a few more freemen who were inside standing in the shop and Semple came in . . . "What will you hold?" says he, "I will hold a pound", says I.'[3] As elsewhere corruption produced a culture and a language of its own. Generous candidates were said to be 'bleeding freely', and 'they had a bye-word "crap"—that's what they called money, which was also designated "twine" '. Everything proceeded upon the 'nod-and-a-wink' principle: sums were only vaguely agreed, cash was never paid on the spot, people did not 'insist' but they did 'expect'. Elections stood outside conventional morality and otherwise respectable people took bribes as a 'matter of course'. 'You are an advocate for justice?—Yes; I am an honest man . . . You are an honest man; and you would sell your vote for £10 and would have liked £30 better?—Certainly.'[4]

[1] R. O'Gorman to W. S. O'Brien, [Feb. 1847], Smith O'Brien Papers MS 441; P. Green to M. J. Blake, 15 July 1852, Blake of Ballyglunin Papers M6936/68; K. Byrne to Blake, 30 Dec. 1852, ibid. M6936/68; D. Considine to Blake, 10 July 1852, ibid. M6936/68; J. to M. J. Blake, 4, 12 Feb. 1859, ibid. M6936/81; E. L. O'Malley and H. Hardcastle, *Reports of the decisions of the judges*, i (1869), pp. 303-4. For further details of Galway politics, see Chapter VI, section I below.

[2] *Copies of Schedule One attached to the judgement of the County Galway election petition 1872; and, Schedules A, B, C, and D attached to the report of the royal commission 1857 appointed to investigate into the existence of corrupt practices in the Town of Galway*, H.C. 1874 (0.1), liii, 743-6.

[3] *Galway Town Corrupt Practices Commission*, H.C. 1857-8 [2291], xxvi, 313-24, 450; also Blake of Ballyglunin Papers M6935/31, 32, and F. S. P. Wolferstan and E.L'E. Dew, *Reports of the decisions of committees of the House of Commons*, pp. 136-44.

[4] D. Donelan to M. J. Blake, 11 Feb. 1847, Blake of Ballyglunin Papers M6936/58; *Western Star*, 6 Mar. 1869; *Cashel election petitions*, H.C. 1868-9 (121), xlix, 160-4; *Report from the select committee on Carrickfergus Borough; with the minutes of evidence and an appendix*, H.C. 1833 (527), viii, 128; *Newry Borough election petition*, H.C. 1833 (76), x, 614.

Implicit codes required that some candidates be let off more lightly than others. George Morris in 1868, though popular, still had to pay 'very liberally. But a stranger would be obliged to pay twice as much.' Amounts could be high. In 1865 Sir Rowland Blenner-hassett handed out £4,000 in bribes, which, if the other three candidates had spent similar sums, would have come to almost £14 for every Galway elector for illegal expenditure alone.[1]

Other leading contenders in the corruption stakes included Cashel, Sligo, Dungarvan, Athlone, Coleraine, Carlow, Clonmel, Carrick-fergus, and Youghal. To the first two (which were actually disfranchised in 1870 because of persistent bribery) wealthy carpet-baggers were attracted like flies to manure. 'Cashel', chortled Lord Donoughmore, 'is in a delightful mess. There are Hemphill, Hughes late solicitor-general, Lanigan, V. Scully, and last but not least John Carden, all hard at it.' In 1859 one candidate reminded the voters of their parish priest's denunciations of bribery. 'Votes is riz', came the unflappable reply, 'they were selling at between £5 and £6 on Saturday, but after Sunday when we heard our souls would be damned for selling them no vote will go under at least £20.'[2] At Sligo, where the going rate was £30 in 1853, 'political principles formed no part of the qualification of a candidate'. Every one of the eight elections between 1852 and 1868 was marked by extensive corruption.[3] In the same way candidates perambulated Kinsale in 1847 and Dungarvan and Cashel in 1868 waving bank deposit slips to prove their financial bona fides. Armagh voters required expensive 'nursing' between elections and Armagh Orangemen were corrupt first and Protestant second. At Coleraine in 1843 nothing could be said to 'go so far as money'. Dublin Tories in 1842 estimated that 'other' expenses would total well over £3,000. Youghal voters kissed their thumbs instead of the Bible while taking the bribery oath. Carlow was unambiguously up for sale 'to the highest bidder'.[4]

[1] Bishop MacEvilly to Archbishop Cullen, 21 June 1868, Cullen Papers; *Western Star*, 6 Mar. 1869 (*sic*). In Kinsale too the more rebarbative the electoral request, the higher the payment demanded—R. More O'Ferrall to Cullen, 27 Nov. 1862, Cullen Papers.

[2] Lord Donoughmore to Naas, 22 Apr. 1859, Mayo Papers MS 11036; Revd P. Leahy to Archbishop Cullen, 8 Mar. 1857, Cullen Papers; J. G. Swift MacNeill, *What I have seen and heard* (London, 1925), pp. 185-6.

[3] D. Power, H. Rodwell, and E. L'E. Dew, *Reports of the decisions of committees of the House of Commons* (1857), pp. 296-9; *Drogheda Argus*, 30 Apr. 1859; *Report of the Commissioners appointed under the act of the 15th and 16th Victoria, cap. 57, for the purpose of making inquiry into the existence of Corrupt Practices at the last election for Sligo*, H.C. 1870 [C 48], xxxii, 621-1054.

[4] *Kinsale election petition*, H.C. 1847-8 (138), xiii, 3-17; *Waterford Citizen*, 23 Oct. 1868; *Cashel Corrupt Practices Commission*, H.C. 1870 [C 9], xxxii, 231-2; Archbishop Beresford to Mr Nugent, 23 Aug. 1855, Pack-Beresford Papers D664/A/617; D. Kerr to Sir H. H. Bruce, 28 Jan. 1843, Bruce Papers D1514/2/6/10; De Grey to Graham, 5 Jan.

A wordly English politician was shaken by a visit to Tralee in 1852. 'They were employing—I believe I am right in saying—ten or twelve people to bribe, some without the slightest discretion . . . It is scarcely a figure of speech to say that they were bribing in the market place at noonday.'[1] The mecca of Irish corruption was probably Athlone, whose voters' heroic dedication was later recalled by T. P. O'Connor. The town's

distinction was that the number of voters was small, and that, therefore, the amount of the bribe was high. The bribe averaged £30 to £40 the vote; and there were tales of a vote having run up to £100 in one of Keogh's elections. With many people the periodic bribe entered into the whole economy of their poor, shrivelled, squalid and weary lives. Men continued to live in houses that had better have lived in lodgings, because the house gave a vote. The very whisper of a dissolution sent a visible thrill through the town, and the prospect of common gain swallowed up amid the people all other passions, religious and political, and united ordinarily discordant forces in amity and brotherhood.[2]

Indeed, simple poverty explains a good deal, for a residuum within the electorate was, especially before the reforms of 1850, invariably poor and distressed. Half the Sligo voters were reckoned 'paupers who will take from £20 to £50 as their price'. G. R. Dawson encountered 'great distress', 'horrid distress', among Derry voters. 'What made you take it?' a Belfast voter was asked, 'Poverty' was the stark reply. Many Kinsale voters spent their whole lives 'in abject misery'.[3] And even if by 1850 corruption had developed sufficient momentum to survive and multiply without such help bribes continued to be

1842, Graham Papers 7/Ir; 'Youghal Protestant Operatives Scrapbook', op. cit.; Lord Downes to Downshire, 8 June 1841, Downshire Papers D671/C/12/786.

[1] G. H. Kinderley to Naas, 31 July 1852, Mayo Papers MS 11019. For some examples from other places, see E. J. Littleton to W. Gossett, 17 July 1833, Hatherton Papers D260/M/01/2 (Carrickfergus); H. J. Perry and J. W. Knapp, *Cases of controverted elections*, pp. 149-61 (Newry), 529-34 (Carrickfergus); Lord Glengall to Sir H. Hardinge, 16 Jan. [1835], O.P. 1835/157, Box 47 (Clonmel); Report of Sub-Inspector Crofton, 23 Jan. 1835, O.P. 1835/150, Box 47 (Newry); G. R. Dawson's election diary T874 (Derry 1837); P. Mahony to O'Connell, 30 July 1837, *Correspondence of Daniel O'Connell*, ed. M. R. O'Connell, vi, 79 (Kinsale); *Northern Whig*, 10 July 1841 (Belfast); *Drogheda election petition*, H.C. 1857 (255 Sess. 2), vi, 184; E. L. O'Malley and H. Hardcastle, *Reports of the decisions of the judges*, i (1869), p. 294 (Youghal), ii (1875), p. 1 (Waterford), p. 21 (Mallow), iii (1881), pp. 101-2 (Dungannon). Numerous further citations are possible.

[2] T. P. O'Connor, *The Parnell Movement*, new edn. (London, 1887), pp. 134-5. On Athlone's heroic corruption, see *Central Conservative Society of Ireland: Report of the Sub-Committee 1859* (Mayo Papers MS 11025); Lord Crofton to Naas, 7 May 1859, ibid. MS 11036; Bishop Gillooly to Revd F. Murphy, [1865], Gillooly Papers Section C; Gillooly to Archbishop Cullen, 6 Feb. 1874, Cullen Papers; also reports on various petitions in H.C. 1842 (548), v; 1843 (317), vi; 1844 (97), xiv; 1852-3 (321), viii; 1874 (144), liii; 1880 (187 Sess. 2) vi.

[3] J. Walker to Palmerston, 22 Nov. 1832, Broadlands Archive 27M60, Box cxxiii; G. R. Dawson's election diary T874; *Belfast election compromise*, H.C. 1842 (431), v, 400; *Kinsale election petition*, H.C. 1847-8 (138), xiii, 155.

substantial in relation to the weekly wages of ten or fifteen shillings (irregularly) received by many skilled artisans.

The mushroom cloud of nineteenth-century electoral corruption produced a fall-out more rich and complex than the crudities of hard cash. Donations, large and small, to local charities, chapels, clubs, societies, brass bands, and religious orders were extracted from candidates with a sleight of hand that would have flattered the most practised of pickpockets. 'I was asked for charity', moaned a clean-picked Captain Trench at Galway in 1872, 'all over the county as soon as I became a candidate.' Even the niceties were bogus. 'I am not', a Galway nun hurriedly concluded her begging letter, 'entirely influenced on this occasion by your being a candidate for the representation of the town, but from your general character.'[1] At Derry in the 1830s candidates were expected to buy large numbers of tickets for religious meetings and bazaars. Tralee members 'always supported' the Royal Western Yacht Club. In August 1868 the Prince of Wales's Hotel at Athlone was 'besieged with the cockneys seeking the honour of representing the ancient borough', all desperate to present expensive silver cups and medals for competition at that month's Shannon boating regatta.[2] Henry Mathews's large gifts to the Dungarvan clergy were greeted with the gratifying response that 'such donations . . . are not normally given by a candidate who has not serious intentions'. A Cashel carpet-bagger, who had already distributed almost £2,000 among the Christian Brothers, the Society of St Vincent de Paul, the Thurles Cathedral Building Fund, and the nuns of Fethard Convent, spoiled the whole costly effect by being heard to mutter more loudly than was nice that 'Holy Mother Church has a very wide mouth'. Clergymen, Protestant and Catholic, were invariably at the head of the queue.[3] The O'Conor Don received a scorching acknowledgement in 1860 from a Roscommon priest

[1] *Galway County election petition*, H.C. 1872 (241-I), xlviii, 539; F. Morgan to M. J. Blake, 7 July 1852, Blake of Ballyglunin Papers M6936/68. See also Miss J. Burrows (of the Ladies Association for Clothing the Poor of Cavan Town) to H. Maxwell, 19 Jan. [1835], Farnham Papers MS 18602: 'The custom of making application to newly elected members of parliament . . . in behalf of charitable institutions is now so well established . . .'

[2] G. R. Dawson's election diary T874; T. O'Connell to T. O'Hagan, 16 May 1863, O'Hagan Papers D2777/6; *Western Star*, 15 Aug. 1868, and *Tipperary Advocate*, 3 Oct. 1868.

[3] *Waterford Mail*, 9 Sept. 1868; *Cashel election petitions*, H.C. 1868-9 (121), xlix, 252, 285-6. For other examples, see A. K. Hanrahan, 'Irish electioneering 1850-72', pp. 126-8; A. Macintyre, *The Liberator*, p. 123; *Ballyshannon Herald*, 21 July 1837; *Clare election petition*, H.C. 1852-3 (595), ix, 781; *Dublin Evening Mail*, 29 Apr. 1857; *Drogheda Argus*, 30 Apr. 1859; Mayo Papers MS 11176; J. Machett to Naas, 12 May 1859, ibid. MS 11036; O'Hagan Papers D2777/6; G. V. Stewart to Lord Belmore, 26 Mar. 1873, Belmore Papers D3007/P/78; J. H. Whyte, 'The influence of the Catholic clergy on elections in nineteenth-century Ireland', *English Historical Review*, lxxv (1960), 249.

for his 'trifling' two-pound donation and a reminder that 'the names of the benefactors are to appear in the public prints together with the sums respectively contributed'. Six years later he was again rebuked by Bishop Gillooly for failing to contribute 'largely' to 'the religious and charitable undertakings of the county'.[1] Captain Bellew's efforts in Galway were publicly denounced as 'miserable'. The O'Gorman Mahon paid dearly at the Ennis election of 1852 for his failure to deliver a promised marble high altar to the parish church.[2] The historian Acton's parsimonious high-mindedness debarred him from ever again standing for Carlow after his un-expected return in 1859, all the more so for his having committed a double solecism by refusing to indulge in those personal genialities which helped many others to weather stormy political seas. Wynd-ham Goold too encountered objections at Limerick in 1850 'that I . . . did not follow the hounds, and that, therefore, I could not be a good representative', while Sir Edward Grogan's refusal to be 'genial' hampered the Conservative cause in Dublin.[3] A more calculating W. H. Gregory tortured his stomach and taste-buds by sailing to America by the Galway Line for fear that other-wise he would offend his leading constituents, many of whom had shares in the local company. Even hostile witnesses agreed that the Nationalist, G. H. Moore, was 'a jolly good fellow and one who always had his wits about him', while the maverick Catholic Tory, Michael Morris, charmed Disraeli by his quick-witted stage-Irishman performances and Galway voters by fluent *badinage* and a readiness to swap jokes with the fishwives of the town.[4] Equally important was an ability to hold liquor, and William Keogh's success at Athlone was in part the result of attend-ance at 'the bedside of the companions of his debauch the next morning with a brandy-and-soda in his hand and the Christian name of the scarcely recovered inebriate in his mouth'. In contrast, an English contender for the same borough had to be shipped home 'in a violent fit of delirium tremens', while Serjeant Barry at Dungarvan

[1] Revd. P. Galvin to The O'Conor Don, 1 Nov. 1860, Clonalis .Papers 9.3.HS.309; Gillooly to The O'Conor Don, [c.19 May 1866], Gillooly Papers Section C.
[2] *Western Star*, 17 July 1852; D. Gwynn, *The O'Gorman Mahon: Duellist, Adventurer, and Politician* (London, 1934), p. 168.
[3] J. J. Auchmuty, 'Acton as a member of the House of Commons', *Bulletin of the Faculty of Arts: Farook I University of Alexandria*, v (1950), 31–46; *D.E.P.* 12 Dec. 1850; *C.C.* 14 Feb. 1863.
[4] *Sir William Gregory, K.C.M.G., formerly member of parliament and sometime gover-nor of Ceylon. An Autobiography*, ed. Lady Gregory (London, 1894), pp. 201–2 ('bad fare, worse company, and still worse ships'); Mrs Houston, *Twenty years in the wild west: or, life in Connaught* (London, 1879), p. 36; Maud Wynne, *An Irishman and his Family: Lord Morris and Killanin* (London, 1937), pp. 10–44.

complained of how he was 'expected to imbibe large quantities of punch, day and night, with successive batches of electors; and [how] failure in this terrible duty would seriously imperil his popularity'.[1]

Few aspects of life remained untouched by electoral gold. Loafers received scatterings of coin in the streets or payments to start a riot. Workhouse inmates were given meat teas.[2] Newspaper proprietors grew fat on direct bribes and inflated political advertising. A Co. Down candidate who did not even go to the poll in 1852 paid £232 for advertisements. Serjeant Barry paid £225 at Dungarvan in 1865, Chichester Fortescue £380 at Louth, and Sir A. E. Guinness £1,425 at Dublin in 1868.[3] Candidates advertised in the most unlikely journals: tenant-righters in the virulently Tory *Londonderry Sentinel* in 1859, fierce Conservatives in the *Nation* of 1852, even a clutch of Dublin Conservatives in the Fenian *Irish People* of 1865.[4] Local papers (some of which, like the *Limerick Chronicle* in April 1859, consisted almost entirely of election notices) openly touted for advertising in return for the freedom of their editorial columns. The editor of the *Cashel Gazette* claimed 'some influence by my family and otherwise'. The *Londonderry Standard* was indemnified against loss in return for favourable puffs on behalf of G. R. Dawson. The *Dundalk Democrat* trimmed its opinions to suit the patronage of the moment. The proprietors of the *Mayo Constitution*, after they had extracted 'all the blood they could' from G. H. Moore, then attacked him in 1852 'in the hope of extracting more from the other party'.[5] The practice of the *Coleraine Chronicle* in charging so much a line for sympathetic editorials was not uncommon, as a journalist recalled in his autobiography.

---

[1] T. P. O'Connor, *The Parnell Movement*, p. 89; Diary of W. J. O'Neill Daunt for 6 Oct. 1868, MS 3041.

[2] E. L. O'Malley and H. Hardcastle, *Reports of the decisions of the judges*, i (1869), p. 294; *Cashel Corrupt Practices Commission*, H.C. 1870 [C 9], xxxii, 263; *Drogheda Argus*, 30 Apr. 1859. For riots, see Chapter V below.

[3] J. Andrews to Lord Londonderry, 29 Dec. 1852, Londonderry Papers D/Lo/C158; *Returns from the several sheriffs and returning officers of the abstract of expenses incurred by or on behalf of each candidate at the last general election*, H.C. 1866 (160), lvi, 455–92; Fortescue's expenses 1868, Carlingford Papers CPA1/1; *Commissioners [on] . . . the freemen electors of the City of Dublin*, H.C. 1870 [C 93], xxxiii, 19.

[4] *Londonderry Sentinel*, 15 Apr. 1859; *Nation*, 10 Apr. 1852; *Irish People*, 17 June and 15 July 1865.

[5] J. D. White (*Cashel Gazette*) to R. J. Otway, [Feb. 1865], Otway Papers MS 13008; G. R. Dawson's election diary T874; *Dundalk Democrat*, 23 Apr. 1859; G. H. Moore to W. Keogh, 14 June 1852, Moore Papers MS 892. In 1868 Henry Munster at Cashel paid J. D. White £50 'for services other than advertising' (*Cashel Corrupt Practices Commission*, H.C. 1870 [C 9], xxxii, 124).

Everything written and published in favour of a candidate, be it leading article
or letter, was charged and paid for at the same rate as the advertisements. A
paper published three times a week, therefore, made a good thing out of an
election. In Wexford I was told that some proprietors of local newspapers
calculated on the income from this source to enable them to 'live' from one
election to the succeeding one.[1]

Money could also be made by printing the thousands of placards and
leaflets which covered constituencies like confetti during elections and
even by junior journalists using their contacts to secure 'the occasional
insertion of letters and paragraphs in the newspapers, the circulation
of election squibs, and the distribution of humorous pasquinades'.[2]
Of wider interest was the expectation that candidates would act
as one-man employment agencies. The Westenra family in Monaghan
arranged positions in mercantile establishments for voters' sons.
Railway company directors (like John Ennis of Athlone or William
McCormick of Derry) filled clerical and other posts with personal
dependants. William Bernard boasted of his 'interest' in the 'young
men' of Bandon, while the Cork Liberal, F. B. Beamish, lured
artisans away from O'Connellism by giving them jobs in his brewery.
R. S. Guinness modestly reminded Kinsale voters in 1847 of his
being 'very largely connected through his family' and of the 'great
number of situations that were', as a result, 'to be had'.[3] But it was
as channels of influence between constituents and government
rather than as direct employers that most politicians satisfied the
aspirations of their electorates. Senior ministers concerned themselves with the smallest details of patronage and received letters
of application by the daily sackful. Influential supporters (or potential
supporters) got a better hearing than most, and some jobs were
traditionally regarded as at the disposal of sympathetic MPs. Tide-
waiterships, positions in lunatic asylums, clerkships of the peace,
resident magistrateships, police cadetships, inspectorships under
the poor-law commission, all—and many more—were grist to
the great mill of patronage.[4] John O'Connell arrived at Athlone

---

[1] F. H. Babington to R. Bourke, 12 July 1852, Mayo Papers MS 11018; A. Dunlop,
Fifty years of Irish journalism (Dublin, 1911), p. 20. For the earlier practice of government subsidy, see B. Inglis, *The freedom of the press in Ireland 1784–1841* (London, 1954).

[2] *Galway County election petition*, H.C. 1872 (241-I), xlviii, 929; B. O'Flaherty to
M. J. Blake, 17 June 1852, Blake of Ballyglunin Papers M6936/68.

[3] H. R. Westenra to—, 20 Feb. 1835, Clogher Diocesan Papers DIO(RC)1/6/27; J. Lee,
'Railway labour in Ireland 1833-1856', p. 14; *C.C.* 3 May 1859; J. Hayes to O'Connell,
14 Aug. 1840, *Correspondence of Daniel O'Connell*, ed. M. R. O'Connell, vi, 352–3; *Kinsale
election petition*, H.C. 1847-8 (138), xiii, 119.

[4] For examples of this, see J. Tyrell to M. J. Blake, 14 July 1847, Blake of Ballyglunin
Papers M6936/58; Naas to Lord Eglinton, Eglinton Papers MS 5334 ('any patronage that is
at our disposal . . . should be carefully kept for those persons that [we] may find it of use
to have for election purposes'); Lord Claud Hamilton to Abercorn, 31 Dec. 1866 and

in 1837 announcing his ability to provide revenue-police posts at ten-and-six a week to any two young men the local Liberal Club might select. In 1852 John Boyd of Coleraine received sixty-two letters in ten days asking for 'all sorts of appointments from livings in the church down to a tidewaitership', and James Whiteside placarded Enniskillen with the claim that he had 'procured government situations for the following young townsmen . . . [five names]. This is a good beginning.'[1] Nothing was sacred from the intrusions of the place-seeker in search of his prey. 'I was much annoyed at bringing up the Revd Mr Judge to you at the races just as you were at luncheon. Had I been aware of it I would at least have tried to find some more fitting moment. You little know what *extreme pressure* has been put upon me in his case by one who interests himself in his regard who is my sheet-anchor in anything like electioneering tactics in this district.' But the rewards for a little discomfort could be great. Palmerston's friend, John Patrick Somers, held the mercurial borough of Sligo for over fourteen years by seeing to it that there was 'not a family in the town' untouched by his patronage, and by obtaining 'appointments for, or otherwise substantially benefitting, a greater number of individuals than compose the present constituency'.[2]

The cost in emotional terms was more than matched by the cost in shillings and pence. The subject is a complicated one and merits more extensive treatment than can be given here. Three things, however, stand out: expenses remained potentially high throughout the period; actual expenses were invariably higher than declared expenses; and, although costs varied widely, the possibility of very substantial sums being required was something few candidates could safely discount. It would be tedious to do anything but list briefly a few of the higher sums spent by *individual* candidates (in two-seat constituencies there were often four) during the half-century after 1832, remembering that such amounts could be required again and again at any of the thirteen general elections or the many by-elections in that period (see Table 15). The official returns of expenses made under the 1854 Corrupt Practices Act were in England unreliable and

[Jan. 1867], Abercorn Papers T2541/VR/113, 124; Lord Hawarden to Abercorn, 4 May 1867, ibid. T2541/VR/164; Sir John Young to J. Dickson, 29 Mar. 1856, Young Letter-Book; J. Spaight to Naas, 23 Oct. 1866, Derby Papers 155/2. On patronage and political parties, see Chapter IV below.

[1] *Athlone Conservative Advocate*, 22 June 1837; J. Boyd to Naas, 5 Apr. 1852, Mayo Papers MS 11018; *Nation*, 20 Mar. 1852.

[2] N. Grehan to The O'Conor Don, 1 Sept. 1861, Clonalis Papers 9.3.HS.226; *Sligo Journal*, 2 Apr. 1852 cited in J. H. Whyte, *The Independent Irish Party 1850–9* (Oxford, 1958), p. 46.

TABLE 15

Election expenses of certain candidates, 1832–78

1832	Co. Waterford	£3,000	J. M. Galwey	R	returned
	Waterford City	£3,000	H. W. Barron	R	returned
1835	Waterford City	£2,400	H. W. Barron	R	returned
	Co. Carlow	£5,000	H. Bruen+	C	returned
	Co. Wexford	£3,000	J. Power	R	returned
1841	Belfast	£3,500	J. E. Tennent+	C	returned
1842	Dublin City*	£8,000	W. H. Gregory	C	returned
1850	Co. Mayo*	£2,500	G. G. O. Higgins	L	returned
1852	Co. Clare	£3,000	Sir J. F. Fitzgerald+	L	returned
	Co. Dublin	£2,172	A. Craven	L	defeated
	Ennis	£5,000	J. D. Fitzgerald	Ind. L	returned
	Co. Louth	£3,500	J. McClintock	C	defeated
	Co. Tyrone	£3,000	B. H. Higgins	L	defeated
1857	Co. Tipperary*	£5,000	L. Waldron	L	defeated
	Co. Tipperary*	£3,000	D. O'Donoghue	Ind. L	returned
	Co. Cavan	£2,000	M. O'R. Dease	L	defeated
	Co. Dublin	£3,002	Sir C. Domvile	L	defeated
	Co. Galway	£4,000	T. A. Bellew	Ind. L	defeated
1859	Athlone	£5,000	R. P. Bayley	C	defeated
	Co. Clare	£10,000	L. White+	L	returned
1865	Cashel	£3,000	J. L. O'Beirne	L	returned
	Co. Cork	£7,053	N. P. Leader	C	returned
	Dublin City	£8,600	J. Pim	L	returned
	Galway Town	£6,000	Sir R. Blennerhassett	L	returned
	King's Co.	£2,000	J. G. King	C	returned
1868	Cashel	£6,000	H. Munster	L	defeated
	Dublin City	£15,000	Sir A. E. Guinness+	C	returned
	Dungarvan	£7,000	H. Mathews	L	returned
	Youghal	£5,000	C. Weguelin+	L	returned
1869	Co. Antrim*	£9,116	H. de G. Seymour	C	returned
	Co. Longford*	£4,825	R. J. M. Greville-Nugent+	L	returned
1872	Co. Galway*	£7,000	W. le P. Trench	C	defeated
	Co. Kerry*	£6,000	J. A Dease	L	defeated
1873	Co. Tyrone*	£4,000	H. W. L. Corry	C	returned
1878	Co. Down*	£13,500	Viscount Castlereagh	C	returned

C = Conservative   L = Liberal   R = Repealer
* By-election   + Unseated on petition
Note All sums are minimum amounts.

in Ireland farcical. Many candidates made no returns at all and others produced accounts so heavily laundered—Blennerhassett's £6,000 at Galway in 1865 was rendered down to £585—as to bring the whole procedure into disrepute.[1] Although some contemporary

[1] *Returns from the several sheriffs and returning officers of the abstract of the expenses*, H.C. 1866 (160), lvi, 455–92 (Ireland). Of the 143 Irish candidates, 56 made no response and the returns of few others carry the ring of truth. Nor did things improve: see the similar *Returns*, H.C. 1874 (358), liii, 32–7, and H.C. 1880 (328–II), lvii, 36–43.

English expenses were even higher, the smallness of Irish borough electorates ensured that costs per voter for individual candidates of £35 at Ennis in 1852, £22 at Athlone in 1859, and in 1868 £18 at Youghal, £23 at Dungarvan, and £30 at Cashel were more than fully competitive.[1] Less affluent candidates either abandoned the fight, raised a subscription, or went into debt. And, especially after the disappearance of O'Connell's various national funds, radicals could find the game simply beyond their means.[2] Even comparatively wealthy landed familes could be driven to humiliating shifts. Madame O'Conor moaned in 1833 how 'there are many little gratifications I would allow myself and many things I would get for myself and the children if the last election debts were paid', while the aristocratic Seymours were forced into the grips of the Northern Bank after the Antrim by-election of 1869.[3] For many the final blow came in the shape of the petitions which formed so predictable a coda to Irish contests. When pursued to the bitter end, the hiring of lawyers, the paying of sleuths to dig out local dirt, and the transporting (as was the case until 1868) of witnesses to London and paying for their food, drink, and lodgings, could make men behave as if there was no financial tomorrow. And in the fifty years after 1832 well over a hundred Irish petitions ran their full course, while three or four times that number, though strangled before completion, still sent many a learned counsel refreshed and heavy laden to the bank. Petitions were a kind of local spin-off benefit, as at Carlow in 1859, where many persons 'in very embarrassing circumstances' were 'most anxious that the petition be prosecuted' in the hope of making 'something by the transaction'.[4] Two thousand pounds was regarded as moderate, and some notorious cases involved one side alone in costs amounting to four or five times that sum.[5]

[1] For England, see N. Gash, *Politics in the age of Peel: A study in the technique of parliamentary representation 1830–1850* (London, 1953), pp. 105–36; H. J. Hanham, *Elections and Party Management: Politics in the time of Disraeli and Gladstone* (London, 1959), pp. 249–61; W. B. Gwyn, *Democracy and the cost of politics in Britain* (London, 1962), pp. 21–92.

[2] See, for example, Sir A. de Vere to Knight of Kerry, 20 Jan. 1835, FitzGerald Papers ('The radical candidates in our district were all men of small income, dreading expense, and ready to retire if seriously opposed'); R. D. Craig to E. Littleton, 30 Aug. 1834, Hatherton Papers D260/M/01/14; J. Boyd to Naas, 27 Mar. 1852, Mayo Papers MS 11018; J. Machett to Naas, 12 Apr. 1859, ibid. MS 11036; *Kilkenny Journal*, 16 Apr., 11 May 1859; J. Blake Dillon to Bishop Gillooly, 3 Mar. 1865, Gillooly Papers Section C; J. H. Whyte, *The Independent Irish Party 1850–9*, pp. 47–50.

[3] Madame O'Conor to The O'Conor Don, 6 Mar. 1833, Clonalis Papers 9.2.HS.161; Seymour of Ragley Papers CR114A/538/6.

[4] Revd. J. Maher to Sir John Acton, 2 July 1859, Acton Papers (Correspondence).

[5] For example, the Tories at Belfast in 1837 (*Belfast election compromise*, H.C. 1842 (431), v, 273); O'Connell at Dublin in 1835 (to P. V. Fitzpatrick, 4 Sept. 1835 and 13 May

IV TOWN AND COUNTRY

The shape of this chapter has been determined by the nineteenth-century division of constituencies into largely rural counties and largely urban boroughs. The distinction was and is important. Yet of course neither personal nor political relationships came to a halt at lines drawn on maps by boundary commissioners. The character and intensity of the linkage between what contemporaries would have called the agricultural and the urban interests did not, however, remain constant, nor did they in all respects grow steadily and universally deeper and more powerful as the century progressed. Thus towns were assuming a more exclusively urban character as the proportion of familes chiefly engaged in agriculture in the parliamentary boroughs declined from 25.1 per cent in 1841 to a mere 5.8 per cent twenty years later. At the same time, those 'rural' voters who still remained in borough constituencies seem, at least until the late 1860s, to have maintained a clearly separate political identity from their urban fellows.[1] They were most evident in the large counties of towns, where, as late as 1859, they generally constituted between a fifth and a third of the electorate.[2] Elsewhere, however, they were a steadily declining force and the rather unsubstantiated Conservative fears that town voters would contaminate the supposedly deferential countryside[3] were never really put to the test until 1885. The only inadvertent blurring resulted from the mixed nature of the eight counties of towns; from the continued rights of certain urban freeholders not in occupation of their properties to vote in the surrounding counties; and from suburban extensions into what had once been green fields. The first was limited to eight constituencies; the second, though important in England, was in Ireland never more than marginal;[4] the third was

1836, *Correspondence of Daniel O'Connell*, ed. M. R. O'Connell, v, 329-31, 371-2); the Liberals at Westmeath in 1837 (*D.E.P.* 18 Jan. 1838); the Repealers at Dublin in 1847 (Circular in Clarendon Papers Box 27).

[1] See, e.g., *D.E.P.* 27 Oct. 1838 (Newry); J. Tyrell to M. J. Blake, 27 Jan. 1847, Blake of Ballyglunin Papers M6936/58, and T. F. Meagher to W. Smith O'Brien, [Feb. 1847], Smith O'Brien Papers MS 440 (Galway); *D.E.P.* 22 Mar. 1851 (Dungarvan); J. Spaight to Dunraven, 8 Feb. 1858, Dunraven Papers D3196, and to Naas, 1, 4 May 1859, Mayo Papers MS 11036 (Limerick); *C.C.* 24 May 1859, and R. B. Tooker to Mayo, 20 June 1868, Mayo Papers MS 11175 (Cork); *Cashel election petitions*, H.C. 1868-9 (121), xlix, 230.

[2] *Returns showing the area, population, income tax, number of occupiers rated at various amounts, number of parliamentary voters etc. in each county in Ireland*, H.C. 1860 (128), lv, 261-70. Dublin had none, Waterford 45.6 per cent, Carrickfergus 61.7 per cent, and the remaining five between 22.3 per cent and 37.6 per cent.

[3] See, e.g., Sir J. Young to Eliot, 12 Dec. 1842, Graham Papers 1/Ir; Lord Farnham's memo of 1850, Clanricarde Papers 35; T. E. Taylor in *Hansard*, cviii, 1298-9 (22 Feb. 1850).

[4] For the number of 'urban freeholders' in 1832, see *Copy of Instructions*, H.C. 1831-2 (519), xliii, 10-13. For the limited survival of their rights after 1832, see E. Molyneux,

pretty well restricted to Dublin and Belfast—and in the latter largely defused by an extension of boundaries in 1868.

Not all towns were parliamentary boroughs, but the impact of those which remained within the county constituencies was limited by their small size and by the higher county franchise maintained until 1884. In 1861 there were only fifty towns with more than 3,000 inhabitants which did not themselves return members to Parliament, and their total population of under a quarter of a million constituted less than one in twenty of all those living in the county constituencies. By the early 1870s (when the borough franchise had been reduced to 'over £4') about half the borough electorate would have been voteless under the county requirements.[1] As a result, the inhabitants of unrepresented towns were much less likely to be enfranchised than their counterparts in parliamentary boroughs. Indeed, because of the way in which holdings of different values and (between 1832 and 1850) leases were distributed, they seem also to have been less well represented even in county electorates than the more strictly rural community. Townspeople provided fewer votes in King's Co. throughout the 1830s than their numbers might have suggested. By 1871, when 8.1 per cent of the population of all county constituencies lived in unrepresented towns of more than 2,000 inhabitants, only 5.0 per cent of county *voters* did so, and in fifteen counties the figure was below even 4.0 per cent.[2] As far, therefore, as electoral affairs were concerned, the boroughs and the counties stood for clearly distinct and separate worlds. This dichotomy came, however, to an abrupt end when the reforms of 1884–5 threw all but nine of the largest boroughs into the new county divisions. At the same time, the household franchise gave the vote to many small farmers and agricultural labourers and increased the electorate from 225,999 to

A practical treatise of the law of elections in Ireland as altered by the reform act (Dublin, 1835), p. 27. Urban freeholders could vote in counties at large out of property in the 'pure' boroughs, but not out of property in the eight counties of towns which were electorally distinct and sufficient unto themselves.

[1] From *Returns as respects each of the parliamentary boroughs in Ireland*, H.C. 1874 (45), liii, 557–68 it can be shown that out of a total borough electorate of 50,185, the county franchise would have excluded (a) 52.4 per cent of all rated occupiers because that proportion of borough tenements was valued between 'over £4' and under £12 = 22,600, (b) lodgers = 532, (c) freemen etc. = 3,981: total = 27,113. But some freemen might have qualified as county occupiers, so that a potential 'disfranchisement' of about half would seem broadly correct.

[2] King's Co.: *Fictitious Votes, Ireland*, 2nd series, 3rd report, pp. 411–12, 434. 1871: *Returns as respects each of the parliamentary boroughs in Ireland*, H.C. 1874 (45), liii, 577–68. Proportions were highest in counties with few or no parliamentary boroughs but with some towns of more than 2,000 e.g. Mayo (7.2 per cent), King's Co. (6.4), Wicklow (6.3), Kildare (5.7), and lowest in constituencies such as Cos. Kilkenny (0.8), Limerick (1.3), and Cavan (1.5).

737,965, the largest expansion of the century. Henceforth the electoral politics of town and countryside were to be inexorably intertwined. The barriers by which the political life of most of the middling towns with populations (in 1881) of between 2,500 and 14,000—such as Portarlington, Dungannon, Ennis, New Ross, Coleraine, Clonmel, Dundalk, Lisburn, and Tralee—had for decades been sheltered, though not isolated, from the concerns and pre-occupations of the rural population, were suddenly and thoroughly dismantled. Now urban voters found themselves going to the same booths, supporting the same candidates, starting the same riots as their country cousins.[1] As regards the style of electoral politics, and in some ways the content too, the town had effectively been swallowed up by its rural hinterland.

[1] In South Wexford division, for example, it was estimated that of the new voters in 1885, a quarter would be townsmen, a third farmers, and just over two-fifths labourers (*Wexford Independent*, 29 Aug. 1885), whereas in 1871-3 only 3.5 per cent of the voters in the old Co. Wexford constituency had come from towns of more than 2,000 people (*Returns as respects each of the parliamentary boroughs in Ireland*, H.C. 1874 (45), liii, 557-68).

II

Landlords, Politics, and Rural Society

The political life of the nineteenth-century Irish countryside was the product of relationships between individuals as such and individuals as members of gentry, farmer, and labourer communities. Traditionally politics had been the preserve of landlords and their associates, with the rest either quiescent or acting walk-on parts as rioters, forelock-tuggers, or sporadic insubordinates. The political history of landlord-ism provides at once a direct image of the varying fortunes of the landed community and a reverse measure of what was happening in the world outside the Big House. It can, however, only make sense in these terms if the men of property are placed within the context of rural society and if their characteristic attitudes and patterns of behaviour are understood and assessed.

I CONTEXT

Rural society was neither changeless nor cohesive. Among farmers, between farmers and labourers, between landlords and tenants, tensions and differences were both pervasive and in flux. Yet, beneath the continuing disputes and the assertions of special interests, ran a countervailing tendency towards greater homogeneity of position, status, and attitude among those who did not themselves possess the broad acres of wealth. Contemporaries drew their lines at different points. Distinctions were made between farmers with twenty-five acres who had 'done well' out of the Famine and those with eight or less who had crashed. Political clubs classified their members into 'poor men', 'small farmers', 'the middle classes', and 'higher farmers'. Others divided society into mud-cabin dwellers and possessors of comfortable dressers and kitchen clocks.[1] The widespread subdivision of farms common before the Famine, concentrated as it probably was amongst holdings already small, did little to reduce the earlier heterogeneous nature of rural society in which the greatest cleavage was that between 'large farmers' with more than about twenty to thirty acres and 'the rest' or rural poor.[2] Inquiries in the 1840s revealed that the 'average' farmer

[1] Printed 'Memorandum on the state of Ireland', 9 Jan. 1847, Royal Archives RA D16/15; *D.E.P.* 18 May 1837; A. D. T. Fay, 'The Parishes of Magherafelt and Ballyscullion 1825–1850: An examination of some aspects of social and economic development' (New University of Ulster M.Phil. thesis, 1974), pp. 132–43.

[2] S. J. Connolly, 'Catholicism and social discipline in pre-Famine Ireland' (New University

of the time worked fourteen acres valued at between eight and nine pounds and paid about twelve pounds rent. This somewhat artificial being and those below him, had, it was widely believed, experienced 'more misery than any other' during the Famine and had long been depressed because rents per acre on small farms had always been disproportionately high.[1] The franchise reformers of 1850 completely excluded such men and fixed their twelve-pound valuation barrier more or less precisely at the major fault line which divided the farmers of twenty to thirty acres and more from the rest of the rural population. The members of this 'better class' saw themselves as both socially and politically distinct from poorer farmers. Their involvement with Repeal exhibited a pace and pattern peculiar to themselves. They often adopted the harshest of tones towards those dependent upon them for work and potato ground.[2] Many supported the poor-law system, served on juries, led demands for rent reduction, constituted the backbone of the Tenant League of the 1850s, and talked nervously of the 'lower orders'.[3] But despite the continuation of hostility between various sorts of landholders throughout this period—and large-scale graziers were to become a particular object of distrust—the general distribution of privilege was fundamentally altered by the changes which took place in the pattern of farm holdings both during and after the Great Famine. What mattered was not so much that deep gulfs still remained —in 1881 the mean valuation of those with thirty acres and less was

of Ulster D.Phil. thesis, 1977), pp. 155-6; S. Clark, *Social origins of the Irish Land War* (Princeton, 1979), p. 40. Of course the acreage required varied with the quality of the soil etc.

[1] Lord Morpeth in *Hansard*, lvii, 1260 (29 Apr. 1841), also Sir John Young in *Hansard*, cx, 1335-9 (10 May 1850) and Lord St Germans in *Hansard*, cxii, 750 (1 July 1850); P. Roebuck, 'Rent movement, proprietorial incomes, and agricultural development, 1730-1830' in *Plantation to Partition: Essays in Ulster History in honour of J. L. McCracken*, ed. P. Roebuck (Belfast, 1981), p. 89, also *Third General Report relative to the Valuations for poor rates, and to the registered elective franchise in Ireland*, H.C. 1841 [329], xxiii, 600-8; *Hansard*, lvi, 1076 (25 Feb. 1841).

[2] M. Tierney to Lord Anglesey, 22 June 1831, O.P. 1831/T31, Box 1842; T. Bolton to Lord Stanley, 15 and 24 June 1843, Derby Papers 107/3.

[3] G. C. Lewis to G. Grote, 11 Jan. 1843, G. F. Lewis, *Letters of the Right Hon. Sir George Cornewall Lewis Bart. to various friends* (London, 1870), pp. 127-30; W. L. Feingold, 'The Irish boards of poor law guardians, 1872-86: A revolution in local government' (University of Chicago Ph.D. thesis, 1974), pp. 80-4; *Minutes of evidence taken before the select committee of the House of Lords, appointed to inquire into the state of Ireland since the year 1835 in respect to Crime and Outrage*, H.C. 1839 (486), xi and xii, Q. 10, 918; *Report from the select committee on Outrages (Ireland); with proceedings of the committee, minutes of evidence, appendix and index*, H.C. 1852 (438), xiv, 63; T. Kennedy to Lady Bath, 27 Sept. 1848, Bath Papers Irish Box; *Nation*, 24 Apr. 1852, and K. T. Hoppen, 'National politics and local realities in mid-nineteenth century Ireland' in *Studies in Irish History presented to R. Dudley Edwards*, ed. A. Cosgrove and D. McCartney (Dublin, 1979), p. 216; Carlingford Papers Diary of C. Fortescue I (25 Sept. 1854).

eight pounds as compared with forty-nine pounds for men with larger holdings—but that more and more farmers were finding it possible to improve their positions in the ladder of agrarian life. And however misleading it may be to exaggerate the collapse of the landscape into tiny fields before 1845, there can be no doubt of the importance of the changes which occurred during the four decades thereafter.

Some of the statistics of farm size, shown in Table 16, are familiar, but no less dramatic for that. Despite obvious and important regional differences, it cannot be doubted that it was precisely the middling

TABLE 16

Proportion of all Irish farms of more than one acre (a) above 15 acres,
(b) above 30 acres, (c) above 50 acres, 1841–91

	1841	1844*	1851	1861	1871	1881	1891
				(percentages)			
Above 15	—	36.0	50.9	52.6	54.7	56.1	57.4
Above 30	17.3	—	26.1	27.7	29.3	30.3	31.5
Above 50	—	9.2	13.8	15.0	15.9	16.6	17.2

*The 1844 data relate to 'persons holding land' rather than 'farms' or 'holdings'.

to upper ranks that were everywhere assuming a higher prominence. By 1881 almost a third of such holdings above one acre were over thirty acres and almost a quarter between thirty and a hundred. And as some farmers worked several holdings at once, the proportion of *farmers* in these categories must have been higher still. New calculations comparing valuation levels before and after the Famine add (notwithstanding certain technical difficulties, for which see the Appendix) regional and financial flesh to the inherently vague skeleton of mere acreage. They suggest that a fundamental shift was taking place and that in social and economic terms the Famine was of greater consequence than it is now sometimes fashionable to suppose (see Table 17). With a twelve-pound valuation franchise in the counties after 1850, the proportion of farmers constituting the public political class of the Irish countryside grew significantly to about a third by 1866 and probably nearer two-fifths by the time of Parnell's first electoral successes of the early 1880s.[1] The general influence of these more substantial farmers stemmed partly from their growing relative

[1] *Mean* provincial valuation per acre indicates that a man with a fifteen-pound valuation in 1866 (27.1 per cent of all *holdings* being above that figure) would occupy 25–30 acres in Munster, Leinster, and Ulster, and 45 acres in Connacht (T. W. Grimshaw, 'On some comparative statistics of Irish counties', *Journal of the Statistical and Social Inquiry Society of Ireland*, viii (1882-3), 444-5, Table I).

TABLE 17

Percentages by provinces of 'predominantly agricultural' holdings rated for poor-law purposes
(a) at £10 and above, (b) at £15 and above, (c) at £20 and above, (d) at £50 and above—1841, 1866, 1891

	Ireland			Leinster			Munster			Ulster			Connacht		
	1841	1866	1891	1841	1866	1891	1841	1866	1891	1841	1866	1891	1841	1866	1891
£10 and above	25.2	39.9	—	32.6	48.1	—	33.3	51.0	—	24.6	39.7	—	9.6	20.8	—
£15 and above	16.2	27.1	31.7	23.6	36.0	42.6	24.4	37.8	41.8	13.2	24.4	31.2	4.6	12.1	13.4
£20 and above	11.6	19.5	—	18.3	28.1	—	18.8	28.6	—	8.1	15.8	—	2.3	8.3	—
£50 and above	3.6	5.8	—	6.9	10.8	—	5.9	8.6	—	1.4	3.1	—	1.2	2.9	—

presence in rural society and partly from the obvious fact that they occupied the overwhelming bulk of agricultural property. Thus, by 1871, although holdings above thirty acres constituted 29.3 per cent of all holdings above one acre, they actually contained no less than 74.7 per cent of farming land.[1] And, as relatively more men found themselves amidst the middle reaches of farming wealth, so there emerged a more 'cohesive rural society' in which 'patterns of behaviour' regarding agricultural practice as well as adjustment to economic change were becoming steadily more similar among all but the smallest and largest operators.[2] Contemporary criticism notwithstanding, there can be little doubt that, as a group, Irish farmers responded at once 'rationally' and in much the same way to the fluctuating economic climate of the later nineteenth century.[3]

Already before the Famine the collapse of the domestic textile industry had reduced the non-agrarian sector in the countryside and made it less possible to combine farm work with spinning and weaving.[4] This and the subsequent decline of the skilled artisan helped produce that increasing 'agriculturization' which was to become so notable a feature of rural life in Ireland, as elsewhere. Even more was the post-Famine apotheosis of the farmer the result of the changing fate and experience of that large body of either completely or almost completely landless men who went under the names of agricultural labourers or cottiers.[5] Before 1845 labourers had been simply so

[1] R. O. Pringle, 'A review of Irish agriculture', *Journal of the Royal Agricultural Society of England*, 2nd series viii (1872), 21. See also T. W. Grimshaw, 'Comparative statistics of Irish counties', pp. 444–58, and W. E. Vaughan, 'An assessment of the economic performance of Irish landlords, 1851–81' in *Ireland under the Union: Varieties of tension: Essays in honour of T. W. Moody*, ed. F. S. L. Lyons and R. A. J. Hawkins (Oxford, 1980), p. 195.

[2] W. E. Vaughan, 'Agricultural Output, Rents, and Wages in Ireland, 1850–1880' in *Ireland and France 17th–20th Centuries: Towards a comparative study of rural history*, ed. L. M. Cullen and F. Furet (Paris, 1980), pp. 89–90; J. P. Huttman, 'Institutional factors in the development of Irish agriculture, 1850–1915' (University of London Ph.D. thesis, 1970), pp. 127 ff.

[3] C. Ó Gráda, 'Supply responsiveness in Irish agriculture during the nineteenth century', *Economic History Review*, 2nd series xxviii (1975), 312–17 and sources there cited; also J. P. Huttman, 'The impact of land reform on agricultural production in Ireland', *Agricultural History*, xlvi (1972), 354.

[4] L. M. Cullen, *An economic history of Ireland since 1660* (London, 1972), pp. 108–20; E. L. Almquist, 'Pre-Famine Ireland and the theory of European proto-industrialization', *Journal of Economic History*, xxxix (1979), 699–718; *Selection of Parochial Examinations relative to the destitute classes in Ireland, from the evidence received by His Majesty's Commissioners for enquiring into the condition of the poorer classes in Ireland* (Dublin, 1835), p. 266; P. Connell, 'An Economic geography of Co. Meath 1770–1870' (St Patrick's College Maynooth MA thesis, 1980), pp. 31, 54–5.

[5] G. C. Lewis, *On local Disturbances in Ireland, and on the Irish Church Question* (London, 1836), pp. 251–3 (references to the Cork reprint of 1977). For an explanation of the different regional meanings of the term 'cottier' (usually a labour-service renter of potato ground, but also sometimes a small farmer holding from a middleman, or simply a 'cottager') and the term 'conacre' (parcels of land up to two acres let either plain or manured

numerous and so deeply locked in economic and social conflict with farmers as to sabotage any hope for effective, widespread, and sustained political mobilization. Distinctions cannot of course be pressed too firmly. Some of the smallest farmers shared with labourers 'the same feelings . . . and the same sympathies'.[1] Kin relationships easily meandered across social boundaries, and landlords could find it difficult, for example, to eject squatters claiming family connection with respectable tenants.[2] But that at some point within hailing distance of the labourer/farmer divide there lay a profound if shifting gulf can hardly be denied.

Evidence of conflict is almost confusingly plentiful. The move away from tillage after 1815 did not unite farmers and labourers into a common bond of grievance, quite the reverse. Tillage farmers sought to maintain their living standards by economizing on wages; cattle farmers by definition needed little hired help. Employment opportunities collapsed, not only because of population growth, but because of changes in the rural economy.[3] Only the renting of potato ground in conacre for a single season allowed most labourers to augment erratic wages towards something approaching subsistence levels. Farmers provided such ground and exploited the increasing demand with a dexterity not often shown by their own landlords. Conacre rents were pitched at such a point (in Tipperary mostly about eight and sometimes up to fifteen pounds per Irish acre) that even the smallest hazard of weather or infestation invariably undermined the whole speculation. 'The great majority, therefore, of their bargains for land commence in extortion on one side and fraud on the other. One asks

for either money or labour rent by the season, usually for potatoes), see M. R. Beames, 'Cottiers and Conacre in pre-Famine Ireland', *Journal of Peasant Studies*, ii (1975), 352–4.

[1] *Poor Inquiry (Ireland). Appendix (H)—Part II. Remarks on the evidence taken in the Poor Inquiry (Ireland) contained in the Appendices (D) (E) (F) by one of the commissioners* [J. E. Bicheno], H.C. 1836 [42], xxxiv, 660; Lord Stanley in *Hansard*, lvi, 814–16 (22 Feb. 1841). See also M. [R.] Beames, *Peasants and Power: The Whiteboy Movements and their control in pre-Famine Ireland* (Brighton, 1983), pp. 16–17, and 'Rural Conflict in pre-Famine Ireland: Peasant Assassinations in Tipperary 1837–1847', *Past and Present*, No. 81 (1978), 88.

[2] A. M. Tod, 'The Smiths of Baltiboys: A Co. Wicklow family and their estate in the 1840s' (University of Edinburgh Ph.D. thesis, 1978), pp. 187–8, 203, citing Elizabeth Smith's journal.

[3] P. Connell, 'Economic geography of Co. Meath', pp. 72–4, 11–12; J. A. Edwards, 'The landless in mid-nineteenth century County Louth', *Journal of the Louth Archaeological Society*, xvi (1965–8), 103–4; S. H. Cousens, 'Emigration and Demographic Change in Ireland, 1851–1861', *Economic History Review*, 2nd series xiv (1961), 284. P. J. Duffy ('Irish landholding structures and population in the mid-nineteenth century', *Maynooth Review*, iii (1977), 7–8) rightly points out that landless labourers were also 'characteristic of regions where there was already considerable population pressure due to minuscule farms'. See also *Devon Index*, pp. 241 and 246 to the effect that a 600–700-acre grass farm would scarcely give *constant* work to two labourers.

more than he knows he can get and the other offers more than he has
any intention of paying.'[1] In Limerick and Cork during the 1830s
farmers set wages as low and conacre rents as high as they dared.
In desperation the labourers promised 'a rent they are utterly unable
to pay, and it is common to seize upon the potatoes in the ground
for the rent'. On one large northern estate the thousand-odd tenant
farmers recouped more than a fifth of their own rents from conacre
lettings. They paid on average 22s. an acre and let for 96s., a differential no amount of free manure and preparation (the usual justifications for high conacre rents) could render anything but exploitative.[2]
Farmers were also generally thought bad employers, rarely paying
'proper wages—and what they profess to pay—they give in kind'.
A substantial Meath farmer kept his labourers 'in due order and
subjection' by methods 'learned from General Washington's . . . manner
of treating his negroes'.[3] Small farmers too were often ready to
exploit labourers little different from themselves 'in education and
sentiment'. The Devon commissioners were told again and again in
1844 how labourers were 'oppressed by farmers', made 'dependent
as slaves', 'more wretched than the Fellahs of Egypt or the blacks
of Cuba', and how the jealousy between farmer and labourer was 'much
stronger' than that between landlord and tenant.[4] As a Louth
witness commented, 'Every class in this country oppresses the class
below it, until you come to the most wretched class . . . There is no
exaction practised by their superiors that they do not practise upon
those below them.' About the same time an experienced Cork
magistrate claimed never to have 'sat a court day without witnessing
some act of oppression on the part of the farmer on his labourer'.[5]

[1] For general rent levels, see *Devon Index*, under 'Conacre'; Lord Mulgrave (Viceroy)
to Lord Melbourne, 22 Feb. [1836], Melbourne Papers 99/120—'A peasant can no more
exist without his potato garden than cattle can without a patch of pasture.'

[2] *Selection of Parochial Examinations* (1835), p. 262; J. S. Donnelly Jr., *The Land
and the People of nineteenth-century Cork: The Rural Economy and the Land Question*
(London, 1975), pp. 17–18; Lord Anglesey to Earl Grey, 15 Apr. 1831, Anglesey Papers
D619/28A; H. J. Porter, 'Paper on the condition of cottiers', 10 Feb. 1844, in *Appendix
to the minutes of evidence taken before Her Majesty's Commissioners of Inquiry into
the State of the Law and Practice in respect to the Occupation of Land in Ireland* [hence-
forth *Devon Commission*], part iv, H.C. 1845 [672], xxii, 140–1.

[3] T. Bolton (agent) to Lord Stanley, 24 June 1843, Derby Papers 107/3; B. Currey
(agent) to Duke of Devonshire, 30 Nov. 1840, Devonshire Papers 25/2; Meath farmer cited
in P. Connell, 'Economic geography of Co. Meath', p. 44.

[4] *Devon Commission*, part iv, H.C. 1845 [672], xxii, 130; *Devon Index*, pp. 243, 242,
233, 234, 236, 251, 252, 254 (evidence from Limerick, Cork, Tyrone, Waterford, and
Wexford); J. Bagwell to R. Pennefather, 1 June [1846], Newcastle Papers Ne c 9340b (Tipperary).

[5] *Devon Commission*, part i, H.C. 1845 [606], xix, Witness 62 Q. 24 (W. O'Reilly);
Ordnance Survey Memoir for the Parish of Donegore (1838), ed. W. G. Simpson *et al.*
(Belfast, 1974), p. 41; J. S. Donnelly Jr., *The Land and the People of nineteenth-century
Cork*, pp. 17–18.

Just as farmers and labourers maintained different attitudes to marriage, family size, and provision for the future, so they followed different political cultures which only occasionally overlapped on issues like Emancipation or Repeal. Farmers combined with priests to issue loud demands for obedience, respect for law, and even, on occasion, for coercion.[1] O'Connellite activists were encouraged to inform labourers of the Liberator's hatred of combinations in general and agricultural combinations in particular. The General Association reproved a branch in Kildare for wanting to allow poor agricultural labourers to sit on its committee. In the county constituencies Repeal supporters were invariably depicted as 'honest and respectable *farmers*'.[2] And although of course labourers must have bulked large at O'Connell's monster meetings, their assigned role was that of cannon-fodder, no more. Little wonder that in Waterford, for example, 'the labouring classes steeped to the lips in poverty and ignorance' met the 'cry for agitation by asking "What has O'Connell done for us?"'[3]

The considerable downward mobility of many pre-Famine farmers signified movement rather than a sense of growing identity. 'If once thrown out of our holdings', said some Cork farmers in 1846, 'we consider our station in life completely lost, and we know we never could raise our heads again in the community.'[4] Those directly involved had little time for 'experts' who talked glibly of the 'happiness' small farmers might experience as wage-labourers.[5] Leaving aside the so-called (and usually unmarried) farm servants who lived on the

[1] Lord Eliot to Sir James Graham, 15 Nov. 1843, Graham Papers 11/Ir; T. Bolton to Stanley, 15 and 24 June 1843, Derby Papers 107/3; Lord Clare to Lord Clarendon, 19 Aug. 1847, Clarendon Papers Box 8 (Limerick); Report of Chief Constable Hutton, 13 Feb. 1832, O.P. 1832/255, Box 2175 (Wicklow); printed notice of July 1832, O.P. 1832, Box 2192 (Kildare); Clarendon to Sir G. Grey, 27 Nov. 1847, and to Lord John Russell, 3 Dec. 1847, Clarendon Papers L.-Bs. I and II; William (Limerick farmer) to Charles Hogan, 4 Mar. 1848, ibid. Box 23; T. F. Uniacke, JP to *Crime and Outrage Committee*, H.C. 1839 (486), xi and xii, Qs. 6523–7.

[2] *D.E.P.* 24 Jan. and 18 May 1837; *Kilkenny Journal*, 4 Jan. 1837.

[3] P. Q. Barron to T. M. Ray, 25 Oct. 1841, O'Connell Papers N.L.I. MS 13623.

[4] Cork farmers' petition of 10 Oct. 1846 in O'Connell Papers N.L.I. MS 13649. See also *Selection of Parochial Examinations* (1835), pp. 221 and 247; Timothy P. O'Neill, 'Poverty in Ireland 1815–45', *Folklife*, xi (1973), 26; P. J. Duffy, 'Irish landholding structures and population in the mid-nineteenth century', pp. 23–4.

[5] The 'reduction' of small farmers to labourers became almost government policy, see G. C. Lewis, *On local Disturbances*, pp. 258, 267–8; Lord Bessborough (Viceroy) to Lord J. Russell, 3 Nov. [1846], Russell Papers 30/22/5E; Clarendon to Lord Brougham, 10 Aug. 1847, Clarendon Papers L.-B. I; Russell to Clarendon, 9 July 1848, ibid. Box 43; J. Wynne (member of Devon Commission) to Sir R. Peel, 4 Apr. 1849, *Sir Robert Peel from his private papers*, ed. C. S. Parker, 3 vols. (London, 1891–9), iii, 510–11. On the real-life consequences of decline to labourer status, see *Fictitious Votes, Ireland*, 2nd series, 3rd report, pp. 241–2; *Selection of Parochial Examinations* (1835), p. 247; D. A. Nolan to Earl Fitzwilliam, 26 Jan. [1846], Chaloner Papers ZFM/318; Printed Memorandum for the Cabinet by Sir T. Redington, Under-Secretary, 25 Oct. 1846, Royal Archives RA D15.

premises and often enjoyed tolerable situations, the economic distinctions between labourers and farmers as a whole seem to have widened in this period. All had suffered during the post-Napoleonic depression, but witnesses before the Devon Commission were virtually unanimous that, while in more recent years farmers—especially in Leinster and Munster—had held their own, labourers—especially in Munster and Connacht—had crashed utterly. It is possible to summarize the evidence by weighting unambiguous replies on the matter at two points for 'improving', one for 'stationary', and zero for 'deteriorating'. The result, shown in Table 18, is clear enough. Other witnesses spoke simply of the labourers' condition as 'wretched', 'desperate', or 'pitiful'. Farmers with anything more than five acres

TABLE 18

Analysis of oral evidence to the Devon Commission on the conditions of farmers and labourers, 1844

	Farmers score	(N)	Labourers score	(N)
Leinster	1.1	(123)	0.6	(59)
Munster	1.0	(143)	0.4	(68)
Ulster	0.8	(152)	0.6	(74)
Connacht	0.7	(65)	0.1	(27)
Ireland	1.0	(483)	0.5	(228)

or so simply had different expectations from life. Many already knew the insides of savings banks, but few—in normal times at any rate—had much personal experience of the workhouses established after 1838. Of the 9,946 men with known occupations relieved in workhouses during the first quarter of 1844, 4,599 were 'peasants and common labourers', 734 were 'manufacturing labourers', but as few as 79 were 'farmers'.[1]

Such distinctions were reinforced by the widespread contemporary belief that it was 'the poor who helped the poor'. More prosperous farmers were of course sometimes prominent in their charity, but perhaps no more so than in their ability to adjust the poor-law apparatus to their own ends.[2] Most of those who did the helping were

[1] *Selection of Parochial Examinations* (1835), p. 268; *Tenth Annual Report of the Poor Law Commissioners with appendices* (London, 1844), pp. 580–3. In all, 11,224 men aged fifteen and upwards were relieved in this period in 103 of the 107 workhouses already fully operational (four failed to supply returns). Some *small* farmers must of course have been included among the 'peasants'.

[2] Revd R. Carey and Father T. Mullany to T. L. Kelly, May 1846, N.L.I. Trant Papers; *The Diary of Humphrey O'Sullivan*, ed. M. McGrath, 4 vols. (London and Dublin 1936–7), ii, 291 (25 June 1830); *First Report of the County of Kildare Independent Club* (Dublin,

themselves cottiers and labourers, who thus supported each other as
well as the many 'beggars' and 'vagrants', who, before the Famine
at least, formed a distinct group at the very bottom of the social
pyramid. Mayo farmers blowing their own charitable trumpets were
driven off-key by local accusations that they 'would not give the poor
man his conacre crop if he wanted by half-a-crown of his rent'.[1] By
contrast, landlords, though far from being the universal employers
of surplus labour as their apologists liked to claim, were often prepared, on large estates especially, to pay wages to more men than they
needed, while even a farmer admitted in 1837 that labourers would
never be asked to work as hard for a landlord as for 'a man of my
description'.[2] Farmers with more than thirty acres—and many above
twenty—survived the Famine remarkably well. Landlords in all parts
of the country found such men paying their rents no less regularly than
before. In Tipperary the 'more substantial tenant farmers of the low-
lands remained for the most part unaffected'. In Cork they 'strengthened their position' with livestock numbers increasing on farms
above thirty acres and even smaller holdings maintaining their cattle
stocks. All the more, therefore, did Cork labourers resent prospering
farmers who condemned compassionate magistrates for dismissing
cases against labourers accused of stealing turnips to feed their starving
families. In Meath too commercial farming did well. Men with thirty
acres and more were not only pulling away from the rest, but becoming
relatively more numerous within the farmer class as a whole.[3]

After the Famine the labourers' lot improved less quickly than that
of the farmers. Before 1845 unemployment had been as serious a
cause of distress as low wages. Averagely healthy and skilful labourers
in Meath probably only worked for about 122 days a year. The ninety-
three farmers with ten acres and more in an east Cork parish together
provided only sixty man-years of work for more than 250 labourers;

1848), pp. 10–16—copy N.L.I. P432; *Selection of Parochial Examinations* (1835), p. 203;
Kerry Evening Post, 11 Aug. 1847.

[1] A. D. T. Fay, 'The Parishes of Magherafelt and Ballyscullion 1825–1850', p. 144.
Witnesses before the Poor Inquiry Commission of the 1830s were adamant about the differences between labourers and mendicants (*Selection of Parochial Examinations*, pp. 291,
308, 315, 321–2, 330, 362, 381, 393, 418); Mayo farmers, ibid. 203.

[2] *Fictitious Votes, Ireland*, 2nd series, 3rd report, p. 151. On landlords' patchy employment record, see J. Evatt (agent, Bath estate) to Lord Ashburton, 10 Feb. 1846, Bath
Papers Irish Box; W. M. Thackeray, *The Irish Sketch Book of 1842* (London, 1879), pp. 32–4;
P. Connell, 'Economic geography of Co. Meath', pp. 45, 69–70; *Devon Index*, pp. 234, 236,
243, 244, 248, 251, 252; *Selection of Parochial Examinations*, pp. 258–9, 262, 264, 273.

[3] Clarendon to Lord Clanricarde, 16 Oct. 1847, and Clanricarde to Clarendon, 19 Oct.
1847, Clarendon Papers L.-B. I; W. J. Smyth, 'Estate records and the making of the Irish
landscape: An example from County Tipperary', *Irish Geography*, ix (1976), 46; J. S.
Donnelly Jr., *The Land and the People of nineteenth-century Cork*, pp. 77–9, 87–9, 101;
P. Connell, 'Economic geography of Co. Meath', pp. 164, 184–5.

the smaller farmers almost no work at all.[1] Labourers appearing before the Poor Inquiry commissioners in 1835 were agreed that casual work was virtually unobtainable in the months of December, January, February, March, June, and July, and at best erratic during the rest of the year. The commissioners themselves concluded that some 585,000 men with 1,800,000 dependants (almost a third of the population) were out of work for at least thirty weeks in every year.[2] The employment situation after 1850 was a matter of debate. In the 1860s several expert witnesses denied farmers' complaints that emigration had unduly reduced the supply of labour and increased wages, though shortages did now sometimes occur in the harvesting months of September and October. Large farmers especially were making more efficient use of labour and employed fewer men.[3] Opinions differed as to whether employment opportunities improved after 1870 or whether they actually worsened with the shrinkage of the commercial tillage regions.[4] Post-Famine wage levels (a Serbonian bog for all students of the period) do not seem to have risen any faster than did the labourers' living expenses. Reduced provision by employers of free diet clawed back much of the seeming increase in money wages.[5] Although national figures hide many local peculiarities, a reasonable estimate of weekly wages for men would indicate a rise by 1860 of about half-a-crown on the 4s. 6d. paid in 1844 (see Table 19). Even by the 1850s agricultural wages were still substantially below those of artisans—half those of tailors and shoemakers, a third those of carpenters and masons.[6] And, assuming that labourers spent seven-tenths

[1] P. Connell, 'Economic geography of Co. Meath', pp. 74–8; *Selection of Parochial Examinations* (1835), pp. 239–57 (Killeagh Parish). See also A. M. Tod, 'The Smiths of Baltiboys', p. 201; *Fictitious Votes, Ireland*, 2nd series, 3rd report, pp. 153–6.

[2] *Selection of Parochial Examinations*, pp. 193–278; J. S. Donnelly Jr., *The Land and the People of nineteenth-century Cork*, pp. 19, 22; G. Nicholls, *A History of the Irish Poor Law* (London, 1856), pp. 133–4.

[3] F. Purdy, 'On the earnings of agricultural labourers in Scotland and Ireland', *Journal of the Statistical Society*, xxv (1862), 451–3; *Reports from the Poor Law Inspectors on the Wages of Agricultural Labourers in Ireland*, H.C. 1870 [C 35], xiv, 10–16, 26–30; P. G. Lane, 'On the General Impact of the Encumbered Estates Act of 1849 on Counties Galway and Mayo', *Journal of the Galway Archaeological and Historical Society*, xxxii (1972–3), 53–4; R. M. Barrington, 'The prices of some agricultural produce and the cost of farm labour for the past fifty years', *Journal of the Statistical and Social Inquiry Society of Ireland*, ix (1887), 149; R. O. Pringle, 'Illustrations of Irish farming', *Journal of the Royal Agricultural Society*, 2nd series ix (1873), 404.

[4] A. L. Bowley, 'The statistics of wages in the United Kingdom during the last hundred years (Part III) Agricultural Wages—Ireland', *Journal of the Royal Statistical Society*, lxii (1899), 398; D. Fitzpatrick, 'The Disappearance of the Irish Agricultural Labourer, 1841–1912', *Irish Economic and Social History*, vii (1980), 78–9.

[5] See F. Purdy, 'On the earnings of agricultural labourers in Scotland and Ireland', p. 450, and D. Fitzpatrick, 'The Disappearance of the Irish Agricultural Labourer, 1841–1912', p. 80.

[6] *Sixth Annual Report of the Commissioners for administering the laws for relief*

TABLE 19

Weekly wages of farm labourers, 1844, 1860, 1893

	1844	1860	1893	Percentage increase 1844–60
Leinster	4s. 9d.	7s. 0d.	9s. 5d.	47.4
Munster	4s. 0d.	6s. 9d.	10s. 0d.	68.8
Ulster	5s. 1d.	7s. 3d.	9s. 10d.	42.6
Connacht	3s. 9d.	7s. 0d.	8s. 2d.	86.7
Ireland	4s. 6d.	7s. 0d.	9s. 5d.	55.6

of their incomes on food and clothing, the price data of commodities purchased by workhouses in 1849 and 1869 suggest a rise of at least 30 per cent in relevant costs, to which must be added the additional expense of moving to a more mixed and often less satisfactory diet than the potato fare of earlier times.[1] Only perhaps in the mid- and late-1850s did real incomes improve and even then absolute levels remained low in comparison with the earnings of agricultural workers in England and Scotland.[2] Only over-excited farmers could even try to argue that the luxuries of twice-weekly tea-drinking and verbal 'impertinence' were sure signs of indolent prosperity. But whether the movement in real standards between the early 1840s and 1860 was slightly up or slightly down, no very dramatic change took place to lift labourers substantially above their long experience of hardship and poverty.

The continuing shrinkage of tillage and the increasing proportion of work done by farmers' relatives eroded the benefits which might have accrued from heavy labourer emigration. Long hours continued

of the poor in Ireland, H.C. 1852-3 [1645], 1, 317–22. See also MS 'Return of rates of wages in some of the principal agricultural districts [in Ireland] 1831-66', Mayo Papers MS 11164; Memo by W. N. Hancock in Gladstone Papers Add. MS 44613, fos. 98–104; F. Purdy, 'On the earnings of agricultural labourers in Scotland and Ireland', p. 483.

[1] For workhouse data, see *Reports from the Poor Law Inspectors on the Wages of Agricultural Labourers in Ireland*, H.C. 1870 [C 35], xiv, 10–16, 26–30 (augmented for 1859 by W. N. Hancock's Memo of 7 Feb. 1870 in Gladstone Papers Add. MS 44613, fos. 98–104. See also C. Ó Gráda, 'Post-Famine Adjustment: Essays in nineteenth-century Irish Economic History' (Columbia University Ph.D. thesis, 1973), p. 149.

[2] See remarks on diet by W. P. O'Brien in *Royal Commission on Labour. The Agricultural Labourer. Vol. IV Ireland*, H.C. 1893-4 [C 6894-XIX], xxxvii, 67, and by A. W. Fox on tea addiction etc. in ibid. [C 6894-XXI], xxxvii, 22; also J. Macaulay, *Ireland in 1872: A tour of observation, with remarks on Irish public questions* (London, 1873), pp. 26–7, and (for a more favourable view) H. S. Thompson, *Ireland in 1839 and 1869* (London, 1870), p. 10. On comparative wage levels, see F. Purdy, 'On the earnings of agricultural labourers in Scotland and Ireland', pp. 456–61, 465–6, and T. E. Kebbel, *The Agricultural Labourer: A short summary of his position*, new edn. (London, 1893), pp. 1–55, 235–40.

to be the rule and many labourers still had no continuity of employment and often worked for only half the available days each year.[1]
Housing too, though it improved, remained wretched and, according to
a poor-law inspector in 1869, 'a disgrace to the charity and civilization
of the country. If the farmers have claims for an improvement in their
status, the labourers have a hundred times stronger claims.' In 1870
eight of the eleven poor-law inspectors reported firmly that labourers
were 'not content', one that they were 'fairly content', and only two
that they were 'content'.[2] Ballads sung by labourers in the 1860s
stressed their failure to share in post-Famine prosperity and clothed
the past in colours of counterfeit affection and artificial delight.[3]

A. Its not like days in good olden times
   When the servant and master together did dine
   But now that the farmers has riches to make
   He sends now to the Saxon his butter and milk.

B. The servants wages now must rise since beef and butter got so high
   Ther are hens eggs sold at pence a peice and turkey eggs 3 half pence
   The paper states the London price wheat and oats and bacon dry
   And Gladstone seeking tenant right is now in contemplation.

The issues which galvanized farmers between the Famine and the Land
War left the labourers indifferent. Tenant-right meetings were broken
up by cries of 'The farmers are well enough off, far better than the
labourers' and 'First give the labourer an acre of ground and a free
house and then we'll talk about the tenant farmers'.[4] Sympathetic
landlords pointed to the way in which 'the labouring classes' had been
'utterly ignored', and some were prepared to employ additional hands
and to treat them with a generosity unequalled by most other sections
of the community.[5] But the transparently self-interested attempts of
Tory candidates in constituencies such as Cos. Londonderry, Cork,

[1] D. Fitzpatrick, 'The Disappearance of the Irish Agricultural Labourer, 1841–1912',
pp. 78–80; L. Kennedy, 'Traders in the Irish Rural Economy, 1880–1914', *Economic History Review*, 2nd series xxxii (1979), 209; W. E. Vaughan, 'Agricultural Output, Rents, and
Wages in Ireland, 1850–1880', p. 87; *Royal Commission on Labour*, H.C. 1893–4 [C 6894–
XIX], xxxvii, 5–21, 43, 119.
[2] *Reports from the Poor Law Inspectors on the Wages of Agricultural Labourers in
Ireland*, H.C. 1870 [C 35], xiv, 1–36.
[3] Both in a volume of ballad sheets in B. L. Pressmark C.116.h.3. It was a popular
theme.
[4] W. S. Trench to Mr Grey, 6 Dec. 1869, Gladstone Papers Add. MS 44423; *The Times*,
30 Nov. 1869.
[5] Lord Portarlington to Sir J. Gray, 10 Dec. 1869, Strathnairn Papers Add. MS 42829.
On landlord employers, see *Freeman's Journal*, 14 Nov. 1861, 28 May 1862, 1 Mar. and
14 May 1863; *Irish Farmers' Gazette*, 14 Dec. 1861, 1 Mar. and 13 Sept. 1862; R. Cassidy
to Lord Londonderry, 19 Dec. 1851, Londonderry Papers D/Lo/C160; Lord Dunraven's
Memo Book (Dunraven Papers D3196/F/17/22) recording visits in the 1850s to the Caledon
and Waterford estates.

and Limerick to arouse the anger of unenfranchised labourers against
enfranchised farmers had no more than a momentary and passing
success.[1] Unlike the Land League, which was at least able to secure
the labourers' acquiescence and even support, the Tenant League
remained so firmly, indeed arrogantly, wedded to the sectarian
imperatives of farmers alone, that other sections of rural society felt
themselves entirely excluded.[2]

But however much traditional antagonisms survived the Famine,
there is force in the suggestion that in some respects (especially land
occupation) labourers were becoming 'less rather than more distinct
from Irish farmers'. Evidence concerning the post-Famine availability
of conacre is contradictory and points in no very obvious direction.[3]
Certainly the number of households in rural areas without any land
declined much more dramatically than did the population as a whole.[4]
And, while the proportion of agricultural holdings of one acre and less
fell between 1847 and 1851, it thereafter rose steadily and by 1891
reached what was then the record figure historically of 9.7 per cent.
Increasingly the farmers' own 'assisting relatives' were replacing hired
hands, so that in this respect too a blurring of distinctions may well
have occurred. Perhaps the labouring class—never in any case rigidly
homogeneous—fractured anew into various subgroups: some drifting
closer to farmers, others (relatively poorer than ever) remaining frozen
in attitudes of traditional antagonism.[5] Perhaps too it was developments such as this which helped give the post-Famine period its peculiar
atmosphere of simultaneous friction and integration. Already by the
early 1870s attitudes seem to have become less rigidly fixed, so that
even the endemic labourer–farmer tensions in so regularly disturbed

---

[1] See *Londonderry Sentinel*, 16 July 1852, 6 and 20 May 1859, 24 Nov. 1868; *C.C.*
7 Feb. 1861; *Limerick Reporter*, 12 Apr. 1859.

[2] See, e.g., *D.E.P.* 22 Oct. 1850; J. H. Whyte, *The Independent Irish Party 1850-9*
(Oxford, 1958), pp. 1-13; T. P. Cunningham, 'The Cavan Tenant-Right Meeting of 1850',
Breifne, iii (1969), 417-42 (where labourers were notably absent); *Nation*, 17, 24 Apr.
1852; *Kilkenny Journal*, 27 Apr. 1859; *Banner of Ulster*, 12 Feb. 1857; *Dundalk Democrat*, 21 May 1859.

[3] See D. Fitzpatrick's critique (in 'The Disappearance of the Irish Agricultural Labourer,
1841-1912', pp. 76-7) of S. Clark (*Social origins of the Irish Land War*, pp. 114-16) for
concentrating the post-Famine labourer decline exclusively among 'labourer-landholders'
or cottiers; also *C.C.* 7 Sept. 1861; P.Connell, 'Economic geography of Co. Meath', p. 195;
Mayo Constitution, 27 Dec. 1859; C. Ó Gráda, 'Post-Famine Adjustment', p. 150; *Reports
from the Poor Law Inspectors on the Wages of Agricultural Labourers in Ireland*, H.C.
1870 [C 35], xiv, 31-2; 'One late an Agent', *Landlordism in Ireland with its difficulties*
(London, 1853), pp. 10-11.

[4] The number of households without land declined by 45 per cent 1851-81 (W. E.
Vaughan, 'Agricultural Output, Rents, and Wages in Ireland, 1850-1880', p. 92), while the
rural population fell by 27 per cent in the same period.

[5] For an interesting, if somewhat different, attempt to distinguish between various
groups among labourers, see *Minutes of evidence taken before Her Majesty's Commissioners
on Agriculture*, H.C. 1881 [C 2778-I], xv, 599.

a county as Westmeath began to fade somewhat in the face of a growing contempt for large cattle-grazing ranchers shared by labourers and small to middling farmers alike.[1]

Although collective action is not in any sense an automatic or mechanical consequence of social structure, in nineteenth-century Ireland the two were often related and sometimes closely so.[2] And what distinguished the post-Famine decades from earlier times was as much the changing structure of agrarian society as the shifting alignments within it. Before the Famine labourers had loomed so large and had generated so many of Ireland's characteristic patterns of violence and combination that farmers had not been able to establish the political and social dominance which was to underpin the nationalist politics of later years. Preoccupied with looking over their shoulders, the politically crucial farmer class of twenty to thirty acres and about fifteen pounds valuation had constituted only one element within a countryside made up of several strong and mutually antagonistic forces. Although farming, as time went on, was able to support a somewhat decreasing proportion of the total population, yet the crucial rural areas—outside towns of 2,000 and more inhabitants—remained as fully agrarian as they had ever been (see Tables 20 and 21).

TABLE 20

Occupied male farming population as a percentage of total occupied male population by provinces, 1841–81

	1841	1851	1861	1871	1881
Leinster	64.0	57.1	50.7	49.1	48.5
Munster	75.2	69.6	64.1	61.7	61.0
Ulster	67.6	64.3	62.7	62.0	61.0
Connacht	83.8	80.6	80.3	80.2	79.2
Ireland	71.8	66.3	62.7	61.3	60.5

Farming = farmers plus labourers (see Appendix).

However, after 1845 or so this consistently agrarian-dominated society experienced profound changes as the increasing prominence within the farmer community of middling and larger operators was matched by a severe decline in the absolute and relative size of the labourer class. Between farmers and labourers proper stood an

[1] *Report from the select committee on Westmeath etc. (Unlawful Combinations); together with the proceedings of the committee, minutes of evidence, and appendix*, H.C. 1871 (147), xiii, 642–3.

[2] See D. Fitzpatrick's review of S. Clark's *Social origins of the Irish Land War* in *Irish Economic and Social History*, viii (1981), 138–42, and Clark's book itself.

TABLE 21

Rural occupied male farming population as a percentage of total rural
occupied male population by provinces, 1841 and 1881

	1841	1881
Leinster	73.9	73.7
Munster	81.6	76.7
Ulster	71.8	77.2
Connacht	86.5	85.8
Ireland	77.9	77.8

Rural = outside towns of 2,000 and more inhabitants.

indeterminate category of farmers' 'assisting relatives'. Although the
task of separating these from the mass of labourers (among whom
they were in the main buried by the census commissioners of 1841–71
and even to some extent thereafter) involves some heroic assumptions,
the task is important, because, while not themselves occupiers, they
commonly shared many of the outlooks and preoccupations of their
more prosperous kin (see Table 22).

During the four decades after 1841, therefore, the social composition of the agrarian world was turned upside down. Labourers proper
became a clear minority. Farmers strictly so defined achieved a significantly more prominent position. With numbers as well as wealth now
on their side, farmers and their close kin were able to dominate the
countryside in a manner and to a degree that had not hitherto been
possible. All this, however, took time. The real demographic breakthrough did not occur until the 1850s. The translation of possible
into actual advantage was necessarily further delayed. And in the
interstices created by this period of adjustment, the landlords of
Ireland were able to mount a vigorous political revival, only to be cut
down by the eventual mobilization of an increasingly powerful and
unchallenged community of tenant farmers.

What cannot, indeed, be doubted is the general apotheosis of the
farmer and his progress towards greater acreage and economic substance. By 1881 almost one in three of *all* occupied males in the rural
districts was a farmer strictly defined and almost one in two a farmer
or assisting relative; in 1841 the proportions had been, respectively,
a fifth and a third.[1] It was these farmers, more and more numerically

---

[1] For categories used etc., see Appendix—Tables 20, 21, and 22. In the present case
it was not possible to remove from male 'farmer' or 'assisting relative' categories those
living in towns of 2,000 and more (as was done for the total male farming population in
Table 21), so that the number of farmers and assisting relatives in *all* districts is expressed

TABLE 22

Male farmers and 'assisting relatives' as percentage of total occupied male farming population by provinces, 1841–81

	1841		1851		1861		1871		1881	
Leinster	22.2	(33.7)	26.5	(37.0)	29.0	(44.0)	31.7	(48.1)	32.9	(49.8)
Munster	42.3	(36.5)	23.5	(35.3)	28.7	(43.1)	32.8	(49.3)	33.9	(50.9)
Ulster	34.5	(53.2)	41.1	(60.0)	45.7	(66.7)	46.1	(67.3)	45.1	(65.8)
Connacht	23.3	(35.7)	29.1	(44.6)	36.2	(55.5)	39.6	(60.8)	37.8	(73.3)
Ireland	27.0	(40.3)	30.6	(45.7)	35.8	(53.4)	38.4	(57.4)	40.2	(60.1)

First column = farmers only.
Second column (in parentheses) = farmers and (before 1881, estimated) 'assisting relatives'.

significant and far more likely to have the vote after the Franchise Act of 1850, who, because of a constellation of legislative, social, and economic changes, were soon able to exercise a direct stranglehold over the electorates of the various county constituencies. Even if a twelve-pound franchise allowed only a minority of farmers the vote— though in Munster and Leinster almost half were qualified—this was enough to swamp the registers. A calculation, which, if anything, understates the farmers' dominant position, is possible for the years around 1870, and is shown in Table 23. Potential power must, however, be translated into effective power, and the history of the post-Famine period shows how the interplay of retarding and accelerating influences

TABLE 23

Farmers and the county electorate by provinces, c.1866–71

	Male farmers	Percentage likely to have vote	County electorate	Percentage of electorate consisting of farmers
Leinster	67,972	43.2	45,070	65.2*
Munster	85,169	45.8	46,774	83.4
Ulster	157,898	33.6	67,041	79.1
Connacht	81,212	17.4	17,890	79.0
Ireland	392,251	34.6	176,775	76.8

*The lowness of this figure was largely caused by Dublin City's already considerable suburban sprawl into the surrounding county constituency.

as a proportion of the occupied male population in 'rural' districts only. The distortions will be slight because the number of farmers in such towns was small. The precise figures are: 1841 = 22.2 per cent farmers (33.2 per cent farmers and assisting relatives), 1881 = 31.9 per cent (47.8 per cent).

was able to affect the timing of the emergence of these agrarian angels from the marble of prosperity, localism, deference, and insecurity.

Landlords represented the third important group in rural society. Though fewer than farmers and labourers, they were individually more wealthy, more prominent, and more articulate. Sales of bankrupt land under the Encumbered Estates Act of 1849 gave added impetus to an already existing tendency towards the redistribution and consolidation of rural property. Among the purchasers, landlords who had survived the Famine were at least as important as urban speculators.[1] And calculations which allow some tentative comparisons to be made between 1847–8 and 1873–4, though not without their problems, strongly suggest that this process of consolidation continued to gather force throughout the third quarter of the century, as shown in Table 24. In economic, political, and electoral terms, therefore, the landed community was able to present a notably stronger front: fewer small owners, more resources, and more voters under the direction of the wealthiest and most significant proprietors.

Taking five hundred acres as in general the lowest admission ticket to the 'landed community', we find that in 1873–4 somewhat less than 6,461 proprietors owned 87.8 per cent of all rural and urban land. The rest was in the hands of something like ten times as many persons.[2] If the ticket were raised to a thousand acres, the number admitted would fall to less than 3,745. Looking only at the countryside, the concentration was even more extreme, with 89.7 per cent of land belonging to some 6,437 proprietors[3] distributed as in Table 25. It is at once obvious from the table that the stronger farmers of Munster and Leinster faced a somewhat less substantial body of wealthy proprietors

[1] A Macintyre, *The Liberator: Daniel O'Connell and the Irish party 1830–1847* (London, 1965), p. 104 citing memorandum of 1834 in the Wellesley Papers; J. S. Donnelly Jr., *Landlord and Tenant in nineteenth-century Ireland* (Dublin, 1973), p. 51, and *The Land and the People of nineteenth-century Cork*, p. 131; P. G. Lane, 'General Impact of the Encumbered Estates Act of 1849 on Counties Galway and Mayo', pp. 44–74. The ownership of about a quarter of all agricultural land was transferred during the thirty years after 1849, the great bulk of it in the 1850s.

[2] See figures in *Thom 1888*, p. 721 based on so-called 'Domesday' data (see Appendix —Table 24). As all estates were split at county boundaries, the total number of owners was obviously somewhat less. Urban property could give influence in borough constituencies and increase overall ability to indulge in active political campaigning. Of course some landlords had valuable estates under 500 acres and others worthless ones larger than that, but the figure seems a reasonable (if low) minimum.

[3] Printed Confidential 'Return showing the Names of Proprietors, and the Area and Valuation of all Properties in the several counties in Ireland, held "in fee", "in perpetuity", or "on long leases at chief rents", and classified according to area; but omitting all cities and towns' dated 5 Feb. 1870 with MS notes by J. Ball Greene (Commissioner of Valuation) in Gladstone Papers Add. MS 44613, fos. 86–91, obviously based on an earlier inquiry (also at county level).

TABLE 24

Comparison of percentage of land (by valuation) owned by proprietors of various valuation categories in five counties in 1847–8 and 1873–4

Proprietors with valuations	'Co. Kerry'*		'Co. Cork'		'Co. Leitrim'		'Co. Longford'		'Co. Carlow'	
	1847–8	1873–4	1847–8	1873–4	1847–8	1873–4	1847–8	1873–4	1847–8	1873–4
£5,000 and over	14.3	32.5	8.6	20.0	0.0	21.0	9.2	27.9	10.9	19.9
£2,000 and under £5,000	16.3	25.3	20.1	12.0	14.4	28.5	23.8	21.5	19.2	19.5
£500 and under £2,000	43.5	22.2	41.2	27.8	49.3	26.0	34.8	24.6	43.0	30.9
Under £500	25.9	20.0	30.1	40.2	36.3	24.5	32.2	26.0	26.9	29.7

*Reasons for inverted commas are given in the Appendix.

TABLE 25

Provincial and national distribution of landlords outside cities and towns by acreage and valuation, c.1869–70

Proprietors with acres	Ireland			Leinster			Munster			Ulster			Connacht		
	N	Total acreage per cent	Total valuation per cent	N	Total acreage per cent	Total valuation per cent	N	Total acreage per cent	Total valuation per cent	N	Total acreage per cent	Total valuation per cent	N	Total acreage per cent	Total valuation per cent
10,000 and over	303	33.6	26.2	58	23.8	19.1	76	29.1	20.6	103	43.3	36.1	66	39.0	31.6
5,000 and under 10,000	438	15.2	14.2	94	13.5	12.3	126	15.1	14.1	119	15.8	15.6	99	16.6	15.7
2,000 and under 5,000	1,225	18.9	19.2	337	21.8	22.0	364	19.0	19.3	266	15.9	15.9	258	19.5	20.0
1,000 and under 2,000	1,788	12.5	13.7	534	15.6	16.1	581	13.9	15.4	335	8.9	9.9	338	11.3	13.3
500 and under 1,000	2,683	9.5	11.3	830	12.3	13.2	913	11.1	13.4	519	6.9	8.3	421	7.3	9.5
500 and over	6,437	89.7	84.6	1,853	87.0	82.7	2,060	88.2	82.8	1,342	90.8	85.8	1,182	93.7	90.1

than did their counterparts in Connacht and Ulster, something which
can hardly have been entirely unconnected with the landed community's more lasting control over the county constituencies of the
north and west. Overall, however, power was held in few hands, even
fewer in fact that the figures in Table 25 suggest, for these make no
allowance for the ownership of property in more than one county by a
single wealthy individual. Indeed, the 303 proprietors with 10,000
acres or more in Ireland *as a whole* owned 34.7 per cent of all rural and
urban land (and 23.7 per cent of its valuation). But because *constituency* power was limited to individual counties, the table does in fact
provide an accurate portrait of the distribution of proprietorial influence in the particular world of local politics and parliamentary
elections.

Less than eight hundred landlords owned half the country and were
clearly able to pull strings out of the reach of their smaller colleagues.
Some also owned land in Britain or even (like William Scully) in the
United States. In 1844 Richard Griffith defined a 'great' landowner
in Ireland as 'a gentleman with from 6,000 to 10,000 acres of good
arable land', while contemporaries in England (where ownership was
notably less concentrated) talked of 'great estates' of over 10,000
acres, 'greater gentry estates' between 3,000 and 10,000, and 'estates
of the squirearchy' between 1,000 and 3,000.[1] The extent of the
effective landowning class varies with the criteria of selection employed. Because of their inability to perform *personal* political and
social activity on the ground, absentees might seem to demand exclusion. But many absentees were large landowners who could only reside
on one section of a scattered set of estates, but who frequently visited
outlying parts, maintained sophisticated bureaucratic structures, and
deservedly received plaudits for being more generous than many less
opulent resident landlords anxious to extract the last penny from
tenants constantly before their eyes.[2] Indeed, wealth rather than

---

[1] Griffith in *Report from the select committee on Townland Valuation of Ireland*,
H.C. 1844 (513), vii, 485; F. M. L. Thompson, *English Landed Society in the nineteenth
century* (London, 1963), pp. 32, 113–17. L. P. Curtis Jr. ('Incumbered Wealth: Landed Indebtedness in post-Famine Ireland', *American Historical Review*, lxxxv (1980), 332–67)
divides Irish estates into: Small (£100–£1,000 valuation), Medium (£1,000–£5,000), Large
(£5,000–£15,000), and Great.
[2] For a mixed bag of similar comments, see *Devon Commission*, part iii, H.C. 1845
[657], xxi, Witness 855 Q. 99; *Devon Index*, under 'Landlords'; H. D. Inglis, *A Journey
throughout Ireland during the Spring, Summer, and Autumn of 1834*, 5th edn. (London,
1838), p. 68; T. Carlyle, *Reminiscences of my Irish journey in 1849* (London, 1882), p. 109;
Memo by Chichester Fortescue (after talking to Marcus Keane, agent), 1 Oct. 1869, Gladstone Papers Add. MS 44121; 'Ireland in 1874: Journal of Charles P. Daly (1816–1899)',
ed. M. K. Neville, *Eire–Ireland*, xiv (1979), 47; F. Dun, *Landlords and Tenants in Ireland*
(London, 1881), pp. 13–19, 30–42; T. Macknight, *Ulster as it is or Twenty-Eight years'
experience as an Irish editor*, 2 vols. (London 1896), i, 81.

residence is a reasonably reliable indicator of a landlord's general decency and benevolence.[1] Problems of definition aside, a comparison of the relevant sections of the rather over-precise government residence returns of 1870 with data for the first decade of the century from Armagh, Donegal, Mayo, and Tyrone suggests a fairly static rate of 'absenteeism' during the intervening period.[2] By 1870 the situation was broadly as displayed in Table 26.

TABLE 26

Resident and absentee landlords by provinces, 1870

	Residents		Semi-residents		Absentees	
	percentage of pro-prietors	percentage of valuation held by these	percentage of pro-prietors	percentage of valuation held by these	percentage of pro-prietors	percentage of valuation held by these
Leinster	44.5	50.4	41.6	28.0	13.9	21.6
Munster	48.4	52.2	37.7	25.8	13.9	22.0
Ulster	44.7	48.3	41.9	25.2	13.4	26.5
Connacht	48.3	51.9	39.6	28.8	12.1	19.3
Ireland	46.4	50.4	40.2	26.7	13.4	22.9

Whatever its other effects, absenteeism reduced the pool from which many of the unpaid but essential county functionaries were drawn. As a result, the effective size of local 'society' was often dangerously small if ascendancy flag-waving was to be anything more than a disjointed charade. At its zenith Co. Clare 'society' recognized no more than eighty families. In pre-Famine Cork, with only some 1,500 proprietors of any financial standing (no more than half of whom—if later figures can be relied on—were in permanent residence), it cannot have been easy to find reliable worthies to man the twenty-three-strong grand

[1] Lord Anglesey to Lord Grey, 15 Apr. 1831, Anglesey Papers D619/28A; Sir A. de Vere to Knight of Kerry, 20 Jan. 1835, FitzGerald Papers; Lord Glengall in *Fictitious Votes, Ireland*, 1st series, 2nd report, pp. 30–8; Memo by Lord Clanricarde, Apr. 1841, Russell Papers 30/22/7B; *Third General Report relative to the Valuations*, H.C. 1841 [329], xxiii, 595–6, and Printed Confidential Cabinet Paper, *c.* Dec. 1843, Derby Papers 32 (on lowness of rents on large properties); *Devon Index*, under 'Estate Management', 'Landlords', 'Agents'; Lord Fortescue to Russell, 4 Nov. 1846, Russell Papers 30/22/5E; Memo by C. Fortescue, 1 Oct. 1869, Gladstone Papers Add. MS 44121; Tipperary farmer in *Minutes of evidence taken before Her Majesty's Commissioners on Agriculture*, H.C. 1881 [C 2778-I], xv, 473; P. J. Duffy, 'Irish landholding structures and population in the mid-nineteenth century', pp. 17–18.

[2] Figures for 1802–4 are given from the relevant Royal Dublin Society county surveys in G. E. Christianson, 'Landlords and Land Tenure in Ireland, 1790–1830', *Eire–Ireland*, ix (1974), 33; for 1870 in *Return, for the year 1870, of the number of landed proprietors in each county, classed according to residence, showing the extent and value of the property held by each class*, H.C. 1872 (167), xlvii, 775–84 (applies only to property in rural districts and to proprietors of 100 acres and more). Levels seem to have risen slightly in Armagh and Donegal, fallen substantially in Tyrone, and remained stable in Mayo, with a mean of somewhere between 40 and 50 per cent in both periods.

jury and the eleven (after 1850, seventeen) poor-law boards or to bring the magistrate's bench up to its complement of 257 in 1841.[1] Hence the modest landed 'wealth' of many Cork grand jurymen. Hence the inclusion of agents, parsons, and eldest sons. In some counties, such as Armagh and Carlow in the mid-1870s, there were actually fewer proprietors with a thousand acres than magistrates on the bench. In others, the percentage of justices with at least five hundred acres varied widely: Mayo 60.4, Limerick 48.2, Tyrone 28.2. More important still, the crucial Anglo-Irish *gentry* class (which effectively excluded peers, absentees, Catholics, and sub-thousand-acre men) could probably never muster more than 2,500 families in all to keep the rural ship of state supplied, manned, and in full sail.[2]

The effectiveness of such limited manpower depended crucially upon the relationship between receipts (mainly rent) and expenditure. Rent movements before the Famine are uncertain.[3] Official inspectors, who toured the country in 1840–1 in connection with possible franchise changes, concluded that *actual rents paid* were *in general* not much above the average level of poor-law valuations, and that these valuations in turn were informally related to some concept of 'fair rent', or, in other words, 'the rents of the proprietors in the district whose rents are lowest'.[4] And although there was general agreement that smaller landlords were particularly demanding, net incomes among such men were comparatively low.[5] Broadly speaking, it is probably true that rents, after rising during the late eighteenth and

[1] L. P. Curtis Jr., 'The Anglo-Irish Predicament', *Twentieth Century*, No. 4 (1970), 57 (Clare). In 1847–8 Co. Cork had 1,775 estates with a poor-law valuation of £100 or more and 1,366 at £200 and more (see H.L. Paper cited in Appendix—Table 24). For size of bench, see Pettigrew and Oulton's *The Dublin Almanac . . . for the year of Our Lord 1841* (Dublin, n.d.), pp. 205–7. Membership of the non-elected Irish grand juries (which enjoyed certain local government functions until 1898) was restricted to those possessed of freehold land valued at £50 or more or leasehold land valued at £100 or more above the amount of rent.

[2] D. M. Nolan, 'The County Cork Grand Jury, 1836–1899' (University College Cork MA thesis, 1974), pp. 50–3. Other figures obtained by tracing magistrates listed in *Thom 1876* to Domesday sources. For the size of the gentry class, see L. P. Curtis Jr., 'The Anglo-Irish Predicament', pp. 37–8.

[3] For a 'high' view, see H. Vivian to Lord Fitzroy, 13 Aug. 1831, and to Sir T. Arbuthnot, [Aug. 1831], Vivian Papers No. 10; Lord Eliot (Chief Secretary) to Sir J. Graham, 9 Nov. 1842, Graham Papers 1/Ir. For a 'fair' view, see Lord Palmerston to Lord Minto, 19 Nov. 1847, Minto Papers MS 12073; J. Casserly (Repeal agent) to W. Finn, 1 June 1838, Broadlands Archive 27M60, Box cxxxiii; Lord Morpeth (Chief Secretary) in *Hansard*, lvi, 284–7 (4 Feb. 1841); *Fictitious Votes, Ireland*, 2nd series, 3rd report, p. 214.

[4] *Third General Report relative to the Valuations*, H.C. 1841 [329], xxiii, 594–5.

[5] *Fictitious Votes, Ireland*, 2nd series, 3rd report, pp. 262–3, 420, and P. J. Duffy, 'Irish landholding structures and population in the mid-nineteenth century', p. 20. Even the efficient Colonel Smith of Baltiboys was in 1841 only able to generate a net income of £630 (£100 of it from the home farm) out of his 1,300-acre Wicklow estate, less than twice his East India pension (A. M. Tod, 'The Smiths of Baltiboys', p. 161).

early nineteenth centuries, fell back after 1815, though the process was complicated by the gradual elimination of middlemen who had taken large tracts on long leases for subletting to smaller farmers. Rents actually received seem to have risen modestly after the mid-1820s until they reached a level immediately before the Famine rather higher than that of the post-Napoleonic depression.[1] The Shirley estate in Monaghan registered an increase of 23.9 per cent between 1833 and 1842 and Lord Palmerston's unsettled properties in Sligo and Dublin one of 23.6 per cent between 1828 and 1840. Rent collected on the Gosford estates in Armagh and Cavan rose by 4.5 per cent between 1830–33 and 1840, and by 13.7 per cent between 1840 and 1845. The aggressive absentee, Sir John Benn-Walsh, screwed up his Cork and Kerry rents by 55 per cent in the period 1829–47. The increase of a third recorded on the Downshire properties in Down, Wicklow, and King's Co. between 1815 and 1845 came almost entirely from the non-renewal of middleman leases. On the large Fitzwilliam estates in Wicklow, Wexford, and Kildare the actual rents received (allowing for abatements and arrears) rose by 28.2 per cent in the two decades after 1822.[2] These were all very large or very well run properties, most were both. But already by 1844 at least 1,322 other estates with a rental of £904,000 were being managed by the courts, usually in preparation for sales to pay off creditors. Many probably belonged to men like the Tipperary landlord barricaded into his house for fear of the bailiff, who, a visiting official recorded, 'spoke to me from a window which he ultimately raised up and invited me to join him at breakfast. It was then near noon—bottles and glasses were scattered about the room and by way of explanation of such disorder, [he] said that some friends had spent the night.'[3]

---

[1] See D. Large, 'The wealth of the greater Irish Landowners, 1750–1815', *Irish Historical Studies*, xv (1966), 21–47; J. S. Donnelly Jr., *Landlord and Tenant in nineteenth-century Ireland*, pp. 33–5, and *The Land and the People of nineteenth-century Cork*, pp. 48–53; P. Roebuck, 'Rent movement, proprietorial incomes, and agricultural development, 1730–1830', pp. 82–101; W. A. Maguire, *The Downshire estates in Ireland 1801–1845* (Oxford, 1972), pp. 28–64; R. D. Crotty, *Irish agricultural production: Its volume and structure* (Cork, 1966), pp. 305–6; C. Ó Gráda, 'Post Famine Adjustment', pp. 112–27.

[2] Shirley: Shirley of Ettington Papers CR229/113 (loose) and 97; Palmerston: Broadlands Archive 27M60, Box cxix; R. S. Gourlay, 'The social and economic history of the Gosford estates 1610–1876' (Queen's University Belfast M.Sc.(Econ.) thesis, 1973), p. 316; 'The Journals of Sir John Benn-Walsh relating to the management of his Irish estates, 1823–64', ed. J. S. Donnelly Jr., *Journal of the Cork Historical and Archaeological Society*, lxxx (1974), 89; W. A. Maguire, *The Downshire estates in Ireland 1801–1845*, pp. 32–4; Fitzwilliam: Rentals N.L.I. MSS 6007–50, recalculated so that Adjusted Rent = Rent due ± change in arrears in following year minus Abatements in same year by C. Ó Gráda in 'Post-Famine Adjustment', pp. 122–4.

[3] J. S. Donnelly Jr., *The Land and the People of nineteenth-century Cork*, p. 68, and *Landlord and Tenant in nineteenth-century Ireland*, p. 18; *A Young Irishman's Diary (1836–1847) Being extracts from the early journal of John Keegan of Moate*, ed. W. Clare (March, Cambs., 1928), p. 26.

Thus a picture emerges of a landed class in which the already sensible and efficient kept their heads above water, while the extravagant and lackadaisical crashed mightily into ruin. Overall, however, a rise in property prices as measured by years' purchase at current rents suggests increasing confidence in the investment potential of landed property in general. By 1834 average prices had reached twenty-one-and-one-half years' purchase. Five years later information collected from leading agents recorded some substantial rises in the previous two decades: Galway land from 20 to 26 years' purchase during 1824–39; Limerick, Cork, and Tipperary from 17 to 22 during the same period; Armagh, Down, Antrim, Louth, and Fermanagh from 24 to 29 in the 1830s alone. Prices also recovered swiftly after the Famine, so that by 1855 estates in Cavan were selling at 25 years' purchase in comparison with the 20 years' ruling in 1839.[1]

The situation after 1850 is altogether less opaque. On the whole landlords allowed rents to fall behind the rise in agricultural prices. Specific examples, again mostly from bigger properties (now covering a substantially larger slice of land and therefore more important as rent markers), are numerous and convincing. The Duke of Abercorn's rents for smaller tenants remained stable between 1837 and 1867. Lord Bath's rents fell in the 1850s and did not rise in the following decade. D. S. Ker consciously kept rents in the 1850s below prices. Rent collected on the Gosford properties rose by only 8.8 per cent between 1850 and 1870; on those of the Fishmongers' and Grocers' Companies in Londonderry by only 2.9 per cent and 8.1 per cent respectively during the twenty years after 1841. Lord Londonderry's rents, it was said in 1880, had been 'reduced in the Famine years and never raised since'. Lord Downshire's massive rental remained stationary for 'many years'. Even the allegedly avaricious Law Life Insurance Company had, by 1859, only raised rents on the former Martin estate in Galway by 15 per cent above the levels of 1837. In Co. Cork rents generally lagged well behind prices. In Mayo Lords Dillon and Clanmorris kept rents 'unchanged for thirty years'. Even on the small thousand-acre Donegal estate of Major McNeill rents remained static throughout the forty years before 1879.[2]

---

[1] MS Memo in Melbourne Papers 103/34 gives figures for each county and was clearly based on information collected from the gentry *c.*Jan. 1834 (ibid. 97/40–55). For movements up to 1839, see Morpeth in *Hansard*, xlvii, 287–90 (18 Apr. 1839). In 1834 the provincial figures (unweighted county averages) were: Ulster 22.7 (range 20–5), Leinster 21.4 (20–4), Connacht 20.0 (19–21), Munster 20.0 (18–22). For Cavan, see W. Smith to R. Brady, 15 May 1855, Close (Richardson of Drum) Papers D2002/C/48.

[2] Abercorn: J. W. Humphrey to Abercorn, 22 July 1867, Abercorn Papers T2541/VR/169; Bath: W. S. Trench to Lady Bath, 12 Feb. 1851, Bath Papers Irish Box, and G. Morant to E. P. Shirley, 30 Oct. and 6 Dec. 1865, Shirley of Ettington Papers CR229/115/7; Ker:

Valuable recent work by W. E. Vaughan relates the matter firmly to movements in agricultural output and prices, as shown in Table 27.

TABLE 27

Agricultural output, rents, cost of labour, and gross farming profits, 1852–74

	Agricultural output	Rents	Cost of labour	Gross farming profits
	£ million	£ million	£ million	£ million
1852–4	28.70	10.00	9.00	9.70
1872–4	40.50	12.00	11.35	17.15
per cent increase	41	20	26	77

The mainly casual largesse by which almost two-thirds of increased output was allowed to become absorbed into gross farming profits did not, however, make landlords any more popular. The very largest farmers probably absorbed a quite disproportionate amount of it, while many tillage farmers found even small rent increases difficult to meet. At the same time, as Vaughan has pointed out, the erratic and sudden manner in which rent increases were often implemented caused anger and resentment out of all proportion to the long-term amounts involved.[1] Incomprehensible differences existed between neighbouring estates and 'the greatest dissimilarity' could be found 'between the rents paid by different tenants' with identical

Banner of Ulster, 4 Apr. 1857; R. S. Gourlay, 'The social and economic history of the Gosford estates', p. 316; O. Robinson, 'The economic significance of the London companies as landlords in Ireland during the period 1800–1870' (Queen's University Belfast Ph.D. thesis, 1957), p. 209; Londonderry: *Copy of the shorthand writer's notes of the judgement and evidence on the trial of the Down County election petition*, H.C. 1880 (260–II), lvii, 740; Downshire: *Minutes of evidence taken before Her Majesty's Commissioners on Agriculture*, H.C. 1881 [C 2778–I], xv, 590–1, also W. A. Maguire, *The Downshire estates in Ireland 1801–1845*, pp. 32–4, and F. Dun, *Landlords and Tenants in Ireland*, p. 15; Martin: P. G. Lane, 'The management of estates by financial corporations in Ireland after the Famine', *Studia Hibernica*, No. 14 (1974), 77–8; J. S. Donnelly Jr., *The Land and the People of nineteenth-century Cork*, pp. 187–200; Dillon and Clanmorris: F. Dun, *Landlords and Tenants in Ireland*, pp. 206, 214; McNeill: J. Harvey to W. E. Hart, 5 Nov. 1879, Hart Papers D3077/H/8/14. On part of the Connolly estate in Donegal (rental *c*.£1,080) the rent was not raised between 1818 and 1879 (A. I. Shand, *Letters from the west of Ireland 1884* (Edinburgh, 1885), pp. 55–7). See also B. L. Solow, *The land question and the Irish economy 1870–1903* (Cambridge, Mass., 1971), pp. 71–2, and (for further examples) W. E. Vaughan, 'An assessment of the economic performance of Irish landlords, 1851–1881', pp. 176–8.

[1] W. E. Vaughan, 'Agricultural Output, Rents, and Wages in Ireland, 1850–1880', pp. 88–9, and 'An assessment of the economic performance of Irish landlords, 1851–1881', pp. 176–80.

holdings.[1] As long as prices continued to rise, such illogicalities caused no more than muttered complaint; when once they dropped, resentment—however 'low' the general level of rents—became at once bitter and explosive.

Gross rents were of course substantially reduced by investment and other estate expenses. The astonishing expenditure of 55.4 per cent of the £388,658 received by the Mercers' Company between 1831 and 1874 on 'necessary' expenses (agents, taxes, rates), investment (drainage, buildings, and so on), and 'charities' (churches, schools, dispensaries)[2] could not, however, be matched by individual proprietors carrying the heavy additional burdens of annuities and mortgage payments. Investment expenditure, while higher than traditional critiques allow, was generally modest, probably on average around 5 per cent of rent, though on bigger estates often considerably more. For most landlords non-agricultural investments would have yielded better returns, and in this, as also in their often financially foolish desire to increase the size of estates, proprietors showed little pressing concern for the maximization of profits.[3] Indeed, it was the farmer and not the landlord who was the true economic man of the post-Famine countryside.

More important was the indebtedness caused by mortgages and the like, often incurred to pay jointures to those widows, sisters, and cousins with whom most landlords were so bountifully endowed. In a fairly 'typical' position between heroic spendthrifts like Lord Milltown (whose four-figure racing 'investments' had by 1852 produced encumbrances of £106,131 on a nominal rental of £6,287) and steely-eyed financiers such as Sir John Benn-Walsh, Lord Inchiquin

[1] The O'Conor Don to W. E. Forster, [Jan. 1881], Gladstone Papers Add. MS 44158. The point was widely made, see *Third General Report relative to the Valuations*, H.C. 1841 [329], xxiii, 594; *Minutes of evidence taken before Her Majesty's Commissioners on Agriculture*, H.C. 1881 [C 2778-I], xv, 600-1; F. Dun, *Landlords and Tenants in Ireland*, p. 11; A. I. Shand, *Letters from the west of Ireland 1884*, p. 96.

[2] M. C. Diamond, 'The Irish estates of the Mercers' Company 1609-1906' (New University of Ulster M.Phil. thesis, 1974), p. 229.

[3] C. Ó Gráda, 'The investment behaviour of Irish landlords 1850-75: Some preliminary findings', *Agricultural History Review*, xxiii (1975), 139-55; Debate between Ó Gráda and R. Perrin on 'The landlord and agricultural transformation, 1870-1900', ibid. xxvii (1979), 40-6. The arguments for higher investment by J. S. Donnelly Jr. (*The Land and the People of nineteenth-century Cork*, pp. 167-9) and B. L. Solow (*The land question and the Irish economy 1870-1903*, pp. 77-85) apply more accurately to large landlords, for some examples of whose investment expenditure, see F. Ponsonby (agent) to Revd J. Redmond, 19 Nov. 1868, Cullen Papers, and F. Dun, *Landlords and Tenants in Ireland*, pp. 30-42 (Fitzwilliam); Petworth House Archives PHA/1720 (Wyndham/Leconfield in Limerick); Sandwich Papers Hinch/5/188 and 192 (Sandwich in Limerick); F. Dun, *Landlords and Tenants in Ireland*, pp. 24-5 (Duke of Leinster); W. S. Trench, *Realities of Irish Life*, 4th edn. (London, 1869), pp. 133, 349 (Lansdowne and Bath). For enlarging estates, see R. S. Gourlay, 'The social and economic history of the Gosford estates', pp. 62-4; W. A. Maguire, *The Downshire estates in Ireland 1801-1845*, pp. 20-7.

found himself actually receiving only half the gross rental of his 20,000 acre Clare estate in the period 1851–80, with the rest split evenly between interest charges and investments, taxation, allowances, and so on.[1] The important findings of L. P. Curtis, Jr. reveal not only that some post-Famine landlords were well acquainted with financial grief, but that debt burdens stood in inverse proportion to the size and value of estates. But despite all this, the landlords of the 1850s and 1860s were operating from a far less exposed point of economic departure than had been the case in earlier years. Even the gloomiest analysis does not place many estates valued over a thousand pounds anywhere near the danger level at which net income was less than 30 per cent of rents received and it became difficult to maintain a style of life appropriate to the gentry class.[2] Smaller landlords were, admittedly, sometimes forced to grant out of weakness what the grandees allowed out of *noblesse oblige*, so that the most generous rent abatements during the depression of the early 1860s seem to have been given on estates valued above £10,000 and below £2,000, the meanest on those between £5,000 and £10,000.[3] But even if many yielded to the post-Famine 'temptations of prosperity', the showiest temptation of all— the building of houses, castles and the like—was resisted with an almost iron will. Thus, while after the slump of 1815, construction had continued at a furious pace, the number of country houses built or rebuilt after 1850 was 'very low by comparison with the first half of the century'. Of the 731 major nineteenth-century Irish houses listed in Mark Bence-Jones's pioneering (if incomplete) *Guide*, 512 can be confidently assigned to the period before and only 113 to the period after 1850.[4] And with a few splendid exceptions like Humewood

[1] On Milltown, see A. M. Tod, 'The Smiths of Baltiboys', pp. 56–64; on Benn-Walsh, 'The Journals of Sir John Benn-Walsh', ed. J. S. Donnelly Jr., pp. 86–123 and 15–42; on Inchiquin, W. E. Vaughan, 'An assessment of the economic performance of Irish landlords, 1851-1881', pp. 188–90.

[2] L. P. Curtis Jr., 'Incumbered Wealth: Landed Indebtedness in post-Famine Ireland', pp. 332–67. This brilliant piece of detective work still leaves some loose ends, in particular the very different and unreconciled levels of debt revealed by the Representative Church Body and the Land Commission data.

[3] In an admittedly small sample, 63 abatements noted in the *Freeman's Journal* for 1862 and 1863 (an unsympathetic source) were (as regards proprietors) traced in U. H. H. de Burgh, *The Landowners of Ireland. An alphabetical list of the owners of estates of 500 acres or £500 valuation and upwards, in Ireland* (Dublin, [1878]); under £2,000 valuation = 30.2 per cent abatement; £2,000 to under £5,000 = 22.8 per cent; £5,000 to under £10,000 = 19.9 per cent; £10,000 and above = 30.8 per cent.

[4] Obtained by analysis of the 2,000-odd houses described in M. Bence-Jones, *Burke's Guide to Country Houses Vol. I: Ireland* (London, 1978). Some 56 were noted merely as 'nineteenth century'. The 50 described as 'Victorian' were probably mostly built after 1850. Very substantial remodelling has been included. England is quite different, with a study of 1835–89 showing a high-point of building in 1870–4 (M. Girouard, *The Victorian Country House*, revised edn. (London, 1979), pp. 8–9).

and Dromore (both 1867-70), with their defensive features to avert Fenian attack, the heroic extravagances of earlier years—Norman Gosford and Glenstal, Nash's machicolated Lough Cutra, the Pains' vast Mitchelstown Castle—were universally shunned by the sterner landlords of Ireland's Victorian age, which, in this respect (as in so many others), began, not in 1837, but some dozen years thereafter.

II ATTITUDES

The effectiveness of political power in nineteenth-century Ireland was determined by habits of thought and outlook as well as by economic considerations. Between paternalism and deference on the one hand, and the mutual antagonism of landlord and tenant on the other, lay an untidy range of implicit beliefs. Central to the gentry's political behaviour were a strong ruralism, a contempt for mere intelligence, firm support for accepted modes of conduct, and an iron belief that blood is thicker than water.

A distrust of towns was something landlords shared with many others: priests, romantic nationalists, men of letters. In 1857 the Down gentry expressed a 'desire to have as little to do with Belfast as possible'. Cork gentlemen tried hard to bar even Protestant merchants from the county club.[1] Landowners in general thought nationalism, with its 'sharp operators', a thoroughly greasy and urban phenomenon. 'I am not fond', noted Martin Ross, 'of anything about towns.'[2] Decent men hunted and shot and eschewed febrile intellectualism. The earlier tradition of well-maintained country-house libraries fell into neglect. The richer gentry, with the help of awesomely tuned antennae, saw to it that their sons missed Trinity College Dublin's brief period of late-Victorian brilliance in favour of the more social delights of Oxford and Cambridge.[3] What was correct in politics was simply what was correct in social relationships. Landlords possessed 'rights' over tenants simply as landlords. Ideally such things were implicit, for sermons were usually a sign of unease. 'It cannot', preached Lord Courtown in 1840, 'be supposed that any landlord will quietly offer himself to be stripped of the *fair* and *legitimate* influence which

[1] See printed election letters of 1857 in Perceval-Maxwell Papers D3244/G/1/239; I. d'Alton, *Protestant Society and Politics in Cork 1812-1844* (Cork, 1980), p. 30.

[2] L. P. Curtis Jr., 'The Anglo-Irish Predicament', pp. 59-60.

[3] W. J. Lowe, 'Landlord and Tenant on the estate of Trinity College Dublin, 1851-1903', *Hermathena*, cxx (1976), 20; J. P. Mahaffy, 'The Irish Landlords', *Contemporary Review*, xli (1882), 170-1; I. d'Alton, *Protestant Society and Politics in Cork 1812-1844*, pp. 24-8; R. F. Foster, *Charles Stewart Parnell: The Man and his Family* (Hassocks, 1976), pp. xviii, 117-18. See John Betjeman, *Ghastly Good Taste*, 2nd edn. (London, 1970), p. 8 on the universality of library decay.

property . . . confers upon him.' The same few words and phrases were endlessly repeated like some Anglican mantra to ward off the evil eye. As 'just and legitimate claimant of the votes and support of his tenantry' C. W. Cooper intoned his 'rights' in 1857. E. P. Shirley despised the 'ungentlemanly' behaviour of his Monaghan opponent in 1865. The jumped-up Catholic landlord, William Scully, got no sympathy from his fellows for having 'undertaken in his own person the duties of a common bailiff'. Smaller landlords were touchy at any hint of dictation from richer colleagues.[1] All were touchy if tenants were canvassed without permission.[2] Adept government wire-pullers invariably treated estates as independent kingdoms demanding the full range of diplomatic flattery. Even chief secretaries were for ever being obliged to jump through the hoops of 'delicacy', 'reserve', and 'sensitivity' in their circuitous pursuit of county support.[3]

Politics, however hysterical, remained only an appendage to real life. A certain insouciance persisted almost to the end. The Commons was a training ground for estate management, not the reverse; cheating on the turf a more heinous sin than rigging an election.[4] Family and friendship were the greatest rocks of all, for, as the Whig Colonel Westenra demanded of a rabid Tory, what 'have politics to do with port?' Politics were regularly 'merged in personal friendship' or merely regarded as a tedious 'interruption of friendly intercourse'. Close relatives, however antagonistic, rarely indulged in outright electoral combat.[5] The Repeal candidate for Clare in 1841 was catapulted to the top of the poll because he had 'amongst the Conservatives several personal friends'. G. Hely Hutchinson, though an enthusiastic Repealer, refused to stand for Tipperary, his Tory brother Lord Donoughmore's

[1] E. P. Shirley to Revd P. Carolan, PP, 25 Apr. 1866, Shirley of Ettington Papers CR229/115/9; H. E. Socolofsky, *Landlord William Scully* (Lawrence, Kan., 1979), pp. 46–8; Lord Clanwilliam to Lord Londonderry, 12 Mar. and 14 Apr. 1852, Londonderry Papers D/Lo/C166; J. V. Stewart to Londonderry, 6 Feb. 1852, ibid.; J. Martin of Ross to Lord Clanricarde, 22 July [1852], Clanricarde Papers 78; Abercorn to Lord Belmore, 14 Mar. 1873, Belmore Papers D3007/P/17; S. Knox to Belmore, 16 Mar. 1873, ibid. D3007/P/31.

[2] James Daly to Sir R. Peel, 4 Aug. 1837, Peel Papers Add. MS 40424; I. T. Hamilton to Sir C. Domvile, 2 May 1865, Domvile Papers MS 9365.

[3] Sir T. F. Fremantle to G. R. Dawson, 13 Apr. 1841, Fremantle Papers 88/18; Lord Ebrington to Lord Portarlington, 7 June 1841, Fortescue Papers 1262M/LI203; Clarendon to Russell, 27 Oct. 1850, Clarendon Papers L.-B. VI; Derby to Lord Roden, 5 Feb. 1852, Roden Letter-Book T2647/43; R. U. Bayly to Lord Naas, 5 Oct. 1866, Mayo Papers MS 11143.

[4] Hon. F. Ponsonby to Duke of Leinster, 18 June 1847, Leinster Papers D3078/3/34; Lord Granville to Lord Carlisle, 17 Mar. 1857, Carlisle Papers L.-B. 84; Lord Fitzwilliam to R. Chaloner, 3 Mar. 1845, Chaloner Papers ZFM/318; Clarendon to Lord Carew, 3 Aug. 1852, Shapland–Carew Papers MS 4021.

[5] H. R. Westenra to Lord Rossmore, 7 Jan. 1835, Rossmore Papers T2929/8/14; R. Brady to Sir J. Young, [c.1 May 1851], Close (Richardson of Drum) Papers D2002/C/27/6; Lord Clare to Peel, 14 July 1837, Peel Papers Add. MS 40423; R. P. Maxwell to his uncle, 29 Mar. 1857, and to W. B. Forde, [1857], Perceval-Maxwell Papers D1566/2/1; J. W. Maxwell to Lord Downshire, [27] Mar. 1852, Perceval-Maxwell Papers D3244/G/1/131.

'own county, of which he is lieutenant . . . Such a course would
be unworthy of a gentleman and ruinous to my private peace.'
Many candidates attracted support largely 'on account of their
relationships and friendships', for, as a fierce Kerry reactionary
observed, 'in elections I never mind politics I always vote for friends'.
As late as 1872 the bitterly opposed candidates for Co. Galway
managed, as fellow Army men, to meet amicably 'at the races' and
have an occasional 'chat'. Lord Downshire followed the same code
by being at once prepared to beat an electoral opponent 'into a jelly'
and wanting 'to shake hands with him after'.[1] 'We owe the Tory
party *nothing*', noted a Kildare Whig in 1852, 'they have played (as
they often have played) a short-sighted stupid game . . . Still, they
are gentlemen, mean well to the county, and have an important stake
in it.' The most damning comments were that a candidate was no
gentleman, a stranger to the county, or—worst of all—both at
once; the beau ideal was 'a resident county gentleman of fortune,
of position, and of character, respected by his own class and a favourite
with the people'.[2] Well-used phrases of disapprobation bounced
across the country and across the years: 'a vulgar rich squatter
of farmer origin', 'a man without a foot of property', 'has not
landed property whatever in the county', 'without one penny
in property', 'does not possess as much land in the county as would
supply "a sod for a lark" '.[3] At moments of high tension even
gentlemen adopted the demotic mode. 'He came next to Mr
Daly', shouted a landlord at the Galway hustings of 1852, 'who had
the audacity to come into the Barony of Kiltartan, accompanied
by whom? James Lambert of Creggelare and Martin Staunton of
Tullyra. Mr Lambert had not a single vote of his own and Mr Martin
[Staunton] had one (hear, hear and laughter). He had his own vote
for he farmed a portion of his own property.'[4]

[1] R. Scott to O'Connell, 9 July 1841, O'Connell Papers N.L.I. MS 13649(10); G. Hely
Hutchinson to O'Connell, 19 Dec. 1844, Smith O'Brien Papers MS 434; *Report from the select
committee on Bribery at Elections*, H.C. 1835 (547), viii, 305; Judge Day to Knight of Kerry,
28 Dec. 1832, FitzGerald Papers; *Copy of the evidence taken at the trial of the Galway County
election petition*, H.C. 1872 (241-I), xlviii, 540, 823; W. S. Crawford Papers D856/D/116.

[2] Sir W. Hort to Duke of Leinster, 23 June 1852, Leinster Papers D3078/3/38. See also,
e.g., Knight of Kerry to Duke of Wellington, 6 Dec. 1832, *Despatches, Correspondence, and
Memoranda of Field Marshal Arthur Duke of Wellington K.G.*, ed. [2nd] Duke of Wellington,
8 vols. (London, 1867–80), viii, 477–9; Lord St Germans (Viceroy) to Lord Aberdeen, 22 Feb.
1854, Aberdeen Papers Add. MS 43208; Bishop Kilduff to Archbishop Cullen, 28 Feb. 1862,
Cullen Papers; J. A. Dease to Cullen, [Jan. 1872], ibid.; *C.C.* 30 May 1863 on Sir George
Colthurst.

[3] H. H. McNeile to Lord Cairns, 10 Feb. 1874, Cairns Papers 30/51/16; Judge Day to
Knight of Kerry, 27 Oct. 1831, FitzGerald Papers; Sir J. A. Stewart to Abercorn, 8 Oct.
1868, Abercorn Papers T2541/VR/317; Lord Leitrim to Naas, 28 Apr. 1867, Mayo Papers
C.U.L. MS 7490/30; *Londonderry Sentinel*, 9 July 1852.

[4] *Galway Vindicator*, 31 Mar. 1852.

All this was reinforced by shared experiences of school, university, and social life, while the three key environments for the maintenance of common culture—gentlemen's clubs, the hunting field, and the turf —all bound men together and provided a ladder of communication between grandees and the middling and lesser gentry. By the 1870s at least eleven clubs flourished in Dublin and thirteen (many of them long established) in provincial towns like Belfast, Cork, Limerick, and Waterford, as well as in smaller places like Nenagh, Parsonstown, and Tralee. Forty years later a definitive list included a further dozen locations.[1] Pre-eminent stood the Kildare St. Club, the landowners' chief metropolitan watering-hole. Even some provincial clubs were almost as grand, notably the Cork Club built in 1826 for £4,000 with entablature, enormous dining-rooms, reading, billiard, and card rooms so lavish that even the sybaritic sixth Duke of Devonshire was taken aback by its luxury and 'swagger'.[2] Membership and exclusion marked out the limits of the gentry's social ground.[3] Grand jury meetings too had all the qualities of club life, with coffee rooms to make things more comfortable. Magistrates used quarter sessions as much for tribal solidarity as for law enforcement.[4] Those with wider horizons joined London clubs. Many so liked the life they joined a multitude: William Stacpoole, with 7,441 acres in Clare, belonged not only to the Ennis County Club but to two Dublin and four London establishments.[5]

The worlds of the club and the hunting-field overlapped, so that, for example, the landed profiles of the Limerick Hunt and the Limerick Club were very similar. Obviously the bulk of those involved were very small proprietors or sons and brothers (often Army officers) and other relations. But at the core stood men of substance (see Table 28).

Hunting, as any reading of Lever, Maxwell, or Trollope will quickly

[1] For 1870s, see clubs listed against landowners' names in U. H. H. de Burgh, *The Landowners of Ireland*. The other centres were Clonmel, Galway, Ennis, Armagh, Wexford, and Boyle. *Thom 1916*, p. 1400 adds Downpatrick, Dundalk, Fermoy, Enniskillen, Kilkenny, Kilrush, Londonderry, Castlebar, Newry, Sligo, Strabane, and Omagh.

[2] Diary, 10 Dec. 1850, Devonshire Papers. For a description, see S. Lewis, *A Topographical Dictionary of Ireland*, 2nd edn., 2 vols. (London, 1847), i, 397.

[3] M. J. Foley to Knight of Kerry, 29 Dec. 1834, and Knight of Kerry to C. Gallwey, 3 Jan. 1835, FitzGerald Papers. Yacht clubs also had notable social and political functions (T. O'Connell to T. O'Hagan, 16 May 1863, O'Hagan Papers D2777/6).

[4] J. Andrews to Londonderry, 26 Apr. 1851, Londonderry Papers D/Lo/C158; *Minutes of evidence taken before the select committee on the Mayo County election petition*, H.C. 1857 (182 Sess. 2), vii, 11; T. W. Field to C. Fortescue, 17 July 1861, Carlingford Papers CP3/26; R. Gambleton to T. E. Taylor, 16 July 1868, Mayo Papers MS 11166; H. Corry to Belmore, [c. 10 Mar. 1873], Belmore Papers D3007/P/11; E. Mahony, *The Galway Blazers; Memoirs* (Galway, 1979), p. 121.

[5] U. H. H. de Burgh, *The Landowners of Ireland*, p. 423. Annual gatherings like the famous Ballinasloe Fair also provided opportunities for contact and mutual back-slapping. A temporary club was set up at Ballinasloe each year to give gentlemen shelter 'from drunken intrusion and impertinent familiarity' (*D.E.P.* 11 Oct. 1838).

TABLE 28

Landlords with estates valued at £500 and over as members of the
Limerick County Club (c.1860) and the County Limerick Hunt (1879)

Valuation	Club	Hunt
	percentage of total membership*	
£5,000 and over	3.3	6.3
£2,000 to under £5,000	8.2	11.6
£1,000 to under £2,000	14.2	16.1
£500 to under £1,000	12.6	13.4

*The total membership of the Club was 183 (ordinary members), and of the Hunt 112.

reveal, was as central to gentry life in Ireland as in England, more so perhaps. Clubs might be far away but packs were usually close at hand. By 1875 all but three counties could boast at least one of the sixty-six or more mounted packs then in existence, while numerous trencher-fed foot harriers attracted a less exclusive following. Hunts moved between the mansions in their areas, with 'lawn meets' of sometimes lavish hospitality.[1] Lord Fitzwilliam's agent, Robert Chaloner, hunted on ten days during November 1852 alone, would have been out more but for the weather, and made his remaining time tolerable by coursing and shooting over the estate. The limbless Carlow landlord, Arthur MacMorrough Kavanagh, was even more energetic. Sir John Fermor Godfrey kept a private pack in Kerry and was out sixty-three times during the 1863–4 season, when he also attended numerous steeple-chases, other races, horse and dog shows, and was actively shooting, fishing, and coursing as well.[2] Charles Stewart Parnell kept up his hunting connections throughout the Land War. 'All' the friends of the Cork landowner Robert Bowen, hunted and 'all his friendships had this basis of the hunting field'.[3] Wearing the 'club button . . . carried considerable authority with it', and even hardened anti-intellectuals were driven to verse by the death of a favourite horse.[4] Point-to-points and hunt balls constituted fall-out, as it were from the

[1] C. A. Lewis, *Hunting in Ireland: An Historical and Geographical Analysis* (London, 1975), pp. 53–7 (Kerry must be added to Lewis's list—further research is badly needed here); E. Mahony, *The Galway Blazers*, pp. 5–6, 37.
[2] Diaries of Robert Chaloner, Chaloner Papers ZFM/317; D. McCormick, *The incredible Mr Kavanagh* (London, 1960), p. 155; V. M. Barry, 'The hunting diaries (1863–1881) of Sir John Fermor Godfrey of Kilcoleman Abbey, Co. Kerry', *Irish Ancestor*, xi (1979), 107–19, and xii (1980), 13–25.
[3] R.F. Foster, *Charles Stewart Parnell*, pp. 189–90; Elizabeth Bowen, *Bowen's Court* (London, 1942), p. 257.
[4] *Memoir of the Kilkenny Hunt, compiled by one of its Members* (Dublin, 1897), pp. 60–1, 120–1: 'In the corner of the stable there's a lone and empty stall | There's a snaffle and a breastplate hanging idle on the wall . . . .'

main activity, and provided opportunities for chats and betrothals and for the swapping of private jokes and hermetic gossip.[1] A good deal of informal political and electoral business was transacted before, after, even during the chase. Not to hunt was 'the certain sign of a fool or an ass', for, as Lord Dunsany remarked, 'any man who is utterly unconnected with the fox lives a little apart'.[2] Inveterate political opponents hunted together, and G. H. Moore (the leader of the Independent Party of the 1850s) was hailed by Whigs and Tories alike as 'a jolly good fellow' on a horse. Race courses too were neutral ground and provincial meetings provided one of the few regular contacts between gentry and populace *en masse*.[3]

> It's there you'd see the confectioners with sugarsticks and cakes
> To accommodate the ladies and to mollify their taste
> The gingerbread and lozenges and spices of all sorts
> And a big pigscrubeen for 3d. to be picking till you get home.[4]

More private or less widely supported were shooting——on the whole pretty rough[5]——fishing, amateur theatricals, and cricket. At Naas town hall in 1874 the sons of local landowners appeared in *To Paris and Back for £5* with 'Hon. Algernon Bourke as Mr Samuel Snozzle'. Cricket flourished in unlikely places. Parnells of various political persuasions played it with passion. The touring Ookatiwaikatangua Indians, despite the 'quickness and promptitude of the Darky umpire', went down to defeat at Ballinasloe in 1868.[6] The importance of all this to gentry morale was widely recognized. Hunting was a prime

---

[1] 'An alphabet on the Galway Hunt Ball, February 8th, 1878', N.L.I. Clonbrock Papers; E. Mahony, *The Galway Blazers*, p. 6.

[2] J. P. Mahaffy, 'The Irish Landlords', p. 162; Dunsany quoted in C. A. Lewis, *Hunting in Ireland*, p. 160. See *D.E.P.* 12 Dec. 1850 on the shocked reaction of Co. Limerick society to a Whig parliamentary candidate who did not hunt; also Folklore Commission MS 1194; W. E. Reilly to Downshire, 4 Jan. 1835, Downshire Papers D671/C/2/605.

[3] M. G. Moore, *An Irish Gentleman: George Henry Moore: His Travel, His Racing, His Politics* (London, [1913]), pp. 82-110, 302-15; also Palmerston to Naas, 31 July 1865, Palmerston Letter-Book Add. MS 48583; *Galway County election petition*, H.C. 1872 (241-I), xlviii, 540; *Sir William Gregory, K.C.M.G., formerly member of parliament and sometime governor of Ceylon. An Autobiography*, ed. Lady Gregory (London, 1894), pp. 118-20, 129-30, 147-151; L. M. Cullen, *The emergence of modern Ireland 1600-1900* (London, 1981), p. 244.

[4] 'A New Song on the Sporting Races of Kanturk' (in a Ballad Collection B.L. Press-mark C.116.h.3)——one of many on the subject.

[5] See the rabbit- and snipe-dominated bags recorded in the game-books of the Shirley estate for the 1870s (Shirley of Ettington Papers CR229/113); also G. Rooper, *A Month in Mayo, comprising characteristic sketches (sporting and social) of Irish life* (London, 1876), p. 29; A. I. Shand, *Letters from the west of Ireland 1884*, pp. 13-14, 28.

[6] *Leinster Express*, 24, 31 Jan. 1874; *Clare Freeman*, 16 Apr. 1864; R. F. Foster, *Charles Stewart Parnell*, pp. 114-16; *Western Star*, 19 Sept. 1868.

target for anti-landlord activists at all periods,[1] though the full force of attack was not felt until the Land War when the *Nation* carried weekly reports of popular sabotage.[2] 'The inhuman sport or practice, called fox-hunting', announced the suddenly fastidious farmers of South Kilkenny in 1883, 'tends to debase and denationalize the ignorant and the vain.'[3] The attack on the hunt was, indeed, an epitome of the attack on landlordism. In the end, however, hunting survived the disappearance of its traditional social habitat. The plumage, as so often, had outlived the dying bird.

Far more limited in their impact upon the attitudes of the landowning class were sectarian considerations. Obviously there was a good deal of tribal Church of Irelandism, but there is no evidence, for example, that the old Catholic proprietors treated their tenants in any particularly Catholic style. By the 1830s between a tenth and a fifth of the land was in Catholic hands, mostly in counties like Galway, where, appropriately, the proportion of Catholic magistrates was well above the national average of 10.7 per cent.[4] Forty years later things had changed less than excitement over Encumbered Estates Act sales might suggest: about 6 per cent of Sligo rents were being received by Catholics, just over a quarter of those in Galway.[5] Most Catholic proprietors were, it is true, Whigs rather than Tories, but so were many Protestants. Radicalism was far from their thoughts. They supported Vesey Fitzgerald against O'Connell at Clare in 1828, were hammers of even the mildest 'extremism', and busily issued reprimands to insufficiently deferential priests, many of whom (a Tipperary agent noted in 1843) were in any case seldom 'upon good terms' with the

[1] *Committee on Bribery at Elections*, H.C. 1835 (547), viii, 327; Lord St Lawrence to Mayo, 22 Apr. [1869], Mayo Papers C.U.L. MS 7490/30; *Galway County election petition*, H.C. 1872 (241-I), xlviii, 251.

[2] See, e.g., Report of Sub-Inspector Noonan, Ballyshannon, 3 Dec. 1880, Gladstone Papers Add. MS 44158; Minute Book of Rathvilly Land (and National) League Branch, N.L.I. MS 842; Lord Spencer to Gladstone, 26 Dec. 1882, Gladstone Papers Add. MS 44309; *Freeman's Journal*, 20 Nov. 1885; *C.C.* 16 Dec. 1885; Colonel Wyndham-Quin, *The Fox Hound in County Limerick* (Dublin, 1919), pp. 144-50; V. M. Barry, 'The hunting diaries (1863-1881) of Sir John Fermor Godfrey', *passim*.

[3] *United Ireland*, 3 Nov. 1883. Poaching too increased above even its usual intensity (A. I. Shand, *Letters from the west of Ireland 1884*, pp. 28-9, 72).

[4] See the 'official' land estimate *c.* 1834 in Wellesley Papers Add. MS 37307. Magistrate figures for Dec. 1833 in Hatherton Papers D260/M/01/980-1036: Waterford 32.7 per cent, Galway 32.0 per cent, Cork 7.8 per cent, Queen's Co. and Tyrone zero. Using unweighted county means, we obtain: Ulster 2.8 per cent, Leinster 10.6 per cent, Munster 15.5 per cent, Connacht 19.5 per cent.

[5] Sligo, see W. Kernaghan to Mayo, 27 June 1868, Mayo Papers MS 11168. The Galway figure has been produced from the lists of Catholic proprietors in *Galway County election petition*, H.C. 1872 (241-I), xlviii, 536-7, 821: Of the 95 included (and there must have been others) the holdings of the 69 which could be traced amounted to 19.6 per cent of the county's total valuation. The Catholic 'proportion' must, therefore, have been more than a quarter.

'better class of Roman Catholics'.[1] The old penal gentry, with their 'marks of ancient Catholicity' and 'pictures of ancestors in Austrian uniform', were the very last to make concessions. 'If it be necessary', said one in 1870, 'to evict every tenant who refuses to pay his rent in full—whatever be the consequences—I will take that course.'[2] Archbishop Cullen was rightly suspicious of the Catholic gentry's 'soundness' on education and social questions in general.[3] After the Famine some even became public Tories, Viscount Gormanston being in 1868 rewarded with an English peerage for his pains. In Galway they all looked to Lord Clanricarde for electoral leadership and were, as a Protestant neighbour commented in 1871, 'not at all priest-ridden'; indeed, they gave overwhelming support to the ultra-Tory Captain Trench at the by-election held in 1872.[4]

The majority of proprietors were, in any case, social rather than spiritual Protestants. Religious in no offensive sense of the term, they exhibited a curious mixture of bigotry and tolerance. Thus the fiercest flames of the evangelical revival inaugurated in the 1820s burned in urban rather than rural breasts. A handful of landlords were admittedly converted to Jesus and began to transform their estates into foreshadowings of the Kingdom. But they were a small minority, prominent, above all, for their idiosyncracy. The Shirley estate in Monaghan was awash in the 1830s with Bible 'inspectors' who astonished tenants with earnest citations proving the wickedness and blasphemy of the Mass. But when in 1856 a still devout but more temperate Shirley came to inherit, the policy was quietly dropped and grants once again given to Catholic chapels and parochial houses.[5] A few landowners, notably the sixth Duke of Manchester (d. 1855), the fifth Baron Farnham (d. 1838), and the trustees of the Annesley estate in the 1840s, experimented with the introduction of a 'moral agent' to complement the secular activities of the land agent. Manchester forced even his land agent to abandon 'frivolities' such as membership of the Flax Improvement Society and the British Association

---

[1] T. Kelly, 'Ennis in the nineteenth century' (University College Galway MA thesis, 1971), p. 70; Revd P. Leahy to Archbishop Cullen, 1 Mar. 1857, Cullen Papers, Bishop O'Brien to Cullen, 18 Mar. 1857, ibid., Domvile to Cullen, 9 July 1865, ibid.; T. Bolton to Stanley, 24 June 1843, Derby Papers 107/3.

[2] Morpeth to Melbourne, 4 Aug. 1841, Melbourne Papers 98/130 (after a visit to R. M. O'Ferrall's house); G. H. Moore to Revd P. Lavelle, 4 Feb. 1870, Moore Papers MS 895.

[3] Cullen to Bishop Moriarty, 7 Oct. 1862, Monsell Papers MS 8319; Cullen to Revd T. Kirby, 11 Dec. 1863, Kirby Papers 1863(322).

[4] *Sir William Gregory . . . An Autobiography*, ed. Lady Gregory, p. 161; W. J. Digby to C. W. O'Hara, 28 Feb. 1871, O'Hara Papers MS 20356; Bishop MacEvilly to Cullen, 7 Feb. and 27 Apr. 1872, Cullen Papers; Bishop Duggan to Revd Monsignor McCabe, 9 Mar. [1872], ibid.; *Galway County election petition*, H.C. 1872 (241-I), xlviii, 536-7, 821.

[5] See the ten holograph journals kept by such men in Shirley of Ettington Papers CR229/16/2; also E. P. Shirley to Revd P. Carolan, 25 Apr. 1866, ibid. CR229/115/9.

in order to devote himself to 'the more important truths which concern eternal things'. Farnham genuinely cleaned up the estate corruptions of earlier years (bribery of bailiffs and so forth) and installed a moral agent to be 'the main spring of the machine' and to train the tenants 'in habits of piety, industry, and strict sobriety'. Farnham's personal memoranda are scattered with energizing texts ('In the Lord I have righteousness and strength') and his printed 'Addresses' to his tenantry are full of denunciations of 'dances, ball-alleys, cock-fights, and all other scenes of dissipation'.[1] Colonel Crichton in Fermanagh distributed hortatory leaflets announcing 'A Drunkard Will Not Inherit the Kingdom of Heaven' and 'If a Man Will Not Work Neither Will He Eat'. Others ordered tenants to 'keep animal impulses under the control of reason'.[2] But despite such efforts and those of Lords Roden, Caledon, Clancarty, Gosford, De Vesci, and Lorton, despite even the Plymouth Brethren meetings at Powerscourt House, most landlords remained unmoved. Disappointingly few, for example, were prepared to fight the good fight in Co. Cork. More often than not, indeed, the enterprise collapsed amidst derision, as when one moral agent revealed himself in 1839 as an astute embezzler and an intimate of 'the prostitutes and women' of the neighbourhood.[3] What remained was something at once less heroic and more pervasive: Lord Erne battling against drink in the 1850s with the help of estate coffee rooms or Edward Saunderson, horse fanatic, yacht enthusiast, and billiard player, delivering sermons to his household and enthusing over the Bible, Spurgeon's evangelism, and the Orange Society.[4]

Gentry attitudes towards the Catholic priesthood often exhibited a mingled fear and contempt, with religious abuse serving as little more than code for the expression of social and political distrust. Some landlords raised ambivalence to a fine art and combined general hatred with personal warmth. Archdeacon Redmond of Arklow was 'esteemed friend' to Lord Carysfort who often sought 'his advice in important matters connected with the estate'. Sir William Hort and Lord Ross-

---

[1] H. J. Porter to Duchess of Manchester, 28 Dec. 1843, Manchester Papers ddM10/15/4; R. J. McGhee to Duke of Manchester, 12 June 1841, ibid. ddM10/11/14; *A Statement of the Management of the Farnham Estates* (Dublin, 1830)—copy N.L.I. Ir333 f 10; E. McCourt, 'The Management of the Farnham Estates during the nineteenth century', *Breifne*, iv (1975), 546–58.

[2] Crichton Broadsheet of 1840 in C. U. L. Bradshaw Collection Hib.0.840.1; Shirley Handbill of 1842 cited in W. G. Broehl Jr., *The Molly Maguires* (Cambridge, Mass., 1964), p. 45.

[3] I. d'Alton, *Protestant Society and Politics in Cork 1812–1844*, pp. 71–2; 1839 case cited in H. F. Kearney, 'The estate as social community in the early 19th century' (unpublished paper).

[4] See Lord Dunraven's comments in his notebook (Dunraven Papers D3196/F/17/22) on visits to the Erne and Caledon estates; R. Lucas, *Colonel Saunderson M.P.: A Memoir* (London, 1908), pp. 12–17.

more frequently consulted the clergy on politics in Kildare, Monaghan, and King's Co.[1] Lord Clanricarde regularly talked 'with many good priests and men of the middle class'. The Sligo Tory, Sir Robert Gore Booth, was friendly with Bishop Gillooly who thought him—as he did not think the Catholic landlord, The O'Conor Don—a 'kind and generous proprietor'.[2] Another strong Conservative, Viscount Gough, could not 'speak too warmly' of the priests of south Galway. Priests were not infrequently granted free plots of land and even houses by proprietors of all persuasions. So generous a donor to the Carrickma-cross Chapel Fund did Lord Bath prove himself, that his agent was placed on a prominent 'chair inside the altar railings along with priests' during a special mass celebrated in 1874.[3] But this sort of thing was often combined with patronizing hauteur, a particular speciality of the third Marquess of Downshire, whose 'friendly disposition' was strictly conditional on the regular delivery of 'acquiescence and support' from the priests on his various estates.[4] Outright social hostility was perhaps most widespread of all. To many landlords the priest was in truth the dark figure at the gate, the articulator, or so they (sometimes wrongly) thought, of the even less perfectly understood aspirations and discontents of an undifferentiated peasantry. Lord Westmeath's denunciations of 1865 mark the limits of public abuse: 'No member of my family would ever propose at a public meeting "Three cheers for the Priests"—animals, who, although nurtured upon the public stirabout and buttermilk of Maynooth, have ... assumed to themselves, *by means peculiarly their own*, to be the patrons of the county representation.'[5]

Party political divisions among the gentry were no less complicated

[1] Lord Carysfort to Revd J. Dunphy, 27 May 1877, Cullen Papers; Sir W. Hort to Duke of Leinster, 2 Mar. 1852, Leinster Papers D3078/3/80; Clogher Diocesan Papers DIO(RC)1/6, and Rossmore Papers T2929/4/40, 44, and T2929/8/14, 16.

[2] Clanricarde to Clarendon, 16 Aug. 1847, Clarendon Papers Box 9; Gore Booth to Gillooly, 7 July 1865, and reply, 10 July 1865, also Gillooly to O'Conor Don, 19 May 1866, all Gillooly Papers Section C.

[3] *Galway County election petition*, H.C. 1872 (241-I), xlviii, 408; G. Morant to E. P. Shirley, 13 Jan. 1874, Shirley of Ettington Papers CR229/115/19. See also *Committee on Bribery at Elections*, H.C. 1835 (547), viii, 270-1; N. W. Senior, *Journals, conversations, and essays relating to Ireland*, 2nd edn., 2 vols. (London, 1868), ii, 22; *Sir William Gregory ... An Autobiography*, ed. Lady Gregory, p. 167 and *passim*; also (for free plots etc.) J. Casserly to W. Finn, 1 June 1838, Broadlands Archive 27M60, Box cxxii; Earl Fitzwilliam to R. Chaloner, 30 Oct. 1843, Chaloner Papers ZFM/318; Sir J. Young to W. Donnelly, 8 July 1856, Young Letter-Book; *Freeman's Journal*, 24 Mar., 31 July 1862, 28 Feb. 1863; H. de F. Montgomery Papers D627/295, 297e, 328a.

[4] Downshire to Revd J. Colgan, 10 Nov. 1829, Downshire Papers D671/C/254/58.

[5] *Westmeath Guardian*, 10 Aug. 1865. See also *D.E.P.* 10 Aug. 1837 (Edward Cooper of Markree); R. and J. R. Miller to E. Lawford, 18 Feb. 1852 and 14 Mar. 1853, Drapers' Company L.-B. Irish 1848-57; Bishop Denvir to Revd T. Kirby, 12 Apr. 1854, Kirby Papers 1425; Printed Cabinet Memo on Crime by C. Fortescue, 19 Jan. 1870, Gladstone Papers Add. MS 44613, fos. 16-40 on the Queen's Co. landlord Richard Warburton; *Wexford Independent*, 31 Oct. 1885.

and diverse. Yet, as in all matters, few rejected the overarching values of their class as a whole. The iron rule was that no one was allowed more than one transgression. A handful might not drink or even hunt, a few become pious, a few——such as Smith O'Brien and Parnell——go politically native, but in every other respect such men are usually 'typical' enough. Within gentry politics the only divide that mattered was between Tories and Whigs and even that becomes blurred when external threats demanded a closing of ranks. Because of this, cross-party solidarity was often a sign of weakness rather than strength, as elections for Kerry in 1835 and 1872, Louth in 1865, and Galway in 1872 amply illustrate.[1] At bottom Irish Whigs, though radical towards the past, were conservative towards their own day.[2] They were also, or so accepted wisdom had it, in a distinct minority. But while the many claims to this effect by contemporaries and by later historians are true enough,[3] it would be misleading to overlook the existence of a sizeable Whig interest until the last quarter of the century.[4] A study of the political clubs to which Irish landlords belonged in the late 1870s reveals a significant——though by then largely sentimental——Whig presence (see Table 29). Whatever about the future, it is clear that in former years Irish Toryism (though always the majority creed of country gentlemen) had never entirely had matters its own way. However cautiously such figures must be interpreted, the Whig presence among the smaller landlords is still remarkable. By contrast, the great Whig estates of Fitzwilliam, Devonshire, and Clanricarde were obviously isolated establishments. But while Table 29 suggests that traditional loyalties lingered longer than might have been expected

[1] Catherine FitzGerald to Mrs C. T. Vandeleur, 26 Jan. 1835, FitzGerald Papers; Knight of Kerry to T. Spring Rice, 24 Sept. 1835, ibid.; G. Lyne, 'Daniel O'Connell, intimidation, and the Kerry elections of 1835', *Journal of the Kerry Archaeological and Historical Society*, No. 4 (1971), 74–97; C. H. Foster to C. Fortescue, 5 July 1865, Carlingford Papers CP3/41; B. Ó Cathaoir, 'The Kerry "Home Rule" by-election, 1872', *Journal of the Kerry Archaeological and Historical Society*, No. 3 (1970), 154–70; *Galway County election petition*, H.C. 1872 (241-I), xlviii.

[2] Rossmore to Revd C. McDermott, 20 Jan. 1833, Clogher Diocesan Papers DIO(RC)1/6/19. See also Lord Kenmare to Knight of Kerry, [Apr. 1831], FitzGerald Papers.

[3] See, e.g., Lord Charlemount to Anglesey, 7 Dec. 1832, Anglesey Papers D619/32N; Lord Oranmore to Lord Fortescue, 8 Aug. 1841, Melbourne Papers 98/132; Lord Carew to Clarendon, 27 Sept. [1851], Clarendon Papers Box 8; Lord Gosford to Lord Carlisle, 10 Apr. 1857, Carlisle Papers L.-B. 85; J. Machett to Naas, 12 Apr. 1859, Mayo Papers MS 11036; N. W. Senior, *Journals, conversations, and essays relating to Ireland*, ii, 112; T. Macknight, *Ulster as it is*, i, 54, 89; M. Hurst, *Maria Edgeworth and the public scene* (London, 1969), pp. 85–6; J. H. Whyte, 'Landlord influence at elections in Ireland, 1760–1885', *English Historical Review*, lxxx (1965), 748.

[4] See A. Macintyre, *The Liberator*, p. 103; H. D. Inglis, *A Journey throughout Ireland*, pp. 357–8; Domvile Papers MSS 9361 and 9365 (Co. Dublin, 1857). Co. Waterford had a strong Whig interest: Lord Stuart de Decies, Duke of Devonshire, the Musgraves, the Esmondes, etc. (*Waterford Mail*, 17 Jan. 1877). For Louth, see *Drogheda Argus*, 21 May 1859.

TABLE 29
Party affiliations of Irish landlords as reflected in London club membership,
c.1878–82

Valuation	percentage Tory	percentage Whig/Liberal	N
	A		
£5,000 and over	74.8	25.2	135
£2,000 to under £5,000	63.2	36.8	68
Under £2,000	55.3	44.7	85
Total	66.3	33.7	288
	B (alternative source)		
Ireland: £5,000 and over	74.4	25.6	172
Britain: £5,000 and over	71.5	28.5	747

and that the post-Famine influx of new proprietors included a number of Catholics reluctant to adopt public Toryism, it remains the case that, although the gentry were able to dominate Irish Toryism, they played only a subsidiary role in even the most 'respectable' of the other political movements of the time.

III METHODS

The political wishes of the landowning class were not made manifest by mere example or sympathetic telepathy. Intentions could become effects only after passing through a series of generators and filters which reinforced, altered, or weakened the original impulse. Chief among these were the actual relationship between landlord and tenant, the precise methods used in the transmission of 'orders' from estate offices, and the organizational pattern of local political life.

The incidence of eviction after the early 1850s, though somewhat higher than writers like Barbara Solow allow, was none the less remarkably low.[1] Even before the Famine many large estates had only

---

[1] B. L. Solow, *The land question and the Irish economy 1870–1903*, pp. 51–7. The exclusion of evictions by magistrates' warrants to special bailiffs under Cardwell's Act of 1860 (23 & 24 Vict., c. 154) and by summary jurisdiction of magistrates against certain 'town' tenants under 14 & 15 Vict., c. 92 of 1851 depressed the official returns available from 1849. If the 1868 ratio of executed warrants under Cardwell's Act to families evicted and not readmitted—151 to 515—was constant for 1861–80, and if Solow's over-generous estimate of caretaker readmissions for 1870–9 as a third was reduced (on the evidence of 1860–9) to a fifth, the total net evictions in 1861–80 would be increased by 38.6 per cent or from 12,872

evicted tenants owing heavy accumulated arrears of rent.[1] At no time did the large number of ejectments and notices to quit issued bear much relation to actual evictions, and even many of these latter were defused by readmitting farmers as either tenants or caretakers. Tenants skilled in delay, obfuscation, and legalistic argument regarded notices to quit at best as warnings over bad farming or other infringements and at worst as preliminary shots in a potentially lengthy and winnable war of nerves.[2] In the 1830s notices to quit were scattered like confetti over properties such as those of Lord Bath and Lord Palmerston, often to little purpose, leaving the landlord a choice of ignominious defeat or the adoption of sterner measures.[3] After 1855 their use must be placed within a context where annual evictions amounted to less than a quarter of a per cent of all agricultural tenants. The post-Famine horror stories of evictions by such as Lord Leitrim, William Scully, and J. G. Adair stand out precisely because of their rarity.[4] Generally, notices to quit were used chiefly to gain 'control', for, as one landlord pointed out, 'It is a sort of habit. The people themselves say, "Oh, such-and-such a one is a character" and has got the name of what they call a "tough lad", and he won't pay unless he is served with an ejectment.'[5] On many estates evictions were minimal and usually for non-payment: a mere eight on the 27,000-acre Drapers' Company estate during the period 1857-62; none at all on the 3,735-acre Dawson property in Cavan and Londonderry 1856-9; none save for non-payment on the 47,000-acre Herbert property in Kerry 1866-74;

---

to 17,841, to which must then be added the unknown number of summary 'town' evictions. On this and the 1868 figure, see W. N. Hancock's Memo of 7 Feb. 1870, Gladstone Papers Add. MS 44613, fos. 98-104.

[1] W. A. Maguire, *The Downshire estates in Ireland 1801-1845*, p. 20; P. J. Duffy, 'Irish landholding structures and population in the mid-nineteenth century', p. 20; *Minutes of evidence taken before Her Majesty's Commissioners on Agriculture*, H.C. 1881 [C 2778-I], xv, 854 (Portsmouth estate); A. M. Tod, 'The Smiths of Baltiboys', p. 162; A. D. T. Fay, 'The Parishes of Magherafelt and Ballyscullion 1825-1850', p. 16; *D.E.P.* 18 Jan. 1838 (Kingston estate).
[2] W. E. Vaughan, 'Landlord and Tenant Relations in Ireland between the Famine and the Land War 1850-78' in *Comparative aspects of Scottish and Irish economic and social history 1600-1900*, ed. L. M. Cullen and T. C. Smout (Edinburgh, [1977]), p. 219.
[3] J. Evatt to Lord Bath, 2 July 1832, Bath Papers Irish Box; J. Walker to Palmerston, 18 Dec. 1835, Broadlands Archive 27M60, Box cxxiii.
[4] Even Scully and Adair in the famous Ballycohey (1868) and Derryveagh (1861) evictions actually put out a grand total of sixty-five families (without readmission) between them. See H. E. Socolofsky, *Landlord William Scully*, pp. 51-2, and L. Dolan, *Land War and eviction in Derryveagh 1840-65* (Dundalk, 1980), p. 197.
[5] A MacM. Kavanagh in *Minutes of evidence taken before Her Majesty's Commissioners on Agriculture*, H.C. 1881 [C 2778-I], xv, 647, also evidence of Colonel Cooper in ibid. 565. See E. Galwey (agent) to R. Dundas, 7 Aug. 1856 on serving notices 'in order that I should thereby have that control over them that I found to have been requisite' (Dundas of Arniston Papers); also *Nation*, 24 Apr. 1852 (M. J. Blake estate in Galway).

three on Lord Downshire's vast and varied estates 1870-9; three on Lord Portsmouth's estate in Wexford between—incredibly—1843 and 1880; about thirty without readmission throughout the 1870s on the Lansdowne estates which covered 121,000 acres in six counties.[1] This reluctance to evict was not, however, based on formal tenurial security, but rather on custom, lethargy, and the economic realities of the time. Indeed, by 1870 the long trend away from the granting of leases had produced a situation in which, of the 682,237 agricultural holdings in Ireland, 77.2 per cent were held yearly or 'at will', 5.1 per cent in fee or on leases renewable for ever (an Irish speciality), and only 17.7 per cent on some form of normal terminable lease.[2] With evictions rare and farms often passing more or less automatically from father to son,[3] it is clear that practical security or insecurity had little direct or necessary connection with changes in tenurial arrangements. But men do not live contentedly on favours alone. With notices to quit being showered 'like snowflakes' or being distributed as 'a matter of course' on polling days to remind tenants of their 'obligations', it is hardly surprising that the velvet glove of actual security was not always capable of hiding the mailed fist of retained authority. As Alexander Richey, Professor of Law at Trinity College Dublin, pointed out in 1880, 'every notice to quit brought home to the tenant the power of the landlord to evict him; every use by a landlord of his legal power for the purpose of raising the rent . . . was a conclusive proof that this power might be harshly and inequitably used'.[4]

Carrots were often more useful than sticks in helping landlords retain a measure of electoral influence and usually took the form of consistency of behaviour, generosity in adversity, and the maintenance of 'fair' rents. However, the tenants' picture of the ideal proprietor rarely coincided with that of the landlords' themselves.

---

[1] R. and J. R. Miller to W. H. Sawyer, [Oct. 1863], Drapers' Company L.-B. Irish 1857-67; *Londonderry Sentinel*, 20 May 1859 (Dawson); *Cork Examiner*, 2 Feb. 1874 (Herbert); *Commissioners on Agriculture*, H.C. 1881 [C 2778-I], xv, 588-98 (Downshire); ibid. 854 (Portsmouth); ibid. 726-31 (Lansdowne).

[2] See printed memorandum of 5 Feb. 1870 in Gladstone Papers Add. MS 44613 (also Hancock's MS Memorandum of 27 Apr. 1870 in ibid. MS 44614). Already by 1842 almost two-thirds of the tenants on a sample of ten large properties held without lease (see Confidential Print in Derby Papers 32).

[3] M. C. Diamond, 'The Irish estates of the Mercers' Company', p. 175; Rossmore to Clarendon, 30 May 1850, Clarendon Papers Box 48; *Minutes of evidence taken before the select committee on the Clare election petition*, H.C. 1852-3 (587), ix, 607-8 (Conyngham); J. W. Humphrey to Abercorn, 22 July 1867, Abercorn Papers T2541/VR/169; *Londonderry Sentinel*, 22 Dec. 1868 (Goold estate, Co. Limerick); *Galway County election petition*, H.C. 1872 (241-I), xlviii, 406-9 (Clancarty); ibid. 132 (Sir T. Burke); ibid. 493 (Clonbrock).

[4] Lord Granard to Carlisle, 18 Apr. 1857, Carlisle Papers L.-B. 85 (Leitrim estate), and *Banner of Ulster*, 2 Apr. 1857 (Hertford estate); A. G. Richey, *The Irish Land Laws* (London, 1880), p. 60.

On matters of uncontroversial benevolence alone was there general agreement.[1] The 'munificence' made manifest on estates such as those of Earl Fitzwilliam, Lord Portsmouth, the London companies, David Ker of Montalto, Lord Caledon, Lord Downshire, Lord De Vesci, and Lord Palmerston (with their reasonable rents, subsidized farm buildings, drainage grants, support for schools and chapels, free manure, and agricultural training) received bland, though not unconditional, acknowledgement.[2] Few generosities, however, lacked either intended or imagined barbs. The six months or more by which Irish tenants were generally permitted to delay rent payments (the so-called hanging gale), though it provided free credit to farmers, gave landlords a useful reserve weapon against the recalcitrant. Like so many other boons the favour was informal and could—as happened to those on Lord Londonderry's estate who voted for the tenant-right candidate in 1852—be withdrawn at any time.[3] Even in the case of well-established concessions, such as the Ulster custom by which (not only in the north) farmers received payments from their successors for peaceable departure, tenants could never be entirely sure that sporadic landlord criticisms and complaints might not be transformed into some form of creeping emasculation. And though the campaigns of the Tenant League in the 1850s tended to obscure the point, here too there was a price to be paid, for, not only were landlords able to exercise a measure of control over the way in which the custom was implemented, but farmers on strong Ulster custom estates were often notable for their general subservience to proprietorial influence.[4]

[1] Some general bromides to this effect can be found in Printed Statement referring to Henry Meredyth of Meath, 26 Nov. 1855, Cullen Papers; Bishop Furlong to Cullen, 7 Oct. 1861 (about John George of Wexford), ibid.; Printed poster concerning David Ker of Co. Down, 20 Mar. 1857, Perceval-Maxwell Papers D3244/G/1/239.

[2] F. Ponsonby to Revd J. Redmond, 19 Nov. 1868, Cullen Papers (Fitzwilliam); Lord Portsmouth to Gladstone, 2 Apr. 1870, Gladstone Papers Add. MS 44426; M. C. Diamond, 'The Irish estates of the Mercers' Company', p. 157; *Banner of Ulster*, 4 Apr. 1857 (Ker); Lord Dunraven's notebook *c.*1855, Dunraven Papers D3196/F/17/22 (Caledon); W. A. Maguire, *The Downshire estates in Ireland 1801–1845*, pp. 81–2; *Committee on Bribery at Elections*, H.C. 1835 (547), viii, 295 (De Vesci); J. Casserly to W. Finn, 1 June 1838, Broadlands Archive 27M60, Box cxxiii (Palmerston).

[3] Londonderry Papers D/Lo/C164 (also J. Evatt to Lord Bath, 11 Aug. 1837, Bath Papers Irish Box; A. D. T. Fay, 'The Parishes of Magherafelt and Ballyscullion 1825–1850', p. 21). On abatements, see above, note 3 p. 115; also *Fictitious Votes, Ireland*, 2nd series, 3rd report, pp. 110–14; K. J. Buggy to T. M. Ray, 15 Oct. 1841, O'Connell Papers N.L.I. MS 13623; B. Currey to Duke of Devonshire, 29 Oct. 1846, Devonshire Papers 25/41. On 'non-contractual privileges', see S. Clark, *Social origins of the Irish Land War*, pp. 164–71.

[4] *Freeman's Journal*, 29 Mar. 1860. For some examples of the custom's various forms (payments were much bigger in Ulster than in the south), see H. Anderson to J. A. Beck, 10 Aug. 1852, Ironmongers' Company Irish Correspondence Received 1846–54 (it results in landlord weakness); *C.C.* 7 Sept. 1862 (Devonshire estates); *Irish Farmers' Gazette*, 13 Sept. 1862 (common in Kilkenny); F. Dun, *Landlords and Tenants in Ireland*, pp. 130–1 (in 51 cases in Limavady district of Co. Londonderry 1873–80 the payments equalled almost two-fifths

Thus it was precisely those landlords who behaved most 'generously' who thereby put themselves into a position to take the most severe action against social and political recalcitrants. It was also those landlords most single-mindedly intent on advancing agricultural efficiency who incurred especial suspicion and distrust. Such reactions slid imperceptibly from attacks on obvious targets like Alan Pollock (who brusquely though expensively 'cleared' his Galway estate after 1853)[1] to a distrust of any landlord with new ideas. Really forceful 'improvers' —not infrequently Catholic in religion and Liberal in politics—provided assassins with targets often difficult to resist.[2] The evidence is overwhelming that, both before and after the Famine, the most intense distrust was reserved for those proprietors and their staff who sought to change existing habits and cover the landscape with squared fields, drainage ditches, and neat houses. It was often by contrast (as astonished observers uncomprehendingly reported) the most 'neglectful' proprietors who were the most popular, for at least they eschewed minute interference and patronizing zeal.[3]

This *mélange* of attitudes was further influenced by those reciprocal considerations of paternalism and deference which cut across reactions to improvement, expenditure, and management. Although paternalism and deference existed as much in the eyes of contemporary beholders as in the world of hard knocks, yet certain patterns of behaviour, both unconscious and calculating, can best be so described. Paternalism, even when it was something more than profit dressed up in sentimentality, was always a double-edged affair and often involved its

of annual rent per acre). Despite the views of B. L. Solow (*The land question and the Irish economy 1870–1903*, pp. 26–30) it is not yet entirely clear that Ulster Custom payments were ultimately at the expense of the landlord (the incoming tenant supposedly being able to afford a lower rent because of them). See J. Mokyr, 'Uncertainty and Prefamine Irish Agriculture', in *Ireland and Scotland 1600–1850: Parallels and Contrasts in Economic and Social Development*, ed. T. M. Devine and D. Dickson (Edinburgh, 1983), pp. 94–8.

[1] See P. G. Lane, 'An attempt at commercial farming in Ireland after the Famine', *Studies*, lxi (1972), 54–66.

[2] Clarendon to Russell, 17 Nov. 1847, Clarendon Papers L.-B. I on Major Mahon; 'A Magistrate of the County', *The present state of Tipperary as regards agrarian outrages, their nature, origin, and increase, considered* (Dublin, 1842), pp. 5–7 on Robert Hall (copy in C. U. L. Bradshaw Collection Hib.7.843.8); Printed Memorandum on Irish crime, 19 Jan. 1870, Gladstone Papers Add. MS 44613, fos. 16–40v; M. R. Beames, 'Rural Conflict in pre-Famine Ireland', pp. 75–91, especially 78–9.

[3] Only a pot-pourri of evidence can be offered: *Fictitious Votes, Ireland*, 2nd series, 3rd report, pp. 261–2; *A Young Irishman's Diary (1836–1847)*, ed. W. Clare, pp. 30–1; *The Irish Journals of Elizabeth Smith 1840–1850*, ed. D. Thomson and M. McGusty (Oxford, 1980), p. 142; F. R. Bertolacci to Sir C. Trevelyan, 21 Nov. 1848, Broadlands Archive 27M60, Box cxix; 'The Journals of Sir John Benn-Walsh', ed. J. S. Donnelly Jr., pp. 89, 26; C. W. O'Hara to I. Butt, 20 Jan. 1865, O'Hara Papers MS 20353; F. Dun, *Landlords and Tenants in Ireland*, pp. 9, 20–1; G. Pellew, *In Castle and Cabin or talks in Ireland in 1887* (New York and London, 1888), pp. 131, 191.

recipients in having to sing humiliatingly for both their metaphorical and literal suppers. The hectoring tone of many self-styled paternalists grated on the ear, and the issuing of niggling instructions was not confined to evangelicals and their moral agents. The Mercers' Company's insistence that tenants 'Be Prosperous and Happy', Lord Courtown's reminders about the 'Influence which Property duly Exercised conferred upon him', Lord Downshire's stress that tenants 'Be Punctual and Regular' were revealing in more things than their use of capitals. Colonel Crichton droned on about 'Cleanliness' and 'Manure'. The third Marquess of Londonderry issued periodic manifestos virtually telling his tenants what to *think* about current politics.[1] Lord Palmerston insisted that no books be used in estate schools not 'signed in the inner cover' as approved by himself. Many agents intervened minutely in family quarrels among the tenantry. Mr Batt in Down would accept none on his estate without a 'certificate of character'. E. J. Shirley forbade 'improvident marriages'. On parts of the Lansdowne estate it was, among much else, forbidden in the 1850s to marry or to lodge strangers without permission.[2] Two ruggedly insensitive examples —both perpetrated by men of Liberal politics—make it seem marvellous that so few landlords were actually abused. Sir Charles Domvile forbade smoking near his house, and, while paying his labourers well, obliged them to wear full 'estate dress' of 'laced Boots, leather Gaiters . . . Corduroy Breeches and Waistcoat, Neck Tie, and Smock Frock, with Black Felt Hat'. Their 'whole time', he announced, 'is mine': they must not 'leave home without permission, as each man is liable to be called in at night in case of fire'. Less aloof but even more irritating was the politically amiable H. A. Herbert of Muckross, who was

wont frequently to visit his tenants, to walk over their fields with them, to keep them up to the mark, to see that pigs were not lodged in the parlour . . . Occasionally he would beg a brush, and with his own hand proceed to sweep down offending cobwebs. On the top of a hill with an opera-glass, at four or five on a spring morning, he would turn out to see which of his tenants made the earliest start.[3]

---

[1] M. C. Diamond, 'The Irish estates of the Mercers' Company', p. 175; Printed Paper of 25 Nov. 1840, Courtown Papers; W. A. Maguire, *The Downshire estates in Ireland 1801-1845*, p. 173; Crichton's broadsides in C. U. L. Bradshaw Collection Hib.O.840.1, 2; for Londonderry, see the pamphlet in Clarendon Papers Box 18, also Lord de Ros to Clarendon, 28 Aug. [1850], ibid. Box 23.

[2] *The Letters of the Third Viscount Palmerston to Laurence and Elizabeth Sulivan 1804-1863*, ed. K. Bourne (London, 1979), p. 203; W. E. Vaughan, 'Landlord and Tenant Relations in Ireland between the Famine and the Land War', p. 219, and *Devon Index*, pp. 1-6; ibid. 150; W. G. Broehl Jr., *The Molly Maguires*, pp. 44-5; J. Godkin, *The Land War in Ireland* (London, 1870), pp. 411-14.

[3] Notices issued (c.1859-64) on Domvile estate in N.L.I., *The Landed Gentry: Facsimile*

The continuance of this kind of thing was made possible, not only by coercive power, but because of the survival on some estates of attitudes which depicted proprietors as far more than mere receivers of rent. The phrase *in loco parentis* was often on the lips of those anxious to see estates as a series of happy families.[1] This particularly 'Tory' ideal found more frequent expression in print than in reality. Yet it related to something more than pious hypocrisy and provided at least a counter-rhetoric to liberalism's emphasis on the cash nexus unadorned.[2] 'The staunch principle of firm allegiance to the family' was not without its impact. The thousands of marching men who turned out for their landlords at the great Protestant gathering at Hillsborough in 1834 were no sycophantic or press-ganged automata.[3] Landlords disappointed by electoral disloyalty reminded farmers that if they continued to insist on political individualism, then economic individualism in the shape of higher rents would be their reward.[4] There were proprietors who adjudicated in family disputes, provided dowries for daughters and pensions for indigent widows, who were (? ingratiatingly) asked to help control erring children and feckless relatives, and who used their influence to obtain jobs, grants, loans, and introductions for the tenants on their properties.[5] Some went so far as to perambulate the fields with coins, blankets, and warm clothes for immediate distribution. Some put their money where their mouths were and treated desmesne labourers with uncommon generosity. Owen Wynne of Hazlewood in Sligo introduced, it was said, so much 'comfort among his cottagers, that their neighbours enviously

Documents (1977); F. Dun, *Landlords and Tenants in Ireland*, p. 80. For Lord Dunraven's minute personal enquiries into tenants' farming techniques, see his Adare notebook for the 1850s (Dunraven Papers D3196/F/17/21).

[1] *Crime and Outrage Committee*, H.C. 1839 (486), xi and xii, Qs. 8460-1; *The Times*, 6 Dec. 1842.

[2] *Dublin Evening Mail*, 26 Dec. 1832; *Committee on Bribery at Elections*, H.C. 1835 (547), viii, 662-3, and *Crime and Outrage Committee*, H.C. 1839 (486), xi and xii, Qs. 8268 ff. For the 'liberal' view, see Archbishop Whately cited in B. O'Reilly, *John MacHale, Archbishop of Tuam. His Life, Times, and Correspondence*, 2 vols. (New York, 1890), ii, 297, and A. G. Richey, *The Irish Land Laws*, pp. 57-8.

[3] Rossmore to Clarendon, 30 May 1850, Clarendon Papers Box 48; 'One late an Agent', *Landlordism in Ireland*, p. 24; Lord Clanwilliam to Duke of Wellington, [2 Nov. 1834], *The Prime Ministers' Papers: Wellington Political Correspondence*, ed. J. Brooke and J. Gandy (London, 1975-   ), i, 712.

[4] *Banner of Ulster*, 2 Apr. 1857; *Galway County election petition*, H.C. 1872 (241-I), xlviii, 348-55; T. Duffy to Lord M. Hill, 9 Jan. 1833, Downshire Papers D671/C/12/484.

[5] E. Wakefield, *An Account of Ireland, Statistical and Political*, 2 vols. (London, 1812), ii, 749-50; J. Fleming to H. R. Westenra, 11 May 1835, Rossmore Papers T2929/4/42; G. Wyndham to C. Reddan, 6 Feb. 1840, Petworth House Archives PHA/736; C. W. Cooper to Sir R. Gore Booth, 5 Aug. 1852, O'Hara Papers MS 20353; *Tipperary Advocate*, 13 Oct. 1866; *Galway County election petition*, H.C. 1872 (241-I), xlviii, 547-50; F. Dun, *Landlords and Tenants in Ireland*, p. 190; D. McCormick, *The incredible Mr Kavanagh*, p. 156.

nicknamed them the "golden knockers", a golden knocker being all they wanted, in popular opinion, to reach the heights of absurdity'.[1] Even amidst post-Famine respectability a few landlords maintained a curious chumminess, part genuine, part romantic imitation of what they considered should be the proper filiation between high and low. The very correct Marquess of Clanricarde drank 'goblets of raw whis- key' with local 'characters', while Christopher St George of Galway received the ultimate benediction: 'Sure there is not a place he goes where he does not give a drink.'[2] Yet, in the end, to interpret such alcoholic versions of a generally more frigid paternalism as reliable signs of mutual regard, is to overlook the virtual impossibility of authen- tically relaxed associations between, as some landlords revealingly put it, 'masters and their servants'.

Circuses were provided as well as bread (and booze), usually to help massage the landlords' sense of vanity and position. Self-styled 'clan chiefs' at the head of 'groaning tables' and surrounded by well- lubricated tenants found it easy to believe that all was for the best in the best of all possible worlds. The sixth Duke of Devonshire—a keen organizer of firework displays—spent £2,249 on one grand Lismore party alone. The Drapers' Company gave endless tenant dinners. In 1857 Lady Londonderry provisioned hundreds of Antrim tenants amidst a forest of 'flowers, evergreens, and banners' proclaiming 'God Save the Queen', 'Céad Míle Fáilte', and 'Live and Let Live'—all popu- lar estate slogans. Lord Gosford dispensed gallons of beer, wine, and punch, as well as non-stop music. Lord Bath's visit to Carrickmacross in 1865 drove local newsmen into paroxysms of nervous recollection: 'The dinner was of the most recherché character ... the wines too were of the most excellent quality, champagne flowed . . . a band, toasts, priests in constant attendance.'[3] Small landlords providing more modest entertainment found themselves, like Sir J. F. Godfrey in 1878, the victims of every sponging free-loader in the district lurchingly anxious to compliment 'an ancient and popular house'.[4] Even the

[1] F. Dun, *Landlords and Tenants in Ireland*, p. 13 (Downshire); *Freeman's Journal*, 1 Jan. 1861 (De Freyne); *Londonderry Sentinel*, 6 May 1859 (Heygate); A. I. Shand, *Letters from the west of Ireland 1884*, pp. 84–5 (Wynne). For a further sample, see *Freeman's Journal*, 14, 28 Nov. 1861, 18 Feb., 26 and 29 Apr. 1862 (Hacket, Levinge, Dillon, Ely, Burton, Westby), ibid. 6 May, 2 June 1862, 23, 27, 31 Jan., 16 Feb., 17 Mar. 1863 (Sadlier, Magennis, Hope, Hope-Scott, Erne, O'Callaghan, Lane Fox, Tottenham); *C.C.* 11 Feb. 1863 (Bernard).

[2] Clanricarde to Clarendon, [Nov. 1847], Clarendon Papers Box 9; *Galway County election petition*, H.C. 1872 (241–I), xlviii, 155–7.

[3] Clarendon to Russell, 27 Oct. 1850, Clarendon Papers L.-B. VI, and Devonshire Papers 25/81A (Devonshire); R. and J. R. Miller to E. Lawford, 18 Feb. 1852, Drapers' Company L.-B. Irish 1848–57, and *Londonderry Sentinel*, 18 June 1852 (Drapers'); *Banner of Ulster*, 29 Sept. 1857 (Londonderry); R. S. Gourlay, 'The social and economic history of the Gosford estates', p. 252; W. S. Trench, *Realities of Irish Life*, pp. 368–92 (Bath).

[4] V. M. Barry, 'The hunting diaries of Sir John Fermor Godfrey', p. 22; also *Londonderry*

careful Downshires lashed out for the wedding of Lord Hillsborough in 1837 on 3,500 guests at thirty-four tables, roast oxen, 8,000 flowers, and 'viands of every description'. Years later, when Hillsborough himself had inherited the title, he claimed to know all his Edenderry tenants personally: 'I am as intimate with them as it is possible to be. Whenever I go we have a ball every night . . . and then there is *real happiness* because there is no . . . pride as I dance all night with high and low.'[1] The obverse has been too often depicted to need elaboration. On many small absentee estates relationships were simply expressed in cash. Some resident landlords took pride in their lack of 'intercourse with the lower orders'. Many of the tenant witnesses before the Devon Commission knew pathetically little about the owners of their farms. Even well-intentioned men laboured under revealing illusions, like Mr Lane Fox, who, 'supposing the County of Waterford, and the tastes and wants of its people to resemble those of New Zealand or California', descended on his property in the 1830s 'with pockets full of beads, little mirrors, brooches, and other gew-gaws of a like kind'.[2]

'Deference' is the name given to the tribute paid by dependants to paternalists. In rural Ireland the concept—notable always for its obscurity—is less helpful than in England. Yet versions of the art did flourish in suitably Hibernian metamorphosis. At elections 'good' landlords were more (though not inevitably) successful than 'bad', sometimes extravagantly so, as when the tenants of J. J. Kelly berated their landlord's Home Rule opponents with sticks, stones, and pitchforks at the Limerick election of 1874. Lord Conyngham's tenants, surrounded at Ennis in 1852 by a roaring mob, stuck firm to their Tory promises and shouted 'You may command our bodies, but you cannot command our tongues.' A Galway tenant thought it only right in 1872 to pay a 'good landlord' a 'small compliment by voting for his friends'. Kilrush electors who opposed the local Tory candidate laid themselves open to revenge from his tenants, while Tipperary farmers in 1857 attacked a radical priest for leading the opposition to their landlord's politics. 'We would', announced two Longford tenants in 1870, 'go with our landlord whatever priest put up against him, and

Sentinel, 17 Apr. 1857 (Sir R. Bateson); Carlingford Papers Diary of C. Fortescue II (12 Apr. 1857): 'The dear aunt had a bonfire in the field . . . and beer and whiskey distributed . . . boys and girls danced . . . by the light of the bonfire and cheered for all the family.'

[1] *Belfast Newsletter,* 20 Oct. 1837 cited in A. McClelland, 'Festivities at Hillsborough', *Ulster Folk and Transport Museum Year Book* 1973–4, p. 7; Downshire to Derby, 23 July 1852, Derby Papers 124/6. For a later Downshire beano, see *The Irish Journals of Elizabeth Smith,* ed. D. Thomson and M. McGusty, pp. 227–9.

[2] H. D. Inglis, *A Journey throughout Ireland,* p. 195 (and p. 36); P. J. Duffy, 'Irish landholding structures and population in the mid-nineteenth century', pp. 20, 26; *The Irish Journals of Elizabeth Smith,* ed. D. Thomson and M. McGusty, p. 6.

always will: we like him.'[1] Certain estates built up distinct feelings of
social and political *esprit de corps* which cut across most other barriers
and distinctions.[2] Of course much of this was strictly for show, as
shrewd agents realized more quickly than Panglossian proprietors.
Lord Derby's agent knew that he was told many things merely 'for the
purpose of pleasing me'. Another recognized how 'wonderfully prone
are the lower classes in Ireland to secure the good will of a newcomer
amongst them'. Steuart Trench noted wryly how days after Lord
Bath's tenants had shaken his hands 'till the blood nearly spouted out'
he was obliged to travel the estate with 'double-barrelled pistols' at the
ready.[3] Indeed, both 'paternalism' and 'deference' could be endlessly
manipulated by all concerned, as (almost) all concerned knew well
enough. Daylight sycophants often became moonlight marauders, and
commonplace amiability of the 'God bless you, Sir' variety was no
guarantee that rents would be punctually paid.[4] But when Davitt
denounced the degrading charade of 'manly looking men, young and
old, doffing their hats and cringing in abject manner to any person
connected with an estate' he was certainly catching an authentic aspect
of rural relationships, an aspect typified by Archdeacon Goold, who,
though charging low rents, supporting tenant-right, and calling for
three cheers for the Catholic priests, went into fits of rage if heads
were not instantly bared as he and his passed by.[5] Yet there was more
to it than this, and well into the second half of the century bad landlords, not landlordism *per se*, constituted the main objects of attack.[6]

---

[1] *Daily Express*, 20 Jan. 1874; *Clare election petition*, H.C. 1852-3 (587), ix, 569;
Galway County election petition, H.C. 1872 (241-I), xlviii, 202; *Clare petition*, pp. 128,
179, 201, 205, 209, 232-3; *Tablet*, 21 Mar. 1857; J. H. Whyte, 'Landlord influence at
elections in Ireland, 1760-1885', p. 753. See also A. Montgomery to Earl Fitzwilliam, 12
July 1837, Wentworth Woodhouse Muniments G35; T. Bolton to Stanley, 24 June 1843,
Derby Papers 107/3; C. W. Cooper to Sir R. Gore Booth, 5 Aug. 1852, O'Hara Papers MS
20353; Lady Rossmore to Carlisle, 28 Mar. 1857, Carlisle Papers L.-B. 85; *Londonderry
Sentinel*, 17 Apr. 1857 and 20 May 1859.
[2] Folklore Commission MS 1194 (Co. Limerick); *Clare election petition*, H.C. 1852-3
(587), ix, 638; J.H. Whyte, 'Landlord influence at elections in Ireland, 1760-1885', pp. 744-7.
[3] T. Bolton to Stanley, 8 Nov. 1850, Derby Papers 107/3; 'One late an Agent', *Landlordism in Ireland*, p. 35; W. S. Trench to Lady Bath, 12 Feb. and 18 Dec. 1851, Bath
Papers Irish Box.
[4] D. Fitzpatrick, *Politics and Irish Life 1913-1921: Provincial experience of War and
Revolution* (Dublin, 1977), p. 50; F. Dun, *Landlords and Tenants in Ireland*, pp. 214-17.
See also the over-ripe scene in Chapter Ten of the popular anonymous novel of 1844 *Bob
Norberry; or, Sketches from the Note Book of an Irish Reporter*, where Lord Strangeway
listens to his tenants' petitions—both parties thinking they are 'doing' the other.
[5] M. Davitt, *The Fall of Feudalism in Ireland or the story of the Land League Revolution* (London, 1904), p. 165. On Goold, see *Londonderry Sentinel*, 22 Dec. 1868, and
Folklore Commission MS 1194.
[6] See Ballad on 'Battle of Ballycohey' (1868) in Bradshaw Collection C.U.L. Hib.1.867.1;
also J. Lee, 'The Ribbonmen' in *Secret Societies in Ireland*, ed. T. D. Williams (Dublin, 1973),
p. 33; M. [R.] Beames, *Peasants and Power*, pp. 129-34; *Banner of Ulster*, 17 Feb. 1857.

Popular memory could be tenaciously sentimental when harnessed to the remembrance of 'good' landlords driven by generous bankruptcy to an early grave. Tributes too could come from unlikely sources: Archbishop MacHale, local priests, even presidents of politicized Farmers' Clubs.[1]

The disillusionment which followed the eventual breaking of rosy-tinted spectacles was, therefore, often as profound as it was inevitable. 'Had you', one landlord was asked, 'any reason to suppose before this [attack] you were unpopular in your neighbourhood?—No, indeed I had not; I flattered myself it was the very reverse.'[2] Some placed the collapse of deference in the 1830s and 1840s; others, more realistically, in the late 1860s and the 1870s. By 1868 even so official an observer of events as Major-General McMurdo, commander of the First Infantry Brigade in Ireland, was moved to comment on the almost total collapse of 'old family attachments' apparent in the behaviour of the tenants he so frequently 'escorted' to the polls. 'When my father', recalled Martin Ross in an account of the Galway by-election of 1872, 'came home that afternoon, even the youngest child of the house could see how great had been the blow. It was not the political defeat, severe as that was, it was the personal wound, and it was incurable'.[3] Deference, perhaps, had rarely in Ireland been much more than hostility repressed or delayed. Yet contemporary perceptions often saw what was desired, saw surfaces rather than realities. And as surface phenomena of considerable importance, paternalism and deference helped for a time to shape both the conduct and the language of rural relationships.

Of course at the heart of the matter lay questions of power. The methods used by landlords to translate political opinions into electoral results and the behaviour of their instruments—agents, stewards, bailiffs, and the like—make this abundantly plain. Belonging to a notably beleaguered profession, the agent stood at the point of intersection between landlord and tenant, a location at once exposed and potentially dangerous. The disappearance after 1815 of middlemen,

---

[1] James Berry, *Tales from the West of Ireland*, ed. G. M. Horgan (Dublin, 1975), p. 150; *Galway Vindicator*, 24 July 1852; *Nation*, 24 July 1852; *C.C.* 15 Mar. 1880.

[2] *Minutes of the proceedings of the select committee on the Cork County election petition*, H.C. 1842 (271), vi, 142. For similar cases, see Carlingford Papers Diary of C. Fortescue I (25 Sept. 1854) and II (16 Sept. 1856); *Mayo County election petition*, H.C. 1857 (182 Sess. 2), vii, 10-11; Lord Shannon to Abercorn, 9 Mar. 1867, Abercorn Papers T2541/VR/145; *Galway County election petition*, H.C. 1872 (241-I), xlviii, 260, 347, 406-9; B. L. Fleming and H. A. Herbert to W. E. Forster, 27 Oct. and 6 Nov. 1880, Printed Cabinet Papers CAB37/3/68.

[3] *Report from the select committee on parliamentary and municipal elections*, H.C. 1868-9 (352), viii, 296; E. Œ. Somerville and Martin Ross, *Irish Memories* (London, 1917), p. 27 (also *Galway County election petition*, H.C. 1872 (241-I), xlviii, *passim*).

who, whatever their faults, had acted as social intermediaries, brought landlords and agents into a more direct and possibly corrosive confrontation with the farming community as a whole.[1] Irish agents came from a wide variety of backgrounds. Most were themselves either minor landlords or lawyers.[2] The former (often actually related to their employers) were supposedly skilled in the arts of country life, the latter in the arts of rent collection. Inevitably, however, men who themselves owned land were rarely willing to reside elsewhere save for very substantial returns. A few owned almost as much land as— occasionally even more than—their principals, but, having fallen on hard times, were trying to restore their finances.[3] Training was neither demanded nor available, though the new more expert men hankered after professional exclusivity and loudly but ineffectively stressed the importance of agricultural and commercial education.[4] The widespread practice of allowing agencies to descend within family dynasties lost on the swings of genetic incompetence what it gained on the roundabouts of acquired experience.[5] Given the bewildering variety of proprietors, it is not surprising that agents were often plucked almost casually from an erratically relevant range of social and occupational backgrounds. Some were themselves farmers, one was a former brewer, several—even after 5 Geo. IV, c. 91 had ostensibly forbidden the practice—were clergymen.[6] The mother of Sir John

[1] L. M. Cullen, *The emergence of modern Ireland 1600–1900*, pp. 22, 103–4; also D. Dickson, 'Middlemen' in *Penal Era and Golden Age: Essays in Irish History, 1690–1800*, ed. T. Bartlett and D. W. Hayton (Belfast, 1979), pp. 162–85.

[2] See, e.g., *Fictitious Votes, Ireland*, 2nd series, 3rd report, pp. 5–7; R. Cassidy to Lord Londonderry, 31 Mar. 1852, Londonderry Papers D/Lo/C166; 'One late an Agent', *Landlordism in Ireland*, pp. 27–33; Naas to Derby, 3 Apr. [1857], Derby Papers 155/1; Lord Portarlington to Naas, 11 Oct. [1866], Mayo Papers MS 11145; S. M. Hussey, *The Reminiscences of an Irish Land Agent*, ed. H. Gordon (London, 1904), *passim*. On the whole question, see J. S. Donnelly Jr., *The Land and the People of nineteenth-century Cork*, pp. 178–84.

[3] H. Anderson to J. A. Beck, 21 June 1852, Ironmongers' Company Irish Correspondence Received 1846–54; Chaloner Papers ZFM/318B; W. Smith (agent) to R. Brady, 28 Mar. and 1 Apr. 1857, 1 Feb. 1858, Close (Richardson of Drum) Papers D2002/C/48; *Londonderry Sentinel*, 11 May 1859.

[4] W. Blacker, *Prize Essay, addressed to the agricultural committee of the Royal Dublin Society, on the management of landed property in Ireland; the consolidation of small farms, employment of the poor, etc. etc., for which the gold medal was awarded* (Dublin, 1834), p. 2; 'One late an Agent', *Landlordism in Ireland*, pp. 27–33.

[5] *Devon Commission*, part ii, H.C. 1845 [616], xx, Witness 356 Q. 26. Wainwright Crowe, a substantial (3,126 acres at £2,022 PLV) Clare landlord (for a picture of his house, see M. Bence-Jones, *Burke's Guide to Country Houses Vol. I: Ireland*, p. 53), 'inherited' the Wyndham agency from his brother (G. Wyndham to Naas, 1 Apr. 1851, Mayo Papers MS 11017). On the Fishmongers' estate, Revd G. V. Sampson was succeeded by his son. The Drapers employed in turn a father, son, and grandson; the Grocers and the Ironmongers a father and son (O. Robinson, 'The economic significance of the London companies as landlords in Ireland', pp. v–vi). Lord Dillon employed a father and son (F. Dun, *Landlords and Tenants in Ireland*, p. 201), as did Sir John Benn-Walsh ('The Journals of Sir John Benn-Walsh', ed. J. S. Donnelly Jr., p. 102).

[6] A. W. Rutherford to Anglesey, 30 June 1852, Anglesey Papers D619/23/B/370; N.

Young's agent in 1856 'kept a shop and bakery and made a good deal of money'. Colonel Smith of Baltiboys employed a flour miller, R. J. M. St George of Headfort Castle a local shopkeeper who dealt in 'drapery, grocery, everything'. Others preferred bank managers or engineers. In 1851 the Royal College of Physicians of Ireland considered twenty-four applicants for the agency of its Waterford property, thirteen of them already agents, the others valuators, lawyers, medical practitioners, farmers, or 'agriculturalists'.[1] Three Irish agents (one admittedly a Guinness) managed, like the Duke of Sutherland's famous 'auditor', James Loch, to become Members of Parliament. At the other extreme were men like Arthur Baker, agent in 1841 for Mrs Digby's Carlow property and master of staccato prose: 'Sir, It is folly to be asking time, it is to be supposed O'Connell and his party will pay all for you . . . You voted against the exprest interest and desire of your landlady, such been the case you need not be writing to her or me.'[2]

As the century progressed more and more estate business was given to solicitors or to large offices in Dublin and Cork. Pluralist agents had always been common, but with the appearance of firms like Stewart and Kincaid in the 1820s and the spectacular post-Famine expansion of Hussey and Townsend (who by 1880 collected £250,000 annual rent from 88 estates) land management adopted an unprecedentedly commercial tone.[3] Yet, despite the complaints of a Kilkenny farmer in 1859 that 'lawyers and attorneys' were replacing country gentlemen, it does in general seem to have been the case that Irish agents were of higher social status than their counterparts in England.[4] The shift

Kelly to Rossmore, 30 Apr. 1833, Rossmore Papers T2929/7/49. Dean Stannus, Lord Hertford's agent for over half a century until about 1870, was the most famous clerical agent, others being Revd Somers Payne in Cork (J. S. Donnelly Jr., *The Land and the People of nineteenth-century Cork*, p. 18), Palmerston's Revd Chambers (*Letters of the Third Viscount Palmerston*, ed. K. Bourne, p. 104), and the Fishmongers' Revd G. V. Sampson (O. Robinson, 'The economic significance of the London companies as landlords in Ireland', pp. v–vi).

[1] Sir J. Young to Lord Headfort, 11 June 1856, Young Letter-Book; A. M. Tod, 'The Smiths of Baltiboys', p. 160; *Galway County election petition*, H.C. 1872 (241-I), xlviii, 948–51; *Minutes of evidence taken before Her Majesty's Commissioners on Agriculture*, H.C. 1881 [C 2778-I], xv, 515, 825–52; MS Committee Journal Book IX, pp. 118–19 (Archives of the Royal College of Physicians, Dublin).

[2] Cited in — to T. M. Ray, 11 Sept. 1841, O'Connell Papers N.L.I. MS 13622. The three MPs were R. S. Guinness (Kinsale 1847–8 and Barnstaple 1854–7), Peter Quin (Newry 1859–65), and Tristram Kennedy (Louth 1865–8). The first two were Tories.

[3] Hart Papers D3077/G/15/30; Incorporated Society Papers MS 5290; Drapers' Company L.-B. Irish 1848–57; G. Blackburne to Naas, 5 Oct. 1866, Mayo Papers MS 11143; *Letters of the Third Viscount Palmerston*, ed. K. Bourne, pp. 104–5; *Devon Index*, pp. 1–6; *Minutes of evidence taken before Her Majesty's Commissioners on Agriculture*, H.C. 1881 [C 2778-I], xv, 515, 626–42; F. Dun, *Landlords and Tenants in Ireland*, p. 249; W. A. Maguire, *The Downshire estates in Ireland 1801–1845*, p. 252; J. S. Donnelly Jr., *The Land and the People of nineteenth-century Cork*, pp. 182–5.

[4] *Kilkenny Journal*, 29 June 1859; 'One late an Agent', *Landlordism in Ireland*, p. 27;

away from payment by results (that is, rent collected) towards fixed salaries was evidence of growing professionalism, though the large conglomerate firms continued to work on percentage terms. Spectacular dishonesty and corruption—such as the extraction of bribes from tenants in return for favours—were gradually eliminated, together with much of the casual generosity of earlier times.[1] Successful agents of large properties were well paid. A normal rate was 5 per cent of rent collected, while fixed salaries of £800 or even £1,000 from *single* estates were not unknown. Extensive fringe benefits in the shape of free houses, servants, horses, produce, and so on made the incomes of many resident agents go further still.[2] 'The Dysart agency', noted Somerville and Ross in *The Real Charlotte* (1894), 'had always been considered to confer brevet rank as a country gentleman upon its owner, apart from the intimacy with the Dysarts which it implied . . . Mr Lambert possessed . . . a new house at least a mile from the town, built under his directions and at his employer's expense, Lismoyle placed him unhesitatingly at the head of its visiting list.'

Such rewards reflected the belief that resident agents should be able to 'maintain the position of a gentleman'.[3] And despite much criticism, the actual functions of most agents, while hardly burdensome, were more complex than critics liked to admit. More than a hundred witnesses before the Devon Commission in 1844 answered questions as to what agents actually did; together they provided 232 specific references to the six main tasks, among which rent collection was only one.[4]

J. S. Donnelly Jr., *The Land and the People of nineteenth-century Cork*, p. 178; E. Richards, 'The Land Agent' in *The Victorian Countryside*, ed. G. E. Mingay, 2 vols. (London, 1981), ii, 439–56.

[1] See Lord Stuart de Decies to Clarendon, 25 Jan. and 20 July 1850, Clarendon Papers Box 10; J. S. Donnelly Jr., *The Land and the People of nineteenth-century Cork*, pp. 173–5; E. Wakefield, *An Account of Ireland, Statistical and Political*, i, 297–8; J. E. Bicheno's 'Remarks' in *Poor Inquiry (Ireland). Appendix (H)—Part II*, H.C. 1836 [42], xxxiv, 687–8; W. A. Maguire, *The Downshire estates in Ireland 1801–1845*, pp. 194–6.

[2] Some examples: William Blacker more than £1,000 from various agencies in 1830s (R. S. Gourlay, 'The social and economic history of the Gosford estates', p. 138); £677 for a *half*-year in 1843–4 as 5 per cent on Shirley estate (Shirley of Ettington Papers CR229/16/2A); £800 salary on Curraghmore estate of Lord Waterford in 1856 (Dunraven Papers D3196/F/17/22); London company agents (some of whom were pluralists) moved generally to a fixed salary after mid-century and by c.1860 were receiving between £424 and £800 from the companies alone (O. Robinson, 'The economic significance of the London companies as landlords in Ireland', p. 209). For incomes in various other fields, see Chapter III, section IV below.

[3] 'One late an Agent', *Landlordism in Ireland*, pp. 27–33.

[4] Based on an analysis of 129 witnesses and 232 references in *Devon Index*, pp. 1–6. Provincial percentages show most emphasis on rent collection in Leinster and Connacht, least in Ulster; most on settling disputes in Ulster, least in Connacht. The other figures differ less markedly.

	per cent
Rent collection	50.4
Improving agriculture	12.5
Settling tenant disputes	12.1
Setting land etc.	11.2
'Management of estate'	7.3
Looking after tenants	6.5

It was also repeatedly claimed that things were better done on large than on small properties, though where the border between the two lay was seldom revealed. 'The appointment', Lord Anglesey's new agent was told in 1841, 'includes not only the duties of the receipt of rents . . . but a close investigation into and a general superintendance of the agricultural concerns of the tenantry.'[1] Tristram Kennedy, whose political radicalism (he sat at Westminster 1865-8) makes him a valuable witness, was kept fully stretched while acting for Lord Bath in 1849. In addition to routine duties he busied himself with

The infant state of our poor laws, the total want of harmony and unanimity amongst the gentry, the difficult crisis through which we have I trust passed, the recourse necessary to government aid through the Board of Works, Drainage Commissioners, and other public measures for relief, the establishment of schools in connexion with the Education Board for industrial purposes and general education, the introduction of improved husbandry, the adjustment of the railroad question on behalf of both proprietor and tenant, the facilitating emigration, and the endeavour to establish manufacture.[2]

However, just as the landlords themselves, so did many agents develop a highly patronizing tone, talking of tenant voters as if they were cattle and openly referring to 'the gaping multitude', 'the ignorant and excited peasantry', and the 'characteristic ingenuity of the Irish peasant to evade the truth'.[3] A well-developed sense of *amour propre* could lead to ludicrous confrontations, as when Lord Hertford's agent, Dean Stannus, became embroiled in a heroic Clochmerle-type dispute over the location of a urinal on estate property. The fact that most agents were Episcopalians created further barriers (not only in the south), although the growing minority of Catholic agents was not popularly regarded with any greater enthusiasm than were Catholic landlords, and Gladstone, for example, had no more bitter enemy—a

[1] T. Beer to A. W. Rutherford, [Feb. 1841], Anglesey Papers D619/23/B/1.
[2] T. Kennedy to Lady Bath, 2 Feb. 1849, Bath Papers Irish Box.
[3] T. Murray to Downshire, 19 Feb. 1841, Downshire Papers D671/C/9/681; Naas to J. Inglis, 20 Dec. 1852, Eglinton Papers MS 5341; H. Anderson to J. A. Beck, 9 July 1852, Ironmongers' Company Irish Correspondence Received 1846-54; T. Kennedy to Lady Bath, 2 Feb. 1849, Bath Papers Irish Box.

pretty extreme claim—than J. H. Blake, Lord Clanricarde's Catholic agent in 1872.[1]

Coming from the backgrounds they did, many agents treated employers with a certain chummy equality. 'I always like to say what I think', remarked one in 1875 after delivering himself of a savage critique of his master's attitudes. 'It is a fearful thing', quipped another, 'that the country is at the mercy of that jaunty joker Lord Palmerston.' John Andrews swapped local political abuse with Lord Londonderry. Sir John Young treated his Cavan agent to maudlin reminiscences of his 'dear gentle mother . . . never was there a truer homester or more trusted friend'.[2] So generally uncringing a tone suited the agent's important functions within local politics, society, and administration. Resident agents—persons the 'gentry of the county would look upon with respect and esteem'—served as magistrates, poor-law guardians, town commissioners, and grand jurymen;[3] so much so that in 1838 and again in 1852 Dublin Castle vainly issued circulars to prevent the active magistracy being thus quite overrun.[4] Agents for great and often absentee proprietors like the London companies, the Shirleys, Earl Fitzwilliam, Lord Londonderry, the Duke of Devonshire, and Lord Downshire played a leading part in the politics of their areas and often enjoyed powers of a more than viceregal kind. They attended, even chaired, party meetings and exercised proconsular functions at those informal gatherings from which 'acceptable' election candidates emerged.[5] In counties such as Monaghan and Londonderry, where almost all the large landlords were absentees, agents exercised virtually full proprietorial rights over the land and its

---

[1] S. Adams, 'Relations between landlord, agent, and tenant on the Hertford estate in the nineteenth century', *Journal of the Lisburn Historical Society*, ii (1979), 5; *Galway County election petition*, H.C. 1872 (241-I), xlviii, 348-59; Rossmore to Lord Ashburton, 2 May 1846, Bath Papers Irish Box; Lord Shannon to Derby, 4 Apr. 1852, Derby Papers 150/11; [A Mayo Conservative] to Naas, 27 July 1852, Mayo Papers MS 11018; Archbishop Cullen to K. Digby, 19 Apr. 1864, Cullen Papers L.-B. 4.

[2] J. G. M. Harvey to G. V. Hart, 30 Mar. 1875, Hart Papers D3007/G/15/22; G. Morant to E. P. Shirley, 13 June 1859, Shirley of Ettington Papers CR229/115/1; J. Andrews to Londonderry, 9 Feb. 1851, Londonderry Papers D/Lo/C158; Sir J. Young to T. Chambers, 31 Oct. 1856, Young Letter-Book.

[3] R. Miller to W. H. Sawyer, [Oct. 1863], Drapers' Company L.-B. Irish 1857-67. For such public duties, see N Kelly to Rossmore, 30 Apr. 1833, Rossmore Papers T2929/7/49; E. Littleton to R. Westenra, 17 Oct. 1834, Hatherton Papers D260/M/01/14; W. L. Feingold, 'The Irish boards of poor law guardians 1872-86', pp. 49-52; O. Robinson, 'The economic significance of the London companies as landlords in Ireland', p. 128; 'One late an Agent', *Landlordism in Ireland*, pp. 27-33; *Thom 1844* etc., *passim*.

[4] Thomas Drummond's circular of 4 May 1838 was reissued by Naas on 28 Oct. 1852 (*Galway Vindicator*, 6 Nov. 1852).

[5] *D.E.P.* 3 Jan, 1835, 6, 25 July 1837; C. Knox to R. B. Towse, 21 July 1852, Clothworkers' Company Copy L.-B. 1840-73; *Londonderry Sentinel*, 27 Mar. 1857; Lismore Papers MSS 7182-91; Fitzwilliam Papers N.L.I. MSS 3987 and 8816-17; Shirley of Ettington Papers CR229/115/1-28; W. A. Maguire, *The Downshire estates in Ireland 1801-1845*, pp. 205-7.

people.[1] Within county society they formed a subgroup of their own, dining together, exchanging news of their employers, and pumping up their spirits with mutual backslapping about their own 'firmness, gentleness, and scrutinizing eye'.[2] Some agents were even permitted to pursue idiosyncrasies of a peculiarly compelling kind, so that those exhibited by Lord Lansdowne's Townsend Trench—sketcher of landscapes, Plymouth Brother, ardent bicyclist, inventor of the TTT (Trench's Tubeless Tyre), expert sculler, amateur anatomist and skeleton owner, and exponent of the art of shooting china plates with a revolver while peddling at speed down desmesne avenues—must be regarded as distinguished by their number rather than their oddity.[3]

In politics too agents could prove surprisingly independent. Many of course maintained a decorous probity and constantly referred to headquarters. William Wann in 1852 dutifully supported the Liberal candidate for Armagh on Lord Gosford's estate and the Tory for Tyrone on that of the Dungannon School property. Agents like Robert Chaloner (Fitzwilliam) and F. E. Currey (Devonshire), though too responsible to indulge individual crotchets, were quite prepared to interpret instructions in ways congenial to themselves.[4] The Millers *père et fils* worked with chameleon cunning, telling their main employer, the high-minded Drapers' Company, to allow tenants electoral independence, while frenziedly urging lesser principals to sweep recalcitrants off the face of their estates.[5] Many, particularly Tory agents working for Liberal employers, simply defied orders. Agents for properties in chancery ran their affairs virtually unsupervised, while in some cases the 'politics' of estates changed, not with the succession of a new owner, but with the appointment of a new

---

[1] T. Macknight, *Ulster as it is*, i, 259; A. D. T. Fay, 'The Parishes of Magherafelt and Ballyscullion 1825-1850', pp. 14-16; H. R. Westenra to Rossmore, 7 Jan. 1835, Rossmore Papers T2929/8/14; Major Brownrigg to T. Redington, 1 Feb. 1852, Royal Archives RA D21/61a: 'There are very few landed proprietors [in Monaghan]—it is in truth nothing more or less than a county of agents.'

[2] R. and J. R. Miller to E. Lawford, 7, 18 Feb. 1852, Drapers' Company L.-B. Irish 1848-57; H. Anderson to J. A. Beck, 21 June 1852, Ironmongers' Company Irish Correspondence Received 1846-54. The motto agents liked to accord themselves was of course *Sauviter in modo, fortiter in re* ('One late an Agent', *Landlordism in Ireland*, p. 27).

[3] Marquess of Lansdowne, *Glanerought and the Petty-Fitzmaurices* (London, 1937), pp. 136-41.

[4] W. Wann to T. Grant, 10 July 1852, to J. Pirie, 21 July 1852, to Sir W. Verner, 17 Mar. 1857, Gosford Papers D1606/5A/1, 5/3, 5A/2; R. Chaloner to A. H. Gun Cunningham, 17 Dec. 1846, Fitzwilliam Papers N.L.I. MS 3987 (and Wentworth Woodhouse Muniments and Chaloner Papers—*passim*); F. E. Currey to J. C. Browne, 1 Apr. 1852, Lismore Papers MS 7184, and to W. Currey, 1 June 1865, ibid. MS 7192 (and Lismore and Devonshire Papers—*passim*).

[5] R. and J. R. Miller to various correspondents, Feb.-Aug. 1852, Drapers' Company L.-B. Irish 1850-60. This actually seems to have been the Millers' private letter-book which somehow found its way into the company's archives.

agent.[1] Many of the routine duties were of course done by bailiffs, stewards, agriculturalists, and the like: often farmers themselves, these constituted a curiously spatchcocked breed, sometimes adopting the persona of deputy warder in a penal establishment, sometimes that of trusted prisoner. They often did the really dirty political work: driving farmers to the poll, or threatening, warning, and punishing face-to-face. Like many of the agents, they too were unreliable instruments of their superiors' political beliefs, and their socially exposed position led, when necessary, to a circumspection which would have impressed the Vicar of Bray. Thus a Longford steward, who, in 1869 privately urged the tenants of his Liberal landlord to vote Nationalist, publicly adorned his own kitchen mantle with a photographic triptych made up of his own employer, a prominent Irish Tory politician, and the bearded Fenian Jeremiah O'Donovan Rossa.[2]

In the end, both agents and landlords—sometimes together, sometimes apart—were deeply engaged in the business of 'influence'. An amorphous term at the time, 'influence' could range from 'legitimate' to 'undue' or even 'illegal'. In the case of Ireland the most active ingredient, notwithstanding paternalism and the like, was always power. Power of one kind or another informed, even if it did not always control, the nature of political language and action. The most significant stage for its exercise was the election platform; the handing down of election 'orders' its most significant linguistic manifestation. Of course there were landlords who from principle or expediency did not 'interfere' at all. But even many of these could not resist delivering lectures on the wonders of 'our constitution' and fairness all round.[3] In any case, the men of principle were also the men most anxious to deluge tenants with didactic advice which made up in long-winded propriety what it lacked in harsh imposition.[4] Tenants much preferred

[1] Lord Mulgrave to Melbourne, 31 July [1837], Melbourne Papers 100/41; Memo by Downshire, c.July 1841, Downshire Papers D671/C/12/777; Lord Shannon to Derby, 4 Apr. 1852, Derby Papers 150/1·1; [A Mayo Conservative] to Naas, 27 July 1852, Mayo Papers MS 11018; *Banner of Ulster*, 17 Feb. and 25 Apr. 1857; Naas to Derby, 3 Apr. [1857], Derby Papers 155/1; *Londonderry Sentinel*, 22 Apr. 1859; *Kilkenny Journal*, 25 May and 15 June 1859; *Irish People*, 3 June 1865. See also *Nation*, 1 May 1852, and *D.E.P.* 3 Mar. 1838 (Chancery estates); Sir J. Young to Lord Monck, 16 Mar. 1857, Young L.-B. (Headfort estate changing politics with new agent).

[2] Draft letter of W. S. Crawford (c.1855), Crawford Papers D856/D/124; *Galway County election petition*, H.C. 1872 (241-I), xlviii, 141-2; *Devon Index*, pp. 29-31; 'One late an Agent', *Landlordism in Ireland*, pp. 34-7; *Copy of the shorthand writer's notes of the judgement delivered by Mr Justice Fitzgerald, and of the minutes of evidence taken at the trial of the Longford election petition*, H.C. 1870 (178), lvi, 353.

[3] See, e.g., R. Brady to W. Smith, 31 Mar. 1857, Close (Richardson of Drum) Papers D2002/C/48; Report of Sub-Inspector Croker, 23 Dec. 1832, O.P. 1832/2243, Box 2192 (also *Kilkenny Journal*, 14 Dec. 1832).

[4] See, e.g., *D.E.P.* 5 Aug. 1837 (Bishop Sandes); *Galway Vindicator*, 14 Apr. 1852

the genuine apathetics (mostly members of the *après moi le déluge* school or sporting fanatics with, like the third Marquess of Waterford, time only for 'mastiffs, bull-dogs . . . fights and yachts') or the few patricians so rarefied that, like the third Duke of Leinster, they disdained the mundáne electoral world even when close relatives were running for Parliament.[1] But the characteristic pose was one of engagement rather than non-interference. When the landlords standing around the Tory candidate for Clare in 1852 were asked to 'let their tenants vote as they wished' all but three blankly refused. Of the fifty-three Galway proprietors circularized by Lord Dunkellin at the 1865 election only three declined to put pressure on their tenants. Even the London companies, which generally eschewed open involvement, became electorally active in the 1850s when they believed tenant-right candidates were beginning to threaten their own legal and economic rights.[2]

Tones of voice and unconscious behaviour reveal much about proprietorial sentiments. 'He is a kind man to his tenants', remarked a Catholic bishop in 1872 of a Galway landlord, but 'fearfully despotic. His letters . . . addressed to his tenants were the most menacing I ever heard . . . It seems to be the settled impression of the landlords, that if they told their tenants to vote for Mazzini or Garibaldi, they should in gratitude do so.' Landlords were 'shocked' by the suggestion that they might be prevented from doing what they liked with 'their own'. A Mayo magistrate referred casually in 1857 to voters and 'their masters'. In Longford an agent briskly told tenants that 'of course, of course' they must do as they were told.[3] Colonel Bruen was genuinely amazed when criticized in 1835 for evicting Carlow farmers with large arrears on electoral rather than economic grounds. Lord Powerscourt admitted quite openly that all landlords used what he called 'force' at Wicklow elections.[4] After a show of independence at the Carlow

(Lord Dufferin); *Freeman's Journal*, 6, 26 July 1852 (G. O. Wilson and Lord Massereene); Printed Address of 1857 in Marlay Papers My 4076 (C. B. Marlay); *Northern Whig*, 7 Sept. 1868 (Earl Russell); *Sixty years' experience as an Irish landlord: Memoirs of John Hamilton D.L. of St. Ernan's Donegal*, ed. H. C. White (London, [1894]), pp. 269-70.

[1] E. B. Purefoy to R. J. Otway, 25 Feb. 1865, Otway Papers MS 13008; *D.E.P.* 13 July 1837; Speech on Kildare hustings 1847, Leinster Papers D3078/3/38.
[2] *Clare election petition*, H.C. 1852-3 (587), ix, 699-700; letters in Clanricarde Papers 49; Clothworkers' resolution of 30 June 1852, MS Irish Estate Committee Proceedings; Ironmongers' resolution of 26 June 1852, MS Minute Book of Irish Committee. The Fishmongers continued to hold aloof (resolution of 8 July 1852, Court of Assistants Ledger MS 5571).
[3] Bishop MacEvilly to Archbishop Cullen, 11 May 1872 (Cullen Papers) about G. L. Lynch-Staunton of Clydagh with 2,129 acres at £1,028 PLV in Galway and Mayo; W. Pidgeon to P. Keefe, 20 July 1852, Incorporated Society Papers MS 5290; *Mayo County election petition*, H.C. 1857 (182 Sess. 2), vii, 11; *Fictitious Votes, Ireland*, 2nd series, 3rd report, p. 8.
[4] *Committee on Bribery at Elections*, H.C. 1835 (547), viii, 562-602, 618-34; *Hansard*, liv, 352 (18 May 1840).

polls of 1840, Lord Courtown assembled his tenants, addressed them on their 'duties', extracted a humiliating act of contrition avowing 'sincere sorrow for the opposition which most of us have . . . given to your lordship's political principles', and saw to it that at the next election they did exactly as they were ordered.[1] Sir Roger Palmer was blunter still in hoping after the Mayo election of 1852 that 'upon future occasions my tenants will consider that *those* who refuse to comply with my reasonable requests and . . . directions . . . and who act in direct opposition to my wishes, can expect neither favours nor indulgences'. In 1872 the Whig Sir Thomas Burke's printed 'manifesto' was handed out by bailiffs in Galway: it asked voters 'to recollect, when the election is over, you have no one to expect any favours from but your landlord or his agent'.[2]

So widespread was the use—by landlords less brutally frank—of codes and hints that voters and dependants needed always to construe words carefully to ensure that no hidden meanings had been overlooked. Phrases combining respect for constitutional proprieties with clear electoral instructions were selected from extensive and well-worn linguistic stocks. Lord Listowel was 'most anxious' for the Whig cause in 1837. In 1852 the Clothworkers' agent hoped tenants would give the company's opinions 'such weight as they thought right', while Lord Anglesey felt bound to 'let them know what candidates I would recommend for their choice'.[3] Nudges and winks were endlessly transmitted in 'requests', 'wishes', 'hopes', 'anxious desires', in 'asking' rather than 'pressing'.[4] Vincent Scully of Tipperary was 'always ready to give advice'. A Catholic landlord in Galway would 'be very much obliged'. In Mayo James Hope-Scott 'let' tenants 'know' his 'general feelings'. A large Antrim proprietor distributed printed circulars which read 'Dear Sir, Enclosed is a note from Captain Seymour, the Conservative candidate. I hope you will not find it inconsistent with your duty to give him your vote.'[5] In W. S. Crawford's jaundiced

[1] Printed sheet dated 25 Nov. 1840, Courtown Papers; *The Reign of Terror in Carlow, comprising an authentic detail of the Proceedings of Mr O'Connell and his followers* (London, 1841), p. 11—copy in R. I. A. Halliday Pamphlets 1817; Downshire's Memo, c.July 1841, Downshire Papers D671/C/12/777.

[2] Palmer to P. Gallagher, 14 Jan. 1853, Moore Papers MS 842; *Galway County election petition*, H.C. 1872 (241-I), xlviii, 135.

[3] *D.E.P.* 8 Aug 1837; C. Knox to R. B. Towse, 10 July 1852, Clothworkers' Company Copy L.-B. 1840–73; Anglesey to A. W. Rutherford, 22 Apr. 1852, Anglesey Papers D619/23/B/364.

[4] Bishop Kilduff to Archbishop Cullen, 28 Feb. 1862, Cullen Papers; Palmerston to F. Macdonagh, 26 June 1865, Palmerston L.-B. Add. MS 48583; W. Wann to T. Grant, 10 July 1852, Gosford Papers D1606/5A/1; Ker's printed circular, L'Estrange & Brett Papers D1905/2/3; E. Curling (agent) to Devon tenants, 17 Jan. 1871, Dunraven Papers D3196; Carlingford Papers Diary of C. Fortescue II (8 Apr. 1857).

[5] *Tipperary Advocate*, 13 Oct. 1866; R. Power to Revd J. Kemmy, 22 Jan. 1872, in *Galway*

view, when agents or bailiffs gave 'an intelligent hint of the consequence of disobedience', few tenants would transgress, 'in fact, no threat is required'.[1]

Yet frequently things were driven further. The necessity of moving beyond hints and even threats into actual punishment was a sign of weakness, as was the common 'concession' of asking in two-member constituencies for 'only one' of the tenants' votes.[2] The road to naked coercion traversed along its route a large grey area where nods could be seen developing into St Vitus's Dance and winks into tics douloureux. The flavour of this twilight world (where, for example, one agent was told to show sympathetic candidates round the estate 'but never to open his lips') is accurately caught in the examination in 1838 by the Fictitious Votes Committee of the Longford agent, Thomas Courtenay, who began by admitting that rent arrears were more generously tolerated in those who otherwise did what they were told.[3]

Do you call that persecution?—I do not.
Has there ever been any persecution of tenants for voting against the inclination of their landlords?—I do not know what is meant by persecution . . . .
Did you ever know a tenant menaced or threatened, if he did not vote as the landlord chose?—I have said to them myself, that if they did not vote as the landlord chose, perhaps they would be sorry . . . .
That you would make them sorry?—That is right.

Coercion proper consisted of unambiguous threats and their execution. The effectiveness of such threats depended upon the general circumstances of the time, the tenants' ability and motivation to organize resistance, changing perceptions of landlord–tenant relations, and the economic and social coherence of landlords as a class. Although it is impossible to give more than a few examples, there can be no doubt that electoral intimidation was much more widespread than J. H. Whyte, the leading authority on the subject, has allowed.[4] Threats of the most unvarnished kind—that rents would be raised, arrears briskly collected, favours withdrawn, even evictions

---

County election petition, H.C. 1872 (241-I), xlviii, 118; J. Hope-Scott to J. J. Blake (agent), R. Ornsby, *Memoirs of James Robert Hope-Scott*, 2nd edn., 2 vols. (London, 1884), ii, 190; T. Macknight, *Ulster as it is*, i, 208.

[1] Draft letter of W. S. Crawford (*c.* 1855), Crawford Papers D856/D/124.
[2] Lord Kenmare to C. Gallwey, 3 Jan. 1835, FitzGerald Papers; *Galway Vindicator*, 1 Sept. 1852; Lord Leconfield to W. Crowe, 1 June 1859, Petworth House Archives PHA 748/4; *Dundalk Democrat*, 28 May 1859; Lord Clonbrock to Naas, 22 Apr. 1859, Mayo Papers MS 11036; Lord Massereene to C. Fortescue, [22 Aug. 1865], Carlingford Papers CP3/73.
[3] G. Knox to R. B. Towse, 21 July 1852, Clothworkers' Company Copy L.-B. 1840-73; *Fictitious Votes, Ireland*, 2nd series, 3rd report, p. 39.
[4] J. H. Whyte, 'Landlord influence at elections in Ireland, 1760-1885', pp. 748-50.

implemented—were issued at county elections throughout Ireland
between 1832 and 1885. The style alone varied. Few gentlemen were
quite so personally prepared to buckle to the task as the landlord's son,
who, in 1837, travelled from house to house and 'cursed and swore in
the most vehement manner and said that "He would be revenged of
them, that he would cant the blankets off their heads; that as soon as
the time of their leases would be expired they would be turned out . . .
that his and his father's displeasure would be visited on them to the
fourth generation" '.[1] More usually, messages were handed down to
the effect that something extremely nasty would happen if votes were
not given as demanded.[2] At the Co. Cork election of 1852 farmers
were told at the poll to 'remember the 25th of March' (rent day); others
were 'advised' to 'mind what you are about'; some got a letter asking
them to meet their landlord 'at nine o'clock in the morning at the hotel
in Kanturk. Wait there for him, if you do not meet him . . . he will be
very angry with you.' The nuts and bolts stand out unusually clearly
in a letter to the bailiff on a Wexford estate in 1859.

I enclose you some notices for the Ferns tenants, asking them to give me one
vote for my friend Mr George; deliver them as soon as you can and tell each man
that if he won't give Mr George one vote, at least, he must stay at home, and
not vote at all for any man. Who comes in and votes entirely against my friend Mr
George, he may expect no favour from me . . . If I have time I will go to each man
myself before the election—do this well for me and I will send you 10s.[3]

'I shall', a Sligo landlord bluntly told his tenants in 1868, 'watch carefully how every man votes; it will greatly influence me in all future
transactions with you.' 'On the principle of self-preservation', announced the Tory *Carlow Sentinel* in 1835, 'the landlords MUST AND
WILL encourage those only whose fidelity and character they can place
reliance on when the hour of contest arrives.' Lord Londonderry
sent bailiffs to take the names of all tenants attending tenant-right
meetings on the grounds that 'I certainly would not allow those who
were present and are in arrears to escape with impunity'. At election
meetings in Clare 'landlord emissaries might be seen hovering around
the outskirts . . . in order to transmit an account of the proceedings

---

[1] T. O'Mara to W. S. O'Brien, 13 Feb. 1838, Smith O'Brien Papers MS 429.

[2] For a small garland of cases, see *Committee on Bribery at Elections*, H.C. 1835
(547), viii, 292 (Queen's Co.); *Fictitious Votes, Ireland*, 2nd series, 3rd report, pp. 39–41
(Longford); *Athlone Conservative Advocate*, 1 June 1837 (Galway); *Freeman's Journal*, 22
May 1852 (Antrim); Londonderry to Downshire, 6 June 1852, Downshire Papers D671/C/
377/62 (Down); Lord Granard to Lord Carlisle, 18 Apr. 1857, Carlisle Papers L.-B. 85 (Long-
ford); Revd J. Redmond to Archbishop Cullen, 11 Nov. 1868, Cullen Papers (Wicklow); Bishop
MacEvilly to Cullen, 11 May 1872, ibid. (Galway);—to C. Brett, 5 Feb. 1874, L'Estrange &
Brett Papers D1905/2/3 (Down).

[3] *Nation*, 27 Mar. 1852; *Weekly Register*, 26 Apr. 1859; *Freeman's Journal*, 13 May
1859.

to their employers'.[1] Polling booths were usually as full of agents and bailiffs as of priests. At the Kerry election of 1835 one agent's 'There, slap an ejectment on him' greeted departing tenant voters, while at Carlow another could be heard shouting 'So help me God, I will extirpate themselves and their families; if it were in twenty years to come, I will have revenge of them.'[2]

The implementation of such threats functioned as smoothly as it did because of the wide variety of non-contractual concessions which tenants received from all but the steeliest proprietors: rent abatements, turbary rights, extended arrears, occasional employment, and so on. A few landlords even planned such concessions with this end in view, like those in Kildare and Carlow, who, in the 1830s, entered abatements as 'arrears' in their books so as to keep tenants permanently open to legal proceedings. Lord Erne used them to apportion rewards and punishments on his Donegal estate in 1852: 15 per cent abatements to tenants who had voted for both Tory candidates, 7½ per cent for those who had voted for only one, nothing at all for the rest.[3] Electoral evictions were, therefore, rare (*all* evictions were rare between 1854 and 1880) because so many other forms of punishment were available and because landlords of all kinds—Catholic Liberals, Protestant Whigs, Protestant Tories—could retain informal control by regularly requiring agents to submit details of how tenants had actually voted on the day. In 1852 Lord Londonderry's sophisticated estate bureaucracy produced a list with the names of 229 disobedient tenants and notes on the amount of rent oustanding in each case. That even in prosperous Down almost half were in arrears is a measure of the latent power at the disposal, not only of Lord Londonderry, but of the generality of landlords throughout Ireland.[4]

Withdrawal of the hanging gale was one of the commonest retributive acts. Rents too were raised. 'There is', remarked Lord Clanricarde in 1852, 'a theory abroad that the tenants have nothing to do but pay

---

[1] *Committee on parliamentary and municipal elections*, H.C. 1868-9 (352), viii, 330; *Carlow Sentinel*, 10, 13 Jan. 1835; R. Kelly to Londonderry, 21 Oct. 1851, Londonderry Papers D/Lo/C164; *Nation*, 10 Jan. 1852.

[2] *Committee on Bribery at Elections*, H.C. 1835 (547), viii, 459-60, 563. See also ibid. 473 (Meath); *Nation*, 27 Mar. 1852 (Cork); J. Greer to Belmore, 31 Mar. 1873, Belmore Papers D3007/P/93 (Tyrone); E. Gardener to W. Montgomery, 4 Feb. 1874, L'Estrange & Brett Papers D1905/2/3 (Down); *Down County election petition*, H.C. 1880 (260-II), lvii, 577-8.

[3] *Hansard*, xxxiii, 1027 (17 May 1836); *Freeman's Journal*, 6 Nov. 1852. In 1841 some Carlow landlords fixed enormous rents and granted large informal abatements, thus keeping tenants in constant arrears (K. J. Buggy to T. M. Ray, 15 Oct. 1841, O'Connell Papers N.L.I. MS 13623).

[4] Lord Kenmare to C. Gallwey, 3 Jan. 1835, FitzGerald Papers; *Committee on Bribery at Elections*, H.C. 1835 (547), viii, 471; R. Chaloner to A. Symes, 6 May 1848, Fitzwilliam Papers MS 3987; P. Byrne to W. Reeves, 29 Mar. 1854, Smith Barry Papers MS 8819; Londonderry list in Londonderry Papers D/Lo/C164 No. 165.

their rents ... that is not the feeling upon which I have gone for the last 45 years; but, however, if that is the principle to be adopted for the future, I think that I ought to get a fair and equitable rent for my land.'[1] Anything from eviction itself to a refusal to allow the local race committee to use estate land was grist to the proprietorial punishment machine.[2] E. P. Shirley's hawkish agent, George Morant, put the matter plainly in 1865.

The iron hand without the velvet glove is the thing just now ... The tenants are I believe in considerable alarm as to our future conduct to them—it is well to let the evil conscience press them heavily ... I am making out a list of those whom it will be best to single out as ringleaders and raise their rent.[3]

'Very considerable terror', reported Lord Londonderry's solicitor with satisfaction in 1852, had been caused by his serving a 'large number' of ejectments and processes among those who had disobeyed orders.[4] At no time, it should be said, do landlords seem to have been especially sensitive to publicity. Those prepared to evict were prepared to stand by their actions. And just as a Monaghan landlord happily sent to the press for publication a series of savage letters to electorally disobedient tenants, so Sir Roger Palmer retorted 'Publish and be damned' to threats to reveal details of his fifteen evictions after the Mayo election of 1852.[5]

---

[1] *Galway County election petition*, H.C. 1872 (241-I), xlviii, 348-55; also ibid. 936, and Lord Hertford to Dean Stannus, 27 Dec. 1852, in B. Falk, *'Old Q's' Daughter* (London, 1951), p. 206.

[2] In addition to cases cited elsewhere, a further sample must epitomize the whole (general = general withdrawal of concessions): G. Morant to E. P. Shirley, 10 Oct. 1865, Shirley of Ettington Papers CR229/115/7 (race-course refusal—Monaghan); *Committee on Bribery at Elections*, H.C. 1835 (547), viii, 322, 341 (general, arrears—Cashel, Clare); ibid. 472-3 (gale, covenants—Meath); ibid. 525-41 (general, ejectments—Queen's Co.); *D.E.P.* 5 Aug. 1837 (ejectments—Newry); E. M. Kelly to Downshire, 14 Aug. 1837, Downshire Papers D671/C/12/690 (leases—King's Co.); H. D. Inglis, *A Journey throughout Ireland*, p. 90 (arrears—Cork); C. Conyngham to O'Connell, 13 May 1843, O'Connell Papers N.L.I. MS 13625 (general—Dublin); R. O'Gorman to W. S. O'Brien, 18 Feb. 1847, Smith O'Brien Papers MS 438 (house demolished—Galway); F. R. Bertolacci to Sir C. Trevelyan, 21 Nov. 1848, Broadlands Archive 27M60, Box cxix (leases—Roscommon); *Galway Vindicator*, 24 Apr. 1852 (rent—Cork); *Nation*, 1 May 1852 (abatement—Wexford); *D.E.P.* 11 Sept. 1852 (abatement—Carlow); *Freeman's Journal*, 4 Oct. 1852 (abatement—Down); R. Cassidy to Londonderry, 24 Dec. 1852, Londonderry Papers D/Lo/C160 (arrears—Down); F.E. to W. Currey, 4 Apr. 1857, Lismore Papers MS 7188 (general—Cork, Waterford); *Banner of Ulster*, 2, 16 Apr. 1857 (arrears, ejectments, rent—Antrim, Lisburn); *Londonderry Sentinel*, 22 Apr., 6 May 1859 (general—Londonderry); W. Crowe to Lord Leconfield, 19 May 1859, Petworth House Archives PHA 1668/3 (rent, arrears—Limerick); *Drogheda Argus*, 3 June 1865 (arrears, gales —Louth); *Tipperary Advocate*, 29 July 1865 (arrears, distraint—Cashel). See also J. H. Whyte, *The Independent Irish Party 1850-9*, pp. 63-81.

[3] G. Morant to E. P. Shirley, 8, 21, 24 Aug. 1865, Shirley of Ettington Papers CR229/115/7. Morant and Shirley agreed to raise the rents on all those electoral divisions which had returned 'unsuitable' poor-law guardians.

[4] R. Kelly to Londonderry, 19 Dec. 1852, Londonderry Papers D/Lo/C161.

[5] J. H. Whyte, *The Independent Irish Party 1850-9*, pp. 65-6; Palmer to P. Gallagher,

Against this the tenant had only the weapons of deference and obedience, on the one hand, or numbers and organization, on the other. The law was of little help. Most landlords did nothing overtly illegal, and although intimidation of electors could provide grounds for bringing a petition, it was extremely difficult to prove. Thus, while twenty-seven of the 109 or so petitions pursued between 1832 and 1881 contained allegations of priestly intimidation, only four— Kerry in 1837, Clare and Roscommon in 1859, Down in 1880 —included similar allegations against landlords and only in the last case were these eventually upheld.[1] Occasional attempts were made under O'Connell and in the 1850s to establish national funds to compensate tenants who had suffered electoral coercion. But these invariably collapsed under the pressure of demand, not least from unscrupulous tenants claiming fictitious martyrdoms. The fact that most of the money was ultimately destined for landlords' pockets in the shape of arrears and the like made fund-raising more difficult than it might otherwise have been.[2] Very occasionally tenants felt strong enough—because of their landlord's nature, the shortage of reliable tenants, or some hold over a bailiff—to bargain votes against new leases, larger abatements, or lower rents. Rich farmers were obviously more independent and could even take financial revenge on, for example, solicitors who had executed a landlord's threats. For the generality of farmers, however, the best security lay in numbers. When almost everyone disobeyed, there was little landlords and agents could do.[3] But, as the long survival of landed electoral influence shows, this was as difficult to organize as it was easy to perceive.

14 Jan. 1853, Moore Papers MS 892. See also the publication in *Freeman's Journal*, 28 July 1852, of letters from Sir Robert Keane's Waterford agent.

[1] E. L. O'Malley and H. Hardcastle, *Reports of the decisions of the judges*, iii (1881), p. 115. Even here the meat of the case concerned illegal transport payments and the secret ballot. In the Kerry case no evidence was actually offered, while Clare and Roscommon turned principally on the question of bribery.

[2] *Committee on Bribery at Elections*, H.C. 1835 (547), viii, 441; E. B. Roche to W. J. O'Neill Daunt, 17 Nov. 1841, O'Neill Daunt Papers MS 8048; *Pilot*, 28 July 1841; D. Supple to O'Connell, 9 Aug. 1841, *The Correspondence of Daniel O'Connell*, ed. M. R. O'Connell, 8 vols. (Dublin, 1972–80), vii, 110; Revd E. Sheridan to T. M. Ray, 25 Aug. 1841, O'Connell Papers N.L.I. MS 13622;—to Ray, [Aug.] and 11 Sept. 1841, ibid.; R. Kelly to Londonderry, 2 Oct. 1852, Londonderry Papers D/Lo/C161.

[3] R. Kelly to Londonderry, 28 Mar. 1852, Londonderry Papers D/Lo/C166; R. Cassidy to Londonderry, 25 May 1852, ibid. D/Lo/C160; Naas to J. Inglis, 20 Dec. 1852, Eglinton Papers MS 5341; Palmerston to J. Kincaid, 29 June 1865, Palmerston L.-B. Add. MS 48583; G. Morant to E. P. Shirley, 30 Oct., 3 Dec. 1865, Shirley of Ettington Papers CR229/115/7. On effective tenant action, see *Committee on Bribery at Elections*, H.C. 1835 (547), viii, 278, 335–6 for comments on Kerry in 1835 and Clare in 1828.

IV RESULTS

The potential extent of proprietorial influence, whatever its basis, was set by the size of the electoral interests at the landlords' command. Before 1850, when leasing policy determined the number of county voters, this was seldom directly proportional to total acreage or valuation. Thereafter, although variations in the distribution of holdings and in the stability of farmer communities could still affect the issue, the relationship between valuation and electoral strength was comparatively unambiguous. Within this context, landlordism was most dominant in those counties where a high proportion of the soil was owned by a small oligopoly of proprietors. The presence of a *single* enormous estate was less important, while a wide distribution of ownership was a feature of counties where landlord interests were most successfully challenged. Reliable valuation figures for 1873–4 help identify those counties in which the ten most substantial proprietors owned A: a third or more, and B: less than a fifth of all the land.[1]

A	per cent	B	per cent
Longford	49.9	Meath	18.6
Monaghan	46.3	Limerick	14.7
Fermanagh	45.8	Tipperary	13.4
Wicklow	41.7	Cork	13.4
Leitrim	37.7		
Sligo	36.3		
Mayo	33.5		
Carlow	33.4		

In six of the eight counties where property was most concentrated, landlords were notably dominant until well in the 1860s, and even in the two others (Longford and Mayo) they were at least sporadically effective. In Cork, Tipperary, Limerick, and Meath, however, their electoral position was far less strong. Of course it was easier to control small counties like Carlow than large ones like Cork, but size alone does not explain the degree of difference involved.[2] Provincial

[1] All proportions (by value) calculated from *Return of owners of land of one acre and upwards in the several counties, counties of cities, and counties of towns in Ireland*, H.C. 1876 [C 1492], lxxx, 61–394: individual proprietors only. Areas are for counties at large, which exclude counties of cities etc., but include pure parliamentary boroughs. The only figure seriously affected is that for Antrim, which, though below a fifth at 19.8 per cent, has therefore been excluded.

[2] See *Parliamentary Election Results in Ireland, 1801–1922*, ed. B. M. Walker (Dublin, 1978). It is notable that in 1871 the average population of the three largest county *constituencies* with high concentrations was greater than that of Meath, Limerick, and Tipperary (B. M. Walker, 'The Irish Electorate, 1868–1915', *Irish Historical Studies*, xviii (1973), 380–1).

unweighted county means reveal that the highest concentration of ownership was in Ulster (30.6 per cent), where proprietorial power was strong, and the lowest (21.9 per cent) in Munster, where it was generally weak. Indeed, Ulster was remarkable for the way in which particular families were able to annex the county representation until at least the 1870s and sometimes beyond. In Fermanagh, where an Archdall sat from 1801 to 1885 and a Cole for 1801-23, 1831-40, and 1854-80, not a single election was contested during the four decades beginning in 1832. Elsewhere too in the north a handful of families monopolized matters by judicious alliances and sheer expertise. Even in certain southern counties, notably Wicklow, Sligo, Leitrim, Carlow, Dublin, and Kerry, family dynasties retained a forceful if less vicelike grip.

The identification of the electoral interests at the disposal of landlords large and small formed a recurring theme in the correspondence of politicians and proprietors alike. Monaghan elections in the 1830s were seen as revolving around a complicated set of interlocking relationships between Whig Westenras, Tory Leslies and Shirleys, and 'popular' forces under the O'Connellite banner. Antrim in 1833 and again in 1841 was agreed to be in the hands of 'three great families'; in 1852 Lord O'Neill was strong enough to 'command' one seat; in 1869 the same things were still being said in the same way.[1] Electoral soothsaying depended upon an appreciation of the power of such as Lord Bellew in Louth, Lord Stuart de Decies in Waterford, Lord Farnham in Cavan, Lord Kenmare in Kerry, the Lane Foxes and the Godleys in Leitrim, upon knowing how Lord Abercorn had 'sewn up' Donegal, upon charting the fortunes of the four great Tory proprietors who together owned a seventh of all Co. Clare, upon detecting how the tergiversations of Lord Bath at the Monaghan election of 1865 allowed in the first Whig for twenty years.[2] Inheritance across the party divide could change the political complexion of whole counties, so that the second Viscount Lorton's succession in 1854 temporarily depressed the Tory interest in Roscommon, while the passage of certain Wexford estates in the opposite direction allowed the Tories to win seats in the 1850s and 1860s which they had last held in 1832.[3]

[1] H. R. Westenra to Rossmore, 7 Jan. 1835, Rossmore Papers T2929/8/14; Downshire to W. E. Reilly, 4 May 1833, Downshire Papers D671/C/2/493 (Lords Antrim, O'Neill, Hertford); *Northern Whig*, 17 Apr. 1841; Derby to Lord Roden, 5 Feb. 1852, Roden L.-B. T2647/43; Seymour of Ragley Papers CR114A/538.

[2] Lord St Germans to Lord Aberdeen, 6 Jan. 1854, Aberdeen Papers Add. MS 43208; Bishop O'Brien to Archbishop Cullen, 18 Mar. 1857, Cullen Papers; R. H. Southwell to H. Maxwell, 7 Jan. 1835, Farnham Papers MS 18602; *Cork Examiner*, 4 Jan. 1872; E. K. Tenison to Lord Carlisle, 18 Mar. 1857, Carlisle Papers L.-B. 84; *Londonderry Sentinel*, 12 July 1860; J. Machett to Naas, 12 Apr. 1859, Mayo Papers MS 11036; *Freeman's Journal*, 16 July 1865.

[3] Lord Crofton to T. E. Taylor, 10 Apr. 1859, Mayo Papers MS 11036; *Central Conservative*

The dramatic and well-publicized acrimony which surrounded the nomination of Conservative candidates for Down in 1852 showed what could happen when personal jealousies outstripped class cohesion. In Down the lesser gentry had long been crushed by their wealthier colleagues, and, indeed, the county representation had become entirely divided between the two great houses of Stewart (Marquess of Londonderry) and Hill (Marquess of Downshire). The third Marquess of Londonderry was not popular with the county gentry who found his haughty arrogance at once unpleasing and inappropriate in one who held, by 1851, only the third interest in the constituency.[1] Let down by his own son, Londonderry determined to keep things in the family by supporting the candidature of his nephew, David Ker, who was himself second only to Lord Downshire as the largest landowner in the county. However, Ker later decided to stand 'on his own bottom'; Londonderry become choleric, tried to run another more loyal relative, but was eventually obliged by pressure from the Tory proprietors as a whole to withdraw into sullen rage, while Ker and Downshire's eldest son went on to annihilate the lone tenant-right candidate at the polls. Bitter words had been exchanged and Downshire had vowed that he would 'not forget' Londonderry's conduct on the various private occasions at which they had discussed the matter.[2] Worst of all, the whole 'incredible mess', as Londonderry called it, culminated in the publication of a small pamphlet containing Ker's private electoral correspondence, with star billing given to letters from Londonderry which broke all accepted conventions with their brazen references to 'the family seat' and the writer's position as 'patron' and controller of county affairs.[3] Such public bickering was, however, rare. The great majority of similar disputes were kept from vulgar eyes, and the gentry's mastery at combining private savagery with public harmony

Society of Ireland: Report of the Sub-Committee 1859 (Mayo Papers MS 11025). By 1859 the eight leading Tory proprietors in Wexford owned 16 per cent of the constituency's land (see lists in J. George to Naas, 16 Apr. 1859, Mayo Papers MS 11036, and to Sir W. Jolliffe, 18 Apr. 1859, Hylton Papers Box 24).

[1] M. Forde to J. W. Maxwell, 30 June 1830, Perceval-Maxwell Papers D3244/G/1/63; P. Jupp, 'County Down elections, 1783–1831', *Irish Historical Studies*, xviii (1972), 177–206; Londonderry to Downshire, 1 Aug. 1829, Downshire Papers D671/C/12/400; Londonderry to Lord Hillsborough, 21 Apr. 1845, ibid. D671/C/12/934; Lord de Ros to Clarendon, 28 Aug. [1850], Clarendon Papers Box 23; List of Down proprietors and voters 1851-2, Londonderry Papers D/Lo/C164 No. 14.

[2] Downshire to Londonderry, 21 Apr. [1852], Londonderry Papers D/Lo/C166, to J. W. Maxwell, 20 Apr. 1852, Perceval-Maxwell Papers D3244/G/1/160. See also ibid. D3244/G/1/188; J. V. Stewart to Downshire, [Apr. 1852], Londonderry Papers D/Lo/C166; Sir T. Bateson to Londonderry, 15 Apr. 1852, ibid.

[3] Londonderry to Downshire, 6 June 1852, Downshire Papers D671/C/377/62; Printed 'Correspondence between Lord Londonderry and David Stewart Ker Esq.' in Martin & Henderson Papers D2223/21/7.

helped to preserve their electoral influence even when—as happened so often in Fermanagh for example[1]—knives were flashing in smoke-filled rooms. Indeed, for all but copper-bottomed cholerics like Londonderry, it was a point of honour to keep up at all times the appearance of 'personal friendly intercourse', for by such characteristics could a gentleman best be recognized by his tribe.[2]

Such disputes highlighted the importance of *combined* action. The influence of the great magnates was rendered geometrically greater still by the support of flotillas of lesser men who accepted guidance from the 'natural' leaders of county society. Such leadership required both geniality and *gravitas*. Already as a young man the Whig first Marquess of Clanricarde had 'preserved his self-respect even in the midst of . . . riotous licence. Although full of the wildest fun, he never allowed the slightest liberty to be taken with him.' As Galway's 'natural' leader he received the support of many Tory proprietors and himself expected no less 'looking to my conduct . . . and my distribution of patronage with little regard to local politics and petty party feelings'.[3] But the middling and lesser gentry could be as prickly as the greater men, and concessions—in the escalating shape of condescension, flattery, consultation, or a share in the representation itself—were often necessary to keep the landed forces in harmonious unity. The Duke of Abercorn made frequent (if rather cynical) obeisances to those in Donegal and Tyrone who owned less land than he did. Lord Donoughmore's mini-flotilla in Tipperary was typically kept afloat by regular injections of patronage and good manners. In Monaghan Lord Rossmore's reliance on a set of allied families was recognized by all. At the Kerry election of 1835 a vast Whig-Tory armada of proprietors set sail under Lords Kenmare and Ventry to do battle with O'Connell and, in this case, go down with all hands.[4]

---

[1] See the correspondence of Mar. 1852 between Lord Enniskillen, Lord Erne, and Mervyn Archdall in Erne Papers D1939/21/5j.

[2] See, e.g., Lord Rossmore's Memo of 1832, Rossmore Papers T2929/4/33 (Monaghan); Clanricarde to Lord Dunsandle, 13 July 1852, Clanricarde Papers 83 (Galway); W. R. Ormsby Gore to C. W. Cooper, 6 Apr. 1857, O'Hara Papers MS 20355 (Sligo); H. Anderson to J. A. Beck, 7 Apr. 1857, Ironmongers' Company Irish Correspondence Received 1855–68 (Londonderry); W.F. to Sir G. F. Seymour, [11 Aug. 1869], Seymour of Ragley Papers CR114A/538(3) (Antrim).

[3] *Sir William Gregory . . . An Autobiography*, ed. Lady Gregory, p. 42; Clanricarde to Clarendon, 8 Aug. 1847, Clarendon Papers Box 9; Clanricarde to D. Daly, 1 July 1847, Clanricarde Papers 29; Lord Clonbrock to Clanricarde, 9 and 10 Apr. 1857, ibid. 40; Letters to and from Lord Dunkellin about the 1865 election, ibid. 49; *Galway County election petition*, H.C. 1872 (241-I), xlviii, 118, 137; Clanricarde to Clonbrock, 15 Aug. 1852, Clanricarde Papers 37.

[4] *Londonderry Guardian*, 25 Nov. 1857, 16 Aug. 1859, 10 Sept. 1861, Abercorn to Belmore, 14 Mar. 1873, and S. Knox to Belmore, 16 Mar. 1873, Belmore Papers D3007/P/17,

Although ultimately all landlord influence, whether successful or unsuccessful, single-handed or combined, depended upon the number of voters on particular estates, precise information on this is usually available only in a form so scattered as to defy contextual analysis. In the early 1830s Lords Rossmore, Blayney, and Bath were together landlords to more than two-fifths of Monaghan's 2,100 voters; Lords Kenmare and Ventry to almost a third of Kerry's 1,200.[1] In Cavan Lord Farnham alone held sway over a fifth; in Waterford the two Whigs, Lord Stuart de Decies and the Duke of Devonshire, over a quarter. On the other hand, a reluctance to grant leases had reduced the voters on the considerable estates of Lord Courtown in Carlow and Lord Downshire in Wicklow to forty and twenty-five respectively.[2] By the 1850s and 1860s, when such disparities had ceased to be possible, almost a fifth of the Longford electorate was provided by the King-Harman estate; almost a tenth of Monaghan's by Lord Rossmore; a twentieth of Tipperary's 9,000 and more voters by Lords Glengall and Dunalley; almost a tenth of Louth's by Lord Clermont; a fifteenth of Clare's by Lord Leconfield.[3] At the Antrim by-election of 1869 the ten leading Tories were together able to muster two out of every five electors.[4] Fortunately, however, amidst such bits and pieces it is possible to obtain a more generally useful view from the very detailed figures of proprietorial voting strength which survive for four county constituencies, two before and two after the Franchise Act of 1850. This view is shown in Table 30. Clearly the potential for dominance by a small élite was present everywhere and the number of tenurially independent voters was generally small. Equally clearly the extent to which power was concentrated does not seem to have had any necessary connection with the size of the constituency. Down's electorate,

31; Lord Donoughmore to R. J. Otway, 15 Feb. 1865, Otway Papers MS 13008; H. R. Westenra to Rossmore, 7, 13 Jan., 6 Feb. 1835, Rossmore Papers T2929/8/14, 16, 20, *Freeman's Journal*, 2 Aug. 1852; Knight of Kerry to T. Spring Rice, 24 Sept. 1835, FitzGerald Papers.

[1] Rossmore to Anglesey, 28 Dec. 1832, Anglesey Papers D619/32N (*c*.400); H. R. Westenra to Rossmore, 17 Jan. 1835, Rossmore Papers T2929/8/17 (Blayney *c*.100); J. Evatt to Lord Bath, 4 Dec. 1832, Bath Papers Irish Box (*c*.450). On Kerry, see D. Thompson and M. J. Foley to Knight of Kerry, 27 and 29 Dec. 1834, FitzGerald Papers.

[2] A Macintyre, *The Liberator*, p. 105; P. M. Egan, *Guide to Waterford* (Waterford, 1892); Printed papers of 25 Nov. 1840, Courtown Papers; List of voters on Downshire Wicklow estate in 1837, Downshire Papers D671/C/214/342.

[3] Bishop Kilduff to Archbishop Cullen, 28 Feb. 1862, Cullen Papers; St A. Lennard to Rossmore, 4 Apr. 1857, Rossmore Papers T2929/11/38; *D.E.P.* 13 Mar. 1857, and W. Spaight to Naas, 23 Oct. 1866, Derby Papers 155/2; R. to S. McClintock, 28 Feb. 1854, Mayo Papers MS 11017; W. Crowe to Lord Leconfield, 24 Apr. 1859, ibid. MS 11025.

[4] The number of voters on the Hertford (*The Times*, 23 Aug. 1869) and Macartney (Seymour of Ragley Papers CR114A/742/2) estates are known. By applying their combined voter/valuation ratio to the other leading Tory proprietors (ibid. CR114A/538/3), a figure of 4,654 or 39.7 per cent of the electorate is obtained.

TABLE 30

*Distribution of voters among the leading landed proprietors
in four county constituencies, 1832-65*

	Armagh 1832	Leitrim 1832	Down 1851–2	Louth 1865
	(percentage of total electorate)			
Top proprietor	13.7 (14.5)*	12.0	15.0	7.0 (8.8)*
Top 5 proprietors	54.2 (57.4)	33.5	32.2	18.6 (23.4)
Top 10 proprietors	67.9 (71.9)	47.0	43.8	28.6 (36.0)
Top 20 proprietors	80.2 (84.9)	66.7	56.1	43.0 (54.1)
Top 30 proprietors	85.6 (90.6)	76.3	64.8	50.7 (63.8)
Total electorate	3,210+	1,318	10,028	2,441

*Data for Armagh and Louth include some independent freeholders. The figures in parentheses have been recalculated to ensure comparability with Leitrim and Down.
+As given in source used, though 3,342 is probably the correct figure.

in 1852 the second largest among Irish counties, was in fewer hands than that of Louth, the second smallest. Yet, despite such variations, there can be no doubt that in all four counties the number of leading proprietors in a position to influence more than half the voters could easily have fitted into any moderately sized drawing room. In Armagh only five men would have been needed, in Leitrim a dozen, in Down fifteen, and in Louth about twenty. That this was not untypical is shown by the case of Roscommon at the first registry of voters after Catholic Emancipation, when—of those newly admitted to the rolls —fully a quarter held from the leading landlord, almost a half from the leading five, and three-fifths from the leading ten.[1] And the potential power of these charmed circles was made all the stronger by their very permanence: in Down the ten largest interests remained virtually unchanged between 1808 and the very different world of 1852.[2] So continuously recognizable a political landscape allowed the fruits of paternalism to be the more readily harvested, class cohesion the more readily maintained, and electoral skills learned earlier at the ancestral knee. Here, as in most matters, flux was the enemy of proprietorial influence, stability its friend.

Practically speaking, the electoral impact of the landed classes manifested itself not only through numbers, but through moods, feelings, and atmosphere. The ever-changing climate of tension, worry,

[1] List in Clonalis Papers 9.2.ES.026.
[2] Compare the listing for 1808 in *Letters of a great Irish landlord: A Selection from the estate correspondence of the Third Marquess of Downshire*, ed. W. A. Maguire (Belfast, 1974), pp. 157–61, with that for 1851–2 in Londonderry Papers D/Lo/C164 No. 14.

concern, and (more often than is sometimes supposed) sheer indifference which marked the electors' attendance at the polls had a profound and elusive impact upon political opinion. That voters were often under great strain cannot be doubted. That private turmoil must have been deeper and more common than the evidence of occasional public breakdowns suggests is equally certain. At the Kerry election of 1835 O'Connell's speeches reduced audiences to wild weeping, men met in excited clusters for mutual support, one voter desperately went into hiding to escape both proprietorial and clerical coercion only to be discovered by a priest who 'gave him two glasses of brandy and then took him to vote'. 'I am', cried another to his landlord, 'the fourth generation of my family living under the Herbert family. I have 16 children, and my life and theirs will be taken away if you ask me to vote for your friend and my property burned. Yet, Sir, if you choose to ask me, I will vote for the Knight [of Kerry].'[1] Estates became visibly disturbed places during particularly bitter contests and the 'vile feelings stirred up' could never be entirely erased.[2] Some tenants tried to avoid the franchise altogether. Others would blame their disobedience on the priest as one 'out of the power of the landlord'. In Down in 1852 some 'took ill' and retired to bed. In Louth a Liberal landlord recorded the facial evidence of consciences torn between fear and conviction as 'positively painful to see'.[3] Sir Robert Gore Booth was told by a frightened Sligo voter in 1868, 'I have to choose between Damnation and Eviction.' At the Galway election of 1872 one voter who was literally being chased by priests and agents sought refuge by standing on the polling table and frenziedly shouting his support for both candidates. Another, recalled a landlord, 'ran over and put his arms round me and kissed me, and said "Oh Master, Master, I will do anything for you; I will let them murder me if you wish, but they will murder me unless I vote for Nolan". "Well", said I, "I cannot protect you, you are here now, vote as you like".'[4] Tenants

---

[1] G. Lyne, 'Daniel O'Connell, intimidation, and the Kerry elections of 1835', p. 84; Lady Kenmare to Knight of Kerry, 13 Jan. 1835, FitzGerald Papers; *Committee on Bribery at Elections*, H.C. 1835 (547), viii, 280–2; T. Dumas to Knight of Kerry, 26 Jan. 1835, FitzGerald Papers.

[2] Marquess of Anglesey, *One-Leg: The life and letters of Henry William Paget First Marquess of Anglesey K.G. 1768–1854* (London, 1961), p. 199; *Galway County election petition*, H.C. 1872 (241-I), xlviii, 347; J. Evatt to Lord Bath, 10 June 1833, Bath Papers Irish Box; G. Morant to E. P. Shirley, 6 Aug. 1865, Shirley of Ettington Papers CR229/115/7.

[3] *Fictitious Votes, Ireland*, 1st series, 2nd report, pp. 30–8, 59; *Committee on Bribery at Elections*, H.C. 1835 (547), viii, 331; R. Blakiston-Houston to J. W. Maxwell, 24 May 1852, Perceval-Maxwell Papers D3244/G/1/199; Carlingford Papers Diary of C. Fortescue II (30 June 1852) and I (30 Dec. 1854).

[4] Sir R. Gore Booth to Abercorn, 3 Dec. 1868, Abercorn Papers T2541/VR/314; *Galway County election petition*, H.C. 1872 (241-I), xlviii, 434–5, 443–6.

already in the booths would seek to extricate themselves by acting the fool; and even if some of this was consciously sophisticated evasion, it was humiliating all the same. When asked for their preference they would misunderstand, mispronounce crucial words, or declare their support for ineligibles such as 'Mr Vigors and my priest' (Co. Carlow, 1835), 'O'Connell, Mullins, and the parish priest' (Kerry, 1835), 'G-d's blud-an-ouns . . . the Master' (Co. Cork, 1852), 'My landlord' (Down, 1857), or 'The Law Life' Insurance Company (Co. Galway, 1872).[1]

Not that any single set of emotions was aroused at all elections. In many cases a genuine indifference or total lack of understanding on the part of rural voters produced confusion rather than agony. In 1832 many Tipperary farmers still stood quite outside the world of formal politics. At the Down election of 1857 many tenants were 'perfectly careless and quiescent'.[2] The select committee inquiring into the Clare election of 1852 examined two enfranchised farmers (with twenty and thirty-three acres respectively), whose cast of mind was probably less unusual than might be supposed.

No. 1
Then did you know anything about Colonel Vandeleur?—I did not . . . .
Did you know what his politics were?—I do not understand you . . . .
Do you know the meaning of the word politics?—No . . . .
You knew nothing about Colonel Vandeleur?—Nor did I know anything about the candidates, one way or the other.

No. 2
You have no particular politics of your own?—No . . . .
Did you know anything about Colonel Vandeleur?—I never knew anything of the gentlemen who were there.[3]

Yet authentic feelings that 'good' landlords deserved electoral support were not confined to landlords themselves. Especially in quiet times, many tenants saw no reason why they should not go along with the wishes of proprietors on whose generosity they hoped to depend. 'Votes with his landlord who butters his bread' reads one comment in a Sligo canvasser's notebook. Nor were remarks such as 'Any man must obey his landlord when he has a good landlord' (Clare, 1852), 'I should not like to go against his wishes' (Co. Dublin, 1857), 'I did not care what any man did and I never cared if any man spoke against

---

[1] *Fictitious Votes, Ireland*, 2nd series, 1st report, p. 172; *Committee on Bribery at Elections*, H.C. 1835 (547), viii, 661; A. B. Rowan to Knight of Kerry, 23 Jan. 1835, Fitz-Gerald Papers; *Galway Vindicator*, 20 Mar. 1852; Martin & Henderson Papers D2223/21/11; *Galway County election petition*, H.C. 1872 (241-I), xlviii, 377 (The Law Life Insurance Company owned the tenant's estate).
[2] M. Fallon to R. Earle, 11 Nov. 1832, Melbourne Papers 95/110; A. Rowan Hamilton to Lord Dufferin, [Apr. 1857], Dufferin Papers Mic. 22 Reel 1/Vol. vii.
[3] *Clare election petition*, H.C. 1852-3 (587), ix, 607-8, 633-6.

Mr Greville or the County of Longford, I would support the County of Longford and an honest man's son' (Longford, 1869), or 'The man that gives me a good living, I wish to compliment him' (Co. Galway, 1872) either uncommon or—save in a very general sense—insincere.[1]

No sustained contemporary attempt to analyse the nature of electoral choice was ever made in Ireland. Those sympathetic to the gentry tended to argue that tenants, if left alone, would 'naturally' wish to go with their landlords and that 'good' landlords generally obtained the most support.[2] Others simply turned this on its head: sympathy for Repeal, Independence, or Home Rule was 'natural', tenants would always wish to go with their priests, proprietorial power alone held men back from voting for their rightful Nationalist leaders.[3] In truth, the actual voting behaviour of tenant farmers was rarely constant or predictable. It changed from time to time, county to county, from one estate to another. But, while borough constituencies developed a coherent localist culture of their own, the political life of the counties was shaped by the impact of traditional power relationships, on the one hand, and by the national issues of the farmer community, on the other. Thus the pace and pattern of political change were at least as crucially affected by the willingness—for whatever reasons—of farmers to support proprietorial candidates as by the inherent strength of those national campaigns which have so long constituted the main staple of historical concern. Until the 1870s it is as easy, if not easier, to find instances of tenant obedience as of defiance and rebellion. Landlord defeats, such as those in Clare in 1828, Cork and Longford in 1832, and Kerry in 1835,[4] were more than matched by Lord Clare's ability to win over his tenants between 1832 and 1847, by the utter submission of the Bruen and Kavanagh tenantry at the Carlow election of 1835, by the success of Donegal Toryism in preventing serious challenge for almost half a century after 1832, and by the

---

[1] Sligo Liberal canvasser's notebook 1868, Clonalis Papers 9.4.HS.264; *Clare election petition*, H.C. 1852-3 (587), ix, 633-6; P. Early to A. Spencer, 12 Apr. [1857], Domvile Papers MS 9361; *Longford election petition*, H.C. 1870 (178), lvi, 412-13; *Galway County election petition*, H.C. 1872 (241-I), xlviii, 199.

[2] *Fictitious Votes, Ireland*, 1st series, 2nd report, pp. 32-4; ibid. 2nd series, 3rd report, p. 40; H. Lloyd to Downshire, 2 May 1841, Downshire Papers D671/C/12/783; *The Reign of Terror in Carlow* (1841), pp. 35-7, 81-4; *Galway Vindicator*, 24 Mar. 1852; Lord Eglinton to S. Walpole, 22 July 1852, Eglinton Papers MS 5337; Lord Inchiquin to Naas, 18 Apr. 1859, Mayo Papers MS 11036.

[3] P. Taaffe to The O'Conor Don, 3 Jan. 1835, Clonalis Papers 9.2.HS.265; *Fictitious Votes, Ireland*, 2nd series, 3rd report, p. 195; *Clare election petition*, H.C. 1852-3 (587), ix, 633; Wilson to Lady Londonderry, 13 Apr. 1857, Londonderry Papers D/Lo/C163; *Kilkenny Journal*, 15 June 1859.

[4] J. A. Reynolds, *The Catholic Emancipation Crisis in Ireland, 1823-1829* (New Haven, 1954), pp. 156-60; A. Macintyre, *The Liberator*, pp. 101-3 (Cork and Longford); G. Lyne, 'Daniel O'Connell, intimidation, and the Kerry elections of 1835', pp. 74-97.

enforcement of strict electoral obedience by landowners such as Villiers Stuart at Waterford in 1832, the Catholic Conservative, Henry Lambert, at Wexford in 1834, Roscommon proprietors as a whole in 1835, Lord Charleville at King's Co. and several Cork landlords (who found their wishes obeyed with almost alarming alacrity) in 1841.[1] In such cases, Conservative landlords were as successful as any and Liberalism in itself guaranteed neither personal popularity nor political success.

Perhaps the most striking measure of the deep roots which proprietorial influence had grown in the electoral culture of rural Ireland is provided by the way in which the gentry weathered the storm of 1852, when tenants, galvanized by the specifically farmer issue of tenant-right, defied their landlords to a hitherto unprecedented degree and succeeded in returning more Independent Party members than had been elected on the Repeal ticket even in the balmy days of 1832. Reports of refusals to vote for landed candidates survive for almost all parts of the country. In the north the London companies faced serious tenant opposition. Westmeath landlords were largely abandoned. Tenants in Down were markedly less 'obedient' than in former years. Lord Bellew was in trouble in Louth. In Tipperary landlord power was lower than it had ever been. Farmers in the rural parts of the Cork City constituency refused to walk the well-trodden paths of deference and submission. In Leitrim, where Liberal magnates had long called the electoral tune, a curious combination of 'outs' managed to return one Tory and one Radical.[2] Yet, even in 1852, the Clare tenants of Lord Conyngham violently resisted attempts to divert them away from their landlord's Tory preferences, while Tory landlords in Leitrim (unlike their Liberal colleagues) were able to mobilize an unusually high level of electoral support.[3] And although the following fifteen years marked the Indian summer of landlord politics,

[1] Lord Clare to Clarendon, 19 Aug. 1847, Clarendon Papers Box 8; *Dublin Evening Mail*, 19 Jan. 1835; *Ballyshannon Herald*, 28 Dec. 1832, and D. Murphy, *Derry, Donegal, and Modern Ulster 1790-1921* (Londonderry, 1981), pp. 82-4, 134-40; H. Villiers Stuart to W. S. O'Brien, 23 Dec. 1832, Smith O'Brien Papers MS 427; H. Lambert to E. Littleton, 1 July 1834, Hatherton Papers D260/M/01/12; P. Taaffe to The O'Conor Don, 3 Jan. 1835, Clonalis Papers 9.2.HS.265; Lord Charleville to Sir T. Fremantle, [Apr. 1841], Fremantle Papers 88/18; *Cork County election petition* H.C. 1842 (271), vi, 99-109, 142.

[2] C. Knox to R. B. Towse, 21 July 1852, Clothworkers' Company Copy L.-B. 1840-73; H. Anderson to J. A. Beck, 10 Aug. 1852, Ironmongers' Company Irish Correspondence Received 1846-54; W. Swann to W. Pidgeon, 20 July 1852, Incorporated Society Papers MS 5848; J. Andrews to Londonderry, 15 Mar. 1852, Londonderry Papers D/Lo/C166; List of voters, ibid. D/Lo/C164 No. 165; Carlingford Papers Diary of C. Fortescue II (22 July 1852); J. Hare to Lord Normanton, 25 July 1852, Normanton Papers 21M57, Box xvii; *Report from the select committee on the Cork City election petition*, H.C. 1852-3 (528), xi, 34, 43-4, 97-9. See also J. H. Whyte, *The Independent Irish Party 1850-9*, pp. 63-81.

[3] *Clare election petition*, H.C. 1852-3 (587), ix, 569; L. McNiffe, 'The 1852 Leitrim election', *Breifne*, v (1977-8), 223-52.

the voting patterns of that period were not so much unprecedented as an intensification of what had long gone on before. The most convincing evidence for the durability of the electoral influence of the landed community comes from these years. Earl Fitzwilliam's tenants followed his complex political gyrations with limpet fidelity, as did, for example, those of Lord Farnham in Cavan, Lord Stuart de Decies in Waterford, and Sir Nugent Humble in the ruralized borough of Dungarvan.[1] Indeed, from all parts of the country landlords sent each other encouraging reports of the willingness of tenants to 'go the right way', regardless of where that way might lead.[2]

Evidence from a number of county elections in this period for which results are available on a baronial or other local basis demonstrates the effectiveness of landed estates as political communities. Thus the variation in Leitrim of the Conservative proportion of the vote in 1852 between 49 per cent in the northern baronies of Drumahaire and Rosclogher and 9 per cent in southern Mohill occurred largely because the former belonged to predominantly Tory, the latter to Whig, gentlemen.[3] A similar patterning can be found elsewhere: at the Co. Dublin election of 1852 when the Liberals obtained 74 per cent of the vote in the three northern baronies, but only 37 per cent elsewhere; at Wicklow in 1857 when Lord Milton got more than twice as many votes as the other candidates in Shillelagh (where his father's enormous estates lay), but was in a distinct minority in the 'Conservative' north-west; at Galway in 1857 when W. H. Gregory (as one of three candidates) collected 59 per cent of the vote in his home barony of Kiltartan, but only 18 per cent in the Tuam polling district further north;[4] at Tipperary in 1857 and 1865; Kilkenny in 1859; and even —in a residual and much attenuated form—at the 1872 Kerry and

---

[1] A. K. Hanrahan, 'Irish Electioneering, 1850–1872' (University College Dublin MA thesis, 1965), pp. 22–4; *Report from the select committee on the Dungarvan election petition*, H.C. 1854 (162), viii, 579–82.

[2] For example—Limerick: J. Spaight to Naas, 13 May 1859, Mayo Papers MS 11036; Cavan: W. Smith to R. Brady, [July 1852], Close (Richardson of Drum) Papers D2002/C/48; Antrim: Wilson to Lady Londonderry, 15 Apr. 1857, Londonderry Papers D/Lo/C163; Armagh: S. Blacker to T. Carleton, 3 Jan. 1856, Carleton, Atkinson, & Sloan Papers D1252/42/4; Wicklow: *Central Conservative Society of Ireland: Report of the Sub-Committee 1859* (Mayo Papers MS 11025); Longford: Lord Granard to Cullen, 11 Jan. 1870, Cullen Papers; Kilkenny: *Kilkenny Journal*, 28 May and 1 June 1859; Tipperary: *Dublin Evening Mail*, 13, 16 Mar. 1857; Galway: *Galway County election petition*, H.C. 1872 (241-I), xlviii, 118; Sligo: C. Witton to C. W. Cooper, 14 Apr. 1857, O'Hara Papers MS 20355.

[3] L. McNiffe, 'The 1852 Leitrim election', pp. 237–40. Here, and in immediately subsequent calculations respecting two-member constituencies, party strength has been calculated either as a mean of the two candidates on each side (where this was a realistic course) or as a percentage of the total vote disregarding plumpers and split votes. In by-elections such devices were not required.

[4] K. T. Hoppen, 'National politics and local realities in mid-nineteenth century Ireland', p. 212.

Galway by-elections which otherwise heralded the ultimate disintegration of proprietorial influence as such.[1] Captain Nolan, the Home Rule victor at Galway, still instinctively saw landlordism as the underlying basis of electoral power. 'I think', he remarked of another candidate who later withdrew, 'where I found his influence extended I should say is, if you drew a line from Ballynamore through New Forest, which is his property, up to the town of Mount Bellew, and then went straight to the Roscommon boundary . . . beyond that limit I did not find that he had any . . . influence.'[2] The very personal nature of such influence at the high noon of landlord success can best be seen by comparing the Co. Cork by-elections of 1860 and 1861. At both, a Liberal was opposed by a Tory or crypto-Tory, but the percentage Conservative vote in particular baronies shifted dramatically according to whether or not candidates were able to draw upon the support of friends and relations in individual local communities.[3]

	Conservative percentage of total vote	
	1860	1861
Condons and Kinnataloon (polling at Fermoy)	80.8	38.2
Duhallow (polling at Kanturk)	44.7	90.2
Bantry and Bear	4.4	76.5
Whole County	37.4	69.3

And although it would be wrong to say that these and other similar patterns were entirely the products of a single cause, there can be little doubt that in this period landlord influence was a generally crucial consideration. Where, for example, it is possible to break down baronial votes both by religion and the location of estates it is almost invariably the latter which emerges as the more decisive. At elections for the Counties of Donegal in 1852, Wicklow in 1857, and Dublin in 1865 it was, for example, the most Catholic areas which were the most Conservative—a sure sign of successful proprietorial activity.[4] Even in a county like Down, where Catholic voters in 1852 proved themselves

[1] *Dublin Evening Mail*, 13, 16 Mar. 1857, and *Tipperary Advocate*, 4 Mar., 22 July 1865; *Kilkenny Journal*, 28 May, 1 June 1859, and *Dundalk Democrat*, 21 May 1859; *Cork Herald*, 10, 13 Feb. 1872, and *Cork Examiner*, 10 Feb. 1872 (Kerry); *Galway County election petition*, H.C. 1872 (241-I), xlviii, 382-425, 725.

[2] *Galway County election petition*, op. cit. 814.

[3] *Nation*, 10 Mar. 1860; *C.C.* 28 Feb. 1861. The 1860 result was undoubtedly also affected by divisions among the Catholic clergy—see Chapter III, section V below.

[4] See Chapter I, p. 36 above.

notably more inclined than Church of Ireland or Presbyterian voters to support tenant-right, a really determined proprietor could achieve a great deal. Thus in the Barony of Kinelarty (for which unusually detailed information survives), where almost all the voters held from either David Ker (who stood as a Tory in 1852 and a Liberal in 1857) or the Forde family (who were neutral in 1852 but strongly Tory in 1857), more than nine out of ten electors dutifully followed the opposite and cancelling political movements of their masters.[1] Religion, in other words, though always important, could sometimes suffer almost complete electoral neutralization. Particularly was this the case in the 1850s and 1860s when intense localism in the boroughs and potent landlord influence in the counties proved at least as important in moulding electoral behaviour as did the national politics of the day. Uniquely comprehensive information for the by-election of April 1865 in Co. Louth (a constituency not without a history of agrarian radicalism) reveals how all-pervasive could in certain circumstances be the impact of landed property upon the distribution of the vote. Just over three-fifths of all the 2,441 electors held farms on the forty-three estates able to muster ten or more votes. But on only two of these estates was the vote at all evenly split. On all the rest the majority for either Liberals or Conservatives was large, decisive, and overwhelming, never falling below two to one and in *twenty-two* cases exceeding nine to one. And all this seems to have been entirely personal, for the extent of the majorities did not in any way vary according to whether proprietors were Tories or Liberals or according to the size of particular estates.[2]

Even as an isolated case—and it can hardly have been entirely untypical—the Louth result demonstrates the potential power of the landed community and the extreme lengths to which that power could at times be extended. With the important social and agrarian changes which were to help fashion so powerful an instrument out of the new electorate of 1850 still under way and incomplete, and with the boroughs generating a strong sense of inward-looking parochialism, it was possible for a landed class, purged of its weaker elements in the

[1] Derived from the MS poll books for Co. Down in 1852 and 1857 in Downshire Papers D671/02/5–8 (recatalogued). Only the religion of voters in certain baronies in 1852 is noted. In a sample of 1,214 Presbyterians, 546 Episcopalians, and 184 Catholics in Lower Iveagh, Upper Castlereagh, and Newry, the percentage of those voting who voted the straight Tory ticket was: Presbyterians 72.9, Episcopalians 77.1, Catholics 16.5 (which says little for the supposed radicalism of northern Presbyterians). For the valuation profile of these voters, see Chapter I, note 1 p. 35 above.

[2] Obtained from *An analysis of the parliamentary register of voters for the County of Louth* (Dublin, 1865). The percentage majority (either way) was 85.9 for estates with thirty or more and 85.7 for those with less than thirty voters. It was 87.7 for Liberal and 85.5 for Conservative estates.

furnace of famine, to recapture political territory it had once thought irretrievably lost. Strong and entrenched landlords made substantial purchases among the five million bankrupt acres sold under the Encumbered Estates Act of 1849. The fittest replaced the weakest and emerged ready to benefit from a new era of generally well-paid rents.[1] By not maximizing their rent incomes in the 1850s and 1860s landlords were, in effect, buying political influence with hard cash, while the drastic post-Famine clearance of labourers and cottiers permitted a comparatively smooth transition from tillage to grazing and thus reduced the general conflicts of rural life.[2] By 1857 landlords were rhapsodizing the 'excellent times', with 'country quiet, prices good, farmers prospering, rents well paid'.[3] Politics, they were relieved to find, were becoming 'much more respectable'. In all parts of the country gentlemen were exerting themselves electorally as they had not done for twenty years and more. An initial push in 1852 was fully sustained, so that by 1857–9 the Irish Tories (the chief standard-bearers of gentry politics) were enjoying unprecedented electoral success. A vigorous Conservative Registration Society reported in 1859 on dramatic advances in no less than nineteen counties.[4] In 1859 Ireland returned a unique Tory majority at the polls: 55 seats out of 105. At the same time, the great Whig landlords, such as Devonshire, Clanricarde, Fitzwilliam, Lansdowne, and Kenmare, were also able to consolidate their own electoral positions against radical attack. Everywhere both the private correspondence of individual proprietors and the newspaper press recorded a remarkable willingness by farmers to support 'respectable' landed candidates and resist the blandishments of Independent Opposition in all its chameleon forms.[5]

Even at the time, however, there were signs that all this might eventually run into the sands. The shrill note of hysteria which had

[1] J. S. Donnelly Jr., *The Land and the People of nineteenth-century Cork*, p. 131.

[2] C. Ó Gráda, 'Post-Famine Adjustment', p. 127. See also L. M. Cullen, *An economic history of Ireland since 1660*, p. 116.

[3] Sir J. Young to S. E. Vernon, 17 Mar. 1857, Young L.-B.

[4] Lord Carew to Clarendon, 28 June [1851], Clarendon Papers Box 8; *Galway Vindicator*, 24 Mar. 1852; Naas to Derby, 31 July 1852, Derby Papers 155/1; *Daily Express*, 10, 28 Feb. 1853; Naas to Derby, 3, 18 Apr. 1857, Derby Papers 155/1; *Central Conservative Society of Ireland: Report of the Sub-Committee 1859* (Mayo Papers MS 11025).

[5] See, e.g., Lord Shannon to Derby, 31 Mar. [1852], Derby Papers 150/11; Lord Donoughmore to Derby, 1 Apr. 1856, ibid. 158/6; J. Ball to Carlisle, 7 Mar. [1857], Carlisle Papers L.-B. 84; *Londonderry Sentinel*, 17 Apr. 1857; 'Statement' by G. H. Moore on Mayo election of 1857, Moore Papers MS 893; *Dundalk Democrat*, 9 Apr. 1859; Lord Crofton to T. E. Taylor, 10 Apr. 1859, Mayo Papers MS 11036; Lord Inchiquin to Naas, 9, 18 Apr. 1859, ibid. MS 11026; J. Delaney to Naas, 24 Apr. 1859, ibid. MS 11025; J. Spaight to Naas, 13 May 1859, ibid. MS 11036; *C.C.* 21, 22 Feb. 1861.

risen from the gentry in 1852—when denunciations of 'communism', 'socialism', and 'daylight robbery' had shown that proprietors had little to learn from priestly vituperation against 'in-
differentism', 'secret societies', and 'spoilation'—had already
revealed a dangerous sense of insecurity at the heart of landlord
mentalities. But even after the fevered memories of the revolutions
of 1848 had subsided, the landed community seldom took its analysis
of agrarian questions much beyond uncomprehending abuse.
By the early 1870s, when Home Rule too was being seen as no more
than 'theft' and 'communism', such reactions had become even
more inadequate than they had been in earlier and balmier
days.[1] By keeping rents low, by eschewing evictions, and by
frequently turning a blind eye to the widespread infringement of
lease covenants and estate rules,[2] Irish landlords had in effect,
sacrificed profits for a quiet time. By the late 1860s and the
1870s individual proprietors were openly trading economic
indulgence for political support. As, however, concession slowly
gave way to extraction, so—fatally, from the landlord point of
view—did what had once been a favour become an expectation.
Financially troubled proprietors, such as the Countess of Kingston,
felt themselves virtually obliged to accommodate their tenants,
with the result that estate relations 'could hardly have been friendlier'
and political influence weaker. Within a decade of the high success
of 1859 the Central Conservative Society had replaced erstwhile
optimism with stoic resolve.[3] And the forceful defence of landlord
rights which had marked both public and private communications
during the two immediately post-Famine decades was rapidly fading

[1] See, e.g., *Banner of Ulster*, 17 May 1850; R. and J. R. Miller to E. Lawford, 25 June
1852, Drapers' Company L.-B. Irish 1848–57; C. Knox to R. B. Towse, 21 July 1852, 29 Mar.
1857, Clothworkers' Company Copy L.-B. 1840–73; *Londonderry Sentinel*, 8 Apr. 1859;
B. Cahir, 'Irish National By-Elections 1870–1874' (University College Dublin MA thesis,
1965), pp. 81, 102.

[2] *Telegraph or Connaught Ranger*, 27 Jan. 1869 (G. H. Moore's Mayo estate); C. W.
O'Hara to I. Butt, 20 Jan. 1865, O'Hara Papers MS 20353; *Galway County election petition*,
H.C. 1872 (241-I), xlviii, 491–3; G. F. Stewart to Lord Leitrim, 19 Dec. 1878, Stewart
L.-B.; *Minutes of evidence taken before Her Majesty's Commissioners on Agriculture*, H.C.
1881 [C 2778-I], xv, 1024; B. L. Solow, *The land question and the Irish economy 1870–1903*,
pp. 45, 137–8.

[3] *Tipperary Advocate*, 22 July 1865 (Charles Moore of Mooresfort); G. Morant to
E. P. Shirley, 30 Oct., 6 Dec. 1865, Shirley of Ettington Papers CR229/115/7 (Bath
estate); J. Holland to E. P. Shirley, 16 May 1879, ibid. CR229/115/25 (Shirley estate);
L. M. Geary, 'The Land War on the Kingston Estate, 1879–1888' in *Bulletin of the
Irish Committee of Historical Sciences: Thesis Abstracts No. 2* (1980), p. 33. Compare
*Central Conservative Society of Ireland: Reports by agents of the revisions at the registra-
tion sessions of 1867* (Mayo Papers MS 11161) with the *Report of the Sub-Committee 1859*
(ibid. MS 11025).

into nervous silence on the part of some and hysterical apoplexy on the part of others.[1]

The position of the Irish landed class had, in any case, long been undermined by the critical reactions which its activities and opinions had often evoked in Britain and among British politicians in particular. Many Scots and English proprietors tended to regard Irish landlords with suspicion, superiority, even contempt. Before, after, and especially during the Famine a belief had grown that Irish owners should be 'made to pay' for Irish troubles and thus relieve the imperial exchequer of a burden at once inequitable and excessive—though how this view could be reconciled with the existence of a Union was usually left unexplained.[2] Lord John Russell, with that instant moralism which marked his character, believed that twenty 'gentlemen like those we have in Hampshire and Sussex' would set the Irish countryside aright. Lord Clarendon saw Irish landlords as 'the real obstacle to improvement'. Lord Spencer in 1869 was convinced that agrarian discontent flowed largely from the landlords' 'power to madden a people who have deluded notions about their rights'.[3] Much of this merged into a generalized distaste for all things Irish. Clarendon, for example, who thought the people's 'idleness and helplessness' could 'hardly be believed', had doubts as to the probity even of landed men like W. H. Gregory who had come 'from the centre of civilization' (that is, Harrow School). Derby described Irish landlords as a bunch of hotheads and reminded his lord lieutenant in 1858 of 'the intense moral cowardice which is characteristic of Irishmen'. To Sir James Graham Ireland seemed little more than a nursery for violence. As Chief Secretary in 1855, Edward Horsman expressed the view that 'outrageous' landlords virtually 'deserved to be murdered'.[4] The eventual culmination of all this came in 1881,

---

[1] *Londonderry Sentinel,* 30 July 1852, 6 Mar., 10 Apr., 13 June 1857; C. W. Cooper to J. Gorman, 14 Mar. 1857, O'Hara Papers MS 20353; *Western Star,* 6 Mar. 1869; E. L. O'Malley and H. Hardcastle, *Reports of the decisions of the judges,* ii (1875), pp. 54–5; Naas to Abercorn, 30 Apr. 1867, Abercorn Papers T2541/VR/85/18.

[2] See, e.g., J. Fawcett to Miss Pleydall, 19 Feb. 1828, Morley Papers Deposit 69; Lord Lansdowne to Downshire, 1 Nov. 1829, Downshire Papers D671/C/12/414; H. Vivian to Lord Fitzroy, 13 Aug. 1831, Vivian Papers No. 10; Lord Fortescue to Russell, 4 Nov. 1846, Russell Papers 30/22/5E; Lord Bessborough to Russell, 3 Jan. 1847, ibid. 30/22/6A; Clarendon to Russell, 30 Dec. 1847, Clarendon Papers L.-B. II; A. de Tocqueville, *Journeys to England and Ireland,* ed. J. P. Mayer (London, 1957), p. 135. See N. Lebow, British Images of Poverty in pre-Famine Ireland' in *Views of the Irish Peasantry 1800–1916,* ed. D. J. Casey and R. E. Rhodes (Hamden, Conn., 1977), pp. 73–7.

[3] Russell to Clarendon, 3 Dec. 1847, Clarendon Papers Box 43; Clarendon to Peel, 2 Sept. 1849, *Sir Robert Peel from his private papers,* ed. C. S. Parker, iii, 517; Lord Spencer to Gladstone, 26 Mar. 1869, Carlingford Papers CP1/43.

[4] Clarendon to H. Reeve, 19 July 1847, H. Maxwell, *The Life and Letters of George William Frederick, Fourth Earl of Clarendon,* 2 vols. (London, 1913), i, 280; Clarendon to

for the Land Act of that year 'was really less a considered policy than a wholesale income-maintenance' programme, a relief programme for the people 'at the expense not of the government but the [Irish] landlords'. At the same time Dublin Castle virtually withdrew support from 'bad' landlords 'who were no longer supplied with troops and police to enforce the letter of their legal rights'.[1] Although sections of the landed community were still able to fight a determined rearguard action during the 1880s, external attack and internal malaise combined more and more to divorce a continuing gentry style of life from its essential economic base. And although some landlords seem to have shed their political responsibilities with little more than a resigned shrug, many others sought refuge in a fierce Unionist Anglophobia which had almost as much contempt for English betrayal as for Catholic Irish victory.

A growing realization in the 1870s that the political power of the landed class was receding in the face of an increasingly strong and coherent farmer electorate induced both pessimism and a closing of ranks. Fenianism (however inept in its early days), the Amnesty movement, the growing confidence of organized Catholicism, the seeming hostility of Gladstone and the Liberal party, all reinforced such trends. With a few notable exceptions like Arthur MacMorrough Kavanagh of Carlow, landlords combined a business-as-usual approach with deepening electoral gloom.[2] Even in places where landlord power was still strong, such as Monaghan and Mayo, few could be found to stir themselves. Elsewhere—Tipperary, Longford, Limerick, King's Co., Queen's Co.—landlords seem, by 1870 or thereabouts, largely to have withdrawn from the electoral world.[3] For one

Russell, 25 July 1847, Clarendon Papers L.-B. I; Derby to Eglinton, 1 May 1852, 3 Dec. 1858, Eglinton Papers MSS 5332, 5344; Sir J. Graham to Lord Heytesbury, 16 Nov. 1844, Graham Papers 18/Ir; Carlingford Papers Diary of C. Fortescue I (22 Nov. 1855) recording a conversation with Horsman.

[1] B. L. Solow, *The land question and the Irish economy 1870–1903*, p. 198; C. Townshend, 'Modernization and Nationalism: Perspectives in recent Irish History', *History*, lxvi (1981), 235.

[2] A. MacM. Kavanagh to R. Hall Dare, 5 Nov. 1868, cited L. P. Curtis Jr., 'The Anglo-Irish Predicament', p. 45. I. d'Alton's argument ('Southern Irish Unionism: A study of Cork Unionists, 1884–1914', *Transactions of the Royal Historical Society*, 5th series xxiii (1973), 80–2) that confidence fully survived until 1898, while a useful antidote to the retrospective death-wish theory foisted on the landed community by its twentieth-century descendants, overlooks too much political retreat in the 1870s and 1880s.

[3] G. Morant to E. P. Shirley, 9 Apr. 1868, Shirley of Ettington Papers CR229/115/11 (Monaghan); P. J. Judge to G. H. Moore, 27 Oct. 1868, and Moore to A. H. Sullivan, 25 Nov. 1868, Moore Papers MS 895 (Mayo); Naas to Derby, 22 Oct. 1866, and J. Spaight to Naas, 23 Oct. 1866, Derby Papers 155/2 (Tipperary); *Longford election petition*, H.C. 1870 (178), lvi, 292; *Limerick Reporter*, 22 Sept. 1871, and *Committee on parliamentary and municipal elections*, H.C. 1868–9 (352), viii, 215 (Limerick); ibid. 493–4 (King's Co., Queen's Co.); F. P. Dunne to Mayo, 9 Aug. 1868, Mayo Papers MS 11164 (King's Co.).

landlord the writing appeared on the wall in letters of fire when, at the Kerry by-election of 1872, two hundred farmers he had wined and dined before the poll suddenly responded to a signal, rose from their tables, and handed him a signed refusal to support the estate candidate.[1] In Ulster too the 1870s were a bad time for landed candidates, while in Wicklow the benevolently Whiggish Earl Fitzwilliam was shouted down at the 1874 election, much to the distress of elderly priests who had always supported the family's political line. The heavily rural electorate of Galway City defied local landlords and came out for Home Rule. In Co. Wexford the Conservative candidate was able to do little more than mobilize the Protestant vote.[2] Over the longer run, the early effectiveness of landlord power and its widespread dissolution after about 1868 are revealed by the comparatively low and steady proportion of contested county elections until that date and the dramatic increase thereafter. Thus, while 39.5 per cent of such elections were contested between 1832 and 1852 and 38.5 per cent between 1852 and 1868, no less than 69.9 per cent were contested in the period starting immediately after the General Election of 1868 and ending immediately before that of 1885.[3] By 1880 the number of political activists among the gentry was steadily diminishing and the retreat to the north-east no longer reversible. At about the same time the landed grip on the composition and leadership of the poor-law boards—increasingly important as arenas for the manifestation of power and the distribution of patronage—was being finally loosened by a similar erosion in the face of attacks from the stronger elements within the farmer community.[4]

In the light of such defeats, landlords abandoned the luxury of political pluralism. The sizeable minority which had generally supported the Whigs, the Liberals, even sometimes the Repealers or Independents, moved—unsteadily and rather helplessly—into the Tory fold.[5] Yet at first the resulting Unionism was, among the

---

[1] *Annual Register . . . for the year 1872*, p. 15.

[2] Revd J. Redmond to Cullen, 3 Feb. 1874, Cullen Papers (Wicklow); Bishop MacEvilly to Cullen, 24 Mar. 1874, ibid. (Galway); E. Carr to Lord Courtown, 19 Feb. 1874, Courtown Papers (Wexford). For Ulster, see Chapter IV below.

[3] Calculated from *Parliamentary Election Results in Ireland 1801–1922*, ed. B. M. Walker (Dublin, 1978). The earlier periods run (a) from the General Election of 1832 to the last by-election before the General Election of 1852, (b) from the General Election of 1852 to that of 1868 (inclusive).

[4] See *Limerick Chronicle*, 18 Mar. 1880 on Munster; *Daily Express*, 13 Apr. 1880 on Wicklow, Armagh, Tyrone, and Cavan; J. G. Gibbon to Lord Courtown, 15 Apr. 1880, Courtown Papers (Wexford); D. McCormick, *The incredible Mr Kavanagh*, pp. 189–90; W. L. Feingold, 'The Irish boards of poor law guardians 1872–86', pp. xi–xii, 40–1, 79–93, 267.

[5] See, e.g., Archbishop Kieran to Cullen, 1 June 1868, Cullen Papers (Louth); Revd R. Galvin to Cullen, 12 Nov. 1868, ibid. (Wicklow); G. Morant to E. P. Shirley, 5 July 1871,

landed classes at any rate, no more than an anaemic foreshadowing
of the tough and dogged intransigence of later years. 'When riches
increase, they are increased that eat them, and what *good* is there
to the owners thereof, save the beholding them with their eyes' was
one landlord's gloomily scriptural reaction to the land legislation
of the time. 'Under Messrs Gladstone and Co.', another thought it
'likely that, what of us is left after giving to the Fenians and other
communists, will be made into a mere Jew-paying machine.' Soon
Parnell had become a 'fiend' and Gladstone, it was hoped, would
'follow the example of a former . . . minister, Lord Castlereagh' and
cut his throat with a penknife.[1] Energy was giving way to apoplexy,
the surest sign of disintegration. Yet what is in the end remarkable
about the landed gentry of nineteenth-century Ireland is not the fact
that its power outside Ulster fell into ruins during the 1870s and
1880s, but that, by a generally acute maximization of advantages,
it was able to retain a strong voice in political and electoral affairs
for as long as it did.

Shirley of Ettington Papers CR229/115/16 (Monaghan); Lord Dartrey to Lord Hartington,
29 June 1871, Devonshire Papers 340/466 (Monaghan); *Irish Times*, 10 Feb. 1874 (Louth);
Waterford Mail, 18 Dec. 1876 (Waterford); also Chapter IV below.

[1] W. J. Digby to C. W. O'Hara, 7 Jan. 1870, O'Hara Papers MS 20356; W. to G. V.
Hart, 7 Nov. 1879 and 10 May 1882, Hart Papers D3077/F/6/149, 201.

III

Priests and People

I MANPOWER AND TRAINING

The role and influence of the Catholic clergy are among the great and central realities of modern Irish life. The relationship between priests and people was not, however, strung out along a one-way wire; rather, it both influenced and was itself influenced by that shifting grid of social, political, and economic developments which constituted the nineteenth-century Irish experience. The essential preliminary framework was that of manpower and ecclesiastical resources, which in turn functioned within a changing pattern of outlook, belief, and communal location. Much of what was to happen throughout the century depended ultimately upon simple numerical change. The number of secular priests grew steadily from 1800 onwards, while the demographic collapse of the Famine had a dramatic impact upon the ratio of parochial clergy to Catholic laity, as shown in Table 31. The number of regulars is harder to establish, but, after something of a collapse in the late eighteenth century, there were by 1850 about 312 members of the major male orders as well as Christian and Presentation Brothers and the like, while the world of the female religious had experienced dramatic growth from 122 in 1800 to

TABLE 31

Number of parochial clergymen and ratio to Catholic population, 1800–1901

	Bishops	Parish priests	Curates	Total parochial clergy	Number of Catholics for each parochial clergyman
1800	26	986	628	1,614	2,676
1835	27	993	1,166	2,159	2,991
1845	28	1,008	1,385	2,393	2,773
1851	29	1,014	1,354	2,368	2,214
1861	33	1,036	1,491	2,527	1,783
1871	32	1,080	1,733	2,813	1,476
1881	27	996	1,745	2,741	1,445
1891	32	1,015	1,821	2,836	1,251
1901	29	1,022	1,916	2,938	1,126

Map B Roman Catholic Provinces and Dioceses

over 1,500 half a century later.[1] As, however, with so much else in Ireland, the distribution of spiritual personnel was highly uneven, and, although ratios improved everywhere, they did so at a varying pace.

Number of Catholics for each parochial clergyman		
	1835	1871
Armagh Province	2,805	1,489
Cashel Province	3,227	1,611
Dublin Province	2,451	1,219
Tuam Province	3,569	1,949

That nineteenth-century Ireland experienced a 'Devotional Revolution', as a result of which new forms of religious observance, improved clerical discipline, and modern ecclesiastical government were introduced, is now widely accepted. But to present the matter too firmly in terms of sharp discontinuities is to simplify what was, in reality, a slow and uneven process. In particular, there can be no doubt that, long before the arrival of Paul Cullen as archbishop and papal legate in 1850, the nature of Irish religious life had already undergone profound changes which were to help shape the pattern of subsequent events. Just as Irish politics were heavily determined by local considerations, so local initiatives—however haphazard and inchoate—exercised important and lasting influences upon ecclesiastical and religious matters. Both clergy and laity responded, not simply to the intentions and impact of a single individual, but to a much wider and more complex set of changes within society as a whole.

With the establishment of St Patrick's College, Maynooth, in 1795 the training of the clergy became more centralized. Fewer men went to study on the Continent. By the early 1850s over half the secular clergy and all but a handful of the bishops had been educated at Maynooth, which then contained some two-thirds of all the seminarians being trained for the Irish mission.[2] Although Maynooth recruited predominantly from the farmer

---

[1] For male regulars, see the Return in Clarendon Papers Box 33. For nuns, see E. Larkin, 'The Devotional Revolution in Ireland, 1850-75', *American Historical Review*, lxxvii (1972), 626.

[2] In 1853, 53.3 per cent of priests and 23 of the 28 bishops were Maynooth men (*Report of Her Majesty's Commissioners appointed to inquire into the management and government of the College of Maynooth*, H.C. 1854-5 [1896], xxii, 34-5, 205-6). As early as 1826 some 60 per cent of clerical students were at Maynooth (*Eighth Report of the Commissioners of Irish Education Inquiry*, H.C. 1826-7 (509), xiii, 544-5). Between

class, there is considerable uncertainty as to the precise wealth and standing of the families in question. A good deal of impressionistic gossip contrasted the gentlemanly French- or Spanish-educated priests of earlier times with the supposedly raw-boned sons of toil who flocked to Maynooth. Trollope's Fr. McGrath, 'a man of good family' whose 'French manners' fitted him 'to mix in society', winced at his Maynooth-trained curate's 'dirt and untidiness' and violent 'little farmer' politics.[1] Lever's senior clergy, notably Fr. Malachi Brennan in *Harry Lorrequer* (1839) and Fr. Tom Loftus in *Jack Hinton* (1843), were as 'rollicking' (and as two-dimensional) as his gentry; and the same stereotypes appeared in Edgeworth's *Ormond* (1817), Lover's *Rory O'More* (1837), and Lady Morgan's *The Wild Irish Girl* (1806). Inveterate travellers, such as Henry Inglis and the Hall duo, also bemoaned the decline from drawing-room to farmyard, while in 1844 the unsympathetic Viceroy, Lord De Grey, dismissed the new priests as 'born in poverty and want' and impervious to 'the misery of dirt and poor fare during their period of education'.[2]

The social origins of the eighteenth-century clergy are obscure, although there can be little doubt that the bishops at least had often come from the few remaining (and usually minor) Catholic landed families. Seminary fees alone, especially before 1845, must have excluded large sections of the rural poor. In 1826 the minimum required to complete the six- to eight-year course was seventy pounds and the college president believed that in consequence 'our students are generally the sons of farmers, who must be comfortable in order to meet the expenses . . . [or] of tradesmen, shopkeepers; and not a very small proportion of them are the children of opulent merchants, and rich farmers and graziers'.[3] This may have been gilding the lily a little; but certainly cash acted as a filter, both from the point of view of fees and, at least in the early years, because of the Church's inability to

1846 and 1861 Maynooth produced 875 ordinands (*Return of the number of persons who have completed their education at the College of Maynooth*, H.C. 1862 (137), xliii, 555).

[1] *The Macdermots of Ballycloran* (1847), Chapter Five.
[2] H. D. Inglis, *A Journey throughout Ireland during the Spring, Summer, and Autumn of 1834*, 5th edn. (London, 1838), pp. 388–94; Mr and Mrs S. C. Hall, *Ireland: Its Scenery, Character etc.*, 3 vols. (London, 1841–3), ii, 279–81; Lord De Grey to Sir James Graham, 27 Feb. 1844, Graham Papers 14/Ir.
[3] *Eighth Report . . . Commissioners of Irish Education*, H.C. 1826–7 (509), xiii, 593. For fees in the 1830s and early 1840s, see H. D. Inglis, *A Journey throughout Ireland*, p. 393, and Mr and Mrs S. C. Hall, *Ireland*, ii, 278; for later years, see J. Healy, *Maynooth College: Its Centenary History* (Dublin, 1895), pp. 415–19.

raise sufficient income to support the newly ordained curates.[1] The problem was not one of recruits, but one of resources.

Even if, however, the wilder denunciations that Maynooth was filled with the 'dregs of the people' can be disregarded, precise division of the students into neat packages remains impossible. A Westmeath land agent in 1839, while allowing that younger priests were 'selected from, I will not say the lowest order, but the next grade', thought many of their older colleagues well able to handle cutlery without distress at the tables of Protestant gentlemen.[2] Some, including the Whiggish Catholic, Thomas Wyse, talked loosely of men 'taken from the lower orders', only to be contradicted by another Catholic, who pointed instead to the 'middle class', though not 'the wealthiest sections of it'.[3] The most elevated claims came from two students themselves, who spoke respectively of the 'middling order . . . the agricultural . . . or the commercial order' and of 'the sons of persons in business and trade . . . of the comfortable, middle, and humble farmers in the country'.[4] 'Humble' farmers, however defined, seem, indeed, to have represented the lowest stratum from which aspiring priests could emerge in any numbers. Tocqueville in 1835 was told, reasonably if imprecisely, that most secular priests were from the 'tenant class', and there is some evidence that the small number of really prosperous candidates were disproportionately mopped up by the various religious orders.[5] As the Catholic bourgeoisie grew in size and wealth, so increasingly did a clerical career become only one among an expanding range of attractive employment opportunities. By the middle of the century

[1] For the social backgrounds of students in 1808, see *Papers presented to the House of Commons relating to the Royal College of St. Patrick, Maynooth*, H.C. 1812-13 (204), vi, 644–65. On expenses and resources, see also É. Ó Doibhlin, *Domhnach Mór (Donaghmore): An outline of parish history* (Omagh, 1969), pp. 214, 219.

[2] Cornwallis to Duke of Portland, 18 Apr. 1799, in *Correspondence of Charles, First Marquis Cornwallis*, ed. C. Ross, 2nd edn., 3 vols. (London, 1859), iii, 91; T. F. Uniacke in *Minutes of evidence taken before the select committee of the House of Lords, appointed to inquire into the state of Ireland since the year 1835 in respect to Crime and Outrage*, H.C. 1839 (486), xi and xii, Qs. 6426 ff.

[3] Wyse to Lord John Russell, 10 Aug. 1847, Russell Papers 30/22/6E; Anthony Blake to Lord Stanley, 4 Nov. 1844, Derby Papers 37/1. See also W. M. Thackeray, *The Irish Sketch Book of 1842* (London, 1879), p. 238; B. W. Noel, *Notes of a short tour through the midland counties of Ireland, in the Summer of 1836* (London, 1837), p. 339.

[4] Charles Cassidy in *Eighth Report . . . Commissioners of Irish Education*, H.C. 1826-7 (509), xiii, 969; John Harold, CC in *Report of Maynooth Commissioners*, H.C. 1854-5 [1896], xxii, 406.

[5] A. de Tocqueville, *Journeys to England and Ireland*, ed. J. P. Mayer (London, 1958), p. 133; J. A. Murphy, 'Priests and People in Modern Irish History', *Christus Rex*, xxiii (1969), 251; G. Pellew, *In Castle and Cabin or talks in Ireland in 1887* (New York and London, 1888), pp. 37–41. It is significant that a man of aristocratic background like Theobald Mathew should have joined the Capuchins.

the pressure on places for the study of law and medicine was considerable and increasing.[1]

The scattered evidence available suggests that, although bishops came from a range, if generally a narrow range, of backgrounds, only an outsider, like the sixth Duke of Devonshire, should have been surprised to discover, as he noted in his diary, that 'the Catholic Bishop of Ross [William Keane], concerning whose grand consecration at Cork, a great breeze arose, is [the] brother of my *gardener* at Lismore'.[2] Murray of Dublin (1809–52) came from 'substantial farming stock', the father of Doyle of Kildare and Leighlin (1819–34) was a 'respectable' though latterly an indigent farmer, that of MacHale of Killala and Tuam (1825–81) 'kept a large family business', Crotty of Cloyne's (1833–46) father was a weaver, Slattery of Cashel (1834–57) sprang from 'well-to-do farming stock in Tipperary', Murphy of Cork (1815–47) from a 'long-tailed mercantile family', Derry of Clonfert's (1847–70) father owned a 'house of business' in Ballinasloe, Cullen of Armagh and Dublin (1849–78) was related to middlemen farmers in Leinster, Dixon of Armagh's (1852–66) parents were 'middle class', Furlong of Ferns's (1857–75) father was a 'landholder' in Wexford, McGettigan, of Raphoe's (1820–61) a farmer, MacEvilly of Galway and Tuam (1857–1902) came from 'the respectable farming class', Leahy of Cashel's (1857–75) father was a civil engineer, Duggan of Clonfert (1871–96), who triumphantly announced himself at the Galway election hearings of 1872 'a peasant born and taught',[3] was the son of a farmer evicted in the 1850s, Croke of Cashel (1875–1902) the son of a land agent whose family owned a general store in Tralee, while McCabe and Walsh of Dublin (1879–85 and 1885–1921) came respectively from 'a poor Dublin family' and from that of a city watchmaker.[4]

[1] L. Kennedy, 'The Roman Catholic Church and Economic Growth in Nineteenth-Century Ireland', *Economic and Social Review*, x (1978), 53. For the considerable Catholic presence after 1845 in the Queen's Colleges (notwithstanding episcopal condemnation), see K. Flanagan, 'The Godless and the Burlesque: Newman and the other Irish universities' in *Newman and Gladstone: Centennial Essays*, ed. J. D. Bastable (Dublin, 1978), pp. 239–77.

[2] The sixth Duke's red morocco diary for 8 Feb. 1851, Devonshire Papers.

[3] *Copy of the evidence taken at the trial of the Galway County election petition*, H.C. 1872 (241–I), xlviii, 595.

[4] The dates are for episcopates. See J. Healy, *Maynooth College, passim*; W. J. Fitzpatrick, *The Life, Times, and Correspondence of the Right Revd Dr Doyle, Bishop of Kildare and Leighlin*, new edn., 2 vols. (Dublin, 1890), i, 5–6; P. K. Egan, *The Parish of Ballinasloe* (Dublin, 1960), p. 243; E. R. Norman, *The Catholic Church and Ireland in the Age of Rebellion 1859–1873* (London, 1965), pp. 4–13; *Paul Cullen* [see above, Abbreviations], i, 339; *Londonderry Sentinel*, 13 Aug. 1852; M. Murphy, 'Repeal, Popular Politics, and the Catholic Clergy of Cork, 1840–50', *Journal of the Cork Historical and Archaeological Society*, lxxxii (1977), 45; M. Tierney, 'Catalogue of Letters relating to the Queen's Colleges, Ireland, 1845–50', *Collectanea Hibernica*, ix (1966), 83–120; C. J. Woods, 'The Catholic Church and Irish Politics 1879–92' (University of Nottingham Ph.D. thesis, 1968),

One firm conclusion stands out amidst the ambiguities of the evidence: very few priests came from any section of rural society below that of 'modest farmer'. When, therefore, observers talked of a clergy springing from 'the masses' or from 'the peasantry',[1] these terms should not be interpreted as comprehensive or all-embracing. Families were, of course, prepared to scrimp and go short to prepare a boy for the priesthood and to elevate and cherish him above his brothers (as Carleton's story of 'Denis O'Shaughnessy going to Maynooth' makes clear), but by no means all farmers (let alone lesser men) could even begin to think of embarking on such a course. Hard times, frequent enough between the end of the Napoleonic Wars and the Famine, made matters worse, so that in the 1840s, for example, a farmer near Macroom occupying the 'grass of seven cows' (at a time when the average dairy herd in Co. Cork consisted of less than five animals) 'had not anything like the means neces-sary for such a venture'.[2]

Before the Famine, therefore, when farmers of all kinds and their 'assisting relatives' constituted only two-fifths of the male agricul-tural labour force, the mass of the clergy's closest and most direct family relationships were drawn from a distinct minority of a rural population which otherwise consisted predominantly of cottiers and landless labourers. This sectional identification exercised a powerful effect upon clerical outlook and behaviour, which were, as a result, reinforced rather than fractured by post-Famine changes in the structure of rural society. Farmers became increasingly prosperous and relatively more and more were pulled into that sector which might reasonably be expected to contribute to the pool of clerical manpower. Their particular support for the new piety provided the essential context and encouragement for the consolidation of devotional and ecclesiastical reform.[3] Before the Famine many priests had themselves been directly engaged in farming, so that the relationship between clergy and farmers had operated at a direct

p. 47; *idem*, 'The Politics of Cardinal McCabe, Archbishop of Dublin, 1879–85', *Dublin Historical Record*, xxvi (1973), 101; P. J. Walsh, *William J. Walsh, Archbishop of Dublin* (Dublin, 1928), p. 1.

[1] Lord O'Hagan to Earl Spencer, 9 Mar. 1869, O'Hagan Papers D2777/8/1; S. M. Hussey, *The Reminiscences of an Irish Land Agent*, ed. H. Gordon (London, 1904), p. 116.

[2] P. Ó Laoghaire, *My Own Story*, trans. from the Irish by Sheila O Sullivan (Dublin, 1973), pp. 1–6; Ó Laoghaire was eventually able to enter St Colman's College, Fermoy, only because of the Bishop of Cloyne's decision to waive the annual thirty-pound fees for a 'very few . . . boys of *exceptional* ability'. For the size of herds and 'the grass of a cow' in 1841, see J. S. Donnelly Jr., *The Land and the People of nineteenth-century Cork: The Rural Economy and the Land Question* (London, 1975), pp. 41, 142.

[3] E. Hynes, 'The Great Hunger and Irish Catholicism', *Societas*, viii (1978), 137–56.

as well as at an inherited level of experience. The wide variety of service obligations paid by rural parishioners to their clergy—the collection of oats, the cutting of turf, harvesting, threshing, and so on—reflected the importance of the priests' agricultural activity. In the 1830s 'farming, jobbing, buying, and selling priests' were, as Archbishop Curtis angrily noted, 'common all over the diocese of Meath'.[1] Bishop Murphy of Clogher himself owned a 'small farm'; Archbishop MacHale of Tuam leased a 'small farm' in the 1830s; Dean Lyons of Killala was involved in large-scale agricultural operations; many priests in Kildare 'speculated in farming and made money by it'. The parish priest of Ballinasloe rented thirty acres in 1825, his colleague at Dungarvan twenty in 1844, another on the Coolattin estate in Wicklow held a fair-sized farm on favourable terms from Earl Fitzwilliam in 1843.[2] Soon after his appointment to Kildare in 1819, Bishop Doyle (who was later to accuse the bursar of Maynooth of knowing 'more about bullocks than bulls') tried to limit his priests to fourteen acres. Under Archbishop Murray, Dublin promulgated a statute in 1831 drawing the line at fifteen acres. Further legislation was passed in 1850 by the Synod of Thurles, in 1854 by the provincial Synod of Armagh, and in 1875 by the national Synod of Maynooth.[3] The impact of all this was, however, fragmentary and delayed. During the 1850s the Bishop of Elphin was locked in combat with priests guilty of concubinage, simony, and obsessive concern for profitable farming; two Cavan priests were able to buy 210 acres for almost £8,000; in Louth several priests rented 'farms from Lord Clermont'; the parish priest of Ahamlish in Co. Sligo held an extensive farm, while his colleague

---

[1] *The Diary of Colour-Sergeant George Calladine 19th Foot 1793–1837*, ed. M. L. Ferrar (London, 1922), p. 195 (June 1836); Curtis to Christopher Boylan (Rector, Irish College Rome), 1 June 1830, cited in J. H. Whyte, 'The Appointment of Catholic Bishops in nineteenth-century Ireland', *Catholic Historical Review*, xlviii (1962), 20.

[2] S. Ó Dufaigh, 'James Murphy, Bishop of Clogher, 1801–24', *Clogher Record*, vi (1968), 452; B. O'Reilly, *John MacHale, Archbishop of Tuam. His Life, Times, and Correspondence*, 2 vols. (New York, 1890), i, 304–5, 373 (MacHale and Lyons); Archbishop Crolly to Cullen, 16 Nov. 1836, Irish College Rome, Cullen Papers, and W. J. Fitzpatrick, *Dr Doyle, Bishop of Kildare and Leighlin*, i, 104, 138–9; P. K. Egan, *The Parish of Ballinasloe*, p. 166; F.E. to B. Currey, 26 Oct. 1844, Lismore Papers MS 7183/1 (Dungarvan); Earl Fitzwilliam to R. Chaloner, 30 Oct. 1843, Chaloner Papers ZFM/318.

[3] W. J. Fitzpatrick, *Dr Doyle, Bishop of Kildare and Leighlin*, ii, 315, and i, 138; *Second Report from the select committee of the House of Lords appointed to inquire into the collection and payment of tithes in Ireland*, H.C. 1831–2 (663), xxii, 277–8; *Decreta Synodi Plenariae Episcoporum Hiberniae apud Thurles* (Dublin, 1851), 'De Parochis' dd. 15, 16, 17; J. Ahern, 'The Plenary Synod of Thurles II', *Irish Ecclesiastical Record*, lxxviii (1952), 7; P. C. Barry, 'The Legislation of the Synod of Thurles, 1850', *Irish Theological Quarterly*, xxvi (1959), 149; E. Larkin, 'Economic Growth, Capital Investment, and the Roman Catholic Church in nineteenth-century Ireland', *American Historical Review*, lxxii (1966–7), 863.

at Bailieborough was in a similar position.[1] In the early 1870s Sir Thomas Burke of Galway still allowed 'the curates grazing' and all his farms had 'a priest's ground', while Bishop MacDevitt of Raphoe was himself involved in land transactions. Ten years later a French visitor contrasted the 'French curés . . . who can scarcely distinguish a beetroot and a turnip' with the 'great many' Irish priests who themselves ran 'a small farm'.[2]

Open and effective clerical action on behalf of labourers was rare —and notable for its rarity. Archbishop O'Reilly's *Catechism*, which still circulated widely in the mid-century, did, indeed, list 'defrauding the labourer of his wages' among the four sins which 'cried to heaven for vengeance' (the others included sodomy and murder), but this was more like the Church's theoretical condemnation of usury than a matter of pressing and immediate morality. Two Kildare priests found themselves totally isolated among their brethren, when, in July 1832, they tried to organize a meeting 'for the avowed purpose of increasing the wages of the labourers and of compelling every farmer and landowner, who possesses or holds twenty acres of land, to give up one acre for the benefit of the poor'.[3] Five years later it was a curate, who, together with representatives of O'Connell's General Association, 'persuaded' labourers to abandon a series of anti-farmer demonstrations in Co. Meath and was loudly heckled for his pains. The widespread labourer unrest during the 1830s was, even when it eschewed violence, greeted with marked clerical hostility. A Wicklow priest blamed paid agitators and warned that higher wages would increase the burden of tithes, while a Kildare priest plastered his parish with placards telling labourers 'to obey the law, if not, your cause will not prosper'.[4] Bishop Doyle gave labourers a lecture on the tribulations of their

[1] Bishop Browne to Tobias Kirby (Rector, Irish College Rome), 2 Nov. 1855, Kirby Papers 1668; Browne to Propaganda, 8 Oct. 1855, Propaganda Archives Rome, Acta 1856, 11; Revd W. Fagan to Cullen, 5 and 15 June 1857, Cullen Papers; *Dundalk Democrat*, 23 Apr. 1859; Lord Palmerston to Joseph Kincaid, 19 July 1852, Broadlands Archive 27M60, Box cxix, and J. Lynch to Kincaid, 6 Apr. 1857, ibid. Box clxix; Sir John Young to W. Donnelly, 8 July 1856, Young L.-B.

[2] Burke's evidence in *Galway County election petition*, H.C. 1872 (241-I), xlviii, 140-2; MacDevitt to Revd M. Curtain, 27 Mar. 1873, MacDevitt L.-B.; E. de Mandat-Grancey, *Paddy at Home* (London, 1887), p. 181.

[3] Reminiscences of Co. Cavan in Folklore Commission MS 1209; Lord Melbourne to Lord Anglesey, 25 July 1832, Melbourne Papers 94/32; Major Tandy to W. Gossett, 22, 29 July 1832, O.P. Private Index 1832/1341 cited in B. Cahill, 'The Impact of the Catholic Clergy on Irish Life 1820-45' (University College Galway MA thesis, 1975), pp. 137-8.

[4] *D.E.P.* 24 Jan. 1837 (O'Connellite organizations were notably unsympathetic to labourers: see, for example, *Pilot*, 26 Apr. 1837); Report of Chief Constable Hutton, Dunlavin, 13 Feb. 1832, O.P. 1832/255, Box 2175; printed notice dated July 1832, ibid. 1832, Box 2192.

masters: 'Consider the rents . . . look to the tithes . . . calculate the county cesses, the vestry cesses, the charges to maintain your own clergy and places of worship, and ask yourselves when the farmer has paid all these rents, tithes, taxes, and charges . . . what remains to him?' Repeated clerical condemnations of rural violence appealed especially to the 'respectable farmers', the men enrolled by a Kilkenny priest as special constables during the disturbances of May 1832, the men assured by Bishop Doyle that they might safely dismiss all labourers who failed 'in the duties they owe to God and to their employers'. In 1847 the 'principal farmers' of Limerick joined the local clergy in a desire for strong coercive action to reduce the disorder of the countryside.[1] After the Famine, though labourers ceased to occupy quite the demonic role of former times, attitudes changed only slowly and sometimes not at all. Bishop Moriarty warned the farmers of Kerry in 1872 that Home Rule meant labourer rule, and, although Archbishop Croke tried to draw attention to 'the sad case' of the labourers, priests in general were notable for their aloofness from the labourer agitation of the 1890s at a time when their prominence on tenant and Nationalist platforms was a matter of common report.[2]

If the relationship between clergy and labourers was at best distant and at worst antagonistic, the very large farmers or graziers, with their highly commercialized and increasingly capitalistic enterprises, were also often distrusted by sections of the priesthood. Not that financial considerations could be totally ignored. During the 1830s the 'large householders' in a rural Tipperary parish paid two pounds a year in dues, 'small householders' about two to five shillings, while 'more than a third of the parishioners' paid nothing at all. Gifts of a hundred guineas or of 'a fine horse, saddle, and bridle, a beautiful suit of silk vestments, and a purse containing twenty sovereigns' were difficult to overlook.[3] Occasional bonanza funerals could lift a priest from modest competence to modest luxury. In the mensal parish of Monaghan, for example, no less than a fifth and a third respectively of the total incomes for 1866 and 1877

[1] Pastoral of Nov. 1829 in W. J. Fitzpatrick, *Dr Doyle, Bishop of Kildare and Leighlin,* ii, 170; *Report from the select committee on the State of Ireland,* H.C. 1831-2 (677), xvi, 506, 600-1; Lord Clarendon (reporting G. J. Goold, RM of Rathkeale) to Lord John Russell, 3 Dec. 1847, Clarendon Papers L.-B. II.

[2] *Annual Register . . . for the year 1872,* p. 12. For Croke, see his Emly speech of July 1882 in D. B. King, *The Irish Question* (London, 1882), pp. 338–41. See also L. Kennedy, 'The early reponse of the Irish Catholic Clergy to the Co-opèrative Movement', *Irish Historical Studies,* xxi (1978), 70–1, and his unpublished paper 'The Irish Rural Social Structure: Elements of Stability and Change 1880–1914'.

[3] P. K. Egan, *The Parish of Ballinasloe,* p. 166; *Catholic Directory 1846,* pp. 212–15.

were produced by only three such funerals which between them yielded no less than £457.[1] As retailing grew in size and respectability, so large shopkeepers took on an increasing proportion of the burden. Patrick MacGill's picture of Donegal in the 1890s, with gombeen traders giving £250 each Christmas to a priest who responded from the altar with a loud 'That's the man for you', embroidered rather than counterfeited reality. And the clergy's success in stopping the spread of the co-operative movement into retailing marked the reciprocal side of a mutually beneficial relationship.[2] But sheer force of numbers, combined with the late-century sharpening of romantic feeling for 'peasant' culture, helped to attach the clergy most closely to the general class of small to middling farmers. In 1847 a Limerick observer saw such men combine with priests in alarm 'at the encroachment of the masses'. As clerical incomes plummeted in response to Famine hardship so some priests supported Protection in order 'to court popularity with the farmers', while others saw tenant-right as good, not only for farmers, but for ecclesiastics as well.[3] By 1871 Bishop Nulty of Meath had decided upon whose shoulders Holy Ireland must rest.

The purest, the holiest, and the most innocent of society in this country, at least, certainly belong to the class of small farmers. They are high enough, in the social scale, to be above the temptation of extreme want and poverty; and they are below the reach of the seductive and demoralising influences of great wealth and affluence.[4]

During the Galway by-election of 1872 the administrator of Ballymacward parish denounced those big farmers or 'landsharks' who swallowed 'up the little tenants, buying up all their little neighbourhoods', only to be contradicted by loud assertions from the 'popular' and Catholic candidate, Captain Nolan, to the effect that 'strong farmers . . . in the grazing line' (men with 80 to 400

---

[1] 'Accounts and Receipts received in the Parish of Monaghan April 1865–December 1886', Clogher Diocesan Papers DIO(RC)1/11D. Mensal parishes were those which provided the bulk of bishops' incomes.

[2] Patrick MacGill, *Children of the Dead End: The Autobiography of a Navvy* (London, [1914]), pp. 4–5 (In Folklore Commission MS 1209 it is noted that, while the shopkeepers of small Cavan towns gave a couple of pounds, 'small' farmers gave five shillings); L. Kennedy, 'The early response of the Irish Catholic Clergy to the Co-operative Movement', pp. 63–72.

[3] Lord Clare to Clarendon, 19 Aug. 1847, Clarendon Papers Box 8; *Nation*, 17 Jan. 1852; Clarendon to Russell, 9 May 1851, Clarendon Papers L.-B. VII. Already the depression of the early 1840s had cut clerical incomes (B. Molloy to W. S. O'Brien, 17 Dec. 1845, Smith O'Brien Papers MS 435). Tenant-right priests, such as Frs. O'Shea and O'Keefe, were specifically seen as defenders of the middling farmers of Kilkenny (Bishop Walsh to Cullen, 20 Nov. 1854, Cullen Papers), while the more 'moderate' priests were accused of being men 'whose fathers never held an acre of land in the county' (*Kilkenny Journal*, 25 June 1859).

[4] *Letter of the Most Revd Dr Nulty, Bishop of Meath, addressed to Lord Hartington, Chairman of the Westmeath Committee* (Dublin, 1871), p. 7—copy in Gladstone Papers Add. MS 44616.

acres) were peculiarly independent and radical of mind.[1] By the late
1870s and early 1880s a distinct, though by no means universal,
distrust of the larger agrarian capitalists had become a dominant
theme. In 1879 Bishop MacEvilly saw the modest farmers of the west
as the backbone of religion and soon the Connacht clergy were
widely engaged in the popular activity of grazier-denunciation.
A Cavan priest eulogized 'small farmers' as members of 'a class socially
the most beneficial, politically the most pure, and morally the
most virtuous'. By the end of the century the clergy were prominent in the anti-grazier movement and the bishops had come
down firmly for the redistribution of 'the great grass plains that are
at present worthless to their owners'.[2] In their attitude to women
('Go in, ma'am', said a Galway curate to a landlord's wife in 1872,
'this is no affair of yours; you don't understand such things; go into
your house; go in ma'am, out of that'),[3] in their ruralist suspicion
of the town and of urban values,[4] in their curious combination of
cute worldliness and distrust of simple material betterment,[5] many
priests reflected, and in their turn reflected back upon, the values of
those from whom they had sprung. Fr. Walter McDonald, from 1881
a professor at Maynooth, recognized, with unusual clarity, that
priests did 'not spring from the labouring class' and failed to 'sympathize with labourers as much as with farmers'. As a student at
St Kieran's College, Kilkenny, in the 1860s McDonald had been
shocked by the few city boys in the place: 'their spirit was not like
ours; they were not as simple, reverent, honest, pure; they spoke
of things that were almost unknown to [us] . . . A tenant-farmer's

---

[1] *Galway County election petition*, H.C. 1872 (241-I), xlviii, 743-4, 815, 840.
[2] MacEvilly to Kirby, 11 Dec. 1879, 'Irish College, Rome: Kirby Papers', ed. P. J.
Corish, *Archivium Hibernicum*, xxx (1972), 90 (a three-part calendar of these papers,
henceforth cited as *Arch. Hib.* xxx, xxxi, or xxxii); P. Bew, *Land and the National Question
in Ireland 1858-82* (Dublin, 1978), p. 88; *Drogheda Argus*, 27 Mar. 1880. For the later
period, see L. Kennedy, 'The early response of the Irish Catholic Clergy to the Co-operative
Movement', p. 57; D. S. Jones, 'Agrarian Capitalism and Rural Social Development in
Ireland' (Queen's University Belfast Ph.D. thesis, 1977), pp. 109-11.
[3] *Galway County election petition*, H.C. 1872 (241-I), xlviii, 444.
[4] Two comments are germane: (a) that of a Meath PP praising Frederick Lucas for
remaining uncorrupted 'by the immorality of that Babylonian metropolis, London' (F. B.
Head, *A Fortnight in Ireland* (London, 1852), p. 310); (b) Cullen to Kirby, 12 June
1872 (*Arch. Hib.* xxxii, 58) to the effect that in country districts the people 'are very
good, but in the city they are corrupted by drink and strikes'. See also L. Kennedy,
'The Roman Catholic Church and Economic Growth in nineteenth-century Ireland',
pp. 56-7; D. W. Miller, *Church, State, and Nation in Ireland 1898-1921* (Dublin, 1973),
pp. 70-6; P. O'Farrell, *Ireland's English Question: Anglo-Irish Relations 1534-1970*
(London, 1971), pp. 170-1.
[5] The former is well documented; for the latter, see the comments of a Limerick priest
in the ?1870s recorded in Mary Carbery, *The Farm by Lough Gur: The Story of Mary
Fogarty* (Cork, 1973), p. 208.

son, all my natural inclination was to act with the class to which
I belonged.'[1]

The education provided at Maynooth and elsewhere reinforced
rather than broadened such attitudes. Discipline (though not untypical of the age) was harsh and often disintegrated amidst complaints of bad food, refusals to sit examinations, and general
discontent. The staff remained rigidly aloof.[2] The course of
studies was designed to produce a narrow, well-drilled, and obedient
priest with all the strengths and weaknesses of the type. On paper
the syllabus, especially before the withdrawal of the government
grant in 1871, seemed wide and liberal, but much of it was totally
ignored.[3] The status of those staff who taught 'secular' subjects—
natural sciences, Irish, English, and so on—was low, and Fr. Nicholas
Callan (1799-1864), the pioneer of electromagnetism and the most
distinguished professor of nineteenth-century Maynooth, was forced
to spend long hours 'in making available in English the simple
devotions of St. Alphonsus Liguori'.[4] As a powerhouse of ideas,
Maynooth and the whole Irish Church was a failure. This did not,
however, prevent recommendations of candidates for the episcopacy
being sent to Rome thick with inflated claims of intellectual
achievement,[5] nor the official *History* of the college produced
in 1895 from dripping with platitudes about the scholarly virtues
of alumni and staff, many, it seems, sadly barred from publication
by fastidiousness and perfectionism alone. Most of the small
garland of religious books and pamphlets produced by Maynooth
professors were either enormous collections of antiquarian bits
and pieces or derivative pot-boilers like the scriptural studies of
Archbishop Dixon hailed by his hagiographer as 'a triumphant
refutation of Protestant calumny' and happily devoid 'of all dangerous

---

[1] W. McDonald, *Reminiscences of a Maynooth Professor*, ed. D. Gwynn (London, 1925), pp. 334, 23, 169.

[2] See Revd P. F. Moran to Kirby, 25 Aug. 1865, *Arch. Hib.* xxx, 49; 'Resolutions adopted by the Trustees of St. Patrick's College, Maynooth', June, Oct. 1871, Cullen Papers; Draft Report to the College Council, 12 Jan. 1877, Walsh Papers 368/5; J. Healy, *Maynooth College*, pp. 467, 496-7, 521; W. McDonald, *Reminiscences of a Maynooth Professor*, pp. 61-2; Revd E. J. O'Reilly to Kirby, 23 July 1839, *Arch. Hib.* xxxi, 2-3.

[3] D. A. Kerr, *Peel, Priests, and Politics: Sir Robert Peel's Administration and the Roman Catholic Church in Ireland, 1841-1846* (Oxford, 1982), pp. 237-8; H. D. Inglis, *A Journey throughout Ireland*, p. 388.

[4] P. J. McLaughlin, 'Nicholas Callan' in *Dictionary of Scientific Biography*, ed. C. C. Gillispie, 15 vols. (New York, 1970-8), iii, 17-18. Callan depended on private cash for his research into the induction coil and self-excitation in dynamo-electrical machines.

[5] See, e.g., Propaganda Archives, Acta 1833, 335 (Cashel); 1834, 778 ff. (Tuam); 1837, 20 (Derry); 1837, 158 (Waterford); 1843, 8 and 138 (Clogher); 1847, 36-8 (Cork); 1849-50, 672 (Ross); 1852, 489 (Armagh); 1852, 508 (Kilmacduagh); 1856, 657 (Galway); also Scritture riferite nei Congressi Irlanda 31, 410-12 (Ardagh 1853).

speculations'.[1] And even if the more independent writings of Patrick Murray (especially the *Tractatus de Ecclesia Christi* of 1860-6) constitute a partial exception,[2] there can be little doubt that the college ignored the intellectual currents of the time, refusing, for example, to consider even the work of the more exciting orthodox theologians such as J. B. Franzelin. 'We were', recalled Walter McDonald, 'educated in a fool's paradise . . . our strong, childlike faith kept us safe in the middle ages.'[3] Even as the century wore on and increasing prosperity might have allowed more clerical leisure, there is little evidence of mental concern or curiosity among the clergy at large. Those that had the means for extra-parochial activities, seem, in early days, to have been more interested in the hunt or even the turf, while the later emphasis on moral control left many with little time for more considered pursuits.[4] Here too the bishops were fairly typical. A few read widely, but these were often men who stood apart from their colleagues over a large range of political and other issues, such as Moriarty of Kerry (1854-81) with his contacts among English and continental Catholic intellectuals, Murphy of Cork (1815-47) with his enormous private library, or Ryan of Limerick (1825-64) whose reading encompassed not only the challenging work of contemporary Catholic theologians like Johann Möhler but also the writings of Anglican scholars and of philosophers of all persuasions.[5] In general, however, the Irish church, not without reason, set a premium on bureaucratic rather

[1] J. Dixon, *A General Introduction to the Sacred Scriptures*, 2 vols. (Dublin, 1852); see *The Life of the Most Revd Joseph Dixon, D.D. Primate of All Ireland* (London, [1878]) 'By the Author of "Jews and Jerusalem" ', pp. 76-7.

[2] K. McNamara, 'Patrick Murray's teaching on tradition' in *Volk Gottes: Festgabe für Josef Höfer*, ed. R. Bäumen and H. Dolch (Freiburg, 1967), pp. 455-79.

[3] W. McDonald, *Reminiscences of a Maynooth Professor*, pp. 30-67. McDonald's recollections were clouded by his own unhappy experience with the ecclesiastical censor.

[4] See D. O. Croly, *An Essay Religious and Political on Ecclesiastical Finance, as regards the Roman Catholic Church in Ireland* (Cork, 1834); W. J. Fitzpatrick, *Dr Doyle, Bishop of Kildare and Leighlin*, i, 104; J. H. Whyte, 'The Appointment of Catholic Bishops in nineteenth-century Ireland', p. 28. For the enforcement of strict sexual morality, see K. H. Connell, 'Catholicism and Marriage in the century after the Famine' in *Irish Peasant Society: Four Historical Essays* (Oxford, 1968), pp. 113-61. Archbishop Cullen was condemning 'foreign' dances and 'immodest and scandalous pictures' within two years of his appointment to Dublin in 1852 (*Paul Cullen*, ii, 157).

[5] On Murphy, see J. G. Kohl, *Ireland, Dublin, the Shannon, Limerick, Cork, and the Kilkenny Races* (London, 1843), p. 108 (he stood aloof from O'Connell and Repeal Banquets etc.—*C.C.* 25 May 1843). For Ryan, see *Catalogue of Books to be sold by unreserved auction at the Auction Mart, No. 6 Rutland-Street, Limerick, on Tuesday, 30th August Instant, the Select Library of the late Right Rev. Dr Ryan, Bishop of Limerick* (Limerick, [1864])—copy in C.U.L. Bradshaw Collection Hib.5.864.5. Ryan was a high Whig, see *The Letters and Diaries of John Henry Newman*, ed. C. S. Dessain and others, 26 vols. to date (London and Oxford, 1961-), xvi, 63; Lord Lismore to —, [Oct. 1833], Melbourne Papers 96/52.

than intellectual talents. 'In Ireland', wrote one exasperated scholar, 'administrators are as thick as blackberries . . . is there to be no honour for bookmen?' Typical, therefore, was Bishop Cantwell of Meath (1830-66), 'not a man of books, but rather a man of action'. Paul Cullen too, as Archbishop of Armagh 1849-52 and of Dublin 1852-78, though far from unsophisticated, was suspicious of the currents of the age.[1] Admittedly Chichester Fortescue was impressed in 1854 by the parish priest of Collon's 'odd collection of books which he had picked up—including Massillon, Bossuet, Hooker, Burke, Byron, Swift, Ben Jonson, etc.', but then Fr. Cavanagh was 'above the average of the P.P.s in intelligence and cultivation' and a staunch *opponent* of tenant-right. A querulous Carlyle, on the other hand, would allow a Donegal priest in 1849 only 'some approach to civilization: a book or two—unfortunately only mass books, directories or the like'.[2] And certainly not grossly untypical were the western priests pictured by a sympathetic Tocqueville in 1835 amidst religious engravings, coloured prints of Jesus, the Virgin, the Pope, with only newspapers or a breviary for reading matter, or the Kerry priest of the 1880s seen by another observer surrounded by pious objects, with two cats on the armchair, and a lone copy of a *Life of Pius the Ninth* on the table. Nor, especially in later years, was this the invariable result of financial difficulties, but rather of attitudes by then implicit in the very framework of clerical life. As Paul-Dubois noted, the Maynooth priest 'installed and isolated in his country presbytery, often showed very little intellectual activity and little taste for study . . his library was poor and his pen unfruitful'.[3]

Despite all this, there was considerable distrust of Maynooth in senior clerical circles, fostered not only by fears of residual scholarly independence, but also by political differences and suspicions concerning the college's Gallican origins. Cullen in particular saw these as connected dangers and believed that political radicalism and doubts as to papal authority grew from the same bush. Programmed by his long years in Rome to see the worst, he latched on to the evidence given by some of the staff to the Royal Commission of 1853, evidence which he denounced as perfectly Gallican.[4] To less

[1] W. McDonald, *Reminiscences of a Maynooth Professor*, pp. 202-3; J. Healy, *Maynooth College*, p. 556; Cullen to Kirby, 17 Apr. 1863, Kirby Papers 1863(121).

[2] Carlingford Papers Diary of C. Fortescue I (25 Sept. 1854); T. Carlyle, *Reminiscences of my Irish journey in 1849* (London, 1882), p. 247.

[3] A. de Tocqueville, *Journeys to England and Ireland*, pp. 162, 186; W. S. Blunt, *The Land War in Ireland being a personal narrative of events* (London, 1912), p. 116; L. Paul-Dubois, *Contemporary Ireland* (Dublin, 1908), p. 504.

[4] Cullen to Kirby, 9 Sept. 1854, *Arch. Hib.* xxx, 43; Cullen to Kirby, 24 Feb. 1854,

jaundiced eyes, the Gallicanism of Maynooth (which had never amounted to much), would, in the 1850s, have seemed a withered plant indeed.[1] But although some other bishops tried to give Rome a more balanced view, Cullen was able to obtain condemnations of some of the textbooks used at the college, and, after a 'tense and painful meeting' with the staff in 1855, to impose savage and humiliating demands upon Maynooth's leading theologians, George Crolly and the sea-green ultramontane Patrick Murray. The following year the hierarchy introduced further reforms: discipline was tightened and Roman devotions ordered to be performed with a new lavishness and enthusiasm, although a rearguard refusal to replace Gregorian chant with Palestrina helped nurture the continuation of mutual suspicion.[2]

As regards political orientation, Cullen and his supporters also maintained hostile views of Maynooth. Officially there had long been a desire to surround the place with a species of political cordon sanitaire. Newspapers were, rather unsuccessfully, banned, and in the 1820s the students' political interests had been narrowly focused on the quasi-religious issue of Emancipation and articulated through ringing manifestos of loyalty to the throne.[3] Twenty years later many of the staff had become firm, if circumspect, Repealers, still anxious, however, not to encourage enthusiasm. Their worries were a little arcane, for, inward-looking and isolated, they had not perceived the growth of considerable Young Ireland sympathies amongst the student body as a whole.[4] To both Tory and Whig governments the college presented a self-interestedly amiable front. The Viceroy, Lord Heytesbury, seems, in 1845, to have enjoyed

---

ibid. xxxi, 51. See also Cullen to Vice-Rector of Irish College, 30 Dec. 1853, cited in J. H. Whyte, 'The Appointment of Catholic Bishops in nineteenth-century Ireland', p. 29.

[1] P. J. Corish, 'Gallicanism at Maynooth: Archbishop Cullen and the Royal Visitation of 1853' in *Studies in Irish History presented to R. Dudley Edwards*, ed. A. Cosgrove and D. McCartney (Dublin, 1979), pp. 176–89; C. Boylan to J. Ennis, Maynooth 1820, in S. Ó Dufaigh, 'James Murphy, Bishop of Clogher, 1801–24', pp. 488–91; J. Healy, *Maynooth College*, p. 325.

[2] P. J. Corish, 'Gallicanism at Maynooth', op. cit.; Cullen to Kirby, 15 May 1856, *Arch. Hib.* xxxi, 90; Cullen to Kirby, [Oct. 1856], ibid. 62. Palestrina (or even ersatz Palestrina) had intimations of Romanità for Cullen, who opened the Synod of Thurles in 1850 with 'the old Irish College [Rome] mass in four parts quite in the Palestrina style' (Revd L. Forde to Kirby, 22 Aug. 1850, cited E. Larkin, *The Making of the Roman Catholic Church in Ireland, 1850–1860* (Chapel Hill, 1980), p. 27).

[3] For newspapers, see *Report of Maynooth Commissioners*, H.C. 1854–5 [1896], xxii, 38, and J. Healy, *Maynooth College*, p. 450; for the 1820s, see ibid. 361, 370. MacHale was among those who signed a loyalty manifesto.

[4] Revd P. Murray to O'Connell, 26 Mar. 1843, *The Correspondence of Daniel O'Connell*, ed. M. R. O'Connell, 8 vols. (Dublin, 1972–80), vii, 194–7; J. Healy, *Maynooth College*, pp. 450–1.

a remarkably jolly visit, while his successor, Lord Clarendon, was pleased to notice the president's (somewhat aspirational) comments that 'no allusion' to politics 'was ever permitted, nor was the introduction of a newspaper allowed . . . the young men are constantly admonished to abstain from politics in after life and to inculcate in their flocks obedience to the laws'.[1] In fact, the political results of a spell in the college are difficult to assess, although there is, for example, no evidence that Maynooth-trained bishops were any more likely to take up Repeal than colleagues who had been trained elsewhere.[2]

Why Cullen, who arrived in Ireland from Rome in 1850 determined to introduce ecclesiastical reforms, should have felt quite so agitated is difficult to determine. He himself was an O'Connellite of sorts, with, however, a chronic distrust of Young Ireland and of the public demonstrations for tenant-right which in the 1850s attracted a good deal of clerical support. As Cullen tightened his political grip, so the signs of disaffection grew.[3] Patrick Leahy, soon to be appointed archbishop of Cashel and a close supporter, complained in 1857 of the 'violent Young Ireland' priests produced by Maynooth, while, four years later, the students blatantly chanted a requiem for the 1848 rebel, Terence Bellew MacManus, an act of direct and open defiance.[4] Other seminaries proved little better. St Colman's, Fermoy, harboured sympathy for Fenianism's attempt to 'smash the first heretical power on the globe'. The students of the Irish College in Paris cheered John Mitchel on a visit in 1866 ('It strikes me that if they cheer *me* so warmly, they cannot be very earnestly loyal . . . Maynooth, I hear, is no better, that is, no worse'), while St Jarlath's, Tuam, was widely regarded as a 'nest' of Fenianism.[5] What, however, Cullen denounced as revolutionary seemed to

---

[1] Lord Heytesbury to Graham, 30 July 1845, Graham Papers 22/Ir; Clarendon to Russell, 31 July 1847, Clarendon Papers L.-B. I.

[2] Accepting the political labels given the episcopate in the mid-1840s in O. MacDonagh, 'The politicization of the Irish Catholic Bishops, 1800–1850', *Historical Journal*, xviii (1975), 47 (as amended by E. Larkin, 'Church, State, and Nation in Modern Ireland', *American Historical Review*, lxxx (1975), 1249–50), and connecting these with information as to education (see J. Healy, *Maynooth College*, pp. 631–4), the result is: Maynooth-educated = 18 (10 'Repealers', 8 'non-Repealers'), non-Maynooth-educated = 10 (6 'Repealers', 4 'non-Repealers'). Of course the former had been to Maynooth in its early days.

[3] See Cullen to Propaganda, 18 Mar. 1854, *Paul Cullen*, iii, 194; Archbishop Dixon to Kirby, 27 Oct. 1857, *Arch. Hib.* xxxi, 21.

[4] Patrick Leahy (then vicar-capitular of Cashel) to Cullen, 8 Apr. 1857, Cullen Papers; E. R. Norman, *The Catholic Church and Ireland in the Age of Rebellion 1859–1873*, p. 98.

[5] Revd J. O'Leary to Kirby, 5 Oct. 1865, Kirby Papers 1865(218); W. Dillon, *Life of John Mitchel*, 2 vols. (London, 1888), ii, 247. On St Jarlath's, see MacEvilly to Kirby, 14 Jan. 1878, *Arch. Hib.* xxx, 82, and M. Ryan, *Fenian Memories* (Dublin, 1945), pp. 25–9.

Fenians themselves no more than drawing-room radicalism. Cork Fenians suspected all Maynooth priests of being British loyalists, while Fr. Peadar Ó Laoghaire, who, at Maynooth in the 1860s, 'hated the English' and 'thrilled' to the rising of 1867, was distressed to find that the local boys at Macroom regarded him and all May-nooth men as tainted with a profoundly anti-national spirit.[1] But however vicarious Maynooth nationalism may have seemed to the men of the IRB, to Cullen it was profoundly disturbing. For his own diocese he sought to preserve seminarians from danger by, in 1859, establishing the College of the Holy Cross at Clonliffe along unremit-tingly Roman lines. At Clonliffe the staff was, if anything, even less distinguished, but the place was certainly orthodox: the students wore 'soutane, Roman collar, and clerical cap' from the start, and Tongiorgi, Knoll, Perrone, and Gury ruled supreme in dogmatics and morals, with the result that by the early 1880s nearly three hundred priests of ultramontane mould had been injected into the parishes of the metropolitan see.[2]

Although Cullen's impact elsewhere was tangential, his influence at the Vatican and his qualities of persistence, clarity of vision, and administrative skill made him the key figure of his time. More emotionally sensitive than is often supposed, Cullen was, none the less, a remarkably resilient man whose motto might well have been 'Never apologise, never explain'. After thirty years in Rome, his first pastoral in 1850 expressed characteristically continental fears of revolution, socialism, communism, sedition, bad books, 'harmful' systems of education, and proselytism, not all of them, perhaps, germane to the contemporary Irish experience. After burning his fingers with too enthusiastic an endorsement of the brittle and wily lawyer, William Keogh (upon whose electoral ambitions at Athlone he had poured the 'protection of the Immaculate Mother of our Redeemer'), he developed deep suspicions of any form of politics devoid of a thoroughly clerical dimension.[3] Religion was, indeed, literally for him the sum of politics, and preferences were to be developed above all upon the basis of loyalty to the Church. He never attended government levees as his predecessor at Dublin, Archbishop Murray, had done, and he tried to stay aloof from both 'Castle dinners *and* . . . patriots'.[4] Inflexible and narrow of mind,

---

[1] E. R. Norman, *The Catholic Church and Ireland in the Age of Rebellion 1859–1873*, p. 99; P. Ó Laoghaire, *My Own Story*, pp. 61–2.

[2] Cullen to Kirby, 13 Sept. 1859, *Arch. Hib.* xxxi, 72; [R. Sherry], *Holy Cross College, Clonliffe, Dublin: College History and Centenary Record* (Dublin, 1962), pp. 50–3, 74–7.

[3] *Paul Cullen*, ii, 43; Cullen to Revd M. O'Neill (PP, Athlone), 22 Oct. 1851, ibid. ii, 101–3.

[4] J. J. Taylor to Kirby, 5 Jan. 1854, *Arch. Hib.* xxxi, 15; Cullen to Kirby, 16 Feb.

he yearned to inflate the 'Index', was ready to see conspiracies (especially masonic or 'Young Ireland' conspiracies) behind every movement of which he disapproved, and was so prone to view all things through a remorselessly denominational lens that even the Crimean War became, above all else, a great and essentially Catholic crusade.[1] In the end, however, Cullen's intransigence was overlaid by a political flexibility both surprising and un-Roman. Conscious of the difference between English and Italian liberalism, he located the dangers of 'libertà alla Mazziniana' within Fenianism rather than within the Liberal Party at Westminster. Adherence to constitutional nationalism did not prevent secret meetings with leading Whigs who found him 'a quiet, simple-mannered, self-collected man'. A vigorous distrust of Palmerston and Gladstone on Italian (and other) grounds and a strong dislike of virtually all Englishmen (and of English Catholics especially) did not stand in the way of alliances over the issues of land and disestablishment.[2] Above all, however, order must be maintained, for the 'first duty of every Catholic was to support the government unless it attacked the Church'. And, as in secular affairs, so in ecclesiastical, the duty of the ruler was to rule. Not long after his appointment as Coadjutor Bishop of Kerry, David Moriarty received the following advice: 'I hope you will not distress yourself too much in hearing confessions . . . Every priest can hear confessions but the bishop must *govern*'.[3]

Thus for Cullen the nature of the episcopate lay at the centre of the church's well-being, and, as a result, he was to spare no efforts to secure the appointment of loyal men. Above all, that most noticeable characteristic of the pre-1850 bench—fissiparous free-wheeling

1853, ibid. xxxi, 45; Cullen to Propaganda, [1857], *Paul Cullen*, iii, 250; Cullen to Kirby, 13 Apr. 1875, Kirby Papers 1875(197). On levees, see Cullen to Kirby, 16 Jan. 1854, *Arch. Hib.* xxxi, 82; Revd W. Walsh to Kirby, 18 May 1885, ibid. xxxii, 3.

[1] For his sectarian dining habits, see letter to Kirby, 28 July 1865, Kirby Papers 1865 (171); for the Index, letter to Kirby, 10 Jan. 1851, *Arch. Hib.* xxxi, 37–8; for Young Ireland priests (among much else), letter to Kirby, 2 Jan. 1867, Kirby Papers 1867(2); for Freemasons, letter to Cardinal Fransoni, 19 Feb. 1852, *Paul Cullen*, iii, 110, to Kirby, 5 Apr. 1867, Kirby Papers 1867(128), and Revd P. F. Moran to Kirby, 29 July and 11 Aug. 1868, Kirby Papers 1868(227A and 238A); for his 'spiritual imperialism', letter to Propaganda, 28 July 1855, *Paul Cullen*, ii, 199; for Crimean War, Pastoral of 21 Apr. 1856, summarized ibid. ii, 215.

[2] Cullen to Kirby, 3 Dec. 1863, Kirby Papers 1863(316); Carlingford Papers Diary of C. Fortescue II (28 Mar. 1857); Cullen to Kirby, 16 Mar. 1860, *Arch. Hib.* xxxi, 75; Cullen to Revd B. Woodlock, 17 Mar. 1868, *Paul Cullen*, iv, 232; E. D. Steele, 'Cardinal Cullen and Irish Nationality', *Irish Historical Studies*, xix (1975), 254. At the Dublin City election of 1868 Cullen brought himself to vote for the Protestant Liberal: 'I suppose no cardinal ever voted for a Quaker before ' (to Kirby, 18 Nov. 1868, Kirby Papers 1868(355)).

[3] E. Lucas, *The Life of Frederick Lucas M.P.*, 2 vols. (London, 1886), ii, 123; Cullen to Moriarty, 20 Jan. 1855, *Paul Cullen*, ii, 188.

in politics and church government—seemed to Cullen to require immediate reversal along centralized and Roman lines. A complete *Gleichschaltung* was, of course, impossible, given the personalities involved—most toweringly that of Archbishop MacHale of Tuam. But Cullen's eventual success was remarkable, though not in every sense permanent. As early as 1850 he had, like some ecclesiastical actuary, informed Rome of the advanced age, ill-health, and imminent demise of bishops unsympathetic to the cause, and by the middle of the decade had already consolidated an effective majority by means of influence at Rome over crucial appointments in the dioceses of Armagh, Achonry, Ardagh, and Ross.[1] The deep splits of the 1840s over the university question were allowed a final flowering at the Synod of Thurles in 1850 when Cullen's denunciation of the Queen's Colleges was only very narrowly carried. Thereafter, however, they were overcome, partly because the death of Archbishop Murray of Dublin in 1852 left the opposition leaderless and partly because of Cullen's impact on episcopal appointments.

The short-term effect of all this should not, however, be exaggerated. In the first place, difficulties and disputes over other matters continued; in the second, there is no evidence that an increasingly united bench exercised greater influence over national or political affairs than had been the case during the O'Connellite era. Indeed, bereft of effective secular leadership, the bishops wallowed in the rudderless and localist atmosphere of the 1850s and early 1860s like so many sleek and well-armed men o' war, fully-crewed perhaps, but without compass, sextant, or chart. As permanent apostolic delegate, Cullen's national powers were limited to the implementation of the Thurles decrees, so that even the reorganized system of regular episcopal meetings, of which much had been expected, too often degenerated into angry, bitter, and unproductive argument.[2] Divisions continued, with MacHale's free-booting obstructionism, the 'unsoundness' of bishops like Moriarty of Kerry and Delany of Cork on the education question, and a widespread lack of enthusiasm for Cullen's new Catholic University maintaining the unhappy traditions of earlier years. Although by 1861 Cullen was beginning to think the whole business a waste of time, his steady attrition in the face of MacHale's refusal to sign letters or even to attend meetings did eventually bring about a sense of uneasy calm and make

---

[1] E. Larkin, *The Making of the Roman Catholic Church in Ireland, 1850–1860*, pp. 42–3 and Chapters Two to Five.

[2] On the position of the delegate, see Cullen to Kirby, 3 June 1869, *Arch. Hib.* xxxi, 71, and [Mar. 1861], ibid. xxxii, 48. On the complicated matter of bishops' meetings, see S. Cannon, *Irish Episcopal Meetings, 1788–1882: A juridico-historical Study* (Rome: Pontifical University of St Thomas, 1979).

possible the consolidation of the work of Thurles at the Synod of Maynooth in 1875. However, soon after Cullen's death in 1878 it became clear that 'cohesion' had depended upon personality rather than upon reformed institutions, and for a time meetings reverted to the relaxed free-for-alls they had been in pre-Cullen days.[1] Cullen's efforts to avoid disunity were therefore only partially and sporadically successful. Several bishops blatantly refused to follow his guide-lines on how the clergy should behave in matters of public politics, and while he himself (in this following Archbishop Murray, with some of whose attitudes he had more in common than is often supposed) was able to keep his own Dublin priests in check,[2] others were either less successful or of a quite opposite disposition. Some, like Cantwell of Meath, openly and enthusiastically backed the cause of Independent Opposition. Others, like Butler of Limerick and Murphy of Ferns, were men of a generally Whiggish frame of mind. Others again had no hesitation in making their private dislike of Cullen's activities widely known, not least among sympathetic Protestant landlords.[3]

Even had all between bishop and bishop suddenly become as sweet as sugar, effective action would still have depended upon the relationship between individual bishops and their clergy. And here episcopal authority was increasing only very slowly, and there is no evidence that, for example, bishops were becoming any more successful in controlling, guiding, or containing the political proclivities of the priesthood at large. The experiences of the so-called 'moderate' bishops of the 1840s, who had suffered a cut-back in dues and had 'been treated with the utmost insult' after suspending priestly activists, were repeated throughout the following decades. Cautious bishops realized that they 'could not take a prominent part against the feelings of the majority of the priests' and that often persuasion was the only (rather feeble) weapon in their armoury.[4] Some, indeed, continued to hold relaxed views of the whole business and

---

[1] Cullen to Kirby, 15 Feb. 1861, 29 Mar. [1861], *Arch. Hib.* xxxii, 47-8; Cullen to Kirby, 15 Apr. 1862, ibid. xxxii, 54; S. Cannon, *Irish Episcopal Meetings*, pp. 83-6; Bishop Moran to Kirby, 19 July 1880, *Arch. Hib.* xxx, 95; Bishop Power to Kirby, 29 Mar. 1881, ibid. xxx, 103.

[2] C. J. Woods, 'The Politics of Cardinal McCabe', pp. 101-10; Jacqueline Hill, 'The Role of Dublin in the Irish National Movement 1840-48' (University of Leeds Ph.D. thesis, 1973), pp. 50-2, 89; D. A. Kerr, *Peel, Priests, and Politics*, pp. 89-92.

[3] Cantwell to Kirby, 1 Oct. 1852, Kirby Papers 1049; Butler to Kirby, 5 Feb. 1862, ibid. 1862(22); Lord Carew to Clarendon, [25 Nov. 1851], Clarendon Papers Box 8; Lord Rosse to Lord Naas, 6 May 1859, Mayo Papers MS 11036.

[4] Clarendon to Russell, 1 Oct. 1847, Clarendon Papers L.-B. I, and 3 May 1848, L.-B. II; P. Joyce to M. J. Blake, 18 July 1857, Blake of Ballyglunin Papers M6936/78, apropos MacEvilly of Galway; Furlong of Ferns to Cullen, 26 June 1857, Cullen Papers.

(to Cullen's dismay) confined themselves to amused hopes that electoral contests would pass without too much 'sacerdotal knight errantry'. Even admirers, like Leahy of Cashel, were driven to dismaying feebleness: 'I was simply in the chair [for an election meeting of Cashel priests]. I was pressed to hold the meeting, and I do assure you on my oath, that I had rather to follow than to lead.'[1] Lurid views of rampant episcopal power bear little relation to reality. Nearer the truth was the Kerry land agent, Sam Hussey: 'The fact is, his bishop can do very little with a treasonable man when once he has been inducted a parish priest.'[2] Curates could, indeed, be moved from the scene of electoral action and some were certainly exiled to remote and undesirable parishes. Cullen, for example, removed a Louth curate in 1852 after altar denunciations of a particularly savage kind. In 1872 Moriarty peremptorily sent a Home Rule priest to a parish described as 'the Siberia of the diocese', while Delany despatched two curates from comfortable Cork City parishes to more rural parts.[3] But this was nothing new. Ten years before Cullen's arrival, Bishop Foran of Waterford (not himself 'a working patriot') had 'inflicted a sentence of transportation to mountain districts on two of the best priests in the diocese . . . for the active part they took at the late Dungarvan Repeal meeting'.[4] The ways in which authority was exercised depended upon inclination and upon the individual's view of episcopal duties and rights. Here the dividing lines cut across distinctions based on simple loyalty to the new Archbishop of Dublin. Cullen's closest, if rather spineless, ally, Dixon of Armagh, specialized in despairing jeremiads about the awfulness of it all, interspersed with unconvincing promises to be tough and ruthless with priests who preferred 'miserable politics' to 'practical religion'.[5] By contrast, another Cullenite, MacEvilly of Galway, was prepared to issue from the altar of his cathedral a rallying cry to the priests of his diocese: 'The everlasting Gospel which they are commanded to preach embraces not merely spiritual

[1] Walshe of Kildare and Leighlin to Cullen, 3 Apr. 1857, Cullen Papers; *Minutes of evidence taken before the select committee on the Tipperary election*, H.C. 1867 (211), viii, 194.

[2] S. Brooks, *Aspects of the Irish Question* (Dublin, 1912), p. 187; S. M. Hussey, *Reminiscences of an Irish Land Agent*, p. 118.

[3] Cullen to Kirby, 13 June 1852, *Arch. Hib.* xxxi, 43, and Lord Bellew to Cullen, 4 May 1852, Cullen Papers; B. Ó Cathaoir, 'The Kerry "Home-Rule" by-election, 1872', *Journal of the Kerry Archaeological and Historical Society*, No. 3 (1970), 161; C. J. Woods, 'The Catholic Church and Irish Politics 1879–92', pp. 68–70.

[4] P. Q. Barron to T. M. Ray, 25 Oct. and 13 Nov. 1841, O'Connell Papers N.L.I. MS 13623.

[5] Dixon to Cullen, 21 Feb. 1854, Cullen Papers; Dixon to Kirby, 13 Apr. 1857, Kirby Papers 1925 A.

doctrines, but duties of a temporal nature . . . the legitimate influence of the clergy has been at all times the firmest bulwark of society.' And when in 1869 the administrator of a Galway parish returned from the pulpit of his own chapel one Sunday he was met by Mac-Evilly, who had been listening to his failure to preach with sufficient vigour in the Gladstonian cause, and sent smartly back to try again.[1] A similarly tough response was shown by the orthodox Cullenite, Bishop O'Brien of Waterford, who successfully 'silenced the [clerical] brawlers on both sides' at the General Election of 1859, by the Whiggish and anti-Cullenite Bishop Ryan of Limerick, who, while locked in a bitter dispute with his reformist coadjutor, none the less adopted an extremely energetic policy towards politically inclined clerical subordinates, and by Moriarty, many of whose views diverged widely from those of Cullen but who forbade priests from entering election towns 'under pain of suspension *ipso facto*' and thought nothing of forcing recalcitrant priests to 'beg pardon on bended knees'.[2] In short, those who followed Cullen's high view of authority, especially in relation to political priests, did not necessarily follow his line on other matters. Slattery of Cashel, who generally supported Cullen, was feeble and weak in his response to clerical indiscipline in political affairs. Browne of Elphin, a devotee of MacHale, tried far harder to act as episcopal governor, though admittedly without much success.[3] Indeed, practical authority was by no means proportional to the efforts and intentions involved. Browne found himself ignored by his clergy when he enjoined abstinence from politics in 1853; Fallon of Kilmacduagh (a disciple of MacHale) simply closed his eyes to local nastiness; Walsh of Ossory had little success in swinging his clergy behind the 'moderate' candidate in 1859; Duggan of Clonfert (a man of radical agrarian views) was following as much as leading his priests at the Galway by-election of 1872; McGettigan of Armagh failed totally in 1874 to push his priests in the required electoral direction.[4] It

---

[1] *Western Star*, 14 Nov. 1868, 6 Mar. 1869; MacEvilly to Kirby, 1 Aug. 1869, Kirby Papers 1869(219); Lord Strathnairn to Duke of Grafton, 22 Mar. 1869, Strathnairn Papers Add. MS 42825; MacEvilly to Cullen, 9 Apr. 1872, Cullen Papers.

[2] O'Brien: O'Brien to Kirby, 7 May 1859, Kirby Papers 2354. Ryan: *C.C.* 13 Apr. 1859; J. Spaight to Naas, 4 May 1859, Mayo Papers MS 11036; C. B. Lyons to Cullen, 19 Apr. 1859, Cullen Papers; Cullen to Kirby, 7, 10, 19 Feb., 27 Mar., 11, 17 Apr. 1863, and to Propaganda, 27 Apr. 1863, *Paul Cullen*, iv, 134–42. Moriarty: Moriarty to Lord Denbigh, 20 Jan. 1867, Derby Papers 155/3; Moriarty to Cullen, 10 Feb. [1872], Cullen Papers.

[3] Cullen to Kirby, 9 Dec. 1853 and 16 Mar. 1857, *Arch. Hib.* xxxi, 50, 63; Browne to Kirby, 14 Sept. 1853, Kirby Papers 1259, and 2 Nov. 1855, ibid. 1668.

[4] Browne to Kirby, 14 Sept. 1853, Kirby Papers 1259; Evidence about Fallon by Cornelius O'Brien MP in *Minutes of evidence taken before the select committee on the*

remains, therefore, the case that factions within the hierarchy shifted and changed from one issue to another and that the touchstone of general sympathy for Cullen's approach to church and religion cannot be used as an invariable indicator of outlook and response. In this, as in so much else, Cullen's most authentic forerunner was the despised Archbishop Murray, whose view of episcopal authority and political action so closely foreshadowed that of his successor in the metropolitan see.[1]

Cullen's impact upon the structure—as opposed to the views—of the hierarchy proved, in general, short-lived. Under the new regulations for the appointment of bishops introduced in 1829 by which the parish priests of a vacant diocese met to select three names for submission to Rome, ordinaries had tended to come from the local area, to have themselves been parochial clergymen, and, increasingly, to have attended (or even taught at) Maynooth.[2] In Cullen's view this had exacerbated the inward-looking, localist, and sometimes scandalously unreformed nature of the Church, and the cumulative effect of the appointments made during his ascendancy in Ireland —when, as papal delegate he often managed to circumvent formal procedures—was to diminish local influence, inject outsiders into moribund dioceses, and reduce the impact of Maynooth. This is shown by an analysis of episcopal appointments between 1816 and 1895.

	Maynooth-educated		Educated elsewhere	
	number	per cent	number	per cent
1816–35	18	54.5	15*	45.5
1836–55	19	79.2	5	20.8
1856–75	18	64.3	10	35.7
1876–95	28	87.5	4	12.5

* Includes three ex-members of Maynooth staff.

Clare election petition, H.C. 1852–3 (595), ix, 791; for Walsh, *Kilkenny Journal*, 16 Apr., 14 May 1859 (while 25 priests supported Walsh's man, 46 supported the more radical candidates Moore and Greene); for Duggan, *Galway County election petition*, H.C. 1872 (241-I), xlviii, 222–3; for McGettigan, L. J. McCaffrey, 'Irish Federalism in the 1870s: A Study in Conservative Nationalism', *Transactions of the American Philosophical Society*, new series lii, part 6 (1962), 20; D. Thornley, *Isaac Butt and Home Rule* (London, 1964), p. 181.

[1] For an instance of Murray's views, see Clarendon to Russell, 1 Feb. 1848, Clarendon Papers L.-B. II. On Murray, see D. A. Kerr, *Peel, Priests, and Politics, passim.*
[2] J. H. Whyte, 'The Appointment of Catholic Bishops in nineteenth-century Ireland', pp. 12–32.

Cullen, therefore, only momentarily stemmed the rising tide of Maynooth men which was to reach levels after his death higher even than those that had so disturbed him on his arrival.[1] Similarly, Cullen's attempts to check the promotion to the hierarchy of local priests ('accustomed to live among the abuses so common in rural parishes') were quickly reversed after his death, the relevant proportions of such men being roughly: 1800-49—50 per cent, 1850-78 —33 per cent, 1879-1900—50 per cent.[2]

II ORGANIZATION AND PRACTICE

There can be little doubt that patterns of clerical behaviour, standards of Church organization, and levels of adhesion to ultramontane practices and beliefs did not remain constant throughout the nineteenth century. However, the changes involved were slow, and far from even, as to either time or place. It was not, in other words, a case of a rank and weed-overgrown garden startled to reformed and devotional life by the stern Roman gardener dispatched to Ireland by Pius IX in 1849. Certainly, the discipline and moral standards of some of the clergy in the early years of the century left much to be desired. Greed, drink, and (to a much lesser extent) women were too often found in clerical company.[3] The episcopate on Cullen's arrival included at least two topers and several others whose life-styles had become relaxed to the point of abandonment. The clergy of Ardagh were, many of them, heavy drinkers and an episcopal candidate for that diocese was 'involved' with his 'serving woman', drank like a fish, and owned a racehorse.[4] Furthermore, the peripatetic nature of episcopal life in certain sees reflected the still primitive state of diocesan organization.[5] Most spectacular of all,

---

[1] Cullen to Kirby, 12 Mar. 1854, *Arch. Hib.* xxxi, 84. Between 1836 and 1849 not one non-Maynooth bishop was appointed; between 1858 and 1877 not one ex-member of staff was appointed. Indeed, of the twenty-three staffmen elevated 1816-95, only two were elevated during Cullen's time. And even if Maynooth in 1878 was not the Maynooth of 1830, Cullen, to the end, remained suspicious of the place.

[2] Cullen to Propaganda, 23 July 1855, cited J. H. Whyte, 'The Appointment of Catholic Bishops in nineteenth-century Ireland', p. 30; ibid. 29-31.

[3] E. Larkin, 'Church and State in Ireland in the Nineteenth Century', *Church History*, xxxi (1962), 294-306, and 'The Devotional Revolution in Ireland, 1850-75', pp. 627-30. On drink, see J. E. Bicheno, *Ireland and its Economy: being the result of observations made in a tour through the country in the Autumn of 1829* (London, 1830), pp. 190-1.

[4] Cullen to Propaganda, 28 Sept. 1851, cited J. H. Whyte, 'The Appointment of Catholic Bishops in nineteenth-century Ireland', pp. 24-5; ibid. 25-6. See also D. Bowen, *Souperism: Myth or Reality: A Study in Souperism* (Cork, 1970), pp. 54-65, and P. J. Murphy, 'The papers of Nicholas Archdeacon', *Arch. Hib.* xxxi, 130.

[5] For example, the bishops of Clonfert oscillated between Loughrea and Ballinasloe during the early-nineteenth century (P. K. Egan, *The Parish of Ballinasloe*, pp. 243-4);

perhaps, were the occasional, but noisy and extremely embarrassing, apostasies which took place among the priesthood. In 1836 half-a-dozen cases were known to a well-informed observer, among them those of the articulate and able Fr. David Croly and of the Crotty cousins who had undertaken a double abandonment.[1] Croly, a parish priest in Cork, left with a bang in the shape of a startling pamphlet on *Ecclesiastical Finance, as regards the Roman Catholic Church in Ireland* (Cork, 1834) in which he made a number of (by no means fanciful) revelations regarding his colleagues' inflated financial aspirations. But while Croly headed speedily for England, Michael and William Crotty remained at Birr in King's Co. (where the former had been curate) ministering to a schismatic congregation of parishioners who openly supported them against the Bishop of Killaloe.[2] Others acquired a more local renown: the Killala priest who turned Anglican in 1845 after money differences with his bishop, Fr. Denis Brasbie of Dingle who fled into the arms of the evangelicals in 1848, Revd T. W. Dixon who was driven from his native north Mayo after attempts to serve the area as parson, Fr. Mulholland, who, after a row with the Archbishop of Armagh in 1834, set up a schismatic congregation in the diocese of Cloyne.[3] But even the statistics collected by Protestant proselytizers (the maximum tide-mark in the matter) were relatively modest and the Priests Protection Society (founded in 1844 to provide financial and moral support for disaffected Catholic clergymen) claimed to have helped no more than fourteen priests and twenty-four 'reformed Romanist students intended for the priesthood' in the first seven years of operation, and this at a time when there were about 2,400 secular priests in Ireland and after a blanket distribution of no less than 202,910 of the society's propagandist leaflets.[4]

Elphin was ruled from both Roscommon and Athlone by Bishop Plunkett (1815–27) and later from Sligo (Plunkett to Propaganda, 6 Feb. 1826, cited E. Larkin, 'Church and State in Ireland in the Nineteenth Century', p. 299); the bishops of Killaloe moved between Limerick, Newmarket-on-Fergus, Quin, Castleconnell, Sixmilebridge, Birr, Nenagh, and Killaloe, and did not settle at Ennis until the late 1880s (T. Kelly, 'Ennis in the Nineteenth Century' (University College Galway MA thesis, 1971), p. 45).

[1] Revd E. Barron to Cullen, 16 Sept. 1836, Irish College Rome, Cullen Papers. The most detailed account of Croly and the Crottys is in D. Bowen, *The Protestant Crusade in Ireland, 1800–70: A Study of Protestant–Catholic relations between the Act of Union and Disestablishment* (Dublin, 1978), pp. 144–52.

[2] See also N. W. Senior, *Journals, conversations, and essays relating to Ireland*, 2nd edn., 2 vols. (London, 1868), ii, 26–8; *Diary of Colour-Sergeant George Calladine*, ed. M. L. Ferrar, pp. 194–5.

[3] *Catholic Directory 1846*, p. 218; P. de Brún, 'An tAthair Brasbie', *Journal of the Kerry Archaeological and Historical Society*, No. 2 (1969), 38–58; D. Bowen, *The Protestant Crusade in Ireland, 1800–70*, p. 144; Cullen to Propaganda, [1844], *Paul Cullen*, iii, 29–30.

[4] *Fifth Report of the Priests Protection Society* (Dublin, 1851)—copy in C. U. L. Bradshaw Collection Hib.5.851.11. The society's income for 1844–50 was £5,388.

The pre-Famine church, in other words, though still far from the perfection which must be the (unattainable) aim of all religious institutions, was not experiencing that haemorrhage of personnel which might have been expected to flow from spiritual or physical decrepitude and chaos. It is, indeed, important to overlook neither the substantial expansion of plant and reforms in discipline and devotional practice which had been implemented during the first half of the century, nor the continued existence of problems of all kinds in the later period. Although, with a few exceptions, the evidence is inevitably impressionistic, there can be little doubt as to the substantial and fundamental nature of the reforms introduced throughout the years before the Famine. Cullen's long absence in Rome after 1820 distorted his view of contemporary Irish realities and led him to see only the rough and nothing of the smooth. In 1833 he wrote to his sister of the 'truly edifying' devotion of the Italians to the Blessed Virgin, of the churches dedicated to her, and of the ubiquity of the rosary, all in sad contrast to the supposed state of things at home.[1] In fact, devotions of a similar flavour, whether to Mary or other saints, had long been a feature of Irish Catholicism, and the Archdiocese of Dublin (where Murray—seen by Cullen as representing the spirit of cisalpine particularism—ruled) long the centre of this new ultramontane style. The *Catholic Directory* for 1821 reveals a vigorous religious life in both the urban and the extensive rural parts of the archdiocese. The rosary and stations of the cross were regularly recited and benediction given in many chapels. The range of sodalities, confraternities, and societies was impressively large: Trinitarian Orphan Societies, a Virgo-Marian Orphan Society, Purgatorian Confraternities, Sodalities of the Most Sacred Heart of Jesus, Confraternities of the Sacred Scapular of Mount Carmel, of the Cord of St Francis, of the Blessed Virgin Mary, of the Sacred Rosary, and of the Sacred Cincture of the Blessed Virgin of Consolation. Catechism classes were held in each chapel by the members of the Confraternity of the Christian Doctrine. This last organization, founded during the Counter-Reformation, was widespread throughout Ireland by the 1820s and included both men and women who took communion monthly and pledged themselves to a 'vigilant superintendence of one another's moral conduct and the duty of teaching catechism at the parish chapel on Sundays'.[2] The enthusiastic devotions to the Blessed Virgin and

---

[1] Cullen to Margaret Cullen, 25 July 1833, *Paul Cullen*, i, 206–7. See also Cullen to Michael Cullen (brother), 9 July 1836, ibid. i, 223.

[2] P. Cunningham, 'The Catholic Directory for 1821', *Reportorium Novum: Dublin Diocesan Historical Record*, ii (1960), 324–63; P. K. Egan, *The Parish of Ballinasloe*, p. 126;

the widespread saying of the rosary which had been a feature of penal days were continued unbroken into the emancipated Church of the early nineteenth century.[1] Nor were pious confraternities confined to Dublin. Bishop Young of Limerick told Rome in 1802 of the flourishing confraternities established by his predecessor. The raising of the eighteenth-century feast of the Sacred Heart to the rank of a Greater Double in Ireland in 1831 encouraged the foundation of sodalities dedicated at that devotion. By 1845 confraternities of the Immaculate Heart of Mary had spread as far as the western diocese of Clonfert. Bishop Doyle did much to encourage religious societies in Kildare and Leighlin between 1819 and 1834 and extended the work of his predecessor, Bishop Delaney (1787–1814), who had already built large churches furnished in Roman style, established processions of the Blessed Sacrament during the octave of Corpus Christi, and founded a Perpetual Adoration Confraternity. Maynooth too in the 1830s supported many sodalities—or 'nurses of bigotry' in the sour words of a Protestant observer.[2] Archbishop Murray, in particular, had, on becoming metropolitan, been anxious to propagate Marian devotions in both extent and intensity and had introduced to Dublin the feast of the Seven Dolours, had urged his priests to recite various Marian offices, had set up the 'Month of Mary' in 1840, and had encouraged the formation of circles of the 'living rosary'.[3]

The Association for the Propagation of the Faith, founded in France in 1822 to support missionary work, was extended to Ireland in 1838 by Murray and spread rapidly throughout the country. In 1844 the St Vincent de Paul Society (founded in France in 1833) began its activities in Dublin. It too spread rapidly and was a mark of the Church's increasing involvement in large-scale and practical

I. Murphy, 'Primary Education' in *A History of Irish Catholicism*, ed. P. J. Corish, V, Fascicule 6 (Dublin, 1971), pp. 2–3; Evidence of Archbishop Murray in *First Report of the Commissioners of Irish Education Inquiry*, H.C. 1825 (400), xii, 887–914.

[1] J. Brady and P. J. Corish, 'The Church under the Penal Code' in *A History of Irish Catholicism*, ed. P. J. Corish, IV, Fascicule 2 (Dublin, 1971), pp. 72–3.

[2] Bishop Young to Propaganda, 29 Nov. 1802, cited E. Larkin, 'Economic Growth, Capital Investment, and the Roman Catholic Church in nineteenth-century Ireland', p. 855; T. P. Cunningham, 'Church Reorganization' in *A History of Irish Catholicism*, ed. P. J. Corish, V, Fascicule 7 (Dublin, 1970), p. 29; P. K. Egan, *The Parish of Ballinasloe*, p. 264; W. J. Fitzpatrick, *Dr Doyle, Bishop of Kildare and Leighlin*, i, 116–18, ii, 517–19. For Maynooth, see Mr and Mrs S. C. Hall, *Ireland*, ii, 285.

[3] W. Meagher, *Notices of the Life and Character of His Grace Most Revd Daniel Murray, late Archbishop of Dublin* (Dublin, 1853), pp. 131–5. The 'living rosary' did not reach rural Limerick until the 1860s (another example of devotional patchiness) when it caused some confusion: 'I'd like ye to tell me, if I join it, will I get a higher place in Heaven then me mother have? She wasn't belongin' to any society' (Mary Carbery, *The Farm by Lough Gur*, pp. 64–5).

charity work among the poor.[1] And although many church leaders remained ambivalent and even hostile towards the powerful temperance campaign of Fr. Mathew in the 1830s and 1840s, here was another sign of vigorous moral and spiritual organization among the Catholic population; and, however much Fr. Mathew tried to separate himself from the Repeal agitation, the two campaigns inevitably crossed each other, and neutral observers and government agents alike were convinced of the reality of the connection.[2] Not that there was any particular political pattern in episcopal enthusiasm, with, in 1840, the various available combinations spread broadcast among the hierarchy: Temperance Repealers (Browne of Galway, Coen of Clonfert, Foran of Waterford, Kennedy of Killaloe, Blake of Dromore, Feeny of Killala, Keatinge of Ferns, Cantwell of Meath), Temperance non-Repealers (Ryan of Limerick, Murray of Dublin, Haly of Kildare and Leighlin, Browne of Kilmore, Kernan of Clogher, Kinsella of Ossory, McGettigan of Raphoe), non-Temperance Repealers (MacHale of Tuam, MacNicholas of Achonry, Burke of Elphin, French of Kilmacduagh and Kilfenora, Higgins of Ardagh, MacLaughlin of Derry, Slattery of Cashel), and fully negative non-Temperance non-Repealers (Crolly of Armagh, Denvir of Down and Connor, Egan of Kerry, Murphy of Cork, Crotty of Cloyne and Ross).[3] None the less, it was certainly possible to harness temperance to devotional reform, and later movements, such as the League of the Cross, the sodalities dedicated to the Sacred Heart and Sacred Thirst, and the Pioneer Total Abstinence Association, were inextricably identified with the growing Catholic triumphalism of the time.[4]

---

[1] *D.E.P.* 20 Sept. 1838; *Catholic Directory 1846*, p. 186 (in 1844 Ireland provided almost a twentieth of the association's total receipts); W. Meagher, *Most Revd Daniel Murray*, p. 146; T. P. Cunningham, 'Church Reorganization', p. 31; Timothy P. O'Neill, 'The Catholic Church and Relief of the Poor 1815–45', *Arch. Hib.* xxxi, 132–45.

[2] J. G. Kohl, *Ireland*, p. 59; Printed Notice (?Dec. 1842) in Downshire Papers D671/C/12/822; Downshire to Dr J. Sheil, 3 Dec. 1842, ibid. D671/C/12/821; T. G. Stoney, *A Short Address as a word of advice to the small farmers and peasantry of the County of Tipperary* (Dublin, 1843), pp. 17-18; *The Irish Journals of Elizabeth Smith 1840–1850*, ed. D. Thomson and M. McGusty (Oxford, 1980), p. 15 (18 June 1840); *D.E.P.* 15 July 1837; Replies to government circular of 1840 on connections between temperance and Repeal (O.P. 1840 131/10) cited H. F. Kearney, 'Fr. Mathew: Apostle of Modernisation' in *Studies in Irish History*, ed. A. Cosgrove and D. McCartney, pp. 164–75; Elizabeth Malcolm, 'Temperance and Irish Nationalism' in *Ireland under the Union: Varieties of tension: Essays in honour of T. W. Moody*, ed. F. S. L. Lyons and R. A. J. Hawkins (Oxford, 1980), pp. 69–114.

[3] Kinsella *privately* favoured a form of Repeal. Feeny was technically apostolic administrator of Killala, Bishop O'Finan having been decanted to Roman retirement. See also Munster Bishops to Propaganda, 1847, Propaganda Archives, Acta 1847, 386.

[4] Elizabeth Malcolm, 'Temperance and Irish Nationalism', pp. 103–14. The later

Substantial progress was also made by the pre-Famine Church in the business of education at all levels. New diocesan colleges enlarged the provision of seminary training and acted as feeder establishments for Maynooth. By the early 1820s nuns and teaching brothers ran seventy schools for the middling classes, while 352 free day schools—frequently attached to chapels—and 9,352 pay schools with 394,732 pupils catered for a wider market. The introduction of the National System by the Whig administration in 1831, despite all suggestions to the contrary, greatly increased clerical control. Many of the 'new' national schools were merely old pay schools now subsidized by the Government, and, in general, public finance was channelled through the hands of the clergy.[1] The growth of religious publishing reflected the increasing literacy and confidence of the Catholic population. In the period 1809–45 publishers in Dublin, Belfast, and Newry alone *sold* some 279,000 copies of Catholic Bibles and Testaments.[2] By the mid-1840s Dublin suported four major Catholic publishers as well as numerous booksellers supplying a vast range of religious literature from the decrees of the Council of Trent to William Graham's *Complete Manual of Catholic Piety* (1845). Depositories and warehouses stocked and sold ecclesiastical goods—crucifixes, fonts, statues, beads, medals, 'lawn and linen albs, and cinctures, embroidered mitres, in gold and silver cloth, and . . . pontifical shoes and gloves'.[3] Murray's efforts were augmented by, among others, those of Crotty, who encouraged religious orders and revitalized liturgical practices in Cloyne and Ross during the 1830s and 1840s, of O'Reilly, who, as early as 1801, reformed the system of visitation in Armagh, of Plunkett, with his energetic introduction of confraternities, clerical meetings, Christian teaching, and a modern approach to confirmation in Elphin between 1814 and 1827, and

temperance campaign was not without political overtones. The Ballinasloe movement, for example, was infiltrated by Fenians and maintained a highly political library and meeting hall (P. K. Egan, *The Parish of Ballinasloe*, pp. 274–5), while, during the 1880s, the numerous western branches of the League of the Cross provided not only billiards, skittles, and bands, but nationalist newspapers, prints, and cartoons (G. Pellew, *In Castle and Cabin*, pp. 50–6).

[1] Mary Daly, 'The Development of the National School System, 1831–40' in *Studies in Irish History*, ed. A. Cosgrove and D. McCartney, pp. 150–63. See also I. Murphy, 'Primary Education', and S. V. Ó Súilleabháin, 'Secondary Education' in *A History of Irish Catholicism*, ed. P. J. Corish, V, Fascicule 6 (Dublin, 1971), pp. 1–83; M. de L. Fahy, *Education in the Diocese of Kilmacduagh in the Nineteenth Century* (Gort, 1972); M. Brenan, *Schools of Kildare and Leighlin 1775–1835* (Dublin, 1935).

[2] *Catholic Directory 1846*, pp. 176–8. Many more were published in Cork or imported from abroad.

[3] Ibid. 453–567.

of Murphy, who could report to Rome in the early years of the century the 'astonishing progress in acquiring a competent knowledge of the Christian doctrine' shown by the laity in the diocese of Clogher.[1] At the same time, Doyle inaugurated a local devotional revolution in Kildare and Leighlin, with reforms of clerical standards, liturgical practice, and educational provision. In Ossory there was no shortage of priests and a modern attachment to the sacraments was being introduced. In 1840 Waterford Cathedral could boast 600 communicants on the first Sunday of every month. A priest could tell Tocqueville in 1835 of the 'religious fervour of the people' in a Mayo parish where regular confession was the universal norm.[2] When Dublin's pro-cathedral was dedicated in 1825, the 'sustained dignity and splendour' and the 'rigid adherence to every liturgical direction' impressed the faithful and marked a new and real point of ceremonial departure. The papal jubilee was celebrated with massive devotional enthusiasm: throngs at communion, multitudes renewing their baptismal vows 'with uplifted hands and streaming eyes [as] they literally shouted aloud their eternal renunciation of Satan'. In Ossory too there were daily jubilee sermons at Callan and regular nightly sermons during Lent, practices, which, by 1839, had spread to the neighbouring diocese of Ferns, where at New Ross the Revd Mr Murphy ('a fine preacher') 'lectured during Lent on the commandments'. Special Marian devotions during May were common, not only in Dublin, but also in Cork, Waterford, Clonmel, Carrick-on-Suir, and elsewhere, while novenas for St Patrick were said in various southern towns.[3]

Cullen did, of course, give added impetus to such existing tendencies. Armagh Cathedral was soon awash with Palestrina. Cullen himself presided over the Synod of Thurles in cope of crimson and gold cloth and mitre of white satin and silver tissue decorated with the cross and paschal lamb in raised bullion and set with diamonds, rubies, amethysts, and emeralds. The Dublin provincial synod of 1853 was more splendid still: 'the clergy of all orders, chaunting the hymns and psalms prescribed . . . all attired in surplices, soutanes and caps . . . the parochial secular dignitaries and clergy and the Very

---

[1] J. Healy, *Maynooth College*, p. 401; É. Ó Doibhlin, *Domhnach Mór (Donaghmore)*, pp. 211-12; S. Ó Dufaigh, 'James Murphy, Bishop of Clogher, 1801-24', pp. 479-82, 423, 459-60, 464.

[2] *Catholic Directory 1840*, p. 301; W. J. Fitzpatrick, *Dr Doyle, Bishop of Kildare and Leighlin*, i, 106-18; A. de Tocqueville, *Journeys to England and Ireland*, pp. 142, 145, 191.

[3] W. Meagher, *Most Revd Daniel Murray*, pp. 98-9, 106-7; *The Diary of Humphrey O'Sullivan*, ed. M. McGrath, 4 vols. (London and Dublin, 1936-7), ii, 203, 243; *A Young Irishman's Diary (1836-1847) Being extracts from the early journal of John Keegan of Moate*, ed. W. Clare (March, Cambs., 1928), p. 19; *Catholic Directory 1846*, pp. 220, 227, 229.

Revd the Secretaries of the synod robed in surplices . . . the deacon in chasuble of crimson tissue, worn over alb, amict, and soutane, with cincture and stole over one shoulder.'[1] But such positively eye-splitting brilliance was in no sense out of line with the existing ultra-montane rituals of the Dublin archdiocese, rituals which had also for some time been energetically—if more modestly—implemented throughout the country as a whole. That, indeed, the impact of Cullen must be seen within an evolutionary context is emphasized by a survey of the state of affairs just before the outbreak of the Famine. Dublin, of course, was in the lead, with its many societies, its Archconfraternity of the Immaculate Conception (to which twenty-five churches throughout Ireland were attached), its twenty-six nunneries, priests' library, asylums for 'penitent Magdalens', and its enormous range of liturgical provision: novenas, devotions, adorations, expositions.[2] But other dioceses too were making substantial progress. Derry had schools and confraternities in every parish, many with libraries. Clogher's 'grand diocesan seminary' was almost complete, while devotions to the Sacred Heart and the Virgin were, together with numerous sodalities, widespread throughout the diocese. Raphoe had a large number of temperance societies and a 'classical seminary'; Down and Connor a college in 'flourishing condition'; Kilmore many chapels and a seminary opened in 1839; Ardagh a new cathedral under construction; Dromore 'several elegant churches'; Ossory numberless confraternities; Ferns religious book societies in 'almost every parish' as well as the usual devotional organizations. Kerry had Christian Doctrine Confraternities, circulating libraries, and schools. Tuam boasted St Jarlath's College, convents, monasteries, and the Third Order of St Francis. In Clonfert the rosary was widely said, Purgatorial Societies were replacing traditional wakes, and individual sodalities could claim over 900 members. And the gradually evolving nature of the process is further revealed by the chronology of developments in such vital areas as parochial missions, church music, clerical dress, ecclesiastical building, and the vexed question of 'stations'.

Parochial missions, given usually by Dominicans, Vincentians, or Redemptorists, were used by Cullen as a vehicle for religious

---

[1] Revd L. Forde to Kirby, 22 Aug. 1850, cited E. Larkin, 'The Devotional Revolution in Ireland, 1850–75', p. 645; *Freeman's Journal*, 23 Aug. 1850; *Catholic Directory 1854*, pp. 121–2. It should, however, be noted that MacHale's attire when consecrating Tuam Cathedral in 1836 had been far from dingy: 'beautiful long rich white satin, overlaid with gold, in a pattern of chaste and splendid execution . . . a variety of diamonds . . .' (B. W. Noel, *Notes of a short tour through the midland counties of Ireland*, pp. 175–6).

[2] *Catholic Directory 1846*, pp. 176–8, 186, 247–326 for this and subsequent information.

revival, and there are many references to them in his early Irish correspondence. But the practice had in fact been introduced by Murray with the help of the Vincentians at Athy in 1842 and had spread rapidly in the neighbouring dioceses. When, by 1869, almost every parish in the country had experienced at least one visitation, the effort had been supported, not only by 'reformers' like Moriarty, but also by men of very different stamp, such as O'Donnell of Galway and MacHale himself.[1] Similarly, Cullen's advocacy of musical reform, which had more to do with Romanità than artistic sensibility, depended ultimately upon the lively and demotic, if often unsophisticated, traditions of earlier times. By the 1820s an enthusiastic choirmaster in Co. Wexford could already report

I have two fine choirs in the two chapels and music to no end, and we sing the Mass and Office of the Dead . . . in grand stile on every corpse . . . We do have great work here on festivals. On Corpus Christi we have a procession of the Blessed Sacrament, on Palm Sunday a procession of palm, on 15th of August, our patron day, a grand solemn mass and procession of candles. Every Sunday in Lent we sing round the Stations, and on other festivals we have a benediction of the Blessed Sacrament, all which serve very much to excite devotion in the people.[2]

At Callan the chanting of Tenebrae during Holy Week took place in 'a very beautiful chapel' recently decorated with ornamental plaster work, while the chapel at Bagenalstown in Carlow boasted a uniformed band which played at Mass and also provided entertainment for voters incarcerated during the 1841 election to prevent them polling against the Catholic and Repeal candidates.[3] As in other matters, the early foundations were slowly extended under Cullen, though often with more enthusiasm than expertise. Moriarty's consecration in 1854 was done to 'pure Gregorian chant'. For Cardinal Wiseman's attendance at the consecration of St Michael's, Ballinasloe, in 1858 'Ilari's mass was chaunted in a solemn and effective manner by a choir of clergymen, assisted by some accomplished amateur

[1] Cullen to Kirby, 6 June 1852, 20 Mar., 8 June 1853, 23 Nov. 1855, *Arch. Hib.* xxxi, 43, 46, 47, 56; T. P. Cunningham, 'Church Reorganization', pp. 31-2; E. Larkin, 'The Devotional Revolution in Ireland, 1850-75', pp. 637-8; K. O'Shea, 'David Moriarty (1814-77): Reforming a Diocese', *Journal of the Kerry Archaeological and Historical Society*, No. 4 (1971), 112-13; Cullen to Kirby, 13 June 1852, 28 Jan. 1853, *Arch. Hib.* xxxi, 43, 45. See also E. Hosp, 'Redemptorist Mission in Enniskillen, 1852', *Clogher Record*, viii (1975), 268-70.

[2] J. Brady and P. J. Corish, 'The Church under the Penal Code', pp. 65-7; M. Wall, *The Penal Laws 1691-1760* (Dundalk, 1961), p. 59; B. P. Keegan to M. Doyle, OFM, 14 Jan. 1822, in P. Ó Súilleabháin, 'Sidelights on the Irish Church, 1811-38', *Collectanea Hibernica*, ix (1966), 74-6.

[3] *The Diary of Humphrey O'Sullivan*, ed. M. McGrath, i, 241, 243; *The Reign of Terror in Carlow, comprising an authentic detail of the Proceedings of Mr O'Connell and his followers* (London, 1841), pp. 57-8.

vocalists'. Ennis pro-cathedral shared the conducting skills of a Signor Nono with the local brass band.[1] Not until 1888, however, did Maynooth appoint a (German) priest to teach 'organ and Gregorian chant', and certainly the general standard of musical performance remained, well into the twentieth century, unimpressive, timid, and saccharine.

Sartorial reform was capable of more rigorous resolution, but here too changes pre-dated the Famine and their extension continued long thereafter. Already at the end of the eighteenth century some priests had begun to replace the frieze of the peasantry or the wig and buckled shoes of the urban bourgeoisie with sober black. But Tocqueville still found priests in 1835 dressed 'like a layman',[2] while Carleton's *Traits and Stories of the Irish Peasantry* (1830-3) reveal as keen an eye for textiles as for place, personality, and mood.

Father Philemy [continental-trained PP] had long hair according to the old school . . . His coat had large double breasts, the lappels of which hung down loosely on each side . . . his black small-clothes had silver buckles at the knees, and the gaiters, which did not reach up so far, discovered a pair of white lamb's-wool stockings, somewhat retreating from their original colour. Father Con [Maynooth-trained CC] had a coat which though not well made, was of the best glossy broadcloth, and his long clerical boots went up about his knees like a dragoon's.

('The Station')

The Bishop wore black silk stockings, gold knee-buckles to his small-clothes, a rich ruby ring on his finger, and a small gold cross, set with brilliants, about his neck . . . his manner altogether impressive and gentlemanly.

('Denis O'Shaughnessy going to Maynooth')

By the 1840s, although the Capuchin, Fr. Mathew, was still sporting an outfit 'plain and scrupulously neat . . . nothing ultra-clerical', many priests were already noticeable for their obviously religious attire. Indeed, an observer at a Cork election, when asked how he knew certain men at the booths to be priests, answered, 'They wear a very remarkable dress, and I took them to be so from their dress.'[3] But, even though the wearing of formal clerical uniform was made

---

[1] *Paul Cullen*, ii, 189; *The Sermons, Lectures, and Speeches delivered by His Eminence Cardinal Wiseman, Archbishop of Westminster, during his tour of Ireland in August and September 1858* (Dublin, 1859), p. 16; *Clare Freeman*, 21 Jan. 1861, 4 Jan. 1862, cited T. Kelly, 'Ennis in the Nineteenth Century', p. 272.

[2] J. Brady and P. J. Corish, 'The Church under the Penal Code', p. 53; A. de Tocqueville, *Journeys to England and Ireland*, p. 162.

[3] J. Birmingham, *A Memoir of the Very Reverend Theobald Mathew, with an Account of the Rise and Progress of Temperance in Ireland* (Dublin, 1840), p. 26; J. Smyth, *The Elector: Containing a true and faithful picture of the awful state of the representation of parts of the Counties of Tipperary and Waterford* (Dublin, [1853]), p. 61; *Report from the select committee on the Cork City election petition*, H.C. 1852-3 (528), xi, 13.

compulsory by the Synod of Thurles, other witnesses still found it impossible to distinguish priests by costume alone at the Clare election of 1852, while, six years later, the Ballinasloe police arrested an English monsignor and 'other priests in Roman attire' in the act of ringing the bell of the Convent of Mercy at 4.30 a.m.—thinking them, from their dress, to be a 'group of evangelicals' out to cause a pre-breakfast riot. Indeed, it was many years before all priests wore even the Roman collar.[1] Similarly, in the parallel matter of nomenclature, changes were promoted by a desire to increase the 'separation' of the priest behind special uniforms and titles. Although the laity in general had long referred to all priests as 'Father', the formal usage of ecclesiastical authority had reserved that term for members of religious orders, preferring to call seculars and students 'Mister', the English equivalent of the Latin 'Dominus'. By the 1870s, however, things had changed. William Walsh (the future Archbishop of Dublin) saw to it that Maynooth students applied 'Father' in all cases, while the bishops in general had already silently elevated themselves from 'Right' to 'Most Reverend', the latter title having been previously reserved (as in the Anglican church) for metropolitans alone.[2]

Perhaps the most impressive of the achievements of the Church before 1850 was its enormous investment and progress in building work. During the period between 1817 and 1847 alone some four million pounds was probably spent on building. Under Murray (1823–52) the Dublin diocese acquired some £1,200,000 worth of property, of which £700,000 represented expenditure on no less than ninety-seven churches.[3] In 1825 Tuam, with 106 congregations, had only fifteen slated chapels complete and some eighty inadequate thatched chapels so small that worshippers were often driven out of doors. Within twenty years no less than sixty new chapels and a cathedral had been built.[4] Patrick McGettigan, Bishop of Raphoe 1820–61, took his diocese from a period when

---

[1] 'A Barrister', *Observations on Intimidation at Elections in Ireland by Mob Violence and Priestly Intimidation* (Dublin, 1854), p. 29; P. K. Egan, *The Parish of Ballinasloe*, p. 251.

[2] W. McDonald, *Reminiscences of a Maynooth Professor*, pp. 31–2. See the change in episcopal nomenclature between the 1859 and 1860 issues of the *Catholic Directory*.

[3] E. Larkin, 'Economic Growth, Capital Investment, and the Roman Catholic Church in nineteenth-century Ireland', pp. 856–8; W. Meagher, *Most Revd Daniel Murray*, p. 146.

[4] Evidence of Archbishop Kelly in *Report from the select committee appointed to inquire into the State of Ireland, more particularly with reference to the circumstances which may have led to disturbances in that part of the United Kingdom*, H.C. 1825 (129), viii, 255–6; *Cork Examiner*, 10 Apr. 1843, cited J. Coombes, 'Catholic Churches of the Nineteenth Century: Some Newspaper Sources', *Journal of the Cork Historical and Archaeological Society*, lxxxi (1975), 2.

it had not a single church of any substance to one of ample pro-vision.[1] Clogher experienced a building revolution between 1786 and 1814 when thirty 'good chapels' were erected. By 1841 Elphin already had seventy-two chapels, among which twenty-six of the forty-four slated ones had been put up since 1825. Of the hundred or so chapels in Co. Clare just before the Famine, more than a quarter had been built during the 1820s and 1830s, while at least eighty chapels were built or substantially renovated in Co. Cork between 1805 and 1848.[2] Near Tuam Tocqueville saw a typical example of a chapel, which, however modest, marked an enormous advance: 'a small building roughly built in stone and with a slate roof, whose mode of construction could be studied from the inside as it had neither vault nor ceiling; the floor is of beaten earth, the altar was of wood . . . the nave was cut in two by a wooden platform . . . [to accommodate] a large number of people without increasing the size.' But even by then such places already represented the lower reaches of a lengthy architectural continuum. Newspaper accounts of many of the Co. Cork churches built at the time indicate (even allowing for the inflations of local pride) substantial investment: 'Handsome Gothic', 'lately erected beautiful and commodious', '£2000 to date', 'six or seven thousand pounds', 'Gothic pilasters', 'spacious', '£4500', 'magnificent'.[3] Constructional metamorphoses had become common. St Patrick's in Cavan Town was built in 1823 for £1,000, a plain oblong building 80 by 44 by 29 feet. Early in the 1850s the place was refurbished and extended, and with a poor-law valuation increased from £44 to £72 now left both the Presby-terian meeting-house (£20) and the Anglican church (£57) far behind. In 1862 it became Kilmore's cathedral and remained such until replaced by Ralph Byrne's extraordinary neo-classical edifice in the 1940s. In Ballinasloe the simple whitewashed plain-glassed chapel of 1807 was 'improved' in 1826; then money was collected in the 1840s for a replacement, which, designed by Pugin and J. J. McCarthy, was consecrated in 1858 with a nave more than 153 feet long, marble altar, and stained glass. Further embellishments, including the addition of a spire and pine pitch seating, were carried out in the 1870s and 1880s.[4]

[1] Cullen to Propaganda, 3 May 1861, *Paul Cullen*, iv, 93. Many must obviously have been built before 1850.

[2] S. Ó Dufaigh, 'James Murphy, Bishop of Clogher, 1801–24', p. 422; *Catholic Directory 1842*, p. 322; A. MacLochlainn, 'Social Life in County Clare, 1800–1850', *Irish University Review*, ii (1972), 64–6; Cork figures calculated from J. Coombes, 'Catholic Churches of the Nineteenth Century', pp. 6–12.

[3] A. de Tocqueville, *Journeys to England and Ireland*, pp. 168–9; J. Coombes, 'Catholic Churches of the Nineteenth Century', pp. 6–12.

[4] T. P. Cunningham, 'Cavan Town in 1838, I', *Breifne*, iii (1969), 528–51; P. K. Egan,

Pre-Famine building was not, however, confined to the simplest and the simple.[1] The few unobtrusively handsome urban churches built before 1800—of which St Patrick's, Waterford is a beautiful and rare survivor—were added to in something approaching a flood. A few samples give the flavour. In 1810 the Augustinians at Callan built a new church costing £4,000. Dublin's splendid pro-cathedral was slowly completed at a cost of £50,000, while at least seven *major* churches were built in Dublin between 1830 and 1845 alone. The attractively Gothic Carlow Cathedral was completed in the 1830s for £30,000.[2] The interior of Cork's pro-cathedral was substantially rebuilt in 1820 with fancy lierne vaulting and the outside subjected to prolonged Gothicization. St Malachy's Cathedral at Belfast was completed in 1844 along stylishly romantic lines with fan-vaulting based on the Henry VII Chapel in Westminster Abbey. Handsome classical churches appeared at Cork in the shape of St Patrick's (1836) and St Mary's on Pope Quay (1839). Pugin is credited with Ramsgrange and Bree churches in Wexford (both 1838) and certainly designed St Michael the Archangel, Gorey (begun 1839), St Peter's, Wexford (begun 1840), and various other Wexford churches, though his most notable effort was Killarney Cathedral, which had cost over £20,000 by the time its very incomplete state was consecrated in 1855. A further host of much less successful— though far from inexpensive—cathedrals was launched during the twenty years before the Famine: at Ballina (for which MacHale collected £12,000), Tuam, Ennis, Longford, Armagh, and Kilkenny. St Eugene's, Derry, was started in 1851 and dedicated in 1873 after an expenditure of £40,000. Archbishop Leahy had little trouble on begging tours in the 1860s for the heavy Lombardo-Romanesque Cathedral of the Assumption completed at Thurles in 1872.[3] During the twenty-eight years of his episcopate (1865-93) Bishop Donnelly of Clogher raised almost £100,000 towards the capital costs of a new cathedral, seminary, and hospice, quite apart from annual collections for Peter's Pence (about £8,400 per decade), special collections for Maynooth (£1,177 in 1882) or the Pope's

---

The Parish of Ballinasloe, pp. 162, 247-9, 282, and *Sermons . . . by . . . Cardinal Wiseman . . . during his tour of Ireland*, pp. 10-12.

[1] In what follows I rely (unless otherwise stated) on T. P. Kennedy, 'Church Building' (thin on dates) in *A History of Irish Catholicism*, ed. P. J. Corish, V, Fascicule 8 (Dublin, 1970); B. de Breffny and G. Mott, *The Churches and Abbeys of Ireland* (London, 1976), Chapters 7 to 10; personal observation.

[2] M. Craig, *Dublin 1660-1860* (Dublin, 1969), p. 293; A. de Tocqueville, *Journeys to England and Ireland*, p. 134.

[3] Leahy to Daunt, 2 Oct. 1866, O'Neill Daunt Papers MS 8046.

jubilee (£728), and the usual parochial receipts from annual dues and from baptisms, weddings, and funerals.[1]

The laity could not fail to be impressed by these new citadels of faith.

> The grand description the stain'd glass windows,
> And most amazing for to beho'd,
> And the bells melodiously sounding daily,
> To call'd the people to save their souls,
> The splendid organ construo' in order,
> Before the Alter is most complete,
> With a choir of chanters to sing most charming,
> Saying Gloriu in Excelses Deo.[2]

But whatever the physical conspicuousness of post-Famine building, the crucial provision of accommodation for the faithful had been largely supplied by 1850. Of course replacements and extensions continued, but the actual number of churches (admittedly for a shrinking population) increased little between 1845 and 1891.[3]

Year	No. of churches
1845	2,218
1851	2,197
1861	2,339
1871	2,349
1881	2,380
1891	2,410

Of the 2,339 churches in Ireland in 1861 about 2,000 had been built since 1800, the great bulk of them clearly before 1850.[4] Architecturally, therefore, the Cullen era must essentially be seen as one of gilding (and all too often garishly gilding) the lily of substantial pre-Famine achievement.

One of the reforms Cullen was most anxious to effect was the abolition of 'stations' or the holding of confession and Mass (usually twice yearly) in selected private houses throughout rural parishes. Introduced originally because of the shortage of Mass houses, the practice had become encrusted with jovial secularity in the shape of heavy eating and drinking and with expensive competition between families for the privilege of clerical visitation. It represented, in

[1] Donnelly's 'Book of Accounts', Clogher Diocesan Papers DIO(RC)1/11C.

[2] 'A New Song in Praise of the Catholic Church of Kanturk' (?1860s), sheet in B. L. Pressmark C.116.h.3.

[3] T. P. Kennedy, 'Church Building', p. 1; Figures taken from the *Catholic Directory* one year later than the year given.

[4] *The Church Establishment in Ireland: The Freeman's Journal Church Commission* (Dublin, 1868), p. 377.

starkest form, that peculiarly Hibernian mingling of the sacred and profane so repugnant to Cullen's religious sensibilities. But here too, not only had serious attempts at reform been made during the years immediately after 1800, but Cullen's own interventions were to prove far from irresistible or decisive.[1] Admittedly, the Dublin province eventually adopted strict legislation, but substantial loopholes long allowed a flexible interpretation.[2] Archbishop Slattery of Cashel, with strong support from Delany of Cork and even from the Cullenite Keane of Ross, blandly ignored the spirit of the new rules.[3] Keane, who in 1857 was translated with Cullen's approval to the important see of Cloyne, did not hesitate to defend stations to Rome on the grounds that they alone allowed the priest to cover the whole of a parish, not merely 'peccatores reconciliantes et panem vitae distribuentes', but also 'scandala si quae sint removentes, dissentiones componentes, amicitiam et charitatem cum omnibus colentes, consiliarorum munere fungentes'.[4] In the Clonfert of the early 1870s stations also remained 'frequent' and recalcitrant voters were threatened with withdrawal from the list should they reject the priest's political line.[5] Thus, although extreme abuses were, indeed, brought under control—save in Tuam where they continued unabated—stations survived Cullen's onslaughts throughout the provinces of Cashel, Tuam, and Armagh, and even in the diocese of Kildare in the province of Dublin.[6]

Institutional change is usually a slow process and so it was in the case of the Irish Church. Many of the traditional 'problems' continued a lively and far from underground existence. Priests continued quite simply to go mad. They continued to cause scandal by playing cards for money and fighting in public. They continued to be involved in unfortunate liaisons with women. Above all, they continued to drink. Bishop Fallon of Kilmacduagh (whose appointment had been supported by Cullen in 1852) was, it seems, so keen an imbiber that

---

[1] Cullen to Kirby, 28 Jan. 1853, *Arch. Hib.* xxxi, 45; W. J. Fitzpatrick, *Dr Doyle, Bishop of Kildare and Leighlin*, i, 105-6; J. A. Murphy, 'The Support of the Catholic Clergy in Ireland, 1750-1850', *Historical Studies*, v (1965), 111-12. For a fictional account, see Carleton's 'The Station' in *Traits and Stories of the Irish Peasantry* (1830-3),

[2] J. Ahern, 'The Plenary Synod of Thurles II', pp. 4-5; P. C. Barry, 'The Legislation of the Synod of Thurles, 1850', pp. 139-42.

[3] See the various letters from Cullen and others in Propaganda Archives, Acta 1854, 267-318; also Revd D. O'Brien to Kirby, 20 Sept. 1853, *Arch. Hib.* xxxi, 14; Keane to Kirby, 2 Nov. 1853, ibid. xxxi, 15; Cullen to —, [1853], ibid. xxxi, 47; Cullen to Kirby, 17, 20 Oct. 1853, 7 Jan. 1854, ibid. xxxi, 48-51.

[4] Keane to Propaganda, 4 Jan. 1854, Propaganda Archives, Acta 1854, 305ᵛ.

[5] *Galway County election petition*, H.C. 1872 (241-I), xlviii, 150-1. See also K. O'Shea, 'David Moriarty (1814-77)', pp. 123-4.

[6] Cullen to Kirby, 6 Apr. 1875, *Arch. Hib.* xxx, 78; to Leahy, 26 Oct. 1875, *Paul Cullen*, v, 218; to Kirby, 12 Nov. 1876, *Arch. Hib.* xxxii, 59.

Bishop MacEvilly was dispatched in 1863 to call casually to see if drink was evident in bottle or on breath.[1] The Cashel clergy were still drinking too much on Croke's appointment in 1875. Eight years later Croke suffered agonies when one of his priests had to be carried, in full view of hostile Protestant witnesses, from a carriage at Mallow railway station after having smashed the windows in a fit of loud and alcoholic rage. Moriarty thought drink the main source of clerical scandal, while Cullen's successor, McCabe, had long drawn-out problems with drunken priests.[2] Change in every sense proved complicated and ambiguous. Tuam, so often and rightly denounced as the epicentre of traditional particularism, could, none the less, at MacHale's funeral in 1881 muster all the spectacular manifestations of ultramontane liturgy: gorgeous ceremonial and a procession with convent children, boys from the Christian Brothers' schools, members of the Female Sodality of the Sacred Heart and of the Burial Society, Children of Mary, the Brotherhood of the Sacred Heart ('a host in itself'), members of the Third Order of St Francis, and many more. Yet, as late as 1880 episcopal meetings were still often confused, angry, disorganized, and ineffective.[3] Liturgical reform too proceeded only in fitful bursts: even attendance at Sunday Mass could still be casually overlooked by small Galway farmers in 1872.[4] Many churches continued to present a primitive appearance: 'There was no music or any other art [at Spiddal, Co. Galway in the 1870s and 1880s]. Nor were there benches or chairs, just a mud floor . . . the country people knelt in the body of the church on their haunches and heels, women on one side, men on the other, the children playing about quietly in and out.'[5] Nor by the late 1860s had the devotional revolution hit Patrickswell near Limerick City, where a plain chapel could still boast 'no singing, no incense,

---

[1] Bishop O'Brien to Kirby, 16 May 1857, Kirby Papers 1939, H. A. Herbert to T. Larcom, 30 June 1857, Larcom Papers MS 7578; Dean Kieran to Archbishop Dixon, 30 Mar. 1854, Dixon Papers VII/2, Cullen to Kirby, 3 July 1863, *Paul Cullen*, iv, 148; Bishop Ryan (Coadjutor Killaloe) to Cullen, 13 Jan. 1876, Cullen Papers; MacEvilly to Cullen, 14 Aug. 1863, ibid., also Propaganda Archives, Acta 1852, 501–11.

[2] M. Tierney, *Croke of Cashel: The Life of Archbishop Thomas William Croke, 1823–1902* (Dublin, 1976), p. 71; Croke to Archbishop Walsh, 2 Jan. 1883, Walsh Papers 350/3; K. O'Shea, 'David Moriarty (1814–77)', p. 122; McCabe to Fr. J. Slattery, 8 Dec. 1883, 17 Jan. 1885, Walsh Papers 350/5.

[3] MacEvilly to Cullen, 12 Jan. 1878, Cullen Papers; MacEvilly to Kirby, 10 Feb. 1878, 20 Oct. 1879, *Arch. Hib.* xxx, 81, 87; B. O'Reilly, *John MacHale, Archbishop of Tuam*, ii, 690–1; Bishop Moran to Kirby, 19 July 1880, *Arch. Hib.* xxx, 95.

[4] M. Tierney, *Morroe and Boher: The History of an Irish Country Parish* (Dublin, 1966), p. 45; *Galway County election petition*, H.C. 1872 (241-I), xlviii, 737–8.

[5] Maud Wynne, *An Irishman and his Family: Lord Morris and Killanin* (London, 1937), p. 15. See also the account by a Kilmacduagh PP of the state of his chapel about 1868 in *Galway County election petition*, H.C. 1872 (241-I), xlviii, 846.

no candles, no pictures nor stations of the cross'. In 1880 parts of Connemara contained people 'who have never received any religious instruction', while six years later Wilfrid Scawen Blunt found Mass in rural Kerry 'a very old-fashioned business . . . the altar was very simple, not to say slovenly, and the priest's vestments put on all awry'.[1]

III THE SACRED AND THE PROFANE

Religious life does not, in any case, change course merely in response to episcopal command. Revolutions in outlook and behaviour, in practice and belief, depend ultimately upon deeper shifts in the practices of a community and in the relationships within it. Such shifts are almost always slow. Yet real they were in this instance and without them little lasting institutional reform would have been possible at all. It is not necessary to establish a precise genealogy for certain forms of popular religious behaviour to be able to assert the pervasive presence throughout the early nineteenth century of practices not recognized by the canon of Tridentine, let alone neo-ultramontane, Catholicism. Some aspects of the semi-formal rural celebration of seasons, of seedtime and harvest, had indeed remained entirely unconcerned with any form of Christian influence.[2] Nor had the vigorous realm of fairies, of magical cures, semi-professional 'healers', the evil eye, changelings, and curses yet yielded to the enervating clasp of national religion and reformed manners. None the less, the massive fairy emigration following the last of their great assemblies in 1839 marked (in the end a disastrous) cowardice in the face of modernization.[3] The hidden became more hidden still. Those who had once been both numerically dominant and the chief proponents of popular esotericism (labourers, cottiers, itinerants, and the like) maintained only the latter role after 1850. Of the servants on a two-hundred-acre Limerick farm, the farmer's daughter noted that, 'although they were thankful for holy days and went to mass, they were really more interested in the old Irish world where fairies, witches, and banshees took the place of our angels and

---

[1] Mary Carbery, *The Farm by Lough Gur*, pp. 26, 99; B. H. Becker, *Disturbed Ireland: Being the letters written during the winter of 1880–81* (London, 1881), p. 80; W. S. Blunt, *The Land War in Ireland*, p. 115.

[2] Thus, of the 104 known hill and lakeside assemblies for Lughnasa (beginning of harvest) celebrations still active in the early-nineteenth century, 82 had no known religious connection (Máire MacNeill, *The Festival of Lughnasa: A Study of the Survival of the Celtic Festival of the Beginning of Harvest* (Oxford, 1962), pp. 68 ff.).

[3] W. G. Wood-Martin, *Traces of the Elder Faiths of Ireland: A Folklore Sketch*, 2 vols. (London, 1902), ii, 4.

saints'. Some pre-Famine observers, though still recording both
the picturesque activities of 'sybilline dealers in pishogues' and
the killing of children by parents who thought them fairy changelings, none the less believed that national schools and Fr. Mathew's
temperance campaign were jointly eroding fairy power. Others were
still impressed by vigorous belief and by the mirrored relationship
between the here and the beyond: 'You hear of the Limerick fairies,
and the Donegal fairies, and the Tipperary fairies, and the fairies of
two adjoining counties have their faction fights.'[1] 'Fairy-doctors'
enjoyed extensive practices. Concealed significance and hidden
signatures required formal understanding. Magic powers called forth
rebuttal and defence. Conscious use of the evil eye and the malign
potential of 'unlucky folk' were still, it seems, equally to be feared
and averted.[2]

This manner of reflecting the transcendence of things in action
and belief did not, of course, remain hermetically separated from the
preoccupations of formal Christianity. Spread as it was throughout
the country it inevitably attracted the attention of clergymen,
Protestant[3] as well as Catholic. In addition, the Catholic priest
was himself sometimes seen, and on occasion is known to have
acted, as a species of superior magician calling on a particular set of
supernatural weapons for the implementation of particular ends.
The implications behind a good deal of electoral cursing were not
lost on countrymen at large. In 1840 a Carlow priest announced
from the altar that 'the parties were all damned . . . that they walked
the earth as accursed beings'. Various priests threatened to turn
recalcitrant voters into 'goats', 'puck-haunes', or, less specifically,
into 'amphibious animals'. Fr. Hickey of Waterford rode along the
Ardmore strand on a white horse and shouted at electors on a ship
chartered by the Tory candidates, 'My curse and the curse of God
upon you all . . . mark me, I will raise such a storm around that

[1] Mary Carbery, *The Farm by Lough Gur*, p. 158; Mr and Mrs S. C. Hall, *Ireland*,
iii, 31, 237, 248-9, 269; J. G. Kohl, *Ireland*, pp. 33-5; H. D. Inglis, *A Journey throughout
Ireland*, pp. 165-6.

[2] W. R. Le Fanu, *Seventy Years of Irish Life, Being Anecdotes and Reminiscences*
(London, 1928), p. 39 (first published 1893); William Wilde in *The Census of Ireland for
the year 1851. Part V*, H.C. 1856 [2087-I], xxix, 719 (see also T. Crofton Croker, *Researches
in the South of Ireland illustrative of the Scenery, Architectural Remains, and the Manners
and Superstitions of the Peasantry* (London, 1824), pp. 78-99); R. P. Jenkins, 'Witches and
Fairies: Supernatural Aggression and Deviance among the Irish Peasantry', *Ulster Folklife*,
xxiii (1977), 33-56.

[3] See *Ordnance Survey Memoir for the Parish of Antrim* (1838), ed. B. Trainor (Bel-
fast, 1969), pp. 70-3; *Ordnance Survey Memoir for the Parish of Donegore* (1838), ed.
W. G. Simpson *et al.* (Belfast, 1974), pp. 18-19; O. Davies, 'Folklore in Maghera Parish',
Ulster Journal of Archaeology, 3rd series viii (1945), 63-5; D. W. Miller, 'Presbyterians and
"Modernization" in Ulster', *Past and Present*, No. 80 (1978), 66-90.

vessel as will keep her at sea for six weeks, and then she will split in two before reaching Dungarvan.'[1] In 1832 a priest told his parishioners that he would keep his cold, clear, and effective eye upon their every electoral action. At the Clare election of 1828 Fr. Murphy allegedly terrorized voters with powerful sacerdotal 'stares'. The parish priest of Cashel in 1835 threatened to 'put the sickness' on those who voted against his wishes.[2] The meaning of this was clear enough and could be reinforced by less ambiguous messages of a more directly Christian slant: refusal of sacraments, orthodox anathemas, invocation of particularly powerful saints, intimations of hell. But even the waving of portable crucifixes at the Carlow election of 1841 or the Tipperary priest who 'wheeled . . . a piece of the holy palm . . . over his head' while 'advising voters in the chapel yard',[3] however superficially Christian the materials involved, were ritual usages well beyond the experience of the Roman schools. Such things were possible because of the enormous and mysterious powers ascribed to priests in pre-Famine Ireland, 'that the visible and invisible world is under their control, that they can at their will and pleasure make sick or well again, give prosperity or adversity, damnation or salvation'. Certain priests thought peculiarly adept were prepared to undertake 'cures' of a distinctly esoteric kind, though such men seem often to have been of a disreputable, marginal, and overly alcoholic disposition. Orthodox priests, most notably Fr. Mathew, could also, however, be assigned magical and positively hermetic powers. Crowds rushed after Fr. Mathew to touch his clothing or to obtain temperance medals to protect them against sickness or ill-fortune. The lame and maimed threw themselves in front of his path, for many believed he possessed

---

[1] *The Reign of Terror in Carlow* (1841), pp. 17–18; J. Smyth, *The Elector*, p. 45; J. Lord, *Popery at the hustings: foreign and domestic legislation* (London, 1852), p. 63; *Daily Express*, 9 Aug. 1852. For what it is worth, Carleton, in 'The Station', had no hesitation 'in asserting that the bulk of the Irish peasantry really believe that the Romish priests have this power . . . [to] translate all the Protestants into asses', while S. M. Hussey (*Reminiscences of an Irish Land Agent*, p. 94) noted how 'in those days it was generally believed that the priests had power to change men into frogs and toads'. See S. J. Connolly, *Priests and People in pre-Famine Ireland 1780–1845* (Dublin, 1982), pp. 100–20.

[2] Sub-Inspector Battersby to Gossett, 19 Dec. 1832, Melbourne Papers 95/112; T. Kelly, 'Ennis in the Nineteenth Century', p. 72; *Report from the select committee on Bribery at Elections*, H.C. 1835 (547), viii, 320–1.

[3] *The Reign of Terror in Carlow* (1841), p. 52 (for another example in Cork in 1852, see J. Lord, *Popery at the hustings*, p. 32); Revd P. Leahy to Cullen, 8 Apr. 1857, Cullen Papers. In 1837 Carlow priests 'visited the electors, bearing large crucifixes and lighted tapers and asking the electors were they going to vote against "God Almighty" ' (*Athlone Conservative Advocate*, 24 Aug. 1837), while Tipperary priests canvassed in 1835 carrying crucifixes (Lord Glengall to Sir H. Hardinge, 16 Jan. [1835], O.P. 1835/157, Box 47).

'the power to heal diseases and preserve his followers from all spiritual and physical danger'.[1]

In general, however, the pre-Famine clergy became increasingly involved in intermittently successful attempts to give rural beliefs a more acceptably Christian aspect. At the same time the close inter-meshing of, on the one hand, the religious and the magical, and, on the other, the ecclesiastical and the secular, left many of the clergy stranded, their power shared, their role uncertain and unclear. Especially was this the case in those areas where Gaelic culture was still vigorous and strong and where, indeed, attendance at Mass in the 1830s would seem to have been significantly lower than it was in either the towns or the English-speaking countryside.[2] The half-century before the Famine sees the clergy struggling to resolve such ambiguities; that thereafter witnesses their ultimately successful attempt to acquire a virtual monopoly of supernatural power and to secure an institutional and ideological base that could serve as a sure fortress from which to mount skirmishing expeditions into the worlds of secular politics and moral behaviour.

The two most distinctive occasions for such cleansing operations were provided by the wakes held after death and by the celebrations associated with pattern or patron days held at specific places (wells, mountains, lakesides) ostensibly to mark the feast days of saints venerated in particular localities. While rites of passage in general could still operate outside clerical norms—a traveller in Kerry about 1830 was astonished to observe a 'pagan' marriage ceremony held alfresco with symbolic greenery and bonfires and 'a wild chorus of dancers and singers'—the coming to terms with death most power-fully resisted sacerdotal assimilation and monopoly.[3] The Church objected, not only because of its exclusion from rituals so central to peasant (indeed to all) life, not only because of the flamboyant

---

[1] D. O. Croly, *An Essay Religious and Political*, pp. 67–8, also W. G. Wood-Martin, *Traces of the Elder Faiths of Ireland*, ii, 13; Lady Gregory, *Visions and Beliefs in the West of Ireland*, new edn. (Gerrards Cross, 1970), pp. 38, 39, 44, 82, 97, 295 ff.; T. Crofton Croker, *Researches in the South of Ireland*, p. 170. On Fr. Mathew, see J. Birmingham, *A Memoir of the Very Reverend Theobald Mathew*, p. 27; J. G. Kohl, *Ireland*, pp. 36, 57–9; Mr and Mrs S. C. Hall, *Ireland*, i, 43; J. F. Maguire, *Father Mathew: A Biography* (London, 1863), pp. 526–34; H. F. Kearney, 'Fr. Mathew: Apostle of Modernisation', pp. 169–70. W. R. Le Fanu (*Seventy Years of Irish Life*, pp. 121–2) recalled how medals blessed by Fr. Mathew were 'tied to the back of a man's hand to cure a boil, and I have seen ophthalmia treated by hanging two or three medals over a girl's eyes'.

[2] D. W. Miller, 'Irish Catholicism and the Great Famine', *Journal of Social History*, ix (1975), 81–98; S. J. Connolly, 'Religion and History', *Irish Economic and Social History*, x (1983), 66–80.

[3] W. G. Wood-Martin, *Traces of the Elder Faiths of Ireland*, ii, 33–4; S. Ó Dufaigh, 'James Murphy, Bishop of Clogher, 1801–24', p. 469; *Catholic Directory 1846*, pp. 228, 325; Mr and Mrs S. C. Hall, *Ireland*, i, 224–6; *Catholic Directory 1840*, p. 244.

drinking and dancing, but, above all, because of the extraordinary wake 'games' in which priests were caricatured, mock rosaries of potatoes worn, travesties of Christ's Passion enacted, and much of the Church's teaching publicly and precisely ridiculed. Just as remarkable were those 'games' of high sexuality only delicately reported by astonished Victorian commentators, particularly that called 'Making the Ship' with its 'several parts of "laying the keel", forming the "stem and stern", and erecting "the mast" ', the latter of which was done by a female using 'a gesture and expression proving beyond doubt that it was a relic of pagan rites'.[1] Patterns presented a different (though not unrelated) set of problems, for here the Church was not excluded, but rather in danger of being overwhelmed and tainted by a characteristic combination of demonstrative religiosity and unambiguously secular merriment in the shape of dancing, eating, singing, and drinking. Above all, the pattern revealed that species of close intermingling of the sacred and profane which was so marked a feature of much pre-Famine 'religious practice' and which at once diluted and muddied the clear waters of ecclesiastical authority. Croagh Patrick in Mayo attracted enormous numbers, many climbing the mountain on bare knees 'suffering severe pain, wounded and bleeding in their knees and feet, and some of the women shrieking with the pain'. On the summit in the mid-1820s could be found, not only 'an immense number of small relics, such as buttons, pieces of rag, bits of wood, shells, and a number of small articles . . . deposited there by the superstitious peasantry', but also elderly females engaged in various Marian devotions. Priests supervised the accompanying pattern, which, after the pain and the ecstasy, ended with visits to the many stalls selling mutton, bread, pigsfeet, ginger beer, biscuits, with 'dancing and love-making', with 'everybody . . . happy'.[2] The experience was broadly similar throughout the country. 'There were', wrote a schoolmaster of St James's pattern at the holy well near Callan, 'gooseberries and currants and cherries for the children: ginger bread for grown girls: strong beer and maddening whiskey for wranglers and busybodies: open-doored booths filled with lovers: bag-pipers and risp-raspers

---

[1] J. G. A. Prim, 'Olden Popular Pastimes in Kilkenny', *Journal of the Royal Society of Antiquaries of Ireland*, ii (1853), 333–4 ('to spare the feelings of the modest reader, if written at all, they should be confided to the guardianship of a dead language'); also W. G. Wood-Martin, *Traces of the Elder Faiths of Ireland*, i, 314–22.

[2] See Thackeray's account of a visit in 1842 (*Irish Sketch Book*, pp. 224–7); *Diary of Colour-Sergeant George Calladine*, ed. M. L. Ferrar, pp. 127–8. Displays of votive rags, buttons, etc. survived until much later. In 1851, e.g., the well near Mothel Abbey (Waterford) had 'offerings of rags, nails, buttons, pins' (W. G. Wood-Martin, *Traces of the Elder Faiths of Ireland*, ii, 94).

[fiddlers] making music there for young folks: and pious pilgrims making their stations around the well.'[1] The scene depicted in Joseph Peacock's panoramic painting exhibited at the Royal Academy in 1817 and entitled *The Patron, or Festival of St Kevin at the Seven Churches, Glendalough* (now in the Ulster Museum) catches the atmosphere: fairground and business, hustle and bustle, calm contemplation and fierce ecstasy. Much the same happened elsewhere: at Mount Brandon and Cloghane in Kerry, at Arboe on Lough Neagh, at Knocknadobar in Kerry again, at St Declan's pattern held near Ardmore in Waterford, at the great pattern of Mám Éan in Galway. All were marked by fighting, dancing, drinking, gambling, by abandoned asceticism and spiritual excitement, by the telling of rosary beads and by 'red and yellow dresses on the green sward'.[2] Theoretical irreconcilables were thrown into cheek-by-jowl relationships, as at the holy well near Letterkenny where the lame and sick left crutches and rags both to the saint and to the nearby fairy whose assistance also demanded formal acknowledgement.[3] And while patterns were perhaps especially attractive to the poor, stations enabled the prosperous farmer to see confession and eucharist comfortable in his own kitchen—a matter of some annoyance to labourers, who resented not only clerical dues, but also the lavishness of station entertainment. Baptisms and marriages too were often held in private houses amidst the usual juxtaposition of piety and enjoyment.[4]

The whole atmosphere of pre-Famine Catholicism was one of ambiguity. Church buildings were, not only for reasons of necessity, happily used for a wide variety of secular purposes, and political meetings continued to be held in them even after the episcopal regulations of 1834 had ostensibly banished such things to the yard. Repeal registration agents were allowed to use chapels in Sligo in 1841. Anti-tithe meetings (with farmers in the chair) were held in Queen's Co. chapels in 1834 to select parliamentary candidates with lots of 'speeching . . . intemperate and violent'. Emancipation meetings took place in churches and chapels, with, in some cases, platforms being erected in front of the altar. At Youghal in 1835 coalfactors, small farmers, and fishermen assembled for entirely

[1] *The Diary of Humphrey O'Sullivan*, ed. M. McGrath, ii, 183 (1829).

[2] H. D. Inglis, *A Journey throughout Ireland*, pp. 225–8; M. MacNeill, *The Festival of Lughnasa*, pp. 104–5, 107–12, 257–8, 137–9, 123–8; Mr and Mrs S. C. Hall, *Ireland*, i, 284–5.

[3] F. and E. Ponsonby, 'Diary of a Tour of Donegal, 1837', *Donegal Annual*, x (1973), 286.

[4] J. S. Donnelly Jr., 'The Rightboy Movement 1785–8', *Studia Hibernica*, No. 17/18 (1977–8), 166–7; Slattery to O'Connell, 8 Apr. 1842, *Correspondence of Daniel O'Connell*, ed. M. R. O'Connell, vii, 148–51; T. P. Cunningham, 'Church Reorganization', pp. 16–20.

secular purposes in the town's chapel, and much the same happened
in Waterford. Regular election meetings were held in Co. Carlow
chapels throughout June and July 1841 and meetings to protest
against O'Connell's imprisonment in Cork City chapels during the
summer of 1844.[1] Not only were the great men like O'Connell
to be found in chapels, 'cravat loose . . . waistcoat unbuttoned',[2]
but minnows too were allowed entrance.

I observed . . . a mob assembled round the chapel . . . Within, there was a meeting
of Radical Reformers; a tall man was pouring forth a philippic from the altar
. . . The gist of his oration went to prove, that Catholic Emancipation was a
humbug—concession a farce—and luck, or grace, would never visit this unhappy island until Mr Cornelius Cassidy, of Killcooney-house, was sent to
represent us in the Imperial Parliament.[3]

Priests, indeed, often adopted a comparatively relaxed approach in
front of their congregations, which in turn expressed 'their sympathy
with the preacher, as the Methodists in England do, by a deep and
audible breathing'. Suggestions that altar pronouncements on purely
'temporal concerns' might be unedifying were met with blank
astonishment. Kerry priests aroused tumult with denunciations of '
Conservatism—'the people shouted, and said they would vote for
him [O'Connell] and groaned the Knight of Kerry in the chapel'[4]
—while Carleton's Fr. Philemy M'Guirk (in 'The Station') took
a break during Mass to exchange broad-humoured *badinage* with his
assembled flock. Throughout the 1830s and 1840s few county
elections were complete without gangs of parishioners attacking
unpopular voters at worship, smashing their pews, and beating their
relatives. In early 1835 agitated reports poured into Dublin Castle:
in Rathoe Chapel 'a most respectable farmer' was violently attacked
at Mass; in Queen's Co. Conservative voters were dragged out of
chapels and left bleeding; at Rossmore in Cork an elderly gentleman
was assaulted and his pew smashed; at Edgeworthstown three pews
were dismantled; in Carlow Town 'a riotous and tumultuous mob of

[1] S. Murphy to T. M. Ray, 22 Oct. 1841, O'Connell Papers N.L.I. MS 13623; Report
of Chief Constable Wright, Ballickmoyler, 29 Dec. 1834, O.P. 1835/152, Box 47; *The Diary
of Humphrey O'Sullivan*, ed. M. McGarth, i, 207, ii, 93; P. K. Egan, *The Parish of Ballinasloe*, p. 163. See also *Clare Journal*, 23 June 1828; *C.C.* 17 Feb. 1835; *Committee on
Bribery at Elections*, H.C. 1835 (547), viii, 446; *The Reign of Terror in Carlow* (1841),
p. 30; M. Murphy, 'Repeal, Popular Politics, and the Catholic Clergy of Cork, 1840-50',
p. 46. They were also used as schools (I. Murphy, 'Primary Education', pp. 1-52).
[2] J. A. Reynolds, *The Catholic Emancipation Crisis in Ireland, 1823-1829* (New Haven,
1954), p. 37.
[3] [W. H. Maxwell], *Wild Sports of the West. With Legendary Tales, and local Sketches*,
2 vols. (London, 1832), i, 23.
[4] J. E. Bicheno, *Ireland and its Economy*, p. 173; *Committee on Bribery at Elections*,
H.C. 1835 (547), viii, 274, 501-8; *Cork City election petition*, H.C. 1852-3 (528), xi, 387.

at least twenty persons entered the chapel [with] . . . calls of "put
him out until we pull his guts out" '.[1] After the Co. Carlow by-
election of 1840 one victim recalled: 'I was surrounded by a crowd,
dragged out of chapel . . . when some persons leaped on me . . . I was
saved by the police. Mass was going on at the time.'[2]

However individual priests may have behaved, significant efforts
were made during the half-century before the Famine either to
suppress such practices as wakes and patterns or to reform them in
the direction of contemporary theological respectability. Archbishop Laffan of Cashel found on visitation in 1828 that 'a great
many gave themselves up . . . for fighting, witchcraft, not attending
their duty, etc. etc.', and pioneering Gaelic scholars like John
O'Donovan in 1837 bemoaned that 'the priests, I am sorry to see and
to say, [are] inclining very much to Protestant notions, are putting
an end to all . . . venerable old customs'. Other, not unperceptive,
observers also thought many churchmen altogether too eager to put
on the robes of modernization in company with the agencies of
government and of British influence.[3] Such priests were often
labelled 'Protestant' priests and a Catholic friend of the antiquarian,
William Wilde, could write in 1849: 'The tone of society in Ireland is
becoming more and more *"Protestant"* every year; the literature is
a Protestant one, and even the priests are becoming more Protestant
in their conversations and manners. They have condemned all the
holy wells and resorts of pilgrimage, with the single exception of
Lough Derg, and of this they are ashamed.'[4] And while this may
have been an exaggeration, it undoubtedly recorded a growing
reality. Lough Derg in Donegal had long been the only pilgrimage
countenanced by the northern bishops, whose efforts to transform
it into something more acceptable to modern practice—by the provision of regular confessors and the formal teaching of the catechism

[1] Report of Sub-Inspector Battersby, 5 Feb. 1835, O.P. 1835, Box 34; W. Molony
to Sir John —, [Jan. 1835], ibid. 1835/152, Box 47; Constable D. Dwyer to Capt.
Grant, 26 Jan. 1835, ibid. 1835, Box 46; Report of Chief Constable King, 20 Feb. 1835,
ibid. 1835, Box 46; Information of Luke and George Nolan, [Feb. 1835], ibid. 1835,
Box 34; Report of Chief Constable Hawkshaw, 8 Feb. 1835, ibid. 1835, Box 34. For
additional cases, see *Committee on Bribery at Elections*, H.C. 1835 (547), viii, 255, 291,
494-5, 654-6.

[2] *The Reign of Terror in Carlow* (1841), pp. 13-14, 89-90, 93, 98, 100, 118. For
further examples in other counties, see P. O'Donoghue, 'Opposition to Tithe Payment in
1832-3', *Studia Hibernica*, No. 12 (1972), 94 (Longford); J. Lord, *Popery at the hustings*,
p. 20 (Clare); T. P. Cunningham, 'The Burrowes-Hughes by-election', *Breifne*, iii (1967),
205 (Cavan).

[3] Laffan and O'Donovan cited in S. J. Connolly, *Priests and People in pre-Famine
Ireland 1780-1845*, pp. 112-13; *D.E.P.* 29 July 1837; W. R. Wilde, *Irish Popular Superstitions* (Dublin, 1852), pp. 34-9.

[4] R. and J. R. Miller to E. Lawford, 14 Mar. 1853 (writing about the 1840s), Drapers'
Company L.-B. Irish 1848-57; W. R. Wilde, *Irish Popular Superstitions*, p. 16.

—had not been without effect.[1] Indeed, after the Famine the pilgrimage became so fully absorbed into respectability that in 1879, for example, the place was almost overwhelmed by ecclesiastical dignitaries: Archbishop Croke of Cashel, Archbishop Lynch of Toronto, the Bishops of Clogher, Elphin, and Achonry, and the president of Maynooth. This process of absorption on the one hand, and simple suppression on the other, constituted the twin prongs of reformist strategy. Significantly, in the case of Lough Derg, the whole business resulted in a catastrophic fall in numbers. Attendances of 60,000 in the 1820s, 19,000 in the 1830s, 15,000 in the 1850s gradually declined to an average of 2,700 in the 1880s, while at the same time there occurred a noticeable shift from the 'humbler' to 'the better-off classes, including many foreigners and priests of every order'.[2]

In general, patterns and seasonal festivals were slowly strangled or left to decay in the unsympathetic atmosphere of post-Famine religiosity. The process was a continuous one and had begun many years earlier.[3] The celebrations associated with the festival of Lughnasa or the beginning of harvest have been studied in unusual detail and their history is an epitome of a wider transformation. As early as the 1830s attempts were made to subsume the whole business under the feast-day of the Assumption on 15 August. Priests inveighed against 'pagan' practices and removed objects of traditional devotion—sacred trees, hallowed stones, and the like. Associated patterns were heavily laundered and emasculated. By mid-century some of the greatest patterns in the land were in chronic decay: Slieve Donard, Church Mountain in Wicklow, Mount Brandon in Kerry.[4] Carlyle heard a Mayo priest denounce a local pattern in 1849 (a sentiment in which his Young Ireland guide, Gavan Duffy, heartily concurred) and noted the decay of another tradition in the keening at Killarney where 'there was no sorrow

---

[1] Bishop Murphy to Propaganda, 1804 and 8 Oct. 1814, in S. Ó Dufaigh, 'James Murphy, Bishop of Clogher, 1801-24', pp. 458, 462; D. O'Connor, *St. Patrick's Purgatory, Lough Derg. Its history, traditions, legends, antiquities, topography, and scenic surroundings*, enlarged edn. (Dublin, 1910), pp. 177-90.

[2] D. O'Connor, *St. Patrick's Purgatory*, p. 238. For the 1820s, see J. Glassford, *Notes of three tours in Ireland, in 1824 and 1826* (Bristol, 1832), p. 95; the 1830s, H. D. Inglis, *A Journey throughout Ireland*, p. 298; the 1850s, J. Fraser, *Hand-Book for Travellers in Ireland*, 5th edn. (Dublin, [1859]), p. 580; the 1870s and 1880s, D. O'Connor, *St. Patrick's Purgatory*, pp. 194-7. The pilgrimage lasts from 1 June to 15 August.

[3] 'In the year 1780 the priests discontinued their attendance, but the patrons . . . still continued the same, and to this day attract all the country for ten or twenty miles round (J. Carr, *The Stranger in Ireland: Or a tour in the southern and western parts of that country in the year 1805* (London, 1806), p. 255).

[4] M. MacNeill, *The Festival of Lughnasa, passim*. Smaller patterns followed the same trend.

whatever ... idle women ... hoh-hoh-ing with a grief quite evidently hired and not worth hiring'. State, gentry, and Church were agreed on this if on little else. 'Mr Galvin', noted a Wicklow landlord's wife of a new curate in 1847, 'is a real blessing; he preaches upon the moral virtues, tries to instil principle [*sic*] ... encourages a spirit of industry and checks the idle love of wakes and patterns.'[1] At Athea in Co. Limerick the local proprietor (a wealthy Church of Ireland clergyman) expelled the pattern from his estate; soon it was finally suppressed by the parish priest 'on account of all the drinking and other abuses that followed it'. Landlords had little sympathy for popular traditions. They 'derange the village outlines; its festal anniversaries have now [1873] no votaries, its holy wells and cherished traditions are alike ignored. The Catholic clergy too have lent their aid to obliterate those vestiges of once important institutions.'[2]

Already in the 1830s priests had kept a wary eye upon the local magic woman and by the end of the century 'it was all you could do to get to Biddy Early with your skin whole, the priests were so set against her ... the friars are gone and there are missioners come in their place and all they would do for you is to bless the holy water'.[3] Of course everything did not come to a complete or sudden halt. Vague clerical hints that the limblessness of the Carlow Tory politician and landlord, Arthur MacMorrough Kavanagh, derived from a mixture of religious perversion and magical influences enjoyed vigorous currency in the late 1860s, while Mayo priests remained happy and eager to trade politically upon the extraordinary powers they were still accorded by many of their parishioners.[4] Court cases allow continuing glimpses into an increasingly secret world. At Riverstown Petty Sessions in 1868 one woman charged another 'that she had held constant communication with the fairies'. In Louth in the 1890s another tried to murder a neighbour by sympathetic magic. Near Clonmel a woman was killed in 1895 by relatives in the belief that she was a fairy, the parish priest revealingly defending his lack of intervention by saying 'the priest is very often

[1] T. Carlyle, *Reminiscences of my Irish journey in 1849*, pp. 207, 130; *The Irish Journals of Elizabeth Smith*, ed. D. Thomson and M. McGusty, p. 140 (23 Apr. 1847).
[2] C. Ó Danachair, 'Faction Fighting in County Limerick', *North Munster Antiquarian Journal*, x (1966), 50; J. Hogan, 'Patron Days and Holy Wells in Ossory', *Journal of the Royal Society of Antiquaries of Ireland*, xii (1873), 267.
[3] Lady Gregory, *Visions and Beliefs in the West of Ireland*, pp. 42, 296, also pp. 33-6, 39, 41-2, 47, 49, 83, 97, 99, 300. For the 1830s, see Mr and Mrs S. C. Hall, *Ireland*, ii, 269.
[4] J. Pope Hennessy to Disraeli, 23 Oct. 1866, Hughenden Papers B/XIII/198; G. Rooper, *A Month in Mayo, comprising characteristic sketches (sporting and social) of Irish life* (London, 1876), p. 57; *Galway Vindicator*, 24 July 1852 (on a speech by MacHale); *Minutes of evidence taken before the select committee on the Mayo County election petition*, H.C. 1857 (182 Sess. 2), vii, 7-8 and *passim*.

the last to hear of things like that'.[1] As late as 1 May 1890 virtually all the houses in Sligo Town were decorated with blooming gorse to please 'the good people', while the county infirmary regularly admitted patients wearing 'straining strings' designed to cure dislocated limbs.[2] Indeed, well into the twentieth century Travellers (or Tinkers) could find a market for cure-alls made of wood from Lourdes blessed by a 'curing priest'—a potent amalgam of religious power and their own esoteric arts.[3]

Such things were, however, seeping towards the margins—both socially and mentally—of Irish life, for in reality assimilation meant eventual death. In 1868 Bishop Moriarty unsuccessfully attempted a great modernization of the Mount Brandon pilgrimage, with confraternity processions, a series of Masses, benediction, 'a selection of sacred music with delicious effect'.[4] The history of one of the few successful 'survivals' makes the point, for the decline of Croagh Patrick during the late nineteenth century suggests that the 'driving force in its secular popularity had been commemoration of a seasonal festival'. The appointment of Archbishop Healy in 1903 introduced enthusiastic episcopal support, but the subsequent pilgrimage was a heavily sanitized and artificial revival of what had by then become a far from vigorous tradition.[5] Events which had previously contained that intermingling of the Catholic and the 'pagan', the secular and the sacred, which had been so marked a feature of pre-Famine religion, now either disappeared or were unscrambled into their constituent parts. Like Croagh Patrick, devotions at wells near Castlekeeran in Meath, at St Mullins in Carlow, at Tobernalt in Sligo, near Kilmainham River in Meath, at Oran in Roscommon, and at many other places became more or less swiftly transformed into unambiguously Catholic events with only the vaguest hints of a more complex paternity. Near Lacken Church in Wicklow a change in nomenclature from St Boden's

[1] *The Times*, 1 Aug. 1868; R. P. Jenkins, 'Witches and Fairies', pp. 40-1, 47-8.

[2] W. G. Wood-Martin, *Traces of the Elder Faiths of Ireland*, i, 299-302, ii, 29, 262, 72-3, also i, 325-7. See also J. MacDevitt, *The Most Reverend James MacDevitt D.D. Bishop of Raphoe: A Memoir* (Dublin, 1880), p. 314; W. H. Hurlbert, *Ireland under Coercion: The diary of an American*, 2 vols. (Edinburgh, 1888), i, 221; A. I. Shand, *Letters from the west of Ireland 1884* (Edinburgh and London, 1885), pp. 110-11.

[3] G. Gmelch and B. Kroup, *To Shorten the Road* (Dublin, 1978), p. 28. See also L. Kennedy, 'Profane images in the Irish popular consciousness', *Oral History*, vii (1979), 42-7.

[4] *Nation*, 4 July 1868; *The Times*, 1 July 1868, M. MacNeill, *The Festival of Lughnasa*, pp. 101-4.

[5] E. E. Evans, 'Peasant Beliefs in nineteenth-century Ireland' in *Views of the Irish Peasantry 1800-1916*, ed. D. J. Casey and R. E. Rhodes (Hamden, Conn., 1977), p. 53; also M. MacNeill, *The Festival of Lughnasa*, pp. 79-80.

to Fr. Germaine's Well labelled the metamorphosis.[1] Totally new centres of devotion of the most modern kind filled the gap, notably at Knock in Mayo, where in 1879 a thirteen-year-old described experiences fully in accord with ultramontane iconography. 'I distinctly beheld the Blessed Virgin Mary, life size . . . clothed in white robes, which were fastened at the neck . . . she appeared to be praying . . . she wore a brilliant crown on her head, and, over the forehead, where the crown fitted the brow, a beautiful rose.'[2]

The priests of post-Famine Ireland, however much they still from time to time used chapels for secular purposes, however much they continued to issue general guide-lines from the altar,[3] were more and more being fashioned into the clear role of purely religious specialists. And the more autonomous the priests' role became, the more successfully were the clergy able to maintain their identity amidst the powerful national and secular political movements of the 1880s and beyond.[4] Increasingly the priest retreated into a physical and mental state of distinctiveness, set apart, not only by literacy (as had long been the case), but by his formal dress, his parochial house,[5] his improving standard of living, by his own reformed image of himself as community guide and mediator of the supernatural. To pre-Famine visitors such as Thackeray Irish Catholicism had often presented 'strange, wild' scenes 'so entirely different . . . from the decent and comfortable observances of our own church'.[6] Thereafter, however, we find a 'diminished reality', a change reflected starkly in the different prisms of imagination ground by Carleton in the 1830s and George Moore more than half a century later: 'The sense of vitality, of masses of people lined up for a faction fight, crowding to midnight mass, attending stations, going on pilgrimage, getting married, abducting teachers, drinking, courting, being evicted, emigrating, dying, is missing from Moore's

---

[1] M. MacNeill, *The Festival of Lughnasa*, pp. 260–3, 263–8, 607, 638, 632–3, 185–7; *The Irish Journals of Elizabeth Smith*, ed. D. Thomson and M. McGusty, p. 268.

[2] J. MacPhilpin, *The Apparitions and Miracles at Knock* (Dublin, 1880), p. 32. By the 1870s pilgrimages to Lourdes itself were already popular (K. O'Shea, 'David Moriarty (1814–77)', p. 122).

[3] Many examples could be cited, including the denunciation from the altar of a man for burying his cow in the churchyard—'this man won't be here this time twelvemonths' (*Londonderry Sentinel*, 3 Nov. 1868) and fierce electoral denunciations of a 'magical' kind (ibid. 28 July 1865; F. B. Head, *A Fortnight in Ireland*, pp. 283, 367, 370, etc.).

[4] P. Bew, *Land and the National Question in Ireland 1858–82*, pp. 68–9, 128–9.

[5] Priests had earlier mostly lived in thatched cabins, and had, as a result (according to Major Willcock's evidence to a parliamentary committee in 1824) been 'very much more at the mercy of the population, than others who live in houses of a different description' (cited G. C. Lewis, *On local Disturbances in Ireland and on the Irish Church Question* (London, 1836), p. 114—references to the Cork reprint of 1977).

[6] W. M. Thackeray, *The Irish Sketch Book of 1842*, pp. 132–4.

world, as it is from that of his contemporaries'.[1] And just as the wakes and the patterns declined, so the world of the pre-Famine prophecy men and the millenarian texts of 'Pastorini' and 'Colmcille' (so typical of an oppressed but still vigorous culture) diminished into the harmless sands of *Nugent's* and *Old Moore's Almanac*.[2] The casual lack of prudery which had long maintained itself in country districts also succumbed to the same processes of secular and ecclesiastical modernization. Bursts of hysterics concerning nude bathing, had, in earlier years, been confined to peers, magistrates, tourists, and anonymous letter-writers.[3] Tocqueville and many others had noticed the juxtaposition of high chastity with the fact that 'women take less trouble to hide themselves than in any other country in the world, and men seem to have no repugnance to showing themselves almost naked'.[4] The large proportion of single people in the post-Famine population and the increase of postponed marriages encouraged, even obliged, the church to accentuate a more overt, conscious, indeed legalistic, view of sexuality in general. Steady, remorseless, and occasionally ludicrous pressures could the more easily be applied by a clergy firing its moral ammunition from the cleared redoubts—separate, secure, unambiguous— of post-Famine professionalism. And parents too were ready to respond to the Pastoral Address of the Maynooth Synod of 1875 condemning 'fast dances'—the waltz and the polka.[5] The success of the priesthood in achieving a virtual monopoly in the spiritual sphere *and* in unscrambling a once powerful intermingling of sacred and profane was, however, neither inevitable nor inconsiderable. In north-west Scotland, for example, the Presbyterian clergy continued

[1] M. Harmon, 'Aspects of the Peasantry in Anglo-Irish Literature from 1800 to 1916', *Studia Hibernica*, No. 15 (1975), 118-19.

[2] P. O'Farrell, 'Millenialism, Messianism, and Utopianism in Irish History', *Anglo-Irish Studies*, ii (1976), 45-68; J. S. Donnelly Jr., 'Propagating the Cause of the United Irishmen', *Studies*, lxix (1980), 15-20.

[3] *D.E.P.* 5 Nov. 1825; A MacLochlainn, 'Social Life in County Clare', p. 62 (poster advertising a meeting at Kilkee in 1833 to protest against 'indecent exposures' and 'the shameful custom which prevails, of naked men riding horses through the water'); *Galway Vindicator*, 31 July 1852 (letter denouncing 'the hideous sights that are hourly to be seen [at Salt Hill] . . . naked men perched like statues . . . exposing themselves in a manner which would bring a blush over the most barbarous subject of King Dahomy').

[4] A. de Tocqueville, *Journeys to England and Ireland*, p. 191. The incidence of illegitimacy etc. seems to have been low in pre-Famine Ireland—see K. H. Connell, 'Illegitimacy before the Famine' in *Irish Peasant Society*, pp. 78-82, and S. J. Connolly, 'Illegitimacy and pre-nuptial pregnancy in Ireland before 1864: The evidence of some Catholic parish registers', *Irish Economic and Social History*, vi (1979), 5-23.

[5] *Pastoral Address of the Archbishops and Bishops of Ireland assembled in National Synod at Maynooth* (Dublin, 1875)—copy in Cullen Papers: 'Dangerous amusements in theatres . . . improper dances . . . imported into our country from abroad . . . innumerable souls are suffering eternal punishment for sins they have committed in dancing.'

to face a powerful rivalry from *na daoine* ('the men'), self-selected preachers of crofter origin, indebted to an 'older faith', wearing hair and clothes in a recognized 'uniform', and spreading a millennial puritanism of prophetic allegory and power. Again, a Mediterranean version of the pattern survives energetically in modern Malta and carries with it all the complex ambiguities of early-nineteenth-century Ireland: 'I was in the church during a particularly solemn moment in the service of worship. Suddenly there was a nerve-shattering burst of fireworks from the roof of the church. Then, slowly, the sharp smell of burning gunpowder began to drift in through the open doors and mingle with the pungent odour of candles and incense. After that I ceased to be aware of separateness, and realized that both incense and gunpowder were ingredients basic to the celebration of a festa.'[1]

IV INCOME AND STATUS

Within the wider limits set by general developments in religious culture and organization was played out the precise choreography of relations between priests and people. Money constituted a crucial point of friction. Although no satisfactory indices exist for the cost of living in nineteenth-century Ireland, there can be little doubt that the clergy became steadily better off. Reasonably reliable figures for 1801 suggest that the average gross annual *ecclesiastical* incomes of parish priests fell into the following categories.[2]

Income	per cent
Under £50	15.5
£50 to under £100	58.6
£100 to under £150	19.9
£150 and over	6.0

[1] J. Hunter, *The Making of the Crofting Community* (Edinburgh, 1976), pp. 100–1; J. Boissevain, *Saints and Fireworks: Religion and Politics in Rural Malta*, revised edn. (London, 1969), pp. 59–60.

[2] Calculated from 'Abstract of the Returns of the several Roman Catholic Bishops of Ireland', January 1801, in *Memoirs and Correspondence of Viscount Castlereagh*, ed. Charles Vane, Marquess of Londonderry, 4 vols. (London, 1848-9), iv, 97–173, but (for reasons of omission or statistical inadequacy) based on only 18 of the 26 dioceses and (for these and other reasons) on only 55.8 per cent of the parishes. Payment in kind (oats, hay, free labour, etc.) and free hospitality at stations etc. must be added (see T. Wyse, *Historical Sketch of the late Catholic Association of Ireland*, 2 vols. (London, 1829), ii, pp. cv–cx).

As compared with the £40-60 of the 1780s,[1] the bulk of the priests probably had about £70 or £80 a year clear. Theoretically, curates living apart were supposed to receive one-third of the parochial income, but this was at best irregularly the case until the middle of the century.[2] Curates who lodged with the parish priest subsisted on erratic hand-outs amounting to perhaps ten pounds a year. After 1801 the information available, though patchy, suggests that parish priests received in general about £100 a year in the 1820s, perhaps £130 in the 1830s, and somewhat more in the 1840s. After the Famine incomes rose substantially to between £250 and £400 in the 1880s, by which time curates too had increased their average earnings from the very low levels of earlier times to £150 or thereabouts.[3] Individual cases illuminate local and temporal peculiarities. Some priests found themselves on totally static earnings for almost thirty years. Others, like the parish priest of Kenmare in Kerry, had incomes which fluctuated substantially: 1839—£250, 1840—£270, 1841—£340, 1842—£280.[4] Priests and laymen often accused bishops of operating a form of 'spoils' system in which the subservient were rewarded and the independent punished.[5] Even in poorer areas individual parishes could produce substantial revenues: Oughaval (Westport) was worth £500 in 1860, Burtonport in Donegal £560 during the 1880s. In large urban parishes the expenses of church maintenance and episcopal subsidy could be unusually high, so that for example at St Paul's, Arran Quay,

[1] J. S. Donnelly Jr., 'The Rightboy Movement 1785-8', pp. 164-5.

[2] For the theory, see T. Wyse, *Historical Sketch of the late Catholic Association*, ii, pp. cv-cx, and *Minutes of evidence taken before the select committee of the House of Lords appointed to inquire into the State of Ireland, more particularly with reference to the circumstances which may have led to disturbances in that part of the United Kingdom*, H.C. 1825 (181, 521), ix, 231 (Dr Doyle); for the practice, see *Pilot*, 18 Sept. 1835, and S. Ó Dufaigh, 'James Murphy, Bishop of Clogher, 1801-24', pp. 452-3.

[3] These averages disguise considerable fluctuations and are based on: *Lords' Committee appointed to inquire into the State of Ireland*, H.C. 1825 (181, 521), ix, 231 (Bishop Doyle: see also W. J. Fitzpatrick, *Dr Doyle, Bishop of Kildare and Leighlin*, i, 285-6), 369 (Fr. John Kiely, PP), 256 (Archbishop Curtis), 366-7 (Archbishop Kelly), 66 (J. L. Foster, MP: 'It is a question which I asked everywhere'); J. E. Bicheno, *Ireland and its Economy*, p. 176; D. O. Croly, *An Essay Religious and Political*, pp. 29-30; A. de Tocqueville, *Journeys to England and Ireland*, p. 174; T. C. Anstey to Propaganda, 17 Nov. 1843, cited E. Larkin, 'The Devotional Revolution in Ireland, 1850-75', p. 634; Clarendon to Russell, 15 Nov. 1849, Clarendon Papers L.-B. V (reporting Bishop MacGettigan); *The Church Establishment in Ireland*, pp. 377-87; E. de Mandat-Grancey, *Paddy at Home*, p. 175; P. H. Bagenal, *The Priest in Politics* (London, 1893), p. 42.

[4] P. K. Egan, *The Parish of Ballinasloe*, p. 164; B. Cahill, 'The Impact of the Catholic Clergy on Irish Life 1820-45', p. 248 citing the diary of Fr. John O'Sullivan, who—free of debt—thought his lot better than that of many minor gentlemen.

[5] See the 'Memorial' of 1855 to the Pope by certain priests cited E. Larkin, *The Making of the Roman Catholic Church in Ireland, 1850-1860*, p. 278; *Kilkenny Journal*, 13 Apr. 1859 on Fr. J. Aylward.

in Dublin, only £646 was left out of gross annual receipts of £1,900 in 1885–6.[1]

Bishops' incomes remain in even greater obscurity. In general these derived from mensal parishes, annual levies (the cathedraticum) on parish priests of between two and ten pounds, and (decreasingly) from licences to marry without banns. Clearly much depended on the wealth of individual dioceses. In tiny Kilmacduagh and Kilfenora, for example, with only nineteen parishes, parochial levies were modest and the two mensal parishes yielded no more than £80 in 1853, hardly a recipe for lavish living. Even in Armagh, Archbishop Dixon's receipts from Drogheda parish were small and legalistically defined: his board, lodgings, coals, candles, and transport were provided while in residence, but wine was strictly extra.[2] In 1801 the national average had been just over £300, with little obvious geographical patterning, Dublin's £320 being exceeded in six dioceses, while bishops in Kilmacduagh (£100), Clonfert (£117), and Kilmore (£147) rubbed along on less than many parochial clergymen.[3] Twenty-five years later things had obviously improved. All northern bishops received between £500 and £600, Kildare and Leighlin yielded £450–500, another Leinster bishop got £700, while some in Munster got even more. By the mid-1830s the upward tendency was still evident with incomes falling between £500 and £1,000: the Bishop of Ossory on the former amount considered himself 'rich enough . . . Sometimes I can give friends dinner. I have a gig and a horse.'[4] Occasionally incomes could even hit £1,300 (as in Kerry between 1837 and 1847),[5] but unpredictable fluctuations must have caused serious problems and acute embarrassment. Raphoe, for example, yielded £200 in 1801, £500 in the 1830s and early 1840s, £200 during the Famine, and (for income tax purposes at any rate) £275 in 1871–2.[6] To some extent, of course, life-styles depended on

[1] Revd B. Bourke to Kirby, 11 June 1860, *Arch. Hib.* xxxi, 28; W. H. Hurlbert, *Ireland under Coercion*, i, 135–7; Revd F. J. Maguire to Archbishop Walsh, 20 Nov. 1886, Walsh Papers 402/5 (split £344 to the PP and £151 to each of two curates).

[2] Cullen to Propaganda, 12 July 1853, *Paul Cullen*, iii, 178 (see *Thom 1859*, p. 538); Dixon's Memorandum of 1860, Dixon Papers VII/1.

[3] Calculated from 'Abstract' in *Memoirs and Correspondence of Viscount Castlereagh*, ed. Charles Vane, Marquess of Londonderry, iv, 97–173.

[4] *Lords' Committee appointed to inquire into the State of Ireland*, H.C. 1825 (181, 521), ix, 231, 255; A. de Tocqueville, *Journeys to England and Ireland*, pp. 133, 145.

[5] This was the vicar-general's estimate, cited from his diary in B. Cahill, 'The Impact of the Catholic Clergy on Irish Life 1820–45', p. 209.

[6] 1801 from 'Abstract' in *Memoirs and Correspondence of Viscount Castlereagh*, ed. Charles Vane, Marquess of Londonderry, iv, 112; 1830s and 1840s from Clarendon to Russell, 15 Nov. 1849, Clarendon Papers L.-B. V; 1871–2 from Bishop MacDevitt to G. Ogilvy (Surveyor of Taxes), 17 Jan. 1873, MacDevitt L.-B. Bishop Donnelly of Clogher probably received gross about £507 in 1883, of which £307 was 'expenses' (carriage and

inclination as well as income, and bishops like MacCormack of Achonry and Duggan of Clonfert were in the 1880s pursuing rigid frugality as good in itself.[1]

What does seem to be clear is that overall clerical incomes improved substantially during the post-Famine decades, even though the percentage of (low-paid) curates rose steadily from 38.9 in 1801 to 57.9 in 1845 and 63.7 in 1881.[2] There had, of course, been extravagant—even gargantuan—styles of living in earlier times, but in general things had been simple and plain. 'Priests' breakfast and equipment' had been 'nothing special; that of a poor school-master or the like, living in lodgings with a rude woman and her niece or daughter.'[3] That by the 1880s some priests (however untypical) were to be seen at the best hotels, eating à la carte, and drinking fine wines, was a measure of the changes which had taken place.[4] Considering, therefore, the bachelor status of the clergy, the general level of incomes received by parish priests after the Famine was surprisingly high and placed a heavy burden upon the supporting laity.[5] It compared well with that of Presbyterian ministers, and, as time went on, even with that of Church of Ireland incumbents.[6] The gap between Church of Ireland bishops and their parsons had traditionally been large, but the enormous erosion of bishops' incomes throughout the nineteenth century narrowed the difference both there and between Catholic and Protestant

coachman £130, secretary £100, etc.) and £200 declared to the Inland Revenue ('Book of Accounts', Clogher Diocesan Papers DIO(RC)1/11C). The total income of one of his mensal parishes—Monaghan—fluctuated 1866-85 between £412 and £770 (average £535). The bishop received half of this ('Accounts and Receipts', DIO(RC) 1/11D).

[1] W. S. Blunt, *The Land War in Ireland*, pp. 58, 63, 66-7, 71.

[2] W. McDonald, *Reminiscences of a Maynooth Professor*, p. 204; A. I. Shand, *Letters from the west of Ireland 1884*, p. 225; Mrs Houston, *Twenty Years in the wild west; or, life in Connaught* (London, 1879), pp. 204, 252.

[3] For salmon and asparagus dinners in the 1820s, see *The Diary of Humphrey O'Sullivan*, ed. M. McGrath, i, 287, 311; ii, 13, 89, etc. But see also T. Carlyle, *Reminiscences of my Irish Journey in 1849*, p. 93; A. de Tocqueville, *Journeys to England and Ireland*, pp. 162, 186; Carlingford Papers Diary of C. Fortescue III (30 Apr. 1859).

[4] 'Philippe Daryl' [Paschal Grousset], *Ireland's Disease: Notes and Impressions* (London, 1888), pp. 218-20.

[5] In the 1860s the annual cost of clerical 'wages' along was estimated at £395,480 (*The Church Establishment in Ireland*, p. 387), which is almost certainly too low.

[6] In the late 1830s Synod of Ulster ministers seemed to be getting about £148 to £167, Secession Synod ministers £85, Remonstrant Synod (Unitarian) ministers £155, Methodist minister £20 plus keep (*Ordnance Survey Memoir for the Parish of Antrim* (1838), ed. B. Trainor, pp. 18-22, 63-5, 95, and *Ordnance Survey Memoir for the Parish of Donegore* (1838), ed. W. G. Simpson *et al.*, pp. 6-7, 15-16). The mean income of Church of Ireland incumbents in 1832 was £375—with 50.5 per cent receiving under £300—and in 1867 £242—with 70.8 per cent receiving under £300 (calculated from D. H. Akenson, *The Church of Ireland: Ecclesiastical Reform and Revolution 1800-1885* (New Haven, 1971), pp. 87, 221).

bishops.[1] In the 1860s parish priests earned as much as the thirty-odd county inspectors of constabulary (£220-50), more than assistant masters in the larger Protestant grammar schools (£150-200), probably a little less than most of the local agents for the Bank of Ireland (£300-400) or the inspectors of the Local Government Board (£350-450).[2] Financially, therefore, they stood much closer to medium-ranking officials, modest land agents, or senior bank representatives than to groups such as clerks, national schoolmasters, or manual workers of any kind. Even curates received more than these and all priests inhabited an economic world far distant from that of agricultural labourers—still in the 1860s lucky to earn as much as seven or eight shillings a week.[3] Nor did rising money incomes fail to benefit from the drop in prices after the mid-1820s, the general steadiness between the mid-1850s and mid-1870s, and the subsequent substantial fall. In every sense, therefore, the thousand-odd parish priests constituted a comparative élite.

An accelerating programme of parochial house-building further improved clerical life-styles and imposed an increasing separation between priests and people. During the 1850s many rural priests still lived in lodgings and continued to do so in remoter parts such as Donegal for another twenty years.[4] But encouragement from the Synod of Thurles helped improve the situation and between 1800 and 1867 at least 600 houses were built at an average cost of £500.[5]

---

[1] Church of Ireland bishops' mean incomes declined from £5,855 in 1831 (22 bishops) to £4,526 in 1867 (12 bishops) and to £1,724 in 1919 (13 bishops). The last figure cannot have been a great deal higher than that received by their celibate Catholic brothers (D. H. Akenson, *The Church of Ireland*, pp. 84, 223, 321).

[2] *Report of the commission directed by the Treasury to inquire into the state of the Constabulary Force in Ireland, with reference to their pay and allowances*, H.C. 1866 [3658], xxxiv, 167-90 (the 265 sub-inspectors received £120-50); R. B. McDowell, *The Church of Ireland 1869-1969* (London, 1975), p. 12. In 1858 clerks of poor-law unions received £88 and workhouse masters £50 (N. W. Senior, *Journals, conversations, and essays relating to Ireland*, ii, 112-15). For the earnings of the larger land agents, see Chapter II, note 2 p. 140 above; for medical earnings, see J. Fleetwood, *History of Medicine in Ireland* (Dublin, 1951), pp. 175, 183, 186, 203.

[3] For labourers, see Chapter II, Table 19 above and associated text; for clerks, P. Lynch and J. Vaizey, *Guinness's Brewery in the Irish Economy 1759-1876* (Cambridge, 1960), p. 234. National school salaries: 1830s = £6-15, 1850s = £13-35, 1870s = £25-58 (Mary Daly, 'The Development of the National School System, 1831-40', p. 160; *Thom 1852*, p. 197; *Thom 1876*, p. 660).

[4] Cullen to Pius IX, 31 Jan. 1852, *Paul Cullen*, iv, 49; J. MacDevitt, *The Most Reverend James MacDevitt*, pp. 181-2; M. Tierney, *Morroe and Boher*, pp. 80-1; P. K. Egan, *The Parish of Ballinasloe*, pp. 174, 289; Archbishop Slattery to O'Connell, 8 Apr. 1842, *Correspondence of Daniel O'Connell*, ed. M. R. O'Connell, vii, 148-50.

[5] J. Ahern, 'The Plenary Synod of Thurles II', p. 7; *The Church Establishment in Ireland*, pp. 386-7. The Glebe Loans (Ireland) Act of 1870 (33 & 34 Vict., c. 112) provided until 1875 government loans for the erection of glebe-houses to 'ministers of any religious denomination whatsoever'. Despite criticism, it was welcomed by many priests.

By the last decades of the century, comfort, dignity, and gentility had replaced the demotic conditions of earlier years. 'Fr. McFadden's house [in Gweedore] is . . . smart and new, like a villa at Horley.' In Youghal the priest enjoyed 'an extremely good house . . . well placed in the most interesting part of the town'. In Clogher the bishop's representative reported witheringly that no priest should be expected to live in a house which 'might satisfy the wants of a small farmer' but was 'altogether insufficient as a residence for a *gentleman*'. 'We all', spoke George Moore's Fr. MacTurnan, 'live better than our parishioners . . . [they] eat yellow meal, and I eat eggs and live in a good house.'[1]

Instances of substantial wealth, prominent rather than typical, could reinforce popular stereotypes, however undeservedly. Fr. Hickey of Doon amassed £20,000 in the 1860s with £13,000 of it sitting in the local Savings Bank. Bishops like Ryan of Limerick, with his £30,000 gifts to charities in the 1860s, Feeny of Killala, described as 'rich' by Cullen in 1872, Power of Waterford, who died in 1889 leaving £10,000 to his relatives, even Croke of Cashel, whose £19,000 inheritance from an uncle in 1857 allowed him—'for he had a good business head'—to live in 'a substantial residence' with a team of servants, were none of them, however spotless their behaviour, notable exemplars of holy poverty.[2] Again, Fr. Peter Daly of Galway, chairman of the corporation and the gas company, president of the Commercial Society and owner of the Lough Corrib Steam Company, not only, like the good and faithful servant, allowed his one pound to gain ten, but persuaded thirteen other Galway priests (as well as the local Sisters of Mercy) to invest in J. O. Lever's highly speculative Atlantic Royal Mail Steam Navigation Company of the late 1850s. He died leaving 'vast means', not to the Church, not 'for either masses or . . . charities', but to his friends.[3] In a similar mould was the parish priest of Milford in Donegal, who

[1] W. S. Blunt, *The Land War in Ireland*, pp. 54-5 (on McFadden's house, see also W. H. Hurlbert, *Ireland under Coercion*, i, 159-60, and P. MacGill, *Children of the Dead End*, p. 22); W. H. Hurlbert, op. cit. ii, 62; Revd K. McKenna to Bishop Donnelly, 10 Mar. 1882, Montgomery Papers D627/328a; 'A Letter from Rome' in Moore's *The Untilled Field* (London, 1903).

[2] Fr. J. Maher to Cullen, 2 Jan. 1842, Irish College Rome, Cullen Papers (see also Colonel H. Bruen in *Committee on Bribery at Elections*, H.C. 1835 (547), viii, 631, and W. J. Fitzpatrick, *Dr Doyle, Bishop of Kildare and Leighlin*, i, 286); Cullen to Kirby, 11 Apr. and 18 May 1863, *Paul Cullen*, iv, 139, 144 (Hickey); Cullen to Kirby, 10 Feb. 1863, ibid. iv, 135 (Ryan); Cullen to Gillooly, 16 Mar. 1872, ibid. v, 184 (Feeny); Croke to Walsh, 25 June 1889, cited E. Larkin, *The Roman Catholic Church in Ireland and the Fall of Parnell 1888-1891* (Liverpool, 1979), p. 76 (Power); M. Tierney, *Croke of Cashel*, pp. 28, 32.

[3] The final share register (P.R.O. BT31/363/1333) records Catholic clerics as purchasers of 198 £10 shares, while two local Protestant ministers bought only three between them; also Bishop MacEvilly to Cullen, 5 Oct. 1868, Cullen Papers.

died in the 1880s 'possessed not only of a farm at Ardara, but of cash on deposit in the Northern Bank to the very respectable amount of £23,711'.[1] The point here is not that such men were typical or even in many cases grasping, but that their very existence underlined an undoubted general rise in clerical incomes. The increasingly 'bourgeois' nature of the clergy's social status is confirmed by the success with which priests were infiltrating electoral rolls, impossible between 1850 and 1884 without occupation of property to the poor-law value of at least £12 in counties and £8 (after 1868 'over £4') in parliamentary boroughs. At Athlone in 1868 five of the six priests were on the register; in Tipperary 'many' of the parish priests had the vote in 1866; while at Limerick City in 1859 no less than fourteen priests voted, all of them for the Liberal candidates.[2] At Newry efficient organization ensured success: all six clergymen were registered as voters, the Bishop of Dromore out of his 'palace' valued at £90 and the five resident priests out of a shared house valued at £46 or £9. 4s. each, sufficient for the borough franchise.[3] Exceptionally detailed information for the county constituencies of Mayo (1857) and Armagh (1870) suggests a level of enfranchisement among parish priests of between a half and three-fifths, below that of Church of Ireland incumbents but ahead of Presbyterian and other dissenting ministers.[4]

As priests grew more prosperous, so the extraction of dues and other payments became an altogether smoother and less disputatious operation. After the Famine, when the spiritual and the secular parts of the clerical role had become untangled and separated, when

[1] W. H. Hurlbert, *Ireland under Coercion*, ii, 305.

[2] Compare copy of Athlone Registry for 1868 in Burgess Papers with local clergy listed in *Thom 1870*; Archbishop Leahy in *Committee on the Tipperary election*, H.C. 1867 (211), viii, 196; Revd James Reynolds in *Copy of the shorthand writer's notes of the judgement delivered by Mr Justice Fitzgerald, and of the minutes of evidence taken at the trial of the Longford election petition*, H.C. 1870 (178), lvi, 452; *Limerick Chronicle*, 7 May 1859.

[3] *Newry Election. An alphabetically arranged list of electors who voted, and those who did not, at the election held in Newry, on the 20th of November 1868* (Newry, n.d.), and *Thom 1870*. Three of the four Anglicans, none of the three Presbyterians, one of the two Unitarians, the one Independent, and neither of the two Wesleyan ministers were registered. The Bishop of Dromore's residence was unusually substantial. Cullen's house at 55 Eccles St., Dublin had a valuation of £75 (*Thom 1859*, p. 1069), while Bishop Durcan of Achonry's house at Ballaghadereen had one of only £12. 10s. (Electoral Register for Costello Barony, Mayo, 1857, P.R.O.I. M3447).

[4] In Armagh the level of enfranchisement and the mean PLV of the holdings of those enfranchised in 1870 was: Church of Ireland incumbents 73.8 per cent (£76), PPs 58.8 per cent (£20), Presbyterian ministers 54.5 per cent (£25). In five Mayo baronies in 1857 the proportion of PPs enfranchised was 52.6 per cent (£23). See Co. Armagh electoral register (P.R.O.N.I. T2883) and registers for Mayo baronies of Tyrawley, Gallen, Costello, Clanmorris, and Kilmaine (P.R.O.I. M2782-4 and M3447-8).

moral judgements and political judgements involved a different set of distinct specialities, the priest's position in society more and more began to resemble that of a ship constructed of watertight compartments designed to limit damage in the event of flooding or explosion. Thus, while politically the clergy were never immune from criticism or simple disobedience, other aspects of their activities were steadily moving out of the sphere of debate and into that of acceptance. In addition, agricultural prosperity after the mid-1850s and the relatively increasing presence of the farmer class reduced the potential demands upon the poorest sections of the community. For decades before 1850 rural secret societies had included the question of excessive clerical dues among their demands.[1] In the 1840s too strong efforts to hold down dues and fees had been made and priests had been obliged to seek police protection against threats of violence from organized parishioners.[2] Of course stories and instances of clerical greed did not disappear after the Famine, nor did resentment die away.[3] But there can be little doubt that the money rolled in more easily than before, despite the fact that a falling population produced fewer births, deaths, and marriages, all of them prime fund-raising occasions for the priesthood.[4] By the 1850s the usual western fees of twenty shillings (for the 'very poorest') and upwards for marriages, half a crown for baptisms, and Easter and Christmas dues between a shilling and a pound, were being paid, if not cheerfully, at least regularly and universally. In parts of Leinster priests were successfully demanding

[1] See, e.g., J. Soden to Palmerston, 1 Oct. 1830, Broadlands Archive 27M60, Box cxxiii; Bishop Plunkett to Propaganda, Feb. 1826, cited E. Larkin, 'Church and State in Ireland in the Nineteenth Century', pp. 298-300; also J. S. Donnelly Jr., 'The Rightboy Movement 1785-8', pp. 163-7; J. A. Murphy, 'Priests and People in Modern Irish History', pp. 235-59.

[2] See various letters from priests and reports in O.P. 1843/21/1735, 5997 cited B. Cahill, 'The Impact of the Catholic Clergy on Irish Life 1820-45', pp. 246-7; also M. Murphy, 'Repeal, Popular Politics, and the Catholic Clergy of Cork, 1840-50', p. 43; *The Irish Journals of Elizabeth Smith*, ed. D. Thomson and M. McGusty, p. 12 (17 Apr. 1840); Fr. J. Maher to Cullen, 21 Feb. 1843, Irish College Rome, Cullen Papers.

[3] K. H. Connell, 'Catholicism and Marriage in the Century after the Famine' in *Irish Peasant Society*, p. 153; Mary Carbery, *The Farm by Lough Gur*, p. 26; W. H. Hurlbert, *Ireland under Coercion*, i, 162-3; S. M. Hussey, *Reminiscences of an Irish Land Agent*, p. 120. Carlingford Papers Diary of C. Fortescue I (16 Jan. 1853) records how 'when the men of the Drogheda [Railway] Bridge, masons etc. are paid weekly, a set of priests stand at the door of the pay office and demand dues out of the pay, which they receive from all—Protestants and some Englishmen included'.

[4] C. Lee and D. MacCárthaigh, 'Certain Statistics from the United Parishes of Knockainy and Patrickswell (Diocese of Emly, Co. Limerick) for the years 1819-1941', *Journal of the Cork Historical and Archaeological Society*, xlvii (1942), 1-8. In the Parish of Monaghan 1866-85 the *average* annual take from baptisms, marriages, etc. was £259 and on Easter and Christmas dues £154. Annual curate collections produced £52 ('Accounts and Receipts', Clogher Diocesan Papers DIO(RC)1/11D).

ten pounds for marriages in the 1860s, although in cities like Dublin (where mass production raised total incomes) individual fees were much lower. Seasonal dues were regularly paid and parishes like Ennis and Rathkeale were easily able to raise sums of £142 and £170 at either Easter or Christmas alone.[1] Economic reasons, there-fore, as well as arguments of principle, allowed the clergy to refuse the occasionally proffered poisoned cup of state payments with ever-increasing firmness and confidence as the century wore on.

V POLITICS

Increased lay acquiescence in clerical views of morality and finance was not, however, accompanied by a similar deference in the field of politics. Enthusiastic clerical involvement in the post-Famine world of political localism made the priest merely one among many wheeler-dealers, suppliers of favours, and orchestrators of pressure groups.[2] 'Ecclesiastical clans', families which specialized in the production of priests who were then bound, not only to one another, but to a large farming, commercial, or professional kinship, connected powerful clerical groupings with particular and often partisan local interests. Fr. James Maher of Carlow, with Cullen as nephew, Arch-bishop Moran as cousin, two sisters and eighteen nieces as nuns, was one ecclesiastical patriarch.[3] Revd Matthew Kelly, professor at Maynooth from 1841 to 1858, was blessed with a priest as brother, a nun as sister, a bishop as uncle, and a dean as granduncle. Walter McDonald of Maynooth had two uncles, one granduncle, a brother, and two cousins in the priesthood. Two of Archbishop Croke's brothers, as well as an uncle, were priests, two sisters were nuns, and a granduncle was a bishop. All the parish priests of Morroe in Co. Limerick from 1814 to 1922 had clergymen amongst their near relatives.[4] The 'priest as boss' was not, indeed, a new phenomenon, but the three decades after 1850 undoubtedly constituted the

---

[1] F. B. Head, *A Fortnight in Ireland*, pp. 129, 163; Cullen to Kirby, 6 Oct. 1862, *Paul Cullen*, iv, 120; J. Kenny to —, Ennis [1863], O'Hagan Papers D2777/6; Cullen to Kirby, 17 Apr. 1863, *Paul Cullen*, iv, 140 (Rathkeale). See also Folklore Commission MS 1209, and note 4 p. 231 for Monaghan.

[2] See, e.g., *Galway County election petition*, H.C. 1872 (241-I), xlviii, 179–81; Lord Donoughmore to R. J. Otway, 9 Feb. 1865, Otway Papers MS 13008; J. Hodnett to Daunt, 10 Apr. 1870, O'Neill Daunt Papers MS 8046; K. T. Hoppen, 'National politics and local realities in mid-nineteenth century Ireland' in *Studies in Irish History*, ed. A. Cosgrove and D. McCartney, pp. 190–227; also Chapter VI below.

[3] D. Bowen, *The Protestant Crusade in Ireland, 1800–70*, p. 101.

[4] J. Healy, *Maynooth College*, p. 594; W. McDonald, *Reminiscences of a Maynooth Professor, passim*; M. Tierney, *Croke of Cashel, passim*; M. Tierney, *Morroe and Boher*, pp. 80–3.

heyday of the type. Dean Bourke of Tuam actually referred to himself as Mayo's 'political godfather', while Fr. Peter Daly virtually ruled Galway, conducted negotiations with government ministers over shipping contracts, and exercised considerably greater political influence than the bishop.[1] Fr. Jeremiah Halley occupied an even more permanent position in Dungarvan.[2] At Kinsale the parish priest and his curate 'controlled' thirty-four (or almost a quarter) of the votes and conducted energetic negotiations with the local MP. In the 1850s Tralee passed from the influence of Revd Dr J. M'Ennery, PP to that of Revd John Mawe, PP, both of them regarded as 'prevailing and paramount'.[3] In Cashel the clergy were highly clannish and partisan. In Wicklow Archdeacon Redmond acted dictatorially in the selection and nomination of parliamentary candidates. At Waterford the priests operated as political allies of the local drink interest.[4] In rural districts too clerical strong-men emerged, though their electoral authority was necessarily more diffused in county constituencies. The 'able domineering' Fr. Daniel Corcoran, who, as parish priest of Mullinahone from 1846 to 1862, took 'over many of the functions of a local magistrate', or the priests who organized mobs of non-voting inebriates at Mullingar in 1865 were obviously men of local weight.[5] The type was pinned down with lepidopterist precision by M. F. Mahony in his novel *The Misadventures of Mr Catlyne Q.C.* of 1872.

Canon Ingomar . . . domineered over the constituency . . . [and] possessed a fine social disposition, jocular, florid, familiar. He did not mistrust his powers of

[1] *Galway Vindicator*, 24 July 1852; J. B. to M. J. Blake, 12 Feb. 1859, Blake of Ballyglunin Papers M6936/81; MacEvilly to Cullen, 14 June 1864, Kirby Papers 1864(115); Naas to Disraeli, 8 June 1859, Hughenden Papers B/XX/Bo/13; E. R. Norman, *The Catholic Church and Ireland in the Age of Rebellion 1859–1873*, p. 16.

[2] Halley to Naas, 28 Nov. 1855, 15 Apr. 1859, Mayo Papers MSS 11023, 11036, Naas to Halley, 6 Apr. 1859, ibid. MS 11036; Bishop O'Brien to Kirby, 30 May 1865, Kirby Papers 1865(99); Revd G. Commins to Kirby, 25 Sept. 1868, ibid. 1868(283); Bishop Power to Cullen, 2 Apr. 1877, Cullen Papers; K. T. Hoppen, 'National politics and local realities in mid-nineteenth century Ireland', pp. 209–10.

[3] Revd Dr Coveny to T. O'Hagan, 24 Dec. 1862, O'Hagan Papers D2777/6; O'Hagan to Mawe, 6 May 1863, ibid.; D. Shine Lawlor to G. H. Moore, 30 June 1853, Moore Papers MS 892.

[4] Cullen to Kirby, 15 and 18 May 1863, *Paul Cullen*, iv, 143–4 (Cashel); Revd D. Kane, PP to Archbishop McCabe, 1 Apr. 1880, McCabe Papers 337/8 (Wicklow); Myles O'Reilly to Cullen, 21 Nov. 1868, Cullen Papers (Waterford); *Dublin Evening Mail*, 30 Apr. 1852, 30 Mar. 1857. See also *Clare Journal*, 13 July 1865 (Ennis); J. J. Auchmuty, 'Acton's Election as an Irish Member of Parliament', *English Historical Review*, lxi (1946), 394–405 (Carlow); *Dublin Evening Mail*, 30 Mar. 1857 (Dundalk).

[5] R. V. Comerford, *Charles J. Kickham: A Study in Irish Nationalism and Literature* (Dublin, 1979), p. 41; *Westmeath Guardian*, 20 July 1865 (cutting P.R.O.N.I. T3069/G/5B). In the three southern provinces at the 1852 General Election priests appeared on 82.6 per cent of hustings in county constituencies but on only 34.8 per cent in boroughs (calculated from F. B. Head, *A Fortnight in Ireland*, pp. 281–3).

charming in society . . . He possessed . . . not only the confidence of his bishop in Ireland, but of 'the bishops' . . . A judge of cookery and wine [he] . . . gave cosy dinners in a quiet, decorous way . . . If not sneering directly at purely scholastic attainments, he had an off-hand, jocular way of referring to such subjects which did not suggest respect . . . . He would have made an excellent tradesman or business manager, active, intelligent, acute, overbearing.[1]

Such operators depended, however, as much on native wit and nimble footwork as on the inherent power of the priestly position. Indeed, after the Famine, politics in the broadest sense provided the only relatively acceptable channel for disagreement between clergy and people. As a result, all the energy which had previously been diffused was now concentrated within the political arena alone, which, in consequence, was to exhibit a bitterness and individuality quite out of line with the growing deference elsewhere. And despite Cullen's administrative ascendancy and his efforts to circumscribe the role of the 'priest in politics', the years of his episcopate were, above all, those in which the clergy managed most successfully to let a hundred political flowers bloom.

Episcopal huffing and puffing had gone on ever since the 1820s. In the five years after Emancipation the bishops, both jointly and individually, had issued a flurry of letters and statements enjoining loyalty, quiescence, thankfulness, forbidding the use of chapels for political gatherings, and ordering priests to abandon political clubs and refrain from 'acting as chairmen or secretaries at political meetings'.[2] But the impetus of the 1820s could not be stopped and such exhortations and regulations were widely ignored, not least by their own authors. Bishop Blake of Dromore delivered a political harangue beside his own cathedral. Bishop Nolan of Kildare and Leighlin (allegedly a 'moderate') hoisted the flag of 'modification by circumstances' to oppose 'an administration which is determined to check the progress of salutary improvement'. Abraham of Waterford rallied his troops against the Beresford interest. Keatinge

---

[1] 'Matthew Stradling' [Martin Francis Mahony], 'The Misadventures of Mr Catlyne Q.C.', *Fraser's Magazine*, new series v (1872), 753–5. This work, serialized in five parts, was published in book form in 1873.

[2] In Feb. 1830 a joint letter urged withdrawal from politics after the winning of Emancipation. In Oct. 1830 Murray and Kinsella of Ossory individually reiterated the point. In July 1831 the Dublin provincial synod passed statutes forbidding the use of chapels etc. In Jan. 1834 the annual general meeting of bishops (in the only detailed set of instructions issued by the *hierarchy* before the Famine) laid down remarkably restrictive ground rules: 'Resolved that our chapels are not to be used in the future for the purpose of holding therein any public meeting, except in cases connected with charity or religion', and priests to be reminded 'most earnestly to avoid in future any allusion at their altars to political subjects and carefully to refrain from connecting themselves with political clubs' (*Ballyshannon Herald*, 31 Oct. 1834). See J. F. Broderick, *The Holy See and the Irish Movement for the Repeal of the Union with England 1829–1847* (Rome, 1951).

of Ferns urged his priests into electoral involvement. Browne of Galway thought chairmanship at political banquets in no way 'incompatible with the sacred office which I fill'. MacHale delivered two-hour harangues at Mayo elections.[1] The Repeal agitation of the 1840s attracted substantial episcopal support, and clerical infringement of the rules of 1834 was frequent and widespread, culminating in Bishop Higgins's famous expression of 'unbounded contempt' for all aristocrats at the Mullingar monster meeting of May 1843.[2] In general the clergy adopted one of two stances throughout the 1830s and 1840s: support for O'Connell's constitutional nationalism or political quietism. Admittedly, a few Whiggish clerics rose to the surface in episcopal garb or as local political chiefs. Bishop Kinsella declared for 'those who have *something*' as against 'those who have *nothing*' at the Kilkenny by-election of February 1831,[3] and parish priests at Dungarvan and Youghal preferred the house of Devonshire to O'Connell's rough wooing. But by 1841 it was the Repeal platforms that were collapsing under the weight of clerical enthusiasm.[4] Even bishops like Crotty, Murphy, Egan, and Denvir, who stood aloof from Repeal itself, were, none the less, ardent supporters of O'Connell as Catholic tribune, while most of the clergy were enthusiasts and 'sound at heart'.[5] Not only, indeed, do letters, impressions, and accounts drive home the point of involvement,[6] but detailed government

[1] J. F. Broderick, *The Holy See and the Irish Movement for the Repeal of the Union*, pp. 61-2 (Blake), 113-14 (Browne), 115 (MacHale); *D.E.P.* 13 Jan. 1835, and *Committee on Bribery at Elections*, H.C. 1835 (547), viii, 672-3 (Nolan); J. Sheehan to O'Connell, 14 Jan. 1835, *Correspondence of Daniel O'Connell*, ed. M. R. O'Connell, v, 259 (Abraham); J. H. Whyte, 'The influence of the Catholic clergy on elections in nineteenth-century Ireland', *English Historical Review*, lxxv (1960), 242 (Keatinge).

[2] *Nation*, 20 May 1843. For detailed accounts of activities in the 1830s and 1840s, see J. F. Broderick, *The Holy See and the Irish Movement for the Repeal of the Union*, *passim*, and K. B. Nowlan, 'The Catholic Clergy and Irish Politics in the Eighteen Thirties and Forties', *Historical Studies*, ix (1974), 119-36.

[3] Kinsella to Murray, [Feb. 1831], Melbourne Papers 93/110 (sent in Murray to —, 28 Feb. 1831, ibid. 93/109). See also Kinsella to Murray, [1833], ibid. 94/69 (in Anglesey to Melbourne, 27 Feb. 1833, ibid. 94/67) favouring coercion.

[4] Melbourne to Littleton, 30 Oct. 1833 and 22 May 1834, Hatherton Papers D260/M/01/8, 11; F. E. Currey to Duke of Devonshire, 26 July 1847, Devonshire Papers 25/54; *Freeman's Journal*, 18 Jan. 1841. None the less, more bishops joined the short-lived General Association of 1836-7 than the Repeal Association (G. Lyne, 'The General Association of Ireland, 1836-7' (University College Dublin MA thesis, 1968), pp. 117-18).

[5] M. Murphy, 'Repeal, Popular Politics, and the Catholic Clergy of Cork, 1840-50', pp. 46-7; Bishop Egan to O'Connell, 28 Sept. 1840, *Correspondence of Daniel O'Connell*, ed. M. R. O'Connell, vi, 367-8; Gavan Duffy to O'Connell (on Denvir), 18 Oct. 1840, ibid. vi, 373. Others, at first cautious, soon joined the Repeal Association: O'Connell to Slattery, 17 Jan. 1841, and Slattery to O'Connell, 19 Jan. 1841, ibid. vii, 7-10. See P. O'Donoghue, 'Opposition to Tithe Payments in 1830-31', *Studia Hibernica*, No. 6 (1966), 89-90, and 'Opposition to Tithe Payment in 1832-3', pp. 83, 93.

[6] See, e.g., Clarendon to Russell, 5 July 1847, Clarendon Papers L.-B. I; Lord Stuart

questionnaires distributed in May 1843 to county constabulary
inspectors and stipendiary magistrates elicited replies to the effect
(a) that the majority of priests favoured Repeal and (b) that clerical encouragement outstripped all other factors—the depression,
the press, municipal reform, and so on—as a manufacturer of
enthusiasm.[1]

On Cullen's return in 1850 he found, therefore, a clergy with
strong political tastes but with, after O'Connell's death, no effective
affiliation. The time, it seemed, was ripe for new attempts to improve
discipline and make a reality of previous unsuccessful efforts (notably
by Archbishop Murray) to assert episcopal control. Between 1850
and 1854 various regulations were produced, though, because of the
usual compromises, the final version of 1854 was less restrictive
than had at first been hoped. On the one hand, priests were 'strictly'
forbidden from discussing 'merely secular' matters or elections at
Mass or within chapels, on the other, enormous loopholes were
opened up by exhortations to condemn bribery and perjury, to
maintain the rights of the Church, and to be 'solicitous' in having
Parliament and poor-law boards stocked with 'men of integrity and
favourable to the Catholic religion'.[2] Cullen's own position varied
as circumstances changed. Neither a relentless hunter of political
priests, nor a consistent and sea-green upholder of Irish nationalism,
Cullen seems in general to have functioned politically with a mixture
of realistic pragmatism and flexible principle. Quite prepared in 1852

de Decies to Clarendon, 8 Apr. 1848, ibid. Box 10; T. Bolton to Stanley, 15 June 1843,
Derby Papers 107/3; Lord Heytesbury to Graham, 1 Oct. 1845, Graham Papers 24/Ir;
Nation, 18 May, 8 June 1844; *Committee on Bribery at Elections*, H.C. 1835 (547), viii,
666–7; *Fictitious Votes, Ireland*, 2nd series, 3rd report, pp. 173–4; A. de Tocqueville,
Journeys to England and Ireland, p. 130; K. B. Nowlan, 'The Catholic Clergy and Irish
Politics in the Eighteen Thirties and Forties', *passim*, and *The Politics of Repeal: A Study
in the Relations between Great Britain and Ireland, 1841–50* (London, 1965), pp. 65–6,
110, 156, 166, 177–8, 180, 208; A. Macintyre, *The Liberator: Daniel O'Connell and the
Irish party 1830–1847* (London, 1965), pp. 14–15, 111–17; J. F. Broderick, *The Holy
See and the Irish Movement for the Repeal of the Union, passim*.

[1] Printed Questions and Replies in Derby Papers Box 34. Every single county inspector
recorded clerical enthusiasm for Repeal, the usual phrases being 'to a man', 'generally',
'without exception'.

[2] For the crucial Latin text, see E. Larkin, *The Making of the Roman Catholic Church
in Ireland, 1850–1860*, p. 498, also p. 240 for a detailed history of the matter. The Dublin
provincial rules of 1853 had, at Cullen's instigation been altogether stricter (*Paul Cullen*,
i, 395), more so certainly than the Thurles decrees ('De Parochis' dd. 18 and 19) which were
in places rather unclear (P. C. Barry, 'The Legislation of the Synod of Thurles, 1850',
p. 150). For Catholic theory, see *Report of Maynooth Commissioners*, H.C. 1854–5 [1896],
xxii, 379, 402, 423, 432, 452, 467, 530, also J. Healy, *Maynooth College*, pp. 177–8.
Patrick Murray, in particular, stressed that political activity should be rare: 'The rule was
—stick to the sanctuary, the altar, the pulpit, the confessional, the sick-bed.'

to remove a Louth priest for delivering a political sermon or to demand in 1853 that priests 'mind their own business' and stay out of the Tenant League,[1] he was, none the less, capable of considerable mental dexterity in the matter. The restrictive tone of 1855— 'the business of a priest was to confine himself to his spiritual duties' —was effortlessly transformed into a partisan circular to the Dublin clergy during the General Election of 1857.[2] By the mid-1860s, when he himself was deeply involved in the highly political National Association, he was to show little sympathy for those who objected to clerical involvement in electoral affairs.[3] At the General Election of 1874 he was asked for help by certain Home Rule candidates: ' "Well", said the cardinal [as he by then was], "I have never issued any orders against the clergy sympathising with the people . . . if you can get a man or two men who are up to your standard on the questions of land and Home Rule, and who are up to my standard on education, let me know and I shall make arrangements that you shall get every facility in this contest." '[4] Other bishops boxed the compass with even greater energy. O'Brien of Waterford thought the synodical rules too lax, Moriarty thought them wonderfully apt, Slattery more or less ignored them, Furlong thought they created nothing but resentment, Walsh ordered his Ossory priests to withdraw from political action of any kind, Browne of Kilmore celebrated the first anniversary of the 1854 statutes by addressing his Easter Sunday congregation in favour of a by-election candidate, Leahy circularized the decrees around his diocese, the Meath clergy were encouraged by Cantwell to ignore them, while MacHale so completely flouted rules to which he had of course himself agreed that, almost two decades later, few Tuam priests seem even to have heard of them.[5]

[1] Cullen to Kirby, 13 June 1852, *Arch. Hib.* xxxi, 43; 9 Dec. 1853, ibid. xxxi, 50; also [Oct.] 1855, *Paul Cullen*, ii, 208.

[2] E. Lucas, *The Life of Frederick Lucas M.P.*, ii, 124; 1857 Circular cited E. D. Steele, 'Cardinal Cullen and Irish Nationality', p. 248; also Cullen to Kirby, 7 Jan. 1854, *Arch. Hib.* xxxi, 51.

[3] Cullen to Sir C. Domvile, 10 July 1865, Domvile Papers MS 9365.

[4] Recollections of a meeting with Cullen concerning the Co. Dublin by-election of Mar. 1874 in *The Material for Victory: Being the Memoirs of Andrew J. Kettle*, ed. L. J. Kettle (Dublin, 1958), p. 18.

[5] O'Brien to Kirby, 16 May 1857, Kirby Papers 1939, O'Brien to Cullen, 8 Mar. 1857, Cullen Papers, O'Brien to Cullen, 14 May 1857, ibid.; Moriarty to Kirby, 26 Apr. 1855, Kirby Papers 1577; Cullen to Kirby, 16 Mar. 1857, *Arch. Hib.* xxxi, 63 (Slattery); Furlong to Cullen, 26 June 1857, Cullen Papers; *Kilkenny Journal*, 8 and 25 June 1859 (Walsh); T. P. Cunningham, 'The Burrowes-Hughes by-election', pp. 199–200 (Brown); Leahy's printed leaflet of 3 Apr. 1857, Cullen Papers; Cullen to Kirby, 23 Nov. and 10 Dec. 1855, *Arch. Hib.* xxxi, 57 (Meath); Cullen to Kirby, 27 July 1857, ibid. xxxi, 65, MacEvilly to Cullen, 2 May 1872, Cullen Papers (MacHale). See also Cullen to Kirby, 28 Mar. 1857, *Arch. Hib.* xxxi, 63 for situation as a whole.

The failure to enforce even the modest regulations of 1854 helped produce a reversal of the pre-Famine situation: then fragmented clerical mores but united politics, now united mores but fragmented politics. Ecclesiastics high and low could be found actively supporting men and policies of virtually every kind, and Cullen's attempt to encourage a line of moderate reformism and general opposition to Toryism proved only fitfully successful. Episcopal irreconcilables, such as MacHale, Derry, Cantwell, Nulty, and Dorrian, were quite prepared to join in the national game of nose-cutting and facespiting in order to keep Palmerstonian Whiggism at bay. During the late 1850s and early 1860s significant sections of Catholic opinion swung to the Tories as the lesser evil on both religious and secular grounds and the sweeping Tory gains at the General Election of 1859 owed much to clerical support.[1] Bishop Walshe of Kildare and Leighlin, who saw 'no reason to be thankful' to the Liberal Government, revelled in his reputation for 'Conservative leanings— a very wholesome tendency after all'. The Meath clergy produced a notorious 'Address' pledging themselves 'deeply and passionately' against 'Lord John Russell and . . . the Whig Party' and insisting that 'from the Tory side there was never danger to the independence of the Irish Party'.[2] Bishop Keane of Cloyne, who shared all Cullen's devotional attitudes, intervened in a series of Cork elections on the Tory side, while Delany of Cork, who distrusted many of Cullen's reforms, believed, none the less, that only Liberals could promote 'in some degree the important interests that are dear to us, and that cannot be attained but slowly and gradually'.[3] Even in the mid-1860s, when Cullen's National Association managed for a time to swing opinion at least on 'religious' questions like education and

[1] *Tablet*, 19 Mar. 1859. On this episode in general, see K. T. Hoppen, 'Tories, Catholics, and the General Election of 1859', *Historical Journal*, xiii (1970), 48–67; also, for further examples of pro-Tory action by priests and bishops, *Tablet*, 23 Apr., 14 May 1859; *Nation*, 23 Apr. 1859; *The Times*, 12 May 1859; *Dublin Evening Mail*, 27, 29 Apr. 1857; *Drogheda Argus*, 7 May 1859; *C.C.* Feb. and Mar. 1860, Feb. 1861; *Roscommon Journal*, 30 Apr. 1859; *Freeman's Journal*, 12 June 1865; T. McDermot to O'Conor Don, 13 May 1859, Clonalis Papers 9.3.H.145; MacEvilly to G. H. Moore, [May 1857], Moore Papers MS 893; *Mayo County election petition*, H.C. 1857 (182 Sess. 2), vii, 3, 236.

[2] Walshe to Cullen, 3 Apr. 1857, Cullen Papers; Address in *Freeman's Journal*, 23 Apr. 1859—reprinted as an electoral pamphlet, copy in Cullen Papers.

[3] Keane to Cullen, 29 Feb. 1860, Cullen Papers; Delany to Cullen, 1 Feb. 1861 (also Keane's pastoral of Feb. 1861), ibid. See also *C.C.* 10 May 1859; T. Joyce to M. J. Blake, 20 Apr. 1859, Blake of Ballyglunin Papers M6936/81; Speech by Revd P. Leahy (later Archbishop of Cashel) in cutting in Vatican Secret Archives, Seg. di Stato 1852/278; Stephen de Vere's Diary 1854–7, Trinity College Dublin MS 5066; F. Lucas to Cullen, 10 May 1852, Cullen Papers; Revd A. Roche to Sir C. Domvile, 30 Mar. 1857, Domvile Papers MS 9361; *Clare election petition*, H.C. 1852–3 (587), ix, 791; *Minutes of evidence taken before the select committee on the Clare election petition*, H.C. 1860 (178), xi, 87–152; *Drogheda Argus*, Apr. and May 1859; *Kilkenny Journal*, 25 June 1859.

disestablishment behind the Liberal party, unity was neither universal nor more than skin-deep. The Meath clergy still canvassed the primacy of the land question, while men like Bishop Dorrian 'would have nothing to do with those Liberal Catholics who make the confidence of bishops the way to advance themselves'.[1] Disestablishment, of course, attracted widespread support, but the ecstasies of those who saw it as inaugurating the end to all 'the sighs and tears and blood of the poor faithful Irish'[2] were soon tempered by Gladstone's fierce denunciations of Vaticanism.

Active episcopal involvement in the National Association made it more difficult than ever to set effective limits to political action. If Archbishop Leahy could claim the 'right' as ecclesiastic and Irishman to demand social and political change,[3] so, by legitimate extension, could any curate or parish priest. Thus Fr. Patrick Lavelle pranced across the 1860s as propagandist for the 'Catholic doctrine of the right to revolution'; Fr. Peter Conway denounced Cullen as selling Ireland for a university charter; Fr. Mullen of Mullingar attended Fenian council meetings; Fr. Ryan (self-styled 'man of peace') exulted that at Tipperary elections the aggrieved tenant 'goes out, he takes his revolver, and he tumbles the landlord'; Wexford priests joined in hissing the national anthem; and Fr. James Anderson and others defiantly offered public Masses for the souls of the Manchester Martyrs.[4] By the late 1860s the fate of the Manchester Martyrs and the Fenian prisoners had, indeed, elicited a good deal of both positive and forced clerical sympathy.[5] Even Cullen helped gain a reprieve

[1] Dorrian to Kirby, 6 Nov. 1865, Kirby Papers 1865(263). See also Nulty to Cullen, 10 Feb. 1866, Cullen Papers—'The Whigs hate our race and religion more violently and rancorously even than the Tories.' On the National Association, see E. R. Norman, *The Catholic Church and Ireland in the Age of Rebellion 1859-1873*, Chapter Four, and P. J. Corish, 'Cardinal Cullen and the National Association of Ireland', *Reportorium Novum*, iii (1962), 13-61.

[2] Bishop McGettigan to Kirby, 3 Nov. 1868, Kirby Papers 1868(342).

[3] As he did in his Address to the Aggregate Meeting of Dec. 1864 (E. R. Norman, *The Catholic Church and Ireland in the Age of Rebellion 1859-1873*, p. 148).

[4] For Lavelle, see P. J. Corish, 'Political Problems 1860-78' in *A History of Irish Catholicism*, ed. P. J. Corish, V, Fascicule 3 (Dublin, 1967), pp. 5-23, Cullen to Kirby, 21 June 1863, Kirby Papers 1863(171), Lavelle's letter of 'retraction' of 25 Jan. 1864, ibid. 1864(14), Cullen to Kirby, 8 Mar. 1864, ibid. 1864(50), E. R. Norman, *The Catholic Church and Ireland in the Age of Rebellion 1859-1873*, pp. 111-12. See also Cullen to B. Woodlock, 23 Mar. 1868, *Paul Cullen*, iv, 234 (Conway); E. R. Norman, op. cit. 113 (Mullen); *The Times*, 25 Nov. 1869 (Ryan); *Londonderry Sentinel*, 1 Dec. 1868 (Wexford); C. M. Dwyer, 'James Augustine Anderson O.S.A.', *Seanchas Ardmhacha*, vii (1974), 215-58.

[5] R. V. Comerford, *Charles J. Kickham*, pp. 68-9, 185; Cullen to Kirby, 3 Jan. and 24 Mar. 1869, *Arch. Hib.* xxxii, 55; Cullen to Dr Spratt, 14 May 1867, *Paul Cullen*, iii, 479; E. R. Norman, *The Catholic Church and Ireland in the Age of Rebellion 1859-1873*, pp. 120-1, 127-8; Earl Spencer to Gladstone, 30 Mar. 1869, Gladstone Papers Add. MS 44306; T. Ó Fiaich, 'The Clergy and Fenianism, 1860-70', *Irish Ecclesiastical Record*, cix (1968), 81-103; Mayo to Derby, 3 Jan. 1868, Derby Papers 155/4.

for Thomas Burke in 1867; nor did he approve of Moriarty's notorious announcement that hell was not hot enough nor eternity long enough for the Fenian malcontents.[1] But here, as throughout Irish history, the clergy as a body had only thrown the revolutionaries a lifeline upon their reaching dry land: 'the clergy will preach against rebellion on account of the evils it will bring on the people, but I am sure that their almost unanimous opinion is that if there was a fair chance of success it would be lawful nay *dulce et decorum*.'[2]

Such confusions help explain the continuation of strong resistance to priestly influence in political matters at a time when clericalism was deeply affecting almost all other aspects of Irish life. Politics, indeed, came to constitute the lightning-conductor which helped channel criticism away from the main edifice of social and moral control. Whereas in the 1830s and 1840s disagreements over dues, the conduct of stations, tithes, patterns, or personal morality might have called forth a political response,[3] thirty years later politics had become a separate self-regarding activity, handled directly and in its own terms. As the cottier and labourer sections of society declined and as reducing levels of violence required less potentially irritating intervention by the priesthood, so possible political tensions assumed a more direct and unavoidable prominence. And the evidence is overwhelming that post-Famine laymen, however deferential in other respects, were, if pushed too hard, quite prepared to bite the hand that was by them fed. Already in the 1850s priests, whether 'Whigs' or 'Tories' or supporters of Independent Opposition, were having their windows smashed, being offered violence in the streets, being reported to their bishops for abusing laymen and for threatening, as recorded in 1855, to 'ball me off in real earnest from the altar', being manhandled by election mobs, having to face open and bitter electoral defiance, and having sometimes even to plead with landlords to protect them against their politically recalcitrant

---

[1] E. R. Norman, *The Catholic Church and Ireland in the Age of Rebellion 1859–1873*, pp. 126–7; Cullen to Kirby, 22 Feb. 1867, *Paul Cullen*, iv, 212. Also, some 'Cullenite' bishops like Gillooly, O'Hea, and Pius Leahy, and even the Whiggish Butler gave some support to the Amnesty Movement (T. Ó Fiaich, 'The Clergy and Fenianism, 1860–70', p. 95).

[2] Moriarty to Monsell, 2 Mar. 1868, in J. H. Whyte, 'Bishop Moriarty on Disestablishment and the Union, 1868', *Irish Historical Studies*, x (1956), 198.

[3] See, e.g., the accounts of an assault on a Limerick priest (J. O'Reagan to Lord Dunraven, 22 Dec. 1832, Dunraven Papers D3196), of Bishop Foran's problems in Waterford (Revd J. Sheehan to O'Connell, 30 Oct. 1845, *Correspondence of Daniel O'Connell*, ed. M. R. O'Connell, iv, 345–6), of the way in which one of two Catholic 'factions' in Kilorglin, angered by some new regulations introduced by the clergy, supported the Tory candidate at the Kerry election of 1837 (Report of Chief Constable Smith, 14 Aug. 1837, O.P. 1837/620/32, Box 52), of the assaults on various bishops and priests in the early 1830s (*Hansard*, xxiii, 38 (25 Apr. 1834)). See also *Committee on Bribery at Elections*, H.C. 1835 (547), viii, 308, 335–41, 473–7, 504, 542.

flocks.[1] At the Tipperary election of 1857 priests were heckled by 'women, boys, and butchers . . . who put out their tongues . . . Scarcely had the Revd gentlemen retired when a volley of stones . . . came bang in through the windows of the committee-rooms, and it was with much difficulty that Fr. Collins escaped unhurt.' Five years earlier much the same had happened in Limerick City, Co. Kilkenny, and Louth.[2] Voters defiantly resisted threats that they would not be helped at 'the day of death' and publicly announced that they had voted Conservative as a protest against clerical pressure to do the opposite.[3] Some were prepared to stand up in chapel and denounce the advice being dispensed from the altar, as happened at Meath in 1855, on several occasions two years later in Mayo (where priests responded with threats to deluge interrupters with 'a certain liquid got under the beds'), at Dungarvan in 1868, Co. Galway in 1872, and Kerry in 1880.[4] Dramatic walk-outs from Mass had also already become that last gesture of the denounced which they were long to remain.[5] Not, of course, that there was much of principle in the matter, for only a very few anticlericals like James Stephens could claim consistent support for the slogan 'No Priest in Politics —Ever'.[6] Most men, whether Fenians, Whigs, Liberals, Nationalists, Tories, voters, rioters, bribers, or bribed, spoke simply for the moment.[7] The savage abuse at hustings and canvass, the cries of

[1] *D.E.P.* 15 June 1852—cutting in Vatican Secret Archives, Seg. di Stato 1852/278 with note that story confirmed by New Ross police; Folklore Commission MS 1194, fos. 360 ff. (Limerick 1859); C. S. Farrell to Bishop Cantwell, 29 Nov. 1855, copy in Cullen Papers; A. C. O'Dwyer to Cullen, 10 Mar. 1857, ibid. (Clonmel); *Clare election petition*, H.C. 1852-3 (587), ix, 179, 201; E. O'Brien to W. Crowe, [4] May 1859, Mayo Papers MS 11036 (Limerick); *The Times*, 2 May 1859 (Roscommon); Sir R. Lynch Blosse to Naas, 18 Nov. 1858, Mayo Papers MS 11021 (Balla).

[2] *Dublin Evening Mail*, 6 Apr. 1857; *Londonderry Sentinel*, 16 July 1852; *Galway Vindicator*, 28 July 1852; *Freeman's Journal*, 6 July 1852.

[3] *Minutes of evidence taken before the select committee on the Mayo election petition*, H.C. 1852-3 (415), xvi, 48; *Cork City election petition*, H.C. 1852-3 (528), xi, 105, 109.

[4] C. S. Farrell to Cantwell, 29 Nov. 1855, copy in Cullen Papers; *Mayo County election petition*, H.C. 1857 (182 Sess. 2), vii, 118-24, 150-62; *Irishman*, 20 Sept. 1868 ('Oh! God forgive him, this is awful' cried out a Dungarvan layman from the back of the church); *Galway County election petition*, H.C. 1872 (241-I), xlviii, 136; Fr. J. O'Leary, PP to W. E. Forster, 26 Oct. 1880, in Printed Cabinet Papers CAB37/3/68.

[5] For examples, see *Galway County election petition*, H.C. 1872 (241-I), xlviii, 573; B. Ó Cathaoir, 'The Kerry "Home Rule" by-election, 1872', pp. 161, 168; *Nation*, 14 Feb. 1874; C. J. Woods, 'The Catholic Church and Irish Politics 1879-92', pp. 141-5. See J. A. Murphy, 'Priests and People in Modern Irish History', p. 257.

[6] An excellent account of the 'Fenian view' is given in R. V. Comerford, *Charles J. Kickham*, especially Chapter Four.

[7] See *C.C.* 6 Mar. 1861; *Tipperary Advocate*, 16 Feb., 4 Mar., 29 July 1865; E. R. Norman, *The Catholic Church and Ireland in the Age of Rebellion 1859-1873*, p. 457; *Daily Express*, 28 Feb. 1870; *Longford election petition*, H.C. 1870 (178), lvi, 291; Revd M. J. Brady to Archbishop McCabe, 21 Mar. 1880, McCabe Papers 337/8; Lord Emly to

'mind your own business' at Monaghan or 'No priest in politics' and 'Go back to Paul Cullen' at Tipperary in 1865, the resonant shouts of 'Hurrah for Bismarck . . . Hurrah for Oliver Cromwell' at Mayo in 1874, while disclosing strong reservoirs of feeling, defy meticulous exegesis.[1] The slow and erratic growth of Home Rule gave rise to many suggestions that the clergy were being dragged unwillingly behind an increasingly politicized laity,[2] an analysis which was underpinned by scattered clerical admissions and by the early history of the New Departure.[3] Bishop Butler of Limerick, on being reminded in the 1880s of his earlier denunciations of Home Rule, replied simply 'We must go with the people.'[4] What is, however, above all the conclusion to be drawn from any comparison between such developments in the 1880s and in earlier post-Famine decades is the fundamental continuity of the period as a whole. Thus, the cries of 'No priest in politics' at the Thurles Home Rule meeting chaired by Dean Quirke in March 1880 or the famous set piece at Macroom in April the same year when Andrew Kettle and Lysaght Finigan announced ideological and family descent from the rebels of earlier times while stick-brandishing clerics cursed Parnell's men as Friday meat-eaters and Garibaldians, were, it is clear, enacted within a still living and active tradition which had already been evolved to its highest pitch throughout the previous thirty years.[5]

The manner in which the clergy sought, in the half-century before the Land War, to exercise a political voice produced so many tensions

W. E. Forster, 3 Nov. 1880, in Printed Cabinet Papers CAB37/3/68; Archbishop Croke to Kirby, 1 Mar. 1884, in M. Tierney, *Croke of Cashel*, p. 160.

[1] G. Morant to E. P. Shirley, 8 Aug. 1865, Shirley of Ettington Papers CR229/115/7; *Nation*, 22 July 1865, *Clonmel Chronicle*, 15 July 1865, and *Irish People*, 22 July 1865; *Daily Express*, 9 Feb. 1874. Bismarck was then engaged in his *Kulturkampf* with the Catholic Church.

[2] J. A. Dease to Monsell, 9 June 1871, Monsell Papers MS 8319; R. Osborne to C. Fortescue, 4 Nov. 1869, Carlingford Papers CP3/96 R. Lalor to K. Digby, 19 Jan. 1871, Lalor Papers MS 8566.

[3] MacEvilly to Cullen, 16 Feb. 1872, Cullen Papers: 'We cannot afford to go against them [the people]'; MacEvilly to Kirby, 11 Dec. 1879, cited E. Larkin, *The Roman Catholic Church and the Creation of the Modern Irish State, 1878–1886* (Philadelphia and Dublin, 1975), p. 29; Croke to Kirby, 19 Dec. 1880, cited ibid. 52; Revd J. Bourke to Kirby, 22 May 1881, cited ibid. 113–14; Bishop Donnelly to Kirby, 1 July 1883, cited ibid. 191; R. V. Comerford, *Charles J. Kickham*, p. 115; C. J. Woods, 'The Catholic Church and Irish Politics 1879–92', p. 255; S. Clark, *Social origins of the Irish Land War* (Princeton, 1979), pp. 284–90.

[4] T. Macknight, *Ulster as it is or Twenty-Eight years' experience as an Irish editor*, 2 vols. (London, 1896), i, 232–3: 'These', noted Macknight (editor of the *Northern Whig*), 'are very significant words. They ought to be well considered by all who would really understand Ireland.' See also Bishop Gillooly to O'Conor Don, 14 Aug. 1883, Clonalis Papers 9.4.HS.204.

[5] *Limerick Chronicle*, 20 Mar. 1880; *Drogheda Argus*, 17 Apr. 1880. See also C. J. Woods, 'The Catholic Church and Irish Politics 1879–92', pp. 82, 103–4.

within the priesthood itself that an overspill of dispute and wrangling into the world at large was, perhaps, inevitable. Not only that, but eager involvement in political clubs[1] and in the selection of candidates, while at the beginning often a response to the existence of local vacuums, became as time passed a matter of struggle and rivalry. Clerical involvement in voter registration between 1832 and 1850[2] was made less important by the Franchise Act of 1850, so that enthusiasm could be diverted towards the considerably more contentious business of selecting candidates at parliamentary and other elections. Although priests had long played a part in the matter, it was the 1852 election, conducted within a fiercely sectarian atmosphere and without the benefit of O'Connellite organization, that marked the point of a deeper and more decisive intervention.[3] Exclusively clerical gatherings began to meet so as to help preserve a united front and, if possible, face constituencies with a series of accomplished facts.[4] But the very necessity of such tactics reflected the profoundly fragmented nature of clerical politics throughout the three decades between the Famine and Parnell.[5] Selection meetings

[1] See, e.g., R. Westenra to W. Gossett, 1 Oct. 1834, Hatherton Papers D260/M/01/14; *Fictitious Votes, Ireland*, 2nd series, 3rd report, p. 224; *D.E.P.* 13 Oct. and 29 Dec. 1838; J. M. Fallon to T. M. Ray, 10 Oct. 1841, N. L. I. O'Connell Papers MS 13622.

[2] M. Fallon to R. Earle, 11 Nov. 1831, Melbourne Papers 95/110; J. Walker to Palmerston, 22 Nov. 1832, Broadlands Archive 27M60, Box cxxiii; J. Evatt to Marquess of Bath, 11 Apr. 1836, Bath Papers Irish Box; G. Lyne, 'The General Association of Ireland, 1836-7', pp. 70-3; *D.E.P.* 27 Apr. 1837, 2 Nov. 1841; T. McDermot to T. M. Ray, 30 Aug., 3 Sept. 1841, N. L. I. O'Connell Papers MS 13622; S. Murphy to T. M. Ray, 28 Sept. 1841, ibid. MS 13622; Revd J. Coghlan to O'Connell, 15 Oct. 1841, ibid. MS 13623; printed circular concerning meeting 'Of the Clergy and other Reformers of Sligo County' (1841), ibid. MS 13622; mimeographed O'Connellite Circular to Clergy, 19 Dec. 1845, Smith O'Brien Papers MS 435.

[3] Events in the following constituencies make the point: Queen's Co. (*Nation*, 1 May 1852), Co. Cork (Report of Stipendiary, 4 July 1852, Mayo Papers MS 11037, *Nation*, 13 Mar. 1852), Cork City (*Cork City election petition*, H.C. 1852-3 (528), xi, 14), Limerick City (cutting in Vatican Secret Archives, Seg. di Stato 1852/278, *Nation*, 20 Mar. 1852), Mayo (Cutting in Seg. di Stato 1852/278), Galway Borough (*Galway Vindicator*, 13 Mar. 1852), Co. Galway (ibid. 27 Mar. 1852), Westmeath (*Freeman's Journal*, 25 June, 24 July 1852, F. B. Head, *A Fortnight in Ireland*, p. 187), Tipperary (ibid. 301, *Freeman's Journal*, 2 July 1852), Longford (ibid. 24 Apr. 1852), Louth (*D.E.P.* 14 May 1852), King's Co. (*Freeman's Journal*, 1 July 1852), Meath (*Dublin Evening Mail*, 24 Apr. 1852), Co. Wexford (*Freeman's Journal*, 19 May, 6 June 1852), Co. Waterford (*Waterford News*, 25 June, 13 July 1852).

[4] J. H. Whyte ('The influence of the Catholic clergy on elections in nineteenth-century Ireland', pp. 249-50) suggests that this practice only started in 1855, but for its existence in 1852, see the references in the previous note for Queen's Co., Limerick City, and Tipperary. In the three decades thereafter the practice became common: see, e.g., references to Wexford, Westmeath, Clare, and Mayo in 1857 in *Freeman's Journal*, 26, 28 Mar., 4 Apr. 1857.

[5] For continued clerical involvement, see: Tipperary (Revd P. Leahy to Cullen, 1 Mar. 1857, Cullen Papers, G. Ryan to R. J. Otway, 16 Feb. 1865, Otway Papers MS 13008),

became, as often as not, arenas for recrimination and for the settlement of local scores between priest and laity and among the priesthood itself. Local unity, though sometimes achieved——as at Meath in 1852, Tipperary in 1857, and the dioceses of Ferns in 1857, Kilmacduagh in 1859, Cashel in 1866, and Ardagh in 1869[1]——was always fragile in the extreme. More 'normal' was a state of affairs in which discord rather than harmony tended to prevail. At Louth in 1854 and 1857 priests savaged each other on the public hustings. At New Ross in 1852 parish priest and curate (each reinforced by neighbouring clergymen) violently supported different candidates. Meath priests were involved in open fisticuffs at Navan in 1855. Bishop O'Brien noted in 1857 how 'our clergy, unfortunately, are as much divided as those of Cashel and Kildare'. At Kilkenny in 1859 priests were bitterly divided.[2] The list could be extended almost indefinitely throughout the period.[3] At the Limerick election of 1858 both candidates were Catholic Liberals,

Yet the clergy . . . are . . . fiercely divided and as bitterly hostile as if there were some principle involved. Dean Butler, Father William Bourke, a lot of the curates and, it is said, the Bishop . . . on Ball's side, while Father Mat. O'Connor, Father Raleigh, Fathers Darrac, Casey, and another lot of curates, take the side of Gavin . . . The reason of all this uproar is not simply a difference in opinion on the merits of the two candidates, but a pre-existing cause of jealousy

Co. Wexford (Bishop Furlong to Cullen, 31 Mar. 1857, Cullen Papers, H. Hennessy to Cullen, 24 Oct. 1866, ibid.), Co. Cork (F. E. Currey to F. J. Howard, 4 Apr. 1857, Lismore Papers MS 7191), Co. Sligo (*Dublin Evening Mail*, 8 Apr. 1857), Co. Limerick (ibid. 1 Apr. 1857), Longford (*Drogheda Argus*, 16 Apr. 1859, Lord Granard to Cullen, 27 Jan. 1874, Cullen Papers), Louth (*Drogheda Argus*, 23 Apr. 1859), Limerick City in 1859 (Mayo Papers MS 11036), Sligo Borough (*Sligo Champion*, 15 Aug. 1868, cutting in N.L.I. MS 14335), Mayo (*Telegraph or Connaught Ranger*, 12 Aug. 1868), Galway City (*Western Star*, 7, 14 Nov. 1868), Meath (J. A. Dease to Monsell, 9 June 1871, Monsell Papers MS 8317), Kildare (*Daily Express*, 30 Mar. 1880), King's Co., Queen's Co., and Westmeath (ibid. 19, 20, 22, 23 Mar. 1880), also Gillooly's Circular to his Clergy, 28 Dec. 1876, Clonalis Papers 9.4.HS.094.

[1] Cantwell to Kirby, 1 Oct. 1852, Kirby Papers 1049; Revd P. Leahy to Cullen, 1 Mar. 1857, Cullen Papers; Bishop Furlong to Cullen, 31 Mar., 1 Apr. 1857, ibid.; Bishop Fallon to Kirby, 12 May 1859, Kirby Papers 2356; *Committee on the Tipperary election*, H.C. 1867 (211), viii, 195-6; *Longford election petition*, H.C. 1870 (178), lvi, 343.

[2] Fr. J. Powderley to Kirby, 25 Feb. 1854, Kirby Papers 1377, and Dixon to Kirby, 13 Apr. 1857, ibid. 1925A; *D.E.P.* 15 June 1852; Cullen to Kirby, 23 Nov., 2 Dec. 1855, *Arch. Hib.* xxxi, 56-7; O'Brien to Cullen, 2 Mar. 1857, Cullen Papers; C. B. Lyons to Cullen, 19 Apr. 1859, ibid.

[3] See, e.g., *Clare election petition*, H.C. 1852-3 (587), ix, 791; W. Crowe to Naas, 20 Apr. 1859, Mayo Papers MS 11025; W. H. Gregory to Clanricarde, [8 Apr. 1857], Clanricarde Papers 40; A. C. O'Dwyer to Cullen, 10 Mar. 1857, Cullen Papers; Lord Campden to Naas, 23 Apr. [1859], Mayo Papers MS 11025; *Dundalk Democrat*, 21 May 1859; Revd R. Galvin to Cullen, 12 Nov. 1868, Cullen Papers; *C.C.* 5, 8 June 1863; Revd Fr. Crean to Bishop O'Brien, 24 Sept. 1868, Cullen Papers; *Waterford Citizen*, 23 Oct. 1868; Lord Granard to Cullen, 10 Jan. 1871, Cullen Papers; Gillooly to Cullen, 16 Mar. 1874, ibid.

at Father Butler having been made dean. This fact created immense soreness on the part of those who saw themselves better entitled to such a dignity . . . and so we have the people canvassed and re-canvassed, making promises and breaking them.[1]

Equally destructive were those inter-diocesan conflicts encouraged by local patriotism and by a desire to use external attack as a means of suppressing internal disunity.[2] Here individual bishops seemed positively to relish the clash of rivalry and distrust. MacHale and Gillooly, who overlapped in the Galway and Roscommon constituencies, were locked in permanent conflict. In King's Co. wrangling broke out between the clergy of Killaloe, Ardagh, and Meath. Tuam and Galway disputed the Galway County constituency. In Co. Limerick there was fierce rivalry between the priests of Cashel and those of Limerick itself. W. H. Gregory records how clerical attitudes at the Galway election of 1857 were dictated by loyalty to the respective dioceses of Tuam, Galway, Clonfert, and Kilmacduagh. Most notable of all was the famous clash of the Co. Cork by-election of 1860 between the dioceses of Cloyne, Cork, and Ross.[3]

The very nature of electoral contests—often bitter, fierce, local, corrupt—called forth a matching response which grew especially intense in the decades immediately after the Famine. Few county hustings were complete without a substantial clerical presence,[4] while the number of formal allegations of, and unseatings of MPs for, spiritual intimidation was much higher in the period 1852-81 (18 and 6 respectively) than it had been in 1832-51 (9 and 2).[5]

[1] D. Griffin to Earl of Dunraven, 29 Jan. 1858, Dunraven Papers D3196; also J. Ball to Dunraven, 21 Feb. [1858], ibid.; *Limerick Reporter*, 15 Apr. 1859; W. Spaight to Naas, 4 May 1859, Mayo Papers MS 11036; *C.C.* 21 Apr. 1859.

[2] See Walter McDonald's account of student life in the early 1870s: 'Football and hurling were not allowed; lest, it was said, an inter-diocesan and inter-provincial faction-spirit should be raised, and we should kill one another' (*Reminiscences of a Maynooth Professor*, pp. 48-9); also J. Healy, *Maynooth College*, p. 466: 'The general rule at Maynooth then [1850s] was, as it is still, that after breakfast and dinner the students of each diocese associated with themselves alone during their walks at recreation'.

[3] Gillooly to Kirby, 26 Oct. 1862, *Arch. Hib.* xxx, 31, and to McCabe, 10 June 1880, McCabe Papers 346/1; Bishop Power to Cullen, 9 Aug. 1868, Cullen Papers; MacEvilly to G. H. Moore, [May 1857], Moore Papers MS 893; J. Elland to Butt, 7, 12 Jan. 1874, Butt Papers MS 8696; *Sir William Gregory, K.C.M.G., formerly member of parliament and sometime governor of Ceylon. An Autobiography*, ed. Lady Gregory (London, 1894), pp. 162-3. For Cork, see below, pp. 250-1.

[4] In 1852 priests were present on 19 of the 23 county hustings outside Ulster (see F. B. Head, *A Fortnight in Ireland*, pp. 281-3). See also the cuttings on the 1852 election collected by the Government and presented to the Vatican in Vatican Secret Archives, Seg. di Stato 1852/278.

[5] The number of petitions presented (and pursued) and the number of those resulting in voidance equalled 55 and 28 in 1832-51, and 54 and 19 in 1852-81 (calculated from

Politics now offered one of the few spheres in which priests could still behave as if distinctions between the religious and the profane had not yet achieved effective definition. Involvement in the most clearly secular aspects of electioneering—treating, bribery, the encouragement of mobs, acting as personation agents—continued, sometimes openly sometimes covertly, to form a significant strand in the clergy's concerns. Wild mêlées were garnished with clerical agitators made incoherent by the frenzy of it all: Fr. Bourke got 'very excited', rushed about flourishing 'a whip with a lash to it [and shouting] . . . "Boys fight for your religion", "God", "Traitors" '.[1] At the same time the comparatively casual use of what was pejoratively known as 'spiritual intimidation' seems to have reached its climax during this period. Perspective, as in everything, is all important. Yet, making every allowance, it would be impossible to deny that even Judge Keogh's vituperative masterpiece after the Galway election of 1872 was not entirely without foundation.

Fr. Lavelle is still an officiating priest, who goes to the altar, and who . . . does not perform but desecrates the renewal of that *tremendum mysterium* which was consecrated upon Calvary . . . As to Revd Peter Conway, all I can say of him is *splendide mendax* . . . what an odious exhibition he made of himself . . . as he swelled and fumed, talked and raged . . . [Dreadful was] the organized system of intimidation which has pervaded this county in every quarter, in every direction, in every barony, in every town, in every place. I shall report to the House of Commons that the Archbishop of Tuam, the Bishop of Galway, the Bishop of Clonfert,

---

information in the relevant parliamentary papers on individual petitions, various legal handbooks, *The Irish Franchise and Registration Question* (London, 1841), *Return of the election petitions alleging Bribery and Corruption*, H.C. 1866 (77), lvi, 515–28, *Return of all election petitions alleging Intimidation or Undue Influence*, H.C. 1866 (114), lvi, 529–36, *Returns of the number of petitions complaining of Undue Returns*, H.C. 1880 (69), lvii, 63–8).

[1] *Clare election petition*, H.C. 1852–3 (587), ix, 574, 594, 671, 742, and *Copies of the several inquisitions removed from the Court of Queen's Bench . . . and transferred to the County of Clare*, H.C. 1852–3 (313), xciv, 112. For a sample of similar cases, see *Galway Vindicator*, 20, 26 Mar. 1852; Eglinton to S. Walpole, 22, 24 July 1852, Eglinton Papers MS 5337; *Cork City election petition*, H.C. 1852–3 (528), xi, 13; Cullen to Kirby, 16 Jan. 1854, *Arch. Hib.* xxxi, 82; D. Power, H. Rodwell, and E. L'E. Dew, *Reports of the decisions of committees of the House of Commons in the trial of controverted elections during the sixteenth parliament of the United Kingdom* (London, 1857), p. 247; *Mayo County election petition*, H.C. 1857 (182 Sess. 2), vii, 175; *Dublin Evening Mail*, 20 Mar. 1857; *Clare election petition*, H.C. 1860 (178), xi, 144–8; *Westmeath Guardian*, 20 July 1865; H. Armstrong to Naas, 15 Oct. [1866], Mayo Papers MS 11142; *Report of the Commissioners appointed for the purpose of making inquiry into the existence of Corrupt Practices at the last election for Cashel; with minutes of evidence*, H.C. 1870 [C 9], xxxii, 178–9, 336–8; Lord Strathnairn to Under-Secretary, 1 Mar. 1869, Kilmainham Papers MS 1062; Strathnairn to Duke of Grafton, 22 Mar. 1869, Strathnairn Papers Add. MS 42825; *Longford election petition*, H.C. 1870 (178), lvi, 283–6, 301; E. L. O'Malley and H. Hardcastle, *Reports of the decisions of the judges for the trial of election petitions in England and Ireland*, ii (London, 1875), p. 11.

all the clergymen whose cases I have gone through . . . have been guilty of an organized attempt to defeat the free franchise and the free votes of the electors.[1]

And although, of course, many elections were entirely innocent of such excesses, the Galway case was, none the less, a not unnatural outcome of the way in which the clergy were prepared to wield their spiritual weapons: threatened refusal of sacraments, altar denunciations, quasi-religious cursing, the giving of religious sanction to participation in local rivalries and mundane disputes. Priests in Kilkenny pointedly reminded their parishioners that 'You cannot give half your soul to God and the other to the Devil. It is a moral essence; it is indivisible; it will all go to Hell or to Heaven.' In Limerick they locked the chapel doors and urged a captive flock to 'keep their baptismal vows and . . . renounce the Devil' by voting for one Catholic Liberal rather than another. In Mayo Fr. Conway could be heard announcing 'My curse as a priest, the curse of God, the curse of the church and people be upon you if you vote for Colonel Higgins.'[2] Priests threatened to withhold sacraments, certainly in Kerry, Louth, Cork, Tipperary, Mayo, Longford, and Dublin, and almost certainly in many other places as well.[3] The clergy of King's Co. called down a 'visible curse . . . on the man who votes for John Pope Hennessy'. Those in Longford hoped that obstinate voters would rot 'till the maggots and worms eat you, and after that you may go to Hell'.[4]

The involvement was undoubted—for example in 1859 over two-thirds of the priests in Co. Kilkenny and four-fifths of those in

---

[1] *Galway County election petition*, H.C. 1872 (241-I), xlviii, 17–70. Keogh 'specially reported' three bishops and thirty-one priests. Of these, twenty-eight priests came from the dioceses of Tuam, Galway, Clonfert, and Kilmacduagh, and, although large parts of the first two lay outside the constituency, these clerics still constituted 16.2 per cent of *all* the priests in these four dioceses (*Catholic Directory 1873*). The prosecutions failed and the government was, indeed, usually reluctant to take legal action against priests save in the most outrageous cases (A. Brewster to Lord St Germans, 20 June 1853, Aberdeen Papers Add. MS 43207).

[2] Report on Kilkenny, 18 July 1852, Mayo Papers MS 11184; J. Ball to Dunraven, 21 Feb. [1858], Dunraven Papers D3196 (Limerick); *Telegraph or Connaught Ranger*, 24 Feb. 1858, and *Mayo County election petition*, H.C. 1857 (182 Sess. 2), vii, 7–8, 41. Conway was immediately thereafter promoted from curate to parish priest by MacHale.

[3] *Londonderry Sentinel*, 30 July 1852; Dean Kieran to Dixon, 26 Feb. 1854, Dixon Papers VII/2; *C.C.* 15 July 1852; *Daily Express*, 24 July 1852; Cullen to Kirby, 5 Feb. 1858, *Arch. Hib.* xxxi, 66; Report on Longford, 7 Aug. 1852, Mayo Papers MS 11037; J. Lord, *Popery at the hustings*, p. 40.

[4] *Irish People*, 1 July 1865; *Longford election petition*, H.C. 1870 (178), lvi, 301; also Lord Bellew to Cullen, 4 May 1852, Cullen Papers; C. S. Farrell to Cullen, 26 Nov. 1855, ibid.; E. O'Brien to W. Crowe, [4] May 1859, Mayo Papers MS 11036; Strathnairn to Lord De Vesci, 3 Dec. 1868, Strathnairn Papers Add. MS 42828; *Daily Express*, 23 Mar. 1853; *Western Star*, 6 Mar. 1869; Gillooly's 'Suggestions as to the Clergy relative to the approaching [Roscommon] Election', 1859, Clonalis Papers 9.3.HS.034; *Report from the select committee on parliamentary and municipal elections*, H.C. 1868-9 (352), viii, 264–6.

Louth signed their names to electoral placards, flysheets, and mani-festos[1]—the effect, however, altogether more ambiguous. Con-temporary views are not always helpful. On the one side, animus rather than assessment lay behind the many frantic suggestions for legislation against priestly 'interference'.[2] On the other, senti-mental recollections of an electoral Soggarth Aroon, of priestly supermen, or of Archbishop MacHale as western Napoleon sur-rounded by a staff of priests, 'generals in fact, who were the bravest of the brave', distort rather than illuminate.[3] Not only, however, were commentators not unanimous about the effectiveness of it all, but the endemic disagreements and disputes within the Church served to lessen its overall impact as a national vehicle of political influence and power. Some thought that clerical leverage would be increased, others that it would be diminished, by the Franchise Act of 1850.[4] For every fear that the Church's power was growing, there were suggestions that it was 'diminishing and that people think and act much more for themselves than they did'.[5] Observers pointed to the failure of particular electoral interventions: in Co. Cork and Queen's Co. in 1852, Cashel throughout the 1850s, Co. Sligo in 1857, Limerick City in 1858, Queen's Co. in 1868, and, above all, at the important series of 'national' by-elections between 1869 and 1872.[6] Priests, it

[1] Calculated by comparing clergy listed in *Thom 1859*, pp. 713–34 with various signed statements in (a) *Kilkenny Journal*, 16 Apr., 14 May 1859, (b) *Drogheda Argus*, 23 Apr. 1859.

[2] See, e.g., Glengall to Derby, 19 Oct. 1852, Derby Papers 120/2; Eglinton to Walpole, 23 Oct. 1852, Eglinton Papers MS 5337; Sir M. Barrington to Derby, 6 Sept. 1852, Derby Papers 125/4; A. C. Innes MP to Mayo, 16 Mar. 1868, Mayo Papers MS 11168. While the 1854 Corrupt Practices Act (17 & 18 Vict., c. 102) omitted all mention of 'spiritual in-timidation', that of 1883 (46 & 47 Vict., c. 51, s. 2) referred to 'any temporal *or spiritual* injury, damage, harm, or loss upon or against any person in order to induce or compel such person to vote or refrain from voting'.

[3] James Berry, *Tales from the West of Ireland*, ed. G. M. Horgan (Dublin, 1975), p. 12 ('A Parliamentary Election'); Folklore Commission MS 1194, fos. 318 ff.

[4] Clarendon to Russell, 17 Feb. 1851, Clarendon Papers L.-B. VI; Stanley to Down-shire, 16 Mar. 1850, Derby Papers 178/2; Lord Sligo to G. H. Moore, [late 1850], Moore Papers MS 891. See also a clerical speech of 1851: 'We have too, in our own hands . . . an instrument of terror—the new elective franchise; with this . . . we can tumble governments like ninepins' (cutting in Vatican Secret Archives, Seg. di Stato 1852/278).

[5] Clarendon to Russell, 29 Nov. 1851, Clarendon Papers L.-B. VII.

[6] Lord Shannon to Derby, 31 Mar. [1852], Derby Papers 150/11 (Cork); R. Miller to E. Staples, 29 Apr. 1852, Drapers' Company L.-B. Irish 1850-60 (Queen's Co.); Revd P. Leahy to Cullen, 8 Mar. 1857, Cullen Papers (Cashel); *Dublin Evening Mail*, 8 Apr. 1857 (Sligo); J. Ball to Dunraven, 21 Feb. [1858], Dunraven Papers D3196 (Limerick); *Free-man's Journal*, 15, 17 Aug. 1868 (Queen's Co.). On the later by-elections, see *Daily Express*, 21 Sept. 1871; *Cork Herald*, 13 Feb. 1872; B. Cahir, 'Irish National By-Elections 1870-1874' (University College Dublin MA thesis, 1965); *idem*, 'Isaac Butt and the Limerick By-Election of 1871', *North Munster Antiquarian Journal*, x (1966), 56–66; *idem* [as B. Ó Cathaoir], 'The Kerry "Home Rule" by-election, 1872', pp. 154–70.

was widely remarked, were only successful when articulating the implicit preferences of their flocks or when canvassing topics (denominational education most notably) for which the mass of the laity had little burning concern.[1] But such views, even if true, disguise the distinction between broad national influence, on the one hand, and local influence, on the other. Aspiring candidates of appropriate hue rarely thought twice before swarming around the clerical honey-pots of their own constituencies. Priests, secular and regular, were usually the first ports of call, and clerical co-operation in matters of organization and canvassing was always highly prized.[2] While in the eighteenth and early-nineteenth centuries the rural priest had still faced an amount of rivalry within the community from such comparatively independent figures as poets and school-masters,[3] thereafter he was to stand virtually alone until the arrival of shopkeeper allies produced a sharing, though hardly a diminution, of status. National schoolteachers were kept firmly under control and the Irish clergy never faced the strident opposition which their colleagues in even so Catholic a part of France as Brittany experienced at the hands of that 'pillar of the Republic', the village schoolmaster.[4]

In the end, the immediate extent of the clergy's political and electoral influence can only rarely be assessed with any exactitude. The potential was certainly substantial. Smaller boroughs with electorates of one to four hundred were generally part of only a single parish, and while some rural parishes might have as few as seven or eight voters country priests more commonly had between thirty and eighty enfranchised parishioners 'at their disposal'.[5] O'Connell's

[1] [W. G. Ward], 'The Priesthood in Irish Politics', *Dublin Review*, new series xix (1872), 276; Lord Anglesey's Memo for the cabinet of 30 Dec. 1831, Anglesey Papers D619/32E; *D.E.P.* 2 July 1835; *Nation*, 10 Apr. 1852; *Cork City election petition*, H.C. 1852-3 (528), xi, 412; R. Osborne to C. Fortescue, 4 Nov. 1869, Carlingford Papers CP3/96; J. A. Dease to Monsell, 25 Aug. 1872, Monsell Papers MS 8917.

[2] For endless applications, see Cullen Papers; also O'Connell to Daunt, 9 Sept. 1842, *Correspondence of Daniel O'Connell*, ed. M. R. O'Connell, vii, 173-4; Sir W. Hort to Duke of Leinster, 2 Mar. 1852, Leinster Papers D3078/3/80; *Galway Vindicator*, 27 Mar. 1852; Bishop Cantwell to Cullen, 3 Apr. 1852, Cullen Papers; Stephen de Vere's Diary 1854-7, MS 5066; Carlingford Papers Diary of C. Fortescue I (20, 29 Jan. 1854); Sir J. Young to Lord Monck, 16 Mar. 1857, Young Letter-Book; *Limerick Reporter*, 12, 26 Apr. 1859; Clogher Diocesan Papers DIO(RC)1/11A/1-37; J. H. Whyte, *The Independent Irish Party 1850-9*, pp. 77-8.

[3] T. Ó Fiaich, 'Irish Poetry and the Clergy', *Léachtái Cholm Coille* [Maynooth], iv (1975), 30-56; L. M. Cullen, 'The Hidden Ireland: Re-assessment of a Concept', *Studia Hibernica*, No. 9 (1969), 23.

[4] B. B. Singer, ' "Pillar of the Republic": The Village Schoolmaster in Brittany 1880-1914' (University of Washington Ph.D. thesis, 1971), especially Chapter Two. Hence some of the clerical apprehension of the lay-led Land League (M. Davitt, *The Fall of Feudalism in Ireland or the story of the Land League Revolution* (London, 1904), p. 466).

[5] The numbers 7, 34-6, 60, 80, and 80 again occur in *Galway County election petition*,

movement had depended heavily on the clergy's support, for, as the Chief Secretary had commented in 1845, 'whenever the priests came forward and collected their parishioners a large force was brought into the [meetings] . . . but from those parishes in which no such influence was used, few persons attended'.[1] The result of the Donegal election of 1852 shows that the tenant-right vote depended more on clerical activism than on the mere local presence of a Catholic electorate.[2] At Wicklow in 1857, where the Conservative candidate obtained clerical support only in the eastern Talbotstown baronies, these alone placed him at the head of the poll. Two years later in Co. Kilkenny, when the clergy were split between the Whiggish Catholic, William Shee, and two uncompromising Independent tenant-righters, John Greene and G. H. Moore, although the latter attracted most support, Shee undoubtedly did best in those areas where the clergy were least opposed to his cause.[3] Monaghan priests successfully 'turned round' substantial numbers of voters in 1865, while at the Co. Galway by-election of 1872 many tenants who had promised for one side were persuaded to 'change their minds'.[4] Again, at Kerry in 1872, although the bulk of the clergy under Bishop Moriarty failed to prevent a Home Rule triumph, it is clear that the victorious candidate did much better in those baronies where a significant number of maverick priests had defied their bishop and canvassed on his behalf.[5]

By isolating one element—clerical influence—in a complex equation, such examples beg as well as answer questions. Thus, Shee's Kilkenny vote in 1859 may have depended crucially on the location of his own landed property and Hume's Wicklow result of 1857 upon the distribution of landed support in general. Yet the results of two by-elections in Co. Cork—a constituency pleasingly

H.C. 1872 (241-I), xlviii, 899, 636, 677, 755, and *Longford election petition*, H.C. 1870 (178), lvi, 523-4. Archdeacon Redmond (PP Arklow) claimed to 'have' 150 voters in Co. Wicklow and 100 in Co. Wexford, though that they would have been all in his own parish is unlikely (to Cullen, 11 Nov. 1868, Cullen Papers).

[1] T. F. Fremantle to Peel, 10 Oct. 1845, Peel Papers Add. MS 40476.

[2] Information on the baronial patterning of the vote in *Belfast Newsletter*, 2 Aug. 1852; on the religious distribution of the population in the *Census* of 1861, H.C. 1863 [3204-III], lx, 45-54; on the localized activism of the clergy kindly supplied by Desmond Murphy, Esq.

[3] *Dublin Evening Mail*, 15, 22 Apr. 1857; *Kilkenny Journal*, 16 Apr., 14, 18 May 1859.

[4] *Londonderry Sentinel*, 28 July 1865; *Galway County election petition*, H.C. 1872 (241-I), lxviii, 858, also 176-7, 187-8, 250-1, 407, 469-72.

[5] Notably in Iraghticonnor and Clanmaurice (polling at Listowel) where the Home Rule vote was 87.4 per cent (49.9 per cent in the rest of the county): see B. Ó Cathaoir, 'The Kerry "Home Rule" by-election, 1872', pp. 165-6.

divided between the jurisdictions of the Bishops of Cloyne, Cork, Ross, and Kerry—reinforce the evidence from other places. When in 1852 the Cloyne priests 'imposed' their candidate upon the Liberal machine, the effect upon polling figures was dramatic, for the boundary between the areas of Liberal and Conservative majorities at once became strikingly aligned to the boundaries of Cloyne.[1]

	Liberal per cent	Conservative per cent
Whole County	56.0	44.0
Cloyne Baronies	65.0	35.0
Other Baronies	41.0	59.0

Eight years later, with the Cloyne clergy fervently backing the crypto-Tory carpet-bagger, Lord Campden, and the rest equally strong in support of his Liberal opponent, Rickard Deasy, the situation was clearer still.[2]

	Deasy per cent	Campden per cent
Whole County	62.6	37.4
Cloyne Baronies	47.3	52.7
Other Baronies	86.5	13.5

At a by-election in the following year, when diocesan loyalties were not at stake, the patterning of the vote followed the distribution of landlord rather than clerical influence.[3]

It was eventually in the furnace of Home Rule and the Land War that the clergy's political status was tempered and reassessed. Previously, although most priests had of course 'supported' tenants rather than landlords, their varied positions on the land question had—apart from a clear identification with farmers rather than labourers—defied overall characterization. Certainly, both before and after the Famine one can find public and private denunciations of landlords as 'the cause of all our miseries', as 'anxious to wallow up to their knees in human blood', as 'tyrants and . . . exterminators of the poor'.[4]

---

[1] *Cork Southern Reporter*, 23 Mar. 1852.

[2] *C.C.* Feb. and Mar. 1860. See also Chapter II above, p. 163.

[3] *C.C.* 6, 10, 26, 28 Feb. 1861.

[4] A. de Tocqueville, *Journeys to England and Ireland*, p. 164; *Committee on Bribery at Elections*, H.C. 1835 (547), viii, 650–2; F. B. Head, *A Fortnight in Ireland*, p. 370. See also Lord Courtown to Clarendon, 14, 17 Dec. 1847, Clarendon Papers Box 8; cuttings in Vatican Secret Archives, Seg. di Stato 1852/278; Moore Papers MS 899.

The priests of Meath in particular remained true to the cause of land reform throughout the 1850s and 1860s at a time when, in the eyes of many churchmen, such a course seemed neither popular nor profitable. The majority, however, were less extreme. Cullen, who had clear ideas about agrarian reform, distrusted Bishop Nulty of Meath's exuberance and believed that violent priests merely provoked landlord retaliation.[1] On the whole the bishops adopted a moderate tone throughout the 1860s. When in August 1869 they issued a set of ten resolutions on public affairs, nine concerned education and only one, which combined strong rhetoric with impenetrable vagueness, touched on 'the one topic which engages the attention of the people'.[2] By then individual clergymen had, in any case, already propounded elaborate distinctions between bad landlords and good,[3] and the amount of fraternization had become considerably greater than is often imagined. Especially on larger estates, priests were rarely reluctant to accept financial and material favours or gifts from landed hands.[4] Warm electoral compacts were concluded and by no means always on the priest's terms.[5] Landlords, indeed, were sometimes prepared to write polite letters to Catholic bishops in order to encourage such collaboration.[6] One Louth priest was even willing in 1865 to announce publicly that local tenants were, contrary to their own denials, quite prosperous enough to pay the arrears of rent demanded by their landlords.[7] A Limerick

---

[1] Cullen to Kirby, 10 Mar. 1865, Kirby Papers 1865(52). See E. D. Steele, 'Cardinal Cullen and Irish Nationality', pp. 239-60.

[2] *Daily Express*, 4 Sept. 1869, cited E. R. Norman, *The Catholic Church and Ireland in the Age of Rebellion 1859-1873*, pp. 392-3, also pp. 144 ff.

[3] See, e.g., Revd D. M. Collins, PP to O'Connell, 2 June 1841, *Correspondence of Daniel O'Connell*, ed. M. R. O'Connell, vii, 82-3; *Nation*, 24 Jan. 1852; *Galway Vindicator*, 1 Sept. 1852.

[4] Downshire to Revd J. Colgan, 10 Nov. 1829, Downshire Papers D671/C/254/58; Lord Devon to Lord Ebrington, 26 Mar. 1839, Fortescue Papers 1262M/LI26; Earl Fitzwilliam to R. Chaloner, 30 Oct. 1843, Chaloner Papers ZFM/318; F. E. to W. Currey, 14 Apr. 1851, Lismore Papers MS 7186; Revd M. Brennan to J. Kincaid, 20 June, 2 July 1852, Kincaid to Brennan, 19, 25 June 1852, Palmerston to Kincaid, 19 July 1852, Broadlands Archive 27M60, Box cxix; Downshire to Derby, 23 July 1852, Derby Papers 124/6; Sir C. Domvile to Revd C. Rooney, 7 Aug. 1865, Domvile Papers MS 9365.

[5] Revd. J. McHugh to Palmerston, 23 Apr. 1829, Broadlands Archive 27M60, Box cxxiii; Lord Clare to Clarendon, 19 Aug. 1847, Clarendon Papers Box 8; R. Chaloner to Revd J. McKenna, 12 July 1847, 13 Apr. 1848, and to Revd P. Morrin, 30 Apr. 1852, Fitzwilliam Papers MS 3987; Revd A. Roche to Sir C. Domvile, 30 Mar. 1857, Domvile Papers MS 9361; *Drogheda Argus*, 21 May 1859; Bishop Fallon to Lord Dunkellin, 13 July 1865, Clanricarde Papers 49; Clogher Diocesan Papers DIO(RC)1/6/15-51.

[6] Lord Desart to Clarendon, 11 Dec. 1849, Clarendon Papers Box 10; Lord Oranmore to Clarendon, 20 July [1850], ibid. Box 21; Sir C. Domvile to Cullen, 20 Apr. [1865], Cullen Papers; Cullen to Domvile, 13 May 1865, ibid. L.-B. 4; Domvile to Cullen, 9 July 1865, ibid.

[7] *Irish People*, 3 June 1865.

landlord could demand 'three cheers' for the local parish priest in return for co-operation in bringing defaulters to justice. To Bishop Egan the Knight of Kerry was an 'old friend'. From Archdeacon Redmond Lord Carysfort's death in 1868 called forth a eulogy of eager generosity.[1] Landlords, though probably less often as time went on, had priests to dine, a kindness sometimes repaid by sermons on the sins of poaching.[2] A few superfine clerics simply loved a lord. The unfortunate Duke of Devonshire was pursued around Lismore in the 1850s and 1860s by the Uriah Heepish figure of Fr. Pat Fogarty, VG, anxious for 'a word', anxious that he might do himself 'the high honour of paying your grace my personal respects', while the social and culinary activities of the ghastly Fr. Healy of Little Bray, guest at Blenheim, Hatfield, and Gladstone's breakfasts, are well known.[3]

Such men, though far from typical, were but the extreme manifestations of a living tradition. Bishops like Moriarty, with his belief that land agitation struck at the 'foundations of property' and the roots of society,[4] may, indeed, have been unusual, but they did not spring from the void. And the presence of such a tradition—and of much simple indifference too—severely fractured the Church's initial response to the new agrarian and political demands of the 1870s and 1880s. The Orange tinge of Home Rule in its early days alarmed Church leaders confused by the swiftness of contemporary political realignments.[5] A few bishops of the older radical school, like MacHale, O'Hea, and Keane, were, without fully realizing the potential of the movement, more welcoming. So were a handful of more recent appointments, such as Duggan, Nulty, and Dorrian. Most, however, seem simply to have regarded the whole business as yet another attempt to push 'the people' away from the Church

[1] Folklore Commission MS 1194, fos. 372 ff., and *Londonderry Sentinel*, 22 Dec. 1868; ibid. 11 July 1865, 6 Oct. 1868; Egan to Knight of Kerry, 11 May 1831, FitzGerald Papers; Redmond to Cullen, 11 Nov. 1868, Cullen Papers.

[2] P. Ó Mórdha, 'Some Notes on Monaghan History (1692–1866)', *Clogher Record*, ix (1976), 47; N. W. Senior, *Journals, conversations, and essays relating to Ireland*, ii, 22; G. Rooper, *A Month in Mayo*, pp. 54–5.

[3] Fogarty pursued both the sixth and the seventh Dukes (Fogarty to Devonshire, 5 Aug. 1848 and 22 Mar. 1851, Devonshire Papers 207/0 and 1; seventh Duke's Diary, Vol. XIII for 5 May 1859, and Vol. XVII for 25 Apr. 1865, ibid.); [W. J. Fitzpatrick], *Memoirs of Father Healy of Little Bray* (Dublin, 1896). See also W. McDonald, *Reminiscences of a Maynooth Professor*, p. 82, on certain Maynooth professors.

[4] Moriarty to Archbishop Leahy, 10 Feb. 1864, in 'Correspondence concerning the Disestablishment of the Church of Ireland 1862–1869', ed. M. Tierney, *Collectanea Hibernica*, No. 12 (1969), 122; Moriarty to Monsell, 2 Mar. 1868, Gladstone Papers Add. MS 44152; Moriarty to Revd W. Walsh, 23 Jan. 1877, Walsh Papers 350/3.

[5] Revd P. Moran to Kirby, 25 Aug. 1871, Kirby Papers 1871(190A); Cullen to Kirby, 28 Oct. 1873, ibid 1873(403); Cullen to Cardinal Manning, 13 Oct. 1871, *Paul Cullen*, v, 167; Leahy to Daunt, 14 Feb. [1871] and 3 Aug. 1872, O'Neill Daunt Papers MS 8046.

and towards a merely secular social and economic culture.[1] Yet there are clear signs that a significant number of priests were, for reasons ranging from ideological conviction to the changing demands of a local *Realpolitik*, running ahead of the episcopate.[2] And however amorphous and many-splendoured the ideas of Home Rule and land reform may have remained throughout the decade, this combination of political conversion and energetic bandwagon jumping revealed a good deal of unsettled nervousness, which, when combined with the survival of more conservative tendencies, did much to shape clerical reactions to the New Departure and the Land War in general. Confusion and disagreement were the keynotes here, with marooned Whigs like Walshe of Kildare still puffing up 'the great Liberal Party', Croke and Dorrian enthusiastic for Parnell, Warren of Ferns finding everything 'very delicate and difficult', Moran calling 'attention to the want of union among our body in this matter of promoting Parnell', Donnelly of Clogher 'standing aloof' from the Land League, with the staff of Maynooth split along a line reaching from 'old-fogy Liberals' to agrarian radicals,[3] with indeed, the clergy as a whole replicating, in the changed circumstances of the 1880s, their earlier divided, complicated, and contradictory reactions to the politics of tenant-right and Independent Opposition. Priests in 1880 dashed energetically in all political

[1] See, e.g., Bishop McCabe of Ardagh's statement in *Freeman's Journal*, 13 Dec. 1869; *Nation*, 20 Aug. 1870; R. Lalor to K. Digby, 19 Jan. 1871, Lalor Papers MS 8566; G. Morant to E. P. Shirley, 29 June 1871, Shirley of Ettington Papers CR229/115/16; J. A. Dease to C. Fortescue, [1871], Carlingford Papers CP3/130; J. Ferguson to Butt, 14 Nov. 1872, Butt Papers MS 8694; Moriarty cited in *Annual Register . . . for the year 1872*, p. 12; Cullen to Kirby, 23 Nov. 1873, Kirby Papers 1873(425); Archdeacon Redmond to Cullen, 16 Jan. 1874, Cullen Papers; Gillooly to Cullen, 25 Jan. 1874, Bishop McGettigan to Cullen, 30 Jan. 1874, Bishop Walshe to Cullen, 1 Feb. 1874, all ibid.

[2] MacEvilly to Cullen, 1 Feb. 1874, Cullen Papers; R. Osborne to C. Fortescue, 4 Nov. 1869, Carlingford Papers CP3/96; Revd U. J. Kenny, CC to Gladstone, 20 Feb. 1870, Gladstone Papers Add. MS 44425; Cullen to Revd G. Conroy, 22, 23 Mar. 1870, *Paul Cullen*, v, 91; Bishop Donnelly to Lord O'Hagan, [July 1871], Clogher Diocesan Papers DIO(RC)1/11A/26; *Galway County election petition*, H.C. 1872 (241-I), xlviii, 312–13; J. Elland to Butt, 7 Jan. 1874, Butt Papers MS 8696; *Cork Examiner*, 31 Jan. 1874; *Daily Express*, 13 Jan., 3 Feb. 1874; *Leinster Express*, 7, 17 Feb. 1874; *Irish Times*, 10 Feb. 1874; E. Carr to Lord Courtown, 19 Feb. 1874, Courtown Papers; E. O'Brien to Lord Carlingford, 22 Nov. 1875, Trinity College Dublin O'Brien Papers MS 3633; Minute Book of the Wexford Independent Club for the 1870s (N.L.I. Microfilm Positive 4026).

[3] Walshe to McCabe, 30 Dec. 1880, McCabe Papers 346/1, and to Kirby, 27 Mar. 1880, *Arch. Hib.* xxx, 93; Croke to Kirby, 21 Nov. 1879, 28 Mar. 1881, ibid. xxx, 88–9, 102–3; Dorrian to Kirby, 24 Nov. 1879, 14 Apr., 1 Nov. 1880, ibid. xxx, 89, 93, 96; Warren to Kirby, 28 Mar. 1880, 7 Apr. 1881, ibid. xxx, 93, 104; Moran to Kirby, 19 Apr. 1880, ibid. xxx, 93; Donnelly to M. de F. Montgomery, 28 Dec. 1880, Montgomery Papers D627/297e; W. McDonald, *Reminiscences of a Maynooth Professor*, p. 83. For the line-up on the Land League in late 1879, see E. Larkin, *The Roman Catholic Church and the Creation of the Modern Irish State, 1878–1886*, p. 24, where the hierarchy is divided into: Supporters 5, Sympathetic 5, Hostile 9, Neutral 9, Incapacitated 1.

directions.[1] 'Our country has been ground down and cruelly oppressed by an alien nation for the last seven hundred years' announced one Kildare priest. 'Rent is essentially a contract and I cannot see how one party to the contract [tenants] can justly fix the terms of the contract without any reference to the other' insisted his near neighbour.[2] Musical bands were engaged and bonfires lit by a Mayo priest to celebrate attacks on process-servers and to encourage tenants to withhold rent, while in Kerry Fr. O'Leary demanded government help to support those of the 'Catholic clergy as counsel peace and moderation [and] are held up to public scorn'.[3] Bishops of all opinions asserted that diocesan religious fervour was directly related to their own political attitudes.[4] Soon, however, the bulk of the clergy was sucked into the new movement —many willingly, many not. Numerous Land League and National League branches began to operate under clerical guidance,[5] although on a national scale the central Home Rule *Apparat* was, despite cosmetic appearances, able to exclude the clergy from any effective voice in the selection of parliamentary candidates.[6] By entering into an alliance with Parnell's party, the episcopate, although in some ways reinforcing its position in Irish life, was also bending with the wind.

In the end, 'clerical influence' must, as a concept, remain imprecise as to both nature and extent. It cannot only mean the simple alteration of votes, but must also be related to the gradual moulding of opinion.[7] It did not rise and fall in neat temporal packages. Its impact depended, not only on the carrots of popular identification

[1] *Daily Express*, 19, 20, 22, 23, 30, 31 Mar. 1880; *Kilkenny Journal*, 13, 20 Mar. 1880; *Drogheda Argus*, 20 Mar., 17 Apr. 1880; *C.C.* 29 Mar. 1880; Revd D. Kane, PP to Archbishop McCabe, 1 Apr. 1880, McCabe Papers 337/8 ('We were not, here [Wicklow], at all events, yet prepared to submit even to Mr Parnell'); *Limerick Chronicle*, 20 Mar. 1880.

[2] Printed Address of Revd J. Nolan, 9 Mar. 1880, McCabe Papers 337/8; Kildare PP to Revd W. Walsh, [1880], Walsh Papers 350/5.

[3] Printed Cabinet Papers CAB37/3/68: this also gives similar information on other areas.

[4] See, e.g., Gillooly to Kirby, 12 Sept. 1881, McCabe to Kirby, 12 Oct. 1881, Woodlock to Kirby, 28 Oct. 1881, Nulty to Kirby, 10 June 1881, Power to Kirby, 29 Mar. 1881, McCarthy to Kirby, 18 Feb. 1881, all *Arch. Hib.* xxx, 102–8; Duggan to Revd W. Walsh, 24, 27 Jan. 1882, Walsh Papers 350/3.

[5] P. Bew, *Land and the National Question in Ireland 1858–82*, pp. 128–9; C. J. Woods, 'The Catholic Church and Irish Politics 1879–92', pp. 138–9; G. Pellew, *In Castle and Cabin*, pp. 132, 138, 148, 185, 203, 206, 229–30, 285; Minute Book of the Rathvilly Branch of the National League, N.L.I. MS 842 (especially 27 Jan. and 10 Mar. 1884); W. S. Blunt, *The Land War in Ireland*, p. 44.

[6] C. C. O'Brien, *Parnell and his Party 1880–90*, corrected impression (Oxford, 1964), pp. 130–2; Lord Carnarvon to H. Rochfort, 26 Oct. 1885, Carnarvon Papers P.R.O. 30/6/66; *Daily Express*, 25, 28 Nov. 1885; *Freeman's Journal*, 19, 21, 24, 25 Nov. 1885; *C.C.* 13 Oct. 1885.

[7] For an outstanding discussion of such matters at a slightly later date, see C. J. Woods,

and sympathy, but upon the sticks of outright intimidation and spiritual coercion. It functioned most effectively when constricted and directed by powerful external political forces, such as those led by O'Connell and Parnell, and most feebly when freed of significant rivalry. Invariably the Church's position in Irish life was shaped by the interaction between internal and external forces and of these the latter were almost always the more important. Certainly the devotional revolution was central to the manner in which religious attitudes were made materially manifest. But, not only were its pace and scale highly uneven, but profound changes in the nature of ambient popular culture were of equal, if not greater, importance in rearranging the relationship between life and belief. By internal reform, by the selection of individuals, by the way in which seminarians were trained, the Church fashioned itself anew. But it was social changes, such as the post-Famine apotheosis of the farmer, cultural changes, such as the decline in the 'magical' beliefs of the countryside, economic changes, such as those which made possible an increase in clerical incomes, which drew the contours within which the new forces were obliged to operate. The earlier wide variety of friction points was, as regards public criticism and resistance at any rate, refined down into the political sphere alone. And the intensity of the conflict in this sphere was exacerbated by the localist politics of the years immediately after the Famine, when the clergy, released from the simple choice of O'Connellism or apathy, were faced with a bewildering range of possible alternatives. Clericalism is not the issue here, but rather the confessional nature of Irish life, something which, despite (and perhaps even to some extent because of) the critiques offered by fringe groups such as Young Ireland or the Fenians, deepened as the century progressed. With the Church increasingly the only interpreter of the mysterious and the eternal, the religious element in Irish culture became at once more orthodox and more regulated. That ecclesiastical demands were often rejected and that, as time went on, priests were increasingly 'expected to be adjutants, not generals',[1] affected only the workings not the centrality of the matter. As guardian of this sectarian and confessional tradition the Church was able to transcend profound social, cultural, and economic upheavals, internal disputes, political resistance, and the attentions of Rome and Westminster. In this lay its most outstanding achievement.

'The General Election of 1892: The Catholic Clergy and the defeat of the Parnellites' in *Ireland under the Union*, ed. F. S. L. Lyons and R. A. J. Hawkins, pp. 289–319.

[1] D. Fitzpatrick, *Politics and Irish Life 1913–1921: Provincial experience of War and Revolution* (Dublin, 1977), p. 90.

IV

Political Parties and Their Activities

In recent years a series of excellent studies by Macintyre, Nowlan, Whyte, Thornley, and O'Brien has laid bare the manner in which the various 'nationalist' political parties sought to pursue their goals between the 1830s and the 1880s.[1] Not only, however, is this no more than part of the story, but the chronological completeness of the historical account has itself tended to produce a misleading impression of continuity throughout the period. In reality, it was above all nationalist politics which experienced sharp breaks and which developed more by abrupt saltations than by any predictable or steady progression. O'Connell's party was a very personal affair and never managed to overcome the electoral problems of its time. The Independent Party was a chaotic adjunct to discrete agrarian and religious agitations, which, in their own reciprocal destruction, destroyed it also. The later politics of Home Rule depended for their success upon yet another discontinuity in the shape of the New Departure. Historical attention, perhaps unconsciously, has let the victory of nationalism divert it from other significant, and notably less fluid, groups making up the political world of nineteenth-century Ireland: the Whigs or Liberals and the Tories or Conservatives. Only at that moment in the last quarter of the century when the former disappeared and the latter were transformed into Unionists have either attracted much sustained analysis.[2] Yet the importance of Irish Toryism, not merely as a punch-bag against which nationalists might hurl their blows, but as an authentic, lively, and influential tradition, cannot be denied, while Irish Liberalism's long capacity for dingy but tenacious survival makes it, at very least, interesting as an example of effective political parasitism.

[1] A. Macintyre, *The Liberator: Daniel O'Connell and the Irish party 1830–1847* (London, 1965); K. B. Nowlan, *The Politics of Repeal: A Study in the relations between Great Britain and Ireland, 1841–50* (London, 1965); J. H. Whyte, 'Daniel O'Connell and the Repeal party', *Irish Historical Studies*, xi (1959), 297–316; idem, *The Independent Irish Party 1850–9* (Oxford, 1958); D. Thornley, *Isaac Butt and Home Rule* (London, 1964); C. C. O'Brien, *Parnell and his Party 1880–90*, corrected impression (Oxford, 1964).

[2] A partial exception must be made for passages in R. B. McDowell's pioneering *Public Opinion and Government Policy in Ireland, 1801–1846* (London, 1952).

I LIBERALS

In nineteenth-century Ireland the term 'Liberal' had two chief meanings: either it referred to almost anyone not actually a Tory or it was used more narrowly to designate those who simultaneously opposed the Tories and upheld the Union. The essentially negative characteristic of anti-Toryism lay, therefore, at the heart of both groups. But the spasmodic unity between them which marked the 1830s in particular—when O'Connell actually established an Anti-Tory Association—was thereafter only recaptured under the transient force of immediate circumstances. Even in these early days, Irish Liberalism kept itself alive chiefly by a vampire-like ability to obtain vicarious sustenance from the popularity of O'Connell's campaigns. In addition, practical inefficiency encouraged a species of 'political drift' by means of which the more active and extreme sections of O'Connell's organizations often became enervated and absorbed by more lethargic and moderate elements. Many local clubs and societies, though ostensibly supporting Repeal or some other identifiably O'Connellite cause, refused to implement even the loose tests of loyalty favoured by O'Connell himself and were in consequence often converted into little more than mild, if noisy, reformist pressure groups.[1] Irish Liberals, narrowly defined, depended however for their survival not only upon such parasitic absorption, but upon their place within the wider world of British Liberalism and particularly upon the partisan activities, when in power, of Liberal ministers in Dublin Castle and the viceregal lodge. In 1831 the Whigs maintained a 'secret committee' for Irish elections and gave grants to Irish candidates through the London-based Loyal and Patriotic Fund Committee.[2] A year later the Chief Secretary raised money to subsidize non-O'Connellite Liberals, with, however, only indifferent success. In 1837 Thomas Drummond, then Under-Secretary, controlled election matters in Ireland, his chief, Lord Morpeth, being otherwise engaged in a vigorous election campaign in West Yorkshire. As usual, subsidies were carefully confined to candidates unsullied by Repeal, despite the fact that O'Connell's many and substantial political funds invariably assisted men and

---

[1] *Third Report from the select committee appointed to inquire into the nature, character, extent, and tendency of Orange Lodges, Associations, or Societies in Ireland,* H.C. 1835 (476), xvi, 4–11; M. Murphy, 'Municipal Reform and the Repeal Movement in Cork 1833–44', *Journal of the Cork Historical and Archaeological Society,* lxxxi (1976), 16–17; J. H. Whyte, 'Daniel O'Connell and the Repeal party', pp. 297–316; A. Macintyre, *The Liberator,* pp. 79–82, 90.

[2] Lord Anglesey to Lord Stanley, 7 Aug. 1831, Anglesey Papers D619/31C; W. H. Ord to R. S. Carew, 13 May 1831, Shapland-Carew Papers MS 4020.

causes only feebly loyal to the Liberator's own brand of public politics.[1] Some years later the Irish Whig, Lord Duncannon, was among the official managers of a United Kingdom fund which provided significant sums for Irish candidates and was used to augment a separate Irish fund to which the Viceroy alone had subscribed more than a thousand pounds.[2] However, the precise relationship between Liberals in England and in Ireland depended on little more than private interest and personal initiative. In 1831 Edward Ellice, the Chief Whip, received daily election reports from Ireland. In 1835 he helped co-ordinate a 'quiet committee' in London which was in touch with Irish ministers on electoral matters. In 1841, however, all was confusion. Committees in London clashed with a viceroy's committee in Dublin, and the Viceroy himself, Lord Ebrington, protested, not only against ignorant external interference in the affairs of 'those who are devoting their whole time and energies to the subject and possess the confidence generally of the Liberal Party in Ireland', but against the chief English organizer's reiterated determination, 'on principle', never to trust 'Irishmen' of any kind.[3]

After 1847 the activities of government ministers and sporadic help from England constituted just about the whole extent of national Liberal organization in Ireland, something which cannot have been entirely unresponsible for the comparative electoral success of the Tories in 1857, 1865, and especially 1859. In this sense the Liberal Party in Ireland evolved quite unambiguously into an 'official' party, no more and no less. As such it survived largely because Liberal administrations were almost continuously in office between 1846 and 1874 and were able to supply a somewhat fitfully competent band of viceroys and chief secretaries to stoke the electoral engines with organization, patronage, and cash. None, however, of the eleven Liberal office-holders appointed between 1852 and 1874 (only three of whom were actually themselves Irish) possessed the sheer electoral knowledge and skill of Lord Naas, Tory Chief Secretary in 1852, 1858-9, and 1866-8, and only one approached him even as to dedication and zeal. This was the seventh Earl of Carlisle (Lord Lieutenant 1855-8 and 1859-64), who not only knew

---

[1] Stanley to Sir H. Taylor, 25 Nov. 1832, Derby Papers 169; N. Macdonald to Lord Morpeth, 31 July 1837, Carlisle Papers L.-B. 27; A. Macintyre, *The Liberator*, pp. 120-2.

[2] Lord Ebrington to Lord Duncannon, 13 June 1841, and E. Ellice to Ebrington, 29 June 1841, Fortescue Papers 1262M/LI204, 205.

[3] Stanley to Lord Melbourne, 19 May 1831, Melbourne Papers 95/88; E. Littleton to R. D. Craig, 30 Nov 1834, Hatherton Papers D260/M/01/4; Ebrington to Morpeth, 5 June 1841, Carlisle Papers L.-B. 43; J. Parkes to E. Ellice, 15 July 1841, 25 Dec. 1852, Ellice Papers MS 15041.

a good deal about Irish matters—having been Chief Secretary between 1835 and 1841, and having actually contested the Dublin City by-election of 1842—but was unusually prepared to roll up his own electoral sleeves. But while his diaries record a long attention to election duties, they also reveal a general passivity which rarely moved beyond the collection and exchange of information. He relied too much for advice on a rarefied Whig circle of aristocrats and for practical assistance on the unpopular Catholic Attorney-General, 'Single-Finger' Jack Fitzgerald, so named on account of a bogusly genteel habit of presenting only one finger in place of a handshake.[1] Carlisle was also long past his prime, had never quite fulfilled an early political promise, and spent too much time in dancing the night away at viceregal balls and in making undignified attempts to curry favour by, for example, appearing on St Patrick's day virtually engulfed in 'an extra-enormous bunch' of shamrock.[2] Just as had Ebrington in 1841, so Carlisle suffered from breakdowns in communication between Dublin and London. Prominent Irish Liberals, like Lord Fermoy, demanded electoral autonomy to counter the possibility of an alliance between the Tories and the Independent Party under G. H. Moore. Others, like John Ball, the member for Carlow and Under-Secretary for the colonies, urged the appointment of a professional election supremo in Dublin prepared to do the detailed work it was 'not seemly' for the Viceroy to concern himself with.[3] Nothing, however, was done.

Most of the other Liberal ministers in Ireland were considerably less energetic, though even when lethargically led the official machine was always capable of pumping out significant amounts of electoral influence and patronage. Cardwell thought the post of chief secretary between 1859 and 1861 a part-time affair, a view shared by his mentor Gladstone. Horsman during the period 1855-7 knew 'very little' about Irish politics, did not endear himself by referring to Irish MPs as 'the shabbies', constantly threatened to resign, and conducted most of his business with his wife prominently ensconced in a corner of the room.[4] The Irishmen, Sir John Young

---

[1] See Carlisle's Diaries (among Carlisle Papers), especially for Mar. and Apr. 1857; also J. G. Swift MacNeill, *What I have seen and heard* (London, 1925), p. 157.

[2] 'A Native', *Recollections of Dublin Castle and of Dublin Society* (London, 1902), pp. 39-40, 62-3; Carlisle's Diaries (op. cit.) for 17 and 19 Mar. 1857.

[3] Lord Fermoy to Carlisle, 17 Mar. 1857, Carlisle Papers L.-B. 84; J. Ball to Carlisle, 7 Mar. 1857, ibid.

[4] A. B. Erickson, 'Edward T. Cardwell: Peelite', *Transactions of the American Philosophical Society*, new series xlix, part 2 (1959), 27; Lord St Germans to Lord Aberdeen, 27 Feb. 1855, Aberdeen Papers Add. MS 43208; E. Horsman to Lord Palmerston, 3 Nov. 1855, and to Carlisle, 3 Dec. 1855, 1 Aug. 1856, Ramsden (Bulstrode) Papers Horsman L.-B. 1855-8. See also his own Occasional Diary 1850-66 and his wife's Diary 1855, ibid.

and H. A. Herbert (Chief Secretaries 1853–5 and 1857–8), who converted lethargy into principle by trying to remain 'free from local and personal association', also did little to help the Liberal cause. Indeed, so chronic was Young's indecisiveness that even his far from resolute successor, Chichester Fortescue (1865–6 and 1868–71)—whose own appointment Disraeli cattily denoted 'rather social than political'—was driven to thinking him at best 'very unsatisfactory'.[1] Strangest of all was Sir Robert Peel (third baronet), whose period as Chief Secretary between 1861 and 1865 was marked by choleric incompetence, lack of application, and burst blood vessels all round. That Palmerston should have kept so manifestly absurd a man in so important an office—a man whose 'repeated follies' he himself had often condemned—suggests a profound contempt, not only for most things Irish, but for the Irish Liberal Party in particular.[2] Gladstone too, when offering the Chief Secretaryship to one of the very few really able Liberals to hold that office, told Lord Hartington in 1870 that no 'vast or exhausting efforts' need be made to keep 'Irish members in humour' and that no more than occasional brief trips across the Irish Sea would ever be required.[3] The Liberal successes in Ireland at the General Election of 1868 were, therefore, the outcome of Gladstonian promises rather than efficient organization. As in 1865 a small low-powered Dublin committee collected subscriptions (some of which found their way to the perennially corrupt pockets of the electors of Cashel) and undertook to report progress weekly to the Chief Whip in London. It consisted of Fortescue, the law officers, one old-style Protestant Whig, and an unlikely Catholic duo in the shape of The O'Conor Don, a Roscommon landlord, and The O'Donoghue, the impecunious heir (his begging letters abound in the manuscript remains of almost all Victorian politicians) to what was left of the O'Connellite tradition.[4] By 1874, when things had become much more desperate,

[1] H. A. Herbert to Carlisle, 27 May 1857, Carlisle Papers L.-B. 86; Carlingford Papers Diary of C. Fortescue I (31 May 1853); Disraeli to Lord Derby, 24 Nov. 1865, Derby Papers 146/1.

[2] Palmerston to Lord Clarendon, 16 Jan. 1857, in H. E. Maxwell, *The Life and Letters of George William Frederick, Fourth Earl of Clarendon*, 2 vols. (London, 1913), ii, 137–8; to Carlisle, 11 Apr. 1857, Carlisle Papers L.-B. 85; Lord Stanley's Diary for 22 Nov. 1865, in *Disraeli, Derby, and the Conservative party: Journals and memoirs of Edward Henry, Lord Stanley 1849–1869*, ed. J. Vincent (Hassocks, 1978), p. 241.

[3] Gladstone to Lord Hartington, 5 Dec. 1868, 26, 31 Dec. 1870, Devonshire Papers 340/386, 445, 450. Hartington was presumably reluctant to spend much time in Ireland partly because he could not take the Duchess of Manchester with him.

[4] *Report of the Commissioners appointed for the purpose of making inquiry into the existence of Corrupt Practices at the last election for Cashel*, H.C. 1870 [C 9], xxxii, 433–5; Gladstone to C. Fortescue, 10 Jan. 1870, Carlingford Papers CP1/86; W. Monsell to Fortescue, 7 Jan. 1869, ibid. CP3/74; B. Osborne to Fortescue, 4, 29 Nov. 1869, ibid. CP3/96, 98.

an even less adequate electoral organization failed miserably to stem the early and variegated tides of Home Rule.[1] By then it was, in any case, too late, for Spencer as Viceroy and Hartington as Chief Secretary were in 1874 the last Liberal ministers to hold office during a general election seriously contested by Liberal candidates in Ireland.

Despite themselves, however, even lukewarm ministers could not stand entirely aside from the main method by which party cohesion was maintained in Ireland. With policy in such short supply after the Famine, patronage alone helped to sustain the attachments created by family ties, social rank, and personal inclination. The increasingly centralized nature of Irish government placed an expanding number of posts in ministerial hands; and although some Liberals were unusually prone to thinking it necessary to adopt superior attitudes—'When a man', noted Lord Clarendon in 1847, 'catches a cold here or is not seen for a few days, he is voted dead or as good as by a crowd of applicants who ask for his place'—others were prepared to rattle the pork-barrel with well-tuned discrimination and considerable effect.[2] But for Liberals far more than for Conservatives patronage continually posed the problem of religion. 'Respectable' Catholics of all kinds were rabid for jobs and honours, the more so because they had entered the race furlongs behind their Protestant rivals. In 1833 only a quarter of JPs were Catholics, only three out of thirty-three assistant barristers, four out of thirty-seven Crown Counsels, and two out of forty-three stipendiaries.[3] Yet, at first, even prime ministers like Melbourne (otherwise prepared to enter into informal alliance with O'Connell) harboured such peculiar fears of antagonizing extreme Protestants beyond even their normal state of paranoia,[4] that not until the late 1840s and the 1850s did Catholics receive as much as half the major positions available, although even this was as water in the desert to men who had been virtually ignored under the Tory administration of 1841-6.[5] But, while Tory ministers

[1] J. Bagwell to Fortescue, 21 Feb. 1874, Carlingford Papers CP3/137; T. H. Bourke to Hartington, 28 Feb. 1874, Devonshire Papers 387/162. See also G. G. Glyn to Hartington, 24 Jan. 1872, ibid. 340/485.
[2] Clarendon to Lord Normanby, 2 Aug. 1847, Clarendon Papers L.-B. I; J. Hatchell to Carlisle, 12 Jan. 1860, Carlisle Papers L.-B. 99 (on Cardwell); Morpeth to Melbourne, 24 May 1841, Melbourne Papers 98/125; G. H. Moore's Memo on the Mayo election of 1850, Moore Papers MS 893; H. Brand to Palmerston, 3 Dec. 1864, Palmerston Papers General Correspondence.
[3] Hatherton Papers D260/M/01/980-1036.
[4] Lord Mulgrave to Melbourne, 29 Jan. 1836, and Melbourne to Mulgrave, 7 Feb. 1837, Melbourne Papers 99/113 and 100/18.
[5] Clarendon to Sir G. Grey, 17 Feb. 1851, Clarendon Papers L.-B. VI. During the

were invariably more business-like in such matters—they managed to appoint two-fifths of Dublin's magistrates between 1841 and 1866 even though they were in office for only a quarter of the period—the Liberals undoubtedly benefited from an understandable feeling among job-hungry lawyers, influential clergymen, and possessors of local influence that, especially after 1846, Tory governments did not last.[1]

After the General Election of 1859, when many Irish Catholics had voted Tory, Palmerston adopted a curious course. He reversed the existing policy of generosity to Catholics in the matter of official posts and repeatedly told his Irish ministers to favour the 'large and respectable body' of Liberal Protestants, a body larger in his imagination that it was in real life.[2] Yet the accumulated appointments of Melbourne, Russell, and Aberdeen ensured that Protestant Liberals continued to feel themselves increasingly isolated. They warned Carlisle that Catholics were 'bad stuff to lean upon—willing to make use of you and predetermined to throw you over at any fitting opportunity'. In places like Wicklow and most of Ulster, where they still had a powerful voice in Liberal affairs, they relentlessly prevented the adoption of Catholic candidates, and even in so obviously 'Catholic' a constituency as Limerick City were able—by their determined cohesion and wealth—to ensure the regular return of one Protestant member throughout the period 1852–74.[3] Nationally, the remarkable success of Protestant Liberals in maintaining an electoral presence out of all proportion to their numbers is shown in Table 32. What in essence the Protestant Liberals of Ireland were especially good at was cross-channel propaganda. They played to a particularly receptive audience when voicing fears of ultramontane Catholicism. They made much of their parliamentary loyalty, though in fact this was not a great deal more impressive than that of their Catholic Liberal colleagues at Westminster.[4] At the same time,

first twenty-two months of Peel's second administration Catholics received less than a tenth of civil and constabulary appointments in Ireland (Lord Eliot to Sir J. Graham, 15 July 1843, Graham Papers 63).

[1] Figures concerning Dublin magistrates in Mayo Papers MS 11145. See also W. Bonsall to Judge Crampton, 6 May 1859, ibid. MS 11036.

[2] Palmerston to Carlisle, 7 Jan. 1862, Palmerston L.-B. Add. MS 48582; Palmerston to Fortescue, 15 Sept. 1864, Palmerston Papers General Correspondence. On the 1850s, see Lord Eglinton to Derby, 23 May 1858, Derby Papers 148/3; also K. T. Hoppen, 'Tories, Catholics, and the General Election of 1859', *Historical Journal*, xiii (1970), 48–67.

[3] Carlisle to Palmerston, 11 Jan. 1862, Palmerston Papers General Correspondence; Lord Gosford to Carlisle, 10 Apr. 1857, Carlisle Papers L.-B. 85; Horsman to Carlisle, [31 Mar. 1857], ibid.; *Limerick Reporter*, 5, 15 Apr. 1859. In 1861 only four of the dozen common-law judges were Protestants (E. Cardwell to Palmerston, 12 Jan. 1861, Palmerston Papers General Correspondence).

[4] D. T. Horgan, 'The Irish Catholic Whigs in Parliament, 1847–1874' (University of Minnesota Ph.D. thesis, 1975), pp. 24–38, 128–39.

TABLE 32

*Catholic and Protestant Liberal and 'Nationalist' MPs returned
at various general elections, 1832-85*

	Catholic MPs	Protestant Liberal or 'Nationalist' MPs
1832	26	49
1837	29	44
1847	33	31
1852	43	22
1857	35	24
1859	31*	20
1865	31	27
1868	36	30
1874	51	19
1880	55	23
1885	75	10

Total number of MPs: 1832-70 = 105; 1870-85 = 103
*Includes one Catholic Conservative; otherwise all Catholics were Liberals or 'Nationalists'.

however, their view of themselves as the 'gentlemen' of Irish politics eternally locked in combat with 'players' in the shape of Catholics and Conservatives made them extremely vulnerable to changes in the political atmosphere. Lacking a well-defined constituency, they found themselves ill equipped to deal with the increasing polarization of southern politics, so that, by the early 1870s, when registration experts and voters alike no longer thought it useful to allow even for the possibility that any Protestant might be a Liberal or any Catholic a Conservative, their effectiveness as a national force had simply faded away.[1]

Only in Ulster did the Liberal Party experience an Indian summer, but even that, though greeted by some as the dawn of a new age, was built upon foundations too subject to sectarian animosity to last for more than a decade. Ulster Liberalism had always been a rather separate affair, and had held aloof from O'Connell while articulating a rigorous unionism and an almost philosophical radicalism based upon demands for efficient government and 'logical' franchise reforms.[2] Thus, while eighteen of the twenty-five southern

[1] *Report from the select committee on registration of parliamentary voters, Ireland,* H.C. 1874 (261), xi, 209, 239.

[2] Ebrington to Morpeth, 17 Jan. 1841, Carlisle Papers L.-B. 41; *Report on the registration and election laws of the United Kingdom as prepared by a sub-committee of the Ulster Constitutional Association* (Belfast, 1840)—copy in Derby Papers 20/9; *The Repealer Repulsed: A correct narrative of the use and progress of the Repeal invasion of Ulster* (Belfast, 1841).

Whig MPs had joined O'Connell's General Association of 1836-7, only two of their nine Ulster colleagues had been prepared to do so.[1] The most obvious feature of Liberal activity in Ulster was its dependence upon Presbyterian leadership and Catholic numbers. This was an essentially pragmatic collaboration based on two un-complicated realities: many Presbyterians felt excluded by Church of Ireland Toryism, while Catholics, in the absence of organized northern nationalists, had no one else to support. Yet, despite all their efforts and complaints, Presbyterians were for a long time remarkably unsuccessful in sending men of their own denomination to Parliament. Twenty of the twenty-five Liberals returned for Ulster constituencies between 1832 and 1857 were members of the established Church, one was a Quaker, and only four were Presby-terians.[2] Presbyterian resentment over this led eventually to the foundation in the 1850s of the Presbyterian Representation Society to agitate for the adoption of denominational candidates and to mobilize support on the hustings.[3] Although the number of Presby-terian MPs rose as a result (probably a dozen or more sat between 1857 and 1885), this in turn was paralleled by increasing disenchant-ment on the part of the Catholic community which still felt itself excluded from the spoils of political influence, particularly as Catholics had generally been more loyal to, if not always more enthusiastic about, the northern Liberal cause. Presbyterian ambi-valence on the matter had a long history. Already by 1830 the question of the Liberal connection had become a strongly disruptive force within a Presbyterianism increasingly subject to internal conflict between those led by Revd Henry Cooke, who in a sermon of 1837 had equated Toryism with divine truth, and those (often of more 'moderate' theological views) who identified the chief target for attack amidst the ranks of Episcopalian Toryism.[4] Apart from the land question, the only great issue upon which Presbyterians and Catholics shared a measure of agreement was that of the dis-establishment of the Church of Ireland, although even here leaders

[1] G. Lyne, 'The General Association of Ireland, 1836-7' (University College Dublin MA thesis, 1968), pp. 171-4.

[2] Leonard Dobbin (Armagh Bor. 1832-7), William Kirk (Newry 1852-9 and 1868-71), S. M. Greer (Co. Londonderry 1857-9), James Gibson (returned Belfast 1837 but unseated). In addition one Presbyterian (John Boyd: Coleraine 1843-52 and 1857-62) sat as a Con-servative in this period. See *Banner of Ulster*, 11 Apr. 1857.

[3] *Banner of Ulster*, 17 Feb. 1857. Although its headquarters seem to have been in Dublin, it naturally intervened most frequently in Ulster elections, in 1857 supporting Greer in Londonderry (the first Presbyterian ever returned for a county seat) as 'an elder and son of the manse'.

[4] R. F. Holmes, 'Henry Cooke 1788-1868' (University of Dublin M.Litt. thesis, 1970), pp. 418-19, 489, 517, 519, 541; *Banner of Ulster*, 11 July 1843.

like Cooke did all they could to create a pan-Protestant alliance to defeat the political onslaughts of Rome.[1] The feelings and attitudes which Cooke so vociferously articulated were not, in any case, his own creation, but lay deeply embedded within the whole mentality of Ulster Presbyterianism. Thus, although particular issues such as tenant-right and disestablishment could from time to time produce moderately effective alliances with Catholics, significant sections of Presbyterian opinion remained hostile to such collaboration, against which they wielded arguments of attachment and emotion incomparably stronger than those of pragmatism and opportunity.

However much, therefore, occasional populist mavericks like Revd ('Roaring') Hugh Hanna might try to denounce Tory candidates as 'soft on Rome' and back Presbyterian Liberals for rock-like adhesion to Calvinist 'doctrines and policy', the common Presbyterian heritage of anti-Catholicism was increasingly able to overwhelm such deviations.[2] Under its shadow both evangelicals like Cooke and 'moderates' like Revd Henry Montgomery were, for example, united in reaction to the so-called 'Papal Aggression' of 1850.[3] With, therefore, the Conservatives enthroned as the 'natural' party of Protestantism in general, the result was, that, long before Parnellism drove Anglicans and Presbyterians into a final and total collaboration, Presbyterian voters could rarely be relied upon to support Liberal candidates with unanimity or resolve. Even during the 1850s, when the 'League of North and South' allegedly united all hearts in pursuit of tenant-right, Presbyterian congregations often refused to follow their own ministers' urgings to vote for the radical Liberal candidates standing for Ulster constituencies.[4] Catholics, on the other hand, remained electorally attached to the Liberal cause. Until the 1870s they were effectively cut off from 'nationalist' politics. Nor, in the sectarian atmosphere of the north, did they ever feel inclined to follow those of their southern co-religionists, who, in 1859 especially, moved temporarily into the Tory camp. With Presbyterianism, therefore, almost always divided, the Liberal Party in Ulster became increasingly and dangerously dependent on the Catholic vote alone.

[1] Cooke to Lord Naas, 5 June 1852, Mayo Papers MS 11018; *Londonderry Sentinel*, 27 Feb. 1857, 27 Oct. 1868.

[2] *Banner of Ulster*, 26 Mar. 1857.

[3] R. F. Holmes, 'Henry Cooke 1788–1868', pp. 556–8; *Banner of Ulster*, 18 Nov. 1851.

[4] See, e.g., *Londonderry Sentinel*, 3 Apr. 1857, 28 July 1865; *Banner of Ulster*, 4 Apr. 1857; Lord Talbot de Malahide to Carlisle, 4 Apr. 1857, Carlisle Papers L.-B. 85; Lord C. Hamilton to Duke of Abercorn, 22 Jan. 1867 (*sic*), Abercorn Papers T2541/VR/128; C. Gavan Duffy, *The League of North and South: An episode in Irish History 1850–1854* (London, 1886).

Already in 1832 the bulk of Liberal backing at Belfast elections was coming from Catholics, who, it was noticed, 'act more determinately together, and have more determination to vote for their own side [and] a stronger political feeling'.[1] In Armagh too the victorious Liberal in 1837 depended heavily on Catholic votes to defeat the Orange party, whereas the Presbyterians of Coleraine seemed happy to support Conservative candidates. By the 1850s Catholics had come to form the clear numerical backbone to the electoral survival of Ulster Liberalism; Presbyterians, on the other hand, were proving themselves more and more favourable to the Conservatives.[2] This was evident everywhere in 1852, while at later elections, such as those at Downpatrick in 1857 and Armagh in 1859 and 1865, the solidity of the Catholic Liberal vote contrasted starkly with the fragmented politics of the Presbyterians.[3] Angry recriminations inevitably followed, and one Antrim priest felt driven to denounce 'the base desertion of the Presbyterian voters . . . from this section of the community we are not in Ireland to reckon on sympathy or co-operation . . . There is not on the face of the globe a greater tyrant over a dependant than a Calvinist nor a greater more base sycophant to a superior.'[4] And just as tenant-right had failed to mobilize the Presbyterian vote as a whole, so disestablishment too proved something of a disappointment, to the extent that at Newry in 1868 only 15 per cent of Presbyterian electors voted for their own Gladstonian co-religionist, the local business man William Kirk.[5]

That this was far from unusual is demonstrated by the electoral

[1] R. B. McDowell, *Public Opinion and Government Policy in Ireland, 1801–1846*, p. 135; *Report from the select committee on the Belfast election compromise*, H.C. 1842 (431), v, 312–13.

[2] *D.E.P.* 5 Aug. 1837; J. M. Greer (Secretary to the 'Presbyterian Association' of Coleraine) to Sir H. H. Bruce, 20 Feb. 1843, Babington & Croasdaile Papers D1514/2/6/22; MS Autobiography of A. J. H. Moody (Presbyterian elder and grocer of Coleraine) T2901/4/1.

[3] J. H. Whyte, *The Independent Irish Party 1850–9*, p. 84. For Downpatrick, see Martin & Henderson Papers D2223/21/10; for Armagh, *List of Voters who recorded their votes at the Armagh Borough election, in 1859*—copy in Armagh Museum No. 22–76—showing that 108 of the 112 Catholic voters supported the more 'liberal' of two Conservatives; also, for 1865, 'Armagh Borough Election File' (Armagh Museum) showing that 70 per cent of the Liberal vote came from Catholics.

[4] Revd D. Curoe to G. H. Moore, 5 Jan. 1853, Moore Papers MS 892. For further evidence of Catholic electoral solidarity and Presbyterian fragmentation, see C. Knox to R. B. Towse, 21 July 1852, Clothworkers' Company Copy L.-B. 1840–73; H. Anderson to J. A. Beck, 9 July 1852, Ironmongers' Company Irish Correspondence Received 1846–54; R. and J. R. Miller to E. Lawford, 25 June 1852, Drapers' Company L.-B. Irish 1848–57.

[5] *Newry Election. An alphabetically arranged List of Electors who voted, and those who did not, at the election held in Newry, on the 20th of November 1868* (Newry, n.d.)—copy P.R.O.N.I. T2336/1 (also *Londonderry Sentinel*, 8 Dec. 1868). Almost 97 per cent of the Catholics voted for Kirk, who was narrowly victorious.

histories of Belfast and Derry City. In both towns Catholics lived within a fully articulated system of denominational politics. Belfast was especially known for its sectarian riots and for the long domination of the Tory Party in municipal affairs.[1] Even so, the Belfast Liberal Party, such as it was, made few formal concessions to Catholic feelings. Enthusiastic in the 1850s and early 1860s for Palmerston, it seems organizationally to have revolved around the Presbyterian Representation Society, despite the fact that Catholic numbers alone provided it with any real chance of success.[2] Steadily between 1857 and 1868 Catholic voters constituted about a fifth of the electorate and provided much the most coherent bloc of potential Liberal support in the constituency. In 1865 the Liberal agent calculated that any party candidate would probably obtain almost half his total vote from Catholics, a quarter from orthodox Presbyterians, an eighth from Unitarians, and the rest from 'other Protestants'. By 1868 it was estimated that dependence upon the Catholic vote had become greater still.[3] With, therefore, Presbyterians decreasingly reliable and with Belfast Catholics still largely excluded from positions of social and economic influence,[4] the Liberal alliance was becoming more fragile by the year. Even the dramatic capture of a seat at the General Election of 1868 (the first victory in Belfast for more than twenty years) was based on some quite untypical success in exploiting divisions between the populist and 'respectable' wings of local Conservatism. And although such divisions did not thereafter disappear, Liberals never again showed either the ability or the inclination to profit from their enemies' mistakes. Instead, they themselves returned to their old splintering ways, and acrimonious wrangles between candidates and agents further weakened their already enfeebled position in local political life.[5]

The case of Derry demonstrates the importance of the Catholic vote even more clearly. As early as 1837 almost a third of the electors were Catholics, while by 1868 Catholics constituted 40.4 per cent

---

[1] I. Budge and C. O'Leary, *Belfast: Approach to Crisis: A Study of Belfast politics 1613–1970* (London, 1973), pp. 41–100.

[2] *Banner of Ulster*, 10, 21 Mar., 4 Apr. 1857. See also R. Davison to R. Bourke, 21 June 1852, Mayo Papers MS 11018; *Northern Whig*, 9 Apr. 1857; J. Rea to Mayo, 7 Mar. 1868, Mayo Papers MS 11172.

[3] For 1857, see 'Census of Belfast' by the United Protestant Committee (*Banner of Ulster*, 27 Oct. 1857); for 1865, 'Report of the Presbyterian Sub-Committee' of the Liberal Party, L'Estrange & Brett Papers D1905/2/142/2; for 1868, ibid. D1905/2/17A/5, and *Belfast Newsletter*, 13 Oct. 1868.

[4] The 'Census of Belfast' (op. cit.) shows, for example, that all 48 bank directors were Protestants, 186 out of 194 members of the chamber of commerce, 42 out of 46 linen merchants, and 63 out of 70 solicitors.

[5] L'Estrange & Brett Papers D1905/2/210A.

of the voters, Presbyterians (of all types) 37.2 per cent, and Episcopalians 22.4 per cent.[1] From 1830 until his death in 1860 Catholics had supported the wealthy and largely apolitical Sir Robert Ferguson, but the weakness of Derry Liberalism became apparent when all but two of the eight contested elections held after 1860 were won by the Conservatives.[2] That Conservatives should have been so successful in a town where members of the Church of Ireland (their traditional electoral bedrock) constituted less than a quarter of the electorate, shows how weak had become the effective foundations of Ulster Liberalism. The detailed figures available for the isolated Liberal victories of 1868 and 1870 (the high point of Presbyterian support in Derry) clearly reveal the shape of things to come (see Table 33). By the time the Tories recaptured the seat in 1872 it is

TABLE 33

Voting by denomination in Derry City, 1868 and 1870

	percentage of all voting		percentage voting Liberal		percentage of Liberal vote	
	1868	1870	1868	1870	1868	1870
Episcopalians	22.0	24.8	4.5	4.7	1.8	2.2
Presbyterians	32.7	30.5	39.0	36.9	23.6	21.0
Dissenters, etc.*	5.2	3.6	38.2	31.1	3.7	2.1
Roman Catholics	40.1	41.1	95.6	97.1	70.9	74.7

*i.e. various breakaway 'Presbyterian' groups (Unitarians, etc.) and other Dissenters.

probable that no less than 83.6 per cent of the Liberal vote was coming from Catholic sources.[3] This was highly dangerous. It meant that any major shift in Catholic politics would entirely annihilate the Liberal Party in Ulster, for Catholic voters also represented significant blocs in the county constituencies. For counties such as Donegal and Cavan this can be readily supposed; for other counties reliable contemporary information makes the point with mathematical

[1] C. Walsh to O'Connell, 10 July 1837, *The Correspondence of Daniel O'Connell*, ed. M. R. O'Connell, 8 vols. (Dublin, 1972-80), vi, 59-60. The information here and below for 1868 is taken from *List of Voters, showing for whom each elector polled at the late general election for the City of Londonderry, distinguishing the religion of each voter* (Londonderry: Sentinel Office, [1868])—copy P.R.O.N.I. D1935/6, and *State of the Poll at the general election held for the City of Londonderry, 20th November 1868* (Londonderry: John Hempton, [1868])—copy P.R.O.N.I. D1509/10.

[2] See D. Murphy, *Derry, Donegal, and Modern Ulster 1790-1921* (Londonderry, 1981), pp. 110-34.

[3] Ibid. 127.

precision: Londonderry 1852—25.6 per cent, Tyrone 1857—
47.3 per cent, Monaghan 1883—47.3 per cent, North Armagh
1885—22.4 per cent.[1]

Despite the Conservative triumphs at Derry and Belfast in 1874,
that year marked what to many seemed a real, if modest, Liberal
advance in Ulster. After a period in which adhesion to the cause
had carried with it 'many social drawbacks and a great deal of mis-
representation and abuse',[2] the winning of six out of the twenty-
nine Ulster seats seemed to represent at worst survival and at best
hope. The major force behind both the three gains in Cos. Down
and Londonderry and the victory of the radical Conservative, J. W.
Ellison Macartney, in Tyrone, was the renewed excitement generated
by the land question. Whereas in the south the crucial electoral
breakthrough against landlord power of 1869–72 had preceded the
introduction of the secret ballot, it would seem that Ulster radicalism's Indian summer required secrecy of voting to flourish. For
a time traditional Conservatives were disturbed by an (as it ensued
temporary) alliance between populist Orangemen and radical land
reformers. They need not have worried, for the whole business was
built on inevitably shifting sands, as was shown by the contemporary
adjectival gymnastics required to describe the victors in Tyrone:
'the democratic or Fenian Orange Party'.[3] At the same time it
became clear that Catholic voters in rural Ulster were moved to
enthusiasm by land reform alone and stood aloof from candidates,
however supported by Isaac Butt or radical Orangemen, who had
nothing to say on agrarian matters.[4] Despite the exertions of a new
Ulster Liberal Society and despite architectural explosions in the
shape of a new Ulster Reform Club in Belfast, success had, in any
case, been the outcome more of Tory failure than of Liberal achievement. Indeed, honours in this respect were more or less even, with
the casual ignorance of the Disraeli government's approach to Ulster

---

[1] *Londonderry Sentinel*, 9 July 1852; ibid. 29 Apr. 1859 (*sic*); *The Times*, 30 June
1883; Carleton, Atkinson, & Sloan Papers D1252/42/3/48—this last for the post-1884
Reform Act period when counties were split into divisions, North Armagh being the least
Catholic division in that county.

[2] T. Macknight, *Ulster as it is or Twenty-Eight years' experience as an Irish editor*,
2 vols. (London, 1896), i, 54–5.

[3] T. Dickie to Lord Belmore, 20 Mar. 1873, Belmore Papers D3007/P/52; also M. Hurst,
'Ireland and the Ballot Act of 1872', *Historical Journal*, viii (1965), 349. A Conservative
Presbyterian (in a letter forwarded to an uninterested Disraeli) thought 'it is a great mistake
to put down the agitation in favour of tenant-right as Irish dissatisfaction alongside with
Fenianism etc. The Orangemen and respectable gentlemen farmers are its strongest advocates'
(Revd H. P. Charleton to Lord Hamilton, 18 June 1874, Hughenden Papers B/XXI/H/38A).

[4] J. Madden to I. Butt, 6 Mar. 1874, Butt Papers MS 8696; *Londonderry Journal*,
2 Feb. 1874.

in particular and Ireland in general being more than matched by the energetic myopia of Gladstone's tour of Ireland in 1877, when, apart from one brief third-class railway journey to 'hear the poorer people', the great tribune spent all his time in the unrevealing country houses of aristocratic friends.[1]

At the General Election of 1880 the Liberals won nine seats in Ulster, their best result since 1835. In some areas the improved organizational apparatus built up in the years of optimism undoubtedly helped. Elsewhere, notably in Donegal, the agricultural depression produced gains in hitherto alien territory. Liberals made much of the Tories' land record (or lack of it), but their own success was to prove, as soon became clear, a highly fragile phenomenon.[2] Because only two Home Rulers had stood in Ulster, the Catholic vote had, as usual, been pointed in the direction of Liberal candidates. While Catholics, however, had only voted Liberal for want of anything better, the shrinking band of Presbyterian Liberals, now fortified by the anti-Catholic outbursts of Gladstone's *Vaticanism* pamphlets, had done so out of conviction. The Land League was perceptive enough to see the possibilities of such a state of affairs. Work began in Ulster during the summer of 1880 and proceeded in careful stages. The first electoral advance took place in the peripheral county of Monaghan, where, in 1883, Tim Healy gained a remarkable victory. But, although Healy's colours had been those of Parnellite Home Rule, his campaign had been almost entirely based on the land question and the defects of Gladstone's Land Act of 1881.[3] The derisory vote obtained by the Liberal candidate (less than 6 per cent) revealed the depths to which Protestant Liberalism in the county had fallen. Now at last Catholics had an alternative which offered a sense of denominational identity, a nationalist philosophy, and (most importantly) a more attractive agrarian programme. By 1885, when it was too late, Liberal leaders acknowledged that 'hitherto all Liberal members returned from Ulster have been largely indebted for their position to the Roman Catholic party' and bemoaned how the 'Catholic voters in the

---

[1] T. Macknight, *Ulster as it is*, ii, 28, and *Copy of the shorthand writer's notes of the judgement and evidence on the trial of the Down County election petition*, H.C. 1880 (260–II), lvii, 702–4 (Liberal Society); A. B. Cooke, 'A Conservative party leader in Ulster: Sir Stafford Northcote's diary of a visit to the province, October 1883', *Proceedings of the Royal Irish Academy*, Section C, lxxv (1975), 61–84 (Tory ignorance); T. Macknight, op. cit. i, 338–9 (Gladstone).

[2] D. Murphy, *Derry, Donegal, and Modern Ulster 1790–1921*, pp. 138–9; Leaflet produced by Down Liberals entitled 'Words of Reason to Reasoning Men', Perceval-Maxwell Papers D1556/23.

[3] J. Magee, 'The Monaghan election of 1883 and the "Invasion of Ulster" ', *Clogher Record*, viii (1974), 147–66.

country districts of Ulster are, with exceptions that one may count
on one's fingers, [now] all enrolled in the National League'.[1] On
the eve of the 1885 election a well-informed agent estimated that in
the North Armagh division voters could be divided into Catholics
(22 per cent), Protestant Conservatives (56 per cent), 'Orange'
(12 per cent), and, last and very much least, Liberal Protestants
(10 per cent).[2] In Ulster as a whole the election resulted in the
return of seventeen Nationalists, sixteen Conservatives, and no
Liberals at all.

Quite apart from more general developments, the franchise changes
of 1884–5 had also hurt the Liberals. The small farmers and labourers
given the vote for the first time proved unsympathetic, and, in many
areas, as Tim Healy provokingly pointed out, Liberals were ground
down between 'Orange labourers and Catholic farmers'. Nor were the
Conservatives unprepared to outbid Liberals in the matter of land
reform, their candidate for Mid-Armagh demanding nothing less
than compulsory purchase.[3] The simultaneous redistribution of
seats, by splitting two-member county constituencies (as well as
Belfast) into single-member divisions, allowed the now Nationalist
Catholics to mobilize their local strength to much greater effect than
before. All this had the result of further accelerating the existing
tendency towards pan-Protestant political solidarity. Disappointed
anti-Tory candidates denounced the 'dog-faced Presbyterian clergymen' for encouraging their congregations to espouse the Conservative (now effectively the Unionist) cause, and, indeed, all the northern
constituencies went strictly according to their denominational compositions, save only South Derry where a three-cornered fight split
the Protestant vote.[4] In Tyrone the president of the Liberal Association defected to the Conservatives, and joint meetings of Protestant

---

[1] R. MacGeagh to J. Bryce, 14 Dec. 1885, Bryce Papers, and H. de F. Montgomery in
Northern Whig, 29 Aug. 1885, both cited F. Thompson, 'The Armagh elections of 1885–6',
Seanchas Ardmhacha, viii (1977), 370.

[2] Carleton, Atkinson, & Sloan Papers D1252/42/3/48. The Liberals' attention to voter
registration in Ulster had also declined notably after 1880 (B. M. Walker, 'Party Organization in Ulster, 1865–92: Registration Agents and their Activities' in *Plantation to Partition:
Essays in Ulster History in honour of J. L. McCracken*, ed. P. Roebuck (Belfast, 1981),
pp. 191–209).

[3] E. T. Herdman to H. de F. Montgomery, 9 Mar. 1888, Montgomery Papers D627/
428/34, and Healy in *Daily Express*, 16 Dec. 1885 (also T. Macknight, *Ulster as it is*, ii,
56). For Mid-Armagh, see F. Thompson, 'The Armagh elections of 1885–6', p. 372.

[4] *C.C.* 9 Dec. 1885; *Return showing the religious denominations of the population,
according to the census of 1881 in each constituency formed in Ulster by the Redistribution of Seats Act, 1885*, H.C. 1884–5 (335), lxii, 339–42. On the Land League, see
P. Livingstone, *The Fermanagh Story* (Enniskillen, 1969), pp. 261–2, also R. W. Kirkpatrick, 'Origins and Development of the Land War in mid-Ulster, 1879–85' in *Ireland under
the Union: Varieties of tension: Essays in honour of T. W. Moody*, ed. F. S. L. Lyons
and R. A. J. Hawkins (Oxford, 1980), pp. 201–35.

'gentry, farmers, shopkeepers, and tradesmen' were held to mobilize opposition to Parnell. The same happened in Down, in Monaghan, in virtually all the constituencies.[1] By 1886 it was recognized that 'the rank and file' Liberals had virtually all gone over to Unionism. The local leaders were not far behind, their views epitomized by those of a prosperous Tyrone flax spinner who had once been an 'ardent Gladstonian' and who now talked dourly of resisting the 'uncultivated ignorant people' of the Catholic south and proudly of his own preference for employing Protestant workers in his mills.[2]

In the south it had of course always been more likely that the bulk of Catholic voters would eventually be diverted from the negative and merely governmental Liberal Party of 1847–65, even though the powerful localism of the 1850s and 1860s had done much to preserve a body of rather dubiously 'Liberal' MPs at Westminster. The diaries of Chichester Fortescue (later Lord Carlingford), the Protestant Liberal landowning MP for Louth from 1847 to 1874, are unusually revealing as regards the gulf which existed between many (especially Protestant) Liberals and their electoral supporters. In 1855 he attended the local poor-law board: 'Speaking of atrocious Ribbon murder of Miss Hinds in Cavan, I said it made one ashamed of one's country, upon which I saw a couple of tenant-right guardians whispering and looking at me, as if I had committed myself.' He himself had no doubts that, should the fragile edifice of Irish Liberalism ever suffer serious rupture, he would be 'left in the lurch between the landlords' man and the priests' man'.[3] And the narrowness of the reliable support that could be depended upon was neatly encapsulated in an advertisement for a leading 'moderate' newspaper, the Cork *Southern Reporter*, which in 1870 claimed to be the 'sole organ in the south of Ireland of the moderate Liberal Party, *the upper middle classes*'.[4]

On the surface, however, such things were not always apparent, especially during the few years in the late 1860s when Gladstone's dexterity produced a temporary but impressive unity among anti-Conservatives in Ireland. The number of Irish seats won by Liberals rose from fifty in 1859 to sixty-six in 1868, the product of an alliance of priests, farmers, and some of the urban middle class around the issues of disestablishment and land reform. What made

---

[1] *Daily Express*, 26 Nov., 1 Dec. 1885; *Northern Standard*, 12 Sept., 5 Dec. 1885.

[2] R. MacGeagh to J. Bryce, 5 Feb. 1886, cited F. Thompson, 'The Armagh elections of 1885-6', p. 377; G. Pellew, *In Castle and Cabin or talks in Ireland in 1887* (New York and London, 1888), pp. 240-2.

[3] Carlingford Papers Diary of C. Fortescue I (6 Nov. 1855) and III (30 Apr. 1859).

[4] C. Mitchell, *The Newspaper press directory for 1870* (London, [1870]), p. 115; my italics.

it all work was the marriage of the two issues; alone, their impact would have been far less decisive. For a time it seemed almost as if Irish politics were becoming more and more Anglicized. There was even a fleeting Irish Reform League, which favoured cross-channel co-operation and dispatched its unlikely leader, The O'Donoghue, to attend Hyde Park demonstrations, before suddenly collapsing into irrelevant obscurity.[1] But, whereas franchise reform, at least imperially, had been 'solved' in 1867–8 and disestablishment been laid to rest in 1869, the land question was something very different —a Pandora's box, which, once opened, was capacious enough to swallow much larger concessions than British ministers were ever likely to be prepared to make. For this and other reasons the early years of Gladstone's first ministry saw the revival of a form of politics not seen since the days of O'Connell and with it the creaking death of southern Liberalism. In 1874 Fortescue was overwhelmed in Louth, despite the efforts of the Catholic Archbishop of Armagh. At Galway Town F. H. O'Donnell defeated a local Liberal with the support of a band of 'healthy strong young men' discovered, to the ineffective chagrin of the bishop, one Friday 'eating meat . . . at the hotel and the servants and all concerned with the hotel scandalized by them'. In Co. Wexford the bitter tears of 'respectable Catholics' did not protect the incumbent Catholic Liberal from humiliating defeat. 'Think', wrote a hitherto powerful priest, 'of a good young man, exemplary in life and heir to a fine property, spent at home, a soldier of the pope, who never gave a corrupt vote, rejected for a young [Home Rule] man from another county without a shilling in his pocket.'[2]

Outside Ulster the 1874 election was a disaster for the Liberals. Only four were returned, two of them for the small boroughs of Bandon and Tralee. Of course many of the sixty Home Rulers elected were palpable trimmers: one candidate had even written to the Liberal Chief Secretary to excuse a mildly separatist address, 'for it is my only chance. I do not think any one can make much of my Home Rule.'[3] Yet, however tentative many Home Rulers may

[1] See the papers of the (English) Reform League in the George Howell Collection at the Bishopsgate Institute, London, especially Minutes of the Executive Council for 5 Dec. 1866, 2 Jan. 1867, and of the General Council for 8 May 1867, 8 Jan., 11 Mar. 1868; also *D.E.P.* 27 Mar. 1867, and *Londonderry Standard*, 8 Dec. 1867.

[2] Louth: Archbishop McGettigan to Archbishop Cullen, 30 Jan. 1874, Cullen Papers; Galway: Bishop MacEvilly to Cullen, 24 Mar. 1874, ibid.; Wexford: Revd J. Redmond to Cullen, 19 Feb. 1874, ibid.; also E. Carr to Lord Courtown, 19 Feb. 1874, Courtown Papers.

[3] A. W. F. Greville to Hartington, 26 Jan. 1874, Devonshire Papers 340/564. Greville eventually stood more as a Liberal than a Home Ruler.

have been, they none the less demonstrated a remarkable degree of voting cohesion on Irish issues in the Parliament of 1874–80, unlike the 'great Liberal Party', which rarely proved itself able to present a united front on matters connected with Ireland.[1] An indication of popular disenchantment is provided by the changing image of Gladstone presented in the ballads of the time. In 1868 the picture was unambiguously that of a man offering popular reforms.[2]

> The hour is come for Irishmen
> To right their native land,
> When all that's pure in Parliament
> Extends to us the hand;
> Since Gladstone gave the word that sent
> Glad tidings to our shore
> The Irish Church Establishment
> Must cease for evermore.

Rather more ominous, however, were the mingled hopes and promises expressed in a ballad sung at the November elections.

> The tenant right is now at hand
> We can improve our native land
> They'll give a lease to every man
> As Gladstone had propos'd it
> No more Unlawful tax we'll pay
> Tho' long the breed o'Tudor claim'd
> They are pamper'd by the sweat of slaves
> With mutton beef and bacon.

But, although Gladstone survived as hero in ballads written for the Kerry by-election of 1872 when a Liberal went down to overwhelming Home Rule defeat ('Brave Gladstone won't refuse to sign for us home rule / In the year of seventy-two, says the Shan Von Vocht'), the tone was changing and it was not long before cheap collections of songs were adopting a very different stance.[3]

> We've got some noble heroes to advocate our cause
> Who know that Ireland is oppressed by cruel and alien laws
> There's Counsellor Butt our noble chief determined to stand
> And to do his best to free the sons of poor old Ireland

---

[1] J. C. Hamilton, 'Parties and voting patterns in the parliament of 1874–80' (University of Iowa Ph.D. thesis, 1968), pp. 110–11, 171.

[2] 'The Hour is Come for Irishmen' circulated in Co. Sligo etc., copy in Clonalis Papers 9.2.HS.161; followed by 'A New Song on Captain Flanagan's Victory over the Tories', copy in N. L. I. Ballad Collection, Pressmark J39988(1).

[3] Kerry Ballad 'Belimner Hassits [*sic*] Address to Kerry on Home Rule', copy in Bradshaw Collection C.U.L. Hib.2.867.2; *The Home Rule Songster: Being a choice collection of the newest and best songs* (Dublin, [?1874]), copy in ibid. Hib.2.867.2.

There's Gladstone the Prime Minister who the Irish Church Bill plann'd
He thought that it would satisfy the sons of Paddy's land
But Pat he wants to rule himself and be free from all his foes
Then the sun of happyness will shine where the little Shamrock grows.

By the time of the Land League Gladstone had been entirely dropped
from the canon—a significant fact, for the writers and printers
involved knew well the tastes and opinions of their public and
depended for their livelihoods upon an accurate assessment of
popular feelings. And what met the mood of the early 1880s were
songs about 'Parnell's Progress through America', 'The Arrest of
Messrs Davitt, Healy, and Quinn', and very practical ballads about
'Griffith's Valuation'.[1]

The crucial electoral confirmation of these changes occurred in
1880 and in the years immediately thereafter. Parnell entered the
General Election with no machinery and little money. The Catholic
hierarchy was deeply divided. Only five of the twenty-eight bishops
were willing to give the League any support at all. Some of the others
denounced Parnell's desire to become 'universal dictator' and
prophesied that his 'popularity might at any moment burst before
the indignant spirit of Irish faith and fatherland'.[2] There were
attacks also from Fenian irreconcilables and 'moderate' Home
Rulers as well as from Liberals and Conservatives. But despite all
this, the voters returned sixty-three Home Rulers, no less than
twenty-seven of whom (more than a quarter of all Irish MPs) were
already committed 'Parnellites'. For the first time since O'Connell
an Irish party at Westminster had managed to increase both its
strength and its militancy from one election to another. A measure
of the movement which had occurred is provided by the case of
Keyes O'Clery, the member for Wexford. Considered so radical by
the local clergy and gentry in 1874 when he had replaced a Catholic
Liberal, in 1880 he was in turn successfully opposed by Parnellite
candidates and attacked by Parnell himself on the grounds that his
'Whiggish' tendencies made him unfit to represent the 'people'.[3]
During the four years after 1880 Parnell achieved a real control
over Irish politics, and the by-election victories of this period show
that franchise changes were, in this case at least, not a necessary

[1] Copies of all three in Bradshaw Collection C.U.L. Hib.1.867.1.
[2] A. O'Day, *The English face of Irish Nationalism: Parnellite involvement in British politics, 1880–86* (Dublin, 1977), pp. 11–12; F. S. L. Lyons, *Charles Stewart Parnell* (London, 1977), p. 117; E. Larkin, *The Roman Catholic Church and the Creation of the Modern Irish State, 1878–1886* (Philadelphia and Dublin, 1975), p. 24; *C.C.* 10 Apr. 1880 (quoting Bishop MacCormack of Achonry).
[3] *C.C.* 29 Mar. 1880, and F. S. L. Lyons, *Charles Stewart Parnell*, pp. 119–21 (for 1880). For 1874, see note 2 p. 274.

prerequisite for success, the electorate still being very largely that of the Franchise Act of 1850. As Parnell freed himself from left-wing agrarian demands, so his lieutenants built up an impressive electoral machine in the shape of the National League, which, though different from the suppressed Land League in its lack of independence from central party control, was, for obvious reasons, based on a predominantly continuing membership.[1] Particularly noteworthy was the National League's dramatic growth in the six months leading up to the General Election of December 1885 when its branch network increased from 818 to 1,261.[2] Also by 1885 a National Registration Association had been established and local registration societies (that in Dublin had nineteen branches) were energetically acting as agents for the League itself.[3]

The 1885 election produced an overwhelming Nationalist victory. Eighty-five seats went to Parnell, the remaining eighteen to the Conservatives. Already five years earlier the anti-Nationalist press had argued that only two parties—Home Rulers and Conservatives —had any future.[4] By 1865 the shrinking band which still thought of itself as Liberal, had, under the force of circumstances, effectively lost its identity within a Conservative-led Unionist coalition. 'I am a Liberal', announced a prominent Tipperary landlord, 'but party politics are necessarily in abeyance at this juncture, and I am ready to vote for anyone who will vote against Mr Parnell.'[5] The Liberal Party had simply ceased to exist. Squeezed between Nationalists and Unionists, its loyal remnant lashed desperately about for some issue to make its own. But the efforts of certain candidates to rouse urban artisans against the rural selfishness of contemporary Irish politics were practically fanciful and entirely ineffective. Organizational neglect had, in any case, long eroded what little electoral machinery the party had ever possessed in the south.[6] Liberals were not even being attacked any more—a sure sign of rigor mortis. Nationalists fought sixty-eight contests and obtained 290,006 votes,

---

[1] See, e.g., how the Minute Book of the Land League branch at Rathvilly (Co. Carlow) simply carries on as that of the National League branch (N.L.I. MS 842); also T. Macknight, *Ulster as it is*, ii, 22.

[2] Figures are for 1 July 1885 and 1 Jan. 1886 (from C. C. O'Brien, *Parnell and his Party*, pp. 132–3).

[3] *C.C.* 2 Oct. 1885; *Northern Standard*, 12 Sept., 10 Oct. 1885; *Wexford Independent*, 16 Sept. 1885; *Daily Express*, 1, 2, 6 Oct. 1885; J. Magee, 'The Monaghan election of 1883', p. 158; F. Thompson, 'The Armagh elections of 1885–6', p. 379.

[4] *Daily Express*, 17 Mar. 1880.

[5] *Daily Express*, 26 Nov. 1885; also *Freeman's Journal*, 26 Nov. 1885.

[6] *Freeman's Journal*, 16 Nov. 1885. For neglect of registration etc., see *Northern Standard*, 12 Sept., 10 Oct. 1885; *Daily Express*, 1, 2, 10 Oct. 1885; *Freeman's Journal*, 17, 26 Oct. 1885.

Conservatives sixty-five contests for 109,393 votes, Liberals only twenty-three contests for a mere 35,713 votes.[1] Deprived between 1874 and 1880 of its essential lifeline—government patronage—an already weakened party was simply unable to come to terms with the new politics of the time. Like a parasite deprived of its host, it lacked those reserves of faith and sectarian cohesion which allowed the Conservatives to survive even in the darkest days. Whatever the degree of permanence or the precise nature of the changes wrought in the 1880s upon the deep structures of Irish politics, the demise of the Liberal Party was final and complete.

II CONSERVATIVES

Irish Conservatism followed a rougher trade. Its most remarkable characteristics during the half-century after 1832 were tenacious survival, an ability to develop reserves of social and religious cohesion, and success in retaining a grip upon the jugulars of political life. After 1859 Conservatives briefly became the largest Irish group at Westminster. Even as late as 1879 they held more seats than they had done in 1832. Crucial to their success were the lessons learned during the reform years of 1829-32, when the party first realized how energizing could be the effects of unyielding reaction followed by rapid adjustment and organizational drive. During the reform crisis itself Irish Tories lashed even English ultras for faintness of spirit,[2] and the Grand Orange Lodge cracked its whip over the few recalcitrant populists who criticized the gentry's opposition to change of any kind.[3] Yet, once the Reform Bill was passed, the characteristic tendency of Irish Toryism to make the best of a bad job led to speedy efforts to operate the new system as advantageously as possible. This was a viable course because Toryism in Ireland, defining as it did a man's role within a largely hostile world and setting limits to acceptance and mutual recognition, was much

---

[1] See cutting in South Co. Dublin Scrapbook (1885), N.L.I. MS 5946. Had the Liberals fought as many forlorn hopes as the Conservatives their average local vote would have been much lower. Two Independent Nationalists obtained 2,889 votes, while twenty Nationalists and four Conservatives were returned unopposed.

[2] Judge Day to Knight of Kerry, 28 Dec. 1832, FitzGerald Papers; *Hansard*, xiii, 128-30 (25 May 1832), xiv, 757-71 (26 July 1832); also Lord Anglesey to Grey, 13 June 1832, Anglesey Papers D619/28A; M. Tierney to Anglesey, 22 June 1831, O.P. 1831/T31, Box 1842.

[3] Revd H. Waring to J. W. Maxwell, 19 Sept. 1828, Perceval-Maxwell Papers D3244/G/1/58; *First Report from the select committee appointed to inquire into the nature, character, extent, and tendency of Orange Lodges, Associations, or Societies in Ireland*, H.C. 1835 (377), xv, 214-15, 146; H. Senior, *Orangeism in Ireland and Britain 1795-1836* (London, 1966), pp. 250-1.

more than a political movement alone. Private jokes and hermetic language reflected its implicit attitudes. Kerry landlords referred casually to O'Connell as 'O'Horrid'. Semaphore phrases such as 'law and order' signalled agreement across hostile political territory. 'I believe', said a newspaper editor about a Tory candidate in 1835, 'he is for the preservation of life and property in Ireland, and all such are Conservatives.'[1] Protestantism, more than anything else, reinforced a tribal loyalty transcending class, status or geographical origin. 'Our politics', noted a Wicklow land agent in 1832, 'are a curious commodity. They are mere county politics and have little or nothing to do with any general principle or feeling save that of Catholic versus Protestant.' Hence the peculiar fierceness poured over Protestant Liberals.[2] Hence too the denial of all politics save sectarian politics, as when a Cork magistrate told an election committee in 1842 that he considered 'the word "Tory" . . . an extraordinary word, I do not well know what it means: I will tell you what I have supported; I have supported the Protestant interest of the county'.[3]

The strength of the loyalties involved meant that Tory renegades were among the rarest exotics of the Irish political landscape. In 1845 the *Newry Telegraph* prepared a journalistic *auto-da-fé* for 'skulkers' who supported Peel on Maynooth and reminded them that 'Protestant constituents will avenge themselves on those who have treated with contempt sympathies and prejudices which they formerly resorted to for party purposes'.[4] It was for such reasons also that the Irish Peelites had so brief a history. The few who survived the butterfly years between 1846 and 1852 were soon harried back into the capacious arms of Derby and Disraeli.[5] Only in the late 1850s and early 1860s did 'moderation' make any kind of appearance on the Irish Conservative stage, and even then it was a fleeting business of anonymous pamphlets demanding 'enlightened Conservative progress' and cosmetic appeals to 'true consistent progress' by unlikely figures such as the authentically reactionary lawyer, James Whiteside, and the future Tory Chief Whip, Colonel T. E. Taylor, a man of

[1] Lord Kenmare to Knight of Kerry, 8 Jan. 1835, FitzGerald Papers; *Report from the select committee on Bribery at Elections*, H.C. 1835 (547), viii, 654.

[2] R. Chaloner to Lord Milton, 13 Oct. 1832, Wentworth Woodhouse Muniments G35; Melbourne to Mulgrave, 7 Feb. 1837, Melbourne Papers 100/18; Lord Farnham to Eglinton, 26 July 1852, Eglinton Papers MS 5343.

[3] *Minutes of the proceedings of the select committee on the Cork County election petition*, H.C. 1842 (271), vi, 75.

[4] Cited in *The Times*, 29 May 1845.

[5] See, e.g., Sir J. Young to Gladstone, 10 Aug. 1852, Gladstone Papers Add. MS 44237; Lord Enniskillen to Archbishop Beresford, 21 Mar. 1855, Pack-Beresford Papers D644/A/586; Sir J. Young to Gladstone, 7 May 1859, Gladstone Papers Add. MS 44237.

otherwise impeccably bluff and traditional manner and outlook.[1] In truth, this was no more than fashionable froth, for, as Nassau William Senior was rightly told in 1858, 'an Irish Tory is a very different person from an English Tory. He is a real Tory—an enemy to everything popular [that is, progressive].'[2] The tone was established in the 1830s and 1840s when Protestantism ceased to be simply a badge of loyalty and became an explicit propellant of action. The O'Connellite assault and the opening of closed boroughs called forth overt and general political activity. Morale, badly dented in 1829 and 1832, was accorded immediate and vigorous restoration.

The Irish Protestant Conservative Society founded in 1831 constituted the first practical response to the new politics. Well before the General Election of December 1832 it drew up detailed plans for local clubs, registration drives, and sectarian solidarity in employment and patronage. Substantial sums were collected in the form of a 'Protestant Rent'. Although at first the society was dominated by populist urban Tories led by Revd Charles Boyton, its success in attracting country gentlemen and parliamentarians helped to establish the (sometimes uneasy) coalition which was to make Conservatism so vital a political force.[3] Both Boyton and many Tory MPs realized the importance of keeping 'alive the spirit of the poor . . . Protestants', and all knew that the party would 'quickly lose our counties if we can't keep our lower orders tied to us'.[4] The thirty seats won in 1832 came as a bitter disappointment after so much effort.[5] Unlike the Liberals, however, the Tories, whose whole life revolved around their 'minority' status, were able to draw paradoxical strength from the years of opposition between 1830 and 1841. Comparative defeat led to increased electoral activity. The Conservative Society gave detailed attention to the registries,

---

[1] 'Feeva', *A Psalter of Derry: Letters of 'Conservator-Elector' on the political condition and parliamentary representation of the county* (Dublin, 1859)—the work of R. P. Dawson (Co. Londonderry MP) who was just about the only genuine 'progressive' Conservative in Ireland; see also ibid. 50–1 for Whiteside and Taylor.

[2] N. W. Senior, *Journals, conversations, and essays relating to Ireland*, 2nd edn., 2 vols. (London, 1868), ii, 112 (said by his brother, an Irish poor-law commissioner). See also *D.E.P.* 21 May 1859: 'Toryism in England is comparatively mild . . . in Ireland Toryism is Orange Ascendancy.'

[3] Circular from Captain E. Cottingham (Secretary), 17 June 1832, Farnham Papers MS 18610(7); T. Lefroy to Farnham, 4 June 1832, ibid. MS 18611(3).

[4] T. Lefroy to Farnham, 12 June 1831, ibid. MS 18611(2); Boyton to Farnham, 2 Dec. 1831, ibid. MS 18609(3).

[5] Cottingham (to Farnham, 17 Oct. 1832, ibid. MS 18610(3)) had hoped for 50 to 60 seats. For organizational preparations locally and through a Dublin committee, see *Bally-shannon Herald*, 12 Oct. 1832; *Report from the select committee on the Carrickfergus election petition*, H.C. 1833 (181), viii, 11, 20, 23, 37 ff.; T. Lefroy to Farnham, 4 June 1832, Farnham Papers MS 18611(3); Cottingham to Farnham, [Oct. 1832], ibid. MS 18610(7).

while local registration clubs established a network of provincial and county organizations which was to form the long-term basis of party work and solidarity. Registration societies in Co. Armagh co-ordinated baronial committees and collected accurate information about Protestant tenant voters. Active Conservative societies existed, for example, in Ballymena, Banbridge, and Cavan, often under the control of Church of Ireland clergymen. In Monaghan the grand jury (itself a Tory monopoly) put a prominent land agent in charge of the county Conservative Association. In Belfast began the long reign of the solicitor, John Bates, whose unscrupulous administrative skills kept the town under virtually permanent Tory domination. Bates was a master of registry matters and employed teams of architects to swear down the values of houses occupied by Liberal claimants to the vote.[1] In the south, where only four county and three borough seats had been won in 1832, an even greater effort was made. Registration was regularly supervised in constituencies such as Waterford Co. and Borough, Queen's Co., Tipperary, Westmeath, Co. Carlow, Kerry, and Longford, often by permanent societies.[2] In Kildare a 'Freedom of Election Society' founded in 1835 collected large sums from landlords, and protected voters against agrarian and political violence.[3] In King's Co. a central Registration Society controlled the work of twelve baronial sub-committees. Mullingar had a 'Conservative Club Room', Co. Cork a regular organization complete with paid valuators, while the Queen's Co. Conservative Society published leaflets warning farmers who 'swore up' the value of their land in order to get the vote that they would be charged that value in rent by their respective proprietors.[4]

[1] Co. Armagh Society circular, 25 Aug. 1837, Chambré Papers M7035/24; [R. M. Sibbett], *Orangeism in Ireland and throughout the Empire*, 2nd edn., 2 vols. (London, [1939]), ii, 239; J. Withers to Lord Downshire, 20 Dec. 1837, Downshire Papers D671/C/12/700; Revd M. Beresford to Farnham, 12 Jan., 1 Feb. 1837, Farnham Papers MS 18608; P. Ó Mórdha, 'Some Notes on Monaghan History (1692-1866)', *Clogher Record*, ix (1976), 35-6; on Bates, see [D. Dunlop], *A brief historical sketch of parliamentary elections in Belfast from the first general election under the Reform Act till 1865* (Belfast, [1865]), pp. 11-12; J. E. Tennent to Sir T. Fremantle, Nov. 1841, cited R. Stewart, *The Foundation of the Conservative party 1830-1867* (London, 1978), p. 137; *Fictitious Votes, Ireland*, 1st series, 1st report, pp. 29, 53, 62, 113-14.

[2] J. Alcock to Stanley, 29 June 1840, Derby Papers 20/9 (Waterford); Lawyer's Notebook for 1840, Trinity College Dublin MS 4590e (Queen's Co.); *Hansard*, liv, 221 (18 May 1840), ii (19 June 1840), also *Fictitious Votes, Ireland*, 1st series, 2nd report, p. 25 (Tipperary); *Hansard*, liv, 426-7 (20 May 1840) (Westmeath); *Minutes of evidence taken before the committee on the Carlow County election petition*, H.C. 1837 (307), x, 17; *Fictitious Votes, Ireland*, 2nd series, 3rd report, pp. 13, 48 (Longford); *D.E.P.* 2 Jan. 1841 (Kerry).

[3] Society's leaflet of 17 July 1837, Downshire Papers D671/C/214/351; Circular of 14 Apr. 1840, N.L.I. Pressmark P2188 No. 6.

[4] King's Co.: Lord Charleville to Fremantle, [Mar. 1841], Fremantle Papers 88/18;

Parish clubs and active election societies set up in Waterford, Bandon, Youghal, and Sligo proved particularly successful in attracting support from Protestant artisans.[1] In many counties, such as Tipperary, Cavan, Wicklow, and Donegal, Tory landlords and their agents established quasi-permanent election organizations to supervise the registries, pay the travel expenses of sympathetic voters, and manipulate the granting of leases according to the changing demands of local politics.[2]

The metropolitan conspicuousness of the Tory revival in Dublin City and County—and to a lesser extent in Cork City—led its opponents into the propaganda of exaggeration.[3] Not that the Dublin revival was insubstantial, for, while all twelve of the parliamentary vacancies there between 1832 and 1837 were filled by Liberals or Repealers, all but three of the thirty-two seats contested between 1838 and 1868 were won by Conservative candidates. Dublin was the headquarters of the Irish Metropolitan Conservative Society, which, in 1836, replaced the Protestant Society. Ostensibly less extremist, it still demanded 'Protestantism in Ireland . . . by every means in our power'. With rooms in fashionable Dawson Street and the support of two leading Conservative intellectuals (rare birds in Ireland), Isaac Butt and Mountifort Longfield, it co-operated actively with the more specialized Conservative Registration Society.[4] Money was sent to the provinces and in 1841 an 'Anti-Intimidation Committee' indemnified 'the poorer electors, Catholic and Protestant, who may have been made the victims of mob violence'.[5] Such formal political structures, which attracted the support of professional and mercantile men as well as of landowners, were underpinned by open sectarian bodies like the Irish

E. M. Kelly to Downshire, 9 July, 14 Aug. 1837, Downshire Papers D671/C/12/781; *Fictitious Votes, Ireland*, 2nd series, 3rd report, pp. 319–20, 405. Others: *D.E.P.* 1 Aug. 1837; *C.C.* 23 Oct. 1832; *Hansard*, liv, 361 (19 May 1840), 425–6 (20 May 1840), 1341 (19 June 1840); *Committee on Bribery at Elections*, H.C. 1835 (547), viii, 541.

[1] *Kilkenny Journal*, 26 July 1832; J. Wheeler to Peel, 1 Jan. 1835, Peel Papers Add. MS 40409; R. N. Rorke to T. Ray, 6 Nov. [1841], O'Connell Papers N.L.I. MS 13623; 'Youghal Protestant Operatives Scrapbook 1829–48' (Bradshaw Collection C.U.L. Hib.1. 844.1); *Ballyshannon Herald*, 17 Mar. 1837.

[2] M. Fallon to R. Earle, 11 Nov. 1832, Melbourne Papers 95/110; J. Fawcett to J. Dicken, 24 Nov. 1832, Morley Papers Deposit 69; Lord Powerscourt to Downshire, 13 Nov. 1836, Downshire Papers D671/C/12/632; *D.E.P.* 6 July 1837.

[3] *D.E.P.* 19 July 1836; *Freeman's Journal*, 26 Aug. 1836; *Hansard*, lii, 635 (25 Feb. 1840).

[4] R. B. McDowell, *Public Opinion and Government Policy in Ireland, 1801–1846*, p. 117; *D.E.P.* 22 July 1837; *Fictitious Votes, Ireland*, 1st series, 3rd report, pp. 257, 282–3, 290–4, 352–6.

[5] *Report of the Outrages and Intimidations at the late Elections* (Dublin, 1841), pp. 29–30—copy U.C.D. Pamphlets 6201; *Hansard*, xxviii, 782–3 (15 June 1835).

Protestant Association of 1836, which co-ordinated charitable work among poor Protestants and encouraged them to register as voters, and the Clerical Society and Lay Association, which together raised large funds (£8,000 from a handful of magnates alone) to help clergymen sue for the recovery of unpaid tithes. It all showed, as one Tory observed, that 'under no circumstances, however adverse, or appearances, however dispiriting, ought a party who possess in themselves the means and elements of success, to abandon their hopes or relax their efforts'.[1] In Cork too teams of 'objectors' helped the Tory cause at the revisions of 1832 and 1835 and a broadly based society drew support from 'almost every class from the estated gentleman to the tradesman [and] . . . poor apprentices'.[2] In 1840 municipal reform suddenly ended Cork Corporation's long subjection to the Protestant 'Friendly Club' and evoked a powerful Tory response in the shape of Anti-Repeal Clubs and Protestant Operative Associations dedicated to galvanizing the sectarian freeman vote and to castigating Peel for weakness in the face of popish imperialism. And, indeed, within eight years, Tory representation on the reformed corporation rose from a dispiriting seven (out of sixty-four) to a remarkable twenty-two—a considerable and morale-boosting achievement.[3] A similar post-1840 recovery took place in Dublin, where, although the Tories lost control of the corporation, they steadily increased their seats on the council and retained their grip upon the guilds which in Dublin played an important role in parliamentary as well as in local politics.[4]

By 1837 the Tories were nationally strong enough to mount a vigorous election campaign and to run candidates simply to annoy the enemy and consolidate their own support, for, as one pointed out, 'in Ireland either fighting or drinking together is the real bond of union'.[5] Helped by Tory cohesion and Whig disunion in the

---

[1] *First Report of the Irish Protestant Association* (Dublin, 1836)—copy R. I. A. Halliday Pamphlets 1677; Littleton to Lord Brougham, 17, 30 Oct. 1834, Hatherton Papers D260/M/01/4; G. Lyne, 'The General Association of Ireland', pp. 18–27; *Report of the City of Dublin Conservative Registration Committee, June 1842* (Dublin, 1842)—copy Halliday Pamphlets 1842.

[2] *Hansard*, xxx, 774–5 (20 Aug. 1835); *Fictitious Votes, Ireland*, 2nd series, 1st report, pp. 123, 274–5, 281.

[3] M. Murphy, 'Municipal Reform and the Repeal Movement in Cork', pp. 16–18; G. Shea to Peel, 28 Feb. 1844, Peel Papers Add. MS 40540. See also *Municipal Corporations (Ireland). Appendix to the First Report of the Commissioners Part I*, H.C. 1835 [27 & 28], xxvii, 29; *Fictitious Votes, Ireland*, 2nd series, 1st report, pp. 21–2; Anglesey to Melbourne, 13 Aug. 1832, Melbourne Papers 94/40.

[4] *D.E.P.* 22, 29 July 1837; Jacqueline Hill, 'The role of Dublin in the Irish national movement 1840–48' (University of Leeds Ph.D. thesis, 1973), p. 206.

[5] Mulgrave to Melbourne, 7 Aug. [1837], Melbourne Papers 100/43; Graham to Peel, 1 Jan. 1842, Peel Papers Add. MS 40446.

United Kingdom as a whole, the Irish Tories managed not only to obtain in 1837 an important legal decision on the franchise question, but to pursue no less than thirty-one election petitions between 1832 and 1840 as against the Whigs' nine and the Repealers' six. The victory of 1841 acted like a blood transfusion to an already reviving patient, for, as the liberally minded Tory Chief Secretary, Lord Eliot, somewhat fearfully reported, 'a strong Protestant, almost Orange feeling has burst forth, which, however useful it may be on the present occasion, will be difficult to deal with hereafter'.[1] Peel's efforts to conciliate the Catholics produced in Ireland, not Protestant disunion but Protestant wrath, while the Protectionist split of 1846–52 proved a very minor episode. Indeed, small-scale Peelite defections were more than balanced by a spectacular victory at the Cork City by-election of 1849 and an extremely respectable result at Cork Co. in March 1852. Not that Protectionism *per se* ever gained much of a foothold. Many farmers saw it as no more than a 'high rent dodge', while most Irish 'Protectionists' cared 'more about Protestantism than agriculture' and reacted favourably to Derby's willingness in 1851–2 to countenance the 'Protestant Cry' he had so worryingly ignored in 1847.[2] The fact that the 1850s and 1860s mark the high-point of Conservative success in Victorian Ireland—forty seats won in 1852, forty-six in 1857, fifty-five in 1859, forty-seven in 1865—is a tribute to the foundations laid down after 1832. The continuing work of consolidation was substantially extended by the establishment in February 1853 of the Central Conservative Society of Ireland, perhaps the single most important development in the history of the party's electoral and political machinery. And although English Conservatism was at the time not entirely bereft of administrative orchestration, the Irish Society clearly predates the emergence of similar bodies in England in 1867 and Scotland in 1882. Begun by a private caucus of prominent Conservatives (including fourteen MPs, ten peers, and many land-owners and professional men), the society was soon actively engaged in all types of political organization: registration, the collection of statistics, exchanging information, maintaining links with England, and encouraging Irish Tories to work effectively together at

---

[1] *The Irish franchise and registration question* (London, 1841), pp. 18–23—copy R. I. A. Halliday Pamphlets 1816; Lord Eliot to Peel, 20 Jan. 1842, Peel Papers Add. MS 40480.

[2] Fitzwilliam to Milton, 1 Apr. 1852, Wentworth Woodhouse Muniments T2; Clarendon to Russell, 5 Jan. 1850, and to Sir C. Wood, 20 Jan. 1850, Clarendon Papers L.-B. V; Clarendon to Russell, 5 Aug. 1847, ibid. L.-B. I; Derby to Roden, 5 Feb. 1852, Derby Papers 179/1; R. Stewart, *The Politics of Protection: Lord Derby and the Protectionist party 1841–1852* (Cambridge, 1971), pp. 91, 181.

Westminster.[1] In these respects, therefore, it anticipated the later workings of Ulster Unionism, which, far from marking a new departure in Irish Tory affairs, were no more than a logical continuation in one province of what had formerly been the case in the country as a whole.

A general mixture of loyalty, apprehension, and disdain towards England and English Conservatism marks another connecting link between the Unionism of the 1880s and 1890s and the Toryism of earlier years. Already in the 1850s many leading Irish Tories had little faith in the backbone of the English leadership when faced with demands for tenant-right.[2] At times such fears led men into vigorous bouts of political suttee, as when maddened ultras in the late 1840s determined to break with English party structures or when a handful of Protestant landlords temporarily threw themselves upon the pyre of the Home Government Association in the early 1870s. Invariably, however, such efforts at self-immolation foundered upon the realistic recollection that 'our only hope in the present crisis is in English connexion, English councils, English assistance, English sympathy'.[3] Not that the love–hate relationship with England was ever far distant from the heart-strings of Irish Toryism, especially when it came to religious questions. Sir Joseph ('Holy Joe') Napier, MP for Dublin University 1848–58 and sometime Attorney-General and Lord Chancellor of Ireland, was a notable propagandist of Ireland's special Protestant culture. Convinced as he was that 'the Protestantism of Ireland . . . is worth contending for', he hammered home the necessity of solidarity in the face, not only of ultramontane Catholicism, but of English indifference also. 'I am', he told Lord Naas in 1853,

More than ever impressed with the importance of having our Irish Party kept together, and that you should communicate with each and every of them and endeavour to arrange a united action and regular conference . . . Without political influence and power any class is treated as a cypher . . . [and] Ireland is treated as a mere political convenience for English parties.[4]

---

[1] Full details in *Daily Express*, 3, 7, 28 Feb., 1, 29, 30 Mar. 1853.

[2] Lord Desart to Eglinton, 9 Dec. 1852, Eglinton Papers MS 5343; Lord Clonbrock to Naas, 22 Apr. 1859, Mayo Papers MS 11036.

[3] Lord Clare to Farnham, 9 Jan. 1847, Leinster Papers D3078/3/34; also Sir T. Redington to Clarendon, 27 June 1847, Clarendon Papers Box 24; L. J. McCaffrey, 'Irish Federalism in the 1870s: A Study in Conservative Nationalism', *Transactions of the American Philosophical Society*, new series lii, part 6 (1962), 11; also Naas to Abercorn, 30 Apr. 1867, Abercorn Papers T2541/VR/85/18.

[4] Sir J. Napier to Naas, [25 June 1853], Mayo Papers MS 11017; also to Sir W. Jolliffe, n.d., cited R. Stewart, *The Foundations of the Conservative party 1830–1867*, pp. 296–7; A. C. Ewald, *The Life and Letters of the Right Hon. Sir Joseph Napier Bart.*, revised edn. (London, 1892), p. 42.

English insouciance increased Irish suspicions. 'We are sick', remarked a well-meaning Lord Stanley (later fifteenth Earl of Derby) in 1852, 'of the old story—true as it undoubtedly is—of election riots and priestly intimidation.'[1] Nor did Disraeli's undifferentiated meteorological suggestions that Irish character was shaped by life 'on an island in a damp climate, and contiguous to the melancholy ocean' exhibit either the sympathy or the vigour expected by his political followers in Ireland. Unsurprisingly, the parliamentary resistance to Gladstone's disestablishment proposals of 1868–9 struck Irish Tories as insufficiently energetic, for they saw the Church question as merely the start of a reformist procession which would soon include the 'hereditary peerage', the 'Horse Guards', and even 'the Throne'.[2] In the end, however, the British party provided the only possible refuge. All else was self-delusion. Derby, for all his puzzlement over Irish affairs, talked a political language at least comprehensible, if not always soothing, to Irish Tory ears. His comments of 1852 blaming the Famine upon the 'incurable taint' which would never allow Ireland 'to be prosperous while it is Roman Catholic' were profoundly reassuring. Certainly the rumour in 1855 that Gladstone might join a future Conservative administration produced 'a strong remonstrance' from Ireland and threats that, in such an event, the 'Protestant party' would entirely abandon the cause.[3]

The Central Conservative Society of 1853 fell fully into this general tradition, for it had among its patrons the Earl of Enniskillen (the Orange Grand Master) and as its Secretary, Samuel Yates Johnstone, another senior Orangeman and a prominent barrister. What distinguished it, however, from earlier groups were staying-power and a sense of continuing application. The real work was done by a group of young lawyers with a dynamic sense of purpose and a zeal to spread the gospel into the constituencies. Help, for example, was sent to Armagh during the by-election of 1855 and also to secure an unexpected Tory gain at Athlone in 1856.[4] The society's report of January 1859 shows it giving useful technical advice to constituencies

---

[1] Stanley to Naas, 30 Aug. 1852, Mayo Papers MS 11020; also F. R. Bonham to Peel, 5, 9 Aug. 1837, Peel Papers Add. MS 40424.

[2] W. F. Moneypenny and G. E. Buckle, *The Life of Benjamin Disraeli*, 6 vols. (London, 1910–20), v, 91; W. W. F. Dick (MP for Wicklow) to Mayo, 13 Apr. 1868, Mayo Papers MS 11164.

[3] Derby to Eglinton, 2 Oct. 1852, 6 June 1858, Eglinton Papers MSS 5332, 5344; Stanley's Diary for 31 Jan. 1855, in *Disraeli, Derby, and the Conservative party*, ed. J. Vincent, p. 132.

[4] G. A. Hamilton to Derby, 26 June 1855, Derby Papers 150/9; J. Napier to Archbishop Beresford, [20 Nov. 1855], Pack-Beresford Papers D664/A/641; Revd T. Kilroe to Cullen, 12 Apr. 1856, Cullen Papers.

with good local organizations (such as Dublin City and County, Cork City, Co. Carlow, Bandon, Co. Sligo, and Co. Londonderry) and elsewhere sending agents to attend revisions, give legal assistance, and rekindle dying Tory fires.[1] After the dramatic electoral success of 1859 attempts were made to increase the society's financial resources and circulars were sent to all Irish Tory MPs and 'Conservative members of the House of Lords connected with Ireland' on the principle that '£5 spent upon looking after the registry goes further than £100 spent upon a contest'.[2] Gladstone's victory in 1868 led to a broadening of the society's aims to include agitation of 'the great political questions of the day . . . through the medium of the press' and to ambitious (and largely unfulfilled) plans for a 'London Committee' to watch over Irish interests at Westminster.[3] Additional registration agents were also employed and in 1870 the society published (for private circulation) an unusually useful handbook written in prose so translucent that even dim-witted locals could through it begin to understand the Neoplatonic mysteries of Victorian election law.[4]

In many constituencies local clubs and societies were also active. As before, Dublin City and County formed the brightest jewels in the crown, and not until 1855 did Liberals in the latter even attempt a counter-organization. Dublin City's Conservative Association was particularly impressive and involved itself, not only in registration, but in the selection of candidates and the management of elections in general. Symbolically its national importance was profound.[5] In the run-up to the 1868 election it spent almost £3,000 in compiling 'complete lists of the [12,899] voters in Dublin, with their names and addresses . . . with their political opinions marked opposite each name'.[6] The substantial Protestant working-class electorate

---

[1] *Central Conservative Society of Ireland: Report of the Sub-Committee 1859*— copies Mayo Papers MS 11025 and Hylton Papers Box 24.

[2] Lord Donoughmore to Lord Leconfield, 7 Feb. 1860, and S. Y. Johnstone to Leconfield, 24 Apr. 1861, Petworth House Archives PHA/1668/6, 7; also *Daily Express*, 31 Jan. 1861.

[3] Leaflet headed 'Central Conservative Registration Society for Ireland' (1869), Perceval-Maxwell Papers D1556/23.

[4] D. Plunket to E. Gibson, 12 Aug. 1869, Ashbourne Papers T2955/B119/7; *Notes and Hints upon the Registration of Voters, for the guidance of Agents* (Dublin, 1870)— copy in Dungannon Borough Revision Papers D847/8, Box 24.

[5] For the county, see Liberal circulars etc. in Domvile Papers MS 9361, and *Committee on registration of parliamentary voters, Ireland,* H.C. 1874 (261), xi, 267. For the city, see ibid. 229; letter from the Association, 8 July 1857, Incorporated Society Papers MS 5849; J. Vance, MP to Mayo, 6 July [1868], Mayo Papers MS 11175.

[6] *Report of the Commissioners appointed by the act of the 32nd and 33rd Victoria, cap. 65, for the purpose of making inquiry into the existence of Corrupt Practices amongst the freemen electors of the City of Dublin,* H.C. 1870 [C 93], xxxiii, 923–33.

in Dublin (substantial because of the survival of an effectively
sectarian freeman franchise) was further mobilized by a variety
of quasi-social organizations designed to elevate religious identity
above class distinction. Some, such as the Protestant Registration
Office, were private-enterprise offshoots of business ventures, in this
case of the Protestant Servants Registry Office owned by John and
James Frederick. Others were primarily charitable associations.
Others again were long-established clubs like the Aldermen of Skinner's
Alley whose meetings allowed prosperous Conservatives of extreme
views to mix with their more modest co-religionists. The Aldermen
included the rabble-rousing parson, Revd Tresham Dames Gregg,
as well as genteel ultra lawyers like J. D. Jackson, Peel's Irish legal
adviser and later a judge of the common pleas. Poor Protestant
voters were canvassed and flattered, the 'Protestant ascendancy
in church and state' defended, and excited meetings of freemen
organized during general elections under the inspiring gaze of a 'unique
marble statue of King William III'.[1]

After the Famine Tory organization in Ulster was further refined.
Lisburn Borough provides a typical example. Apart from a brief
Liberal interlude between 1852 and 1857, the seat was in Tory hands
from 1832 until its disfranchisement in 1885. The influence of the
local Tory landowner, Lord Hertford, was augmented by a Protestant
Conservative Registration Society, the activities of which included
the provision of 'intellectual treats' in the shape of lectures by
Revd Henry Cooke attended by artisans, shopkeepers, merchants,
and gentlemen alike. Its membership overlapped with that of the
Orange Institution and the inclusion of various clergymen reflected
its success in creating a local pan-Protestant consciousness. Speakers
emphasized the power of the 'united loyal Protestants' in repelling
'all the assaults of unprincipled Whiggism, levelling radicalism, and
rampant Romanism'. And during the brief years of Tory government
the society helped to distribute the minor local patronage which
kept the rank and file at once expectant and disciplined.[2] Much the
same happened elsewhere. Newry had a Conservative Registration
Society as active in 1868 as it had been in 1829. At Dungannon
the registry was closely watched and information exchanged with the
Central Society in Dublin.[3] In the 1860s Derry City boasted a

---

[1] J. Frederick to —, 31 July 1865, Domvile Papers MS 9365 (The Protestant Servants
Registry Office had a long life, see *Thom 1852*, p. 789 and *Thom 1876*, p. 1366); Minute
Book of the Aldermen of Skinner's Alley 1842–59, R.I.A. MS 23/H/52, and *Saunders'
Newsletter*, 27 Mar. 1857.

[2] *Belfast Newsletter*, 22 Oct. 1864; D. Beatty to Naas, 24 Nov. 1866, Mayo Papers
MS 11143.

[3] *Newry Commercial Telegraph*, 25 Oct. 1864; A. C. Innes to Mayo, 16 Mar. 1868,

Working Men's Protestant Defence Association occupying reading rooms, providing lectures, and, again, acting as a link between the more affluent magistrates, physicians, ministers, and parsons and the mass of Protestant electors in the borough. Non-voters too were as welcome here as in the similar societies which existed in Coleraine, Enniskillen, Armagh, and almost certainly throughout nearly all the northern borough constituencies.[1] In Belfast also the Conservatives retained an iron grip after 1847 with the single and dramatic exception of 1868. Even after the downfall of their organizational genius, John Bates, in the 1850s, their determination stood in stark contrast to the endemic divisions of their opponents. The 1870s witnessed the rise to influence of Edward Finnigan, Secretary to the Antrim and Down Constitutional Association of 1874 and to the Ulster Constitutional Union of 1880. Indeed, despite some temporary set-backs in Ulster about this time, Belfast Conservatives were able to raise almost £10,000 for the building of a Constitutional Club opened by Sir Stafford Northcote in 1883.[2] Even in the counties, where landlord influence operated through less formal channels, local Conservative clubs helped to increase electoral efficiency. The shock of a Liberal gain in Down led to the establishment of a County Constitutional Association in 1874, while in Antrim, Tyrone, and elsewhere, Protestant Associations emerged from time to time to weld together Church of Ireland and Presbyterian farmers into a united Conservative bloc.[3]

What is, however, above all noteworthy is how the early southern thrust of organized Conservatism was maintained after 1850.

	Conservative seats won in Ireland	Conservative seats won outside Ulster	Conservative seats won in single-member boroughs outside Ulster
1852	40	14	3
1857	46	20	4
1859	55	26	5
1865	47	20	2
1868	39	14	2
1874	33	12	1
1880	25	7	2

Mayo Papers MS 11168; J. N. Gerrard to [a Dungannon solicitor], 24 Oct. 1871, Dungannon Borough Revision Papers D847/8.

[1] *Londonderry Sentinel*, 24 Apr. 1857, 3 June 1859, 6, 20 Oct., 6, 10 Nov. 1868; *Londonderry Guardian*, 10 Oct. 1867; *Committee on registration of parliamentary voters, Ireland*, H.C. 1874 (261), xi, 250, 278; *Londonderry Standard*, 19 Oct. 1867; Archbishop Beresford to G. Dunbar, 13 Sept. 1855, Pack-Beresford Papers D664/A/620.
[2] [D. Dunlop], *A Brief historical sketch of parliamentary elections in Belfast*, pp. 32, 35; *Northern Whig*, 6 Oct. 1857; I. Budge and C. O'Leary, *Belfast: Approach to Crisis*, pp. 43–65; *Belfast Newsletter*, 5 Oct. 1883; A. B. Cooke, 'A Conservative party leader in Ulster', p. 78.
[3] *Down County election petition*, H.C. 1880 (260-II), lvii, 593; G. Brush to W. B. Forde, 22 Aug. 1876, Perceval-Maxwell Papers D1556/23; *Daily Express*, 10 Feb. 1853.

Tory success until the late 1860s was, therefore, spread through all types of constituency. It was not confined to small southern boroughs, the most notoriously venal of which (Athlone, Kinsale, Cashel, Youghal, and the like) were in any case strongholds of localist 'Liberalism'. Nor was the ultimate withdrawal into the northern laager as early a development as has often been supposed.

In the south formal organization was strongest in places where some kind of Protestant community was able to maintain a separate cultural identity. Thus, although Tories won four of the eleven Mayo seats filled between 1852 and 1868, this was achieved entirely by the informal efforts of landlords and their agents. In neighbouring Co. Sligo, however, where almost one in ten of the people was Protestant, the situation was very different. There the county's chief town (with 21.7 per cent of its population Protestant in 1861) acted as a centre for political action throughout the area, and this modest demographic base, when combined with the prosperity of the Protestant community, yielded a Protestant element within the electorate of very considerable size: 48.8 per cent in the borough in 1852 and 36.3 per cent in the county.[1] An active Registration Society co-ordinated local election work, watched the revisions, and saw to it that no more than forty of the 663 Protestant county voters in 1852 could in any sense be designated 'anti-Tory'.[2] The two Conservative candidates in 1857 and the nine substantial proprietors who sat on the society's committee together owned over a quarter of the county's total land surface as well as property elsewhere in Ireland.[3] And this combination of landlord power, organizational efficiency, and significant Protestant numbers proved so irresistible that only two non-Tories were returned for the county between 1832 and 1874. Even in the comparatively corrupt borough, with its substantially lower franchise levels, the Conservatives were able to win four of the six contested elections held between 1856 and 1868.

Elsewhere too organizational activity followed the Protestant flag. Youghal and traditionally 'Protestant Bandon' had energetic

---

[1] *Galway Vindicator*, 27 Mar. 1852; *Daily Express*, 15 Oct. 1852. As late as 1859 and 1868 the proportions of Protestant voters in Sligo Borough were 52.8 per cent and 50.2 per cent respectively (*Central Conservative Society of Ireland: Report of the Sub-Committee 1859; Waterford Mail*, 9 Oct. 1868). The denominational figures for the population are taken from the 1861 census.

[2] Sir W. Jolliffe to Naas, 22 Dec. 1858, Mayo Papers MS 11023; *Central Conservative Society of Ireland: Report of the Sub-Committee 1859*; E. Pollock to C. W. O'Hara, 21 Oct. 1868, O'Hara Papers MS 20348.

[3] List of committee members in C. W. Cooper (later O'Hara) to E. J. Cooper, 31 July 1856, O'Hara Papers MS 20353. See also U. H. H. de Burgh, *The Landowners of Ireland* (Dublin, [1878]).

registration clubs.[1] In Cork City the sectarian enthusiasm which almost alone underpinned Tory activism during the long years of local defeat after 1852 was rewarded by a shock Conservative gain at a by-election in 1876. Throughout the period a variety of registration societies meeting in the Protestant Hall and the winning of seats in municipal and poor-law elections kept the cause sufficiently alive to ensure that the revisions were still being actively watched as late as 1885.[2] But, while Cork City was well supplied with political organizations, the very size of the county made it difficult for any party to provide more than fleeting clubs or occasional teams of revision lawyers to fight the autumnal battles in the courts. Indeed, regular registration work constituted the most common form of Tory organization in the south, and the Central Society was able to report in 1859 upon impressive activity in Cos. Dublin, Wicklow, Carlow (where Conservative landlords retained the representation until 1880), Mayo, Louth, Sligo, Leitrim, Waterford, and Queen's Co., and in the boroughs of Dublin, Clonmel, Mallow, Portarlington, Carlow, Drogheda, Athlone, Sligo, Cork, Bandon, Dungarvan, Waterford, and Tralee. So lively a collaboration between urban and landed Conservatives helped to produce a great victory at the General Election of 1859, and it was precisely in those counties where the gentry remained apathetic, such as Kilkenny, Longford, and Clare, that organizational deficiencies first exacerbated and then reflected the ominous psychological collapse of later years.[3]

Less public was the work of informal committees of influential Conservatives and government ministers, though the rarity of Tory administrations after 1846 meant that many men who would otherwise have been in office became, *faute de mieux*, fund-raisers and cheer-leaders during the years of opposition. Particularly prominent were the second Earl of Glengall (1794-1858) and the fourth Earl of Donoughmore (1823-66), who played important parts both in general political co-ordination and in the management of the twenty-eight Irish representative peers who sat in the House of Lords. When a vacancy in the peerage occurred, party leaders consulted widely and, virtually without exception in the period 1832-85, were able

---

[1] F. E. to W. Currey, 11 June 1851, 3 June 1863, Lismore Papers MSS 7186, 7190; *C.C.* 29 Oct. 1859, 20 Oct. 1860.

[2] *C.C.* 12 May, 17 Sept., 1 Oct. 1859, 18 Oct. 1860; Lord Bandon to Naas, 13 Aug. 1866, Mayo Papers MS 11143; R. B. Tooker to T. E. Taylor, 20 Aug. 1868, ibid. MS 11174; *Committee on registration of parliamentary voters, Ireland*, H.C. 1874 (261), xi, 197; I. d'Alton, 'Cork Unionism: Its role in parliamentary and local elections, 1885-1914', *Studia Hibernica*, No. 15 (1975), 146.

[3] *Central Conservative Society of Ireland: Report of the Sub-Committee 1859* (Mayo Papers MS 11025).

to secure the return of one reliably orthodox Conservative after another.[1] So efficient was Tory organization, that special Irish magistrates (who alone could tender the necessary oath to prospective noble electors) were dispatched on complicated tours of English stately homes to help sympathetic peers with Irish titles to register their votes. The development of active canvassing also helped the best-organized party, and Tory dominance survived undiminished as the century wore on.[2] In the 1860s Lord Derby, as leader of the party, was still encouraging Donoughmore to sort out rival claims by means of informal meetings among peers, while in the 1870s the task was taken over by the Duke of Abercorn, himself Viceroy of Ireland in the years 1866-8 and 1874-6.[3]

More generally, Glengall played a vital role in preparing the party for the General Election of 1852, issuing technical notes, encouraging constituency activism, recommending candidates, obtaining funds from the Tory government of the day, and acting as agent for a small committee of MPs then meeting under the chairmanship of the Chief Secretary at the usually rather sleepy Irish Office in Westminster.[4] After the election Glengall stridently catalogued his many services: 'This I do say, for 25 or 30 years I have fought for our party. I have spent £26,000 in elections—have filled the *Quarterly, Blackwood*, and *Fraser*, the *Herald, Standard, Morning Post, Mail* with articles and never asked a favour for myself (nor ever shall).' And even if the boasted 'restraint' was no more than old Irish humbug ('Lord Glengall's communications', noted one Chief Secretary, 'must always be viewed *cum grano*'), the contribution was undoubted. Indeed, Glengall's plans for the provision of English funds to help fight the new electoral registers established by the Irish Franchise Act of 1850 probably marked one of the first moves towards the eventual foundation of the Central Society in 1853.[5]   By 1857,

---

[1] D. Large, 'The House of Lords and Ireland in the Age of Peel, 1832-50', *Irish Historical Studies*, ix (1955), 69-71; Downshire to Dunraven, 16 Apr. 1839, Downshire Papers D671/C/12/723; F. R. Bonham to Peel, [July 1841], Peel Papers Add. MS 40485. The electorate consisted of all those with Irish peerages (many of whom also had English, Scots, British, or UK titles) who had taken the trouble to register their names.

[2] Lord Downes to Duke of Wellington, 23 Jan., 23 Feb., 8, 30 Mar. 1833, *The Prime Ministers' Papers: Wellington Political Correspondence*, ed. J. Brooke and J. Gandy (London, 1975-), i, 39-41, 91-2, 112-13, 149-52; Lord Clonbrock to Downshire, 12 Apr. 1841, Downshire Papers D671/C/12/782; Aberdeen to St Germans, 19 Apr. 1854, and St Germans to Aberdeen, 20 Apr. 1854, Aberdeen Papers Add. MS 43208.

[3] Derby to Belmore, 15 Oct. 1862, 2 Jan. 1864, Belmore Papers D3007/J/7, 11; Lord Hawarden to Belmore, 14 Jan. 1874, ibid. D3007/J/26.

[4] Glengall to Naas, 30 June, [July], 8 Aug. 1852, Mayo Papers MS 11019; J. Elliott to W. Pidgeon, 12 June 1852, Incorporated Society Papers MS 5848; Naas to Eglinton, 30 Mar. 1852, Eglinton Papers MS 5334.

[5] Glengall to Eglinton, 29 July 1852, Eglinton Papers MS 5343; Eliot to Graham, 21 Oct. 1843, Graham Papers 6/Ir; Naas to Derby, 29 June [1852], Derby Papers 155/1.

Donoughmore (already long active in registration work in Tipperary, Cork, and Waterford) had taken over with the help of another *ad hoc* committee formed to make Tory capital out of the 'ruin of the Sadleir faction' of corrupt Liberals in 'the south of Ireland'.[1] Two years later, with the Tories briefly in office, Donoughmore became President of the Board of Trade and the centre of an extending network of senior politicians—Disraeli, Colonel Taylor, Lord Naas (as Chief Secretary), Lord Eglinton (as Viceroy), and the Whip, Henry Whitmore—actively raising money for Irish elections, directing official patronage into appropriate Irish channels, encouraging Conservative landowners to bring their tenants to the poll, and coordinating the work of special teams of election experts working from central offices in London and at the Sackville St. Club in Dublin.[2]

The party in Ireland was even more fortunate in having in Lord Naas (Chief Secretary 1852, 1858-9, 1866-8) and Colonel T. E. Taylor (Whip 1855-9, Chief Whip 1859-68 and 1873-4) two men of standing, in touch with the leadership, and prepared to involve themselves in the details of electoral and constituency business. Both were precisely the kind of efficient, loyal, and dedicated politicians of the second rank without whose constant hard work the tedious chores so necessary for success tend to remain undone. In 1866 Naas was admitted to the cabinet and in 1868 (as sixth Earl of Mayo) appointed Viceroy of India, while Taylor became Chancellor of the Duchy of Lancaster. Both stood in stark contrast to the procession of dilatory Liberals who held the leading Irish offices between 1846 and 1874. Even before 1852 the Conservatives had usually thought it important to have at least one Irish whip in the Commons, and, although Naas's Tory predecessors as Chief Secretary had all been Englishmen, they too, both in office and in opposition, had actively encouraged registration work, found posts for the more energetic Irish agents employed by the party, negotiated patronage in return for local influence, and intervened directly when elections seemed in danger of being lost.[3] Thereafter, Naas and Taylor, assisted especially by the Scots Earl of Eglinton and the

---

[1] Naas to Derby, 3 Apr. [1857], Derby Papers 155/1; Donoughmore to Derby, 3 Apr. [1857], ibid. 158/6. The bankruptcy and suicide of John Sadleir, MP in 1856 had broken up an important (and corrupt) 'Liberal' political faction in Munster (see J. H. Whyte, *The Independent Irish Party 1850-9*, pp. 161-3).

[2] Donoughmore to Naas, 8, 12, 22 Apr. 1859, Mayo Papers MS 11036; Eglinton to Derby, 25 Apr. 1859, Derby Papers 148/3.

[3] For the Irish activities of Sir Thomas Fremantle (both as Chief Whip 1837-44 and Chief Secretary 1845-6), see Fremantle Papers 88/18; Fremantle to Peel, 1 Dec. [1844], Peel Papers Add. MS 40476; Peel to Heytesbury, 16 Aug. 1844, ibid. Add. MS 40479.

Irish Marquis (later Duke) of Abercorn as Lords Lieutenant in 1852, 1858–9, 1866–8, and 1874–6, gave the necessary continuity to Tory leadership and management in Ireland. Eglinton ignored Peel's curious doctrine of 1844 that viceroys should be largely non-political and combined lavish benevolence with partisan adhesion to the cause. A generally shrewd operator, in political terms he was anything but the extravagant nonentity which his flamboyant 'medieval' tournament of 1839 or oft-repeated jokes about his Dublin statue (now destroyed) having its eyes fixed permanently on the card-room of the University Club might lead one to suppose.[1] His splendid entertainments delighted Irish 'society' and his generous charities contrasted starkly with the parsimonious rule of his Whig predecessor, Lord Clarendon, and showed a proper appreciation of the truth, that largesse, like flattery, is best laid on with a very large trowel indeed.[2] His authorship of the 'Eglinton Clause' (in 11 & 12 Vict., c. 108) effectively forbidding the reception of papal envoys at the Court of St James's and his donation of funds to distinctly sectarian charities such as the Dingle Mission (designed to pervert Catholics to the Church of Ireland) ensured popularity among Protestants, while Lady Eglinton's heroic visitations with open purse to St Vincent de Paul bazaars mollified the politer sections of the Catholic community.[3] And although Eglinton commissioned Sir Francis Head to write a book exposing the doings of the priesthood at the elections of 1852 and was himself convinced that 'the whole misery of Ireland is owing to the thraldom of the priests', he was a rugged realist in political matters and was always anxious to make the best of any job upon which he was engaged.[4] Occasional public acts of the *noblesse oblige* sort, such as asking a priest to say grace at a Galway cattle-show banquet, were invariably well chosen and shrouded him in the character of one 'friendly to Ireland and no foe to religious freedom'. More important still was his role as racehorse owner, and his running of 'Pelopidas' at the Curragh excited even opposition newspapers into admitting him a 'ruler who really identifies himself

[1] Peel to Heytesbury, 1 Aug. 1844, Peel Papers Add. MS 40479; I. Anstruther, *The Knight and the Umbrella: An Account of the Eglinton Tournament 1839* (London, 1963); R. B. McDowell, *The Irish Administration 1801–1914* (London, 1964), p. 53.

[2] Derby to Eglinton, 12 Apr. 1852, Eglinton Papers MS 5332 ('Your style of living and of reception is on an *unnecessarily* liberal scale. This is undoubtedly an error on the right side . . .'); H. Maxwell, *The Life and Letters of George William Frederick, Fourth Earl of Clarendon*, i, 302–5.

[3] Details of charitable activities and donations in Eglinton Papers MS 5354.

[4] Head's researches resulted in the publication of *A Fortnight in Ireland* (London, 1852), partly based on anonymous insights into official files—see Eglinton to Derby, 4 Aug. 1852, Eglinton Papers MS 5333, and Head to Naas, 2 Oct. 1852, Head Letters N.L.I. MS 18513. See also Eglinton to Derby, 10 Sept. 1852, Eglinton Papers MS 5333.

with, not only the political affairs, but with the national prosperity and amusements of the people'.[1] Eglinton, who, while refusing to meet Cardinal Wiseman at public dinners, had many 'agreeable conversations . . . with Bishop Moriarty' ('a particularly gentlemanlike person'), acted, therefore, as the genial and public 'front-man' for Conservative rule in Ireland. At the same time, he intervened effectively in disputes within the party and gave Naas valuable support in resisting Disraeli's wilder demands that the temporary flirtations of the 1850s with anti-Whig Catholics be cemented by a deluge of Catholic appointments and patronage.[2] Abercorn, himself the head of a large Conservative tribe and owner of 63,557 Ulster acres, continued Eglinton's good work on the charitable front and was necessarily even more concerned with the details of power in the various constituencies. Indeed, in 1868 he joined Taylor and Mayo (as Naas had then become) in a triumvirate to undertake preliminary arrangements for the elections then pending in Ireland.[3]

Taylor and Naas did the really important work however. Taylor, as befits a whip, is the more shadowy figure. A typical country gentleman with almost 8,000 acres in Dublin and Meath, his long tenure of office betokens popularity as well as efficiency, though an illegible hand must have impaired his accuracy as a disseminator of information. First returned for Co. Dublin in 1841, he rose to prominence in the 1850s as an opposition whip and held office in the next three Conservative administrations. In 1857 he helped conduct secret negotiations with G. H. Moore to secure an anti-Whig coalition between Tories and Independents in certain constituencies. In 1859 he joined Naas, Donoughmore, the then Chief Whip Sir William Jolliffe, and G. A. Hamilton who had just resigned his Dublin University seat to become head of the Treasury, to disburse central Conservative funds among promising Irish candidates.[4] In 1865 he played a key role in reconciling discordant elements in a number of

---

[1] *Galway Vindicator*, 28 Apr., 25 Aug. 1852.

[2] Eglinton to Derby, 2 Apr. 1858, Derby Papers 148/3; to Naas, 10 July 1858, Mayo Papers MS 11031; Sir R. Bateson to J. W. Maxwell, 7 May [1852], Perceval-Maxwell Papers D3244/G/1/165; Eglinton to Disraeli, 11 May 1859, Hughenden Papers B/XXI/E/110.

[3] Abercorn Papers T2541/VR/40; Mayo to Disraeli, 18 Aug. 1868, Hughenden Papers B/XX/Bo/71.

[4] Taylor to Moore, 2 Apr. [1857], Moore Papers MS 893; to Naas, [Apr.], 26 Apr. 1859, Farnham to Taylor, 8 Apr. 1859, J. McClintock to Taylor, 8 Apr. 1859, all Mayo Papers MS 11036; Taylor to Jolliffe, 22 Apr. 1859, Hamilton to Jolliffe, 23 Apr. [1859], Hylton Papers Box 24. Hamilton had been on an earlier committee working with Markham Spofforth, the party's first agent in England (R. Stewart, *The Foundation of the Conservative party 1830–1867*, p. 280). Philip Rose (Disraeli's solicitor and unpaid party 'agent') also intervened sporadically in Irish affairs (J. Spaight to Jolliffe, 16 Apr. 1859, J. George to Jolliffe, 18 Apr. 1859, J. Whiteside to Jolliffe, 28 Apr. 1857, all Hylton Papers Box 24), though Jolliffe's constituency notebooks (ibid.) completely ignore Ireland.

troubled constituencies. In 1868 he poured the balm of patronage
over warring Conservative factions, and was, in the event, left in
charge of Irish arrangements as a result of Mayo's departure for
India. As always, he combined effectiveness with the tact required
of any central official daring to 'meddle' in the affairs of sensitive
local party leaders and organizations.[1] Throughout the 1870s he
continued to apply good sense to difficult situations (especially
with regard to the tangled Conservative politics of Co. Tyrone)
and to help John Gorst's Central Office distribute 'Carlton Club
money' to constituency organizations in various parts of Ireland.[2]

More important still to the Tories' success in mid-century Ireland
was Lord Naas, contemporary estimates of whose talents hover
between the hostile and the patronizing. 'Fat, steady, country
gentleman' was the *Nation*'s ill-informed assessment of 1852.
Lord Kimberley (Palmerston's opinionated Lord Lieutenant in
the mid-1860s) denied him anything approaching 'first-rate
powers' and was irritated when assassination in India in 1872
'raised him to a pedestal of fame altogether beyond his merits'.[3]
Others, like Thomas Macknight, editor of the *Northern Whig*, and
the Galway MP, W. H. Gregory (who was to follow a similar path
to Asian proconsulship), moved from initial suspicion to ultimate
respect. In fact, Naas's handling, for example, of the Fenian
crisis of the 1860s was firm and sensible. His one major mistake—over the Orange marches of 1867 in defiance of the Party
Processions Act—stemmed from an increasing reluctance to
abide by the strictly sectarian tenets of traditional Toryism.[4] More
orthodox in his younger days, he had, as early as 1852 at the age
of thirty, been busy reinforcing party cohesion among Irish
MPs and peers in London and co-operating with the Under-
Secretary, John Wynne, in mounting a coherent election campaign in

---

[1] Abercorn Papers T2541/VR/85/37, 38; Donoughmore to R. J. Otway, 17 Feb. 1865,
Otway Papers MS 13008; Mayo to Abercorn, 1 Mar. 1868, Abercorn Papers T2541/VR/
85/34; Mayo to Disraeli, 18, 25 Aug., 17 Sept. 1868, Hughenden Papers B/XX/Bo/71,
72, 79.

[2] E. J. Feuchtwanger, *Disraeli, Democracy, and the Tory Party: Conservative leadership
and organization after the Second Reform Bill* (Oxford, 1968), p. 55; E. Macnaghten to
Taylor, 10 Aug. 1869, Seymour of Ragley Papers CR114A/724(1); D. Plunket to E. Gibson,
4 Sept. 1876, Ashbourne Papers T2955/B119/14; Taylor to Belmore, 2 Mar. [1873],
H. Corry to Belmore, 25 July, 5 Aug. [1877], Belmore Papers D3007/P/2, 179, 181; Taylor
to Lord Courtown, [5 Feb. 1874], R. W. Hall-Dare to Taylor, 4 Feb. 1874, Courtown
Papers.

[3] *Nation*, 28 Feb. 1852; Kimberley's 'A Journal of Events during the Gladstone
Ministry 1868–1874', ed. E. Drus, *Camden Miscellany XXI*, Camden 3rd series xc (1958), 27.

[4] T. Macknight, *Ulster as it is*, i, 93; *Sir William Gregory, K.C.M.G., formerly member
of parliament and sometime governor of Ceylon. An Autobiography*, ed. Lady Gregory
(London, 1894), pp. 245–6.

Ireland.[1] After obtaining a result almost as good as that of 1841
Naas became the undisputed expert on Irish affairs. He ensured that
Irish Conservatives 'kept together' by means of 'united action and
regular conferences', and the fact that over the next decade party
growth was considerably greater in Ireland than in Britain was
the measure of his success.[2] As Chief Secretary he conducted an
astonishingly extensive and careful correspondence, spent a substantial amount of time actually in Ireland, and, through his relatives
in both the Irish and English aristocracy (his mother was kin to the
ultra Lord Roden and his wife a daughter of the extremely wealthy
Lord Leconfield), enjoyed direct access to the highest echelons of
landed society. A bluff, heavy-jowled, and red-faced exterior disguised a shrewd mind, so that by 1859 he had become, in Philip
Rose's view, the undisputed 'manager in Ireland', a position he unusually combined with both high office and powerful connections.
Taylor too saw Naas, 'surrounded as he is with advice from all places
where fights are possible', as central to the party's campaigns and
successes. Derby invariably consulted him on Ireland, and Naas
himself was not slow to contrast his own Irish victories in 1859
with the much less dramatic results obtained in England. The fact
that Naas and Eglinton worked harmoniously together—a rare state
of affairs between Viceroy and Chief Secretary—added greatly to
their joint effectiveness and to the fortunes of the Irish Conservative
Party as a whole.[3] It was also Naas who took the leading part in the
delicate negotiations which secured limited agreement between the
Conservatives and sections of the Independent Party under G. H.
Moore. At the Mayo election of 1857 Moore appealed openly for
voters to unite behind the Conservative 'Captain Palmer and myself'.
In Clare the Independents obtained funds through Taylor to oppose
a 'thoroughgoing Whig'. At the Tipperary by-election of March
1857 Glengall and Donoughmore mobilized Tory landlords behind
The O'Donoghue's defeat of another Whig candidate,[4] while pacts

[1] Naas to Eglinton, 16 June [1852], Eglinton Papers MS 5334; various letters from
Wynne to Naas, May and June 1852, Mayo Papers MS 11029.

[2] Derby to Naas, 16 Jan. 1854, Napier to Naas, [25 June 1853], Mayo Papers MS
11017. Taking the most optimistic view of British and the most pessimistic view of Irish
Tory affiliations it would seem that the percentage of Irish members in the total Westminster party rose from 12.2 in 1852 to 18.0 in 1859 (and was still 16.0 in 1865).

[3] P. J. Mayne to Rose, 8 Apr. 1859, Mayo Papers MS 11036 (endorsed by Rose);
Taylor to S. Fitzgerald, [Apr. 1859], ibid.; Derby to Naas, 16 Mar. 1859, ibid. MS 11025;
Naas to Eglinton, 14, 16 June [1859], Eglinton Papers MS 5352; Eglinton to Naas, 16 June
1859, Mayo Papers MS 11031.

[4] Printed Circular of 31 Mar. 1857, Moore Papers MS 893; Naas to Derby, 18 Apr.
1857, Derby Papers 155/1; cutting in Dunboyne Scrapbook N.L.I. MS 3377, p. 52; *Dublin
Evening Mail*, 13 Mar. 1857; Moore to Archbishop MacHale, 14 Mar. 1857, Moore Papers
MS 893.

in constituencies such as Co. Wexford, Sligo, New Ross, and Co. Cork certainly increased the number of Conservatives returned.[1] Already in 1856 Catholic priests and voters in Sligo had announced their intention to support 'Mr Wynne, the Orange candidate', while in Athlone 'a good deal' of Catholic support had swung behind a Conservative candidate normally best known for his 'rampant anti-Catholic declarations'.[2] Three years later the 'alliance' was in the fullness of its flowering. Independent members were busily applying for patronage, and modest legislative concessions kept a united anti-Whig front in tenuous but effective existence.[3] Naas's triumph was highlighted by the Commons division which finally brought down Derby's government in June 1859, when the Irish members as a whole split sixty-three to thirty-eight in favour of the Conservatives, a degree of support at once remarkable and unprecedented.

Gradually after 1859 the *rapprochement* with the Independents faded away. In 1864 several 'gentlemen connected with the Independent Irish Party' were still attending Tory meetings at Lord Salisbury's house in London to organize opposition to Palmerston's Danish policy, and occasional local pacts continued to be made at by-elections in 1863 and 1866.[4] By then, however, even Disraeli, formerly so anxious to pursue almost any kind of parliamentary compact, had come to accept Naas's policy of disengagement from 'unnatural' alliances.[5] By 1868 virtually all the threads of party management had come together in the Chief Secretary's experienced hands. As early as June, Mayo (of whom Disraeli now had a very high opinion) was drawing up lists of constituencies in need of party funds and establishing a committee of members of the Kildare St. and Sackville St. Clubs in Dublin to advise the authorities on liaison with local party functionaries.[6] Unfortunately the sudden call to

[1] Whiteside to Taylor, 1 Apr. [1857], Taylor to Moore, 2 Apr. [1857], Moore Papers MS 893; J. Robinson to Moore, 28 Mar. [1856], ibid.; *C.C.* 2, 6, 7 Mar. 1860.

[2] J. P. Somers to Cullen, 4 Mar. 1856, Cullen Papers; Revd T. Kilroe to Cullen, 12 Apr. 1856, ibid. Both by-elections produced Tory gains.

[3] J. F. Maguire to Naas, 25 Sept. 1858, Mayo Papers MS 11024; Donoughmore to Naas, 12 May 1859, ibid. MS 11036; Naas to Eglinton, 11 June 1859, Eglinton Papers MS 5352; F. E. Currey to Duke of Devonshire, 22 Apr. 1859, Lismore Papers MS 7190. For a detailed account, see K. T. Hoppen, 'Tories, Catholics, and the General Election of 1859', *Historical Journal*, xiii (1970), 48–67.

[4] *Tablet*, 2 July 1864 (In the 'Schleswig-Holstein' division of July 1864 Palmerston received only 27 Irish votes and pairs, the Tories received a remarkable 74—see ibid. 16 July 1864); *Speech of the Right Hon. Thomas O'Hagan, MP Attorney-General for Ireland, at the hustings of Tralee, on the 15th of May 1863* (Dublin, 1863), pp. iv–v; J. Bolton to Derby, 10 Oct. 1866, Derby Papers 107/2 (concerning Tipperary).

[5] R. Stewart, *The Politics of Protection*, pp. 160, 207, 227; J. H. Whyte, *The Independent Irish Party 1850–9*, p. 95; Disraeli to Mayo, [5 Aug.] 1868, Mayo Papers MS 11164; Mayo to Disraeli, 5 Aug. [1868], Hughenden Papers B/XX/Bo/69.

[6] List in Mayo Papers MS 11239; Hamilton to Lord C. Hamilton, 3 June 1868, and

India removed him from the scene well before polling began, and his replacement, the Englishman John Wilson-Patten, only took the job after obtaining the curious assurance that he need 'have nothing to do with the elections'.[1] That, despite this and despite the powerful impact of Gladstonian promises concerning disestablishment, education, and land, the Tories still managed to retain thirty-nine Irish seats (fourteen of them outside Ulster) is a tribute to the work undertaken by Naas and his associates throughout the previous twenty years.

If the engine of the vehicle that was Irish Conservatism was constructed out of various local and national organizations and the driver furnished by ministers, whips, and other officials, the necessary fuel was produced in the refinery of Protestant solidarity and the oil to secure smooth and continuous operation formulated out of a mixture of patronage and hard cash. If too during the 1830s and 1840s no other group in Irish politics managed to raise the vast sums of money collected by O'Connell—£91,800 between 1829 and 1834 and £48,706 in 1843 alone[2]—the Tories (and to a much lesser extent the Whigs) were able to mobilize much unpaid help from a network of landlords and their agents as well as support from wealthy Conservative merchants such as the Guinnesses of Dublin, the Spaights of Limerick, the Carrolls of Cork, and the Corrys and Ewarts of Belfast. Not that the Tories ever seem to have been particularly short of cash. Already in 1831 special Irish funds of £12,500 and more were being sent over from London by the 'Charles St. Gang' to augment the much larger sums available in Ireland itself, where Tory peers had subscribed fifty pounds each for the Dublin City petition alone. In addition, some portion of the enormous donations garnered in England—£80,000 from Lord Dudley and £100,000 from the Duke of Northumberland, it was said—found its way across the Irish Sea.[3] In 1832 large sums were available

---

C. Hamilton to 'Charlie', 7 June 1868, Mayo Papers MS 11167. See Disraeli to Derby, 27 Sept. 1866, Derby Papers 146/2 ('I think him eminent for judgement . . . and eminent judgement, with a complete understanding of Ireland is a choice combination for a chief secretary'), and Disraeli to M. Corry, 16 Apr. 1866, Hughenden Papers B/XX/D/22 ('Men like Naas and Taylor, and especially the former, who is a most able . . . and enlightened man').

[1] H. J. Hanham, *Elections and Party Management: Politics in the time of Disraeli and Gladstone* (London, 1959), p. 297.

[2] A. Macintyre, *The Liberator*, p. 121.

[3] C. Arbuthnot to Farnham, 4, 6 May 1831, Farnham Papers MS 18606; T. Lefroy to Farnham, 1 Aug. 1831, ibid. MS 18611; A. Perceval to Farnham, 11 Oct. [1831], ibid. MS 18612; Lord Sandon to Lord Harrowby, 3 May 1831, cited J. N. Odurkene, 'The

to fight elections in Dublin City and University, £3,000 at least from England. Centrally the Irish party was also able to amass funds considered 'cheering' from wealthy supporters and through local collecting agents working on a 5 per cent commission basis.[1] In 1835 the party nationally was prosperous enough to pay arrears of municipal tax for Tory voters in danger of disfranchisement. In 1837 it was able 'to threaten a contest everywhere' in order to make opposing candidates 'spend money': £2,400 arrived from London for Dublin City alone and prominent supporters gave generously on both sides of the Irish Sea.[2] Locally too the gentry were prepared to put their money where their opinions lay: in Leitrim £4,000 was promised in a couple of days, at a Cork meeting £1,200 materialized within twenty minutes. The party in Belfast was able to promise an initial sum of £3,200 in 1841 to augment the candidates' own contributions, even though £10,000 had just been spent on a petition; the Liberals in contrast found it difficult to scratch together even £1,800.[3] In counties such as Kerry, Kildare, and Sligo, party organizers never had any difficulty in raising money for registration or elections,[4] and there is no reason to suppose that their experience was untypical. Help from England continued to arrive throughout this early period, most notoriously in the shape of the famous Spottiswoode Fund raised by the Queen's Printer in 1837 to help Tories attack their opponents by means of election petitions, especially in Ireland.[5] Five years later a crucial by-election at Dublin City (crucial because the Whig candidate was none other than the

British General Elections of 1830 and 1831' (University of Oxford B.Litt. thesis, 1977), p. 131. See also *Three early nineteenth-century diaries*, ed. A. Aspinall (London, 1952), pp. xlv–lii.

[1] Anglesey to 'My dear Sir', 11 Dec. 1832, Anglesey Papers D619/38G; *Three early nineteenth-century diaries*, ed. A. Aspinall, pp. xlviii–xlix; Anglesey to Grey, 23 Nov. 1832, Anglesey Papers D619/28A; E. Cottingham to Farnham, 17 Oct., [Oct.] 1832, Farnham Papers MS 18610. Over £2,000 was quickly raised to enable poor clergymen to poll at the university election.

[2] R. D. Craig to Littleton, 16 Jan. 1835, Hatherton Papers D260/M/F/5/27 (see also T. M. Ray to M. O'Connell, 8 Aug. 1845, U. C. D. O'Connell Papers Box E); D. O'Connell to P. Mahony, 14 July 1837, *Correspondence of Daniel O'Connell*, ed. M. R. O'Connell, vi, 64; Hardinge to Peel, 20 July [1837], Peel Papers Add. MS 40314; *D.E.P.* 27 July 1837.

[3] *Athlone Conservative Advocate*, 3 Aug. 1837; I. d'Alton, *Protestant Society and Politics in Cork 1812–1844* (Cork, 1980), p. 218; *Belfast election compromise*, H.C. 1842 (431), vi, 273, 284, 294–5, 389–91.

[4] S. M. Hickson to Knight of Kerry, 1 Jan. 1835, FitzGerald Papers; Sir W. Hort to Duke of Leinster, 21 June 1852, Leinster Papers D3078/3/38; Memo of 1857, O'Hara Papers MS 20355.

[5] R. Stewart, *The Foundation of the Conservative party 1830–1867*, p. 140; Lord F. Egerton to Peel, 29 Sept. 1837, Peel Papers Add. MS 40424; Graham to Bonham, 9 Oct. 1837, ibid. Add. MS 40616. Two seats were gained as a result and party morale boosted at a bad time.

former Chief Secretary, Lord Morpeth) produced an avalanche of cash from all sides: £4,000 from the Tory candidate, several thousands from the Chief Whip in England, £500 from the Viceroy, and appropriate levies from junior ministers and 'a good many lawyers and merchants' with Conservative views.[1] Even after the Peelite split, an 'Irish Protestant Election Fund' was established in London to transfer money across the sea to help Protectionist and Protestant candidates.[2]

With the arrival of Naas as Chief Secretary in 1852 a more regular (though secret) system of central funding was established. Naas well realized that, while local donations (like Lord Lucan's £1,000 in Mayo) were easy enough to obtain, it was never easy to raise money 'from any quarter for *general* purposes'.[3] He therefore did what he could with what little remained of the secret-service monies of yesteryear. Although in England the Government Whip's secret-service grant of £10,000 remained unchanged between the early 1830s and its abolition in 1886, the Irish fund was cut from £21,000 in 1832 to £9,000 in 1834. Its great advantages, however, remained: prompt availability and no questions asked. Indeed, until a late date it was still so generally regarded as available for utterly partisan purposes that Lord Hartington in 1874 briskly transferred a balance of £5,106 into his own personal bank account to prevent it falling into the hands of his Tory replacement as Chief Secretary. It provided a modest but useful subsidy for electioneering, and, though the Liberals were generally in power after 1846, the Tories were fortunate in finding themselves in office during the important general elections of 1852, 1859, and 1868.[4] Quite apart from secret-service money, Naas had, as early as 1852, other sources of finance at his disposal, enough to send several sums of £600 or £1,000 to constituencies needing help. Some of this may have come from the £20,000 collected in England and controlled by a committee (with G. A. Hamilton as Irish representative) which pointedly never 'kept lists or names or anything like that'.[5] In 1859, when the party in England 'produced

[1] Graham to Eliot, 7 Jan. 1842, De Grey to Graham, 5, 7 Jan. 1842, Graham Papers 7/Ir; Eliot to Peel, 8, 20 Jan. 1842, Peel to Eliot, 10 Jan. 1842, Peel Papers Add. MS 40480; N. Gash, *Politics in the age of Peel: A study in the technique of parliamentary representation 1830–1850* (London, 1953), p. 132.

[2] *Kerry Evening Post*, 30 Apr. 1847 citing *Morning Herald*.

[3] J. Macalpine to Naas, 18 July 1853, Mayo Papers MS 11017 (on Lucan); Derby (reporting Naas) to Eglinton, 27 May, 1 June 1852, Eglinton Papers MS 5332.

[4] N. Gash, *Politics in the age of Peel*, p. 326; H. J. Hanham, *Elections and Party Management*, pp. 369–70 (after 1875 some of the English monies were sent to Ireland); *An Account of the public income and expenditure of the United Kingdom, for the years ended 5th January 1833, 1834, and 1835*, H.C. 1835 (302), xxxvii, 155; Hartington's black-strapped folder, Devonshire Papers.

[5] J. Wynne to Naas, 19 May 1852, Mayo Papers MS 11029; Lord Colville to Eglinton, [15 June 1852], Eglinton Papers MS 5343.

the most concerted electoral effort of the Palmerston years', as much as £50,000 may have been collected centrally, with an additional £8,000 or so being sent to Ireland, where Naas was also able to wheedle large sums from prominent supporters like Lord Downshire, Lord Waterford, and Stanley McClintock, all of them also generous local donors in 'their own' counties of Down, Kildare, Wicklow, King's Co., Waterford, and Louth.[1] The mere whiff of cash sent up the usual howls for indiscriminate largesse. But Naas, as always, chose the recipients for his modest bounty with care, and helped only those Tory *and* Independent candidates most likely to defeat potentially damaging onslaughts from the opposition. Although in essence subsidies were no more than pump-priming investments and quite distinct from local efforts such as the £1,600 subscribed by Cork City candidates or the much greater sums spent by landed Conservatives, they were a reminder that Conservatism was a national movement as well as useful gilt upon the essential gingerbread of constituency fund-raising. Much the same seems to have happened in 1865 and 1868, although (as in England) money was seldom collected between elections, save to support bodies like the Central Society. In 1874 too cash was sent from London to help Conservative candidates in various Irish constituencies.[2]

Perhaps even more important than the availability of cash was the control and distribution of patronage, a sphere in which the Tories exercised an iron discrimination tempered only by Peel's insistence on 'balance' and Disraeli's brief opportunist attempts to mollify Catholic opinion in the 1850s. Most commonly patronage concerned individual jobs, though it could also furnish concessions or assistance to whole groups or localities. In practice the Tories were much less fastidious than their opponents. Even the ritual moans of Peel about 'gross [jobs] . . . according to the most approved old Irish practice' signified little more than moral 'tone'.[3] Of course

---

[1] R. Stewart, *The Foundation of the Conservative party 1830-1867*, pp. 330-1; Naas to Disraeli, 2 Apr. 1859, Hughenden Papers B/XX/Bo/9; G. A. Hamilton to Jolliffe, 23 Apr. [1859], Taylor to Jolliffe, 22 Apr.1859, Hylton Papers Box 24; Notes of Money Paid (1859), and Donoughmore to Naas, 12 Apr. 1859, Mayo Papers MS 11036; K. T. Hoppen, 'Tories, Catholics, and the General Election of 1859', p. 66. On the three Irish donors, see R. Wingfield to Naas, 26 Apr. 1859, Downshire to Naas, 5 May [1859], McClintock to Naas, 26 Apr. 1859, all Mayo Papers MS 11036.

[2] *Drogheda Argus*, 16 Apr. 1859; Donoughmore to R. J. Otway, 15 Feb. 1865, Otway Papers MS 13008; Mayo's Notes on Constituencies (Summer 1868), Mayo Papers MS 11239; R. W. Hall-Dare to Courtown, 5 Feb. 1874, Taylor to Courtown, 3 Feb. [1874], Courtown Papers.

[3] Peel to Heytesbury, 16 Aug. [1844], Peel Papers Add. MS 40479; Peel to De Grey, 23 Nov. 1841, ibid. Add. MS 40477. Still less convincing were the conscience-salving protestations of Tory Chief Secretaries such as Eliot (to Peel, 17 Aug. 1844, ibid. Add. MS 40480) and Viceroys such as Eglinton (to Derby, 8 Dec. 1852, Eglinton Papers MS 5333).

the unwearying attention which the business demanded could wear down even the toughest mentality, though strong men like Naas rarely lost their sense of humour: 'I am literally', he noted in 1867, 'torn to pieces by these infernal places and am nightly insulted by half a dozen men . . . [but] we are at last landed in the Blessed Position of having a resident magistracy vacant.' Superior Anglo-Saxon attitudes were as unjustified as they were patronizing, and Pilate-like hand-washing rarely more than a disguise for practical acquiescence. Dr Malcomson's percipient remarks about an earlier period apply fully to this period also: 'The important point is that there are two sides to a bargain, not to say a corrupt transaction; and post-Union British governments had no right to moralize unless they dismantled the Irish patronage system. Like Maria Theresa, they wept, but they pocketed the advantages all the same.'[1]

What the Tories recognized more deeply than any one else was the cohesive effectiveness of patronage properly applied. 'Party', wrote a Wicklow Conservative in 1868 to Naas (then Earl of Mayo), 'cannot—has not—nor ever will be kept together by sentiment. It is but human nature in men to expect that they will not be neglected when those whom they have laboured to put in high places have it in their power to reward them.'[2] Knowing when to yield and when to resist was one of the distinguishing marks of a good manager. And only intimate knowledge could minimize the dangers involved in the bluff-calling so necessary to chief secretaries armed with but few loaves with which to feed so hungry a multitude. Naas usually got it right.

Your statement that you must contest the seat for Lisburn on Liberal principles unless you are appointed to be Sessional Crown Prosecutor now vacant in the County of Antrim, renders it quite impossible that I can entertain your proposal for a moment. You are quite mistaken if you suppose that a threat of that nature would have the smallest effect upon the disposition of patronage.[3]

This was, of course, hog-wash, and more important blackmailers could not be so easily dismissed. The endless demands of the Presbyterian wire-puller, John Boyd (who owned most of Coleraine and arranged Naas's own return for that borough in 1852), were handled at the highest levels, with Eglinton and Derby desperately searching for something lucratively suitable for a septuagenarian unable 'to

[1] Naas to Abercorn, 23 Mar., 4 May 1867, Abercorn Papers T2541/VR/85/13 and 20; A. P. W. Malcomson, *John Foster: The Politics of the Anglo–Irish Ascendancy* (Oxford, 1978), p. 245.
[2] W. W. F. Dick to Mayo, 13 Apr. 1868, Mayo Papers MS 11164. See also Eglinton to Derby, 27 July 1852, Eglinton Papers MS 5333.
[3] Mayo to S. Kennedy, 4 Aug. 1868, Mayo Papers MS 11168. Mayo's bluff succeeded.

face hard work or bad climate'.[1] Again, Edward Grogan, the member
for Dublin City 1841–65, was able to extract a baronetcy almost as
and when he wanted. Powerful local families like the Coles in Enniskillen required careful handling, not least when their demands for
a taxing mastership for a valetudinarian hanger-on, who spent all his
time in bed, raised the business to new and higher stages of complicated 'delicacy'.[2] 'Difficult' men, like the third Earl of Portarlington, required verbal soothing, perhaps an even more exhausting
business than the distribution of jobs and cash.[3] At times the Tories'
practice of 'looking after their own' was almost touching in its
fierce contempt for either qualifications or ability. Broken-down
newspaper hacks were appointed sub-inspectors in the constabulary,
while in the 1830s wealthy Whig proprietors were briskly ignored
in the search for suitably loyal high sheriffs in the various counties.
Officials in renewable posts were dismissed at the smallest sign of
independence, and Conservatives were never slow to demand that the
interest of obedience be regularly paid on the capital of patronage.[4]
'Every man receiving the pay of the crown', wrote the 'high-minded'
Sir James Graham of the Dublin by-election of 1842, 'should be
required to vote in favour of the government candidate.' It was,
therefore, perhaps hardly surprising that ministers so effectively
ignored Peel's pleas for the appointment of 'respectable Roman
Catholics' that seventy-four of the eighty-three 'substantial' positions
filled during the first twenty-two months of his second administration were given to Protestants.[5]

For the Conservative interest in Ireland, both organization and
patronage acted, therefore, primarily as a species of binding cement
holding together a number of otherwise potentially antagonistic
elements: the rural gentry, the urban professional classes, and what
might best be called the 'populist' element within the Protestant
community. The symbiotic relationship between Conservatism
and the landed classes remained, of course, a key to Irish politics

---

[1] Eglinton to Derby, 12 Sept. 1858, Derby Papers 148/3.
[2] Grogan: Eglinton to Naas, 28 Mar. 1858, Mayo Papers MS 11031; Eglinton to Derby,
3 May 1859, Derby Papers 148/3. Coles: Mayo to Abercorn, 1 Mar. 1868, Taylor to Abercorn, 5 Feb. 1868, W. A. Dane to Mayo, 5 Feb. 1868, H. Corry to Abercorn, 7 Feb. 1868,
Abercorn Papers T2541/VR/85/54, 37, 38, T2541/VR/197.
[3] Portarlington to Derby, 5 May 1852, Derby Papers 156/7; Naas to Eglinton, 11 June
[1858], Eglinton Papers MS 5352. The Earl had an important say in the return of members
for Portarlington Borough.
[4] M. Brophy, *Sketches of the Royal Irish Constabulary* (London, 1886), pp. 80–9;
D.E.P. 19 Nov.–15 Dec. 1835; Glengall to Graham, 11 Oct. 1841, Graham Papers 8/Ir.
[5] Graham to Peel, 1 Jan. 1842, Peel Papers Add. MS 40446; De Grey to Graham,
28 Dec. 1841, Graham Papers 8/Ir; Peel to Graham, 16 July [1843], Eliot to Graham,
15 July 1843, ibid. 63.

throughout the period, as one of O'Connell's correspondents from Wexford pointed out in 1832.

There is a *very strong* . . . ultra-bigoted high church and ascendancy party in this county. They form the majority of the aristocracy of the county, but there is also a very formidable Protestant tenantry, strongly tinctured and linked to this aristocracy . . . The ultra high church party are *all united* thorough-going bigots.[1]

In Monaghan in 1839 the grand jury was virtually a Conservative club at whose dinners members 'Hip! Hip! Hurrayed enough to crack the drums of our ears' in favour of 'the Conservative interest of the county'. The 'Conservative tendency of the greatest part of the gentry and squireens' of Armagh was equally evident, while in Kerry those opposing O'Connell (Whigs as well as Tories) mustered a rental of £158,000 against a mere £5,000 for the other side.[2] In Wicklow until 1874, although the massive Whig Fitzwilliam interest regularly claimed one of the county seats, the other as regularly went to the mass of Tory proprietors who invariably managed to 'set' the electoral 'tone' of the county, so much so, that in 1868 even the son of Earl Fitzwilliam could get no Protestant gentleman to propose him on the hustings.[3] Indeed, throughout the period it was the Tories who presented the most united county front. As in Armagh, Monaghan, Wexford, Kerry, and Wicklow, so in Sligo, whence an unhappy Whig explained to Palmerston (himself a local proprietor) that, 'from the activity of the Tory Party and the want of union among those friendly to the government . . . the representation has been monopolized and used as a triumph by the Tories'.[4] The sheer size of the Conservative interest in Sligo has already been noted, but the same was true elsewhere. After the Famine, for example, Wexford Tories were able to win seats in 1852, 1859, 1865, and 1866, largely because their proprietorial power—in 1859 the candidate's nine principal supporters owned 15 per cent of the county's land surface—no longer faced a united or organized opposition.[5] The five leading 'High Orange and Protectionist'

---

[1] C. A. Walker to O'Connell, 8 Nov. 1832, *Correspondence of Daniel O'Connell*, ed. M. R. O'Connell, iv, 466-8. 'High Church' here means ultra-Protestant, not Anglo-Catholic.

[2] N. Ellis to Sir T. Barrett-Lennard, 7 Aug. 1839, in P. Ó Mórdha, 'Some Notes on Monaghan History', p. 36; Lord Charlemount to Anglesey, 7 Dec. 1832, Anglesey Papers D619/32N; Catherine FitzGerald to Mrs Crofton Vandeleur, 26 Jan. 1835, FitzGerald Papers.

[3] Powerscourt to Downshire, 13 Nov. 1836, Downshire Papers D671/C/12/632; Fr. R. Galvin to Cullen, 26 Nov. 1868, Cullen Papers.

[4] C. O'Hara to Palmerston, 1 Oct. 1836, Broadlands Archive 27M60, Box cxxiii.

[5] J. George to Naas, 16 Apr. 1859, Mayo Papers MS 11036. See U. H. H. de Burgh, *The Landowners of Ireland*.

gentlemen of Co. Down in 1851 owned 17 per cent of the county
acreage and had almost a fifth of all the voters as tenants on their
estates.[1] In Connacht too, politically active Liberal proprietors
were few and far between. Co. Cavan was for a time virtually a fief
of the ultra Lord Farnham.[2] Without the energetic Tory gentlemen of Galway and Louth, Conservative candidates could not have
mounted their occasionally successful raids into what might otherwise have seemed the most unpromising of territories.[3] And even if
most counties were not without a substantial complement of Whig
and Liberal proprietors (as Table 29 in Chapter II reveals), the unity
and drive of the Tory gentry were often able to turn a significant
numerical advantage into an overpowering electoral one. 'Marginal'
victories like those in Galway and Louth provided the essential additional strength, which, when combined with that of the Ulster
heartlands and traditional Conservative areas like Dublin, Carlow,
Sligo, and Bandon, helped to maintain the party as a national force
well into the 1870s. 'Our men', wrote Naas to Derby in 1852,
'behaved magnificently, every county gentleman in Ireland of our
side went into the struggle with a will.' Not that so heavy a reliance
upon the landed community was without its dangers should ever that
community's nerve begin to crack, and by the late 1860s Naas's
well-tuned political antennae were already beginning to reverberate
to worrying erosions of confidence in many parts of the south.[4]
Having, as it were, staked all upon the Big House, rural Conservatism
was eventually to find itself unable—outside Ulster—to extend its
power-base into other sections of society, so that, as the county
gentlemen lost heart and influence, so did the party which had for
so long represented their interests and depended upon their support.

In towns, however, the party presented a somewhat different
picture. In Dublin, where lawyers played a key role, Conservatism
reflected their aspirations as well as those of the Protestant mercantile
class.[5] In Cork too most of the wealthy merchants were sympathetic

[1] J. Andrews to Lord Londonderry, 9 Feb. 1851, Londonderry Papers D/Lo/C158;
Holdings listed in D/Lo/C164 No. 14. There was also an enormous 'Orange squirearchy'
(Andrews to Londonderry, 26 Apr. 1851, ibid. D/Lo/C158).

[2] Lord Oranmore to Lord Fortescue, 8 Aug. 1841, Melbourne Papers 98/132; Johnston and Fawcett (agents) to J. Dicken, 4 Aug. 1847, Morley Papers Deposit 69.

[3] *D.E.P.* 13 May 1837, 13 Apr. 1841; T. Redington to Lord Clanricarde, 24 June
1847, Clanricarde Papers 29; Conservatives won seats in Galway in 1832 and 1847, and in
Louth in 1857.

[4] Naas to Derby, 31 July 1852, Derby Papers 155/1; Naas to Derby, 14, 23 Oct. 1866,
ibid. 155/2; Naas to Disraeli, 30 Oct. [1866], Hughenden Papers B/XX/Bo/23.

[5] Eliot to Peel, 8 Jan. 1842, Peel Papers Add. MS 40480; Jacqueline Hill, 'The role
of Dublin in the Irish national movement 1840-48', p. 171; *Committee on registration of
parliamentary voters, Ireland*, H.C. 1874 (261), xi, 267.

and provided the majority of candidates at municipal elections.[1]
Not that urban Conservatives spurned support from the countryside.
Indeed, occasional frictions apart, a degree of co-operation between
country and town was a particular feature of Conservative strength.
Landed proprietors exercised considerable influence in the rural
districts attached to the various counties of cities and towns (notably
in the cases of Cork, Galway, and Limerick) as well as in some of the
smaller 'pure' boroughs such as Bandon, Lisburn, and Portarlington.
By the middle of the century Cork Toryism as a whole had, for
example, reached a state of equilibrium between its once suspicious
components in town and country, so that a joint registration society
was active in 1832, the city elections of 1835 were fought with
strong landed support, and the selection as candidates in 1859
of Colonel Andrew Wood, a county gentleman, and Barcroft Carroll,
a merchant and shipowner, showed how two-member urban constituencies could allow parties to balance the various interests of
which they were often composed.[2] Again, at the Co. Londonderry
by-election of 1857 the Tory candidate came forward 'at the
unanimous request of the landed gentry and indeed the nearly
unanimous call of the mercantile interest of Derry, Newtownlimavady,
and . . . Coleraine'. In Kinsale too the party relied heavily on the
services of Dr Edward Jago, whose sources of income (two-thirds
from medical fees and one-third from landed property) neatly
epitomized the rural–urban alliance which often (though not always)
gave added strength to the Conservative cause.[3]

Only in the one large Irish town to develop a modern industrial
base, namely Belfast, did borough Toryism proceed upon exclusively
urban lines. Here the traditional landed interest—that of the
Marquess of Donegall—had been Whig, so that from the start Belfast
Conservatism had constituted an anti-proprietorial bloc. Donegall's
financial collapse in the 1820s and 1830s, together with serious
divisions among the Liberals, helped produce a long period of Conservative domination in which men of commerce and industry
played the leading part.[4] The respective compositions of the Liberal

[1] Alderman T. Lyons to O'Connell, 11 July 1846, *Correspondence of Daniel O'Connell*,
ed. M. R. O'Connell, viii, 65–6; I. d'Alton, *Protestant Society and Politics in Cork 1812-
1844*, p. 187; idem, 'Southern Irish Unionism: A study of Cork Unionists, 1884–1914',
Transactions of the Royal Historical Society, 5th series xxiii (1973), 73.

[2] *Fictitious Votes, Ireland*, 2nd series, 1st report, p. 281; I. d'Alton, *Protestant Society
and Politics in Cork 1812–1844*, p. 169 (also pp. 30, 140); *C.C.* 7, 9 Apr. 1859.

[3] C. Knox to R. B. Towse, 21 Feb. 1857, Clothworkers' Company Copy L.-B. 1840–
73; *Minutes of evidence taken before the select committee on the Kinsale election petition*,
H.C. 1847–8 (138), xiii, 157.

[4] *Belfast election compromise*, H.C. 1842 (431), v, 263–414; I. Budge and C. O'Leary,
Belfast: Approach to Crisis, pp. 41–100.

and Conservative election committees in 1857 reflect the growing differences between the parties in Belfast. Although on the surface the two groups seem similar enough, on closer examination it becomes apparent that the important shipping interest was entirely Tory and that, whereas a third of the Liberals were country gentlemen or professional men, only an eighth of the Conservatives can be so categorized.[1] And this ability to attract men in newer fields like shipping and engineering, which was to become an increasingly important feature of Belfast Conservatism during the next twenty-five years, contrasted sharply with Liberalism's continued reliance on a rather inward-looking collection of families engaged in the more entrepreneurially traditional textile business.[2] As regards Ulster's second city, Derry, it has been possible to identify almost all the seventy-nine men on the Conservative election committee of 1868, both as to occupation and religion. A comparison (in Table 34) of their backgrounds with those of all the Derry electors who voted

TABLE 34

Percentages of various occupational and denominational groups among members of the Conservative election committee and Conservative voters as a whole in Derry City, 1868

	Committee	Voters
Gentlemen	16.2	3.3
Professionals	25.7	13.6
Merchants, etc.	37.8	26.4
Shopkeepers	16.2	19.2
Drink interest	—	3.3
Artisans	4.1	22.6
Others	—	11.6
Episcopalians	62.7	45.7
Presbyterians	30.7	43.4
Dissenters, etc.*	6.6	7.0
Roman Catholics	—	3.9

* i.e. various breakaway 'Presbyterian' groups (Unitarians, etc.) and other Dissenters.

[1] Liberal Committee (39 members) listed in *Banner of Ulster*, 7, 10 Mar. 1857; Tory Committee (40 members) in ibid. 12 Mar. 1857. Occupations traced in *The Belfast and Province of Ulster Directory for 1858–9* (Belfast, 1858).

[2] See the analysis of Belfast party leaderships for 1885 in P. Gibbon, *The Origins of Ulster Unionism: The formation of popular Protestant Politics and Ideology in nineteenth-century Ireland* (Manchester, 1975), pp. 105–6. An analysis of the Belfast Liberal Association committee of 1870 (list in L'Estrange & Brett Papers D1905/2/17A/5 traced to *The Belfast and Province of Ulster Post-Office Directory* (Belfast, 1870)) also supports this general view.

Conservative shows in concrete terms both the nature of a Tory borough élite and the unsurprising differences between it and the party's following at large. The impression given in the table that substantial numbers of shopkeepers and artisans (in an electorate comprising over a quarter of the adult males in the borough) were willing and prepared to vote Conservative is strengthened by the fact that even in 1868 when the Liberals won a handsome victory by 704 to 599, no less than 38.0 per cent and 48.1 per cent respectively of the enfranchised members of these occupational groups supported the Conservatives at the polls.

Irish Conservatism's most interesting—certainly its most lively—support came from the Tory populists. Heroically Protestant, they played an important role in the revival of party fortunes after the defeats of 1829 and 1832. Contemporary indications that poor Protestants had become disenchanted with Conservative orthodoxy[1] led to the organization in the 1830s of great morale-boosting public meetings to unite the party across the class divide. The ultra Lord Roden travelled the country on propaganda tours (at Cork he was met by 'a noble Protestant spirit'), while the huge Co. Down meeting of 1834 was, as Lord Clanwilliam reported to Wellington, notable for

The organization . . . by which we brought a very large proportion of the people to Hillsborough in bodies headed by the larger proprietors, who started at the head of their tenants and met bodies of 'neighbours and friends' at points announced by printed circular placards. Lord Roden thus came in with . . . eight thousand, and all of us in proportion. I am quite certain that this will, for a long time to come, be a band of union available between me and the 2000 who made my tail . . . Another local result from the meeting will be the making the orthodox Presbyterians more steadily draw together with the Church of England.[2]

In the south, of course, popular Protestantism was predominantly an urban phenomenon, and as such, was heavily influenced by the nature of the political structures made possible by the first Reform Act. At Bandon, for example, the cosy private compact between the Duke of Devonshire and the Earl of Bandon to alternate Whig and Tory members was smashed when corporation electors were

[1] T. Lefroy to Farnham, 7 Sept. 1830, 12 June 1832, Farnham Papers MS 18611; Knight of Kerry to Wellington, 5 Mar. 1832, *Despatches, Correspondence, and Memoranda of Field Marshal Arthur Duke of Wellington K.G.*, ed. [2nd] Duke of Wellington, 8 vols. (London, 1867-80), viii, 239-53.

[2] Lord Roden to Wellington, 4 Jan. 1833, *The Prime Ministers' Papers: Wellington Political Correspondence*, ed. J. Brooke and J. Gandy, i, 12-13; Roden's various reports in letters to Lord Downshire of 1834, 1836, and 1837 (Downshire Papers D671/C/12/510, 517, 530-7, 666, 668); Clanwilliam to Wellington, [2 Nov. 1834], *The Prime Ministers' Papers*, p. 712.

replaced. by ten-pound householders. For the next thirty-five years *only* Conservatives were returned and the corporation (until its abolition in 1840) was transformed from Lord Bandon's creature into a propaganda vehicle for the 'lower middle class Protestant element in the town'. Protestants, in other words, split by the 'defeat' of 1829, were enabled by the second 'defeat' of 1832 to construct a set of genuinely popular local political movements. Much the same happened in Kinsale, where the estate of the former Whig Patron, Lord de Clifford, was sold in 1834 and the now-liberated corporation became both the centre of Protestant electoral organization and the instrument for the return of Conservative members in 1835 and 1847.[1] Another Cork borough, Youghal, provides a particularly well-documented example of this move from Whig patronage to Conservative 'democracy'. There the Duke of Devonshire had returned steady Whigs since gaining control from Lord Shannon in 1822. But while he was successfully able to force Catholic freemen on the town in 1829, the Reform Act greatly reduced his authority and created the possibility of success for an organized and popular Protestant Toryism. And even if electoral victory proved elusive until 1852, the dangerous campaigns mounted, especially in 1835 and 1837, against the united Whig and Repeal forces greatly helped to forge a sense of common identity within the Protestant community.[2] The establishment in 1835 of a Protestant Protection Society increased sectarian solidarity: henceforth Tories dealt only with Tory shopkeepers and regular meetings ensured that all could participate in what amounted to mutual political revivalism. In 1837 Devonshire's nominee, the Hon. Frederick Howard, was loudly interrupted on the hustings by Tory cries that the 'House of Cavendish has no right to support . . . What benefit are they to the perishing artisans?' Local Tory virtue, in other words, was being pitched against established Whig cosmopolitanism. Liberals were élitist, Repealers were rabble, Tories were honest folk ground down by privilege and revolution alike. Howard's hustings pronouncement to the effect that 'large proprietors who have property at stake' were quite entitled to 'see representatives sent to parliament with principles in accordance with theirs' was welcome grist to this particular

[1] I. d'Alton, *Protestant Society and Politics in Cork 1812–1844*, pp. 102–3, 108–9 —d'Alton's view that the Whig purchaser of the De Clifford estate, J. I. Heard, was immediately able to 'control' Kinsale is incorrect. Not until the 1850s did Heard enjoy anything like a total (and, as it ensued, extremely brief) domination.

[2] A. Barry and K. T. Hoppen, 'Borough politics in O'Connellite Ireland: The Youghal poll books of 1835 and 1837', *Journal of the Cork Historical and Archaeological Society*, lxxxiii (1978), 106–46, and lxxxiv (1979), 15–43.

mill,[1] which was further sharpened by Protestant ballads of fiercely sectarian hue. One atavistic example sung at the 1835 election lampooned the Catholic sentiments of 'two Reverend Bums'.

> When you walk thro' the town—and Protestants meet,
> Or pass nigh their dwellings along in the street,
> Ev'n hoot them, and shove them, and spit in their face,
> But don't at your peril infringe on the pace!
>> Sing Ballynamona Oro etc.
>> True Christian-like feeling for me.

Insult and abuse, however, require support from self-righteousness, and in 1837 the Tory candidate, William Nicol, was provided with shining armour.

> His Bible, will his shield be seen—
>> His faith, a trusty sword
> His watch-word, Nicol, Church and Queen—
>> His strength, his God, his Lord.[2]

Not long after the delivery of these warblings a Protestant Operative Association was set up. As mutual-aid society and defender of the settlement of 1688 it attracted support, not only from artisans at a penny a fortnight, but also from wealthier men at higher subscriptions. It was open to Protestants of all denominations, held meetings, distributed literature, organized elections, and was popular enough to attract over three hundred to its 'anniversary soirée' in 1843 when tea and seed-cake helped inflame both preachers and audience into mutual political and religious enthusiasm.[3]

Irish Protestant operative societies, even more sectarian than their English counterparts,[4] were, indeed, a notable feature of post-Reform politics. Their readiness to be extreme and to be critical of respectable Conservative leadership provided a social safety-valve and paradoxically strengthened the sense of overall religious identity. Cork City had its Protestant Operative Association and Reformation Society which denounced Peel over Maynooth and issued manifestos from its 'Cumberland Room and Protestant Hall'. In Derry, artisans were by far the liveliest element within local Conservatism. Sligo's Protestant Operative Brotherhood expanded rapidly in 1837 and attracted Presbyterians and Wesleyans as well as members of the

---

[1] 'Youghal Protestant Operatives Scrapbook 1829–48' (Bradshaw Collection C.U.L. Hib.1.844.1); *D.E.P.* 14 Feb. 1835; *C.C.* 7 Feb. 1835. Cavendish is the Duke of Devonshire's family name.

[2] Both ballads in 'Youghal Protestant Operatives Scrapbook 1829–48', op. cit.

[3] Ibid. It attracted as patrons the usual bevy of ultra peers: Lords Winchelsea, Lorton, Kenyon, Roden, Farnham, etc. The total population of Youghal in 1841 was only 9,939.

[4] See R. L. Hill, *Toryism and the people 1832–1846* (London, 1929), pp. 47–57.

Church of Ireland.[1] Some clubs, such as the Belfast Protestant Operative Society of the 1840s, were little more than Orange lodges which had changed their names after the rather bogus dissolution of the order in 1836.[2] Thus, whereas in England the parliamentary and municipal reforms of the 1830s gave a boost to liberal and non-conformist elements, in Ireland they simultaneously allowed O'Connell to make a few electoral gains *and* liberated popular Conservatism from some at least of the moderating shackles hitherto placed upon it by aristocratic magnates and political leaders alike.

The first great centre of organized working-class Protestantism was Dublin, not Belfast. There Revd T. D. Gregg and his numerous organizations—chief among them the Dublin Protestant Operative Association and Reformation Society—rode out to do battle with the Scarlet Woman of Rome. Gregg, who in 1866 was to receive divine intimation of his own immortality, constantly in the 1830s and 1840s demanded crusades to 'root Popery out of our land', to expel Catholics from Parliament, to make men 'treat Ireland as a *missionary* country', and to 'effect a legislative separation between Christianity and Idolatry'.[3] A Protestant Operative Union organized the overwhelmingly Protestant freeman electorate and encouraged exclusive dealing with Conservative shopkeepers and tradesmen. In 1837 the city's poorer Protestants, enraged by electoral defeat, gathered outside Conservative Party headquarters to shout and hiss at Liberal passers-by, an event notable, not only as evidence of enthusiasm, but as a reflection of the lingeringly village-like quality of even metropolitan life which made it possible to recognize the perambulating manifestations of one's animosities and dislikes. Gregg, who exercised imperial sway over branch societies in Belfast and Cork, had by the 1840s made himself crucial to electoral success.[4] At the 1842 Dublin by-election he engineered massive demonstrations

---

[1] G. Shea to Peel, 28 Feb. 1844, Lady De Grey to Peel, [Feb. 1844], Peel to Lady De Grey, [29 Feb. 1844], all Peel Papers Add. MS 40540; *Londonderry Sentinel*, 10 July 1841; *Ballyshannon Herald*, 17 Mar. 1837.

[2] S. E. Baker, 'Orange and Green: Belfast, 1832–1912' in *The Victorian City: Images and Realities*, ed. H. J. Dyos and M. Wolff, 2 vols. (London, 1973), ii, 795. The order had come under parliamentary attack and investigation.

[3] 'Address to the Protestants of Ireland', *Athlone Conservative Advocate*, 17 Aug. 1837. For Gregg's career in general, see D. Bowen, *The Protestant Crusade in Ireland, 1800–1870: A Study of Protestant-Catholic relations between the Act of Union and Disestablishment* (Dublin, 1978), pp. 108–13, and for an excellent account of the pre-Famine Dublin scene, see Jacqueline Hill, 'The Protestant response to Repeal: The case of the Dublin working class' in *Ireland under the Union*, ed. F. S. L. Lyons and R. A. J. Hawkins, pp. 35–68.

[4] *Ballyshannon Herald*, 8 Sept. 1837; *A Voice from the Protestants of Ireland to the Revd Tresham Dames Gregg, the faithful and intrepid Defender of Protestant Truth and Liberty* (Dublin, 1846), pp. 36–7—copy R. I. A. Halliday Pamphlets 1982.

to the tunes of 'The Boyne Water' and 'Croppies lie Down'. These and his other speciality—marching into Catholic meetings and bawling out his own opinions at high intensity and great length—turned him into a Protestant folk hero, beloved for an ability to 'get up the steam' and licensed to issue warnings to politer leaders tempted to talk of compromise and moderation. In 1845 he attacked those 'coroneted brows' which countenanced Peel's 'Romeward tendencies'. In 1846 he told a soirée of his

Great respect for leaders, the free consistent nobility of Ireland, such as Lords Roden and Lorton; but . . . I would tell them, that we have our own interests to protect, and that we will not wait on their bidding, that we will stand up for our own rights (loud cheers); and furthermore, that in any movement concerning our interests, we will have the substantial voice.[1]

But already by 1852, though Gregg still held election audiences spellbound, signs of his later vintage idiosyncrasy were beginning to show. Bitter arguments with a hostile ecclesiastical superior, Archbishop Whately, did little to stabilize his mind. Indeed, increasing obsessions with eschatological speculation and the connections between morality and optics, while not lessening his standing as honorary sage and hero, undoubtedly impaired his general effectiveness as political agitator and Protestant steam-engine.[2]

Gregg's various societies continued, none the less, to act as gadflies to the Tory establishment and as lightning-conductors diverting attention from class to sectarian divisions. Meetings continued to thrill to demands for Protestantism above all else: 'They should have nothing of Conservatism without Protestantism (hear, hear)— otherwise it would be like acting the play without the principal characters.' The Dublin Protestant Association and similar bodies in Down, Tyrone, Newry, and elsewhere, continued to demand unity in the face of the common enemy, Catholicism.[3] Predominantly charitable societies also did much to promote solidarity, and ranged from large national groups like the Association for the Relief of Distressed Protestants to specialized bodies like Gardiner's Charity founded to apprentice poor Protestant boys to Protestant masters.[4]

[1] *Sir William Gregory . . . An Autobiography*, ed. Lady Gregory, pp. 59–66; *Kerry Evening Post*, 15 Feb. 1845; *Soirée of the Dublin Protestant Association and Reformation Society at Whitefriars Hall, January 14, 1846* (Dublin, [1846]), p. 10—copy R. I. A. Halliday Pamphlets 1814.

[2] *Londonderry Sentinel*, 16 July 1852; *Daily Express*, 11 Feb. 1853; Whately to Carlisle, 10 Mar. 1857, Carlisle Papers L.-B. 84; D. Bowen, *The Protestant Crusade in Ireland*, pp. 111–12.

[3] *Banner of Ulster*, 21 Mar. 1857; *Dublin Evening Mail*, 27 Mar. 1857; *Londonderry Sentinel*, 1 May 1857, and *Daily Express*, 10 Feb. 1853.

[4] *First Report of the Irish Protestant Association* (Dublin, 1836)—copy R. I. A.

A typical mixture of eleemosynary and political activities was maintained by the Dublin Protestant Freemen's Fellowship Society set up in 1852 to bring 'Protestants together, in order that by a firm union they might not only be the means of doing good to each other, but of keeping the political enemy at bay'. In part a friendly society and in part a sponge for the donations of wealthy Protestants, it aimed to make the 'heart of an aged freeman rejoice . . . to find that he is remembered—that he is cared for. Then with pleasure he will recount how often by his vote he served the good cause.' Cash was carefully filtered downwards by the president, a shoemaker, whose 'local knowledge' enabled him 'to assist the Conservative Registration Committee with the particular abode of all who changed their residence'.[1] In Yougal, Lisburn, and Derry working men were also enrolled in similar societies.[2] Protestant voters in Galway Town acted as a coherent bloc and could sometimes, as in 1852, decide the outcome of elections.[3] At Youghal the 'grand distinction' was entirely a religious one. Bandon's 'strong Protestant and Tory' element rendered void the Whig influence of the enormously wealthy Duke of Devonshire and briskly reminded one candidate billing himself as a 'Conservative of a progressive caste' that by 'Conservatism *we* mean . . . Protestantism'.[4] Only a tiny handful of Protestant voters in constituencies as different as Co. Sligo, Limerick City and Co., Kinsale, Queen's Co., Meath, and Clare ever showed even the feeblest inclination to vote for other than Conservative candidates,[5]

Halliday Pamphlets 1677; *Society for the Relief of Distressed Protestants, First Annual Report* (Dublin, 1838)—copy Halliday Pamphlets 1712. See the list of such bodies in *Thom 1859*, pp. 993–1011, not overlooking the Protestant Asylum for Aged Governesses and Respectable Females.

[1] *Daily Express*, 13 Dec. 1853; *Address, Rules, and Object of the Protestant Freemen's Fellowship Society, with a list of Patrons, Officers etc.* (Dublin, 1855), *Report of the Protestant Freemen's Fellowship Society with Abstract of Accounts and a list of Subscribers for the year 1854* (Dublin, 1855), the same *for the year 1855* (Dublin, 1856)—copies U.C.D. Pamphlets 3730. The donors were mainly gentlemen (39.4 per cent), professional men (22.5 per cent), clergymen (18.3 per cent), and merchants and shopkeepers (12.7 per cent), more than half of them occupying houses worth £50 and more. See also F. S. P. Wolferstan and E. L'E. Dew, *Reports of the decisions of committees of the House of Commons in the trial of controverted elections during the seventeenth parliament of the United Kingdom* (London, 1859), pp. 320–1.

[2] A. Merry to I. Butt, 24 July 1865, Butt Papers MS 8687; *Belfast Newsletter*, 22 Oct. 1864; *Londonderry Sentinel*, 22 Oct., 6, 10 Nov. 1868.

[3] Lord Dunkellin to W. H. Gregory, [July 1852], Clanricarde Papers 109; also Clanricarde to Clonbrock, 15 July 1852, Clonbrock to Clanricarde, 18 July 1852, ibid. 37.

[4] F. E. to W. Currey, 16 May 1849, 26 Feb. 1851, Lismore Papers MSS 7183/2, 7186; F. E. Currey to Carlisle, 9 Mar. 1857, and to Devonshire, 15 Apr. 1859, ibid. MSS 7189, 7190; *C.C.* 14, 22 Feb. 1861.

[5] *Galway Vindicator*, 27 Mar. 1852; *Limerick Reporter*, 3 May 1859; J. Spaight to Naas, 13 May 1859, Mayo Papers MS 11036; *Kinsale election petition*, H.C. 1847–8 (138), xiii, 145–9, and List of Kinsale electors *c*.1863, O'Hagan Papers D2777/6; Sir C. Coote to

because, when it came to an appeal to Protestant instincts, the Liberals had few cards to play. Lord John Russell's contortions over the 'Papal Aggression' of 1850-1 repelled Catholics without attracting Protestants, and Conservative leaders were, in any case, quite prepared to outbid Russell in order to retain 'legitimate Protestant feeling on our side'.[1]

Lord Derby's unswerving dislike of Catholicism ensured that Disraeli's acrobatics never permanently alienated Irish Protestants from the cause. Popery, Derby announced in 1857, was 'religiously corrupt and politically dangerous'. Seven years later he happily took part in Garibaldi's English visit, and in 1865, during a Lords debate on the Catholic Oaths Bill, suddenly launched into an unvarnished metaphor which must have paid ample dividends among the Protestants of Ireland.

If a man comes to me with a dog with a muzzle on and says, 'Take the muzzle off this poor creature, he will do us no harm, he is quite harmless, and, besides, the muzzle is half-rotten and affords no great protection', I understand him; but if he says, 'This is a most vicious animal, and nothing prevents him pulling you and me to pieces except the muzzle which is put round his nose, and therefore I want you to take it off', I am inclined to say, 'I am very much obliged to you, but I had rather keep the muzzle on'.[2]

Eglinton, Naas, and Abercorn represented, albeit usually more politely, the same tradition, realizing as they did that the influential core of Catholic leadership could never permanently be won to the Conservative side.[3] The handful of Irish Catholics who did try to make political careers as Conservatives were all, in the end, ground to dust between the prejudices of their co-religionists and those of their chosen associates. Only John Pope Hennessy, who represented King's Co. from 1859 until his defeat in 1865, had any success. And even he was finally driven from the field at a by-election in Wexford in 1866, during which the local Catholic bishop pronounced his landed Protestant opponent to be much the less 'objectionable

Jolliffe, 6 Apr. 1859, Mayo Papers MS 11036; *Committee on Bribery at Elections*, H.C. 1835 (547), viii, 473; J. Machett to Naas, 12 Apr. 1859, Mayo Papers MS 11036.

[1] Disraeli to Stanley, 7 Dec. 1850, W. F. Moneypenny and G. E. Buckle, *Life of Benjamin Disraeli*, ii, 272. In 1852 Antrim Conservatives had no difficulty in depicting local Liberals as cat's-paws of Rome (Ballad Sheet in Antrim Election Songs etc., P.R.O.N.I. T1104).

[2] Derby to H. Lambert, 23 Mar. 1857, Derby Papers 183/2 (also E. Horsman to Carlisle, 17 Mar. 1857, Carlisle Papers L.-B. 84); Cullen to Revd T. Kirby, 15 Apr. 1864, Kirby Papers 1864(86)—Derby's meeting with Garibaldi was a 'frightful disgrace'; *Hansard*, clxxx, 790 (26 June 1865).

[3] Naas to Eglinton, 9 July [1858], Eglinton Papers MS 5352. See also Disraeli to Naas, 12 May [1859], Mayo Papers MS 11036.

of the two'. Sensing the way the wind was blowing, Pope Hennessy wisely accepted the governorship of unhealthy Labuan, only to emerge phoenix-like in 1890 as Nationalist MP for Kilkenny North.[1]

It is ironic, therefore, that, just as the attempts to conciliate Catholic opinion were fading into the mists of illusion, the Conservative Party should have experienced a period of internal turmoil caused by Ulster populists whose radicalism could not be so easily defused as that of their southern counterparts. The key figure here was the bankrupt Down landlord, William Johnston of Ballykilbeg (1829–1902), whose helter-skelter career sheds interesting light upon the Orange Institution of which he was a prominent member. An extreme evangelical Church of Ireland man, Johnston was already by the mid-1850s Deputy Grand Master of the Grand Orange Lodge of Ireland, founder of the Down Protestant Association, and moving spirit behind the vitriolic *Downshire Protestant* newspaper. After some earlier limbering-up, 1857 was the first *annus mirabilis* of Johnston's political career, marking as it did his candidature for Downpatrick and the publication of his novel *Nightshade* in which Ribbonmen, 'prowling Jesuits', and 'liberal Protestants' are combined in a lurid demonology of the damned. Johnston's election committee was almost entirely made up of artisans, shopkeepers, and publicans, most of them Episcopalians, though with enough Presbyterians and Unitarians to reflect a wide measure of inter-denominational support.[2] On the hustings Johnston attacked the milksop Protestantism of his opponent, Richard Ker, brother of the local landlord, product of Eton and Oxford, and a former Peelite lapsing into open Palmerstonianism. Ker desperately riposted by demanding state inspection of nunneries, but visibly wilted under Johnston's bitter characterization of his views—'Oh, Bother the electors of Downpatrick; sure my brother owns all them niggers.' In the end, however, Johnston was forced to withdraw in the face of proprietorial power, Ker smoothly informing voters that, in the Commons, any talk of 'niggers' or any 'throwing of the arms would never do'.[3] However, throughout the 1860s Johnston steadily emerged as the leading campaigner against the unpopular Party Processions

[1] Bishop Furlong to Cullen, 6 Dec. 1866, Cullen Papers; Hennessy's speech at Wexford, and Hennessy to Disraeli, 25 Apr. 1867, Hughenden Papers B/XIII/195B, B/XXI/H/491.

[2] Committee list in Martin & Henderson Papers D2223/21/10 which also contain a voters' list with poor-law valuations and religious affiliations marked in pen. Occupations traced in *The Belfast and Province of Ulster Directory for 1858-9* (Belfast, 1858). The eighteen committee men occupied houses with an average value of £17. 10s.; the average for all electors was £20. 1s.

[3] *Banner of Ulster*, 10 Feb. 1857; MS copy of Ker's speech in Martin & Henderson Papers D2223/21/10. Johnston was a physically energetic speaker.

Act of 1850 and, as such, expressed the increasing dissatisfaction of rank and file Orangemen at what they believed to be their leadership's timid respectability. In July 1866 he held a great jamboree on his estate. In 1867 he led a parade from Newtownards to Bangor in defiance of the Act. In February 1868 a two-month jail sentence made him the undisputed hero of Orangeism and popular Protestantism alike. As Chief Secretary, Lord Mayo had desperately tried to prevent this, but, faced with cabinet ignorance and Johnstonian intransigence, he had been obliged to stand helplessly by as Johnston chose to cash in on his martyrdom by standing as an independent Conservative for Belfast at the General Election of November 1868.[1] And whereas in the south minority status made Protestant solidarity virtually inevitable, in Belfast the denominational imperatives were reversed and the climate potentially less static. Already in June 1867, 4,000 working men had met to demand parliamentary reform. Under the leadership of Thomas Henry, master printer, Orange district secretary, and anti-Catholic agitator, they had hissed the Conservatives for their aristocracy and the Liberals for their adhesion to *laissez-faire*, had turned themselves into a Protestant Working Men's Association with an artisan committee, and had denounced the 'betrayal' and compromises of 'respectable' Conservatism.[2]

By making overtures to the somewhat emaciated forces of Belfast Liberalism Johnston was able to strengthen his position further and, above all, to obtain the cash he so desperately needed. Secret negotiations unlocked Liberal coffers and, with the Liberals showing unusual good sense in nominating only a single (Presbyterian) candidate, the two Church of Ireland Conservatives faced a difficult task. The normally fastidious *Northern Whig* printed blatant Johnstonian puffs. Populist steam was raised by open-air meetings, by canvassing along the Protestant strongholds of Sandy Row and the Shankill Road, by unofficial Orange support, and by the excited afflations of Revd ('Roaring') Hugh Hanna, who also helped draft Johnston's radical address demanding reform, the ballot, and concessions to the 'peculiar interests of labour'. Johnston's father-in-law, the famous and fiercely evangelical Revd Thomas Drew, added his support with public letters denouncing wealthy northern landlords (he was then rural dean of Lecale West) on whose estates 'the screw

---

[1] Mayo to Abercorn, 15 Feb. 1868, Abercorn to Mayo, 3, 4 Mar. 1868, Abercorn Papers T2541/VR/85/47, 58, 59.

[2] *Freeman's Journal*, 17 June 1867; I. Budge and C. O'Leary, *Belfast: Approach to Crisis*, pp. 92, 99; *Northern Whig*, 5 Mar. 1868; P. Gibbon, *The Origins of Ulster Unionism*, p. 95. A similar group was set up in Derry (*Londonderry Guardian*, 12 Mar. 1868).

is never withdrawn from its circuitous and oppressive work'.[1] With considerable dexterity Johnston danced around the one issue—disestablishment—which might have upset his curious alliance, 'repeatedly declaring it to be a large [question] . . . and somewhat mysteriously intimating that if he list to speak he might say something about it not very pleasant'. The official Conservatives lurched from incomprehension into confusion. 'HE IS NO CONSERVATIVE', they placarded the town; 'HE WOULD PANDER TO THE ARIAN, THE ROMANIST, THE WILDEST RADICAL'.[2] But on this occasion radicalism was grist to the populist mill, and Johnston shouted from the hustings that he 'did not appear here today as the nominee of an oligarchy, self-constituted, self-elected, professing an authority to nominate candidates in your name . . . The working classes . . . have the power and the right . . . to return two members for the borough.' And they did, with Johnston heading the poll and the two Tories trailing third and fourth.[3] Johnston's strength had been concentrated in the 'heavily working-class Orange districts', though in Smithfield (then the most Catholic of the city's five wards) he polled almost as well as did the Liberal, Thomas McClure.[4]

Yet, once the victory had been achieved, the fundamental fragility of the whole affair was soon evident. At Westminster Johnston sat with the Conservatives, became more and more obedient as his need for money increased, and declaimed a curiously insistent admiration for Disraeli, to whom he had already accorded the title 'genius' in an issue of the *Downshire Protestant* in 1862.[5] At the 1874 election Belfast Conservatives wisely adopted Johnston as an official candidate, and he, in return, diluted his radicalism into acceptably Protestant appeals to the Orangemen of Down to oppose the Liberal

---

[1] See the cryptic entries in Johnston's Diary for 11 Sept.–10 Oct. 1868, Johnston of Ballykilbeg Papers D880/2/20; also his address in *Northern Whig*, 12 Sept. 1868; A. McClelland, 'Johnston of Ballykilbeg' (New University of Ulster M.Phil. thesis, 1977), pp. 53–5; for Drew's letter, see *Tipperary Advocate*, 26 Sept. 1868, and also I. Budge and C. O'Leary, *Belfast: Approach to Crisis*, pp. 78–80.

[2] T. Macknight, *Ulster as it is*, i, 164–5; *The Belfast Election*, 30 Sept., 3, 7 Oct. 1868 (a file of this Conservative news-sheet is in the B.L.).

[3] *Northern Whig*, 18 Nov. 1868. Johnston obtained 5,975 votes, the Liberal 4,202, the Tories 3,540 and 1,580 (the second Tory withdrew during polling in a vain effort to boost his colleague).

[4] F. Wright, 'Protestant ideology and politics in Ulster', *Archives Européennes de Sociologie*, xiv (1973), 255; detailed ward figures in Johnston's Diary D880/2/20. See E. Jones, *A Social Geography of Belfast* (London, 1960), pp. 191–2. It should be noted, however, that while almost a third of the *population* of Belfast was Catholic in 1871, only 17.4 per cent of the *electorate* was in 1868 (*Belfast Newsletter*, 13 Oct. 1868).

[5] Cutting from *Downshire Protestant* in Johnston to Disraeli, 7 June 1862, also Johnston to Disraeli, 20 Jan. 1871, Hughenden Papers B/XXI/J/64, 70. The correspondence goes back to 1854.

tenant-right blandishments of James Sharman Crawford.[1] And despite overtures from Gladstone himself and despite a continuing ability to (as one Tory put it) 'play the very devil with us in Ulster', Johnston remained 'fairly loyal to the Conservative Party' and was rewarded in 1878 with an inspectorship of fisheries at £700 a year.[2] Not that populist Protestantism was dead. Johnston himself was soon dismissed from his post for political invective, and reappeared at Westminister in 1885, though once again he was quickly reabsorbed into the fold. By then the party had, in any case, become sufficiently adept in such matters that it was able to annihilate Robert Seeds's appeals (with the help of the Orange and Protestant Working Men's Association) to the Belfast electorate in 1878 and 1880 and to defuse by assimilation the Johnstonian electoral performances of the populist slum landlord, E. S. W. de Cobain (later, to mixed embarrassment and relief, expelled from the Commons for 'gross and criminal acts of indecency'), in 1885 and 1886.[3] What all these and later efflorescences, such as the Independent Orange Order of T. H. Sloan or the Unionist socialism of William Walker, showed, was not so much the splintering impact of Protestant populism as the rapidity with which it could be absorbed and defused. Protestant working-class political culture was, indeed, autonomous, but it was not at this time prepared to deviate consistently from the orthodox path. What was to happen almost a century afterwards shows, however, that latent potentialities have a habit of appearing on stage when they are least expected.

It was, of course, Orangeism that provided Johnston with a ready-made rhetoric as well as a substantial following. The Orange Order, established in the 1790s, had found the reforms of 1829-32 a stimulus to involvement in Conservative politics and electoral organization. The Derry election of 1832 was marked by Orange discussions concerning the merits of rival candidates. Newry Orangemen appeared armed to 'encourage' Conservative victory. Cavan lodges 'came forward with zeal' to work the registers. As County Grand Master, the MP for Donegal, Sir Edmund Hayes, received enthusiastic support,[4] and on the order's 'dissolution' in 1836 at least a dozen Irish

---

[1] Johnston to E. Gardner, 4 Feb. 1874, L'Estrange & Brett Papers D1905/2/3.

[2] Sir T. Bateson to Disraeli, 24 Nov. 1874, Hughenden Papers B/XXI/J/83; Sir M. Hicks-Beach to Disraeli, 29 Dec. 1875, ibid. B/XXI/J/94A.

[3] P. Gibbon, *The Origins of Ulster Unionism*, pp. 82, 102, 129; *Journals of the House of Commons*, cxlvii, 67 (26 Feb. 1892); M. Stenton and S. Lees, *Who's Who of British Members of Parliament*, 4 vols. (Hassocks and Brighton, 1976-81), ii, 93.

[4] *Londonderry Sentinel*, 17 Nov., 22 Dec. 1832; *Committee on Bribery at Elections*, H.C. 1835 (547), viii, 431-5; J. Fawcett to J. Dicken, 24 Nov. 1832, Morley Papers Deposit 69; Farnham to R. Bell (County Grand Master), 10, 14 Sept. 1832, and Bell to Farnham, 12 Sept. 1832, Farnham Papers MS 18612; *Ballyshannon Herald*, 18 Jan. 1833.

MPs and several peers were active members.[1] Already in 1835 Orangemen had started serious election riots in Armagh, where they had forced Catholics to flee the town and had battled with armed Ribbonmen until the appearance of infantry and a six-pounder brought matters to a halt. In Belfast thousands of Orangemen had 'paraded the streets for three days' during the election 'with drums and fifes playing party tunes'.[2] Further south, Meath Orangemen had marched through Trim brandishing pistols, had killed two Catholics, and been thanked by the Conservative candidates for their support. At Abbeyleix in Queen's Co., a successful Conservative had been chaired by a mob 'decorated with Orange ribands and Orange banners', while Wexford Orangemen had been no less enthusiastic.[3] Nor did the purely formal 'dissolution' of 1836 produce any slackening of endeavour at the General Election of 1837, when Orangemen were (to say the least) active in constituencies such as Dublin City, Monaghan, Armagh, Longford, and Portarlington. Cork City Conservatives chose a grand master as one of their parliamentary candidates and regularly—until the municipal reforms of 1840—saw to it that mayors were elected who could be relied upon to announce their public willingness 'to drive the Catholics into the sea'.[4]

This demotic tradition stretching from 'Thrashy' Gregg (himself a Deputy Grand Chaplain) to Johnston of Ballykilbeg was, however, interwoven with the rather different attitudes of sympathetic landowners and aristocrats anxious to mobilize the 'lower orders' behind what might otherwise have seemed unattractive causes like the royal prerogative and the regular payment of tithes.[5] But if the nature of class relationships was a complex matter, there can be few doubts as to the resonant power of Orange argument and language. No less than thirty-two lodges were active in Belfast in 1835 and probably 90 per cent of the 1,400 or so lodges of the period were to be found

---

[1] See list in [R. M. Sibbett], *Orangeism in Ireland and throughout the Empire*, ii, 218.

[2] *D.E.P.* 22 Jan. 1835; Lord Gosford to W. Gossett, 17 Jan. 1835, O.P. 1835, Box 45; also *Proceedings had at an investigation held in Armagh on the Transactions which took place in that town and neighbourhood on the 15th January last*, H.C. 1835 (101), xlv, 461-87; J. Hancock to E. J. Littleton, 1 Feb. 1835, Hatherton Papers D260/M/F/5/27.

[3] *Third Report . . . Orange Lodges*, H.C. 1835 (476), xvi, 1-11; R. B. O'Brien, *Thomas Drummond Under-Secretary in Ireland 1835-40* (London, 1889), pp. 119-20; Report of Sub-Inspector Despard, 25 Jan. 1835, O.P. 1835, Box 47; *D.E.P.* 29 Jan. 1835; *Committee on Bribery at Elections*, H.C. 1835 (547), viii, 262.

[4] Revd C. McDermott to —, 18 Aug. 1837, Clogher Diocesan Papers DIO(RC)1/6/41; *Fictitious Votes, Ireland*, 2nd series, 3rd report, p. 250; *D.E.P.* 25 July, 5, 8 Aug. 1837; M. Murphy, 'Municipal Reform and the Repeal Movement in Cork', p. 5; *Third Report . . . Orange Lodges*, H.C. 1835 (476), xvi, Appendix pp. 36, 54.

[5] *Correspondence relating to a meeting of the Inhabitants of . . . Dungannon*, H.C. 1835 (120), xlv, 511-14; *Copies of Extracts of Reports . . . with reference to riotous proceedings . . . in the Village of Ballykelly*, H.C. 1835 (345), xlv, 489-92.

in the northern province. The main centres outside Ulster were Leitrim (29), Cork (21), Wicklow (20), and Dublin (17). Total membership probably hovered somewhere not far above 100,000, though agitated contemporaries (O'Connell among them) often inflated the figure to as much as 250,000 or more.[1] And while numbers probably fell during the 1850s, they rose again thereafter as a result of Johnston's efforts and the threats of Home Rule.[2] The nature of this membership varied both as to time and place. By the late 1820s gentry involvement was temporarily lessening in Armagh and recruitment was coming predominantly from among 'the lower orders, farmers and cottiers' and the many small weavers of the county. Around Strabane most of the gentry and 'the respectable farmers and yeomanry class' remained aloof. Yet even unsympathetic Conservative landlords such as Lord Caledon in Tyrone still found it politic to speak soothingly of the Orangemen's steadfastness and support.[3] Whig sources, torn between feelings of fear and superiority, generally adopted an uneasily haughty tone typified by references to the 'few beggarly little shoneen Orangemen' of Youghal or the 'rag, tag, and bob-tail' enrolled in Limerick.[4] In fact, things were far from as simple as this. In Cork City, where Orangeism before 1832 had been very much a 'lower middle class' affair, the impact of reform brought about the adhesion of Lord Bandon and a flotilla of lesser gentlemen. Thereafter, the local Tory leadership openly identified itself with the order and an Orange-inspired political association founded in 1835 acquired extensive aristocratic support, so much so, that, for the first time, Cork Orangeism became a 'blanket institution for the political defence of Protestantism' as a whole.[5] In Monaghan too the gentry were well to the fore, and even Stewart Blacker, the Orangeman who had thought Armagh lodges full of 'the lower orders', insisted that district masters often came from 'the highest rank of life ... Many [are] grand jurors and magistrates ...

[1] *First Report ... Orange Lodges*, H.C. 1835 (377), xv, 113, and Appendix pp. 35–69; M. W. Dewar, J. Brown, and S. E. Long, *Orangeism: A new Historical Appreciation* [Belfast, 1967], p. 129. Dewar etc. estimate 100,000, while the consensus among witnesses before the committee would suggest an average lodge membership of about eighty or a total maximum membership of 112,000 (though some lodges were probably moribund). R. M. Sibbett's pietistic *Orangeism in Ireland and throughout the Empire* presents unresolved figures of between 150,000 and 250,000 for this period. These are certainly too high.

[2] A. McClelland, 'The later Orange Order' in *Secret Societies in Ireland*, ed. T. D. Williams (Dublin, 1973), p. 126.

[3] Revd H. Waring to J. W. Maxwell, 19 Sept. 1828, Perceval-Maxwell Papers D3244/G/1/58; *First Report ... Orange Lodges*, H.C. 1835 (377), xv, 129, 277, 349, 368–78; Lord Caledon to Peel, 10 Aug. 1837, Peel Papers Add. MS 40424.

[4] *D.E.P.* 18 July, 3 Aug. 1837. 'Shoneen' means a gentleman in a small way; a would-be gentleman who puts on superior airs. Always used contemptuously.

[5] I. d'Alton, *Protestant Society and Politics in Cork 1812–1844*, pp. 204–10.

but the generality of them belong to the class of the upper rank of substantial farmers.' In the country as a whole, it was claimed by the deputy treasurer of the Grand Lodge of Ireland, '120 gentlemen of the first rank' had joined to express political and religious solidarity, while similar sentiments lay behind the considerable growth of Orangeism in areas such as Cork, Wexford, and Queen's Co.[1]

What seems clear is that, although increasingly after 1830 the order was able to attract an influential crust of gentry, the heart of the movement continued to be supplied by the substantial farmers who predominated as local leaders or by men like the ironmaster's clerk who presided over matters in Clonmel throughout the 1830s. Of course, outside the north and a few southern districts (for instance west Cork, Wicklow, Sligo, Leitrim) Protestant farmers were few in number, but the very smallness of the Protestant community in the Catholic south forcibly united its various elements in a manner which was less necessary in the north-east.[2] At the same time the more respectable members tended, throughout Ireland as a whole, to stand apart from (though often to encourage) the wilder physical demonstrations which formed so important a part of Orange life. Genteel candidates may have happily had themselves carried through their constituencies by Orange mobs, but 'gentlemen', merchants, and professional men were notable for their absence in the various excited Orange marches, which, for example, took place around Dungannon in 1830 and 1831 and were watched and recorded by the police. Again, at the local rural level, lodges seem predominantly to have attracted younger men, who, almost by definition, can hardly have included many influential country gentlemen.[3] The precise nature of the influence exercised by the leadership is unclear. Certainly men like Lords Enniskillen and Roden tried hard to stop trigger-happy public displays, but just as certainly 'our poor Protestant supporters of the humbler class' regularly ignored them. But even if Liberal critics like William Sharman Crawford shuddered at the predominance of 'a class that ought to be in their beds preparing to work in the morning' (a revealing phrase), none could

[1] A. McClelland, 'Orangeism in County Monaghan', *Clogher Record*, ix (1978), 393; *First Report . . . Orange Lodges*, H.C. 1835 (377), xv, 113, 198, 201.
[2] *Fictitious Votes, Ireland*, 1st series, 1st report, pp. 222–45; 2nd series, 3rd report, pp. 195, 250.
[3] *Third Report . . . Orange Lodges*, H.C. 1835 (476), xvi, 105, 117. The ages of the fifty-eight members of L.O.L. 614 (East Cavan) are given in R. M. Hassard to Clarendon, 9 Apr. 1848, Clarendon Papers Box 17: 86.2 per cent were thirty or younger. See also *First Report . . . Orange Lodges*, H.C. 1835 (377), xv, 129; Farnham to Graham, 13 July 1845, Graham Papers 22/Ir.

deny the order's ability to attract members from right across the social scale.[1]

After the 'dissolution' of 1836 Belfast lodges continued to meet in public houses and regrouped under the banner of the Belfast Protestant Operative Society, while in Fermanagh activity increased rather than diminished.[2] In August 1846 the Grand Lodge of Ireland was formally revived and immediately extended the respectable election work of the order which had in the past been overshadowed by its marches, riots, flag-waving, and intimidation. Elections, it was found, greatly boosted morale and involved a wide range of members in Orange meetings and organization.[3] Samuel Yates Johnstone, a key figure in the Central Conservative Society of 1853, was a leading Orangeman; indeed, that society may well have developed out of the special electoral subcommittee set up by the Grand Lodge in November 1851 with Johnstone, Revd Dr Drew, and two MPs as its most prominent members. The 1852 election, falling as it did in the sacred Orange month of July, was marked by the forceful intervention a 'respectable' Orangeism, especially against Sharman Crawford's tenant-right campaign in Co. Down.[4] And not without effect, for, as Lord Londonderry's law agent admitted, the Tories were indebted for many of their votes to 'the Orangemen determined to put out Crawford'. In the mean time, however, 'the lower orders of [Down] Orangemen', sorely tempted by the promises of the Tenant League, resorted to 'great violence' of a generally anarchic kind. In neighbouring Antrim (where the County Grand Master, Lord Dungannon, was an altogether more elevated being than the respectably modest William Beers of Down) much the same happened and the county lodge felt it necessary to bring its followers into line by issuing strong public calls for Protestant solidarity behind the Conservative candidates, who were, in the event, returned unopposed.[5]

---

[1] Roden to Downshire, 11 July, 19 Nov. 1834, Downshire Papers D671/C/12/510, 542; *First Report... Orange Lodges*, H.C. 1835 (377), xv, 330.

[2] S. E. Baker, 'Orange and Green: Belfast, 1832–1912', p. 795. [R. M. Sibbett], *Orangeism in Ireland and throughout the Empire*, ii, 308, and *First Report . . . Orange Lodges*, H.C. 1835 (377), xv, Appendix pp. 35–69 show that the number of Fermanagh lodges probably increased between 1834 and 1844. See also A. McClelland, 'Orangeism in County Monaghan', pp. 392–3.

[3] *First Report . . . Orange Lodges*, H.C. 1835 (377), xv, 358. Not that electoral and registration matters had formerly been ignored—indeed land surveyors had even been organized to 'swear down' the value of Catholic farms and so reduce the Catholic electorate. See ibid. 49, 104; *Fictitious Votes, Ireland*, 2nd series, 3rd report, pp. 48–81.

[4] [R. M. Sibbett], *Orangeism in Ireland and throughout the Empire*, ii, 309, 438; printed address of R. W. Phaire to Lord Enniskillen, 4 Dec. 1848, Clarendon Papers Box 36; W. Johnston to J. W. Maxwell, 3, 30 Apr. 1852, Perceval-Maxwell Papers D3244/G/1/149, 164; *Londonderry Sentinel*, 2 July 1852.

[5] R. Cassidy to Londonderry, 30 Aug. 1852, Londonderry Papers D/Lo/C160; Report

The increasing organizational co-ordination between Orangeism and the Conservative Party owed much to Yates Johnstone, who, for example, was sometimes able to act as soothing mediator between Colonel Taylor and Johnston of Ballykilbeg. Such contacts helped create dramatic electoral coups like that at Downpatrick in 1859, while the Grand Lodge's formal endorsements and circulars to local lodges in 1859, 1865, and again in 1868 did much to boost the party nationally.[1] At the same time it would seem that Orange violence had declined. A brief flurry occurred in 1852, and the heartlands of Armagh continued to experience large and disorderly demonstrations, but elsewhere the more careful advice of the Grand Lodge had its effect.[2] Conservative leaders welcomed this, for what they wanted was a polished Orangeism which could still produce support but without the tribal savagery of the unvarnished article. They did all they could to get Orange chiefs like Enniskillen and Roden (both directly approachable through the old-boy network) to keep things reasonably quiet. And indeed Enniskillen, for one, saw the institution primarily as a 'compact among Protestants . . . that will admit the lower orders being brought into closer connection with . . . their natural and legitimate guides'. Yet, as time went on, even he was driven to what might best be called a controlled extremism in order to preserve his popular influence. Indeed, in the face of Johnston of Ballykilbeg, polished Orangeism disappeared momentarily from the centre of the stage.[3] This is not to say that conventional *respectability* was at any time entirely banished from the movement in general. Typical of this important strand of Orange gentility were, for example, the polite teas, which, in the 1860s, formed so large a part of the social life of Revd James O'Hara, Church of Ireland curate of Coleraine, a man whose fierce Orange and temperance loyalties represented a certain type of Protestant culture

of G. Fitzmaurice, 23 July 1852, O.P. 1852/8/292, Box 1217; *Londonderry Sentinel*, 25 June 1852.

[1] Johnston of Ballykilbeg's Diary D880/2/11 (2–10 May 1859); *Londonderry Sentinel*, 22 Apr., 11 May 1859; J. Hill to Sir H. H. Bruce, 6 Apr. 1859, J. Hill to W. Macartney, 21 Apr. 1859, Circular of Apr. 1859, all L.-B. of Grand Lodge of Ireland D2947/1/B3; I. Budge and C. O'Leary, *Belfast: Approach to Crisis*, p. 128; *Londonderry Sentinel*, 23 Oct. 1868.

[2] Bishop MacNally of Clogher to Cullen, 19 July 1852, Cullen Papers; Revd E. Moore to Revd G. Kirkpatrick, 31 July 1852, Kirkpatrick Papers D1604/109; Lord G. Beresford to Mrs Harriet Dunbar, 6, 9 Oct. 1855, Pack-Beresford Papers D664/A/624, D664/D/74B; W. Wann to J. C. Stronge, 7 Mar. 1857, Gosford Papers D1606/5A/2.

[3] Derby to H. Lambert, 23 Mar. 1852, Derby Papers 180/1; Eglinton to Derby, 28 June 1852, Eglinton Papers MS 5333; Naas to Eglinton, 4 June 1852, ibid. MS 5334; Eglinton to Naas, 20 Mar. 1858, Mayo Papers MS 11031; Eglinton to Derby, 3 May 1858, Eglinton Papers MS 5345; Enniskillen to Heytesbury, 10 Sept. 1845, Graham Papers 23/Ir.

common in country and town alike. Of course lodge gatherings themselves provided regular opportunities for letting off steam—often it seems a very audible activity—and for jovial horseplay of an unsophisticated and sectarian kind.[1]

Yet the *official* 'moderation' of post-Famine Orangeism so infuriated sections of the movement that some even made curious overtures to the Liberals. Others, more logically, backed Johnston of Ballykilbeg, whose candidature at Belfast in 1868 simultaneously evinced strong local Orange support and extreme prevarication from Grand Lodge headquarters in Dublin.[2] Surveying the near-defeat of the official Tory candidate at the Tyrone by-election of 1873, the Grand Master, Enniskillen, noted that 'Orangeism has not been fashionable of late years, and the gentry, with very few exceptions, have withdrawn . . . The masses of the Orangemen have felt this deeply, and have often complained about it.' But this obscures as much as it reveals. The great magnates may well have stood aloof, but, at the level of local activism, there seems in fact to have been a shift of leadership after 1850 towards lesser gentlemen and (where appropriate) the middle classes, and away from the substantial farmers of the 1830s. The backgrounds of the district grand masters in 1855 suggest as much, while the leaders of Tyrone Orangeism in the early 1870s consisted of three small landlords, two landlord kin, a land agent, a flax buyer, and an insurance agent.[3] The rank and file probably continued to come from the same strata that had supplied the movement's main strength throughout the 1830s and 1840s. And, despite dissensions and disputes, the order as a whole probably grew in size throughout the decade after 1865. In Belfast, membership trebled between 1851 and 1870, the number of Orange halls rose from one in 1853 to five in 1886, while the officers became notable for their lower-middle-class respectability—commercial travellers, woollen drapers, occasional clergymen.[4] In smaller provincial centres, artisans, shopkeepers, and farmers were especially prominent, as the combined membership of the Enniskillen Royal

---

[1] O'Hara's Diary for 1868–73 N.L.I. MS 14911; *The Diary of Colour-Sergeant George Calladine 19th Foot 1793–1837*, ed. M. L. Ferrar (London, 1922), p. 134.

[2] Horsman to Carlisle, 28 Mar. 1857, Carlisle Papers L.-B. 85; *Belfast Election*, 28 Oct., 11 Nov. 1868; *Northern Whig*, 22 Oct. 1868. The Grand Lodge's instructions of July 1856 to 'abstain from any outward display' had caused great resentment ([R. M. Sibbett], *Orangeism in Ireland and throughout the Empire*, ii, 450).

[3] Enniskillen to Belmore, 24 Mar. [1873], Belmore Papers D3007/P/72; P. Gibbon, *The Origins of Ulster Unionism*, p. 141; R. C. Brush to Belmore, 14 Mar. 1873, Belmore Papers D3007/P/19.

[4] M. J. Dewar, J. Brown, and S. E. Long, *Orangeism*, p. 142; I. Budge and C. O'Leary, *Belfast: Approach to Crisis*, p. 93. In 1864 Belfast was at last raised to the status of a county grand lodge.

Black Preceptory (an associated organization) in 1868 and 1873 would seem to suggest.[1]

Occupation	per cent
Gentlemen	1.3
Merchants etc.	10.7
Clerks etc.	9.3
Artisans and Shopkeepers	40.0
Farmers	18.7
Soldiers	6.7
Others	13.3
(N = 75)	

Although the same data have been used to argue that the movement was predominantly one in which the 'downwardly mobile sections of society' found solace for shrinking prestige and economic power,[2] the main conclusion to be drawn is that things had changed little over the previous fifty years. Landowners would not, in any case, have joined small town preceptories, while professional men did not appear in large numbers until somewhat later

Orangeism in Dublin remained a more consistent and less troubled vehicle for Protestant solidarity. Its characteristic attitudes reflected a membership in which shopkeepers, artisans, and clerks formed the predominant part. Admission lists for Dublin No. 1 district demonstrate the importance of such men.[3]

Occupation	1861–4 per cent	1881–4 per cent
Gentlemen	2.8	1.6
Professional men	6.7	11.1
Merchants etc.	5.3	3.2
Clerks etc.	19.5	33.0
Artisans	16.7	17.6
Shopkeepers	32.6	16.5
Labourers and Servants	11.1	10.7
Others	5.3	6.3

(N Admitted: 1861-4—359, 1881-4—476)

---

[1] Minute Book of the Royal Black Preceptory, Enniskillen, D1360/2A. Technically distinct, the RBPs of the Grand Black Chapter were in practice closely intertwined with Orangeism (A. McClelland, 'The Origin of the Imperial Grand Black Chapter of the British Commonwealth', *Journal of the Royal Society of Antiquaries of Ireland*, xcviii (1968), 191-5).

[2] P. Gibbon, *The Origins of Ulster Unionism*, p. 115.

[3] Dublin District Orange Lodge No. 1 Minute Books 1860-7 and 1867-84, D2947/3/A1, A2. The 'districts' did not recruit exclusively from particular parts of the city. As *admission* lists, these naturally exclude members of long standing.

Much the same was probably true of other southern towns, with the growing interest shown by clerks, book-keepers, and accountants—the commercial storm-troopers of the late-Victorian *petit bourg*—reflecting the changing aspirations of the Protestant lower class.

The future, however, lay in the north, and it was there that the problems raised by Johnston of Ballykilbeg had to be resolved. Even Ulster Tories who distrusted Johnston agreed with his (correct) analysis that the leaders of Irish Conservatism still looked mainly to Dublin and London rather than to Belfast. 'Many of them', wrote one northern MP to Mayo in 1868, 'feel sore that their country [*sic*], which gives little or no trouble, is peaceful, prosperous, and contented, is included in the exceptional legislation for the south and west.' English party leaders made matters worse with their sneers at the 'foul Ulster Tories' (Lord Randolph Churchill), distrust of Ulster Toryism's sporadic radicalism on land questions (Disraeli), and comments that northern MPs found 'loyalty to the party' no 'very fierce passion just now' (Salisbury).[1] Indeed, of the seven Irishmen whom Salisbury included in his first administration, only one came from Ulster. Yet, as regards its own internal political strength, Ulster Conservatism can be seen paradoxically to have benefited rather than suffered from the freebooting populism of Johnston and his supporters. A new seriousness and realism were called into being by the realization that Johnston was not alone. M. R. Dalway, for example, the maverick member for Carrickfergus from 1868 to 1880, found enough support among radical Orangemen to set up an Independent Orange Association. A few northerners even joined the Protestant day-trip to Home Rule which so excited Nationalists in the early 1870s and led to co-operation between Catholics and 'rabid Orangemen' at the Monaghan by-election of 1871. More serious still were the powerful radical attacks mounted by the Orange-supported landowner, J. W. Ellison Macartney, at the Tyrone by-election of April 1873. Macartney mobilized support from Orange farmers, who wanted an extension of Gladstone's 1870 Land Act, and from retailing and mercantile elements in places like Cookstown, where Brother W. J. Devlin, a prominent flax buyer and future embezzler of Orange funds, was chairman of the poor-law board and of the town commissioners.[2]

---

[1] Sir F. W. Heygate to Mayo, 8 Jan. 1868, Mayo Papers MS 11167; Churchill to Salisbury, 16 Nov. 1885, cited F. Thompson, 'The Armagh elections of 1885–6', pp. 381–2, Beaconsfield (Disraeli) to Salisbury, 27 Dec. 1880, and Salisbury to Churchill, 16 Nov. 1885, cited A. B. Cooke, 'A Conservative party leader in Ulster', p. 62.

[2] J. C. Lowry to Belmore, 15 Mar. 1873, J. Greer to Belmore, 15 Mar. 1873, J. F. Lowry to Belmore, 24 Mar. 1873, Belmore Papers D3007/P/23, 24, 68; W. Wilson to J. W. Ellison Macartney, 25 Jan., 19 Feb. 1877, Ellison Macartney Papers Nos. 15, 16; *Thom 1876*, pp. 1154, 1221.

But, as with Johnston, de Cobain, and others, so Macartney too was eventually reabsorbed into the mainstream of Ulster Conservative Unionism and given formal blessing as an official candidate at the subsequent General Election held in 1874.

In other counties, such as Armagh, Antrim and Fermanagh, Conservative candidates owed their success to Orange solidarity in the face of the Liberal challenge, for, although the Liberals achieved some impressive (though very fleeting) victories, Orange populism almost invariably found the maverick Toryism of a Macartney or a Johnston more to its taste. The conclusion to be drawn, according to the *Belfast Newsletter*, was not that the order should be shunned for its radicalism, but that 'it would be well . . . if the Conservative gentry, commercial classes, artisans, and farmers in Ulster would join its ranks and make it still more powerful in the land, and still more useful in promoting the interests of Protestantism'. The mavericks actually increased the power of Orangeism and this in turn eventually added stature and impact to the official Conservative and Unionist cause. Already in 1868 observers had noticed a substantial increase in the numbers 'walking' on 12 July. Allied bodies, such as the Apprentice Boys of Derry, were also moving decisively from a merely sectarian attitude to one in which Conservative partisanship played an important part.[1] And in the end, this Orange revival was harnessed to Conservatism because most Orangemen saw social issues as secondary to the great issue of religion and because orthodox leaders in the north allowed realism to defeat apprehension by themselves adopting flexible views on the land question and other matters of popular concern. In 1876 an Ulster Tory caucus at Westminster discussed the land question at length, while the success of the Presbyterian solicitor selected to contest Donegal in the same year was undoubtedly connected with his long devotion to the tenant-right movement of earlier times.[2] Many of the eighteen Ulster Conservatives returned in 1880 adopted virtually Gladstonian positions on the matter, and during the main Commons divisions on the 1881 Land Bill thirteen Ulster Tory votes went with the Bill (there were four abstentions), 'while in the Lords the "Ulster feeling" helped to paralyse every attempt made by the massive Conservative majority to undo Gladstone's handiwork'. Some Tyrone landlords even considered holding a county conference

---

[1] *Belfast Newsletter*, 3 Mar. 1874; *Londonderry Guardian*, 16 July 1868; *Report of the Commissioners of Inquiry, 1869, into the Riots and Disturbances in the City of Londonderry*, H.C. 1870 [C 5*], xxxii, 82. The Governor of the Apprentice Boys in 1868 was a prominent member of the Tory election committee (*Londonderry Sentinel*, 24 Nov. 1868).

[2] *Irish Times*, 13 Feb. 1874; H. Corry to Belmore, 8 Feb. 1876, Belmore Papers D3007/P/169; *Londonderry Journal*, 18 Aug. 1876; T. Macknight, *Ulster as it is*, i, 367.

with 'representatives of the tenant farmers' to agree a common policy on the matter.[1] As a result, the Grand Lodge of Ireland had little difficulty in mobilizing a united Conservative front at the elections held in 1880, which were, indeed, marked by powerful Orange demonstrations on behalf of particularly favoured candidates, such as those in the counties of Fermanagh and Armagh. In Belfast too, despite occasional tensions in 1885, Orangeism and Conservatism grew closer together, in both the personnel of their leaderships and the attitudes of their supporters. Not only did many Johnstonites now support official candidates, but the County Grand Lodge itself intervened decisively on the official side.[2]

In an important sense, therefore, the politics of Ulster Conservatism in 1880 still ran along normal lines, with a multiplicity of issues —land, law, religion—exercising both leaders and led. Southern Conservatism, however, had already entered a new political world. Landlords had finally lost all electoral power. Outside the University, only seats in the small boroughs of Bandon and Portarlington, a single seat in Co. Leitrim, and two seats in the increasingly suburbanized county of Dublin remained in Conservative hands, and even these were soon to be swept away. The thud of towels being thrown in could be heard throughout the land. 'In truth', as the *Limerick Chronicle* reported, 'the gentry . . . are now the worst represented class in the community . . . [Among] the landed proprietors, great and small, is to be found apathy, complete want of cohesion, and an utter absence of a rallying cry.' The ability to coerce or attract Catholic electors, whether as tenants or as men expecting custom and patronage, had disappeared, with the result that the Tory vote was picked to its irreducible and ineffective Protestant bone. Arthur MacMorrough Kavanagh was able to count only eighty Catholics among his 714 Co. Carlow voters in 1880. In Co. Wexford all but fifty of the lone Tory candidate's 847 votes were plumps, a certain sign that only the Protestants had been mobilized.[3] In boroughs too appeals from Protestant employers, however generous and however wealthy, that voters should concentrate on bringing 'plenty and comfort to . . . hearths and homes' fell on deaf ears, for 'prosperity' was also the stock-in-trade of Home Rulers and could by them be wrapped in more attractive

[1] A. B. Cooke, 'A Conservative party leader in Ulster', p. 68; J. C. Lowry to Belmore, 19 Oct. 1880, Belmore Papers D3007/P/183.

[2] *Daily Express*, 15, 23, 26, 29 Mar. 1880; F. Thompson, 'The Armagh elections of 1885-6', p. 361; I. Budge and C. O'Leary, *Belfast: Approach to Crisis*, pp. 103, 128; P. Gibbon, *The Origins of Ulster Unionism*, p. 104.

[3] *Limerick Chronicle*, 18 Mar. 1880; *Daily Express*, 13 Apr. 1880; U. Hatton to Courtown, 7 Apr. 1880, and J. G. Gibbon to Courtown, 15 Apr. 1880, Courtown Papers.

packages.[1] The Irish Loyal and Patriotic Union's support for a host
of no-hope candidates at the General Election of 1885 was simply
whistling to keep one's spirits up. Certainly the few remaining
Protestant Liberals were driven into Unionist unity, but with fifty-
two Loyalist candidates in the south obtaining 31,772 votes against
231,454 for their Home Rule opponents (who also convincingly
claimed the bulk of the 111,974 electors left unpolled), the
southern laager was made to seem very small indeed.[2] The whole
business had become little more than a census of the faithful. 'My
dear good Sir John', remarked one Protestant landlord's wife, 'made
a gallant fight . . . Of course he never expected to win. He fought
to call the muster roll of the loyalist Protestants and well did they
respond—so well that he almost can name the few absent ones.'[3]
Even the charmed circle of lively Dublin Unionist intellectuals which
had buzzed around Lord Randolph Churchill's early excursions into
Irish politics now found itself stranded with nothing left but its
charm. As a result, apart from odd victories caused by Nationalist
splits (as in South Co. Dublin and Dublin St Stephen's Green in
1892 and 1895) and a last ineffectual presence on county grand
juries until 1898, the stream of Protestant energy was henceforth
to flow almost entirely into the maintenance of a separate social
identity—witness the extraordinary success in the south of the
Primrose League—and into a strategic defence of economic interests.
The 'more the gentry's economic power shrank, the more important
the comforting sense of status became', so that, within the world
of hunt balls, tea-parties, and bazaars, an increasingly particular and
minute appreciation of hierarchy was demanded and obtained.[4]
In major towns, where Protestants still loomed large in commerce
and the professions (the 1901 census shows that more than half
Dublin's doctors and more than a third of its bankers and merchants
were Protestants, Cork's proportions being two-fifths in both cases),
a pattern of life was continued which rarely necessitated any real

[1] *Limerick Chronicle*, 1 Apr. 1880.
[2] See *Wexford Independent*, 11, 14 Nov. 1885; *Daily Express*, 12, 15 Dec. 1885;
P. Buckland, *Irish Unionism: The Anglo-Irish and the new Ireland 1885–1922* (Dublin,
1972), p. 3.
[3] Lady Leslie to Salisbury, 2 Dec. 1885, cited D. C. Savage, 'The Origins of the Ulster
Unionist party, 1885–6', *Irish Historical Studies*, xii (1961), 186. This was actually said
about the Monaghan election.
[4] R. F. Foster, 'To the Northern Counties Station: Lord Randolph Churchill and the
prelude to the Orange Card' in *Ireland under the Union*, ed. F. S. L. Lyons and R. A. J.
Hawkins, pp. 237–87; I. d'Alton, 'Cork Unionism: Its role in parliamentary and local
elections, 1885–1914', pp. 151–4; *idem*, 'Southern Irish Unionism: A study of Cork
Unionists, 1884–1914', pp. 71–88; D. Fitzpatrick, *Politics and Irish Life 1913–1921:
Provincial experience of War and Revolution* (Dublin, 1977), pp. 52–3.

breach in the sectarian divide. But what there remained of 'confident opposition'[1] was becoming neither very active nor very confident. The journey to quietism had begun, a journey which was to transform the vitality of traditional Protestant solidarity into a shallow stand-offishness sustained chiefly by rigorous endeavours to employ only Protestant gardeners and by remaining seated at the Dublin Horse Show (for political not aesthetic reasons) while the Free State's national anthem was being played.

As northern Conservatism, always a separate force, transformed itself into provincial Unionism, so the links with the Protestants of the south became ever more tenuous. In this respect the 'border' existed long before 1921. By the early 1880s Orangeism, while continuing to act as a safety-valve for rural radicalism, was fully and successfully engaged in mobilizing Protestant forces against the Land League. Arms were procured and distributed. Colonel Saunderson, an erstwhile Liberal now emerging as an increasingly important Unionist leader, demanded in 1882 that 'within the Orange Association a body of men should be enrolled who would adopt a uniform and be drilled as far as the law would permit'.[2] And even as English Conservatives hesitated, so Ulster militants welcomed Sir Stafford Northcote's visit to Belfast in 1883 with meetings of 40,000, vitriolic attacks upon the Catholic community, and demands that MPs 'take off their coats and go to work'.[3] When, in February 1885, Northcote confessed that, during inter-party discussions on the Redistribution Bill, he and Salisbury had 'forgotten all about Ulster', this, combined with the electoral death of southern Unionism, helped to direct the Protestant politics of the north into channels ever more distinct and separate. In a constituency such as North Armagh, Colonel Saunderson was able to depend upon organized Orangeism, working through the Lurgan District Working Men's Constitutional Association and the Portadown Constitutional Association, to help him replace an incumbent Conservative candidate of less fiercely Unionist views, even though Orangemen constituted no more than an eighth of the

---

[1] P. Buckland, in *Irish Unionism: The Anglo-Irish and the new Ireland 1885–1922*, pp. 1–28, calls 1885–1914 the period of 'confident opposition'. While this is a useful corrective to over-threnodic retrospective gloom, it seems, none the less, to mistake the appearance for the substance.

[2] Revd D. C. Abbott to H. de F. Montgomery, 18 Dec. 1880, Montgomery Papers D627/428/7; J. Magee, 'The Monaghan election of 1883', p. 151.

[3] Lord Carnarvon to Lord Cranbrook, 2 Sept. 1885, cited A. O'Day, *The English face of Irish Nationalism*, p. 100; Northcote's Diary, 6 Oct. 1883, printed A. B. Cooke, 'A Conservative party leader in Ulster', pp. 79–80; Northcote to Lord Crichton, [1883], cited P. M Bottomley, 'The North Fermanagh elections of 1885 and 1886', *Clogher Record*, viii (1974), 170; *Belfast Newsletter*, 8 Oct. 1885.

electorate.[1] At the same time, a combination of assimilation and legerdemain kept Protestant agrarian radicalism at bay. In Fermanagh Tory agents insisted that 'the *less landlords* we have [on the platform] the *better*, but we must have some; farmers are the *correct cards* if we can get them'. In Mid-Armagh the Secretary of the Constitutional Association demanded nothing short of the compulsory purchase of landed estates.[2] And even if some local associations were still inefficient, the actual MPs returned must have warmed the heart of the Armagh County Grand Chaplain who had called for men 'not ashamed to wear the Orange colours'. Ten of the sixteen Ulster Conservatives were now Orangemen,[3] and under Saunderson the group as a whole adopted a distinct political identity underpinned by the Orange Institution, various provincial and local organizations, and grass-roots sectarianism.[4] Tensions of course remained. Populist mavericks, beadily searching for the slightest sign of weakness (such as Saunderson's parliamentary vote against compulsory inspection of convent laundries) continued to be a feature of Ulster politics. Yet, in a real and effective sense, the events of the 1880s had managed to impose upon the traditional ingredients of Irish Conservatism—religion, economic power, social cohesion—a new binding agent in the shape of *explicit* (rather than merely latent) Unionism.

III THE MEMBERS RETURNED

The formal object of elections was the return of members to Parliament. The representation of Ireland before the Famine had lain largely with men drawn from the nobility and the landed gentry. Even a stringent definition of 'aristocratic' (sons, brothers, and nephews of peers, baronets and their sons) leaves thirty-one of the 105 men returned in 1832 in so elevated a category. Among Tories

[1] Carleton, Atkinson, & Sloan Papers D1252/42/12; W. J. Locke to J. B. Atkinson, 15 Sept. 1885, J. Monroe to J. B. Atkinson, 18 Sept. 1885, J. B. to J. Atkinson, 18 May 1885, J. Ellis to 'My dear Sir', 20 Aug. 1885, ibid. D1252/42/3/33, 36, 22, 30; calculations by J. B. Atkinson in ibid. D1252/42/3/48; J. Johnston to J. B. Atkinson, 19 Oct. 1885, ibid. D1252/42/3/46; F. Thompson, 'The Armagh elections of 1885-6', pp. 364-7. North Armagh covered the Orange heartlands: Portadown alone had 33 lodges, while a further 157 operated within a nine-mile radius (G. Pellew, *In Castle and Cabin*, pp. 289-95).

[2] P. M. Bottomley, 'The North Fermanagh elections of 1885 and 1886', p. 175; F. Thompson, 'The Armagh elections of 1885-6', p. 372.

[3] P. Buckland, *Irish Unionism Two: Ulster Unionism and the origins of Northern Ireland 1886-1922* (Dublin, 1973), p. 5; Revd T. Ellis, *The Action of the Grand Lodge of the County of Armagh (and the reasons thereof) on the 6th of July, 1885* (Armagh, 1885), p. 4—copy in Carleton, Atkinson, & Sloan Papers D1252/42/3/47; A. McClelland, 'The later Orange Order', p. 131.

[4] D. C. Savage, 'The Origins of the Ulster Unionist party, 1885-6', pp. 185-208.

and Whigs even the 'non-aristocratic' members were, with the exception of a group of lawyers, as often as not, either owners of or heirs to landed property, while no less than thirty-one of the thirty-nine Repeal members of 1832 were landowners 'or men who derived their incomes in whole or in part from the ownership of land'.[1] Repeal, however, seems to have attracted especially strong support from what might best be termed the 'mere' or the declining gentry of the time: men like Dillon Browne (MP for Mayo 1836-50), who was constantly 'embarrassed', addicted to sherry, and sometimes obliged to borrow suits of clothes before appearing in the Chamber, Joseph MacDonnell (MP for Mayo 1846-7), who rarely ventured outside Doo Castle for fear of being arrested for debt, or Feargus O'Connor (MP for Cork 1832-5), the scion of an old but impoverished and declining family in the county.[2] As a result, landed origins did little to endear Repeal members to other MPs at Westminster. And even if a few observers believed Repealers preferable to the new men returned by English boroughs after 1832 'who talk of the " 'ustings" and the " 'ouse" ', most thought them 'wretched specimens . . . their morals . . . [even] judged by Irish standard . . . of the lowest kind'.[3] O'Connell's residually Gaelic life-style repelled English politicians who liked to think themselves 'fastidious'. His followers, wrote one such politician,

are not [a] very creditable looking set. Feargus O'Connor has the appearance of a country attorney. He was involved some time ago in a charge of robbing the mail . . . Daunt and O'Dwyer have more of the ruffian about them. Lalor shews that he has never been in gentlemen's society before . . . Some of the others are not a whit better. They are understood to subsist on O'Connell. His large house in Albermarle Street is their hotel. They live there free of expense, much, as I hear, in the savage style of their own country.[4]

Such hypocritical disdain formed the staple of English attitudes. Even sympathetic Whigs, like Edward Littleton (Chief Secretary 1833-4), bleakly thought that no more than six Irish MPs were worth much consideration. Lord Clarendon, when Viceroy 1847-52, denounced Irish members who gave 'themselves landlord airs' while not possessed of 'a shovelful of land' and patronizingly

[1] J. H. Whyte, 'Daniel O'Connell and the Repeal party', pp. 297-316; A. Macintyre, *The Liberator*, pp. 74, 308.

[2] *Correspondence of Daniel O'Connell The Liberator*, ed. W. J. Fitzpatrick, 2 vols. (London, 1888), ii, 372.

[3] John to George Campbell, 29 Mar. 1833, cited Mrs Hardcastle, *Life of John, Lord Campbell, Lord High Chancellor of Great Britain*, 2 vols. (London, 1881), ii, 34; [D. O. Madden], *Ireland and its Rulers* (London, 1843), cited J. H. Whyte, 'Daniel O'Connell and the Repeal party', p. 297.

[4] *Three early nineteenth-century diaries*, ed. A. Aspinall, p. 314 (Diary of Denis Le Marchant for early Mar. 1833).

recommended one member to Russell as 'a very ridiculous but not ill-disposed savage [who] . . . is quite ready to be your confidential Irish whipper-in'.[1] All of this was part of that great English misunderstanding which ensured that, whenever Ireland should have been seen as another country where things followed a different path it was in fact viewed as an appendix of England, and whenever it should, indeed, have been seen as an appendaged reflection it was regarded as wild, *sui generis*, and remote. 'People', wrote the Under-Secretary, Thomas Larcom, in 1858, 'who come to this country and travel through it, and visit in the houses of the nobility and gentry, and see but the outside, find the same manners, the same habits, the same education, as those to which they are accustomed in England . . . and seeing this they are slow to believe that a different mode of government is necessary.' Peel, on the other hand, referred to 'the gross exaggerations of suffering and distress in Ireland' and believed too readily that Irishmen measured 'privation by a standard of their own'.[2]

With the collapse of the Repeal Party, the Irish parliamentary presence became less threatening, so that fear was replaced by contempt alone. 'None of the impassioned orators of the moment', announced *The Times* in 1852, 'are anything but broken-down black-legs . . . they have run up scores with the waiters of their clubs, and with as many unfortunate tradesmen as they could find silly enough to give them credit.' In Ireland itself, however, candidates were at the same period beginning to find it useful to stress 'popular' elements within their own ancestry. Patrick O'Brien, the eldest son of a baroneted merchant and minor landowner, faced his King's Co. electorate in 1859 with assurances that 'he had sprung from the people—that he was the grandson of a tenant farmer', remarks which produced wails from the genteel to the effect that respectable Conservatives were being defeated by 'a whiskey-seller, whose uncle, the head of the family, still lives in a cabin'.[3] Irish 'Liberals' in general offered a wealth of social contradictions, and ranged from upper-crust Whigs like the Hon. Leopold George Frederick Agar-Ellis (MP for Co. Kilkenny 1857–74), heir to the fifth Viscount Clifden and nephew of both the Earl of Carlisle and the Duke of Sutherland, to haunted bankrupts who were obliged, like

---

[1] Littleton to Anglesey, 2 July 1833, Hatherton Papers D260/M/01/02; Clarendon to Sir C. Wood, 14 Dec. 1849, and to Sir G. Grey, 7 July 1848, Clarendon Papers L.-Bs. V and III; Clarendon to A. R. Blake, 26 July 1847, and to Russell, 20 Nov. 1847, ibid. L.-B. I.

[2] T. Larcom to Naas, Mar. 1858, Larcom Papers MS 7504; Peel to Knight of Kerry, 4 Apr. 1833, FitzGerald Papers.

[3] *The Times*, cited in *Londonderry Sentinel*, 13 Aug. 1852; *Dundalk Democrat*, 21 May 1859; N. W. Senior, *Journals, conversations, and essays relating to Ireland*, ii, 22.

The O'Donoghue, to beg from colleagues, or, like Serjeant Murphy, to locate themselves 'at Boulogne for several months' to escape their creditors. Even less straitened MPs found it difficult sometimes to break into the London clubland which still provided the main clearing-house for privileged political discourse.[1] It was, for example, not only Quakerism which kept the Ulster linen merchant, J. J. Richardson (MP for Lisburn 1853-7), modestly in his two-guinea-a-week London lodgings, nor yet the wholesome presence there of 'good milk, cream, and butter which is not everywhere to be met with in London'. Even the incontrovertibly propertied Catholic landowner, Denis Maurice O'Conor (MP for Co. Sligo 1868-83), found his few visits to the Reform Club embarrassingly cheerless and spent most of his time in London (when not at daily Mass) playing pool and cards for modest stakes at the Catholic Stafford Club. Regular letters home to Bishop Gillooly of Elphin were a lifeline as much as a duty, while the reading of *Phineas Finn* provided O'Conor—a Liberal and then a Home Ruler in no offensive sense of the term—with his only glimpse of a high political world from which he seems so obviously to have been excluded.[2]

Already, however, before the advent of effective Home Rule politics, the landed grip upon the Irish representation was being modestly relaxed. By 1868 no less than seventeen men with predominantly commercial backgrounds were returned, and even so staunchly Conservative a paper as the *Cork Constitution* had long thought it 'excessively silly, in a day like this, to reproach an attorney with presumption because he chooses to aspire to the representation of his native town'.[3] Overall the landed element among MPs declined from 70 per cent in the period 1832-59 to 56 per cent in 1859-85, and the trend (shown in Table 35) was discernible among all political groups. But, whereas the Conservatives never ceased to be the party of broad acres, their more and more nationalist opponents were moving towards a world in which the men of the Bar and of the bar-room were increasingly to constitute the Westminster representatives of a largely agrarian electorate: and this despite the ritual attacks of nationalist newspapers on self-seeking lawyers, and the demands that 'independent, intelligent, and respectable tenant farmers' be

---

[1] Glengall to Stanley, 16 Oct. 1849, Derby Papers 120/2; The O'Donoghue to C. Fortescue, 27 Mar. [1868], Carlingford Papers CP3/65, and to Archbishop McCabe, 11 Nov. 1881, McCabe Papers 346/8; A. E. Pease, *Elections and Recollections* (London, 1932), p. 101.

[2] J. J. Richardson to W. Kirk, 1 Mar. 1854, Kirk Papers D1185/1; Diary of D. M. O'Conor for 1869, N.L.I. Microfilm Positive 5485.

[3] D. Thornley, *Isaac Butt and Home Rule*, p. 207; *C.C.* 25 Feb. 1863.

TABLE 35
Occupations of Irish MPs, 1832–85

| | 1832–59 | | 1859–85 | | 1832–85 |
| | Tories | Others | Tories | Others | All |
	per cent		per cent		per cent
Landed	81.2	65.1	63.0	45.1	62.6
Professional	11.8	17.9	15.3	26.1	19.1
Mercantile	4.8	15.7	9.0	19.5	13.4
Other	2.2	1.3	12.7	9.3	4.9

returned by rural constituencies.[1] In fact, the decline of Irish Conservatism and the collapse of the Liberals actually reduced the number of Members with a direct knowledge of agricultural affairs. At the General Election of 1859 no less than 87 of the 105 Members returned held land, 65 of them more than 2,000 acres and 29 more than 10,000 acres each. Catholic Members, though they owned smaller estates, were hardly less 'landed' than their Protestant colleagues. Even the difference between those who adopted a Whiggish line and those wedded to the Independent Party, though real, was not so large as to involve serious social cleavage.[2] The crucial shift in the representation (as in the nature) of Irish politics occurred between 1868 and 1874. The parliamentary Home Rule Party of 1874, however bogus the ideological credentials of many of its adherents, represented something undeniably new. Now only the Conservatives (despite the populist support on which they often depended) kept the proprietorial flag aloft, for the shrinking band of Liberals was dominated by merchants, Presbyterian divines, and lawyers, as can be seen from Table 36. The gap created by the departure of the landlords was filled, not so much by the purple of commerce (there were actually fewer merchants, financiers, and newspaper proprietors in 1874 than in 1868), but by professional men. Throughout the previous fifty years Irish lawyers in general and barristers in particular had displayed a clear disposition to support whichever group could promise the most patronage. That

[1] *Nation*, 31 Jan. 1874, cited L. J. McCaffrey, 'Irish Federalism in the 1870s', p. 19.

[2] If one divides the amount and valuation (obtained from U. H. H. de Burgh, *The Landowners of Ireland*, and other sources) of land held, by the *total* number in each group and (in parentheses) by the total number holding land in each group, the result is: Catholic MPs 8,122 acres at £3,617 (9,325 at £4,154); Protestant Liberal MPs 8,699 acres at £5,154 (10,223 at £6,063); Protestant Conservative MPs 11,707 acres at £6,337 (14,703 at £7,957); Catholic Independent MPs 3,757 acres at £2,745 (4,592 at £3,355); Catholic Liberal MPs 15,674 acres at £5,667 (all held land); Catholic 'uncertain' MPs 3,197 acres at £1,995 (3,730 at £2,328).

fifteen of the nineteen lawyers returned in 1874 were Home Rulers (at Westminster Home Rulers were the most lawyer-ridden party)[1] is evidence that Ireland's most acute and subtle political seismographs had already registered the rumblings of violent and far-reaching earthquakes ahead.

The work begun in 1868 and 1874 was completed at the elections of 1880 and 1885. Political collapse, in other words, preceded economic retreat. By 1885 even the Conservative Party's complement of proprietors had declined (Table 37): among its eighteen MPs were five lawyers, an apothecary, a local government official, and a retired soldier. Although, in a sense, Dr O'Brien is right to point out that 'from the purely statistical point of view . . . all that happened to the balance of classes [in the Home Rule Party] at the 1880 election was the "replacement" of about ten landlords by the same number of individuals from . . . the lower middle class', contemporary observers were not simply indulging in social hysterics when they believed that fissures were appearing in the composition of the political community. The aged recollections of a disgruntled Frank Hugh O'Donnell—'Penny-a-liners from New York and Lambeth, from Mallow and Drumcondra; out-of-works from half a dozen modest professions . . . [like] the sparkish ranks of the gay and desperate disclassees around Lucius Sergius Catilina'—need not be taken too seriously,[2] but more immediate reactions were no less violent and no less understandable. Conservative newspapers sang a hypocritically bitter threnody of how 'gentlemen who, though Liberals, Roman Catholics, and Home Rulers, were at the same time men of property and position' had been replaced by 'commercial travellers, journalists, non-descript losels of all sorts'. Parnell himself emphasized the difficulty of 'obtaining a sufficient number of gentlemen of a national and honest type'.[3] And when Home Rule meetings were regularly addressed by bakers, publicans, and grocers; when Lysaght Finigan (returned for Ennis in 1879) openly boasted at election meetings 'I am the grandson of a rebel of '98. I am the son of a rebel of '48 . . . I will stand or fall by the [green] flag'; when Parnell loudly denounced The O'Conor Don as 'a sample of West Britishism in Ireland', it was not difficult to believe that one was witnessing the introduction of new rules into the political game.[4]

---

[1] J. C. Hamilton, 'Parties and voting patterns in the parliament of 1874–80', p. 56.

[2] C. C. O'Brien, *Parnell and his Party 1880–90*, p. 19; F. H. O'Donnell, *History of the Irish Parliamentary party*, 2 vols. (London, 1910), i, 467–8: 'Gone were all the colleagues who symbolized the union of Ireland under Isaac Butt; gone Lord Francis Conyngham, our genial whip; gone O'Conor Don, gone Lord Robert Montague, P.C. . . . .'

[3] *Daily Express*, 17, 23 Mar. 1880.

[4] *Daily Express*, 7 Apr., 26 Mar. 1880; *Drogheda Argus*, 17 Apr. 1880.

TABLE 36

The landed element among Irish MPs returned in 1868 and 1874

| | 1868 | | | 1874 | | | |
	Conservatives	Liberals	Total	Conservatives	Liberals	Home Rulers	Total
	per cent			per cent			
Landowners	64.1	43.9	51.4	63.6	42.8	30.0	40.8
Sons of Landowners	25.6	13.6	18.1	15.1	–	8.4	9.8
Total	89.7	57.5	69.5	78.7	42.8	38.4	50.6
(Total N)	(39)	(66)	(105)	(33)	(10)	(60)	(103)

TABLE 37

The landed element among Irish MPs returned in 1880 and 1885

| | 1880 | | | | 1885* | | |
	Conservatives	Liberals	Home Rulers	Total	Conservatives	Nationalists	Total
	per cent				per cent		
Landowners	48.0	20.0	15.9	24.3	33.3	5.9	10.7
Sons of Landowners	20.0	6.7	–	5.9	22.2	1.2	4.8
Total	68.0	26.7	15.9	30.2	55.5	7.1	15.5
(Total N)	(25)	(15)	(63)	(103)	(18)	(85)	(103)

* No Liberals returned in 1885.

The increase in the number of Catholic MPs from thirty-one in 1865 to seventy-five in 1885 added a religious counterpoint to social and economic change. The message was driven home when an official return of March 1885 revealed that only forty-two of the 103 Irish MPs still served on grand juries,[1] and when the General Election later the same year brought forth an eighty-six-strong Nationalist group at Westminster which included seventeen journalists, seventeen lawyers, nine merchants, seven licensed traders, six farmers, five landlords (with more than £1,000 valuation), and four physicians, as well as single representatives of occupations not hitherto thought acceptable in such a context: tailor, grocer, draper, cattle dealer, teacher, money-lender, and manager of an aquarium at New Brighton.[2] The irony, of course, was that such a party was quite unrepresentative, not only of the 'people' at large, but even of its own grass-roots activists. In particular, the failure to recruit farmers—in 1895 they still constituted only a tenth of the parliamentary membership—made the Westminster party seem remote and excessively metropolitan to many of its rural supporters.[3]

Transformations within parties and the rise of new parties act as markers to point the fundamental changes which took place between 1832 and 1885. The Liberals, lacking a permanent or 'natural' constituency, none the less demonstrated a remarkable and parasitic resilience. The triumph of 1868 was achieved because, to the well-tried ingredients of patronage and cash, were fleetingly added the potent symbols of Gladstonian concern. But such fragile pillars proved unable to bear the strains which the decline of localism, and the eventual mobilization of the homogeneous electorate established in 1850, were beginning to place upon the general fabric of Irish politics. The very different history of the Irish Conservatives shows that no constitutional movement in nineteenth-century Ireland could endure without a sectarian base. The popular Protestant revival of the 1830s and 1840s gave a biting edge to what had previously been a rather flabby and unrealistically self-satisfied group. But, if Protestantism was the party's strength, it was also both its particular and its general weakness, for it caused sporadic

---

[1] *Return of members serving in the present parliament for counties and boroughs in Ireland who were not summoned at the recent Spring Assizes by the High Sheriffs to serve as Grand Jurors*, H.C. 1884–5 (277), lxiii, 263–8.

[2] For some useful information and comments, see A. O'Day, *The English face of Irish Nationalism*, pp. 10–50. The group included one MP returned by an English constituency.

[3] P. J. Bull, 'The Reconstruction of the Irish Parliamentary movement, 1895–1903: An analysis with special reference to William O'Brien' (University of Cambridge Ph.D. thesis, 1972), pp. 281–90.

dissension and ensured a virtually permanent minority status in the
country as a whole. What is remarkable is not that the party eventually
shrank into little more than a north-eastern rump, but that this
process was so long delayed. Amidst, however, the changes of the
1880s it is important not to lose sight of the continuities. Although
the Liberal Party no longer existed as an organized force in Ireland,
there were still many, who, *faute de mieux*, entered the ranks of the
new Nationalism, not as enthusiastic apostles of Parnell (or Redmond, or Pearse, or De Valera), but because the Home Rule and
similar movements now offered the only political career open to
ambitious Catholics. And the history of the Irish Parliamentary
Party, especially after 1890, shows how such men continued to
enjoy both power and influence. Indeed, some at least of the old
Liberals never died—they merely faded into the fancy dress of
Home Rule.

V

Violence and Its Modes

I METHODS AND MANPOWER

However circumscribed was the formal authority of landlords, agents, priests, and other public men, the tensions which existed, now strongly now flickeringly, within nineteenth-century Irish society were often sharp enough to persuade many Irishmen that violence alone could redress their grievances. Ever since the Whiteboy outbreaks of the 1760s the intermittent discontents of the countryside had become increasingly patterned into a particular tradition of action characterized at its most developed by almost theatrical styles and repertoires: white shirts and straw caps and 'murders, robberies, burnings of houses, houghing of cattle, serving of threatening notices, [and] severely beating obnoxious persons'. By 1845, when the authorities had officially begun to distinguish between those peculiarly Irish categories of crime called 'outrages' and 'agrarian outrages', the 673 offences which occurred in Roscommon alone were pigeon-holed under no less than twenty-two headings, of which homicide, firing at the person, appearing armed, attacking houses, turning up land, maiming cattle, and sending threatening notices were only the most visible.[1] In counties like Tipperary violence developed a self-generating tradition, and local observers could talk almost casually of 'three or four murders committed on the townland . . . several attacks . . . [the] murder of two bailiffs'. Spasmodic lurches into real cruelty—roasting alive, mutilation by nails, ear cropping of man and beast—added a fearful counterpoint to what was usually a highly formal tune.[2] Comparisons with the Thugs of India, warnings not to travel unarmed, and predictions of universal

[1] G. C. Lewis, *On local Disturbances in Ireland, and on the Irish Church Question* (London, 1836), pp. 33, 185 (references to the Cork reprint of 1977); J. S. Donnelly Jr., 'The Whiteboy Movement 1761-5', *Irish Historical Studies*, xxi (1978), 29. For Roscommon, see the Return in Graham Papers 28/Ir for the period 1 Mar. 1845-17 Mar. 1846.

[2] See the summary of evidence of four Longford witnesses in *Devon Index* (where eleven pages are devoted to 'Outrages, Agrarian'), pp. 298-9; also Lord De Grey to Sir J. Graham, 27 May 1842, Graham Papers 7/Ir. For cruelty in general, see G. C. Lewis, *On local Disturbances*, pp. 88, 95, 119-20, 183-4; *D.E.P.* 14 Nov. 1837; *Evidence taken before Her Majesty's Commissioners of Inquiry into the State of the Law and Practice in respect to the Occupation of Land in Ireland* [henceforth *Devon Commission*], parts ii and iii, H.C. 1845 [616, 657], xx and xxi, Witness Nos. 684, 823; Graham to Lord Heytesbury, 16 Nov. 1844, Graham Papers 18/Ir.

chaos constituted a common discourse among the comfortable classes. Viceroys envisaged rivers of blood, magistrates reported 'profound terror', Crown solicitors thought the people 'demoralized', landlords drilled servants into private armies to protect their estates.[1]

Yet the fact that perceptions, however important to the actors involved, were often distorted, did not go entirely unnoticed even at the time, for, in reality, the violence of pre-Famine Ireland was both less constant and less universal than has often been supposed. Even in 1847, when 'total outrages' reached their peak, the summer quarter sessions and assizes at Tralee in Kerry were devoted almost entirely to minor larcenies, sheep-stealing, or 'the passing of base coin'.[2] 'The fact is', wrote the Chief Secretary in 1833, 'that with the exception of tithes, there have been no more outrages here for a month past than in the best part of England.' And a decade later the gloomy majority of witnesses with 'views' on violence appearing before the Devon Commission was challenged by a substantial minority from twenty-three counties who repeatedly mentioned the 'rarity' and 'fewness' of local outrages and the calm and peace which pervaded their respective districts.[3] Violence, however, there undoubtedly was, and whatever its precise incidence in pre-Famine Ireland—for which certain *crime* levels must often stand historical surrogate—its nature, the manner in which it mediated between social groups, and its geographical distribution reflected the tensions within Irish society in general and rural society in particular. As there is no evidence to suggest that towns were especially disturbed (indeed the contrary is argued below), it is clear that, with in 1841 less than 14 per cent of the population living in towns of 2,000 or more inhabitants and less than 18 per cent even in places with 500 or more,[4] most violence was almost certainly of a *rural* (if not always

---

[1] Lord Hillsborough to Sir R. Peel, [May 1839], Downshire Papers D671/C/12/745; W. Moloney to—, [Jan. 1835], O.P. 1835/152, Box 47; Various reports of 1833 in Melbourne Papers 94/86–95; Lord Clarendon to Lord John Russell, 12, 15, 19 Nov. 1847, Clarendon Papers L.-B. I; J. Carden to Lord Donoughmore, 10 Nov. [1844], Graham Papers 18/Ir; Lord Roden to Lord Eliot, 21, 25 Sept. 1843, ibid. 5/Ir.

[2] *Kerry Evening Post*, 3, 21 July 1847.

[3] E. Littleton to Lord Melbourne, 2 Oct. 1833, Melbourne Papers 96/40. See *Devon Commission*, Witness Nos. (by counties): Antrim (99); Armagh (79, 86); Carlow (965, 967); Clare (571, 574, 591, 592, 600, 601, 605, 606, 608); Cork (704, 715, 741, 798); Donegal (158, 181, 186, 203, 278); Down (90); Galway (513, 542); Kerry (668, 692); Kilkenny (16, 881, 882, 884, 890, 894, 897); King's Co. (1005); Leitrim (381, 398); Limerick (614, 615, 641); Londonderry (163); Longford (408); Monaghan (239, 249, 324, 327); Queen's Co. (867, 986); Tipperary (830, 843, 852); Tyrone (213); Waterford (824, 828, 903); Westmeath (417, 426); Wexford (924, 931); Wicklow (960, 1019, 1021). These include landlords, agents, farmers, priests, parsons, ministers, lawyers, etc.

[4] 2,000 and more = 13.9 per cent; 500 and more = 17.8 per cent (*Irish Historical Statistics:*

of an agrarian) character. As such, it tended to spark off in almost all directions and to create animosities and alliances between almost every group. In this respect, the recent scholarly emphasis upon the fundamental rift between labourers, cottiers, and the smallest farmers on the one hand, and more substantial men on the other, should not obscure other realities: that many of the latter participated in or sympathized with violent acts, that large farmers used violence against the poor, that violent contact between labourers and landlords could bypass intermediate groups, that, as a lingua franca among all classes, violence sometimes cut across the obvious economic and social patternings of rural life.

The substantial body of contemporary opinion which stressed the 'wretchedness' of those involved in rural crime and pointed to the prominence of labourers, cottiers, and small farmers, is tempered, though not overturned, by evidence of the sporadic participation of more prosperous farmers and of the importance of land occupation (essentially but not exclusively a farmer issue) as the central problem of rural conflict. Throughout the quarter-century before the Famine, witnesses at government inquiries, leading administrators, and articulate men in general kept reminding one another that those who committed violent crimes were 'of the lowest description; persons who have no homes' (1824), 'of the very lowest class' (1832), the 'lowest dregs' (1837), 'persons having very small tenures of land and farm servants . . . the very lowest orders' (1841).[1] Certainly the bulk of Irishmen transported to Australia were rural labourers. Certainly the literacy levels of those committed at assizes and quarter sessions in the 1840s give some support to the notion of a set of

---

Population, 1821–1971, ed. W. E. Vaughan and A. J. Fitzpatrick (Dublin, 1978), p. 27, and H. Mason, 'The development of the urban pattern in Ireland 1841–1881' (University of Wales Ph.D. thesis, 1969), p. 104.

[1] G. C. Lewis, *On local Disturbances*, pp. 148–9; *Fictitious Votes, Ireland*, 2nd series, 3rd report, p. 229; *Minutes of evidence taken before the select committee of the House of Lords, appointed to inquire into the state of Ireland since the year 1835 in respect to Crime and Outrage*, H.C. 1839 (486), xi and xii, Q. 322; Mr and Mrs S. C. Hall, *Ireland: Its Scenery, Character etc.*, 3 vols. (London, 1841–3), ii, 126–7. For further linguistic variations on this theme, see *Minutes of evidence taken before the select committee appointed to examine into the nature and extent of the disturbances which have prevailed in those districts of Ireland which are now subject to the provisions of the Insurrection Act*, H.C. 1825 (20), vii, 38, 75; *Minutes of evidence taken before the select committee of the House of Lords appointed (in 1824) to examine into the nature and extent of the disturbances which have prevailed in those districts of Ireland which are now subject to the provisions of the Insurrection Act*, H.C. 1825 (200), vii, 532–3, 637, 644–5; *Report from the select committee on the State of Ireland*, H.C. 1831–2 (677), xvi, 105–6; D. O'Connell to Lord Duncannon, 14 Jan. 1833, *The Correspondence of Daniel O'Connell*, ed. M. R. O'Connell, 8 vols. (Dublin, 1972–80), v, 3; M. Greene to W. Gossett, 6 Mar. 1835, O.P. 1835/166, Box 47; *Crime and Outrage Committee*, H.C. 1839 (486), xi and xii, Qs. 322, 6303, 7452, 14450; *Devon Commission*, Witness Nos. 547, 1051, 1101. See also note 1 p. 345 below.

lumpen marauders.[1] Certainly the comparative youth of those who committed outrages, those tried in court, those killed in agrarian clashes with the police or involved in election riots, rural Ribbonism, Orangeism, and Fenianism, suggests that comfortable farmers were not especially prominent.[2] Certainly many of the demands most commonly made reflected the aspirations of labourers and cottiers: employment, higher wages, potato plots at reasonable rents.[3] And as the conditions of the labourer class grew steadily worse, so all these issues helped widen the gap between the more prosperous farmers and those beneath them. On the other hand, even the conacre problem made a highly erratic appearance on the platform of contemporary complaints. In some areas at some times, for example Clare and Roscommon in the early 1830s, lack of conacre was the single most important propellant of rural violence, with thousands assembling to dig up pasture land at night so that potatoes might be grown upon it.[4] Here farmers were the prime objects of attack and were to be found loudly denouncing the 'lower classes', demanding coercion, even organizing their own secret violence to depress wages and keep inferiors in their place.[5] The whole relationship seems,

---

[1] L. L. Robson, *The Convict Settlers of Australia: An enquiry into the origin and character of the convicts transported to New South Wales and Van Dieman's Land 1787–1852* (Melbourne, 1965), pp. 10–70; *Thom 1852*, p. 201; J. Haughton, 'The social and moral elevation of our working classes', *Journal of the Statistical and Social Inquiry Society of Ireland*, ii (1857), 63–72.

[2] See, e.g., *D.E.P.* 27 Dec. 1834 (victims of Rathcormac 'massacre'); G. C. Lewis, *On local Disturbances*, pp. 146 ff.; *Devon Commission*, Witness No. 570; lists of those tried by special commissions 1848 in Clarendon Papers Box 75; *Report from the select committee on Outrages (Ireland)*, H.C. 1852 (438), xiv, Qs. 146–9, and Carlingford Papers Diary of C. Fortescue II (16 Sept. 1856) (Ribbonism); J. M. Wilson, *Statistics of Crime in Ireland, 1842–1856* (Dublin, 1857), pp. 14–16, 32–7; R. M. Hassard to Clarendon, 9 Apr. 1848, Clarendon Papers Box 17 (Orangeism); H. H. van der Wusten, 'Iers verzet tegen de staatkundige eenheid der Britse eilanden 1800–1921' (University of Amsterdam Doctorate thesis, 1977), pp. 91–2 (Fenianism). For election riots, see Reports of Constable Causion, 2 Aug. 1852, O.P. 1852/15/264, Box 1218; of E. Collins, RM, 8 May 1859, R.P. 1859/4340, Box 808; *Banner of Ulster*, 4 Apr. 1857; T. P. Cunningham, 'The Burrowes-Hughes by-election [in Cavan, 1855]', *Breifne*, iii (1967), 201.

[3] *Athlone Conservative Advocate*, 17, 31 Aug. 1837; *Devon Commission*, Witness No. 39; J. Young to Palmerston, 10 Jan. 1828, Broadlands Archive 27M60, Box cxxiii.

[4] S. J. Connolly, 'Catholicism and Social Discipline in pre-Famine Ireland' (New University of Ulster D.Phil. thesis, 1977), pp. 597–601, and *idem, Priests and People in pre-Famine Ireland 1780–1845* (Dublin, 1982), pp. 237–9; *D.E.P.* 1831, *passim*; Co. Clare Witnesses in *Devon Commission*, Nos. 571, 572, 574, 579, 586, 625; Co. Limerick Witness in ibid., No. 652; G. C. Lewis, *On local Disturbances*, pp. 70, 91, 180, 184; A. de Vere to Lord Ebrington, 9 June 1840, Fortescue Papers 1262M/LI148; 'A Magistrate of the County', *The present state of Tipperary as regards agrarian outrages, their nature, origin, and increase, considered* (Dublin, 1842), p. 21.

[5] *Committee of the House of Lords appointed to examine into . . . the disturbances of Ireland*, H.C. 1825 (200), vii, 593, 707; Report of J. Sandys, 13 Dec. 1831, O.P. 1835/572, Box 1842; *Papers relating to the State of Ireland*, H.C. 1834 (459), xlvii, 424–5; G. C. Lewis, *On local Disturbances*, p. 92; *Crime and Outrage Committee*, H.C. 1839 (486), xi and xii,

indeed, to have resembled nothing so much as an agrarian version of the psychological condition of *folie à deux* in which two parties drive each other to manic instability by their very proximity and the intensity of their mutually destructive attitudes.[1]

On closer examination, however, this simple picture of an all-pervasive labourer–farmer antagonism melts into the same complicated historical chiaroscuro which some time ago overtook the notion of tenant–landlord conflict as the sole key to the realities of Irish rural life. The harder one looks the more do single explanations dissolve into an almost impenetrable fusion of impressionistic complexities. Thus, however important wages, employment, and conacre were as issues of conflict, the occupation of land seems to have overwhelmed all other concerns in the minds of those embarking on acts of agrarian violence. And although 'occupation' was not without its interest for men with conacre, it was predominantly a matter of *direct* concern to tenant farmers of all kinds. Motivations were naturally often mixed. The agrarian secret societies of Queen's Co. in the 1830s made socially comprehensive demands and 'endeavoured to procure a rise of wages, to prevent people being turned out of their holdings, and to lower the rents'. In Monaghan, farmer demands for tithe reform and cottier demands for low conacre rents merged into an uneasy local unity.[2] But the evidence is overwhelming that occupation stood at the core of discontent. 'The leading objects', Colonel Miller of the constabulary told the Devon Commission, 'are to regulate arbitrarily the letting and holding of land, and to sustain, under all circumstances, the tenant, whatever his irregularities or breaches of covenant may be.'[3] Some 200 unambiguous reasons for

---

Qs. 6523–5, 13413–14; Clarendon to Russell, 26 Jan. 1848, and Russell to Clarendon, 28 Jan. 1848, Clarendon Papers L.-B. II and Box 43; Lord Carew to Clarendon, [Apr. 1848], ibid. Box 8; J. Lee, 'The Ribbonmen' in *Secret Societies in Ireland*, ed. T. D. Williams (Dublin, 1973), pp. 29–30, and *idem*, 'Patterns of rural unrest in nineteenth-century Ireland: A preliminary survey' in *Ireland and France 17th–20th Centuries: Towards a comparative study of rural history*, ed. L. M. Cullen and F. Furet (Paris, 1980), p. 225; D. Fitzpatrick's review of S. Clark's *Social origins of the Irish Land War* in *Irish Economic and Social History*, viii (1981), 140–1.

[1] Lord Mulgrave to Melbourne, 22 Feb. [1836], Melbourne Papers 99/120 (cited above in Chapter II, pp. 94–5). For a recent account of early-nineteenth-century agrarian violence which adopts a rather different view of social relationships and tensions in the countryside, see M. [R.] Beames, *Peasants and Power: The Whiteboy Movements and their control in pre-Famine Ireland* (Brighton, 1983).

[2] G. C. Lewis, *On local Disturbances*, p. 62 (Queen's Co.); J. Evatt (agent) to Lord Bath, 1 June, 7 Nov. 1832, Bath Papers Irish Box (Monaghan). On the broad distinction (even rivalry) between the tithe and the conacre agitations, see P. O'Donoghue, 'Opposition to Tithe Payments in 1830–31', *Studia Hibernica*, No. 6 (1966), 90–3, who does, however, allow that 'in some places they merged and here the [tithe] opposition was generally more violent' (p. 92).

[3] *Devon Commission*, Witness No. 1101. See also, e.g., Lord De Grey to Graham,

TABLE 38

Reasons for outrages given by witnesses before the
Devon Commission, 1844

	Occupation of land per cent	Conacre and employment per cent	Other reasons per cent	N
Leinster	62.2	2.2	35.6	45
Munster	57.3	13.6	29.1	103
Ulster	48.6	0.0	51.4	37
Connacht	13.3	46.7	40.0	15
Ireland	53.5	11.0	35.5	200

rural violence were given by the 234 witnesses examined by the Commission on the matter. Outside Connacht (where the number of cases was small) few doubted that occupation was far more important in driving men to violent acts than conacre and employment put together (Table 38). A decade earlier more than half of the serious crimes with assignable causes committed in Munster were calculated by the police to have been concerned with occupation, tithes, rents, and taxes, and less than a sixth with the employment and wages of labourers.[1]

The substantial involvement of farmers' sons in agrarian outrages provided a bridge between those labourers engaged in rural violence and the farmer community as a whole. Particularly at times of distress farmers hovered between open encouragement of violence and tacit sympathy. Smaller farmers (variously defined as those with less than ten or twenty acres) were widely thought to furnish the *leadership* of secret societies, while even larger men with 300 acres could sometimes prevaricate uneasily between admiration and fear.[2] Already in the 1780s the Rightboys had sometimes been led by

27 May 1842, Graham Papers 7/Ir; Lord Eliot to Graham, 11 Sept. 1843, ibid. 5/Ir (reporting a Tipperary stipendiary); G. C. Lewis, *On local Disturbances*, pp. 87 ff.; M. R. Beames, 'Rural Conflict in pre-Famine Ireland: Peasant Assassinations in Tipperary 1837-1847', *Past and Present*, No. 81 (1978), 85-8.

[1] G. C. Lewis, *On local Disturbances*, pp. 84-7, 281-5.

[2] Clarendon (reporting a Limerick stipendiary) to Russell, 3 Dec. 1847, Clarendon Papers L.-B. II; T. Garvin, *The evolution of Irish nationalist politics* (Dublin, 1981), p. 42; also *Devon Commission*, Witness No. 15; *Crime and Outrage Committee*, H.C. 1839 (486), xi and xii, Q. 10782. On the importance of farmers' sons, see 'A Magistrate of the County', *The present state of Tipperary*, Appendix 2; *Devon Commission*, Witness Nos. 16 (Kilkenny lawyer) and 547 (King's Co. agent); J. Lee, 'The Ribbonmen', pp. 28-9. On the involvement of farmers of all sorts, see T. Garvin, op. cit. 37; *D.E.P.* 16, 30 Dec. 1834 (Armagh, Queen's Co.); G. C. Lewis, *On local Disturbances*, pp. 146-9; *Crime and Outrage Committee*, op. cit. Qs. 1391-3; *Devon Commission*, Witness Nos. 869 (Queen's Co. agent) and 1051 (Tipperary solicitor); Printed Memorandum for Cabinet by Sir T. Redington, Under-Secretary, 25 Oct. 1846, Royal Archives RA D15.

farmers and had developed an eclectic programme appealing to virtually all classes. And as Cornewall Lewis pointed out in 1836, many countrymen, 'though they may not have a present, yet they may have a future interest in the matter [of farming]; though they may not be personally concerned, yet their kinsmen and fellows are concerned'.[1] In such ways could aspirations, on the one side, and mingled sympathy and fear, on the other, lead to a confluence as well as to an antagonism of attitudes and behaviour. An experienced land agent thought three-hundred-acre farmers encouraged Tipperary outrages in the 1840s, a local lawyer that farmers sustained servants known to be violent, a landlord that 'strong' farmers in economic difficulties protected midnight marauders, a shopkeeper that farmers benefited most from rural intimidation. The apocalyptic expectations of Protestant annihilation during the 1830s were common to labourers and farmers alike. 'Intimidation', it was claimed in 1845, 'is everywhere and amongst all classes.' 'I do not', a police officer remarked in 1839, 'make any distinctions; I think the peasantry generally [involved] . . . There have been farmers convicted; but generally speaking I think I would say the lower classes.'[2] Farmers fearful of losing their land could see in rural violence—even when it was not concerned with occupation and even perhaps when it was directed against their own kind—a bulwark against modernization and change. As a shopkeeper observed in 1844, 'You may execute a decree upon them, and sell the last farthing, but touch the farm, and turn them out, and they get frantic and wild—the mind gets changed, and there is sure some misfortune to follow from that.'[3] An unusually direct insight into the ambivalence of the more prosperous is given in a letter from a substantial Limerick farmer to his brother, a military clerk in the Army.

The visit of the Rockites did not alarm me when I found they only wanted arms . . . Certainly the fools were not disposed to do any damage . . . I know many unfortunate fellows who I am sure are engaged in this trade and word has been conveyed to us not to be at all apprehensive as that no injury will be done us . . . If I ever knew the fellows who called on me I would not prosecute them, they acted kindly under the circumstances.[4]

[1] J. S. Donnelly Jr., 'The Whiteboy Movement 1761-5', pp. 34-9, and 'The Rightboy Movement 1785-8', *Studia Hibernica*, No. 17/18 (1977-8), 127, 137-43; G. C. Lewis, *On local Disturbances*, p. 154.

[2] *Devon Commission*, Witness Nos. 8, 15, 30, 567; —to W. Gossett, 11 Jan. 1833, O.P. 1833, Box 2454, Bundle 1; Heytesbury to Graham, 29 May 1845, Graham Papers 21/Ir; *Crime and Outrage Committee*, H.C. 1839 (486), xi and xii, Qs. 1391-3.

[3] *Devon Commission*, Witness No. 567.

[4] William to Charles Hogan, 7 June 1847, Clarendon Papers Box 23 (sent by Lord de Ros). See also de Ros to Clarendon, 13 Mar. 1848, and W. to C. Hogan, 4 Apr. 1848, ibid.

No simple picture, therefore, can emerge of either the victims or the perpetrators of rural violence. The occupation of land may well have been predominantly a farmer 'matter', yet the victims of the outrages in which it was a prime concern were usually farmers themselves, more specifically farmers who had taken land from which others had been evicted or to which others were assumed to have a more substantial 'claim'. Labourers too took action against other labourers who offered to pay higher conacre rents or to work for lower wages. Victims and executants changed from place to place and time to time. The great majority of those tried for largely agrarian offences by the special commissions in Clare and Limerick in January 1848 (67 out of 80) were labourers, and most had been involved in attacks on farmers.[1] But while farmers were also the most likely targets for serious violence in the six most disturbed counties in early 1846 (for which unusually full information is available, as shown in Table 39), they suffered more because of disputes over the occupation of land than because of conflicts concerning labour or conacre. Violence, it seems, was mounted by farmers and labourers in very roughly similar proportions. But

TABLE 39

Victims and motives of serious 'agrarian' outrages, January to May 1846, in the six most disturbed counties: Clare, Leitrim, Limerick, Longford, Roscommon, Tipperary

	Victims per cent	Main grievances against
Farmers	61.3	Occupation of land
Labours and servants	14.3	Employment
Gentlemen and agents	13.1	Occupation and employment
Bailiffs, etc.	5.2	Rent
Others	6.1	—
	Motives per cent	
Occupation of land	35.2 ⎱	43.5 (?Farmers)
Rent	8.3 ⎰	
Employment and wages	17.6 ⎱	32.3 (?Labourers, etc.)
Conacre	14.7 ⎰	
Obtaining arms	15.3	
Other	8.9	

N = 1,027

[1] Lists of prisoners in Clarendon Papers Box 75. The mean age of the labourers was twenty-six and a half, of the farmers thirty-one. Two-thirds of the Limerick prisoners were unmarried. See also J. Lee, 'The Ribbonmen', p. 29.

although farmers seem to have been particularly prominent as victims of assaults etc. in all of these counties, labourers were much more likely to suffer murder or attempted murder both there and in Ireland as a whole, as Table 40 indicates.

TABLE 40

Victims (by occupation) of homicide and attempted homicide in A: Ireland 1842-5, and B: Clare, Leitrim, Limerick, Longford, Roscommon, Tipperary 1842-5

	A (N = 874) per cent	B (N = 384) per cent
Farmers	19.8	26.8
Labourers and servants	45.9	39.3
Gentlemen and agents	6.6	7.6
Bailiffs, etc.	6.8	·8.3
'Poor Persons'	6.9	6.0
Others	14.0	12.0

Now, although not all such homicides were agrarian,[1] what cannot be doubted is that landlords and agents constituted only secondary targets. Indeed, not only were farmers and labourers the leading producers and consumers of violence, but both aimed their acts as often against fellow-farmers and fellow-labourers as across the social boundaries of the time. The activities of the various agrarian secret societies reflected this state of things. Their endlessly changing names reveal essentially local concerns, even though the so-called 'Ribbon' element was occasionally able to undertake political forays beyond the economic heartlands of the dominant Whiteboy tradition. Overall, however, it is difficult to make clear distinctions[2] and only

[1] M. R. Beames, 'Rural Conflict in pre-Famine Ireland', pp. 75-91. Although only about a sixth of the actual murders in these years were adjudged 'agrarian' by the authorities (*Return of Outrages reported to the Royal Irish Constabulary Office from 1st January 1844 to 31st December 1880*, H.C. 1881 [C 2756], lxxvii, 887-914), more detailed police reports emphasize the broadly agrarian or quasi-agrarian nature of many of them (*Extracts made by Colonel M'Gregor from the police reports, stating the particulars of the principal homicides in Ireland in the years 1845 and 1846*, H.C. 1846 (179), xxxv, 261-72).

[2] T. Garvin, 'Defenders, Ribbonmen and others: Underground political networks in pre-Famine Ireland', *Past and Present*, No. 96 (1982), 133-55, and M. R. Beames, 'The Ribbon Societies: Lower-class nationalism in pre-Famine Ireland', ibid. No. 97 (1982), 128-43 do make some convincing distinctions, but see Sir H. Vivian (Commander of the forces in Ireland) to Sir T. Arbuthnot, 19 July 1831, and to Lord Fitzroy, 13 Aug. 1831, Vivian Papers No. 10; E. Stanley to Melbourne, 26 Mar. 1833, *Lord Melbourne's Papers*, ed. L. C. Sanders (London, 1889), pp. 193-4; *First report from the select committee appointed to inquire into the nature, character, extent, and tendency of Orange Lodges, Associations, or Societies in Ireland*, H.C. 1835 (377), xv, 322; *Crime and Outrage Committee*, H.C. 1839 (486), xi and xii, Qs. 328, 612; *Devon Commission*, Witness Nos. 15, 27, 38; G. C. Lewis, *On local Disturbances*, pp. 62, 88; extracts from various official inquiries made for Lord Clarendon, Clarendon Papers Box 67 (especially Papers E and F).

a handful of generalizations carry much conviction: that the societies recruited mostly labourers, cottiers, and small farmers; that they could be very large and comparatively open in their activities; that they probably declined somewhat after the late 1830s.[1] Nor does it seem, from the disturbed state of Tipperary in the pre-Famine decades, that their extensive presence was a necessary precondition for the existence of local violence. They helped the orchestration but they did not write the tune.[2]

Though none of this undermines earlier comments regarding the tensions in rural Ireland between farmers and labourers, it would be misleading to ignore the existence, before the Famine especially, of a 'peasant class' made up of labourers, cottiers, and small farmers, with even many substantial farmers obtaining occasional honorary membership. In relation to the 'traditional rights' of conacre and undisturbed occupation this 'class' simultaneously exhibited those hallmarks of solidarity (protection of 'class' values) and dissension (punishment of the *many* transgressors who restricted conacre or took evicted land) which were its most distinctive characteristics. Solidarity was expressed by a moral rhetoric which declared 'killing no murder'; by a general approval of outrages (many of which were committed quite openly before appreciative audiences); by the integration of activists within the local community and their protection from the authorities; ultimately by the considerable effectiveness of the business as a whole.[3] Thus, although the common opinion that most outrages occurred at night is true enough, a substantial number were not thought to need nocturnal concealment.[4] Of the (mostly agrarian) outrages committed in Tipperary and Leitrim in 1846 to which precise times can be assigned, about a third were 'daylight' events, as were two-fifths of the 673 which took place in Roscommon between 1 March 1845 and 17 March 1846.[5]

---

[1] Clarendon Extracts (see note 2 p. 349) Paper G; *Fictitious Votes, Ireland*, 2nd series, 3rd report, p. 229; J. Evatt to Lord Bath, 4 Dec. 1832, Bath Papers Irish Box, Hon. A. Westenra to W. Gossett, 3 Jan. 1833, O.P. 1832/90, Box 2173, *D.E.P.* 16 Dec. 1834, *Report from the select committee on Bribery at Elections*, H.C. 1835 (547), viii, 363-4, *First report . . . Orange Lodges*, H.C. 1835 (377), xv, 24, *Crime and Outrage Committee*, H.C. 1839 (486), xi and xii, Qs. 2296, 2315, 2349, *Papers relating to an investigation held at Castlewellan into the occurrences at Dolly's Brae, on the 12th July 1849*, H.C. 1850 [1143], li, 331-83; *Devon Commission*, Witness Nos. 89, 143, 558, 592, 965, 972.

[2] De Grey to Graham, 27 May 1842, Graham Papers 7/Ir; Major E. Priestly, RM to Lord Eliot, 30 Sept. 1843, ibid. 6/Ir; *Fictitious Votes, Ireland*, 1st series, 1st report, p. 376.

[3] See comments about Co. Kilkenny in 1832-3 by a local stipendiary cited in Printed Cabinet Papers CAB37/7/26; Report of Chief Constable Meredith, 23 Jan. 1835, O.P. 1835, Box 46; *Devon Commission*, Witness No. 547; G. C. Lewis, *On local Disturbances*, p. 184.

[4] *Athlone Conservative Advocate*, 31 Aug. 1837; *Devon Commission*, Witness Nos. 547 (King's Co. agent), 567 (Tipperary shopkeeper), 643 (Limerick farmer), 657 (Limerick agent).

[5] Newcastle Papers Ne c 9539 (Tipperary and Leitrim); Lord Crofton to Heytesbury, 17 Mar. 1846, Graham Papers 28/Ir (Roscommon). Much the same continued to be the

The pressures to 'go with the tide' were also clearly great.[1] Men not at all directly involved in disputes were still prepared actively to punish offenders against the communal code.[2] Virtually universal was a broad feeling of sympathy towards violence, something which drove men of property into apoplectic rage: 'It is not to be wondered at, that murder stalks abroad in the glare of day, to commit his foul deeds, when every cottage is his sanctuary [and] . . . the epithet "informer" is looked on as being far more derogatory than that of "murderer".'[3]

Despite, therefore, the loose contemporary use of the term 'banditti' to describe those who committed rural outrages,[4] it is clear that in the popular mind such men were not criminals and were in no sense separated from their local communities, for, as an experienced Munster lawyer remarked in the 1830s, 'very soon after disturbances have ceased . . . they have become quiet and peaceable, and have returned to their former occupations'.[5] Indeed, the pseudo-legal formularies used by secret societies both generally and in their threatening notices (which combine the languages of Dracula and the judiciary in pretty equal proportions) as well as the alternative 'courts' set up to 'try' transgressors against the popular code show a profound wish to operate, not outside law as such, but merely outside the corrupt laws of a distant and questionably legitimate authority. The aims most constantly kept in view were limited, socially conservative, and above all realistic—lower tithes, smaller rents, more potato ground, more work, more security—not jackpot

case in the 1860s (Lord Mountmorres to Sir T. Larcom, 29 Oct. 1868, Larcom Papers MS 7762; Printed Memorandum on Irish Crime, 19 Jan. 1870, Gladstone Papers Add. MS 44613, fos. 16-40ᵛ).

[1] *D.E.P.* 30 Dec. 1834, 3 Jan. 1835. 'They have matters so organized that I could not live amongst them, buy or sell or get my work done unless I did in some degree go with the tide' (E. Parke to E. Ashley, 20 Nov. 1880, Broadlands Archive 27M60, Box clxxiv). See also *Minutes of evidence taken before the select committee on the Galway Town election petition*, H.C. 1857 (187 Sess. 2), vi, 556.

[2] *Devon Commission*, Witness Nos. 15, 30, 547, 560, 1051, 1101; G. C. Lewis, *On local Disturbances*, p. 182; *A Young Irishman's Diary (1836-1847) Being extracts from the early journal of John Keegan of Moate*, ed. W. Clare (March, Cambs., 1928), p. 32; M. R. Beames, 'Rural Conflict in pre-Famine Ireland', p. 86.

[3] 'A Magistrate of the County', *The present state of Tipperary*, pp. 13-14. See Eliot to Graham, 9 Nov. 1841, Graham Papers 8/Ir; De Grey to Graham, 27 May 1842, ibid. 7/Ir; T. Garvin, *The evolution of Irish nationalist politics*, p. 37; *Devon Commission*, Witness Nos. 8, 15, 567, 1051, 1094.

[4] As in Thomas Murray (agent) to Lord Downshire, 23 Nov. 1834 (Downshire Papers D671/C/9/402), also describing 'real' banditti in what had clearly become boggy 'badlands' around Edenderry; Lord Clanricarde to Clarendon, 29 Nov. 1847, Clarendon Papers Box 9; Mulgrave to Melbourne, 23 Feb. [1836], Melbourne Papers 99/121; *Ballyshannon Herald*, 22 Sept. 1837.

[5] M. Barrington cited in G. C. Lewis, *On local Disturbances*, p. 183 (also p. 192); Sir T. Redington (Under-Secretary) in *Further Correspondence on the Subject of Convict Discipline and Transportation*, H.C. 1850 [1285], xlv, 88-9; printed 'Memorandum on the State of Ireland', 9 Jan. 1847, Royal Archives RA D16/15; J. Lee, 'The Ribbonmen', pp. 31-2.

demands of immediate riches for all.[1] Sometimes careful distinctions
were even made between 'deserving' and 'undeserving' tenants, so
that farmers who had been excused large arrears and given emigration money by their landlords were not always supported with any
extremity of zeal. 'Good' (which is to say non-interfering, non-
modernizing, low-rent-charging) landlords were often recognized as
such and no general wish was expressed until much later for the
abolition of landlordism in general. 'Believe me', wrote a Tipperary
secret society boss to a landlord in 1841, 'I hold a greater esteem for
you than to put you on a level with Tyrents. I respect the law . . .
What I want to put down is what you can't get at by the law of the
land—that is Tyrents of all descriptions—wicked rich men that is
denounced in the Criptures, when their own bellies is pampered, has
no compassion for the poor.'[2] Bad men, rather than bad institutions,
were blamed for the evils of the social order. 'If there were Catholic
lords' in Parliament, the Irish-speaking draper and schoolmaster,
Humphrey O'Sullivan, told a Kilkenny meeting in 1832, 'the present
swadlers could not be calumniating us.' Thus 'acceptable' conacre
rents were often computed and there were few demands of free plots
for all.[3] At the same time, acts of violence were presented as instru-
mental, not only in obtaining general protection, but in redressing
the specific grievances of the poor such as retail profiteering or the
abduction of young girls by wealthy libertines.[4] But because the Irish
tenants' belief in their prescriptive claims to land was part of a highly
developed and often individualistic sense of property rights in everything from profit and jobs to poor relief and pitches at fair grounds,
such expressions of communal solidarity often stood in destructive
tension against the undoubted hostility and suspicions which existed

---

[1] See, e.g., *First report . . . Orange Lodges*, H.C. 1835 (377), xv, 24; W. G. Broehl Jr.,
The Molly Maguires (Cambridge, Mass., 1964), p. 25; W. S. Trench, *Realities of Irish Life*,
4th edn. (London, 1869), plate No. 3 between pp. 46 and 47; T. Garvin, *The evolution of
Irish nationalist politics*, pp. 37–40; W. H. Curran to Lord Anglesey, 4 Apr. 1833, Melbourne
Papers 94/101 (on 'courts' known as 'committees of association' in east Galway); G. C. Lewis,
On local Disturbances, pp. 80–1 (citing Viceroy Wellesley in 1834 on there being 'a com-
plete system of *legislation*, with the most prompt, vigorous and severe executive power . . .
established in almost every district'), 179–82; O. MacDonagh, 'Irish Famine Emigration to
the United States' in *Perspectives in American History*, x, ed. D. Fleming and B. Bailyn
(Cambridge, Mass., 1976), p. 385.

[2] 'A Magistrate of the County', *The present state of Tipperary*, Appendix 3 (the copy
in Bradshaw Collection C.U.L. Hib.7.843.8 has a MS note by the author stating this was
sent to him). In 1862 Queen's Co. Ribbonmen followed precisely the same practice (N. W.
Senior, *Journals, conversations, and essays relating to Ireland*, 2nd edn., 2 vols. (London,
1868), ii, 217). See also *Devon Commission*, Witness Nos. 17, 847, 849, 853, 854.

[3] *The Diary of Humphrey O'Sullivan*, ed. M. McGrath, 4 vols. (London and Dublin,
1936–7), iv, 113–14 (8 July 1832); *Devon Commission*, Witness No. 1101.

[4] W. G. Broehl Jr., *The Molly Maguires*, pp. 31, 18–20, and Mr and Mrs S. C. Hall,
Ireland, ii, 126–7; also *Committee on Outrages (Ireland)*, H.C. 1852 (438), xiv, Qs. 196–7.

between labourers and cottiers, on the one hand, and farmers, on the other. Not that the traditions in question were anything but pervasive and durable, with the Land League in the 1880s achieving some of its greatest successes by means of the 'different varieties of highly legalistic strategies' which had been pioneered by Whiteboys and Rightboys in the second half of the eighteenth century.[1]

The seasonal patterning of outrages provides further evidence of their perpetrators' integration within the local community. While summer was always the hungriest time, most agrarian outrages were committed in the winter, not only because nights were longer, but because farming tasks were few, labourers had little to do, and 'the winter time is generally the time for setting the lands'.[2] In the early 1830s troops were disproportionately called out in aid of the civil power between January and March. In 1836 the Viceroy noted that the December police reports were always especially bad. A fifth of the serious outrages committed in Munster in 1833 occurred in January and February, less than a tenth in June and July. Similar patterns occur in the agrarian assassination figures for Tipperary between 1837 and 1845 and in the detailed outrage returns available for the Barony of Kilmacrenan in Donegal from 1851 to 1860. And while officially designated 'non-agrarian' outrages in years such as 1865 and 1880 were spread fairly evenly throughout the seasons, three-fifths and three-quarters respectively of 'agrarian' outrages were committed between October and March.[3]

The difficulty of obtaining evidence against the perpetrators of outrages was another reflection of communal solidarity, whether voluntary or enforced. The comment of the Limerick lawyer, Matthew Barrington, in 1832 that 'there is a kind of chivalrous feeling in thinking it an honour to protect any man who is charged with an offence' was echoed again and again by police, magistrates, and

[1] B. L. Solow, 'A new look at the Irish Land Question', *Economic and Social Review*, xii (1981), 301-14; J. Lee, 'Patterns of rural unrest in nineteenth-century Ireland', p. 229; J. S. Donnelly Jr., 'The Whiteboy Movement 1761-5', p. 30, and 'The Rightboy Movement 1785-8', p. 159; P. Bew, *Land and the National Question in Ireland 1858-82* (Dublin, 1978), p. 221.

[2] M. MacNeill, *The Festival of Lughnasa: A Study of the Survival of the Celtic Festival of the Beginning of Harvest* (London, 1962), pp. 44, 69; Captain G. Talbot, RM in *Report from the select committee on Westmeath etc. (Unlawful Combinations)*, H.C. 1871 (147), xiii, 573, 584.

[3] Sir H. Vivian to *Committee on the State of Ireland*, H.C. 1831-2 (677), xvi, 83-4; Mulgrave to Russell, 16 Jan. 1836, Carlisle Papers L.-B. 22; G. C. Lewis, *On local Disturbances*, p. 283 (Munster 1833); M. R. Beames, 'Rural Conflict in pre-Famine Ireland', p. 85; *A Return of the Outrages specially reported by the constabulary as committed within the Barony of Kilmacrenan, County Donegal, during the last ten years*, H.C. 1861 (404), lii, 585-98; S.P.O. Irish Crime Records (Printed but not published). See also R. Pennefather to Lord Lincoln (Chief Secretary), 2 June [1846], Newcastle Papers Ne c 9340.

civil servants.[1] Witnesses, it was claimed, were prepared to (and actually did) hang themselves rather than give evidence in court, so that 'the universal sympathy with crime, the general intimidation which prevails render all the efforts of the authorities fruitless'.[2] This combination of solidarity and fear provided the inchoate and generally disorganized world of rural discontent with considerable protection against official attack. The early police detectives of the 1840s (whose work preceded the formal establishment of detective branches in the Royal Irish Constabulary and the Dublin Metropolitan Police by more than thirty years) were not notably successful in penetrating agrarian secret societies. Known as 'disposable men' because of public hostility towards 'any approach to a system of [detective] espionage', their numbers gradually increased and by the 1860s their activities were producing some useful arrests and helping to counter the constant complaints that the constabulary's essentially military style of operation stood in the way of sophisticated detection techniques. It was, however, only when *formal* 'secret' societies such as the Irish Republican Brotherhood (or the earlier United Irishmen) appeared on the scene, that spies, informers, and detectives ever had much success. And until well into the 1880s this important aspect of police work continued to be hampered, not only by the network of silence offered by the rural population at large, but by the suspicions of unsteadily fastidious political leaders in Westminster and Dublin alike.[3]

[1] Cited G. C. Lewis, *On local Disturbances*, p. 205. See also G. Jackson to Lord Sligo, 3 Jan. 1833, O.P. 1832/47, Box 2173; T. Dumas to Knight of Kerry, 20 Feb. 1835, Fitz-Gerald Papers; M. Barrington to Lord Lansdowne, 17 Mar. 1839, Melbourne Papers 19/46; Clarendon to Lord Brougham, 10 Aug. 1847, and to Russell, 19 Nov. 1847, Clarendon Papers L.-B. I; Major Brownrigg to T. Redington, 1 Feb. 1852, Royal Archives RA D21/61a; Report on Longford outrages in O.P. 1852/19/302, Box 1219; Reports of E. Collins, RM, 1, 8 May 1859, R.P. 1859/3993, 4340, Box 808; Lord Mountmorres to Sir T. Larcom, 29 Oct. 1868, Larcom Papers MS 7762; Lord Spencer to Gladstone, 26 Mar. 1869, Carling-ford Papers CP1/43; Spencer (citing Co. Limerick police inspector) to Lord O'Hagan, 2 Feb. 1871, O'Hagan Papers D2777/8/45; Printed Cabinet Papers CAB37/4/71.

[2] Memorandum on Irish Crime, 19 Jan. 1870, Gladstone Papers Add. MS 44613: in Meath witnesses were so terrified 'the perspiration was literally rolling from their faces'. See also Spencer to Gladstone, 9 Mar. 1870, ibid. Add. MS 44306.

[3] This account of a matter requiring urgent investigation is based on: Heytesbury to Graham, 5 Dec. 1844, Graham Papers 19/Ir; de Ros to Duke of Leinster, Feb. 1851, Larcom Papers MS 7618; Major Brownrigg to T. Redington, 1 Feb. 1852, Royal Archives RA D21/61a; F. B. Head, *A Fortnight in Ireland* (London, 1852), pp. 49–50; Lord Carlisle to Sir G. Grey, 26 Mar. 1864, Larcom Papers MS 7619; Lord Strathnairn to Under-Secretary, 1 Mar. 1869, Kilmainham Papers MS 1062; Strathnairn to Colonel L. Smyth, 22 Mar. 1869, Strathnairn Papers Add. MS 42825; Spencer to Gladstone, 9 Mar. 1870, Gladstone Papers Add. MS 44306; Spencer to C. Fortescue, 18 Mar. 1870, Carlingford Papers CP2/8; R. [A. J.] Hawkins, 'Government versus Secret Societies: The Parnell Era' in *Secret Societies in Ireland*, ed. T. D. Williams, pp. 100–12; *Standing Rules and Regulations for the government and guidance of the Royal Irish Constabulary*, 3rd. edn. (Dublin, 1872), ss. 599–616; and, for general criticisms and difficulties: Lord Oxmantown to E. Littleton, 9 Apr. 1834,

The effectiveness of outrages in preventing landlords and many farmers from taking those actions which economic considerations alone might otherwise have dictated is difficult to measure but easy to detect and describe. In the broadest sense it is of course unlikely that the evolution of Irish agriculture was ever seriously affected, although, as Joseph Lee has pointed out, 'the speed with which live-stock numbers rose in the immediate aftermath of the Famine provides some indication of the disincentive effects of the pre-Famine Ribbon activity'.[1] But in the shorter term the evidence for success in forcing down rent, restricting evictions, and even providing more conacre land (farmers were probably harder nuts to crack than land-lords) is not difficult to find. As the admission that 'intimidation' or fear have changed one's mind is not a noble one to make, the cases in which this is known to have happened must stand examples for the many others hidden beneath the silence of injured pride. Ros-common landlords in 1832 felt 'obliged to promise to reduce their rents, and to submit to . . . dictation. No one dared to work for a landlord who would not comply.' And throughout the 1830s and 1840s similar concessions over rents, wages, and evictions on the part of proprietors and conacre-letting farmers are known to have been made intermittently in King's Co., Queen's Co., Tipperary, Limerick, and Westmeath, and almost certainly in many other counties also.[2] J. E. Bicheno, one of the acutest observers of the pre-Famine scene, believed 'the fear of exciting the hostility of the people' to be the 'chief cause' preventing the consolidation of farms. 'The small farmers', it was claimed in 1831, 'are of opinion that but for those outrages their lands would be taken from them.' A prosperous Tipperary farmer told the Devon Commission that 'in some districts, and in some cases, I would not like to take the land of a person put out as a bad tenant'. Plaintive agents became unnerved by having, as they thought, to patrol the countryside with a military

in *Papers relating to the State of Ireland*, H.C. 1834 (459), xlvii, 435; De Grey's Memoran-dum of 31 Aug. 1843, Graham Papers 5/Ir; Clarendon to Russell, 3 Dec. 1847, Clarendon Papers L.-B. II; black-strapped folder in Devonshire Papers detailing difficulties in buying information from informers; *Committee on Westmeath etc. (Unlawful Combinations)*, H.C. 1871 (147), xiii, 630–1; H. A. Blake to Chief Secretary, 19 June 1880, in Printed Cabinet Papers CAB37/2/31; H. Jephson's Memorandum of 20 Apr. 1882, ibid. CAB37/7/26.

[1] J. Lee, 'The Ribbonmen', p. 33.

[2] The O'Conor Don cited in G. C. Lewis, *On local Disturbances*, p. 193; also ibid. 92 (Queen's Co.), 193 (King's Co.); *Fictitious Votes, Ireland*, 2nd series, 3rd report, p. 353 (King's Co.); *Crime and Outrage Committee*, H.C. 1839 (486), xi and xii, Qs. 6380–4 (Westmeath); M. R. Beames, 'Rural Conflict in pre-Famine Ireland', pp. 88–9 (Tipperary); *Devon Commission*, Witness Nos. 545 and 991 (Tipperary), 652 (Limerick), 1101 (King's Co.).

force 'from 10 to 11 hours each day'.[1] Even after the Famine,
threats of violence and their associated theatricalities could still
cause a drawing-back on the part of rent-raising landlords and employing farmers alike.[2] In 1862 Nassau William Senior bemoaned the fact
that 'Ribbon conspiracies' prevented Irish landlords from emulating
the 'beneficial' example of the Duke of Sutherland, and Westmeath
farmers were successfully resisting attempts to evict tenants unable
to pay rents because of the agricultural depression of the time.
Indeed, Lord Derby, who in 1859 was himself forced into rapid
retreat over the famous 'Doon' evictions on his Tipperary estate,
was convinced that 'the bulk of landlords dare not, and therefore do
not, attempt to remove even the most disorderly, idle, and objectionable tenant'.[3] And while this was certainly an exaggeration, it is clear
that only the Famine relieved many landlords and middling to large
farmers from having to steel their nerves in what otherwise would
have been an unprecedented battle of wills and determination
against those below them.

In such a context it is not surprising that similar techniques should
have been applied to the public politics of electoral contests. Given
the social ambience within which voters found themselves, it is equally
unsurprising that actions which frightened landlords, bailiffs, farmers,
and labourers should have frightened voters and candidates as well.
Irish electoral violence was a complicated phenomenon and reveals
as much about its practitioners as about its victims. But of its intermittent 'success' there can be no doubt. And just as it is a mistake
to imagine that rural Ireland was in every sense a more peaceful
place in the decades immediately after the Famine than it had been
in the 1830s and 1840s, so it is a mistake to detect any notable
decline in the violence of public constitutional politics throughout
the same period. Authenticated cases in which electors 'changed
their minds', candidates withdrew, or voters fled into the under-
growth as a result of intimidation were as numerous after as they
had been before 1850. The effective terror stalking Carlow in 1830,

[1] *Poor Inquiry (Ireland) Appendix H—Part II* [by J. E. Bicheno], H.C. 1836 [42],
xxxiv, 681; *Committee on the State of Ireland*, H.C. 1831 (677), xvi, 398; *Devon Commission*, Witness No. 846; J. Evatt to Lord Bath, 4 Dec. 1832, Bath Papers Irish Box.
[2] See, e.g., Clarendon to Sir G. Grey, and Major Brownrigg to T. Redington, 1 Feb.
1852, Royal Archives RA D21/61a; Carlingford Papers Diary of C. Fortescue II (16 Sept.
1856); *Committee on Outrages (Ireland)*, H.C. 1852 (438), xiv, 11–13, 193–4; J. Godkin,
The Land War in Ireland (London, 1870), p. 417; Strathnairn to Spencer, 20 Mar. 1870,
Strathnairn Papers Add. MS 42826.
[3] N. W. Senior, *Journals, conversations, and essays relating to Ireland*, ii, 266–7;
W. N. Hancock's Memorandum, 14 Feb. 1870, Gladstone Papers Add. MS 44613, fos. 120–6;
E. D. Steele, *Irish Land and British Politics: Tenant-Right and Nationality 1865–1870*
(Cambridge, 1974), p. 16.

the enforced desertions at the Co. Cork elections of 1841 and 1842, the efficacious violence in Kerry in 1835 and Louth in 1830,[1] can be matched and matched again during the 1850s and 1860s—those supposedly quiescent decades in Irish political life. In particular, the scenes of clanging cudgels and breaking skulls at the General Election of 1852 induced voters to exhibit to the full that mesmerized caution with which they had long learned to face agrarian intimidation. Indeed, election and agrarian outrages were often the work of the same men. 'I am in great trouble that I cannot vote for your friend Mr Otway', wrote a Tipperary tenant to his landlord, 'as I could not find myself safe in doing so.' In Sligo 'the houses of voters were visited either by night or day by large parties with fire-arms, and . . . many [voters] hid in the fields and in holes and corners'. The sheer weight of such documentation overwhelms both the undoubtedly tendentious nature of some stories and the fact that tenants occasionally invented and even invited intimidation in order to conceal the exercise of their own electoral preferences.[2] Quite apart, therefore, from the actual survival of agrarian violence throughout the period, the continuing vigour of electoral intimidation shows how the tradition of rural outrage endured also in surrogate form, and how popular memories gave a sustained edge to the activities of political mobsters of all persuasions—Orange, Green, or Mainchance.[3]

[1] For what is only a garland of examples, see *Committee on Bribery at Elections*, H.C. 1835 (547), viii, 634-5; *Minutes of the proceedings of the select committee on the Cork county election petition*, H.C. 1842 (271), vi, 66-72, 81; Lady Kenmare to Knight of Kerry, 13 Jan. 1835, FitzGerald Papers, and G. Lyne, 'Daniel O'Connell, intimidation, and the Kerry elections of 1835', *Journal of the Kerry Archaeological and Historical Society*, No. 4 (1971), 74-97; W. Armstrong to Lord Anglesey, 19 Sept. 1830, Anglesey Papers D619/23/A/228.

[2] *Daily Express*, 24 July, 4 Aug. 1852. For similar cases of *successful* violence in 1852, see *Report from the select committee on the Cork City election petition*, H.C. 1852-3 (528), xi, 43, 106-9, 144-8, 159-60; *Minutes of evidence taken before the select committee on the Clare election petition*, H.C. 1852-3 (595), ix, 56, 62, 78, 100-1; *Minutes of evidence taken before the select committee on the Mayo election petition*, H.C. 1852-3 (415), xvi, 253-8, 264-70; *Minutes of evidence taken before the select committee on the Sligo Borough election petition*, H.C. 1852-3 (600), xviii, 659, 668, 672; D. Power, H. Rodwell, and E. L'E. Dew, *Reports of the decisions of committees of the House of Commons in the trial of controverted elections during the fifteenth parliament of the United Kingdom* (London, 1853), p. 198 (New Ross); H. Anderson to J. A. Beck, 7 July 1852, Ironmongers' Company Irish Correspondence Received 1846-54 (Londonderry). For asking to be 'intimidated', see *Clare election petition*, op. cit. 152; *Minutes of evidence taken before the select committee on the Tipperary election*, H.C. 1867 (211), viii; *Copy of the evidence taken at the trial of the Galway County election petition*, H.C. 1872 (241-I), xlviii, 822.

[3] For an assortment of post-1852 examples, see Lord Carlisle's Diary for 7 Apr. 1857 (Carlisle Papers) on demoralized state of many candidates; *Londonderry Sentinel*, 10 Apr. 1857 (Drogheda); J. Spaight to Lord Naas, 4, 5 May 1859, Mayo Papers MS 11036 (Limerick); *Londonderry Sentinel*, 28 July 1865 (Louth and Monaghan); *D.E.P.* 5 July 1865 (Dungarvan); *Freeman's Journal*, 2 Aug. 1852, and *Daily Express*, 24 July 1865 (Monaghan); Revd C. Fry to W. Armstrong, 28 Dec. 1866, Mayo Papers MS 11144 (Co. Waterford);

The broad patterns established before the Famine continued thereafter. Many outrages were still undertaken as 'a stern vindication of supposed popular rights against the violators of those rights, of whatever class and whatever creed'. The repertoire too—and also the occasionally savage cruelty—remained the same: 'assaults on houses . . . night visits and administering unlawful oaths . . . attempts to murder by firing bullets through the windows . . . and cases in which inmates have been "carded" ' by having their flesh torn with nails.[1] But while farmer involvement was substantial in the Ribbon outbursts in Armagh, Monaghan, and Louth during the early 1850s (after which 'Ribbonism' replaces 'Whiteboyism' as the portmanteau label for violent agrarian unrest), this soon melted away and rural outrages became more than ever before the preserve of the declining labourer and cottier class.[2] The Ribbonism of these years—in the midlands in 1858, more generally during the depression of the early 1860s, even the dramatic appearance at Louth elections of Ribbon leaders on white horses actively directing the Liberal 'street agents and supporters'[3]—was almost entirely staffed by labourers, 'farmers' boys', and a 'low class of person' generally.[4] Increasingly farmers became the prime targets of attack. They constituted twelve of the victims of agrarian murder in 1850-1 as against four labourers and two landlords. Two-thirds of the threatening notices posted between October 1858 and January 1859 were aimed at farmers and less than a quarter at landlords. Incendiarism exhibited an even more marked

Report from the select committee on parliamentary and municipal elections, H.C. 1868–9 (352), viii, 333 (Co. Sligo); Strathnairn to Duke of Abercorn, 29 Nov. [1868], Strathnairn Papers Add. MS 42828 (estimating that twenty of the thirty-eight uncontested constituencies were left thus because of outrage and intimidation).

[1] Printed Cabinet Memorandum, 13 Dec. 1869, Gladstone Papers Add. MS 44612; H. A. Blake, RM to Chief Secretary, Tuam, 19 June 1880, Printed Cabinet Papers, 29 June 1880, CAB37/2/31.

[2] See W. S. Trench to Lady Bath, 18 Dec. 1851, Bath Papers Irish Box; Major Brownrigg to Sir T. Redington, 1 Feb. 1852, Royal Archives RA D21/61a; R. Miller to E. Lawford, 4, 18 Feb. 1852, Drapers' Company L.-B. Irish 1848-57; Lord Rossmore to Lord Eglinton, 26 Aug. 1852, Eglinton Papers MS 5243; *Committee on Outrages (Ireland)*, H.C. 1852 (438), xiv, Qs. 712-28, 2060.

[3] Report of B. Warburton, RM, 26 July 1852, O.P. 1852/8/305, Box 1217; Dean Kieran to Archbishop Dixon, 26 Feb. 1854, Dixon Papers. See also *Dublin Evening Mail*, 20 Apr. 1857 (Co. Sligo election).

[4] T. O'Hagan to W. Monsell, 29 May 1862, O'Hagan Papers N.L.I. MS 17871. See also Report of H. Pollock, RM, 5 July 1852, O.P. 1852/15/152, Box 1218; Report of G. Fitzmaurice, RM, 23 July 1852, O.P. 1852/8/292, Box 1217; *Committee on Outrages (Ireland)*, H.C. 1852 (438), xiv, Qs. 146-9, 3137-40; Lord Bandon to Naas, 18 Nov. 1858, Mayo Papers MS 11021; Revd J. Halley to Naas, 28 Nov. 1858, ibid. MS 11023; Reports of N. Kelly, RM, and H. G. Curran, RM, Dec. 1858, ibid. MS 11027; T. L. D'Arcy to Naas, 17 Jan. 1859, ibid. MS 11025; Reports of E. Collins, RM, 1, 8 May 1859, R.P. 1859/3993, 4340.

social discrimination.[1] Comparing the victims of agrarian outrage in Kilmacrenan Barony (Donegal) in 1846 and 1861, farmers increase from two-fifths to more than half, 'gentlemen' decline from a fifth to a twelfth and labourers from a sixth to nothing at all.[2] During the 1860s as a whole discontented labourers 'intended to strike their first blow at the farmers and take possession of their land'. None of this means that farmers were the only magnets for rustic violence. 'Ferocious-looking' mobs in Co. Kilkenny in 1852 were happy enough to notch up a very mixed bag of victims: one baronet, two deputy lieutenants, another magistrate, two priests, and two 'gentlemen'.[3] But when violence had any aim beyond simple bravado, it seems to have developed an increasingly pronounced anti-farmer bias. Even during the outbreaks in Meath and Westmeath between 1869 and 1872, when hatred of large graziers managed to unite most sections of rural opinion against them, the underlying labourer–farmer tensions were never far below the temporarily ecumenical surface of events.[4]

What did, however, cut across the traditional nature of post-Famine violence was the Fenian movement. Yet it too was never quite the sea-green novelty it often pretended to be. Fenianism found the bulk of its members among urban artisans, shop assistants, and clerks, that 'class above the masses', as the percipient Commander of the Forces in Ireland, Lord Strathnairn, called it in 1869.[5] Its outer penumbra of sympathizers also had similar backgrounds, as is shown

[1] F. B. Head, *A Fortnight in Ireland*, p. 386; 'Return of agrarian outrages reported by the constabulary', 1858/9, Mayo Papers MS 11027.

[2] Obtained by comparing the more or less agrarian crimes in *A Return of all aggravated assaults; of all assaults endangering life; of all incendiary fires; of every demand or robbery of arms; of all cases of persons appearing armed; of all unlawful oaths administered or tendered; of all threatening notices or letters delivered or posted; of all malicious injuries to property; and of all firings into dwellings . . .*, H.C. 1846 (369), xxxv, 181–234 for the first five months of 1846 in Kilmacrenan with those for the same period of 1861 in *A Return of the Outrages . . . committed within the Barony of Kilmacrenan*, H.C. 1861 (404), lii, 585–98. Spot checks for 1851 and 1856 in the latter source support the general trend.

[3] Strathnairn to Under-Secretary, 1 Mar. 1869, Kilmainham Papers MS 1062; *Galway Vindicator*, 28 July 1852.

[4] See Printed Cabinet Memorandum, 13 Dec. 1869, Gladstone Papers Add. MS 44612; S. Seed (Crown Solicitor) to Attorney-General, 27 Nov. 1869, in Memorandum on Irish Crime, 19 Jan. 1870, ibid. Add. MS 44613; Reports of Tipperary Crown Solicitor and of John Julian (King's Co.), ibid.; breakdown of victims of agrarian murders and firings 1 Dec. 1868–7 Jan. 1870, ibid.; Strathnairn to Colonel L. Smyth, 22 Mar. 1869, Strathnairn Papers Add. MS 42825; Waller to Fortescue, 6 Dec. 1869, Carlingford Papers CP1/76; G. Fitzgibbon, *Ireland in 1868, The battle-field for English party strife* (London, 1868), pp. 6–7; *Committee on Westmeath etc. (Unlawful Combinations)*, H. C. 1871 (147), xiii, 549, 573, 606, 629, 642.

[5] Strathnairn to Spencer, 19 Dec. 1869, Strathnairn Papers Add. MS 42826. For further evidence, see Report of Chief Inspector Ryan, 23 Dec. 1858, Mayo Papers MS 11187; Lord Wodehouse to Sir G. Grey, 3 Sept. 1865, Palmerston Papers GC/Gr/2577; A. J. Semple, 'The Fenian Infiltration of the British Army', *Journal of the Society for Army Historical Research*, lii (1974), 142; M. Murphy, 'Fenianism, Parnellism, and the

by a comparison in Table 41 of A: those arrested under the Habeas Corpus Suspension Act of 1866, B: a hard core of Fenian convicts still imprisoned in mid-1870, and C: the urban participants in a large parade mounted in Limerick on 8 December 1867 to publicize the cause of the lately executed 'Manchester Martyrs'. This was certainly new enough. At the same time, however, and despite what to a cynic might have seemed the leadership's best efforts, Fenianism was not entirely an urban phenomenon. To begin with, and contrary to the opinions of several contemporaries, its most notable impact was to be found, not only in the cities, but also in the smaller towns dotted around the Irish countryside. The small towns of Co. Monaghan (none of them with more than 3,632 inhabitants in 1871) were strongholds, while twenty-six of the thirty-one schoolmasters arrested for Fenianism in 1865-6 came from towns with populations under 2,000.[1] In the countryside itself Fenians were significantly linked with traditional conflicts and traditional antagonisms. Already in 1856, as James Stephens tramped the roads to assess the possibility of founding a secret political society, he had been struck by 'the apathy of the farmers, the pigheadedness of the bourgeoisie; but the labourers . . . were very sympathetic'. And throughout the 1860s the bulk of rural support came from labourers (many of them migrant harvesters moving between Ireland and Britain), who saw in the Brotherhood a means of reversing their own relatively declining economic position *vis-à-vis* the farmer community. Most farmers already hostile, became more hostile still.[2] In the south Ulster borderlands, where Fenianism merged into the still-living remnants of Ribbonism, the resulting 'Ribbon–Fenianism' represented a notable

Cork Trades 1860-1900', *Saothar*, No. 5 (1979), 28; R. V. Comerford, 'Patriotism as pastime: The appeal of Fenianism in the mid-1860s', *Irish Historical Studies*, xxii (1981), 239-42.

[1] Strathnairn to Duke of Cambridge, 18 Aug. 1865, Strathnairn Papers Add. MS 42821 W. Bence Jones, *The life's work in Ireland of a landlord who tried to do his duty* (London, 1880), pp. 62, 67; B. Mac Giolla Choille, 'Fenians, Rice, and Ribbonmen in County Monaghan, 1864-67', *Clogher Record*, vi (1967), 221-52; *Return of all Schoolmasters arrested in Ireland for Ribbonism, Sedition, or connected with the Fenian Conspiracy, from 1st January 1860 to 12 March 1866*, H.C. 1866 (455), lviii, 475-8.

[2] D. Ryan, *The Fenian Chief: A biography of James Stephens* (Dublin, 1967), p. 80 (also p. 65); Reports of F. J. Davys, RM, and Sub-Inspector Potter, 19 Sept. and 6 Oct. 1858, Mayo Papers MS 11187 (Phoenix Society); Memorandum for the Cabinet by Lord Strathnairn, *c.*May 1867, ibid. MS 11188(5); Strathnairn to Under-Secretary, 1 Mar. 1869, Kilmainham Papers MS 1062; Sir R. Blennerhassett to Lord Acton, 10 Nov. 1869, Acton Papers (Correspondence); R. B. Osborne to C. Fortescue, 29 Nov. 1869, Carlingford Papers CP3/98; Spencer to Gladstone, 13 Sept. 1870, ibid. CP2/15. Kerry Fenianism attracted labourers, artisans, shopkeepers, and some *sons* of 'comfortable' farmers (S. Ó. Lúing, 'Aspects of the Fenian Rising in Kerry, 1867' (III), *Journal of the Kerry Archaeological and Historical Society*, No. 5 (1972), 109).

TABLE 41

Occupations of Irish Fenians and their supporters, 1866–70

	A (N = 1,081) per cent	B (N = 26) per cent	C (N = 418) per cent
Gentlemen and professionals	6.0	19.2	0.2
Mercantile and commercial	3.9	11.5	5.3
Clerks	5.3		12.2
Artisans	31.6*	38.5	36.6
Shopkeepers and assistants	23.6	11.5	27.8
Drink interest	3.8	0.0	3.8
Labourers	12.1	3.9	4.5
Farmers	5.7	0.0	0.0
Others	8.0	15.4	9.6

* The largest groups here were shoemakers and tailors.

if rough-hewn foreshadowing of the New Departure(s) of the 1870s.[1] Just as Ribbonmen had involved themselves, however tangentially, in the electoral politics of the 1850s, so did Ribbon-Fenians provide many of the canvassing, rioting, and organizing shock-troops who made possible the important nationalist breakthroughs which took place at the by-elections held between 1869 and 1872.[2] The Land War of Davitt and Parnell was to show how explosive could be the conjuncture of agrarian, revolutionary, and constitutional agitations. But, whereas the 'agrarianism' of 1879–82 was farmer-dominated, that of 1869–72 involved mostly labourers, and this at a time when it was already obvious that no national movement could hope for success without the substantial involvement of farmers large and small. None the less, even though large sections of Fenianism remained untouched by Ribbon sentiment, the remarkable spread of the Brotherhood in the west of Ireland during the 1860s and early 1870s was at once novel and full of import for the future.[3]

[1] *Committee on parliamentary and municipal elections*, H.C. 1868–9 (352), viii, 496; Printed Cabinet Memorandum, 13 Dec. 1869, Gladstone Papers Add. MS 44612; S. Seed to Attorney-General, 27 Dec. 1869, in Memorandum on Irish Crime, 19 Jan. 1870, ibid. Add. MS 44613; C. Fortescue to Queen Victoria, 12 Apr. 1870, Royal Archives RA D27/45; B. Mac Giolla Choille, 'Fenians, Rice, and Ribbonmen', pp. 225–7; S. Ó. Lúing, 'A Contribution to the study of Fenianism in Breifne', *Breifne*, iii (1967), 156–61; P. Bew, *Land and the National Question in Ireland 1858–82*, p. 41; T. Garvin, *The evolution of Irish nationalist politics*, pp. 59–65.

[2] Strathnairn to Colonel North, 7 Dec. 1868, Strathnairn Papers Add. MS 42828; *Committee on parliamentary and municipal elections*, H.C. 1868–9 (352), viii, 209; Lord Granard to Archbishop Cullen, 25 Nov. 1869, Cullen Papers; *Copy of the shorthand writer's notes of the judgement delivered by Mr Justice Fitzgerald, and of the minutes of evidence taken at the trial of the Longford election petition*, H.C. 1870 (178), lvi, 506–7; Lord Kenmare to Lord Hartington, 14 Jan. 1872, Devonshire Papers 340/483; Bishop Moriarty to Hartington, 1 Feb. 1872, ibid. 340/491; also Strathnairn to Abercorn, 23 Jan. 1867, Strathnairn Papers Add. MS 42823.

[3] Spencer to Gladstone, 30 Mar. 1869, Gladstone Papers Add. MS 44306; *Committee*

II TRENDS AND LOCATIONS

Save for the matter of farmer–labourer antagonism, the contours of rural violence remained broadly similar throughout the period. Even the incidence of 'crime', 'violence', 'disorder'—call it what you will —changed less than is often supposed. Of course any attempt to measure unrest in nineteenth-century Ireland is hampered by statistical problems both general and particular. From the early 1830s the police produced returns of 'specially reported' crimes or outrages. These were vaguely defined as 'serious', but at first erratically included many trivial offences 'not affecting in any manner the public peace, such as forgery, uttering base coin etc., larcenies, common assaults, [and] . . . trespasses'. Despite attempted improvements in 1833, the existence of separate provincial police forces introduced powerful regional, let alone temporal, peculiarities into the criminal data.[1] Only with the constabulary reforms of 1836 did relatively reliable figures become available; and not even the heroic attempts of Whig reformers like Thomas Drummond (Under-Secretary 1835–40) to prove that 'moral' government provoked less crime make it convincingly possible to connect the reliable data beginning in 1837 with the non-comparable statistics of earlier years. Superficially there was indeed an overall drop, but this may well have flowed entirely from a decision of 1835 to exclude much of the trivial crime previously included in the returns, while even the raw figures still contain several awkward 'increases' in crimes like robbery of arms and assaults with intent to murder. In addition, expanding governmental involvement in criminal prosecutions distorts all long-term series either of committals or convictions, while grave doubts were often entertained throughout the period as to whether anything like the totality of serious crime was in fact consistently known to the police at all.[2] The use of general categories could also disguise significant

on *Westmeath etc. (Unlawful Combinations)*, H.C. 1871 (147), xiii, 634; P. Bew, *Land and the National Question in Ireland 1858–82*, pp. 41–4; S. Ó. Lúing, 'Fenianism in Breifne', pp. 160–1, 173–4. The actual size of the organization in the 1870s possibly fluctuated between 24,000 and 40,000 according to sources of notorious unreliability (P. Bew, op. cit. 47, also Devoy Papers MS 18036).

[1] Lord Mulgrave in *Hansard*, xxxix, 228 (27 Nov. 1837); Thomas Drummond in *Crime and Outrage Committee*, H.C. 1839 (486), xi and xii, Q. 13132; E. Littleton to Melbourne, 2 Oct. 1833, Melbourne Papers 96/40; Melbourne to Littleton, 27 Dec. 1833, ibid. 97/16.

[2] Drummond in *Crime and Outrage Committee*, H.C. 1839 (486), xi and xii, Qs. 13065–138 and immediately subsequent appendices; also Major G. Warburton in ibid. Qs. 915–23; Mulgrave to Russell, 16 Jan. 1836, Carlisle Papers L.-B. 22; *Hansard*, xxxix, 228 (27 Nov. 1837); *D.E.P.* 10 May 1838; G. Locker Lampson, *A Consideration of the State of Ireland in the nineteenth century* (London, 1907), pp. 238–40. For the police's supposedly limited knowledge, see Report of Sub-Inspector Battersby, 5 Feb. 1835, O.P. 1835, Box 34; *Committee on Bribery at Elections*, H.C. 1835 (547), viii, 268; 'A Magistrate of the County',

trends. 'Common assaults' in the 1830s covered an enormous range, while during the Famine, offences like cattle-stealing were transformed from manifestations of 'agrarian conspiracy' into mere signs of starved desperation.[1] Even after 1836 the authorities continued to dabble in the bad old practice of trying to record the gravity of crime by means of weighted entries, so that the returns for 1869-70 (let alone for the years before 1837) are often hopelessly distorted.[2] The case, therefore, for seeing the late 1830s and early 1840s as substantially less disturbed than earlier decades is neither obvious nor provable. Indeed, even Drummond's dashing efforts to show that, taking population into account, things were better in 1836-8 than they had been in 1826-8 must remain almost as unconvincing as they were ingenious.

Another complication appeared in 1844 when outrages adjudged 'agrarian' in character began to be listed separately. As before, the statistics were based entirely on constabulary reports. Local sub-inspectors first wrote out 'the facts', but then (and this is crucial) the actual sorting into various categories was wholly undertaken by central officials in Dublin.[3] Now, although it has been suggested that the Castle tended to exaggerate the proportion of crime accounted 'agrarian', the very opposite would seem to have been the case. Indeed, as time went on the bureaucrats became so exclusive in their judgements, that various viceroys and chief secretaries (who had regular access to the files) became convinced that many outrages not so designated were in fact 'agrarian' by any reasonable definition of the term. It is, however, unfortunately not possible to trace the precise development of the highly exclusive criteria known to have been well established by the 1880s, criteria which required that, to be classed as 'agrarian', a crime must not only have arisen 'out of social disorganization consequent . . . upon agrarian discontent', but also 'be directly traceable to some specific motive connected with land', and which, as a result, excluded much cattle-stealing and maiming, 'firing into houses, moonlighting, and raiding for arms' from the 'agrarian' pantheon. With, therefore, uncertain criteria

---

The present state of Tipperary, Appendix 1; *Committee on Westmeath etc.* (*Unlawful Combinations*), H.C. 1871 (147), xiii, 563-4; 3rd edn. of Constabulary's *Standing Rules and Regulations* (1872), ss. 963-7.

[1] Mulgrave to Russell, 16 Jan. 1836, Carlisle Papers L.-B. 22; printed 'Memorandum on the State of Ireland', 9 Jan. 1847, Royal Archives RA D16/15; Clarendon to Grey, 27 Nov. 1847, Clarendon Papers L.-B. I.

[2] *Crime and Outrage Committee*, H.C. 1839 (486), xi and xii, Qs. 915-23; *Return of Outrages reported to the Royal Irish Constabulary Office from 1st January 1844 to 31st December 1880*, H.C. 1881 [C 2756], lxxvii, 901.

[3] *Crime and Outrage Committee*, H.C. 1839 (486), xi and xii, Qs. 915-23; *Devon Commission*, Witness No. 1101 (Colonel W. Miller, Deputy Inspector-General of constabulary).

uncertainly applied, it is hardly possible to regard the returns of 'agrarian outrages' as a full or accurate reflection of the state of serious agrarian crime.[1]

Perhaps, therefore, it might be best to concentrate upon the *total* outrage returns. These of course cover the whole country (with the exception of the Dublin Metropolitan Police District) and thus include urban as well as rural incidents. But preliminary findings suggest that towns experienced substantially less serious crime (that is, 'outrages') than the countryside,[2] so that, in what was in any case a predominantly rural nation (excluding Dublin City, only 11.2 per cent of the people in 1841 and 18.5 per cent even in 1871 lived in towns with more than 2,000 inhabitants), the general outrage figures can be safely regarded as a rough-and-ready guide to levels of 'rural' —in many ways a more useful concept than 'agrarian'—violence and crime. And what emerges most notably from any examination of outrage data measured against population over the half-century after 1836 (Table 42) is the general consistency of the overall levels of the time. Taking population into account, it is clear from the Table that levels of serious crime in general and of particular types of serious crime (some of them with obvious 'agrarian' connections) only fell significantly below their immediately pre-Famine levels

---

[1] W. E. Vaughan, 'A Study of Landlord and Tenant Relations in Ireland between the Famine and the Land War, 1850-78' (University of Dublin Ph.D. thesis, 1974), pp. 203-5, also S. Clark, *Social origins of the Irish Land War* (Princeton, 1979), p. 74. But see Cabinet Memorandum by C. Fortescue, 31 Jan. 1870, Gladstone Papers Add. MS 44613, fos. 45-7; Spencer to Gladstone, 9 Mar. 1870, ibid. Add. MS 44306; *Memorandum* [by A. J. Balfour] *as to the Principle upon which Outrages are recorded as agrarian*, H.C. 1887 (140), lxviii, 25-6. See also note 1 p. 349.

[2] It is possible to distinguish between the cities of Cork, Limerick, and Waterford, and their surrounding 'rural' counties. Reducing (a) all outrages, (b) all outrages *excluding* agrarian, to ratios per 10,000 population for the eight regularly separated periods of 1844, 1849-50, 1854-5, 1859-60, 1864-5, 1874-5, 1879-80, 1884-5 (1845 is not available and 1869-70 unreliable) and denoting the city levels in each case as = 100, we find for the eight periods taken together: 'rural' Co. Cork (a) = 183 (b) = 147; 'rural' Co. Limerick (a) = 171 (b) = 224; 'rural' Co. Waterford (a) = 167 (b) = 150, though there is some evidence that cities were catching up in the 1870s and 1880s. To find the rural areas so obviously ahead in even 'non-agrarian' crime is remarkable. (Sources: 1844—*Devon Commission*, part iii, Appendix 36, H.C. 1845 [657], xxi; 1849-85—S.P.O. Irish Crime Records). Furthermore, while the figure per 10,000 population for homicides/attempted homicides in Cork City 1842-5 was 0.1, in 'rural' Co. Cork it was 0.9 and for Munster as a whole 1.6 (*A Return of all murders that have been committed in Ireland since the 1st day of January 1842; specifying the county, and the barony of the county, where each murder was committed; the name and condition of the person so murdered . . . Similar Return of attempts to murder attended with bodily injuries*, H.C. 1846 (220), xxxv, 293-306). Viceroy Wellesley considered rural Ireland much more violent than the towns (to Melbourne, 15 Apr. 1834, in *Papers relating to the State of Ireland*, H.C. 1834 (459), xlvii, 419-22). Ribbonism was stronger on a per capita basis in 'rural' Co. Sligo than in Sligo Town (figures in *Crime and Outrage Committee*, H.C. 1839 (486), xi and xii, Qs. 2296, 2315, 2349). Townsmen arrested under the Protection of Persons and Property Act of 1881 had notably less 'violent' records than their rural counterparts (S. Clark, *Social origins of the Irish Land War*, pp. 270-2).

TABLE 42

Incidence of all and of selected types of specially reported outrages per 10,000 population for two-year periods, 1837–82

	Homicides and serious assaults	Cattle and sheep stealing and maiming	Threatening letters and notices	Incendiary fires	All outrages
1837–8	13.6	8.0	6.8	5.6	72.8
1839–40	10.2	9.4	6.1	5.1	59.4
1841–2	10.2	13.3	9.6	5.4	72.4
1843–4	10.3	9.1	10.9	6.1	73.9
1851–2	14.9	50.4	11.4	11.7	132.0
1853–4	13.1	25.2	4.9	6.1	82.3
1855–6	12.8	16.3	3.9	4.6	69.5
1857–8	13.9	11.5	4.4	4.4	63.7
1859–60	13.7	10.4	4.4	3.9	61.2
1861–2	12.4	15.3	6.9	4.3	71.6
1863–4	9.9	13.7	6.1	4.7	59.9
1865–6	8.1	7.1	3.5	3.5	41.1
1867–8	8.5	5.9	3.4	3.8	41.8
1871–2	13.0	6.7	6.5	3.4	57.9
1873–4	10.4	5.9	3.8	2.8	41.1
1875–6	10.9	4.4	2.8	3.6	38.4
1877–8	11.7	5.8	4.0	3.7	45.7
1879–80	12.0	9.1	23.7	7.6	87.8
1881–2	11.0	9.4	54.6	11.4	137.2

Note The Famine years 1845–50 were particularly heavily disturbed and have been omitted, as have 1869–70 when returns were constructed on non-comparable principles.

during a brief interlude in the late 1860s and the 1870s, itself interrupted by the disturbed years of 1869–72.[1] The Famine of course recorded a uniquely large number of outrages. But these were overwhelmingly confined to starvation crimes, notably sheep- and cattle-stealing and the like, which alone constituted half the 223.8 outrages per 10,000 inhabitants committed in 1847–8. By contrast, the outrages of the Land War were clearly the product of more than economic distress. Cattle-stealing rose little. Threatening letters and notices (*not* a species of outrage to be dismissed lightly) increased substantially, as did other serious crimes such as firing at the person and into dwellings, injury to property, and demand for or robbery of arms. Leaving aside, therefore, the aberrant years of 1847–50, it is clear

[1] The differently constructed returns for 1869–70 suggest strongly that outrage levels were even higher then than in 1871–2, and that for the four years as a whole levels were not far short of those for 1837–44.

that the Land War at its height produced more outrages per head than any other period since at least 1837 and possibly earlier. At the same time those supposedly decisive reductions in serious crime and violence which have so often been identified as a particular feature of immediately post-Famine society seem, on closer examination (as when the mean of 64.2 for 1853–82 is compared with that of 69.6 for 1837–44), to have been far from immediate and only haltingly decisive.

Admittedly, statistics which include a far wider range of less serious offences (such as those recording all cases brought before assizes and quarter sessions) do seem to indicate a significant reduction from about the mid-1850s onwards. But these present even greater methodological snares, with 'breaks' not only in the 1830s, but also in 1865, and with almost insuperable problems of shifting categorization. For what little it is worth, such committal returns do not, however, show any substantial changes between the late 1820s and the 1830s as a whole.[1] Pending more detailed examination it would seem, therefore, that, while 'trivial' offences were generally less common after than before the Famine, the same cannot be said for outrages regarded as serious and worthy of 'special report'. In such a perspective, the Land War involved not only a new set of rural alliances, but an extremely serious wave of disturbances after a long period, not so much of calm, but of enervating and demanding levels of outrage throughout large parts of Ireland.[2] Not only, therefore, were many of the social tensions of the pre-Famine countryside carried over into the 1850s and 1860s, but they continued to manifest themselves in degrees of violence neither particularly unprecedented nor in general particularly low.

Trends in violent rural crime bear some relation to the incidence of economic hardship, although in the period before the 1830s any detailed correlation depends more upon imaginative speculation than quantifiable information.[3] Although there was widespread

[1] On this complicated problem it is worth examining the 'Abstract of the number of committals and convictions returned in the appendix to the annual reports of the Inspector General of Prisons in Ireland from 1826 to 1838', Clarendon Papers Box 67; *Thom 1852*, p. 199; *Thom 1870*, p. 811; *Thom 1876*, p. 664; *Thom 1888*, p. 571; T. W. Grimshaw, *Facts and Figures about Ireland Part I* (Dublin, 1893), Summary Table VI; J. M. Wilson *Statistics of Crime in Ireland, 1842–1856* (Dublin, 1857); Memorandum on Crime (1857), Larcom Papers MS 7562; detailed analysis by W. N. Hancock (Superintendent of judicial and criminal statistics) for Gladstone in Dec. 1869, Gladstone Papers Add. MS 44798. Some of these sources, notably the last two, contain some heroic attempts to compare Irish crime levels with those of England, France, and Belgium.

[2] While in the autumn of 1837 some 41 persons were accorded special police protection, the numbers in Jan. 1870 and Nov. 1880 were 23 and 80 respectively (Returns in Carlisle Papers Irish Box, and Harcourt Papers 106). On relative levels of outrage, see also Printed Cabinet Papers (Memorandum by W. E. Forster, 16 Nov. 1880), CAB37/4/71.

[3] See J. Lee, 'Patterns of rural unrest in nineteenth-century Ireland', pp. 223–37.

contemporary agreement that depressions increased crime, a few brawny heretics were sufficiently struck by what they believed to be the exclusion of the *really* poor from active agrarian crime and by the diminution of outrages during the hungry months of each year to feel uneasy about making any direct or all-inclusive connections between distress and crime.[1] Certainly during the two major post-Famine depressions in the early 1860s and just before and during the Land War, both agrarian and total outrages increased. But they did not do so in direct and equivalent step with economic deterioration, the impact of the later depression being disproportionately severe.[2] At certain times economic stress seems, indeed, to have affected the nature of crime more than its extent, although not always in the same way. Depressions in pre-Famine Tipperary shifted criminal activity sharply towards non-violent crimes against property and away from violent crimes against the person. During the Famine itself, outrages connected with the possession of land declined in favour of attempts to regulate employment, wages, and poor relief, while offences against the person slumped in comparison with hunger-induced offences against property.[3] During the Land War, however, things were very different, with relative falls in both categories in the face of a substantial increase in those outrages designated as 'affecting the public peace' (Tables 43 A and B). The Land War was marked, therefore, not only by an increase in all forms of

[1] For connections, see, e.g., various witnesses of the 1820s and 1830s cited in G. C. Lewis, *On local Disturbances*, pp. 51-60, 67; Eliot to Graham, 20 Aug. 1842, Graham Papers 1/Ir; N. W. Senior, *Journals, conversations, and essays relating to Ireland*, ii, 183-4; T. O'Hagan to W. Monsell, 29 May 1862, O'Hagan Papers N.L.I. MS 17871; Diary of 7th Duke of Devonshire XVI (30 Sept. 1863), Devonshire Papers; A. I. Shand, *Letters from the west of Ireland 1884* (London, 1885), pp. 222-3. For modern concurrence, see F. D'Arcy, 'Dublin artisan activity, opinion, and organization, 1820-1850' (University College Dublin MA thesis, 1968), p. 47; W. E. Vaughan, 'A Study of Landlord and Tenant Relations in Ireland between the Famine and the Land War', p. 226; J. Lee, 'Patterns of rural unrest in nineteenth-century Ireland', p. 223. For doubts, see *Devon Commission*, Witness No. 1101; *Crime and Outrage Committee*, H.C. 1839 (486), xi and xii, Q. 1393; G. C. Lewis, *On local Disturbances*, pp. 71-2.

[2] For outrage data, see *Return of Outrages reported to the Royal Irish Constabulary Office from 1st January 1844 to 31st December 1880*, H.C. 1881 [C 2756], lxxvii, 887-914; for other crime, M. S. O'Shaughnessy, 'On Criminal Statistics, especially with reference to population, education, and distress in Ireland', *Journal of the Statistical and Social Inquiry Society of Ireland*, iv (1864), 91-104, and T. W. Grimshaw, *Facts and Figures about Ireland Part I*, Summary Table VI. For differing views on the comparative 'objective' severity of the two depressions, see J. S. Donnelly Jr., 'The Irish agricultural depression of 1859-64', *Irish Economic and Social History*, iii (1976), 33-54, and J. Lee, 'Patterns of rural unrest in nineteenth-century Ireland', pp. 223-37. Available annual estimates 1851-83 of changes in the value of agricultural output (in T. W. Moody, *Davitt and Irish Revolution 1846-82* (Oxford, 1981), p. 569) would certainly not explain so different an effect.

[3] J. W. Hurst, 'Disturbed Tipperary 1831-1860', *Eire-Ireland*, ix (1974), 54; Printed Memorandum for Cabinet by Sir T. Redington, Under-Secretary, 25 Oct. 1846, Royal Archives RA D15.

specially reported outrage, but also by a move away from less and towards more serious crime. Furthermore, while during the Famine the proportion of outrages designated 'agrarian' had fallen from 15.8 per cent of the whole in 1844 to 3.0 per cent in 1847, the depression of the early 1860s registered a modest contrary trend, while the proportions rose dramatically from 11.9 per cent to no less than 57.0 per cent between 1878 and 1881.

TABLE 43A

Movements in specially reported outrages during the Great Famine and the Land War

	Against the person		Against property		Against public peace	
	N	percentage of total	N	percentage of total	N	percentage of total
1844	1,700	26.9	2,321	36.7	2,282	36.1
1847	1,498	7.1	15,901	75.8	3,555	16.9
1878	917	36.3	924	36.6	601	23.8
1881	1,148	14.7	1,631	20.9	4,917	63.1

Note The small balance is made up of 'other offences'.

TABLE 43B

Movements in offences during the Land War, distinguishing indictable cases not disposed of summarily from minor charges disposed of summarily

	Indictable cases not disposed of summarily	Minor charges disposed of summarily
1878	6,959	269,000
1880	8,607	240,000
1881	11,915	206,000

The leaky nature of comprehensive explanations for the movement of crime and violence is further emphasized by the relative failure of preliminary attempts to link the regional and local distributions of unrest to any particular set of social and economic characteristics. For the Land War period itself Andrew Orridge has, indeed, been able to find some significant correlations between early (1879–80) crime levels and the local existence of a poor, backward, and small-farmer economy, and also between later (1881–2) levels and the location of more prosperous farming communities.[1] But my own

[1] A. W. Orridge, 'Who supported the Land War? An aggregate-data analysis of Irish agrarian discontent 1879–1882', *Economic and Social Review*, xii (1981), 203–33.

comparatively unsophisticated attempts to use county data during the period 1844-80 to calculate correlation coefficients between either all outrages or agrarian outrages alone and (a) percentages of holdings under five, and under fifteen acres or valued at £4 and under, and under £8, and (b) the proportion of land in pasture, both for Ireland as a whole and (to eliminate possible distortions) for the three southern provinces only, have in general yielded a string of weak and 'insignificant' relationships.

This does not, of course, necessarily imply a lack of geographical patterning to rural unrest. Both contemporary comment and such relatively reliable data as are available agree broadly as to the counties most prone to violence of one kind or another. The various Whiteboy and Rightboy outbreaks of the late eighteenth century were concentrated upon Tipperary, Limerick, Waterford, Cork, King's Co., Queen's Co., and Kilkenny; Defender unrest in this and later periods upon the south Ulster borderlands and across the north midlands.[1] The severe disturbances of 1811 and 1813-16 and the districts proclaimed as a result were again mainly to be found in Tipperary, Limerick, Waterford, King's Co., Kilkenny, Longford, and Westmeath. Roughly similar locations marked the Rockite troubles of 1821-4 and the Terry Alt outbreaks of 1829-31. Even the rather separate Tithe War of the early 1830s was at its most intense in these areas.[2] Connacht, it was widely agreed, was second to Protestant Ulster for quietness, calm, and lack of disturbance.[3] Tipperary, on the other hand, enjoyed a general contemporary reputation as the 'worst' and most 'dangerous' place in Ireland. Indeed, something approaching an upper-class folklore existed on the subject, and the mere mention of Tipperary made—and the results are still visible— some men's hands shake as they wrote.[4] The county origins of those

[1] S. Clark, *Social origins of the Irish Land War*, p. 84; *Copy of a dispatch from His Excellency the Lord Lieutenant of Ireland, to Lord Viscount Sidmouth: dated 5th June 1816:—viz. A Statement of the nature and extent of the disturbances which have recently prevailed in Ireland*, H.C. 1816 (479), ix, 479-603.

[2] P. O'Donoghue, 'Causes of the opposition to Tithes, 1830-38', *Studia Hibernica*, No. 5 (1965), 8, *idem*, 'Opposition to Tithe Payments in 1830-31', ibid. No. 6 (1966), 79-80, *idem*, 'Opposition to Tithe Payment in 1832-3', ibid. No. 12 (1972), 81; Sir H. Vivian to Lord Fitzroy, 25 Dec. 1831, Vivian Papers No. 10.

[3] Lord Wellesley to Lord Sidmouth, 3 Jan. 1822, Wellesley Papers Add. MS 37298; E. Littleton to Melbourne, 12 Dec. 1833, Melbourne Papers 97/8; Melbourne to Littleton, 30 Dec. 1833, ibid. 97/22; *Papers relating to the State of Ireland*, H.C. 1834 (459), xlvii, 419-22; *Crime and Outrage Committee*, H.C. 1839 (486), xi and xii, Qs. 6658 ff.; *Devon Commission*, Witness No. 1101; Heytesbury to Graham, 29 May, 2 Sept., 14 Nov. 1845, Graham Papers 21/Ir, 23/Ir, 24/Ir; Memorandum by J. R. Godley, 27 June 1845, ibid. 22/Ir.

[4] See Mulgrave to Melbourne, 23 Feb. [1836], Melbourne Papers 99/121; J. Carden to Lord Donoughmore, 10 Nov. [1844], Graham Papers 18/Ir; Graham to Heytesbury, 16 Nov. 1844, ibid. 18/Ir; Heytesbury to Graham, 21 Nov. 1844, ibid. 18/Ir; *Devon*

transported to Australia for 'agrarian' offences in the 1820s and
1830s, as also the locations of the most serious armed clashes between
police and civilians between 1830 and 1846, again produce few sur-
prises, with Tipperary, Kilkenny, Westmeath, Limerick, and Longford well to the fore.[1] The first two major outbreaks of rural violence
after the Famine occurred around south-east Ulster (Armagh,
Monaghan, and Louth) in the early 1850s and Westmeath and its
surroundings between 1869 and 1871.[2]

Locations, indeed, seem to have changed little throughout the
decades before the Land War.[3] In this matter provinces are too large
for useful analysis and even counties sometimes exhibited extreme
internal localisms of violence which must add a note of caution to
conclusions based on county data alone. It is, in any case, far from
easy to display succinct evidence of the relative amount of violent
unrest in various counties over long periods. Two indirect measures
are, however, available which reveal general and official perceptions
rather than the actual incidence of violence itself. The 234 witnesses
who made specific comments to the Devon Commission in 1844 on
the state of rural unrest in their respective counties (see Table 38
above) constituted about a fifth of all the county witnesses to appear
before the Commission. Assuming that the intensity of comment
reflected the intensity of the problem, it is possible to identify those
counties in which A: more than 30 per cent of witnesses commented,
and B: between 20 and 30 per cent commented, and to list them
in descending order.[4]

A	B
Tipperary	Longford
Armagh	Wexford
King's Co.	Limerick
Waterford	Leitrim
Cavan	
Kilkenny	
Monaghan	

Commission, Witness No. 1101; Palmerston to Lord Minto, 19 Nov. 1847, Minto Papers
MS 12073; also J. W. Hurst, 'Disturbed Tipperary 1831–1860', pp. 44–59.

[1] A. G. L. Shaw, *Convicts and the Colonies: A Study of Penal Transportation from
Great Britain and Ireland to Australia and other parts of the British Empire* (London, 1966),
pp. 180–1; *Return relative to the persons who have been killed or severely wounded in
affrays with the constabulary force in Ireland, since 1st December 1830, specifying their
names, date, place of occurrence*, H.C. 1846 (280), xxxv, 237–60.
[2] See, e.g., R. and J. R. Miller to E. Lawford, 4 and 7 Feb. 1852, Drapers' Company
L.-B. Irish 1848–57; *Committee on Outrages (Ireland)*, H.C. 1852 (438), xiv, 1–690; Spencer
to Gladstone, 28 Dec. 1869, Gladstone Papers Add. MS 44306; Strathnairn to Spencer, 23

[*See opposite page for n. 2 cont. and nn. 3 and 4*].

Similarly, the dispositions of the national constabulary established in 1836 can be taken as a rough reflection of what were perceived to be local needs or levels of criminal activity. Shown in Table 44, the rank order of the ten most policed counties (taking population into account) provides some insight into those districts from which violence and crime were thought most likely to arise. Counties appearing at least three times out of a possible four selected occasions are given in italics.

TABLE 44

The most heavily policed counties, 1837, 1845, 1869, 1886

	1837	1845	1869	1886
1st	*Kilkenny*	*Tipperary*	*Tipperary*	*Westmeath*
2nd	*Kildare*	*Kildare*	*King's*	Kerry
3rd	*Queen's*	*King's*	*Meath*	*Meath*
4th	*Westmeath*	*Kilkenny*	*Kilkenny*	Limerick
5th	*King's*	*Queen's*	*Westmeath*	*Tipperary*
6th	Galway	*Westmeath*	Leitrim	Galway
7th	*Meath*	Carlow	Limerick	*King's*
8th	*Tipperary*	*Meath*	*Queen's*	Clare
9th	Carlow	Wicklow	Longford	*Kilkenny*
10th	Louth	Louth	*Kildare*	Longford

percentage of total population in above	24.9 (1841)	24.9 (1841)	20.2 (1871)	26.4 (1881)
percentage of police in above	45.5	37.9	30.7	42.5

Apart from the appearance of Kildare (caused by the large military camp at the Curragh), the counties in Table 44 generally match those traditionally regarded as unruly since the middle of the eighteenth century. The absence (with the fleeting exception of Louth) of the south Ulster borderlands is the result of lower—but not low—levels of violence in that area as reflected in the repeated positioning in eleventh or twelfth place of counties such as Cavan and Monaghan. Indeed, the locations of constabulary *stations* in 1852 and 1871 reveal extremely heavy concentrations, not only in the Limerick-Tipperary-King's Co.-Queen's Co.-Westmeath-Longford area, but

Mar. 1869, Strathnairn Papers Add. MS 42825; *Committee on Westmeath etc. (Unlawful Combinations)*, H.C. 1871 (147), xiii, 547–818.

[3] I have not in general been able to detect Joseph Lee's 'westward shift of chronic unrest since the mid-eighteenth century' ('Patterns of rural unrest in nineteenth-century Ireland', pp. 223–5).

[4] *Devon Index*, under 'Outrages, Agrarian'.

around the southern border between Leinster and Ulster also.[1] Overall, therefore, the distribution of police manpower and the analysis
of outrages themselves (in Tables 45 A and B) demonstrate the
'stability' of the disturbed districts and highlight the significantly
novel emergence in the early 1880s of certain western counties, such
as Mayo, Kerry, and Sligo, not hitherto noted for either the persistence or the intensity of their violence. Tables 45 A and B indicate
—for both all specially reported outrages and for officially defined
agrarian outrages alone—the rank order of the ten most disturbed
counties (measured, not only for *all* outrages against *total* population, but also for *agrarian* outrages against '*rural*' population outside
towns of 500 and more inhabitants) during eight two-year periods
between 1844 and 1885. The results obtained are consolidated for
the period as a whole and for 1844-60 and 1864-85 by means of a
percentage figure based on the maximum 'score' each county might
have achieved had ten points been attached to the 'worst' county in
each two-year period, nine to the second 'worst', and so on. Although
cumbersome, this procedure is comparatively immune from aberrant
fluctuations and makes it possible, therefore, to assess *relative*
positions over long periods. Separate ranking for 1879-80 and
1884-5 highlights the contrast between these later years and the
distribution of violence in earlier times.

In general terms Tables A and B match well enough. Kildare's
claim disappears once the doings of the licentious soldiery are
removed in the agrarian figures. Of the remaining nine 'most disturbed'
counties for the period as a whole, all but two appear among the
ten 'most disturbed' agrarian counties. But before discussing the
character of this core area, it is well to emphasize both the intensity
and the comparative transience of the Land War's success in awakening the west. In the thirty-five years before 1879 only Leitrim made
any consistent appearance in the annals of disturbance. But although
all this changed dramatically in 1879-80,[2] even then it was not long
before the traditionally disturbed counties began once more to
reassert their old predominance. This later shift in the focal point
of the Land War away from the west and towards those parts of
the country with longer experience of the cultural atmosphere of

[1] Map in F. B. Head, *A Fortnight in Ireland*, frontispiece; list in *Returns of the number on the register of parliamentary electors: of the names of the places where petty session courts are held: And, of the names of the constabulary stations in each county in Ireland*, H.C. 1871 (373), lvi, 579-88.

[2] For additional analyses of *agrarian* outrages per 10,000 of *total* population for 1879-82, see D. Fitzpatrick, 'The geography of Irish nationalism 1910-1921', *Past and Present*, No. 78 (1978), 138; also, for 1880-2, see E. Rumpf and A. C. Hepburn, *Nationalism and Socialism in twentieth-century Ireland* (Liverpool, 1977), p. 52.

TABLE 45A

*Counties with the highest relative incidence of all
specially reported outrages, 1844–85*

	1844–85 'Score'*	1844–60 'Score'	1864–85 'Score'	Position 1879–80	Position 1884–5
Longford	76.3	90.0	62.5	8th	2nd
Westmeath	58.8	47.5	70.0	4th	4th
Tipperary	58.8	75.0	42.5	—	5th
King's Co.	45.0	47.5	42.5	5th	9th
Kildare	45.0	55.0	35.0	9th	—
Limerick	40.0	45.0	60.0	3rd	3rd
Leitrim	31.3	35.0	37.5	10th	—
Galway	28.8	—	45.0	1st	10th
Kilkenny	20.0	—	22.5	—	—
Clare	17.5	22.5	—	—	6th
Wicklow	—	22.5	—	—	—
Carlow	—	20.0	—	—	—
Kerry	—	—	35.0	7th	1st
Mayo	—	—	—	2nd	—
Sligo	—	—	—	6th	—
Queen's Co.	—	—	—	—	7th
Waterford	—	—	—	—	8th

* Maximum possible 'score' = 100.

specially reported outrages was noticed at the time and more recently by Paul Bew in his sparkling study of the Land War and its migrations.[1] For two counties—Galway and Cork—it is actually possible to disentangle the outrages of the agriculturally backward western parts from those of the more advanced east (Table 46). And this too shows that, after a striking western efflorescence, the weight of outrage and violence had already by 1885 returned to its traditional more eastern orientation. That already in 1846 a similar tendency can also be discerned for agrarian violence to be located in the more prosperous parts of other western counties—south rather than north Leitrim, south-east rather than north-west Roscommon, east rather than west Clare—suggests that broad generalizations connecting poverty with unrest require modification.[2]

In any case, those counties which consistently emerge as the

[1] W. E. Forster to Gladstone, 25 Oct. 1880, Gladstone Papers Add. MS 44157; Printed Cabinet Papers (Memorandum by W. E. Forster, 16 Nov. 1880), CAB37/4/71; P. Bew, *Land and the National Question in Ireland 1858–82*, Chapter Six.

[2] J. Lee, 'Patterns of rural unrest in nineteenth-century Ireland', pp. 225–7. The food riots which broke out in Co. Cork at the beginning of the Famine were concentrated in the more prosperous east (J. S. Donnelly Jr., *The Land and the People of nineteenth-century Cork: The Rural Economy and the Land Question* (London, 1975), p. 91).

TABLE 45B

*Counties with the highest relative incidence of specially
reported agrarian outrages, 1844–85*

	1844–85 'Score'*	1844–60 'Score'	1864–85 'Score'	Position 1879–80	Position 1884–5
King's Co.	78.8	95.0	62.5	6th	8th
Tipperary	68.8	80.0	57.5	—	2nd
Westmeath	66.3	70.0	62.5	8th	9th
Longford	57.6	60.0	55.0	—	5th
Leitrim	51.3	70.0	32.5	5th	—
Limerick	33.8	30.0	37.5	4th	4th
Kerry	22.5	—	45.0	3rd	1st
Galway	18.8	—	37.5	1st	—
Cavan	17.5	15.0	—	—	—
Donegal	17.5	35.0	—	—	—
Kilkenny	—	17.5	—	—	—
Roscommon	—	17.5	—	—	—
Clare	—	—	27.5	10th	3rd
Mayo	—	—	22.5	2nd	—
Sligo	—	—	—	7th	—
Cork	—	—	—	9th	7th
Queen's Co.	—	—	—	—	6th
Waterford	—	—	—	—	10th

* Maximum possible 'score' = 100.

TABLE 46

*Percentages of county outrages (adjusted for population) in the
west ridings of Cos. Cork and Galway, 1865, 1880, 1885*

	All outrages		Agrarian outrages	
	Cork	Galway	Cork	Galway
1865	45.3	47.3	33.5	49.0
1880	56.4	74.6	55.3	75.6
1885	44.5	43.5	47.4	45.5

most disturbed throughout the period—Limerick, Tipperary, King's
Co., Westmeath, Longford, Leitrim, with lesser outliers in Kilkenny,
Roscommon, and Cavan—form a kind of intermediate buffer, geographically and to some extent economically, between the extremes
of east and west.[1] Contemporary explanations as to why this area
should have been particularly disturbed fall into three categories.
Some analysts favoured highly local reasons: bad landlords, absentees,

---

[1] It is notable that by 1878 (when urban Fenianism had receded) Leitrim, Roscommon,
and Cavan were among the five strongest Fenian counties (T. Garvin, *The evolution of Irish
nationalist politics*, p. 63).

bad farming, or 'some great oppression for which the law afforded
no protection'.[1] Some simply expressed themselves baffled: 'I am',
confessed Colonel Miller of the constabulary, 'unable to assign a
reason for the prevalence of crime in Tipperary . . . but it would
appear that in all history Tipperary has been remarkable for the
lawless character of its peasantry.'[2] A few attempted more general
explanations. The commonest, that based on race, was favoured by
many intelligent observers. It did not, as might be supposed, blame
violence upon Celtic hotness of temper, quite the reverse. Cornewall
Lewis thought Kerry quiet in 1836 because the Celts were a cowed
people and Tipperary violent because many of its inhabitants were
Anglo-Saxons, 'large limbed and fair-haired'. In 1852 the land agent,
W. S. Trench, attributed Tipperary's violence to the peasantry's
'Cromwellian' blood. A poor-law inspector blamed 'an infusion of
Teutonic blood. They will not lie down under the handicap endured
by my Donegal neighbours.' Thirty years later, an American, Professor David King, thought the 'mixture of English blood' made
peasants 'more obstinate'. In 1870 the Irish Government's chief
statistician, W. N. Hancock, turned things on their head by telling
Gladstone that Tipperarymen were genetic heirs to 'the bravest races
of Celtic Irishmen', that Westmeath and Longford were stocked with
people of the ancient 'ruling Irish race', and that King's Co. had
always resisted the earliest 'Anglo-Saxon government'.[3] Lewis and
Hancock were, however, unusual in venturing beyond such fashionable analysis. Lewis's book *On local Disturbances* (1836) was carefully organized to lead to the conclusion that disturbances 'prevail
most where the peasantry are bold and robust, and one degree
removed above the lowest poverty'. And just as outrages were
scarcest in the hungriest months, so, Lewis believed, were they
scarcest in the hungriest counties. Hancock identified Tipperary,

[1] R. M. O'Ferrall to N. Macdonald, [Oct. 1838], Carlisle Papers L.-B. 32; also, e.g.,
Heytesbury to Graham, 29 May 1845, Graham Papers 21/Ir; T. Garvin, *The evolution of
Irish nationalist politics*, p. 36; *A Young Irishman's Diary (1836–1847)*, ed. W. Clare,
pp. 30–3 (1840).

[2] *Devon Commission*, Witness No. 1101, Q. 8. See also Major Brownrigg of the constabulary in *Committee on Outrages (Ireland)*, H.C. 1852 (438), xiv, Qs. 1386 ff. and
W. S. Trench's reference in 1852 to 'the better management of Queen's Co. over King's Co.'
as 'a lucky accident, which is the same as saying that I cannot explain it' (N. W. Senior,
Journals, conversations, and essays relating to Ireland, ii, 16–17).

[3] G. C Lewis to E. W. Head, 9 Apr. 1836, *Letters of the Right Hon. Sir George Cornewall Lewis Bart. to various friends*, ed. G. F. Lewis (London, 1870), pp. 49–50; N. W. Senior,
Journals, conversations, and essays relating to Ireland, ii, 16–17, 46 (Trench and poor-law
inspector); D. B. King, *The Irish Question* (London, 1882), p. 224. James Macaulay (*Ireland
in 1872: A tour of observation, with remarks on Irish public questions* (London, 1873),
p. 140) blamed religion instead of race, pointing to contemporary Scots Highlanders as
very 'loyal and orderly and exemplary'. See MS Memorandum by Hancock, Feb. 1870,
Gladstone Papers Add. MS 44613, fos. 70–85, continued fos. 120–6.

Westmeath, Longford, Meath, Leitrim, and King's Co. as persistently disturbed and produced a mass of statistics to show that all of them had experienced unusually high rates of eviction, farm consolidation, transfer of tillage to pasture, low rates of waste-land reclamation, and substantial declines in 'rural' population.[1] Sadly, however, such heroic generalizations keep breaking down on the hidden rocks of local events and circumstances. The evidence that evictions led to outrages is highly variable and weaker in the 1850s and 1860s than during the Land War. And, in any case, three of Hancock's counties experienced perfectly average rates from 1849 onwards when reliable eviction returns begin.[2] Again, the decline in rural population was near the mean in Westmeath and Leitrim, though far above it in King's Co. and Tipperary. The rates of decrease in tillage varied widely between the six counties. Nor even did Hancock's own estimates of consolidation between 1841 and 1866 (vitiated as they were by unreliable figures for 1841) make counties like Longford and Leitrim stand out in any way from national trends.

Returning to the rather different set of persistently disturbed counties identified earlier and dividing it into two geographically coherent blocks consisting of A: King's Co., Tipperary, Limerick, and Kilkenny, and B: Westmeath, Longford, Leitrim, Roscommon, and Cavan, it is possible to test more accurately some of the views put forward by Hancock and by more recent students of the matter (Table 47). What emerges most strongly is the remarkably 'normal' nature of the disturbed counties. Of course some differences stand out, especially Group A's higher eviction rate in 1850. But no general pattern is apparent and in some matters, such as farm size and valuation, the two groups stand at opposite sides of provincial and national averages. Even before the Famine and certainly thereafter, it can hardly, therefore, be said that unrest was necessarily greatest in 'areas with a significant number of bigger farms, with relatively high proportions of labourers and farm servants, where market forces were influential but not yet triumphant'. Undoubtedly the nine persistently disturbed counties fall largely into L. M. Cullen's middle region of 1841, marked, he suggests, by particularly sharp

[1] G. C. Lewis, *On local Disturbances*, pp. 72-3; W. N. Hancock's Memorandum of Feb. 1870, op. cit.

[2] T. Garvin, *The evolution of Irish nationalist politics*, pp. 76-8; A. W. Orridge, 'Who supported the Land War?', p. 221. Evidence to the contrary—that outrages led to evictions —has not been produced in any but isolated cases. See also W. E. Vaughan, 'Landlord and Tenant Relations in Ireland between the Famine and the Land War, 1850-78' in *Comparative aspects of Scottish and Irish economic and social history 1600-1900*, ed. L. M. Cullen and T. C. Smout (Edinburgh, [1977]), p. 220. The 'average' Hancock counties were Longford, Meath, and Westmeath.

TABLE 47
Economic and social characteristics of the most disturbed districts compared with provincial and national trends, 1841–81

		Group A		Group B		All Munster and Leinster		All Ireland	
I Size of holdings (percentage of all holdings more than 1 acre)		1–5 acres	1–15 acres	1–5 acres	1–15 acres	1–5 acres	1–15 acres	1–5 acres	1–15 acres
	1847	26.5	53.0	19.2	63.1	20.0	48.7	19.0	56.0
	1850	19.5	45.5	14.3	54.3	16.4	41.1	15.5	49.7
	1865	17.2	39.4	12.9	49.0	15.6	37.1	14.7	46.5
	1880	15.2	36.0	11.1	46.2	13.7	34.3	12.3	43.1
II Valuation (percentage of all agricultural holdings)		£4 and below	Under £8	£4 and below	Under £8	£4 and below	Under £8	£4 and below	Under £8
	1866	25.8	43.2	28.1	55.9	25.3	43.5	24.8	50.8
III Number of farm labourers (to every farmer)	1841	3.0		3.1		3.3		2.7	
	1851	2.8		2.2		3.0		2.3	
	1861	2.3		1.9		2.5		1.8	
	1881	2.0		1.4		2.0		1.5	
IV Gross evictions (per 1,000 holdings of more than 1 acre)	1850	70.9		33.5		50.9		33.6	
	1865	2.1		2.1		2.2		1.7	
	1880	5.5		5.5		5.6		4.0	
V Percentage of non-waste land in pasture								(3 southern provinces only)	
	1851	59.9		61.6*		57.3		59.9	
	1881	67.3		69.8*		65.2		67.5	

* Excluding Co. Cavan

contrasts 'between farmer and other rural classes'.[1] And one may speculate that labourers in such places had more to envy than their western and less to expect than their eastern brothers; that farmers felt neither sufficiently secure nor sufficiently indigent to behave with the confidence or the camaraderie essential for either disciplined or relaxed relationships; that the *process* of integration into the market was more unsettling than the existence of either a sophisticated or a primitive economy. But, in the end, rural unrest remains a profoundly mysterious phenomenon. Its locus was remarkably stable over long periods. It involved labourers and cottiers, in opposition to and sometimes in uneasy alliance with, farmers. It was driven by distress but generally absent from the most distressed counties and seasons—until suddenly in 1879 the most distressed counties exploded into a short concentrated burst of unprecedented violence. It declined less markedly after the Famine than has often been supposed, and, while shifting its social texture, remained constant to long-hallowed techniques and procedures. Above all, it furnished a highly varied repertoire for those anxious to pursue group, class, or local solidarity. And as such, it provided a model set of examples which could easily be followed in other, less directly agrarian, contexts: social or spiritual reform, sectarian strife, politics, and electioneering.

III AGRARIAN VIOLENCE AND POLITICAL ACTION

The connection between agrarian disorder and formal political mobilization (for the geography of the latter, see Chapter VI and especially Table 56 below) was always far from constant. Neither the motivation nor the result of rural outrages was generally regarded as even vaguely political by those involved in such matters.[2] The objects were agrarian, and political compliance with the 'popular' cause did not—as several victims of assassination in Tipperary and many land-grabbing O'Connellites found out to their cost—ensure immunity from either verbal or physical attack.[3] Not that the Ribbon

---

[1] J. Lee, 'Patterns of rural unrest in nineteenth-century Ireland', p. 225; L. M. Cullen, *An economic history of Ireland since 1660* (London, 1972), pp. 111-12.

[2] See, e.g., Sir H. Vivian to Sir T. Arbuthnot, 19 July 1831, Vivian Papers No. 10; J. S. Kennedy to Melbourne, 18 Oct. 1837, Melbourne Papers 100/60; *Fictitious Votes, Ireland*, 2nd series, 3rd report, p. 230; Eliot to Graham, 9 Nov. 1841, Graham Papers 8/Ir; De Grey to Graham, 27 May 1842, ibid. 7/Ir; Printed Memorandum for Cabinet by Sir T. Redington, Under-Secretary, 25 Oct. 1846, Royal Archives RA D15; Clarendon to Russell, 29 Jan. 1850, Clarendon Papers L.-B. V; Major H. Brownrigg to Redington, 1 Feb. 1852 (copy), Royal Archives RA D21/61a.

[3] M. R. Beames, 'Rural Conflict in pre-Famine Ireland', pp. 75-91; G. C. Lewis, *On local Disturbances*, pp. 143-4; Report of Chief Constable Trant, 7 Dec. 1835, O.P. 1835, Box 34.

(as opposed to the Whiteboy) tradition did not sustain overtly political goals, but then its direct connections with rural life were often overwhelmed by more urban concerns.[1] In the 1830s and 1840s, as in the 1860s, scattered Ribbon groups spent as much time on electoral canvassing, intimidation, and rioting as upon wages or the price of land.[2] Monaghan Ribbonmen thought it worth while to appear in 1834 at reform meetings called to petition Parliament 'in great numbers; several shots were fired; they were decorated with ribands and other emblems'. But the motivation behind such involvement is far from clear, nor should the distinction between Ribbonism and Whiteboyism be pressed too far. In 1837 a Longford priest angrily denounced local Ribbonmen for being 'hostile to the Liberal interest' and supporting Conservative candidates, while in Kerry rival agrarian factions used elections as no more than another excuse for mutual assault and recrimination.[3] Many of those who perpetrated outrages felt bitter and disappointed by O'Connell's false political dawns. 'I have', recalled a priest in 1832, 'often heard their conversations, when they say, "What good did Emancipation do for us? Are we better clothed or fed, or our children better clothed or fed?"' And although some observers could never shake off a belief in hidden connections between O'Connell and rural crime, O'Connell's ceaseless denunciations of secret societies were certainly as genuine as they were ineffective. O'Connell disliked rural combination as much as he did labour unions, and it is notable that the peaks and troughs of labour unrest in Dublin had little or nothing to do with the intensity or otherwise of Repeal politics.[4] In general, however, such —mainly impressionistic—evidence as exists suggests that periods of national political excitement often coincided with low levels of rural outrage.[5] Certainly before the Famine, O'Connell seems to have appealed to a constituency which overlapped with that drawn upon

[1] T. Garvin, 'Defenders, Ribbonmen and others', pp. 133-55; M. R. Beames, 'The Ribbon Societies', pp. 128-43; Clarendon to Grey, 29, 31 May 1849, Clarendon Papers L.-B. IV.

[2] *Committee on Bribery at Elections*, H.C. 1835 (547), viii, 363-4; *Crime and Outrage Committee*, H.C. 1839 (486), xi and xii, Qs. 673-6, 2296; *Papers relating to ... Dolly's Brae*, H.C. 1850 [1143], li, 374. In Dublin City, however, urban Ribbonmen 'never' interfered in elections (*Crime and Outrage Committee*, op. cit. Qs. 5059 ff.).

[3] *First report ... Orange Lodges*, H.C. 1835 (377), xv, 24; *Fictitious Votes, Ireland*, 2nd series, 3rd report, p. 230; Report of Chief Constable Smith, 14 Aug. 1837, O.P. 1837/ 620/32, Box 52; G. C. Lewis, *On local Disturbances*, pp. 89-90.

[4] F. Blackburne to E. Stanley, 21 Dec. 1832, Melbourne Papers 102/45; *Devon Commission*, Witness Nos. 357 (Sligo farmer) and 986 (Queen's Co. agent); Lord Glengall in *Fictitious Votes, Ireland*, 1st series, 2nd report, pp. 25-7; F. D'Arcy, 'Dublin artisan activity, opinion, and organization 1820-1850', p. 47.

[5] G. C. Lewis, *On local Disturbances*, pp. 142-5; Major E. Priestly to Lord Eliot, 30 Sept. 1843, Graham Papers 6/Ir; Graham to Heytesbury, 16 Nov. 1844, ibid. 18/Ir;

by the secret societies. Probably, however, it was the exhilaration generated rather than O'Connell's efforts at rural 'pacification'[1] that helped to absorb or divert the perpetrators of rural outrage into less overtly violent activities. Yet the actual relationship between political and agrarian excitement remains uncertain. To some extent, elections, with their opportunities for mass demonstration and public pressure, provided the more sophisticated Whiteboys (the term is used generally) with attractive opportunities for carrying on their struggle by other means, and certainly elections often acted as generators of increased and *continuing* violence in what had previously been comparatively peaceful communities. On the other hand, in counties such as Monaghan, the fiercest election mobs were regularly recruited from those districts most noted for their addiction to outrages of every kind.[2]

The striking success of the New Departure of the 1870s in simultaneously harnessing and controlling agrarian unrest is highlighted by the very different alignments which existed between outrages and political action in the 1840s and the 1860s. In 1843 all but one of the thirty-five county police inspectors saw no connection between the Repeal campaign and rural unrest and only six believed that 'secret meetings' had been held in their areas in favour of O'Connell's agitation. If anything, they thought there was more *political* danger to be feared from the temperance movement than from agrarian secret societies.[3] Nor was there any consistent convergence between counties of known Repeal strength (as measured, for example, by contributions to O'Connell's National Annuity in 1833 or degrees of attendance at the 'monster' meetings of 1843) and counties most notable in 1844 for either outrages as a whole or agrarian outrages in

W. R. Le Fanu, *Seventy years of Irish Life* (London, 1928), pp. 36-7; J. A. Reynolds, *The Catholic Emancipation Crisis in Ireland, 1823-1829* (New Haven, 1954), pp. 137-9; P. O'Donnell, *The Irish Faction Fighters of the 19th Century* (Dublin, 1975), pp. 45-6.

[1] P. Holohan, 'Daniel O'Connell and the Dublin Trades: A Collision 1837/8', *Saothar*, No. 1 (1975), 11 (and sources cited). On the activities of Repeal 'Pacificators', see *Kilkenny Journal*, 6 Mar. 1833; *Pilot*, 10 Aug., 16 Nov. 1836, 5 July, 23 Aug. 1837. See also O'Connell to Duncannon, 14 Jan. 1833, *Correspondence of Daniel O'Connell*, ed. M. R. O'Connell, v, 3; *Crime and Outrage Committee*, H.C. 1839 (486), xi and xii, Qs. 13413-14.

[2] E. Stanley to Melbourne, 19 May 1831, Melbourne Papers 95/88; M. Tierney (Carlow farmer) to Anglesey, 22 June 1831, O.P. 1831/T31, Box 1842; Anglesey to Grey, 28 Nov. 1832, Anglesey Papers D619/28A; *Crime and Outrage Committee*, H.C. 1839 (486), xi and xii, Qs. 6658 (King's Co. JP), 10601 ff. (P. Finn), 263-99 (former police inspector-general), 11667-71 (RM); Eglinton to Derby, 10 Sept. 1852, Eglinton Papers MS 5333; Lord Rosse to Naas, 26 Oct. 1852, ibid. MS 5352; *Committee on parliamentary and municipal elections*, H.C. 1868-9 (352), viii, 312-14; P. O'Donoghue, 'Opposition to Tithe Payment in 1832-3', p. 93.

[3] See Printed Questionnaire (Derby Papers 34) Section B: 'Secret and Confidential. Ireland. Questions addressed by order of the government to the county inspectors of the constabulary with Precis of the Answers received from the officers. 1843'.

particular. Only Cork and Tipperary appear among the ten leading counties in all four lists, which otherwise differ very markedly, with, for example, Wexford, Waterford, Meath, and Louth high in the ranks of Repeal but altogether less so in those of disorder.[1] Some four decades later, however, the situation had changed dramatically. Whatever the formal connections between Land League activities and the perpetration of outrages—and although the Government could find little evidence it harboured the darkest suspicions[2]—the close geographical alignment between the two marked the measure of a changed political world. The correlation coefficients between League meetings and (a) *agrarian* and (b) *all* specially reported outrages in 1879–80 are quite remarkably high at + 0.90 and + 0.89 respectively.[3] Apart from the dramatic efflorescence of the west (where incidentally Leitrim, not Mayo, led the way), it was the traditionally 'disturbed' counties which stood out as epicentres of League strength —Westmeath, Longford, Tipperary, and King's Co.—an early harbinger of the later shift in emphasis away from Connacht and towards the less impoverished farmers of the central counties. But, more importantly, the relationship between political action and rural unrest had developed beyond a largely random one into a structured configuration by which both were transformed. The Land War and its aftermath, far from establishing constitutionalism or *de facto* Irish states, finally welded formal politics and rural violence together into a practical union of a fundamentally new and powerful kind.

The ultimate coming together could not, however, have taken place without much previous mingling, however haphazard. The way in which the traditional methods of the secret societies were increasingly carried over into formal politics helped to create that common culture which was to prove amenable to joint mobilization when the time came. Especially notable is the translation of the agrarian 'threatening letter' into political and specifically electoral

[1] Contributions 1833: *Detailed Report of Contributions (Parochial and Personal) to the O'Connell National Annuity for the year 1833* (Dublin, 1834)—copy in Hull University Library Pressmark DA 950.2 01; estimated attendance at meetings; Confidential Print, Derby Papers 33/2; outrages: *Devon Commission*, part iii, Appendix No. 36, H.C. 1845 [657], xxi. High-outrage counties such as Roscommon, Leitrim, and King's Co. make no appearance in the O'Connellite top ten. See also Chapter VI, Table 56 below.

[2] See, e.g., H. A. Blake, RM to Chief Secretary, 19 June 1880, in Printed Cabinet Papers (1880), CAB37/2/31; Memorandum by W. E. Forster, 16 Nov. 1880, ibid. CAB37/4/71; Gladstone to Queen Victoria, 13 June 1881, Royal Archives RA D31/99.

[3] Calculated on a population basis in each case from *Return showing for each month of the years 1879 and 1880 the number of Land League meetings held and agrarian crimes reported to the Inspector General of the Royal Irish Constabulary in each county throughout Ireland*, H.C. 1881 (5), lxxvii, 793–803 (with total outrage data from S.P.O. Irish Crime Records). Of course League meetings only really got under way in the summer of 1879.

contexts. Its style—hovering between demotic vigour and lumpen intellectualism—was often the product of disgruntled schoolmasters, many of whom (whether self- or state-employed) were to be found in pre-Famine Ireland organizing secret societies, tithe disturbances, O'Connellite politics, and electoral pressure groups. As all-purpose demagogues, they attended 'places of public resort, chapels, schools, forges, and, making use of the most inflammatory language', spouted meanderingly about Brian Boru, electoral confrontations, the evils of Protestantism, and the particular crotchets of each place.[1] Later they were so active in Fenianism that the Government pressured the Board of Education into demanding declarations from new teachers that they did not belong 'to any secret society whatsoever', despite which no less than thirty-two teachers were arrested for Ribbonism, sedition, or Fenianism during seven months in 1865-6 alone.[2] Some schoolmasters found it impossible to restrain or disguise their own characteristically quirky learning when making speeches or penning the threatening letters which oiled the machine of agrarian outrage. The tenant-right candidate for Co. Limerick in 1850 was backed by one local educational casuist who talked passionately of moral philosophy (or how to break promises given to landlords) and of Cicero and Epictetus from the balcony of Cronin's Hotel. Documents found in Tipperary referred to magistrates as surpassing 'Diocletian's or Nero's cruelty'. At the Meath election of 1835 'Captain Rock' distributed letters comparing Tory voters unfavourably with 'Epaminondas, that famous Theban... or Leonidas, the great Lacedemonian prince'. A poster found in a Longford chapel yard in 1847 signed 'Molly Anne Maguire' denounced landlords and agents as 'worse than Nero, Maxentius, or Caligula'.[3] More common was the threatening notice in 'illiterate' or disguised hand promising torture, death, or ostracism, and often embellished with crude drawings of gallows,

[1] Revd S. Payne to Sir H. Hardinge, 17 Jan. 1835, O.P. 1835, Box 35B. See *Diary of Humphrey O'Sullivan*, ed. M. McGrath, i, 207, 301, ii, 25-7, iv, 109-15; *Athlone Conservative Advocate*, 24 Aug. 1837; Mr and Mrs S. C. Hall, *Ireland*, i, 259; P. O'Donoghue, 'Opposition to Tithe Payments in 1830-1', pp. 80-1; J. S. Donnelly Jr., 'The Whiteboy Movement 1761-5', p. 40; T. Garvin, *The evolution of Irish nationalist politics*, pp. 17, 28, 49. In 1860 hedge-schoolmasters were still working on the Shirley estate in Monaghan (Shirley of Ettington Papers CR229/115/2).

[2] Eglinton to Naas, 16 Mar. 1859, Mayo Papers MS 11036; Government to Board of Education, 6 Apr. 1859, Larcom Papers MS 7793. See R. D. FitzSimon, 'The Irish Government and the Phoenix Society' (University College Dublin MA thesis, 1965), pp. 28, 31, 42, 133; *Return of all Schoolmasters arrested in Ireland for Ribbonism, Sedition, or connected with the Fenian Conspiracy*, H.C. 1866 (455), lviii, 475-8.

[3] Folklore Commission MS 1194, fos. 318 ff.; T. Garvin, *The evolution of Irish nationalist politics*, pp. 17-18; *Committee on Bribery at Elections*, H.C. 1835 (547), viii, 344; Maria Edgeworth to Clarendon, 19 Dec. 1847, Clarendon Papers Box 11. On the ubiquity of schoolmasters as penmen of threatening letters, see *Committee on Outrages (Ireland)*, H.C. 1852 (438), xiv, Qs. 65-7, 129-30.

pistols, graves, coffins, and other icons of destruction.[1] The debt owed by the numerous threatening election letters to agrarian models is clear enough. The same Gothick horrors were promised, the same irregular orthography presented, the same very specific orders given and responses demanded. And like their agrarian originals, they ranged from barely controlled frenzy ('i will tear ye asunder for year coffin is made') to an even more chilling civil-service formality ('Dear Sir, I have to inform you that I have to pay you a visit on the night of the 16th Inst. with regard to your vote . . . ').[2] Such letters, which continued to be a feature of rural elections throughout the century,[3] sometimes even appeared in printed form, while that specifically electoral sub-species—the list of voters who had 'gone the wrong way' and were to be shunned, assaulted, or otherwise abused—was usually run up by jobbing printers for sale in the streets by ballad singers and other men 'of uncertain employment'.[4] Threatening letters, the most common form of specially reported outrage, were, however, notoriously difficult to enumerate accurately. One stipendiary with sixteen years' experience estimated in 1871 that no more than a third were known to or reported by the police.[5] Bearing this in mind, the continuing vigour of the official statistics throughout the period, shown in Table 48, bears impressive testimony to the persistent liveliness of the genre. And if instances reported were but the tip of a much larger iceberg, so equally were threatening letters far from the comparatively innocuous rural art-form they might at first seem to have been. Indeed, many knowledgeable farmers, policemen, and government ministers were convinced that a substantial number of

[1] G. C. Lewis, *On local Disturbances*, pp. 82, 179–81. For illustrations, see ibid., and 'A Barrister', *Observations on Intimidation at Elections in Ireland* (Dublin, 1854), pp. 57–8; J. Lord, *Popery at the hustings: foreign and domestic legislation* (London, 1852), p. 36; *Saunders' Newsletter*, 24 July 1852; P. O'Donoghue, 'Opposition to Tithe Payments in 1830–1', p. 93; J. S. Donnelly Jr., 'The Whiteboy Movement 1761–5', p. 29.

[2] Mayo Papers MS 11037 (1852); F. B. Head, *A Fortnight in Ireland*, p. 379.

[3] For a pot-pourri of examples, see *Ballyshannon Herald*, 11 Jan. 1833; Report of Chief Constable Valentine, 15 Jan. 1835, O.P. 1835, Box 34; G. Warburton to W. Gossett, 29 May 1835, ibid.; *Athlone Conservative Advocate*, 31 Aug. 1837; *The Reign of Terror in Carlow, comprising an authentic detail of the Proceedings of Mr O'Connell and his followers* (London, 1841), pp. 16–17, 34–5, 92; police reports, 17 July 1852, Mayo Papers MS 11037; J. W. Chamberlin to Naas, 22 July 1852, ibid. MS 11018; *Freeman's Journal*, 25 Nov. 1869; *Committee on Westmeath etc. (Unlawful Combinations)*, H.C. 1871 (147), xiii, 563–4, 573.

[4] Petition of Clonakilty Magistrates, 31 Jan. 1835, O.P. 1835, Box 46; G. C. Lewis, *On local Disturbances*, p. 180; 'A Barrister', *Observations on Intimidation*, pp. 57–8. For lists of ostracized voters, see R. Fitzgibbon to Under-Secretary, 24 Dec. 1832, O.P. 1832/ 2264, Box 2192; Report of Sub-Inspector Clarke, 16 Jan. 1835, O.P. 1835, Box 46; Report of Chief Constable Daly, 20 Jan. 1835, O.P. 1835/152, Box 47; Petition of Kildare Magistrates, 27 Jan. 1835, O.P. 1835, Box 34; also Chapter I above.

[5] Captain G. Talbot, RM in *Committee on Westmeath etc. (Unlawful Combinations)*, H.C. 1871 (147), xiii, 563–4, 573.

TABLE 48
Threatening letters and notices, 1837–81

	Total letters, etc.	Percentage of total outrages	Total agrarian letters, etc.	Percentage of agrarian outrages
1837	685	10.1	n.a.	n.a.
1844	862	13.6	417	41.7
1851	686	7.5	66	26.3
1861	260	6.7	105	45.9
1871	363	12.5	173	46.4
1881	2,862	36.7	2,191	49.4

letters were, if disregarded, likely to be swiftly followed by violent action of a thoroughly unpleasant kind.[1]

A similar, if more general, kinship between the exercise of agrarian and of political pressure can be found in the common tradition of hyperbole in which both were often expressed. Just as the Widow Ryan of Rathcormac tithe fame was described as having dropped to her knees 'and prayed to the great God to hear the blood of the widow's son' with 'eyeballs like two burning coals', so priests promised to 'melt' voters 'off the face of the earth . . . to put the sickness on them' or see them 'fester in their corruption'. Election propaganda was spattered with words and phrases like 'slave', 'plague', 'grovelling creatures', 'Orange Catholic traitors', 'reptiles', men 'not fit to be kept alive', 'demons of hell', and 'exterminating blood-suckers'.[2] Those shouts that could be heard above the electoral mayhem owed many debts to the colourful traditions of popular violence: 'Bastards and whores', 'Take home your bastard Englishman', 'Dowse for ever and Clod's a bugger', 'Down with the Orange buggers', 'Tear the guts out of the — Orangemen'. Official pens quivered as they recorded the election speech delivered in 1872 by a farmer pointing at the Athenry Railway Station lavatories— 'I would go in there and s——t, and take it in my hand, and ram it down the throat of any fellow or man who would vote for a Trench.'[3]

[1] *Devon Commission*, Witness Nos. 846, 1101; Printed Cabinet Papers (by W. E. Forster, 16 Nov. 1880), CAB37/4/71.

[2] Information of H. Griffith, 17 Jan. 1835, O.P. 1835, Box 47; T. Pennefather to G. Fitzgerald, 17 Feb. 1835, O.P. 1835, Box 46; 'A Clergyman of the Established Church' [G. Dwyer], *Popery unmasked at the recent elections in Ireland* (London, [1852]), pp. 23–4. For phrases etc., see Printed Poster for Meath election, O.P. 1835/148, Box 47; N. Ross, 'Two nineteenth-century election posters', *Journal of the County Louth Archaeological Society*, xvi (1968), 224–32; Report of Sub-Inspector Despard, 5 July 1852, Mayo Papers MS 11037; *Londonderry Sentinel*, 16 July 1852; *Tipperary Advocate*, 16 Feb. 1865.

[3] Martin, King, French, & Ingram Papers D1550/81; *Report of the Outrages and Intimidations at the late Elections* (Dublin, 1841), p. 14; *Copy of the Depositions taken before the Coroner at the Inquests held at Dungarvan . . . on . . . William O'Brien and Bartholomew Keily, killed at the last Waterford County election*, H.C. 1867 (200), lvi, 230;

At times, colourful tableaux of various agrarian horrors—evictions, police brutality, and so on—were even wheeled around on carts during election campaigns while priests moved about carrying vast crucifixes, uttering curses in Irish and English, and distributing leaflets denouncing 'The Walpoles, Drummonds, Jocelyn Otways, and other earth-stoppers of the DERBY PRIEST-HUNTING BLOOD-HOUNDS'.[1]

Sectarian jealousies formed yet another connecting link between certain types of rural unrest and the contours of political violence. These jealousies, which had long lain behind the outrages of the south Ulster borderlands and behind a good deal of anti-landlord feeling, were translated into an urban electoral environment in towns such as Derry, Newry, and Belfast. In the south too agrarian unrest could from time to time be informed by strong sectarian under-tones, as during the anti-Protestant millenarian enthusiasms of the 1820s or in counties such as Longford, Clare, King's Co., and Sligo throughout the 1840s. But, although in 1844 the constabulary believed that the nature of agrarian crime was sometimes 'modified by sectarian prejudices', sectarianism was rarely more than a secondary or marginal aspect of crime in the countryside of the south.[2] Rather it was in those parts of south Ulster where both Catholics and Protestants maintained a considerable presence, notably Cavan, Monaghan, and Armagh, that religious and agrarian antagonisms were most markedly intermingled. Rank and file Ribbon-men and Orangemen may well have had similar economic interests, but the very occasional *rapprochements* between them (which frightened the life out of the 'respectable' classes as much in the 1870s as in the 1830s)[3] were invariably overwhelmed in the hotter

Lord C. J. Hamilton to Mayo, 22 Sept. 1868, Mayo Papers MS 11167; *Londonderry Sentinel*, 15 Feb. 1870; *Galway County election petition*, H.C. 1872 (241-I), xlviii, 125-6.

[1] W. Miller to Sir H. Hardinge, 15 Jan. 1835, O.P. 1835, Box 46; Lord Glengall to Hardinge, 15 Jan. 1835, O.P. 1835/157, Box 47; *Dublin Evening Mail*, 30 Jan. 1835; *Fictitious Votes, Ireland*, 2nd series, 1st report, p. 172; *Saunders' Newsletter*, 14 July 1852; J. Going to J. Wynne, 19 July 1852, O.P. 1852/27/493, Box 1220; *Copies of the several inquisitions removed from the Court of Queen's Bench . . . and transferred to the County of Clare . . . in relation to any of the cases of homicide etc. alleged to have been committed at the Town of Sixmilebridge, in July last, at the time of the general election*, H.C. 1852-3 (313), xciv, 96-8; *Minutes of evidence taken before the select committee on the Mayo County election petition*, H.C. 1857 (182 Sess. 2), vii, 7-8, 19; *Telegraph or Connaught Ranger*, 24 Feb. 1868; T. Greene to Under-Secretary, 9 Nov. 1868, R.P. 1868/15364, Box 1778.

[2] *Devon Commission*, Witness No. 1101; also *Devon Index*, under 'Outrages'; G. C. Lewis, *On local Disturbances*, pp. 95-6, 102 ff.; T. Murray to E. Reilly, 14 Aug. 1841, Downshire Papers D671/C/9/692; Printed Cabinet Memorandum, 13 Dec. 1869, Gladstone Papers Add. MS 44612.

[3] See M. FitzGerald to Lord Downshire, 27 Nov. 1830, Downshire Papers D671/C/12/445; H. Corry to Lord Belmore, 27 Mar. [1873], Belmore Papers D3007/P/79.

anger of religious distrust. 'All day long', reported a Cavan landowner in 1845 of a manifestation already hallowed by tradition, fourteen hundred armed Orangemen

paraded the roads in defiance, with flags, music etc. without meeting their enemies who remained overawed and quiet and at about 4 o'clock peacefully dispersed. No sooner had they done so, when, under the pretence of outrages committed by the Orange party . . . the Ribbonmen began in their turn to assemble, armed with pikes, guns, scythes, pitchforks etc.[1]

By then such demonstrations of tribal identity had already been imported into industrial Ulster by rural migrants whose obsessive concern for territorial imperatives became, in the narrower confines of the towns, almost all-consuming in its nit-picking intensity. Belfast Protestants needed to assert themselves against growing Catholic numbers—up from less than a twelfth to more than two-fifths in the century or so before 1848. An endless succession of marches, processions, and demonstrations ('walking' was the term favoured by participants) was interspersed only by increasingly desperate legislative attempts—in the form of Party Processions Acts—to reduce sectarian temperatures. Invariably, however, the 'walkers' continued to brandish guns, pistols, and swords, and to step out to the repetitive rhythms of sectarian fifes and drums. The long campaign to repeal the Act of 1850 (13 & 14 Vict., c. 2) raised Johnston of Ballykilbeg into a provincial hero, gave new vigour to an Orangeism which might otherwise have faltered, and, when repeal came in 1872, released in unprecedented strength the Ulsterman's passion for sectarian display. Between then and early 1879 as many as 1,400 of the 1,520 party processions recorded nationally by the constabulary took place in Ulster, 792 of them 'Orange' and 608 'Nationalist'. Together they required the attention of no less than 37,837 policemen and 3,111 troops.[2]

Such pointed sectarianism inevitably found for itself an especially attractive venue upon the field of electoral battle. The scattered clumps of Orange lodges in the south, the Protestant enclaves in towns like Dublin, Cork, and Bandon, and occasional pockets of rural Protestantism, helped provide southern elections with sporadic

[1] Memorandum by J. R. Godley, 27 June [1845], Graham Papers 22/Ir. See also *Crime and Outrage Committee*, H.C. 1839 (486), xi and xii, Qs. 9006–8; *Devon Commission*, Witness No. 1101; *Papers relating to . . . Dolly's Brae*, H.C. 1850 [1143], li, 331–83; Lord Rossmore to Eglinton, 26 Aug. 1852, Eglinton Papers MS 5343; W. Wann to J. C. Stronge, 7 Mar. 1857, Gosford Papers D1606/5A/2; Memorandum on Irish Crime, 19 Jan. 1870, Gladstone Papers Add. MS 44613.

[2] *Returns, as far as are practicable, of all party processions, whether Orange, Nationalist, Amnesty, 'Martyr', or other, specifying those which did not suffer molestation, which have taken place in Ireland since the repeal of the Party Processions Act in 1872*, H.C. 1880 (380 Sess. 2), lx, 395–432.

sectarian riots, demonstrations, and popular festivals. These were, however, largely a feature of pre-Famine times. The events of the 1835 election, when anti-Protestant mobs smashed churches in Kerry, drunken Orangemen fired guns to celebrate the return of their man for Queen's Co., and lethal sectarian clashes took place in Meath and Drogheda, the 1837 religious disturbances at Dublin, Portarlington, and Cork, and the 1841 brawls in Co. Cork, were repeated again only in 1852.[1] In that year an unusual combination of circumstances —the so-called 'Papal Aggression' and anti-Catholic riots in England —generated intense sectarian convulsions in the southern constituencies, notably Cork, Clare, Tipperary, and Leitrim. Enthusiastic rioting in Roscrea produced a clear sectarian result with 296 Protestant but only 44 Catholic windows smashed in an overwhelmingly Catholic town.[2] But after 1852, though occasional elections like that at Drogheda in 1868 were still marked by religious violence and while of course religious distrust remained, southern political life largely confined its rampant sectarianism to the prejudices of the parlour, the chapel, the club, and the employment office.

In contrast, Belfast and Derry continued the tradition of sectarian violence apparent at Ulster elections in the 1830s and 1840s, and preserved in the aspic of urban confrontation the bitterness of the countryside.[3] At least nine of Belfast's eleven contested elections between 1832 and 1868 were marked by more or less savage religious violence. 'Thousands of Orangemen', it was noted of the comparatively mild events of 1835, 'paraded the streets for three days with drums and fifes playing party tunes . . . to terrify and beat all who were inclined to follow their own inclinations.' Gun clubs were active at the election of 1847. 'Screams of women', 'insane wretches', 'savage conflict', and 'horrors transcending description' featured at that of 1852. In 1857 places of worship were

[1] Memorial of Pierce Butler, 13 Jan. 1835, O.P. 1835, Box 46; *D.E.P.* 29 Jan. 1835; Report of Sub-Inspector Despard, 25 Jan. 1835, O.P. 1835, Box 47, and *Third report . . . Orange Lodges*, H.C. 1835 (476), xvi, 1–11 (Meath and Drogheda); *D.E.P.* 5, 8 Aug. 1837 (Dublin, Portarlington, Cork); *Cork County election petition*, H.C. 1842 (271), vi, 93.

[2] *Londonderry Sentinel*, 30 July 1852 citing *C.C.*; *Clare election petition*, H.C. 1852–3 (587), ix, 574, and *Copies of the several inquisitions removed from the Court of Queen's Bench . . .*, H.C. 1852–3 (313), xciv, 63–170; police reports on Tipperary and Leitrim, July 1852, Mayo Papers MS 11037 (also J. H. Whyte, *The Independent Irish Party 1850–9* (Oxford, 1958), pp. 59–62); Report of J. Atkins, JP, 23 July 1852, Mayo Papers MS 11037 (Roscrea windows).

[3] See, e.g., Revd C. McDermott, PP to 'My dear Sir', 18 Aug. 1837, Clogher Diocesan Papers DIO(RC)1/6/41; Lord Gosford to W. Gossett, 17 Jan. 1831, O.P. 1835, Box 45, *D.E.P.* 22 Jan. 1835, *Proceedings had at an investigation held in Armagh on the Transactions which took place in that town and neighbourhood on the 15th January last*, H.C. 1835 (101), xlv, 476 (all Armagh); *Committee on Bribery at Elections*, H.C. 1835 (547), viii, 431–5, and *Copies of Correspondence between the lieutenants of counties . . . and the Irish government, previously to and during the late elections*, H.C. 1835 (170), xlv, 390–1.

reciprocally destroyed to 'Three cheers for Dan O'Connell' and a
whistled juxtaposition of 'Croppies lie Down', 'Kick the Pope before
you', and various Catholic fighting songs.[1] In Derry the conflicts of
the 1830s were revived more bitterly still in the 1860s and 1870s
when Catholics began to assert themselves after years of relative
electoral subordination.[2] The accidental timing of the General
Elections of 1852 and 1865 in the month of July made bad situations worse.[3] Feelings eventually became so excited that the great
communal riots of 1864, 1872, and 1886 in Belfast and 1869 in Derry
needed no electoral spark, and the physiognomic claims of Belfast's
Police Committee Chairman in 1864—'I could tell a man's religion
by his face'—no longer seemed either incongruous or bizarre.[4]

IV ELECTORAL VIOLENCE

If sectarian riots were a northern speciality, violent electioneering
in general knew no boundaries. Here too agrarian models were
applied to overtly political ends. And just as rural unrest maintained
a lively presence after the Famine, so there can be no doubt that
electoral violence, which often involved the same people and discontents, diminished not at all as the century wore on. Collections
of electoral horror stories became almost a literary form, with the
1852 election producing a particularly throbbing set of accusatory
pamphlets from English and Irish pens alike.[5] In an atmosphere in
which electoral violence—itself often the continuation by other
means of fights between farmers, landlords, priests, and labourers—
was merely part of a greater disorder, certain mechanical features of

---

[1] J. Hancock to E. Littleton, 1 Feb. 1835, Hatherton Papers D260/M/F/5/27/10;
S. E. Baker, 'Orange and Green: Belfast, 1832–1912' in *The Victorian City: Images and
Realities*, ed. H. J. Dyos and M. Wolff, 2 vols. (London, 1973), ii, 796 (which see generally,
pp. 789–814); Eglinton to S. Walpole, 15 July 1852, Eglinton Papers MS 5337; *Banner of
Ulster*, 4, 7 Apr. 1857.

[2] *D.E.P.* 22 Jan. 1835; *Londonderry Standard*, 22 July 1868; *Londonderry Guardian*,
23 July 1868; *Report of the Commissioners of Inquiry, 1869, into the Riots and Disturbances in the City of Londonderry, with minutes of evidence and appendix*, H.C. 1870
[C 5*], xxxii; D. Murphy, *Derry, Donegal, and Modern Ulster 1790–1921* (Londonderry,
1981), pp. 39–59, 110–34. See also Chapters I and IV above.

[3] Eglinton to Naas, 24 June 1852, Mayo Papers MS 11031; Memorandum from Quarter-
Master General, 2 July 1867, ibid. MS 11202.

[4] I. Budge and C. O'Leary, *Belfast: Approach to Crisis: A Study of Belfast politics
1613–1970* (London, 1973), pp. 83, and 73–100 generally.

[5] See, e.g., (shortened titles only): *Report of the Outrages and Intimidations at the late
Elections* (Dublin, 1841)—U.C.D. Pamphlets 6201; *The Reign of Terror in Carlow* (London,
1841)—R.I.A. Halliday Pamphlets 1817; J. Lord, *Popery at the hustings* (London, 1852)
—B.L. 3942.b.38; *Freedom of election in Ireland, or violence and intimidation illustrated*
(Carlow, [1853])—C.U.L. Hib.5.853.5; F. B. Head, *A Fortnight in Ireland* (London, 1852);
John Smyth, *The Elector: Containing a true and faithful picture of the awful state of the
. . . Counties of Tipperary and Waterford* (Dublin, [1853])—Halliday Pamphlets 2145;
'Eladrius', *Thoughts on the late general election in Ireland* (Dublin, 1853)—Halliday

the business were often enough to trigger off almost instant turmoil and unrest. Until 1850 each county constituency had only one polling place and the long journeys this often entailed provided endless opportunities for ambush, on the one hand, and prevarication, on the other.[1] The Franchise Act of that year increased the number of polling places in county constituencies to between three and six, while the County Election Act of 1862 (25 & 26 Vict., c. 62) allowed the Viceroy to specify even more on petition from local magistrates.[2] Inevitably, the selection of locations became so highly political, that, for example, the various interests in Wicklow were prepared to fight a long battle to ensure the proximity of polling places to the estates of their respective chief supporters.[3] As late, however, as 1868 some voters in Donegal still had to travel twenty-five miles to the poll and some in Wexford up to fifteen miles. And the continuing dangers of such long journeys for electors obliged to traverse politically hostile territory were not finally brought to an end until the General Election of 1874, when 640 county polling places were provided as compared with the 155 of 1868, the 134 between 1850 and 1862, and the mere 32 of earlier years.[4] The leisurely pace of polling in Ireland could also increase the opportunities for rioting and other disorder. Whereas the English Reform Act of 1832 allowed only two days for polling (later reduced to one for boroughs in 1835 and for counties in 1853), its Irish equivalent allowed no less than five. Only in 1847 was this reduced to one day for boroughs, while counties were more tenderly limited to two days in 1850 and to one not until 1862.[5] Such long periods not only allowed candidates to manufacture impressive bandwagon effects by releasing voters to poll at specified intervals, but also gave

Pamphlets 2144; 'A Barrister', *Observations on Intimidation at Elections in Ireland* (Dublin, 1854)—Halliday Pamphlets 2163.

[1] Graham to Eliot, 26 Oct. 1841, Graham Papers 8/Ir; Lord Stuart de Decies to Clarendon, 14 Aug. 1847, Clarendon Papers Box 33; Lord Carew to Clarendon, 27 Oct. [1847], ibid. Box 8; Clarendon to Russell, 15 Jan. 1848, ibid. L.-B. II. Some Co. Galway voters had to travel 75 miles to the poll (*Hansard*, ix, 616—19 Jan. 1832).

[2] Further changes were made in the Ballot Act (35 & 36 Vict., c. 33) and the Polling Districts (Ireland) Act (36 Vict., c. 2) of 1873. On the later history of the matter, see J. R. Mahon to W. S. Fitzgerald, 27 Apr. 1859, Mayo Papers MS 11036; Donoughmore to Derby, 13 Mar. 1860, Derby Papers 98; *Freeman's Journal*, 15 July 1868; T. H. Bourke to Hartington, 15 Feb., 4 Mar. 1871, 26 Apr. 1872, Devonshire Papers 387/2, 6, 36.

[3] R. Chaloner to Sir R. Howard, 5 Mar. 1849, Fitzwilliam Papers MS 3987; M. Toomey to W. Owen, 31 May 1850, [June 1850], Downshire Papers D671/C/373/80, 81.

[4] Memorandum by T. H. Bourke, 28 Jan. 1874, Kilmainham Papers MS 1067. See also the Duration of Elections in Ireland Act of 1850 (13 & 14 Vict., c. 68, Schedule A).

[5] See 2 & 3 Will. IV, c. 88, s. 52 (1832); 10 & 11 Vict., c. 81 (1847); 13 & 14 Vict., c. 68, s. 1 (1850); 25 & 26 Vict., c. 62 (1862). The polls usually opened at 8 a.m. or 9 a.m. and closed at 4 p.m. or 5 p.m.

full rein to the notorious laxity of officials in permitting booths to be crowded with noisy groups of landlords, agents, priests, and rough-necks, all energetically 'influencing' electors and acting as brokers between the activities of the rioters outside and the wavering voters within.[1]

Behaviour like this was made effective by the ever-present possibility and the frequent actuality of electoral violence in Ireland. As with rural unrest, the actuality may often have been sporadic, but the possibility was rarely far from the minds of those whose decisions might be thought subject to external pressure of various kinds. Many elections were quiet enough, but the surprised tone in which such news was usually reported reveals that it was the absence rather than the presence of violence which seems to have been thought worthy of comment and explanation.[2] Nor was there any consistent pattern in the location of electoral calm. Trouble might realistically be expected at any time and in any form. The almost obligatory violent election scenes in contemporary Irish novels were exaggerated only in the sense that they distilled into a single moment a multitude of usually separate and distinct events.[3] A retired Army officer present at the Carlow election of 1841 had no doubt about the warmth of the temperature: 'I have served in all quarters of the globe, and faced danger in every shape . . . but as a soldier, I am not ashamed to confess that I was never placed in such bodily fear as when [I was] dragged out of Her Majesty's mail and saw myself surrounded by a body of inhuman savages.'[4]

[1] For bandwagoning, see A. Symes to Lord Fitzwilliam, 28 Apr. 1848, Wentworth Woodhouse Muniments G83 No. 435 (Wicklow); P. M. Gartlan to C. Fortescue, 22 Feb. 1854, Carlingford Papers CP3/3 (Louth); *Banner of Ulster*, 7 Mar. 1857 (Co. Londonderry); *C.C.* 8 June 1863 (Kinsale); *The Belfast Election*, 18 Nov. 1868. For crowded booths, see Revd A. B. Rowan to Knight of Kerry, 23 Jan. 1835, and J. Hurly to Knight of Kerry, 29 Jan. 1835, FitzGerald Papers (Kerry); *Dublin Evening Mail*, 28 Jan. 1835 (Meath); *Committee on Bribery at Elections*, H.C. 1835 (547), viii, 552 (Clonmel); *Clare election petition*, H.C. 1852-3 (595), ix, 724; *Dublin Evening Mail*, 13 Mar. 1857 (Tipperary); *Mayo county election petition*, H.C. 1857 (182 Sess. 2), vii, 176; 'Instructions for Deputies of Sheriffs and other returning officers', Longfield, Kelly, & Armstrong Papers D847/8.
[2] See, e.g., Report of J. Vignoles on Co. Clare, [Dec. 1832], O.P. 1832/2258, Box 2192; Reports on Tyrone and Westmeath, 21 Jan. 1835, O.P. 1835/159, 162, Box 47; Mulgrave to Melbourne, 13 Sept. [1837], Melbourne Papers 100/48. In 1837 reports suggesting that twelve of thirty-four contested constituencies were 'quiet' were clearly considered remarkable by the authorities (O.P. 1837/620/8, 11, 12, 13, 17, 33, 34, 36, 37, 40, 42, 44, 48, 49, 52, 57, 61, 65—all Box 52).
[3] For a mixed bag, see Miss H. L. Martin's *Canvassing* (1832), [P. B. Kelly's] *The Manor of Glenmore* (1839), [Revd. G. Brittaine's] *The Election* (1840), Charles Lever's *Charles O'Malley* (1841), William Johnston of Ballykilbeg's *Nightshade* (1857), 'Allen H. Clington's' [D. P. Conyngham] *Frank O'Donnell* (1861), 'Matthew Stradling's' [M. F. Mahony] *The Misadventures of Mr Catlyne Q.C.* (1873), 'J. T. Listado's' *Civil Service* (1874), and W. H. Maxwell's famous quasi-novel *Wild Sports of the West* (1832).
[4] *The Reign of Terror in Carlow* (1841), p. 77. These 'savages' were in fact 'canvassers'.

Although disturbances had graced Irish elections between the Union and the First Reform Act—indeed twenty-six people were killed at Kerry in 1826—it was the mobilization achieved by O'Connell and the franchise changes of 1832 which together turned what had once been an occasional into a more regular excitement. 'The thing', noted a Carlow farmer, 'is kept up . . . [with] angry feeling and animosity . . . It is frightful to contemplate', and, indeed, the General Election of 1832 itself was pioneeringly agitated and unruly.[1] Also, the way in which this newly intensified electoral violence manifested itself owed everything—save perhaps the pure action of mass rioting itself—to agrarian models. The broad pattern was laid down between 1832 and 1847. Just as agrarian violence provided sections of the rural population with protection against their 'exploiters', so electoral violence allowed the voteless a voice and enabled them to bring countervailing pressures against the influences of property, money, and patronage. In rural constituencies the classic pattern began with midnight intimidation, continued with rioting during the poll, and concluded with revenge against those who had disobeyed. Intimidation could involve anything from a couple of men with sticks to several hundred with guns, lighted tapers, and dressed in the traditional costume of the secret societies. Before the Monaghan election of 1835 one voter's house was attacked at nine in the evening by a dozen men who fired shots, beat up father, mother, and son 'in a cruel and savage manner', broke all the windows, and stole a gun. In Mayo 'a large party of men disguised by wearing white shirts with straw round their bodies and sounding horns attacked' several voters' houses about midnight, breaking doors and windows, and wrecking furniture. Two years later at the King's Co. election 'a band of ruffians patrolled the county during the night, visiting such of the Catholic tenantry as had promised to go with their landlords . . . and setting fire to the dwellings of such as showed a lingering inclination to fulfil their promises'.[2] The theme had many variations: beatings of docile priests at the Limerick Co. election of 1832; minatory hay-rick burning and the dragging of 'trembling freeholders' from their beds in Kerry in 1835; nocturnal bayoneting in Queen's Co. (1835); large bands roaming Mayo 'swearing in the freeholders not to vote for any of the

---

[1] *Copies of Correspondence between the lieutenants of counties . . . and the Irish government, previously to and during the late elections*, H.C. 1835 (170), xlv, 393; *Crime and Outrage Committee*, H.C. 1839 (486), xi and xii, Q. 10658; Anglesey to Grey, 8 Dec. 1832, Anglesey Papers D619/28A.

[2] Report of Chief Constable Mansfield, 4 Jan. 1835, O.P. 1835/149, Box 47; of Chief Constable Meredith, 23 Jan. 1835, O.P. 1835, Box 46; E. M. Kelly to Downshire, 14 Aug. 1837, Downshire Papers D671/C/12/690.

Brownes' (1832).[1] There were bloody night attacks in King's Co. by 'demons in the shape of women', five-hundred-strong groups foot-loose in Meath, and three hundred with sticks reclaiming the night in Co. Wexford under the command of local priests.[2]

The actual rioting, sometimes a direct consequence of nocturnal visitations, sometimes an independent phenomenon, boasted, by its very nature, a more limited repertoire. Sensible men boarded up their houses on polling day when skulls were cracked, windows smashed, and insults exchanged with an enthusiasm that varied in intensity rather than style. Even big cities like Cork were said at times to be 'in the possession of the mob', while large gangs—often of country people—regularly took control of smaller places like Bandon, Cashel, Clonmel, Dundalk, or Downpatrick. 'I reached Youghal', wrote Feargus O'Connor in 1835, and 'found the town in a state of siege, full of horse, foot, and police.' Kenmare Town and its hinterland were, the police reported, 'in a state of perfect dis-order and confusion; the hills and mountains were in a blaze'. In 1841 a Cork candidate wrote how 'one of my voters after giving his vote was murdered, another lies at the point of death from a com-pound fracture of the skull; many have been cruelly beaten, their houses fired, others destroyed and the furniture burned before the doors'.[3] Similar accounts in almost unvarying language crowd the pages of contemporary Blue Books, official and private correspon-dence, parliamentary debates, and newspapers.[4] Even the polling at Dublin University was punctuated by injuries and explosions,

[1] J. O'Reagan to Lord Dunraven, 22 Dec. 1832, Dunraven Papers D3196; T. A. Ponsonby to Peel, 31 Jan. 1835, Peel Papers Add. MS 40412, and Lady Kenmare to Knight of Kerry, 12 Mar. 1835, FitzGerald Papers (both Kerry); Report of Chief Constable Williams, 8 Jan. 1835, O.P. 1835/152, Box 47; Report of Chief Constable Shaw, 10 Dec. 1832, O.P. 1832/2229, Box 2192.

[2] *Athlone Conservative Advocate*, 17 Aug. 1837; *Dublin Evening Mail*, 23 Jan. 1835; *Committee on Bribery at Elections*, H.C. 1835 (547), viii, 251-2.

[3] F. O'Connor, *A series of letters from Feargus O'Connor Esq. Barrister at Law; to Daniel O'Connell Esq. M.P. containing a review of Mr O'Connell's conduct* (London, 1836), p. 6; *Committee on Bribery at Elections*, H.C. 1835 (547), viii, 269; J. C. Chatterton to Peel, 10 July 1841, Peel Papers Add. MS 40485.

[4] See, e.g., Reports of Chief Constable Mahony, 16, 17 Dec. 1832, O.P. 1832/2194, Box 2192 (Dungarvan); of Sub-Inspector Crofton, 26 Dec. 1832, O.P. 1832/2202, Box 2192 (Newry); *Ballyshannon Herald*, 11 Jan. 1833, and *Athlone Conservative Advocate*, 17 Aug. 1837 (Co. Limerick); Report of Chief Constable Watkins, 15 Jan. 1835, O.P. 1835, Box 45 (Bandon); of Chief Constable Cummins, 19 Jan. 1835, O.P. 1835, Box 46 (King's Co.); J. Wilcox to Major Miller, 23 Jan. 1835, O.P. 1835, Box 46 (Clonmel); *D.E.P.* 15 Jan. 1835 (Coleraine); Revd C. McDermott to 'My dear Sir', 18 Aug. 1837, Clogher Diocesan Papers DIO(RC)1/6/41 (Co. Armagh); G. R. Dawson's MS election diary, 1837, T874 (Derry City); Reports of N. Power etc., 2, 7 Aug. 1837, O.P. 1837/620/57, Box 53 (Tipperary); *The Reign of Terror in Carlow* (1841), pp. 62-4; D. Power, H. Rodwell, and E. L'E. Dew, *Reports of the decisions of committees of the House of Commons* (1853), p. 90 (Dundalk 1847).

while nervous election agents in constituencies such as Queen's Co., Mayo, and Wicklow carried loaded pistols as they sought to influence the democratic will.[1] The general atmosphere of commotion was often much prolonged by the revenge visited upon voters who had not done as they were told. Tenants had privileges withdrawn by landlords, shopkeepers their businesses destroyed by customers, farmers unwilling to bow to the will of secret societies their property burned, their cattle maimed, and themselves and their families injured and attacked. Fairs and markets became places as dangerous for those whose electoral behaviour had proved unpopular as for those who had dared occupy land from which others had been evicted.[2] Death and serious injury were a feature of elections as much as of agrarian crime in general. Complete statistics were not collected, but it is known, for example, that ten of the thirty civilians killed in clashes with the police during the four general election years between 1832 and 1841 died in election affrays, while scattered evidence quite incidentally discovered in the course of other research shows that killings or near-fatal injuries occurred at the following pre-Famine contests.[3]

1832	Dungarvan, Co. Carlow, Co. Mayo
1835	Clonmel, Cork City, Co. Meath, Co. Westmeath
1836	Co. Longford
1837	Galway Town, Co. Kerry, King's Co., Co. Longford, Co. Sligo, Co. Tipperary
1841	Cork City, Co. Tipperary
1846	Co. Mayo

[1] Anglesey to the Provost, 12 Dec. 1832, Anglesey Papers D619/32H, and Report of G. Neville, 19 Dec. 1832, O.P. 1832/2204, Box 2192 (University); H. J. Porter to Lord Farnham, 10 Jan. 1833, Farnham Papers MS 18612, W. Moloney to—, [Jan. 1835], O.P. 1835/152, Box 47, *D.E.P.* 24 Jan. 1835.

[2] See Chapters I and II above; also W. Armstrong to Anglesey, 19 Sept. 1830, Anglesey Papers D619/23/A/228 (Louth); Report of Chief Constable Lewis, 27 Dec. [1832], O.P. 1832/2231, Box 2192, and *Ballyshannon Herald*, 4 Jan. 1833 (Mayo); ibid. 11 Jan. 1833, 1 Sept. 1837, *Committee on Bribery at Elections*, H.C. 1835 (547), viii, 289 (Queen's Co.); R. Fitzgerald to Knight of Kerry, 29 Jan. 1835, FitzGerald Papers (Kerry); Reports of Chief Constables Ponsonby and Watkins, 22, 24 Jan. 1835, O.P. 1835, Box 46 (Co. Cork).

[3] *Return relative to persons who have been killed or severely wounded in affrays with the constabulary*, H.C. 1846 (280), xxxv, 237-60. For 1832: Report of Chief Constable Mahony, 17 Dec. 1832, O.P. 1832/2194, Box 2192; G. Jackson to Lord Sligo, 3 Jan. 1833, O.P. 1832/47, Box 2173; *Hansard*, xxvi, 905-6 (12 Mar. 1835). 1835: Lord Glengall to Sir H. Hardinge, 16 Jan. [1835], O.P. 1835/157, Box 47; *C.C.* 17 Jan. 1835; *D.E.P.* 24 Jan. 1835; *Hansard*, xxxvi, 905-6 (12 Mar. 1835). 1836: *Fictitious Votes, Ireland*, 2nd series, 3rd report, p. 313. 1837: Report of G. Fitzgerald, RM, 10 Aug. 1837, O.P. 1837/620/57, Box 53; of Sub-Inspector Lewis, 12 Aug. 1837, O.P. 1837/620/30, Box 52; of Chief Constable Smith, 14 Aug. 1837, O.P. 1837/620/32, Box 52; *Athlone Conservative Advocate*,

Not only, however, did such incidents often involve more than one killing (no less than fourteen at the Carlow election of 1832), but many deaths must obviously remain hidden in the sources. Electoral assaults in general, as a senior policeman noted in 1835, were often concealed from the constabulary for fear of further reprisals,[1] so that what is known cannot be more than a fraction of the whole. Sometimes, however, election violence was intense enough to persuade local officials to keep detailed accounts, if only to frighten Dublin Castle. In one report alone, the Inspector-General of Constabulary for Munster recorded twenty separate incidents in Co. Cork at the 1835 General Election of major riots, assaults, damage to property, and the throwing of vitriol. Two years later the Westmeath police noted seven major election outrages in one district even before the polls had opened, while further assaults and attacks took place thereafter.[2] Cos. Longford and Sligo too had traditions of both agrarian and electoral violence. In 1837 alone the Sligo elections notched up eight cases of destruction of shopkeepers' goods, forty houses with broken windows, nine 'severe' and five 'other' assaults, 'several' threatening notices, 290 barrels of turf and 150 hundredweight of straw burned, widespread exclusive dealing, the smashing of three carriages, the maiming of cattle, asses, and sheep, and the revival of the old rustic torture of 'carding' by which a spiked board was raked across the victim's back 'literally tearing the flesh from his bones'.[3] Carlow too was both a comparatively unruly county in general and noted for the intensity of its electoral disturbances, especially in 1841 when its roads were jammed with armed men 'calling themselves O'Connell's police', and vast mobs (100,000 strong in the opinion of a hysterical Conservative) rioted angrily around the polling booths set up in the county town.[4]

17 Aug. 1837; *D.E.P.* 14 Nov. 1837; *Minutes of evidence taken before the committee on the Longford County election petitions*, H.C. 1837 (319), x, 201-2. 1841: J. C. Chatterton to Peel, 10 July 1841, Peel Papers Add. MS 40485; *Report of the Outrages and Intimidations at the late Elections* (1841), p. 18. 1846: Heytesbury to Graham, 6 Mar. 1846, Graham Papers 28/Ir.

[1] *Committee on Bribery at Elections*, H.C. 1835 (547), viii, 268.

[2] W. Miller to Sir H. Hardinge, 19 Mar. 1835, O.P. 1835, Box 46; Report of Chief Constable Dobbyn, 12 Aug. 1837, O.P. 1837/620/62, Box 53; *Ballyshannon Herald*, 15 Sept. 1837.

[3] For Longford: *Ballyshannon Herald*, 4, 11 Jan. 1833; *Fictitious Votes, Ireland*, 2nd series, 3rd report, pp. 40, 310-13; Reports of N. Carney and others, 2, 20, 24 Apr. 1835, O.P. 1835, Box 46; *Athlone Conservative Advocate*, 21 Sept. 1837. For Sligo: *A Return of all reports made to the inspector general of police by the constabulary officers, during the late elections for the County and Borough of Sligo*, H.C. 1837-8 (166), xlvi, 555; *Ballyshannon Herald*, 18 Aug., 8, 22 Sept. 1837; *Athlone Conservative Advocate*, 17 Aug. 1837.

[4] *The Reign of Terror in Carlow* (1841), pp. 40-6, 53-4, 63-4, 66-8. See also *Committee on Bribery at Elections*, H.C. 1835 (547), viii, 634-5; *Copies of Correspondence*

What was most remarkable about the quarter-century after the Famine was how closely electoral violence continued to follow the patterns laid down in earlier years. And just as outrage levels in general only fell for comparatively short periods, so election disturbances showed no sign of diminution. The same preliminary intimidation, the same rioting, the same retribution flourished during the 1850s and 1860s as they had before. Even supposedly 'quiet' elections such as those of 1859 and 1865 were in fact marked by widespread disorders of a traditional kind.[1] Between 1868 and 1874 there were extremely serious disturbances in Sligo Co. and Borough, Drogheda, Limerick Co., Derry City, Queen's Co., and Cos. Mayo, Wexford, Cork, Waterford, Carlow, Longford, Kerry, and Galway,[2] all in addition to the 'normal' physical excitements experienced in these and almost all other contested constituencies. Widespread and violent assaults were a feature also of by-elections, such as those of 1854 in Co. Louth, 1862 in Co. Longford, 1863 in Bandon, and 1866 in Co. Waterford.[3] Witnesses were sometimes simply overwhelmed by what they saw. 'Oh Lord', exclaimed a small farmer in 1857, 'I see the town [Ballinrobe] in a blaze, groaning, and fighting and killing.' Journalists rummaged *Roget* to do justice to a heightened reality: at Mallow in 1859 the air was pierced by

between the Roman Catholic priests of Borris, Robert Doyne Esq., and the lord lieutenant of Ireland, on alleged attendance of military at the Roman Catholic chapels, H.C. 1835 (198), xlv, 493–510; Report of Sub-Inspector Battersby, 22 Jan. 1835, O.P. 1835/149, Box 47.

[1] For claims of comparative quietness, see R.P. 1859/4052, 4056, 4270, 4275, 4439, 4440, 4519, 4567, 4575, 4617, 4730, 4812—all Box 808, and Sir H. Rose to Duke of Cambridge, 23 July 1865, Strathnairn Papers Add. MS 42821. But see R.P. 1860/16926; Reports of E. Collins, RM, 1, 8 May 1859, R.P. 1859/3993, 4340, Box 808; F. S. P. Wolferstan and S. B. Bristowe, *Reports of the decisions of election committees during the eighteenth parliament of the United Kingdom* (London, 1865), pp. 66–70; J. Spaight to Naas, 2, 4, 5 May 1859, Mayo Papers MS 11036; *C.C.* 5 May 1859; *Limerick Chronicle*, 13, 15, 22 July 1865; *Westmeath Guardian*, 20 July 1865; *Londonderry Sentinel*, 28 July 1865; *Tipperary Advocate*, 15, 29 July 1865; *Committee on parliamentary and municipal elections*, H.C. 1868–9 (352), viii, 216–17.

[2] Strathnairn to H. Fitzwilliam, 19 Nov. 1868, and to Major-General Borton, 2 Dec. 1868, Strathnairn Papers Add. MS 42828, *D.E.P.* 20 Nov. 1868, Lord Mountmorres to Sir T. Larcom, 29 Oct. 1868, Larcom Papers MS 7762 (Sligo); Strathnairn to Larcom, 5 Dec. 1868, R.P. 1868/17385, Box 1780, and E. L. O'Malley and H. Hardcastle, *Reports of the decisions of the judges*, i (1869), pp. 252–3 (Drogheda); *Daily Express*, 20 Jan., 6 Feb. 1874 (Limerick); *Londonderry Sentinel*, 24 Nov. 1868 (Derry); Strathnairn to Lord de Vesci, 9 Nov. 1868, Strathnairn Papers Add. MS 42828 (Queen's Co.); Strathnairn to J. Wilson-Patten, 11 Dec. 1868, ibid. Add. MS 42828 (next six counties); Lord Granard to Archbishop Cullen, 11 Jan. 1870, Cullen Papers; Spencer to C. Fortescue, 30 Mar. 1870, Carlingford Papers CP2/13; Lord Kenmare to Hartington, 26 Jan. [1872], Devonshire Papers 340/486 (Kerry); *Galway County election petition*, H.C. 1872 (241–I), xlviii, 103.

[3] Dean Kieran to Archbishop Dixon, 26 Feb. 1854, Dixon Papers VII; Bishop Kilduff to Cullen, 28 Feb. 1862, Cullen Papers; *C.C.* 27 Feb. 1863; Letters etc. of Dec. 1866, Mayo Papers MS 11210.

shoutings, hissings, tumults, barking, bleating, yells, clamour, groans, howling, hooting, cries, roaring, cheers, all of them 'tremendous', 'prolonged', and 'great'. At Cashel in 1865 'young and old' were to be found 'shouting, whistling, groaning, dancing, and foaming with irrepressible rage'.[1] In 1852 the three principal towns of Co. Longford each sported a mob of 8,000 or so 'uttering the most savage yells—many of them in a state of excitement bordering on absolute frenzy'. Things were so bad in the weeks before the Waterford City by-election of 1870 that departing trains were full of 'respectable voters' seeking refuge elsewhere. Election injuries were so common in Sligo that the local paper listed the names and addresses of those killed, maimed, or left for dead with the casual sang-froid normally reserved for petty sessions reports.[2] Deaths and fatal woundings were as common as ever and are known to have occurred at the following electoral contests, which, as before, must be regarded as no more than representative of a greater totality.[3]

1852	Cork City, Downpatrick, Limerick City, Co. Clare, Sligo Borough and Co., Co. Westmeath
1859	Limerick City and Co.
1865	Belfast, Co. Monaghan
1866	Co. Tipperary, Co. Waterford
1868	Drogheda, Co. Sligo
1874	Co. Limerick

Just as the General Elections of 1859 and 1865 were 'quiet' only in an Irish manner of speaking, so that of 1857, though gentler than its immediate predecessor, was by any other standard well up to the mark of former times. The matter-of-fact tone in which the Duke of Devonshire's agent reported his missile-accompanied entry into Dungarvan that year shows how certain things had almost ceased to

---

[1] *Mayo County election petition*, H.C. 1857 (182 Sess. 2), vii, 104; *C.C.* 5 May 1859; *Tipperary Advocate*, 15 July 1865.

[2] 'A Clergyman of the Established Church' [G. Dwyer], *Popery unmasked at the recent elections in Ireland* (London, [1852]), p. 33; P. H. Bagenal, *The Life of Ralph Bernal Osborne M.P.* (London, 1844), p. 285; *Sligo Journal* cited in 'A Barrister', *Observations on Intimidation at Elections*, p. 68.

[3] 1852: J. Lord, *Popery at the hustings*, pp. 23, 82; 'A Barrister', *Observations on Intimidation at Elections*, pp. 48, 68; P. Barron, RM to Under-Secretary, 12 July 1852, Mayo Papers MS 11037; Folklore Commission MS 463; Sir J. Young to Gladstone, 27 Apr. 1852, Gladstone Papers Add. MS 44327. 1859: *Nation*, 7 May 1859; J. Spaight to Naas, [May 1859], Mayo Papers MS 11036. 1865: I. Budge and C. O'Leary, *Belfast: Approach to Crisis*, p. 77; *Londonderry Sentinel*, 28 July 1865. 1866: Strathnairn to Comte de Jarnac, 30 Dec. 1866, Strathnairn Papers Add. MS 42823; *Copy of the Depositions taken before the Coroner . . . at Dungarvan*, H.C. 1867 (200), lvi, 209 ff. 1868: Strathnairn to Under-Secretary, 1 June 1869, Kilmainham Papers MS 1062; Strathnairn to H. Fitzwilliam, 19 Nov. 1868, Strathnairn Papers Add. MS 42828. 1874: *Daily Express*, 6 Feb. 1874.

shock: 'I was never without an escort of police. I escaped myself, but the person next me was twice struck and . . . I was only saved from a violent blow at the head with a stick, by a mounted police-man who warded it off with his sword.'[1]

There can be no doubt that, throughout the century, elections not only borrowed a style of violence from existing traditions of disorder, but contributed substantially to the general calendar of crime and outrage. Witnesses before the Crime Committee of 1839 repeatedly blamed them for boosting the activities of 'agrarian malcontents'. Notably high crime returns for 1832 and 1835 were almost certainly election-induced, while the whole of the increase which 1841 registered over 1840 was concentrated in the six months during and after the General Election held in July.[2] Detailed returns reveal distinct upswings for the months during which general elections were held in 1852, 1859, 1865, 1868, and (to a lesser extent) 1857.[3] In April 1857 the 116 election outrages constituted more than half of all outrages in the fifteen electorally active counties, while only eighteen agrarian outrages were recorded for the whole of the country. The figures for May 1859 are very similar.[4] In 1852 a strong wave of sectarianism combined with considerable rural unrest to produce one of the most violent of all nineteenth-century Irish elections. Serious disorders were reported from an astonishingly wide range of constituencies. Indeed, many more than half those contested are *known* to have been generally disturbed, which, considering the random and incomplete nature of the evidence to hand, can safely be assumed to indicate a virtually universal violence.[5]

---

[1] F. E. Currey to F. J. Howard, 4 Apr. 1857, Lismore Papers MS 7191. See also, e.g., W. Wann to J. C. Stronge, 7 Mar. 1857, Gosford Papers D1606/5A/2; D. Power, H. Rodwell, and E. L'E. Dew, *Reports of the decisions of committees of the House of Commons in the trial of controverted elections during the sixteenth parliament of the United Kingdom* (London, 1857), pp. 21-4, 206-13; *Banner of Ulster*, 4, 7 Apr. 1857; *Londonderry Sentinel*, 10 Apr. 1857; *Dublin Evening Mail*, 6, 8, 17 Apr. 1857; H. A. Herbert to T. Larcom, 9 July 1857, Larcom Papers MS 7578.

[2] *Crime and Outrage Committee*, H.C. 1839 (486), xi and xii, Qs. 263-99, 722-4, 11667-71, 13014-22; Mulgrave in *Hansard*, xxxix, 224-50 (27 Nov. 1837); *A Return of Outrages reported by the constabulary in Ireland during the years 1837, 1838, 1839, 1840, and 1841: A like Return of Outrages during each month of the year 1842*, H.C. 1843 [460], li, 149-68, especially 152-3. Thus, Jan.-June 1840 = 2,553, and ditto 1841 = 2,447; July-Dec. 1840 = 2,073, and ditto 1841 = 2,913. See also the views of J. S. Kennedy (Inspector-General of Constabulary) writing to T. Drummond, 12 Oct. 1837, Carlisle L.-B. 28, and of W. Miller (Deputy Inspector-General), *Devon Commission*, Witness No. 1101.

[3] See *Return of Outrages reported to the Royal Irish Constabulary Office from 1st January 1844 to 31st December 1880*, H.C. 1881 [C 2756], lxxvii, 887-914; on p. 913 the compiler specifically assigns the increase in 1868 to the election. The election of 1847 occurred in mid-Famine, that of 1874 at unusually short notice.

[4] S.P.O. Irish Crime Records 1857-63. In May 1859 the seventy-four election outrages constituted 48 per cent of all outrages in the nine relevant counties.

[5] See note 3 p. 399.

In Longford alone sixty-two persons complained to the police of nocturnal intimidation, and arrests were made after more than a dozen separate riots.[1] For the twelve months ending 30 September 1852, when specially reported outrages were still running at the high 'Famine' rate of 8,006, no less than 666 were designated 'electoral' as compared with the 943 designated 'agrarian'. The election contribution is in fact actually more striking still, because, while agrarian outrages were generated nationally throughout a full year, their electoral counterparts occurred in only the forty-three contested constituencies for a period of a few months before, during, and immediately after the election itself. Nor in any sense were election outrages less serious than outrages as a whole, quite the reverse. And while in July 1852 the elections were the source of a half—and agrarian matters of only one-twenty-fifth—of all outrages, even in August the proportion was still a third—and agrarian matters a tenth.[2] Indeed, even the comparatively modest fall in total outrage levels after the Famine was not matched by any diminution in electoral violence. Rather, if the frequency with which intimidation and riot were mentioned in petitions for undue return is any guide, electoral violence actually increased after 1850.[3]

Another comparatively constant feature of the matter was the generally rural rather than urban origins of electoral violence. Although the evidence is impressionistic, it seems clear that, especially in the pre-Famine period, the reservoirs from which such violence drew its strength lay overwhelmingly in the countryside. Of course the bulk of the population lived there, but, as polling itself invariably took place only in the larger towns, a high level of commitment and enthusiasm was required if rural rioters wished to attend the scenes of constitutional choice. Contemporaries were convinced that election mobs made up of countrymen were particularly dangerous.[4]

---

[1] Report in O.P. 1852/19/302, Box 1219.

[2] Based on Crime Reports 1850-2 in Mayo Papers MS 11033, Memorandum in ibid. MS 11019(E), and S.P.O. Irish Crime Records. The year ending 30 Sept. 1852 also included two contested by-elections. The constabulary returns exclude all outrages committed in the Dublin Metropolitan Police district. During the 1852 General Election *five* geographical counties experienced no contested elections for either county or borough seats: Armagh, Fermanagh, Queen's Co., Wicklow, and Roscommon (save for the *part* of Athlone within the county boundaries).

[3] The percentage of petitions mentioning riot etc. rose from 30.9 in the period 1832-51 to 55.6 in 1852-81. The number of such petitions *per general election* rose from 3.5 to 4.5. See sources given in Chapter III, note 5 p. 245.

[4] Report of Chief Constable Shaw, 10 Dec. 1832, O.P. 1832/2229, Box 2192; of Sub-Inspector Croker, 23 Dec. 1832, O.P. 1832/2243, Box 2192; Sir H. Hardinge to Peel, 12 Jan. 1835, Peel Papers Add. MS 40314; Heytesbury to Graham, 23 June 1845, Graham Papers 22/Ir; T. Jones, JP to J. Wynne, 8 July 1852, O.P. 1852/26/83, Box 1220; *Galway County election petition*, H.C. 1872 (241-I), xlviii, 499-504.

And just as O'Connell's campaigns found their real electoral dynamic outside the towns, and just as enthusiasm for the remote and 'sophisticated' cause of revolution in 1848 was as much a rural as an urban phenomenon,[1] so electoral violence had its strongest roots in country districts. Again and again the mobs which filled the streets as canvassing or polling took place were predominantly rural in composition.[2] Generally too violence was greater in county than in borough constituencies: at the elections of 1852 eighteen of the twenty-two contested counties are known to have been marked by serious disorder as compared with eleven of the twenty-one contested boroughs.[3] Of course townsmen also rioted, but urban mobs were generally less large, less fierce, and notably more venal.[4] Townsmen rioted for money; countrymen, however lubricated by alcohol, rioted for principles.

Increasingly until 1885 the mob represented the chief electoral power of the poor, for, whereas the electorate established in 1832 had included a significant proportion of random indigents, that produced by the Franchise Act of 1850 was based on principles of rigid economic exclusion. Of course many riots were orchestrated

[1] K. T. Hoppen, 'Politics, the law, and the nature of the Irish electorate 1832–1850', *English Historical Review*, xcii (1977), 772–3; Ann Barry and K. T. Hoppen, 'Borough politics in O'Connellite Ireland: The Youghal poll books of 1835 and 1837', *Journal of the Cork Historical and Archaeological Society*, lxxxiii (1978), 117; 'Extracts of Reports from different counties', 1848, Royal Archives RA D17/23.

[2] Only a sample can be given of the *vast* amount of supportive evidence: Report of Sub-Inspector Crofton, 26 Dec. 1832, O.P. 1832/2202, Box 2192 (Newry); of Magistrate Jones, 28 Dec. 1832, O.P. 1832/2232, Box 2192 (Castlebar); of Chief Constable Watkins, 15 Jan. 1835, O.P. 1835, Box 45 (Bandon); *Copies of Communications relative to the marching of people during the Kerry elections*, H.C. 1835 (197), xlv, 433–4; Report of Sub-Inspector Haly, 7 Aug. 1837, O.P. 1837/620/33, Box 52 (Athy); of Sub-Inspector Lewis, 12 Aug. 1837, O.P. 1837/620/30, Box 52 (Galway); S.P.O. Stipendiary Magistrates' Diaries No. 30, for 12 July 1841 (Longford); *Cork County election petition*, H.C. 1842 (271), vi, 80; Affidavit of R. English, 15 July 1852, O.P. 1852/15/170, Box 1218 (Tullamore); *Galway Vindicator*, 21 Apr. 1852 (Ennis); *Westmeath Guardian*, 20 July 1865 (Mullingar); *Waterford Mail*, 18 Sept. 1868 (Dungarvan); *Daily Express*, 3 Feb. 1874 (Kildare).

[3] Based on the collections made from newspapers etc. in 'A Barrister', *Observations on Intimidation at Elections*, pp. 20–75, and J. Lord, *Popery at the hustings*, pp. 1–87. See also 'Eladrius', *Thoughts on the late general election in Ireland*, pp. 11–12.

[4] *Cork County election petition*, H.C. 1842 (271), vi, 113; Revd E. Moore to Revd G. Kirkpatrick, 31 July 1852, Kirkpatrick Papers D1604/9/1; J. Bolton to Derby, 10 Oct. 1866, Derby Papers 107/2. On venality of urban mobs, see *Cork City election petition*, H.C. 1852–3 (528), xi, 36–8; *Report from the select committee on the Dungarvan election petition*, H.C. 1854 (162), viii, 497–8; *Report of the Commissioners appointed to investigate into the existence of corrupt practices in elections of members to serve in parliament for the County of the Town of Galway*, H.C. 1857–8 [2291], xxvi, 318; *Daily Express*, 14 Apr., 15 July 1865; *Limerick Chronicle*, 13, 15, 22 July 1865; *Committee on parliamentary and municipal elections*, H.C. 1868–9 (352), viii, 207–18; *Report of the Commissioners appointed for the purpose of making inquiry into the existence of Corrupt Practices at the last election for Cashel*, H.C. 1870 [C 9], xxxii, 289.

and paid for by candidates or their more prosperous supporters. But even then the manipulation was not always one-sided, for payers were as subject to short-term exploitation as were recipients. Those who became accustomed to augmenting generally miserable earnings with payments for rioting acquired a vested interest in the continuation of the practice, which, like so much agrarian discontent, developed a culturally conservative orientation: belief in tradition, dislike of change, opposition to 'progress'. In many places candidates were obliged to deal with popularly recognized mob leaders who negotiated pay and contracted to supply crowds as and when required. At Nenagh in 1852 each 'leader' provided twenty men. At Cashel in 1868 Mary Glasgow 'ruled forty women during the election; speeched and agitated day and night six weeks in the interest of O'Beirne . . . and begs to submit to him a bill of £3'.[1] Mob 'captains' acted as wholesalers of violence in many places, such as Antrim, Limerick, Clare, Longford, and Tipperary. They could earn up to six pounds for a few days' work, while rank and file rioters could expect anything between one and five shillings a day, occasionally more.[2] Given low pay and fitful employment, such sums as the forty shillings each netted by twenty Castlebar nailers in 1857 or the five pounds each earned by twenty-six Ennis artisans in 1859 constituted a substantial if erratic part of the economy of the poor.[3] This was the poor man's equivalent of the voter's election bribe, and, as such, enjoyed a similar quasi-formal recognition. Rioters openly sued for unpaid fees, even receiving (as at Kilrush in 1852) legal help from the local stipendiary. And when arrested, they were generally treated with unusual leniency by courts not otherwise remarkable for their benevolence.[4] Men regularly banded together into free-lance mobs to offer themselves to the highest bidder. At the Co. Sligo election of 1857 the local Ribbonmen

[1] *Galway Vindicator*, 7 Aug. 1852; *Minutes of evidence taken at the trial of the Cashel election petitions*, H.C. 1868-9 (121), xlix, 202.

[2] See W. R. A. Gore to Sir G. F. Seymour, 15 Sept. 1869, and Dean Stannus to Seymour, 20 Sept. 1869, Seymour of Ragley Papers CR114A/538/1; E. L. O'Malley and H. Hardcastle, *Reports of the decisions of the judges*, i (1869), pp. 260-1; *Galway Vindicator*, 7 Aug. 1852; *Clare election petition*, H.C. 1852-3 (587), ix, 661-8; *Longford election petition*, H.C. 1870 (178), lvi, 455; *Committee on parliamentary and municipal elections*, H.C. 1868-9 (352), viii, 209. On pay in general, see L. Drennan to W. Andrews, 10 Dec. 1852, Andrews Papers; Affidavit of R. English, 15 July 1852, O.P. 1852/15/170, Box 1218; *Minutes of evidence taken before the select committee on the Clare election petition*, H.C. 1860 (178), xi, 140; *Cashel election petitions*, H.C. 1868-9 (121), xlix, 250.

[3] *Mayo County election petition*, H.C. 1857 (182 Sess. 2), vii, 421; *Clare election petition*, H.C. 1860 (178), ix, 114.

[4] For suing, see *Galway Vindicator*, 7 Aug. 1852; *Clare election petition*, H.C. 1852-3 (587), ix, 750; *Londonderry Sentinel*, 27 Nov. 1868. For lenient punishment, see *Tipperary Advocate*, 29 July 1865; *Londonderry Sentinel*, 24, 27 Nov., 11 Dec. 1868, 22 Feb., 4 Mar. 1870.

boosted lodge funds by marketing their well-honed talents in return for hard cash.[1] Not that all this implied total venality. At many elections all the candidates were expected to have a mob—'our mob behaved with great propriety' remarked a Belfast Liberal smugly in 1835—so that rioters could pick and choose. Some mobs, such as those in Cos. Galway, Cork, and Limerick, were famous for their independent spontaneity: money could only move them in certain limited and congenial directions. And the Derry rioter who caused amusement in court by shouting 'I follow Liberal principles and I will fight for them till I die' was speaking truer than his audience supposed.[2]

Fairs, markets, crossroad entertainments, rural hurling contests, and faction fights in earlier years, all provided ample opportunities for collecting people together, as did pattern days and similar observances.[3] In the weeks before, during, and after elections such gatherings provided a ready source of casual violence. Many unemployed people were ready to drift with the crowd. 'I had no employment', remarked one east Cork labourer in 1834, 'and I went with the people.' Another, knowing little of politics, 'went down the bohreen because the crowd went'. Excitement was easily generated, and elections, in the comparative absence of demotic sports, provided frequent and potentially profitable occasions for excitement on the part of men and women with time on their hands. In the interval between the decline of faction fighting and the rise of organized Gaelic games, elections fulfilled an acutely unsatisfied need. The

---

[1] *Dublin Evening Mail*, 20 Apr. 1857; also Requisition of Lord Rosse, 17 July 1852, Mayo Papers MS 11176; *Cork City election petition*, H.C. 1852-3 (587), xi, 36-8; *Sligo Borough election petition*, H.C. 1852-3 (600), xviii, 626-8; *Dungarvan election petition*, H.C. 1854 (162), viii, 497-8; *Galway Town corrupt practices commission*, H.C. 1857-8 [2291], xxvi, 318; J. Spaight to Naas, [2 May 1859], Mayo Papers MS 11036; *Cashel corrupt practices commission*, H.C. 1870 [C 9], xxxii, 289.

[2] J. Hancock to E. Littleton, 1 Feb. 1835, Hatherton Papers D260/M/F/5/27/10; also T. H. Babington to R. Bourke, [1852], Mayo Papers MS 11176; *Cashel election petitions*, H.C. 1868-9 (121), xlix, 170-1; E. L. O'Malley and H. Hardcastle, *Reports of the decisions of the judges*, i (1869), pp. 260-1; Spencer to C. Fortescue, 30 Mar. 1870, Carlingford Papers CP2/13; *Londonderry Sentinel*, 27 Nov. 1868; also *Cork County election petition*, H.C. 1842 (271), vi, 98, 115; R. O'Gorman to W. S. O'Brien, 18 Feb. 1847, Smith O'Brien Papers MS 438; *Committee on parliamentary and municipal elections*, H.C. 1868-9 (352), viii, 209.

[3] M. Tierney to Anglesey, 22 June 1831, O.P. 1831/T31, Box 1842; *Committee on Bribery at Elections*, H.C. 1835 (547), viii, 289; G. C. Lewis, *On local Disturbances*, p. 99; *Fictitious Votes, Ireland*, 2nd series, 3rd report, p. 41; E. Priestley, RM to Eliot, 30 Sept. 1843, Graham Papers 6/Ir; F. S. P. Wolferstan and E. L'E. Dew, *Reports of the decisions of committees of the House of Commons in the trial of controverted elections during the seventeenth parliament of the United Kingdom* (London, 1859), p. 15; *Commissioners of Inquiry, 1869, into the Riots and Disturbances in the City of Londonderry*, H.C. 1870 [C 5*], xxxii, 91; J. Elland to I. Butt, 7 Jan. 1874, Butt Papers MS 8696; *Daily Express*, 20 Jan. 1874. See Chapter III above for patterns etc.

large reservoirs of poverty, the desperate inhabitants of shanty
suburbs, the men of 'no occupation' who hung around towns like
Clonmel, the many beggars noticed by travellers as late as the 1880s,
all supplied a ready source of rioters with little to lose and (relatively)
much to gain.[1] 'He said', recalled a Mayo constable of what a
frenzied rioter had yelled at Ballinrobe in 1857, 'he did not care if
he lost his life.' And there can be no doubt that most election and
other mobs were substantially composed of poor labourers (urban
and agricultural), declining artisans, and men even more marginal
—'the habits of beggars are much worse than those of labourers',
a parson noted in 1834.[2] Expert evidence comes from all sides:
from social analysts—'the most ragged, rejected creatures' (Clonmel
1835), 'the rags and wretchedness which usually congregates whenever there is a crowd' (King's Co. 1852); from moralists—'all the
scum of the population willing to shout and curse and fling all sorts
of filth' (Co. Longford 1869); from psychologists—'the lowest
type and character' (Co. Clare 1852); from sartorialists—'barragan
jackets and smock frocks' (Cork City 1852), 'half-naked' (Co. Louth
1865); from phrenologists—'a very large . . . head' (Co. Clare 1852);
and from physiognomists too—'wild-looking frantic men, who put
out their tongues' (Co. Tipperary 1857).[3] A Mayoman struggling
for the *mot juste* in 1857 summed up the prevailing view.

Were they farm people, labourers or people of the town, and that sort of thing;
artisans?—It is difficult to know . . . but they were all the same class of persons;
they were either the mob of the town or the neighbourhood of the town, the
humbler classes . . . They were the lower class, the labouring poor . . . What we
call in Ireland the peasantry.[4]

The occupations of those charged with rioting after the Derry
election of 1868 and those killed or injured during the Belfast riots
of 1864 and 1886 provide an urban confirmation of such views,
with two-thirds of them labourers, artisans, and factory workers.

[1] *Selection of Parochial Examinations relative to the destitute classes in Ireland, from
the evidence received by His Majesty's Commissioners for enquiring into the condition of
the poorer classes in Ireland* (Dublin, 1835), pp. 344, 327, 308, also 315, 321, 340, 390;
K. T. Hoppen, 'National politics and local realities in mid-nineteenth century Ireland',
in *Studies in Irish History presented to R. Dudley Edwards*, ed. A. Cosgrove and D. Mc-
Cartney (Dublin, 1979), pp. 191–2; *Fictitious Votes, Ireland*, 1st series, 2nd report, p. 19;
D. B. King, *The Irish Question*, pp. 21–2.

[2] *Mayo County election petition*, H.C. 1857 (182 Sess. 2), vii, 48; *Selection of Parochial Examinations* (1835), p. 393.

[3] *Committee on Bribery at Elections*, H.C. 1835 (547), viii, 552; Report of H. Pollock,
RM, 5 July 1852, O.P. 1852/15/152, Box 1218; *Telegraph or Connaught Ranger*, 12 Jan.
1870; J. P. Brown, JP to Naas, 16 July 1852, Mayo Papers MS 11018; *Cork City election
petition*, H.C. 1852–3 (528), xi, 58; *Londonderry Sentinel*, 28 July 1865; *Clare election
petition*, H.C. 1852–3 (587), ix, 722–6; *Dublin Evening Mail*, 6 Apr. 1857.

[4] *Mayo County election petition*, H.C. 1857 (182 Sess. 2), vii, 60.

Youth too was a characteristic of election and other rioters alike, as it was also of those most active in the perpetration of rural outrages.[1]

Being so much smaller than, for example, O'Connell's monster meetings or even the organized demonstrations of the Fenian and Amnesty movements, election mobs were probably socially far less mixed and tactically far more coherent and manœuvrable. Estimates in this respect are notoriously unreliable. A single crowd at the Co. Londonderry election of 1859 was thought to number 2,000 by one side and 300 by the other, while a Fenian demonstration in Limerick in 1867 attracted 11,000 marchers according to one estimate and 4,100 according to the police.[2] However, even allowing for a substantial margin of error, there can be little doubt that election mobs generally varied in size between about one and five thousand. Smaller subgroups can of course also be identified, while mobs of up to eight thousand and more were not unusual in the larger constituencies. Occasional higher estimates—up to 20,000 at Mallow in 1841 (total population 6,851), Limerick in 1852, and Kerry in 1872, and even 100,000 at Carlow in 1841—were probably exaggerated or included onlookers as well as participants. Thus the average election mob was large enough to intimidate and destroy but small enough to retain a high degree of mobility, energy, and social cohesion. The scene at the Cavan by-election of 1855 was typical: 'A body of stout active young fellows, numbering some five or six thousand and each brandishing an enormous cudgel, came down the streets and advanced to the court house, roaring vociferously.'[3]

[1] For occupations, see *Londonderry Sentinel*, 24, 27 Nov., 11 Dec. 1868; *Minutes of evidence and appendix to the report of the Commissioners of Inquiry, 1864, respecting the magisterial and police jurisdiction arrangements and establishment of the Borough of Belfast*, H.C. 1865 [3466–I], xxviii, Appendix 18; *Report by one of the Commissioners* [W. B. M'Hardy] *of Inquiry, 1886, respecting the origin and circumstances of the Riots in Belfast*, H. C. 1887 [C 5029], xvii, Supplement. For ages, see *Belfast Newsletter*, 17 July 1835; Memorial of J. Duffy, 2 Aug. 1852, O.P. 1852/15/264, Box 1218; *Banner of Ulster*, 4 Apr. 1857; *Londonderry Sentinel*, 22 Feb. 1870.

[2] Lord Ebrington to Lord Normanby, 24 Jan. 1840, Fortescue Papers 1262M/LI21; *Londonderry Sentinel*, 6 May 1859; B. Mac Giolla Choille, 'Mourning the Martyrs: A Study of a demonstration in Limerick City, 8 December 1867', *North Munster Antiquarian Journal*, x (1967), 180. See *Sunday Times* (London), 5 Apr. 1981 for equally unreliable modern techniques.

[3] *Anglo-Celt* (Cavan), 12 Apr. 1855. For the 'larger' mobs, see Report of D. E. Jennings, 5 Dec. 1868, R.P. 1868/17392, Box 1780; *Athlone Conservative Advocate*, 31 Aug. 1837; B. Cahir, 'Irish National By-Elections 1870–1874' (University College Dublin MA thesis, 1965), p. 104; *The Reign of Terror in Carlow* (1841), p. 66; J. Lord, *Popery at the hustings*, pp. 97–8; *Report of the Outrages and Intimidations at the late Elections* (1841), p. 14. For the more usual smaller mobs, see Report of W. P. Walker, 5 May 1831, O.P. 1831/M63; of Sub-Inspector Crofton, 26 Dec. 1832, O.P. 1832/2202, Box 2192; of Sub-Inspector Battersby, 4 Jan. 1835, O.P. 1835, Box 46; W. Miller to Sir H. Hardinge, 19 Mar. 1835,

Violence or its threat being the *raison d'être* of election mobs, it is hardly surprising that behaviour was rarely restrained. Neither the need for payment nor the occasional bureaucratic efficiency—at Carrick-on-Suir there were separate mobs for adults and juveniles, each subdivided into 'light', 'semi-light', and 'heavy brigades'[1]— necessarily implied any lack of enthusiasm. The full cycle of activity usually began with hooting, continued with hitting (spitting was an optional extra), and concluded with shooting. 'Any men that would interfere for Vandeleur', the Liberal mob at the Clare election of 1852 was told, 'to strike them, and knock them down as fast as ever they could . . . and kick them for falling, too.'[2] Most mobs, however, developed a momentum of their own as violence became virtually an end in itself. 'Kill Him! Finish Him!', yelled a Belfast mob around a Protestant victim already felled by a cleaver in 1832. 'Frenzied . . . their hair all about them', a large mob of countrymen tornadoed through Ballina in 1857. At the Derry election of 1868 a wild-eyed labourer was arrested waving a knife and shouting he would 'rip open the first man' he saw. In 1859 the Mallow mob, though paid by one candidate, got so excited it smashed the skulls of friend and foe alike. The various mobs collected by opposing Nationalists and clericalists at the Co. Longford by-election of 1869 were required to be 'up to anything and prepared for any kind of violence', and, indeed, they were soon to be found cutting down trees 'to get terrible big sticks' and 'leaping and jumping and threatening', just as their local predecessors—'many of them in a state of excitement bordering on frenzy'—had done in 1852.[3]

The variety of weapons used ensured that such energy rarely went to waste. Sticks and cudgels were particularly common. Connoisseurs discussed the relative merits of ash, oak, and holly, of size and shape. In 1852 seven hundred cudgels were removed at one Co. Down

---

ibid.; *D.E.P.* 20 June 1835; Report of G. Fitzgerald, 10 Aug. 1837, O.P. 1837/620/57, Box 53; *Cork City election petition*, H.C. 1852-3 (528), xi, 12; *Minutes of evidence taken before the select committee on the Drogheda election petitions*, H.C. 1857 (255 Sess. 2), vi, 15; Reports of E. Collins, RM, 1, 8 May 1859, and N. Bourke, 8 May 1859, R.P. 1859/ 3993, 4340, 4420—all Box 808.

[1] J. Smyth, *The Elector* (1853), p. 34. See also J. Evatt to Lord Bath, 4 Dec. 1832, Bath Papers Irish Box; G. Fitzgerald to W. Gossett, 30 Dec. 1832, O.P. 1832/2261, Box 2192; *Clare election petition*, H.C. 1852-3 (587), ix, 569-70; Report by a major of the 12th Lancers, 30 Dec. 1866, Mayo Papers MS 11210; *Committee on parliamentary and municipal elections*, H.C. 1868-9 (352), viii, 296.

[2] *Clare election petition*, H.C. 1852-3 (587), ix, 677.

[3] S. E. Baker, 'Orange and Green: Belfast 1832-1912', p. 792; *Mayo County election petition*, H.C. 1857 (182 Sess. 2), vii, 197, 209; *C.C.* 5 May 1859; *Londonderry Sentinel*, 24 Nov. 1868; *Longford election petition*, H.C. 1870 (178), lvi, 285-6, 292, 329, 455, 492, 499; 'A Clergyman of the Established Church' [G. Dwyer], *Popery unmasked at the recent elections in Ireland* (1852), p. 33.

polling station and two hundred from a band of 'agitators' entering Ennis.[1] Such basic equipment was augmented by an almost endlessly ingenious battery of other instruments: crutches, spikes, hatchets, knives, axes, cleavers, and skewers at Belfast in 1832; sword canes at Cork the same year; loaded whips and sticks at Longford in 1841; pikes at Tipperary in 1852 and paving stones in 1857; iron bars and bottles at Drogheda and half-pound weights with straps at Newry in 1868. One group marching towards Newry in 1852 was alone relieved of 500 bludgeons, fifty rounds of ammunition, forty spare balls, sixteen pistols, a bayonet, a dagger, and a set of loaded whips.[2] Guns of various kinds were easily obtained and made crackling appearances at elections throughout the period. Given their condition, they were often more frightening than dangerous, but the sound of gunfire at elections like those at—to name only a few—Newry in 1832, Armagh and Mayo in 1835, Tipperary in 1837, Longford in 1841, Dundalk in 1847, Leitrim in 1852, Limerick and Louth in 1865, Drogheda in 1868, and Limerick again in 1874 created considerable alarm and often drove the forces of law and order into premature displays of marksmanship with their own more lethal carbines and 'rifles.[3] Although injuries were often extensive rather than dangerous, the presence of effective weapons could, when combined with a high degree of mob excitability, produce bloody and horrendous results. The Limerick election riots of 1852 ended in much human destruction, while the 327 people killed or injured during the Belfast riots of 1864 included 107 gunshot, 214 contusion, and five stabbing cases,

[1] P. O'Donnell, *The Irish Faction Fighters*, pp. 15-18; C. Ó Danachair, 'Faction Fighting in County Limerick', *North Munster Antiquarian Journal*, x (1966), 47-55; 'A Barrister', *Observations on Intimidation at Elections*, p. 49; *Copies of the several inquisitions removed from the Court of Queen's Bench* . . ., H.C. 1852-3 (313), xciv, 73-5. For their use elsewhere, see, e.g., Report of Chief Magistrate Jones, 28 Dec. 1832, O.P. 1832/ 2232, Box 2192; *D.E.P.* 8 Aug. 1837; J. Going to J. Wynne, 19 July 1852, O.P. 1852/27/ 493, Box 1220; Report of Inspector Curtis, 25 July 1852, Mayo Papers MS 11037; *Dublin Evening Mail*, 6 Apr. 1857; *Westmeath Guardian*, 20 July 1865.

[2] S. E. Baker, 'Orange and Green: Belfast 1832-1912', p. 791; *D.E.P.* 5, 8 Aug. 1837; S.P.O. Stipendiary Magistrates' Diaries No. 30 (Major P. C. Howley) for July 1841; J. Going to J. Wynne, 19 July 1852, O.P. 1852/27/493, Box 1220; *Dublin Evening Mail*, 6 Apr. 1857; *Londonderry Sentinel*, 27 Nov. 1868; Strathnairn to Duke of Grafton, 2 Dec. 1868, 22 Mar. 1869, Strathnairn Papers Add. MS 42825. For the Newry incident, see F. B. Head, *A Fortnight in Ireland*, p. 381.

[3] *Committee on Bribery at Elections*, H.C. 1835 (547), viii, 431-5; *D.E.P.* 22, 24 Jan. 1835; Revd N. Power to T. Drummond, 7 Aug. 1837, O.P. 1837/620/57, Box 53; S.P.O. Stipendiary Magistrates' Diaries No. 30, for July 1841; D. Power, H. Rodwell, and E. L'E. Dew, *Reports of the decisions of committees of the House of Commons* (1853), p. 90; L. McNiffe, 'The 1852 Leitrim Election', *Breifne*, v (1977-8), 234; *Limerick Chronicle*, 13, 15, 22 July 1865; *Londonderry Sentinel*, 28 July 1865; Strathnairn to Duke of Cambridge, 22 Nov., 5 Dec. 1868, Strathnairn Papers Add. MS 42825; *Daily Express*, 6 Feb. 1874.

as well as one man who—understandably enough—had died from 'mania caused by fright'.[1]

Election mobs can be seen, therefore, to have offered a variety of roles within the wider world of politics to many of those without the vote, not least to that 'half the human race, women'. Occasionally, individual women achieved positions of local political influence: Miss Forrest of the Gort Hotel (described in 1872 as the MP Sir William Gregory's 'right-hand man'), Anne Brien, the tough Dungarvan mob leader of 1868, the Claddagh fishwives who constituted the praetorian guard of Michael Morris in Galway, or the businesslike women of Newry who negotiated their husbands' bribes in 1832. Occasionally, appeals were issued by candidates to 'the fair sex' for help in persuading spouses to vote in the right direction.[2] Occasionally, it must even have struck people that women enjoyed enough economic power (that is, they occupied enough houses of the required value) to have been able, in 1874 for example, to wield an eighth of the Irish borough vote had the law allowed it.[3] Occasionally, indeed, the obvious enthusiasm and commitment of women at certain elections, such as those at Cork City in 1835, King's Co. in 1837, Co. Louth in 1859, and Co. Tipperary in 1869, actually attracted nervous contemporary comment.[4] But far and away the most common outlet for women's political feelings, as for those of the disenfranchised generally, was provided by election riots and disorders. The phenomenon of women taking a prominent, sometimes even a leading, part in riots—and doing so with a vigour second to none—though common before the Famine, became dramatically so thereafter. Perhaps, with the narrowing range of female job opportunities caused by the collapse of the domestic textile industry and the more and more onerous household duties demanded by the 'modernized'

[1] *Londonderry Sentinel*, 22 Feb., 4 Mar. 1870; P. Barron, RM to Under-Secretary, 12 July 1852, Mayo Papers MS 11037; *Commissioners of Inquiry, 1864, respecting the magisterial and police jurisdiction arrangements and establishment of the Borough of Belfast*, H.C. 1865 [3466-I], xxviii, Appendix 18.

[2] *Galway County election petition*, H.C. 1872 (241-I), xlviii, 539; *Waterford Mail*, 18 Sept. 1868; M. Wynne, *An Irishman and his Family: Lord Morris and Killanin* (London, 1937), p. 10; *Report from the select committee on the Newry Borough election petition*, H.C. 1833 (76), x, 612. For appeals, see Ebrington to Morpeth, 8 May 1840, Carlisle Papers L.-B. 38; *Londonderry Sentinel*, 6 Mar., 17 Apr. 1857.

[3] Women were particularly prominent in this respect in Clonmel (18.2 per cent), Waterford (17.5 per cent), and Wexford (14.6 per cent)—calculated from information on proportions of tenements 'over £4' occupied by women in 19 of the then 31 parliamentary boroughs in *Returns for each city, town and township . . . of the number of female rated occupiers*, H.C. 1875 (455), lxiv, 47-61, and *Returns from each city, town, and borough in Ireland . . . of the number of male persons rated*, H.C. 1875 (424), lx, 493.

[4] *Dublin Evening Mail*, 18 Feb. 1835; *Athlone Conservative Advocate*, 17 Aug. 1837; Carlingford Papers Diary of C. Fortescue III (12 May 1859); *Freeman's Journal*, 29 Nov. 1869.

men of late-nineteenth-century Ireland, poorer women increasingly found that riots provided one of the few available and public roles of equality in a world in which churches, political parties, clubs, and Orange lodges alike assigned them either no role at all or restricted them to the making of tea and the saying of prayers. The result was that purely female mobs made their appearance, that women led and organized mobs composed mostly of men, that thousands of lethal stones were carried about at elections in female aprons, that at Cork women rioters were especially sought after, that in Kilrush women rioters were especially inebriated, that, again and again, women were described as the most violent and savage of all. 'By G——, Smith', yelled one women at Cork in 1852, 'if you attempt to vote I'll rip your bloody Protestant guts out', at which another 'female demon seized one of his hands in her mouth and tore it with her teeth'. At Cashel in 1865 'well-looking well-dressed girls, one a perfect Amazon, bared their arms, wound their shawls tightly around them, and rushed with the mêlée'. When at Dungarvan in the same year one unfortunate candidate stepped from his carriage 'a woman of the town rushed at him and assaulted him. He retired to his hotel, where he remained during the day.'[1] Such examples could be multiplied and caused all right-thinking men to join with a Catholic schoolmaster in 1828 and a Protestant stipendiary in 1874 in respectively disapproving of women attending O'Connellite meetings and finding it 'disgraceful to think that women should descend to such disgraceful acts'.[2] But, however complicated the motives and experiences of female rioters may have been, there can be no doubt that this aspect of electioneering provided far more women with political opportunities of a sort than did all the Quaker teacups rattled by the genteel Irish suffrage reformers of the 1860s and 1870s. It is also notable that only one of the seven Irish MPs who signed Woodall's suffrage amendment of 1884 was a Catholic, and that the few ministers of religion who supported the movement were all Protestants of one sort or another.[3] With the Catholic Church

[1] *Londonderry Sentinel*, 30 July 1852 (Cork); *Tipperary Advocate*, 15 July 1865 (Cashel); *D.E.P.* 5 July 1865 (Dungarvan). For a sample of similar incidents, see T. Kayne to J. Wynne, 15 July 1852, O.P. 1852/17/291, Box 1219 (Limerick); Memorial of J. Duffy, 2 Sept. 1852, O.P. 1852/15/264, Box 1218 (Donegal); R. Corbett to C. H. Frewen, [11 July 1852], Mayo Papers MS 11019 (Cork female rioters especially sought after); *Clare election petition*, H.C. 1852-3 (587), ix, 749 (Kilrush inebriates); *C.C.* 27 Feb. 1863 (Bandon); *Waterford Mail*, 18 Sept. 1868 (Dungarvan); *Annual Register . . . for the year 1872*, p. 15 (Kerry); W. E. Forster to Gladstone, 27 May 1881, Gladstone Papers Add. MS 44158.

[2] *Diary of Humphrey O'Sullivan*, ed. M. McGrath, ii, 25-7; *Daily Express*, 23 Jan. 1874.

[3] Rosemary Owens, 'Votes for Women: Irishwomen's Campaign for the Vote' (University College Dublin MA thesis, 1977), pp. 5-11. For participants at a meeting of the

not simply hostile like Gladstone and Parnell, but massively indifferent to women as anything other than cooks, mothers, and
saints, the enterprise shown by so many Irishwomen in identifying
riots as one of the few available opportunities for equality of expression and action was at once realistic and shrewd.

V LAW ENFORCEMENT

When agrarian and electoral disorder are held up as mirrors to society
they catch the light of many other aspects of life and experience.
Notably they make it possible to see how violence created certain
kinds of reactions and stresses among the forces of law and order,
and how—for large sections of the population—violence occupied
a recognized place within the wider world of celebration, enjoyment,
and festivals.

The ever-present possibility of unrest of all kinds in Ireland drew
forth a much more visible government response than was the case in
England or Scotland. The increasing use after 1814 of full-time
stipendiary magistrates—there were fifty-nine by 1841 and seventy-
three by 1860—to 'assist' and replace local justices, as well as the
police reforms which led to the establishment of a national constabulary in 1836, reveal a level of centralized commitment and
control altogether absent in the rest of the United Kingdom. Stipendiaries were regularly employed at elections and upon their individual
abilities could depend the difference between excitement and chaos.
At the Co. Waterford by-election of 1866, for example, no less than
seventeen were imported to supervise the conduct of the poll.[1] However, their failures at election after election, and their timidity,
inefficiency, and (in early days) partiality show them to have been
unsteady instruments of Dublin Castle's will. With certain exceptions
they swung between lethargy and panic. At the 1858 Limerick by-
election one spoke wildly of Balaclava as he ordered the dragoons to
clear the streets. At a series of elections in the 1850s and 1860s their
general lack of resolution did little to prevent injury and disturbance.[2]

Women's Suffrage Association in the Dublin home of a Church of Ireland curate, see *Daily
Express*, 18 Mar. 1880.

[1] *Copies of all orders or requisitions to General or other Officers for Troops to escort
voters on any day or days previous to the day of polling, at the last election for the County
of Waterford . . . with the names of the magistrates in charge*, H.C. 1867 (216), lvi, 237–50.
See also some of the official diaries which stipendiaries were required to complete in the
1830s and 1840s, e.g. S.P.O. Stipendiary Magistrates' Diaries Nos. 22 and 30; also *Banner
of Ulster*, 10 Feb. 1857; T. Larcom to Naas, 14 May 1858, Mayo Papers MS 11190.

[2] W. Spaight to Lord Dunraven, 8 Feb. 1858, Dunraven Papers D3196; also C. F. Johnson to R. Bourke, 7 July 1852, Mayo Papers MS 11019; J. C. Chatterton to Naas, 13 July
1852, ibid. MS 11018; Eglinton to Walpole, 15 July 1852, Eglinton Papers MS 5337;

Viceroys and chief secretaries often thought them 'totally indifferent' or 'nearly all . . . useless'. The lack of job specifications and the generous pay (£350 to £685 in 1851) made the position especially attractive to well-connected incompetents, to (as Lord Rosse put it) 'elderly roués with broken fortunes and damaged reputations'.[1] There were of course exceptions, such as P. C. Howley who controlled the dangerous Longford election of 1841 with courage and skill. But it is none the less striking how, when in 1843 the Government circularized stipendiaries and county police inspectors for their views on the Repeal agitation, the policemen's invariably sensible and well-informed replies contrasted sharply with the alternatively vapid and hysterical responses of the 'professional' magistrates.[2]

Indeed, the constabulary was one of nineteenth-century Ireland's most remarkable success stories. A quasi-military force in dark green uniforms, armed with bayonets, carbines, and (later) rifles, living in barracks, largely unmarried, with no member 'allocated to his native county or to any county in which he is connected by marriage', the constabulary replaced and greatly improved upon the chaotic and separate forces of earlier years.[3] Its enormous range of duties, as reflected in minutely detailed regulations which moved majestically through Agricultural Statistics, Auctions, Dog Acts, Drill, Elections, Funerals, Inflammatory Placards, and much else to Vagrancy and Wrecks (stopping only to insist that 'Men in uniform are not to carry umbrellas'), quickly intruded its members into every sphere of Irish life.[4] And, despite occasional criticisms that the force was too military and too obsessed with spit and polish, there can be no doubt that, until the temporary failure of nerve of the

S. A. Dickson to Naas, 2 May 1859, Mayo Papers MS 11036; W. C. Talbot to Naas, 28 Dec. 1866, ibid. MS 11210; Strathnairn to Naas, 29 Dec. 1866, Strathnairn Papers Add. MS 42823; Strathnairn to Under-Secretary, 1 Mar. 1869, Kilmainham Papers MS 1062.

[1] Wellesley to Peel, 27 Sept. 1822, Wellesley Papers Add. MS 37299; Eglinton to Derby, 19 June 1852, Derby Papers 148/2; Carlingford Papers Diary of C. Fortescue I (12 Nov. 1855—reporting Horsman); N. W. Senior, *Journals, conversations, and essays relating to Ireland*, ii, 30 (reporting Rosse). On pay, see *Abstract of a statement of the amount of constabulary force employed in each county, county of a city, and county of a town, in Ireland*, H.C. 1851 (214), 1, 379–82.

[2] Howley's Diary, S.P.O. Stipendiary Magistrates' Diaries No. 30 (July 1841); various Confidential Printed Reports etc. in Derby Papers 34. See also Naas to Derby, 31 July 1852, Derby Papers 155/1.

[3] J. S. Kennedy, *Standing Rules and Regulations for the government and guidance of the Constabulary Force in Ireland* (Dublin, 1837), ss. 126 and 127. The rules regarding localism became even stricter in the 1870s and 1880s (I am indebted to R. A. J. Hawkins for this information). See also F. B. Head, *A Fortnight in Ireland* (1852), pp. 42–65.

[4] *Standing Rules and Regulations for the government and guidance of the Royal Irish Constabulary*, 3rd edn. (Dublin, 1872)—see s. 838 for umbrellas; also *Devon Commission*, Witness No. 1906 (Inspector-General McGregor), and Mr and Mrs S. C. Hall, *Ireland*, i, 420.

early 1880s, the constabulary was generally loyal, efficient, and effective.[1] Even in the difficult year of 1882, there was, as always after the early days, a large core of experienced men: more than half the constables and head constables had served for twenty years and even a quarter of the sub-constables had served for ten.[2] In the present context the most remarkable aspects of the constabulary were its size, social and religious composition, and its pattern of recruitment. From the start, numbers were larger than the total of previous forces, and thereafter they rose steadily. And as the number of soldiers did not show any matching decline, it is clear that Ireland was a much more heavily 'policed' country in Parnell's than it had been in O'Connell's time, especially if movements in population are taken into account. Indeed, Gladstone, while on his brief visit in 1877, was 'astonished' by the 'superfluous number' of policemen, and characteristically blamed Peel for having taken 'the whole charge on the consolidated fund'.[3] In fact, of course, this increase reflected not only increased duties and typical bureaucratic drift, but a perception on the part of informed authorities that a changing agrarian and political situation required more rather than less surveillance and control. As numbers in the national force rose from 7,633 in 1837 to 12,592 in 1882, so did the proportion of Catholics—from 53.4 per cent in 1842 to 63.4 per cent in 1852—until in 1882 the religious composition of the constabulary reflected that of the country as a whole. It remained, however, the case that Catholics were always more common in the lower ranks, though even among head constables the Catholic proportion did rise from one-third to two-thirds during the three decades after 1852.[4]

---

[1] On spit and polish, see T. O'Hagan to W. Monsell, 29 May 1862, O'Hagan Papers N.L.I. MS 17871; Sir G. Grey to Carlisle, 22 Mar. 1864, Larcom Papers MS 7619. On efficiency etc., see Mr and Mrs S. C. Hall, *Ireland*, i, 418, and ii, 420; Memorandum by Viceroy De Grey, 31 Aug. 1843, Graham Papers 5/Ir; Graham to Eliot, 3 Sept. 1843, ibid.; Confidential Printed Reports of 1843 in Derby Papers 34; Memorandum on Irish Crime, 19 Jan. 1870, Gladstone Papers Add. MS 44613; Lord Carnarvon to Sir R. A. Cross, 25 July 1885, Carnarvon Papers P.R.O. 30/6/62.

[2] *Report of the Committee of Inquiry into the Royal Irish Constabulary*, H.C. 1883 [C 3577], xxxii, 756. Details in R.I.C. Records HO184/54 indicate an annual turnover (for all reasons) of about a tenth between 1842 and 1882. See also F. B. Head, *A Fortnight in Ireland*, p. 53.

[3] Gladstone to W. E. Forster, 25 Oct. 1880, Gladstone Papers Add. MS 44157. For the ubiquity of police and troops, see Table 51 below.

[4] See R.I.C. Records HO184/54. The percentage of Catholics among (a) head constables, (b) constables, (c) sub-constables, (d) all three ranks together was as follows:

	(a)	(b)	(c)	(d)
1842	n.a.	n.a.	n.a.	53.4
1852	31.0	51.9	66.9	63.4
1882	64.0	69.2	74.8	73.6

In social terms also the constabulary reflected the changing face of rural Ireland. Strict entry requirements—literacy, 'good character', height, possession of a 'suit of plain clothes and a hat' and two pounds in money—barred the poor. And, despite claims that slippage in pay in the 1860s was producing a 'lower class' of recruit, official sources make it clear that, as in so many other aspects of Irish life, farmers and their sons were in fact dramatically replacing labourers among the ranks of the police.[1] Already in 1852 the new entrants being trained at the Dublin depot were mostly 'the sons of deserving small farmers . . . fine handsome intelligent lads', an impression borne out by the official registers, which show that the occupational composition of the force kept steady pace with the profound social changes taking place within the rural population as a whole. The overall picture given in Table 49 is, however, significantly qualified by equally dramatic changes in the locations from which the force drew the bulk of its recruits, for the farmers who were replacing the pre-Famine labourers were not in the main the sons of well-to-do men in the midlands or the east but of the struggling small farmers of the west. In 1842 the four provinces provided recruits roughly in proportion to their populations; by 1862 Ulster and Munster were falling behind; by 1882 only Connacht (with 15.9 per cent of the population and 28.4 per cent of the recruits) was exceeding its share. Indeed, by 1882 the five Connacht counties and Cavan, Monaghan, Longford, and Kerry, with together a quarter of the country's people, provided more than half of its police recruits. Such social and geographical shifts constitute a somewhat idiosyncratic reflection of two rather different developments within the general community: the lasting triumph of the farmer and the more transient westward movement of serious outrage and violence. And just as more literate and educated policemen—one was encountered near Clifden in the 1850s reading Adam Smith, Josephus, the *Saturday Magazine*, and Chalmers's *Discourses*—reacted to their tasks in new ways, so did men who were simultaneously identified with and exiled from the world of the western farmer view the tenant agitation of the 1870s and 1880s through lenses very different from those through which the labourer policemen of the 1830s and 1840s had

---

[1] F. B. Head, *A Fortnight in Ireland*, pp. 174-5. On pay etc., see T. O'Hagan to W. Monsell, 29 May 1862, O'Hagan Papers N.L.I. MS 17871; *Report of the commission directed by the Treasury to inquire into the state of the Constabulary Force in Ireland*, H.C. 1866 [3658], xxxiv, 177-8. Already in 1847 the same point had been made (Clarendon to Grey, 22 Nov. 1847, Clarendon Papers L.-B. I). The annual pay of a constable was £32 until 1848, then £36 until 1866, then £49, and £73 from 1872 (*Report of the Committee of Inquiry into the Royal Irish Constabulary*, H.C. 1883 [C 3577], xxxii, 755). The Inspector-General got £1,500, county inspectors about £250, and sub-inspectors about £150.

TABLE 49
Social backgrounds of policemen enlisting in 1842, 1882, Jan.–Mar. 1913

	1842 per cent	1882 per cent	1913 Jan.–Mar. per cent
Farmers	24.4	55.8	60.0
Labourers	59.4	25.6	19.0
Artisans	9.6	6.2	7.0
Shop assistants, clerks, others	6.6	12.4	14.0

seen the agrarian troubles of earlier times. 'Who are the policemen?' shouted a radical candidate at the Tipperary by-election of 1865, 'they are the sons of . . . farmers; they were the best sons of the plough too . . . If the policemen had farms they would stay at home in the fork of the plough.'[1]

The other major law-enforcement agency in Ireland was the Army. It led an equivocal existence uneasily combining defence duties with long-stop policing. Its fluctuating size of between 15,000 and 30,000 was determined by availability and by the authorities' perception of trouble. The rankers were mostly unskilled industrial and agricultural workers, who enlisted for life (until 1847), suffered bad pay and worse conditions, and were altogether less well situated than their constabulary counterparts. Already by 1851 their backgrounds (especially in the cavalry) were predominantly urban, though of course the substantial proportion recruited in Ireland came largely from 'the lower agricultural and labouring classes', as Lord Strath-nairn, the Commander of the Forces in Ireland, put it in 1869.[2] Ireland supplied more recruits than its population warranted, for Irish agricultural labourers alone could objectively regard Army pay as better than their own. But, as Ireland's share of United Kingdom population fell, so did its contribution to Army numbers and so did the proportion of Catholics in the ranks (Table 50). Among the officers—an increasingly middle-class group—Irishmen were not disproportionately common, though Protestant Irishmen were.[3] With Protestants forming the bulk of troops stationed in

[1] F. B. Head, *A Fortnight in Ireland*, pp. 175–6; *Tipperary Advocate*, 18 Feb. 1865.

[2] Strathnairn to Under-Secretary, 1 Mar. 1869, Kilmainham Papers MS 1062. For pay, conditions, and background, see A. R. Skelley, *The Victorian Army at Home: The Recruitment and Terms and Conditions of the British Regular, 1859–1899* (London, 1977), pp. 192–3, 289–92, 296, 310, also 21–84.

[3] P. E. Razzell, 'Social Origins of Officers in the Indian and British Home Army: 1758–1962', *British Journal of Sociology*, xiv (1963), 248–68; H. J. Hanham, 'Religion and Nationality in the mid-Victorian Army' in *War and Society: Historical essays in honour and memory of J. R. Western 1928–1971*, ed. M. R. D. Foot (London, 1973), p. 162.

TABLE 50

The Irish and Catholic presence in the British Army, 1830–85

Irish NCOs and men Year	per cent	Catholic NCOs and men Year	per cent	Irish in UK population Year	per cent
1830	42.2			1831	32.3
1840	37.2			1841	30.6
1868	30.4	1861	28.0	1861	20.0
1875	23.1	1875	22.6	1871	17.5
1880	21.1	1880	23.1	1881	14.8
1885	17.4	1885	21.3	1891	12.5

Ireland—almost three-quarters, one expert estimated in 1844[1]— problems of loyalty were divided between dangers in the 1820s and 1830s of Orange and in the 1860s of Fenian infiltration. Neither was negligible, but both fell short of the optimistic exaggerations of Brunswickers and Republicans alike.[2] More persistently irritating to the authorities was the work of Catholic parochial clergymen in allegedly undermining military authority. After 1859, however, the 'concession' of appointing full-time Catholic chaplains kept the troops away from the unsupervised clutches of priests not amenable to Army control.[3]

The widespread use of the Army in aid of civil authority made large demands on manpower, and both the military and the police maintained a consistently more substantial presence in Ireland than elsewhere. Table 51 shows that on a population basis (and despite defective *British* police returns for earlier years) the differences were always striking and sometimes dramatic. During the eleven months ending in May 1832 troops were called out 677 times to assist the Irish civil authorities in arms searches, riot control, and other work. And although the police reforms of 1836 reduced the demand for military involvement in keeping order at fairs, escorting

[1] Eliot (reporting General Blakeney) to Graham, 17 Nov. 1844, Graham Papers 18/Ir.

[2] For the pre-Famine situation, see Sir H. Vivian to General Macdonald, 13 Jan. 1833, Vivian Papers No. 11; *D.E.P.* 5 May 1835; Printed General Order No. 522 of 31 Aug. 1835 on Orangeism (Melbourne Papers 103/31) referring to earlier circulars of 1822 and 1829; Eliot to De Grey, 29 Jan. 1844, Graham Papers 69B; H. Senior, *Orangeism in Ireland and Britain 1795–1836* (London, 1966), p. 268; *The Diary of Colour-Sergeant George Calladine 19th Foot 1793–1837*, ed. M. L. Ferrar (London, 1922), p. 134. On the 1860s, see A. J. Semple, 'The Fenian Infiltration of the British Army', pp. 133–60.

[3] W. Miller to Sir H. Hardinge, 19 Mar. 1835, O.P. 1835, Box 46; Duke of Wellington to F. Maule (Secretary at War), 30 Nov. 1850, and Maule to Wellington, 29 Nov., 1 Dec. 1850, Panmure Papers GD45/8/20; Major-General E. Fleming to Deputy Adjutant-General, 13 July 1852, Mayo Papers MS 11037; Colonel Egerton to Colonel Park, 4 Jan. 1860, Seaton Papers; A. R. Skelley, *The Victorian Army at Home*, pp. 165–6.

prisoners, and discovering illegal weapons, yet the disturbed state of
Tipperary in 1844, for example, persuaded the Army to renew the
practice of joint patrolling, while in Cavan and Monaghan the separate
and highly military Revenue Police (concerned with illicit distillation, and disbanded in the 1850s) was often obliged to take up
general constabulary duties to augment the regular force.[1] During
the Fenian and agrarian disturbances of 1867–70 joint patrolling was
again revived and a number of military 'flying columns' formed to
ensure that self-sufficient reserves could be speedily deployed to
suppress 'disturbances, seditious meetings, or processions'. Ten years
later the Army found itself involved in Land War duties, which,
though not unprecedented, had rarely before been necessary in so
concentrated and frequent a form: escorting sheriffs, process-servers,
and bailiffs, augmenting the police in protecting threatened individuals, quelling riots, breaking boycotts, and providing 'overawing
force'.[2]

TABLE 51

Ratios of police and soldiers to population in Britain and Ireland, 1830–81

	Police		Soldiers	
	Britain	Ireland	Britain	Ireland
1830	—	—	1 to 599	1 to 388
1835	1 to 3,203	1 to 942	1 to 647	1 to 418
1842	1 to 1,611	1 to 791	1 to 747	1 to 491
1851	1 to 1,387	1 to 480	—	—
1862	—	—	1 to 347	1 to 262
1864	1 to 1,063	1 to 449	—	—
1871	—	—	1 to 335	1 to 195
1881	1 to 833	1 to 374	1 to 455	1 to 194

Given the military's peace-keeping role, a complex set of rules
was drawn up in a vain attempt to afford useful guidance to officers
commanding detachments 'in aid of the civil power'. These rules
changed little after 1832 and were generally high on theory and low
on utility. The problem of course was, that while in such cases the
Army was ultimately acting under civil control, yet the officers in

[1] *Committee on the State of Ireland*, H.C. 1831–2 (677), xvi, 83–4. For reductions
in duties, see *Crime and Outrage Committee*, H.C. 1839 (486), xi and xii, Qs. 9751–2, also
Devon Commission, Witness No. 1096. For Tipperary etc., see Heytesbury to Graham,
5 Dec. 1844, 5 July 1845, Graham Papers 19/Ir, 22/Ir. For the thousand-strong Revenue
Police, see F. B. Head, *A Fortnight in Ireland*, pp. 133–4, and R. B. McDowell, *The Irish
Administration 1801–1914* (London, 1964), pp. 137–9.

[2] Strathnairn to Duke of Cambridge, 27 Apr. 1870, Strathnairn Papers Add. MS
42826; R. [A. J.] Hawkins, 'An Army on Police Work, 1881–2: Ross of Bladensburg's
Memorandum', *The Irish Sword*, xi (1973), 75–117.

charge were still responsible for the maintenance of good order and discipline. This circle was never satisfactorily squared. The rules of 1832 and 1847 insisted that officers act only under the orders of a magistrate, but went on to talk vaguely of 'exceptional' cases and 'immediate' dangers.[1] Officers, the Commander of the Forces insisted in 1835, must *always* obey accompanying magistrates, but also *never* disperse detachments or act contrarily to military rules. In 1852 one expert feebly concluded that 'there is no fixed rule on the subject'.[2] And this was about the truth of it, for, although in some cases discretion was extremely limited (the Army could not, for example, refuse a magistrate's call for an escort detachment), yet in the end no instructions could cover every eventuality, as the Chief Secretary admitted, when, in 1868, he sent his stipendiaries forth on election duty with the piously useless instruction to 'keep the peace'.[3]

What cannot be disputed, however, is that the most common military duty 'in aid of the civil power' was the prevention of election disorder, so much so, that in 1859 the Inspector-General of Constabulary imposed even more contradictory advice upon his Army colleagues by producing yet another memorandum 'for the guidance of officers commanding corps . . . at the approaching election'. In the end the dilemma was insoluble, for electoral circumstances were as changeable as the experience of officers unacquainted with Ireland was limited: in England troops marched out of towns as polling took place, in Ireland they marched in.[4] Englishmen found this at once shocking and amusing, proof of Paddy's coterminous violence and hot-headed charm. In fact, however, even in England troops were sometimes discreetly moved near towns where election disturbances might reasonably be

[1] 'Copy of the general orders for the guidance of the troops, in affording aid to the Civil Power, and to the Revenue Department in Ireland' in *Orders and Regulations for the Army serving in Ireland* (Dublin, 1832); *General Orders for the guidance of the troops in affording aid to the Civil Power, and to the Revenue Department in Ireland* (Dublin, 1847) —copies in possession of author. The latter is in handy pocket format and reprints the Riot Act.

[2] Sir H. Vivian to Major-General Sir J. Douglas, 11 May 1834, and to Sir T. Arbuthnot, 14 Jan. 1835, Vivian Papers Nos. 12 and 13 (see also the fourteen-point 'Instructions for the information and guidance of officers when called out in command of troops for the maintenance of the public peace in aid of the Civil Authorities', 27 Mar. 1835, Hardinge Papers); Colonel R. P. Douglas (Assistant Adjutant-General) in *Copies of the several inquisitions removed from the Court of Queen's Bench . . .*, H.C. 1852-3 (313), xciv, 72-3, and *Londonderry Sentinel*, 6 Aug. 1852.

[3] *Committee on parliamentary and municipal elections*, H.C. 1868-9 (352), viii, 501, 462-4, also 491.

[4] Dated 25 Apr. 1859 in R.P. 1859, Box 808. For an account of the various statutes etc. governing English practice, see 'Memorandum on the removal of Her Majesty's troops from towns and cities during assizes or elections held therein', Jan. 1868, War Office Papers W033/19.

expected.[1] But the scale of military and police commitment in Ireland was on an altogether higher level. Policemen regarded election work as among their 'principal' duties. The Commander of the Forces was unceremoniously 'required' to be in the country as the nation went to the polls. In 1852 extra troops were specially sent from England. In 1852, 1859, 1865, and almost certainly at other times also, the whole of Ireland was divided into five or six election districts each under the command of an officer of proven worth.[2] Anxious generals held endless consultations with anxious chief secretaries and drew up ever-changing lists of the dates of nomination and polling in the various constituencies. The Inspector-General had a special questionnaire printed on which local inspectors could provide details of their requirements: it repeatedly reminded them to ask for as few men as they safely could.[3]

Although Irish elections had long enjoyed a reputation for boisterousness, it was probably the late 1820s and early 1830s which marked a significant shift towards that widespread and sometimes brutal violence which was so often to require the attentions of troops and police.[4] Already by the mid-1830s it had become a matter of surprised remark if no troops were to be seen when polling took place.[5] And just as electoral violence did not decline during the supposedly corpse-like years of the 1850s and 1860s, so did demands upon the constabulary and Army remain consistently high. At the same time, changing military attitudes and the dangers of Fenianism made the Army ever less enthusiastic about splitting its forces into the many small detachments required for election duty. Senior officers ceaselessly demanded 'concentration' on grounds of efficiency

[1] On attitudes, see Anglesey to Grey, 9 Dec. 1832, Anglesey Papers D619/28A, and Colonel Evans in *Hansard*, xxvi, 907 (12 Mar. 1835); On realities, see *Diary of Colour-Sergeant George Calladine*, ed. M. L. Ferrar, pp. 163, 170-1 (Calladine served in both countries).

[2] F. B. Head, *A Fortnight in Ireland*, p. 176; Strathnairn to Duke of Cambridge, 24 June 1865, Strathnairn Papers Add. MS 42819; Colonel E. R. Wetherall to General Lord Seaton, 11 May 1859, Seaton Papers; S. Walpole to Eglinton, 26 June 1852, Eglinton Papers MS 5336, and Eglinton to Derby, 10, 16 July 1852, Derby Papers 148/2 (extra troops); Eglinton to Derby, 1 June 1852, ibid.; Military Secretary to Under-Secretary, 27 Apr. 1859, R.P. 1859/3831; Strathnairn to Major-General Ridley, 6 July 1865, Strathnairn Papers Add. MS 42819.

[3] Strathnairn to Mayo, 4 Aug. 1868, Mayo Papers MS 11173; Lord Seaton's list of nomination dates etc. in 1859, Seaton Papers; questionnaire of 9 Apr. 1859, Mayo Papers MS 11025.

[4] P. Jupp, *British and Irish elections 1784-1831* (Newton Abbot, 1973), pp. 156, 173-4; *Cork County election petition*, H.C. 1842 (271), vi, 76, 79-80; *Mayo County election petition*, H.C. 1857 (182 Sess. 2), vii, 288; *Fictitious Votes, Ireland*, 2nd series, 3rd report, p. 310.

[5] Report of J. Vignoles, [Jan. 1833], O.P. 1832/2258, Box 2192; *Fictitious Votes, Ireland*, 1st series, 1st report, p. 221.

and security. Politicians constantly demanded the opposite on grounds of law and order.[1] Elections, indeed, faced both the constabulary and the Army with something akin to an ever-changing mosaic, in which duties altered, contests appeared and disappeared, trouble could erupt unexpectedly, and the complications posed by a numerically fixed force and the exigencies of transport made peace depend as much on railway timetables and swiftness of march as upon anything else. The movement orders drawn up to cope with the long succession of individual contests typical of Victorian elections combined the rushed chaos of musical chairs with the procrustean rigidity of the Schlieffen plan.[2] Although the successive use of detachments in different places makes numerical assessment difficult, it is clear that the proportion of the total military force in Ireland employed on election duty was about two-thirds in 1835, four-fifths in 1852 (when almost half the constabulary was also *moved* to support colleagues already stationed at polling places), two-thirds or more in 1865, while in 1868 every single cavalry and infantry unit (apart from a lone regiment in Dublin) was detached on election duty of one kind or another.[3] Even allowing for the fact that standards of peace-keeping had changed since 1835, it is still remarkable that, despite an improved constabulary and a falling population, levels of violence at elections in the 1850s and 1860s were actually thought to demand a greater commitment of police and soldiers than had formerly been the case. In 1865 and 1868 every single polling place was crammed with troops and police.[4]

[1] Sir H. Vivian to Sir T. Arbuthnot, 17 Oct. 1831, and to W. Gossett, 9 July 1832, Vivian Papers No. 10; Memorandum to Cabinet by Sir H. Hardinge of 1853, War Office Papers WO33/3/5516; Strathnairn to Duke of Cambridge, 23 July, 18 Aug. 1865, 5 Dec. 1868, Strathnairn Papers Add. MSS 42821, 42825.

[2] See, e.g., T. Larcom to Naas, 22, 23, 25 Apr. 1859, Mayo Papers MS 11190; Memorandum by the Commander of the Forces, 25 Apr. 1859, Seaton Papers; T. Larcom to Colonel E. R. Wetherall, 5 May 1859, ibid.; Strathnairn to Abercorn, 9 Nov. 1868, Strathnairn Papers Add. MS 42828, and to Cambridge, 17 Nov. 1868, ibid. Add. MS 42828 ('My whole time is taken up by receiving and answering continual reports, telegraphs, communications with the government'). The unusually heavy use of the railway—troops normally marched—indicates the urgency of election duties.

[3] 1835: *Copies of Correspondence between the lieutenants of counties . . . and the Irish government previously to and during the late elections*, H.C. 1835 (170), xlv, 385–431—figures based on a mean between a high estimate for the actual size of cavalry troops and infantry companies (35 and 70) and a low estimate (30 and 60) with deductions for double counting. 1852: *A Return of the number of Troops, Constabulary, and Police at each polling place in Ireland, during the days of polling at the last general election*, H.C. 1852-3 (325), xciv, 699–704. 1865: Return of Troops in motion by the Quartermaster-General's Office, Mayo Papers MS 11170 (almost one-third were 'in motion' and another third or more were already appropriately stationed). 1868: Strathnairn to Cambridge, 5 Dec. 1868, Strathnairn Papers Add. MS 42825.

[4] Strathnairn to Sir R. Airey, 21 July 1865, Strathnairn Papers Add. MS 42821; to Abercorn, 9 Nov. 1868, ibid. Add. MS 42828.

Vulnerable constituencies were repeatedly swamped. The Limerick City contest of 1852 saw cavalry, infantry, and artillery at the Court House, Custom House, South Barracks, and Potato Market. Six years later, 500 constables, 500 infantry, 200 cavalry, and six stipendiaries were sent to the town. The Co. Limerick election of 1859 required over 2,000 soldiers with substantial reinforcements not far away.[1] At the Co. Longford election of 1862 the regularly stationed police force was increased from 416 to 1,189 and the troops from 98 to no less than 818, all under the control of eleven stipendiaries, one county and eighteen sub-inspectors, thirteen Army captains, twenty-three subalterns, and a senior commanding officer. Even at general elections, when resources were stretched, substantial detachments could be scratched together in a crisis, as at Co. Sligo in 1868 when joint Army and police numbers were increased from 297 to 1,977 virtually overnight.[2] Although the Ballot Act persuaded the authorities to experiment with lower forces in 1874, the Army returned to its traditional role at the General Election of 1880, albeit on a somewhat smaller scale. Almost simultaneously, however, the repeal of the Party Processions Act in 1872 sucked large numbers of police as well as some soldiers into supervising the 1,520 processions known to have been held between then and the end of the decade.[3]

Election duties, therefore, posed major problems for constabulary and Army alike. Sometimes a positively warlike response was preferred, with fully-equipped artillery units appearing at various elections, marines entering Dungarvan in 1832, and gunboats positioned off the coasts of Waterford in 1868 and Kerry in 1872.[4]

---

[1] P. Barron, RM to Under-Secretary, 12 July 1852, Mayo Papers MS 11037; T. Larcom to Naas, 14 May 1858, ibid. MS 11190; Larcom to Colonel Wetherall, 5 May 1859, and Wetherall to Seaton, 12 May 1859, Seaton Papers. For some other figures, see Memorandum by G. D'Aguilar (Deputy Adjutant-General), 28 July 1837, O.P. 1837/620/12, Box 52 (Dublin City); *Telegraph or Connaught Ranger*, 4 Mar. 1846 (Mayo); Lord Ingestre to Naas, 9 May 1859, Mayo Papers MS 11036 (Co. Waterford); Naas to Derby, 14 Oct. 1866, Derby Papers 155/2 (Tipperary).

[2] *Return of the number of Cavalry, Artillery, and Infantry ordered to, or stationed in the County of Longford for the late election*, H.C. 1862 (239), xliv, 3–5; *Correspondence with the Irish government, complaining of the use of military and police forces in the County of Sligo previous to the late election*, H.C. 1868–9 (180), 1, 227–8.

[3] D. N. Haire, 'In Aid of the Civil Power, 1868–90' in *Ireland under the Union: Varieties of tension: Essays in honour of T. W. Moody*, ed. F. S. L. Lyons and R. A. J. Hawkins (Oxford, 1980), p. 125; R.P. 1880/8263 (I owe this reference to R. A. J. Hawkins); *Returns, as far as are practicable, of all party processions*, H.C. 1880 (380 Sess. 2), lx, 395–432.

[4] For artillery, see *Copies of Correspondence between the lieutenants of counties . . . and the Irish government previously to and during the late elections*, H.C. 1835 (170), xlv, 391; *The Reign of Terror in Carlow* (1841), p. 64; P. Barron, RM to Under-Secretary, 12 July 1852, Mayo Papers MS 11037; *Committee on parliamentary and municipal elections*, H.C. 1868–9 (352), viii, 271; *Freeman's Journal*, 29 Nov. 1869. For marines, Report of

More commonly, the many complexities of crowd control produced inconclusive debates among all concerned. Civilian politicians, for example, always naïvely believed that masses of cavalry were a sovereign remedy for any riot. Experienced officers (notably Lord Strathnairn) rightly believed that in confined streets horses were virtually useless and that, because Army horses were only taught to jump tightly held on the curb by a regulation hand over a single bar in a riding school, cavalry was not even very successful across open country in many parts of Ireland.[1] As regards weapons, amateurs favoured quick fusillades over a crowd's head (something guaranteed to increase panic), while professionals preferred to hold back as long as possible and then to fire in earnest. As always, politicians were more bloodthirsty than Army or constabulary officers, who, despite occasional disagreements, generally co-operated well. Particularly admired was the constabulary's ability to respond flexibly to disturbances. Between a third and a half of all policemen usually carried only truncheons even on riot duty, and constables were of course far more experienced than soldiers in arresting trouble-makers.[2] Some military experts, notably Major-General McMurdo in 1868, argued that not all soldiers should actually carry arms, that 'light sticks' be issued, and that the really lethal forces be kept well in the background. Others tried to reduce injuries by ordering their men to shoot but once and then only in limited sections. But in the heat of riot such cool theory ignited into confusion, as when, at Sixmilebridge during the Clare election of 1852, a desperate officer with blood streaming down his face despairingly yelled at a frantic priest-led mob 'For God's sake, men, mind what you are at; my men are all loaded'. And being so, they opened fire and six rioters fell dead.[3]

Chief Constable Mahony, 16 Dec. 1832, O.P. 1832/2194, Box 2192; and gunboats, C. M. Dwyer, 'James Augustine Anderson O.S.A.', *Seanchas Ardmhacha*, vii (1974), 232, and Lord Kenmare to Hartington, 27 Jan. 1872, Devonshire Papers 340/487.

[1] For the cavalry issue, see D. Browne to Anglesey, 9 Dec. 1832, Anglesey Papers D619/32N; Sir E. Blakeney to Eglinton, 25 June 1852, Eglinton Papers MS 5342; Naas to Eglinton, 2 June 1858, ibid. MS 5352; Strathnairn to Naas, 29 Dec. 1866, and to Comte de Jarnac, 30 Dec. 1866, Strathnairn Papers Add. MS 42823, to Cambridge, 3 Aug. 1868, ibid. Add. MS 42828.

[2] Anglesey to W. Gregory, 27 June 1828, in Marquess of Anglesey, *One-Leg: The life and letters of Henry William Paget First Marquess of Anglesey K.G. 1768–1854* (London, 1961), p. 372; *Clare Journal*, 9 June 1842; *Copies of the several inquisitions removed from the Court of Queen's Bench* . . ., H.C. 1852-3 (313), xciv, 78; *Report* . . . *into the state of the Constabulary Force in Ireland*, H.C. 1866 [3658], xxxiv, 183–8; E. Cooper to Sir T. Larcom, 22 Nov. 1868, Larcom Papers MS 7762; *Copy of General Instructions issued to the Royal Irish Constabulary in reference to carrying and using their firearms*, H.C. 1868-9 (388), li, 523–4; Strathnairn to Under-Secretary, 1 Mar. 1869, Kilmainham Papers MS 1062; R. [A. J.] Hawkins, 'An Army on Police Work, 1881-2', pp. 80–1.

[3] McMurdo in *Committee on parliamentary and municipal elections*, H.C. 1868-9 (352), viii, 290–1, 299 (Strathnairn, however, disapproved—pp. 493–4); Colonel Douglas

The task upon which the soldiers at Sixmilebridge had been
engaged was among the most important of all election duties: the
escorting of (often unwilling) voters from landed estates to polling
places. At virtually every election, detachments of police and soldiers
criss-crossed the countryside to take sometimes frightened, frequently drunk, and occasionally grateful farmers to cast their votes
in the nearest large town. Escorts could not be refused if required by
a magistrate—twenty-four were organized at the 1868 Co. Sligo
election alone[1]—and the whole business developed more often than
not into a running battle between escorts, on the one hand, and
aggressive rural mobs, on the other. 'On approaching the town',
noted a Clonmel stipendiary in 1837, 'we perceived *thousands* of
people collected on the surrounding hills; they had, in a short space
of time, erected several barricades, and so completely covered the
direct road with large stones that a passage . . . was found impracti-
cable.' Between Nenagh and Cashel 'walls were built across the road
in some places; in others broad pits were dug, and then filled with
bushes and covered'. Colonel Dickson thought it had been easier
to relieve Lucknow than guide escorts safely to the poll at Limerick
in 1859. At the Co. Waterford by-election of 1866 a series of escorts
was overwhelmed, and dead horses, broken carts, and abandoned
weapons left in the fields. Serious injuries occurred—sometimes
soldiers were killed—at every general election between 1832 and
1880.[2] By 1868 things were so bad that many escorts were not
allowed out until equipped with cavalry assistance, cars carrying
spades, axes, saws, and entrenching tools, and quite extravagantly
large numbers of infantry and police—each voter, it was reckoned,
required the presence of at least one soldier.[3] The rapidity with
which voters fled, if given the opportunity, showed, however, not
only that abhorrence of coercion which popular politicians so frequently emphasized, but a high and uncomplicated sense of self-
preservation from soldiery and mob alike.

and Captain Eagan in *Copies of the several inquisitions removed from the Court of Queen's
Bench* . . ., H.C. 1852–3 (313), xciv, 72–3, 112.

[1] *Committee on parliamentary and municipal elections*, H.C. 1868–9 (352), viii,
331–2.

[2] Report of G. Fitzgerald, 10 Aug. 1837, O.P. 1837/620/57, Box 53; E. M. Kelly to
Downshire, 14 Aug. 1837, Downshire Papers D671/C/12/690; Colonel Dickson to Naas,
8 May 1859, Mayo Papers MS 11036; Revd C. Fry to W. Armstrong, 28 Dec. 1866, ibid.
MS 11144. For a sample of other incidents, see *Cork County election petition*, H.C. 1842
(271), vi, 39; Heytesbury to Graham, 6 Mar. 1846, Graham Papers 28/Ir (Mayo); W. Swan
to W. Pidgeon, 20 July 1852, Incorporated Society Papers MS 5848 (Westmeath); Report
of J. Little, RM, 23 July 1852, O.P. 1852/3/75, Box 1217 (Co. Carlow); W. Wann to J. C.
Stronge, 7 Mar. 1857, Gosford Papers D1606/5A/2 (Armagh).

[3] *Committee on parliamentary and municipal elections*, H.C. 1868–9 (352), viii, 290;
Clare election petition, H.C. 1852–3 (587), ix, 593.

Although it is difficult to prove, there can be little doubt that this vast investment of manpower (and the many injuries suffered by soldiers and police on election duty—three times as many casualties were sustained in 1868 at Drogheda alone as in the whole Abyssinian campaign[1]) did help to reduce the overall level of violence at Irish elections. This was widely believed at the time and certainly policemen and soldiers were often successful in containing riots, diverting the mob towards excited but harmless shouting and fist-waving, and protecting voters from lethal attack. In 1832, when troops were little used, fourteen people were killed in Carlow alone; in 1835, when soldiers swamped the constituencies, only one fatality occurred in the country as a whole.[2] Again, it was the temporary withdrawal of the police at Limerick in 1852 which really set the town alight.[3] Popular attitudes, however, were often selective and usually predictable. In particular the police were widely disliked, especially before the reforms of 1836. By contrast, the regular Army was becoming more popular. Priests praised soldiers at the expense of policemen and even invited officers on election duty to dine. Army recruiting was neither difficult nor socially exclusive. Even after 1836 the very permanence of the constabulary's presence diverted feelings of dislike away from the more transient military.[4] As a result, although troops were less expert in riot control, they were sometimes more effective because red uniforms caused less gut opposition than green. Billeting and brothels, both of them military specialities, were as much a source of friendship as resentment, at least in certain quarters. Nor did 'nice girls' ever seem to have neglected the soldiers. In some contexts, such as Protestant Belfast, the Army was always

[1] Strathnairn to A. C. Innes, 2 Dec. 1868, Strathnairn Papers Add. MS 42828. No less than twenty-nine of a fifty-strong police detachment at Limerick in 1859 were, e.g., seriously wounded (two rioters were killed and four badly wounded), while nine of the sixteen lancers in one part of Dungarvan in 1866 suffered extensive contusions and cuts (J. Spaight to Naas, 5 May 1859, Mayo Papers MS 11036; *Copy of the reports of the proceedings at the inquests held at Dungarvan in the month of January last*, H.C. 1867 (237), lix, 467).

[2] *Hansard*, xxvi, 905-6 (12 Mar. 1835) for the comparison between 1832 and 1835. See also *Committee on Bribery at Elections*, H.C. 1835 (547), viii, 265; *Copies of Correspondence between the lieutenants of counties . . . and the Irish government previously to and during the late elections*, H.C. 1835 (170), xlv, 411-27; *Cork County election petition*, H.C. 1842 (271), vi, 93; T. Murray to Downshire, 14 Mar. 1841, Downshire Papers D671/C/9/686; *Banner of Ulster*, 10 Feb. 1857; *C.C.* 7 May 1859; H. Keogh to Under-Secretary, 18 Feb. 1870, R.P. 1870/3336.

[3] T. Kayne to J. Wynne, 15 July 1852, O.P. 1852/17/291, Box 1219.

[4] See *Diary of Humphrey O'Sullivan*, ed. M. McGrath, i, 299 (10 July 1828); Anglesey to Grey, 15 Apr. 1831, Anglesey Papers D619/28A; Sir H. Vivian to Lord Fitzroy, 13 Aug. 1831, Vivian Papers No. 10; *Committee on the State of Ireland*, H.C. 1831-2 (677), xvi, 62; *Committee on Bribery at Elections*, H.C. 1835 (547), viii, 334 (priest praises troops); *Hansard*, xxvi, 906-7 (11 Mar. 1835); Lord de Ros to Duke of Leinster, Feb. 1851, Larcom Papers MS 7618; *Cork County election petition*, H.C. 1842 (271), vi, 94 (recruiting popular); *Galway County election petition*, H.C. 1872 (241-I), xlviii, 677-9 (priest invites officer).

preferred to the 'Catholic' constabulary.[1] Naturally enough many rioters disliked the Army—'Down with the Lancers, Down with the Horse Soldiers, Down with the Orange Buggers' was the cry at Waterford in 1866—and occasional ballads record uncompromising antagonism.

> Then like wolves bloodthirsty that lost their prey,
> Those vile assassins without delay
> Commenced to fire, the Cromwellian corps,
> And left them weltering all in their gore.[2]

But a matching fraternity often balanced such bitterness: working-class women cheering the troops at the Cork City election of 1852 and yelling 'God bless you' to General Maunsell; dragoons and civilians of all classes amicably joining in dances to fiddle and flute at the Galway election of the same year; soldiers giving well-received theatrical shows at Ballinasloe in 1868.[3] Only a few scattered traces survive of what the ordinary rankers thought of it all. Catholic police constables showed little reluctance to report priests for 'inflammatory' sermons and one in retirement put on record his belief that the 'peasantry' were often indecently violent over matters of trivial importance.[4] The unique reminiscences of an English colour-sergeant of the 19th Foot serving in Ireland during the 1820s and 1830s reveal a man with a strong Protestant dislike of 'superstition', a strong contempt for idle Church of Ireland clergymen, a warm sympathy for the poor whose poteen stills he was often obliged to smash, and a hearty dislike of having to perform election duties. So universal was this dislike that Sir Hussey Vivian quickly noticed it when commanding the forces in the 1830s, while the unpublished diary of Lieutenant George Lamb of the 49th Regiment records the Waterford election of 1852 in terms of mingled distaste and anthropological fascination. In 1868 General McMurdo summed up the military view. 'Do you know', he was asked, 'whether the troops

---

[1] Paper on Irish billeting, 22 Feb. 1847, Panmure Papers GD45/8/27. On brothels, see *Fictitious Votes, Ireland*, 1st series, 1st report, pp. 443-4 (Clonmel), and H. Shane to Under-Secretary, 18 June 1852, O.P. 1852/15/130, Box 1218 (Banagher). On 'nice girls', see D. Fitzpatrick, *Politics and Irish Life 1913-1921: Provincial experience of War and Revolution* (Dublin, 1977), p. 30. On Belfast, see S. E. Baker, 'Orange and Green: Belfast 1832-1912', p. 806, and D. N. Haire, 'In Aid of the Civil Power, 1868-90', p. 134.

[2] *Copy of the Depositions taken before the Coroner . . . at Dungarvan*, H.C. 1867 (200), lvi, 209-35; 'A Lament written on the Dreadful Massacre of Sixmilebridge' (1852) in G.-D. Zimmermann, *Songs of Irish Rebellion* (Dublin, 1967), pp. 243-4.

[3] *Cork City election petition*, H.C. 1852-3 (528), xi, 54; *Galway Vindicator*, 24 July 1852; *Western Star*, 2 May 1868.

[4] Sir T. Arbuthnot to Sir H. Vivian, 23 Mar. 1833, Melbourne Papers 94/88; Lord Courtown to Clarendon, 17 Dec. 1847, Clarendon Papers Box 8; Michael Corduff's reminiscences in Folklore Commission MS 1243.

dislike the [election] service?' 'They are', he replied, 'perfectly frantic about it and they call out "Are we brought here to be murdered".'[1]

VI SONGS AND CELEBRATIONS

Agrarian and electoral violence were predominantly practical, realistic, and (metaphorically as well as physically) hard-headed. They were aimed at particular goals: repossession, security of tenure, lower rents, provision of conacre, or the victory of one candidate over another. Both also possessed a self-generating quality and often provided concrete occasions for communal displays, mass participation, even enjoyment of a kind. In the quarter-century before the Famine the complex connections between the realistic and the carnival aspects of violence were themselves shaped and influenced by a powerful, if intermittent, millenarianism which predicted, especially in the 1820s and on the basis of the so-called prophecies of Pastorini and Colmcille, the imminent overthrow of Protestantism and English rule.[2] The unrealistic expectations created by the Emancipation and Repeal campaigns and the transformation of O'Connell himself into a species of earthy demigod—'O'Connell be with you' said voters at the Clare by-election of 1828, while others, recalled an old man, thought O'Connell 'would stream gold into their pockets', and many labourers equated Repeal with an acre of potato ground for all—show how easily political campaigns could become encrusted with both homespun millenarianism and Gaelic nostalgia.[3]

[1] *Diary of Colour-Sergeant George Calladine*, ed. M. L. Ferrar, pp. 116-17, 127-8, 151, 122, 138-9, 163; Diary of Lieutenant George Lamb, N.L.I. MS 7323 (6-24 July 1852); *Committee on parliamentary and municipal elections*, H.C. 1868-9 (352), viii, 294-5. See also M. Brophy (ex-Sergeant RIC), *Sketches of the Royal Irish Constabulary* (London, 1886), pp. 31-2.

[2] See *Diary of Colour-Sergeant George Calladine*, ed. M. L. Ferrar, p. 132; *Committee appointed to examine into the nature and extent of the disturbances which have prevailed in . . . Ireland*, H.C. 1825 (20), vii, 143-4; G. C. Lewis, *On local Disturbances*, pp. 58, 102-26, 170; Courtown to Clarendon, 6 June 1848, Clarendon Papers Box 8; P. O'Farrell, 'Millenialism, Messianism, and Utopianism in Irish History', *Anglo-Irish Studies*, ii (1976), 45-68; B. Cahill, 'The Impact of the Catholic Clergy on Irish Life 1820-45' (University College Galway MA thesis, 1975), pp. 77-80; J. S. Donnelly Jr., 'Pastorini and Captain Rock: Millenarianism and Sectarianism in the Rockite Movement of 1821-4' in *Irish peasants, violence, and political unrest 1780-1914*, ed. S. Clark and J. S. Donnelly Jr. (Manchester, 1983), pp. 102-39; also William Carleton's powerful novel set in 1817-22, *The Black Prophet* (1846-7). Pastorini's prophecies derived from an analysis of the Apocalypse published in 1771 by the English Catholic bishop, Charles Walmesley.

[3] Baron Tuyll to Anglesey, 29 June-4 July 1828, Marquess of Anglesey, *One-Leg*, p. 199; *Mr Gregory's Letter-Box 1813-1830*, ed. Lady Gregory (London, 1898), p. 267; *Devon Commission*, Witness No. 969. Even cautious Tipperary farmers began to think they might soon own their farms (T. Bolton to Lord Stanley, 24 June 1843, Derby Papers 107/3). See also Local Confidential Printed Reports of 1843 in Derby Papers 34; Graham

In Ireland, however, even the apocalypse had its practical side and
the awaited climacteric was seen, 'not in terms of throwing back
the process of anglicization—this was tacitly accepted as a
triumphant force—but rather in terms of a role reversal in which
Catholics would replace Protestants in wielding power and possessing
property and wealth'.[1] In any case, although occasional quasi-
millenarian survivals were still to be found in the 1850s and 1860s,
and although similar expectations could be aroused by elections
as late as 1892, the deification of Parnell was an altogether different,
more consciously wrought, and fundamentally more modern phenomenon.[2]

This irreversible shift in outlook is particularly evident in the
changing tone and style of ballads—those blurred and filmy reflec-
tions of the popular mind. Traditional ballads continued to be widely
sold and sung until at least the 1880s, although by then the professional ballad singer no longer occupied the central social role he
(or sometimes she) had enjoyed before 1850.[3] On the surface, just
as many ballads would seem to have continued to be produced, with
their stories of love and humour, electoral battle, political aspirations, and of the wickedness of criminals, landlords, and agents alike.
Elections both before and after the Famine provided balladeers with
obvious and sometimes lucrative employment. Tailor-made songs
were produced for the highest bidder and combined 'the poetry of
unlimited abuse', maudlin sentimentality, and collapsing rhyme
in just about equal proportions. Villiers Stuart had teams of 'Irish
bards' 'humouring' (as the highly artificial enunciation of the singers
was known) on his behalf at Waterford in 1826, while O'Connell's
return for Clare in 1828 was accompanied by energetic and threatening music in the streets.[4] And so it continued pretty well without

to De Grey, 17 Oct. 1843, Graham Papers 66B; Report of J. G. Jones, RM, 26 Sept. 1845,
ibid. 23/Ir; Clarendon to Russell, 19 Nov. 1847, Clarendon Papers L.-B. I; T. Garvin, *The
evolution of Irish nationalist politics*, pp. 18, 28, 46-8.

[1] O. MacDonagh, 'The Irish Famine Emigration to the United States', p. 376; also
P. O'Farrell, 'Millenialism, Messianism, and Utopianism in Irish History', pp. 52-3; G. Ó.
Tuathaigh, *Ireland before the Famine 1798-1848* (Dublin, 1972), pp. 67-8.

[2] D. Ryan, *The Fenian Chief: A biography of James Stephens*, p. 74; Revd. R. Noble
to 'My Lord', 11 Sept. 1857, Larcom Papers MS 7578; Printed Memorandum for the
Cabinet by Strathnairn (1867), Mayo Papers MS 11188(5)—verse found on Fenian soldier;
Reminiscences of Michael Corduff (formerly of the RIC) of the 1892 North Mayo election,
Folklore Commission MS 1243.

[3] M. Murphy, 'The Ballad Singer and the role of the Seditious Ballad in nineteenth-
century Ireland: Dublin Castle's View', *Ulster Folklife*, xxv (1979), 79-102 (I owe much
to this invaluable essay); G.-D. Zimmermann, *Songs of Irish Rebellion*, p. 23; Folklore
Commission MS 1209.

[4] W. Barry, 'The current Street Ballads of Ireland', *Macmillan's Magazine*, xxv (1872),
199; J. J. Auchmuty, *Sir Thomas Wyse 1791-1862: The Life and Career of an Educator
and Diplomat* (London, 1939), p. 92; Baron Tuyll to Anglesey, 29 June-4 July 1828,

a pause for the next fifty years. The Co. Limerick by-election of 1850 was typical, with its battle of the ballads echoing and encouraging the battle at the polls.[1]

> Michael Ryan stout and true
> Is the boy for me and you.
> When we bear him to the hustings our hurraws for the cause
> Will scare them like a flock of jackdaws.

> *versus*

> All bluster and swagger see Ryan appear
> That he would be popular candidate 'tis clear
> With murderous epithets ready at hand
> He swears that the owner's no right to his land . . .
> Hurrah then for Dickson . . . .

Sung by itinerant performers who often travelled great distances, such songs were highly elastic and could easily be adapted to local needs. In good times ballad singers could make a reasonable living —up to three shillings a day on sheets bought from printers for a penny a dozen and sold for a halfpenny each. In bad times they starved. But, although their presence was a feature of Irish life throughout the period, the law-and-order authorities moved from an attitude of distinct apprehension before about 1850 to one of relaxed ↘ acceptance thereafter.[2]   In part this reflected a growing

Marquess of Anglesey, *One-Leg*, p. 199. For 'humouring', see F. Scullion, 'The relative gravity of Irish music', *Ulster Folk and Transport Museum Year Book* (1976-7), pp. 21-3.

[1] Limerick ballads in Folklore Commission MS 1194. For a sample of other election ballads, see 'Cuthbert's Lamentation for the loss of Kinsale election', 'A new election song in praise of O'Connor and Barry' (Co. Cork), 'A new song on the County of Cork election', 'O'Connell's Glorious Victory' (Meath)—all in O.P. 1833, Box 2454, Bundle 1; 'Martin Blake and Ireland for Ever' (Galway Town) in O.P. 1835/139, Box 46; 'A new song called Browne now lie down', 'A new song called the Sweets of Liberty', 'The Shan Van Vocht's Address to her Friends' (all Mayo)—all in O.P. 1835/147, Box 46; 'The Defeat' (Monaghan 1852) in T. Bell, 'The Revd David Bell', *Clogher Record*, vi (1967), 259; 'Blinkin Jack The Mimber for Athlone' (1859) in author's possession; 'A Song on the expected triumph of Sir Dominick Corrigan' (Dublin City 1868), 'The Glorious Victory of Richard Dowse MP' (Derry City 1868), 'A new song on Captain Flanigan's Victory over the Tories' (Sligo Borough 1868), 'Lines written on the Glorious Victory gained by our Bishop and Catholick Clergy' (Galway Town 1868)—all in Collection of Ballads N.L.I. Pressmark J39988; 'The Hour is come for Irishmen' (Co. Sligo 1868) in Clonalis Papers 9.2. HS. 161; 'A new song on Election of Meath and the Return of John Martin' (1871) in Bradshaw Collection C.U.L. Hib.1.867.1.

[2] For earnings and travelling, see G. Ó. Dúghaill, 'Ballads and the Law 1830-1832', *Ulster Folklife*, xix (1973), 39, and M. Murphy, 'The Ballad Singer', pp. 88-92. For the authorities' view, see also Report of Sub-Inspector Battersby, 13 Feb. 1835, O.P. 1835, Box 46; St C. O'Malley to W. Gossett, 14 Feb. 1835, O.P. 1835/147, Box 46; *Hansard*, xxxiv, 1004-10 (28 June 1836); *Galway County election petition*, H.C. 1872 (241-I), xlviii, 327-9. Potentially severe penalties were available under 47 Geo. III, Sess. 2., c. 13, s. 26 (1807), 3 Geo. IV, c. 1, s. 10 (1822), and 1 & 2 Will. IV, c. 44, s. 3 (1831). See also *Standing Rules . . . of the Royal Irish Constabulary*, 3rd edn. (1872), s. 760.

maturity in official minds, in part the changing nature of ballads themselves. Certainly if the task of election songs was to 'set them wild', then pre-Famine ballads were notably more successful.[1] Indeed, across the whole spectrum of political ballads a distinct slackening of drive and softening of tone becomes apparent in the second half of the century. Early ballads were often bilingual, incomprehensible to outsiders ('obscurely emblematic', thought Carlyle), and steeped in half-remembered Jacobite aspirations. They included vague millenarian and revolutionary references. Above all, they often expressed themselves in savage imagery and muscular tones.[2]

A large fleet is coming over from France, with young
O'Connell with them as their leader, and then we will have
Bonfires over the country for joy
And beat them to hell.

> ('A New Song Coish Ariglen', 1833—contemporary
>   translation from the Irish)

And of ministers we will make labourers
    each day for our endustry
To earn 4 pence wages to teach them frugality,
Of their churches we will make stables
    and places of fidelity,
And we will plant a tree in Erin and the
    name it takes is Liberty.

> ('Poor Erin', 1835)

Who could desire to see better sport
Than Peelers groaning among the rocks
Their skulls all fractured, their eye balls broken
Their fine long noses and ears cut off.

> (Untitled, 1832)

Placemen and police who soon must away
With corporate despots to go and hawk pisspots.

> ('Freedom, dear Freedom will carry the
>   day', 1831)

---

[1] M. Murphy, 'The Ballad Singer', pp. 83, 93–4; T. M. Sloane to W. Gossett, 31 Dec. 1832, O.P. 1833, Box 2454, Bundle 1 (also letters from Killaloe, Kinsale, Skibereen, Clonmel, Mallow, and Waterford, in ibid.); *Hansard*, xxxiv, 1004–10 (28 June 1836) about a singer in Mayo producing 'savage yells, blasphemous vociferations, and rebellious defiance'; De Grey to Graham, 27 June 1843, and Graham to De Grey, 29 June 1843, Graham Papers 4/Ir. Many singers *sang* 'much more inflammatory songs' than they *sold* in printed sheets (E. Huntly to Gossett, 14 Jan. 1833, O.P. 1833, Box 2454, Bundle 1).

[2] Thomas Carlyle, *Reminiscences of my Irish Journey in 1849* (London, 1882), p. 140. The ballads that follow are in: O.P. 1833, Box 2454, Bundle 1; Report of F. Vokes,

Cheer up Roman Catholics we will shortly gain the day
M'Auliffe in his prophecy made mention of the same
You will see those Tory Orangemen in swarms dying in agony
And the devil die along with them I have no more to say.

('Distress of Erin', 1843)

Numerous ballads expressed an intense interest in prophecies and the 'showers of honey' which would engulf the land upon O'Connell's triumph.[1] So vivid and demotic was their imagery that Repeal leaders—intent as always on respectability—felt obliged to festoon their gatherings with placards to the effect that 'NO BALLAD SINGERS SHALL BE ALLOWED TO INTERFERE IN THE MEETING'.[2] After the Famine, however, the language of songs became so laundered as to render them (if not their reciters) almost acceptable in the most bourgeois of surroundings. A kind of indirect neutering had spread out from Young Ireland's genteel warblings and from the artificial 'literary' ballads increasingly popular in nineteenth-century drawing-rooms.[3] Strong views were now made to dress for dinner. Even the woodcuts which decorate many ballad sheets assumed a sentimental style: crucifixes, crosses with inter-twined flowers, wreaths, endless harps, shamrocks, and all the other 'antiquarian' impedimenta of modern nationalism. The simultaneous appearance of cheap patriotic song books, such as the *Home Rule Songster* of around 1874 ('country shopkeepers and dealers supplied on the shortest notice and most reasonable terms'), and the extensive sale of so-called 'Irish National Literature' on railway bookstalls and elsewhere completed the process. Even election ballads were now published in cheap pamphlets designed to meet the demand of those who preferred Paddywhackery to enraged abuse.[4]

Limerick, 6 Feb. 1835, O.P. 1835/139, Box 46; O.P. 1832/2268 cited in P. O'Donoghue, 'Opposition to Tithe Payment in 1832–3', p. 101; O.P. 1831/D82 cited in G. Ó Dúghaill, 'Ballads and the Law', p. 39; T. Bolton to Lord Stanley, 15 July 1843, Derby Papers 107/3.

[1] See, e.g., G.-D. Zimmermann, *Songs of Irish Rebellion*, pp. 19, 29–31, 34, 231–3; G. Ó Dúghaill, 'Ballads and the Law', pp. 39–40; M. Murphy, 'The Ballad Singer', p. 83; — to W. Gossett, 11 Jan. 1833, O.P. 1833, Box 2454, Bundle 1.

[2] Report of J. G. Jones, RM, 26 Sept. 1845, Graham Papers 23/Ir.

[3] G. Gavan Duffy, *Young Ireland Part II, or Four Years of Irish History 1845–49* (Dublin, 1887), p. 24. Although one contemporary claimed that Thomas Davis's songs were far less popular in the 1860s than even the neutered 'genuine' ballads, Davis's ballads were certainly sung (W. Barry, 'The current Street Ballads of Ireland', pp. 190–9, and M. Murphy, 'The Ballad Singer', p. 92).

[4] Copy of *The Home Rule Songster* in Bradshaw Collection C.U.L. Hib.2.867.2; copy of *Songs for the Hustings* by 'Paudeen Tory-Throuncer' (1868) in U.C.D. Pamphlets 102. For railway stations, see J. Macaulay, *Ireland in 1872*, p. 322. See also M. Murphy, 'The Ballad Singer', p. 92.

> Band with the people, rise with the nation;
> Be not the sheep of a landlord's pen;
> Respond to the country's just indignation—
> They shall not brand the backs of Irishmen.

('A Ballad of Two Bs', 1865)

> The standard of Erin is now unfurl'd
> In the person of Peter Gill;
> And the news is spread all over the world
> Of his eloquent tact and skill
> In describing the state of Ireland now,
> How her people are trodden down;
> With the colour of misery on their brow
> Instead of an Emerald Crown.

('Peter Gill', 1865)

> There is one golden gleam of solace
> Sustaining me thro' anguish alone
> You're dying for your country
> With sacred Young Emmet and Tone
> And like the Heroine Miss Curran
> My spirit shall fly to thee soon
> For I'll sink broken-hearted
> And breathe my last sigh at your tomb.

('Mrs O'Donovan Rossa's Lament for
her Husband', 1869)[1]

Few changes, of course, are ever complete, and, just as there had been lace-curtain ballads in the 1830s, so powerful invective did not entirely disappear in later years.[2] But the general drift towards polish and self-consciousness is clear enough, as much in the lively school of Orange–Tory ballad writing as in the majority tradition.[3] Not that this implied any necessary reduction in impact or effect. A changing and culturally laundered society was being provided with appropriately changed and laundered songs. The growing moral hegemony of the Catholic Church made what had once been acceptable no

---

[1] The above to be found in: Moore Papers MS 898; *Tipperary Advocate*, 25 Feb. 1865; Bradshaw Collection C.U.L. Hib.2.867.2.

[2] As denunciations of the assassinated Lord Leitrim make clear in 1878: '. . . This old debaucher left his den / He left bailiffs, bums, and harlots in the Castle of Lough Rynn' (A. L. Lloyd, 'On an unpublished Irish ballad' in *Rebels and their Causes: Essays in honour of A. L. Morton*, ed. M. Cornforth (London, 1978), p. 178).

[3] Compare, e.g., some of the sprightly Protestant ballads distributed during Youghal elections of the 1830s ('Youghal Protestant Operatives Scrapbook 1829-48', Bradshaw Collection C.U.L. Hib.1.844.1) with later electoral efforts in P.R.O.N.I. T1104 (Antrim 1852), Seymour of Ragley Papers CR114A/538/3 (Antrim 1869), Carleton, Atkinson, & Sloane Papers D1252/42/2 (Tyrone 1873), and Perceval-Maxwell Papers D1556/23 (Down 1880), though this last is genuinely funny.

longer so. The relative collapse of the labourer and cottier class probably reduced the demand for the fiercer and cruder type of song. More and more were the increasingly dominant farmers becoming the arbiters of both action and taste—in politics, in agriculture, in the nature of violence, in popular ballads. Growing literacy in English made men uncomfortable with the strongly Gaelic atmosphere of much pre-Famine ballad writing. Yet, even though ballads had become only one among a number of vehicles for the transmission of popular feelings, they still elicited a response, and Fenians, Land Leaguers, and their successors continued to use songs to encourage solidarity and (often unconsciously) to express the changing nature of their own values and aspirations.

Just as ballads were 'cleaned up', so the once frequent opportunities for mass public enjoyment and celebration became increasingly formalized and controlled. Wakes, patterns, and their associated amusements were transformed into shadows of their former vibrant selves. The enormous and chaotic meetings of O'Connell gave way to generally smaller and more efficiently marshalled affairs. Even the often spontaneous Orange and Ribbon marching of the 1830s and 1840s was succeeded by organized parades, though in this case organization was no guarantee of peace. The 'holiday outing' atmosphere of Parnell's meetings was but a genteel reflection of the harsher joys made manifest at the large gatherings of country folk demonstrating for Emancipation in 1828, at the so-called 'Peace League' marches of the 1820s, at Ulster Ribbon parades and St Peter's Eve celebrations in the 1830s, or at the many energetic patterns of pre-Famine times.[1] Within this atmosphere of gathering respectability, elections constituted a striking anachronism. And just as electoral violence maintained itself at a high pitch well into the second half of the century, so the associated carousals and revelry (which often hovered uncertainly between mere disorder and open chaos) continued largely unchanged. Elections could not simply be abolished. Their incidence could not be controlled either by Church or even ultimately by state. High-minded candidates could always be outbid by less fastidious opponents. Bribes actually left voters, canvassers, shouters, and rioters in pocket, while the entertainments on offer were free, lavish, and virtually irresistible.

The fuel which powered the carnival was alcohol. 'Treating',

---

[1] F. S. L. Lyons, *Charles Stewart Parnell* (London, 1977), pp. 95–6; J. A. Reynolds, *The Catholic Emancipation Crisis in Ireland*, pp. 149–50; *Diary of Humphrey O'Sullivan*, ed. M. McGrath, ii, 25–7; *First report ... Orange Lodges*, H.C. 1835 (377), xv, 24, 27 (also *Third Report*, H.C. 1835 (476), xvi, 105–17); *D.E.P.* 29 July 1837; S. J. Connolly, *Priests and People in pre-Famine Ireland 1780–1845*, p. 140. See also Chapter III above.

as it was called, constituted the great auxiliary to bribery[1] at Irish as at English elections. Though expensive, it did two things for the price of one: mollified the powerful Irish publicans and gratified the expectations of electors and non-electors alike. These expectations —of free food and entertainment as well as drink—were usually substantial, often heroic. 'Several of the freeholders came in from the country. I had to treat them, I could not avoid it' explained a Mayo election agent in 1847. A few examples accurately reflect the general atmosphere. All the pubs were open all of the day at Donegal and endless 'Johnnys' of rum handed out at Newry in 1832. At Clonmel in 1835 there was free drink, free food, and free dancing with 'immoral women'. The open pubs of Downpatrick in 1837 were thronged day and night with dancers (and eventually lurchers) to fiddle and flute. An early-morning barber called to Sisk's public house at Kinsale in 1847 to spruce up forty voters before the poll found them all 'discharging their stomachs over a bucket' after a night of 'ale and rum and brandy and wine' and before an election breakfast of 'beef steaks and mutton and bacon and tea and eggs and . . . spirits of all kinds'. At the Longford election of 1869 one publican alone had 300 inebriates simultaneously staggering around his backyard too drunk even to riot.[2] Open barrels of beer on the streets and alfresco canvassers (priests often among them) ladling whiskey into tumblers were a common sight. At Cashel, where the voters got 'lots' of drink and music in 1865 and 1868, wild masculine 'dances' were held from which women were strictly excluded. The same happened at the Co. Galway by-election of 1872, after which one exhausted voter intoned a litany of the delights which had been available at Daly's Hotel.[3]

Had you any sherry?——I suppose I had.
Had you any brandy?——Likely that I had.
Had you ale?——Yes.

[1] For bribery (as opposed to treating), see Chapter I above.

[2] R. Mullet to G. H. Moore, 26 July 1847, Moore Papers MS 890; *Sixty years' experience as an Irish landlord: Memoirs of John Hamilton D.L. of St. Ernan's Donegal*, ed. H. C. White (London, [1894]), p. 146; *Newry Borough election petition*, H.C. 1833 (76), x, 587; *Fictitious Votes, Ireland*, 1st series, 1st report, pp. 466-9 (Clonmel); *D.E.P.* 25 July 1837; *Minutes of evidence taken before the select committee on the Kinsale election petition*, H.C. 1847-8 (138), xiii, 5, 18, 26-32; *Longford election petition*, H.C. 1870 (178), lvi, 400-2.

[3] T. Sheile to W. H. Gorton, 4 Oct. 1847, Mayo Papers MS 11028 (Kildare); *Clare election petition*, H.C. 1852-3 (587), ix, 735; *Dungarvan election petition*, H.C. 1854 (162), viii, 469-612; *Mayo County election petition*, H.C. 1857 (182 Sess. 2), vii, 199; F. S. P. Wolferstan and S. B. Bristowe, *Reports of the decisions of election committees* (1865), pp. 102-13 (Roscommon 1859); *Tipperary Advocate*, 8 July 1865, and *Cashel election petitions*, H.C. 1868-9 (121), xlix, 137-9; *Galway County election petition*, H.C. 1872 (241-I), xlviii, 551, 954.

Had you malt?—Yes.
Had you dinners?—Yes.
Had you breakfasts?—Yes.

Pubs were often deliberately chosen as party headquarters, and candidates too were expected to demonstrate geniality by constant potations with voters and other thirsty men of importance. Chichester Fortescue staggered home after a day's canvassing 'full of whiskey and bad wine'. An English candidate for Athlóne had to be shipped home 'in a violent fit of delirium tremens', defeated by William Keogh's bottomless capacities. Serjeant Barry of Dungarvan dreaded the 'terrible duty' of having to drink 'large quantities' of powerful election punch.[1] A whole science of electoral drunkenness was established, with experts able to gauge the various levels and degrees involved. 'When I say drunk', noted a Kinsale practitioner, 'there are different stages'. Fellow *cognoscenti* in Mayo talked of voters being 'drunk' but not 'drunk in that way . . . not lying upon the ground', and, when asked 'If you can lie on the ground without holding, do you think yourself drunk?', answered briskly, 'Oh, an Irishman can drink more than that.'[2]

All this naturally cost money. One candidate at Derry in 1832 spent £600 (almost a fifth of his total expenditure) on drink. One publican at Longford in 1869 single-handedly distributed £200 worth of beer and spirits. At the Clare election of 1859 the aptly named Charteris Brew Maloney had a thousand pounds available to treat on behalf of the Liberal candidates. Such sums, high but not unusual, could buy enough drink to keep a whale afloat.[3] A single Kinsale dealer supplied the Conservative side in 1847 with 108 gallons of whiskey, rum, and brandy—the equivalent, he calculated, of 10,368 tots of one-twelfth of a pint each. At Tulla, Co. Clare, in 1859 £96 cash bought (even at inflated 'election' prices)

[1] For pubs as headquarters, see H. J. Perry and J. W. Knapp, *Cases of controverted elections in the eleventh parliament of the United Kingdom* (London, 1833), pp. 151-2 (Newry); J. W. Knapp and E. Ombler, *Cases of controverted elections in the twelfth parliament of the United Kingdom*, pp. 2-3 (Dungarvan); F. S. P. Wolferstan and S. B. Bristowe, *Reports of the decisions of election committees* (1865), pp. 102-13 (Roscommon); *Clare election petition*, H.C. 1860 (178), xi, 128. For candidates' capacities, see Carlingford Papers Diary of C. Fortescue I (20 Jan. 1854); K. T. Hoppen, 'National politics and local realities in mid-nineteenth century Ireland', p. 201.

[2] *Kinsale election petition*, H.C. 1847-8 (138), xiii, 33-4; *Mayo County election petition*, H.C. 1857 (182 Sess. 2), vii, 171, 411. 'They beat me sober . . . I may drink to be drunk, but I am not a blackguard' (ibid. 410).

[3] G. R. Dawson's Derry City MS Election Expenses T1048/4; E. L. O'Malley and H. Hardcastle, *Reports of the decisions of the judges*, ii (1875), pp. 10-11 (Longford); F. S. P. Wolferstan and S. B. Bristowe, *Reports of the decisions of election committees* (1865), pp. 138-43 (Clare). See also *Report from the select committee on Carrickfergus Borough*, H.C. 1833 (527), viii, 113; O'Hara Papers MS 20355 (Co. Sligo); *Committee on parliamentary and municipal elections*, H.C. 1868-9 (352), viii, 273 (Limerick City).

19 flitches of bacon, £21 worth of bread, 60 dozen biscuits, 35 lb. mutton, 4 bottles pickle, 15 gallons spirits, 43 gallons ale, 31 gallons porter, 15 dozen lemonades (a posthumous tribute, no doubt, to Fr. Mathew), 11 dozen bottles of porter, and 9 dozen bottles of ale. Yet this light collation was designed for no more than fifty voters and further supplies were necessary to ensure that all were able to eat and drink 'morning, noon, and night' as the polling days passed by.[1] Similar offerings constituted the standard means of turning mere idlers into an active election mob. 'Take them to the pub and they will', claimed one experienced agent, come out 'in a body . . . flourish their sticks . . . and go in a most excited way along the streets.' Prospective rioters were in the normal course of events several degrees below par and needed totting up, like those in Co. Galway in 1872, who, a landlord noted, emerged with their cudgels from a pub at eight in the morning shouting 'Hey for Nolan' in so listless a manner 'that I did not think they could have had much to drink'.[2] Nearly all election riots were alcohol-based, and degrees proof were directly related to degrees violence. Few contested elections escaped some disorder; fewer still the friendly embrace of the Demon Drink.[3] Official attitudes were generally ambivalent. As late as the 1870s election judges were still remarkably 'understanding', and it was not until the passing of the Corrupt Practices Act of 1883 that 'illegal treating' even began to be seriously regarded in Ireland as anything much worse than raffishly exciting or mildly disreputable.[4]

---

[1] *Kinsale election petition*, H.C. 1847-8 (138), xiii, 65-7; *Clare election petition*, H.C. 1860 (178), xi, 146-8. At the Clare election a gallon of whiskey was supplied for fifteen shillings, a gallon of porter for two shillings, and a bottle of porter for threepence.

[2] *Committee on parliamentary and municipal elections*, H.C. 1868-9 (352), viii, 266; *Galway County election petition*, H.C. 1872 (241-I), xlviii, 400-1; also *Cork City election petition*, H.C. 1852-3 (528), xi, 36-8; *Dungarvan election petition*, H.C. 1854 (162), viii, 497-8. For female drinkers, see *Kinsale election petition*, H.C. 1847-8 (138), xiii, 36, and *Clare election petition*, H.C. 1852-3 (587), ix, 749.

[3] On the relationship between corruption and violence, see G. F. Blomfield to Mayo, 30 June 1868, Mayo Papers MS 11162. For a few examples of drunken mobs etc., see Lady Kenmare to Knight of Kerry, 17 Jan. 1835, FitzGerald Papers; *Report from the select committee on the Belfast election compromise*, H.C. 1842 (431), v, 279; Carlingford Papers Diary of C. Fortescue II (30 June 1852—Louth); Report of E. Collins, 1 May 1859, R.P. 1859/3993, Box 808 (Co. Limerick); *Committee on parliamentary and municipal elections*, H.C. 1868-9 (352), viii, 206-7, 266, 273 (Limerick City); *Western Star*, 21 Nov. 1868 (Galway Town).

[4] For a garland of inconsistent Irish judicial opinions, see E. L. O'Malley and H. Hardcastle, *Reports of the decisions of the judges*, i (1869), pp. 260, 265-8; ii (1875), pp. 10-15, 22-3; iii (1881), pp. 91-2, 162-77. Before 1883 'corruption' was required not merely to be 'contrary to law' but to involve 'corrupt intention'. The necessity to prove 'agency' (a candidate's *direct* involvement) wrecked many petitions. The parliamentary committees which tried petitions before 1868 were even more relaxed, e.g. the Dungarvan Committee of 1854 reported in D. Power, H. Rodwell, and E. L'E. Dew, *Reports of the decisions of committees of the House of Commons* (1857), pp. 319-20.

If the joys of whiskey underpinned the electoral carnival, drinking was not its only public pleasure. Solidarity was displayed, misery forgotten, and high spirits released by the burning of tar-barrels through the streets, the illumination of windows, the lighting of bonfires, by activities which neatly translated the illegal incendiarism of the countryside into acceptable electoral brilliance.[1] Small boys knew that elections provided good cover for intensified raids on apple orchards. Candidates organized donkey races to attract the crowds. Members of the gentry, high on politics and drink, horse-played around their country clubs with more than usual enthusiasm. Elections, a sour Mayo solicitor admitted in 1857, were regarded by 'the lower classes' as *'great fun'*: or, as a countryman on his way to the polls put it in 1872, 'We are just going there on a spree, Sir . . . We are to have a spree tomorrow in Tuam.'[2] Apart from drink, the commonest accompaniments to and outward signs of electoral exhilaration were music and flags, banners, arboreal arches, and the like. Music was often provided by the crowd itself, or, more formally, by either itinerant pipers and fiddlers or local bands of varying skill and size. Payments to street musicians provided another outlet for electoral largesse and no doubt the members of the Galway Band whose instruments were released from pawn by John Lever's agents in 1859 did their very best on his behalf. Some bands played to order, others were themselves partisan and played appropriately. Anyone hearing the distant notes of 'God Save Ireland' or 'Croppies lie Down' could instantly identify the politics of the approaching parade.[3] Music, indeed, could be overtly aggressive (it was also sometimes used to drive opponents into nocturnal insomnia) or, as when the Ennis Brass Band played a selection of bouncy melodies

---

[1] Report of Sub-Constable Irwin, 24 Jan. 1835, O.P. 1835, Box 45 (Newry); of Chief Constable Ponsonby, 26 Jan. 1835, O.P. 1835, Box 35B (Co. Cork); of Chief Constable Trant, 31 May 1835, O.P. 1835, Box 34 (Carlow); Diary of Lieutenant George Lamb, N.L.I. MS 7323 (9 July 1852—Co. Waterford); *Galway Vindicator*, 24 July 1852 (Co. Galway); Report of N. Bourke, 8 May 1859, R.P. 1859/4420, Box 808 (Cork City); *Londonderry Sentinel*, 24 Nov. 1868 (Derry City).

[2] Folklore Commission MS 107; *D.E.P.* 19 July 1865; H. Corry to Belmore, [Apr. 1873], Belmore Papers D3007/P/110. Quotations from *Mayo County election petition*, H.C. 1857 (182 Sess. 2), vii, 24, and *Galway County election petition*, H.C. 1872 (241-I), xlviii, 525.

[3] B. Jackson to H. Brownrigg, 4 Feb. 1859, Mayo Papers MS 11025 (Galway). On the use of (a) pipers and fiddlers, see C. FitzGerald to Knight of Kerry, 26 Jan. 1835, Fitz-Gerald Papers; *D.E.P.* 25 July 1837 (Downpatrick); *Galway Vindicator*, 24 July 1852 (Co. Galway); *Drogheda Argus*, 21 May 1859 (Louth); (b) bands, see *D.E.P.* 16 June 1835 (Co. Carlow); *D.E.P.* 3 Aug. 1837 (Carrickfergus); Report of Constable Robinson, 9 Aug. 1837, O.P. 1837/620/36, Box 52 (King's Co.); *Telegraph or Connaught Ranger*, 4 Mar. 1846 (Mayo); Report of P. Whelan, 8 July 1852, O.P. 1852/26/87, Box 1220 (Sligo Borough); *Dublin Evening Mail*, 13 Mar. 1857 (Tipperary); *Daily Express*, 3 Feb. 1874 (Kildare); *Kilkenny Journal*, 24 Mar. 1880 (Co. Kilkenny).

in a local procession to mark the death of Prince Albert, subversive and even ironic.[1] It was, in every sense, an eclectic medium capable of both power and wit, and, as such, it occupied an important place on the Irish electoral scene. Visually, however, this scene was perhaps most obviously marked by the numerous flags, triumphal arches, and streamers which decorated the buildings, streets, and inhabitants of election towns. Actual election colours on the English model were not, however, much used in Ireland, where orange and green provided all the distinctions generally thought necessary.[2] Many elections took place amidst an overpowering landscape of greenery. Green banners and flags were held aloft. Green boughs woven into arches. Laurels worn in hats. At the Clare election of 1859 a 'very gay and grand' crowd carried 'a cross on a pole over their heads, and this cross was decorated with laurels and flowers'. At Macroom in 1880 the Parnellite candidate appeared, as he put it, 'under the green banner of our country' and waved 'in the air his umbrella from which green streamers were flying'—a sight certain to distress the 'Chief', who combined a superstitious dislike of the colour with a hatred of crowds and profound unmusicality.[3]

All these elements—drink, bonfires, music, banners—when combined with the natural excitement created by elections, helped to produce those massive displays of communal sentiment which many contests were able to elicit. 'It is a kind of triumph', remarked a Cork merchant of the election parades of 1837. At Ennis in 1852 one candidate was greeted by 'the Trades and their respective banners, sixteen in number, the labourers with theirs, and immense crowds of people . . . There were priests . . . electors and non-electors, windows full of ladies, and streets ablaze with burning barrels of tar.' Isaac Butt was conveyed through Youghal in 1859 'in a triumphal procession' with 'hundreds of the townspeople bearing flags and other emblems'. In the same year Major Gavin entered his Jerusalem

---

[1] See *Dublin Evening Mail*, 18 Feb. 1835, and T. Kelly, 'Ennis in the nineteenth century' (University College Galway MA thesis, 1971), p. 272. At the very least, bands helped to collect crowds (J. Spaight to Naas, 26 Apr. 1859, Mayo Papers MS 11036).

[2] *Clare election petition*, H.C. 1852-3 (587), ix, 780; *Galway Town corrupt practices commission*, H.C. 1857-8 [2291], xxvi, 334; *Londonderry Sentinel*, 28 July 1865.

[3] *Clare election petition*, H.C. 1852-3 (587), ix, 669-73, 694-8; *Drogheda Argus*, 17 Apr. 1880 (Macroom). For other examples of triumphal display, see Report of W. P. Walkers, 5 May 1831, O.P. 1831/M63 (Bandon); of Chief Magistrate Jones, 28 Dec. 1832, O.P. 1832/2232, Box 2192 (Mayo); *Communications relative to the marching of people during the Kerry elections*, H.C. 1835 (197), xlv, 433-4; *Cork County election petition*, H.C. 1842 (271), vi, 22, 74-81, 113; *Galway Vindicator*, 21 July 1852 (Co. Galway); Report of Sub-Inspector Ireland, 27 July 1852, O.P. 1852/11/305, Box 1218 (Mayo); Flanagan Scrapbook N.L.I. MS 14335 (Sligo Borough 1868); Folklore Commission MS 463 (Co. Galway 1872). For the stomach-turning greenery of the Dublin O'Connell memorial parade of 1864, see *Northern Whig*, 9 Aug. 1864.

(scilicet Limerick) 'mounted on a white pony . . . headed by a band'. Serjeant Barry's arrival in Dungarvan in 1868 was marked by a forest of flags in green and black (the latter for the Manchester Martyrs) and a procession of 'women dressed in white . . . mounted on open cars, with green bushes in their hands'. Tipperary Town was *en fête* during the O'Donovan Rossa by-election of 1869 'gleaming with a thousand lights, some brilliant and gorgeous coloured, others shining with the lustre of halfpenny dips. Each window was a sheet of flame . . . Tar barrels flamed everywhere and were surrounded by crowds, shouting and dancing.'[1] The fullest description relates to the Co. Limerick election of 1837.

From an early hour this morning, the roads leading in from all the country towns and villages were covered with a dense population, hastening into the election, and preceded by music, each group or cohort rather having a piper or flute player at their head . . . The great and powerful body of farmers . . . arrived shortly after ten o'clock . . . on horseback, the Roman Catholic priests conspicuous before each troop . . . followed by a force of pedestrians, double, if not treble, the number of horsemen . . . Green . . . flags, with laurel branches, were borne by those in the procession, while jaunting-cars, gigs, job-cars etc. tottered under the weight of those who crowded each vehicle.[2]

Such events, which occurred at elections concerned with drains and street lighting as much as at those concerned with Repeal and Home Rule, provided a physical image of that local solidarity which—as much as tension and conflict—lay behind the fruitful turmoil of electoral politics in nineteenth-century Ireland. At the very least elections allowed communities to express themselves in ways not otherwise regularly available. In their violence and disorder, their carnivals and festivals, in the forces mobilized to control them, they constituted an epitome of society at large. And just as violence and outrage as a whole at once mirrored and moulded the fabric of contemporary Irish society, so electoral violence in particular—a microcosm of this greater unrest—at once reflected and influenced the conduct of politics and the identity of each place.

[1] *Fictitious Votes, Ireland*, 2nd series, 1st report, p. 171 (Cork merchant); *Galway Vindicator*, 14 Apr. 1852 (Ennis); *C.C.* 7, 12 May 1859 (Youghal); J. Spaight to Naas, 5 May 1859, Mayo Papers MS 11036 (Limerick); *Waterford Mail*, 18 Sept. 1868 (Dungarvan); *Freeman's Journal*, 29 Nov. 1869 (Tipperary). See also *D.E.P.* 3 Aug. 1837 (Cashel); Carlingford Papers Diary of C. Fortescue II (17 June 1852—Louth); J. to M. J. Blake, 12 Feb. 1859, Blake of Ballyglunin Papers M6936/81 (Galway Town).
[2] *Athlone Conservative Advocate*, 17 Aug. 1837.

Patterns of Change and Continuity

I TOWNS AND POLITICAL LOCALISM

The parish pump has long been the true symbol of the 'hidden Ireland', and its deep and constant importance is best revealed in those periods when it was able to emerge from the closet of national mobilization and nationalist rhetoric into the full light of demotic day. In this sense the 1850s and 1860s, usually dismissed (Fenianism apart) as some kind of embarrassing black hole in the seamless universe of principled politics, constitute a particularly revealing (though far from unique) moment in modern Irish history when underlying forces bubbled energetically to the surface and otherwise whispered verities were shouted lustily for all to hear. Politically, the particular flavour of these years was produced by a constellation of developments—the demographic emergence of urban Ireland, the increasing economic sophistication of the towns, a momentary but powerful landlord revival—which together ensured that the liveliest manifestations of political and electoral life were temporarily to be found in the thirty-three enfranchised boroughs rather than in the overwhelmingly rural county constituencies.

Successive censuses recorded the pace of urbanization. Every geographical county experienced an increase in the proportion of its population living in settlements with either more than 2,000 or (perhaps for Ireland a more realistic lower limit) with more than 500 people. Nationally the percentages moved briskly upwards.[1]

	2,000 and upwards	500 and upwards
	per cent	per cent
1841	13.9	17.8
1861	19.4	23.7
1881	24.1	27.8

The parliamentary boroughs were in the vanguard of change. Nine actually *increased* their population in the periods 1841-61 and 1841-81, while together they grew by 2.9 per cent in the two

[1] *Irish Historical Statistics: Population, 1821-1971*, ed. W. E. Vaughan and A. J. Fitzpatrick (Dublin, 1978), p. 27; H. Mason, 'The development of the urban pattern in Ireland 1841-1881' (University of Wales Ph.D. thesis, 1969), pp. 104 and 638-55 (Appendix Five).

decades after 1841—compared with a drop of almost a third in the rest of the population. By 1861 no less than one in eight Irishmen lived in boroughs which sent Members to Parliament. But outside the north-east there was little correlation between the maintenance of urban and of surrounding county populations. Towns, it seems, were developing along specifically urban lines rather than as mere rural appendages. The relationship between town and country was changing. Before the mid-1840s this had often been particularly personal and direct, many towns having almost a third of their inhabitant families engaged in agriculture. Paupers thronged the streets, part of that band of chronically underemployed which was so depressing a feature of pre-Famine life. The experience of Ennis in Co. Clare, with its squalid suburbs of the 1830s, was typical enough: facilities improved steadily and the proportion of agricultural families declined from 28 per cent in 1841 to a mere 7 per cent twenty years later.[1] The urban–rural relationship began to centre more exclusively upon a money connection, and towns expanded their function as providers of retail trade and services. The increasing flow of mass-produced goods significantly altered employment opportunities in skilled and artisan occupations. Railways hastened the process and transformed the 'tradesman' into, or replaced him by, a shopkeeping retailer. The flow became a flood, when, in the mid-1870s, English manufacturers, facing falling margins at home, 'attempted to capture a larger share of the Irish market'.[2]

As artisans suffered, so shopkeepers prospered.* Before the Famine observers reported that many shops were doing little trade and seemed too big for the business transacted.[3] But already by 1850 the agent for a 'Manchester House' was impressed by the volume of cotton sales at Athlone and by the fact 'that the farmers and their wives were able and willing to pay for better clothing'. Similarly,

---

* For further details of post-Famine retailing and of the political role and influence of shopkeepers, see Chapter I, section II above.

[1] L. M. Cullen, *An economic history of Ireland since 1660* (London, 1972), p. 141; G. Nicholls, *A History of the Irish Poor Law* (London, 1856), pp. 133–4; H. D. Inglis, *A Journey throughout Ireland during the Spring, Summer, and Autumn of 1834*, 5th edn. (London, 1838), pp. 32–3, 53–4, 157; T. Kelly, 'Ennis in the nineteenth century' (University College Galway MA thesis, 1971).

[2] J. Lee, 'The Railways in the Irish Economy' in *The Formation of the Irish Economy*, ed. L. M. Cullen (Cork, 1969), pp. 77–87; *Report from the select committee on Industries (Ireland), with the proceedings, evidence, appendix, and index*, H.C. 1884–5 (288), ix, 814–28.

[3] W. M. Thackeray, *The Irish Sketch Book of 1842* (London, 1879), pp. 37, 46, 76, 141, 266; H. D. Inglis, *A Journey throughout Ireland*, pp. 158, 35, 33; J. Barrow, *A Tour round Ireland, through the sea-coast counties, in the Autumn of 1835* (London, 1836), pp. 265, 278. All these references are to towns that were parliamentary boroughs.

northern towns noted as 'emporia of the linen trade' were reported to be extraordinarily prosperous compared with earlier times.[1] Expansion in demand probably increased the relative number of shopkeepers. Although census data are not consistent over the four decades after 1841, there is little doubt that those groups most clearly associated with modern shopkeeping—bakers, butchers, publicans, and grocers—either grew or (within a substantially declining population) remained numerically stable after the Famine. The number of grocers, publicans, and innkeepers rose from about 15 per 10,000 inhabitants in 1841 to over 45 per 10,000 in 1881, the number of butchers and bakers from 14 to 29 per 10,000.[2] Even in western towns like Galway the number of grocers rose from 50 to 110 or from 1 in 398 to 1 in 133 of the population.[3] And whatever doubts may be thrown upon the total reliability of the occupational information given in the various censuses, there can be little doubt that shopkeepers were becoming an increasingly visible and powerful force in Irish society. They benefited from the shift to pastoral farming and from the decline of local markets (where farmers had dealt directly with customers) in favour of more distant cattle fairs. Retailing became the main urban function. Visitors commented repeatedly upon the 'numerous', 'respectable', and 'extensive' shops of places like Clonmel, Dundalk, Newry, Lisburn, New Ross, Tralee, Galway, and Sligo.[4] Already by 1856 Armagh (1861 pop. 8,969) boasted at least 215 shopkeepers, among them 61 grocers, 31 drapers and haberdashers, and 8 butchers, while its smaller neighbours, Keady (pop. 1,566) and Markethill (pop. 1,164), supported 47 and 42 retailers respectively.[5] Shopkeepers moved into virgin territory. Scariff in Clare, with in 1846 only 'one little shop of the meanest description', contained by the early 1860s 'several thriving and wealthy shopkeepers' stocking 'crinoline, hoops, and other articles of fashionable female attire for the farmers' wives and

[1] Lord Clarendon to Lord John Russell, 24 Mar. 1850. Clarendon Papers L.-B. V; J. E. Tennent to Lord Derby, 5 Dec. 1851, Derby Papers 131/7.

[2] L. Kennedy, 'Farmers, traders, and agricultural politics in pre-Independence Ireland' in *Irish peasants, violence, and political unrest 1780–1914*, ed. S. Clark and J. S. Donnelly Jr. (Manchester, 1983), pp. 339–73; A. W. Orridge, 'Who supported the Land War? An aggregate-data analysis of Irish agrarian discontent 1879-1882', *Economic and Social Review*, xii (1981), 210–12. Orridge's reservations are in part based upon his inclusion of declining artisan occupations among 'traders', though his point about changing census categorization is valid enough. See Chapter I, pp. 51–2.

[3] H. Mason, 'The development of the urban pattern in Ireland 1841–1881', p. 301.

[4] T. W. Freeman, 'The Irish country town', *Irish Geography*, iii (1954), 7; James Fraser, *Handbook for travellers in Ireland*, 5th edn. (Dublin, [1859]), pp. 90, 110, 113, 127, 152, 166, 169, 176, 204, 252, 335, 445, 518, 568, 613, 623, 658.

[5] *Slater's Directory of Ireland* (Manchester and London, 1856), pp. 388–94. Publicans (but not spirit dealers) have been excluded.

daughters'. At Kilrush the number of shops doubled, those with plate-glass windows increasing from one to twelve. Gweedore in Donegal, which knew not retailing in 1838, was, by 1886, able to support 'an extensive shop'. In 1880 Claremorris in Mayo (pop. 1,319) boasted a 'main street . . . full of shops, corn-dealers, drapers, butchers, bakers, and general dealers'. By 1871 an independent-minded Cork landlord was already convinced that 'the goods shown today' in the windows of shops 'in every small town . . . include numbers of articles of comfort and even luxury goods' which it would have been 'silly to ask for . . . twenty years ago', while a public works inspector in the north-west noted the rapid growth of 'permanent shops with meat and bread, where such supplies were only to be procured once a week, on market days, when I first acted for the Board'.[1] By the mid-1870s, and probably earlier, specialized retailing premises had become a notable and obvious feature of all but the smallest hamlets. In twenty-one towns with more than 6,000 inhabitants, no less than one in every twelve buildings was a distinct shop or office (many others served duty both as residence and small shop), while among buildings valued at ten pounds or over the proportion was as high as one in seven.[2]

The increasing significance of retailing reflected the growing social and economic importance of towns and their material betterment. Already by 1861 the quality of urban housing had greatly improved, while a 'hierarchy index' constructed by Dr Hugh Mason to indicate economic, administrative, and social significance, demonstrates a marked upswing in the standing of towns in the decades after the Famine.[3] As the state became more involved in social policy, so the physical products of its concern—workhouses, barracks, hospitals—were placed in the larger towns. These benefited from the

---

[1] H. Coulter, *The West of Ireland: Its condition and prospects* (Dublin, 1862), pp. 30-1, 57; Lord George Hill, *Facts from Gweedore*, 5th edn. (London, 1887), p. 63; B. H. Becker, *Disturbed Ireland: Being the letters written during the winter of 1880–81* (London, 1881), p. 6; W. Bence Jones, *The life's work in Ireland of a landlord who tried to do his duty* (London, 1880), p. 60 (written 1871); J. Macaulay, *Ireland in 1872: A tour of observation, with remarks on Irish public questions* (London, 1873), pp. 26–7 (quoting the public works inspector).

[2] Calculated from *Returns for each city, town, and township in Ireland, the population of which, according to the census of 1871, exceeded 6000, and in which the Acts of Geo. 4, c. 82, 3 & 4 Vict., c. 100, and 17 & 18 Vict., c. 103, and the Acts amending the same, are now in force: 1. Of the number of dwelling houses valued . . .*, H.C. 1875 (455), lxiv, 47–61. For buildings valued at more than £10, the shop and office percentage ranged from 8.1 (Ballymena) to 22.9 (Derry), the mean unweighted figure being 14.0 (8.3 of *all* buildings). Public buildings and townships have been excluded.

[3] H. Mason, 'The development of the urban pattern in Ireland 1841-1881', pp. 582-96, 17–82. The twenty-six index functions include the presence of a dispensary, railway station, workhouse, barracks, newspaper, brewery, physician, lawyer, bank, draper, bookseller, etc.

expenditure generated, shopkeepers most of all. Economic importance led to political importance, something government circles were
quick to recognize. As early as 1852 the Tory Viceroy, Lord Eglinton, was, for electoral reasons, opposing the withdrawal of debased
copper coinage because most of it had 'got into the hands of the
smaller shopkeepers here and as the calling it up [would cause]
some loss and inconvenience to that class, it might tell against our
candidates'.[1] With the collapse of Repeal and its central organization,
smaller local business men, freed from the domination of the larger
traders who had supported O'Connell most actively (Smithwick in
Kilkenny, Delahunty in Waterford, Bianconi in Clonmel, Lyons and
Hays in Cork) and of the now-floundering priesthood, came into a
political inheritance of their own. At the same time, artisans and
tradesmen lost interest in party politics and became ever more
exclusively involved in activities 'geared to catering for their particular concerns as working men'.[2]

Increasing sectionalism led to a concentration upon craft rather
than national or even 'class' issues. Thus, while some observers in
1848 saw tradesmen as 'centres round which the disaffected in the
rural districts would naturally rally', Smith O'Brien's revolutionary
'army' found places such as Cashel so like 'cities of the dead', that,
after encountering the indifference of no less than three towns, it
was obliged 'to fall back on the rural districts'.[3] In Waterford too
shopkeepers were itching to become special constables; at Dungarvan
they were determined 'to defend themselves against those whose
object was plunder'. But, although business men and shopkeepers
were increasingly disturbed by news of the Paris revolution, they
lacked unity of purpose. At Limerick, while knowing 'very well
that the first outbreak [of rebellion] would . . . destroy their stores
at once . . . yet [they] do not in the least merge their differences . . .
but cringe . . . or argue on individual crotchets, or grumble against
the government'.[4] Such incoheren was to characterize the towns
of post-Famine Ireland. Urban politics, setting the tone for the

---

[1] Lord Eglinton to Lord Naas, 11 May 1852, Eglinton Papers MS 5335. The discussion
of localist politics which follows is in part based on my 'National politics and local realities
in mid-nineteenth century Ireland' in *Studies in Irish History presented to R. Dudley
Edwards*, ed. A. Cosgrove and D. McCartney (Dublin, 1979), pp. 190-227.

[2] F. A. D'Arcy, 'Dublin artisan activity, opinion, and organization 1820-1850' (University College Dublin MA thesis, 1968), pp. i, 38-9, 71, 78.

[3] Lord Stuart de Decies to Clarendon, 8 Apr. 1848, Clarendon Papers Box 10; C. Gavan
Duffy, *Young Ireland Part II or Four Years of Irish History 1845-49* (Dublin, 1887),
pp. 235-6.

[4] Clarendon to Sir G. Grey, 2 June 1848, Clarendon Papers L.-B. II; Lord Carew to
Clarendon, [*c.* Apr. 1848], ibid. Box 8; Clarendon to Grey, 7 Mar, 1848, ibid. L.-B. II;
Augustus Stafford to Lord Dunraven, [*c.*1848], Dunraven Papers D3196/F/4.

country as a whole, became at once unusually fragmented and unusually lively. More or less simultaneously the true (if temporarily latent) locus of 'national' as well as 'nationalist' politics was moving decisively out of the streets and into the fields. Even under O'Connell the county voters had provided steadier (if weaker) electoral support than their supposedly more sophisticated urban cousins.[1] Increasingly as time went on support for nationalist movements was to be found in the countryside, something the landlord revival of the 1850s could only delay, not prevent. The distribution of parliamentary seats won by movements with obvious (if sometimes rather muted) nationalist tendencies makes the point.

	percentage of county seats won	percentage of borough seats won
O'Connellites 1832–47	29	35
Independents 1852	45	48
Home Rulers 1874	67	59
Home Rulers 1880	67	54
(Parnellites only 1880	30	13)

More and more did countrymen match their energy and violence as rioters with an equal enthusiasm for electoral radicalism. Already at the Co. Meath election of 1835 three-quarters of the rural voters supported O'Connellite candidates against less than three-fifths of those in the eleven largest 'towns'. At Cork City in the same year the 483 enfranchised farmers and labourers in that constituency's large rural hinterland split three to one for O'Connell, a notably more substantial endorsement than that of the other major occupational groups (shopkeepers, artisans, merchants, and so on), publicans alone excepted.[2] Conservative candidates at elections in Co. Louth in 1852 and 1865 polled significantly better in towns with 500 or more inhabitants than in the rural areas.[3] Impressionistic comments

[1] The percentage of seats won by O'Connellites in boroughs veered wildly between 18 (1841) and 51 (1832); in counties support—at between 20 (1841) and 35 (1832)— was much steadier (Dublin University excluded here and in immediately following figures in text).

[2] Calculated from (a) 'Meath Election. January 1835. Names of those who voted', printed list in O.P. 1835/148, Box 47—all the towns in question (e.g. Navan, Kells, Trim, etc.) were of course not parliamentary boroughs; (b) lists of Cork voters in *The People's Press and Cork Weekly Register*, 17, 24, 31 Jan., 7, 14 Feb. 1835. See also Chapter I, Table 10.

[3] Calculated from *County of Louth Election 1852. A list of the electors of the several baronies of the County of Louth, who voted at the general election of 1852* (Dundalk, 1852), N.L.I. MS 1660—one-in-five sample—and *An Analysis of the parliamentary register of voters for the County of Louth* (Dublin, 1865), N.L.I. P2491. In 1852 the Conservative

make the same point. Radical Co. Limerick supporters of Smith O'Brien bemoaned the anaesthetic intrusions of city 'moderates' in 1847. The anti-Tory vote in the 1850s was, it seems, highest in the most rural parts of constituencies like Co. Dublin and Cork City. Carlow Borough was hardly less Tory than the notoriously Conservative county of which it was the leading town.[1] In 1869, not only were the Whiggish clericalists of Co. Longford strongest in the county town, but Catholic radicalism in Londonderry was most aggressive in the rural hinterland, and Amnesty meetings in Kilkenny attracted little support from the towns.[2] At the Co. Galway by-election of 1872 a disproportionate number of Tory votes came from the various unrepresented towns, while at the Tralee Union poor-law elections of 1881 the farmers proved themselves more radical than did the voters living in the town itself.[3] In certain areas —notably Donegal—Parnellite nationalism was almost entirely confined to the countryside, and, indeed, the Land League's obvious lack of interest in the problems of city tradesmen was symptomatic of that movement's overwhelmingly rural ideology.[4] Throughout the country as a whole it is notable that the counties which contributed most substantially to the Parnell Tribute of 1883 were very markedly more rural in character than those which had been financially most generous to O'Connell in, for example, 1826 and 1833.[5]

The economic and political ascendancy of the towns in post-Famine Ireland meant that public politics were for a substantial period divorced from the increasingly rural drift of radicalism in general. The fact that the Tenant League, for example, was driven

vote in Ardee and Carlingford stood at 50 per cent as opposed to 40 per cent elsewhere. At the 1865 by-election the Conservative vote in all towns with 500 and more inhabitants stood at 57 per cent as opposed to 44 per cent in the rural districts.

[1] M. O'Shaughnessy to W. S. O'Brien, [Aug. 1847], Smith O'Brien Papers MS 440; breakdown of Co. Dublin vote in 1852, Domvile Papers MS 9361; *C.C.* 24 May 1859; H. Conolly to G. H. Moore, [Jan. 1853], Moore Papers MS 892.

[2] *Copy of the shorthand writer's notes of the judgement delivered by Mr Justice Fitzgerald, and of the minutes of evidence taken at the trial of the Longford election petition,* H.C. 1870 (178), lvi, 329; *Londonderry Standard,* 23 Dec. 1869; Lord Spencer to Gladstone, 18 Sept. 1869, Gladstone Papers Add. MS 44306.

[3] *Copy of the evidence taken at the trial of the Galway County election petition,* H.C. 1872 (241-I), xlviii, 352-8. On both the campaign in general and Tralee in particular, see W. L. Feingold, 'The Irish boards of poor law guardians 1872-86: A revolution in local government' (University of Chicago Ph.D. thesis, 1974), pp. xii, 163-72, 267.

[4] Notes by Lord Carnarvon for Cabinet meeting, 6 Oct. 1885, Carnarvon Papers B.L. Add. MS 60823; D. Murphy, *Derry, Donegal, and Modern Ulster 1790-1921* (Londonderry, 1981), pp. 141-5; M. Murphy, 'Fenianism, Parnellism, and the Cork Trades 1860-1900', *Saothar,* No. 5 (1979), 30.

[5] See sources used in Table 56 below. Of the eleven counties which provided the 'eight leading' counties in 1826 and 1833, eight were above the national mean for proportion of population in towns of 500 or more, while only two of the eight leading counties in 1883 were above what was then the mean.

to making a series of acceleratingly desperate appeals to urban opinion shows the gulf between the two. By 1857 a leading supporter of tenurial reform, William Sharman Crawford, admitted 'in despair' that 'the town constituencies appear indifferent to the tenant-right question'.[1] Yet in no sense were the concerns of the boroughs less authentically political, less lively, or less involving. On the contrary, they exhibited, in their glorification of the local and particular, a consuming enthusiasm and passion capable of mobilizing virtually all sections of opinion. And shopkeepers, with their growing numerical, physical, and financial prominence, constituted the single most important political group within the urban community. In the Galway of 1859, for example, no less than 116 of the 475 occupier electors were rated out of shops. In the same year almost two-fifths of Armagh's voters were retailers or publicans. At Derry in 1868 the proportion was a third. Even amidst Dublin City's enormous constituency of 9,905 in 1857 it was almost a fifth. Of Newry's 124 shopkeepers in 1868 no less than 88 were registered as voters, while in Limerick 'small shopkeepers and persons in the same rank of life' formed the majority of the electorate.[2] And because this was the case at a time when neither the 'popular' party nor the establishment Liberals or Tories exercised a monopoly of influence, shopkeeper (and to some extent artisan) sectionalism found itself best served, not by rigid political consistency, but by constant reference and deference to the local demands of customers and others in a position to bring pressure to bear. Not only, therefore, were the 1850s and 1860s a period in which certain successful entrepreneurs were able to pull themselves into positions of political power, but a period also when retailers as a whole felt themselves peculiarly vulnerable to the imperatives of local concern. As a result, post-Famine elections provided unprecedented occasions for exclusive dealing (retailer impotence), for rivalry between shopkeepers (internecine strife), and for economic opportunism (entrepreneurship), as when an Armagh grocer had placards printed to hot up electoral fever and so 'push trade as far as I can'.[3] But in order to retain and increase

---

[1] See *Nation*, 17 Jan., 7 Feb., 3, 17, 24 Apr. 1852; and (for Crawford) *Banner of Ulster*, 19 Mar. 1857.

[2] For Galway, see electoral list in Blake of Ballyglunin Papers M6935/37B; for the others, Chapter I, Table 8. Newry figures obtained by tracing shopkeepers (including grocers who dealt in spirits but not publicans as such) from *The Belfast and Province of Ulster Directory* (Belfast, 1870) to *Newry Election. An alphabetically arranged list of electors who voted, and those who did not, at the election held in Newry, on the 20th of November 1868* (Newry, n.d.)—copy P.R.O.N.I. T2336/1. The enfranchisement level for grocers *and* spirit dealers alone was higher still: 53 out of 65. For Limerick, see *Daily Express*, 21 Sept. 1871.

[3] F. McKee to Revd H. McKee, 11 Nov. 1868, McKee Papers D1821/1/8. For examples

business within the intensely localized atmosphere of provincial Ireland it became more than ever necessary to establish factionalized sets of dependants and associates, who, through the provision of credit, charity, and other advantages, could be tied to the one shop or firm. And it was the vigorous activities of personal cliques such as these which so constantly and effectively asserted the pressing realities of particular communities against the distant and, for a time, anaemic attractions of national politics and national organizations.

Thus did the social characteristics of the time and an increasing prosperity, punctured only by the agricultural depression of the early 1860s, combine to provide a framework for politics which actually encouraged those fissiparous and localist tendencies that were never far below the surface of Irish politics. Local cliques luxuriated, stimulated by the changing nature of urban life. Even the traditional power of landlords, which had provided a certain docile uniformity in some of the smaller boroughs, was reduced or destroyed.[1] With the landlord revival confined to the counties and the clergy more disunited than for many years, power within the town community was to be had for the grasping, and personal followings became both the norm and the decisive element in local affairs.* In Galway, Lord Clanricarde's electoral success depended on the 'many shop-keepers such as Geogheghan, Dooley, Hennessy etc. etc. and R. O'Connor the grocer, all of whom and others have such influence'. Galway, indeed, was representative of a certain type of town constituency, and even its large and corrupt freeman electorate was by no means unique.[2] The occupational composition of these freemen had almost certainly varied little since the 1830s when many had belonged to crafts later to suffer the onslaughts of mass production, such as shoemaking (16.6 per cent), nailmaking (3.8 per cent), and linen weaving (6.2 per cent). In any case, retailers had already infiltrated this section of the electorate and established a 'Trojan

of these various 'styles', see Chapter I, pp. 55-7 above, and K. T. Hoppen, 'National politics and local realities in mid-nineteenth century Ireland', pp. 197-8; also *Banner of Ulster*, 7 Apr. 1857, *Report from the select committee on parliamentary and municipal elections*, H.C. 1868-9 (352), viii, 208, and J. C. Lowry to Lord Belmore, 15 Mar. 1873, Belmore Papers D3007/P/23.

* On local cliques and corruption proper, see Chapter I, sections ii and iii above.

[1] An important technical matter was the growing tendency of landlords to grant long (60 years or more) 'building leases' in towns. This reduced their tenants' dependence (F. E. Currey to Duke of Devonshire, 15 Apr. 1859, Lismore Papers MS 7190). See also Chapter II above.

[2] In 1852 freemen constituted more than 10 per cent of the electorate in nine boroughs: Carrickfergus (67.4), Galway (53.4), Waterford (41.1), Dublin (33.6), Youghal (31.3), Wexford (30.0), Drogheda (18.8), Cork (15.8), Derry (12.2): *Number of electors on the register of 1852-3 in each county, city, and borough in Ireland, distinguishing their qualifications*, H.C. 1852-3 (957), lxxxiii, 413-15. See also Chapter I, pp. 3-5 above.

Horse' for later influence from within.[1] Freemen supported anyone willing to pay, and various occupational groups, such as tailors in 1847 and bakers in 1852, offered themselves for sale *en masse*. In 1857 they submitted 'a scale of prices for plumpers and split votes' and became so frantic at the prospect of an uncontested return, that 'the heads of each trade to the number of thirty in six jaunting cars went out to Kilcornan to invite Sir T. Redington to stand'.[2] Entrepreneurs anxious to capitalize on economic dominance took advantage of situations like this. One was Henry Comerford, magistrate, gaol-board member, and trustee of the Galway Savings Bank, who had 'a great deal of influence among the trades and . . . can *command* the Barna [a district] voters—in fact there are very few of our merchants over whom he cannot exercise vast influence, they are nearly all debtors to him'.[3]

The operation of politics motivated by immediate material considerations, at a time when central organizations were largely ineffective, reinforced the supremacy of local issues and interests. Certain men became centres of patronage and power on the basis, not of leadership of national sentiment, but of what they could 'deliver' to the local community. Hence the extraordinary Galway figure of Fr. Peter Daly, PP, who owed his power to 'the firmly secular base of chairmanship of the corporation and the gas company, presidency of the Mechanics' Institute and the Commercial Society, and ownership of the Lough Corrib Steam Company.[4] In 1859 he formed a compact with the English adventurer, John Orrell Lever, who triumphantly headed the poll. Lever stood as a 'Conservative', something virtually unknown in Galway for more than quarter of a century. But 'party' affiliation was irrelevant to a success based on one consideration and one only: Lever's directorship of the Atlantic Royal Mail Steam Navigation Company. Schemes for opening a packet service to America had long been discussed. Lever's company ran such a service and Lever reaped the electoral harvest. He sold ten-pound shares to a cross-section of the patriotically avaricious in Galway Town and County, where about a third of the shareholders were 'gentlemen', a fifth lawyers, doctors, and the like, and a third business men.[5] Daly became a director (and the owner

[1] Blake of Ballyglunin Papers M6935/5. Some 68 retailers of various sorts were already freemen in the 1830s, more than 10 per cent of the total freeman body.

[2] E. Kelly to M. J. Blake, 27 July 1847, Blake of Ballyglunin Papers M6936/58; K. Byrne to Blake, 30 Dec. 1852, ibid. M6936/67; J. Blakeney to Blake, 27 Mar. 1857, ibid. M6936/78; T. Reid to Lord Clanricarde, 26 Mar. 1857, Clanricarde Papers 40. For further details concerning Galway corruption, see Chapter I, pp. 75-7 above.

[3] J. Blakeney to M. J. Blake, [July 1847], Blake of Ballyglunin Papers M6936/58.

[4] E. R. Norman, *The Catholic Church and Ireland in the Age of Rebellion 1859–1873* (London, 1965), pp. 16-17; *Galway Vindicator*, 22 Sept. 1852.

[5] See the Share Register P.R.O. BT31/363/1333.

of 120 shares). Lever entered the town dramatically accompanied by the contractor for the new floating docks, who, he hinted, would provide a bottomless supply of jobs. A grand ball was held at Corrigan's Hotel for all the 'respectable tradesmen' and their families. Posters appeared reminding citizens that 'Lever, when your town was falling into the last stage of decay and impoverishment, came to your rescue—risking tens of thousands of pounds in an undertaking, which . . . will bring prosperity to the whole community'.[1]

The Tory Government, desperate for support, gave the Galway line a mail contract (something Viceroy Eglinton thought 'must benefit us politically') and even the Catholic bishop, otherwise bitterly opposed to Fr. Daly, felt himself obliged to vote for Lever. As early as 1847 and 1851 the issue had already become 'quite a national one' and ministers had quickly grasped the party gains which might flow from the opening of pork barrels in the west.[2] Palmerston, who returned to office in June 1859, though horrified by the cost, was told by his chief whip that 'Ireland has set its heart upon the contract. This may be very wild and foolish, but . . . if you fail to conciliate Ireland upon this point you will not be able to reckon next session upon *ten* Irish supporters.' Against his better judgement and the moral indignation of his Chancellor of the Exchequer (Gladstone), Palmerston extended the contract and even granted Daly a private interview in London.[3] Success like Lever's could, however, quickly turn to ashes if the promised benefits failed to materialize. The collapse of the Galway line led to Lever's defeat in 1865, despite offers of a £3,000 'gift' to establish a cotton-mill and of money to provide relief work for indigents. Galway, however, merely reverted to a 'purer' localism—the 'clannish disposition of its voters being well known'[4]—and returned, under the suitably ambiguous banner of 'Liberal Conservatism', the inimitable Michael

[1] J. Blake to M. J. Blake, 31 Jan., 4, 12 Feb. 1859, Blake of Ballyglunin Papers M6936/81. Lever's 'politics and principles', the poster continued, were 'all embraced in the advancement of Galway—the erection of a breakwater in its harbour'.

[2] Eglinton to Derby, 22 Feb. 1859, Derby Papers 148/3; Bishop MacEvilly to M. J. Blake, [May 1859], Blake of Ballyglunin Papers M6936/80; Memorandum by the Chief Secretary, Sir William Somerville, Dec. 1847, Somerville L.-B. T2982; Clarendon to Russell, 9 Feb. 1851, Clarendon Papers L.-B. VI.

[3] Henry Brand to Lord Palmerston, 31 July 1861, Palmerston Papers General Correspondence; *The Gladstone Diaries*, ed. M. R. D. Foot and H. C. G. Matthew, 8 vols. to date (Oxford, 1968–   ), vi, 361; *Sir William Gregory, K.C.M.G., formerly member of parliament and sometime governor of Ceylon. An Autobiography*, ed. Lady Gregory (London, 1894), p. 213. See also *Report from the select committee on the Royal Atlantic Steam Navigation Company*, H.C. 1861 (463), xii, 3–13, and W. S. Sanderlin, 'Galway as a transatlantic port in the nineteenth century', *Eire–Ireland*, v (1970), 15–31.

[4] *Nation*, 15 July, 3 Aug. 1865; Bishop MacEvilly to Archbishop Cullen, 30 June, 15 July 1865, Cullen Papers. See also Lever's Address in *D.E.P.* 3 July 1865: 'If you ask me what my politics are? I answer manufactures and commerce'.

Morris on 'independent principles and "Himself" ' (as he was known in the neighbourhood). Morris, whose 'high local position' rendered unnecessary 'any declaration of political opinion', headed the poll more because of much-admired abilities to 'lift the kitchen table with his teeth' than because of any wider principles.[1] Northern boroughs too were 'peculiarly *clannish* and local in their predilections', something only money or patronage could overcome. Thus, the electors of Armagh were reluctant to 'select as a candidate any person locally unconnected with them, *unless* he . . . was . . . possessed of very ample means so as to enable him not merely to meet the first expenses (which would be found to be tolerably heavy) but to continue to reply in a generous manner to unceasing demands from year to year'. And in 1857 the borough's police treasurer stressed that neither he nor the town could back any man 'that would not pledge himself to support the railway between Newry and Armagh'.[2] The construction and routeing of railways were, indeed, of crucial electoral importance. Local opinion generally harboured ecstatic expectations. In 1855 Longford saw itself as about to become 'one of the most flourishing of Irish provincial towns', while a western newspaper asserted the 'well-known fact that a man with a capital of £200 could with such facilities do as much business as a person with £2000 without'. By 1870, however, 'few had a good word to say about the railways', and towns like Youghal, which had expected much, found their hopes unrealized.[3] But the mid-century was a boom time. William McCormick, the successful Tory at the 1860 Derry by-election, was a railway developer who had prevented the Ulster Railway from gaining control of the Enniskillen line and thus, in the eyes of local merchants, rescued the town from the trade monopoly of Belfast. His connections proved in every sense electorally decisive.[4]

Shopkeepers were the prime beneficiaries of railways and welcomed their arrival. But farmers too, especially in the midland counties, laid increasing stress on the importance of communications. So much so,

[1] *D.E.P.* 10 July 1865; Maud Wynne, *An Irishman and his Family: Lord Morris and Killanin* (London, 1937), pp. 29, 44. On the importance of such genialities, see Chapter I, section III.

[2] J. E. Tennent to Derby, 5 Dec. 1851, Derby Papers 131/7; Archbishop Beresford to Mr Nugent, 23 Aug. 1855, Pack-Beresford Papers D664/A/617; *Banner of Ulster*, 31 Mar. 1857.

[3] *Midlands Counties Gazette*, 14 Apr. 1855, and *Tyrawley Herald*, 18 Oct. 1855, both cited H. Mason, 'The development of the urban pattern in Ireland 1841–1881', p. 286; J. Lee, 'The Railways in the Irish Economy', p. 82; A. R. Orme, 'Youghal, County Cork—growth, decay, resurgence', *Irish Geography*, v (1966), 138–9.

[4] *Londonderry Guardian*, 28 Feb. 1860; *Londonderry Sentinel*, 5, 8 Mar. 1860 (References kindly supplied by Desmond Murphy).

that at Roscommon in 1859 several 'R.C. independent farmers' offered to defray the election expenses of the son of the Tory Lord Crofton (who also reported the adherence of 'some of the priests'), all because Crofton had 'been most successful in getting railway accommodation through the county against the opposition of the Great Midlands'. And although in the event Crofton's son did not come forward, Captain Goff was to enjoy the unique distinction of being the only Tory returned for the county in the post-reform period.[1] At Coleraine railways were merely one element in the formation of local influence. There the Presbyterian business man, Dr John Boyd, had 'purchased a great part of the town' and was able to establish a virtual hegemony between the 1840s and his death in 1861. In 1852 he was powerful enough to install the Tory Chief Secretary as Member on the ostensible grounds that so senior a politician could further extend rail communications and improve navigation on the River Bann, an issue which to Coleraine was as the transatlantic packet to Galway.[2] By 1858, however, with navigation improvement languishing, opposition began to emerge and a group of electors agreed to 'sink their politics and private feelings and support *any* good man who will . . . be able to do some good for the town'. As a result, Boyd was threatened with the candidature of Alderman Humphrey, a governor of the Irish Society of London which owned large estates in the area. Humphrey arrived trailing such clouds of expectation that Boyd was driven to promising land for a market (something the Society had long refused) and calling attention to his loss of £4,000 on the Portrush harbour works and his efforts regarding railway extension. He was returned unopposed; and the themes to which he had responded continued to be orchestrated after his death by Sir H. H. Bruce, local landowner and Orangeman, who was also to remind voters of the 'marvels' *he* had performed 'in opening the Bann to navigation', safe in the knowledge that 'there was one thing . . . about which all agreed and that was the promotion of the trade of the town'. Coleraine politics made nonsense of party labels, for, as the local agent of the Central Conservative Society reported in 1868, 'it is long since there was a contest in Coleraine on purely political grounds'.[3]

[1] Lord Crofton to T. E. Taylor, 10 Apr. 1859, and to Naas, 19 Apr. 1859, both Mayo Papers MS 11036.

[2] J. Boyd to Naas, 27 Mar. 1852, Mayo Papers MS 11018B; *Londonderry Sentinel*, 11 June 1852. See S. W. Knox to Naas, 17 Jan. 1854, Mayo Papers MS 11017: 'There is no question so popular, or one on which the Coleraine people have so much set their hearts as on the improvement of the river navigation.'

[3] J. McFarland to Naas, 23 Feb., 22 May 1858, Mayo Papers MS 11024; *Londonderry Sentinel*, 15 Apr., 6 May 1859, 18 July 1865; *Central Conservative Society of Ireland:*

Boyd's long reign was unusual. Elsewhere power followed oligarchical lines or was held by single individuals for briefer periods. At Athlone, the influence of J. J. Ennis (MP 1857–65) was short of overwhelming, although his family controlled large business interests and had acquired the Ballinahown estate in 1834, while Ennis himself was a governor of the Bank of Ireland, Chairman of the Midland Great Western Railway, and a commissioner of charitable bequests. None the less, he had from the start been forced to rely on episcopal support and on the forging of alliances with other important entrepreneurs such as James Murtagh (later Deputy Vice-Chairman of the Athlone poor-law board), who was soon pressurizing *his* dependants into the Ennis camp. Weaker men were torn between different factions. The master of the Protestant School, whose employers were hot for Ennis's opponent, was driven to the admission that he had 'yielded on Saturday evening to Mr Murtagh to whom about five months ago I placed myself under heavy obligation in getting him to become security for one of my sons to the amount of £1000'.[1] Ennis was not, however, popular and had to resort to massive bribery 'without any disguise or concealment',[2] tactics which demonstrated the uncertainty of his position for they represented a move from a patronage system (the mark of confident power) to a naked cash relationship, never a *secure* foundation for electoral success. Opposition developed out of residual Conservatism and revulsion by the 'respectable', so that Ennis was defeated by a fellow 'Liberal' fighting on principles of electoral 'purity'. This was an old game and merely implied a slight readjustment of local alliances as typified by Bishop Kilduff of Ardagh's success in persuading Murtagh to abandon Ennis. As Kilduff told his brother of Elphin, 'I do not attach so much value to the six votes the Murtaghs have in the boro' as I do to the *painful* influence they have over their customers and creditors, the publicans and bankers of Athlone'.[3] By 1869, however, Murtagh's keenly attuned political antennae had convinced him that the future lay elsewhere and that generous financial contributions to the election

Reports by agents of the revisions at the registration sessions of 1867 (Mayo Papers MS 11161).

[1] J. Macnamara to Revd. J. W. Hackett, 4 May 1859, and to W. Pidgeon, 26 Apr. 1859 (respectively Secretary and Agent to the Incorporated Society for Promoting English Protestant Schools in Ireland), Incorporated Society Papers MS 5805. See also J. H. Whyte, *The Independent Irish Party 1850–9* (Oxford, 1958), p. 171.

[2] Bishop Gillooly of Elphin to Revd F. Murphy, PP, [1865], Gillooly Papers Section C. Athlone was partly in the diocese of Elphin and partly in that of Ardagh.

[3] Kilduff to Gillooly, [c.10 July 1865], Gillooly Papers Section C. A colourful account of mid-century·Athlone corruption is given by T. P. O'Connor (*The Parnell Movement*, new edn. (London, 1887), pp. 89–90), who cites a 'highly respected Protestant tradesman': 'I am a Protestant . . . and my father was a Protestant, and his father before him; but the man I want to see returned for Athlone is the man that leaves the money in the town.'

funds of Nationalist candidates might well prove a sound and reward-
ing investment.[1]

Corruption flourished most where power was relatively diffuse.
Cashel was a notorious example. Here blocs of voters, sometimes
grouped along occupational, sometimes along purely *ad hoc* lines,
auctioned themselves in return for communal or individual benefits.
In 1852 more than half the electorate agreed publicly to support
whoever would promise money for railway construction. Weeks
before the 1868 contest one of the candidates (all of them 'Liberals')
deposited £5,000 in a local bank and had his agent parade the town
waving the deposit slip for all to see—a practice far from uncommon
elsewhere.[2] In such a context Archbishop Leahy's remark that voters
could quite 'conscientiously' prefer the candidate who would
'promote the material prosperity' of the town took on meanings
clear to all. Others made the message even less ambiguous. The
voters, according to Fr. John Ryan, PP, were entitled to any money
going, 'they would be very great fools if they refused it'.[3] Only
in private, it seems, was Leahy brave enough to summon up a mood
of moral outrage.

> The men who would determine the election . . . are to a man corrupt. They are
> divided into two parties. If one of them takes up a candidate, the other is sure
> to oppose him. And those parties are Catholics . . . No one would have any
> business in Cashel that would not be prepared to look for places for themselves
> and their children [or] . . . spend money liberally.[4]

Such an atmosphere encouraged the activities of electoral *condottieri*.
Occupational groups voted together, not because issues of importance to particular crafts were at stake, but because occupation
constituted the most obvious basis for association. At Cashel in 1868
twenty-six of the 203 voters were butchers; twenty-five voted for
Henry Munster, not because Munster represented interests congenial
to butchering, but because their support had jointly been purchased
at £30 a head.[5] And such imperatives were all-involving, so much so
that the turn-out of borough voters in these years was exceptionally
high. Individual figures often exceeded 90 per cent on registers which
must have contained their share of the dead and the departed, while
the mean turn-out in all contested one-member boroughs at the

---

[1] Butt Papers MS 10415. See Mr Justice Fitzgerald's comments on Murtagh's continuing
influence in *Longford election petition*, H.C. 1870 (178), lvi, 291.

[2] *Nation*, 10 Apr. 1852; *Report of the Commissioners appointed for the purpose of
making inquiry into the existence of Corrupt Practices at the last election for Cashel*, H.C.
1870 [C 9], xxxii, 7; *Waterford Citizen*, 23 Oct. 1868 (on Dungarvan election).

[3] *Cashel Corrupt Practices Commission*, op. cit. 337, 178.

[4] Archbishop Leahy to Cullen, 8 Mar. 1857, Cullen Papers.

[5] *Cashel Corrupt Practices Commission*, op. cit. 101.

General Elections of 1857, 1859, and 1865 was of the order of 80 per cent or more.[1] Such a degree of involvement makes it clear that considerations quite distinct from those of 'national' politics could and did galvanize men into vigorous electoral activity. In the mid-century boroughs, at least, there can be little doubt that issues such as education, disestablishment, or tenant-right were generally no more than gilt on the gingerbread of immediate and local preoccupations.

An object-lesson is provided by the experiences of the Catholic lawyer, Thomas O'Hagan (later Lord Chancellor), who in the early 1860s held office as Attorney-General for Ireland. Not yet in Parliament, he desperately needed a seat, and approached various constituencies whose members might be induced to resign. In all he met with the same response. At Kinsale he encountered the wealthy but financially troubled Sir John Arnott, a Scotsman with large business interests in Britain and Ireland. Arnott had bought his way into the borough in 1859 when his 'Liberal' agents had chanted a litany of the facts that he employed over 1,100 people in the area and paid them £90,000 a year, that he spent £25,000 annually on work for the poor, that 'the question was, which representative was best calculated to serve their local interests'. The unfortunate Tory, Captain Brine, who had at first seemed eminently suitable because of a military position which could ensure the expenditure of 'a great deal of public money in the town on their fortifications and barracks', found himself hopelessly outgunned. Arnott had crushed Brine with a hustings announcement that 'within the last day or two . . . one of my managers when here told me that he had paid about £1000 a year to the poor of this town for crochet work, but I told him not to be contented with a paltry thousand, but to increase it considerably (immense cheering)'. Such rhetoric determined the politics of the town and although some divided the electorate into 'Liberals' and 'Conservatives' on simple denominational criteria, Arnott was happy to note that half the 'Conservatives' energetically supported him 'for personal and commercial reasons'. Arnott, though a Presbyterian, was on close terms with the local Catholic curate ('it so happens that I have the good fortune of making friends'), who promised to work on his parish priest, who was in turn 'a bosom friend of Dr Delany' the Bishop of Cork.[2] The two priests 'controlled' thirty-four (out of

---

[1] For more general details regarding turn-out, see Chapter I, pp. 71–2 above, especially Table 14.

[2] *C.C.* 3, 5, 10 May 1859. See the list of electors in H. E. O'Donnell to O'Hagan, 29 Dec. 1862, O'Hagan Papers D2777/6, also M. Barry to O'Hagan, 14 Mar. 1862, ibid.; Revd Dr Coveny to O'Hagan, 24 Dec. [1862], and M. Barry to O'Hagan, 20 Mar. 1862, ibid. Cash transcended religion, for, as R. M. O'Ferrall, MP told Archbishop Cullen (27 Nov. 1862, Cullen Papers) neither Protestants nor Catholics would vote for O'Hagan without money.

Patterns of Change and Continuity

the 130) votes, a bloc rivalled only by that of Captain Heard, local landowner and himself Member for the borough between 1852 and 1859. By 1862, however, Arnott's failure to redeem the pledge which had formed the brightest jewel of his electoral crown—the promise to build a waterworks to realize 'the expectations of the Kinsale folk by supplying them with fresh water for their tea'—was encouraging rumours of financial distress.[1] O'Hagan's attraction to local political chiefs lay in his holding office. Kinsale desired a trans-atlantic telegraph station, 'and through this', O'Hagan was told, 'you will be a more useful member particularly in advancing local interest (*and to this we all turn our eyes*), being a member of the govern-ment . . . All other considerations are as nothing when there is a probability of such a thing . . . being obtained.' But O'Hagan had little money of his own, and was obliged to decamp when Arnott made resignation conditional upon the payment of 'a large portion of the cost' of the waterworks promised three years before.[2]

The Attorney-General's subsequent peregrinations must have induced a strong sense of *déjà vu*. Inquiries at Ennis revealed that a third of the voters 'would yield to the influence that may be most powerfully brought to bear' and that the sitting Member, another ostensible 'Liberal', could, as 'a native and constant resident', rely on 'relatives, who are numerous and influential [to] . . . secure for him the Conservative votes'. Eventually O'Hagan came to rest at Tralee, where, 'as a matter of course, government money' and patronage would 'have something to do' with the result and where enfranchised Protestant bootmakers and Catholic grocers unitedly demanded tide-waiterships and postal positions for friends and relatives.[3] O'Hagan was more fortunate here. The sitting Member, Daniel O'Connell (the Liberator's youngest son), resigned in return for an Inland Revenue commissionership and 'bequeathed' the support 'inherited' in 1853 from his brother, Maurice, which included that of important bodies such as the Tralee Chamber of Commerce.

[1] See list referred to in note 2 page 451 above—comments written against the names of voters include 'Will go with the crowd', 'Can be induced to go any way'. Heard had helped build a bridge across the Bandon River, something which had once 'been the battle-cry at every contested election' (O'Donnell to O'Hagan, 5 Jan. 1863, O'Hagan Papers D2777/6). See also Keenan to O'Hagan, 19 Dec. 1862, ibid.

[2] O'Donnell to O'Hagan, 22 Oct. 1862, and Coveny to O'Hagan, [early 1863], ibid. A few years later Lord Dunkellin, Member for Galway, was afraid his constituents would dis-cover his having refused office and thus denied them the services of one 'who they think might have patronage at his disposal' (to W. H. Gregory, 26 Jan. [1865], Clanricarde Papers 109).

[3] J. Kenny to Dr Carolly, [1863], O'Hagan Papers D2777/6; Cullen to Myles O'Reilly, MP, 12 May 1863, O'Reilly Papers MS 17886; E. Murphy to Naas, 6 Apr. 1859, Mayo Papers MS 11036. In 1852 party agents had been 'bribing in the market-place at noonday' (G. H. Kinderley to Naas, 31 July 1852, ibid. MS 11019).

As a result, after pledges that 'no influence which my position . . . can enable me to exert will be wanting the advocacy of the claims to enforce the rights of [Tralee's] . . . port and people' and an address entirely concerned with local issues, O'Hagan was returned un-opposed.[1]

That most boroughs shared—to a greater or lesser extent—the politics of Kinsale, Ennis, and Tralee is a matter not open to statistical proof: only examples can make the point. Waterford in 1852 was 'split' into so many factions pursuing 'each other with invincible hatred' that party labels became meaningless. Powerful blocs, such as publicans fearful of Sunday closing, ignored the supposedly key issues of land and disestablishment.[2] Non-electors too formed pressure groups to squeeze purses, and the conciliation of 'a horny-handed body of quay-porters and pigstickers' was essential if violence was to be avoided. Once crossed, the Waterford mob was promiscuous in its vengeance, attacking in one grand riot the supporters of the successful Gladstonian Liberal, a Dominican Convent, and St Olave's Protestant church. Even at Belfast rioters smashed denominational buildings with ecumenical abandon.[3] At Lisburn, after 'the men of business and shopkeepers' had been asked to ponder carefully 'what would be the result if the name of Richardson were blotted out from the map of the locality' and the £40,000 expended by that candidate's family withdrawn, the election concluded with a riot in which Orangemen and Catholics joined in brotherly amity to crack the skulls of victims chosen according to strictly non-sectarian principles. Sligo too was 'split up into little streets each having their own candidate', so that 'political principles' formed 'no part of the qualification . . . If the gentleman . . . be a good financier, well versed in the quick calculation of pounds, shillings, and pence . . . it matters little what his political principles are.'[4] In 1865 Major Knox of the Protestant *Irish Times* appeared with the qualified blessings of Archbishop Cullen, who recommended him on the (presumably sufficient) ground that he had 'been kind to the poor'. But his 'Liberal'

---

[1] *Nation*, 10 Apr. 1852; O'Hagan to R. Donovan (Chairman of Tralee town commissioners), and O'Hagan's Address of 9 May 1863, both O'Hagan Papers D2777/6. The Donovans were a powerful Tralee merchant family whose support O'Hagan had obtained.

[2] Bishop O'Brien to Cullen, 7 June 1852, Cullen Papers; T. Meagher to —, [1852], ibid.; G. Commins, CC, to Revd T. Kirby, 25 Sept. 1868, Kirby Papers 1868(283); M. O'Reilly to Cullen, 21 Nov. 1868, Cullen Papers.

[3] P. H. Bagenal, *The Life of Ralph Bernal Osborne M.P.* (London, 1884), pp. 261, 267, 285. The same Belfast mob attacked the Methodist Chapel and that of Revd Hugh Hanna (a leading Presbyterian anti-papist) and was only prevented by the police from assaulting St Patrick's Catholic Chapel (*Banner of Ulster*, 4 Apr. 1857).

[4] *Banner of Ulster*, 21 Mar., 4 Apr. 1857; T. Mostyn to [J. Whiteside], 14 Apr. 1859, Mayo Papers MS 11036; *Drogheda Argus*, 30 Apr. 1859.

opponent, Serjeant Armstrong, eventually topped the poll after issuing an address so 'vague' in all but its repeated references to the town's 'quays and fisheries', that, in the words of the local bishop, it could 'mean anything or nothing'.[1] At Youghal, prosperous Tories were happy to ally themselves with the Duke of Devonshire's Whig interest to see 'the Protestant operative section put down who have . . . not in their opinion [advanced] . . . the interests of the town', and the citizens' pragmatic aspirations responded enthusiastically to the wealthy Catholic, Joseph McKenna, who reminded them that 'he could give situations to all the young men in the town' and had persuaded the Government to pass a special act freeing Youghal Bridge from its traditional tolls.[2]

Dungarvan followed equally eclectic lines, though there the parish priest (the extraordinary Fr. Halley) had made himself indispensable by the opportunist manœuvrings of a small faction devoted to him by ties of kinship, sympathy, and dependence. After some free-wheeling preliminaries in the 1840s (which involved extracting large sums of money from the Duke of Devonshire's agents, in part to rebuild and redecorate the Halley residence),[3] he pursued a breath-taking course, supporting now Whigs, now Tories, now Independent Oppositionists. Amidst the enthusiastic local game of political musical chairs, Halley retained a central importance.[4] In 1857 he abandoned Devonshire and was roundly abused by His Grace's agent, only to be wooed again in 1859, when, however, he secured the return of a pro-Tory Independent by means of an alliance with the Conservatives arranged personally with the Chief Secretary himself.[5] All good things, however, come to an end, and eventually Halley's

[1] Cullen to Gillooly, 14 July 1865, Gillooly Papers Section B; Gillooly to Armstrong, 2 Aug. 1865, and Armstrong to Gillooly, 4 Aug. 1865, ibid. Section C; *D.E.P.* 11 July 1865.

[2] F. E. to W. Currey, 11 July 1851, 3 July 1863, Lismore Papers MSS 7186, 7190; J. I. Barry to I. Butt, 28 May 1865, Butt Papers MS 8687; *Tablet*, 5 Sept. 1868. In 1868 McKenna was only defeated because opposed by an even more open-pursed opponent (C. Wegeulin to Butt, 30 Dec. [1868], Butt Papers MS 8710). For the political atmosphere of Youghal in an earlier period, see Ann Barry and K. T. Hoppen, 'Borough politics in O'Connellite Ireland: The Youghal poll books of 1835 and 1837', *Journal of the Cork Historical and Archaeological Society*, lxxxiii (1978), 106–46, and lxxxiv (1979), 15–43.

[3] The saga is laid bare in F. E. to B. Currey, 16 July 1843, 26 Oct. 1844, Lismore Papers MS 7183/1; F. E. to E. Currey, 4 Apr. 1848, ibid. MS 7183/2; F. E. to W. Currey, 5 Sept. 1859, ibid. MS 7190.

[4] F. E. to W. Currey, 13 May 1852, ibid. MS 7191; F. E. Currey to F. J. Howard, 29 Mar. 1857, ibid. MS 7191; F. E. Currey to Duke of Devonshire, 22 Apr. 1859, ibid. MS 7190. See also *C.C.* 17, 31 Mar. 1857, 12, 21 Apr. 1859, 24 June, 7 July 1865.

[5] F. E. to W. Currey, 4 Apr. 1857, 10 Apr. 1859, Lismore Papers MSS 7188, 7190; also Revd J. Halley to Naas, 28 Nov. 1858, Mayo Papers MS 11023 (in which Halley refers to their recent 'familiar chat' and expects that in the event of an election 'you and I will be able to manage things'); Halley to Naas, 15 Apr. 1859, ibid. MS 11036; J. F. Maguire to Disraeli, 4 Apr. 1859, Hughenden Papers B/XXI/M/69.

nimble footwork faltered. In 1868 he supported Serjeant Barry, unpopular for his small alcoholic capacity and his prosecution of the Fenian prisoners. To the end Halley's predilections were determined by anything save general principles and in this case sprang largely from jealousy of the local Augustinian friars (competitors for the money of the faithful), whose prior was hot for the Tory candidate. Halley devoted sermon after sermon to lashing the Augustinians and their lay confraternity of 'belted knights'.[1] But anger led him into error and allowed the Dungarvan Conservatives to achieve a remarkable and overwhelming victory.

Personality clashes were of central importance so long as contests were seen as forums for the settling of scores or as levers for the prising of gain and position. The intimacy of many constituencies produced a heightening of tension. At Kinsale one side thought its letters were being opened by an antagonistic postal official. At Athenry the station-master gossiped about an indiscreet telegraph —'How are you off for soap? If required, lay it on thick'—from Lord Clanricarde to a candidate. In 1868 the parish priest of Enniskillen threatened to withdraw support from the Liberal candidate after a row with the man's brother.[2] The Louth by-election of 1854 produced public confrontations: one between two priests which involved repeated shouts of 'Who stole the bond?', a second at Mass when another two almost came to blows at the altar.[3] Lord Sligo refused to support the Liberal at Mayo in 1850 because the candidate had once fought a duel with one of his relatives. The Tories in Sligo were badly split 'by an unfortunate jealousy between the Booths and Gores'. At Longford, Henry Hughes was forced to retire because, though a Catholic, he had brought up his daughter as a Protestant, and so strong was 'the feeling of the laity' (for which Bishop Kilduff felt moved to 'thank and bless my God') that his hopes of re-election were shattered.[4] The first Limerick City by-election of 1858 was declared invalid because of the intimidation resulting from deep divisions among the clergy, the sole cause of which lay in 'Father Butler having been made dean. This fact created immense soreness on the part of those who thought themselves better entitled to such a dignity.'[5]

[1] Revd M. Crean (Augustinian provincial) to Cullen, 6 Nov. 1868, Cullen Papers; Bishop O'Brien to Cullen, 9 Nov. 1868, ibid.

[2] H. E. O'Donnell to O'Hagan, 10 Jan. 1863, O'Hagan Papers D2777/6; P. F. French to J. Blake, 30 Aug. 1857, Blake of Ballyglunin Papers M6935/33; Revd P. F. Moran to Cullen, 19 Oct. 1868, Cullen Papers (Secretaries' File).

[3] Dean Kieran to Archbishop Dixon, 12, 30 Mar. 1854, Dixon Papers VII.

[4] Lord Oranmore to Clarendon, 16 July [1850], Clarendon Papers Box 21; Naas to Derby, 31 July 1852, Derby Papers 155/1; Bishop Kilduff to Cullen, 29 Mar. 1857, Cullen Papers.

[5] D. Griffin to Lord Dunraven, 29 Jan. 1858, Dunraven Papers D3196/F/5/3.

Thus were elections and politics during the 1850s and 1860s shaped by considerations more pragmatic than ideological. The relationship between 'brokers' and 'clients' more often than not determined the outcome. At Carrickfergus one candidate obtained the support of the enfranchised fishermen solely because he had fought a legal battle of their behalf. The Governor of Sligo gaol told a member of the board of superintendence that, 'as you feel interested for Major Knox, I will abstain from voting for Captain Flanagan'. At New Ross the Liberals came within two votes of upsetting Tory hegemony only because their candidate was manager of the National Bank, a position giving 'a large amount of local influence'. The strongest ties of all were those of kinship, so that at Bandon the 'Sullivans' alone would, it was estimated in 1863, give T. K. Sullivan 'a phalanx'.[1]

II MODERNIZATION

What is perhaps most surprising about the strong localism of mid-century Irish politics is its temporal coincidence with that set of changes normally included under the heading of 'modernization'. In broadly cultural terms Ireland was becoming an increasingly modern and homogeneous society. Yet this development was never easily or permanently translatable into nationally coherent and homogeneous political action.

The connected phenomena of literacy and education recorded remarkable upswings in all parts of the country. Increases after 1841 in the percentage of those aged five and over who were able to read and of those aged six to fifteen actually attending various schools mark the creation of a new society far more open than before to the influence of the printed word (Table 52). By 1881 little more than a sixth of the population could speak Irish and most of these were concentrated in parts of Munster and Connacht, though even in the latter province the proportion was already substantially less than half. The many pre-Famine instances of monoglot Irish-speaking witnesses before election committees needing interpreters or of references to voters unable to understand English greatly declined after 1850 and became confined exclusively to the constituencies of the extreme west.[2] The fact that almost all agrarian threatening notices

[1] *Banner of Ulster*, 14 Mar. 1857; E. Walsh to C. W. O'Hara, 13 Nov. 1868, O'Hara Papers MS 20348; *C.C.* 2 June, 25 Feb. 1863.
[2] See, e.g., Lord Rossmore to Lord Plunkett, [Feb. 1833], Rossmore Papers T2929/7/32; J. W. Knapp and E. Ombler, *Cases of controverted elections in the twelfth parliament of the United Kingdom* (London, 1837), p. 393; *Fictitious Votes, Ireland*, 2nd series, 1st report, p. 15; ibid. 2nd series, 3rd report, p. 77; *Minutes of the proceedings of the select*

had already by 1852 long been written in English is strong evidence
of the utilitarian pressures for linguistic change.[1]

TABLE 52

*Percentages able to read and attending school by provinces,
1841, 1861, 1881*

| | Able to read | | | Attending school | | |
	1841	1861	1881	1841	1861	1881
Leinster	56.0	68.9	79.7	29.8	41.0	63.4
Munster	39.4	53.9	71.5	28.4	41.1	66.3
Ulster	59.4	70.0	79.7	22.9	33.2	52.0
Connacht	27.9	42.9	62.1	14.2	27.2	45.4
Ireland	47.3	61.3	74.8	24.4	36.1	57.1

It was this increasingly Anglicized and literate society which provided the growing audience for newspapers of all kinds. Between
1831 and 1887 the number of titles issued rose from about 71 to
162—the number of dailies from a mere three to nineteen—and
this for a population that had fallen from almost eight to less than
five million. Connacht had ten papers in 1831; twenty in 1869.
Between 1831 and 1854 (the last year for which figures are available)
the number of newspaper stamps sold annually increased from 0.56
to 1.48 per person. Although all political persuasions found themselves more than amply catered for, the strong numerical survival of
the Conservative press is perhaps especially remarkable. Excluding
those papers with no obvious party affiliation, the relative strengths
of the Nationalist/Liberal press, on the one hand, and the Conservative press, on the other, remained more or less stable. Exactly half
the 'political' papers in 1834 were Tory, about 55 per cent in 1853
and about 47 per cent in 1870. The total number of stamps sold
to regular newspapers in 1853 can be divided into 867,000 to
'neutral', 2,806,385 to Nationalist/Liberal, and 2,550,325 to Conservative papers. The press must, therefore, be seen not simply as the
engine of nationalist opinion, but as the reinforcer as much as the
creator of the tribal political loyalties and identities of Irish society
in general. Indeed, what it was most successful in disseminating was

committee on the Cork County election petition, and of the evidence taken before them,
H.C. 1842 (271), vi, 55-60; *Minutes of evidence taken before the select committee on the
Clare election petition,* H.C. 1852-3 (595), ix, 673-6; *Telegraph or Connaught Ranger,*
24 Feb. 1858; *Minutes of evidence taken before the select committee on the Clare election
petition,* H.C. 1860 (178), xi, 105, 123-4.

[1] *Report from the select committee on Outrages (Ireland),* H.C. 1852 (438), xiv, Qs.
129-30.

not so much nationalism as the metropolitan culture of Dublin and indirectly that of London too. Thus, while only seventeen of the eighty-nine newspapers being published in 1853 were produced in the Irish capital, these seventeen between them sold over 55 per cent of all the individual issues bought in the country as a whole.[1]

The very low individual circulations of the 1830s grew steadily, especially in the case of the national press, for local papers often remained content with sales of less than a thousand. By the 1840s and 1850s the *Nation* (with a staff of twenty-eight) was selling between 4,000 and 7,000, by 1859 the *Freeman's Journal* probably about 8,500, by 1882 Parnell's organ *United Ireland* possibly as many as 44,000.[2] Although many copies were read by more than one person (the *Freeman* claimed an average of four)—indeed the tableau of the literate radical reading publicly to his unlettered neighbours was almost as common in reality as in myth—the actual purchasers of papers as different as the *Nation* and the *Galway Vindicator* seem to have been predominantly shopkeepers and the more prosperous farmers.[3] Of course in some places papers as well as books were also sporadically available to those prepared to pay subscriptions for the use of reading rooms. But such institutions were usually short-lived and were neither as successful nor as nationalist in flavour as has sometimes been supposed. The Repeal reading room in Ennis, for example, proved a very transient phenomenon, that

[1] The various statistics in the above passage have been taken or calculated from: MS 'List of Newspapers published in Ireland' of 1834, Melbourne Papers 103/37 (for party affiliations); R. M. Martin, *Ireland before and after the Union with Great Britain*, 2nd edn. (London, 1848), frontispiece and p. xv; *Thom 1870*, pp. 1242, 1275, *Thom 1888*, pp. xlviii, 1292 (number of papers), and *Thom 1859*, p. 586 (stamps in 1854); *A Return of the number of newspaper stamps at one penny issued to newspapers in England, Ireland, Scotland, and Wales for the years 1851, 1852, 1853*, H.C. 1854 (117), xxxix; C. Mitchell, *The Newspaper press directory for 1854* (London, [1854]), and *for 1871* (London, [1871]) —for party affiliations. Of course the number of stamps sold gives only a rough indication of circulation, though A. P. Wadsworth ('Newspaper Circulations, 1800–1954', *Manchester Statistical Society* (1965), 1–40) thinks the figures reasonably accurate after 1836.

[2] *A Return of the number of newspaper stamps at one penny issued to the under-mentioned newspapers in England, Ireland, Scotland, and Wales from the year 1837 to the year 1850*, H.C. 1852 (42), xxviii, and . . . *for the years 1851, 1852, 1853*, H.C. 1854 (117), xxxix; Clarendon to Russell, 25 Sept. 1847, Clarendon Papers L.-B. II; *Nation*, 14 Feb. 1852; *Freeman's Journal*, 25 Apr. 1859; 'Strictly Confidential: *United Ireland*' (1882), Harcourt Papers 106.

[3] *Freeman's Journal*, 25 Apr. 1859; paper on newspaper circulation in Waterford, 1 Mar. 1848, Clarendon Papers Box 76; Evidence of Galway editors in *Galway County election petition*, H.C. 1872 (241-I), xlviii, 438–40, 448, 473–4. For public readings etc., see P. O'Donoghue, 'Opposition to Tithe Payments in 1830–31', *Studia Hibernica*, No. 6 (1966), 84; W. to C. Hogan, 4 Mar. 1848, Clarendon Papers Box 23; R. Kee, *The Green Flag: A History of Irish Nationalism* (London, 1972), pp. 194–5; also Henry MacManus's painting *Reading 'The Nation'* now in the National Gallery of Ireland (reproduced in Jeanne Sheehy, *The Rediscovery of Ireland's Past: The Celtic Revival 1830–1930* (London, 1980), p. 35).

in Carlow was more Liberal than O'Connellite, those in Tallow and Youghal survived largely on Whiggish hand-outs from the Duke of Devonshire.[1] The Kilrush Literary and Scientific Society was kitted out in 1852 by the violently Tory Colonel Vandeleur. The Literary Institute established in Donegal Town in 1853 was supervised by a high-minded local landlord. The reading rooms of the Limerick, Clonmel, and Galway Mechanics' Institutes were biased towards self-improving literature of a Smilesian nature, while Bishop Gillooly manfully saw to it that the reading room of the Catholic Young Men's Society at Boyle in Co. Roscommon was entirely 'free from political or any other feeling'.[2]

By about 1870, however, most towns of any size, such as Tralee, Cavan, or Enniskillen, were capable of supporting two or three newspapers to cater for the various political persuasions present in the local community. Newsagent shops were beginning to appear (hitherto Irish papers had been sold largely by subscription or by street vendors). Ten years later the literate readership had expanded to encompass farmers and labourers in third-class railway carriages not excluding, according to a travelling American physiognomist, either 'rather ragged-looking individuals' or 'even those who looked the least intelligent'.[3] The lack of printed material in the Irish language meant that the popular reading available even in the early years of the century was entirely in English. Pre-Famine commentators such as Hely Dutton, Edward Wakefield, Crofton Croker, W. M. Thackeray, and Mr and Mrs Hall all noticed the widespread diffusion of demotic evergreens like 'The History of Irish Rogues and Rapparees', 'The Life of Captain Freeny Highwayman', and 'The History of Witches and Apparitions'. By the early 1840s, however, the Halls in particular were already convinced that 'a vast improvement in this respect has taken place'. What in fact was happening was that the path was being cleared for the respectable politico-historical productions of the Young Ireland school and its successors.[4] Just as the

---

[1] T. Kelly, 'Ennis in the nineteenth century', p. 208; *Minutes of evidence taken before the committee on the Carlow County election petition*, H.C. 1837 (307), x, 91; F. E. to W. Currey, 14 Apr. 1851, Lismore Papers MS 7186—on Tallow in 1838 and Youghal in 1851.

[2] *Nation*, 10 July 1852 (Kilrush); *Sixty years' experience as an Irish landlord: Memoirs of John Hamilton D.L. of St. Ernan's Donegal*, ed. H. C. White (London, [1894]), p. 285; *Galway Vindicator*, 30 June 1852 (Mechanics' Institutes); *D.E.P.* 24 July 1865 (Boyle).

[3] J. Macaulay, *Ireland in 1872*, pp. 321-2; D. B. King, *The Irish Question* (London, 1882), p. 293. It would, however, be wrong to ignore the fact that many late-nineteenth-century households rarely if ever saw a newspaper (Folklore Commission MS 1209; C. Ó Danachair, 'The death of a tradition', *Studies*, lxiv (1964), 229).

[4] H. Dutton, *Statistical Survey of the County of Clare* (Dublin, 1808), pp. 235-7; E. Wakefield, *An Account of Ireland, Statistical and Political*, 2 vols. (London, 1812), ii, 400; T. C. Croker, *Researches in the South of Ireland* (London, 1824), p. 55;

ballads of the second half of the century were gradually laundered of their earlier anarchic vigour, so the popular reading which was to become increasingly available through outlets such as railway station bookstalls was either entirely English in origin or the product of the new 'Irish National Reading' movement—earnest, patriotic, and ideologically nationalist.[1] Naturally the older favourites lingered on—small Cavan farmers in the third quarter of the century were still reading 'The Life of Quickset'[2]—but the dominant tone had undoubtedly changed. By the early 1880s a well-informed observer was struck by the ubiquity in rural cottages of cheap editions of the prose and poetry of writers such as T. D. Sullivan, Kickham, Davis, Downey, and the like. Threepenny and sixpenny nationalist song books were, he believed, circulating far more extensively than James Duffy's earlier 'Irish Library' had done. Catholic Young Men's reading rooms were stuffed full of the works of A. M. Sullivan, Gavan Duffy, John Mitchel, and Wolfe Tone. They were also, like the extensive network of Land League rooms, attracting far more readers than had ever been prepared to visit the Repeal rooms of the 1840s.[3]

People were not only becoming more literate, but more financially sophisticated as well. This too had the effect of helping to connect not only more parts of the country but also more sections of society to a single national economic network. Banks greatly increased their activities throughout the period. The number of full branches rose from 140 in 1839[4] to 179 in 1859 and 404 in 1879. By 1879 many sub-branches (for which earlier details are lacking) had also been established, and banking provisions had become widely available in all parts of the country, not excluding the west (Table 53). The number of places with banking facilities rose from 90 to 322 between 1845 and 1883. Already by the mid-1870s Ireland's branch network was, on a per capita basis, comparable with that of England and Wales (though not with that of Scotland).[5] Indeed, visitors were

W. M. Thackeray, *The Irish Sketch Book of 1842*, pp. 153–68; Mr and Mrs S. C. Hall, *Ireland: Its Scenery, Character etc.*, 3 vols. (London, 1841–3), ii, 363–4.

[1] See Chapter V, section VI above for ballads; also J. Macaulay, *Ireland in 1872*, p. 322; M. Murphy, 'The Ballad Singer and the role of the Seditious Ballad in nineteenth-century Ireland: Dublin Castle's View', *Ulster Folklife*, xxv (1979), 92.

[2] Folklore Commission MS 1209.

[3] J. Pope Hennessy, 'What do the Irish read?', *The Nineteenth Century*, xv (1884), 920–32.

[4] G. L. Barrow, *The emergence of the Irish banking system 1820–1845* (Dublin, 1975), Appendix 3.

[5] Ibid. (for 1845); J. Dick, 'Banking Statistics: A record of nine years' progress: 1874 to 1883', *Journal of the Institute of Bankers*, v (1884), 347 (for 1883); W. Newmarch, 'The increase in the number of banks and branches in the metropolis: the English counties: Scotland and Ireland, during the twenty years 1858–1878' in *The Banking Almanac, Directory, Year Book, and Diary for 1880* (London, [1880]), pp. 425–48.

TABLE 53

Bank branches per 100,000 people by provinces, 1859 and 1879

	1859	1879	
	Full branches	Full branches	All branches
Leinster	2.8	7.8	9.5
Munster	3.2	8.7	9.7
Ulster	3.8	8.0	12.9
Connacht	1.8	6.0	9.3
Ireland	3.1	7.8	10.6

often surprised by the number of branches 'in pettifogging places like Kilrush or Ennistymon—mere hamlets of some two thousand inhabitants'. As a result, the 'use of money [became] better understood by the rural population' throughout the country.[1] Bank-note circulation increased from about eighteen shillings per person in 1846 to thirty shillings in 1876, while deposits in joint-stock, trustee, and (from 1862) post office banks underwent a dramatic growth from an average of about twenty-three shillings per person in 1841-5 to sixty-one shillings in 1861-5 and 139 shillings in 1881-5.[2] Whatever may or may not have been the case concerning Ireland's supposedly 'dual' pre-Famine economy, there can be no doubt that developments such as these profoundly changed the financial environment of towns and countryside alike.

The simultaneous extension and improvement of transport facilities helped to change men's consciousness of distance and of place. Between 1849 and 1879 the number of miles of railway track rose from 428 to 2,285 and the passengers carried from 6,056,947 to 16,402,397 or from 0.8 to 3.1 per head of population.[3] While in 1840 the Dublin to Belfast coach had taken twelve hours at a cost of fifteen shillings outside, by 1857 the train could do the journey in five hours for nine shillings and four pence second class. Already in 1852 the absentee Cork landowner, Sir John Benn-Walsh, was able to travel from London to his estates in forty-eight hours, something which had taken him seven days or more in 1821.[4] Costs were

[1] B. H. Becker, *Disturbed Ireland*, p. 210; J. Macaulay, *Ireland in 1872*, pp. 26-7.

[2] *Thom 1859*, p. 594; T. W. Grimshaw, *Facts and Figures about Ireland Part I* (Dublin, 1893), p. 43. For certain problems connected with the joint-stock deposit figures, which may not be entirely comparable before and after 1845, see G. L. Barrow, *The emergence of the Irish banking system*, pp. 186-7.

[3] *Thom 1916*, p. 811. Passenger and goods *receipts* rose from £290,604 to £1,360,258 and from £127,462 to £1,212,677 respectively.

[4] K. B. Nowlan, 'Communications' in *Ulster since 1800 Second Series: A Social Survey*,

greatly reduced, especially for the poor who travelled mainly by special trains on market days. And even if at first most people saw the inside of a train little more than once or twice a year,[1] that alone was something new, while the increased number of travellers able to visit the various parts of the country must have reduced the isolation of the remoter areas. A wider set of family and business contacts was also made possible by the enormous extension of postal services. The amount of postal revenue taken in Ennis, for example, tripled in the decade after 1841, while by 1855 letters dispatched from London regularly reached Cork within little more than twenty-four hours.[2] The average annual number of letters posted per head of the population rose from 2.9 in the period 1841-5 to 17.3 in 1881-5, by which time large numbers of packets and postcards were also being sent. By the 1870s newspapers had been granted special tele-graphic rates, and Parnell, for example, was an eager customer of the telegraph service, which in 1880 alone transmitted no less than one and a half million telegrams.[3]

Although, therefore, there can be little doubt that Ireland remained until the end of the century and beyond a country in which even quite short distances could separate the consciousness of men— indeed the ties between Connemara and Boston were probably closer than between Connemara and Donegal—horizons had begun to broaden and geographical perceptions to change. The proportion of the population *not* living in their counties of birth rose from a twentieth in 1841 to more than a tenth in 1881.[4] The gradual replacement of markets by fairs extended the geographical range of those attending, and fair days provided prime opportunities for political as well as social discourse.[5] The decline of ecclesiastical stations extended the neighbourhood unit to encompass the whole of the many very large parishes into which Ireland was divided,

---

ed. T. W. Moody and J. C. Beckett (London, 1957), pp. 138-47; 'The Journals of Sir John Benn-Walsh relating to the management of his Irish estates, 1823-64', ed. J. S. Donnelly Jr., *Journal of the Cork Historical and Archaeological Society*, lxx (1974), 120.

[1] J. Lee, 'The Railways in the Irish Economy', p. 79.

[2] T. Kelly, 'Ennis in the nineteenth century', p. 174; *Report from the select committee on Postal Arrangements (Waterford etc.)*, H.C. 1854-5 (445), xi, 432 (evidence of Anthony Trollope).

[3] T. W. Grimshaw, *Facts and Figures about Ireland Part I*, p. 52; B. R. Mitchell and H. G. Jones, *Second Abstract of British Historical Statistics* (Cambridge, 1971), pp. 109-12.

[4] Calculated from the county statistics in *Thom 1916*, pp. 1127-330. The number of counties with more than a tenth of their residents born elsewhere in Ireland rose from two in 1841 to sixteen in 1881.

[5] T. W. Freeman, 'The Irish country town', pp. 5-14, and J. P. Haughton, 'The live-stock fair in relation to Irish country towns', *Irish Geography*, iii (1955), 109-11; *Longford election petition*, H.C. 1870 (178), lvi, 530-3, and *Galway County election petition*, H.C. 1872 (241-I), xlviii, 137.

a tendency reinforced by the parochial basis of O'Connell's organizations, and, much later, by the 'parish rule' of the Gaelic Athletic Association. And although baronies had never been seen as areas of regional consciousness, yet the GAA's encouragement of inter-county hurling and football matches did much to extend the horizons of loyalty.[1] Naturally this was a slow business. As late as 1880 quite well-to-do farmers from counties such as Kilkenny and Waterford proved themselves staunchly ignorant of anything much beyond the next hill.[2] But the Ireland of pre-Famine times, in which 'different districts' were 'almost as unlike each other as any two countries in Europe' and in which disappointed nationalists could in the 1840s come upon parts of Cork, Kerry, Leitrim, and Sligo where the very name of O'Connell was almost unknown, was inexorably passing away.[3] The same tendency can be seen in the manner in which diet and dress became increasingly dependent upon retail purchase, and, as a result, more standardized. In the 1830s and 1840s it still seems to have been the case that men and women from counties like Kildare and Cork, Limerick and Kerry, Galway and Antrim, could be recognized by their particular apparel, and that within large counties like Cork internal variations were also maintained.[4] And just as these differences became submerged under the increasing tide of manufactured cloth and ready-made clothes, so did imported tea, sugar, and tobacco, mass-produced white bread, and other manufactured foods align Irish diet more closely with that of modern cosmopolitan society as a whole.[5] Less ambiguous an improvement was the virtual disappearance of the pre-Famine mud cabin and the betterment in

[1] W. J. Smyth, 'Continuity and Change in the territorial organization of Irish rural communities (Part II)', *Maynooth Review*, No. 2 (1975), 60-2, 66; *Report from the select committee on Bribery at Elections*, H.C. 1835 (547), viii, 300; T. Jones Hughes, 'Administrative divisions and the development of settlement in nineteenth-century Ireland', *University Review* [Dublin], iii (1962-3), 10; D. Greene, 'Michael Cusack and the rise of the G.A.A.' in *The Shaping of Modern Ireland*, ed. C. C. O'Brien (London, 1960), pp. 80-1.

[2] See, e.g., *Minutes of evidence taken before Her Majesty's Commissioners on Agriculture*, H.C. 1881 [C 2778-I], xv, 515, 529-30.

[3] T. N. Brown, 'Nationalism and the Irish Peasant, 1800-1848', *Review of Politics*, xv (1953), 403, 434.

[4] T. C. Croker, *Researches in the South of Ireland*, p. 221; J. Barrow, *A Tour round Ireland*, p. 261; *Minutes of evidence taken before the select committee of the House of Lords, appointed to inquire into the state of Ireland since the year 1835 in respect to Crime and Outrage*, H.C. 1839 (486), xi and xii, Q. 3792; *Cork County election petition*, H.C. 1842 (271), vi, Qs. 2909-11; L. Jones, 'Dress in nineteenth-century Ireland: An approach to research', *Folklife*, xvi (1978), 42-53.

[5] *Minutes of evidence taken before Her Majesty's Commissioners on Agriculture*, H.C. 1881 [C 2778-I], xv, 445, 495, 628-9, 671; A. I. Shand, *Letters from the west of Ireland 1884* (Edinburgh and London, 1885), pp. 35-6, 81-3, 166; G. Pellew, *In Castle and Cabin or talks in Ireland in 1887* (New York and London, 1888), pp. 232-9; C. Ó Danachair, 'The death of a tradition', p. 223; J. Lee, 'The Railways in the Irish Economy', p. 77; L. M. Cullen, *An economic history of Ireland since 1660*, p. 138.

housing conditions generally. The percentage of families accommodated in the two highest of the four categories of housing identified by the Irish census commissioners rose from 18.5 in 1841 to 56.7 in 1881, while the proportion of the housing stock classified as one-roomed mud cabins fell from 37 per cent to 5 per cent (50 per cent to 6 per cent in Connacht alone) over the same period.[1]

III MOBILIZATION

During the course of the 1860s Fenianism, however haltingly, was able to create a politics which offered an alternative to the localist idioms of the day. And it was through the awakening of a sentiment which saw beyond the boundaries of place and sectionalism and was at least articulated (though often not pursued) within a broader context, that the localism and particularism of the two post-Famine decades were for a time directed towards more national goals. Evidence of potentialities later to be more fully realized can be found in the occasional surfacings of Fenian sentiment in rural politics, as when at the declaration of the Co. Cork poll in 1861 Edward O'Sullivan hailed the return of a Conservative landlord as a triumph over corrupt Whiggery and condemned the hollowness of traditional agitation.

What good has it done? It has sent two millions and a half across the seas (renewed cheering) . . . If you have time and money, go home—buy arms—be prepared to show your arms when the time comes for Ireland's liberation . . . Do what I tell you—go home; buy arms; be ready when the time comes.[2]

Four years later, 'Three cheers for John O'Mahony and the Fenian Brotherhood' were given at a Co. Kilkenny election meeting, while John Blake Dillon was greeted in Tipperary with shouts of 'Dillon the '48 Renegade' and 'Go back to Paul Cullen'.[3]

The crucial politicization of the countryside came about in the late 1860s and during the 1870s and was something which the Fenians, despite doctrinaire refusals to develop an attractive agrarian policy, certainly helped to bring about. The ignominious defeat of

---

[1] *Thom 1870*, p. 786, and *Thom 1888*, p. 631; R. E. Matheson, 'The Housing of the people of Ireland during the period 1841–1901', *Journal of the Statistical and Social Inquiry Society of Ireland*, xi (1904), 196–212. The 'percentage of families accommodated' was calculated by adjusting for multiple occupation of the better houses and is a more realistic figure than that for houses only. Class 4 = mud cabins with only one room; Class 3 = better class of mud buildings with 2–4 rooms and windows; Class 2 = good farm houses (or, in towns, houses with 5–9 rooms and windows, in a side street); Class 1 = all houses of 'a better description'.

[2] *C.C.* 1 Mar. 1861.

[3] *Irish People*, 8, 15, 22 July 1865.

the rising of 1867 led paradoxically to a significant breakthrough in the shape of the Amnesty movement. The Liberal triumph of 1868 disguised a shift in the style of popular politics and the perceptive Lord Strathnairn, Commander of the Forces in Ireland, noted that 'The confederacy of the masses against the law in Ireland which extends to agrarian, religious, electioneering interests etc., were [*sic*] more violent in their action this last election than ever; and what were formerly violent election riots, are now a system of intimidation outrage with Fenian organization.'[1] The Amnesty movement achieved enormous public support in all parts of the country outside the north-east, and worried officials recognized that it represented a new phenomenon within the world of post-Famine politics, encompassing as it did almost all non-Conservative opinion from moderate Liberals to physical force revolutionaries. Almost all the Irish Liberal MPs returned in 1868 felt it wise to join the Amnesty Association, and poor-law boards in hitherto quiescent Mayo publicly supported the movement.[2] What was especially worrying was the large-scale involvement of the rural areas and the particular enthusiasm, in Co. Limerick for example, of the smaller farmers and the labourers.[3] The impact of the Amnesty Association, which between July and October 1869 alone held forty-eight meetings with a total estimated attendance of 638,000, produced a heightened consciousness.[4] No less than eight of these meetings took place in Tipperary and helped to create an atmosphere of excitement immediately before the by-election at which the Fenian prisoner, O'Donovan Rossa, defeated a Catholic Whig by 1,131 votes to 1,028. This was among the most significant contests of post-Famine Ireland and inaugurated a series of by-elections in the next three years which mobilized opinion into patterns increasingly remote from the fragmentation of the previous twenty years. The unusually low poll of 23 per cent reflected indifference to conventional politics. But the comparative vacuum enabled Fenianism to win an astonishing victory. Rossa's support varied enormously from one district to another. But

---

[1] Lord Strathnairn to A. C. Innes, 9 Jan. 1869, Strathnairn Papers Add. MS 42828.

[2] See Spencer to Gladstone, 30 Mar. 1869, Gladstone Papers Add. MS 44306; C. Fortescue to Gladstone, 12 Oct. 1869, ibid. Add. MS 44121; R. B. Osborne to Fortescue, 4 Nov. 1869, Carlingford Papers CP3/96; W. Monsell to Lord Granville, 7 Jan. 1869, and J. F. Maguire to Gladstone, 2 Aug. 1869, ibid. CP3/74, CP1/59; *Leinster Express*, 31 Jan. 1874 (on Liberal MPs in 1869); W. L. Feingold, 'The Irish boards of poor law guardians 1872–86', p. 103 (Mayo boards).

[3] Spencer to Gladstone, 18 Sept. 1869, Gladstone Papers Add. MS 44306; Strathnairn to Spencer, 26 Dec. [1869], Strathnairn Papers Add. MS 42826; Strathnairn to Knight of Kerry, 4 Feb. 1870, ibid. Add. MS 42829.

[4] P. O'Byrne to Butt, 1 Nov. 1869, Butt Papers MS 8691. These figures must be treated with caution. Attendances for two of the meetings are not given, and, if available, would increase the estimate.

the significance of the result lies in the fact that Rossa's *rural* strength outweighed his opponent's support among *town* voters. This happened at the Cashel polling station, while at Tipperary Town it was the 'comfortable farmers' of Clanwilliam Barony who gave Rossa an overwhelming majority of 497 to 10, despite the hostility of local priests.[1] Clearly the new politics were able to attract support, not only from labourers and small farmers, but also from the better-off sections of agricultural society, for, as was shown in Chapter I, all county voters were still required to occupy property with a valuation of twelve pounds or more and with in general, therefore, a minimum rental of not less than fifteen pounds a year. Rossa's victory was greeted by many substantial public demonstrations in traditionally militant counties such as Limerick and Tipperary itself as well as in the long-quiescent west—in Sligo, Clare, Kerry, and the cattle areas of east Galway where 'a strong party of stalwart men, including farmers and their sons, from the neighbourhood of Ballinasloe, Laurencetown, Kiltormer, and Eyrecourt' assembled in enthusiastic force.[2]

The Tipperary election also marks a move away from the personalized politics of the 1850s and 1860s when the patterning of the vote had usually been determined by estate or individual influence. Whereas, for example, the Co. Cork results of 1860 and 1861 had exhibited dramatic internal adjustments caused by shifts in proprietorial affiliations,[3] Rossa stood highest in exactly those areas where the 'popular' candidate had also done best three years before, while, even more significantly, the geographical distribution of his result was substantially duplicated the following year when his Fenian associate, Charles Kickham, fought the by-election caused by Rossa's own disqualification as a felon.[4]

Polling Stations	1869 percentage of vote to Rossa	1870 percentage of vote to Kickham
Tipperary	98.0	96.4
Thurles	73.2	52.0
Cashel	55.5	68.9
Clonmel	25.9	41.8
Nenagh	5.3	11.0

[1] J. Lee, *The Modernisation of Irish Society 1848–1918* (Dublin, 1973), pp. 118–19; *Freeman's Journal*, 29 Nov. 1869.
[2] *Daily Express*, 29 Nov. 1869.
[3] On Cork and other similar cases, see Chapter II, section IV above.
[4] S. H. Goold to Lady Donoughmore, [22 Oct. 1866], Mayo Papers MS 11144. For

The consequent breaking of the electoral log-jam was of great importance. During the three years after Rossa's victory a series of crucial by-elections took place in the counties of Tipperary (again), Longford (twice), Meath, Kerry, Galway, and in the heavily ruralized Cork City constituency. Nationalist candidates were victorious in the last four of these contests, all of which (save that at Cork City) were held *before* the introduction of the secret ballot.[1] Indeed, once a nationalist bandwagon had been started, public voting probably helped to persuade waverers to support the 'popular' cause.[2] A longer perspective even more clearly identifies the watershed nature of the politics of these years. The era of uncontested county returns was coming to an end. Whereas in the period from the 1852 General Election up to and including that of 1868 only 38.5 per cent of *all* county elections had gone to the polls, this figure rises to 69.9 per cent for the period beginning in 1869 and ending with the last by-election before the General Election of 1885.[3] Similarly, if one groups the general elections of 1865 and 1868, on the one hand, and those of 1874 and 1880, on the other, and apportions marks of one to each contested and zero to each uncontested county, the average 'score' rises from 0.5 (out of a maximum of 2.0) in the earlier period to 1.6 in the later. Fenians and their allies were certainly active in providing and organizing support for Nationalists contesting the by-elections of 1869–72,[4] and their arrival on the electoral scene marks not only an early foreshadowing of the New Departure but also a diminution in the influence of the Catholic clergy which had still seemed so powerful in 1868. The priests, reported one candidate, were 'afraid of the Fenian organization'. Another thought them 'afraid to oppose the popular feeling'.[5] A geographical breakdown of the Kerry vote in 1872 shows that the Protestant Home Ruler was able to gain over three-quarters of the vote at Cahirciveen,

the patterning of the votes, see *Freeman's Journal*, 29 Nov. 1869, and *Daily Express*, 28 Feb. 1870. Kickham was narrowly defeated by fourteen votes.

[1] Nationalists were also powerful enough to be returned unopposed for Westmeath and for the ruralized Limerick City constituency in 1871.

[2] See M. Hurst, 'Ireland and the Ballot Act of 1872', *Historical Journal*, viii (1965), 326–52. It is also significant that the important Nationalist capture of the poor-law boards after 1879 took place under an open voting system.

[3] See Chapter II, p. 169 above.

[4] See, e.g., Lord Granard to Cullen, 25 Dec. 1869, Cullen Papers; *Longford election petition*, H.C. 1870 (178), lvi, 506–7; Revd P. F. Moran to Revd T. Kirby, 17 Jan. 1871, Kirby Papers 1871(11A); Lord Kenmare to Lord Hartington, 14 Jan., 13 Feb. 1872, Devonshire Papers 340/483, 494; Bishop Moriarty to Hartington, 1 Feb. 1872, ibid. 340/491; B. Cahir, 'Irish National By-Elections 1870–1874' (University College Dublin MA thesis, 1965), p. 116; also Bishop Conroy of Ardagh to Cullen, 17 Oct. 1872, Cullen Papers.

[5] R. Osborne to C. Fortescue, 4 Nov. 1869, Carlingford Papers CP3/96; J. A. Dease to W. Monsell, 14 June 1871, Monsell Papers MS 8317.

despite strong clerical opposition and despite Bishop Moriarty's jeremiads to local 'farmers' to 'beware' lest they succumb to the rising agitation of 'labourers and servant boys'. Moriarty's defeated Whig candidate prophesied that there would 'be *very few* priests found at the next general election to *oppose* the extreme party. They will *pretend* to *lead*, in truth being *driven*.' The measure of the changes which had taken place can be seen in Co. Limerick. In January 1871 the Catholic Whig, William Monsell, had still been returned unopposed on the basis of localist references to charity work and railway extension.[1] Three years later he dared not even stand, and was lucky to obtain a peerage during the last dying days of Gladstone's administration.

Fenianism and the Amnesty agitation, seen in 1873 by the Viceroy, Lord Spencer, as the determinants of constituency mobilization,[2] were augmented electorally by the widespread dissatisfaction felt in many agrarian circles at Gladstone's feeble Land Act of 1870. Already in 1868-9 the former leader of the Independent Party had realized that 'we have a different people to fight with now from those of twenty years ago', while a knowledgeable land agent in Co. Clare had warned the Chief Secretary that the younger farmers —'far more intelligent and independent and educated in the national schools'—were becoming increasingly militant and would react badly if disappointed in their hopes for substantial reform.[3] In the event, Gladstone's Land Act attracted few admirers in the rural community.[4] And what was especially remarkable was how, within a few years, farmers of all sorts, prosperous as well as indigent, had rallied to the cause of Nationalist candidates in counties as different as Galway and Limerick.[5] At the same time the increasingly political tone adopted by the various Farmers' Clubs throughout the country helped lead the rural tenantry towards involvement with the new agitation. Societies and clubs for farmers had of course

[1] B. Ó Cathaoir [Cahir], 'The Kerry "Home Rule" by-election, 1872', *Journal of the Kerry Archaeological and Historical Society*, No. 3 (1970), 154–70; *Annual register . . . for the year 1872*, p. 12; J. A. Dease to W. Monsell, 25 Aug. 1872, Monsell Papers MS 8317; E. Curling to tenants on the Devon estate (Co. Limerick), 17 Jan. 1871, Dunraven Papers D3196.

[2] Memorandum on Home Rule, 22 Nov. 1873, Devonshire Papers 354/251.

[3] G. H. Moore to A. M. Sullivan, 25 Nov. 1868, Moore Papers MS 895; Memorandum by C. Fortescue of a conversation with Marcus Keane, 1 Oct. 1869, Gladstone Papers Add. MS 44121.

[4] See, e.g., M. J. Kenny to Gladstone, 20 Feb. 1870, Gladstone Papers Add. MS 44425; *Flag of Ireland*, 14 Jan. 1871; *Limerick Chronicle*, 5 Sept. 1871; D. Thornley, *Isaac Butt and Home Rule* (London, 1964), pp. 80–2; E. D. Steele, *Irish Land and British Politics: Tenant-Right and Nationality 1865–1870* (Cambridge, 1974), pp. 312–15.

[5] *Galway County election petition*, H.C. 1872 (241-I), xlviii, 627–32, 815; J. Elland to Butt, 7 Jan. 1874, Butt Papers MS 8696.

a long history, but until the late 1860s had been little more than social organizations concerned with conviviality and improvements in agricultural techniques. The 1870s, however, as Samuel Clark has shown, witnessed a dramatic increase in both the number and politicization of the Farmers' Clubs. Indeed, the movement was if anything even more widespread than he suggests, for among the clubs represented at the National Land Conference in January 1875 were at least eleven not included in his list of thirty clubs active between then and 1878.[1] And although Clark is almost certainly correct in seeing the membership largely in terms of men holding thirty acres or more, there is some evidence that in Limerick, for example, even labourers were not entirely excluded from club activities, while the joint support afforded to Isaac Butt's candidacy for Limerick in 1871 by the Limerick Farmers' Club and the Kanturk Labourers' Club of Co. Cork implies at least sporadic willingness to cross the social divide. At the same time the fact that labourers seem to have been as dissatisfied with the Land Act as farmers helped to prepare the way for the closer solidarity of the Land War years.[2] The clubs performed a number of functions important to the new politics of the 1870s. They kept the Home Rule movement's interest in land reform alive; they helped to increase the political awareness of the farming community; and, by their involvement in electoral activity, prepared the ground for the more dramatic politico-agrarian alliance of Davitt and Parnell. Already in 1868 the Co. Cork Club had debated the merits of rival parliamentary candidates. At the 1871 by-election in Limerick the Farmers' Club, disgruntled by Gladstone's Land Act, helped to secure Butt's unopposed return. A year later, Blennerhassett was first adopted by the North Kerry Farmers' Club, while at Cork the Fenian-backed J. P. Ronayne also received strong support.[3] At the General Election of 1874 clubs were active across the country—in Kerry, Kildare, Wicklow, Limerick, Queen's Co., Armagh, Cork, and almost certainly elsewhere as well.[4]

It is, therefore, the renewed interest in national politics shown by the rural constituencies which differentiates the 1870s from the preceding decades. Whereas in the 1850s and 1860s the politics of

[1] S. Clark, *Social origins of the Irish Land War* (Princeton, 1979), pp. 214–20; *Nation*, 30 Jan. 1875.

[2] *Cork Examiner*, 31 Jan. 1874; *Flag of Ireland*, 14 Jan. 1871, *Freeman's Journal*, 16 Sept. 1871. On labourers, see *Report from the select committee on Westmeath etc. (Unlawful Combinations)*, H.C. 1871 (147), xiii, Q. 1230.

[3] *Tipperary Advocate*, 10 Oct. 1868; B. Cahir, 'Isaac Butt and the Limerick By-Election of 1871', *North Munster Antiquarian Journal*, x (1966), 56–66; *idem*, 'Irish National By-Elections 1870–1874', pp. 82, 116.

[4] *Daily Express*, 14, 19 Jan., 2, 3 Feb. 1874; *Irish Times*, 6, 11 Feb. 1874; *Cork Examiner*, 26, 29, 31 Jan., 2 Feb. 1874.

confrontation had been concentrated in the localist boroughs, by the early 1870s the focus of activity was moving to the counties. The Amnesty movement, dissatisfaction with the Land Act, the failure of Gladstone's government to understand Irish problems, all encouraged increasing political involvement by farmers and the beginnings of a national organization in the (admittedly at first inadequate) shape of the Home Rule League. Thus, when the depression of the late 1870s occurred, rural Ireland was not unprepared for protest. Economic hardship hit both town and country, both farmer and shopkeeper. The compensation clauses in the Land Act had made it easy for tenants to obtain credit. They had borrowed extensively not only from banks but, especially in remoter areas, from money-lending shopkeepers—the ubiquitous gombeenmen—who operated on the twin bases of usury and credit trading. Although banks had greatly increased their lending to farmers in the 1870s, their practice of doing so on three-month promissory notes, which required regular renewal (often at increased discount) and obliged borrowers to seek securities four times a year, made them comparatively unattractive to poorer tenants with modest requirements who were in any case often baffled by the complexities of the paperwork involved. Gombeenmen could either act as such securities or be preferred as lenders because of their willingness to grant extended credit without bureaucratic procedures at, however, invariably higher (if often concealed) rates of interest.[1] With the onset of agricultural depression in the late 1870s both banks and gombeenmen severely curtailed the credit, which, according to universal opinion, they had granted so lavishly during the previous years.[2] Indeed, even before the Land Act, it would seem that credit had become easier and easier to obtain, so that, during the depression of the early 1860s, farmers had already experienced a milder foretaste of what was to occur fifteen years later.[3]

During the late 1870s and 1880s money-lending and credit-trading shopkeepers found themselves, therefore, in a position which

[1] *Committee on Industries (Ireland)*, H.C. 1884-5 (288), ix, 229-34, 321, 564-8, 704-9.

[2] The evidence is extensive. See, e.g., W. Lowe (land agent in Sligo) to E. Ashley, 25 Nov. 1880, Broadlands Archive 27M60, Box clxxiv; *Minutes of evidence taken before Her Majesty's Commissioners on Agriculture*, H.C. 1881 [C 2778-I], xv, 89, 118, 368, 555, 628-9; *Preliminary Report of the Assistant Commissioners* [on Agriculture] *for Ireland*, H.C. 1881 [C 2951], xvi, 1-8; D. B. King, *The Irish Question*, pp. 102-3; A. I. Shand, *Letters from the west of Ireland 1884*, pp. 85-6; G. Pellew, *In Castle and Cabin*, pp. 44-5.

[3] Report drawn up by Mr Murray of the Provincial Bank for Lord Clarendon, 1 Jan. 1850, Larcom Papers MS 7562; N. W. Senior, *Journals, conversations, and essays relating to Ireland*, 2nd edn., 2 vols. (London, 1868), ii, 263 (1862); H. Coulter, *The West of Ireland*, pp. 57-8.

accentuated the Janus-like orientation they had long taken in Irish society. On the one hand, the growing indebtedness of their customers greatly increased their own potential power within the local community. On the other, the general financial hardship of the times affected them also and inclined them towards demonstrations of solidarity with the tenantry as a whole. The precise nature of shopkeeping operations in the more rural parts of the country at this period is not yet entirely clear. A good deal of contemporary polemic suggests the virtually universal and lurking existence of retailing Svengalis, 'hungry of eye', as a typical commentator put it, 'and greedy of claw, sitting in the rear of a gloomy store looking over papers by the light of a miserable tallow dip'. Fattening on the misery of the times, the gombeenman, it was claimed, ground the rural poor into yet further wretchedness and despair. Undoubtedly such figures did exist, especially in the west and especially in those places where the lack of bank branches allowed gombeenmen to flourish unchecked.[1] But increasing competition *within* the retailing sector 'ensured that local monopolies were generally not possible', although, 'in isolated rural areas, mainly in the west . . . probably a not uncommon market form before 1890 was one of a limited number of sellers, each with a degree of monopoly power, and shielded in part by transport and information costs from contiguous markets.'[2] Evidence from the 1890s suggests that the effective rates of interest charged by traders covered a remarkably wide range, but that really high rates (say 15 per cent or more) were largely confined to the remoter parts of the west.[3] In any case, many relationships between even western shopkeepers and their customers continued to involve reciprocal advantages and obligations. Credit was a widely perceived necessity and by no means all retailers were regarded as on the casting list for Scrooge. 'The people', reported one of the inspectors for the Congested Districts Board in Mayo, 'generally deal with the same shopkeeper year after year, keeping a running account. No interest is charged if money is paid within a short period, say

[1] B. H. Becker, *Disturbed Ireland*, p. 208, also *Preliminary Report of the Assistant Commissioners* [on Agriculture] *for Ireland*, H.C. 1881 [C 2951], xvi, 1-8; *Committee on Industries (Ireland)*, H.C. 1884-5 (288), ix, 568.

[2] L. Kennedy, 'Traders in the Irish Rural Economy, 1880-1914', *Economic History Review*, 2nd series xxxii (1979), 206. Kennedy, the best writer on the subject, has been involved in a debate on the beastliness or otherwise of the late-Victorian credit traders: see P. Gibbon and M. D. Higgins, 'Patronage, tradition and modernisation: The case of the Irish "Gombeenman" ', and 'The Irish "Gombeenman": Re-incarnation or Rehabilitation?', and Kennedy's 'A sceptical view of the re-incarnation of the Irish "Gombeenman" ' (respectively), *Economic and Social Review*, vi (1974), 27-44; viii (1977), 313-19; viii (1977), 213-22.

[3] L. Kennedy, 'Retail Markets in Rural Ireland at the end of the nineteenth century', *Irish Economic and Social History*, v (1978), 50-3.

three months . . . Shopkeepers, as a whole, treat their customers leniently, and in bad seasons the amount of credit given is beyond all conception.'[1] Shopkeepers themselves were often indebted to larger merchants, and the financial stresses experienced in the years after 1877 virtually obliged them to proceed cautiously in requiring repayment, and encouraged many to support their customers' demands for reductions in the rents paid to landlords.[2] Although retailers did make periodic efforts to issue civil bill processes for the recovery of debts, the widespread opposition to processes from whatever source discouraged too eager a recourse to legal retribution.[3] In short, the reduction in purchasing power produced by the agricultural depression meant that both farmers *and* traders had, more than ever before, a vital and shared interest in maintaining agrarian incomes as far as was politically possible. The importance of this new alliance was quickly realized by the Land League. As early as the autumn of 1879 Davitt and Parnell publicly urged that debts due to shopkeepers had a higher priority than rents, while some months later the radical Parnellite MP, Lysaght Finigan, declaimed from election platforms in Co. Cork that 'We want' the farmer 'to pay his debts to the shopkeeper, and after that it will be time enough to think of the rent.'[4] For a short period, therefore, farmers and shopkeepers became pragmatically united in a common cause.[5] What was particularly remarkable was how even those retailers who had managed to profit from the troubles of the times could often transform themselves into orchestrators and leaders of nationalist politics in their own particular areas. In north Donegal the Land League depended heavily upon the support of a small number of prosperous retailing barons, while in the west of the county the business of Dungloe was by the mid-1880s dominated by the Sweeney family, whose head was 'not only the great "Gombeen Man" of the

---

[1] Congested Districts Board 'Base-Line Reports' (Trinity College Dublin Library Pressmark A.7.11), p. 381 (though credit prices were higher than cash prices). The Base-Line Reports reveal a wide range of practices in the west of the 1890s—see especially pp. 16, 26, 33, 46, 59, 84, 320, 400, 482.

[2] See J. Holland (agent) to E. P. Shirley, 5 May 1879, Shirley of Ettington Papers CR229/115/25; C. Russell, *'New Views on Ireland'. Or, Irish Land: Grievances: Remedies* (London, 1880), pp. 41, 60; F. Dun, *Landlords and Tenants in Ireland* (London, 1881), p. 227; G. Pellew, *In Castle and Cabin*, pp. 107-9, 173-4; J. S. Donnelly Jr., *The Land and the People of nineteenth-century Cork: The Rural Economy and the Land Question* (London, 1975), p. 245.

[3] B. L. Solow, *The land question and the Irish economy, 1870–1903* (Cambridge, Mass., 1971), p. 87; G. Parkinson, RM of Clifden, Co. Galway, 19 June 1880, in 'Reports on Crime and Disturbances', Printed Cabinet Papers CAB37/2/31.

[4] T. W. Moody, *Davitt and Irish Revolution 1846–82* (Oxford, 1981), p. 417; *Drogheda Argus*, 17 Apr. 1880.

[5] S. Clark, *Social origins of the Irish Land War*, pp. 262-76.

region, but a leading local member of the National League and Her Majesty's post-master'. Such 'domination' was, however, occurring at the same moment as other Donegal traders were nervously subscribing to the League 'through fear of incurring the displeasure of its members and consequent subsequent injury to their trade'.[1] In a curious way, therefore, the 1880s was a decade when both economic weakness and economic strength pushed shopkeepers into some kind of alliance with farmers. As leaders, however, shopkeepers were most prominent in those areas which boasted few large farmers, such as Mayo and Donegal. In more prosperous districts, it was the substantial farmers who played the crucial part,[2] though in the agrarian world as a whole (and not just in the connections between it and retailing) the Land War was to see a greater social cohesion and unity of action than had been the case before or was to be the case thereafter.

In a recent study Paul Bew has emphasized the sometimes conflicting ways in which various sections of the rural community reacted to the early Land War, and how the tactics of the smaller farmers of the west were changed as the main action moved into the central and eastern regions where farmers had more to lose, were more inclined to claim the concessions offered by the Land Act of 1881, and were less intent on the hope of land redistribution. He has stressed too the continuation into the 1880s of the long and bitter conflict between farmers and agricultural labourers.[3] All of this is valuable. Yet, as he himself admits, the continued presence of such 'class divisions' in no fundamental sense negates the undoubted reality of a general anti-landlord alliance.[4] In the longer perspective and the wider view it is, indeed, not the dissensions within the land movement that elicit wonder, but rather (in the light of all that had gone before) the new cohesion and collaboration displayed by the events of 1879–82 and their immediate aftermath.

The possibility of some kind of pragmatic and temporary alliance between labourers and farmers had, of course, been made more likely by a cumulative decline in the relative numerical importance

---

[1] D. Murphy, *Derry, Donegal, and Modern Ulster 1790–1921*, pp. 141–2; W. H. Hurlbert, *Ireland under Coercion: The diary of an American*, 2 vols. (Edinburgh, 1888), i, 126–7; Report of Sub-Inspector Nunan, 3 Dec. 1880, Gladstone Papers Add. MS 44158. In 1879 a Donegal landlord encouraged the establishment of a second shop in his district— 'an opposition shop . . . would be a good thing for the people' (J. G. M. Harvey to W. E. Hart, 18 Sept. 1879, Hart Papers D3077/H/11).

[2] K. T. Hoppen, 'National politics and local realities in mid-nineteenth century Ireland', pp. 222–3.

[3] P. Bew, *Land and the National Question in Ireland 1858–82* (Dublin, 1978), especially pp. 175–6, 217–24.

[4] Ibid. 223. See also S. Clark, *Social origins of the Irish Land War*, pp. 246–304.

of labourers. From constituting three-fifths of the agrarian community in 1841 they had fallen to only two-fifths by 1881, a reduction at once substantial and important.[1] Already this had affected the class nature of rural violence as farmers no longer felt themselves so obviously threatened by labourer numbers.[2] And, just as the labourers' minority status first became readily apparent after 1861, so from that date not only did labourers become more and more likely to occupy land on their own account, but it is also possible to detect a growing integration on their part into the humbler strata of the farmer community.[3] Although open conflicts between labourers and farmers continued to occur during the Land War,[4] Parnell was quick enough to replace his comparative indifference to labourers of 1876 with determined efforts to appeal to them as a group. By 1880-1 the Land League, as part of the delicate and shifting acrobatics it was then performing between the various rural interests it sought to represent, had ceased to ignore the labourer question,[5] and not without result or response. Parnell's repeated speeches on labour problems were no mere sham and even if the League's change of title in September 1881 to the 'Land League and the Labour and Industrial Movement' could not disguise its primary function as a tenants' organization, yet many labourers also felt moved to join, for they too saw in the League the best chance of obtaining redress for their own particular discontents. The many land meetings held between June 1879 and August 1881, though predominantly taken up with farmer problems, did not ignore labourer demands, while the dismissal of labourers by economically troubled landlords showed that little help was to be expected from that quarter.[6] By 1880 Kildare farmers could see the movement as uniting their own interests with those of local labourers; the former chairman of the Limerick Farmers' Club (now absorbed into the League) was prepared to defend labourers' interests; and Parnellite

[1] See Chapter II, Table 22 above (where provincial figures are also provided).

[2] See Chapter V above.

[3] D. Fitzpatrick, 'The Disappearance of the Irish Agricultural Labourer, 1841–1912', *Irish Economic and Social History*, vii (1980), 76–7.

[4] See, e.g., E. O'Brien to W. E. Forster, 4 Nov. 1880, Gladstone Papers Add. MS 44157; *Daily Express*, 27 Nov. 1885 (anti-National League demonstration by Kerry labourers); J. S. Donnelly Jr., *The Land and the People of nineteenth-century Cork*, pp. 236–41; P. Bew, *Land and the National Question in Ireland 1858–82*, p. 142.

[5] See *Freeman's Journal*, 15 Mar. 1876 (on National Land Conference), and, on how attitudes changed thereafter, D. B. King, *The Irish Question*, p. 275; F. S. L. Lyons, *Charles Stewart Parnell* (London, 1977), pp. 87, 97–9 (1879) and 229, 263 (1882–3); P. Bew, *Land and the National Question in Ireland 1858–82*, pp. 142–4 (1885–6).

[6] See the analysis of resolutions passed at meetings in S. Clark, *Social origins of the Irish Land War*, p. 298; also W. Lowe (agent) to E. Ashley, 25 Nov. 1880, Broadlands Archive 27M60, Box clxxiv, and T. Kelly, 'Ennis in the nineteenth century', p. 86.

candidates at the General Election (including Parnell himself) thought it important to reconcile labourers to the cause. In Carlow and Tipperary desperate labourers were inspired by farmer tactics to demand outdoor relief and to threaten to join the League unless granted immediate assistance.[1] Of course much of this was opportunistic, but that in itself does not diminish either its importance or its effectiveness. An American observer articulated the unspoken analyses of many when he wrote: 'The laborers [*sic*] are too poor and weak to agitate effectively. If their cause could be coupled with some other great movement in which the tenants are interested, their chances of success will be better.'[2] What is remarkable is not the divisiveness of the land movement, but the way in which it was at once able to absorb not only labourers, but small, large, and middling farmers as well. Despite the tensions of the April 1880 Land Conference, the movement survived and adapted itself to changing circumstances, so that, for example, at the Tralee poor-law elections of 1881 the small farmers firmly supported their wealthier colleagues at the polls.[3] Tom Garvin has rightly seen both the 'poor and rather better-off' classes as 'involved in the campaign' and has stressed the movement's 'strong cross-class character'.[4] And the fact that evictions seem to have occurred right across the economic spectrum served a warning to all farmers, whatever their preferred tactics of agitation, that none could feel entirely safe. Information on the valuations of those evicted during the first three months of 1881 suggests that, while in Munster and Leinster the middling and larger farmers suffered disproportionately (something which might explain their policy of paying 'rent at the point of the bayonet' rather than offering all-out resistance),[5] no group was excluded and the overall match between the distribution of agricultural holdings by value and of evictions was relatively close. Even more does this become the case when it is remembered that some evictions in the lowest value category were undoubtedly executed under magistrate's warrant and so excluded from the official returns. The proportion of evictions at four pounds and below is, therefore, to some extent understated in Table 54.

That this shared experience was translated into support for and

[1] *Minutes of evidence taken before Her Majesty's Commissioners on Agriculture*, H.C. 1881 [C 2778-I], xv, 493-4; ibid. 906-7; *C.C.* 14 Apr. 1880, and *Drogheda Argus*, 17 Apr. 1880; *C.C.* 4 Mar. 1880, and W. E. Forster to Gladstone, 2 Dec. 1880, Gladstone Papers Add. MS 44158.

[2] D. B. King, *The Irish Question*, p. 278.

[3] P. Bew, *Land and the National Question in Ireland 1858-82*, pp. 101-4; W. L. Feingold, 'The Irish boards of poor law guardians 1872-86', pp. 172-3.

[4] T. Garvin, *The evolution of Irish nationalist politics* (Dublin, 1981), pp. 71, 80. See also J. S. Donnelly Jr., *The Land and the People of nineteenth-century Cork*, p. 252.

[5] See P. Bew, *Land and the National Question in Ireland 1858-82*, pp. 121-6.

TABLE 54

Valuation comparison between evictions in the first three months of 1881 and the distribution of agricultural holdings, by provinces

	£4 and under		Over £4 to £10		Over £10 to £20		Over £20 to £50		Over £50	
	per cent holdings	per cent evictions	per cent holdings	per cent evictions	per cent holdings	per cent evictions	per cent holdings	per cent evictions	per cent holdings	per cent evictions
Leinster	28.5	17.5	23.9	15.0	19.3	5.0	17.3	37.5	11.0	25.0
Munster	29.4	8.2	24.2	16.4	20.0	28.3	18.1	26.6	8.3	20.5
Ulster	29.5	17.5	33.9	41.0	21.8	24.1	12.0	12.6	2.8	4.8
Connacht	47.2	30.0	34.2	50.0	11.2	10.0	4.8	6.6	2.6	3.4
Ireland	33.1	18.4	29.8	35.6	18.7	19.7	12.9	16.8	5.5	9.5

Note If one excludes all holdings at £4 and under, the resulting national percentages of (a) holdings and (b) evictions are as follows: over £4 to £10 = (a) 44.6 (b) 43.6; over £10 to £20 = (a) 27.9 (b) 24.1; over £20 to £50 = (a) 19.2 (b) 20.6; over £50 = (a) 8.3 (b) 11.7.

membership of the Land League is made clear by the surviving records of a number of League branches. The lively branch at Rathvilly in Co. Carlow was, for example, active in the cause of small farmers and labourers alike during both its Land and its National League periods. It demanded that employment be given and potato ground granted. Several of the wealthier members agreed to take on more labourers, and three labourers were elected to the local committee of sixteen. Many farmers of all kinds and labourers as well joined the branch at Bohola near Foxford in the central district of Co. Mayo.[1] More revealing still and more precise are the surviving membership lists for 1880-1 of Land League branches in the very different neighbourhoods of Ballydehob in west Cork and Raheen in Queen's Co. These give the valuations of the holdings rented by farmer members and the subscriptions of those who did not rent any land. As the League had decided that labourers should pay only a shilling a year, it is clear that the great majority of those without land and subscribing such an amount must in these districts have been agricultural labourers. In the case of Ballydehob the 656 members can be divided into 508 farmers, 125 non-farmers paying a shilling (mostly labourers), and 23 non-farmers paying more, while the 469 Raheen members (in an area with no town of any size at all) included 322 farmers, 123 shilling members, and 24 others. These figures far more closely reflect (especially in the case of Ballydehob) the proportions of farmers and labourers in the respective neighbourhoods than most farmer-orientated accounts of the Land War might have led one to expect. Thus, while the Ballydehob branch contained four farmers to every labourer, the surrounding poor-law union of Skull (1881 pop. 12,369) maintained a precisely similar ratio among its male inhabitants. And even the Raheen branch's 2.6 farmers to every labourer was not absurdly greater than the 1.4 ratio of the union of Abbeyleix (pop. 18,181).[2] Just as remarkable was the extraordinarily close match, displayed in Table 55, between the holdings of the farmer members and those in the surrounding unions as a whole. In two very different parts of the country, therefore, the Land League was able to attract a representative cross-section of farmers as well as many labourers. As there is no reason to suppose these branches to have been untypical, it must

[1] Minute Book of the Rathvilly Branch, N.L.I. MS 842; Report of 31 Aug. 1880 in Land League Papers N.L.I. MS 17706(2)—in general a disappointing collection. The Ennis Branch of the National League declared itself open to farmers, labourers, artisans, and traders (T. Kelly, 'Ennis in the nineteenth century', p. 88).

[2] Union figures taken from the *Census* of 1881, Tables VI and XX. Only agricultural labourers proper, not assisting relatives, have been counted. For branch membership lists, see sources referred to in Appendix—Table 55.

TABLE 55

Valuation comparison between holdings of farmer members of the Ballydehob and Raheen branches of the Land League and all agricultural holdings in the unions of Skull and Abbeyleix, 1880–1

	Ballydehob members per cent	Skull holdings per cent	Raheen members* per cent	Abbeyleix holdings per cent
£4 and under	22.0	28.4	24.4	34.1
Over £4 to £10	47.4	42.6	34.2	23.6
Over £10 to £20	26.4	21.8	22.6	19.1
Over £20 to £50	4.0	6.7	14.2	15.3
Over £50	0.2	0.5	4.6	7.9

* The 47 farmers whose valuations are not given in the Raheen membership records have been excluded. They were almost certainly small farmers and their inclusion in this column —had it been possible—would have increased the closeness of the match.

be accepted that the League's appeal was genuinely wider than has often been supposed. Cynical and opportunist reasons for membership no doubt existed, but then, in a sense, the Land League movement as a whole was opportunist if it was anything, while cynicism was hardly the peculiar prerogative of any one section of the rural community.

All this makes the overwhelming success of the Nationalist Party and the National League at the General Election of 1885 far more comprehensible. If farmers alone had been involved in the Land War, or if larger farmers had entirely hijacked the movement in 1880, then how was it that the labourers and the many small farmers enfranchised for the first time in 1884[1] enabled Parnell and his party to capture no less than 85 of the 103 Irish seats? Certainly Parnell had already achieved a crucial breakthrough on the more restricted electorate of the early 1880s, but it was the new voters who confirmed his position with a triumph denied all previous leaders of political opinion in Ireland. Nationalist candidates asked specifically for and received specific support from labourers as well as farmers.[2] The widespread efforts of various 'loyalist' candidates in the south to appeal to labourers (against farmer exploitation) collapsed amidst

[1] Many small farmers as well as labourers were among the new voters in Ireland because previously all farmers below a twelve-pound valuation had been excluded. See B. M. Walker, 'The Irish Electorate, 1868–1915', *Irish Historical Studies*, xviii (1973), 366.

[2] See, e.g., *Daily Express*, 25 Nov. 1885 (Kildare), 30 Nov. 1885 (Louth); *Freeman's Journal*, 24 Nov. 1885 (King's Co., Wicklow, Dublin); *C.C.* 24 Nov. 1885 (Cork); *Wexford Independent*, 29 Aug., 24 Oct. 1885 (Wexford and Wicklow). The Rathvilly National League Branch formally thanked the labourers of Carlow and Wicklow for their electoral enthusiasm (Minute Book, N.L.I. MS 842).

general derision: in the six contested Cork County divisions together they attracted a grand total of 1,703 votes from all sources compared with the 27,692 of their Home Rule opponents.[1] As the Lord Lieutenant had predicted before the election, Parnell succeeded in 'commanding for a time all parties, the clergy, farmers, labourers, many of the towns, the National League, [and] the parliamentary party'. 'To attain an united Irish party', the irascible editor of the *Roscommon Herald* had announced, 'the people must sacrifice their local prejudices and personal likings.'[2] It was Parnell's genius that he was able to absorb personal crotchets into a single campaign in a manner which demanded enough sacrifice to produce effectiveness but not enough to cause disintegration. But then his success was short-lived, and the peculiar moment was soon to pass away.

IV *PLUS ÇA CHANGE*

A number of complex developments helped to change the tone and organization of Irish politics in the late 1870s and 1880s. The accelerated mobilization of the countryside brought about by the Land War was made possible by earlier transformations: the revival of political activity along national lines in the county constituencies during the late 1860s and early 1870s, the failure of nerve on the part of the landlord class, the impact of Fenianism and the Amnesty movement, the changing role of shopkeepers and credit-traders in the smaller towns, the eclipse of the localist patterns of the post-Famine period. Indeed, the counties, where the tradition of violent action had never disappeared, were able, on a franchise unchanged since 1850, to provide Parnellite Home Rule and land reform with the crucial election victories of 1880–4.

But, just as after O'Connell the country had returned to community politics, to drains and cash rather than Repeal and reform, so, after Parnell, an emerging 'peasant' proprietorship reinforced similar but not identical reversions to 'normalcy'. Something of particular importance to the campaign of the early 1880s had been the manner in which the west of Ireland had for the first time become deeply and actively involved in a popular movement, and, perhaps even more significantly, had been able to export, in however transmuted a form, its own mobilization into the countryside as a whole. Previous

---

[1] On this aspect of the loyalist campaign, see *Daily Express*, 23, 30 Nov. 1885, and *C.C.* 23, 26 Nov. 1885 (Cork); *Daily Express*, 1 Dec. 1885 (Waterford); ibid. 27 Nov. 1885 (Westmeath). The Irish Loyal and Patriotic Union vainly published a pamphlet before the election appealing 'to the enfranchised labourers of Ireland' (copy in N.L.I. MS 5946).

[2] Notes by Lord Carnarvon for cabinet meeting, 6 Oct. 1885, Carnarvon Papers B.L. Add. MS 60823; *Roscommon Herald*, 3 Oct. 1885.

popular movements had always been far more successful in Leinster and Munster than in Connacht and had been handicapped as a result. This had been true of O'Connellism, of the Tenant League, even of the Amnesty Association. By contrast, the distribution of Land League meetings in 1879-80 shows how, on this occasion, Connacht led the way. And however defective are sources such as lists of contributions to national appeals (where poorer Connacht ran under obvious disadvantages)[1] or estimates of attendances at meetings, they are all we have as a measure of the regional strength of nineteenth-century popular movements. Standardizing all data by population, and then calculating how each province stood in relation to a national mean of 100 produces figures which chart the peregrinations of enthusiasm (Table 56). The list of the individual

TABLE 56
The geography of certain popular movements, 1826-89

	Leinster	Munster	Ulster	Connacht
Contributions to Catholic Rent 1826	169	137	37	49
Contributions to O'Connell Annuity 1833	176	157	28	20
Attendances at Repeal meetings 1843	164	140	7	99
Contributions to Tenant League Funds 1851	209	118	55	0
Attendances at Amnesty meetings 1869	180	177	8	46
Distribution of Land League meetings 1879-80	79	99	51	251
Membership of National League Jan. 1883	120	119	79	83
Contributions to Parnell Tribute 1883*	170	162	31	35
Contributions to Tenant Defence Fund 1889	127	171	39	77

* See note 1 below.　　　　　　　　　National Mean = 100

counties most active in each of the cases in the Table overlaps with but by no means exactly fits the list of those counties with most outrages given in Chapter V, Table 45. Thus, while the disturbed

[1] However, recalculation of the data in Table 56 relating to the Parnell Tribute of 1883, according to (a) total valuation and (b) agricultural valuation only, merely modifies, but does not change, the picture: thus Leinster (a) 144 (b) 137; Munster (a) 192 (b) 156; Ulster (a) 40 (b) 36; Connacht (a) 55 (b) 44.

King's Co., Tipperary, and Westmeath were among the leading suppliers of O'Connellite cash, so were the relatively peaceful Waterford, Dublin, and Louth. Much the same was true in the case of the Tenant League. By 1879-80, however, the match had become very much closer. Five of the seven most active Land League counties were among the contemporary top ten for agrarian outrages and six were among the leaders for *all* outrages. Yet already by January 1883 the moment had passed and membership of the National League had become dispersed fairly randomly among counties of all kinds, as heavy in the relatively untroubled Louth, Carlow, Wicklow, and Kildare as in the disturbed Tipperary, Limerick, and Westmeath.[1] It can of course be objected that cash subscriptions measure a different kind of commitment than do meetings or membership. But one must make the best of what is available, and what is available suggests that the coming together of political action, on the one hand, and agrarian and general violence, on the other, was a feature peculiar to the early Land War and a development which may help to account for the special success and impact of the events of those years. Although thereafter Connacht did not for long return to the political quiescence of former days—quite the reverse—the focus of activism was henceforth to oscillate according to the particularist aims of the campaigns in question, so that, for example, the United Irish League in its early radical days immediately after 1898 was never able to export its western mobilization with anything like the success which the Land League had been able to achieve.

More important still, the farmer–trader alliance virtually collapsed in the face of conflicts over access to land and over the growing co-operative movement which shopkeepers feared and opposed. Also, by the turn of the century 'the temporary and sometimes uneasy alliance established between large farmers . . . and smallholders during the Land War' had 'given way to strong tensions between the two ends of the farming spectrum'.[2] The dramatic confrontations which broke out in the 1890s between small farmers and graziers (and many graziers were also shopkeepers) once again soured the fragile relationships which had sustained the campaigns of the previous decade, and revived, more strongly than ever before, the long-standing differences between the two groups.[3] The powerful

---

[1] The same was true of contributions to the Parnell Tribute and to the Tenant Defence Fund. County breakdowns of the Repeal and Amnesty attendances of 1843 and 1869 can have little meaning as crowds frequently crossed county boundaries.

[2] L. Kennedy, 'Farmers, traders, and agricultural politics in pre-Independence Ireland', pp. 339–73; also *idem*, 'The early response of the Irish Catholic Clergy to the Co-operative Movement', *Irish Historical Studies*, xxi (1978), 55–74.

[3] M. D. Higgins and J. P. Gibbons, 'Shopkeeper-Graziers and land agitation in Ireland,

clericalist forces which resurfaced in Irish political life during and after the Parnell split of 1890-1 represented a return to the localist traditions of the post-Famine years, with the Healyites the most frenetically virulent exponents of the art. In economic terms the period after the Land War was one in which the regions of Ireland drew further and further apart. Those which had been 'traditionally dominated by agriculture were becoming relatively more so as non-agricultural employment become more concentrated in the neighbourhood of towns', while simultaneously 'there was a growing divergence between regions specializing in commercial farming with its high concentration of hired hands, and regions dominated by small and "uneconomic" holdings sustained through the agency of continuous emigration'.[1] Whereas during the Land War neither the western radicals nor the more substantial farmers of the midlands and east had been allowed to obtain a stranglehold over the movement for land reform and Home Rule, thereafter fragmentation on class and regional lines became once again the normal style of rural politics. And despite much rhetoric about the virtue of small farms and cosy homesteads, despite the violence of occasional outbursts such as the Ranch War of 1906-10 or the labourers' agitation of 1919-20, despite the comparative agrarian radicalism of some early Fianna Fáilers, it would be hard to deny that grazierdom became more triumphant after Independence than it had ever been under British rule.

In a paradoxical way the great combined struggle of the 1880s, though perhaps drawing inspiration from some sense of communal property rights,[2] ultimately ensured the victory of individualism. Though even as owner-occupiers, small farmers, for example, might still share certain group interests, yet these were never to be either as immediate or as encompassing as the common experiences and the common grievances once lived through by large numbers of *tenants* upon particular local estates. Of course there had always been violent disagreements and bitter feuds within the tenant community as a whole and within its constituent families and kinship groups,[3] but in no degree did these diminish with the onset of

1895-1900' in *Irish Studies 2: Ireland: Land, Politics, and People*, ed. P. J. Drudy (Cambridge, 1982), pp. 93-118; also D. S. Jones, 'Agrarian Capitalism and Rural Social Development in Ireland' (Queen's University Belfast Ph.D. thesis, 1977), *passim*.

[1] D. Fitzpatrick, 'The Disappearance of the Irish Agricultural Labourer, 1841-1912', p. 76.

[2] See B. L. Solow, 'A new look at the Irish Land Question', *Economic and Social Review*, xii (1981), 301-14; also T. Garvin, *The evolution of Irish nationalist politics*, p. 71.

[3] D. Fitzpatrick, 'Class, family, and rural unrest in nineteenth-century Ireland', in *Irish Studies 2*, ed. P. J. Drudy, pp. 37-75.

'peasant proprietorship' or with the disappearance of landlords, some of whom at least had been willing and able to referee and defuse disputes upon their properties. Even without romanticizing the past it is possible to see how the increasing penetration of commercial farming multiplied the roles in which farmers stood in competition rather than in community with one another. Sustained conditioning by commercial influences extended market values into areas of life once shaped by other considerations.[1] The fascinating but ultimately misleading work of Arensberg and Kimball has tended to obscure the individualist values and the recurrent jealousies of rural life.[2] And even if many accounts written retrospectively in the twentieth century about the period 1880–1914 have exaggerated the demoralized nature of the countryside and its people, vitality in 'culture, sport, pastimes, and life styles'[3] seems all too often to have coexisted with altogether more depressing experiences. There is some evidence to suggest that once the poor-law system had become firmly established after the Famine 'the sense of communal and kinship responsibilities for victims of age and ill-health was diminished'.[4] Problems with the relevant data cannot disguise the undoubted rises in suicides and in admissions to lunatic asylums which took place in this period. Suicides per 100,000 males more than doubled between 1864–8 and 1904–8 from 2.1 to 5.2 and were probably (if the evidence available from the 1920s is any guide) much higher in rural than in urban areas.[5] Reasonably comparable information for public asylum admissions shows an increase per 100,000 population from 29.8 in 1865–9 to 67.7 in 1900–4. The numbers of the 'insane' in asylums of all kinds, in the mental departments of workhouses, and estimated to be 'at large' in the community, rose from 224.3 per 100,000 in 1855 to 432.3 in 1886. Of course the number of places available also increased, but the trend was undoubtedly

[1] D. S. Jones, 'Agrarian Capitalism and Rural Social Development in Ireland', pp. 307–20.

[2] Some hints can be obtained in J. M. Mogey, *Rural life in Northern Ireland: Five regional studies* (London, 1947), pp. 119, 129; J. Bell, 'Relations of mutual help between Ulster farmers', *Ulster Folklife*, xxiv (1978), 48–58; C. Ó Gráda, 'Primogeniture and Ultimogeniture in rural Ireland', *Journal of Interdisciplinary History*, x (1980), 491–7. Imaginative writers, notably Patrick Kavanagh, make the point more forcefully. The 'classic' account is C. M. Arensberg and S. T. Kimball, *Family and Community in Ireland*, 2nd edn. (Cambridge, Mass., 1968).

[3] L. M. Cullen makes this valid point in his 'Ireland' in *The Victorian Countryside*, ed. G. E. Mingay, 2 vols. (London, 1981), i, 100.

[4] D. H. Akenson, *Between Two Revolutions: Islandmagee, County Antrim 1798–1920* (Don Mills, Ontario, 1979), p. 114.

[5] D. Walsh, 'A century of Suicide in Ireland', *Journal of the Irish Medical Association*, lxix (1976), 144–52. The higher rural rates may have been due to the disproportionate presence of older unmarried people. Walsh suggests that under-recording of suicides was probably constant throughout the period.

upwards in every sense. On the whole, relatives seem to have been extremely eager to have 'difficult' members of the family committed, and had not medical authorities tried to exclude those they considered 'idiotic' (as opposed to 'insane'), the numbers would have been far higher still. After about 1871 western admission rates rose steadily; by 1901 they equalled those of the east; thereafter they exceeded them.[1]

Modernization in the context of late-nineteenth century Ireland adopts a set of unexpected aspects. The growth of towns and their economic importance coexisted with a period of fragmented politics conducted almost entirely on localist lines. The ability to read and to travel had only the most tenuous connections with political development. Certainly the country was becoming culturally more homogeneous. Regional differences diminished, though they did not disappear. But while in its broadest sense Irish culture was becoming steadily more and more modern—and the Gaelic revival in all its linguistic, social, and sporting forms was above all a profoundly *modern* phenomenon—Irish politics after the Land War reverted to their characteristically localist mode. Only haltingly and very briefly was subsequent political life able to transcend this—its 'normal'—state, notably in 1918-21. The 'modern' Irish politician is essentially a broker, a conveyer and distributor of favours, a man for whom attention to the parish pump or the crossroads telephone box counts for more, both intuitively and at election time, than almost anything else.[2] He does not impose this role, but adopts it to meet a widely perceived need among voters 'who expect nothing of their T.D. except that he get them the odd grant; the pension; or that he quash an occasional summons for drunk and disorderly behaviour or driving the Morris Minor without tax or an "audible warning device" '.[3] Irish social habits may change, but politics remain largely immutable, with the immediate and local defining the usual limits of political activity and with the countryside more prepared than the town to make occasional forays into wider agitations and national campaigns.[4]

It is of course true that after Parnell forms of nationalism continued

[1] M. Finnane, *Insanity and the Insane in post-Famine Ireland* (London, 1981), pp. 232 (admission data), 111, 135-6, 145, 161-9; *Thom 1870*, p. 820, *Thom 1876*, p. 674, and *Thom 1888*, p. 666 (for 1855 and 1886 figures).

[2] See, e.g., the work of M. Bax, 'Patronage Irish Style: Irish politicians as brokers', *Sociologische Gids*, xvii (1970), 179-91; *Harpstrings and Confessions: Machine-Style Politics in the Irish Republic* (Assen and Amsterdam, 1976); 'The small community in the Irish political process' in *Irish Studies 2*, ed. P. J. Drudy, pp. 119-40.

[3] *Hibernia*, 7 Jan. 1977.

[4] D. Fitzpatrick, 'The geography of Irish nationalism 1910-1921', *Past and Present*, No. 78 (1978), 125, 130-3.

to dominate the politics of the south and continued also, especially in 1892 and in the years immediately before the Great War, to exercise a powerful impact upon Westminster. But it is equally true that this was achieved at the cost of making constitutional nationalism so capacious a portmanteau that it was at once able and obliged to provide a refuge for men who would as readily have declared themselves Whigs or Liberals in earlier days. At the same time the reactions of Parliament to Ireland were determined as much by the vagaries of party numbers at Westminster as by the nature of politics in Ireland itself. Thus, while the imperatives of political nomenclature had certainly changed (in itself a matter of no small importance), the bones beneath the skin had changed to an altogether lesser degree. In the end it is important to place the matter in perspective. If, instead of seeing every event as an anticipation of events that have not yet occurred and regarding the organized activism of the 1880s as 'normal', and then attempting to explain its absence in earlier or later periods, one regards a situation of fragmented localism as the usual state of affairs, a more convincing view of Irish history may become possible. This is not to equate 'normality' with quiescence or lack of violence. The bitterness and bloody conflict of the sectional tithe affrays of the 1830s or the heightened tensions which raged in the Irish boroughs during the 1850s and 1860s make that clear enough. But what O'Connell and Parnell did was to wrench their countrymen from the ways of sporadic action for local and particular interests into those of national demands and national issues. But although both of their agitations implanted potential time-bombs into Irish life, neither achieved more than a temporary mobilization. In social and economic terms Ireland may have moved in a linear direction. But in politics wheels have always turned around and ultimately they have always turned full circle.

Appendix
Sources and Methods of the Tables[*]

TABLE 1

Calculated from material relating to 47 unions in *Third General Report relative to the Valuations for poor rates, and to the registered elective franchise in Ireland*, H.C. 1841 [329], xxiii, 611–15, 651–3, 662, 689. Rent has been calculated from poor-law valuations by using provincial multipliers based on unweighted averages of the relevant county ratios of PLV to rent which R. D. Crotty (*Irish agricultural production: Its volume and structure* (Cork, 1966), p. 303) has obtained from an analysis of the Devon Commission's minutes of evidence of 1844. For the heavy dominance of the rural and farmer element within county electorates, see above, Chapter I, section IV, also Chapter II, Table 23.

TABLE 2

A: calculated from the distribution of *tenements* in 1848 given in a printed Cabinet paper of 3 Jan. 1860 by the Chief Secretary, Edward Cardwell (Gladstone Papers Add. MS 44590), where figures for 1853 suggest that 1.4 per cent were rated at £200 and above. These figures exclude tenements in counties of cities and towns but include those in 'pure' boroughs, so that they do not entirely reflect the situation in county constituencies. The distortions should be very small. B: based on figures for 1852–3 relating only to the eight counties which contained no parliamentary boroughs (Kildare, Wicklow, Longford, Cavan, Donegal, Monaghan, Mayo, and Leitrim) in *Return of the number of persons in Ireland assessed to the rate for the relief of the poor, made next before the rate collecting in July 1853*, H.C. 1854 (503), lv, 737–8. C: based on data for all county *constituencies* save Galway and Meath in *Number of electors on the register of 1852–3 in each county, city, and borough in Ireland, distinguishing their qualifications*, H.C. 1852–3 (957), lxxxiii, 413–16, and *Abstract of. . . Return of all persons appearing in the revised lists of voters in the several counties, counties of cities, and counties of towns in Ireland, and in parliamentary boroughs*, H.C. 1854–5 (90), xlvii, 605.

TABLE 4

Understatement results from the comparison of the 'lower' Griffith values of 1866 with the poor-law values of 1840 and 1850–1. The 1840 figures are calculated from those relating to a large sample of county electors in *Third General Report relative to the Valuations*, H.C. 1841 [329], xxiii, 613–15; those for 1866 from Griffith's distribution of agricultural holdings in *Thom 1870*, p. 842; those for 1850–1 (the first registration after the Franchise Act) from the distribution of holdings for 1848 in Cardwell's printed Cabinet paper of 3 Jan. 1860 (Gladstone Papers Add. MS 44590). The 1850–1 and 1866 figures, therefore,

[*] No note required for Table 3; Table 32 is based on sources too scattered to allow useful citation.

depend on the (reasonable) assumption that from 1850 the distribution of county voters in general and of farmer voters who supplied more than three-quarters of such voters (see Chapter II, Table 23) followed broadly the distribution of agricultural holdings. The source data are divided at £10 and £15 rather than at £12 (the lowest enfranchising amount allowed under the 1850 Act) and have been recalculated on the assumption that distribution was even throughout the £10-15 range. As comparisons are at issue, this is not likely to produce serious distortions.

TABLE 5

Armagh 1852: Register N.L.I. Pressmark I6551 (baronies of Upper Fews, Upper Orior, and O'Neiland West analysed); Down: MS Poll Book in Downshire Papers D671/02/5 and 6 (now re-sorted) (Dufferin, Kinelarty, Upper Castlereagh, Lower Iveagh, and Newry analysed); Louth (valuation and size): by comparing *County of Louth Election 1852: A list of the electors of the several baronies of the County of Louth, who voted at the general election of 1852* (Dundalk, 1852)—copy in N.L.I. MS 1660—with Griffith's valuation for Louth published in 1854 (every fifth rated occupier in baronies of Lower Dundalk, Ardee, Upper Dundalk, and Louth analysed); Sligo: MS Poll Book with valuations N.L.I. MS 3064 (Tireragh only available); Galway: Register P.R.O.I. M2433 and M3446 (Moycullen, Ross, and Ballynahinch only available); Mayo: Register P.R.O.I. M2782-4 and M3447-8 (Tyrawley, Kilmaine, Gallen, Costello, and Clanmorris only available); Roscommon: Register in Papers of the Incorporated Society for Promoting English Protestant Schools in Ireland MS 5805 (Athlone Barony only available); Armagh 1870: Register P.R.O.N.I. T2883 (Upper Fews, Upper Orior, and O'Neiland West analysed). All figures are for rated occupiers only. The inclusion of other voters would slightly increase the overall 'wealth' of the respective electorates.

TABLE 6

Co. Down Poll Books, Downshire Papers D671/02/5 and 6 (now re-sorted)—baronies of Dufferin, Kinelarty, Upper Castlereagh, Lower Iveagh, and Newry analysed.

TABLE 7

Clonmel: *Fictitious Votes, Ireland*, 1st series, 1st report, pp. 204, 376, 406; Kilkenny: *Kilkenny Journal*, 31 Oct. 1832; Portarlington: G. Damer to —, 18 Jan. 1835, Peel Papers Add. MS 40410; Athlone 1835: list of voters in O.P. 1835, Box 46; Tralee: printed list of voters headed 'Tralee Borough election, January 1835' in O.P. 1835/158, Box 47; Dublin: *Sir William Gregory, K.C.M.G., formerly member of parliament and sometime governor of Ceylon. An Autobiography*, ed. Lady Gregory (London, 1894), p. 75; Kinsale 1847: *Minutes of evidence taken before the select committee on the Kinsale election petition*, H.C. 1847-8 (138), xiii, 12, 145; Athlone 1852: R. B. Lawes to Lord Naas, 10 July 1852, Mayo Papers MS 11019; Limerick 1852: *Londonderry Sentinel*, 16 July 1852; New Ross: *Nation*, 10 Apr. 1852; Waterford: T. Meagher to —, [1852], Cullen Papers; Youghal: *Daily Express*, 15 Oct. 1852; Dundalk: *Tablet*, 23 Apr. 1859; Sligo: *Central Conservative Society of Ireland: Report of the*

Sub-Committee 1859 (Mayo Papers MS 11025); Bandon: F. E. Currey to Duke of Devonshire, 7 Feb. 1863, Lismore Papers MS 7190; Kinsale 1863: MS list of voters (O'Hagan Papers D2777/6); Limerick 1869: *Report from the select committee on parliamentary and municipal elections*, H.C. 1868-9 (352), viii, 270; Cork: I. d'Alton, 'Cork Unionism: Its role in parliamentary and local elections, 1885-1914', *Studia Hibernica*, No. 15 (1975), 145. The percentages for Clonmel, Athlone 1835, and Dublin are of those polling only.

TABLES 8, 9, AND 10

Where calculations are based on a systematic sample, this is indicated. Otherwise the total statistical population has been analysed. For locations of poll books (which are comparatively rare in Ireland), see B. M. Walker and K. T. Hoppen, 'Irish election poll books 1832-72', *Irish Booklore*, iii (1976), 9-13, and iv (1980), 113-19. Cashel, Clonmel, Sligo: *Fictitious Votes, Ireland*, 1st series, 3rd report, Appendix 6; Carrickfergus: *A Return of the names, occupations, and residences of the registered freeholders, leaseholders, and £10 householders, included in the return made to the House of Commons on the 25th day of February 1834, by the clerk of the County of the Town of Carrickfergus*, H.C. 1834 (329), xliii, 549-67; Coleraine: 'A List of the Persons who voted at the Coleraine Borough election, in December 1832, classified, and taken from the list published by the Beresford party' (printed) in O.P. 1832/2188, Box 2191; Belfast: MS Poll Book 1832-7 P.R.O.N.I. D2472/1; Cork: *The People's Press and Cork Weekly Register*, 17, 24, 31 Jan., 7, 14 Feb. 1835 (all those—about two-thirds of total—with designated occupations analysed); Tralee: printed list of voters headed 'Tralee Borough election, January 1835' in O.P. 1835/158, Box 47; Youghal: MS Poll Books among Youghal Corporation Records in keeping of Cork Archives Council and published (with introduction) in Ann Barry and K. T. Hoppen, 'Borough politics in O'Connellite Ireland: The Youghal poll books of 1835 and 1837', *Journal of the Cork Historical and Archaeological Society*, lxxxiii (1978), 106-46, and lxxxiv (1979), 15-43; Dundalk: N. Ross, 'Two nineteenth-century election posters', *Journal of the County Louth Archaeological Society*, xvi (1968), 224-32; Dublin 1832 (one-in-five sample): *A List of the constituency of the City of Dublin, as registered prior to the City of Dublin election, in January 1835; exhibiting the voting at that election, and also at the city election in December 1832* (Dublin, n.d.); Dublin 1837 (one-in-five sample): *A correct List of the poll of voters at the City of Dublin election in August, 1837, compiled by T. M. Ray* (Dublin, 1838); Dublin 1841 (one-in-five sample): *A Mirror of the Dublin election for members to serve in parliament, commencing Monday 5th and ending Saturday 11th July, 1841* (Dublin, 1841); Dublin 1842 (one-in-five sample): *List of voters at the City of Dublin election, for one member in the room of the late much lamented John Beatty West, M.P.* (Dublin, 1842); Dublin 1857 and 1865: *The constituency of the City of Dublin, as revised in the year 1865, arranged in alphabetical order* [Dublin, 1866]—copy N.L.I. Ir94133 d 17 (not a real poll book and my figures based on all those who voted in 1857 and 1865 *and* were still on the register after the 1865 revision); Armagh: printed *List of Voters who recorded their votes at the Armagh Borough election, in 1859*—copy in Armagh Museum (No. 22-76), from which 134 of the 338 who voted were traced as to occupations in *Slater's Directory of Ireland* (Manchester and London, 1856), pp. 388-94; Londonderry 1832: Clerk of the Peace's Book P.R.O.N.I. T1048/3; Londonderry 1868: *List of Voters, showing for whom each elector polled at the late general election for the City of London-derry, distinguishing the religion of each voter* (Londonderry: Sentinel Office, [1868]); Londonderry 1870: *Names of the Voters at the election held in London-derry on Thursday, February 17th, 1870* (Londonderry: Sentinel Office, [1870]).

The author needs no reminding of the imperfections of the data. 'Gentlemen' are at once mysterious and self-appointed. 'Professionals' are perhaps the easiest to handle. 'Merchants, manufacturers, and commercial' include only those with enterprises clearly larger than a small retail outlet, though it is not always possible to separate masters and men (but see Chapter I, pp. 4-5). To distinguish between craft and retail trades is especially difficult: in general, those traders 'more concerned with materials than customers and typically without a shop in the modern sense' have been classified as 'Artisans', while 'Shopkeepers' include those engaged in businesses where 'the customer is as immediate a reference point as the material and where a shop in a modern sense is involved' (T. J. Nossiter, *Influence, opinion, and political idioms in reformed England* (Hassocks, 1975), pp. 211-12). The 'Drink interest' (in a sense a subgroup of Shopkeepers) is clear enough. 'Others' is everyone else: pensioners, town criers, policemen, watermen, etc. 'Farmers' and 'Labourers' were only separately identified when their inclusion among 'Others' might have caused distortion.

TABLE 11

Calculated by comparing *List of voters at the City of Dublin election* (Dublin, 1842) with *Census of Ireland for the year 1841*, H.C. 1843 [504], xxiv, 22 (City of Dublin). The census figures are for males aged fifteen and upwards.

TABLES 12 AND 13

See the coloured map usually bound between Appendices II and III in *Census of Ireland for the year 1841*, H.C. 1843 [504], xxiv. Only streets *clearly* designated have been included, and a sixth category ('third-class mixed streets') has been omitted. Although many voters lived either in these mixed streets or in un-designated areas further from the centre, the party profile of voters in the ninety-one streets analysed (55 per cent Conservative) was roughly similar to that in the constituency as a whole (52 per cent). See poll book for 1841 noted above for Tables 8, 9, and 10.

TABLE 14

Figures are unweighted constituency means to reflect the nature of local experience. The large number of two-member constituencies (where electors could use one *or* two votes) makes the accurate calculation of turn-out impossible without separate information on the actual numbers voting. This is fully avail-able only for 1832, 1835 (but for 1835 rendered useless by unreliable electorate figures), 1857, 1859, and for 32 out of 44 relevant contests in 1852. See *A Return of the electors registered in each county, county of a city, county of a town, and borough in Ireland . . . also the number of voters who polled*, H.C. 1833 (177), xxvii, 289-311, as corrected by *Amended Return . . . so far as relates to County Galway and County Tipperary*, H.C. 1833 (767), xxxiii, 313-14; *Returns of the number of voters which appear on the parliamentary register for each county, city, and borough in the United Kingdom for the year 1858 . . . and of the number of voters who recorded their votes at the general election . . . so far as relates to Ireland*, H.C. 1860 (277-I), lv, 103-8, augmented by *Returns showing the area, population, income tax, number of occupiers rated at various amounts, number of parliamentary voters etc. in each county in Ireland*, H.C. 1860 (128), lv, 261-70. The purely nominal contests in Youghal and Kildare (1832) and Co. Armagh (1857) have been omitted, so that the number of contests used in each year was 42 (1832), 32 (1852), 35 (1857), 27 (1859).

TABLE 15

Sources, in the order presented: 1832—J. M. Galwey to E. Littleton, 7 Feb. 1834, Hatherton Papers D260/M/01/10; Memo by H. W. Barron, Melbourne Papers 19/51; 1835—ibid.; *D.E.P.* 11 July 1837 (*sic*); J. Power to Archbishop Cullen, 15 July 1861 (*sic*), Cullen Papers; 1841—J. E. Tennent to Lord Stanley, 22 July 1841, Derby Papers 131/7; 1842—Lord Eliot to Peel, 8 Jan. 1842, Peel Papers Add. MS 40480; 1850—Lord Sligo to G. H. Moore, 28 July [1850], Moore Papers MS 891; 1852—*Limerick Chronicle*, 4 Sept. 1852; Domvile Papers MS 9361; J. Machett to Naas, 12 May 1859 (*sic*), Mayo Papers MS 11036; J. McClintock to T. E. Taylor, 8 Apr. [1859 (*sic*)] , ibid. MS 11036; Revd E. Moore to Revd G. Kirkpatrick, 31 July 1852, Kirkpatrick Papers D1604/109; 1857—*Banner of Ulster*, 21 Mar. 1857 (both Tipperary figures); W. Smith to W. S. R. Brady, 10 Apr. 1857, Close (Richardson of Drum) Papers D2002/C/48; Domvile Papers MS 9361; T. Burke to Lord Clanricarde, 19 Apr. [1857], Clanricarde Papers 40; 1859—T. McDermot to The O'Conor Don, [1859], Clonalis Papers 9.3.H.145; J. Machett to Naas, 12 May 1859, Mayo Papers MS 11036; 1865—*Report of the Commissioners appointed for the purpose of making inquiry into the existence of Corrupt Practices at the last election for Cashel*, H.C. 1870 [C 9], xxxii, 5; *Returns from the several sheriffs and returning officers of the abstract of expenses incurred by or on behalf of each candidate at the last general election*, H.C. 1866 (160), lvi, 455-92; *Report of the Commissioners appointed . . . for the purpose of making inquiry into the existence of Corrupt Practices amongst the freemen electors of the City of Dublin*, H.C. 1870 [C 93], xxxiii, 19; Bishop MacEvilly to Archbishop Cullen, 21 June 1868 (*sic*), Cullen Papers; F. P. Dunne to Lord Mayo, 9 Aug. 1868 (*sic*), Mayo Papers MS 11164; 1868—*Minutes of evidence taken at the trial of the Cashel election petitions*, H.C. 1868-9 (121), xlix, 231-2; E. L. O'Malley and H. Hardcastle, *Reports of the decisions of the judges for the trial of election petitions in England and Ireland*, i (London, 1869), p. 271; *Waterford Citizen*, 23 Oct. 1868; H. J. Hanham, *Elections and Party Management: Politics in the time of Disraeli and Gladstone* (London, 1959), p. 278; 1869—Seymour of Ragley Papers CR114A/854A/1; *Copy of the shorthand writer's notes of the judgement delivered by Mr Justice Fitzgerald, and of the minutes of evidence taken at the trial of the Longford election petition*, H.C. 1870 (178), lvi, 306-7; 1872— *Copy of the evidence taken at the trial of the Galway County election petition*, H.C. 1872 (241-I), xlviii, 543-4; Lord Lansdowne to Lord Hartington, 27 Jan. 1872, Devonshire Papers 340/489; 1873—J. Greer to Lord Belmore, 9 Apr. 1873, Belmore Papers D3007/P/117; 1878—Downshire Papers D671/G14/15 (now re-sorted).

TABLE 16

The 1841 figure and that for 'above 15 acres' in 1844 are based on recalculations in P. M. A. Bourke, 'The agricultural statistics of the 1841 census of Ireland: A critical review', *Economic History Review*, 2nd series xviii (1965), 376–91, with the addition that, for the former, the number of holdings above one and not exceeding two acres (which Bourke's recalculations 'throw out' of the total number of holdings) has been put back to the sum of 50,355 as given in the general source for 1844 (*Appendix to the minutes of evidence taken before Her Majesty's Commissioners of Inquiry into the State of the Law and Practice in respect to the Occupation of Land in Ireland* [henceforth *Devon Commission*], part iv, H.C. 1845 [672], xxii, 280–9—note the lack of a return for Cahirciveen Union). The 1851–91 figures are taken from the decennial land returns published with the population census reports.

TABLE 17

Although the pre-1852 poor-law valuations operated on different principles from those underpinning Griffith's final valuation (which came into complete force in 1865), the latter was *in general* lower than the former (see Chapter I, pp. 25–6). In that respect the degree of change after 1841 indicated in Table 17 is an *underestimate*. Changes between 1866 and 1891 were caused almost entirely by consolidation, for Griffith's *land* values were never revised. The figures for 1866 (from *Returns (No. 1) showing the number of agricultural holdings, with the area, valuation, and population of the agricultural districts in each county in Ireland: And (No. 2) of all the cities, boroughs, and towns in Ireland omitted in Return (No. 1)*, H.C. 1867 (144), lvi, 517–26) and for 1891 (from T. W. Grimshaw, *Facts and Figures about Ireland Part II* (Dublin, 1893), Table column 34) are for agricultural holdings exclusively and are thus strictly comparable. It was not possible to remove *all* non-agricultural holdings from the 1841 source (*Returns of parliamentary electors; also of tenements valued under the act 1 & 2 Vict., cap. 56 for the relief of the poor in Ireland*, H.L. 1844, xv, 449–628, and H. L. 1847–8, xxi, 661–5), but a large measure of comparability was achieved by extracting from it the holdings in all but five (Gilford, Belturbet, Queens-town, Passage West, Skerries) of the 126 towns and urban areas with populations of 2,000 and over in 1861 (the base population year for the agricultural/urban divisions used by the compiler of the 1866 data). In the case of the thirty-three parliamentary boroughs (which included all the really large towns) this could be done quite cleanly, even to the extent of distinguishing between the urban and rural areas of six of the eight counties of cities and towns—Galway and Carrick-fergus alone proving indivisible. The nature of the 1841 data, however, allowed the 'extraction' of the other towns with populations above 2,000 only by the device of removing the whole of those poor-law electoral divisions of which each town formed the centre. These divisions were, however, small and the resulting loss of agricultural babies with urban bath-water cannot be large. Indeed, this process 'solves' the problem of dealing with the extension of certain town boundaries between 1841 and 1866. It was not realistically possible to remove the non-agricultural holdings in towns of less than 2,000 persons (in 1861). Thus the adjusted 1841 data still include approximately a quarter of all urban hold-ings and exclude a very small number of agricultural holdings. A check calcula-tion throwing into the 1866 figures all holdings in towns which it was not possible to exclude from the 1841 data slightly reduces the rate of change between 1841 and 1866, though the undoubtedly lower Griffith values more than outweigh any such reduction. It should be noted that, whereas Table 16 takes all agricultural holdings *above one acre* as its statistical population, Table 17 takes *all* relevant holdings.

TABLE 18

Devon Index, under 'Farmers' and 'Labourers'. See also J. S. Donnelly Jr., *The Land and the People of nineteenth-century Cork: The Rural Economy and the Land Question* (London, 1975), p. 23.

TABLE 19

Based on unweighted means of county data in the following sources: for 1844 —F. Purdy's analysis of 373 witnesses before the Devon Commission in 'On the earnings of agricultural labourers in Scotland and Ireland', *Journal of the Statistical Society*, xxv (1862), 482; for 1860—*A Return of the average rate of weekly earnings of agricultural labourers in Ireland, for the last 6 months previous to the 1st day of January 1861*, H.C. 1862 (2), lx, 105–12, as adjusted by D. Fitzpatrick, 'The Disappearance of the Irish Agricultural Labourer, 1841–1912', *Irish Economic and Social History*, vii (1980), 90 (note that the Connacht figure would be 6s. 3d. and the national figure 6s. 11d. had not Roscommon returned 10s. 2d. because of high wages created by railway building); for 1893 —Royal Commission on Labour figures as used by D. Fitzpatrick, op. cit.

TABLE 20

Adapted from Table I in D. Fitzpatrick, 'The Disappearance of the Irish Agricultural Labourer, 1841-1912', p. 87. Here and in Table 21 categories similar to those of Fitzpatrick have been used. *Farmers*: 1841, 1851, 1861 = 'Ministering to Food: Farmers; Graziers', including resident dependants so returned; 1871 = 'Agriculturalists: Farmer, Grazier', also probably including dependants so returned, but excluding occupiers of agricultural land engaged in pursuits other than farming; 1881 = 'Farmer, Grazier', excluding resident dependants and also occupiers of land engaged in pursuits other than farming. *Farm Workers/ Labourers*: 1841 = 'Ministering to Food: Servants and Labourers; Ploughmen; Herds', excluding 'Unclassified: Labourers and Porters; Servants (domestic)'; 1851 = 'Ministering to Food: Farmers' Labourers and Servants; Ploughmen; Herds', excluding 'Unclassified: Labourers (not agricultural) and Porters; Servants (domestic)'; 1861 = 'Ministering to Food: Farm Labourers and Servants; Ploughmen; Herds and Drovers', excluding 'Ministering to Furniture: Domestic Servants', but including 'Unclassified: Labourers' (though not porters) except those returned for the major cities and those estimated to have been resident in the 'principal towns' (estimates being the number so returned in 1871); 1871 = 'Agriculturalists: Agricultural Labourer (out-door); Shepherd (out-door); Farm Servant (in-door); Farmer's, Grazier's son, grandson, brother, nephew'; 'General Labourer', excluding those returned for cities and 'principal towns'; 1881 = 'Agricultural Labourer, Cottager; Shepherd; Farm Servant (in-door); Farmer's, Grazier's son, grandson, brother, nephew'; 'General Labourer', excluding those returned for cities and 'principal towns'. (Farmers' relatives excluded those aged under fifteen. Principal towns were generally those with at least 2,000 inhabitants). *Occupied Male Farming Population* = the sum of *Farmers* and *Farm Workers/Labourers*. *Occupied Male Population 1841–81* = persons with specified occupations. Note that in Table 22 and elsewhere farmers' 'assisting relatives' have not *invariably* been aggregated with labourers and the like.

TABLE 21

Categories as in Table 20. 1841: *Census* 'General Summary: Tables of Rural and Civic Districts' gives total number of occupied males aged fifteen and over in rural districts. The occupied males under fifteen given in provincial tables of occupations have been assigned to rural districts according to the proportion of older occupied males in such districts within each province. The occupied male farming population in rural districts has been calculated by allocating the total occupied male farming population in the same proportions as (in each province) the number of families 'chiefly engaged in agriculture' were allocated between rural and urban ('civic') districts. 1881: *Census*. The total occupied male population and the total occupied male farming population were respectively reduced by using the County Tables Sections V, XIXA, and XXI to remove all occupied males and all occupied farming males in towns with populations of 2,000 and over. Of course the list of such towns changed between 1841 and 1881 as did certain urban boundaries.

TABLE 22

The figures for 'Farmers' alone are probably accurate enough in all years (see note to Table 20). Male assisting relatives (excluding those aged under fifteen) are separately noted in the 1881 Census. The earlier figures have been obtained by assuming that the ratio of assisting relatives to farmers was the same (by province and nationally) 1841–71 (the returns of assisting relatives in the 1871 Census are clearly inadequate) as in 1881. As not all assisting relatives were successfully pinned down as such even in 1881, the figures in Table 22 almost certainly underestimate the number of assisting relatives and exaggerate the number of labourers.

TABLE 23

Farmers from 1871 *Census* as defined in note to Table 20. Percentages likely to have the vote calculated according to the distribution of all agricultural holdings by valuation in 1866 (see Table 17 and the notes on its sources) with a new break at twelve pounds as in note to Table 4. County electorate for 1868–9 from *Thom 1870*, p. 779. Understatement is caused because the inclusion among male farmers of a certain number aged under twenty-one is more than outweighed by the fact that many of the occupiers of the smallest agricultural holdings in 1866 (28.7 per cent of which were valued at £4 or less) were probably not returned as 'farmers' in the Census, and because of the multiple occupation of several holdings by individual farmers. An even distribution of holdings held by female farmers throughout the valuation scale has been assumed. A *very small* proportion of the farmers in the 'Male farmers' column would in fact have had votes in counties of cities and towns rather than in county constituencies at large.

TABLE 24

Sources: for 1847–8: 'Appendix H. Return showing the number of estates in the several poor law unions of Ireland, divided into 17 classes, from under £50 to £5000 and upwards; setting forth . . . the values of each class of estate according to the poor law valuation' in *Appendix to minutes of evidence taken before the select committee of the House of Lords appointed to inquire into the operation of the Irish poor law, and the expediency of making any amendment in its enactments*, H.L. 1849 (19 App.), xxxii, 531–2; for 1873–4: *Return of owners of land of one acre and upwards in the several counties, counties of cities, and counties of towns in Ireland*, H.C. 1876 [C 1492], lxxx, 61–394. The values of the estates returned in 1847–8 are 'exaggerated' because the poor-law valuation then in force was higher than Griffith's valuation operative in 1873–4 (see note to Table 17), because some very small properties were almost certainly overlooked, and because a small proportion of land in four of the five 'counties' resisted official attempts to discover ownership (by value, 4.6 per cent in 'Kerry', 15.5 per cent in 'Cork', 2.4 per cent in 'Leitrim', 1.1 per cent in 'Carlow'). However, possibly a strong pull in the opposite direction is caused by the fact that the 1847–8 figures relate initially to poor-law unions and the 1873–4 figures to counties, the latter being substantially larger. The 'splitting' of *some* of the earlier estates at union boundaries must certainly have reduced the number of large estates, though even the 1873–4 figures are not 'national' ones. Two approaches have been adopted in an attempt to overcome this and the associated problem that union and county boundaries are rarely identical. In the case of 'Cork' (11 unions) and 'Kerry' (5 unions) the boundaries are very similar (indeed identical if the two counties are taken as a single unit), but the large number of unions distorts the 1847–8 figures (though the 1873–4 Cork estates are also split into *two* between the county of the city and the county at large). For both 'Longford' and 'Carlow' it has been possible to find a single union of the same name in 1847–8 which, while omitting parts of the county and containing small sections of other counties, fits reasonably well and is of generally similar size to the county proper. 'Leitrim', with only two unions (Mohill and Manorhamilton) covering almost four-fifths of the county (and not extending beyond it), represents a middle position. The general trends are similar in all five areas. The fact that proprietor categories are not national ones naturally reduces the number of large owners but also more accurately reflects the distribution of power within local political units. (Note that poor-law unions were much larger before 1850 than thereafter.)

TABLE 25

Source as in Chapter II, note 3 p. 106. Comparing the material given in the 1870 'Return' and that in the so-called 'Domesday Book' (H.C. 1876 (412, 422), lxxx), it would seem that, of the *total* acreage in Ireland (excluding waste land), 92,973 acres (0.5 per cent), and of the total valuation, £3,228,924 (24.1 per cent) were excluded by 'omitting all cities and towns' in the 1870 data. Thus, their inclusion could not have any significant effect on the land distribution pattern, but might reduce the proportion of the total valuation in the hands of the largest landowners (by size), though many of these also owned substantial urban property.

TABLE 26

Source as in Chapter II, note 2 p. 109. The categories in the *Return* have been allocated as follows: Residents = 'resident on or near property'; Semi-residents = 'resident usually elsewhere in Ireland and occasionally on the property' and 'resident elsewhere in Ireland'; Absentees = 'resident usually out of Ireland but occasionally on the property' and 'rarely or never resident in Ireland'. The small number 'not ascertained' have been excluded, as have proprietors under 100 acres.

TABLE 27

Taken from W. E. Vaughan, 'An assessment of the economic performance of Irish landlords, 1851–81' in *Ireland under the Union: Varieties of tension: Essays in honour of T. W. Moody*, ed. F. S. L. Lyons and R. A. J. Hawkins (Oxford, 1980), p. 187. Output figures exclude potatoes and are three-year averages. Rather different versions of this material are presented in Vaughan's 'Landlord and Tenant Relations in Ireland between the Famine and the Land War, 1850–78' in *Comparative aspects of Scottish and Irish economic and social history 1600–1900*, ed. L. M. Cullen and T. C. Smout (Edinburgh, [1977]), pp. 216–26, and in his 'Agricultural Output, Rents, and Wages in Ireland, 1850–1880' in *Ireland and France 17th–20th Centuries: Towards a comparative study of rural history*, ed. L. M. Cullen and F. Furet (Paris, 1980), pp. 85–97. C. Ó. Gráda, in 'Agricultural Head Rents, Pre-Famine and Post-Famine', *Economic and Social Review*, v (1973–4), 385–92, is less convincing in his higher output estimates for 1852–4 (even allowing for his inclusion of potatoes). Also, his suggestion that landlords were taking a greater share of total output in rent overlooks the growing importance of livestock production and the fact that such extensive forms of agriculture produce a proportionately higher surplus on potential rent than more intensive forms such as tillage (see P. Connell, 'An Economic geography of Co. Meath 1770–1870' (St Patrick's College Maynooth MA thesis, 1980), p. 220).

TABLE 28

List of Club members in Dunraven Papers D3196/F/5/14, and of Hunt members in Colonel Wyndham-Quin, *The Fox Hound in County Limerick* (Dublin, 1919), p. 125. Landholding traced in *Return of owners of land of one acre and upwards in the several counties . . . in Ireland*, H.C. 1876 [C 1492], lxxx, 61–394, and U. H. H. de Burgh, *The Landowners of Ireland* (Dublin, [1878]). Probably about 10–15 per cent of members held smaller estates. Of the 183 ordinary club members, no less than 69 were magistrates in Cos. Limerick and Clare and Limerick City (30 of these *not* having land valued at £500 or more), 6 were peers, 4 baronets/knights, and 7 Church of Ireland clergymen.

TABLE 29

For A: U. H. H. de Burgh, *The Landowners of Ireland* [1878], which includes all with at least *either* 500 acres or £500 valuation; for B: J. Bateman, *The Great Landowners of Great Britain and Ireland*, 4th edn. (London, 1883). Only London clubs have been used, since there was no clearly Whig club in Ireland.

Tory clubs were the Carlton and Junior Carlton, St Stephen's and the Conservative. Liberal clubs were the Reform, Devonshire, and Brooks's. This somewhat inflates the Whig element, as Brooks's included a few notable Tories (Lord Oranmore and Browne, Lord Powerscourt, etc.). Multiple membership adds no weight. Valuation bands refer either to land in Ireland *alone* or (where relevant) in Britain *alone*.

TABLE 30

The rank of proprietors is based on the number of voters on their estates. Armagh: MS 'List of County Interests after 1832 Registry' in Election File in Armagh Museum; Leitrim: *Ballyshannon Herald*, 23 Nov. 1832; Down: 'County of Down landed proprietors, with the extent and valuation of each property and the number of voters under each landlord', Londonderry Papers D/Lo/C164 No. 14; Louth: *An analysis of the parliamentary register of voters for the County of Louth, with the names of the landlords and their tenants on the register of voters, shewing the candidate for whom they voted at the election in April 1865* (Dublin: Peter Roe, 1865)—copy N.L.I. P2491.

TABLE 31

The figures for 1800 are based on 'Abstract of the Returns of the several Roman Catholic Bishops of Ireland', January 1801, in *Memoirs and Correspondence of Viscount Castlereagh*, ed. Charles Vane, Marquess of Londonderry, 4 vols. (London, 1848-9), iv, 97-173, as adjusted in S. J. Connolly, *Priests and People in pre-Famine Ireland 1780-1845* (Dublin, 1982), pp. 33, 36, 282-6; for 1835 on *First Report of the Commissioners of Public Instruction, Ireland*, H.C. 1835 [45, 46], xxxiii, 870-96; for the remaining years on the issues of [Battersby's] *Catholic Directory* published at Dublin one year after the year in question. The Catholic populations in 1845 and 1851 have been estimated at 80 per cent of the total population; thereafter the figures are available in the respective censuses.

TABLE 33

For 1868, see Chapter IV, note 1 p. 269. For 1870, see *Names of the Voters at the election held in Londonderry on Thursday, February 17th, 1870* (Londonderry: Sentinel Office, [1870])—copy in Magee College Library, Derry, as amended by *State of the Poll at the election for the City of Londonderry, 17th February 1870* (Londonderry: John Hempton, [1870])—copy in Queen's University Library, Belfast.

TABLE 34

List of Conservative Committee in *Londonderry Sentinel*, 6 Oct. 1868. Members and voters traced through the two Derry poll books listed in sources for Tables 8, 9, and 10. Percentages are of those identified. All could be identified as to religion, but the occupations of five of the seventy-nine committee members and 144 of the 599 Tory voters could not be traced. The 'gentlemen' were mostly either urban *rentiers* or men with land in the vicinity of the city.

TABLE 35

M. Stenton and S. Lees (eds.), *Who's Who of British Members of Parliament*, 4 vols. (Hassocks and Brighton, 1976-81) has been augmented by a wide range of other sources. The groups are discrete and consist of (a) all sitting 1832-59 who did *not* sit after 1859 and (b) all sitting 1859-85 who did *not* sit after 1885. Length of service is not taken account of. Military men have generally been accounted 'landed'. The *main* 'occupation' has been taken in each case.

TABLE 36

Adapted from table in D. Thornley, *Isaac Butt and Home Rule* (London, 1964), p. 207, save that in 1868 Edward Saunderson (Cavan) has been transferred to the Liberal side and in 1874 Philip Callan has been counted twice having been returned for two constituencies. 'Landowner' here is a man possessed of landed property with a valuation of £1,000 or more.

TABLE 37

Based on a wide variety of sources including U. H. H. de Burgh, *The Landowners of Ireland* [1878], contemporary parliamentary returns, handbooks, etc. (see list in D. Thornley, *Isaac Butt and Home Rule*, p. 206, note 4). To ensure comparability with Table 36 the definition of landowner was kept the same. This produces different results from those for 1880 in C. C. O'Brien, *Parnell and his Party 1880-90*, corrected impression (Oxford, 1964), p. 18, where the looser definition of 1,000 *acres* or more (rather than £1,000 valuation or more) is used (*pace* Thornley, op. cit., who suggests that O'Brien used valuation criteria). In 1880 I count Parnell three times and in 1885 T. M. Healy and E. D. Gray twice, as all enjoyed multiple returns. But for this, the proportion of Home Rule landlords in 1880 would have been smaller still.

TABLE 38

Devon Index, under 'Outrages, Agrarian'. Only reasons given by witnesses examined *as to particular counties* were analysed.

TABLE 39

A Return of all aggravated assaults; of all assaults endangering life; of all incendiary fires; of every demand or robbery of arms; of all cases of persons appearing armed; of all unlawful oaths administered or tendered; of all threatening notices or letters delivered or posted; of all malicious injuries to property; and of all firings into dwellings . . ., H.C. 1846 (369), xxxv, 181-234. Not all of the individual cases in this *Return* were officially assigned as 'agrarian', and a few traditional 'agrarian' crimes, such as levelling of land and maiming of cattle, were not included. Somewhat different figures presented differently for the same counties are given in M. [R.] Beames, *Peasants and Power: The Whiteboy Movements and their control in pre-Famine Ireland* (Brighton, 1983), pp. 225-32.

TABLE 40

A Return of all murders that have been committed in Ireland since the 1st day of January 1842; specifying the county, and the barony of the county, where each murder was committed; the name and condition of the person so murdered . . . Similar Return of attempts to murder attended with bodily injuries, H.C. 1846 (220), xxxv, 293–306. Under 'A' the only significant provincial difference was that the proportion of Labourer/servant victims was especially high in Connacht (49.5 per cent) and Munster (48.7 per cent) and low in Leinster (37.8 per cent). 'Ireland' here excludes the Dublin Metropolitan Police District.

TABLE 41

A: S.P.O. Fenian Papers, Habeas Corpus Act Abstracts of Cases 1866–8; B: *Report of the Commissioners appointed to inquire into the treatment of Treason Felony Convicts in English prisons*, H.C. 1871 [C 319], xxxii, 42–5; C: B. Mac Giolla Choille, 'Mourning the Martyrs: A study of a demonstration in Limerick City, 8 December 1867', *North Munster Antiquarian Journal*, x (1967), 173–205 (police identified about a third of the *urban* participants—few ruralists were identified). Though 'A' is a better source than the rag-bag List of Fenian Suspects 1866–71 (S.P.O. Fenian Papers), an analysis of the latter in S. Clark, *Social origins of the Irish Land War* (Princeton, 1979), p. 203 is fully in line with the above.

TABLE 42

S.P.O. Irish Crime Records (printed but not published)—commencing 1849 (figures for 1837–48 in the Return for 1851). Mid-year population estimates taken from B. R. Mitchell and P. Deane, *Abstract of British Historical Statistics*, new edn. (Cambridge, 1976), pp. 8–9. 'Homicides' = murders and manslaughters only; 'serious assaults' = assaults with intent to murder, aggravated assaults, and assaults endangering life only. The non-exclusion of the *population* of the Dublin Metropolitan Police District should not affect trends.

TABLES 43 A AND B

Table 43A based on S.P.O. Irish Crime Records—from 1849 (see sources for Table 42); Table 43B on T. W. Grimshaw, *Facts and Figures about Ireland Part I* (Dublin, 1893), Summary Table VI.

TABLE 44

For 1837 and 1845: *Devon Commission*, part iv, H.C. 1845 [672], xxii, Appendixes 79 to 83; for 1869: *Thom 1870*, p. 795; for 1886: *Thom 1888*, p. 635.

TABLES 45 A AND B

1844: *Devon Commission*, part iii, H.C. 1845 [657], xxi, Appendix 36; other years: S.P.O. Irish Crime Records. The eight periods analysed are: 1844 only (county division of *agrarian* outrages not available for 1845), 1849–50, 1854–5, 1859–60, 1864–5, 1874–5 (figures for 1869–70 unreliable), 1879–80, and 1884–5. County populations outside towns of 500 or more inhabitants taken from H. Mason, 'The development of the urban pattern in Ireland 1841–1881' (University of Wales Ph.D. thesis, 1969), Appendix Five.

TABLE 46

S.P.O. Irish Crime Records. Both the population and outrages of Cork City are entirely excluded, but Galway Town is included in the county's west riding. The *total* populations of the relevant areas have been used for both calculations. Outrage figures are not presented on a riding basis before 1865.

TABLE 47

To reflect as closely as possible the characteristics of the various individual counties, all figures are the products of unweighted county means. Sections I and V are based on the relevant annual parliamentary papers of *Agricultural Statistics* (for list, see J. S. Donnelly Jr., *The Land and the People of nineteenth-century Cork*, pp. 393-4); Section II on *Returns (No. 1) showing the number of agricultural holdings, with the area, valuation, and population of the agricultural districts in each county in Ireland . . .*, H.C. 1867 (144), lvi, 517-26; Section III is adapted from D. Fitzpatrick, 'The Disappearance of the Irish Agricultural Labourer, 1841-1912', *Irish Economic and Social History*, vii (1980), Table II (where all farmers' assisting relatives are categorized as labourers); Section IV based on *Return by provinces and counties . . . of cases of evictions which have come to the knowledge of the Constabulary in each of the years from 1849 to 1880 inclusive*, H.C. 1881 (185), lxxvii, 725-47.

TABLE 48

S.P.O. Irish Crime Records, and (for 1844 agrarian outrages only) *Devon Commission*, part iii, H.C. 1845 [657], xxi, Appendix 36.

TABLE 49

1842 and 1882 based on R.I.C. Records in P.R.O. H0184/3, 25, and 26 (in 1842 there are gaps in the occupational data); Jan.-Mar. 1913 on D. Fitzpatrick, *Politics and Irish Life 1913-1921: Provincial experience of War and Revolution* (Dublin, 1977), p. 24.

TABLE 50

Based on H. J. Hanham, 'Religion and Nationality in the mid-Victorian Army' in *War and Society: Historical essays in honour and memory of J. R. Western 1928-1971*, ed. M. R. D. Foot (London, 1973), pp. 176-81. For somewhat different figures, see A. R. Skelley, *The Victorian Army at Home: The Recruitment and Terms and Conditions of the British Regular, 1859-1899* (London, 1977), pp. 284-9.

TABLE 51

Soldiers: *A Return of the number of commissioned and non-commissioned officers and men, distinguishing cavalry and infantry, employed in the public service in Great Britain and Ireland, and in the Colonies (exclusive of India), on the 1st Day of January in each of the years 1792, 1822, 1828, 1830, 1835, and 1842*, H.C. 1843 (140), xxxi, 145-9; *General annual Return of the British*

Army for the year 1881, abstracts for the years 1862 to 1881, H.C. 1882 [C 3405], xxxviii, 512. Police: *Abstract of Return for each year, 1835-6 to 1851-2, inclusive . . . of the number of police in England and Wales, Ireland, and Scotland*, H.C. 1852 (260), xxx, 1-4; *Return of the Police Force in England and Wales* [and Ireland and Scotland], H.C. 1864 (409), xxxv, 599-634; *Judicial Statistics 1881*, H.C. 1882 [C 3333], lxxv, 9 (England and Wales), [C 3355], lxxv, 287 (Ireland), [C 3353], lxxv, 390 (Scotland). Dublin Metropolitan Police strength is included in the Irish figures.

TABLE 52

Derived from the respective *Censuses*. School figures are based on attendances during the weeks ending 5 June 1841, 13 Apr. 1861, and 14 May 1881. Pupils *enrolled* in National Schools rose (as a percentage of those aged 6-15) from 13.7 per cent in 1841 to 66.6 per cent in 1861 and 87.1 per cent in 1881.

TABLE 53

The Banking Almanac, Directory, Year Book, and Diary for 1860 (London, [1860]), and *for 1880* (London, [1880]).

TABLE 54

For evictions: printed 'Return showing number and particulars of each eviction from agricultural holdings from 1st January 1881 to 31st March 1881', marked 'Private and Confidential' in Harcourt Papers 106. For holdings: *Return of agricultural holdings in Ireland, compiled by the Local Government Board*, H.C. 1881 [C 2934], xciii, 804-5.

TABLE 55

For memberships: Register of Ballydehob Land League Branch 1880-1, S.P.O. Irish National League Papers Carton 9; Minute and Membership Book of Raheen Land League Branch 1880-1, N.L.I. MS 9219. For holdings in unions: *Return of agricultural holdings in Ireland, compiled by the Local Government Board*, H.C. 1881 [C 2934], xciii, 793-805.

TABLE 56

Catholic Rent: T. Wyse, *Historical Sketch of the late Catholic Association of Ireland*, 2 vols. (London, 1829), ii, pp. cclxx-cclxxi. O'Connell Annuity: *Detailed Report of Contributions (Parochial and Personal) to the O'Connell National Annuity for the year 1833* (Dublin, 1834)—copy in Hull University Library DA 950.2 01. Repeal meetings: for 1 Mar.-1 Oct. 1843 in Confidential Print (copies in Peel Papers Add. MS 40540 and Derby Papers 33/2). Tenant League Funds: *Nation*, 7 Feb. 1852. Amnesty meetings: for 11 July-24 Oct. 1869 in P. Byrne to I. Butt, 1 Nov. 1869, Butt Papers MS 8691. Land League meetings: *Return showing for each month of the years 1879 and 1880 the number of Land League meetings held . . .*, H.C. 1881 (5), lxxvii, 793-803. National League membership: S.P.O. Irish National League Papers Carton 9. Parnell

Tribute: *United Ireland,* 30 Nov. 1883 (this is the last county breakdown I could find and covers 80 per cent of the final sum raised in Ireland). Tenant Defence Fund: reprinted from *Freeman's Journal* in a pamphlet published by the Irish Loyal and Patriotic Union entitled *The Tenants' Defence Fund* (1890)—copy in Bodleian Library John Johnson Collection, Ireland Box 1.

Bibliography

A Manuscript Sources
B Parliamentary Debates and Papers
C Newspapers
D Poll Books
E Reference Works
F Dissertations
G Nineteenth-century Printed Works
H Twentieth-century Printed Works
(Abbreviations as listed at beginning of book)

A MANUSCRIPT SOURCES

Asterisked collections proved especially rich in material, though many of the other sources provided valuable information on particular topics.

Abercorn Papers Papers of 1st Duke of Abercorn (Viceroy 1866–8 and 1874–6): P.R.O.N.I. T2541.

Aberdeen Papers Papers of 4th Earl of Aberdeen: B.L.

Acton Papers Papers (including correspondence) of Sir John Acton, Bt., MP (later 1st Baron Acton): C.U.L.

Aldermen of Skinner's Alley Papers Papers of this Dublin Protestant political and social club: R.I.A.

Andrews Papers Papers of the Andrews family: in possession of Edwin Bryson, Belfast (transcript kindly provided via P.R.O.N.I.).

Anglesey Papers* Political and estate papers of 1st Marquess of Anglesey (Viceroy 1828–9 and 1830–3): P.R.O.N.I. D619.

Antrim Election Songs P.R.O.N.I. T1104.

Armagh Election File Armagh Museum, Armagh (folder of assorted election material on Armagh County and Borough).

Ashbourne Papers Papers of 1st Baron Ashbourne: originals in House of Lords Record Office—copies examined at P.R.O.N.I. T2955.

Ballad Collections B.L. Pressmark C.116.h.3; Bradshaw Collection, C.U.L. Hib. 2.867.1 and 2; N.L.I. Pressmark J39988 (2 vols.); many scattered in *Outrage Papers* in S.P.O. [mostly printed].

Ballydehob Land League Branch Register Book S.P.O. *Irish National League Papers* Carton 9 (see also under *Raheen* and *Rathvilly*).

Bath Papers Papers relating to the management of the Bath estates in Co. Monaghan: Longleat House, Wiltshire.

Belmore Papers* Political and other papers of 4th Earl of Belmore: P.R.O.N.I. D3007.

Blake of Ballyglunin Papers* Papers of M. J. Blake, MP, of Galway: P.R.O.I. M6935 and M6936.

Board of Trade Papers P.R.O. (Share Register of the Atlantic Royal Mail Steam Navigation Company BT31/363/1333).

Broadlands Archive Papers relating to the management of the Irish estates of 3rd Viscount Palmerston: Hampshire County Record Office, Winchester 27M60 (see also *Palmerston Letter-Books* and *Palmerston Papers*).

Bruce Papers Papers of Sir H. H. Bruce, MP: Among Babington & Croasdaile (solicitors) Papers P.R.O.N.I. D1514.

Burgess Papers Papers of an Athlone antiquarian: Longford-Westmeath Library, Athlone.

Butt Papers Papers of Isaac Butt, MP: N.L.I.

Cabinet Papers See *Printed Cabinet Papers*.

Cairns Papers Papers of 1st Earl Cairns: P.R.O.

Carleton, Atkinson, & Sloan Papers Papers of Portadown (Co. Armagh) solicitors: P.R.O.N.I. D1252.

Carlingford Papers Papers and diaries of Chichester Fortescue, MP (later 1st Baron Carlingford): Somerset County Record Office, Taunton.

*Carlisle Papers** Papers of 7th Earl of Carlisle (Chief Secretary—as Lord Morpeth—1835-41, Viceroy 1855-8 and 1859-64): Castle Howard, Yorkshire.

Carnarvon Papers (B.L.) Papers of 4th Earl of Carnarvon (Viceroy 1885-6): B.L.

Carnarvon Papers (P.R.O.) Papers of 4th Earl of Carnarvon (Viceroy 1885-6): P.R.O.

Chaloner Papers Papers of Robert Chaloner, land agent to Earl Fitzwilliam: North Yorkshire County Record Office, Northallerton, in Gisborough Papers ZFM (see also *Fitzwilliam Papers* and *Wentworth Woodhouse Muniments*).

Chambré Papers Papers of the Chambré family of Co. Armagh: P.R.O. M7035.

*Clanricarde Papers** Papers of 1st Marquess of Clanricarde: Leeds City Libraries Archives Department (Sheepscar Branch Library).

*Clarendon Papers** Papers of 4th Earl of Clarendon (Viceroy 1847-52): Bodleian Library, Oxford (refers to the 'Irish Deposit' section of the collection).

Clogher Diocesan Papers Episcopal and other papers of the Roman Catholic diocese of Clogher: P.R.O.N.I. DIO(RC)1.

Clonalis Papers Political and other papers of the family of The O'Conor Don: Clonalis, Castlerea, Co. Roscommon.

Clonbrock Papers Papers of the Barons Clonbrock and their Galway estates: N.L.I.

Close (Richardson of Drum) Papers Estate and other Ulster family papers: P.R.O.N.I. D2002.

*Clothworkers' Company Papers** Papers relating to the Co. Londonderry estates of the company: Clothworkers' Hall, London (see also *Drapers', Fishmongers',* and *Ironmongers' Papers*).

[Congested Districts Board], 'Base-Line Reports' Copy in Trinity College Dublin Library Pressmark A.7.11 (printed but not published).

Courtown Papers Political and other papers of the Earls of Courtown of Co. Wexford: Trinity College Dublin Library.

W. S. Crawford Papers Papers of William Sharman Crawford, MP: P.R.O.N.I. D856.

Cullen Papers [so cited]* Papers of Paul Cullen, Archbishop of Armagh (1849-52) and Dublin (1852-78) and cardinal: Diocesan Archives, Dublin.

Cullen Papers (Irish College, Rome) Papers of the same—mostly as Rector of the College before 1849: Archives of the Irish College, Rome.

G. R. Dawson's Election Diary MS Diary of Derry City election of 1837 by the Conservative candidate: P.R.O.N.I. T874.

G. R. Dawson's Election Expenses MS accounts of Conservative candidate at Derry City election of 1837: P.R.O.N.I. T1048/4.

Derby Papers* Papers of 14th Earl of Derby (Chief Secretary 1830-3 etc.): in keeping of Lord Blake, The Queen's College, Oxford.

Devonshire Papers Political and estate papers of the Dukes of Devonshire, including papers of Lord Hartington (later 8th Duke) as Chief Secretary 1871-4: Chatsworth, Derbyshire (see also *Lismore Papers*).

Devoy Papers Papers of John Devoy: N.L.I.

Dixon Papers Papers of Joseph Dixon, Archbishop of Armagh (1852-66): Diocesan Archives, Armagh.

Domvile Papers Papers of Sir Charles Domvile of Santry House, Co. Dublin: N.L.I.

Downshire Papers* Political and estate papers of 3rd and 4th Marquesses of Downshire: P.R.O.N.I. D671.

Drapers' Company Papers* Papers relating to the Co. Londonderry estates of the company: Drapers' Hall, London (see also *Clothworkers', Fishmongers',* and *Ironmongers' Papers*).

Dublin District Orange Lodge No. 1 Minute Books See *Orange Order Papers*.

Dufferin Papers Estate and other papers of 1st Earl of Dufferin: P.R.O.N.I. Mic.22.

Dunboyne Scrapbooks Scrapbooks of 14th Baron Dunboyne: N.L.I.

Dundas of Arniston Papers Papers relating to small properties in Cos. Limerick and Galway: Miss Dundas of Arniston, Gorebridge, Scotland (via Scottish Record Office, Edinburgh).

Dungannon Borough Revision Papers Part of *Longfield, Kelly, & Armstrong Papers* (Dungannon solicitors): P.R.O.N.I. D847.

Dunraven Papers Estate and other papers of the Earls of Dunraven: P.R.O.N.I. D3196.

Eglinton Papers* Papers of 13th Earl of Eglinton (Viceroy 1852 and 1858-9): Scottish Record Office, Edinburgh.

Electoral Register for Co. Armagh (1852): N.L.I. Pressmark I6551.

Electoral Register for Co. Armagh (1870): P.R.O.N.I. T2883.

Electoral Registers for Co. Galway (1857): P.R.O.I. M2433 and M3446 (Moycullen, Ross, Ballynahinch Baronies only).

Electoral Registers for Co. Mayo (1857): P.R.O.I. M2782-4 and M3447-8 (Tyrawley, Kilmaine, Gallen, Costello, Clanmorris Baronies only).

Electoral Register for Co. Roscommon (1859): *Incorporated Society Papers* MS 5805 (Athlone Barony only).

Ellice Papers Papers of Edward Ellice, MP (1781-1863), Liberal Chief Whip and minister: National Library of Scotland, Edinburgh.

Ellison Macartney Papers Papers of J. W. Ellison Macartney, MP: P.R.O.N.I.

Erne Papers Papers of 3rd Earl of Erne: P.R.O.N.I. D1939.

Farnham Papers Papers of 5th Baron Farnham: N.L.I.

Fenian Papers S.P.O.

Fishmongers' Company Papers Papers relating to the Co. Londonderry estates of the company: Guildhall Library, London (see also *Clothworkers', Drapers',* and *Ironmongers' Papers*).

FitzGerald Papers* Papers of Maurice FitzGerald, Hereditary Knight of Kerry (1774–1849): in possession of Adrian FitzGerald Esq., London (Calendar at P.R.O.N.I.).

Fitzwilliam Papers Papers relating to Earl Fitzwilliam's Irish estates: N.L.I. MSS 3987 and 8816–17 (see also *Chaloner Papers* and *Wentworth Woodhouse Muniments*).

Flanagan Scrapbook Scrapbook respecting Sligo and its elections in the 1860s: N.L.I. MS 14335.

Folklore Commission Manuscripts Reminiscences etc. collected by the Irish Folklore Commission: Department of Irish Folklore, University College, Dublin.

Fortescue Papers Papers of 2nd Earl Fortescue (Viceroy 1839–41): Devon County Record Office, Exeter.

Fremantle Papers Papers of Sir Thomas Fremantle, later 1st Baron Cottesloe (Chief Secretary 1845–6): Buckinghamshire County Record Office, Aylesbury.

Gillooly Papers Papers of Laurence Gillooly, Bishop of Elphin (1858–95; Coadjutor 1856–8): Elphin Diocesan Archives, Sligo.

Sir Thomas Gladstone Papers Among Glynne-Gladstone Papers: St Deiniol's Library, Hawarden.

Gladstone Papers* Papers of W. E. Gladstone: B.L.

Gosford Papers Estate and other papers of the Earls of Gosford: P.R.O.N.I. D1606.

Graham Papers* Papers of Sir James Graham (2nd Baronet): Netherby, Cumbria (examined on microfilm at C.U.L.—also thus available at Bodleian Library, Oxford, and N.L.I.).

Grand Orange Lodge of Ireland Letter-Books See *Orange Order Papers*.

Harcourt Papers Papers of Sir William Harcourt (Home Secretary 1880–5 etc.): Bodleian Library, Oxford.

Hardinge Papers Papers of 1st Viscount Hardinge (Chief Secretary 1830 and 1834–5): McGill University Library, Montreal.

Hart Papers Estate and other Ulster family papers: P.R.O.N.I. D3077.

Hatherton Papers Papers of 1st Baron Hatherton (Chief Secretary 1833–4): Staffordshire County Record Office, Stafford.

Head Letters Letters between Sir F. B. Head, Lord Naas, and others: N.L.I. MS 18513.

Howard Bury Papers P.R.O.N.I. T3069.

Hughenden Papers Papers of Benjamin Disraeli, 1st Earl of Beaconsfield: Bodleian Library, Oxford (examined while still at Hughenden Manor).

Hylton Papers Papers of Sir William Jolliffe 1st Baron Hylton (Conservative Chief Whip 1852–9): Somerset County Record Office, Taunton.

Incorporated Society Papers Papers of the Incorporated Society for Promoting English Protestant Schools in Ireland (including material concerning the Society's estates and electoral activities): Trinity College Dublin Library.

Irish Confederation Papers Papers of the Irish Confederation (1840s): R.I.A.

Irish Crime Records* Various printed but unpublished crime returns compiled by Dublin Castle from 1849 onwards (with some earlier returns): S.P.O.

Irish National League Papers S.P.O.

Ironmongers' Company Papers* Papers relating to the Co. Londonderry estates of the company: Guildhall Library, London (see also *Clothworkers'*, *Drapers'*, and *Fishmongers' Papers*).

Johnston of Ballykilbeg Papers Papers and diaries of William Johnston of Bally-kilbeg: P.R.O.N.I. D880.

Kilmainham Papers Papers of the Irish military headquarters at the Royal Hospital, Kilmainham: N.L.I.
Kirby Papers* Papers of Revd (later Archbishop) Tobias Kirby, Rector of the Irish College, Rome (1849–91): Archives of the Irish College, Rome.
Kirk Papers Papers of William Kirk, MP: P.R.O.N.I. D1185.
Kirkpatrick Papers Papers of Revd George Kirkpatrick, Rector of Craigs from 1840: P.R.O.N.I. D1604.

Lalor Papers Papers of Richard Lalor, MP: N.L.I.
Lamb Diary Diary of Lieutenant George Lamb (1850s): N.L.I. MS 7323.
Land League Papers N.L.I. (a disappointing collection).
Larcom Papers Papers of Sir Thomas Larcom (Under-Secretary 1853–68): N.L.I.
Lawyer's Notebook for 1840 Trinity College Dublin Library MS 4590e.
Leahy Papers Papers of Patrick Leahy, Archbishop of Cashel (1857–75): Cashel Diocesan Archives, Thurles (available on microfilm at N.L.I.).
Leinster Papers Political and other papers of 3rd Duke of Leinster: P.R.O.N.I. D3078.
L'Estrange & Brett Papers Papers of Belfast solicitors (including election material): P.R.O.N.I. D1905.
Lismore Papers* Papers relating to the management of the Duke of Devonshire's Irish estates: N.L.I. (see also *Devonshire Papers*).
Londonderry Papers* Political and estate papers of 3rd and 4th Marquesses of Londonderry: Durham County Record Office, Durham.
Longfield, Kelly, & Armstrong Papers Papers of Dungannon solicitors: P.R.O.N.I. D847.

McCabe Papers Papers of Edward McCabe, Archbishop of Dublin (1879–85) and cardinal: Diocesan Archives, Dublin.
MacDevitt Letter-Book Letter-Book of James MacDevitt, Bishop of Raphoe (1871–9): Diocesan Archives, Armagh.
McKee Papers McKee family (Armagh) papers: P.R.O.N.I. D1821.
Manchester Papers Include material relating to the Duke of Manchester's Co. Armagh estates: Cambridgeshire County Record Office, Huntingdon.
Marlay Papers Include some material relating to the Westmeath estate of Charles Brinsley Marlay (formerly the Belvedere estate): Nottingham University Library.
Martin & Henderson Papers Papers (including election material) of Ulster solicitors: P.R.O.N.I. D2223.
Martin, King, French, & Ingram Papers Papers of Limavady (Co. Londonderry) solicitors: P.R.O.N.I. D1550.
Mayo Papers [so cited]* Papers of 6th Earl of Mayo (until Aug. 1867 known as Lord Naas)—Chief Secretary 1852, 1858–9, 1866–8: N.L.I.
Mayo Papers (C.U.L.) Papers of 6th Earl of Mayo relating mostly but not exclusively to his period as Viceroy of India (1869–72): C.U.L.

*Melbourne Papers** Papers of 2nd Viscount Melbourne: Royal Archives, Windsor Castle.

Minto Papers Papers of 2nd Earl of Minto: National Library of Scotland, Edinburgh.

Monsell Papers Papers of William Monsell, MP (1st Baron Emly): N.L.I.

Montgomery Papers Papers of Hugh de Fellenberg Montgomery of Co. Tyrone: P.R.O.N.I. D627.

Moody Papers Papers of A. J. H. Moody, grocer of Coleraine: P.R.O.N.I. T2901.

*Moore Papers** Papers of George Henry Moore, MP: N.L.I.

Morley Papers Deposit 69 Papers relating to the Pleydall/Dicken/Morley estate in Co. Cavan: Devon County Record Office (West), Plymouth.

Newcastle Papers Papers of 5th Duke of Newcastle (Chief Secretary 1846): Nottingham University Library.

Normanton Papers Include material relating to the 2nd Earl of Normanton's Co. Tipperary estate: Hampshire County Record Office, Winchester 21M57.

O'Brien Papers Papers of Edward O'Brien: Trinity College Dublin MS 3633.

O'Connell Papers (N.L.I.) Papers of Daniel O'Connell and of some of his political organizations: N.L.I.

O'Connell Papers (U.C.D.) Papers of Daniel O'Connell: U.C.D.

O'Conor Diary Diary (1869) of Denis Maurice O'Conor, MP: N.L.I. Microfilm Positive 5485.

O'Hagan Papers (N.L.I.) Papers of Thomas O'Hagan, MP (1st Baron O'Hagan): N.L.I.

O'Hagan Papers [so cited]* Papers of Thomas O'Hagan, MP (1st Baron O'Hagan): P.R.O.N.I. D2777.

O'Hara Diary Diary (1868–73) of Revd James O'Hara, curate of Coleraine: N.L.I. MS 14911.

O'Hara Papers Papers of the O'Hara Family of Co. Sligo, especially of C. W. Cooper, MP (later O'Hara): N.L.I.

O'Neill Daunt Papers Papers and diaries of W. J. O'Neill Daunt: N.L.I.

Orange Order Papers Include nineteenth-century letter-books and minute books of Grand Lodge of Ireland, admission and other records of various Dublin lodges, etc.: P.R.O.N.I. D2947.

Ordnance Survey Letter-Books P.R.O.I.

O'Reilly Papers Papers of Myles O'Reilly, MP: N.L.I. MS 17886.

Otway Papers Papers of the Otway family of Co. Tipperary: N.L.I.

*Outrage Papers** A vast collection produced by the Chief Secretary's and other departments in Dublin Castle: S.P.O. (see also *Registered Papers*).

Pack-Beresford Papers Beresford and Dunbar family papers, including political correspondence etc. of Lord John George de la Poer Beresford, Archbishop of Armagh (1822–62): P.R.O.N.I. D664.

Palmerston Letter-Books Letter-Books (1860s) of 3rd Viscount Palmerston: B.L. Add. MSS 48582-3 (see also *Broadlands Archive* and *Palmerston Papers*).

Palmerston Papers Papers of 3rd Viscount Palmerston: in keeping of National Register of Archives, London (see also *Broadlands Archive* and *Palmerston Letter-Books*).

Panmure Papers Include papers of 11th Earl of Dalhousie (Secretary at War 1846–52 etc.): Scottish Record Office, Edinburgh.

Peel Papers* Papers of Sir Robert Peel (2nd Baronet): B.L.

Perceval-Maxwell Papers Political and other papers of the Perceval-Maxwell family, including those of J. W. Maxwell (MP for Downpatrick 1820–30 and 1832–5): P.R.O.N.I. D1556 and D3244.

Petworth House Archives Contain some papers relating to the Leconfield estate in Co. Limerick: Petworth House, Sussex (via West Sussex County Record Office, Chichester).

Printed Cabinet Papers Collection of Confidential Prints (1880 onwards) prepared for the Cabinet: P.R.O. CAB.

Propaganda Archives Rome Archives of the Sacra Congregatio de Propaganda Fide, Rome (Acta and Scritture riferite nei Congressi, Irlanda series).

Raheen Land League Branch Minute and Membership Book N.L.I. MS 9219 (see also under *Ballydehob* and *Rathvilly*).

Ramsden (Bulstrode) Papers Include material relating to Edward Horsman (Chief Secretary 1855–7): Buckinghamshire County Record Office, Aylesbury.

Rathvilly Land (and National) League Branch Minute Book N.L.I. MS 842 (see also under *Ballydehob* and *Raheen*).

Reform League (English) Papers In George Howell Collection: Bishopsgate Institute, London.

Registered Papers A vast collection produced by the Chief Secretary's and other departments in Dublin Castle: S.P.O. (see also *Outrage Papers*).

Roden Letter-Book Letter-Book of 3rd Earl of Roden: P.R.O.N.I. T2647.

Rossmore Papers Political and estate papers of 3rd Baron Rossmore: P.R.O.N.I. T2929.

Royal Archives Windsor Castle (Victorian Archive).

Royal Black Preceptory, Enniskillen, Minute Book (1867–89): P.R.O.N.I. D1360/2A.

Royal College of Physicians of Ireland Archives Archives relating to the management of the College's landed estates in Co. Waterford: Royal College of Physicians of Ireland, Dublin.

Royal Irish Constabulary Records Among Home Office Papers: P.R.O.

Russell Papers Papers of Lord John (later 1st Earl) Russell: P.R.O.

Sandwich Papers Contain papers relating to the Earl of Sandwich's estate in Co. Limerick: Cambridgeshire County Record Office, Huntingdon.

Seaton Papers Papers of 1st Baron Seaton (Commander of the Forces in Ireland 1855–60): in the possession of J. E. C. Colborne-Mackrell Esq., Beechwood, Sparkwell, Devon (examined through the kindness of the Devon County Record Office (West), Plymouth).

Seymour of Ragley Papers Political and estate papers of the Seymour family and their Antrim estates: Warwickshire County Record Office, Warwick CR114A.

Shapland-Carew Papers Include papers of 1st Baron Carew of Co. Wexford: Trinity College Dublin Library.

Shirley of Ettington Papers* Papers of the Shirley family, including material relating to their Co. Monaghan estates: Warwickshire County Record Office, Warwick CR229.

Smith Barry Papers Papers relating to the Smith Barry estate in Co. Louth: N.L.I. MS 8819.

Smith O'Brien Papers Papers of William Smith O'Brien, MP: N.L.I.

Somerville Letter-Book Letter-Book of Sir William Somerville while Chief Secretary (1847–52): P.R.O.N.I. T2982.

South Co. Dublin Scrapbook (1885): N.L.I. MS 5946.

Stewart Letter-Book Letter-Book of G. F. Stewart, land agent for the estates of Colonel H. T. Clements in Co. Leitrim (1878–80): N.L.I. Leitrim Papers (Packing Crate 156).

Stipendiary Magistrates' Diaries Official duty diaries kept by stipendiaries on government orders in the 1830s and 1840s: S.P.O.

*Strathnairn Papers** Papers of 1st Baron Strathnairn (Commander of the Forces in Ireland 1865–70): B.L.

Trant Papers Papers of the Trant family of Co. Tipperary: N.L.I.

Valuation of Ireland [Griffith's Valuation]: see Section G below, Nineteenth-century Printed Works.

Vatican Secret Archives; Seg. di Stato Archives of the Vatican Secretariat of State: Vatican Secret Archives, Vatican City.

Stephen de Vere's Diary (1854–7): Trinity College Dublin Library MS 5066.

Vivian Papers Papers of 1st Baron Vivian (as Sir Hussey Vivian, Commander of the Forces in Ireland 1831–5): National Army Museum, London.

Walsh Papers Papers of William Walsh, Archbishop of Dublin (1885–1921): Diocesan Archives, Dublin.

War Office Papers P.R.O.

Wellesley Papers Papers of 1st Marquess Wellesley (Viceroy) 1821–8 and 1833–5): B.L.

Wentworth Woodhouse Muniments Papers of the Earls Fitzwilliam, including material relating to their Irish estates: Central Library, Sheffield (see also *Chaloner Papers* and *Fitzwilliam Papers*).

Wexford Independent Club Minute Book (1870s): N.L.I. Microfilm Positive 4026.

Youghal Corporation Records Cork Archives Council (include poll and rate books of the 1830s).

Youghal Protestant Operatives Scrapbook 1829–48 Bradshaw Collection, C.U.L. Hib.1.844.1.

Young Letter-Book Letter-Book (1850s and 1860s) of Sir John Young, later 1st Baron Lisgar (Chief Secretary 1853–5) relating mostly to his period as High Commissioner of the Ionian Islands but containing some Irish material: original in possession of the Seferis family of Greece—copy in possession of Anthony Seymour Esq., zur Talmühle, 8226 *SCHLEITHEIM*, kt. Schaffhausen, Switzerland.

Note It was not possible to obtain access to the Papers of 1st Earl of Kimberley (Viceroy 1864–6) or to those of 5th Earl Spencer (Viceroy 1868–74 and 1882–5).

B PARLIAMENTARY DEBATES AND PAPERS

Papers are listed in section ii, save for census returns which are listed together in section iii.

i Debates

Hansard's parliamentary debates, 3rd series, 1830-91.

ii Papers in Chronological Order

Papers presented to the House of Commons relating to the Royal College of St. Patrick, Maynooth, H.C. 1812-13 (204), vi.

Copy of a dispatch from His Excellency the Lord Lieutenant of Ireland, to Lord Viscount Sidmouth: dated 5th June 1816:—viz. A Statement of the nature and extent of the disturbances which have recently prevailed in Ireland, H.C. 1816 (479), ix.

Minutes of evidence taken before the select committee appointed to examine into the nature and extent of the disturbances which have prevailed in those districts of Ireland which are now subject to the provisions of the Insurrection Act, H.C. 1825 (20), vii.

Minutes of evidence taken before the select committee of the House of Lords appointed (in 1824) to examine into the nature and extent of the disturbances which have prevailed in those districts of Ireland which are now subject to the provisions of the Insurrection Act, H.C. 1825 (200), vii.

Report from the select committee appointed to inquire into the State of Ireland, more particularly with reference to the circumstances which may have led to disturbances in that part of the United Kingdom, H.C. 1825 (129), viii.

Minutes of evidence taken before the select committee of the House of Lords appointed to inquire into the State of Ireland, more particularly with reference to the circumstances which may have led to disturbances in that part of the United Kingdom, H.C. 1825 (181, 521), ix.

First Report of the Commissioners of Irish Education Inquiry, H.C. 1825 (400), xii.

Eighth Report of the Commissioners of Irish Education Inquiry, H.C. 1826-7 (509), xiii.

Report from the select committee on the State of Ireland, H.C. 1831-2 (677), xvi.

Second Report from the select committee of the House of Lords appointed to inquire into the collection and payment of tithes in Ireland, H.C. 1831-2 (663), xxii.

Copy of Instructions given by the chief secretary for Ireland with reference to the cities and boroughs in Ireland, sending representatives to parliament, H.C. 1831-2 (519), xliii.

Report from the select committee on the Carrickfergus election petition, H.C. 1833 (181), viii.

Report from the select committee on Carrickfergus Borough; with the minutes of evidence and an appendix, H.C. 1833 (527), viii.

Report from the select committee on the Newry Borough election petition, H.C. 1833 (76), x.

A Return of the electors registered in each county, county of a city, county of a town, and borough in Ireland . . . also the number of voters who polled, H.C. 1833 (177), xxvii. As corrected by *Amended Return . . . so far as relates to County Galway and County Tipperary*, H.C. 1833 (767), xxxiii.

A Return of the names, occupations, and residences of the registered freeholders, leaseholders, and £10 householders, included in the return made to the House of Commons on the 25th day of February 1834, by the clerk of the County of the Town of Carrickfergus, H.C. 1834 (329), xliii.

Papers relating to the State of Ireland, H.C. 1834 (459), xlvii.

Report from the select committee on Bribery at Elections, H.C. 1835 (547), viii.

First Report from the select committee appointed to inquire into the nature, character, extent, and tendency of Orange Lodges, Associations, or Societies in Ireland, H.C. 1835 (377), xv; *Second Report*, H.C. 1835 (475), xv; *Third Report*, H.C. 1835 (476), xvi.

Municipal Corporations (Ireland). Appendix to the First Report of the Commissioners Part I, H.C. 1835 [27, 28], xxvii.

First Report of the Commissioners of Public Instruction, Ireland, H.C. 1835 [45, 46], xxxiii.

An Account of the public income and expenditure of the United Kingdom, for the years ended 5th January 1833, 1834, and 1835, H.C. 1835 (302), xxxvii.

Proceedings had at an investigation held in Armagh on the Transactions which took place in that town and neighbourhood on the 15th January last, H.C. 1835 (101), xlv.

Correspondence relating to a meeting of the Inhabitants of the County of Tyrone, held in Dungannon, H.C. 1835 (120), xlv.

Copies of Correspondence between the lieutenants of counties . . . and the Irish government, previously to and during the late elections, H.C. 1835 (170), xlv.

Copies of Communications relative to the marching of people during the Kerry elections, H.C. 1835 (197), xlv.

Copies of Correspondence between the Roman Catholic priests of Borris, Robert Doyne Esq., and the lord lieutenant of Ireland, on alleged attendance of military at the Roman Catholic chapels, H.C. 1835 (198), xlv.

Copies of Extracts of Reports from Magistrates or officers of the constabulary, to His Majesty's government, with reference to riotous proceedings which lately took place in the Village of Ballykelly, Parish of Tamlaght-fadagan, County of Londonderry, H.C. 1835 (345), xlv.

Poor Inquiry (Ireland) Appendix D containing baronial examinations relative to earnings of labourers, cottier tenants, employment of women and children, expenditure, H.C. 1836 [36], xxxi.

Poor Inquiry (Ireland) Appendix E containing baronial examinations relative to food, cottages and cabins, clothing and furniture, pawnbroking and savings banks, distillation, H.C. 1836 [37], xxxii.

Poor Inquiry (Ireland) Appendix H—Part II. Remarks on the evidence taken in the Poor Inquiry (Ireland) contained in the Appendices (D) (E) (F) by one of the commissioners [J. E. Bicheno], H.C. 1836 [42], xxxiv.

Minutes of evidence taken before the committee on the Carlow County election petition, H.C. 1837 (307), x.

Minutes of evidence taken before the committee on the Longford County election petitions, H.C. 1837 (319), x.

Select Committee on Fictitious Votes, Ireland, 1st series, 1st report, H.C. 1837 (308), xi, part i, 2nd report, 1837 (335), xi, part ii, 3rd report, 1837 (480), xi, part ii; 2nd series, 1st report, H.C. 1837–8 (259), xiii, part i, 2nd report, 1837–8 (294), xiii, part i, 3rd report, 1837–8 (643), xiii, part ii.

Minutes of evidence taken before the select committee on the Kinsale election petition, H.C. 1837–8 (332), xii.

A Return of all reports made to the inspector general of police by the constabulary officers, during the late elections for the County and Borough of Sligo, H.C. 1837–8 (166), xlvi.

Minutes of evidence taken before the select committee of the House of Lords, appointed to inquire into the state of Ireland since the year 1835 in respect to Crime and Outrage, H.C. 1839 (486), xi and xii.

Third General Report relative to the Valuations for poor rates, and to the registered elective franchise in Ireland, H.C. 1841 [329], xxiii.

Report from the select committee on the Belfast election compromise, H.C. 1842 (431), v.

Minutes of the proceedings of the select committee on the Cork County election petition, and of the evidence taken before them, H.C. 1842 (271), vi.

A Return of the number of commissioned and non-commissioned officers and men, distinguishing cavalry and infantry, employed in the public service in Great Britain and Ireland, and in the Colonies (exclusive of India), on the 1st Day of January in each of the years 1792, 1822, 1828, 1830, 1835, and 1842, H.C. 1843 (140), xxxi.

A Return of Outrages reported by the constabulary in Ireland during the years 1837, 1838, 1839, 1840, and 1841: A like Return of Outrages during each month of the year 1842, H.C. 1843 [460], li.

Report from the select committee on Townland Valuation of Ireland, H.C. 1844 (513), vii.

Returns of parliamentary electors; also of tenements valued under the act 1 & 2 Vict., cap. 56 for the relief of the poor in Ireland, H.L. 1844, xv; and H.L. 1847-8, xxi.

Evidence taken before Her Majesty's Commissioners of Inquiry into the State of the Law and Practice in respect to the Occupation of Land in Ireland, parts i, ii, and iii, H.C. 1845 [606, 616, 657], xix, xx, xxi.

Appendix to the minutes of evidence taken before Her Majesty's Commissioners of Inquiry into the State of the Law and Practice in respect to the Occupation of Land in Ireland, part iv, H.C. 1845 [672], xxii.

Index to minutes of evidence taken before Her Majesty's Commissioners of Inquiry into the State of the Law and Practice in respect to the Occupation of Land in Ireland, H.C. 1845 [673], xxii.

Extracts made by Colonel M'Gregor from the police reports, stating the particulars of the principal homicides in Ireland in the years 1845 and 1846, and forwarded to the Home Office by him, H.C. 1846 (179), xxxv.

A Return of all murders that have been committed in Ireland since the 1st day of January 1842; specifying the county, and the barony of the county, where each murder was committed; the name and condition of the person so murdered . . . Similar Return of attempts to murder attended with bodily injuries, H.C. 1846 (220), xxxv.

Return relative to the persons who have been killed or severely wounded in affrays with the constabulary force in Ireland, since 1st December 1830, specifying their names, date, place of occurrence, H.C. 1846 (280), xxxv.

A Return of all aggravated assaults; of all assaults endangering life; of all incendiary fires; of every demand or robbery of arms; of all cases of persons appearing armed; of all unlawful oaths administered or tendered; of all threatening notices or letters delivered or posted; of all malicious injuries to property; and of all firings into dwellings . . . , H.C. 1846 (369), xxxv.

Minutes of evidence taken before the select committee on the Kinsale election petition, H.C. 1847-8 (138), xiii.

Appendix to minutes of evidence taken before the select committee of the House of Lords appointed to inquire into the operation of the Irish poor law, *and the expediency of making any amendment in its enactments,* H.L. 1849 (19 App.), xxxii.

Further Correspondence on the Subject of Convict Discipline and Transportation, H.C. 1850 [1285], xlv.

Papers relating to an investigation held at Castlewellan into the occurrences at Dolly's Brae, on the 12th July 1849, H.C. 1850 [1143], li.

Copy of a Letter addressed by the Commissioner for Valuation to the Lord Lieutenant of Ireland, H.C. 1851 (4), l.

Abstract of a statement of the amount of constabulary force employed in each county, county of a city, and county of a town, in Ireland, H.C. 1851 (214), l.

Report from the select committee on Outrages (Ireland); with proceedings of the committee, minutes of evidence, appendix and index, H.C. 1852 (438), xiv.

A Return of the number of newspaper stamps at one penny issued to the under-mentioned newspapers in England, Ireland, Scotland, and Wales from the year 1837 to the year 1850, H.C. 1852 (42), xxviii.

Abstract of Return for each year, 1835-6 to 1851-2, inclusive . . . of the number of police in England and Wales, Ireland, and Scotland, H.C. 1852 (260), xxx.

Minutes of evidence taken before the select committee on the Clare election petition, H.C. 1852-3 (595), ix.

Report from the select committee on the Cork City election petition, H.C. 1852-3 (528), xi.

Minutes of evidence taken before the select committee on the Mayo election petition, H.C. 1852-3 (415), xvi.

Minutes of evidence taken before the select committee on the Sligo Borough election petition, H.C. 1852-3 (600), xviii.

Sixth annual report of the commissioners for administering the laws for the relief of the poor in Ireland, H.C. 1852-3 [1645], l.

Number of electors on the register of 1852-3 in each county, city, and borough in Ireland, distinguishing their qualifications, H.C. 1852-3 (957), lxxxiii.

Copies of the several inquisitions removed from the Court of Queen's Bench . . . and transferred to the County of Clare . . . in relation to any of the cases of homicide etc. alleged to have been committed at the Town of Sixmile-bridge, in July last, at the time of the general election, H.C. 1852-3 (313), xciv.

A Return of the number of Troops, Constabulary, and Police at each polling place in Ireland, during the days of polling at the last general election, H.C. 1852-3 (325), xciv.

Report from the select committee on the Dungarvan election petition, H.C. 1854 (162), viii.

A Return of the number of newspaper stamps at one penny issued to news-papers in England, Ireland, Scotland, and Wales for the years 1851, 1852, 1853, H.C. 1854 (117), xxxix.

Return of the number of persons in Ireland assessed to the rate for the relief of the poor, made next before the rate collecting in July 1853, H.C. 1854 (503), lv.

Report from the select committee on Postal Arrangements (Waterford etc.), H.C. 1854-5 (445), xi.

Report of Her Majesty's Commissioners appointed to inquire into the manage-ment and government of the College of Maynooth, H.C. 1854-5 [1896], xxii.

Abstract of . . . Return of all persons appearing in the revised lists of voters in the several counties, counties of cities, and counties of towns in Ireland, and in parliamentary boroughs, H.C. 1854-5 (90), xlvii.

Minutes of evidence taken before the select committee on the Galway Town election petition, H.C. 1857 (187 Sess. 2), vi.

Minutes of evidence taken before the select committee on the Drogheda election petitions, H.C. 1857 (255 Sess. 2), vi.

Minutes of evidence taken before the select committee on the Mayo County election petition, H.C. 1857 (182 Sess. 2), vii.

Returns showing the counties in Ireland in which the tenement valuation has been completed, H.C. 1857 (21 Sess. 2), xlii.

Report of the Commissioners appointed. to investigate into the existence of corrupt practices in elections of members to serve in parliament for the County of the Town of Galway, H.C. 1857-8 [2291], xxvi.

Minutes of evidence taken before the select committee on the Clare election petition, H.C. 1860 (178), xi.

Returns showing the area, population, income tax, number of occupiers rated at various amounts, number of parliamentary voters etc. in each county in Ireland, H.C. 1860 (128), lv.

Returns of the number of voters which appear on the parliamentary register for each county, city, and borough in the United Kingdom for the year 1858 . . . and of the number of voters who recorded their votes at the general election . . . so far as relates to Ireland, H.C. 1860 (277-I), lv.

Report from the select committee on the Royal Atlantic Steam Navigation Company, H.C. 1861 (463), xii.

A Return of the outrages specially reported by the constabulary as committed within the Barony of Kilmacrenan, County Donegal, during the last ten years, H.C. 1861 (404), lii.

Return of the number of persons who have completed their education at the College of Maynooth, H.C. 1862 (137), xliii.

Return of the number of Cavalry, Artillery, and Infantry ordered to, or stationed in the County of Longford for the late election, H.C. 1862 (239), xliv.

A Return of the average rate of weekly earnings of agricultural labourers in Ireland, for the last 6 months previous to the 1st day of January 1861, H.C. 1862 (2), lx.

Return of the Police Force in England and Wales [and Ireland and Scotland], H.C. 1864 (409), xxxv.

Minutes of evidence and appendix to the report of the Commissioners of Inquiry, 1864, respecting the magisterial and police jurisdiction arrangements and establishment of the Borough of Belfast, H.C. 1865 [3466-I], xxviii.

Report of the commission directed by the Treasury to inquire into the state of the Constabulary Force in Ireland, with reference to their pay and allowances, H.C. 1866 [3658], xxxiv.

Return of the election petitions alleging Bribery and Corruption, H.C. 1866 (77), lvi.

Return of all election petitions alleging Intimidation or Undue Influence, H.C. 1866 (114), lvi.

Returns from the several sheriffs and returning officers of the abstract of expenses incurred by or on behalf of each candidate at the last general election, H.C. 1866 (160), lvi; similar *Returns*, H.C. 1874 (358), liii, and H.C. 1880 (382-II), lvii.

Return of all Schoolmasters arrested in Ireland for Ribbonism, Sedition, or connected with the Fenian Conspiracy, from 1st January 1860 to 12 March 1866, H.C. 1866 (455), lviii.

Minutes of evidence taken before the select committee on the Tipperary election, H.C. 1867 (211), viii.

Returns (No. 1) showing the number of agricultural holdings, with the area, valuation, and population of the agricultural districts in each county in Ireland: And (No. 2) of all the cities, boroughs, and towns in Ireland omitted in Return (No. 1), H.C. 1867 (144), lvi.

Copy of the Depositions taken before the Coroner at the Inquests held at Dungarvan . . . on . . . William O'Brien and Bartholomew Keily, killed at the last Waterford County election, H.C. 1867 (200), lvi.

Copies of all orders or requisitions to General or other Officers for Troops to escort voters on any day or days previous to the day of polling, at the last election for the County of Waterford . . . with the names of the magistrates in charge, H.C. 1867 (216), lvi.

Copy of the reports of the proceedings at the inquests held at Dungarvan in the month of January last, H.C. 1867 (237), lix.

Return of the number of occupiers in Irish counties rated at £8 and under £10, and at £10 and under £12, in 1866, H.C. 1867-8 (245), lvi.

Returns in tabular form of the different cities and boroughs in Ireland, in which the freeman franchise at present exists, H.C. 1867-8 (305), lvi.

Report from the select committee on parliamentary and municipal elections, H.C. 1868-9 (352), viii.

Minutes of evidence taken at the trial of the Cashel election petitions, H.C. 1868-9 (121), xlix.

Correspondence with the Irish government complaining of the use of military and police forces in the County of Sligo previous to the late election, H.C. 1868-9 (180), l.

Copy of General Instructions issued to the Royal Irish Constabulary in reference to carrying and using their firearms, H.C. 1868-9 (388), li.

Reports from the Poor Law Inspectors on the Wages of Agricultural Labourers in Ireland, H.C. 1870 [C 35], xiv.

Report of the Commissioners of Inquiry, 1869, into the Riots and Disturbances in the City of Londonderry, H.C. 1870 [C 5*], xxxii.

Report of the Commissioners appointed for the purpose of making inquiry into the existence of Corrupt Practices at the last election for Cashel; with minutes of evidence, H.C. 1870 [C 9], xxxii.

Report of the Commissioners appointed under the act of the 15th and 16th Victoria, cap. 57, for the purpose of making inquiry into the existence of Corrupt Practices at the last election for Sligo, H.C. 1870 [C 48], xxxii.

Report of the Commissioners appointed by the act of 32nd and 33rd Victoria, cap. 65, for the purpose of making inquiry into the existence of Corrupt Practices amongst the freemen electors of the City of Dublin, H.C. 1870 [C 93], xxxiii.

Returns showing the number of agricultural holdings in Ireland and the tenure by which they are held by the occupiers, H.C. 1870 [C 32], lvi.

Copy of the shorthand writer's notes of the judgement delivered by Mr Justice Fitzgerald, and the minutes of evidence taken at the trial of the Longford election petition, H.C. 1870 (178), lvi.

Report from the select committee on Westmeath etc. (Unlawful Combinations);

together with the proceedings of the committee, minutes of evidence, and appendix, H.C. 1871 (147), xiii.

Report of the Commissioners appointed to inquire into the treatment of Treason Felony Convicts in English prisons, H.C. 1871 [C 319], xxxii.

Returns of the number on the register of parliamentary electors: of the names of the places where petty session courts are held: And, of the names of the constabulary stations in each county in Ireland, H.C. 1871 (373), lvi.

Return, in a tabular form, showing the area, population, and valuation of the several counties of cities, counties of towns, baronies, and half-baronies in Ireland, H.C. 1872 (96), xlvii.

Return, for the year 1870, of the number of landed proprietors in each county, classed according to residence, showing the extent and value of the property held by each class, H.C. 1872 (167), xlvii.

Copy of the evidence taken at the trial of the Galway County election petition, H.C. 1872 (241-I), xlviii.

Report from the select committee on registration of parliamentary voters, Ireland, H.C. 1874 (261), xi.

Copies of Schedule One attached to the judgement of the County Galway election petition 1872; and, Schedules A, B, C, and D attached to the report of the royal commission 1857 appointed to investigate into the existence of corrupt practices in the Town of Galway, H.C. 1874 (0.1), liii.

Returns as respects each of the parliamentary boroughs in Ireland . . . [also] as respects each of the counties in Ireland, exclusive of the boroughs or parts of boroughs contained therein, of the following particulars, viz:—area, valuation, population, H.C. 1874 (45), liii.

Returns for each city, town, and borough in Ireland, returning members or a member to parliament (excepting the City of Dublin), of the number of tenements valued over £4 within the parliamentary limits . . . Of the number of male persons rated . . ., H.C. 1875 (424), lx.

Returns for each city, town, and township in Ireland, the population of which, according to the census of 1871, exceeded 6000, and in which the Acts of Geo. 4, c. 82, 3 & 4 Vict., c. 100, and 17 & 18 Vict., c. 103, and the Acts amending the same, are now in force: 1. Of the number of dwelling houses valued . . . Of the number of female rated occupiers . . ., H.C. 1875 (455), lxiv.

Report from the select committee on parliamentary and municipal elections, H.C. 1876 (162), xii.

Copy of a return of the names of proprietors and the area and valuation of all properties in the several counties in Ireland, held in fee or perpetuity, or on long leases at chief rents, H.C. 1876 (412), lxxx.

Summary of the returns of owners of land in Ireland, showing with respect to each county, the number of owners below an acre, and in classes up to 100,000 acres and upwards, with the aggregate acreage and valuation of each class, H.C. 1876 (422), lxxx.

Return of owners of land of one acre and upwards in the several counties, counties of cities, and counties of towns in Ireland, H.C. 1876 [C 1492], lxxx.

Returns of the number of petitions complaining of Undue Returns, H.C. 1880 (69), lvii.

Copy of the shorthand writer's notes of the judgement and evidence on the trial of the Down County election petition, H.C. 1880 (260-II), lvii.

Copies of the shorthand writers' notes, not already printed, of all judgements of the election judges, H.C. 1880 (337–II), lvii.

Returns, as far as are practicable, of all party processions, whether Orange, Nationalist, Amnesty, 'Martyr', or other, specifying those which did not suffer molestation, which have taken place in Ireland since the repeal of the Party Processions Act in 1872, H.C. 1880 (380 Sess. 2), lx.

Minutes of evidence taken before Her Majesty's Commissioners on Agriculture, H.C. 1881 [C 2778–I], xv.

Preliminary Report of the Assistant Commissioners [on Agriculture] *for Ireland*, H.C. 1881 [C 2951], xvi.

Return showing for each month of the years 1879 and 1880 the number of Land League meetings held and agrarian crimes reported to the Inspector General of the Royal Irish Constabulary in each county throughout Ireland, H.C. 1881 (5), lxxvii.

Return by provinces and counties (compiled from returns made to the Inspector General, Royal Irish Constabulary), of cases of evictions which have come to the knowledge of the Constabulary in each of the years from 1849 to 1880 inclusive, H.C. 1881 (185), lxxvii.

Return of Outrages reported to the Royal Irish Constabulary Office from 1st January 1844 to 31st December 1880, H.C. 1881 [C 2756], lxxvii.

Return of agricultural holdings in Ireland, compiled by the Local Government Board, H.C. 1881 [C 2934], xciii.

General annual Return of the British Army for the year 1881, abstracts for the years 1862 to 1881, H.C. 1882 [C 3405], xxxviii.

Judicial Statistics 1881, H.C. 1882 [C 3333] (England and Wales); [C 3355] (Ireland); [C 3353] (Scotland), all lxxv.

Report of the Committee of Inquiry into the Royal Irish Constabulary, H.C. 1883 [C 3577], xxxii.

Return showing with respect to each parliamentary constituency in England, Ireland, and Scotland respectively, the population, the total number of electors on the register then in force, the number of illiterate voters recorded at the general election of 1880, H.C. 1883 (327), liv.

Report from the select committee on Industries (Ireland), with the proceedings, evidence, appendix, and index, H.C. 1884–5 (288), ix.

Return showing the religious denominations of the population, according to the census of 1881 in each constituency formed in Ulster by the Redistribution of Seats Act, 1885, H.C. 1884–5 (335), lxii.

Return of members serving in the present parliament for counties and boroughs in Ireland who were not summoned at the recent Spring Assizes by the High Sheriffs to serve as Grand Jurors, H.C. 1884–5 (277), lxiii.

Report from the select committee on town holdings, H.C. 1886 (213), xii.

Return showing with respect to each parliamentary constituency in England, Ireland, and Scotland respectively, the population, the total number of electors on the register then in force, the number of illiterate voters recorded at the general election of 1885, H.C. 1886 (165), lii.

Return showing with respect to each parliamentary constituency in England, Ireland, and Scotland respectively, the population, the total number of electors on the register then in force, the number of illiterate voters recorded at the general election of 1886, H.C. 1886 (46 Sess. 2), lii.

Report by one of the Commissioners [W. B. M'Hardy] *of Inquiry, 1886, respecting the origin and circumstances of the Riots in Belfast*, H.C. 1887 [C 5029], xvii.

Memorandum [by A. J. Balfour] *as to the Principle upon which Outrages are recorded as agrarian*, H.C. 1887 (140), lxviii.

Royal Commission on Labour. The Agricultural Labourer. Vol. IV Ireland, H.C. 1893-4 [C 6894-XIX], xxxvii.

Royal Commission on Local Taxation, H.C. 1898 [C 8763], xli.

Appendix to minutes of evidence (volume I) taken before the Royal Commission on Local Taxation, H.C. 1898 [C 8764], xlii.

iii Census Returns

1831   *Abstract of Population Returns*, H.C. 1833 (634), xxxix.

1841   *Report of the Commissioners appointed to take the Census of Ireland for the year 1841*, H.C. 1843 [504], xxiv.

1851   *The Census of Ireland for the year 1851*, H.C. 1852-3 [1465, 1553, 1481, 1486, 1488, 1492, 1503, 1496, 1502, 1564, 1527, 1544, 1552, 1550, 1551, 1543, 1554, 1549, 1545, 1546], xci; 1852-3 [1565, 1547, 1563, 1567, 1570, 1574, 1571, 1575, 1579, 1557, 1548, 1542, 1555, 1560], xcii; 1852-3 [1589], xciii; 1854 [1765], lviii; 1856 [2053], xxix; 1856 [2087], xxix and xxx; 1856 [2134], xxxi.

1861   *The Census of Ireland for the year 1861*, H.C. 1863 [3204], liv, lv, lvi, lvii, lviii, lix, lx, lxi.

1871   *Census of Ireland, 1871*, H.C. 1872 [C 662], lxvii; 1873 [C 873, C 876], lxxii; 1874 [C 964, C 1000, C 1106], lxxiv; 1876 [C 1377], lxxxi.

1881   *Census of Ireland, 1881*, H.C. 1881 [C 3042], xcvii; 1882 [C 3148], lxxvii; 1882 [C 3204], lxxviii; 1882 [C 3268], lxxix; 1882 [C 3365], lxxvi.

C NEWSPAPERS

Town of publication given unless contained in title.

Anglo-Celt (Cavan)
Athlone Conservative Advocate
Ballyshannon Herald
Banner of Ulster (Belfast)
Belfast Election
Belfast Newsletter
Carlow Sentinel
Clare Freeman (Ennis)
Clare Journal (Ennis)
Clonmel Chronicle
Cork Constitution
Cork Examiner
Cork Herald
Cork Southern Reporter
Daily Express (Dublin)
Drogheda Argus
Dublin Evening Mail
Dublin Evening Post
Dundalk Democrat
Flag of Ireland (Dublin)

Freeman's Journal (Dublin)
Galway Vindicator
Irish Farmers' Gazette (Dublin)
Irishman (Dublin)
Irish People (Dublin)
Irish Times (Dublin)
Kerry Evening Post (Tralee)
Kilkenny Journal
Leinster Express (Maryborough)
Limerick Chronicle
Limerick Reporter
Londonderry Guardian
Londonderry Sentinel
Londonderry Standard
Nation (Dublin)
Newry Telegraph
Northern Standard (Monaghan)
Northern Whig (Belfast)
People's Press and Cork Weekly Register
Pilot (Dublin)

Roscommon Herald (Boyle)
Roscommon Journal (Roscommon)
Saunders' Newsletter (Dublin)
Sligo Champion
Tablet (Dublin)
Telegraph or Connaught Ranger (Castlebar)
The Times (London)
Tipperary Advocate (Nenagh)

United Ireland (Dublin)
Waterford Citizen
Waterford Mail
Waterford News
Weekly Register (London)
Western Star (Ballinasloe)
Westmeath Guardian (Mullingar)
Wexford Independent

D POLL BOOKS

Listed alphabetically by constituencies. For further details, locations, and other poll books not specifically used in this work, see B. M. Walker and K. T. Hoppen, 'Irish election poll books 1832-1872', *Irish Booklore*, iii (1976), 9-13, and iv (1980), 113-19. *Note* (a) Poll books are much rarer in Ireland than in England; (b) the locations given below are not exhaustive—some poll books survive in several different copies and locations (see Walker and Hoppen). For Electoral Registers, see Section A of this Bibliography.

List of Voters who recorded their votes at the Armagh Borough election, in 1859—copy in Armagh Museum No. 22-76.

MS Belfast Poll Book 1832-7—P.R.O.N.I. D2472/1.

List of electors of the Borough of Belfast who voted at the general election, 1868 (Belfast: H. Adair, 1869)—copy in Belfast Public Library.

'A List of the Persons who voted at the Coleraine Borough Election, in December 1832, classified, and taken from the list published by the Beresford party' (printed)—copy in O.P. 1832/2188, Box 2191.

Lists of voters in *The People's Press and Cork Weekly Register*, 17, 24, 31 Jan., and 7, 14 Feb. 1835 (Cork City election 1835).

MS Co. Down poll books for 1852 and 1857: Downshire Papers P.R.O.N.I. D671/02/5-8 (recatalogued).

A List of the constituency of the City of Dublin, as registered prior to the City of Dublin election, in January 1835; exhibiting the voting at that election, and also at the city election in December 1832 (Dublin: Gerald Crean, n.d.) —copy in B.L. Pressmark 809.g.40(2).

A correct List of the poll of voters at the City of Dublin election in August, 1837, compiled by T. M. Ray (Dublin: Shaw Brothers, 1838)—copy in Trinity College Dublin Library Pressmark Gall.NN.12.16.

A Mirror of the Dublin election for members to serve in parliament, commencing Monday 5th and ending Saturday 11th July, 1841 (Dublin: W. H. Dyott, 1841)—copy in N.L.I. Pressmark Ir94133 d 15.

List of voters at the City of Dublin election, for one member in the room of the late much lamented John Beatty West, M.P. (Dublin: Shaw Brothers, 1842)—copy in N.L.I. Pressmark Ir32341 d 29 (1842 by-election).

The constituency of the City of Dublin as revised in the year 1864, arranged in street order and districts [Dublin, 1864]—copy in N.L.I. Pressmark Ir94133 d 16 (not, strictly speaking, a poll book).

The constituency of the City of Dublin, as revised in the year 1865, arranged in alphabetical order [Dublin, 1866]—copy in N.L.I. Pressmark Ir94133 d 17 (not, strictly speaking, a poll book).

Marked list of voters, Co. Dublin, July 1852 (n.d.)—copy in U.C.D. Pamphlets 5328.

'Election for the Borough of Dundalk 1847': Poster in County Reference Library, Dundalk. Published in N. Ross, 'Two nineteenth-century election posters', *Journal of the County Louth Archaeological Society*, xvi (1968), 224–32.

Analysis of the late election of Limerick, showing the entire list of the poll (Limerick, 1852)—copy of this Limerick City poll book for 1852 in Limerick City Library (Bound Pamphlets kept in Office). Not listed in Walker and Hoppen.

'List of voters at the Lisburn election held on 21st February 1863': P.R.O.N.I. D1763/1.

Clerk of the Peace's Book for Londonderry City election of 1832: P.R.O.N.I. T1048/3.

List of Voters, showing for whom each elector polled at the late general election for the City of Londonderry, distinguishing the religion of each voter (Londonderry: Sentinel Office, [1868])—copy P.R.O.N.I. D1935/6.

State of the Poll at the general election held for the City of Londonderry, 20th November 1868 (Londonderry: John Hempton, [1868])—copy P.R.O.N.I. D1509/10.

Names of the Voters at the election held in Londonderry on Thursday, February 17th, 1870 (Londonderry: Sentinel Office, [1870])—copy in Magee College Library, Derry.

State of the Poll at the election for the City of Londonderry, 17th February 1870 (Londonderry: John Hempton, [1870])—copy in Queen's University Library, Belfast.

County of Louth Election 1852: A list of the electors of the several baronies of the County of Louth, who voted at the general election of 1852 (Dundalk: Patrick Dowdall, 1852)—copy in N.L.I. MS 1660.

An analysis of the parliamentary register of voters for the County of Louth, with the names of the landlords and their tenants on the register of voters, shewing the candidate for whom they voted at the election in April 1865 (Dublin: Peter Roe, 1865)—copy in N.L.I. Pressmark P2491.

'Meath Election. January 1835. Names of those who voted': a printed list in O.P. 1835/148, Box 47.

Newry Election. An alphabetically arranged list of electors who voted, and those who did not, at the election held in Newry, on the 20th of November 1868 (Newry, n.d.)—copy P.R.O.N.I. T2336/1.

Co. Sligo: annotated MS poll book for 1852: N.L.I. MS 3064 (3 vols.).

'Tralee Borough election, January 1835': a printed list in O.P. 1835/158, Box 47.

Youghal MS poll books for 1835 and 1837: Among Youghal Corporation Records, Cork Archives Council. Published in Ann Barry and K. T. Hoppen, 'Borough politics in O'Connellite Ireland: The Youghal poll books of 1835 and 1837', *Journal of the Cork Historical and Archaeological Society*, lxxxiii (1978), 106–46, and lxxxiv (1979), 15–43.

E REFERENCE WORKS

The Annual Register: A Review of Public Events at Home and Abroad, for the year 1872 (London, 1873).

The Banking Almanac, Directory, Year Book, and Diary (London, 1844-) under various titles.

Bateman, J., *The Great Landowners of Great Britain and Ireland*, 4th edn. (London, 1883).

The Belfast and Province of Ulster Directory (Belfast, 1852-) under various titles.

Bence-Jones, M., *Burke's Guide to Country Houses Vol. I: Ireland* (London, 1978).

Burgh, U. H. H. de, *The Landowners of Ireland. An alphabetical list of the owners of estates of 500 acres or £500 valuation and upwards, in Ireland* (Dublin, [1878]).

The Catholic Directory, Almanac, and Registry [Battersby's] (Dublin, 1836-) under various titles.

Dod, C. R., *Electoral Facts from 1832 to 1852*, 2nd edn. (London, 1853).

—, *Parliamentary Companion* (London, 1833-).

Fraser, J., *Hand-Book for Travellers in Ireland*, 5th edn. (Dublin, [1859]).

Lewis, S., *A Topographical Dictionary of Ireland*, 2nd edn., 2 vols. (London, 1847).

Mitchell, B. R. and Deane, P., *Abstract of British Historical Statistics*, new edn. (Cambridge, 1976).

— and Jones, H. G., *Second Abstract of British Historical Statistics* (Cambridge, 1971).

Mitchell, C., *The Newspaper press directory and Advertisers' guide* (London, 1846-) under various titles.

Pettigrew and Oulton's The Dublin Almanac and General Register of Ireland, for the year of Our Lord 1841 (Dublin, n.d.).

Slater's Directory of Ireland (Manchester and London, 1856).

Stenton, M. and Lees, S. (eds.), *Who's Who of British Members of Parliament*, 4 vols. (Hassocks and Brighton, 1976–81).

Thom's Irish Almanac and Official Directory (Dublin, 1844-) under various titles.

Vaughan, W. E. and Fitzpatrick, A. J. (eds.), *Irish Historical Statistics: Population, 1821–1971* (Dublin, 1978).

Walker, B. M. (ed.), *Parliamentary Election Results in Ireland, 1801–1922* (Dublin, 1978).

F DISSERTATIONS

Bull, P. J., 'The Reconstruction of the Irish Parliamentary movement, 1895–1903: An analysis with special reference to William O'Brien' (University of Cambridge Ph.D. thesis, 1972).

Cahill, B., 'The Impact of the Catholic Clergy on Irish Life 1820–45' (University College Galway MA thesis, 1975).

Cahir, B., 'Irish National By-Elections 1870–74' (University College Dublin MA thesis, 1965).

Connell, P., 'An Economic geography of Co. Meath 1770–1870' (St Patrick's College Maynooth MA thesis, 1980).

Connolly, S. J., 'Catholicism and social discipline in pre-Famine Ireland' (New University of Ulster D.Phil. thesis, 1977).

D'Arcy, F. A., 'Dublin artisan activity, opinion, and organization 1820–1850' (University College Dublin MA thesis, 1968).

Diamond, M. C., 'The Irish estates of the Mercers' Company 1609–1906' (New University of Ulster M.Phil. thesis, 1974).

Fay, A. D. T., 'The Parishes of Magherafelt and Ballyscullion 1825–1850: An examination of some aspects of social and economic development' (New University of Ulster M.Phil. thesis, 1974).

Feingold, W. L., 'The Irish boards of poor law guardians 1872–86: A revolution in local government' (University of Chicago Ph.D. thesis, 1974).

FitzSimon, R. D., 'The Irish Government and the Phoenix Society' (University College Dublin MA thesis, 1965).

Gourlay, R. S., 'The social and economic history of the Gosford estates 1610–1876' (Queen's University Belfast M.Sc.(Econ.) thesis, 1973).

Hamilton, J. C., 'Parties and voting patterns in the parliament of 1874–80' (University of Iowa Ph.D. thesis, 1968).

Hanrahan, A. K., 'Irish electioneering 1850–1872' (University College Dublin MA thesis, 1965).

Hill, Jacqueline, 'The role of Dublin in the Irish national movement 1840–48' (University of Leeds Ph.D. thesis, 1973).

Holmes, R. F., 'Henry Cooke 1788–1868' (University of Dublin M.Litt. thesis, 1970).

Horgan, D. T., 'The Irish Catholic Whigs in Parliament, 1847–1874' (University of Minnesota Ph.D. thesis, 1975).

Huttman, J. P., 'Institutional factors in the development of Irish agriculture, 1850–1915' (University of London Ph.D. thesis, 1970).

Jones, D. S., 'Agrarian Capitalism and Rural Social Development in Ireland' (Queen's University Belfast Ph.D. thesis, 1977).

Kelly, T., 'Ennis in the nineteenth century' (University College Galway MA thesis, 1971).

Lyne, G., 'The General Association of Ireland, 1836–7' (University College Dublin MA thesis, 1968).

McClelland, A., 'Johnston of Ballykilbeg' (New University of Ulster M.Phil thesis, 1977).

Mason, H., 'The development of the urban pattern in Ireland 1841–1881' (University of Wales Ph.D. thesis, 1969).

Mitchell, J. C., 'Electoral change and the party system in England, 1832–1868' (Yale University Ph.D. thesis, 1976).

Nolan, D. M., 'The County Cork Grand Jury, 1836–1899' (University College Cork MA thesis, 1974).

Odurkene, J. N., 'The British General Elections of 1830 and 1831' (University of Oxford B.Litt. thesis, 1977).

Ó. Gráda, C., 'Post-Famine Adjustment: Essays in nineteenth-century Irish Economic History' (Columbia University Ph.D. thesis, 1973).

Owens, Rosemary, 'Votes for Women: Irishwomen's Campaign for the Vote' (University College Dublin MA thesis, 1977).

Robinson, Olive, 'The economic significance of the London companies as landlords in Ireland during the period 1800–1870' (Queen's University Belfast Ph.D. thesis, 1957).

Singer, B. B., ' "Pillar of the Republic": The Village Schoolmaster in Brittany 1880–1914' (University of Washington Ph.D. thesis, 1971).

Tod, A. M., 'The Smiths of Baltiboys: A Co. Wicklow family and their estates in the 1840s' (University of Edinburgh Ph.D. thesis, 1978).

Vaughan, W. E., 'A Study of Landlord and Tenant Relations in Ireland between the Famine and the Land War, 1850–78' (University of Dublin Ph.D. thesis, 1974).

Walker, B. M., 'Parliamentary Representation in Ulster, 1868–86' (University of Dublin Ph.D. thesis, 1978).

Woods, C. J., 'The Catholic Church and Irish Politics 1879–92' (University of Nottingham Ph.D. thesis, 1968).

Wusten, H. H. van der, 'Iers verzet tegen de staatkundige eenheid der Britse eilanden 1800–1921' (University of Amsterdam Doctorate thesis, 1977).

G NINETEENTH-CENTURY PRINTED WORKS

[Army], *Orders and Regulations for the Army serving in Ireland* (Dublin, 1832) —copy in possession of the author.

—, *Orders for the guidance of the troops in affording aid to the Civil Power, and to the Revenue Department in Ireland* (Dublin, 1847)—copy in possession of the author.

Bagenal, P. H., *The Life of Ralph Bernal Osborne M.P.* (London, 1884).

—, *The Priest in Politics* (London, 1893).

Bailey, W. F., 'The government valuation of Ireland', *Journal of the Statistical and Social Inquiry Society of Ireland*, ix (1892–3), 651–63.

Barrington, R. M., 'The prices of some agricultural produce and the cost of farm labour for the past fifty years', *Journal of the Statistical and Social Inquiry Society of Ireland*, ix (1887), 137–53.

'A Barrister', *Observations on Intimidation at Elections in Ireland by Mob Violence and Priestly Intimidation* (Dublin, 1854).

Barrow, J., *A Tour round Ireland, through the sea-coast counties, in the Autumn of 1835* (London, 1836).

Barry, W., 'The current Street Ballads of Ireland', *Macmillan's Magazine*, xxv (1872), 190–9.

Becker, B. H., *Disturbed Ireland: Being the letters written during the winter of 1880–81* (London, 1881).

Bence Jones, W., *The life's work in Ireland of a landlord who tried to do his duty* (London, 1880).

Bicheno, J. E., *Ireland and its Economy; being the result of observations made in a tour through the country in the Autumn of 1829* (London, 1830).

Birmingham, J., *A Memoir of the Very Reverend Theobald Mathew, with an Account of the Rise and Progress of Temperance in Ireland* (Dublin, 1840).

Blacker, W., *Prize Essay, addressed to the agricultural committee of the Royal Dublin Society, on the management of landed property in Ireland; the consolidation of small farms, employment of the poor, etc. etc., for which the gold medal was awarded* (Dublin, 1834).

Bowley, A. L., 'The statistics of wages in the United Kingdom during the last hundred years (Part III) Agricultural Wages—Ireland', *Journal of the Royal Statistical Society*, lxii (1899), 395–404.

Brophy, M., *Sketches of the Royal Irish Constabulary* (London, 1886).

Bullen, D., 'Statistics of an improved rural district (the Parish of Kilmurray) in the County of Cork', *Journal of the Statistical Society*, vi (1843), 352–4.

Bullen, E., *Five reports of the committee of the Precursor Association* (Dublin, 1839).

Carleton, J. W., *A Compendium of the practice of elections of members to serve in parliament, as regulated by the several statutes in force in Ireland*, 2nd edn. (Dublin, 1852); also 10th edn. by J. N. Gerrard and T. S. F. Battersby (Dublin, 1885).

Carleton, W., *Traits and Stories of the Irish Peasantry*, 5 vols. (Dublin, 1830-3).

Carlyle, T., *Reminiscences of my Irish journey in 1849* (London, 1882).

Carr, J., *The Stranger in Ireland: Or a tour in the southern and western parts of that country in the year 1805* (London, 1806).

Central Conservative Society of Ireland: Report of the Sub-Committee 1859—copies in Mayo Papers MS 11025 and Hylton Papers Box 24.

Central Conservative Society of Ireland: Reports by agents of the revisions at the registration sessions of 1867—copy in Mayo Papers MS 11161.

The Church Establishment in Ireland: The Freeman's Journal Church Commission (Dublin, 1868).

Civil and religious liberty: Address of the Irish Universal Suffrage Association to the Most Rev. and Right Rev. the Roman Catholic archbishops and bishops of Ireland (Dublin, 1843)—copy in R.I.A. Halliday Pamphlets 1868.

'A Clergyman of the Established Church' [G. Dwyer], *Popery unmasked at the recent elections in Ireland* (London, [1852]).

Coulter, H., *The West of Ireland: Its condition and prospects* (Dublin, 1862).

Croker, T. C., *Researches in the South of Ireland illustrative of the Scenery, Architectural Remains, and the Manners and Superstitions of the Peasantry* (London, 1824).

Croly, D. O., *An Essay Religious and Political on Ecclesiastical Finance, as regards the Roman Catholic Church in Ireland* (Cork, 1834).

'Daryl, Philippe' [Paschal Grousset], *Ireland's Disease: Notes and Impressions* (London, 1888).

Decreta Synodi Plenariae Episcoporum Hiberniae apud Thurles (Dublin, 1851).

Dick, J., 'Banking Statistics: A record of nine years' progress: 1874 to 1883', *Journal of the Institute of Bankers*, v (1884), 317-75.

Dillon, W., *Life of John Mitchel*, 2 vols. (London, 1888).

[Dixon, J.], *The Life of the Most Revd Joseph Dixon, D.D. Primate of All Ireland* (London, [1878]) 'By the Author of "Jews and Jerusalem" '.

[Dublin Conservative Registration Committee], *Report of the City of Dublin Conservative Registration Committee, June 1842* (Dublin, 1842)—copy in R.I.A. Halliday Pamphlets 1842.

[Dublin Protestant Association], *Soirée of the Dublin Protestant Association and Reformation Society at Whitefriars Hall, January 14, 1846* (Dublin, [1846])—copy in R.I.A. Halliday Pamphlets 1814.

Dun, F., *Landlords and Tenants in Ireland* (London, 1881).

[Dunlop, D.], *A brief historical sketch of parliamentary elections in Belfast from the first general election under the Reform Act till 1865* (Belfast, [1865])—copy in Queen's University Library, Belfast Pressmark hJN563/2.

Dutton, H., *Statistical Survey of the County of Clare* (Dublin, 1808).

Egan, P. M., *Guide to Waterford* (Waterford, 1892).

Ellis, T., *The Action of the Grand Lodge of the County of Armagh (and the reasons thereof) on the 6th of July, 1885* (Armagh, 1885)—copy in Carleton, Atkinson, & Sloan Papers D1252/42/3/47.

Ewald, A. C., *The Life and Letters of the Right Hon. Sir Joseph Napier Bart.*, revised edn. (London, 1892).

A Farce. Portarlington Election: Intended in three parts. Part I—The Canvass (Portarlington, 1832)—copy in the Sir Thomas Gladstone Papers.

'Feeva' [R. P. Dawson], *A Psalter of Derry: Letters of 'Conservator-Elector' on the political condition and parliamentary representation of the county* (Dublin, 1859).

Fitzgibbon, G., *Ireland in 1868, The battle-field for English party strife* (London, 1868).

Fitzpatrick, W. J. (ed.), *Correspondence of Daniel O'Connell The Liberator,* 2 vols. (London, 1888).

— *The Life, Times, and Correspondence of the Right Revd Dr Doyle, Bishop of Kildare and Leighlin,* new edn., 2 vols. (Dublin, 1890).

—, *Memoirs of Father Healy of Little Bray* (Dublin, 1896).

Flint, J., *Mr Jonathan Pim and the Dublin Freemen* [Dublin, 1868]—copy in N.L.I. Pressmark J667.

Freedom of election in Ireland, or violence and intimidation illustrated (Carlow, [1853])—copy in Bradshaw Collection, C.U.L. Hib.5.853.5.

Gavan Duffy, C., *Thomas Davis: Memoirs of an Irish patriot 1840-46* (London, 1870).

—, *The League of North and South: An episode in Irish History 1850-1854* (London, 1886).

—, *Young Ireland Part II, or Four Years of Irish History 1845-49* (Dublin, 1887).

Glassford, J., *Notes of three tours in Ireland in 1824 and 1826* (Bristol, 1832).

Godkin, J., *The Land War in Ireland* (London, 1870).

Gregory, Lady (ed.), *Sir William Gregory, K.C.M.G., formerly member of parliament and sometime governor of Ceylon. An Autobiography* (London, 1894).

— (ed.), *Mr Gregory's Letter-Box 1813-1830* (London, 1898). See also Section H below, for twentieth-century work.

Grey, Henry George, [3rd] Earl (ed.), *The Reform Act, 1832. The correspondence of the late Earl Grey with His Majesty King William IV,* 2 vols. (London, 1867).

[Griffith, R.], *Instructions to the valuators and surveyors appointed under the 15th and 16th Vict., cap. 63, for the uniform valuation of lands and tenements in Ireland* (Dublin, 1853). See also under [Valuation of Ireland].

Grimshaw, T. W., 'On some comparative statistics of Irish counties', *Journal of the Statistical and Social Inquiry Society of Ireland,* viii (1882-3), 444-58.

—, *Facts and Figures about Ireland Part I* (Dublin, 1893); also *Part II* (Dublin, 1893).

Hall, Mr and Mrs S. C., *Ireland: Its Scenery, Character etc.,* 3 vols. (London, 1841-3).

[Hamilton, J.], *Sixty years' experience as an Irish landlord: Memoirs of John Hamilton D.L. of St. Ernan's Donegal,* ed. H. C. White (London, [1894]).

Hardcastle, Mrs, *Life of John, Lord Campbell, Lord High Chancellor of Great Britain,* 2 vols. (London, 1843).

Haughton, J., 'The social and moral elevation of our working classes', *Journal of the Statistical and Social Inquiry Society of Ireland,* ii (1857), 63-72.

Head, F. B., *A Fortnight in Ireland* (London, 1852).

Healy, J., *Maynooth College: Its Centenary History* (Dublin, 1895).

Hill, Lord George, *Facts from Gweedore,* 5th edn. (London, 1887).

Hogan, J., 'Patron Days and Holy Wells in Ossory', *Journal of the Royal Society of Antiquaries of Ireland,* xii (1873), 261-81.

The Home Rule Songster: Being a choice collection of the newest and best songs (Dublin, [?1874])—copy in Bradshaw Collection, C.U.L. Hib.2.867.2.

Houston, Mrs, *Twenty years in the wild west: or, life in Connaught* (London, 1879).

Hurlbert, W. H., *Ireland under Coercion: The diary of an American*, 2 vols. (Edinburgh, 1888).

Inglis, H. D., *A Journey throughout Ireland during the Spring, Summer, and Autumn of 1834*, 5th edn. (London, 1838).

The Irish franchise and registration question (London, 1841)—copy in R.I.A. Halliday Pamphlets 1816.

[Irish Loyal and Patriotic Union], *The Tenants' Defence Fund* (1890)—copy in Bodleian Library John Johnson Collection, Ireland Box 1.

[Irish Protestant Association], *First Report of the Irish Protestant Association* (Dublin, 1836)—copy in R.I.A. Halliday Pamphlets 1677.

Kebbel, T. E., *The Agricultural Labourer: A short summary of his position*, new edn. (London, 1893).

Kennedy, J. S., *Standing Rules and Regulations for the government and guidance of the Constabulary Force in Ireland* (Dublin, 1837). See also under [Royal Irish Constabulary].

[Kildare Independent Club], *First Report of the County of Kildare Independent Club* (Dublin, 1848)—copy in N.L.I. Pressmark P432.

[Kilkenny Hunt], *Memoirs of the Kilkenny Hunt, compiled by one of its Members* (Dublin, 1897)—copy in B.L. Pressmark 7921.de.41.

King, D. B., *The Irish Question* (London, 1882).

Knapp, J. W. and Ombler, E., *Cases of controverted elections in the twelfth parliament of the United Kingdom* (London, 1837).

Kohl, J. G., *Ireland, Dublin, the Shannon, Limerick, Cork, and the Kilkenny Races* (London, 1843).

Lewis, G. C., *On local Disturbances in Ireland, and on the Irish Church Question* (London, 1836; reprinted Cork, 1977).

Lewis, G. F., *Letters of the Right Hon. Sir George Cornewall Lewis Bart. to various friends* (London, 1870).

Londonderry, Charles Vane, [3rd] Marquess of, *Memoirs and Correspondence of Viscount Castlereagh*, 4 vols. (London, 1848-9).

Lord, J., *Popery at the hustings: foreign and domestic legislation* (London, 1852).

Lucas, E., *The Life of Frederick Lucas M.P.*, 2 vols. (London, 1886).

Macaulay, J., *Ireland in 1872: A tour of observation with remarks on Irish public questions* (London, 1873).

MacDevitt, J., *The Most Reverend James MacDevitt D.D. Bishop of Raphoe: A Memoir* (Dublin, 1880).

Macknight, T., *Ulster as it is or Twenty-Eight years' experience as an Irish editor*, 2 vols. (London, 1896).

MacPhilpin, J., *The Apparitions and Miracles at Knock* (Dublin, 1880).

'A Magistrate of the County', *The present state of Tipperary as regards agrarian outrages, their nature, origin, and increase, considered* (Dublin, 1842)—copy in Bradshaw Collection, C.U.L. Hib.7.843.8.

Maguire, J. F., *Father Mathew: A Biography* (London, 1863).

Mahaffy, J. P., 'The Irish Landlords', *Contemporary Review*, xli (1882), 160-76.

Mandat-Grancey, E. de, *Paddy at Home* (London, 1887).

Martin, R. M., *Ireland before and after the Union with Great Britain*, 2nd edn. (London, 1848).

[Maxwell, W. H.], *Wild Sports of the West. With Legendary Tales, and local Sketches*, 2 vols. (London, 1832).

Meagher, W., *Notices of the Life and Character of His Grace Most Revd Daniel Murray, late Archbishop of Dublin* (Dublin, 1853).

Molyneux, E., *A practical treatise of the law of elections in Ireland as altered by the reform act* (Dublin, 1835).

Newmarch, W., 'The increase in the number of banks and branches in the metropolis: the English counties: Scotland and Ireland, during the twenty years 1858-1878' in *The Banking Almanac, Directory, Year Book, and Diary for 1880* (London: Waterlow & Sons Ltd., [1880]), pp. 425-48.

Nicholls, G., *A History of the Irish Poor Law* (London, 1856).

Noel, B. W., *Notes of a short tour through the midland counties of Ireland, in the Summer of 1836* (London, 1837).

Notes and Hints upon the Registration of Voters, for the guidance of Agents (Dublin, 1870)—copy in Dungannon Borough Revision Papers P.R.O.N.I. D847/8, Box 24.

[Nulty, T.], *Letter of the Most Revd Dr Nulty, Bishop of Meath, addressed to Lord Hartington, Chairman of the Westmeath Committee* (Dublin, 1871)—copy in Gladstone Papers Add. MS 44616.

O'Brien, R. B., *Thomas Drummond Under-Secretary in Ireland 1835-40* (London, 1889).

O'Connell, D., *Seven letters on the Reform Bill and the law of elections in Ireland* (Dublin, 1835).

O'Connell, J., *Recollections and Experiences during a parliamentary career from 1833 to 1848*, 2 vols. (London, 1849).

[O'Connell National Annuity], *Detailed Report of Contributions (Parochial and Personal) to the O'Connell National Annuity for the year 1833* (Dublin, 1834)—copy in Hull University Library Pressmark DA 905.2 01.

O'Connor, F., *A series of letters from Feargus O'Connor Esq. Barrister at Law; to Daniel O'Connell Esq. M.P. containing a review of Mr O'Connell's conduct* (London, 1836).

O'Connor, T. P., *The Parnell Movement*, new edn. (London, 1887).

[O'Hagan, T.], *Speech of the Right Hon. Thomas O'Hagan, MP Attorney-General for Ireland, at the hustings of Tralee, on the 15th of May 1863* (Dublin, 1863).

O'Malley, E. L. and Hardcastle, H., *Reports of the decisions of the judges for the trial of election petitions in England and Ireland* (London), i (1869), ii (1875), iii (1881).

'One late an Agent', *Landlordism in Ireland with its difficulties* (London, 1853).

O'Reilly, B., *John MacHale, Archbishop of Tuam. His life, times, and correspondence*, 2 vols. (New York, 1890).

Ornsby, R., *Memoirs of James Robert Hope-Scott*, 2nd edn., 2 vols. (London, 1884).

O'Shaughnessy, M. S., 'On Criminal Statistics, especially with reference to population, education, and distress in Ireland', *Journal of the Statistical and Social Inquiry Society of Ireland*, iv (1864), 91-104.

Parker, C. S. (ed.), *Sir Robert Peel from his private papers*, 3 vols. (London, 1891-9).

Pastoral Address of the Archbishops and Bishops of Ireland assembled in National Synod at Maynooth (Dublin, 1875)—copy in Cullen Papers.

Pellew, G., *In Castle and Cabin or talks in Ireland in 1887* (New York and London, 1888).

Perry, H. J. and Knapp, J. W., *Cases of controverted elections in the eleventh parliament of the United Kingdom* (London, 1833).

Plunkett, H. C., 'Co-operative stores for Ireland', *The Nineteenth Century*, xxiv (1888), 410–18.

[Poor Law Commissioners], *Tenth annual report of the Poor Law Commissioners with appendices* (London, 1844).

Pope Hennessy, J., 'What do the Irish read?', *The Nineteenth Century*, xv (1884), 920–32.

Power, D., Rodwell, H., and Dew, E. L'E., *Reports of the decisions of committees of the House of Commons in the trial of controverted elections during the fifteenth parliament of the United Kingdom* (London, 1853); *Reports . . . during the sixteenth parliament . . .* (London, 1857).

[Priests Protection Society], *Fifth report of the Priests Protection Society* (Dublin, 1851)—copy in Bradshaw Collection, C.U.L. Hib.5.851.11.

Prim, J. G. A., 'Olden Popular Pastimes in Kilkenny', *Journal of the Royal Society of Antiquaries of Ireland*, ii (1853), 319–35.

Pringle, R. O., 'A review of Irish agriculture', *Journal of the Royal Agricultural Society of England*, 2nd series viii (1872), 1–76.

—, 'Illustrations of Irish farming', *Journal of the Royal Agricultural Society of England*, 2nd series ix (1873), 400–22.

[Protestant Freemen's Fellowship Society], *Report of the Protestant Freemen's Fellowship Society with Abstract of Accounts and a list of Subscribers for the year 1854* (Dublin, 1855); *the same for the year 1855* (Dublin, 1856)—copies in U.C.D. Pamphlets 3730.

—, *Address, rules, and object of the Protestant Freemen's Fellowship Society, with a list of Patrons, Officers etc.* (Dublin, 1855)—copy in U.C.D. Pamphlets 3730.

Purdy, F., 'On the earnings of agricultural labourers in Scotland and Ireland', *Journal of the Statistical Society*, xxv (1862), 425–90.

The Reign of Terror in Carlow, comprising an authentic detail of the Proceedings of Mr O'Connell and his followers (London, 1841)—copy in R.I.A. Halliday Pamphlets 1817.

The Repealer Repulsed: A correct narrative of the use and progress of the Repeal invasion of Ulster (Belfast, 1841).

Report of the committee, appointed at a public meeting held in Dublin, Thursday, March 19, 1840, to consider the effect of Lord Stanley's Registration Bill (n.d.)—copy in Derby Papers 20/9.

Report of the Outrages and Intimidations at the late Elections (Dublin, 1841)—copy in U.C.D. Pamphlets 6201.

Report on the registration and election laws of the United Kingdom as prepared by a sub-committee of the Ulster Constitutional Association (Belfast, 1840)—copy in Derby Papers 20/9.

Richey, A. G., *The Irish Land Laws* (London, 1880).

Rooper, G., *A Month in Mayo, comprising characteristic sketches (sporting and social) of Irish life* (London, 1876).

Ross, C. (ed.), *Correspondence of Charles, First Marquis Cornwallis*, 2nd edn., 3 vols. (London, 1859).

[Royal Irish Constabulary], *Standing Rules and Regulations for the government and guidance of the Royal Irish Constabulary*, 3rd edn. (Dublin, 1872). See also under Kennedy, J. S.

Russell, C., *'New Views on Ireland'. Or, Irish Land: Grievances: Remedies* (London, 1880).

[Ryan, J.], *Catalogue of Books to be sold by unreserved auction at the Auction*

Mart, No. 6 Rutland-Street, Limerick, on Tuesday, 30th August Instant, the Select Library of the late Right Rev. Dr Ryan, Bishop of Limerick (Limerick, [1864])—copy in Bradshaw Collection, C.U.L. Hib.5.864.5.

Sanders, L. C. (ed.), *Lord Melbourne's Papers* (London, 1889).

Selection of Parochial Examinations relative to the destitute classes in Ireland, from the evidence received by His Majesty's Commissioners for enquiring into the condition of the poorer classes in Ireland (Dublin, 1835).

Senior, N. W., *Journals, conversations, and essays relating to Ireland*, 2nd edn., 2 vols. (London, 1868).

Shand, A. I., *Letters from the west of Ireland 1884* (Edinburgh and London, 1885).

Smyth, J., *The Elector: Containing a true and faithful picture of the awful state of the representation of parts of the Counties Tipperary and Waterford* (Dublin, [1853]).

Society for the Relief of Distressed Protestants, First Annual Report (Dublin, 1838)—copy in R.I.A. Halliday Pamphlets 1712.

A Statement of the Management of the Farnham Estates (Dublin, 1830)—copy in N.L.I. Pressmark Ir333 f 10.

Stoney, T. G., *A Short Address as a word of advice to the small farmers and peasantry of the County of Tipperary* (Dublin, 1843).

'Stradling, Matthew' [Mahony, M. F.], 'The Misadventures of Mr Catlyne Q.C.', *Fraser's Magazine*, new series v (1872), 751–67; vi (1872), 102–16, 185–200, 375–90, 505–23.

Sullivan, T. D., *A. M. Sullivan: A Memoir* (Dublin, 1885).

Thackeray, W. M., *The Irish Sketch Book of 1842* (London, 1879).

Thompson, H. S., *Ireland in 1839 and 1869* (London, 1870).

'Tory-Throuncer, Paudeen', *Songs for the Hustings* (1868)—copy in U.C.D. Pamphlets 102.

Trench, W. S., *Realities of Irish Life*, 4th edn. (London, 1869).

Trollope, A., *The Macdermots of Ballycloran* (1847).

[Valuation of Ireland: Griffith's Valuation], *Valuation of Ireland*: published in parts 1853–65 (N.L.I. has a set). See also under [Griffith, R.].

A Voice from the Protestants of Ireland to the Revd Tresham Dames Gregg, the faithful and intrepid Defender of Protestant Truth and Liberty (Dublin, 1846)—copy in R.I.A. Halliday Pamphlets 1982.

Wakefield, E., *An Account of Ireland, Statistical and Political*, 2 vols. (London, 1812).

[Ward, W. G.], 'The Priesthood in Irish Politics', *Dublin Review*, new series xix (1872), 257–93.

Wellington, [2nd] Duke of (ed.), *Despatches, Correspondence, and Memoranda of Field Marshal Arthur Duke of Wellington K.G.*, 8 vols. (London, 1867–80).

Wilde, W. R., *Irish Popular Superstitions* (Dublin, 1852).

Wilson, J. M., *Statistics of Crime in Ireland, 1842–1856* (Dublin, 1857).

[Wiseman, N.], *The Sermons, lectures, and speeches delivered by His Eminence Cardinal Wiseman, Archbishop of Westminster, during his tour of Ireland in August and September 1858* (Dublin, 1859).

Wolferstan, F. S. P. and Dew, E. L'E., *Reports of the decisions of committees of the House of Commons in the trial of controverted elections during the seventeenth parliament of the United Kingdom* (London, 1859).

— and Bristowe, S. B., *Reports of the decisions of election committees during the eighteenth parliament of the United Kingdom* (London, 1865).

Wyse, T., *Historical Sketch of the late Catholic Association of Ireland*, 2 vols. (London, 1829).

H TWENTIETH-CENTURY PRINTED WORKS

Adams, S., 'Relations between landlord, agent, and tenant on the Hertford estate in the nineteenth century', *Journal of the Lisburn Historical Society*, ii (1979), 3-10.

Ahern, J., 'The Plenary Synod of Thurles', *Irish Ecclesiastical Record*, Part I in lxxv (1951), 385-403; Part II in lxxviii (1952), 1-20.

Akenson, D. H., *The Church of Ireland: Ecclesiastical Reform and Revolution 1800-1885* (New Haven, 1971).

—, *Between Two Revolutions: Islandmagee, County Antrim 1798-1920* (Don Mills, Ontario, 1979).

Almquist, E. L., 'Pre-Famine Ireland and the theory of European proto-industrialization', *Journal of Economic History*, xxxix (1979), 699-718.

Alwill, G., 'The 1841 census of Killeshandra Parish', *Breifne*, v (1976), 7-36.

Andrews, J. H., *A Paper Landscape: The Ordnance Survey in nineteenth-century Ireland* (Oxford, 1975).

Anglesey, [7th] Marquess of, *One-Leg: The life and letters of Henry William Paget First Marquess of Anglesey K.G. 1768-1854* (London, 1961).

Anstruther, I., *The Knight and the Umbrella: An Account of the Eglinton Tournament 1839* (London, 1963).

Arensberg, C. M., *The Irish Countryman: An Anthropological Study* (reprinted Gloucester, Mass., 1959)—first published 1937.

— and Kimball, S. T., *Family and Community in Ireland*, 2nd edn. (Cambridge, Mass., 1968).

Aspinall, A. (ed.), *Three early nineteenth-century diaries* (London, 1952).

Auchmuty, J. J., *Sir Thomas Wyse 1791-1862: The Life and Career of an Educator and Diplomat* (London, 1939).

—, 'Acton's Election as an Irish Member of Parliament', *English Historical Review*, lxi (1946), 394-405.

—, 'Acton as a member of the House of Commons', *Bulletin of the Faculty of Arts: Farook I University of Alexandria*, v (1950), 31-46.

Baker, S. E., 'Orange and Green: Belfast, 1832-1912' in *The Victorian City: Images and Realities*, ed. H. J. Dyos and M. Wolff, 2 vols. (London, 1973), ii, 789-814.

Barrington, T., 'A Review of Irish Agricultural Prices', *Journal of the Statistical and Social Inquiry Society of Ireland*, xv (1927), 249-80.

Barrow, G. L., *The emergence of the Irish banking system 1820-1845* (Dublin, 1975).

Barry, Ann and Hoppen, K. T., 'Borough politics in O'Connellite Ireland: The Youghal poll books of 1835 and 1837', *Journal of the Cork Historical and Archaeological Society*, lxxxiii (1978), 106-46, and lxxxiv (1979), 15-43.

Barry, P. C., 'The Legislation of the Synod of Thurles, 1850', *Irish Theological Quarterly*, xxvi (1959), 131-66.

Barry, V. M., 'The hunting diaries (1863-1881) of Sir John Fermor Godfrey of Kilcoleman Abbey, Co. Kerry', *Irish Ancestor*, xi (1979), 107-19, and xii (1980), 13-25.

Bartlett, T. and Hayton, D. W. (eds.), *Penal Era and Golden Age: Essays in Irish History, 1690-1800* (Belfast, 1979).

Bastable, J. D. (ed.), *Newman and Gladstone: Centennial Essays* (Dublin, 1978).

Bax, M., 'Patronage Irish Style: Irish politicians as brokers', *Sociologische Gids*, xvii (1970), 179–91.

—, *Harpstrings and Confessions: Machine-Style Politics in the Irish Republic* (Assen and Amsterdam, 1976).

—, 'The small community in the Irish political process' in *Irish Studies 2: Ireland: Land, Politics, and People*, ed. P. J. Drudy (Cambridge, 1982), pp. 119–40.

Beames, M. R., 'Cottiers and Conacre in pre-Famine Ireland', *Journal of Peasant Studies*, ii (1975), 352–4.

—, 'Rural Conflict in pre-Famine Ireland: Peasant Assassinations in Tipperary 1837–1847', *Past and Present*, No. 81 (1978), 75–91.

—, 'The Ribbon Societies: Lower-class nationalism in pre-Famine Ireland', *Past and Present*, No. 97 (1982), 128–43.

Beames, M. [R.], *Peasants and Power: The Whiteboy Movements and their control in pre-Famine Ireland* (Brighton, 1983).

Bell, J., 'Relations of mutual help between Ulster farmers', *Ulster Folklife*, xxiv (1978), 48–58.

Bell, T., 'The Revd David Bell', *Clogher Record*, vi (1967), 253–76.

Berry, J., *Tales from the West of Ireland*, ed. G. M. Horgan (Dublin, 1975).

Betjeman, J., *Ghastly Good Taste*, 2nd edn. (London, 1970).

Bew, P., *Land and the National Question in Ireland 1858–82* (Dublin, 1978).

Blunt, W. S., *The Land War in Ireland being a personal narrative of events* (London, 1912).

Boissevain, J., *Saints and Fireworks: Religion and Politics in Rural Malta*, revised edn. (London, 1969).

Booth, C., 'The economic distribution of population in Ireland' in *Ireland: Industrial and Agricultural*, ed. W. P. Coyne (Dublin, 1902), pp. 64–72.

Bottomley, P. M., 'The North Fermanagh elections of 1885 and 1886', *Clogher Record*, viii (1974), 167–81.

Bourke, P. M. A., 'The agricultural statistics of the 1841 census of Ireland: A critical review', *Economic History Review*, 2nd series xviii (1965), 376–91.

Bourne, K. (ed.), *The Letters of the Third Viscount Palmerston to Laurence and Elizabeth Sulivan 1804–1863* (London, 1979).

Bowen, D., *Souperism: Myth or Reality: A Study in Souperism* (Cork, 1970).

—, *The Protestant Crusade in Ireland, 1800–70: A Study of Protestant-Catholic relations between the Act of Union and Disestablishment* (Dublin, 1978).

Bowen, Elizabeth, *Bowen's Court* (London, 1942).

Brady, J. and Corish, P. J., 'The Church under the Penal Code' in *A History of Irish Catholicism*, ed. P. J. Corish, IV, Fascicule 2 (Dublin, 1971).

Breffny, B. de and Mott, G., *The Churches and Abbeys of Ireland* (London, 1976).

Brenan, M., *Schools of Kildare and Leighlin 1775–1835* (Dublin, 1935).

Broderick, J. F., *The Holy See and the Irish Movement for the Repeal of the Union with England 1829–1847* (Rome, 1951).

Broehl, W. G. Jr., *The Molly Maguires* (Cambridge, Mass., 1964).

Brooke, J. and Gandy, J. (eds.), *The Prime Ministers' Papers: Wellington Political Correspondence*, I (London, 1975).

Brooks, S., *Aspects of the Irish Question* (Dublin, 1912).

Brown, T., 'Nationalism and the Irish Peasant, 1800–1848', *Review of Politics*, xv (1953), 403–45.

Brún, P. de, 'An tAthair Brasbie', *Journal of the Kerry Archaeological and Historical Society*, No. 2 (1969), 38–58.

Buckland, P., *Irish Unionism: The Anglo-Irish and the new Ireland 1885-1922* (Dublin, 1972).

—, *Irish Unionism Two: Ulster Unionism and the origins of Northern Ireland 1886-1922* (Dublin, 1973).

Budge, I. and O'Leary, C., *Belfast: Approach to Crisis: A Study of Belfast politics 1613-1970* (London, 1973).

Cahir, B., 'Isaac Butt and the Limerick By-Election of 1871', *North Munster Antiquarian Journal*, x (1966), 56–66. See also under Ó Cathaoir, B.

Cannon, S., *Irish Episcopal Meetings, 1788-1882: A juridico-historical Study* (Rome: Pontifical University of St Thomas, 1979).

Carbery, Mary, *The Farm by Lough Gur: The Story of Mary Fogarty* (Cork, 1973).

Casey, D. J. and Rhodes, R. E. (eds.), *Views of the Irish Peasantry 1800-1916* (Hamden, Conn., 1977).

Christianson, G. E., 'Landlords and Land Tenure in Ireland 1790-1830', *Eire-Ireland*, ix (1974), 25–58.

Clare, W. (ed.), *A Young Irishman's Diary (1836-1847) Being extracts from the early journal of John Keegan of Moate* (March, Cambs., 1928).

Clark, S., 'The social composition of the Land League', *Irish Historical Studies*, xvii (1971), 447–69.

—, 'The political mobilization of Irish farmers', *Canadian Review of Sociology and Anthropology*, xii (1975), 483–99.

—, 'The importance of agrarian classes: agrarian class structure and collective action in nineteenth-century Ireland', *British Journal of Sociology*, xxix (1978), 22–40.

—, *Social origins of the Irish Land War* (Princeton, 1979).

— and Donnelly, J. S. Jr. (eds.), *Irish peasants, violence, and political unrest 1780-1914* (Manchester, 1983).

Comerford, R. V., *Charles J. Kickham: A Study in Irish Nationalism and Literature* (Dublin, 1979).

—, 'Patriotism as pastime: The appeal of Fenianism in the mid-1860s', *Irish Historical Studies*, xxii (1981), 239–50.

Connell, K. H., *Irish Peasant Society: Four historical essays* (Oxford, 1968).

Connolly, S. J., 'Illegitimacy and pre-nuptial pregnancy in Ireland before 1864: The evidence of some Catholic parish registers', *Irish Economic and Social History*, vi (1979), 5–23.

—, *Priests and People in pre-Famine Ireland 1780-1845* (Dublin, 1982).

—, 'Religion and History', *Irish Economic and Social History*, x (1983), 66–80.

Cooke, A. B., 'A Conservative party leader in Ulster: Sir Stafford Northcote's diary of a visit to the province, October 1883', *Proceedings of the Royal Irish Academy*, Section C, lxxv (1975), 61–84.

Coombes, J., 'Catholic Churches of the Nineteenth Century: Some Newspaper Sources', *Journal of the Cork Historical and Archaeological Society*, lxxxi (1975), 1–12.

Corish, P. J., 'Cardinal Cullen and the National Association of Ireland', *Reportorium Novum: Dublin Diocesan Historical Record*, iii (1962), 13–61.

—, 'Political Problems 1860-78' in *A History of Irish Catholicism*, ed. P. J. Corish, V, Fascicule 3 (Dublin, 1967).

— (ed.), 'Irish College, Rome: Kirby Papers', *Arch. Hib.* xxx (1972), 29–115; xxxi (1973), 1–94; xxxii (1974), 1–62.

—, 'Gallicanism at Maynooth: Archbishop Cullen and the Royal Visitation of 1853' in *Studies in Irish History presented to R. Dudley Edwards*, ed. A. Cosgrove and D. McCartney (Dublin, 1979), pp. 176–89.

— (ed.), *A History of Irish Catholicism*: see under Brady, J. and Corish, P. J.; Corish, P. J.; Cunningham, T. P.; Kennedy, T. P.; Murphy, I.; Ó Súilleabháin, S. V.; Whyte, J. H.

Cosgrove, A. and McCartney, D. (eds.), *Studies in Irish History presented to R. Dudley Edwards* (Dublin, 1979).

Cousens, S. H., 'Emigration and Demographic Change in Ireland, 1851–1861', *Economic History Review*, 2nd series xiv (1961), 275–88.

Craig, M., *Dublin 1660–1860* (Dublin, 1969).

Crotty, R. D., *Irish agricultural production: Its volume and structure* (Cork, 1966).

Cullen, L. M., 'The Hidden Ireland: Re-assessment of a Concept', *Studia Hibernica*, No. 9 (1969), 7–47.

— (ed.), *The Formation of the Irish Economy* (Cork, 1969).

—, *An economic history of Ireland since 1660* (London, 1972).

—, 'Ireland' in *The Victorian Countryside*, ed. G. E. Mingay, 2 vols. (London, 1981), i, 94–102.

—, *The emergence of modern Ireland 1600–1900* (London, 1981).

— and Furet, F. (eds.), *Ireland and France 17th-20th Centuries: Towards a comparative study of rural history* (Paris, 1980).

— and Smout, T. C. (eds.), *Comparative aspects of Scottish and Irish economic and social history 1600–1900* (Edinburgh, [1977]).

Cunningham, P., 'The Catholic Directory for 1821', *Reportorium Novum: Dublin Diocesan Historical Record*, ii (1960), 324–63.

Cunningham, T. P., 'The Burrowes-Hughes by-election' [Co. Cavan 1855], *Breifne*, iii (1967), 175–212.

—, 'The Cavan tenant-right meeting of 1850', *Breifne*, iii (1969), 417–42.

—, 'Carlow Town in 1838', *Breifne*, iii (1969), 528–51, and iv (1970), 96–130.

—, 'Church Reorganization' in *A History of Irish Catholicism*, ed. P. J. Corish, V, Fascicule 7 (Dublin, 1970).

Curtis, L. P. Jr., 'The Anglo–Irish Predicament', *Twentieth Century*, No. 4 (1970), 37–63.

—, 'Incumbered Wealth: Landed Indebtedness in post-Famine Ireland', *American Historical Review*, lxxxv (1980), 332–67.

d'Alton, I., 'Southern Irish Unionism: A study of Cork Unionists, 1884–1914', *Transactions of the Royal Historical Society*, 5th series xxiii (1973), 71–88.

—, 'Cork Unionism: Its role in parliamentary and local elections, 1885–1914', *Studia Hibernica*, No. 15 (1975), 143–61.

—, *Protestant Society and Politics in Cork 1812–1844* (Cork, 1980).

Daly, Mary, 'The Development of the National School System, 1831–40' in *Studies in Irish History presented to R. Dudley Edwards*, ed. A. Cosgrove and D. McCartney (Dublin, 1979), pp. 150–63.

—, 'Late nineteenth and twentieth century Dublin' in *The Town in Ireland*, ed. D. Harkness and M. O'Dowd (Belfast, 1981), pp. 221–52.

Daly, S., *Cork: A city in crisis, A history of labour conflict and social misery 1870–1872* (Cork, 1978).

D'Arcy, F. A., 'The artisans of Dublin and Daniel O'Connell 1830–47: An un-quiet liaison', *Irish Historical Studies*, xvii (1970), 221–43.

Davies, G. L. H. and Mollan, R. C. (eds.), *Richard Griffith 1784–1878* (Dublin, 1980).

Davies, O., 'Folklore in Maghera Parish', *Ulster Journal of Archaeology*, 3rd series viii (1945), 63–5.

Davitt, M., *The Fall of Feudalism in Ireland or the story of the Land League Revolution* (London, 1904).

Dessain, C. S. *et al.* (eds.), *The Letters and Diaries of John Henry Newman*, 26 vols. to date (London and Oxford, 1961–).

Devine, T. M. and Dickson, D. (eds.), *Ireland and Scotland 1600–1850: Parallels and Contrasts in Economic and Social Development* (Edinburgh, 1983).

Dewar, M., Brown, J., and Long, S. E., *Orangeism: A new Historical Apprecia-tion* [Belfast, 1967].

Dickson, D., 'Middlemen' in *Penal Era and Golden Age: Essays in Irish History, 1690–1800*, ed. T. Bartlett and D. W. Hayton (Belfast, 1979), pp. 162–85.

Dolan, L., *Land War and eviction in Derryveagh 1840–65* (Dundalk, 1980).

Donnelly, J. S. Jr., *Landlord and Tenant in nineteenth-century Ireland* (Dublin, 1973).

—— (ed.), 'The Journals of Sir John Benn-Walsh relating to the management of his Irish estates, 1823–64', *Journal of the Cork Historical and Archaeological Society*, lxxx (1974), 86–123, and lxxxi (1975), 15–42.

——, *The Land and the People of nineteenth-century Cork: The Rural Economy and the Land Question* (London, 1975).

——, 'The Irish agricultural depression of 1859–64', *Irish Economic and Social History*, iii (1976), 33–54.

——, 'The Rightboy Movement 1785–8', *Studia Hibernica*, No. 17/18 (1977–8), 120–202.

——, 'The Whiteboy Movement 1761–5', *Irish Historical Studies*, xxi (1978), 20–54.

——, 'Propagating the Cause of the United Irishmen', *Studies*, lxix (1980), 5–23.

——, 'Pastorini and Captain Rock: Millenarianism and Sectarianism in the Rockite Movement of 1821–4' in *Irish peasants, violence, and political unrest 1780–1914*, ed. S. Clark and J. S. Donnelly Jr. (Manchester, 1983), pp. 102–39.

Drake, M., 'The mid-Victorian voter', *Journal of Interdisciplinary History*, i (1971), 473–90.

Drus, E. (ed.), 'A Journal of Events during the Gladstone Ministry 1868–1874' by 1st Earl of Kimberley, *Camden Miscellany XXI*, Camden 3rd series xc (1958).

Duffy, P. J., 'Irish landholding structures and population in the mid-nineteenth century', *Maynooth Review*, iii (1977), 3–27.

Dunlop, A., *Fifty years of Irish journalism* (Dublin, 1911).

Dwyer, C. M., 'James Augustine Anderson O.S.A.', *Seanchas Ardmhacha: Journal of the Armagh Diocesan Historical Society*, vii (1974), 215–58.

Dyos, H. J. and Wolff, M. (eds.), *The Victorian City: Images and Realities*, 2 vols. (London, 1973).

Edwards, J. A., 'The landless in mid-nineteenth century County Louth', *Journal of the Louth Archaeological Society*, xvi (1965–8), 103–10.

Egan, P. K., *The Parish of Ballinasloe* (Dublin, 1960).

Erickson, A. B., 'Edward T. Cardwell: Peelite', *Transactions of the American Philosophical Society*, new series xlix, part 2 (1959).

Evans, E. E., 'Peasant Beliefs in nineteenth-century Ireland' in *Views of the Irish Peasantry 1800-1916* ed. D. J. Casey and R. E. Rhodes (Hamden, Conn., 1977), pp. 37-56.

Fahy, M. de L., *Education in the Diocese of Kilmacduagh in the Nineteenth Century* (Gort, 1972).

Falk, B., *'Old Q's' Daughter* (London, 1951).

Fanu, W. R. Le, *Seventy Years of Irish Life, Being Anecdotes and Reminiscences* (London, 1928)—first published 1893.

Ferrar, M. L. (ed.), *The Diary of Colour-Sergeant George Calladine 19th Foot 1793-1837* (London, 1922).

Feuchtwanger, E. J., *Disraeli, Democracy, and the Tory Party: Conservative leadership and organization after the Second Reform Bill* (Oxford, 1968).

Finnane, M., *Insanity and the Insane in post-Famine Ireland* (London, 1981).

Fitzpatrick, D., *Politics and Irish Life 1913-1921: Provincial experience of War and Revolution* (Dublin, 1977).

—, 'The geography of Irish nationalism 1910-1921', *Past and Present*, No. 78 (1978), 113-44.

—, 'The Disappearance of the Irish Agricultural Labourer, 1841-1912', *Irish Economic and Social History*, vii (1980), 66-92.

—, 'Class, family, and rural unrest in nineteenth-century Ireland' in *Irish Studies 2: Ireland: Land, Politics, and People*, ed. P. J. Drudy (Cambridge, 1982), pp. 37-75.

Flanagan, K., 'The Godless and the Burlesque: Newman and the other Irish universities' in *Newman and Gladstone: Centennial Essays*, ed. J. D. Bastable (Dublin, 1978), pp. 239-77.

Fleetwood, J., *History of Medicine in Ireland* (Dublin, 1951).

Foot, M. R. D. and Matthew, H. C. G. (eds.), *The Gladstone Diaries*, 8 vols. to date (Oxford, 1968-).

Foster, R. F., *Charles Stewart Parnell: The Man and his Family* (Hassocks, 1976).

—, 'To the Northern Counties Station: Lord Randolph Churchill and the prelude to the Orange Card' in *Ireland under the Union: Varieties of tension: Essays in honour of T. W. Moody*, ed. F. S. L. Lyons and R. A. J. Hawkins (Oxford, 1980), pp. 237-87.

Freeman, T. W., 'The Irish country town', *Irish Geography*, iii (1954), 5-14.

Garvin, T., *The evolution of Irish nationalist politics* (Dublin, 1981).

—, 'Defenders, Ribbonmen and others: Underground political networks in pre-Famine Ireland', *Past and Present*, No. 96 (1982), 133-55.

Gash, N., *Politics in the age of Peel: A study in the technique of parliamentary representation 1830-1850* (London, 1953).

Gibbon, P., *The Origins of Ulster Unionism: The formation of popular Protestant Politics and Ideology in nineteenth-century Ireland* (Manchester, 1975).

— and Higgins, M. D., 'Patronage, tradition and modernisation: The case of the Irish "Gombeenman" ', *Economic and Social Review*, vi (1974), 27-44.

— and —, 'The Irish "Gombeenman": Re-incarnation or Rehabilitation?', *Economic and Social Review*, viii (1977), 313-19.

Girouard, M., *The Victorian Country House*, revised edn. (London, 1979).

Gmelch, G. and Kroup, B., *To Shorten the Road* (Dublin, 1978).

Greene, D., 'Michael Cusack and the rise of the G.A.A.' in *The Shaping of Modern Ireland*, ed. C. C. O'Brien (London, 1960), pp. 74-84.

Gregory, Lady, *Visions and Beliefs in the West of Ireland*, new edn. (Gerrards Cross, 1970).

Gwyn, W. B., *Democracy and the cost of politics in Britain* (London, 1962).

Gwynn, D., *The O'Gorman Mahon: Duellist, Adventurer, and Politician* (London, 1934).

Haire, D. N., 'In Aid of the Civil Power, 1868–90' in *Ireland under the Union: Varieties of tension: Essays in honour of T. W. Moody*, ed. F. S. L. Lyons and R. A. J. Hawkins (Oxford, 1980), pp. 115–47.

Hanham, H. J., *Elections and Party Management: Politics in the time of Disraeli and Gladstone* (London, 1959).

——, 'Religion and Nationality in the mid-Victorian Army' in *War and Society: Historical essays in honour and memory of J. R. Western 1928–1971*, ed. M. R. D. Foot (London, 1973), pp. 159–81 and 318–20.

Harkness, D. and O'Dowd, M. (eds.), *The Town in Ireland* (Belfast, 1981).

Harmon, M., 'Aspects of the Peasantry in Anglo–Irish Literature from 1800 to 1916', *Studia Hibernica*, No. 15 (1975), 105–27.

Haughton, J. P., 'The live-stock fair in relation to Irish country towns', *Irish Geography*, iii (1955), 107–13.

Hawkins, R. [A. J.], 'An Army on Police Work, 1881–2: Ross of Bladensburg's Memorandum', *The Irish Sword*, xi (1973), 75–117.

——, 'Government versus Secret Societies: The Parnell Era' in *Secret Societies in Ireland*, ed. T. D. Williams (Dublin, 1973), pp. 100–12.

Hepburn, A. C., 'Catholics in the north of Ireland, 1850–1921: The urbanization of a minority' in *Minorities in history*, pp. 84–101 (see next entry).

—— (ed.), *Minorities in history* (London, 1978).

Higgins, M. D. and Gibbons, J. P., 'Shopkeeper-Graziers and land agitation in Ireland, 1895–1900' in *Irish Studies 2: Ireland: Land, Politics, and People*, ed. P. J. Drudy (Cambridge, 1982), pp. 93–118.

Hill, Jacqueline, 'The Protestant response to Repeal: The case of the Dublin working class' in *Ireland under the Union: Varieties of tension: Essays in honour of T. W. Moody*, ed. F. S. L. Lyons and R. A. J. Hawkins (Oxford, 1980), pp. 35–68.

Hill, R. L., *Toryism and the people 1832–1846* (London, 1929).

Holohan, P., 'Daniel O'Connell and the Dublin Trades: A Collision 1837/8', *Saothar: Journal of the Irish Labour History Society*, No. 1 (1975), 1–17.

Hoppen, K. T., 'Tories, Catholics, and the General Election of 1859', *Historical Journal*, xiii (1970), 48–67.

——, 'Landlords, society, and electoral politics in mid-nineteenth century Ireland', *Past and Present*, No. 75 (1977), 62–93.

——, 'Politics, the law, and the nature of the Irish electorate 1832–1850', *English Historical Review*, xcii (1977), 746–76.

——, 'National politics and local realities in mid-nineteenth century Ireland' in *Studies in Irish History presented to R. Dudley Edwards*, ed. A. Cosgrove and D. McCartney (Dublin, 1979), pp. 190–227.

Hosp, E., 'Redemptorist Mission in Enniskillen, 1852', *Clogher Record*, viii (1975), 268–70.

Hunter, J., *The Making of the Crofting Community* (Edinburgh, 1976).

Hurst, J. W., 'Disturbed Tipperary 1831–1860', *Eire–Ireland*, ix (1974), 44–59.

Hurst, M., 'Ireland and the Ballot Act of 1872', *Historical Journal*, viii (1965), 326–52.

——, *Maria Edgeworth and the public scene* (London, 1969).

[Hussey, S. M.], *The Reminiscences of an Irish land agent being those of S. M. Hussey*, ed. H. Gordon (London, 1904).

Huttman, J. P., 'The impact of land reform on agricultural production in Ireland', *Agricultural History*, xlvi (1972), 353–68.

Hynes, E., 'The Great Hunger and Irish Catholicism', *Societas*, viii (1978), 137–56.

Inglis, B., *The freedom of the press in Ireland 1784–1841* (London, 1954).

Jenkins, R. P., 'Witches and Fairies: Supernatural Aggression and Deviance among the Irish Peasantry', *Ulster Folklife*, xxiii (1977), 33–56.

Jones, E., *A Social Geography of Belfast* (London, 1960).

Jones, L., 'Dress in nineteenth-century Ireland: An approach to research', *Folklife*, xvi (1978), 42–53.

Jones Hughes, T., 'Landlordism in the Mullet of Mayo', *Irish Geography*, iv (1959), 16–34.

—, 'Administrative divisions and the development of settlement in nineteenth-century Ireland', *University Review* [Dublin], iii (1962–3), 8–15.

Jupp, P., 'County Down elections, 1783–1831', *Irish Historical Studies*, xviii (1972), 177–206.

—, *British and Irish Elections 1784–1831* (Newton Abbot, 1973).

Kearney, H. F., 'Fr. Mathew: Apostle of Modernisation' in *Studies in Irish History presented to R. Dudley Edwards*, ed. A. Cosgrove and D. McCartney (Dublin, 1979), pp. 164–75.

—, 'The estate as social community in the early 19th century' (unpublished paper).

Kee, R., *The Green Flag: A History of Irish Nationalism* (London, 1972).

Kennedy, L., 'A sceptical view of the re-incarnation of the Irish "Gombeen-man" ', *Economic and Social Review*, viii (1977), 213–22.

—, 'Retail Markets in Rural Ireland at the end of the nineteenth century', *Irish Economic and Social History*, v (1978), 46–63.

—, 'The early response of the Irish Catholic Clergy to the Co-operative Movement', *Irish Historical Studies*, xxi (1978), 55–74.

—, 'The Roman Catholic Church and Economic Growth in Nineteenth-Century Ireland', *Economic and Social Review*, x (1978), 45–60.

—, 'Traders in the Irish Rural Economy, 1880–1914', *Economic History Review*, 2nd series xxxii (1979), 201–10.

—, 'Profane images in the Irish popular consciousness', *Oral History*, vii (1979), 42–7.

—, 'Farmers, traders, and agricultural politics in pre-Independence Ireland' in *Irish peasants, violence, and political unrest 1780–1914*, ed. S. Clark and J. S. Donnelly Jr. (Manchester, 1983), pp. 339–73.

Kennedy, T. P., 'Church Building' in *A History of Irish Catholicism*, ed. P. J. Corish, V, Fascicule 8 (Dublin, 1970).

Kerr, D. A., *Peel, Priests, and Politics: Sir Robert Peel's Administration and the Roman Catholic Church in Ireland, 1841–1846* (Oxford, 1982).

Kettle, L. J. (ed.), *The Material for Victory: Being the Memoirs of Andrew J. Kettle* (Dublin, 1958).

Kirkpatrick, R. W., 'Origins and Development of the Land War in mid-Ulster, 1879–85' in *Ireland under the Union: Varieties of tension: Essays in honour of T. W. Moody*, ed. F. S. L. Lyons and R. A. J. Hawkins (Oxford, 1980), pp. 201–35.

Lane, P. G., 'An attempt at commercial farming in Ireland after the Famine', *Studies*, lxi (1972), 54–66.

—, 'On the General Impact of the Encumbered Estates Act of 1849 on Counties

Galway and Mayo', *Journal of the Galway Archaeological and Historical Society*, xxxii (1972-3), 44-74.

—, 'The management of estates by financial corporations in Ireland after the Famine', *Studia Hibernica*, No. 14 (1974), 67-89.

Lansdowne, [6th] Marquess of, *Glanerought and the Petty-Fitzmaurices* (London, 1937).

Large, D., 'The House of Lords and Ireland in the Age of Peel, 1832-50', *Irish Historical Studies*, ix (1955), 367-99.

—, 'The wealth of the greater Irish Landowners, 1750-1815', *Irish Historical Studies*, xv (1966), 21-47.

Larkin, E., 'Church and State in Ireland in the Nineteenth Century', *Church History*, xxxi (1962), 294-306.

—, 'Economic Growth, Capital Investment, and the Roman Catholic Church in nineteenth-century Ireland', *American Historical Review*, lxxii (1966-7), 852-84.

—, 'The Devotional Revolution in Ireland, 1850-75', *American Historical Review*, lxxvii (1972), 625-52.

—, 'Church, state, and nation in modern Ireland', *American Historical Review*, lxxx (1975), 1244-76.

—, *The Roman Catholic Church and the Creation of the Modern Irish State, 1878-1886* (Philadelphia and Dublin, 1975).

—, *The Roman Catholic Church and the Plan of Campaign in Ireland, 1886-1888* (Cork, 1978).

—, *The Roman Catholic Church in Ireland and the Fall of Parnell 1888-1891* (Liverpool, 1979).

—, *The Making of the Roman Catholic Church in Ireland, 1850-1860* (Chapel Hill, 1980).

Lebow, N., 'British Images of Poverty in pre-Famine Ireland' in *Views of the Irish Peasantry 1800-1916*, ed. D. J. Casey and R. E. Rhodes (Hamden, Conn., 1977), pp. 57-85.

Lee, C. and MacCárthaigh, D., 'Certain Statistics from the United Parishes of Knockainy and Patrickswell (Diocese of Emly, Co. Limerick) for the years 1819-1941', *Journal of the Cork Historical and Archaeological Society*, xlvii (1942), 1-8.

Lee, J., 'The Railways in the Irish Economy' in *The Formation of the Irish Economy*, ed. L. M. Cullen (Cork, 1969), pp. 77-87.

—, 'The dual economy in Ireland 1800-1850', *Historical Studies*, viii (1971), 191-201.

—, *The Modernisation of Irish Society 1848-1918* (Dublin, 1973).

—, 'The Ribbonmen' in *Secret Societies in Ireland*, ed. T. D. Williams (Dublin, 1973), pp. 26-35.

—, 'Railway labour in Ireland 1833-1856', *Saothar: Journal of the Irish Labour History Society*, No. 5 (1979), 9-26.

—, 'Patterns of rural unrest in nineteenth-century Ireland: A preliminary survey' in *Ireland and France 17th-20th Centuries: Towards a comparative study of rural history*, ed. L. M. Cullen and F. Furet (Paris, 1980), pp. 223-37.

Leister, I., *Das Werden der Agrarlandschaft in der Grafschaft Tipperary (Irland)* (Marburg, 1963) Heft 18 in Marburger Geographische Schriften.

Lewis, C. A., *Hunting in Ireland: An Historical and Geographical Analysis* (London, 1975).

Livingstone, P., *The Fermanagh Story* (Enniskillen, 1969).

Lloyd, A. L., 'On an unpublished Irish ballad' in *Rebels and their Causes: Essays in honour of A. L. Morton*, ed. M. Cornforth (London, 1978), pp. 177–207.

Locker Lampson, G., *A Consideration of the State of Ireland in the nineteenth century* (London, 1907).

Lowe, W. J., 'Landlord and Tenant on the estates of Trinity College Dublin, 1851–1903', *Hermathena*, cxx (1976), 5–24.

Lucas, R., *Colonel Saunderson M.P.: A Memoir* (London, 1908).

Lynch, P. and Vaizey, J., *Guinness's Brewery in the Irish economy 1759–1876* (Cambridge, 1960).

Lyne, G., 'Daniel O'Connell, intimidation, and the Kerry elections of 1835', *Journal of the Kerry Archaeological and Historical Society*, No. 4 (1971), 74–97.

Lyons, F. S. L., *Charles Stewart Parnell* (London, 1977).

— and Hawkins, R. A. J. (eds.), *Ireland under the Union: Varieties of tension: Essays in honour of T. W. Moody* (Oxford, 1980).

McCaffrey, L. J., 'Irish Federalism in the 1870s: A Study in Conservative Nationalism', *Transactions of the American Philosophical Society*, new series lii, part 6 (1962).

McClelland, A., 'The Origin of the Imperial Grand Black Chapter of the British Commonwealth', *Journal of the Royal Society of Antiquaries of Ireland*, xcviii (1968), 191–5.

—, 'The later Orange Order' in *Secret Societies in Ireland*, ed. T. D. Williams (Dublin, 1973), pp. 126–37.

—, 'Festivities at Hillsborough', *Ulster Folk and Transport Museum Year Book* (1973–4), 6–8.

—, 'Orangeism in County Monaghan', *Clogher Record*, ix (1978), 384–404.

McCormick, D., *The incredible Mr Kavanagh* (London, 1960).

McCourt, E., 'The Management of the Farnham Estates during the nineteenth century', *Breifne*, iv (1975), 531–60.

MacDonagh, O., 'The politicization of the Irish Catholic Bishops, 1800–1850', *Historical Journal*, xviii (1975), 37–53.

—, 'Irish Famine Emigration to the United States' in *Perspectives in American History*, x, ed. D. Fleming and B. Bailyn (Cambridge, Mass., 1976), pp. 357–446.

McDonald, W., *Reminiscences of a Maynooth Professor*, ed. D. Gwynn (London, 1925).

McDowell, R. B., *Public Opinion and Government Policy in Ireland, 1801–1846* (London, 1952).

—, *The Irish Administration 1801–1914* (London, 1964).

—, *The Church of Ireland 1869–1969* (London, 1975).

MacGill, P., *Children of the Dead End: The Autobiography of a Navvy* (London, [1914]).

Mac Giolla Choille, B., 'Fenians, Rice, and Ribbonmen in County Monaghan, 1864–67', *Clogher Record*, vi (1967), 221–52.

—, 'Mourning the Martyrs: A study of a demonstration in Limerick City, 8 December 1867', *North Munster Antiquarian Journal*, x (1967), 173–205.

McGrath, M. (ed.), *The Diary of Humphrey O'Sullivan*, 4 vols. (London and Dublin, 1936–7).

Macintyre, A., *The Liberator: Daniel O'Connell and the Irish party 1830–1847* (London, 1965).

McLaughlin, P. J., 'Nicholas Callan' in *Dictionary of Scientific Biography*, ed. C. C. Gillispie, 15 vols. (New York, 1970–8), iii, 17–18.

MacLochlainn, A., 'Social Life in County Clare, 1800–1850', *Irish University Review*, ii (1972), 55–78.

McNamara, K., 'Patrick Murray's teaching on tradition' in *Volk Gottes: Festgabe für Josef Höfer*, ed. R. Bäumer and H. Dolch (Freiburg, 1967), pp. 455–79.

MacNeill, Máire, *The Festival of Lughnasa: A Study of the Survival of the Celtic Festival of the Beginning of Harvest* (Oxford, 1962).

McNiffe, L., 'The 1852 Leitrim election', *Breifne*, v (1977–8), 223–52.

MacSuibhne, P. (ed.), *Paul Cullen and his Contemporaries*, 5 vols. (Naas, 1961–77).

Magee, J., 'The Monaghan election of 1883 and the "Invasion of Ulster" ', *Clogher Record*, viii (1974), 147–66.

Maguire, W. A., *The Downshire estates in Ireland 1801–1845* (Oxford, 1972).

—— (ed.), *Letters of a great Irish landlord: A selection from the estate correspondence of the Third Marquess of Downshire, 1809–45* (Belfast, 1974).

Mahony, E., *The Galway Blazers; Memoirs* (Galway, 1979).

Malcolm, Elizabeth, 'Temperance and Irish Nationalism' in *Ireland under the Union: Varieties of tension: Essays in honour of T. W. Moody*, ed. F. S. L. Lyons and R. A. J. Hawkins (Oxford, 1980), pp. 69–114.

Malcomson, A. P. W., *John Foster: The Politics of the Anglo-Irish Ascendancy* (Oxford, 1978).

Matheson, R. E., 'The Housing of the people of Ireland during the period 1841–1901', *Journal of the Statistical and Social Inquiry Society of Ireland*, xi (1904), 196–212.

Maxwell, H., *The Life and Letters of George William Frederick, Fourth Earl of Clarendon*, 2 vols. (London, 1913).

Miller, D. W., *Church, State, and Nation in Ireland 1898–1921* (Dublin, 1973).

——, 'Irish Catholicism and the Great Famine', *Journal of Social History*, ix (1975), 81–98.

——, 'Presbyterians and "Modernization" in Ulster', *Past and Present*, No. 80 (1978), 66–90.

Mingay, G. E. (ed.), *The Victorian Countryside*, 2 vols. (London, 1981).

Mitchell, J. C. and Cornford, J., 'The political demography of Cambridge 1832–1868', *Albion*, ix (1977), 242–72.

Mogey, J. M., *Rural life in Northern Ireland: Five regional studies* (London, 1947).

Mokyr, J., 'Uncertainty and Prefamine Irish Agriculture' in *Ireland and Scotland 1600–1850: Parallels and Contrasts in Economic and Social Development*, ed. T. M. Devine and D. Dickson (Edinburgh, 1983), pp. 89–101.

Moneypenny, W. F. and Buckle, G. E., *The Life of Benjamin Disraeli*, 6 vols. (London, 1910–20).

Moody, T. W., *Davitt and Irish Revolution 1846–82* (Oxford, 1981).

Moore, G., *The Untilled Field* (London, 1903).

Moore, M. G., *An Irish Gentleman: George Henry Moore: His Travel, His Racing, His Politics* (London, [1913]).

Murphy, D., *Derry, Donegal, and Modern Ulster 1790–1921* (Londonderry, 1981).

Murphy, I., 'Primary Education' in *A History of Irish Catholicism*, ed. P. J. Corish, V, Fascicule 6 (Dublin, 1971).

Murphy, J. A., 'The Support of the Catholic Clergy in Ireland, 1750–1850', *Historical Studies*, v (1965), 103–21.

—, 'Priests and People in Modern Irish History', *Christus Rex*, xxiii (1969), 235–59.

Murphy, Maura, 'Municipal Reform and the Repeal Movement in Cork 1833–1844', *Journal of the Cork Historical and Archaeological Society*, lxxxi (1976), 1–18.

—, 'Repeal, Popular Politics, and the Catholic Clergy of Cork, 1840–50', *Journal of the Cork Historical and Archaeological Society*, lxxxii (1977) 39–48.

—, 'The Ballad Singer and the role of the Seditious Ballad in nineteenth-century Ireland: Dublin Castle's View', *Ulster Folklife*, xxv (1979), 79–102.

—, 'Fenianism, Parnellism, and the Cork Trades 1860–1900', *Saothar: Journal of the Irish Labour History Society*, No. 5 (1979), 27–38.

—, 'The economic and social structure of nineteenth century Cork' in *The Town in Ireland*, ed. D. Harkness and M. O'Dowd (Belfast, 1981), pp. 125–54.

Murphy, P. J., 'The papers of Nicholas Archdeacon', *Arch. Hib.*, xxxi (1973), 124–31.

[National Library of Ireland], *The Landed Gentry: Facsimile Documents* (1977).

'A Native', *Recollections of Dublin Castle and of Dublin Society* (Dublin, 1902).

Neville, M. K. (ed.), 'Ireland in 1874: Journal of Charles P. Daly (1816–1899)', *Eire-Ireland*, xiv (1979), 44–51.

Nolan, W., *Fassadinin: Land, settlement, and society in south-east Ireland 1600–1850* (Dublin, 1979).

Norman, E. R., *The Catholic Church and Ireland in the Age of Rebellion 1859–1873* (London, 1965).

Nossiter, T. J., *Influence, opinion, and political idioms in reformed England: Case Studies from the North-East, 1832–74* (Hassocks, 1975).

Nowlan, K. B., 'Communications' in *Ulster since 1800 Second Series: A Social Survey*, ed. T. W. Moody and J. C. Beckett (London, 1957), pp. 138–47.

—, *The Politics of Repeal: A Study in the Relations between Great Britain and Ireland, 1841–50* (London, 1965).

—, 'The Catholic Clergy and Irish Politics in the Eighteen Thirties and Forties', *Historical Studies*, ix (1974), 119–36.

O'Brien, C. C. (ed.), *The Shaping of Modern Ireland* (London, 1960).

—, *Parnell and his Party 1880–90*, corrected impression (Oxford, 1964).

Ó Cathaoir [Cahir], B., 'The Kerry "Home Rule" by-election, 1872', *Journal of the Kerry Archaeological and Historical Society*, No. 3 (1970), 154–70. See also under Cahir, B.

O'Connell, M. R. (ed.), *The Correspondence of Daniel O'Connell*, 8 vols. (Dublin, 1972–80).

O'Connor, D., *St. Patrick's Purgatory, Lough Derg. Its history, traditions, legends, antiquities, topography, and scenic surroundings*, enlarged edn. (Dublin, 1910).

Ó Danachair, C., 'The death of a tradition', *Studies*, lxiv (1964), 219–30.

—, 'Faction Fighting in County Limerick', *North Munster Antiquarian Journal*, x (1966), 47–55.

O'Day, A., *The English face of Irish Nationalism: Parnellite involvement in British politics, 1880–86* (Dublin, 1977).

Ó Doibhlin, É., *Domhnach Mór (Donaghmore): An outline of parish history* (Omagh, 1969).

O'Donnell, F. H., *History of the Irish Parliamentary Party*, 2 vols. (London, 1910).

O'Donnell, P., *The Irish Faction Fighters of the 19th Century* (Dublin, 1975).

O'Donoghue, P., 'Causes of the opposition to Tithes, 1830–38', *Studia Hibernica*, No. 5 (1965), 7–28.

——, 'Opposition to Tithe Payments in 1830–31', *Studia Hibernica*, No. 6 (1966), 69–98.

——, 'Opposition to Tithe Payment in 1832–3', *Studia Hibernica*, No. 12 (1972), 77–108.

Ó Dufaigh, S., 'James Murphy, Bishop of Clogher, 1801–24', *Clogher Record*, vi (1968), 419–92.

Ó Dúghaill, G., 'Ballads and the Law 1830–32', *Ulster Folklife*, xix (1973), 38–40.

O'Farrell, P., *Ireland's English Question: Anglo-Irish Relations 1534–1970* (London, 1971).

——, 'Millenialism, Messianism, and Utopianism in Irish History', *Anglo-Irish Studies*, ii (1976), 45–68.

Ó Fiaich, T., 'The Clergy and Fenianism, 1860–70', *Irish Ecclesiastical Record*, cix (1968), 81–103.

——, 'Irish Poetry and the Clergy', *Léachtaí Cholm Coille* [Maynooth], iv (1975), 30–56.

Ó Gráda, C., 'Agricultural Head Rents, Pre-Famine and Post-Famine', *Economic and Social Review*, v (1973–4), 385–92.

——, 'Supply responsiveness in Irish agriculture during the nineteenth century', *Economic History Review*, 2nd series xxviii (1975), 312–17.

——, 'The investment behaviour of Irish landlords 1850–75: Some preliminary findings', *Agricultural History Review*, xxiii (1975), 139–55 (also debate between Ó Gráda and R. Perrin on 'The landlord and agricultural transformation, 1870–1900', ibid. xxvii (1979), 40–6).

——, 'Primogeniture and Ultimogeniture in rural Ireland', *Journal of Interdisciplinary History*, x (1980), 491–7.

Ó Laoghaire, P., *My Own Story*, trans. from the Irish by Sheila O Sullivan (Dublin, 1973).

Ó Lúing, S., 'A Contribution to the study of Fenianism in Breifne', *Breifne*, iii (1967), 155–74.

——, 'Aspects of the Fenian Rising in Kerry, 1867', *Journal of the Kerry Archaeological and Historical Society*, I in No. 3 (1970), 131–53; II in No. 4 (1971), 139–64; III in No. 5 (1972), 103–32; IV in No. 6 (1973), 172–94; V in No. 7 (1974), 107–33.

Ó Mórdha, P., 'Some Notes on Monaghan History (1692–1866)', *Clogher Record*, ix (1976), 17–63.

O'Neill, Timothy P., 'Poverty in Ireland 1815–45', *Folklife*, xi (1973), 22–33.

——, 'The Catholic Church and Relief of the Poor 1815–45', *Arch. Hib.* xxxi (1973), 132–45.

Orme, A. R., 'Youghal County Cork—growth, decay, resurgence', *Irish Geography*, v (1966), 121–49.

Orridge, A. W., 'Who supported the Land War? An aggregate-data analysis of Irish agrarian discontent 1879–1882', *Economic and Social Review*, xii (1981), 203–33.

O'Shea, K., 'David Moriarty (1814–77)', *Journal of the Kerry Archaeological and Historical Society*, No. 3 (1970), 84–98; No. 4 (1971), 106–26; No. 5 (1972), 86–102; No. 6 (1973), 131–42.

Ó Súilleabháin, P., 'Sidelights on the Irish Church, 1811–38', *Collectanea Hibernica*, ix (1966), 71–8.

Ó Súilleabháin, S. V., 'Secondary Education' in *A History of Irish Catholicism*, ed. P. J. Corish, V, Fascicule 6 (Dublin, 1971).

Ó Tuathaigh, G., *Ireland before the Famine 1798–1848* (Dublin, 1972).

Paul-Dubois, L., *Contemporary Ireland* (Dublin, 1908).

Pease, A. E., *Elections and Recollections* (London, 1932).

Ponsonby, F. and E., 'Diary of a Tour of Donegal, 1837', *Donegal Annual*, x (1973), 281–91.

Prest, J., *Lord John Russell* (London, 1972).

—, *Politics in the age of Cobden* (London, 1977).

Raymond, R. J., 'Pawnbrokers and pawnbroking in Dublin: 1830–1870', *Dublin Historical Record*, xxxii (1978), 15–26.

Razzell, P. E., 'Social Origins of Officers in the Indian and British Home Army: 1758–1962', *British Journal of Sociology*, xiv (1963), 248–68.

Reynolds, J. A., *The Catholic Emancipation Crisis in Ireland, 1823–1829* (New Haven, 1954).

Richards, E., 'The Land Agent' in *The Victorian Countryside*, ed. G. E. Mingay, 2 vols. (London, 1981), ii, 439–56.

Robson, L. L., *The Convict Settlers of Australia: An enquiry into the origin and character of the convicts transported to New South Wales and Van Diemen's Land 1787–1852* (Melbourne, 1965).

Roebuck, P., 'Rent movement, proprietorial incomes, and agricultural development, 1730–1830' in *Plantation to Partition: Essays in Ulster History in honour of J. L. McCracken*, pp. 82–101 and 262–4 (see next entry).

— (ed.), *Plantation to Partition: Essays in Ulster History in honour of J. L. McCracken* (Belfast, 1981).

Ross, N., 'Two nineteenth-century election posters', *Journal of the County Louth Archaeological Society*, xvi (1968), 224–32.

Rumpf, E. and Hepburn, A. C., *Nationalism and Socialism in twentieth-century Ireland* (Liverpool, 1977).

Ryan, D., *The Fenian Chief: A biography of James Stephens* (Dublin, 1967).

Ryan, M., *Fenian Memories* (Dublin, 1945).

Sanderlin, W. S., 'Galway as a transatlantic port in the nineteenth century', *Eire-Ireland*, v (1970), 15–31.

Savage, D. C., 'The Origins of the Ulster Unionist party, 1885–6', *Irish Historical Studies*, xii (1961), 185–208.

Scullion, F., 'The relative gravity of Irish music', *Ulster Folk and Transport Museum Year Book* (1976–7), 21–3.

Semple, A. J., 'The Fenian Infiltration of the British Army', *Journal of the Society for Army Historical Research*, lii (1974), 133–60.

Senior, H., *Orangeism in Ireland and Britain 1795–1836* (London, 1966).

Seymour, C., *Electoral Reform in England and Wales: The development and operation of the parliamentary franchise 1832–1885* (New Haven, 1915).

Shaw, A. G. L., *Convicts and the Colonies: A Study of Penal Transportation from Great Britain and Ireland to Australia and other parts of the British Empire* (London, 1966).

Sheehy, Jeanne, *The Rediscovery of Ireland's Past: The Celtic Revival 1830–1930* (London, 1980).

[Sherry, R.], *Holy Cross College, Clonliffe, Dublin: College History and Centenary Record* (Dublin, 1962).

[Sibbett, R. M.], *Orangeism in Ireland and throughout the Empire*, 2nd edn., 2 vols. (London, [1939]).

Simpson, W. G. *et al.* (eds.), *Ordnance Survey Memoir for the Parish of Donegore* (1838; Belfast, 1974).

Skelley, A. R., *The Victorian Army at Home: The Recruitment and Terms and Conditions of the British Regular, 1859-1899* (London, 1977).

Smyth, W. J., 'Continuity and Change in the territorial organization of Irish rural communities', *Maynooth Review*, Part I in i, No. 1 (1975), 51-78; Part II in i, No. 2 (1975), 52-101.

——, 'Estate records and the making of the Irish landscape: An example from County Tipperary', *Irish Geography*, ix (1976), 29-49.

Socolofsky, H. E., *Landlord William Scully* (Lawrence, Kan., 1979).

Solow, B. L., *The land question and the Irish economy, 1870-1903* (Cambridge, Mass., 1971).

——, 'A new look at the Irish Land Question', *Economic and Social Review*, xii (1981), 301-14.

Somerville, E. Œ. and Ross, Martin, *Irish Memories* (London, 1917).

Stamp, J., *British incomes and property: The application of official statistics to economic problems*, new edn. (London, 1927).

Steele, E. D., *Irish Land and British Politics: Tenant-Right and Nationality 1865-1870* (Cambridge, 1974).

——, 'Cardinal Cullen and Irish Nationality', *Irish Historical Studies*, xix (1975), 239-60.

Stewart, R., *The Politics of Protection: Lord Derby and the Protectionist party 1841-1852* (Cambridge, 1971).

——, *The Foundation of the Conservative party 1830-1867* (London, 1978).

Swift MacNeill, J. G., *What I have seen and heard* (London, 1925).

Thompson, F., 'The Armagh elections of 1885-6', *Seanchas Ardmhacha: Journal of the Armagh Diocesan Historical Society*, viii (1977), 360-85.

Thomson, D. and McGusty, M. (eds.), *The Irish Journals of Elizabeth Smith 1840-1850* (Oxford, 1980).

Thornley, D., *Isaac Butt and Home Rule* (London, 1964).

Tierney, M., *Morroe and Boher: The History of an Irish Country Parish* (Dublin, 1966).

——, 'Catalogue of Letters relating to the Queen's Colleges, Ireland, 1845-50', *Collectanea Hibernica*, ix (1966), 83-120.

—— (ed.), 'Correspondence concerning the Disestablishment of the Church of Ireland 1862-1869', *Collectanea Hibernica*, xii (1969), 102-91.

——, *Croke of Cashel: The Life of Archbishop Thomas William Croke, 1823-1902* (Dublin, 1976).

Tocqueville, A. de, *Journeys to England and Ireland*, ed. J. P. Mayer (London, 1958).

Townshend, C., 'Modernization and Nationalism: Perspectives in recent Irish History', *History*, lxvi (1981), 231-43.

Trainor, B. (ed.), *Ordnance Survey Memoir for the Parish of Antrim* (1838; Belfast, 1969).

Vaughan, W. E., 'Landlord and Tenant Relations in Ireland between the Famine and the Land War, 1850-78' in *Comparative aspects of Scottish and Irish economic and social history 1600-1900*, ed. L. M. Cullen and T. C. Smout (Edinburgh, [1977]), pp. 216-26.

——, 'Agricultural Output, Rents, and Wages in Ireland, 1850-1880' in *Ireland*

and France 17th-20th Centuries: Towards a comparative study of rural history*, ed. L. M. Cullen and F. Furet (Paris, 1980), pp. 85–97.

Vaughan, W. E., 'An assessment of the economic performance of Irish landlords, 1851–81' in *Ireland under the Union: Varieties of tension: Essays in honour of T. W. Moody*, ed. F. S. L. Lyons and R. A. J. Hawkins (Oxford, 1980), pp. 173–99.

Vincent, J. R., *Pollbooks: How Victorians voted* (Cambridge, 1967).

— (ed.), *Disraeli, Derby, and the Conservative party: Journals and memoirs of Edward Henry, Lord Stanley 1849–1869* (Hassocks, 1978).

Wadsworth, A. P., 'Newspaper Circulations, 1800–1954', *Manchester Statistical Society* (1965), 1–40.

Walker, B. M., 'The Irish Electorate, 1868–1915', *Irish Historical Studies*, xviii (1973), 359–406.

—, 'Party Organization in Ulster, 1865–92: Registration Agents and their Activities' in *Plantation to Partition: Essays in Ulster History in honour of J. L. McCracken*, ed. P. Roebuck (Belfast, 1981), pp. 191–209 and 276–8.

— and Hoppen, K. T., 'Irish election poll books 1832–1872', *Irish Booklore*, iii (1976), 9–13, and iv (1980), 113–19.

Wall, M., *The Penal Laws 1691–1760* (Dundalk, 1961).

Walsh, D., 'A century of Suicide in Ireland', *Journal of the Irish Medical Association*, lxix (1976), 144–52.

Walsh, P. J., *William J. Walsh, Archbishop of Dublin* (Dublin, 1928).

Whyte, J. H., 'Bishop Moriarty on Disestablishment and the Union, 1868', *Irish Historical Studies*, x (1956), 193–9.

—, *The Independent Irish Party 1850–9* (Oxford, 1958).

—, 'Daniel O'Connell and the Repeal party', *Irish Historical Studies*, xi (1959), 297–316.

—, 'The influence of the Catholic clergy on elections in nineteenth-century Ireland', *English Historical Review*, lxxv (1960), 239–59.

—, 'The Appointment of Catholic Bishops in nineteenth-century Ireland', *Catholic Historical Review*, xlviii (1962), 12–32.

—, 'Landlord influence at elections in Ireland, 1760–1885', *English Historical Review*, lxxx (1965), 740–60.

—, 'Political Problems 1850–1860' in *A History of Irish Catholicism*, ed. P. J. Corish, V, Fascicule 2 (Dublin, 1967).

Williams, T. D. (ed.), *Secret Societies in Ireland* (Dublin, 1973).

Wood-Martin, W. G., *Traces of the Elder Faiths of Ireland: A Folklore Sketch*, 2 vols. (London, 1902).

Woods, C. J., 'The Politics of Cardinal McCabe, Archbishop of Dublin, 1879–85', *Dublin Historical Record*, xxvi (1973), 101–10.

—, 'The General Election of 1892: The Catholic Clergy and the defeat of the Parnellites' in *Ireland under the Union: Varieties of tension: Essays in honour of T. W. Moody*, ed. F. S. L. Lyons and R. A. J. Hawkins (Oxford, 1980), pp. 289–319.

Wright, F., 'Protestant ideology and politics in Ulster', *Archives Européennes de Sociologie*, xiv (1973), 213–80.

Wyndham-Quin, Colonel, *The Fox Hound in County Limerick* (Dublin, 1919).

Wynne, Maud, *An Irishman and his Family: Lord Morris and Killanin* (London, 1937).

Zimmermann, G.-D., *Songs of Irish Rebellion* (Dublin, 1967).

Index

Peers are generally listed under their final titles with cross-references where appropriate.